ARCHBISHOP FISHER – HIS LIFE AND TIMES

BOOKS BY THE SAME AUTHOR:

Thomas Sherlock 1678–1761, Bishop of Bangor, Salisbury and London. (S.P.C.K., 1936)

Thomas Tenison, Archbishop of Canterbury, His Life and Times. (S.P.C.K., 1948)

The Protestant Bishop being the life of Henry Compton, 1632–1713, Bishop of London. (Longmans Green and Co., 1956)

Cantuar: The Archbishops in their office. (Cassell, London, 1971; New edition: Mowbray, 1988)

That Man Paul: Bishop of London's Lent Book.

Common Sense about Christian Ethics. (Victor Gollancz Ltd, 1961)

The Service of a Parson: sponsored by CACTM, 1965

A House of Kings: The History of Westminster Abbey (Editor & contributor) (Cassell, 1972)

Westminster Abbey – illustrated by David Gentleman. (Weidenfeld & Nicholson, 1987)

AND AS JOINT AUTHOR:

The Nineteenth Century Country parson. With A. Tindal Heart. (Wilding & Son Ltd, 1954)

A History of St Paul's Cathedral. Edited by W. R. Matthews and W. M. Atkins. (Phoenix House Ltd, 1957)

The Archbishop Speaks: Addresses and speeches by the Archbishop of Canterbury selected by Edward Carpenter. (Evans Brothers Ltd, London 1958)

From Uniformity to Unity 1662–1962. Edited by Nuttall and Chadwick. (S.P.C.K., 1962)

The Churches Use of the Bible: Past and Present. Edited by Dennis Nineham. (S.P.C.K., 1963)

Against Hunting. Edited by Patrick Moore. (Victor Gollancz Ltd, 1965)

AS A CONTRIBUTOR:

The English Church: A New Look. Edited by Leslie S. Hunter. (Penguin 1966)

Tradition and Unity: Sermons published in honour of Robert Runcie. Edited by Dan Cohn-Sherbok (Bellew, 1991)

Portrait of Geoffrey Francis Fisher by artist Middleton Todd.

Reproduced by kind permission of His Grace the Archbishop of Canterbury. Copyright reserved to the Church Commissioners and the Courtauld Institute of Art.

Archbishop FISHER

– *His Life and Times*

by

EDWARD CARPENTER

With a Foreword by
Lord Runcie

The Canterbury Press
Norwich

Copyright © Edward Carpenter 1991

First published 1991 by The Canterbury Press Norwich
(a publishing imprint of Hymns Ancient & Modern Limited,
a registered charity)
St Mary's Works, St Mary's Plain,
Norwich, Norfolk, NR3 3BH

British Library Cataloguing in Publication Data
Carpenter, Edward *1910–*
Archbishop Fisher.
1. Anglican churches
I. Title
283.092

ISBN 1-85311-016-7

*Typeset by Cambridge Composing (UK) Ltd, Cambridge
in 11/12½pt Sabon and printed and bound
in Great Britain by Mackays of Chatham plc.*

I dedicate, with affection,
this biography
to my grandchildren –

EMILY

EDWARD

CHARLOTTE

KATE

JAMES

LILY

Maybe – who knows? – one of them,
in the future,
might even read it.

Foreword

WE OWE Dr Carpenter a great debt for his monumental labours in writing the life of Archbishop Fisher, in particular for giving us access to the remarkable range of Fisher papers now deposited at Lambeth. The debt is all the greater because it enables a reassessment of Fisher and his achievements, at a time when distance makes a proper perspective easier to achieve.

Fisher's reputation has often suffered from the obvious differences of style between him and both his predecessor Temple and successor Ramsey (themselves men of very different character): one might draw some comparison with the common view of Clement Attlee, a statesman whom Fisher found congenial. Fisher's talents were not those beloved of headline-writers: for instance, his relish for the task of canon law revision clearly left behind even his episcopal colleagues. In such matters, Fisher was ready to enter where neither fools nor angels were prepared to tread. There cannot be many senior clergy of whom it could be said, as does Dr Carpenter of Fisher, that drawing up a budget for the World Council of Churches 'was an exercise which gave him a great deal of private pleasure'!

If Fisher acquired the image of the busy and omnicompetent headmaster, he largely had himself to blame. To begin with, of course, that was precisely what he was, and it was the role which he played up to, in mischievous mood, at his first informal meeting with the press as Primate. His capacity for work was staggering, setting perhaps unfortunately high standards for other senior churchmen: not all workaholics can stand the pace as long as he did. He had all the virtues, and some of the limitations, of his background: 120 years of clerical forbears in the same country living, and 38 years himself in the equally Anglican setting of school or university. It was a world which bred self-assurance, it does not seem to have had much direct acquaintance with tragedy or disaster, so that Fisher did not always find it easy to enter situations where tragic history produced an intransigence which seemed to him unreasonable. However, it was also a world which distrusted small-minded extremism, while honouring open-mindedness, curiosity and a capacity to learn: qualities which Fisher demonstrated to the full in his years as Primate.

Fisher's zest for administrative detail was one of his great gifts to the postwar Church. There was much to build afresh, often literally, both in his years in war-torn London and afterwards: subsequent tenants at Lambeth and Canterbury have much to thank him for. More than that, there was much to build up with little precedent for guidance: the World Council of Churches, and a host of new Anglican Provinces emerging from English missions to seek new identities. Fisher was performing a work of decolonisation usually a few years in advance of the British secular colonial power. It is said that he wrote a constitition for the Church in Nigeria in his own hand. In this sort of work so many tender egos had to be accommodated, so many forms of words to be devised: fortunate was the Church to find a leader who adored such activities. Nor was this busyness in a vacuum: the world of the Cold War, and of the traumas caused by British imperial decline, generated continual crises affecting the good of the Church and of its people.

Through all these trials, Fisher kept a cool head, although his tongue would occasionally run away with him in conversation, as his pen did in later years; but in many fraught situations he displayed a capacity for pronouncing less than was demanded of him: a talent which many would do well to emulate. That is not to say that he was a coward: his vigorous interventions in the Suez crisis and after the deportation of Archbishop Makarios reveal an independence of mind and a moral determination which did not endear him to the government of the day. In some matters, his opinions now seem echoes from a world long gone: his sustained fierce opposition to the Divorced Wife's Sister Act seemed archaic even at the time, and his comments on the *Lady Chatterley's Lover* case were vulnerable to accusations of philistine narrow-mindedness. Yet his capacity to look forward can be seen in his cautious welcome for the conclusions of the Wolfenden Report on homosexuality; moreover, it was Fisher who presided over the 1958 Lambeth Conference, which put up an important milestone for the future of Christian moral discussion when it bluntly stated that 'it is utterly wrong to urge that, unless children are specifically desired, sexual intercourse is of the nature of sin.' In his personal progress to a broad ecumenism, too, Fisher both reflected the more generous spirit of the 1950s, and gave a lead precisely when it was needed.

Fisher never allowed anything to happen by oversight. In days before Synods, Anglican Consultative Councils, and the Alternative Service Book he was clearly steering the Church of England into new initiatives but within its traditional shape and character.

For many reasons, therefore, we should honour the memory of a great and godly man, whom we see here in an honest and judicious portrait.

28 June 1991

Contents

Foreword by Lord Runcie   *page* vii

List of Illustrations   xiii

Acknowledgements   xvii

Prologue   xix

PART ONE: FORMATIVE YEARS
1. Higham on the Hill, Home and Family   3
2. School and University   8
3. Marlborough College and Headmaster of Repton   15
4. Bishop of Chester   32

PART TWO: A NATION AT WAR
5. Nomination to the Bishopric of London   55
6. Fulham Palace and the Blitz   63
7. Destruction and War Damage   69
8. The City of London Churches   78
9. The Archbishops' War Committee   85
10. Ecumenicity in Wartime   103
11. The Diocese of London   115

PART THREE: PRIMATE OF ALL ENGLAND
12. Moving to Canterbury   129
13. The Cathedral Church of Christ   135
14. The Very Reverend the Dean of Canterbury   140
15. The Diocese   146
16. Peace and its problems in Europe   152
17. The World Council of Churches and Evanston   169
18. The Lambeth Staff   190
19. Clerical Stipends   198
20. Revision of Canon Law   205
21. Bishops, the Establishment and Crown Appointments   215
22. The Coronation of Queen Elizabeth II   245
23. The Archbishop and the Royal Family   268
24. *The Rise of Christianity* and *Lady Chatterly's Lover*   295

PART FOUR: ECUMENICITY AND REUNION
25. The Free Churches and the Methodists   309
26. The Church of Scotland   319
27. The United Church of South India   331
28. Roman Catholics and Catholicism   344

PART FIVE: THE ARCHBISHOP, THE NATION AND SOCIETY
29. The Nuclear Bomb   373
30. Marriage, Divorce and the Family   381
31. Parliament, Politics and Prime Ministers   395
32. The Media – Press, Radio and Television   409
33. Education   428

PART SIX: THE WORLD-WIDE ANGLICAN COMMUNION
34. Visits to Canada and America, 1946   443
35. The Lambeth Conference, 1948   452
36. The Archbishop and Canada, 1954   463
37. The Lambeth Conference, 1958   468

PART SEVEN: ARCHIEPISCOPAL TOURS AND THE SETTING
UP OF PROVINCES
38. Australia   479
39. New Zealand   492
40. West Africa   500
41. Central Africa   509
42. East Africa   520
43. Kabaka Mutesa II and the Buganda   524
44. Uganda   541
45. South Africa   545

PART EIGHT: THE MIDDLE EAST
46. The Holy Land   577
47. The Jerusalem Bishopric   595
48. Egypt   607
49. Cyprus   617

PART NINE: THE FAR EAST
50. Pakistan, India and Hong Kong   639
51. China   648
52. Japan and Korea   668
53. Singapore and a Pacific Province   684
54. The Western Hemisphere   693

PART TEN: A HISTORIC JOURNEY
55. The Preparation   705
56. Jerusalem   713

57. Istanbul 724
58. Rome 730

PART ELEVEN: THE FINAL YEARS

59. Resignation 747
60. An Assistant Parish Priest 751
61. Post-Retirement Ecumenicity 756
62. Requiescat in Pace 762

EPILOGUE: GEOFFREY FISHER – THE MAN AND HIS FAITH 767

Appendices

I. Note on Sources 777
II. Geoffrey and Lady Fisher's last annual circular letter 779
III. Entry in *Who's Who*, 1972 781
IV. List of Books written by Geoffrey Fisher or to which he
   contributed 783
V. Chaplains who served Archbishop Fisher 785
VI. Bishops during Geoffrey Fisher's Archiespiscopate 787
VII. Bibliography 789

Index 793

List of Illustrations

Frontispiece:
Portrait of Geoffrey Francis Fisher by artist Middleton Todd.

Between pages 172 and 173:
Geoffrey Fisher with his parents and family as a small boy.

At Prep School – Lindley Lodge (GF: top row, fourth from left).

Geoffrey Fisher with his family (standing behind parents).

Member of Exeter College, Oxford rowing eight (GF: third from left).

Headmaster of Repton – Speech Day, 1928

Engagement to Rosamond Forman.

With Harry, eldest son (later Sir Henry Fisher).

Rosamond Fisher with her three eldest sons, Harry, Frank and Charles.

Enthronement as Bishop of Chester, 1932.

Enthronement as Bishop of London in St Paul's Cathedral, 1939.

Meeting with Cardinal Hinsley and Archbishop William Temple, London, 1941.

Enthronement as Archbishop of Canterbury, 1945.

Family group at the Old Palace, Canterbury.

With Bishop Krutitsky of the Russian Orthodox Church and Archbishop Garbett, 1945.[1]

With Archbishop Damaskinos of the Greek Orthodox Church.

Between pages 332 and 333:
With the Bishop of Winchester (Mervyn Haigh) and the Bishop of Chichester (George Bell).[2]

The Fishers relaxing during Canadian Tour, 1946.

With H.R.H. Princess Elizabeth in the Canterbury Precincts, 1947.[3]

Wedding of H.R.H. Princess Elizabeth, 1947.

With his chaplain, the Reverend J. S. Long, in the garden of Lambeth Palace, 1950.

On deck *en route* to Australia and New Zealand, 1950.

The Archbishop with the Archbishop of Brisbane (R. C. Halse) during his tour of Australia and New Zealand.[4]

The Archbishop places St Edward's Crown on the Queen's head.[5]

With pages at the Coronation, 1953.[6]

The Archbishop wearing the Coronation Cope and Mitre given him by the Japanese Church.

The Archbishop in his Canterbury study.[7]

The Archbishop and Mrs Fisher with some of their grandchildren.[8]

Between pages 492 and 493:

Assembly of the World Council of Churches, Evanston, USA 1954: The Archbishop of Canterbury and the Right Reverend Henry Sherrill, Presiding Bishop of the Episcopal Church of USA.[9]

The Archbishop and Mrs Fisher with their staff at Lambeth Palace, July 1955.[10]

Rededication of Lambeth Palace Chapel after its restoration in the presence of the Queen, the Royal Family and the Bishops of the Church of England, 19 October 1955.[11]

Greeting African and Indian Ladies in Mbale, Uganda, 1955.

Consecration of four African Bishops in Uganda, Namirembe Cathedral, May 1955.

Mrs Fisher greeting Kikuyu women at Fort Hall, Kenya.[12]

The Archbishop greeting a Sister in East Africa, 1955.[13]

Inauguration of the Province of Central Africa in Salisbury Cathedral, Southern Rhodesia, 8 May 1955.[14]

Sharing a joke with the Archbishop of Cape Town (G. H. Clayton), the Archbishop of Central Africa (E. F. Paget) and the Bishop of Matabeleland (W. J. Hughes), after the inauguration of the Province of Central Africa.[15]

The Archbishop talking to two Nuns.

The Archbishop in Nigeria, 1960.[16]

The Archbishop with the Patriarch of the Armenians in Turkey, 1960.[17]

The Archbishop in Istanbul – greeted by the Oecumenical Patriarch, 1960.[18]

Surveying the Holy Land, 1960.[19]

Between pages 652 and 653:

The Archbishop with the Apostolic Delegate and His Beatitude the Latin Patriarch in Jerusalem.

The Archbishop with the Archbishop in Jerusalem (The Most Reverend A. C. MacInnes).[20]

'This is no Christian camel'[21]

The Archbishop on his way to the Vatican for his historic meeting with Pope John XXIII, 2 December 1960.[22] (*No photographs were allowed within the Vatican*).

With children in the Piazza Navona, Rome, 1960.[23]

The Archbishop in Lambeth Palace Chapel.[24]

The Archbishop and Mrs Fisher relaxing at Lambeth, 1960.[25]

With the gardeners and chauffeur, May 1961, on leaving Lambeth.

The Fishers in retirement with the Archbishop of York and Mrs Coggan at Bishopthorpe.[26]

Combined Golden Wedding and 80th Birthday celebration at Trent 5 May 1967.[27]

Country walk at Trent.[28]

Lady Fisher, in the presence of the Dean of Westminster and Sir Henry Fisher, on 13 October 1977, unveiling a plaque in Westminster Abbey commemorating all those who, Protestant and Roman Cathlic, at the time of the Reformation surrendered their lives for Christ and conscience sake. The suggestion for such a memorial came from Geoffrey Fsher, Archbishop of Canterbury 1945–1961.[29]

List of Illustrations

ACKNOWLEDGEMENTS TO PHOTOGRAPHS

1. Walter Stoneman
2. Fox Photos
3. Fisk-Moore
4. Lambeth Palace Library (LPL)
5. LPL
6. Keystone
7. Russell Westwood
8–18. LPL
19. Daily Express
20. LPL

21. Daily Express
22. LPL
23. Assoc. Press
24. The Times
25. Daily Mail
26. Yorkshire Post
27. Bristol Evg Post
28. Jane Bown
29. Daily Telegraph

Acknowledgements

I AM quite sure that, in company with the anonymous author of the Epistle to the Hebrews, 'the time would fail me' if I were to record my thanks to all those who have helped me in the course of my writing this book. Their number is indeed "legion". They have assisted me in a variety of ways, such as, for example, in sharing their personal experiences of the Archbishop and in giving me their own assessment of his life and work. Indeed, I fear I must have made myself somewhat of a nuisance in seizing any opportunity to interrogate them on this score.

Some people, however, I must mention by name and I do this with a great sense of gratitude. First comes Lady Fisher, than whom no one could have been more helpful both in private conversation and in giving me access to personal papers. I wish also to thank the family as a whole, not least Sir Henry Fisher. Here it is important for me to say that at no time was I pressurised by its members to take any particular point of view. In this family context, perhaps I may be allowed to mention, Miss Priscilla Lethbridge who was Archbishop Fisher's secretary during almost his whole stay at Lambeth. She has helped considerably, to fill in the picture of his working life in the study or more widely. Nor must I forget the lavish help given me by Lord Coggan.

I am deeply indebted to Dr Geoffrey Bill, Librarian at Lambeth and members of his staff in making my daunting task the more easy. I express my thanks to those in charge of the Library at Sion College for their patience and co-operation. It gives me great pleasure to thank the Reverend T. C. Brook, Rector of the Parishes of Over Compton with Nether Compton and Trent, who gave me a fascinating glimpse of the ministry of his assistant curate when released from his archiepiscopal responsibilities. I am equally grateful to Sir Peter Scarlett, Her Majesty's Minister to the Holy See, and Sir Ashley Clarke, British Ambassador to Italy, who did all that they could – and what a considerable all it was – to make the Archbishop's visit to Rome the undoubted success that it was. Their testimony gives a vivid picture of the difficulties they had to contend with and I am indeed fortunate in being able to draw upon it in this biography.

That I was able to make one part of the chapter on 'Post Retirement Ecumenicity' factually significant I owe to Mr Todhunter, a Roman

Catholic layman and Father Alberic Stacpole, both of whom became his close friends.

An author is not usually a good proof reader of his own works and I am therefore particularly grateful to those who volunteered to read the text, some in proof form. These include Mrs Joan Knapp Fisher, Sir Henry Fisher, Dr Coggan, Mr Nadir Dinshaw, Miss Priscilla Lethbridge and my ever faithful secretary of former years, Miss Christine Zochonis; it gives me pleasure to include in these brief 'mentions', my friend from college days, François Piachaud. For the Canterbury chapter, I thank Roger Job, a former boy Chorister and Christopher Ludlow, Precentor from 1949–1954. I also express my appreciation to Bishop Oliver Tomkins and Professor Gordon Dunstan, who are mentioned by name in the text – also to an American friend Judith Scutch Philston.

It was indeed most kind of Lord Runcie to write a Foreword. True I approached him with some diffidence since he had already done precisely this for the reissue of my *Cantuar*. It was, therefore, doubly noble of him to repeat the dose.

Relations between authors and their publishers are in the nature of the case ambivalent. The classic example is that of Lord Byron and John Murray which is writ large in a voluminous correspondence between the two. Today such relations are not 'what they used to be'. Maybe under increasing financial pressures the personal aspect has been largely squeezed out. I wish to say how much I have appreciated the personal approach of The Canterbury Press Norwich, in particular Mr Kenneth Baker and Mr Gordon Knights. They were accessible and always helpful. I must, finally, thank their reader for the meticulous care with which he read the script and the suggestions he made on it. I certainly profited by them.

Lastly, but by no means least, I thank warmly members of my own family for their interest and help. To them Geoffrey Fisher became progressively more than a remote figure from the past, and I hope this will prove equally true of those who read this biography.

EDWARD CARPENTER

Prologue

THIS is my fourth ecclesiastical biography. The first was of Thomas Sherlock (1678–1761), the only bishop ever to decline both the Archbishoprics of York and Canterbury. The second was of Thomas Tenison, Primate of All England from 1695 to 1716. The third was of Henry Compton (1632–1713), Bishop of London, who played a significant part in bringing over from Holland the Duke of Orange at the time of the 'Bloodless Revolution' in 1688.

I call attention to this since the following study of Geoffrey Francis Fisher (1887–1972) is the first biography I have attempted of a contemporary. I have to confess that I was soon made vividly aware of the difference. In respect of the three earlier biographies I think I succeeded in ferreting out what seemed to me all the relevant, extant material bearing upon these eminent ecclesiastics. Hence, I knew, at least appoximately, when I had come to the end of my researches. Of course one cannot rule out that there might be sources hidden away somewhere which I did not discover. This is a risk, however, which every biographer has to take.

In respect of Geoffrey Fisher the extent of the material was such as to be, for all practical purposes, almost inexhaustible. Through the kindness of Archbishop Michael Ramsey I was given free and unfettered access to Dr Fisher's Canterbury Papers at Lambeth. Around this rich mine (about which I say more in the note on sources in Appendix I) the present biography has been largely written, which gives a particular distinction to this book that does not derive in any way from the merits of the author.

My personal hope is that subsequent scholars will from this treasure house at Lambeth Library produce specialised studies such, for example, as Geoffrey Fisher's 'flirtation' in his retirement with a small but responsible group of Roman Catholics for the purpose of promoting a full communion between the two Churches, while respecting the integrity of both.

Some may feel that like Charles II who is said to have apologised for being an 'unconscionable time dying', I have lingered long over the writing of this book. Certainly I could have avoided this if I had followed the example of Alan Don who, on accepting the Deanery of Westminster, a most time consuming appointment, withdrew from his prior commitment to produce a biography of Cosmo Lang. However, in similar circumstances, I decided to push on with Geoffrey Fisher though it meant consuming much midnight oil and rising early to greet the dawn chorus. In arriving at this decision I was not unaware of the fact that an excellent personal portrait of Geoffrey Fisher of some 120,000 words by William Purcell was published in 1969. It was no fault of his that he was denied access to the Canterbury Papers at Lambeth which, as I have already pointed out, form the essential basis of my own biography. I believe that in some ways my book is a better book in that some thirty years separate Dr Fisher's retirement from the date of its publication. True such a brief space of time, in the broader sweeps of history, may seem but 'an evening gone', yet it can be long enough for time's sifting process at least to begin to separate the wheat from the chaff. So it becomes possible for the biographer to look back on the past from the vantage ground of the present. Younger readers of my book – may feel that in part it depicts a vanished age which strikes them as remote, almost alien. Certainly the last thirty years have seen great changes, here in Britain and throughout the world. Yet they did not come as a bolt from the blue. 'The moving finger writes and having writ moves on.' Hence contemporary questions and criticisms levelled at the British Council of Churches, which led to refashioning that institution, were never far below the surface in the thinking and anxieties of Geoffrey Fisher.

Every biographer of a contemporary figure is faced with the problem how best in dealing with the living, to be honest yet not to hurt. I hope I have come near to achieving this twin ambition not least in relation to the chief actor.

When Geoffrey Fisher first heard that I had accepted an invitation to write his biograpahy he welcomed it though adding, with a twinkle in his eye, 'in spite of my treatment of him in *Cantuar*'. Later he expressed the hope that I would enjoy writing his life as much as he had enjoyed living it. It is for the reader to determine how much of this enjoyment has seeped through into this volume.

E.C.

PART ONE:

FORMATIVE YEARS

CHAPTER I

Higham on the Hill, Home and Family

THAT great Englishman, Dr Johnson, assures us that 'whatever makes the past, the distant or the future, predominate over the present, advances us in the dignity of thinking beings.' Taking a different view Archbishop Fisher writes: 'I am not a person who very often looks back to the past. I live very much engaged in what is before me at the moment, entirely concentrated on that.'

In this respect Geoffrey believes himself to resemble his father. However, this cannot mean that his early years were not strongly formative of his character. Indeed, though he confesses that it required 'considerable effort' to remember his childhood, it is remarkable how vividly, upon reflection, memories came flooding back into his consciousness.

The earliest member of the Fisher family who can be traced with any certainty, according to his brother Herbert's researches, is John Fisher, Prior of the Benedictine Abbey at Burton-on-Trent founded by Wulfric, Earl of Mercia. In the fifteenth and sixteenth centuries the family appear as yeoman farmers at Foremark, a small village close to Repton in Derbyshire. Part of the Fisher family migrated to Castle Donington, where one at least prospered, owning Caldicote Hall, close to Nuneaton, until he lost all the family money. 'However,' so Geoffrey reassuringly comments: 'we remained respectable and a great uncle was a solicitor.'

On his mother's side, his pedigree was more distinguished. Her family name was Richmond and among her connections the Reverend Legh Richmond (1772–1827) who wrote one of the best selling moral tracts of the time *The Dairyman's Daughter* which was translated into many languages. Also there was a Bruce Richmond, founder and editor of the *Times Literary Supplement*.

The most significant family event, so far as concerned Geoffrey, was the appointment on 11 September 1772 of his great-grandfather, John Fisher, to the benefice of Higham on the Hill in Leicestershire. He remained there until his death in 1832, the year of the great Reform Bill. He was followed by his son, also John, whom Geoffrey understood to be the original of the most attractive of the clergy in George Eliot's *Scenes of Clerical Life*. Three years after his graduation he was ordained to the priesthood and on his father's death, he also nominated himself to the rectory where he remained till he died at the age of 71 in

3

1868. He was followed by Henry, Geoffrey's father, who continued in office till 1910.

Thus three Fishers held the incumbency for a hundred and twenty years, a period in the history of Britain which saw *inter alia* a radical reform of the Church of England undertaken by the secularly orientated Government of the thirties; the Anglo-Catholic revival of the Oxford Movement, so unpopular in the countryside; and the rise in status of the rural parson, reaching its peak in the eighties when the rectory often became the centre of a revived village life. This Indian summer of clerical influence had not yet spent its force when Geoffrey Francis Fisher was born on 5 May 1887 and was baptised by his father in Higham church ten days later.

Higham on the Hill was a small agricultural village of some three or four hundred people and made no claim to any particular distinction. It was situated on the border of Leicestershire, a mile to the east of Watling Street and three miles distant from the busy market town of Nuneaton.

Geoffrey Fisher was the youngest of ten children, the two eldest dying early and thus known to him only through the recollections of his sisters, Edith and Katie. After these there came the twins, Lucy and Legh – then four brothers, Harry, Herbert, Leonard and Geoffrey. Nineteenth century parsonages, often enlarged to house large families, provided a pattern of civilized living, yet with no excessive creature comforts. Recalling these early days Geoffrey wrote: '. . . we lived together a very happy life . . . each one of us had his own distinct personality and individual character; each was inclined to go his own way and to fashion his own ideas and yet we lived together in complete harmony.' The rectory was an old manor house, with a Georgian front, 'very roomy and comfortable.'

The family soon scattered. Katie, trained as a nurse, went out to Palestine with the Church Missionary Society serving on the east and west banks of the Jordan. Legh became a clergyman serving for a time at Higham on the Hill. Harry, whom Geoffrey greatly admired, was for many years the 'beloved physician' at Atherton. Then there was Herbert and Leonard who, after being an incumbent in England, and a chaplain in the First World War, held two bishoprics in South Africa. He was Geoffrey's favourite and they enjoyed an abiding friendship in spite of geographical separation.

As the brothers and sisters came and went, so the one permanent ingredient was the eldest daughter, Edith, who remained at home helping her mother and becoming almost an unpaid curate in the parish. For most of his early years she and Geoffrey, with of course their parents, constituted the home team. She gave herself to the demands of the rectory without reserve, ministering to one and all.

However, one suspects that she experienced a great deal of inner frustration and like many a sacrificial Victorian daughter would have liked to take wing.

Geoffrey's father, Henry, was a spare man, a scholar, full of interests of every kind, never idle and very much a man for his study. He was born at Higham on the Hill in 1837 and his education was typical of similar middle-class boys, that is public school at Aldenham and Jesus College, Cambridge. After a period of teaching, he finally followed his father as Rector of Higham in 1868 where he was content to labour forty-two years unheralded and unsung.

In spite of a natural shyness, being a man of few words, Henry Fisher was thoroughly integrated into the life of his rural parish. He visited his parishioners regularly, and like Chaucer's *Poor Parson of a Town*, did not forget those on the outlying farms. Typical of Victorian families, Geoffrey seldom penetrated into his father's study but he remembered long evenings in the drawing room, lit in the winter by an oil lamp and a flickering fire. There the family read their own books – Geoffrey Fisher was greatly impressed with Rider Haggard's *The People and the Miser* – and played games. In the pulpit his father's long, old-fashioned sermons were dull and uninspired, except on rare occasions when he got 'worked up,' becoming 'too vehement and violent.'

The general picture here is that of a good man, dedicated to his job and to the care of his parishioners.

Geoffrey describes his mother as 'a very lovely, very handsome woman with a great presence' and sense of humour, who entered into the life of the family joining boisterously in the games of the children. She had married when very young and her first few years, so she confessed, were lonely and frustrating. In herself she was 'simple, unaffected, shrewd, able, and everything except well-read.' Still she was not bereft of inner resources and, to break the monotony, used to do little mathematical sums to keep her mind active. Little by little she found scope for her abilities in the day to day business of running the rectory. She became its centre, 'the presiding genius', 'a great strong-hold in the whole life of the house.'

Such was the household where Geoffrey grew up, a veritable community in itself. He always felt that, as very much the youngest, he had a special relationship with his mother, who spoilt him a great deal though his four brothers would see that he did not get above himself. But by his own admission they were not always around! One suspects that his sheer exuberance on occasions made him somewhat of a nuisance, since he admits to being in and out of the kitchen and about the place generally, 'getting in the way and picking up little bits of information, sometimes gossip about the village, sometimes how to do a bit of cooking'. Perhaps here the child was father to the man!

If his home life in the rectory exercised a strong and lasting influence this was equally true of the village as a whole and the church in particular. His mother, like many Victorian rectors' wives, acted as choir mistress, and when he was very young Geoffrey sometimes sat beside her; but as he grew up he was elevated to the rector's pew. Higham church – as was the case in most villages in those days – reproduced in its seating the social hierarchy of the parish.

The time quickly came, however, when this carefree existence ceased and Geoffrey went to the village school where the headmistress was the 'formidable' Miss Boon, a very good teacher and strict disciplinarian who won the respect of her young pupils.

Geoffrey did not long remain in the village school but it was long enough, he claimed, to teach him 'to keep your own standards and stick to them'. From this academy he was sent on to a local preparatory school, Lindley Lodge, first as a day boy and then as a boarder. His daily trudge to the school, either across the fields or in wet weather by road, left on him a lasting impression. He recalled how his mother used to wrap him up in mufflers against the winter cold for fear of chilblains. Yet this daily trudge, come wind come weather, did something for him in character building if only in forcing him to overcome his fear of straying bulls! Attendance at Lindley Lodge – it educated some forty boys – was the first, if only partial, break with a closely knit local community. Its owner and headmaster was Mr Lee of Rugby and Oxford. This was the golden age of the preparatory school, catering for the educational demands of an extensive and newly emerged middle class. Geoffrey was there for some six years, during which time Queen Victoria's long reign drew near to its close and England blundered into the South African war. Schoolmasters who have the care of children in early and impressionable years usually leave a mark on their pupils. Mr Lee was no exception and Geoffrey's description of him suggests a lifelong gratitude. He was grateful to Mr Lee for introducing him into the exercise of responsibility by placing under his care boys who had difficulties of one kind or another. This had the effect of putting him on the side of authority against the law breaker.

Geoffrey worked consistently throughout his six years at Lindley Lodge as is evident in such school lists as survive. They show that in his first term he was in the bottom three in every subject, suggesting that he had some adjustments to make in a more scholastically orientated environment. Certainly he gradually overcame this. It is interesting that one report reads that often he had to be sent out of the classroom to allow his convulsive laughter 'to subside'. Reassuringly, however, his general conduct is described as 'good'. In 1900 he was top of the school in Latin, Greek, Mathematics, English and French. 'I think probably I was rather a late developer', he himself commented.

We are fortunate in that one of Geoffrey's schoolmates at Lindley Lodge was Bishop Freeth, who died in retirement in Western Australia and remembered him well. 'He did not excel in sports,' he recalled, 'but took part in them all. I think he was half back in the rugby xv. He was a member of the school fife and drum band. At one concert he and I sang 'Two little girls in blue.' This proved the basis of much jealousy!²

As to the influence of those early years at Higham perhaps Geoffrey Fisher may speak for himself. 'I now sum up the whole of my childhood to the age of eight. The first and greatest thing I can say is that the community was the background and the life blood of everything – the community and my family in the rectory; the community of the village and all its doings: the community of the church in which all of us had our place.'

This, of course, is in part an idealised picture born from nostalgia and irradiated by 'the warmth of a sunset's afterglow'.

The differentiation between parish and people, due to the ecclesiastical reforms of the 1830s, and greater mobility in the countryside, led many an incumbent to try to recreate the integrity of the village around the church and rectory. Hence the golden period of the country parson in the 70s and 80s with, *inter alia*, its glee clubs, large surpliced choirs, penny readings and thrift clubs.

'The child is father to the man' and doubtless these early years which Geoffrey Fisher could remember in such detail when he set his mind to it had a profound if subliminal effect upon him throughout life. His deep affection for the Church of England, his seeming self-confidence are, perhaps, among its many concealed effects. Also his desire to live within a structured society, the individual finding his place within it.

CHAPTER 2

School and University

GEOFFREY Fisher always regarded his going from Lindley Lodge to Marlborough College on a Foundation Scholarship in September 1901 as a decisive break with his previous environment into a wider world.

Marlborough, in the early years of this century, was a small market town on the outskirts of Savernake Forest with a population of some three thousand inhabitants. It was not without its historic associations. Samuel Pepys in 1668 eyed with satisfaction its broad High Street. Its parish church contains the huge basalt font in which King John was baptised and within its walls Cardinal Wolsey was ordained.

Marlborough College, housed in a country mansion, was opened in 1843 for the sons of clergymen. The half century which preceded Geoffrey Fisher's entry represented the heyday of English public schools, fed from the sons of the professional classes, many of whom had newly acquired wealth and were prepared to invest it in education. The young men thus produced were for the most part self-assured and conditioned to take their place in an élite class, in a privileged society.

Although Geoffrey Fisher's days at Marlborough cannot have been quite so idyllic as he later supposed, they were certainly happy and fulfilling. He was now beginning to find his feet and he refused to be daunted by a new and unknown environment. When his father proposed to escort him to Marlborough on his first day Geoffrey insisted that he accompany him only so far as Birmingham. 'I'd rather meet this new situation on my own without any protecting wing', so he explained. Perhaps he suspected that so far he had not flexed his own muscles because of his privileged family position in Higham. His first few days at Marlborough, however, turned out in a way he could not possibly have foreseen.

On arrival at the College he sat shivering by a fire in the Common Room of the Junior House until he was taken by the Matron and promptly placed in the Sanatorium where he spent his first week. Still, so he alleged, even this misfortune proved beneficial in encouraging him to be independent since, when he began to mix with his school-mates, he found that the other new boys had already made friends. Thus he had 'to pick up his way by himself'.

The headmaster of the College was G. C. Bell, then approaching the end of his twenty-six years' reign. Apocryphal stories about him inevitably circulated. When meeting a boy he did not immediately recognise he was reputed to say: 'Hi, boy, who are you?' and when given the appropriate information replied: 'Are you the son of your father?'

Geoffrey began in the remove form A, the master of which was the redoubtable and eccentric P. W. Taylor, a 'notorious figure' who earned a reputation for 'hardness, sternness and gruffness'. Many thought, however, that he kept the best house in the school, largely because he ran it in co-operation with the senior boys most of whom were 'considerate, clear-minded and capable'.

Two other masters left a permanent impression upon the receptive Geoffrey – F. B. Malim whose exposition of the Old Testament long remained in Geoffrey's memory, and C. T. Wood, an outstanding preacher, even capable of enthusing schoolboys – no mean achievement!

It did not take Geoffrey long to settle down in his new surroundings, the extrovert side of his character coming to his aid. Indeed he did more than settle down. He determined to leave his mark upon the college – which he did.

Geoffrey's progress through the school was easy and straight-forward, presenting no apparent problems. When he entered the sixth form at the age of fifteen he was asked if he wished to specialise in mathematics. His reply indicates his ability to look objectively at his own aptitude and talent. He enjoyed maths, he admitted, but he always knew that there was a point at which he was out of his depth. This was a shrewd assessment for though Geoffrey Fisher's intellectual brilliance cannot be doubted he yet lacked the imagination which higher flights in mathematics undoubtedly demand.

G. C. Bell was followed as headmaster by Frank Fletcher who was thirty-two years of age and very different from his predecessor. In appearance he was not impressive; nor had he any ready conversation. But as is sometimes the case with a schoolmaster the brilliance of his mind and the great integrity of his character 'got through' and Geoffrey Fisher freely acknowledged a life-long debt. From him he learned 'never to be content with a superficial impression; never to take a thing at second hand but wade through it until [one] found an underlying and satisfying reason so far as there was one to be found.'

Geoffrey Fisher was the first prefect to be appointed under the new régime, an office which he entered into with both zest and relish; and which he was later to reform by removing the dominance of the athletic boys in the life of the school to whom the prefects had been forced to play second fiddle. When things came to a crisis, Geoffrey, as head prefect, acted decisively. After this he never looked back.

Geoffrey Fisher certainly made his mark on the life of the school and himself regarded his years at Malborough as giving him a purposeful and moral training centring on self-discipline. However, he had his disappointments. His first attempt in the debating society was a disaster, a 'mini' reduplication of Disraeli's initiation into the House of Commons. The subject for discussion was Dickens and Thackeray but, on his own admission, Geoffrey's intervention was disastrous and he sat down amid general laughter and personal humiliation.

As to the influence of Marlborough on his spiritual development Geoffrey Fisher saw it as confirming what he had learned in his own home and family. It engendered an unquestioning acceptance of Christ as the master of the good life. 'I learned,' he writes, 'how to tackle everything that came along in what I now recognise was an intelligent Christian way, not borrowing from Christ, but translating into my daily duties and occupations and pleasures the spirit which flowed from His revelation of the Kingdom of God.' This points to an evangelical faith which was simple, uncomplicated and fervent. In its essence this faith accompanied him for the rest of his life. Geoffrey Fisher may certainly claim to have made the maximum use of his school days. He left, scooping up many a prize, in 'a blaze of glory'.

By no means every adult looks back in later years upon his school days as a time of almost unalloyed bliss. Often recollection is darkened by 'the shades of the prison house'. Not so, for a moment, with Geoffrey Fisher. 'Marlborough was wonderful', he claimed later. 'I enjoyed every bit of it from beginning to end and I was enjoying it because in every kind of way I was growing happily and securely.'

The time had now come for him, in more ways than one, to move on. Departing from the family tradition – his grandfather, father and brothers had gone to Cambridge – Geoffrey Fisher proceeded to Exeter College, Oxford. This seat of learning which then consisted of eight Fellows and 182 students was founded in 1314 by Walter Stapeldon, Bishop of Exeter, who in the course of his career held high office of state including that of Lord High Treasurer, before being murdered by a mob while in charge of the City of London. The College – as befits its name – still today retains a connection with Devon. The Rector, during Geoffrey's five years there, was the Reverend W. W. Jackson who held office from 1887 to 1913.

During his last vacation before going up to the University he considered with his usual earnestness how he ought to disport himself on his arrival. Maybe his older brothers had told him something of the kind of life which awaited him. It was the social side which constituted his main concern, in particular how he would fit into it. Ruefully he had to admit that he had 'none of the ordinary social vices which are also graces'. Ought he to smoke or drink? The latter he rejected on the grounds that you have to consider again and again, have I had enough? Smoking, however – this was years prior to any suggestion of a link-up with lung cancer – was different. 'You could smoke as much as you liked and as long as you liked;' so he became an inveterate pipe smoker and was so for forty years until he gave it up while on holiday – suddenly, completely and finally.

The Oxford to which Geoffrey Fisher went up in October 1906 was very different from the Oxford of today. The College then loomed much larger in the life of the undergraduate than did the University. This meant that members of the College knew each other with an intimacy which no longer obtains to the same extent.

The facilities, compared with today, were spartan. There were few bathrooms and hot water had to be fetched from the kitchen to fill the tin baths usually placed in front of the sitting room fire. However, this had its compensations. J. C. Masterman writes that 'lying in a tin bath, in front of a coal fire, drinking tea and eating well-buttered crumpets, is an experience which few can have today'. *O tempora! O mores!*

The standard of living for most undergraduates was conditioned by their income and Geoffrey Fisher's was not large. In those pre-radio, pre-television days students had to provide their own amusements. Clubs proliferated. The Oxford of Geoffrey Fisher's day was in the main still clerically dominated. Compulsory chapel was the order of the day and undergraduates were required to attend one service, matins or evensong, on Sundays and in addition four services during the week. Yet on the whole politics interested them more than religion.

The national background of Geoffrey Fisher's five years at the University may be briefly summarised. In 1908 Asquith had succeeded the less flamboyant Campbell Bannerman, and a period of liberal legislation, long deferred, was set in motion. It is not surprising that on the crest of this wave Oxford itself became a sitting target for radical reformers. In a letter dated 14 February 1909, Geoffrey Fisher informed his family that 'the academic side of Oxford is very much disturbed at present by rumours of reformation to come. First our Chancellor, Lord Curzon, intends to introduce degrees for women and twelve-week terms. Then a report is issued by a committee of dons and labour leaders advocating and pointing the way for working men to come up to Oxford as undergraduates. *That* of course has roused great indignation amongst the useless people here who do nothing else but spend too much money in disreputable ways – *they* could not stand having to consort with working-men.'

We shall not be surprised that having arrived at Exeter Geoffrey Fisher threw himself into the life of the College with his usual enthusiasm, and that it was not long before he became President of the Junior Common Room. An injury to his collarbone made him decide to abandon rugby for the river. In this he followed the example of his brothers at Cambridge who all rowed with some distinction. It was perhaps a surprising choice in view of his meagre ten stones but in spite of this he ended up by being elected captain of boats and rowed in the trial eights. He describes himself as a 'neat oar', 'vigorous and energetic'. Undoubtedly Geoffrey took rowing seriously and on 14 February 1909 duly reported to his parents: '. . . a day or two ago I received a notification that I had been elected to the Leander Rowing Club, and today am appearing resplendent in a pink tie and scarf with a beautiful dark blue waistcoat and gilt buttons'.

To keep busy was, with Geoffrey Fisher, a life-long preoccupation. Of his university days he writes: 'My day is usually fully occupied by one thing or another – matters connected with the Church Union of which I am President, various societies, the river, social engagements – occasionally a little work, though that normally consists of the minimum – lectures and two essays a week for my history and philosophy dons.' This frank admission as to the paucity of his concentrated study hours seems to have become sufficiently serious for his dons to tell him that he must devote the next vacation exclusively to study. This intervention was effective, and back in Oxford his tutors were more or less satisfied with his progress though they seemed, however, to find 'a lack of subtlety' about him. He secured a first class in Moderations in 1908; a first class in Lit. Hum. in 1910; and a first class in Theology in 1911.

Though he could be flippant about the Chapel, this must not mislead us. For most of his residence at Exeter he was in the Chapel at 8 am which brought him into contact with the sub-Rector, Henderson, the Chaplain, Chappie Allen, and later with N. P. Williams, whom he used to help in the Sunday school especially laid on for the choir boys. Geoffrey's brilliant success in Greats did not seem to himself particularly significant. Obviously he had an extremely clear mind, but the more philosophical aspects of his studies did not basically appeal to him and he tended to make light of them. Certainly he lacked the curiosity which excites the quest for truth. Hence he shied away from branches of learning which seemed to have no immediate connection with practical day to day living. This is amusingly shown in his correspondence with his family in a memorandum dated 1 November 1909. 'My last letter contained the intelligence that I had discovered the difference between twoness and threeness: since then I have been illuminated by learning the real inward meaning of outside-of-otherness.' This is good fun but it suggests strongly that Geoffrey Fisher was not sensitive to what at least some philosophical questions are really about. However, the general discipline of Greats he appreciated and much enjoyed. It introduced him to ethical questions, to the main thrust of history and to an appreciation of a correct use of language.

Some of his teachers undoubtedly left an impression upon him as, for example, Bernard Henderson his tutor in Ancient History. Supremely, but surprisingly, N. P. Williams, a born eccentric, became a close personal friend. Geoffrey Fisher's sketch of this brilliant scholar, from which we quote briefly is interesting since it shows a sympathetic understanding of a man with whom, theologically, he had little in common. 'He was a very great scholar; he was a very shy, frightened man who crept about the College, and when you talked to him he kept his eyes almost shut. He had a queer way of speaking as though he was saying prunes and prisms all the time. He was a very distinct Anglo-Catholic.'

The religious atmosphere at Oxford during Geoffrey Fisher's under-graduate days was dominated by certain key figures some of whom co-operated to produce 'Foundations' in 1912 – an attempt to state Christian belief in terms of contemporary thought. Geoffrey Fisher was present in the University Church when Temple replied to the attack on his radicalism by the inimitable Ronnie Knox, with whom Geoffrey Fisher co-operated in promoting the aims of the Oxford University Church Union. Streeter was at the time a Fellow of Queen's College and was already researching into the New Testament synoptic problem. It was an exciting background for young undergraduates who com-bined academic interests with social concerns as pioneered in earlier days by F. D. Maurice, Westcott and Hort.

Geoffrey Fisher's reaction to the prevailing religious mood of the Oxford he knew is not without interest in relation to his later responsibilities. He was not impressed with the teaching in the theo-logical school, though he came out at the end with the inevitable First. His impatience with contemporary biblical scholarship he parodied as follows: 'One could see rival interpretations [by] critics who exploded evidence, or twisted it, or interpreted it to support their own views.' In contrast with this arid teaching was the lively, vigorous searching for truth by people like Streeter and William Temple and Ronnie Knox and many others. Geoffrey Fisher was not attracted to the Anglo-Catholics, the 'Spikes', and resisted the blandishments of Father McKay and Dr Stone of Pusey House who endeavoured to proselytise at his expense. On the other hand he warmed to J. R. Mott, later Chairman of the Committee which called together the famous Edinburgh Confer-ence in 1910, and Joe Oldham, who gave to the movement a world perspective. Geoffrey never played a prominent part in its life, or sought office, but he was greatly influenced by its conferences at Swanwick and Baslow. He was more drawn at the time to the Evangelicals, amongst whom Chavasse was a dominating figure; but their unilateral stress on personal conversion and 'emotional devotion to Christ as Saviour,' were alien to his practical temperament. Basically,

Geoffrey Fisher was never drawn to give his allegiance to particular movements within the Church of England – and to this principle he himself stuck. Geoffrey Fisher left Oxford at the end of the summer term in 1911, having been there just five years. His own summary of this not inconsiderable period in his life is revealing. 'It was a grand time but it did not make an impression on me that Oxford had made on so many people. I think the cause lay in the fact that it was only developing, stabilising, enriching the same attitude to life that I had already acquired before leaving Marlborough.' This is a surprising statement and suggests a degree of impatience with academic study, and the feeling that many of the lectures were remote from ordinary everyday experience. It shows, perhaps, that Geoffrey Fisher would not have made a technical scholar or a good academic.

It was people whom he recalled – they always interested him most – as he grew older, usually because of some idiosyncracy or quirk of character. Such, for example, was Tubby Clayton, with his immense store of knowledge 'about strange and outlandish things'.

A major event took place towards the end of his stay at Oxford, the departure of the family from the rectory at Higham, where Geoffrey had done most of his serious reading for his degree during the vacation. Now it was to cease to be Geoffrey's home. He has left in his own handwriting a somewhat nostalgic account of the last Christmas there when some twenty-four members of the family slept under its roof for the last time. 'Mother was in the seventh heaven. Father found it rather embarrassing when John tolled the dining room bell at intervals of half a minute.' The presence of a number of grandchildren added to the family atmosphere. Some seven months later the Rector retired to Leamington.

The village was given a farewell party at which a sumptuous tea was provided, Aunt Jenny's tartlets being a great success. In the evening 'Father' was presented with a writing desk and chair, 'Mother' with a folding tea table.

Finally Geoffrey and Edith, 'near to tears,' were left alone in the forsaken house. They had their last meal together in the 'Red Room'. During the course of it a faint 'miaow' emanated from the backstairs, and there emerged the family cat with her brood of six weeks old kittens. They were invited to share the meal! So, comments Geoffrey, 'the house was left, the key delivered to Sam, and Higham Rectory was no longer the abode of the Reverend H. Fisher.' It was the end of an age.

CHAPTER 3

Marlborough College and Headmaster of Repton

IT is not surprising that immediately after Geoffrey Fisher had graduated two Colleges approached him with offers of a lectureship as a prelude to his becoming a Chaplain-fellow but he was not tempted. He knew his own mind and maybe here his instinct was a sure one. Thus he wrote later: 'I did not want to have the kind of academic life which the College offered. I did not want to spend my time doing academic theology. I enjoyed it immensely but I knew quite well that to go on with academic theology would mean to go on asking questions to which there was no answer, and spending most of one's time correcting somebody else's answers, . . . so without hesitation I accepted Frank Fletcher's offer and I went back to Marlborough, after five years at Oxford, with delight.'

The choice may not seem imaginative but for him it was probably right.

The years which followed at Marlborough were happy, almost carefree, when compared with what he was to experience during the long stint as headmaster of Repton. He soon discovered that he liked teaching, even mathematics, though a little apprehensive lest he be 'found out'. He made no claim, quite the reverse, to being a first-rate classicist. However, teaching Euripides was for him 'pure joy', as also was 'the challenge of coping with the difficulties confronting the ordinary boy.' All sides of school life appealed to him, even to persuading the new music master, George Dyson, to write a tune to replace that of his predecessor for the end of term hymn: 'Sweet Saviour bless us e'er we go'. However, the Headmaster would not countenance such an unheard of innovation protesting: 'Oh, good heavens, no! Couldn't possibly do it. Break a tradition like this? Why, why, the boys would throw their hymn books at me!' Geoffrey Fisher also supported George Dyson, when he introduced a new tune for the greatly loved 'Welcome' and a near riot ensued.

Life doubtless presented some problems to the young schoolmaster and maybe the presence of members of staff who had been his own teachers was a slight embarrassment. Geoffrey Fisher was a life-long believer in the need for discipline of the right kind. He was not at Marlborough long before the test came when he was required to take charge of some 200 boys in the Upper School. Geoffrey Fisher entered the room only to find it littered with every variety of paper including a lavish display of toilet rolls. He realised that this was a trial of strength and he must act decisively or all would be lost. He peremptorily ordered the senior boys to pick up the paper. There was an agonising pause – but they obeyed and on the following day he kept them hard at work on some trivial ploy. Thus they learnt that on the whole it was better not to engage in conflict with him – such was his conclusion.

His three years at Marlborough were sufficiently encouraging for him to contemplate a permanent career in schoolmastering. As he put it he had 'from the beginning got the hang of the thing. I was absorbed in all my occupations which exhausted me to the limit of my desires and possibilities' – indeed so absorbed was he that he saw himself as without ambitions, entertaining a proper loyalty to Marlborough as 'the only school worth maintaining'. Everything seemed to be set fair for a long stay at the College. However, in 1914 William Temple, headmaster of Repton was nominated to the Rectory of St James's Piccadilly, from which church Dick Sheppard had launched his 'Life and Liberty Movement'. A colleague urged Geoffrey Fisher to apply for the post thus made vacant. 'To me,' he wrote years later, 'it was perfectly ludicrous. I had no idea of doing such a thing, nor had I any kind of idea that I knew how to be a headmaster.' But something must have stirred in him for he wrote to Frank Fletcher, his mentor, and to William Temple, seeking their advice. They both counselled him to make an application. Indeed the latter wrote cordially expressing the hope that Geoffrey would be his successor, and at the same time let it be known in the right circles that though only twenty-seven years of age he 'had the judgement of a man of forty!'

So an application was duly dispatched and Geoffrey Fisher found himself summoned to an interview at the Westminster Hotel situated close to the Abbey in Victoria Street – and now demolished. He had expected to be one of five but to his surprise discovered himself to be the only candidate. His impression was that the Governors were elderly, quite a number being 'already on sticks'. The interview was neither long nor exacting, being confined to a few questions. Did he agree with Dr Pears, the famous headmaster of Repton – and his future wife's grandfather – that mathematics were the foundation of character? Geoffrey, later so adept at impromptu argument, was at a loss for an instant reply, but was helped out by the kindness of the Governors. Later in the interview candour compelled Fisher on his own initiative to make it quite clear that he really wasn't a very good classicist. William Temple, who surprisingly was present throughout, came to his rescue remarking that, like himself, he supposed Geoffrey meant that he didn't know when to use the subjunctive in a conditional clause, at which interjection the Governing body dissolved into laughter.

It is difficult to imagine that the interview could have been conducted at so inconsequential a level as Fisher himself seems to suggest. What is probably true is that the Governors had already made up their minds and that only some disaster could have prevented Geoffrey's nomination.

So Geoffrey Fisher became Headmaster of Repton at the age of twenty-seven! On hearing the news he went to the rooms of a colleague at Marlborough where they relaxed and roared with laughter. 'It was utterly absurd.' Yet, unlike Temple, his predecessor, he had no difficulty or reservation in accepting the offer, 'since by nature,' he claimed, 'I don't like running away from anything.'

Geoffrey was destined to stay at Repton until 1932 – that is for some eighteen years. So long a period, inevitably formative of his character during early manhood, must receive fuller treatment than normally might be expected in the biography of an Archbishop. Geoffrey Fisher knew little of the school before he went there, though he could recall a cycling expedition with his brother through Ashby-de-la-Zouch to Repton village where in the church they found a tablet to a former Fisher, sometime Mayor of Derby.

The origins of Repton go back to 1557 when Sir John Port, Sheriff of Derbyshire and son of a well-known judge, left a bequest for the foundation of a charity school. For the sum of £37.10.0d there was purchased the famous Repton Priory, part of which, including the church, had been destroyed. In its early days its intake was socially mixed but in the nineteenth century it catered for the rising middle classes. Its greatest headmaster, another Arnold, was Steuart Adolphus Pears (1815–1875) who raised the number of pupils from 50 to 300 – and was the grandfather of Geoffrey Fisher's future wife, Rosamond.

So it was that Geoffrey Fisher took over a task difficult enough to daunt even the bravest. He was appointed in June 1914, war breaking out on 4 August before the school re-assembled for the Michaelmas term. This meant that he found himself short of masters, some six having immediately volunteered for the forces. Thus he had no option but to replace them with such temporary staff as he could muster, these being 'often hopeless disciplinarians and valueless in or out of school activities'. Hardly a boy was left in the school over the age of 18, some 60 of them having gone direct into the army. Apart from such practical and immediate problems created by the war there were nervous tensions and occasional depression among the boys engendered by the very fact of war. Canon Charles Smyth, recalling the effects of long years of conflict writes: 'For about half of my time at Repton we lived under the threatening shadow of war. During the winter of 1916–1917 the average expectation of life for a subaltern on the Western Front was estimated at three weeks; and I can well remember boys who had been thus arbitrarily called up at any stage of the school term, coming round the bedders on their last night at Repton and shaking hands with everyone, knowing as we also knew, that in the following term, at the voluntary intercession services in Chapel on Friday evening, we might hear their names read by the Boss in the O.R. casualty list for that week.' The impact of the War on the school may be seen in the earliest sermon which Geoffrey Fisher preached in Repton School Chapel after his appointment. It goes without saying that its language and general approach could not possibly have been used during the Second World conflict. 'The cause of this War is arrogance and, alas, we see the fruit that grows from it. The facts compel us to condemn our enemies of an arrogance that is unchristian and too often inhuman. They arrogate to themselves a superiority of intellectual power which justifies force as the handmaid to increase its dominion . . . we fight because we are fighting for God's cause against the devil's.'

England had been at war just seven weeks at the time that this address was delivered. Obviously the preacher did not envisage a long war though he recognised that there would be extensive casualties. The sermon was printed 'by request of the Prefects' and distributed in the bookshop.

The seemingly uncritical analysis of the causes lying behind the Great War strikes us today as naive in the extreme: but contemporaries did not see things this way. Geoffrey Fisher understood this war in the moral imperatives of black and white.

The specific problems caused by the war were not the only ones which confronted Geoffrey Fisher. William Temple left behind him a school in many ways disorganised, and a Headmaster's House – the Hall – characterised by a lack of discipline, though Canon Smyth probably goes too far in suggesting that one of Fisher's first tasks was the 'cleansing of the Augean Stables'. Of course any institution which had the good fortune to be presided over by William Temple could not but profit from this challenging experience; but it must be admitted that his two and a half years at Repton were by no means an unqualified success.

His personal misgivings as to whether he should have gone to Repton troubled him and may well have sapped his confidence. Referring to his brief stay at the School and conditions in his own House, 'the Hall', Temple's biographer writes: 'His own innocence and chastity were so exceptional that the sexual malpractices of schoolboys lay outside the general scheme of things which had his immediate sympathetic interest.' As Geoffrey Fisher put it, and maybe he had William Temple in mind: 'There's a good deal of ingenuity required for any schoolmaster or anybody who handles schoolboys.'

William Temple certainly recognised that his successor was cast in a different mould, and to David Somervell, a master at Repton, he commented that 'The Hall has had a fearful crop of failures,' but that he expected Fisher to be more successful than he was.

One other factor ought to be noted which did not make these things easier for Geoffrey Fisher during his first years at Repton – I mean his youth and obvious inexperience.

We turn now to Geoffrey Fisher's endeavours to deal with a lack of discipline thought by some to be sufficiently serious as to require drastic remedial action. It did not take Geoffrey long to decide that so far as homosexuality was concerned the Hall was 'very badly astray' and that 'some of the nicest boys at the top of the house were deeply in this trouble'. Today we recognise that when boys are subjected during a particular period of their lives to the somewhat unnatural conditions of single-sex dormitory sleeping, homosexual practices of varying degrees of seriousness can easily creep in, also that some homosexual relations can be loving and caring especially in young people.

1914, however, was a pre-Freudian world and Geoffrey Fisher, not surprisingly, shared a view common to an overwhelming proportion of his fellow headmasters. Hence he decided that 'there was no place in the life of the Hall or the School for homosexual practices. This was not a matter of less or more.' In pursuit of this objective he confesses to have been 'pretty ruthless' expelling two boys not yet quite seniors. These two expulsions led to 'terrible' interviews with their parents, one of whom, a soldier, couldn't accept that it was expedient his boy must go. The result of such extreme measures, Geoffrey Fisher claimed, was a transformation, and though there was 'dirty talk still, nobody would have dreamed of going any further than that'.

It was a basic conviction of Geoffrey Fisher's that no school – and not only a school – could function effectively without the right degree of discipline. However, he himself always denied being 'ferocious' or pre-occupied with this aspect of the School's life. Indeed discipline ought to be taken for granted and to arise naturally out of the general good sense and co-operative spirit of the members of the community as a whole. It was precisely this situation which Geoffrey Fisher believed came to obtain at Repton. To help in achieving this he drew up a book of rules, all very practical, the first of which was: 'Any breach of commonsense is a breach of these rules.' When asked who decided what was commonsense, the answer came back that 'he did and nobody else'.

In most schools at this time beatings were common practice and were administered by the headmaster, housemasters, prefects, even heads of studies. It is quite unfair, however, to regard Geoffrey Fisher as a devotee of the rod. Indeed he writes that during his last eight years at Repton no boy was submitted to a caning. Perhaps it ought to be added that William Temple, according to his biographer, was 'considered no mean adept with the rod, though not so expert as his predecessor'.

One of the difficulties confronting a headmaster, so Geoffrey Fisher confessed, was to maintain discipline in the form room for members of the staff who could not, unaided, secure it. One such at least existed at Repton, a German born in Hanover when it was still under the British crown. The tricks played upon him by the boys were endless even to introducing a sheep into the form room. Finally a *cri de coeur* came from the afflicted schoolmaster for the 'Boss' to come to his aid. But Geoffrey realised that, rather than resorting to punishment, it was a matter of gaining the malcontents' good will and their sympathy and this he succeeded in doing and the persecution ceased.

Geoffrey Fisher always contended that having once dealt firmly with the initial lack of discipline the maintenance of it was never subsequently a problem.

It is necessary at this point to say something about what came to be known as 'the Gollancz-Somervell row,' particularly since such a *contretemps* could not have developed except against the background of war and the increasing state of tension brought with it. The story is a remarkable one, certainly within the context of a public school and sheds a great deal of light on the characters of some of the main participants.

It all began when Geoffrey Fisher, desperately short of a good classics master, applied to an agency and Victor Gollancz, a subaltern in the army, was seconded to the School by the War Office. Here he met up with Somervell, some nine years his senior, a historian of considerable talent and passionately concerned with the world that he lived in. Gollancz, who – in Somervell's opinion – was 'absurdly clever, absurdly amusing, absurdly childish in many ways, absurdly idealistic in his outlook on life, and absurdly affectionate,' threw himself into his new environment with his accustomed enthusiasm. Indeed he waxed lyrical over cricket in the Paddock; and found both challenge and satisfaction in being, as he described it, 'a radical in a hotbed of Toryism'. Promoted to teach the Upper Sixth, he revelled in introducing the by no means unreceptive minds of the young into the philosophy and religion of ancient Greece. This inevitably led to political and sociological discussion on such contemporary issues as the views of the various political parties; the League of Nations; conscientious objection; and imperialism: – indeed the whole gamut of contemporary issues. There was of course some opposition and in company with Somervell, Gollancz waited on the Headmaster contending that it was their bounden duty to give these young Reptonians some idea of the background out of which the present 'ghastly struggle' had arisen. Fisher at once entirely agreed, asking only that he might have time to take a few more soundings from the teaching staff. Finally Gollancz and Somervell were given the 'All Clear'; and the civics class, as it was called, began early in 1917 and survived until the spring of 1918 when Gollancz left. Some 38 boys volunteered to join the class and all but six were accepted. Numbers soon grew. Encouraged by this response Gollancz asked permission to start a paper to be published by the civics class under the title *A Public School looks at the World* – later nicknamed 'Pubbers'. Geoffrey Fisher gave his permission and described the paper as 'a very remarkable production'. He was right! The intention was that each issue should start with a survey *inter alia* of the military situation – the Russian Revolution (here the bias was towards Kerensky); the Irish question; and the peace terms. In Gollancz's eyes, the viewpoint was 'prudent, middle of the road stuff.' Read today this claim is certainly true but not then against the background of the war. Nor did Gollancz commend himself by proclaiming that he was 'cultivating the boys at the expense of the masters'. For him it was a case of 'Bliss was it in that dawn to be alive, but to be young was very Heaven'. Shelleyan dreams of radical reform and the inaugurating of a brave new world – these fired Gollancz's imagination with visions of an England saved by schoolboys from poverty and war. Geoffrey Fisher now sent him a very pointed letter, the intention of which was 'to pull him up before it was too late'.

Relations between the Headmaster and Gollancz were not easy and causes for friction increased.

'Pubbers' meanwhile was going from strength to strength though exposed to increasing opposition from the reactionary members of the staff. Fisher was reluctant to declare himself against it, though he sometimes felt that he must intervene by correcting the slant of articles which he saw as strongly opposed to some of the policies of the British Government. But the volume of opposition, headed by two senior masters, was growing. Nerves were on edge as news came in, with depressing monotony, of Reptonians killed in the trenches. The internal divisions in the School even had repercussions in Repton village. For example, when a Zeppelin dropped a bomb on Burton, only five miles from Repton, and the School watched it slipping 'silver shining down the Trent valley' a member of the staff circulated the story that a colleague had been seen on the roof of his house signalling with a towel to guide the crew of the Zeppelin. This absurd rumour led to a demonstration by the villagers. To add fuel to the already smouldering fire another member of the staff, Angus, contrived to put the latest issue of 'Pubber' on display in Henderson's of Charing Cross Road, popularly known, through its association with left wing propaganda, as 'the bomb shop'. It had not been there long before the War Office was apprised of this disturbing piece of news, the informer adding, for good measure, that the School was a hotbed of pacifism. The authorities now geared themselves into action, and Geoffrey Fisher was given to understand that the War Office would cease to recognise the School's Officer Training Corps if this state of affairs were allowed to continue.

However, it was not only 'Pubber' which caused the Headmaster a growing concern. Behind 'Pubber' was the civics class and here he confessed to feeling in 'a terrible fix'. It would be easy, he admitted, to suppress the civics class, and indeed it was getting to a point when it was difficult not to suppress it. But on the other hand, to do that would be to extinguish what was still a demonstration of liberal thinking on great national questions.

But the pressure for him to act was mounting until most reluctantly he made his decision to bring the civics class to an end; also he wrote to the War Office asking what substance there was in the rumours that it contemplated withdrawing its grant from the Repton Officer Training Corps.

So at long last a sorely tried Headmaster had come to the conclusion that Gollancz must go and he intimated such in a letter, and confirmed it in another after a long personal interview in London. It only remained for him to inform the War Office that he had taken the matter into his own hands and had terminated Victor Gollancz's employment at the school.

Geoffrey Fisher, reflecting years later on this explosive controversy, admitted that he had been faced with a very real problem of immense difficulty and with strong arguments on both sides: on the one hand not to depress liberal attitudes, on the other not to outrage patriotic sentiment during a time of war.

Gollancz was understandably bitterly upset at leaving Repton, though he drew comfort from the innumerable letters he received from Old Reptonians paying enthusiastic tributes to the enlargement of their intellectual horizons which the civics class had brought to them. Understandably, being the man that he was, Gollancz remained critical of his old Headmaster whom he later delighted to refer to as his 'former employer'. He saw him as more concerned with the smooth running of the School than with challenging young people to think creatively and to engage in social comment. This is a superficial view, and reflects the difficulty which Gollancz understandably had at this time in being sensitive to those in situations unlike his own. Yet no-one admired the true worth of Victor Gollancz more than Geoffrey Fisher as his own testimony makes evident. 'He was a brilliant man . . . full of vitality, full of energy, though very sensitive, as though he lacked one skin, with all the best kind of idealism moving him in every single thing that he thought of.' It is indeed to Gollancz's credit that recalling this chapter of his life many years later his final assessment was: '. . . he gave us our chance, and few others would have done so. My major emotion, therefore, is one of gratitude. I am rather surprised about this.'

For every headmaster the quality of the teaching given in the classroom must constitute a high priority, and for this to be seen to be the case it is important for him at times to be in the form room himself. Geoffrey Fisher saw to it that he did a regular if limited stint, teaching Greek texts to the Upper Sixth which he enjoyed. Also he conducted Divinity for the Middle School as well as for the whole Sixth Form – some 80 or 90 boys – on two mornings a week. He admitted that numbers here were too large and on educational grounds ought to have been halved, but it was his only chance of getting into touch with every senior boy, a satisfying personal contact which he felt he must not forego. In his teaching he endeavoured to introduce a modern approach particularly in the breaking down of the material into more primitive sources.

As Headmaster it was, of course, the whole curriculum which he needed to take stock of. This meant consultation with heads of departments as well as with the staff more generally; it also meant keeping a sharp eye to see how it worked in practice. Here most of his own judgements were liberal and instinctive with a sound practical common sense. He himself, on his own admission, knew no science (nor was he competent in any modern language); yet he did recognise, as some headmasters at the time did not, that scientists must have equipment and that they needed longer periods for instruction than the normal three-quarters of an hour.

Geoffrey Fisher had not been many years at Repton when he became convinced that the whole time-table needed to be radically revised so as to incorporate into it modern approaches and ideas. Not all the members of the common room at first welcomed the project with any enthusiasm. Thus, wisely, the Headmaster called the staff together and after he had expounded the principles on which the new time-table was based they co-operated loyally.

Concerning the state of the school as a whole his own view was that in his middle period each department had a first-class man at the head; many scholarships were gained; and the intellectual life was 'very stimulating'. That he did in fact attract good teaching staff is in some measure borne out in the number who later became headmasters themselves.

One of Geoffrey Fisher's strengths – it could at times be a weakness – was a practical cast of mind which enabled him to concentrate on minutiae which can all too easily be ignored. A typical example was his re-naming of the boarding houses. There were in all nine of them, mostly designated after the present masters in charge. The result was that when old boys returned to the School they had to keep up with the changes of staff to identify their own house.

Another change effected during his reign, though the initiative came from elsewhere, was carried through only by his own enthusiasm.

This arose from an Old Reptonian, a prominent figure in Liverpool, coming up with the suggestion that the best possible way of memorializing Old Reptonians killed in the war would be to get the boys out of the Priory and to restore it sensitively, removing all traces of its immediate use. Geoffrey Fisher was immediately excited at the prospect though well aware that this proposed restoration presented many problems. Where, for example, were the present occupants of the Priory to go? However Gurney, formerly on the teaching staff, died leaving his house to the School. It seemed a God-given opportunity to implement the proposal but it still left one question unsolved. Would it be possible to move perhaps the most distinguished house with its remarkable housemaster Henry Vassal from its traditional home? Wisely Geoffrey Fisher bearded the lion in his den and he agreed happily and with alacrity. Indeed he was helpful throughout. The architect, Forsyth, was from London. The stone-mason was Wat Gaskin, whom Geoffrey Fisher described as 'a sprightly man – full of bucolic wisdom', who rallied the village in support of the project. Thus it was local workmen and carpenters who undertook the whole labour of the restoration of this eleventh century building and 'did it superbly'.

In any school it is, of course, the pupils who constitute the *raison d'être* of its very existence. Geoffrey Fisher recognised the need for a school to be a human institution in which the boys were happy, their minds quickened, their horizons widened. Such *desiderata* are not necessarily determined by the number of scholarships and academic awards. On the other hand this is not to assert for a single moment that learning as such is not important. Nor can a school be evaluated solely in terms of illustrious *alumni* who in their several ways left a name behind them. Perhaps the most sensitive appraisal, though not easily arrived at, is the impact which a school makes on its run of the mill pupils, that is those who win no particular awards and remain unknown except to their immediate circle. Perhaps we might call them the 'silent majority'.

It is, I think, when measured according to this latter yardstick, that Geoffrey Fisher would wish his achievements at Repton to be assessed. The evidence here can only finally rest on the testimony of those who came under his care and upon his own honest and restrained estimate. Of himself, he claimed, that his 'abiding interest' the whole time was in each boy and it was 'a delight' to try to get to know as many boys as he could. Thus he would make a point of stopping boys, asking who they were and getting as much information as he could from them. His chief satisfaction, he often said, was success in winning the confidence of the rather slow, shy, slightly reserved, or the eccentric boy, who just did not fit in to the ordinary pattern. Such boys were a challenge and a trustful relationship could only be established individually. With the more forthcoming and brighter boys he made contacts of a different kind. Thus he writes: 'They were easy to talk to if you were prepared to discuss anything with them without any kind of embarrassment, and that I was always ready to do. It meant endless argument and all the fun of the chase.' Canon Smyth, a member of the Hall, delighted to recall the 'Boss's' habit of coming round to see what books the boys were reading before lights out. He would perch on the bed and if he found them reading Dickens or Conrad or H. G. Wells or Masefield or even the *Loom of Youth* he would say 'Splendid! Hurray! Well done!' Randall Ellison, many years later, recalled an incident which, he felt, showed Geoffrey Fisher in a very human but unexpected situation. 'In my last summer at Repton (1922),' he writes, 'a very hot one, we were bathing in the swimming pool (no bathing pants were worn) when G. F. appeared, stripped off his clothes rather to our amazement and dived in, then splashed about with the rest of us!'

There can be no doubt that Geoffrey Fisher's years at Repton did in fact produce distinguished Old Boys as did most of the privileged public schools. Amongst these were two Ambassadors two poets which included Christopher Isherwood, an Air Marshal and two Generals, a church historian and a famous tennis player.

From such *alumni* Geoffrey Fisher drew the conclusion that under 'the free and friendly discipline, full of commonsense and intellectual stimulus, we did our job, producing able people and even more producing boys who were apparently quite ordinary and rather slow and rather shy and making something very good of them.' Every term, boys leaving School came one by one into the Headmaster's study to say goodbye, he himself – so he confesses – seeking for *le mot juste* fitting to send this particular boy on his way. He long remembered one such interview when in near despair he said: 'Well, I think you'll be able to stand up on your own feet all right.' Years later, when as a professional man of 'good standing' he and his former Headmaster met up again, the erstwhile pupil remarked: 'I was a very diffident boy, very frightened of everything, unsure of myself and unsure of what life would do for me ... I came down to say goodbye to you and you shook me by the hand and said: 'Well, you'll be able to stand on your own feet.' And that gave me a confidence which changed the course of my life.'

Geoffrey Fisher was one of a large number of clerical headmasters, four of whom preceded him as Archbishop of Canterbury. His ordination does not seem to have been preceded by agonising doubts or traumas. There was no question of Augustine's 'twice born'. It seemed natural, almost the inevitable thing for him to do. Following the example of his brother Leonard he spent a short time at Wells Theological College when Canon Parsons, later Bishop of Southwark and Hereford was Principal whom he describes as "shy, diffident, stand-offish until you really got to know him'. He was made a deacon by the Bishop of Salisbury in the Cathedral on 2 June 1912 and on the same day was licensed to officiate as an assistant chaplain at Marlborough. He was ordained as a priest on 18 March 1913. He himself regarded his being a Clerk in Holy Orders as central to the discharge of his office. 'For myself,' he writes, 'I have no doubt at all that I couldn't have done my job unless I had felt not only that I was Headmaster of the School in its general social and community life but was also a Headmaster of the religious side of that community life.'

These are significant words – though one may wonder how the Chaplain fared under the arrangement – and imply that he saw the Chapel as basic to the School and his own role within it. His concern was to ensure that the worship offered there in the Chapel was 'alert and alive and fruitful and joyful'. He admitted, realistically, that some of the boys got bored with it but as he comments: 'That doesn't worry me; I've never known anything good that I've enjoyed that hadn't its boring aspects as well.' Chapel was accepted as part of the normal day-to-day life of the School. When Geoffrey Fisher came to Repton the Chapel, if all the School were present, was crowded to the extent of being highly uncomfortable. Thus a new aisle was added. It did not take Geoffrey Fisher long before he came to the conclusion that the routine Chapel services were too much for the ordinary boy. He therefore decided, and believed that he was the first Headmaster to do so, that those who attended the early morning service on Sunday – the time of which he changed to 8.45 am – would be excused from Morning Prayer. However, if they opted for the latter, which lasted half an hour, they would still be required to attend the divinity hour. The result was that during his time, the early Communion service was well attended, and every now and again he conducted Saturday evening classes of preparation.

While he by no means exaggerated his own powers in the pulpit, he felt that, on the whole, the sermons he delivered in the Chapel engaged the boys' interest. Geoffrey Fisher admitted that though he preached regularly, he didn't greatly enjoy it. However, he set himself one rule which he tried to observe strictly, namely to speak intelligently from within his own personal experience. Indeed both Michael Ramsey and Charles Smyth assured him that his addresses were 'worth listening to' but, as he comments, they were probably in a minority. As to the compelling sermon he confessed that he had never converted anyone by his efforts in the pulpit. Some fifty of Geoffrey Fisher's sermons have survived. They show that the themes were usually practical and ethical, as for example, the Christian use of money; Sunday observance; gambling; and a host of other similar topics.

One event which happened while he was at Repton and which brought him happiness and fulfilment throughout life should now be mentioned. The reference is, of course, to his marrying Rosamond Forman whose father had been a housemaster at Repton, dying prematurely in 1905, and whose grandfather was the redoubtable Dr Steuart Adolphus Pears who did for Repton what Arnold did for Rugby. Their courtship in a school, leading to marriage, particularly when the 'wooer' happened to be the headmaster, was bound to attract interest. Here Canon Smyth can take up the story: 'The river had been frozen up for some days and one afternoon in the middle prep. we looked out of the window and observed the Boss, in a black trilby and black overcoat, walking gingerly with the aid of a stick, into the centre of the ice, followed, to our enchanted gaze, by his fiancée on skates. He stood there, a stocky little figure, occasionally rotating on his axis while she skated round him gracefully cutting circles in the ice.' This preliminary encounter, among many others, led to Geoffrey Fisher's marriage to Rosamond on 12 April 1917.

However, there were more excitements to come. The arrival of Henry, their first child, provoked a natural curiosity. Eric Maschwitz in his *No Chip on my Shoulder* relates that the 'Hall' organised a sweepstake, the gamblers having to forecast the sex of the baby, the date and time of arrival. At a penny a boy, this meant that success was rewarded by the princely sum of six shillings and eight pence, for a schoolboy in those pre-inflationary days, a sum not to be despised. Henry Fisher duly arrived on 20 January 1918 and the event was celebrated by a special supper with poached eggs, a great luxury in those days of war-time rationing. That night the Boss, against a background of hardly concealed emotion, conducted prayers as usual in the Hall. As he walked out through the green baize doors which led into the Headmaster's residence, he turned over his shoulder and said: 'I believe I have to congratulate the lucky winner!' Eric Maschwitz writes that this did a power of good in fostering the mutual relations of Geoffrey Fisher and the boys in his house.

With traditions of service behind her and possessing already family ties with Repton the young Mrs Fisher approached her new role with enthusiasm. Had she not married when she did, she would have gone as a missionary to Africa but she now found a vocation different but equally testing. Her husband's words, written long afterwards, consti-tute a just tribute: 'My wife, Rosamond, entered into the life of the

School in all its aspects as to the manner born! She identified herself with the interests of the masters' wives – and did much for the village community.'

It is clear from this account of Geoffrey Fisher's headmastership at Repton that he immersed himself totally in the immediate tasks. It was this priority which, in spite of promptings from Frank Fletcher, disinclined him to get involved in the business of the Headmasters' Conference of which he was a member; he enjoyed meeting other headmasters but was not interested in the 'high politics of education'. Things were to change later.

Undoubtedly to the end of his life Geoffrey Fisher remained interested in and attracted to young people. Often it was mutual. It is difficult to analyse or account for such an appeal though in the course of this biography we shall give numerous instances of it. Canon David Paton, who later passed some years in China, spent his school days in the Hall and conjures up a very vivid impression of the 'Boss'. It used to be Geoffrey Fisher's custom to spend Sunday afternoon doing the Torquemada crossword in *The Observer*, but unfortunately he could no longer bear J. L. Garvin's editorship, with the result that he refused to have the paper in his house. This left him with a problem which he solved by sharing *The Observer* with David Paton, a regular subscriber. The arrangement was that David cut out the crossword and gave it to his headmaster while the latter reimbursed the former with a shilling a term. This led to many conversations on the basis, as Paton explains, of 'commercial equality'. David Paton comments upon his 'quite extraordinary lack of personal side' and goes on: 'This combination of extreme competence and lack of self-concern made him extraordinarily easy and attractive.' In the sanatorium which Geoffrey Fisher visited daily, he once found Paton reading *The Lighter Side of School Life* by Ian Hay. Cheekily he told the Headmaster he was thus engaged in order to understand the staff. 'Oh,' Fisher retorted, 'if you want to know what we are really like I can do you better than that' and he sent him Bradby's *The Lanchester Tradition*.

Doubtless it was this wholehearted giving of himself, and in the process deliberately shutting out other interests, which made Geoffrey Fisher, in the fateful summer of 1932, know in his bones that he had shot his bolt at Repton and that it was necessary for the school and for himself that he find another stimulus in 'fresh woods and pastures new'. This was made plain when at this time 'an awful period' of measles and mastoid hit Repton. So severe was the attack that three boys were taken off to a nursing home in Birmingham and there died. Two others were operated on and only just came through. In earlier years he could have stood up to this ordeal but now he found the strain almost impossible to bear, as was seen in his sending boys to the sanatorium for treatment when it was really quite unnecessary. Accordingly, he unburdened himself to William Temple when the latter came to the school for a meeting of the Governing Body. 'What would you like to do?' he asked, to which Geoffrey replied 'Be a country parson.' William thought for a moment and suggested that he write to a bishop asking for a rural benefice. A somewhat crestfallen Geoffrey Fisher murmured, 'Thank you very much,' to which William Temple responded without a pause, 'The man I want to succeed you is John Christie.' Geoffrey Fisher would have been less than human had he taken this quite in his stride. Indeed he confessed later that he thought to himself: 'Upon my word! Not only does he think I've been here long enough – he's already chosen my successor. Certainly it's time I got out! I'd never felt more deflated than at that moment.'

On the morning of 6 May 1932 Geoffrey Fisher's curiosity was aroused when he saw lying on the hall table a letter with 'Prime Minister' printed in typescript on the outside of the envelope. It contained a formal notice from Ramsay MacDonald, Prime Minister, of his intention to submit to the Crown Geoffrey Fisher's name to succeed Dr H. L. Paget in the Bishopric of Chester. He had done this 'after the most careful consideration', convinced that he could not better serve the interest of the Church than by this nomination.

Rosamond Fisher long remembered that eventful day. 'It was difficult at the Hall,' she recalled, 'to be sure of an uninterrupted private conversation: children, boys, domestics, masters, any of whom might knock at the study door and, if we talked in the sitting-room, come in unannounced. So the only place where we felt sure of an uninterrupted opportunity to talk was the bathroom which Geoffrey shared.'

Geoffrey Fisher was now confronted with a decision which in itself could not have presented any serious difficulty. He knew he must accept and he wrote immediately to William Temple whose frank reply sketched in the background leading to the Prime Minister's offer. It also went a long way to account for the seeming insensitivity of their conversation at Repton. He had, in fact, already put his name before the Crown but could not at that stage anticipate the result. He very much wanted to see him in charge of a diocese, and of all those in the North, Chester would probably suit him best in its combination of town and country, and in its brands of churchmanship. His power of mastering detail without losing sight of the main object of the exercise would be indeed valuable, particularly since the diocese needed 'gearing up' and he could do that splendidly while keeping alive all the spiritual energy which Paget had released. On personal grounds, moreover, it would be delightful to have him in the Northern Province.

This was a powerful and graceful letter but Geoffrey Fisher needed no persuasion and does not seem to have waited for William Temple's reply before accepting. On 10 May the Prime Minister wrote saying that the King had approved the appointment and four days later it was made public.

Letters now flooded in to Repton. Frank Fletcher, then headmaster of Charterhouse and his mentor, confessed that he had thought for some years that he ought to move and that 'promotion' to quote his own words 'ought to involve *harder* work, something that would really extend him, and make a demand on the whole of him as he did not think his happy family at Repton could. For some years he had been giving to a Public School what was meant for the Church.' Two letters must have given Geoffrey Fisher unique personal satisfaction, one from his brother Leonard Fisher, Bishop of Natal in South Africa, who expressed his deep satisfaction that just when he was feeling that he had about finished his work at Repton this call had come to him. As a postscript to a subsequent letter, Mabel, Leonard's wife, struck a feminine and more domestic note: 'May I say that as Geoffrey Fisher was not at all one's pre-conceived idea of a typical headmaster, so "Geoffrey Chester" will never disguise himself as a "High Anglican Church Dignitary"; I am sure a Fisher could not do that.'

Dr Paget, the much-loved retiring Bishop of Chester, went to great pains to express his genuine thanks and pleasure at the news. '. . . my whole heart (for what it is worth!) will be with you,' he wrote. 'I am thankful that the future of a really dear Diocese is – under God – in your hands.' Geoffrey Fisher on his part had already anticipated this letter by inviting his predecessor to take part in his Consecration Service.

Geoffrey Fisher's joining the bench of Bishops inevitably attracted a number of episcopal letters. Perhaps one of them, which came from Hensley Henson, Bishop of Durham, in earlier years a radical theologian, bears minimal quotation: 'It is, indeed, in such ill times as these, hardly possible to offer any man an *unconditional* congratulation on his becoming a Bishop, for the normal difficulties of Episcopal duty have been greatly increased by the unhappy circumstances into which the Church and the Nation have come.'

There now began the protracted and, for Geoffrey Fisher, the painful process of leave-taking from Repton. Though convinced that the time had come for him to go, moving was a wrench. Not only had he been around the campus long years but a cluster of deep emotions centred upon it. He had found there his bride and his children were born there. Professionally, as well as personally, the School was his life. Never again could he expect to spend his days in so closely-knit a community. Perhaps the letters which poured in from Old Reptonians gave him pleasure but increased the pain. 'I can't overcome the selfish feeling' writes one 'that you belong to Repton and have been robbed from us. I am glad for your sake alone that we have been robbed.'

The usual presentations now followed one upon another – the pastoral staff from the boys; his pectoral cross from the staff, with a moving letter from the senior member, H. L. Hayward. There remained two occasions for formal farewells. The first took place in the Chapel to the boys when Geoffrey Fisher spoke with a deep but controlled emotion. He concluded with these words: 'If we have used our time here rightly we have found the best things that life can give us – friendship and loyalty, manifold activities not selfishly enjoyed but shared, the sense of obligation and duty, the exchange of mutual service, the bond of fellowship with others in a common life . . . But wherever we now go, we shall still find such things if we will seek them. Here it was hard to miss them: for they were made manifest in our common life, our ordered discipleship in the very building which speaks to us of such things.'

The second occasion was his address to parents on the annual Speech Day. Here he indulged a veritable orgy of sentiment, concluding with the words 'Being human we perhaps feel in some sense Repton belongs to us. We are almost angry at the thought that others unknown to us and without our leave will pass in and out of the Priory Church and Hall. But we comfort ourselves with the knowledge that on them too Repton will cast a spell and that they will in their turn delight to love and serve her.'

Rosamond Fisher confessed later that leaving Repton was the 'biggest wrench of her life'.

CHAPTER 4

Bishop of Chester

(i)

THE City of Chester founded (probably) by Scapula in AD 48, became an important outpost of the civilising Empire of Rome, and in the reign of the Saxon Athelstan a mint was established here, a significant sign of the city's importance. It is still in spite of the silting up of the Dee estuary in the fourteenth century no mean city.

Chester, hitherto *terra incognita*, was to Geoffrey Fisher for some seven years to become his home. There had been Bishops of Chester since Saxon times, the old Mercian Bishopric being variously designated as Lichfield and Coventry as well as Chester. The Diocese, as newly constituted by Henry VIII, comprised the County of Cheshire and large areas in Cumberland, Yorkshire and Westmorland, not to mention a few scattered parishes in Wales; but by 1880 it was more or less confined to the county of Cheshire.

During the course of its post-Reformation history only a few of Chester's Bishops can legitimately be described as distinguished national figures. The Diocese consisted of two Archdeaconries – Chester and Macclesfield – and thirteen rural Deaneries. The population of the county in 1933 was approximately three million and it was served by three hundred priests. The Cathedral Church, dedicated to Christ and the Blessed Virgin Mary, was until the Reformation the Church of a Benedictine Monastery.

Mrs Fisher drew up a full account of the first night they spent in Chester after Geoffrey's appointment and of their introduction to the retiring Bishop. She confesses to their being really terrified at the prospect ahead of them and remembered vividly getting out of the station and seeing a rather forbidding strange town ahead of them. The reality was to prove far otherwise. No one could have been more welcoming than the Pagets, though Mrs Fisher acknowledged that they were both 'a little bit out of their depth' when confronted with the ideas and conversation of Mrs Paget, a 'brilliant woman'. The Fishers went over the house which was really too small and they made tentative plans to adapt it to the needs of their large family of six sons.

Maybe the Fishers' initial reactions suggest that long years in the enclosed and protected community of a school made them a little apprehensive of the future. The fact was that going to Chester meant for Geoffrey Fisher a radical change in an accustomed pattern of life no matter how much he himself claimed that it entailed 'doing exactly the same thing in a rather different setting'. Perhaps he was to find that it was not quite so straightforward as this. A diocese is not so compact or self-contained as a school: and the incumbent of the thirties, secure in his freehold, enjoyed an independence which even the most entrenched housemaster might well envy. Also, while at Repton, Geoffrey never involved himself in public controversy, ecclesiastical politics, or with the Church's corporate life. The prolonged debates over the 1928 Prayer Book which aroused such interest, anger and emotion seem to have passed him by. As his forebears stuck to their village ministry unknown to the wider world so did Geoffrey Fisher bring a single-minded devotion to his duties as a schoolmaster. It is significant, in this context, that while William Temple found Repton a restriction and did not stick it long, Geoffrey Fisher found it for many years an absorbing fulfilment. Hence Fisher went to Chester almost as one unknown; a little suspect as a headmaster without parochial experience. Indeed one Chester incumbent in his parish magazine commented that he failed to see why he had been appointed, 'since he seemed to lack the particular qualities needed in a Bishop'. 'However,' he went on philosophically 'as they had prayed for the right man and this is what they had got, they must make the best of it.' The sequel was an evening call from a Manchester journalist asking whether this comment in any way affected his attitude to intercessory prayer! The prejudice against the Headmaster-Bishop died hard. The magazine *Truth*, in its edition of 25 May 1932, commented, somewhat acidly, on the 'surprise' appointment of a man who was better known as a dominie than as a divine. The new Bishop felt that the best way of dealing with these initial Diocesan misgivings was frankly to face up to them. Thus he took advantage, as Bishop-designate, of an invitation to write a letter in the August issue of the Diocesan Gazette. He admitted that he found writing such an article difficult since he was still deeply involved at Repton, and perhaps he would be wiser to emulate the diplomat who could say nothing in five different languages. He then turned disarmingly to his critics who were fearful at the prospect of having a Bishop without parochial experience, who was an unmitigated schoolmaster and who had had no time to take part in public affairs of Church or State. No one could be more anxious than he himself but in spite of this unease he truly felt that he ought to accept such a responsibility, confident that so long as he was found 'faithful' he would be given grace to discharge it. Some reassuring words he could, however, say: 'Chester,' he wrote, 'is in the main a rural Diocese . . . I was born in a country rectory and spent the first twenty years of my life in it: at the age of twelve I was (quite unjustifiably) teaching in the village Sunday School children as old as myself! And for the last eighteen years I have lived in a country village. The spectator does see something of the game.' One promise he was ready to make, namely that he would gladly receive instruction, counsel and advice from any who were good enough to give it him; 'but if his own assets were slender, he brought with him seven stronger ones. Mrs Fisher, already President of the Mothers' Union in the Diocese of Derby, and his six small sons.'

On 21 September 1932, Geoffrey Fisher was consecrated Bishop in the glorious Cathedral Church of York Minster and a special train was laid on by the indefatigable Dean Bennett to transport some three hundred people from Chester and Birkenhead to the Cathedral. Two hundred friends, many of them Masters and Old Reptonians, made the journey as well as some fourteen members of the Episcopate. The Dean and Chapter of Chester were, of course, there in force. Dr Paget took part in the laying on of hands, a somewhat unusual procedure but indicative of the goodwill which the new Bishop consistently showed to his predecessor. The city was full of sunshine by the time the Service of Consecration took place in the nave. William Temple wore his cope and mitre and Sir Edward Bairstow, the Minster's organist and master of the choristers, conducted the choir in a performance of his introit 'Jesu the very thought of Thee'.

The preacher was Geoffrey Fisher's eccentric friend from Oxford days, the studious N.P. Williams, now Lady Margaret Professor of Divinity. The choice was due to personal ties rather than to affinity of theological outlook. His sermon was an odd performance and read today makes one wonder what impression it could possibly have made on those in the Minster. There were lavish quotations, *inter alia*, from the Venerable Bede, the Elizabethan poet Shirley and Shelley's *Adonais*. 'It is difficult,' he claimed, 'to imagine a more searching education in the art of Government than is provided by the headship of a famous school, involving as it does the control of high-spirited adolescents and the presidency over colleagues of strong will and brilliant attainments.'

When day was done, Geoffrey Fisher accompanied the party from the Diocese on its homeward journey which gave him his first direct contact with the Church people of Chester. This, coupled with dinner provided by The London Midland and Scottish Railway for half a crown added to the conviviality of a truly memorable day.

Having been consecrated a Bishop, it was now necessary for Geoffrey Fisher to be enthroned in his own Cathedral. This took place on Michaelmas Day 1932 at a service which owed much to the imaginative planning of Dean Bennett. City and County, together with the Diocese, joined in offering a warm welcome. Following custom the Bishop himself was the preacher which provided a unique opportunity for Geoffrey Fisher to introduce himself to the vast congregation which had assembled to greet him. He was himself greatly moved and confessed, years later, that he would never forget the sight of the Cathedral as he entered through the west door. In the course of his address he referred particularly to members of other Churches 'not of our communion' who were yet, as he put it, 'fellow workers with us in this portion of the Catholic Church of Christ;' also he paid tribute to the Church people of the Diocese and to the civic authorities, not least to the Mayor. He concluded: 'Your presence is a courteous act for which I thank you. I trust and believe it is something more; and it also bears witness to the real community of interest and purpose between the religious and civic life of the people.'

There yet remained what the new Bishop regarded as his third introduction to the Diocese. This was at the Diocesan Conference held on 12 October which was, of course, more specifically directed to committed members of the Church of England. In the morning session, with occasional flashes of humour, Geoffrey Fisher outlined what he understood as the Church's duty and function, in the fulfilment of which task each one of those present had his specific part to play.

A Bishop is in the nature of the case no solitary figure. He must work with and through others. The three clergymen with whom Geoffrey Fisher was necessarily brought into close relationship were Selwyn Macaulay Bennett, Dean of the Cathedral; Paige-Cox, Archdeacon of Chester; and Armitstead, Archdeacon of Macclesfield.

Bennett was by any showing a remarkable man and, to use the cryptic phrase of the new Bishop when summarising his achievements, a Dean who had 'freed the Cathedral'. On his arrival in Chester, some twelve years earlier, he was shocked to discover that there were people living under the very shadow of the Cathedral who had never darkened its doors. To them it was a remote place and irrelevant to their daily lives. Bennett not only made the Cathedral a centre of Diocesan life but he did something even more important and far more difficult, he made it 'lovable'. 'Only a visit to Chester Cathedral,' so a *Times* correspondent wrote, 'can properly convey the unusual impression of a Cathedral that is in use and active from end to end.'

No one appreciated all that Bennett had done more than Geoffrey Fisher. This was particularly important since relationships between Bishops and their Deans are by no means always harmonious. Everything depends on the character, and the general approach of the two persons concerned.

Fisher and Bennett were very different characters but they understood one another, with the result that their relations, with a little give and take on both sides, were excellent. The Dean, in his Bishop's eyes, was 'a proper high churchman' while he himself, he confessed, 'positively wasn't'. Yet the Bishop appreciated the Dean's solid work and was happy to indulge an amused tolerance, even when whiffs of incense were gently wafted throughout the building from a remote chapel where Holy Communion was being celebrated with 'all the high jinks that you could imagine'. In one respect, and in one respect only, Geoffrey Fisher proved a disappointment to the Dean – he was not a daily communicant. He celebrated communion in the Cathedral every Sunday morning when at home but apart from this he said his early morning prayers in the palace. Yet despite such differences Bishop and Dean worked together in complete harmony throughout. When Bennett resigned in the summer of 1937 the Bishop was foremost in voicing the feeling of the Diocese for one whose conspicuous service lay in reviving here in Chester 'the pure significance of a Cathedral as a spiritual home'. The Bishop took the initiative in securing for Dean Bennett from the Archbishop of Canterbury a Lambeth Doctorate of Divinity.

The two other ecclesiastics with whom the Bishop necessarily had close personal contacts were the Archdeacons of Macclesfield and Chester. Not long before Geoffrey's arrival, Archdeacon Thorpe, an evangelical of the most conservative kind – an immense 'fighter' – died at a ripe old age and was followed at Macclesfield by Armitstead, Vicar of Sandbach, and a member of a long-established county family. Fisher describes him as one of those 'good, honest, faithful Christians who know how to get on with everybody'. The effect of this change was to bring to an end the former alliance between Thorpe and Paige-Cox, the latter having been Archdeacon of Chester since 1914. However, in 1934 Paige-Cox died after a long illness, the Bishop paying at the funeral service a well-earned tribute to his fifty years of devoted service at the Cathedral. Geoffrey Fisher always did these eulogies well, realising how important they were in the life of a local Church. Paige-Cox's successor was Bishop Tubbs who as assistant Bishop was already familiar with the Diocese and was nominated Dean of the Cathedral. In 1937 Bishop Fisher appointed as his successor in the Archdeaconry the Reverend R. H. Burne, who had considerable experience overseas in Singapore; also as Principal of Knutsford Training College and later as Warden of Hawarden.

So far as letters between the Bishop and members of the Cathedral Chapter are concerned none of any substance seem to have survived. However, as Geoffrey Fisher reflected in retirement on these, by then distant days, two Canons emerged from the mists of time and came vividly before him. One Newbolt, son of a former Canon of St Paul's Cathedral, was a scholar who had just enough eccentricity to attract attention. Strict and meticulous in his devotions it was said of him that if any liturgical omission should occur at Evensong he would immediately on arriving home complete the Office. When leaving a cinema which was formerly a place of worship, he was once seen bowing reverently to the screen! The other Canon was Simpson, an advanced high churchman and also son of a former Canon of St Paul's Cathedral who went off to become Dean of Peterborough.

By and large the Dean, Archdeacon and Canons of Chester, given the vagaries of human nature, managed to work well together, with the Bishop in the background as an eirenic, non-interfering ingredient. It is, perhaps, not without significance that whenever in his Diocesan Letter the Bishop made reference to his preaching in the Cathedral at a special service he was always careful to point out that he did so at 'the request of the Dean'.

An important person in the diocesan structure is the Rural Dean, the voice and representative in the locality of the parish priest both in relation to the Archdeacon and the Bishop. Geoffrey Fisher felt himself fortunate in having inherited 'a quite splendid body of such people'. But as time went on, some left the Diocese and others were anxious to lay down their burdens. After discussion with them he decided that the office should be held for a fixed period of six years. Not least of the benefits of this innovation was the increasing number of clergy who had behind them the invaluable experience which this office brought with it. The Bishop also saw clearly – others may have seen this but been too timid to act – that those alone should be selected who were prepared to discharge this important responsibility seriously rather than regard it as a position of dignity and honour, a reward for services rendered. Difficulties in churchmanship which cut deeply in the thirties did not, fortunately, disrupt overmuch diocesan life in Chester. Geoffrey Fisher always regarded himself as a central churchman, committed to the broad sweep of Anglican doctrine and worship but wedded to no particular party. In this he was doubtless at one with the vast majority of the clergy of the Church of England and it helped him considerably in his first diocese. Fortunately, therefore, churchmanship in the diocese was not a seriously divisive factor. Inevitably, however, though the number was small, there were those, to quote the Bishop's words, who went 'beyond the limit at either end'. Fortunately 'they were not particularly approved of and did not throw their weight about too much.' In respect of High Churchmen, some of whom had been brought into the diocese by Dr Paget, Geoffrey Fisher claimed that he had not criticised or cold-shouldered them, 'nor looked for trouble'. But sometimes complaints came in from aggrieved parishioners. In one case, for example, a congregation was upset by their parish priest insisting on standing for the confession during the service of Holy Communion. Asked by the Bishop to account for this irregularity he was unable to provide a 'proper explanation', thereby evoking a forthright episcopal admonition. The Bishop then expressed his concern that when the people were making their confession to Almighty God, their father and friend should not be willing to kneel with them.

The incumbent, however, proved adamant and there the Bishop wisely left the matter declining any further recrimination.

A further example more directly related to ecclesiastical loyalties and partisanship may be quoted. Very close to the square in which the Bishop lived, there was an advanced High Churchman, so advanced that not once during the Bishop's seven years in the Diocese did he ever ask him to visit his church. Once again, Geoffrey Fisher exercised a commendable restraint. 'I thought it wise,' he commented, 'not to ask myself.' In general where liturgical matters were concerned, Geoffrey Fisher tended to think that in certain areas the solution was to be found in good manners. Such he felt was the case in the vestments appropriate to a Bishop as he went about his Diocese – a subject which was of concern to him years later in connection with the revision of Canon Law. Some Bishops tried to solve the problem by following the Pauline injunction of being 'all things to all men' and adjusting their attire to what they thought were the wishes of the parishes. Geoffrey Fisher, however, did not believe this to be the solution and, after considering the matter soon after he got to Chester, he decided to wear the same 'dress' everywhere in the diocese, no matter what be the churchmanship of the parish he was visiting. But what should this dress be? Here he finally settled for a cope and was gratified to find that both schools of churchmanship thought this compromise reasonable and the attire 'comely'. A cope also had the advantage for the more historically minded of being mentioned in the 1604 Canons as an appropriate garment.

There were occasions when churchmanship meant that Dr Fisher must tread warily. Such was the case when in the second year of his Episcopate there was due to be celebrated the centenary of John Keble's famous Assize Sermon preached in Oxford on 14 July 1833, and which contributed to the birth of the Oxford Movement. It was a commemoration, the Bishop realised, which would be viewed by his clergy with mixed feelings and varying degrees of enthusiasm or lack of it. Wisely he consulted his Rural Deans in the preceding November, and as a result wrote a letter which came up for discussion at each Decanal Chapter. In this he made it quite clear that each parish had complete freedom to decide what it wished to do. Some, in practice, worked through the Deaneries and laid on ambitious programmes of lectures with a special centenary service; others held their own parochial celebrations; some simply ignored it.

As the day of the commemoration approached, the Bishop stated frankly his own views which he summarised as follows in the June number of the Diocesan Gazette. Most would acknowledge some debt to the Movement, greater or less, 'in the quickening of the corporate life and conscience and witness of the Church'. This did not mean 'endorsing every later development which claims to be a consequence of the Movement'. On the actual day of the anniversary the Bishop celebrated at a Choral Eucharist in the Cathedral and preached at Evensong along the lines of his article in the Gazette. Afterwards the Bishop and Mrs Fisher entertained some five hundred guests in the Refectory and Undercroft of the Cathedral.

From the moment of his arrival at Chester, Geoffrey Fisher recognised the need to get to know that part of the diocese, remote from the Cathedral city, where nearly a million people 'lived and moved and had their being'. Within a matter of a few weeks he had visited Stockport, Wallasey and West Kirby at one end of the Diocese and Crewe and Macclesfield at the other, all this in connection with the 'Merseyside Crusade'. In these industrial areas of the Diocese he was now brought face to face with desperate poverty and inhuman social conditions such as, in his sheltered life, he had not hitherto experienced. What struck him most on his initial visit, apart from the remarkable friendliness of the people, was the co-operative relationship which existed between the Church and civic authorities, a relationship which he always did his best to encourage. Particularly was this the case when it came to doing something about the sad plight of the unemployed which distressed him greatly. He was thus painfully made aware that the Church could not remain indifferent to this human tragedy and in his December Diocesan Letter (1933) he made the point forcefully. 'I am sure that our first duty is to show ourselves anxious and ready to help, to get into personal touch with them, and to discuss with them ways and means by which help may be given.'

The Merseyside Crusade which took place in the autumn of 1933, the planning of which had been in process long before the Bishop arrived on the Chester scene, was not essentially a parochial mission as normally understood; but rather, to quote Geoffrey Fisher's own words, 'a collective effort by the Church to plunge into the great industrial areas on both sides of the Mersey and there proclaim the Gospel of Christ boldly to the thousands to whom Christ means nothing and the Church, if it means anything, is utterly misunderstood.'

As a prelude to the Mission, William Temple, Archbishop of York, held a mass meeting in Birkenhead on 17 November 1932 and a similar gathering was brought together in Wallasey's Town Hall. Right from the start Geoffrey Fisher gave the Mission his full and enthusiastic support, unfamiliar as he was with such evangelistic crusades. 'The Church exists to attack,' he wrote, 'and here it is attacking on a large scale one of the biggest of its problems.'

The Mission proper began on 22 September 1933 when the Crusaders were commissioned in St Paul's Church, Birkenhead, this being followed by a procession of witness through the streets of the city. It was certainly an impressive occasion in which there walked together through crowds of silent and wondering men and women, parish choirs, clergy, church councils, numerous lay people, reinforced by Crusaders from various parts of the country. As to himself, Geoffrey Fisher wrote frankly: 'Nothing could have been more remote than my experience up to date as a boy at a Public School, Oxford and then at Repton. When at Oxford I used to go to the Oxford and Bermondsey Mission, as it was then called down in Bermondsey and that was my only touch with the poorer side of industrial life, but that was very little to go on.' He admitted that it was with some trepidation that he committed himself wholly to the Crusade – but commit himself he most certainly did. One great asset Geoffrey Fisher had which compensated for his obvious lack of experience together with his middle-class background. This was a genuine and friendly concern for his fellow human beings whoever they might happen to be – and this went a long way. As to how successfully he made effective personal relations during this Mission, he himself remained doubtful. Reflecting years later on these crusades he was content to express the hope that at least he 'did no harm,' even if, as he suspected, he had 'probably been not more than just adequate'.

It is never easy to estimate the precise effect of such Missions in the long term even if we include the moral boost which they give to those who undertake them. Archbishop Davidson and Bishop Hensley Henson were never enamoured of such enterprises, certainly not at the national level. Geoffrey Fisher gave an interim assessment, while the excitement still ran high. He was pleased that the response of the congregations in Birkenhead and Wallasey showed they accepted 'that it was their Mission and that the Crusaders were active on their behalf'. Also he was impressed with the way in which, night after night, the Crusaders did not primarily appeal to emotional sentiment, but to a reasoned account of Christian faith, rooted in the Incarnation, the Cross and the Resurrection. The Bishop felt that such an appeal did make an impact.

The Bishop, however, believed, with his customary practical approach, that the Crusade could not be left high and dry with only 'mutual congratulations'. It must be followed up and though the main burden involved in doing this must fall on the parishes it was yet necessary to recruit a more highly specialised and trained personnel to prompt initiatives and to give continuing support. The Bishop acted swiftly and began by appointing such a full time trained person.

Geoffrey Fisher tackled in general his new Episcopal duties at Chester with an immediate burst of energy. Indeed the novelty of it all to an ex-schoolmaster, encouraged him to crowd into the minimum amount of time the maximum amount of effort. So much was this the case that by August 1933 he confessed that never before had he so looked forward to his summer holiday – and no wonder! In his first ten months he had driven himself over more than six thousand miles of Cheshire roads; held over one hundred confirmations; instituted some twenty incumbents; conducted four ordinations; and visited over one hundred churches. The result was that he had reluctantly to confess that his 'output' at such a level was excessive and that he could not go on at that rate, since it meant that he had neither time nor energy to spare for work that must be done in his study in relation to wider Diocesan problems. Hence he declared his intention of reducing to seventy the number of centres where he would hold confirmations. What was obviously needed, in line with most dioceses, was the provision of an assistant Bishop, and this, as we have seen, Geoffrey Fisher secured in the summer of 1934 in Bishop Tubbs who, for domestic reasons, had retired to Britain after giving thirty years' service to the Church in India and Burma. Fortunately he was by no means a spent force and the choice was excellent.

A great deal of the work of a Bishop must appear to be of a somewhat routine character and in this respect when all goes smoothly there is little to tell. Such were Confirmations and Institutions when Geoffrey Fisher was seen at his best particularly in giving to each occasion a unique personal flavour. He lingered long; he spoke easily to all and sundry with a genuine warmth; he was witty, often exuberant. In what must necessarily be a brief encounter he always came alive and usually left behind him a vivid and unforgettable impression.

In October 1935 Geoffrey Fisher held his first triennial visitation of the Diocese which he directed to members of Parish Church Councils. Basically his concern was to encourage them to see their responsibilities as important and essential if the Church were to be faithful to its task. Thus he went out of his way to be practical and down to earth; and in preparation for this occasion he sent out a questionnaire to 203 clergy asking in particular how they viewed their PCCs. The Archbishop began his 'Charge' with a brief historical introduction as to how visitations originated and then turned to the claims and challenges of today. The PCC existed as a kind of General Headquarters to promote, in co-operation with the clergy, the basic work of the Church in its worship, teaching and witness to Christ, also to maintain the 'plant' and to provide the finance. As to the last he went into considerable detail but was clear and concise. Geoffrey Fisher was born in a rectory and was thus made vividly aware of the significance and, too often, the plight of the parish clergy. At his Diocesan Conference in May 1936 he observed that since the previous September he had instituted twenty-seven clergy into livings. This made him painfully aware that there were not a few clergy who might feel disappointed and even distressed that in this change-round they had not 'found a place'. Perhaps it would help them to know that he shared their anxiety and was eager to help them. Maybe, he hopefully commented, a 'better system of appointment will emerge.'

Geoffrey Fisher was fortunate in that he had not been at Chester long before a *casus belli* arose which enabled him, thus early, to identify himself with the city and diocese in a matter of urgent concern to them both.

In January 1933 it was suddenly announced by the Board of Supervisors, which looked after the interests of Church Training Colleges, that three such institutions were to cease to function for three years – Lincoln, Fishponds in Bristol and Chester. The closure of the last of these three would affect Manchester, Liverpool and Blackburn from which dioceses many students were recruited. Not surprisingly the unexpected news aroused great dismay and indeed indignation. The College enjoyed a distinguished history going back a hundred years; it held an important place in the life of the city and more widely in the Church of England; and, not surprisingly, it had a large body of near fanatical old students ready to do battle. On hearing the news, the College Council determined to resist the proposal by every means open to it and to do so in co-operation with the other Governing Bodies equally threatened. Therefore it sent deputations to the Boards of Education and made representations to the Archbishops – but all to no avail. The answer was unequivocal, simply that financial exigencies had made the closure inevitable. As a last resort Canon Thomas, Principal of the College, and others concerned for its future, not unnaturally turned for help to their new bishop. It was clear that he could not ignore so urgent and domestic an appeal and equally clear that he must know the facts. Thus with his accustomed efficiency he investigated the problem 'in depth', and publicised the result in the Diocesan Gazette.

The Board of Education, he explained, would lose some £70,000 annual income as a result of an enforced reduction in the number of students. In his (the Bishop's) opinion alternative methods of dealing with the problem should have been explored by the Board of Supervisors and the three Colleges consulted throughout rather than receive the news as a bolt from the blue.

However, Canon Thomas, the Principal, determined not to take this matter lying down, knowing that the College could muster vociferous support in the Church Assembly and elsewhere. In this critical situation and at the last hour he called on the Bishop and told him in no uncertain terms: 'The College must not be shut and it is up to you to save it.'

Geoffrey Fisher realised that he could not decline this challenge, though he admitted frankly that he was little acquainted with the College. However Geoffrey Fisher did his customary homework, visiting the Church Assembly office; entering into discussions with its personnel, and enquiring extensively as to its finances. Figures, he boasted, were always his strong point. So the long awaited day for the debate (Thursday 9 February) came and on the morning Canon Thomas felt that the Bishop might like to know that the first lesson at Matins from Jeremiah contained the words: 'as the partridge sitteth on eggs and hatcheth them not . . .'. Here, surely, was there not an obvious reference to Dr Partridge, Chairman of the Board of Supervisors, who was known to many as 'the Napoleon of Church House?'

The debate began quietly with that conscientious Christian layman, Earl Grey, proposing that the interim report of the Central Board of Finance be received which, if passed, would have the effect of approving the temporary closure of the three training colleges. His arguments in support of this were realistically powerful.

It was now up to Geoffrey Fisher to measure up to the requirements of the brief which Canon Thomas had entrusted to him. It was the first occasion on which he had participated significantly in a debate of this importance in the Church Assembly.

The closures, he began, undoubtedly weakened the educational witness of the Church, particularly in the case of Chester which was a college serving four local dioceses. The question had, therefore, to be faced up to: were such closures necessary on financial grounds? He did not believe that they were and for the following reason. The money involved was £70,000 and this could be found since the Church Assembly had recently voted exactly that sum, not as yet spent, on extensive works of improvements. 'What was more unfair', he asked, 'to deprive certain colleges for the time being of these amenities or to rob three Colleges of their very life and existence?' If there were to be closures, it was imperative that everyone should recognise the equity of the choices. This was certainly not yet the case.

It was a powerfully persuasive speech even if it did not really go to the heart of the financial problems involved. As the Bishop brought his speech to a conclusion William Temple whispered to him, 'You've done it' – and he had!

In Chester the Bishop's decisive intervention in the debate was received with great satisfaction and his stock correspondingly rose. Dean Bennett, newly recovered from a serious illness, wrote in the Gazette that though many had contributed to this result it was 'the very able speech of our own Bishop that carried the day and we shall all feel proud that it was so'. The Bishop must have been gratified with the tributes he received but he was clearly uneasy lest the Chester reprieve should lead to a complacent and inactive optimism. He therefore proceeded to put the matter into a wide perspective in an article published in the March issue of the Gazette. The points that he now made in the article may be listed as follows:

(1)   The Board of Supervisors were doing a first class piece of work on behalf of the Church Training Colleges particularly in persuading the Board of Education to be patient while improvements were slowly being made in church school buildings.

(2)   The provision of the money necessary to keep the three colleges open for a limited period must mean that repair work needing to be done would have to be postponed, an expedient which could not be more than temporary.

(3)   'The mistake,' he commented of the Board of Supervisors, 'was that they assumed too readily that this was the only practical policy and that it would appear so to others. But they did not consult as they ought to have done the Governing Bodies of the Colleges for closure.'

(4)   The Board had undoubtedly now bought time and it was up to the Church Assembly to arrive at an overall policy such as best served the interest of the whole Church and make her contribution to Christian education the more effective.

Geoffrey Fisher certainly added to his popularity in church circles by his seemingly decisive intervention on behalf of the Chester Training College – but he was not really proud of it.

(ii)

As a headmaster of many years standing, Geoffrey Fisher could not be uninterested in national education though his direct experience of the maintained sector ended when he left Higham Village School at the age of eight! As Bishop of Chester he was now brought into close contact with the Church Schools in his diocese. For him this was a significant encounter since it was usually the responsibilities which necessarily arose out of his work which kindled his interest and spurred him on to activity. He believed firmly – it was rooted in the tradition of his family – that the Church must retain a stake in the national educational system as it had done in the independent sector. This meant, in practice, keeping open the Church Schools; making them efficient; and using to the full the opportunities which generous Governments provided for the Church under successive Acts of Parliament. One such opportunity came with the Education Act of 1936 which the Bishop saw as a challenge to the Church of England. Under its terms the school-leaving age was raised to fifteen, a step forward of which he 'highly approved'. The real problem for the Church authorities, as might be expected, arose out of the increase in the number of pupils, due to such recent legislation, with the consequent need to raise a vast amount of additional annual revenue. Equally demanding in this respect was the provision in the Act to set up senior schools for those over eleven years of age, though here the Act generously eased the burden upon the Church by offering a subsidy of seventy-five per cent of the cost on every new building. The Bishop was convinced that this magnanimous treatment must be responded to by the Church with alacrity and energy, since if this opportunity were let slip it might never return and the Church be progressively ousted from the field of national education.

The Bishop certainly sustained his concern and when in 1937 he launched a Diocesan Appeal for one hundred thousand pounds – a vast sum in those days – he saw to it that provision for senior schools was one of its three main objects and the case for this he spelt out in detail.

As Bishop of the Diocese Geoffrey Fisher was also brought into contact with that time-honoured institution – the Sunday School, but the fact that he was an enthusiastic supporter both of the existence and continuance of this nineteenth-century innovation did not prevent his recognising the need to secure greater efficiency in its operation. Thus he wrote in his Diocesan Letter of October 1934: 'If, as we must most earnestly desire, the children are to be firmly rooted in the faith and fear of the Lord, they must learn their faith in the worship of the Church and in the teaching of the Sunday School.' Everything depended on the quality of the instruction given by the teachers and if this were to be upgraded the clergy must play their part in bringing it about. Of late there certainly had been great improvements in the techniques of Sunday School teaching.

One of the inherent difficulties in endeavouring to raise the level of teaching was the fact that if sights were set too high many deserving but somewhat inadequate teachers might feel that they just could not make the grade. This was the danger of a too rigorous introduction of the new school certificate drawn up in 1935 which the Bishop was anxious to commend. It was with great satisfaction that the Bishop announced that by November 1935 over one hundred teachers had registered for courses of study.

There was another area of diocesan life, educational in its broadest context, which commanded the Bishop's interest and where he could legitimately claim long experience though within a privileged class of the nation's youth. In December 1934 he called together a conference of responsible young people to discuss whether there was a need to increase the number of youth councils in the diocese, there being already two in existence. The result was that three further councils were set up and another conference of young people met in the following May. From this there came, in April 1936, the most ambitious Youth Conference yet held in the Chester Training College.

Over one hundred, between the ages of eighteen and thirty, attended and every Deanery but two was represented. The Bishop, who was present throughout, found the whole spirit of it most inspiring and marked not only by great 'friendliness' but also by 'sincerity of purpose and a vital sense of devotion to our Lord and to His Service'. Geoffrey Fisher was in fact concerned to do two things – to encourage spontaneous development yet at the same time to give it a minimal yet recognisable structure within the life of the Diocese. This entailed in the parishes the establishment of Youth Fellowships for the thirteen- to eighteen-year-olds under the friendly guidance of the local incumbent whose concern must be 'to promote study, service and devotion *before* any social activity'. To assist this development and to secure some central direction the Bishop believed that it must be professionalised at least to the extent of appointing a full time secretary for the Diocesan Youth Council. Here he was conscious that he must tread warily since some of the clergy began to feel that their own status in the parish was being undermined.

Education, however, is an ongoing process and should not end at any one period in life. After some two years in the Diocese he appointed a priest in each Deanery to foster religious study among adults and to liaise in doing this with a secretary in each Archdeaconry. This, he hoped, would also have the effect of encouraging corporate learning among the clergy, a consummation devoutly to be desired.

Geoffrey Fisher came to Chester with a high reputation for being a good administrator within the context of a school. Not for one moment did he regard efficient administration as impersonal, that is as a distasteful but necessary chore. Indeed to secure success here demanded a basically pastoral approach: it meant understanding people and helping them to work happily together with each other. The arrival of such a man to Chester was bound to have its effect on diocesan structures and financial organisation.

Every person (we fondly hope!) has his own gifts and Dr Paget, the retired Bishop, had several, but an interest in, and a capacity for, administration was not among them. When Geoffrey Fisher came to Chester the central accountancy work in the Diocese had for many years been in the hands of Mr Andrews who held the office of Secretary to the Board of Finance. He also ran a private practice and used his own staff for diocesan purposes. There can be no doubt that Geoffrey Fisher was the first to recognise that Mr Andrews had served the Diocese, to quote his own words 'with conspicuous ability and faithfulness'; but every year work at the centre was increasing and the burden of discharging it becoming more onerous. The Bishop initiated discussions on the existing way of doing things and was himself the *fons et origo* of proposals for change which were in fact carried into effect. These entailed Mr Andrews becoming Treasurer to the Board of Finance and the appointment of a separate Secretary, responsible to it, and put in charge of the Diocesan Office and its staff. The first Secretary under the new dispensation was the Reverend J. A. Walker.

Inseparably related to diocesan administration must be the handling of its finance. In this respect Geoffrey Fisher was money conscious and he had not been long at Chester before he became convinced that in a changing social scene, where special needs and opportunities challenged the Church, it was no longer financially equipped to deal with them. Glaring examples of this stuck out like a sore thumb. There were districts in which large new centres of population were springing up unshepherded; also parishes of great size and grinding poverty where incumbents, single-handed, faced an almost impossible task. Referring to this daunting and devastating situation the Bishop commented: 'The primary necessity is to provide clergy in newly developed areas to arrive with the new population and to build up a Church life from the start in hard pressed parishes; to bring relief as a possibility in advance. Paganism can only be arrested and defeated by preaching the gospel, by the Church's sacramental life and by unremitting pastoral care.'

It was, unfortunately, abundantly clear that these needs could not be met financially from the slender resources of the Chester Diocesan Church Fund. The Bishop, therefore, shared these problems with his Diocesan Conference and was encouraged to proceed with his plan to launch a Bishop's Appeal Fund. This, it was proposed should be administered by the Bishop in consultation with the Archdeacons together with the Rural Deans; and its scope was inclusive of any special purpose of real importance for the advance of the Church. The Fund was to be permanent since 'in a Diocese of this size and the varied character of Chester the need for it would be equally permanent'. The Bishop addressed the Appeal not to parishes but to individuals in the hope that this would attract generous annual subscriptions from responsible lay churchmen and women. The total sum asked for was £100.000 and the Bishop sent a pastoral letter commending the Appeal which was read in all parish churches. He urged members of Parochial Church Councils to work for a system under which annual income came from a guaranteed source independent of the vagaries of weather and fluctuating church collections. The natural, if regrettable, inward-looking character of many local communities, coupled with the fact that for centuries they had been cushioned by built-in endowments, militated against the kind of enthusiastic response necessary to make the quota system function to its full potential. Fortunately for the Bishop, Mr Bevan, Treasurer of the Diocesan Conference, on whom he leaned heavily, showed in this matter both enthusiasm and conviction. A crucial meeting of the Conference to tackle this thorny problem took place in October 1937. The Bishop stressed that this matter of quotas had come up for discussion simply because during the last ten years there had been large shifts in population. He admitted frankly that the problem was a difficult one and no diocese had succeeded in finding an altogether satisfactory system.

The Bishop was not disappointed with the result of the Conference which as he said, 'accomplished a difficult piece of work concerning Deanery assessments with a unity of spirit which was altogether admirable and encouraging'. This was democracy at work. The Bishop was particularly impressed with Mr Bevan's speech in its 'wide alpine survey of the spirit' and its appeal to members of the Conference 'to fertilise their imaginations'. Not only did Mr Bevan 'put the points at issue with his usual clarity but he lifted the whole question of assessments and quotas to its true spiritual level'.

There was one particular aspect of diocesan finance which gave Geoffrey Fisher considerable uneasiness – the incomes of the parish clergy to which he referred in these words at his Diocesan Conference in May 1936. 'If I were a dictator in these things I should make every living carry the same stipend, which should be in itself adequate but no more, in addition to which from a common fund each incumbent would receive a personal stipend, the amount of which would be according to his length of service in the ministry, the importance of the work which he was at the moment doing and any special claims which ought to be recognised – but we are a long way from that!' True there was a stipend fund to be used to augment incomes, but he feared lest a special appeal for Church Schools and other worthy objects should cause this source of supply to dry up. That this should not happen was particularly important since under the proposed Tithe Act of 1936 a serious inroad would be made on the living standard of many incumbents.

Tithe was a long established contribution to an incumbent's income which he enjoyed as a statutory right. Originally paid in kind it was commuted to a money payment in 1836 and fixed annually, a difficult and often embarrassing exercise. When Geoffrey Fisher first read the precise terms of the new Act he confessed that his immediate reaction was 'to accept the proposals because they would settle the matter once and for all'. Subsequent perusal in detail made him change his mind. 'They impose a really impossible burden upon the Church and especially on tithe-owning clergy;' he wrote, 'they cannot as they stand be called a compromise but simply a great injustice.' The collective effect of these proposals upon the Church as a whole would be, so he reckoned, a loss of property to the tune of eleven million pounds; and for the Pensions Board it meant being mulcted of a million. Nearer to home in the Chester Diocese some one hundred incumbents – over half of them already living on no more than four hundred pounds per annum – would lose sixty pounds a year. Here the Bishop, to use common parlance, did not 'pull his punches'. If no more favourable terms were offered he did not see how the Church could say anything but: 'This is confiscation of the property of the clergy beyond reason and justice and we must resist it.'

The above is an excellent example of how forcefully the Bishop could state a case. Modifications were in fact made though they hardly measured up to his expectations. However, that he should have made his views public undoubtedly helped to bring this compromise about. We shall return to this subject of clerical stipends in a subsequent chapter.

If the stipends received by many clergy were grossly inadequate this situation served to highlight the hardships endured by not a few clerical widows. Most parishes, he reminded churchmen, wanted a married clergyman but few parishes provided an income adequate for an incumbent to care for his wife in the event of his death. Church funds and charities which could be tapped were lamentably insufficient. 'Women who had gloriously served the church by their influence and their labours are too often left to meet widowhood and old age on a bare pittance insecure and hardly obtained.' He therefore requested that sometime during the year every parish would make its contribution and respond to this call.

We have already described Geoffrey Fisher as money-conscious. It was certainly fortunate for the Diocese that he was, since the acute need for additional financial resources to which he called repeated attention constituted a high priority if the Church were to safeguard its regular ministry. It must, therefore, have been a great satisfaction for the Bishop to be able to report, during his last full year at Chester, that the Diocesan Fund had received from the parishes and elsewhere in 1938 enough to pay the grants to diocesan societies as well as the contribution to the Church Assembly Fund in full. This he believed was a matter for great thankfulness and he warmly congratulated the Diocese on it.

Geoffrey Fisher spent his early and formative years in the last two decades of the 19th century when to many it seemed natural to conceive of the expansion of the Empire, together with the splendour of the British Raj, as indicative of the superiority of the Christian faith over all others. That this religion should missionise and that it was in the interest of mankind that it should do so was part of Geoffrey Fisher's spiritual inheritance and make-up. The rectory at Higham on the Hill took the missionary activity of the Church for granted so that evangelism at home and overseas were not separate but twin aspects of one harmonious whole. Geoffrey's years at school, university and

Repton coincided with the pioneering work of the American evangelist
J. R. Mott; pointing to a growing awareness of the implications of a
world-wide Christianity. Shortly after Geoffrey Fisher came to Chester
there appeared the 'Unified Statement of the Needs of the Church
Overseas', published under the title *With One Accord*. This was
followed by a second volume shortly afterwards, *The World-wide
Church*. The Bishop regarded these publications as so significant that
he believed all mature churchmen should be knowledgeable of their
contents and respond to their challenge. Thus he devoted two of his
diocesan letters – April 1933 and August 1934 – to a succinct and
ordered summary of their main themes not least in relation to the eight
areas where the Anglican Communion was at work. From this survey
he drew immediate practical conclusions as to the responsibilities of
Christians in the Diocese of Chester. The Church overseas was facing
'an unparalleled financial crisis', so much so that if help from the
Church of England were withdrawn or diminished this could prove
'disastrous'. It was thus a bounden duty to provide the younger
churches overseas with the trained leadership, the wisdom, the experience and the stability which only a 'veteran' Church could give. The
conclusion of the whole matter, so far as concerned the Diocese of
Chester, was for every Parochial Church Council seriously to discuss
these problems and what should be done about them. To give added
weight to this request he asked the secretaries of PCCs to send him
information concerning 'any resolution passed or action agreed by
their councils in regard to this matter'. This *cri de coeur* by the Bishop
was not without a very practical result. In August 1934 he was able to
report, with a degree of pride, that diocesan contributions for this
purpose had increased to the grand total of £18,062.

Exhortation, of course, was not enough in itself though Geoffrey
Fisher always believed that to express a worthwhile need clearly and
objectively was a necessary pre-requisite of its being met. As Vice-
Chairman of the Church of England Missionary Council – though on
his own admission he took his duties somewhat lightly – he was in a
position to know what was happening in other dioceses and, as a
result, was impressed by a highly successful missionary weekend held
in the Coventry diocese. Thus he encouraged the Chester Missionary
Council of which he was President to sponsor in 1935 three such
weekend 'campaigns' for the rural deaneries of the Wirral, Nantwich
and Middlewich. Taking stock of these later the Bishop felt, in spite of
the few parishes which did not participate, that they had been
successful, both in giving a fresh understanding of the Church's place
in the world and in strengthening the spiritual life of those who
participated.

The Report, later issued, was carefully studied by the Bishop for future use. The references to particular parishes were revealing, typical examples being: 'PCC keen and took handbills to every house.' 'PCC divided the parish into districts and canvassed hard.' 'PCC to appoint a special Missionary Committee.' The group discussions which took place at the end of the Conference led to practical decision-making and helped the less articulate 'to find their tongues'. To some of the more outlying and isolated parishes the Campaign, as a by-product, brought friendship and spiritual refreshment, yet its basic purpose, as the Bishop re-iterated, was to set people thinking and praying and working for the Church the world over. The result of this initial success was that three more campaigns were held in 1935, and the missionary weekend became a staple diet in the life of the Diocese. These demanded much work and planning in the localities. That they were so readily and cheerfully undertaken owed a great deal to the inspiration, enthusiasm and encouragement of the Bishop himself. The general effect was to enlarge horizons and to create new and significant priorities.

Geoffrey Fisher's last few years at Chester were distinguished by three royal events. No one was less sycophantic where royalty was concerned than the Bishop of Chester, though he believed in the monarchy as an institution and felt he owed a loyalty to the Sovereign as a person. However, until he went to Canterbury it was a world to which he was a stranger.

The Silver Jubilee of King George V was celebrated in May 1935 and Geoffrey Fisher suggested to his clergy that instead of a number of 'sectarian' services in each locality, incumbents should seek the co-operation of their Free Church brethren to organise one collective, ecumenical occasion in each area. He himself preached in the Cathedral.

Within a year of these celebrations King George V had died and the Bishop in his monthly letter paid him a simple tribute: 'We cannot be too thankful to Almighty God,' he wrote, 'that we have had such a man to be a King during what has been perhaps the most critical quarter of a century in our national history – a King, steadfast, humble, courageous and with a God fearing devotion to duty.'

Geoffrey Fisher could not have anticipated that before long, uncrowned and a fugitive, the new King Edward VIII would have abdicated the throne. As to his own attitude to these momentous events the Bishop took the opportunity of dilating upon the nature of Christian marriage and the heart-rending manner in which Edward VIII had endeavoured to solve his own personal dilemma. It could never have occured to Geoffrey Fisher, in his wildest imagination, that he would be actively involved in the Coronation of King George VI's daughter Elizabeth. At the prompting of Geoffrey Fisher, the Dean and

Chapter, with the Mayor and the Chester Council of Free Churches, invited all the citizens to the Cathedral for a joint service. Bishop Fisher took the opportunity to issue a pastoral letter which was read on 7 February by all parish priests in their churches. Its basic intention was to appeal to all members of the Church of England in the Diocese to be active in witnessing to their faith; in giving a reason for the hope that was in them; and in participating regularly in Christian worship.

The Bishop's closing years at Chester were clouded by increasing fears of war. Mussolini's fascists raped Abyssinia while the West looked on in impotence. The League of Nations failed to restrain them nor were sanctions applied. Geoffrey Fisher in his Diocesan Gazette sadly reflected that it was 'winter in the history of the world and of man's discontent'. The prospect was 'bleak and cheerless and man's goodwill to peace seems frozen and frustrated'. The tragic loss of the submarine *Thetis* followed by a memorial service at Birkenhead in which the Bishop participated and which moved him greatly, brought the horrors of war nearer, as did also the streets of Chester, usually so quiet, when crowded with refugee children. It was the deep conviction of Geoffrey Fisher, after Munich proved a pyrrhic victory, that Britain had no option but to prepare reluctantly for the possibility of war. 'In the last resort', he wrote in his Diocesan Gazette, 'unjust force can only, as between nations, be met by force to restrain it'. However, Geoffrey Fisher was not destined to spend his wartime years in Chester.

PART TWO:

A NATION AT WAR

CHAPTER 5

Nomination to the Bishopric of London

ON 1 September 1939 the improbable but not entirely unexpected happened. Dr Winnington-Ingram, Bishop of London, having been gently persuaded by his friends, resigned. He had been in office since 1901 when on the strong recommendation of Queen Alexandra he had been nominated to follow the formidable scholar, historian and churchman, Mandell Creighton.

On Wednesday in Holy Week 1939 as the Bishop of Chester was leaving his house to celebrate Holy Communion in the Cathedral he glanced at the letters on the hall table. 'No, I won't look to see what this morning's budget is: it's only disturbing' – so he said to himself. When he returned he noticed a letter marked 'From the Prime Minister' but in spite of the fact of the Bishop of Exeter telling him he was 'top of the lottery' for London he persuaded himself that it was probably a routine communication concerning a Crown living. Thus undisturbed he went into his study for his customary private devotions and, before conducting family prayers, he returned to the hall, glanced at the letters again and saw another marked 'confidential' with a London postmark. Now, to quote his own words he 'got nervous'. And well he might for the letter marked 'Prime Minister' was from Neville Chamberlain, dated 20 April 1939, offering him the see of London in almost identical words as those used on his nomination to Chester. The other – it came from the Archbishop of Canterbury, Cosmo Lang, dated 19 April – was long and persuasive. It merits a fairly full quotation: 'No-one realises more than I do that your heart may well sink at the prospect of a responsibility so great and a burden so heavy. May I earnestly hope that you will be willing to regard it as a very special call.' He would be succeeding a man who had for long years been unable to take a full hold of all that London means; whereas he, Geoffrey Fisher, was in the very prime of his manhood. What was now needed was a man who could come to the problems of London, especially the ecclesiastical problems, with a fresh mind and was not specially identified with any one ecclesiastical party. Also there was a need for a Bishop who had some basis of scholarship and some intellectual gifts. Hence he did not believe that the Bishop would be justified in refusing the Prime Minister's offer.

It would be difficult to imagine a letter which more strongly expressed an archiepiscopal command masquerading under the guise of advice. The Bishop of Chester must now take up the story of how he faced up to this call.

The following days for Geoffrey Fisher, until he finally made up his mind, were days of intense spiritual anguish, fear, apprehension, finally ending in acceptance and dedication. The evidence for this is a diary which he kept at the time and which, probably, he never expected any eye but his own to see. We quote extracts from this unique document: 'As soon as I read [the Prime Minister's and the Archbishop's letters] I knelt down and wept like a child. The thing frightened me and as I knelt in mute prostration before Our Lord the words which came as commentary were Our Lord's: "Father, if it be possible, let this cup pass from me". I was at the end of a very heavy Lent, physically tired, and this proposal seemed to come with all the gravity and inevitability of a death sentence. I could only see the impossibility of my coping with the infinite demands of London, mind and heart and spirit, and yet the inevitable necessity that I should consider whether Our Lord meant me to face this impossible possibility. So I knelt and wept and kept silent before Our Lord'. Rosamund Fisher, when told, was less surprised and as ever calm and calming. In the afternoon he went for a walk on the Peckforton Hills and 'forgot it mostly'.

In the evening Geoffrey Fisher wrote to the Archbishop of Canterbury protesting that this offer filled him with alarm and dismay since he knew himself to be 'inadequate in mind and spirit for such a task'. He also sent off a letter, in a freer vein, to William Temple, Archbishop of York. As no copy of this letter survives, the substance of it can only be inferred from the *aide memoire* which Geoffrey Fisher drew up at the time. Its objectivity is remarkable: 'I assessed my own capacities as pedestrian, useful enough in a family and friendly Diocese like Chester but threadbare in the publicity of London: moreover I am spiritually an amateur and immature disciple of Our Lord, easily and quickly bankrupt, though when I have anything to say I can do it reasonably well. I am no man of ideas and the manufacture of them is to me a laborious process and laboured in the result: I hate pronouncements and statements and preachments such as should go from London. While I can cope pretty well with a limited problem with all the factors known, the more abstract and indefinite a problem becomes, with unknown factors and uncertain factors, the less I become capable of assessing it and the more I find my only wisdom is silence: that is I am no statesman: and intellectual London would very soon place me and dismiss me. There it is and if I must face it, I am thankful that it has come in Holy Week, the right atmosphere for it. The question for me is not "is there a divine call" but "is there a divine compulsion". Everything in me rebels against it – only if it *is* a divine compulsion can I go forward'. To his family he referred to this 'horror of London'.

After he had finished his letters, Geoffrey Fisher spent the rest of the evening reading a detective story!!

There can be no doubt from this evidence that Geoffrey Fisher found the prospect of going to London daunting. Maybe long years in more or less seclusion at Repton, followed by seven happy years in a somewhat remote diocese, disinclined him to make a radical change.

On Good Friday the eagerly awaited reply came from William Temple, the contents of which could not have been unexpected. 'I read your letter', he wrote, 'with the keenest sympathy. With parts of your account of your own capacities I should not disagree . . . [but] You have a clearer *grasp* of any tangle of considerations, once they are before you, than anyone I know; you are always friendly and conciliatory and yet can be quite definite and fair.' The Archbishop concluded his letter with an invitation to talk the matter over with him on the following Tuesday.

Geoffrey Fisher was considerably influenced by William Temple who, though agreeing with Geoffrey Fisher's own self-analysis, yet still advised him to go forward. 'I could take it for granted,' he reflected, 'as William did, that nobody thought I was really adequate for the task, I knew I wasn't and therefore just rebelled against undertaking what I could not do. But if those who were responsible thought that even so I ought to go, then I could begin to think *not* "can I do this" *but* "can I refuse this?"' Geoffrey Fisher spent most of Good Friday morning visiting a parish church, then returning to the Cathedral for the Three Hours Service. Later he sought solace in the silence and the semi-darkness of the Lady Chapel. Was he right to reject the considered view of both Archbishops as well as an obviously careful act by the PM. 'It would mean turning his back on an exhausting and killing work. To go forward would mean to bear a Cross – but could he, on Good Friday, refuse to take it up. Was there not a Divine compulsion?'

Early on Saturday morning before they got up, he discussed the matter at length with Rosamond speaking to her as if refusal was impossible. Easter morning came and 'was filled with a great happiness', the picture that kept coming back into his mind being always that of Peter meeting the Risen Lord who addressed him with a question thrice repeated, 'Lovest thou me?' He recalled God's lifelong goodness to him, his leading him on from step to step, his keeping of 'Ros' and himself for one another, and for a common work in which they were 'each other's helper and source of complete trust and comfort'.

This long period of self-analysis and introspection, wholly out of character, and this 'dead existence between two lives,' was beginning to damp down his natural buoyancy. However, his conscience was now clear that he just could not turn back. 'Do with me what thou wilt and have mercy.'

On Easter Tuesday the Bishop and Rosamond made the long-deferred journey to York – 'a heavenly drive there and back through glorious country in glorious weather' – in order to talk face to face with William Temple. He told Geoffrey Fisher firmly that he could not refuse the offer and that only he and Garbett had been seriously considered for the appointment.

The Bishop now followed up a suggestion – a surprising one – put to him by William Temple that in order to overcome any remaining scruples he might 'reasonably and informally' ask advice of Walter Matthews, Dean of St Paul's, who by virtue of his office would be involved with the Chapter in his nomination. He therefore wrote to the Dean asking whether the Chapter would wish him to accept or not; or even whether, if it came to this, they would be able to elect him without distress of conscience. This was a nicely courteous letter, though it certainly was unconstitutional to consult beforehand the Chapter in this manner. Nor perhaps was it fair to the Dean of St Paul's to lay this responsibility upon him since he could not properly consult his colleagues. One wonders how Geoffrey Fisher would have reacted had the reply been in the negative! The Dean of St Paul's was far too sagacious to put himself in a position which could later prove embarrassing and this is clear in his reply which is a masterpiece of its kind. He had, of course, he wrote, heard Geoffrey Fisher's name mentioned, 'always with approval as of one who would be welcome: whoever came would need health and energy, since he must promote 'a reasonable obedience to authority among the clergy'. There were parts of London where 'not only the Church of England but organised religion of every kind is for all intents and purposes extinct'. He could assure the Bishop that the Dean and Chapter of St Paul's would have no 'distress of conscience' in electing him. Indeed they would give him 'a very cordial welcome'.

The letter was all that the Bishop could have asked for at a time when he could not remain much longer in the half-real world into which the offer of the Bishopric of London had plunged him. However, the prolonged inner struggle was now over, and he was able in a good conscience to write to the Prime Minister accepting the nomination, this being reported in the press a few days later. At no other time in his life does evidence exist of Geoffrey Fisher being in such an agony and travail of spirit.

The general prospect of 'clearing up' persuaded Geoffrey Fisher that he needed a long holiday. This came but it was spent in Chester Infirmary. A sudden twist on a staircase caused something to slip in his knee which made necessary the removal of a cartilage. He was thus forced to make a virtue of necessity. 'If it is not the holiday I planned', he wrote, 'it is very restful to sleep as much as one likes and very enjoyable to read without interruption.'

It is at this point, on the eve of his departure from Chester, that we may ask the question as to whether he was a good Bishop of a rural/urban See? The *Church Times*, on his departure, spoke of him as having proved himself 'an effective evangelist, a man of wide sympathies and becoming modesty; a hard worker, who concentrated his energies upon his own duties and had not run about the country settling or attempting to settle the affairs of everybody but the members of his own flock'. He was, in his character, 'strong and independent' being concerned to apply theological categories to everyday life. This is high praise, particularly when it is borne in mind, that Geoffrey Fisher's churchmanship was hardly that of this illustrious journal at that time. The Editor of the Chester Diocesan Leaflet – Dean Bennett – who could speak from first-hand experience, testified to the high merits of the Bishop as a pastor. The Diocese had always admired his incisiveness and clarity in argument, the flashes of humour which marked his addresses on such occasions as the Diocesan Conferences. The impressions of him that would linger in the minds of countless church folk up and down Cheshire were those of a Bishop sitting on the top of a desk in an infants' school; or chatting away easily to everyone at a tea party after an induction; or standing near a study fire dealing with a clerical problem, and giving his whole mind to its solution. It was indeed his 'friendliness' that they had come to value most of all. Before he came people had feared a schoolmaster but the schoolmaster never came. Instead there came a man singularly sympathetic and understanding and above all, human. Nor must they forget Mrs Fisher who was a 'charming and vigorous leader'. A parish priest wrote to him: 'They will have a job to find us a "boss" under whom I at any rate shall be able to work with such wholehearted respect and affection.'

Leaving Chester entailed the customary presentations – which included a gold watch thus enabling the Bishop on his own confession to return to its original owner a time-piece which he had borrowed some fifteen years earlier; and gifts for Mrs Fisher from the Mothers' Union. So many affectionate tributes made the pangs of parting the more acute. This Geoffrey Fisher expressed movingly in his Diocesan Gazette. 'A transplanting such as this which confronts me is in some ways like a kind of rehearsal of the final transplanting of death. So much that is known and familiar and dear is lost, so much that is unknown and testing lies ahead. But all that is valuable endures and Christ is the Alpha and the Omega, the beginning and the end.'

During the days immediately following the public announcement of his appointment some thirty-six Bishops wrote to Geoffrey Fisher.

Maybe this was a routine operation, yet it is clear from the tone of these letters that the nomination took none of them by surprise and, unless these epistles are simply dishonest, that the appointment enjoyed their full, indeed enthusiastic support. Running through them all is a constant reference to the almost impossible, 'terrifying', nature of the task which awaited him; 'the most difficult job in the Anglican Communion'; and yet their deep conviction that Geoffrey Fisher was the very person with the talent and energy to cope.

A few letters, perhaps, call for special mention. The following from Dr Winnington-Ingram, written in his almost illegible hand, bears witness to his goodwill, but also, alas, to a somewhat egocentric attitude which constituted a pathetic ingredient of his later years.

'I want my letter if possible to be the first to wish you Godspeed as my successor. I am delighted that my great wish is to be granted. I did not have much difficulty in persuading the Archbishop to nominate you to the Prime Minister but one never knows what other influences are being brought to bear on Prime Ministers. However, I got in first with Neville Chamberlain but we must look beyond all these secondary causes to a Higher Power.'

A generous message which must have given Geoffrey Fisher great satisfaction came from Cyril Garbett, Bishop of Winchester – generous because he was a serious contender for the same office. George Bell, Bishop of Chichester, reminded him that Tait said once that London was the key to the Church of England, and that was truer than ever today. 'None who knows *you*', he wrote, 'can doubt that you have the gift and general qualities as well as ability and grit required for the post today.'

Sir Frank Fletcher, now retired but still seeing himself *in loco parentis* where Geoffrey Fisher's career was concerned, could not forbear giving him some 'preliminary advice' and a warning – 'London killed Creighton, don't let it kill you'. Not surprisingly two affectionate and encouraging letters came from brother Leonard in Africa and sister Katie in Palestine.

Dr Winnington-Ingram possessed neither the scholarship nor the tough intellectual equipment of Creighton but he had great personal charm, enthusiasm and dedication to Christian evangelism. But though his physical energy persisted into a ripe old age – his geriatric tennis became legendary – he early declined mentally. Many were the clergy and laymen who complained that there was a lack of order and general discipline in the parishes; that the Prayer Book was being ignored and that many a church was becoming an 'island refuge' for a bewildering variety of liturgical exiles. *The Times* wrote of the London Diocese that 'every party organisation had its headquarters in London and nowhere else were the evils of party spirit in Church affairs so evident'.

To Geoffrey Fisher, however, the London Diocese was almost unknown territory and here his predecessor could not help him in spite of almost a life-time's experiences of the great metropolis.

Dr Fisher's reception by his new diocese was certainly warm and welcoming in spite of the war. In his last Presidential Address to the London Diocesan Conference Dr Winnington-Ingram had referred to the Bishop-designate in his own inimitable light-hearted style. He possessed three advantages over himself, he admitted frankly. The new bishop had three Firsts whereas he had only got one; he had a charming wife but he could boast no treasure even charming or otherwise; he had six sons: he could only produce sixty-five nephews and nieces. More seriously, the Bishop called attention to Geoffrey Fisher as being an excellent speaker, and to his keen sense of humour. On 2 November 1939 the confirmation of Geoffrey Fisher's election took place in the Church of St-Mary-le-Bow which was followed some days later by his enthronement in St Paul's Cathedral. The exigencies of war did not prevent a large congregation assembling though they curtailed some of the splendour customary on such occasions. The Bishop long remembered the day. The service was beautifully ordered by the Dean and Chapter and was made the more impressive by its austere dignity so suitable to the war conditions in which they lived. Immediately after his enthronement and following a long established custom in the Diocese he celebrated Holy Communion; he himself having particularly asked that he be remembered in the parish churches throughout the Diocese on the following Sunday.

Within a few hours of the St Paul's ceremony the Bishop was presiding over his first Diocesan Conference in a crowded Central Hall in Westminster. It fell to the Bishop of Willesden to welcome him formally. They were confident, he said, that he was the right man to take charge and that he would 'quickly bring a vigorous and alert mind to bear upon the work of the Church in London'. Lord Daryngton, Chairman of the House of Laity of the Church Assembly, urged them all to stand firmly behind the Bishop at this great moment in the history of the world. Both speakers welcomed Mrs Fisher with genuine warmth of feeling.

It was now up to Geoffrey Fisher to reply, which he did in his usual efficient manner though he could not, for once, conceal his deep emotion. He recalled that when he was first offered the See of London in Holy Week he received the news with 'great stress of mind' and had finally accepted only under 'a sense of compulsion'. Since then he had lived in a 'disembodied state' having lost his identity with his former Diocese but now he was 'clothed again'.

Introductions, however, were not yet quite over. Through the London Diocesan Leaflet he could address himself to a far wider clientele. His first words to them were Pauline: 'Grace be unto you and peace from God our Father and from the Lord Jesus Christ'. He entered upon his duties, he confessed, as a stranger to London, and he was therefore grateful to have around him the suffragan Bishops and Archdeacons who had carried on so well during the interregnum and who were there to 'teach and advise' him. He asked the Diocese to be patient during his first few months and to leave him without the incumbrance of too many engagements while he was learning the 'layout of his work'. It had taken him as long as seven years to visit the two hundred parishes in Chester, yet London had treble that number. He would try to avoid a haphazard acceptance of invitations but would endeavour to work to a plan, visiting Deaneries first and in due course the parishes.

The departure from Chester; the arrival in London; the farewells and the welcomes; the legal requirement as well as the religious and worshipful ceremonies – these were now behind him. Against the severe and testing background of war, increasingly felt in London, Dr Fisher embarked upon his Episcopal Ministry.

CHAPTER 6

Fulham Palace and the Blitz

THE contrast, of course, between Chester and London was extreme. The former had large rural areas with industrial pockets at Birkenhead and Macclesfield. London, on the other hand, sprawled eastwards into Essex and westwards into Middlesex. The City of London, the East and West End, were diverse in character. Such an amorphous and mixed complex of people, many of them flooding into and out of London day by day, could hardly be expected to regard themselves as members one of another. Thus even Mandell Creighton was forced to confess that he was unable to deal with the very real difficulties of the clergy such as, for example, 'their excessive individualism, isolation, congregationalism, and little intercourse with one another or with the Bishop'.

However, the immediate task confronting the new Bishop of London was not to embark upon any ambitious plans for Diocesan reform – there was a war on – but simply to repair Fulham Palace as rapidly as possible and physically, with his family, get himself into it. Its condition had long given grave cause for anxiety, Bishop Robinson in 1715 complaining that the House was too large for the resources of the Bishopric to maintain. The only practical and immediate way out for the Fishers was the abandonment of the great maze of buildings and taking shelter in the Elizabethan wing. In spite of almost insuperable difficulties the Fishers moved in and were able to establish themselves fairly adequately in the Palace before the blitz and subsequent bombing altered the whole pattern of their lives. London, unscathed after almost a year of what became known as 'the phoney war', suddenly found itself in mid-August 1940 subjected to aerial bombardment. The blitz had begun and was to continue with spasmodic intermissions till near Christmas. Mrs Fisher with the three children who were still at home – the Bishop accompanied her on the journey – reluctantly left Fulham for Minehead in Somerset, where her mother had lived in retirement. Her fourth son Humphrey (Huff) had broken his neck in a cycling accident on Exmoor and particularly needed a mother's care. On 29 August Geoffrey Fisher returned from Minehead to London, arriving at Paddington Station in the blackout where he was greeted by silence and searchlights. A German aircraft, later brought down over Wimbledon Common, suddenly 'zoomed' overhead and when the Bishop finally reached Fulham Palace by car the maids were already in the shelter. He himself went to bed at midnight and the 'All Clear' sounded at 3 am. It was a home-coming which was an augury of the shape of things to come.

To Rosamond Fisher's enforced absence we owe a series of letters from the Bishop which depicted vividly what life was like during a unique period in the long history of London. More than at any other time in his ministry Geoffrey Fisher shared the stresses and strains, the dangers and difficulties, of the ordinary citizens in the great metropolis. Air-raids proved an indiscriminating leveller. As bombing continued, the residents of Fulham Palace adjusted their sleeping quarters to meet new contingencies, moving into the hastily constructed shelter, the cellars or pantry as the situation seemed to require. Parts of the building were shut up and the whole pattern of the Bishop's daily routine was radically changed and gave way to meeting emergent *ad hoc* demands. Typical was a call from the Ministry of Information to broadcast to America giving a picture of London under bombardment. The result of this talk, so he wrote to his wife, was to increase his fan mail by about a dozen letters – one 'dotty', another abusing the President, two which were clearly excuses for sending poems composed by the authors, three from homesick English-born folk, and the rest 'purely appreciative'. On another occasion he regaled Rosamond with a racy description of his visiting the War Office with Lord Horder's Committee whose writ was sex education in the Forces. He found it all 'amusing' and confessed unashamedly: 'I did almost all the talking'.

During the first week in September London Docks with Stepney, Bow and areas along the south bank, were attacked with incendiary bombs. The glow in the sky could be seen right up the river to Fulham. In his regular bulletin to Minehead the Bishop commented: 'We can inflict great losses on their daylight invaders: the weakness is that we (and the Germans too) can do little against the night raiders. Guns go off, but all the same the raiders circle about freely, uninterrupted. And of course last night they had the glare of the fires started in the daylight raid to guide them. What a world!' Turning to matters domestic he added: 'If this goes on I think you had better send Bob and Tim back to school from Minehead and then come back home with Huff'. Very soon the Bishop changed his mind as to the wisdom of her return. All Geoffrey Fisher's natural sympathies and compassion went out to his fellow Londoners and he did his best to comfort and sustain them. At the request of the Rural Dean of Stepney he went down to the East End and was deeply moved – 'poor things', he commented, 'their houses are demolished or full of debris and with all windows blown in: but the actual loss of life was not large'. The Bishop realised that one of his main tasks was to sustain the morale of the clergy, existing as they did under exceptional, almost intolerable, conditions. Hence, he was assiduous in visiting them as well as the homeless who had 'lost everything but their spirit'. His admiration for their courage was unlimited. He was in the Isle of Dogs just after a dreadful visitation, and long remembered conversing with a clergyman from south of the river, a scholar who had lost everything including his greatly beloved books. 'For the first time in my life', he told the Bishop, 'I really feel a free man.' Geoffrey delighted to tell the story of an old lady, isolated at the top of a tall block of flats, who in refusing to be evacuated protested simply: 'Here I am, I say my prayers and I go to sleep, there's no need for the two of us to keep awake'. Another, when she heard a bomb descending, told the Bishop she resorted to divine succour: 'I prayed to God as hard as I could to move it a bit further down the street, and He did'.

So it was that in the early days of the blitz, the Bishop never ceased to be impressed by the 'astonishing adaptability', 'the quiet heroism' and 'persistent humour' of the average Londoner; also the way in which local and public authorities, including the London County Council as well as voluntary agencies, worked together in a co-operative spirit, overcoming delays and untold hazards. However, there came a time when the Bishop began to wonder whether morale in the East End might crack if the blitz continued much longer. On one of his visits he was received with such complaints as 'the Town Clerk is a washout: no one is doing anything: the homeless are sleeping under arches: we can't stand this much longer: there will be a panic'. To his relief when he next visited them he was greeted with the words: 'the Town Clerk has been splendid: everyone has done his bit: we're all right'. The reason for this sudden change, so the Bishop shrewdly surmised, was the fact that the recently instituted barrage, though it had not stopped all the bombers coming through, had removed the sense of being defenceless. Also, the homeless, the invalids and the expectant mothers were all being evacuated. Those who remained felt they could now face anything. So the Bishop was able to write calmly to Rosamond: 'We can stand up to this in London and let our forces go on with their relentless pressures on Germany till we get through'. As to domestic life in Fulham Palace they now had beds for the maids downstairs near their shelter. 'I think we are all reasonably safe', he assured her, 'but it is all disturbing and leaves one a bit restless next day.'

In the midst of these daily trials, the Bishop was suddenly faced with a crisis in the Palace which, short-lived though it proved, caused much unsettlement at the time. On 11 September at 10.20 am the phone rang and a harassed member of the Women's Voluntary Service asked if the Palace could be ready in half an hour to take in some two hundred refugees rendered homeless through the dropping of a stick of time bombs in the proximity of their homes. The Palace personnel were assured that they would have nothing to do but provide accommodation. However, things did not work out that way. The Bishop was not in the Palace and it was over to Peggy Forman, Rosamond's sister, to rally the household which fortunately included Frank and Charles, two of the Bishop's sons. A rapid transformation scene began to take place, which entailed removing the drawing room carpet; opening up the kitchen; and rounding up all available urns and kettles. Everyone 'worked with a will' but before preparations were completed the evacuees began to flock in. Many were in deep distress having lost members of their family and friends; others were suffering such human ills as ear-ache and neuralgia. Among them was one *very* expectant mother. When the Bishop returned home in the afternoon he found the ground floor, including the passages, crowded with people and was greatly impressed with the manner in which the household had rallied round and even the refugees themselves. Charles Fisher in a vivid letter to his mother makes clear that this incursion caused many traumas and that some of the WVS ladies, well-meaning though they were, constituted somewhat of an embarrassment. The Bishop, fearing that there might be another air-raid during the night, wisely laid on two members of the Home Guard to patrol the Palace in case of emergencies. He himself slept next to the telephone but by the following day the refugees had all gone off to a school in the Fulham Palace Road. It was now a matter of clearing up, a process which was completed when a few days later pies and stale potatoes were burnt in the garden. Charles' abiding memory was of the 'prevailing effect of dirt and filth and smell with which we are still burdened and look as though we shall be forever unless we use gallons of Flit to create a diversion'. Maybe this experience was not without its compensations in that it introduced both father and sons to the way in which the other half of the world lived!

After the excitement of the Palace occupation, the Bishop returned to the 'normal abnormality' of the remaining months of the blitz. Within this context he confessed to Rosamond that he felt 'rather at a loose end'. 'I haven't got outside engagements till next week', he informed her, 'a bit of an advantage when so many roads are blocked that John', the very faithful chauffeur, 'has to dodge to and fro to get anywhere.'

The bombing which had begun in the East End was soon extended over different areas of London. Fulham, lying close to the river, was particularly vulnerable and suffered severely during the nights of 25 and 26 September. Geoffrey Fisher writes of his own experience: 'Last night after ten o'clock was fairly peaceful. But for a few minutes about nine thirty the house rocked like a ship at sea! It took us quite by surprise and we were sitting peacefully in my study listening to the news. Peggy's wireless is here and it came all in a moment – and was over before we could move, with one spasm a bit later'. Many windows in the Palace were broken and the front gate unusable. Even the hens had to be removed to the orchard. It was indeed general post for the inhabitants of the Palace while the Home Guard checked up to locate any unexploded bombs. Peggy claimed proudly that 'funnily enough we all slept quite well' but it was bound to take its toll. People became edgy and rumours began to circulate around Fulham. The baker, for example, asserted that a man had been caught who for the previous fortnight had been signalling to German planes by flashing a torch.

Rosamond Fisher's enforced absence was for her husband a sore trial. He greatly wished her at his side yet, though she herself was desperately keen to return, he was adamant that this could not be. His letters concerning this unnatural separation reflect a mood engendered by the frustration of the blitz and a sense of unreality that went along with it. 'It's a queer life feeling that you are almost in a different world, and a great gulf fixed between us! . . . If I go on being at a loose end, I shall probably fill in time by writing long letters to you! I do feel queerly detached from the world, and as a result I really don't (at present) worry but take things as they come. You and I belong to one another in a different order of reality . . . one must just go on and I do the thing that turns up. But the reality of God and trust in Him can't be touched.'

Normally Geoffrey Fisher did not express himself in this way and the somewhat repetitive awkwardness of his language testifies to the depth of his feelings. He usually found himself with too much to do; but now the 'busyness' of a familiar routine which had given a shape and structure to his life over the years had been removed. 'I hope Churchill is right that this month is the crux', he wrote to Rosamond in September, 'and that by the end of it we shall be "through the worst" – though no doubt with plenty still to come. I wish Hitler would try an invasion quickly.' 'I have never (when normally at work)', he wrote again, 'had such a "bitty" unoccupied time. I do what I have to do which only takes a part of the day and then don't want to settle down to anything. I wish Hitler would try an invasion quickly.'

If life was bleak and disorientated for Geoffrey Fisher during the blitz it was even more so for Rosamond, tucked away in the country and the recipient of letters which must have stimulated a more acute desire to return to London and rejoin her husband. It could not, psychologically, have helped her to remain at her post when told by Peggy that the residents in Fulham Palace were by now well acclimatised to danger and could take it in their stride. It was, therefore, understandable that as September wore on Rosamond's desire to return to London intensified, so much so as to induce her to suggest that she and her sister Peggy should 'swap' places. But the Bishop insisted on taking the view that while there were children to look after her place was in the country with them. He was, of course, sensitive to her feelings, particularly as she kept up the pressure, going so far as to threaten at one stage that she was on the verge of returning to London come what may. 'You'll understand that I want you badly', he reiterated, 'but not *here* whilst this is on – least of all while Fulham seems specially to interest Hitler.' Undoubtedly behind Geoffrey Fisher's firmness was the deep and sacrificial conviction that with three of the family still at school, the risk of both parents being killed ought not to be taken. The position was delicate since to reassure Rosamond he tried in some of his letters to play down the danger while he himself recognised how real it was. By 30 September, however, two of the brothers had returned to school and Mrs Fisher was now free to come back to Fulham. In a letter to her of that date the Bishop admitted generously that he had 'probably not thought enough how beastly it was for you being marooned there . . . you know I shall be thankful beyond words to see you again: and you will very soon acclimatise to this life and feel as little conscious of any danger as we do'. True they would be putting one additional egg in the basket but he wanted her back. 'And after all Fulham is a large enough basket and we can spread ourselves about! So I shall expect you as soon as you can leave Huff.'

This letter was the *amende honorable* which must have given Rosamond intense satisfaction. Ever practical, he added that in case she came by road, he was sending her supplementary coupons which arrived *today*.

So Mrs Fisher returned after over a month's absence and this interesting exchange of letters ceased. The blitz continued up to the end of the year and though there was a serious and spasmodic bombing throughout the whole of the war, culminating in the doodle bugs and rockets, yet the three months in London that brought 1940 to a close were unique and will remain deeply embedded in the consciousness of those who suffered its griefs and shared its glories. But the end of the blitz did not for the Fishers remove all their fears. The years of the war remained for them a time of great and sustained personal anxiety. Four of their sons were in the army and widely dispersed. One was reported missing, but after eighteen months as a prisoner of war in Italy he gallantly escaped through the American lines to Africa and got home to England. Geoffrey Fisher said little about these things but confessed that 'the domestic side was difficult and of course my wife was terribly distracted by care for her sons at the front'. But constant busyness and a firm faith enabled them to contain this nagging worry, not least by offering sympathy to others similarly afflicted.

CHAPTER 7

Destruction and War Damage

WE now turn to consider an aspect of Geoffrey Fisher's wartime commitments which is important in relation to his development and his standing in the Church of England. For the first time he was asked to play a major national role which was challenging and bristling with difficulties yet of supreme significance to the Church and country as a whole. To illustrate this will demand a somewhat detailed treatment.

War damage and consequent casualties – some sixty thousand civilians were killed during the course of the Second World War – did not, even at that level, reach the figure seriously estimated by the British Government, let alone the astronomical proportions prophesied by H. G. Wells. But the menace from the air, after the conclusion of the 'phoney war', brought with it destruction on such a scale that Parliament was forced to recognise that the work of reconstruction, whenever undertaken, could not be left to local authorities or private institutions. Where large areas had been devastated the planning of the shape of things to come needed to be envisaged in the widest possible context. Thus the War Damage Act of 1940 accepted the principle that ravaged areas must be treated as a whole; that overall planning, if only on the drawing board, could not be left to the end of the war; and that such future reconstruction must not be prejudiced by premature, unilateral action. The passing of the Act completely changed the situation so far as the Church of England, the Roman Catholic and the Free Churches were concerned, all of whose communities faced severe losses of property and plant. If the Minister of Works and Building was forced to take a comprehensive view, it was equally clear that the Church authorities must do the same. Destruction, which in the early days was local, minimal and spasmodic, increased alarmingly in concentration and intensity, thus bringing havoc to church and ecclesiastical buildings generally. Geoffrey Fisher in the House of Lords described the gravity of the situation in these words: 'In London and other great cities there are whole districts in which hardly a church remains untouched. It is neither possible nor desirable that a very large destroyed church should be rebuilt as it was and where it was. Conditions have changed, old needs have disappeared, new needs have been created and in many parts of our great cities there were before the war too many separate parishes and too many churches.'

To deal with the problems thus delineated an Archbishops' War

Damage Committee was set up in the second year of hostilities consisting of twelve members – eight clergy and four laymen – with Geoffrey Fisher, Bishop of London, as its Chairman, an excellent, almost an inevitable choice. His exceptional capacity to grasp details coupled with the fact that London was to suffer more severely than any other comparable area, made his nomination singularly appropriate. The Committee held its initial meeting on 18 December 1940 and amongst its first acts was to issue a memorandum for the benefit of clergy and churchwardens, letting them know precisely how the War Damage Act affected them in their parishes. It seemed likely, at first, that the War Damage Commission, set up by Act of Parliament, would centralise its work in London, and from there negotiate settlements with the Church of England as a whole. Fortunately neither of these happened. The Commission wisely decided to set up regional offices throughout the country and agreed with the Bishop of London's proposal that the Church would prefer a system by which separate negotiations were entered into by the diocese where damage had occurred. In return the Commission insisted that these diocesan bodies, with which it was to deal, must be brought into existence as rapidly as possible. Most important of all, so far as the Churches were concerned, was the Chancellor of the Exchequer's assurance that religious institutions, on being given their grants, would not necessarily be expected to restore the *status quo ante bellum*.

Thus the first task confronting the Church of England was highlighted at the summer session of the Church Assembly in 1941 (17–19 June) when its members had before them a report from the Archbishops' Committee to which Geoffrey Fisher spoke. In this he proposed for incorporation into the Measure which established the Diocesan Reorganisation Committees up and down the country, that they: (1) act on behalf of the parishes in negotiating claims for compensation and allocating payments; (2) undertake, at a later stage, the comprehensive re-planning of disaster areas. This would almost certainly mean, so the Bishop warned, the alteration of parish boundaries; the holding of benefices in plurality or their union; the reallocation of endowments; and radical changes in pastoral supervision.

The Bishop's report was given general approval and thus began a period of over two years while its main proposals were given the authority of Measures of the Church Assembly. They did not have a uniformly easy passage. It is not surprising that some of the more conservative members of the Church Assembly were alarmed at what they regarded as undue haste; while others resented what one member described as 'a woeful lack of confidence in Church Councils', and the complete by-passing of parish priests in the decision making. The Reverend C. E. Douglas complained that the Measure gave powers which a German gauleiter would 'envy'. Also participating in the debate was Lord Quickswood, devout churchman, lawyer, Provost of Eton and Member of Parliament whose concern was always to do legally as well as to do justly and with whom Geoffrey Fisher was to have many a tussle before he was home and dry.

This was a useful debate so far as the Bishop of London was concerned. It introduced him to the mood of the Assembly and helped him to see clearly that Measures of this kind inevitably trod upon innumerable toes and could easily generate a collective and unreasoning hostility. The lesson that he took away from it and consistently acted upon was, therefore, the need to be as conciliatory as possible consistent with getting the Measure through. Clergy are traditionally jealous of their ancient rights. Thus he was quick to assure the Assembly that the Diocesan War Damage Committees were to consist of not less than ten and not more than twenty members, one third of whom must be clergy and one third laity. In particular three members must be elected by the Diocesan Conference. In his final reply at the end of the debate the Bishop reasserted that there was a great need for haste in the legislation though this was not of the Archbishops' Committee's choosing. Its members did not create the war nor for that matter the damaged churches: but they had to deal realistically with the situation as it was – and to do so straightaway. The Assembly certainly responded, for the Diocesan Reorganisation Committee Measure 1941 was approved in principle and all was soon ready for the Bishop of London to move its final adoption. This he did under three main resolutions: (1) to set up Diocesan Reorganisation Committees to carry through planning proposals; (2) to set up a special appeal procedure; (3) to empower the Estates Committee of the Ecclesiastical Commissioners to negotiate, on behalf of the Dioceses, with the War Damage Commission. The Motion was approved with only a few dissentients.

It was now necessary, in accordance with the Church of England Assembly (Powers) Act 1919 for the Measure to go to Parliament. Hence on 22 July 1941, the Bishop of London proposed in the Upper House that the Diocesan Reorganisation Committee's Measure of 1941 be presented to His Majesty for the Royal assent. He then succinctly outlined the case for it as he had previously done in the Church Assembly, concluding with these words: 'I hope it may be agreed that it is a wise and necessary Measure and that we are doing in regard to Church property what must be done on a wider scale for the nation as a whole.' The Motion was agreed.

The story now moves on to the Assembly's Spring Session of the following year (3-5 February) when Geoffrey Fisher gave the second report of the Archbishops' War Damage Committee and sought increased powers in a new Measure. In commending the Report, which had already been circularised, he promised to confine himself to a few salient points. A Diocesan Reorganisation Committee had been successfully established in all dioceses, and was now actively engaged in defining the areas for replanning. Here he invited members of the Church Assembly to envisage the situation in a great city where two, three, four or five parishes had been destroyed in part or in whole, and the population dispersed. Obviously such an area could not be rebuilt as it was and, therefore, he must ask for a new Measure with greater powers, including the reallocation of income in relation to several parishes as well as matters of patronage.

The ensuing debate followed a not unexpected course. Lord Quickswood indulged his set piece and expressed extreme 'moral indignation' at the 'highwayman' attitude to the dispossessed incumbent. The income given him at his induction belonged to him with the same inalienable right as did his Lordship's watch belong to its owner. The Bishop was not displeased on the whole with the reception of his report and had little difficulty in securing the appointment of a Committee to draft a Measure which it was hoped would be before the Assembly at its winter session in November. The Reverend R. J. E. Boggis, it is true, deplored the passing of any 'revolutionary proposals' while thousands of clergy and millions of the laity were engaged in total war.

To reassure the conservative and fearful, Geoffrey Fisher kept on repeating that it was no purpose of the Committee to initiate a drastic reform of the parochial or patronage system.

Of one thing the Bishop was constantly reminded, as were the members of his Committee, namely that infinite care must be taken to ensure not only that justice was done, but was also seen to be done to those who felt that they had suffered unfairly under the Measures. The faintest intimation that legal and long-established rights were being arbitrarily whittled away was a sure means of making the lawyers rally to the clergy's defence. Everything, therefore, pointed to building effective rights of appeal into the Measures. Here Geoffrey Fisher recognised he would be wise to seek the advice of the Lord Chancellor, Lord Simon, and the Lord Chief Justice, Lord Caldecote. Indeed, the former took the initiative in getting into touch with the Bishop who followed this up with letters to both of these distinguished Law Lords. He explained at length why his Committee had come to the conclusion that it could not adopt, for an appeal procedure, the Privy Council as in the case of the Union of Benefices Act. Indeed his colleagues believed they had arrived at a better solution. The Lord Chancellor and the Lord Chief Justice conferred together – the former describing their meeting as 'short but not perhaps a very conclusive talk' – and both wrote back individually to the Bishop. The Lord Chancellor was cautious. He would do nothing, if the Measure came to the House of Lords, 'to oppose it – quite the contrary'. On the other hand he must insist that he should not be referred to either as publicly or privately expressing any views on the scheme. With this somewhat negative approval from the Lord Chancellor the Bishop had to be content. Lord Caldicott, the Lord Chief Justice, was more positively forthcoming, and volunteered that he entertained 'no difficulty at all' in the present proposals.

Fortified with these two opinions, one it is true more favourable than the other, the Bishop faced the Spring Session of the Church Assembly on 2 March 1943. He gave a lengthy and detailed analysis of the proposed Measure clause by clause which occupied twenty-two pages in the official report, and was later published independently as a pamphlet.

In the course of his speech he stressed that the Measure was dealing with problems which had to be faced. Also that its main purpose was pastoral. He accepted that it 'touches matters which affect deep feelings and intimate associations'. They had tried to secure at every stage 'co-operation and consultation' and if it were to 'bear fruit it will need, wisdom, charity, self-restraint and mutual trust from all concerned'.

There followed a debate in which some fourteen members took part asking predictable questions which the Bishop dealt with efficiently and briefly, such as: 'Why was compensation limited to incumbents? Ought not the Measure to be rigorously confined to dealing with damage arising directly out of the war? Why could not the Assembly rather than the Standing Committee of the Houses of Clergy and Laity nominate members to the Special Tribunal Appeal?' As was expected, when the Bishop of London moved that the Reorganisation Areas Measure 1943 be submitted to an Appointed Committee for drafting, the motion was carried handsomely.

The aftermath of this debate was a frank exchange of views between Lord Quickswood and the Bishop of London arising out of the latter's courteously informing him that the Measure had gone to the printers and inviting him to list such amendments as he himself would wish to propose. These Lord Quickswood itemised as follows, all of which served to restrict the scope of the Measure:
(1) That an area scheme, agreed by the Diocesan Reorganisation Committee should be brought for approval to Parliament. (2) That the Measure should be confined to matters arising directly out of the war. (3) That incumbents should suffer no financial loss if their parishes were suppressed under the Measure. (4) That the Archbishop's nominee to the Special Appeal Committee should be a person who had held 'high judicial office'.

These were serious amendments and in line with Lord Quickswood's consistent position from the beginning. The Bishop consulted his Committee and replied immediately. He was pleased to say that they had unanimously accepted his first amendment so far as opposed schemes were concerned, since it was 'proper' to leave with Parliament the final decision *vis-à-vis* the overruling of objections. However, the Committee found the other three 'considerable amendments' quite unacceptable.

It was not to be expected that the Bishop's reply would satisfy the noble Lord as he demonstrated with firmness in two letters written on 24 and 27 May. As to the dispossessed clergyman he returned to his defence. 'I cannot even now believe that you will defend before the Assembly the proposition that a perfectly blameless incumbent may be deprived of part of the stipend which he had before the war and was assured to him for life according to law'.

This was very emotive language and it must have distressed the Bishop, particularly since there was something of the lawyer in his own make-up and the very thought of abolishing legal rights by *force majeure* must have struck him as distasteful. Also he could not but recognise that Lord Quickswood, as a member of the Ecclesiastical Committee, was in a position of influence and there could be no question but that the Measure would need to go to Parliament.

On 22 June 1943 when the Measure was considered for revision, there began the most critical session in its progress through the Assembly. Now was the last effective opportunity to debate the many amendments which had been tabled. Were it not that Geoffrey Fisher enjoyed the cut and thrust of debate he might well have found dealing with some of the objections a gruelling and somewhat frustrating experience. He had been over it all before! One advantage of a general debate was that of bringing criticisms into the open and thereby, in most cases, diffusing them so far as the rank and file of the membership was concerned. Throughout, the Bishop preserved his accustomed *bonhomie*, always seeking a *via media*, when he could do so with a good conscience. However, he wisely took the opportunity, in his introduction, of uttering these words of caution: 'Of course a point comes when a decision has to be made which might not be acceptable to all the parties concerned.' When that was reached they had provided, as they thought in the best possible way, for some process of co-operation to continue, objections being referred from one body to another until they finally came, not before a court of law, but before a body wisely chosen for the long experience of its members. The debate was an interesting one though it cannot detain us here. Maybe we have space to squeeze in a contribution by the Reverend G. Henneker. 'The danger of these wide proposals', he protested, 'is that they will tend to make England one great urban district, and will almost wipe out, unless they were very careful, the smaller communities'. The Reverend C. E. Douglas commented somewhat acidly that the Bishop was not justified in 'patting himself on the back' for a Measure so 'exceedingly badly conceived'.

Some minor amendments the Bishop, on behalf of the Committee, wisely accepted. Thus he agreed that the Chairman of the Appeal Tribunal must be 'a person of judicial experience nominated by the Archbishop of the Province after consultation with the Lord Chancellor'. On 25 July the Schedule of the Diocesan Reorganisation Areas Measure, with the approval of the Assembly, was referred to a Drafting Committee.

The end of this long drawn-out process, so far as concerned the Assembly, was now in sight. At the winter session, on 16 November 1943, the Bishop of London proposed that the Measure as drafted be finally approved. In a short speech he reminded the Assembly yet once again that the overriding purpose of this 'flexible' measure was 'practical and pastoral'. Lord Quickswood, indulged a last *cri de coeur* and in a long speech accused the Bishop of having broken at least one of the Ten Commandments. The Measure was then passed to the accompaniment of loud applause by an 'enormous' majority.

The Archbishop of Canterbury then fittingly expressed, on behalf of the Assembly, his gratitude to the members of the Committee and the Bishop of London in particular; 'for the great pains they had taken in preparing the Measure, piloting it through, listening to all the points that had been made and doing their very utmost to meet them'. R. D. Denman, a Member of Parliament, stressed how entirely indebted they were to the Bishop of London for his achievements. Without his drive and his mastery of the subject he did not think the Assembly would have had an opportunity of passing this very remarkable Measure.

No words of thanks were ever more deserved!

The Measure, however, was not yet 'home and dry,' since for it to have legal force it must both be 'cleared' by the Ecclesiastical Committee, of which, as we have seen, Lord Quickswood was a member; and then be approved by Parliament.

The Committee gave its clearance, though with obvious hesitation, prompted doubtless by the Provost of Eton. 'Inevitably', so its judgement ran, 'such re-organisation involves widespread interference with the existing constitutional rights of His Majesty's subjects; also of parishioners, incumbents, patrons and others. After considering the measure, the Committee are satisfied that proper regard has been paid to these rights and provision made for compensation on appropriate occasions.'

Lord Quickswood may well have thought that in one aspect at least he had made his point.

The Reorganisation Area Measure (1943), cleared by the Ecclesiastical Committee, then went before Parliament and was debated in the House of Lords on 15 March 1944. The Bishop of London – this was positively his last word on this subject – gave the briefest of summaries of the Measure, confining himself to stating simply what the situation was which had made the Measure necessary and what its main proposals were. His final words had about them an impressive dignity: 'There, I think, we can leave the Measure. It is full of interest in its fifty-seven clauses for those who like to study it. Its purpose is really to re-start parochial life as effectively as possible and as soon as possible in their dislocated areas. It is an unprecedented Measure; and so are the conditions. The Church has, if I may say so, shown great courage and great foresight in tackling this problem boldly and definitively, and so armed itself beforehand to be ready to act the moment the opportunity arises ... The Ecclesiastical Committee described it as urgently needed and expedient and I submit it to your Lordships with every confidence that you will accept it.'

This confidence was not misplaced. There was, it is true, a short debate in which only two members and the Archbishop of Canterbury joined. Lord Hemingford, a convinced churchman, referred to the particular reservations felt by the Ecclesiastical Committee and observed that if this matter 'had been a little more carefully considered from the point of view of the difficulty which the Ecclesiastical Committee had in getting over these particular points, they could have been avoided'. Earl Grey commented that it was significant that his relative Lord Quickswood had more support for his views in the Ecclesiastical Committee than in the clerical members of the Church Assembly. The Motion was agreed, as was later the case in the House of Commons.

It had indeed been a long haul, a mammoth effort and monstrously time-consuming. However, its significance in relation to the post-war life of the Church of England justifies, it is hoped, the space allocated to it. Certainly the passing through the Assembly of the Measure gave the Bishop of London an opportunity of showing his mettle. He never lost his 'cool', even with the Provost of Eton, who in public controversy, though without personal animosity, could be deliberately provocative. Geoffrey Fisher trod warily but firmly a middle path. He eschewed a timid conservatism since he became convinced that a reasonable solution of existing problems must be a radical one. Though he repeatedly denied and fairly, that he and his colleagues were motivated by any desire to reform the parochial structure of the Church of England, he yet, in retirement, lived to see the changes effected under the Measure paving the way for Group and Team Ministries and Guild Churches.

The Bishop's manner of dealing with opposition in the Assembly was to take it seriously; to master his own brief; to expound the Measure clearly and honestly; to make concessions when he and the Committee felt conscientiously able to do so; and to preserve his customary good humour.

No one is indispensable, but it is difficult to see any other member of the Episcopal Bench at the time who could have done better, or as well; or who possessed in such a measure the diverse abilities and the aptitude necessary for the task. Yet Geoffrey Fisher was the first to recognise the great debt which he owed to the lawyers who drafted the Measures; and to fellow Bishops on the Committee, in particular Dr Mervyn Haigh, Bishop of Winchester. Doubtless the experience which the Bishop of London here gained in piloting two Measures through the Church Assembly was not unhelpful to one who was later to chair its meetings, a role which, though it irritated Cosmo Lang and bored William Temple, delighted Geoffrey Fisher.

The excellent John Guillum Scott, who as Secretary of the Church Assembly for nearly fifteen years had unique opportunities of observing Fisher's chairmanship of this sometimes difficult body at first hand, describes his performance as 'outstanding'. 'He had always complete control of the situation', he writes, 'and could quickly and clearly sum up a debate and bring a diffuse discussion to a conclusion. His own speeches, often impromptu, were 'lucid, forceful and often brilliant'. Geoffrey Fisher showed 'remarkable patience'; but on occasions when he felt he had been over severe and irritable he would seek out the Member concerned and apologise or explain to the other where he felt he had gone wrong.

CHAPTER 8

The City of London Churches

(i)
The Bishop's Committee

AMONGST the chief treasures of the City of London are its churches which constitute a rich architectural and religious inheritance. The Great Fire of 1666 grievously reduced their number, eighty-six being destroyed or partially so, of which thirty-five were never rebuilt. Thus there was given to Sir Christopher Wren an opportunity to display his genius. The decreasing residential population in the City, led two Commissions in 1899 and 1919 to recommend a further reduction in their number. The Second World War introduced a new destructive power in concentrated attack from the air. By 1941 twenty-three City churches had been damaged, two or three beyond the possibility of repair. The extent of this damage sparked off a public debate as to what ought to constitute the priorities when the lights went on again and it was time to rebuild. Here opinions differed. There were those who while deploring the disappearance of so many architectural gems yet believed that a unique opportunity was now provided for a rising generation of practitioners to be given the same opportunity as came the way of Sir Christopher Wren. There were others, however, who wished to restore these churches as near to the originals as possible. Both schools of thought were vocal in advocating their views, using the correspondence columns of *The Times* newspaper.

However, Mr W. H. Ansell, President of the Royal Institute of British Architects, struck a more immediate and sombre note in this newspaper when he claimed that the immediate task was one of ensuring that such fragments as remained of bombed churches should not be further damaged or removed by the unregulated use of pick axes and dynamite. Along with this there was the need to secure maximum protection for church buildings exposed to attack from the air.

It was against the background of this debate that Geoffrey Fisher, as diocesan bishop, was required to discharge his own responsibilities for the present and future of these buildings. His belief was that the questions raised by interested parties related to two different aspects of the overall problem and should, therefore, be treated separately. As for the first, which concerned the preservation and repair of existing buildings this could be best handled by a Committee largely, though not exclusively, consisting of churchmen under his own chairmanship. As to the second, which related to the future, this needed a far more widely recruited, high-powered Commission called into existence by himself but under distinguished lay chairmanship.

We turn first to the Bishop's own Committee set up by himself in December 1940. Its terms of reference included the overall protection of churches; the removing of their treasures to places of greater safety; and last but by no means least their pastoral supervision. The Committee, which was kept small so as to be more easily called together, consisted of: Ernest Sharpe, Archdeacon of London – his knowledge over long years was unrivalled; Prebendary Taylor, Rector of St Bride's, Fleet Street; Godfrey Allen, Architect of St Paul's Cathedral; and Prebendary Wellard, its tireless Secretary. Between its setting up at the beginning of 1940 and July 1943 when the extant records of its meetings cease, the Committee came together some twenty times, the Bishop of London never failing to preside on a single occasion. Indeed he himself was its driving force, making contact with the City Fathers and undertaking much of the necessary correspondence in spite of available secretarial help. Though the scope of the Committee's work was wide, yet it was in the main geared to practicalities, the intention being to take decisions in relation to individual churches, and to implement these as rapidly as possible. One of the Bishop's first acts in January 1941, was to write to all City incumbents requiring them to appoint a qualified architect: and informing them of the correct procedure when the church suffered attacks by aerial bombardment. The Bishop was particularly concerned to ensure a proper salvaging of materials and the speedy drawing up of claims for war damage. There could be no question at this stage of making plans for permanent rebuilding.

This letter to City incumbents was followed by his calling together parish priests and architects of some eighteen damaged churches in order that he might be told of their condition, both in respect of the state of the building and the provision of a pastoral ministry. To assist those assembled he made certain points clear; namely, that when a church was damaged a full report must be sent to the Secretary of the Bishop's Committee; demolition should not be undertaken by the parish architect without reference to his Committee, unless the structure was judged dangerous in which case contact must be made with the City Surveyor. The protection of ruined churches against further depredation was of prime importance since nothing ought to prejudice the possibility of future restoration. Here the London County Council offered help in transporting treasures to places of safety. The Bishop, on his part, was prepared to waive, when necessary, the usual provisions relating to Faculties.

The responsibility for safeguarding the City churches was a heavy one, and lay opinion differed as to how effectively ecclesiastics were discharging it. There were those who thought the Church authorities to be slack to the point of negligence; others that whether this was true or not a task of such magnitude was far beyond the Church's financial resources, its manpower and professional skills. This conviction was shared by no less a person than Mr Hiorne, Architect to the London County Council, who by virtue of his office had a specialised interest and responsibility. One practice to which he took grave exception was the locking up of City churches which meant that the Authority was prevented from inspecting them to ensure the clearance of debris and the safety of the public.

The Bishop of London realised that he must take this complaint seriously and he replied at length in what he hoped was a letter of reassurance, pointing out that each City church had its own architect to advise the Bishop's Committee in seeing that all moveable treasures were safely housed and every possible care taken of ruins. As to bombed diocesan churches outside the City they were immediately inspected by an architect. He, the Bishop, would welcome any advice which Mr Hiorne might care to give him.

Mr Hiorne's fears, however, persisted and at a meeting on Thursday 5 June of the Council for the Protection of Ancient Buildings he delivered a strong and 'unfriendly' attack directed against Church authorities, maintaining that many parish priests were indifferent to their responsibilities and often his letters to incumbents had not even been acknowledged.

These were serious charges suggesting gross negligence and made before a responsible body under the Chairmanship of Lord Esher. Prebendary Wellard, Secretary to the Bishop's Committee, felt that he could not let such an attack pass without comment and he frankly admitted that the Church authorities 'had failed in some instances to do everything that would have been desirable'. Yet the sheer number of works of art which had been damaged made it 'humanly impossible' to tackle every instance of damage at once. After the meeting, Mr Hiorne took the opportunity, in a more relaxed way, of intimating to Prebendary Wellard that the London County Council might be prepared, at its own expense, to undertake the immediate task of shoring up dangerous structures in the City if it were called upon to do so. Dr Francis Eels, Secretary of the Central Council for the Care of Churches approached the Bishop of London, as a result of complaints sent to him, and offered storage space in a remote Somerset village for such valuable treasures as could be moved. In acknowledging this offer, the Bishop regretted that owing to the distance and their bulk he was unable to take this up, but he assured him his Committee was in process of transferring treasures to vaults in the City which were safe against anything but a direct hit. It was Dr Eels' opinion that it would be helpful if the Bishop's Committee were to give its work some wider publicity in the Press, particularly in relation to storage of treasures and protection of buildings. The Bishop felt this to be a helpful suggestion and followed it up with Prebendary Wellard.

One letter, to which the Bishop recognised he must give his own personal attention, came from Mrs Inge, wife of a former and distinguished Dean of St Paul's. Her only excuse for writing, she explained, was that for twenty-four years her home was the Deanery, and she 'loved the City as no other place in the world'. After a recent devastating air raid on London she was distressed to hear from the Cathedral Architect, Mr Godfrey Allen, that some incumbents felt it impossible to allow anything to be removed out of their churches such as, for instance, exquisitely carved fonts, pulpits and altar rails.

The Bishop well understood, so he wrote to Mrs Inge, her 'grief and horror' when she heard of the destruction of much of the City and its churches. 'I appreciate every word you say of them. Your intimate knowledge and love of them makes the wound yet deeper.' But much was in fact being done for their protection and he proceeded to acquaint her with the work of the Bishop's Committee. It was indeed true, unfortunately, that the only means of making an inadequate parish priest active was 'persuasion', since the building was legally vested in him and the churchwardens.

In fairness to its members, it needs to be said that the Bishop's Committee was by no means dilatory. True, its work needed to be more widely known, thereby allaying disquiet and maybe attracting grants and donations. Thus Prebendary Wellard wrote an article which appeared in the City Press entitled 'The City Churches, Preserving Their Treasures'.

This publicity did much good in the City, but it was not the only publicity. Sir Eric Maclagan, a very energetic member of the Committee drew up a statement and the Bishop himself also conferred with Canon Anthony Deane, Ecclesiastical Editor of *The Times*.

One general weakness relating to protective measures – and this was by no means confined to City churches – was the inadequacy of the fire-watching. The incendiary bomb demanded immediate attention, and if this were not forthcoming a church could become a total wreck before expert help, usually stretched to the limit, was able to arrive. The need here was for active and trained personnel, particularly as the City was almost depopulated at night, but this the churches, unaided, could not themselves provide. The Bishop of London decided to share this problem with the Lord Mayor which he did in a letter dated 12 June 1941. The situation in the City, he wrote, had changed radically after the last raid on 11 May. Earlier in the war incumbents had been urged to make their own arrangements through voluntary fire-watchers and had responded to this appeal in a 'very satisfactory way'. At the time this seemed adequate, but since then the general position had deteriorated with the increasing intensity of the raids. Also compulsory fire-watching unfortunately removed the sources of a voluntary supply. The Bishop, therefore, made a practical suggestion to the effect that in each section the fire-watchers should be instructed to include any City churches among the buildings for which they were responsible. This led to a fruitful meeting with the Lord Mayor and as a result Mr Godfrey Allen and Prebendary Wellard, in co-operation with the civic authorities, worked out a scheme by which the City was divided into zones with key stations set up in individual churches.

Though it could not be known at the time, and many trials and tribulations were yet to confront the City until peace came, the main brunt of the concentrated bombing attack on London was over. Flying bombs and rockets did considerable damage but these, in their delivery, were more fitful and less targeted. Precautions were maintained and the Bishop's Committee kept in being; but the years of building up a planned system of civil defence lay in the past.

However, it was not only the preservation of bricks and mortar, memorials and treasures, which occupied the mind of the Bishop. He fully appreciated that the parish churches in the heart of the City had a spiritual and pastoral ministry to discharge and that this was the *raison d'être* of their very existence not least in wartime. As Bishop of London he had a unique responsibility to ensure that this pastorate was carried on regardless and that the secular slogan, 'Business as Usual', should equally obtain in matters religious. Thus he was strongly opposed to any unnecessary closure of churches which inevitably meant a weakening of a strong Christian witness when it was most needed. True, under the National Emergency Precautions Measure he, as Bishop, had power 'to direct the closing, either wholly or partially, of any church; or the suspending or limiting of the number of services to be held in them'. These were certainly extensive, almost Draconian powers, and before Geoffrey Fisher had arrived on the London scene his predecessor had taken advantage of them to authorise the closure of a number of City churches because of a shortage of clergy to minister in them. This was a situation which the Bishop believed needed careful watching and in November 1940 he circularised all City churches asking whether such closures as obtained had been authorised under the Measure; and if so did their incumbents wish such closures to continue. He concluded his letter with a specific request, namely that he, as Bishop, should be told at what hours on weekdays their church was open and what weekday services they provided.

The situation in a few churches, it must be admitted, left much to be desired as was apparent from the periodic inspections which the

Bishop's Committee carried out. Prebendary Wellard, accompanied by an architect, visited them regularly and was on occasion greatly disturbed by what he found, particularly when he discovered a building only kept open for a few hours each day. The condition of neglect in some was appalling particularly when the incumbent was absentee. One church, which shall be nameless, Prebendary Wellard described as 'in a most deplorable and filthy state . . . the dust and dirt everywhere is pathetic. Dead flowers in dirty vases are an eyesore'.

With his customary common sense, Geoffrey Fisher recognised how complex the problems in the City were and how urgently they needed to be tackled. As Napoleon believed that an army marched on its stomach, so did a ministry in the City equally need the provision of adequate emoluments. To secure this was not easy since many clergy still received a part of their incomes in tithe which bombing had progressively eroded. Geoffrey Fisher was well aware that the situation varied from parish to parish, but he insisted that every effort must be made, short of going to law, to retain this tithe income. Not a single claim should be allowed to go by default. To emphasise this he called together the City Parish Assessors and he himself presided over a meeting of Tithe Clerks. In addition, he invited the Lord Mayor and other City Fathers to confer on the same subject with a small group of Ecclesiastical Commissioners. Basic to his efforts in this field was his determination that the clergy should not be deprived of their lawful stipends through apathy or neglect. This was important since the plight of a large number of City incumbents was made worse by the fact that they had let their parsonage houses, thereby becoming landlords receiving rent on a leasehold tenure. This had the unfortunate effect that when these houses were rendered uninhabitable by enemy action, no payment was forthcoming since the tenants, understandably, disclaimed the lease even if they could not legally do so. Geoffrey Fisher determined to keep up the pressure and was in some instances successful.

The Bishop's chairmanship of the City Churches' Committee may not have been among the easiest or most spectacular of his wartime activities, but for a time it was a great preoccupation. Certainly it enabled him to do much to preserve to posterity a wealth of historic treasures; to encourage the clergy, against the grim background of war, to minister pastorally to their parishioners; and to receive less inadequate stipends for so doing than if he had not intervened on their behalf.

(ii)

The Commission that Never Was

It was Geoffrey Fisher's intention, as we have seen, that in addition to his own Wartime Committee, there should be established a high-level

Commission to deal with more long-term problems in relation to rebuilding, City re-planning, and general co-ordination. However, owing to a chronic misjudgement on the part of the Bishop of London this Commission proved a damp squib, and after meeting once only was unceremoniously wound up. Our reference to this denouement, therefore, need only be brief.

Geoffrey Fisher's first task was to find a chairman which he did in Lord Merriman, a good churchman and a High Court judge. The membership was a mixed one representing Church and State. Amongst the former were the Deans of St Paul's and Westminster, also the Archdeacon of London. Amongst the latter Lords Crawford and Banks, the Lord Mayor, and Mr H. W. Ansell.

The Commission held its first meeting on 7 October 1940 when the Bishop of London addressed the gathering for some twenty minutes. All went well so long as the inspirational uplift lasted but it soon became clear after this that he was growing uneasy, particularly when he came to the point of declaring that the Commission would not be entirely free on its own to decide policy. There were other interests involved such as the City Improvement Committee and those serving on the War Damage Commission. These cautionary words took Lord Merriman completely by surprise and he returned home bemused and a little angry. How could a statutory body such as the War Damage Commission relate to another, the existence of which derived solely from the will of the Bishop of London? These sentiments Lord Merriman expressed in a long and forthright letter to the Bishop. In his view there was in fact no role whatever for the newly established Commission to discharge. Thus Geoffrey Fisher realised that there was no alternative for him but to eat humble pie; to admit that he should have alerted Lord Merriman earlier concerning the Diocesan Reorganisation Committee; and in addition to write to members of the proposed Commission explaining the circumstances which made necessary its quietus. In fairness to the Bishop it needs to be said that his workload was extremely heavy and on his own admission he was 'very tired'.

One unfortunate consequence of the abortive Commission was the upsetting of the City clergy by their total exclusion from its membership. Nor did the Bishop assuage their injured pride either by his tactless remark that 'there appeared to be no City incumbent who enjoyed the confidence of all his brethren'; or his contention that he did not think the Commission would be 'strengthened' by such an inclusion. Its effect, so claimed Dr McDonald, Vicar of St Dunstan's, Fleet Street – an erudite Church historian if somewhat peppery – was to put City incumbents in a worse position than clergy in areas where they were free to elect their own members to a Consultative Committee.

CHAPTER 9

The Archbishops' War Committee

(i)

WHEN Geoffrey Fisher came to London in 1939 the Second World War had just begun. One of the first requests put to him by Dr Cosmo Lang, Archbishop of Canterbury, was that he become Chairman of the newly established Archbishops' War Committee. The Bishop accepted the invitation and threw himself into its work with enthusiasm. The writ of the Committee was as ill-defined as it was wide-ranging, nothing less than dealing with any matter which affected the Church and was thrown up by a Britain fighting a total war. The Committee was to meet regularly, attended very occasionally in its early days by the Archbishop himself. Basically, however, Lang saw his archiepiscopal wartime function in more patrician terms. Not for him chairing a committee often dealing with minutiae, routine business and domestic chores. Rather he saw his role, when occasion demanded, as one of calling on, or being called upon by, the Prime Minister; interviewing the heads of the Services and sorting things out with them personally. Nurtured in the cautious school of Randall Davidson, his main preoccupation, except in matters of extreme and self-evident concern to the Church, was never to embarrass the Government.

The personnel of the Archbishops' Committee consisted, for obvious reasons, of the Bishops whose Sees were in or near London, though the attendance even of some of these was irregular and spasmodic. The task of the Chairman was certainly no enviable one. It demanded tact, firmness, much letter writing – this was not uncongenial to Geoffrey Fisher – and an efficient way of working. Fortunately, he possessed these abilities in abundance.

The Bishop was not present on 12 October 1939, at the first meeting of the Committee since he was not installed into his new Diocese till 3 November. He was soon to find out that certain matters came up for discussion with regular monotony, one such being the Home Guard. These excellent 'part-timers', immortalised in the television series 'Dad's Army', did not always find obedience to directions from higher authorities easy and were not beyond paying off old scores against an unpopular vicar. One subject relating to their training which remained a bone of contention was the use of Sunday mornings for this purpose. Many were the parish priests who alleged that these volunteer soldiers 'religiously' did their training at 11.00 am, thus preventing those who wished – and quite a few we are assured did so wish – to attend

Morning Service in their parish church. For example, a vicar in the Hampton Deanery told Geoffrey Fisher that the commanding officer refused permission for members of his unit to attend church, even on 23 March 1940 which was set aside as a National Day of Prayer. This was no isolated incident for protests came in to the Bishop of London from various parts of the country telling similar stories. Hence, he sent a personal letter to Lieutenant-General Eastman, Director-General of the Home Guard, in which he acquainted him frankly with the unease of his Committee at the situation which had developed. He fully understood that in present conditions it might not be always possible to avoid such Sunday training but he had reason to believe that some commanding officers did not recognise that it was a thing to be avoided if possible. The consequence was that men were taken away from their religious duties on many occasions when it could easily have been avoided. Consequently, he urged the Lieutenant-General to issue directions to commanding officers only to resort to training on Sunday mornings when there was no alternative.

Lieutenant-General Eastman was himself a churchman and he replied immediately that he would certainly issue instructions to those concerned embodying the Bishop's suggestions. He was sure that they would be observed wherever possible. The Lieutenant-General was as good as his word and a directive to this effect was sent to all commanding officers.

However, it was one thing to issue instructions, quite another for them to be complied with up and down the country. Much of course depended on the local situation and the particular personalities involved. An unpopular incumbent or a forceful commanding officer could be determining factors in what happened. As complaints continued, Geoffrey Fisher circularised all the Bishops informing them of the correspondence with the Lieutenant-General and the assurance he had been given.

The Bishop of London's consistent view was that the Church, which in this context meant the local clergy, should be content with the compromise which had been agreed. Thus when Dr Hunkin, the Bishop of Truro, in his evangelical zeal suggested to Lieutenant-General Eastman that there should be a monthly church parade of the Home Guard, the Bishop of London cautioned that this was unwise and would create unnecessary tensions, a view in which he was upheld by Dr Cosmo Lang.

Yet in spite of an agreement at the highest level between the Bishop and the War Office difficulties did not disappear. In May 1941 Dr Pollock, Bishop of Norwich, complained that it was still the custom to hold parades at 11.00 am on Sundays, even on Easter Day, and similar protests came from the Dioceses of Winchester and Guildford. In these circumstances the Bishop of London requested the Lieutenant-General to re-issue his former instructions which were evidently not being observed. Lieutenant-General Eastman, however, was now posted elsewhere and Lord Bridgeman had for the time being taken over. His reply was sympathetic but somewhat astringent. Before re-issuing directions, he would wish, and he himself was a practising churchman, to remind the Bishop that the Home Guard were carrying out a vitally significant national duty and doing so in addition to other important war work. Matins was not the only Sunday service so could not the Home Guard parade at another time or a special service be laid on for them, possibly much earlier? 'I do feel there is a case to answer here,' Lord Bridgeman maintained, 'and that if we stress the need for churchgoing – more than ever a vital one in these days when prayer means so much – at least the clergy should be asked to recognise the importance of Home Guard duties, and not to insist overmuch on the special value of divine service at one particular hour of the day which, after all, must have had its origin in a very different age.'

The position of the Bishop of London was not easy and only a few days after receiving Lord Bridgeman's letter the Reverend J. B. H. Evans, Rural Dean of Enfield, complained that the training was being held both in the morning and afternoon. Indeed, one Sunday it had occupied the whole of the day thereby preventing some members of the congregation from coming to church at all.

The Bishop replied to Lord Bridgeman in conciliatory vein, though reiterating that the problem was a very real one. For example, one of his incumbents on confronting the Company Commander with Lieutenant-General Eastman's instructions received the reply that no such orders had ever come his way. When shown the Bishop's letter containing them, he was extremely co-operative. The Archbishops' Committee believed that Lieutenant-General Eastman's directions were helpful when liberally and sensibly interpreted but this only proved possible when there was give and take on both sides.

It was not only church attendance which exercised the minds of parish priests in relation to the Home Guard. In the eyes of most of them their own parish church was the focal point of a unique personal responsibility. As a result they brooded over them as a protective hen over her chicks. Times, however, were exceptional and nerves edgy. The threat of imminent invasion in 1941 by German parachutists encouraged the military to look longingly to church towers as observation posts. Constant vigilance and a local warning system became the order of the day. Hence numerous approaches were made by the military, at first informal, for their use as look-out posts; as well as the deployment of churchyards for military purposes. It was to be expected that individual bishops, inundated with enquiries from their parish clergy, should ask for guidance from the Archbishops' Committee rather than they themselves take up the cudgels locally with the Army authorities. Under increasing pressure, the Bishop of London, on 16 May 1940, wrote to Mr Anthony Eden, Secretary of State for War, asking precisely how he saw the situation so far as ecclesiastical property was concerned. In posing this question, the Bishop confessed that he understood the Military to have given an explicit assurance that church towers would not be used by the Army and he, therefore, hoped that this would be adhered to. He himself was not happy at the prospect of church towers being employed to house the paraphernalia of modern war, but found it difficult to advise clergy seeking to prevent such and similar deployment while at the same time permitting their use for look-out purposes.

The concern felt on such issues by parish priests was widespread. Thus the Convocation of York discussed it at length and on 23 May 1940, William Temple wrote to Geoffrey Fisher stating their general view namely that the mounting of searchlights or anti-aircraft guns upon church towers should be avoided. Of course, if the State in the exercise of its own sovereign powers were to commandeer towers, the Church could not in the last resort resist.

Diocesans continued to write to the Bishop of London for guidance on such matters and on 5 June 1940, he informed Mr Eden's secretary that it had become urgent for 'an immediate decision' by the Government. This evoked an almost instantaneous reply in which Mr Eden informed the Bishop that his advisers were 'now of the opinion that in the existing condition of possible invasion, the use of church towers in the country as sites for observation posts would be of considerable military value in obtaining early information of the arrival of enemy parachutists or troop-carrying aircraft'. There was no question, he assured him, of deploying churches as sites for machine guns or other weaponry. The Bishop lost no time in welcoming Mr Eden's clarification of the position and so informed the diocesan bishops.

This ruling did not answer all the points which came to the Bishop of London. For example, Dr Woods, Diocesan of Lichfield, having in mind William Temple's statement, asked whether church towers could simply be commandeered by the State and if this were so what powers remained with the incumbent. He was making this enquiry because a small body of pacifists in the Diocese would most certainly refuse the use of church towers 'if they have the authority to do so'. To this question the Bishop of London replied cryptically: 'The root fact is, I think, that the State under recent Acts has complete power to commandeer everything including churches and church towers'.

As to Mr Eden's regulations the Archbishops' Committee saw them as 'reasonable' and had no desire to resist them. If an incumbent were to prove obstructive the Bishop of the Diocese, so was the Committee's view, should persuade him that resistance was 'fatal' since the War Office had acquired 'full powers'.

The result of this correspondence between the Bishop and Mr Eden was the issue of guidelines by the War Office to all military commands throughout the country. Enlarging on these guidelines, Mr Eden repeated that he was prepared to be accommodating, although it was his consistent view that the defence of the country made it necessary to intrude in this way on consecrated ground. He could, however, give an assurance that churchyards would not be violated except in cases of 'the greatest urgency' and even then there would be consultation with the incumbent.

The issuing of orders from the centre at the request of the Archbishops' Committee though it had beneficial results did not by any means solve all local problems. Maurice Harland, Bishop of Lincoln, in a letter to Geoffrey Fisher on 11 July, related at length what had been happening in a church near Sleaford. Here the constant tramping up and down of members of the Home Guard in their military boots was damaging the lead on the roof, added to which this made a great deal of noise during Divine Service, not to mention their having appropriated the tower to sleep in!

The Archbishops' Committee was certainly kept busy with enquiries arising from what was happening up and down the country. For example, could a local commanding officer insist that he had the right to put a man as an observer on a church tower equipped with a gun? Could the Royal Air Force install navigational lights on the church tower of Bottisford?

Churchyards, particularly in the countryside, sacred to the memory of many 'rude forefathers of the hamlet', were thought of as hallowed ground even in wartime. The Home Office let it be known that whatever the precise legal position under Section 51 of the Defence of the Realm Act regulating the use of consecrated ground, the policy of the Department was not to assume possession without the consent of the appropriate Church authorities. However, some local units of the Home Guard, in their zeal and under the threat of imminent invasion in the summer of 1940, took the law into their own hands merely informing the parish priest, greatly to his consternation, that they proposed to dig trenches in the churchyard even if graves were disturbed in the process. In one case the reason given for such a violation of consecrated ground was the defence of a main road which skirted the church. Block houses and defence works began increasingly to appear in churchyards, without leave asked for or given. So often was this the case that William Temple, whose temperament was always against making a fuss, yet more specifically wrote to the Bishop of

London asking what the position was *vis-à-vis* gun emplacements and the digging of trenches in churchyards. 'Anyone but a soldier', he commented, 'would get into great trouble with the Home Office for doing this (i.e. disturbing graves) quite apart from the question of consecrated ground and the respect due to the bodies that have been buried.' Cosmo Lang also asked what the Archbishops' Committee was doing in this matter, pointing out that there were instances of abuses in his own Diocese.

It was clear that something needed to be done, and the Bishop of London lodged a formal protest to Mr Eden putting the position fairly and squarely before him. 'A churchyard is consecrated ground,' he wrote tersely, 'set apart by law from all profane and common uses for ever. Their uses for military purposes cannot but be repugnant to Christian feelings and also makes them military objectives. We do not wish to present conditions unreasonably but we think that certain safeguards are required.' These, he suggested, should be: (1) That the use of churchyards in this way needed special justification; (2) That the military should obtain the consent of the ecclesiastical authorities before any action was taken; (3) That the applications to undertake such works should go both to the incumbent and the Registrar of the Diocese, thus ensuring rapid and unified action.

The Bishop also consulted the Registrar of his own Diocese, Sir Henry Dashwood, and agreed with him a procedure to implement item No.3 of the above *desiderata*, namely that the Registrar should give the military officer in charge a written authority for passing on to the parish priest who must immediately be informed if, in the course of digging, any human remains were found.

Mr Eden's reply, written on 27 July 1940, was certainly not all Geoffrey Fisher might have desired. He assured the Bishop that the military authorities were placing defence works in consecrated ground only where no alternative course was possible. Also he would undertake that, except in conditions of the greatest urgency, consultation with the incumbent would always take place. As to the particular safeguards proposed in the Bishop's letter they would involve such delay that he could not order their observance.

The deployment of church towers and churchyards for defence purposes certainly aroused opposition; but far more serious to Geoffrey Fisher was the requisitioning of the building itself for purposes other than its primary use for divine worship. There were rumours, and some evidence to substantiate them, that churches might be employed to house the homeless and refugees from disaster area – or as mortuaries. The Archbishops' Committee believed that this was going too far and determined to resist any proposals of this kind on the grounds that they would rule out any provision for public worship. Geoffrey Fisher conceded that in an emergency anything might happen but no such use was in fact resorted to during the war.

The price of maintaining this position against the zeal of local officers and personnel was certainly eternal vigilance. It was not exceptional for incumbents, quite illegally, to receive orders from the Home Guard that their church must be closed because of the exigencies of an Army exercise. The result, when this happened, was a flood of episcopal letters of complaint and enquiries dispatched to Geoffrey Fisher as chairman of the Archbishops' Committee. The most notorious example occurred in Sheffield where the military, in planning a mock invasion, issued orders, without any reference whatever to religious leaders, which required citizens to remain in their homes over the weekend while this exercise was taking place. Leslie Hunter, Bishop of Sheffield, immediately consulted the Roman Catholics and Free Churches prior to sending a telegram to the Regional Commission protesting that none of them had received any information concerning this 'invasion'. After an exchange of letters, together with an approach to the Town Clerk of Sheffield, the original notice was more or less withdrawn. However, it was too late to prevent the *Sheffield Morning Post* on 22 October 1941, requesting all citizens to stay at home.

When the Bishop of London came to hear of this incident he was shocked – it was no isolated case – and he expressed his sentiments frankly to the Bishop of Sheffield: 'The scandal is less, perhaps, the invasion of Sunday than the complete ignoring of Sunday worship as worth consideration or discussion with those who are responsible.' The Bishop of London also took the opportunity of referring in general terms to this grave matter during his Diocesan Conference held on 27 October 1941. It was of vital importance, he claimed, to the moral health of the nation that Christian worship, and all that it stood for, should be maintained, indeed extended and strengthened. Many local organisations and branches of Civil Defence too often paid little regard to the claims of Sunday worship. Yet the Churches had a duty to safeguard the freedom of their members to fulfil their religious obligations.

The Bishop thought this matter in general sufficiently serious to justify his complaining to Sir James Grigg who had now taken over from Lieutenant-General Eastman. In advising him of what had happened in Sheffield, the Bishop admitted that in this case the offending request came from the local and not the central authorities. Sir James Grigg saw the point and immediately dispatched a directive that no such orders to close a church on Sundays because of military exercises should in future be given unless necessary by actual military operations as distinct from training.

This was all that the Bishop could hope for and it seems to have proved effective.

However an extreme request came during the summer of 1942 when the Army authorities proposed that on 20 July four small parishes in the Norwich Diocese should be wholly evacuated in order that the total area might be used as a training ground by the military. The church and churchyard were to be closed and parishioners buried where they died and re-interred after the war in their former parish if the families so desired. Sir Henry Dashwood, the Bishop of London's Registrar, was of opinion that this scheme, though involving a radical uprooting of many local inhabitants in their pattern of life, was legally in order under special powers granted by Parliament to the Government. He advised that incumbents should, from time to time, revisit their churches to determine whether any repair work needed to be done. One of the purposes lying behind this proposal was the provision of facilities for the storing of ammunition during exercises. Geoffrey Fisher, supported by his Committee, reacted violently against Sir Henry's ruling, believing that the intended requisition of four churches should be resisted at all costs; nor were he and the Committee prepared to concede that being situated within a prohibited area made any material difference. 'Our claim,' Geoffrey Fisher asserted, 'which Mr Eden recognised, was based not on the existence of a population around the church but on the nature of the church as a consecrated building.' It was a matter of principle. If the War Office refused to accept this view then the matter must be referred to the Secretary of State and he be invited to negotiate directly with the Archbishops' Committee.

The scheme was in fact never implemented but it was not until the invasion scare became past-history that extreme requests of this kind ceased to alarm the Bishop of London.

It must not be thought, in the light of the complaints which came in to the War Committee, that relations between the Home Guard and local incumbents (or the bishops) were always conducted at the level of mutual recrimination. Relations were in fact often friendly, as may be seen in the number of clergy who wished to enrol in the ranks of the Home Guard. This raised many questions concerning the priority of their parochial duties, so much so that the War Committee was forced to issue a circular for the benefit of the bishops in general. The line that Geoffrey Fisher himself took was set out in a letter to Bishop Duppa, dated 17 May 1940, namely that clergy were exempted from military service on the grounds that they had their own uniquely essential work to do. However, it might be that service in a Local Defence Corps, since it did not remove the clergy from their parishes, might make it possible for them to continue to discharge their pastoral ministry.

In enunciating this view, the Bishop of London admitted frankly that the Committee did not go along with those clergy who believed that military duties were incompatible with the exercise of the priesthood.

This matter became of sufficient concern to engage the interests of the Southern Convocation a week after the Bishop had dispatched his letter to Bishop Duppa. As a result of the debate, Geoffrey Fisher somewhat modified the emphasis suggested in his original statement, and now proclaimed that there was general agreement on the Bench of Bishops that they did not wish to encourage their clergy to join the Home Guard, but did not feel it appropriate to forbid them provided that their parochial ministry did not suffer. In practice some of the bishops were happy to leave the decision entirely to their own clergy; others did their best to dissuade them from enlisting.

The Archbishops' War Committee, it will have been noticed, served as a clearing house for all kinds of problems and enquiries, and it often fell to the chairman to sort them out and to deal personally with them, indeed even with seeming minutiae which he might well have delegated. A random selection from these illustrates how extensive Geoffrey Fisher's preoccupations could be. We quote the following:

The cost of Communion wine; petrol rationing (this led to a vast correspondence and Geoffrey Fisher, in his own handwriting, drew up a lengthy document giving precise details of each bishop's mileage per month; the kind of car that he possessed and the adequacy of the existing allowance); the relaxation of blackout regulations for early morning services on Christmas Day; the sale of intoxicating liquor to very young soldiers in the N.A.A.F.I. canteens; the provision of rationed food for the retreats of ordinands; church railings (here the Bishop drew up a document in November 1941 for circularization to incumbents letting them know precisely what the situation was); the correct procedure for securing marriage licences and their cost; the removal of names of parishes from church notice-boards so long as the threat of invasion remained; what to do when the services were interrupted by air-raid warnings; the financial implication of the death of a chaplain-incumbent and those reported missing; coupons – a vast file – required for vestments; the provisions and contents of Army Service Books; the need for a resident Anglican Bishop to liaise closely with the Deputy Chaplain-General while acting as a Father in God to the chaplains in general and his availability to undertake Confirmations; the omission, for security reasons, in the publication of banns and in the marriage register, of any reference to the unit to which a member of the Forces belonged; Canadian chaplains and marriages conducted by them in Anglican parish churches; the prevention of, and prosecution for, bigamous marriages in the Forces; the legal status of Army camps; munition workers and the opening of shops on Sundays

– here the Bishop of London conferred with the Engineering Industries' Association as well as the National Council of Social Services.

An unhappy consequence of the war was the isolation of widely distributed Christian denominations from each other due to the near impossibility of travel abroad. To overcome this difficulty Geoffrey Fisher corresponded at length with the Archbishop of Canterbury and suggested, as an alternative, that he invited Bishops Manning and Parsons of the Protestant Episcopal Church of America to visit Britain, to preach here and report back. Also would the Archbishop, in co-operation with the Free Churches, invite to Britain leaders of the French Protestant Churches including Pastor Marc Boegner?

The deployment and recruitment of chaplains for the Army, while at the same time maintaining the parochial ministry at home, were matters to which the Bishop of London and the Committee gave much thought and care. Henry Vodden, Bishop of Hull, put forward an interesting suggestion, namely for chaplains to be employed on short service commissions, possibly for one year only, after which they could return to their parishes. This would give many clergy the opportunity of acquiring a particular experience which would serve them well in their post-war ministry. Geoffrey Fisher, after exploding: 'what a letter to discharge on my unhappy head!' replied cautiously to the Bishop of Hull but promised to discuss the matter with his Committee. However, not much came of the Bishop of Hull's suggestion, largely because of an unfavourable reaction from the Chaplain-General.

Christian mission and pastoral oversight do not, of course, depend solely on the ordained ministry, a fact of which the Archbishops' War Committee was forcefully reminded when lay readers, drafted into the Forces, expressed a desire to continue their ministry in their new environment. The Archbishops' War Committee saw the point and engaged in serious discussions as to how these objectives could be secured in practice and what status such wartime lay readers should be given. At first Geoffrey Fisher inclined to the view that they should be licensed only for the duration, but on becoming convinced that 'men passed for this work in the Forces must be exceptionally good people and above rather than below the ordinary standard of "civil" lay readers', he changed his mind. Indeed, many of these men might well go on to ordination to the priesthood. In taking this line he had the support of Dr Blagden, Bishop of Peterborough, chairman of the Lay-Readers' Board; and also of the Archbishop of York who stressed that, though these lay readers came under the Chaplains' Department they were yet enrolled as Readers in the Church. Thus they could wear cassocks, surplices and badges and take them abroad as part of their kit.

The principle thus having been established, the minutiae of its practical application were left to be worked out by the Bishop of London which he did with meticulous care.

The Archbishops' War Committee never lost its zeal in an increasingly unfavourable environment to protect the English Sunday. This was not always easy as we have already seen from Geoffrey Fisher's tussles with the military authorities over the Home Guard. The exigencies of the black-out led the London County Council, understandably, to resort to holding its evening classes over the whole of the weekend. The Bishop of London sympathised with the difficulties which this imposed on the parish clergy, and he complained in forthright terms to the Director of Education at County Hall believing it to be both 'regrettable' and 'unjustifiable' for the LCC Institutes to 'monopolise' Sunday mornings and afternoons.

The Director's reply was moderate in tone. He drew attention to the fact that the early Morning Communion and the Evening Service were not affected. As to the lecturers, their livelihood had already been destroyed which meant that they welcomed the opportunity of giving up some part of Sunday to professional work and earning a little money which would not otherwise come their way.

So matters were left, but after a few months the Director wrote again to the Bishop, doubtless to the latter's surprise, expressing the desire of the Council 'to do away with all Sunday classes'. 'We feel', he wrote, 'that Sunday should be protected completely, as far as this is possible, from all claims of work.' Accordingly, they had transferred all weekend classes as far as possible to the weekday evenings.

Many clergy felt as strongly as did Geoffrey Fisher the need to maintain church-going and Sunday observance. For example, the Rural Dean of Ealing was asked by his brother clergy to sound a note of alarm at the 'ever increasing tendency to devote *Sunday mornings* to meetings and practices which we feel could take place at other times. Could not the Prime Minister or even the King be approached to give a lead in a matter so urgent?'

The result of this approach was a letter on behalf of the Committee from the Bishop of London to Lambeth itemising the various grounds for complaint. On the credit side, however, was the pronouncement, issued by the Navy – always the 'more godly than the other Services' – emphasising that prayers must be said on board all His Majesty's Ships and Stations. 'Is there any possibility', Geoffrey Fisher asked, 'of getting a joint pronouncement by the Prime Minister and by the Heads of the Army and the Air Force on the same lines if not by the King? We are in a strong position to make such a request.'

Cosmo Lang, the Archbishop, was far too astute to risk a negative reply by writing direct to Winston Churchill but, in a personal interview with the Bishop of London, he urged that he undertake the task himself which he accordingly did. The Prime Minister, whose greatest admirers could hardly think of him as a regular church-goer eager to missionise on behalf of Sunday observance, responded to this approach in an epistle which could not have given the Bishop much comfort. He began by pointing out the difficulties in asking employers to provide facilities for Sunday worship while there was a war on. 'I will, however,' he wrote, 'gladly promise to bring to the notice of the Army and Air Force Authorities the form of the Admiralty Fleet Order, and if I can see a suitable way of bringing the Admiralty's action to the notice of the appropriate Civil Departments who employ labour I will do so.' We are fairly safe in assuming, however, that no such 'suitable way' presented itself.

We have called attention earlier to the multiplicity of concerns which came before the Archbishops' War Committee. Some of them, of course, claimed more attention than others. One that seemed to Geoffrey Fisher to demand particular and careful handling was the series of lectures given, with tacit official approval, to officers and training schools by the Army Scripture Readers' Association. These dissertations, he was given to understand, were unashamedly propagandist on behalf of the British Israelites, a situation which he deplored and took up with the Chaplain-General. There was certainly substance in some of the charges made against certain of the lecturers. The Headmaster of Marlborough, for example, called attention to a group of young, intelligent, officers stationed at Colchester who were compelled to attend a lecture at which they were informed by an official of the Army Scripture Readers' Association that the present war and the appropriate strategy to wage it, were foretold in the Scriptures even to the minutest details. Russia was identified by the lecturer – this country had not yet entered the War – with Gog and Magog on the grounds that before hostilities commenced England had imported large quantities of pencils from that country stamped 'Gog'. 'It is deplorable,' commented the Headmaster, 'that such an address should be put before them as a religious and Christian address'. Another talk at a college in Bexhill was even more offensive. Here the young officers were regaled with the news that even the War Cabinet consulted the Bible when planning military tactics.

Suffice to say that the Archbishop intervened – and effectively.

One further preoccupation constraining the attention of the Archbishops' War Committee, as the European conflict drew to a close, arose simply out of the necessity to look ahead to the prospect of peace and with it of general demobilization. The latter, no matter how welcome, was fraught with problems, not least for the Church. Geoffrey Fisher – he was prompted by Cuthbert Bardsley who acted as a liaison between the Church and the Forces – approached the authorities asking for more information concerning what they envis-aged in respect of the chaplains. If they were to stick rigidly to the 'Military Necessity Clause', chaplains might return hastily to their parishes leaving the Army itself chronicly understaffed. Ought they not, therefore, to be encouraged to stay put for the time being?

It was indeed a highly complex problem though at the time when the Bishop of Croydon wrote to Geoffrey Fisher no chaplains were being released except on compassionate grounds. The difficulty, of course, was how to balance the respective claims of dioceses, universities, colleges and the claims of the Army itself. Some means needed to be found for achieving this balance in co-operation with the Bishops. Geoffrey Fisher wisely decided that this was a matter which equally concerned all denominations and that he must consult the Archbishop of Westminster as well as the Moderator of the Free Church Federal Council. The matter of demobilization, which also affected ordinands, was further complicated by the fact that it was linked to National Service. The Bishop came to the conclusion that an efficient machinery must be set up to deal with the many problems arising out of demobilization.

It was obvious, quite apart from a seemingly casual attitude by the more distant Bishops to the responsibility of membership, that the Archbishops' Committee was unable to give the concentrated attention necessary to deal efficiently with so important a matter. Nor had it any properly constituted executive to do so. Thus Geoffrey Fisher informed the Archbishop of Canterbury that there must be a Church Demobili-zation Board to which Lambeth would nominate a few bishops dispersed geographically. In order to secure a working liaison with the Forces, the Bishop of Croydon should be asked to act in the capacity of Advisor with a Secretary from the Church Advisory Council for Training for the Ministry. This new arrangement still meant doing things on a shoe-string but it was more efficient than that which it had replaced.

The Committee was faced with a veritable host of problems resulting from the changeover from war to peace. The de-requisitioning of church property was one of them, particularly as it was natural for the military authorities to be somewhat reluctant to return them immedi-ately to their legal owners.

There were other areas connected with the aftermath of war which gave great concern to some of the laity as well as to the clergy. Thus the Reverend E.T. Killick, better known for his prowess on the cricket field for Middlesex, raised the question of the pensions due to the widows of serving chaplains. Enquiry convinced the Bishop of London that their plight was 'indefensible' and he so informed the Chaplain-General. The fact was that widows under the age of forty received

£130 per annum and those above £150. Thus prompted by a high authority the Chaplain-General was able to see that something was done to alleviate the sad and unjust predicament of these ladies.

(ii)

It was to be expected that the war would bring in its train vast social and moral problems. In a speech delivered on 4 September 1940, pleading for more instruction in health care in addition to what was already provided by the Royal Medical Corps, Geoffrey Fisher stated as follows the general position as he saw it. 'With the weakening of repressive influences, the social and religious sanctions of former years, together with the widening knowledge of contraceptives, meant that men and women who were not more immoral than a previous generation had been rendered defenceless, lacking any inherited or reasoned relation to, or understanding of, the sexual side of life. The danger was made worse by war.'

Thus when the Archbishops' War Committee held its first meeting way back on 12 October 1939 the agenda told its own story as follows: 'the moral life of the Army; the need for sex education to the Forces.'

These items reflected a growing unease early in the war, as to the moral health of those in the Forces uprooted from their homes. Thus Mr A.F.W. Thomas, Chairman of the London Men's Committee of the Diocesan Moral Welfare Council, wrote a severe letter to the Bishop of London expressing the strong conviction that at the earliest opportunity there should be a public statement by the Church authorities on the subject of sex morality and behaviour. There was an 'abundance of unsettling evidence', he maintained, 'that war conditions have thrown up, in acute forms, problems of the relations between men and women, and also that many young people of both sexes are therefore in great need of help and guidance.'

These were serious words from a responsible moral welfare council such as the Archbishop of Canterbury or Geoffrey Fisher must take account of. Indeed the former was stirred to action and made a public statement as to the activities generally of the Church in wartime and in particular the work of the Archbishops' Committee. This was a typical archiepiscopal utterance moderate in tone, reassuring and charitable in content. Yet its restrained but implied criticism of men and women in the Forces led to a scurrilous press campaign against Archbishop Lang reminiscent of a similar attack made against him during the First World War. Writing to the Bishop of London he protested that he had been 'stupidly misunderstood'.

The Bishops in general, not least Geoffrey Fisher, found themselves in an unenviable position. If they criticised behaviour in the Forces they were condemned, while equally responsible people reproached them if they kept silent. In these circumstances the Bishops were called to Lambeth when they agreed, after a lengthy discussion, to issue a statement, leaving it to the Bishop of Winchester, through the Archbishops' War Committee, to draw up a draft. This choice of a script writer was in part somewhat cynically determined by the negative fact that he was 'really against any statement at all' and was, therefore, rather 'a good person' to do it. The briefing given him by the Bishop of London was to embody in the document: (1) an expression of general concern; (2) a statement dealing with the Christian moral view on sex; (3) the difficult political position in which the Army authorities found themselves; (4) the need neither to rush to condemnation nor in any way to give the appearance of condoning promiscuity; (5) to present the Army Authorities' attitude as 'sympathetic and helpful'.

The Bishop of Winchester now got down to the difficult task and by mid-December 1939 was ready with his first draft. There now happened what some suspected from the beginning, namely that most of the bishops from their differing points of view did not like it. It was, for some, too academic, for others much too long and evasive. So it was that when sent to Cosmo Long he rejected it out of hand, and Geoffrey Fisher was spared the labour of writing another draft.

Withdrawing the draft, however, did nothing to diminish the external pressure brought to bear on the Bishop of London to persuade the Episcopate to do something positive about what many regarded as a public scandal. An instance of this was seen when a group of London clergy, attending a course of lectures on 'Problems of Morals and Marriages', passed a resolution which was forwarded to Fulham. In it they voiced their perturbation at the 'official view of the low standard of moral behaviour expected from men and women in the Forces both in England and abroad'. In particular they complained of the *maisons tolérées* established in France and the low standard of entertainment often laid on by ENSA for the Forces. They therefore called upon the Bishop to take whatever action he considered necessary to deal with this 'emergency'.

Geoffrey Fisher felt that he could not allow letters of this kind from some of his own clergy to pass unchallenged. Things were not, in fact, so bad as these complainants suggested – such was the gist of his reply. Lecturers were now improving their standards and the Medical Secretary of the British Hygiene Council had drawn up a model dissertation which had been widely circulated through the instrumentality of the War Office with official approval. He himself was in close touch with the Roman Catholics and Free Churches and together they would continue to press the British Government to secure the closure by the French Authorities of the *maison tolérées*. As to ENSA it had recently been 'very seriously reprimanded' by the Quartermaster-General and one of its concert parties had been sent home.

However, the increasing incidence of venereal disease made serious-minded people think that there was a seeming lack of sustained efforts on many fronts sufficient to combat and halt it. Certainly the Bishop of London did not conceal his sense of the inadequacy of existing preventive measures, due in part, he believed to the failure to place greater emphasis on the need for moral discipline and self-restraint. He deplored the fact, based on the evidence which came his way, that much of the instruction given to the Forces and in the munition factories tended to minimise the serious nature of venereal disease. Too often it was thought of as an illness which could be cured by right treatment. Lecturers needed to concern themselves with the whole moral and social life of the community from which the religious dimension could not be excluded. Uncontrolled and promiscuous sex was a sin and must be both resisted and condemned as inimical to true citizenship and integrity in family life. So the Bishop was forced to ask – and was unhappy with the answers given – what was being done in the Forces to put forward moral as well as prudential reasons for continence?

The Military authorities were not, of course, unaware of their responsibilities and they themselves from time to time laid on teachers and issued pamphlets suggesting practical guidelines, but these were not always of a kind to commend themselves to the Bishop. What was needed, so the Bishop reiterated, was an increase in clinics and almoners dealing with venereal disease, in addition to an educational campaign putting forward the moral case for chastity.

Typical of what made the Bishop of London unhappy in respect of the advice given are the following *ipsissima verba* of one of the lecturers: 'Speaking as a wife and mother I can tell you that pre-marital virginity is something very much worth having when you are married both from your own and your husband's point of view. But I know that there is a war on and times are hard so I would like to say to you – if you feel that you have got to the stage when you must sleep with so and so and marriage is impossible – don't do it in a hurry. Go home and think it out first, then if you decide quietly in your own mind to do this thing, take adequate precautions. See that the man wears a sheath and don't for God's sake land yourself with a pregnancy.'

This extract shows admirably the dilemma which confronted many who were called in to give advice – the desire to help morally and an equal desire to be practical.

It was not only clergymen who were anxious about conditions in the Forces. In 1940 the Bishop of London was asked to join – the Archbishop of York was its Chairman – a group which the dis-

tinguished physician, Lord Horder, had called together to concern itself
with moral problems arising out of the War. Geoffrey Fisher accepted
the invitation and also agreed to serve on its Executive Committee.
This involvement when it percolated through to Lambeth was received
by the Archbishop with 'considerable irritation'. To placate Cosmo
Lang the Bishop of London replied with a calm, informative letter,
explaining the nature of Lord Horder's committee which was intended
to bring together most of the societies chiefly concerned with sex
education and moral welfare. He himself had joined it only after having
first secured the approval of the Archbishops' War Committee. It was
not a 'pressure group' and he himself would now be able to 'keep an
eye on things'. He would appreciate, and here the Bishop was at his
most tactful, the Archbishop passing on to him any information on this
and kindred subjects which he might receive from the Chaplain-General
or any other responsible source. He was hoping that Lord Horder's
committee might serve to short-circuit rather than encourage public
protests.

The reaction of Archbishop Lang to Lord Horder's committee and
Geoffrey's Fisher's membership illustrated again the dislike at Lambeth
for unofficial, self-appointed bodies which tended to recruit enthusiasts.
This did not prevent, however, the Bishop, together with the Arch-
bishop of York, going on a small delegation from Lord Horder's
Standing Conference to the War Office late in the summer of 1940.

It was, of course, easy to state in principle what ought to be done,
but there were many interests involved both within and outside the
Armed Services which it was not easy to encourage to work together.
Thus, it remained the Bishop of London's deep conviction that there
must be a measure of co-ordination between the various agencies at
work.

Mention has frequently been made of the *maisons tolérées* in France
and of the constant agitation to get rid of them through the British
Government bringing pressure to bear upon the French. Geoffrey
Fisher drew up an *aide memoire* on this matter in which he stated
clearly his own views which coincided with those of churchmen
generally and the bishops in particular, namely that something must be
done. The French Government, so the Bishop believed, could do little
unless considerable pressure came from Britain. Already a question had
been asked in Parliament and a public campaign was in process of
being mounted. However, it was, ironically, only the defeat of France
and its subsequent German occupation, which brought this undesirable
situation to an end so far as concerned British soldiers.

Geoffrey Fisher, throughout the course of the war, stuck to his
conviction, formed early, that all efforts should be directed towards
laying on a really comprehensive system of sex education integrated

with a fuller awareness of basic human nature, its needs and its drives to action. In a paper he drew up he stressed that young people born in so unsettling a period in human history needed special sympathy and understanding. Their question 'why shouldn't I?' deserved a serious answer since in the Forces there was much which *seemed* to suggest that 'it' was all right provided disease and illegitimacy were avoided. Prophylactics and contraceptives had knocked the bottom out of most moral propaganda. The Christian ethic, therefore, must win an intellectual assent. Because of this the Church needed to equip itself, and be prepared to co-operate with the War Office in providing an informed lecture programme not concentrating exclusively on sex but seeing this as but one aspect of the personal life. The Bishop believed that such an offer of help would now find ready acceptance from the military authorities. At the Bishops' meeting in 1941 Geoffrey Fisher suggested that they should approach the G.O.C in each command within their diocese, offering to help officers in talking to men along the lines of Major Radcliffe's pamphlet *The Soldier's Welfare* which, unlike most other hand-outs, the Bishop highly approved for its general approach. To forward this project the Bishop made contact with the Church of England Moral Welfare Council for help in providing trained lecturers in various parts of the country whose task would be to help the officers themselves to undertake this necessary task. The implementation of the Bishops' scheme meant for him the writing of innumerable personal letters, but it also led, as the war went on, to an increasing number of well qualified lecturers.

Being Chairman of the Archbishops' War Committee was certainly no light task! It was a daily preoccupation even if Geoffrey Fisher never saw it as a chore. It touched life at too many points for this. Not surprisingly, in 1944, however, the Bishop of London began to ask himself how long this personal commitment would or ought to continue and in a mood of anxiety wrote to Dr Temple, the Archbishop of Canterbury, on 26 October – Cosmo Lang had retired at the end of March 1941 – somewhat ruefully: 'I suppose I shall have to go on'. What he could not know was that on this very day the Archbishop unexpectedly died at Westgate. This tragic event was to change radically the whole shape and pattern of Geoffrey Fisher's life.

CHAPTER 10

Ecumenicity in Wartime

IF the evils attendant upon the Second World War were near absolute, it is yet paradoxically the case that a number of peripheral 'goods' emerged out of it. One of these 'goods' is the subject of this chapter.

War, like the Deity, is no respecter of persons. The good and the bad, the rich and the poor, Christians and non-Christians, are exposed to the same horrors and subject to the same sufferings. The Army chaplain, be he Anglican, Roman Catholic, Presbyterian, Free Church or Jewish finds himself, if he is worth his salt, ministering to the combatants and civilians of all religious persuasion – or of none. Indeed he may be burying the dead of the enemy as well as one of his own countrymen. Such a situation tends, of necessity, to break down barriers and to weaken extreme denominational loyalties.

The total preoccupation with winning the war made some Christians, as a reaction and in order to keep up their own morale, concern themselves the more fervently with the shape of things to come and what the Churches themselves could do to build a world 'closer to the heart's desire'. Thus in August 1940, with the support of a group of Roman Catholic clergy and laity, Cardinal Hinsley after the collapse of France launched the movement known as 'The Sword of the Spirit'. By its title deeds it was pledged to the support of Britain's efforts in fighting a just war; also to the preservation of a Christian Europe; and to the principles of natural law which undergirded it. Those inaugurating the movement further believed that the Roman Catholic Church, as an international society and inspired by Pope Pius XII's five conditions for a just peace, had much to contribute to the process of reconstruction which must perforce follow on the cessation of hostilities. From its inception the movement set out to appeal to men of goodwill among all Christians. Leading lights of the movement in England from the beginning were Miss Barbara Ward (later Lady Jackson), Fr Victor Murray, the Bishop of Lancaster, and A. C. F. Beales, Secretary and Lecturer in Education at the London School of Economics. Though, as we have seen, the movement had official backing at the highest level, its members were not always *personae gratae* in their own communion. Yet their determination to pioneer a new way forward never flagged.

Such a stirring of the spirit, born out of tragedy, was by no means confined here in the United Kingdom to the Roman Catholic Church.

The famous Edinburgh Conference, held so long ago as 1910, had across the years led to an ecumenical outreach which embraced a wide field of Christian endeavour. One such offshoot was the Ecumenical Commission of the Churches for International Friendship and Social Responsibility of which William Temple was for a time both Chairman and inspiration. From its deliberations there came the Life and Liberty Weeks, ecumenical in character so far as this was then possible, and, linked up with the Sword of the Spirit, equally dedicated to the application of Christian principles to individuals and nations. Inevitably by working together, the members of these organisations were brought into ever increasing contact, so much so that to quote Geoffrey Fisher's words: 'It was really difficult for these two mainstreams to continue without some kind of mutual understanding. Events were making it impossible.'

An early indication of this cross-fertilization appeared in a letter sent to *The Times* newspaper in December 1940 signed by the Archbishops of Canterbury and York, Cardinal Hinsley and the Moderator of the Free Church Federal Council which set out the principles for any true peace integrated into a more just social order. To quote again from Geoffrey Fisher: 'That letter greatly promoted a *Fermentation* among Xtian people and, ever since, there has been a vast amount of active thought and discussion about the relevance of Christianity to problems of social, civic, economic and international life. It has gone on in all sorts of ways, among all sorts of people, sometimes in groups, representing all denominations – more often confined to one or two.' This letter was indeed a creative 'breakthrough' and it was followed by the Sword of the Spirit promoting 'new and far-reaching campaigns' directed to members of their own communion. More widely Anglicans and Free Churchmen were also asked to participate. To this end the initiative was taken by the Sword of the Spirit which called a conference representative of their own membership and that of the other Churches. It assembled on 27 November 1940 at the Presbyterian Church House in Bloomsbury.

In order to enable the meeting to get off to a good start, A. C. F. Beales took an initiative in circularising two Schedules, the one, more ambitious, proposing the setting up of a national joint body, the other a more modest structure – a Standing Committee to sponsor joint activities by the participating Churches. Amongst the Anglicans, Free Churchmen and Roman Catholics who attended this conference were the Bishops of London and Chichester, T. S. Eliot, Dr A. C. Craig, Dr T. C. Dunning, Dr William Paton, Richard O'Sullivan, Fr John Murray, Miss Barbara Ward, Fr Douglas Woodruff and A. C. F. Beales. The group got down to business with commendable speed and decided for the less ambitious of the two schemes. It then agreed that the first task was to produce a document outlining the basis and scope of the newly developing co-operation between the various denominations. By 16 December the Committee was in a position to circulate a tentative draft statement on religious co-operation, and a month later it drew up a programme of joint activities which included 'Religion and Life Weeks', 'Spiritual Talks' and Study Groups. Thus encouraged, its members agreed to establish themselves on a permanent basis as a Joint Standing Committee, and it was at its first meeting in this more formal status that it received the news that the Statement on Religious Co-operation had been approved by the Archbishops of Canterbury and York, Cardinal Hinsley and leading Free Churchmen. Things were moving and Geoffrey Fisher was unanimously appointed chairman of the Committee which seemed singularly appropriate since he was already chairman of the Archbishops' War Committee. His acceptance of this nomination met with general satisfaction and Temple, Archbishop of York, wrote to him: 'I am usually taking the line of urging that you should not be asked to do things . . . but I confess that I do hope you can do this. I believe this may be one of the most important moves in the next five or ten years'. He was right. Dr Craig also rejoiced that someone who had 'easy and natural contact with the Archbishops should have taken over this office'.

The Joint Standing Committee was now in business and so far all seemed to be set fair. But the Statement on Religious Co-operation was not to have quite so easy a passage as in the first flush of excitement had seemed likely. This became apparent when Dr Craig received a somewhat disturbing letter from the Reverend M. E. Aubrey, General Secretary of the Baptist Union of Great Britain and Northern Ireland, arising out of a meeting of its Council at which a number of ministers had expressed disquiet at their Church being involved with Roman Catholics through their representation on the Joint Standing Committee. The nub of this criticism was the impropriety of issuing a statement on Religious Co-operation and Liberty without consulting the member Churches of the new Joint Committee in whose name it was sent out. Also there was much in the Statement of which Dr Aubrey's Communion, the Baptists, disapproved. He was careful to point out that his protest did not represent any unfriendliness towards his fellow Christians of other denominations and this included, of course, members of the Roman Catholic Church.

This was a serious yet understandable criticism on a matter of principle and one feels that William Temple was not being either fair or objective when he commented in a letter to Geoffrey Fisher: 'How touchy these Baptists are'. In a sense they were only asking to be put on a level with the Anglicans and Romans and not to be dealt with only through their membership of the Free Church Federal Council.

Dr Aubrey's criticisms were, in due course, reported by Dr Dunning, himself a Baptist, at the next meeting of the Joint Standing Committee. Geoffrey Fisher was in the Chair, and it was decided to postpone publicising the Statement in order 'to allow further time for sounding the Churches represented on the Commission'. The Baptists had successfully made their point and when the Standing Committee next met on 18 April, the Bishop, as Chairman, was able to inform its members that the Commission of Churches meeting at Oxford some three days previously – the Baptists were represented on this body – had given a 'general welcome' to the Statement with only a few minor reservations. It is therefore appropriate at this point to give a brief summary of its main contents.

The Statement began by stressing that there was 'a compelling obligation' on all Christian people in Britain to act together in this critical period in the history of Europe, and to do this in the social, economic and civic spheres, without, for the time being, raising any ultimate questions of church order. The purpose of the Joint Standing Committee was 'to build up a constituency of informed, enthusiastic Christians all over the country prepared to act together on broad lines of social and international policy'. The Statement also admitted that there were difficulties of various kinds which hindered co-operation but they were determined,with the approval of their appointing bodies, to 'stay together' in order to continue joint discussions and to take appropriate action where needed.

In view of misunderstandings the time had now come to give the Statement and what it stood for in Church relations, a launching pad in the presence of a selective audience.

It seemed a natural and easy operation but events proved otherwise. There were differences of opinion as to how this could best be done, and also how to make it conform with the vexed question of ecclesiastical precedent and protocol. Thus who was to preside? Bishop Bell had assumed that it must be the Archbishop of Canterbury and had already asked him. The Roman Catholics demurred to this unilateral initiative. What about the Cardinal?

It was all very embarrassing and it looked as if the irresistible force was meeting the immovable object. Perhaps, however, if something like this were to happen, it had better happen early – and be resolved. Not the least of those who were angry was Bishop Bell. 'I feel that the Church of England', so he wrote to Fulham, 'is the Church of the country ... and must not be treated as simply one third of English Christianity and not the most important third.' To this *cri de coeur* Geoffrey Fisher replied: 'There can be no two opinions about that', adding that he himself would not come if Cardinal Hinsley presided.

This unfortunate *contretemps*, so out of keeping with the whole spirit of the occasion inclined Geoffrey Fisher – and he was not alone in this – to doubt whether it was appropriate to launch the Statement at this high ecclesiastical level. Miss Barbara Ward was also having second thoughts. The Bishop of London was now seen at his best, judicious as well as eirenical. To overcome this crisis he came up with the proposal that, in the circumstances, it was better for the Joint Standing Committee to act as host and for its Chairman, namely himself, to introduce the Statement. This would allow the Archbishop, the Cardinal and Dr Berry to be invited to come as guests and for each to speak.

Such a change of plan was certainly wise and the Bishop of London had little difficulty in persuading the Committee to accept it. More embarrassing was it to break the news to Dr Cosmo Lang, and at the same time to let down as lightly as possible the Bishop of Chichester. This unwelcome task was left to Geoffrey Fisher. Suffice that he did it with courtesy and a sympathetic understanding.

The decks were now cleared for the launching ceremony which took place at the Waldorf Hotel in the afternoon of 28 May 1942. As arranged, the Bishop of London, in the capacity of Chairman, welcomed those present and began by explaining, as carefully as possible, what the occasion was not, as well as what it was. 'This is not a Public Meeting', he was careful to point out. 'We have invited to it chiefly editors and owners of the secular and religious press.' The intention was to secure for the document the 'intelligent interest and understanding' of such 'influential people as themselves'. He then proceeded to give a brief history of the genesis of the Statement, tracing its rise from the joint letter to *The Times* emanating from the Sword of the Spirit and the Commission of Churches.

His concluding words were weighty and designed to reassure the more cautious ecumenicists: 'What we have done and are seeking to do is only a modest thing. We do not wish to claim too much for it. It is co-operation over wide but still on a strictly defined ground. Even so, so far as it goes, it is a notable thing.'

Geoffrey Fisher then read out the Statement word for word after which the Archbishop of Canterbury, Cardinal Hinsley and the Moderator of the Free Church Federal Council added their commendations.

In spite of the grim background of war the press coverage was excellent. Over 100 newspapers and periodicals reported it and many regarded it as sufficiently significant to refer to it in their leading articles. The general mood was one of 'welcome and thanksgiving'. The religious press, in particular, Anglican, Roman Catholic and Free Church, treated the launching ceremony as an historic event of great importance. Only two papers voiced unfavourable comments – *The*

Christian and *The Life of Faith*. (A useful analysis of the press coverage was drawn up by A. C. F. Beales). Nor was such publicity confined to the United Kingdom. The Bishop of Chichester reported that he had seen a copy of the Statement in Scandinavia and had heard that it was being talked about in Sweden. Notices of the launching also appeared in America and Australia.

Read today, some fifty years after its appearance, the Joint Statement does not strike us as a very radical document. It was, in fact, for its time, precisely this. Born out of the travail and frustration of a uniquely destructive war, it derived from the initiative and pioneering enthusiasm of liberal Christians representing the three mainstreams of English Christianity. Geoffrey Fisher's role throughout, not least in the production of the document itself, was pivotal.

The successful launching of the Statement encouraged the members of the Joint Standing Committee to proceed further and to tackle a subject, even more contentious, which had been deliberately omitted from the letter to *The Times* and only briefly referred to in the agreed Statement on Co-operation. The reference is to the complex and potentially divisive issue of religious freedom. That the Joint Committee was prepared to explore this thorny subject was in itself a sign of growing confidence and of more intimate human relations among the group.

This project began by the Committee asking the mainstream Churches to provide it with relevant pronouncements made by them in this field. Thus by the end of 1943 the Committee had before it a great deal of documentation. At the outset Fr Murray made it clear that the Roman Catholic attitude derived from Catholic doctrine regarding the nature of the Church, which he realised was unacceptable to non-Romans. However, he believed that in relation to practical issues it might be possible to arrive at a common mind. Here Geoffrey Fisher was helpful; and his general comment had a point, namely that Fr Victor Murray had established the case for civil liberty but had not really extended this to matters of religious belief and practise.

A cleavage between a Roman and non-Roman view was clearly emerging. Central to this discussion was not the right of religious minorities to exist but their right to proselytize as, for example, in the case of Protestant missions in South America. The Roman view was supported by T. S. Eliot who maintained that there were extreme situations in which this right might be abused, so much so as to undermine the traditional life and indigenous culture of the nation concerned. In such circumstances, a Catholic State might properly feel that it must restrain the actions of a minority.

In these circumstances it was important to keep things moving. Geoffrey Fisher therefore volunteered, in co-operation with Father

Woodruff and Dr Paton, to draw up the final version. The basic intention was to provide a factual analysis which might shed light on the differing traditions and the ultimate problems involved. One subject, for example, much discussed, was the limitation imposed on freedom by such a phrase as 'so far as is consistent with public order'. On 2 December the Bishop of London was able to report that the British Council of Churches had given a 'general welcome' to the Statement as had the Executive Committee of the Sword of the Spirit. Learning from past experience, the Committee decided on Geoffrey Fisher's suggestion, that it would adopt a 'low profile' at the launching, contenting itself with sending it to the Press with a covering letter and later publishing it as a pamphlet.

This document made the following points: (1) The state had a God-given role but its rights over its subjects were not absolute. (2) The state must rightly have regard to considerations of public order but constant vigilance was needed to prevent this right leading to public abuse. (3) It is the civil duty of members of religious bodies to respect the rights of others though majority and traditional religions might by reason of their historical development properly 'enjoy a specific influence within the state'. (4) The same principle held in respect of conversion from one Christian community to another. There could be difficulties when conversion led to cultural division with distressing side-effects. (5) The state should guarantee freedom to all religions including Jewish, Moslem, Hindu and Buddhist and should recognise a right of conversion from one faith to the other.

This document, thought of in terms of those responsible for it, not least *vis-à-vis* Roman Catholics, was indeed radical far more so than that on 'Co-operation'.

The background to the two Statements was a series of meetings of which three took place under the aegis of the Joint Standing Committee in 1942. These were given more 'bite' by their handling of real contemporary political issues even where this meant criticizing the policy of the Allies. These occasions in spite of their difficulties were felt to be sufficiently significant by their sponsors to be continued throughout the course of the war. All however was not plain sailing. Thus the Bishop of Chichester – and no man was more ecumenically minded than he – wrote early in 1942 drawing Geoffrey Fisher's attention to what he regarded as an inherent limitation imposed upon the work of the Committee. 'What troubles me really about our position in regard to co-operation', he confessed, 'is that the Romans always seem to be united and get their way, while the non-Romans are divided amongst themselves ... The Sword of the Spirit has the immense advantage of having a regular organization meeting frequently and shaping their own mind. Either we shall simply be run by them or there will be no co-operation unless we have and keep a mind of our own.'

Dr Bell was here calling attention to a very real problem on the Standing Committee, even if he expressed it in somewhat exaggerated terms. It manifested itself at the local level in the painful question as to how far when Christians of different Churches were brought together Roman Catholics could participate in joint prayer. One concrete example, typical of many others up and down the country, may serve to illustrate the point.

In Nottingham there had been for some years a happy and fruitful relationship between Anglicans and Free Churchmen who worked together to sponsor various public activities. Encouraged by the success of these ventures they wished now to extend them to include Roman Catholics whose Bishop agreed to go along with them and an ecumenical Christian Council was formed, each church or denomination in turn providing the annual President. In spite of occasional friction the Council worked well, and was accepted by the Local Authority as a sounding board for Christian opinion in the City. In June 1942 the Council planned to hold a fully ecumenical 'Religion and Life Week' in the Nottingham Albert Hall. It was duly held but commenting upon it afterwards to the Bishop of London the liberal-minded Dr F. R. Barry, Bishop of Southwell, deplored the 'fearfully high price' which they had to pay for Roman co-operation. The Catholic Bishop laid it down that they must not talk about the Gospel itself, only its application in social life, and that there must be no prayers. It was only after long negotiations they finally got the Roman Bishop to agree that at the end of the last meeting Dr Barry should give a summing up and ask the people to stand in silence, after which he requested the Roman Catholic Bishop to lead them in the Lord's Prayer.

The problem here referred to was serious indeed if co-operation with Romans was to be maintained at public meetings such as those organised by the International Commission for Friendship and Social Responsibility. Thus many were forced to ask: 'Was it really proper or worthwhile, in order to secure a Roman Catholic presence, most desirable as this must be, to distort and frustrate the whole purpose in a Joint Meeting by thus parading differences. Surely to unite in prayer in response to the Gospel was part of the basic intention in coming together.'

This whole matter was brought before the Joint Committee meeting on 3 July when Geoffrey Fisher in opening the discussion declared, applying a little logic to this severe problem, that there were only three possible procedures: (1) no prayer at all; (2) prayers always said by a Roman Catholic – 'hardly a tolerable solution from a non-Catholic standpoint'; (3) To agree beforehand on an acceptable form – 'how much and what?'

To these three possibilities Beales added that there was a fourth – 'silence' – to which Geoffrey Fisher retorted that this was 'tantamount to no prayer at all', though he cautioned against these difficulties being exaggerated or regarded as insurmountable. Indeed, at a Youth Rally in Manchester a Roman Catholic had led the prayers and a Church of Scotland Minister given the Blessing. The Bishop of London's own view remained that these sensitive issues should be left to the localities for decision though the Joint Committee, if approached, should be willing to give advice. His own view was that joint activities ought not to be purchased at the cost of omitting any reference to the very Gospel that had brought them together.

Few at that time could have suspected that in 1979 an 'Ecumenical Prayer Cycle for All God's People' would be published by S.P.C.K. in co-operation with the Catholic Truth Society!

Fairness compels the comment that it must not too easily be assumed that this particular problem derived solely from timid conservatism or crude religious bigotry. In fact the stresses and strains arose from the very desire of churchmen of different denominations to move more closely towards each other. They could not be expected suddenly to annihilate their past and, as some might see it, forswear their inheritance. Particular credit must go to those members of the Sword of the Spirit who courageously sought to discharge two loyalties at the inevitable cost of occasional inconsistencies.

With the coming of 1944 it began to be evident, though there were still set-backs ahead, that the war in the West was painfully drawing to a close. Britain more realistically than hitherto now looked hopefully to the future and not surprisingly the Joint Standing Committee turned its attention to the nature of the peace which must follow upon the cessation of hostilities. In particular, it considered the wisdom, as well as the rightness, of unconditional surrender to which the United Kingdom had committed itself under pressure from America. Geoffrey Fisher suggested, in an address to the British Council of Churches, that the Archbishop of Canterbury should lead a delegation to the Government comprised of the heads of the various religious denominations – including the recently appointed Cardinal Griffin in succession to Hinsley – the intention being to discuss problems relative to the peace. Each member of the delegation should be left free to follow his own individual line. However, the sudden illness of Archbishop William Temple inevitably halted plans for the time being.

The Bishop of London believed strongly that the Joint Standing Committee could be of help in discussions of this kind, and he reminded its members of the memorandum produced by the British Council of Churches which dealt with the political framework which it was hoped would follow the peace, i.e. the freedom of people to choose their own form of government; an equal distribution of the world's resources; the maintenance of fair labour standards; a just colonial policy with respect for cultural minorities; and, in particular, religious freedom for the Jews. The Standing Committee spent much time seeking to clarify its own mind, discussion being geared to contemporary realities. Among the subjects which commanded prolonged attention was securing the four freedoms in relation to Polish Protestants and German Christians in East Prussia; abandonment by the Great Powers in the peace treaty of any territorial ambitions; the necessity to secure the free consent of populations to any change of sovereignty; the constitution of a new League of Nations. Dr Woodruff pleaded that the Government be told that the moral basis of a League of Nations should be written into the peace treaties.

Critics might well say that these deliberations of the Joint Standing Committee tended to be academic and to ignore political realities. Certainly these wider discussions owed much to the Roman Catholic membership – not least to Barbara Ward – with its wider international outreach.

By 1945 the Joint Standing Committee had been in existence for some four years – years of a major national effort geared to the winning of the war. The Bishop of Chichester believed that the time had now come to undertake an appraisal of its successes and failures to date. He himself was convinced that the Committee ought to have been more positively active and not so preoccupied with drawing up and studying documents. The regrettable fact was that while local meetings of the Life and Liberty Weeks and the Sword of the Spirit had increased in both number and influence, the 'central impact of the Joint Standing Committee was not very significant'. Indeed, the general public was unaware of its existence. 'Our functions', Bell argued, 'were not being fulfilled; the threat to the Christian tradition was greater now than ten years ago, especially as reconstruction was being taken seriously on the political plane'.

When this *cri de coeur* came before the Committee the ensuing discussion was not particularly helpful and led only to a re-examination of well-worn themes, namely the imbalance of its membership. T. S. Eliot expressed disappointment that the British Council of Churches had not wished to use the Joint Committee more frequently. The Bishop of Chichester was in favour of organising two more meetings in the New Year but not everyone welcomed the prospect, Dr Denning doubting whether such practical activities came within the Joint Committee's terms of reference. Geoffrey Fisher, as Chairman, adopted a middle position. It was the main task of the Standing Committee to initiate and to 'prod'; but executive action required authorization by the two parent bodies – the Sword of the Spirit and the Commission – also the British Council of Churches. Surely he was right.

If the achievements of the Joint Standing Committee disappointed some of its constituents, it did in practice encourage and challenge Christians of various churches and denominations to work together in the social field, to stimulate a continuing concern for key Christian principles and their application to necessary reconstruction in the post-war world. For Geoffrey Fisher, personally, the Chairmanship of the Joint Standing Committee, if it provided a unique experience yet had proved a heavy burden and, as he looked ahead, he was apprehensive of the claims which it must make on his time and energies. For him, however, the unexpected death of Archbishop Temple on 26 October 1944 and his own translation to Canterbury, entirely changed his personal situation and his resignation from the Committee inevitably followed.

There can be little doubt that in his capacity as Chairman of this Committee Geoffrey Fisher had done well, even if he had not proved the dynamic leader which Dr Bell might have wished. Holding such an office certainly proved helpful to Geoffrey Fisher in his ministry at Canterbury. It brought him into close and intimate contact with a group of intelligent and dedicated Roman Catholics which was for him an entirely novel experience. Hitherto he had been more familiar with a long-established vestigial English attitude which saw Roman Catholics as an alien ingredient making extravagant claims. His time on the Joint Standing Committee introduced him to a new religious world not at the level of acrimonious discussion but of active co-operation in spite of differences. As Chairman it was his responsibility to ensure that all views were given a fair hearing, and that he himself did not adopt the role of a partisan. Maybe it is not over fanciful to suggest that the visit to Rome in 1960 owed something, and is not unrelated to these early tentative days on the Joint Standing Committee – and not least to its efforts to find common ground with English Roman Catholics.

One of the most totally committed members of the Joint Committee was Barbara Ward, Baroness Jackson of Lodsworth, a member of the Sword of the Spirit and a loyal though progressive Roman Catholic. Hence we may allow her to have the last word:

'Perhaps the first point I should make is how unprecedented our degree of ecumenical co-operation seemed, and indeed was, in those days. I think we all felt the need to tread carefully, so that we should not lay ourselves open to the old suspicions and charges of indifferentism. In this particular exercise of tact, Archbishop Fisher was, I recall, absolutely outstanding. He had a profound sympathy "of the heart" for the limits within which Cardinal Hinsley could act and tried to make sure, with, as I recall, almost complete success, that the approach of the Committee – the agenda, the documents, the shape of the discussions – concentrated on all that the various religious communions could comfortably share and bypass the problems which were likely to be divisive. Yet all this was done with a sort of matter-of-fact tactfulness that prevented any embarrassment, or even perhaps the suggestion that special care was required. As I recall it, the easiest, the most straightforward and the most unifying issues concerned the shaping of a post-War settlement. Archbishop Fisher whole-heartedly endorsed this emphasis on Christian responsibility for future peace. We could never have worked together, publicly and in smaller groups, all over the country, if there had been resentments and disagreements at the centre. Cardinal Hinsley was a man of fatherly goodness. In Archbishop Fisher he found a partner of great tact, unobtrusive decisiveness and a profound sense of loyalty and friendship. The role of both men was, I suspect purposely, projected at a modest level. In any case, they were both men of profound humility. But their leadership was decisive and made the whole work possible. I like to think it even played a part in the astonishing ecumenical advance of the last thirty years – a development I thank God I have lived to see.'

Lady Jackson was certainly in a position to know at first hand what she was writing about and her testimony is high praise.

CHAPTER II

The Diocese of London

WE have been concerned so far in this section with the labours and preoccupations of Geoffrey Fisher in the conditions of a Britain at war. The demands made upon him were many and exacting. However, he was during these years a diocesan bishop and it is to his responsibilities in this capacity that we now turn.

To be Bishop of London during the war years must have constituted a unique experience, not least because of the personal and individual problems of the clergy submitted to exceptional strain. Against this testing background of destruction and danger it fell to the Bishop to keep up morale and bring pastoral support when needed. The story of this wartime ministry would make fascinating and instructive reading, but, as explained earlier, it cannot be told and never will be.

We have already seen how once enthroned in St Paul's Cathedral Geoffrey Fisher immediately got down to business. On the following day he consecrated the Church of St John The Baptist in Tottenham, and on the ensuing Monday held a house-warming party at Fulham Palace. A few days later the communicants of All Saints Church, Fulham, met for their annual party in the Bishop's Palace. 'So', Geoffrey Fisher comments, 'the forging of links has happily begun.'

Among his first acts was to confirm the appointment of diocesan officers – the Examining Chaplains, the Suffragan Bishops, the Archdeacons; also to have a long session with Stanley Eley, Secretary of the London Diocesan Fund from 1937 to 1946. Eley loomed large in the politics of the Diocese, being efficient, meticulous in his administration and possessing an intimate knowledge of London parishes, invaluable to an incoming Bishop. So far as his own comfort and easy relations with individual parish clergy were concerned, the choice of his Domestic Chaplain was important. It is perhaps significant that he appointed the Reverend F. C. Synge, a New Testament scholar and Vice-Principal of Queen's College, Birmingham, also a dedicated and liberal evangelical churchman. The Bishop regarded it as a priority to gain some general impressions, to quote his own words, 'of the topography of the Diocese, of the condition of its greatly differing districts and the difficulties created by an order of things which even before the war was in a state of instability'. In such exceptional circumstances it was inevitable that administrative problems cried out for attention. Many clergy had gone into the Forces, leaving vacancies not easy to fill. In some areas bombing was to become so extensive that parochial boundaries almost ceased to exist. Here Geoffrey Fisher's own energy and pastoral gifts uplifted those who worked with him.

It seems somewhat incongruous, against the background of a devastating and brutal European conflict, to turn to differing ecclesiastical loyalties which brought division to the Church in London. As suggested earlier Geoffrey Fisher inherited a situation which many, both clergy and laity, deplored but of which Winnington-Ingram was either blissfully unaware or, if aware, complacently did nothing. The new Bishop accepted the diagnosis, maybe in a too simplistic form, that so far as lawlessness obtained this was largely due to Anglo-Catholic attitudes to the use of the Book of Common Prayer. He recognised gratefully that so far as Diocesan day-to-day administration was concerned these clergy co-operated fully, thus enabling him to keep on good terms with them personally; however, in matters relating to doctrine and worship 'they were a fortress inside which no Bishop was able to enter'. Their London leader was Prebendary Merritt, a man whom Geoffrey Fisher personally in many ways admired. The Bishop had many discussions with him but could not break what he regarded as his theological intransigence. Geoffrey Fisher thus saw the extreme Anglo-Catholics as a law unto themselves – in the non-Pauline sense – making no pretence of conforming to the Book of Common Prayer or even the Deposited Book of 1928. They did more or less what they liked with the Communion Service and also with Reservation and Benediction.

Though Geoffrey Fisher's language here is perhaps exaggerated – it was written some twenty years after the events – there was some substance in his charges of which Mandell Creighton had earlier complained. Such liturgical individualism, though resented by many laymen, particularly churchwardens, was made less objectionable in London by the fact that loyalty to the parish church had been progressively eroded and, as a consequence, incumbents found themselves ministering to 'gathered congregations'. Those to whom it was not congenial voted against it on their feet and went elsewhere – or nowhere.

The situation was one which in the nature of the case must constitute a problem for a diocesan bishop unless he was prepared to be indifferent to lay complaints thereby agreeing, in practice, with his predecessor that there was nothing that needed or could be done. Geoffrey Fisher decided that this state of affairs was one which he ought not passively to accept, though how exactly to cope with it and restore order constituted a major problem not easy of solution. Thus on his arrival in London and having become personally conscious of this situation, the new Bishop felt it a solemn duty to make plain what deviations from the Book of Common Prayer had been authorised in Acts of Convocation. In deciding to do this, he had every reason to believe that, by and large, such a step would be welcomed, particularly by lay people who found their present predicament confusing; also by clergy who were thrown back upon their own judgement in an area where they needed to be acting under authority. Thus in 1940 Geoffrey Fisher began to draw up a first draft of Episcopal Regulations which were not innovative but simply stated what the legal position factually was. However, the advent of the blitz made the time so inopportune that he was forced to abandon his efforts at reform for the time being. A year later, he admitted that the times were still unfavourable but that he could delay no longer since parish priests repeatedly asked him what code of practice they should observe, and which applied to all clergy without exception. The general liturgical situation was further complicated by the dispersal, through air-raids, of congregations who were forced to worship in churches unfamiliar to them. Geoffrey Fisher sensibly recognised that for some clergy to conform to the Regulations which he now progressively issued, particularly in relation to the celebration of Holy Communion, would mean abandoning certain variations from the Book of Common Prayer to which, in the course of years, they had, with their congregations, grown familiar. 'A change of habits', he admitted, is 'always irksome, specially when it is associated with deep feelings.' What Geoffrey Fisher hoped for was that the clergy would encourage their congregations to believe that obedience to properly constituted authority was 'an absolute good for the Church's own life and for its effective witness'. It might help them, in this respect, to know that he, the Bishop, regarded himself as equally subject to the Regulations largely based on Acts of Convocation.

To assist the clergy in making this adjustment the Bishop circularised the 1662 Order of Holy Communion with, attached to it, variations authorised by the House of Bishops in 1929 and also an elucidation of ambiguities as well as obscurities. As we read these permissions today – the omission in certain circumstances of the Creed; the Gloria; the prayer for the Monarch; and the sermon; the exhortation; more positively the joining of the Prayer of Oblation to that of Consecration and the inclusion of a gradual hymn – these certainly do not strike one as world-shattering. This shows, of course, how radical has been liturgical change in the Church of England in recent years, and how much wider is the range of permitted options.

It should, perhaps, be added that the series of Bishop's Regulations were not confined only to variants from the Book of Common Prayer, but concerned the life of the Church generally, for example in respect of confirmations; lay readers; admission to communion; marriage; youth organisations; ministry of women and the table of affinity.

Undoubtedly Geoffrey Fisher saw his Regulations as a tidying-up operation, thus letting both clergy and laity know precisely where they stood so that all things might be done 'decently and in order'. To commend his policy further, Geoffrey Fisher called together a responsible group of High Church clergymen which included, amongst others, Dom. Bernard Clements, Vicar of All Saints, Margaret Street, and Gage-Brown, Vicar of St Cuthberts, Philbeach Gardens. After a friendly and informal discussion they agreed to support the Bishop but asked him not to let this be known for fear of losing their influence with their fellow Anglo-Catholics. The Bishop, however, was forced later to admit, somewhat bitterly, that his concessions had little effect in promoting respect for the law. Indeed, some of the more extreme brethren maintained that if the Bishop could in his permission commit what, strictly speaking, violated the integrity of the Book of Common Prayer, then they themselves were justified in exercising the same personal discretion. The Bishop felt himself forced to come to a somewhat pessimistic conclusion namely that 'They had no desire whatever to return to an ordered church life'.

This first private meeting arose, it should be noted, from an initiative taken by Geoffrey Fisher in order to make contact with a group of High Churchmen of his own choosing. In 1944 he followed this up by responding to an invitation from Prebendary Merritt to have dinner with a few members of the Federation of Catholic Priests, an extreme Anglo-Catholic group. His account of this meeting, recalled years later and therefore subject to this limitation, is in many respects revealing. He was first introduced, so he relates, into 'a vast array of drink', which, being himself a near-teetotaller, did not initially put him at his ease, particularly since he tended to think of Anglo-Catholics as rigid in their beliefs but luxurious in their living. However, undeterred, he prepared after dinner to secure a 'breakthrough' and to make a working agreement with his hosts. However, just as they were beginning to get down to business news came through on the radio that the fateful invasion of Europe had begun. All agreed immediately that they could not continue their deliberations, so as the Bishop comments, 'at that dramatic moment one hope of mine was extinguished and the great hope of a Nation came to life'.

But there were, in fact, further opportunities of achieving a *modus vivendi* though Geoffrey Fisher's imminent departure from London to Canterbury changed the context and perspective. On 5 December 1944, the Bishop received a significant letter from a group of priests which included *inter alios* C. R. Smith, Vicar of St Michael and All Angels, Bedford Park; Donald Harris, Rector of Greenford (the largest parish in the London Diocese); and A. D. Young, Vicar of St Clement's, Fulham.

C. R. Smith apprised the Bishop that for the last two years a number of clergy from different dioceses had been investigating the possibilities of obtaining a greater degree of uniformity in the Celebration of Holy Communion. This, its members felt, was the more necessary since 'the present wide diversity is confusing to the laity, particularly to the uninstructed and is disturbing to those who have to move about frequently'. They reminded the Bishop that though, at the moment, they used the 1662 Prayer Book, 'the Rite is almost universally admitted to need revision' in that it suffered from 'the stress of the times in which it was drawn up, and is to many liturgically and devotionally not wholly satisfying, despite the magnificence of its language'. Yet since it was unlikely that the 1662 Prayer Book would be revised in the near future they had drawn up a 'schedule of deviations from it which had the weight of long and widespread use and were 'in line with ancient Catholic practice'. In terms of strict law, they admitted, no clergyman had any right to deviate by 'a hair's breadth' from 1662 any more, for that matter, than had the Bishop himself. However, they hoped that he might feel able to approve the use for the present in the Diocese of London of these deviations. There was in fact nothing spectacular in these suggestions; indeed most of them were in line with the Bishop's own regulations.

Geoffrey Fisher felt he ought to respond positively to this appeal and he admitted that if they could get 'common action of which they could all approve', an exchange of letters to this effect might be published. He agreed that it was premature to think in terms of a newly revised Prayer Book which would place an obligation on them to recover a far greater degree of uniformity than existed at the moment. Here the clergy could help.

In the meantime Geoffrey Fisher informed Dr Bell of Chichester and Dr Simpson of Southwark as to the approach which had been made to him. The former was encouraged by what he heard since it showed that there were clergy who 'desire some real sacrifice of much present practice'. The Bishop of Southwark was not so interested since he had 'inherited a much more orderly Diocese' on the south side of the River and therefore these matters gave him very little bother.

To pursue matters further there took place another meeting on 18 December with Gage-Brown and his group. The result was an agreement on a document for publication in which, however, so the Bishop explained to Dr Bell, he was not giving permission for anything which he had not already permitted in his published Regulations. Geoffrey Fisher was able to persuade Noel Davey, Editorial Secretary of SPCK to publish this agreement as a pamphlet. It was also reproduced in the *Church Times*.

The Bishop had acted in these deliberations with frankness and common sense, more meritorious since his natural sympathies did not lie with the liturgical stance of High Churchmen. His approach was characteristically pragmatic. Gage-Brown was gratified and delighted with the discussions and the prospects which they seemed to open up. 'It was a great pleasure to us', so he wrote to the Bishop, 'to be able to discuss the matter frankly and straightforwardly and we appreciate your readiness to meet us in every possible way. I personally am in entire agreement with your views upon the desirability of forgetting a good deal of history and starting again from scratch.'

Certainly Geoffrey Fisher found it easier to talk to the Federation of Catholic Priests than the Church Union but it was already too late in the day for the Bishop effectively to follow up these initiatives. Leaving Fulham for Lambeth in the summer of 1945 broke the momentum thus frustrating this promising beginning. His considered judgement, however, was that his eirenic efforts were anyhow doomed to failure since many High Churchmen were not prepared to conform to any agreement which he might make with Gage-Brown and his colleagues in the Federation.

Some will doubtless think that Geoffrey Fisher would have been wiser to adopt the *laissez-faire* attitude of his predecessor without seeking any agreed *modus vivendi*. Protests from lay people and their expectation that a new Bishop would do something about this problem made such inactivity, even if he had approved it, almost impossible. Also it was against his natural temperament to do nothing. The Bishop was by no means opposed to change in itself, recognising fully that the Book of Common Prayer could not be used, and in fact was not being used as it stood, in every jot and tittle. The pragmatist in him was prepared to bow before the logic of facts and thus authorize adaptation to meet new circumstances. Discretion could be allowed to parish priests but it must be a discretion sanctioned by a competent authority. His inability to establish such a pattern in London came as a profound disappointment, particularly as he saw himself a reconciler 'seeking to take a synoptic view and finding a point where agreement was possible'.

At the other end of the ecclesiastical spectrum were 'the real Evangelicals' – the description is the Bishop's – with whom by early upbringing, temperament and conviction he had more in common and greater sympathy. Most prominent amongst these was Archdeacon Sharpe whom Geoffrey Fisher greatly respected as a person but did not regard as a churchman of real significance. If the Anglo-Catholics were an influential, dominant and well organised party, the Bishop regarded the Evangelicals as a 'cowed, beaten, depressed group' needing encouragement. 'They knew that they were kept out of everything by the Anglo-Catholics,' he affirmed 'so they just kept to themselves and ran their own parishes, knowing that they were disapproved of by the

Bishops as a whole.' This situation was one which Geoffrey Fisher greatly deplored, believing it to be prejudicial to the balanced comprehensiveness of the Church of England. To remedy this he called together some of the evangelical clergy and told them bluntly that they really must equip themselves to take their rightful place in diocesan affairs which at the moment they were 'incompetent' to do. He appreciated that by temperament most of the Evangelicals wished to missionise in their own parishes and were not primarily interested in ecclesiastical politics. But they must not forget that they had duties to the Diocese, which meant making themselves competent and pulling their weight in its counsels. The fact was that when Convocations or Bishops set up committees it was easy to select scholarly Anglo-Catholics to play a particular role but almost impossible to find similarly equipped Evangelicals.

This well-intentioned admonition did not fall on deaf ears for some Evangelicals got together to promote positive theological scholarship and to raise general standards. At least the Bishop had succeeded in making it clear that they need no longer think of themselves as 'outcasts', permanently excluded from diocesan responsibilities. Quite the reverse. His desire was that all kinds of churchmanship should be involved in the overall direction of diocesan life. Certainly the founding by Max Warren – so often mentioned in this biography – of the Evangelical Fellowship for Theological Literature into which he recruited such scholars as Donald Coggan, F. W. Dillistone, D. E. W. Harrison was such as to win the Archbishop's approval. Certainly all of them were committed to a nice balance between tradition and liberalism. That J. R. S. Taylor, Bishop of Sodor and Man, could speak of articulate evangelicals within a contemporary development of Christian theology owes much to Geoffrey Fisher's encouragement – and admonition.

Moving from the Northern to the Southern Province meant that Geoffrey Fisher became a member of a Convocation presided over by Archbishop Lang and, after his retirement in 1941, by William Temple. As Bishop of London he was expected to play an important role in its proceedings and serve on some of its committees. Immediately he was struck with the contrast between the two Convocations. The Northern was small; matters to be dealt with were carefully prepared; and it was domestic in the sense that it assembled at Bishopthorpe where the Archbishop acted as host. Hence the general atmosphere was one of informality and the 'get-togetherness' of a family. The Southern Convocation, so Geoffrey Fisher found, lacked any domestic side. There was no discussion beforehand and 'nobody could guarantee what anybody else was going to say'. It was certainly interesting because at that time bishops had not even attempted to get a common mind, as was the case later on when Geoffrey Fisher became Archbishop.

Cosmo Lang, though he often caused the bishops to be restive, dominated the Upper House through his long experience, his magisterial manner and the considerable 'mana' of his unique personality. William Temple was never really at home in Convocation, hence the story, maybe apocryphal, that he wrote some of his best speeches while presiding over its sessions. In particular, he was usually uneasy when any matter affecting the discipline of clergy or laity was on the agenda. Geoffrey Fisher was able to observe at first hand Temple's chairmanship, the more so as he had been enlisted by the Archbishop to oversee the doings of Convocation and thereby to ensure that business went smoothly. Geoffrey Fisher admitted that this practical task 'exactly suited' his temperament and needed to be done because William Temple was 'living on a higher level, spiritually and intellectually'.

When Geoffrey Fisher went to London he had already been for some four years a member of the Church Assembly but, as we have seen, he affected not to take this over-seriously or regard as a real priority his attendance at its deliberations. He seldom intervened in debates, except where some local interest or his membership of a particular committee made this necessary. In this respect, however, moving to London brought a new situation since as the Bishop of a senior see he was expected to play a more prominent role. He now saw himself in the capacity of a watchdog, intervening on many occasions in debates, not to deliver a prepared speech but as he himself put it 'to keep the debate going in the right direction and likely to lead to the right conclusion'.

One of the problems confronting the Bishop in a London at war was communication since evening meetings often had to be abandoned though less so on the perimeter of the diocese. To maintain contact it was the more necessary for the Bishop to make full use of the *London Diocesan Leaflet*. In spite of the blitz and the hazards of subsequent bombing by doodle-bugs and rockets his Letter appeared every month without a single exception. In particular, he endeavoured to curb the spirit of revenge and retaliation, natural though highly undesirable as these might be. He regarded it as among his duties to keep up national morale, not least during the blitz – 'perhaps the most critical months of our history and of world history'.

The Diocesan Conference, which normally met three times a year, had become a stable ingredient in the life of the Church of England as it tried hard to establish a truly democratic system of government. For the Bishop it proved a unique opportunity to address both clergy and laity from the parishes; and to become sensitive to popular feeling in the localities. In this aspect of his episcopal oversight Geoffrey Fisher was excellent. He was a first-class chairman, tolerant, genial, keeping things moving and knowing how to deal kindly but firmly with those who could not overcome the temptation to talk too often and too long. The Diocesan Conferences were held regularly during his episcopate and he presided over them all. Though he cultivated on occasions a lighter touch, in the main these were serious working assemblies. It was a necessary part of the Conference's duties, through the system of parochial quotas, to contribute to the cost of 'running' the Diocese, never easy but more challenging in wartime with its evacuation and widely dispersed destruction. The Conference received regular reports from the London Diocesan Fund and the Bishop took a pride in the fact that though 1939 had ended with a net deficit of £370 and quotas fell collectively by some £9,000 no parish suffered any diminution in its grants; in fact incumbents' stipends were augmented and pensions for clergy and widows maintained. This achievement says much for the morale of the Diocese, especially in the financial ordering of its corporate life. Here the Bishop consistently gave encouragement, and it was a matter of great satisfaction to him that the Church in London was able to sustain this fortunate position throughout the whole of the war years. The Week of Prayer and Giving reached its target figure as was equally the case with the Women's Offering.

As well as keeping the Diocese solvent it was also important that so far as the exigencies of the war made it possible, diocesan activities should not simply fold up. It was the Bishop's policy that they should continue. Thus the Diocesan and Youth Festivals and the Association of Vergers' Annual Gathering, to mention but two, were maintained.

It was one of the Bishop's deepest convictions that it mattered to keep people informed if their co-operation were to be willingly secured. Lay people ought to know what was happening. Thus he was concerned, organisationally, that the manifold responsibilities of the London Diocesan Office and the manner in which it discharged them should be widely understood. Hence, in the Diocesan Leaflet of April 1943 there appeared a schedule of its activities during a week chosen at random, thus illustrating how 'intensely busy but absorbingly interesting' its day-to-day operations were. They included grants to parishes; interviews with clergy and churchwardens; handling the letters which flooded in to the Secretary; administering, for the advantage of assistant curates and lay readers, the block grants received from the Ecclesiastical Commissioners; concerning itself with the daunting task of handling initially war damage claims.

There can be no doubt from his own admission that Geoffrey Fisher was eagerly looking forward to leading the Diocese of London in the work of reconstruction which must inevitably follow the peace. Hence in both the October and the 1945 January leaflets he suggested the way forward and the problems to be tackled. There was the difficult question of diocesan reorganisation; the need for a strong evangelistic centre, staffed by an equally strong, even if small, group who could give their whole time and attention to stimulating the evangelistic spirit throughout the diocese, and to thinking through the special problems which the peculiar conditions of London presented; the securing of a 'rightly ordered and acceptable internal discipline' in the Church's worship and liturgy. That they might do this effectively it was important for them to seek the help of the Holy Spirit that He might deliver them from the 'spiritual ruts and grooves' which too easily 'impede them'.

However, these tasks were not to fall to him as Bishop of London. On 26 October 1944, there came the death of William Temple after only some two and a half years at Lambeth. To Geoffrey Fisher it was a crushing blow, not least at the level of personal friendship. With great feeling, he testified at the Autumn Session of the Diocesan Conference to the loss thus sustained both by Church and Nation. They met, he said 'overwhelmed' by the death of their Archbishop. 'No one knows or can know all that it means, what it will mean, in the years to come. The immense range of his knowledge and of his sympathy; the synoptic power by which he brought everything into direct relation with profound principles of Christian doctrine; the brilliance of his insight and of his expression; the manner with which he related eternal truths of the Gospel to the here and now of social life and personal life, of national or world problems, of the life of the Church; the fact that he was personally known to and trusted by the leaders of almost every Church in both hemispheres.'

The death of William Temple was to mean for Geoffrey Fisher an unexpected and painful severance from a diocese which he had served to the maximum of his capacity during very testing days. His own deep feelings at the time he expressed in a letter produced in the February number (1945) of the Diocesan Leaflet. Perhaps it is proper that this chapter should conclude with an extract from it. He had been with them just over five years and though he came to them as a 'stranger' he had been most kindly received. True the London Diocese was vast so that contacts with parishes and with people must in the nature of the case be 'hurried, superficial and rare'. Yet he had been made to feel at home in their midst. Out of six hundred parishes he had visited about a half and in all these he had found a 'ready welcome, friendship and that evidence of Christian fellowship and zeal which make the Diocese a true family'. He then went on: 'And what years these have been! I have been with you through the days of London's greatest ordeal and of its greatest glory. I have shared the trials of its citizens and shall never cease to be uplifted by the memory of their behaviour in the time of battle. To have been with you at such a time is the greatest privilege of my life. Just as in the darkest days we did not doubt that a victory would be ours, so as the trail of destruction of churches and devastation of parishes grew I always looked forward to the days of reconstruction. In the meantime one had to be content to do the next thing, and I am aware of but little done and much left undone. But it had been my hope to have a share in the great work of resettling the churches and schools and church life of London to meet the needs and great opportunities of the days to come. Last month I mentioned some of the initial stages of that work. It is a grief to me that it must pass from my hands.'

One can understand Geoffrey Fisher's disappointment at having embarked upon a work and being prevented from continuing it till it was 'thoroughly' finished. The disappointment, maybe, was the more acute since to guide the fortunes of the London Diocese in a new world seemed to be an assignment for which he was fully equipped by experience, aptitude and inclination.

PART THREE:

PRIMATE OF ALL ENGLAND

CHAPTER 12

Moving to Canterbury

AT the end of September 1944, Mrs Fisher was staying at the Old Palace in Canterbury and was taken by Mrs Temple to see William her husband who was confined to his bed. 'He was in great pain from his illness', she wrote later, 'and did not really want to talk to anyone. I noticed for the first time how blue his eyes were, because he had no glasses on.'

On 26 October 1944, Geoffrey Fisher was in the House of Lords Robing Room which he shared with the Archbishop of Canterbury. Someone, unknown to the Bishop, came in and almost casually remarked that William Temple had suddenly died. This news came as a complete surprise, though Geoffrey Fisher knew him to be somewhat unwell. His immediate reaction is best conveyed in his own words: 'I knelt down at one of the chairs, and I think I was there for an hour not thinking about anything at all but just trying to assimilate myself to a completely changed world and a completely changed Church'.

William Temple was then 63 years of age; the war was clearly approaching its end; and it was confidently expected that he would lead the Church of England into the post-war years of necessary reconstruction. At his funeral service in Canterbury a rebellious young clergyman, Joseph McCulloch, reflected somewhat ruefully: 'We are burying the hopes of the Church of England'. Leslie Hunter, Bishop of Sheffield, could not contain his grief. 'So much that one hoped for in the Church at home and in the world seemed likely to be stillborn.'

It fell to Winston Churchill, who knew next to nothing about ecclesiastical personnel, to nominate his successor. Three names were widely canvassed, namely – Garbett, Archbishop of York, who had solid virtues, wide experience in three bishoprics, a reputation for sound common sense, and a capacity to work hard, but was generally regarded as somewhat austere, Geoffrey Fisher, Bishop of London, who had won the affectionate regard of his clergy and had displayed marked powers of administration; and George Bell, generally, if uncritically, thought the most likely. As Archbishop Davidson's chaplain and author of his monumental biography he knew Lambeth and its ways with an intimacy which no other contemporary could rival. He had also fostered the cause of Christian re-union, and had thrown himself energetically into the pioneering work which led to the setting up of the World Council of Churches. Before and during the war he had bravely championed the cause of the refugees. In the House of Lords he strongly opposed obliteration bombing, and behind the scenes involved himself in an effort, through Scandinavian intervention, to secure a negotiated peace with the anti-Nazi elements in Germany. No bishop of the Church of England, with the single exception of William Temple, enjoyed such a reputation on the Continent. He was 61 years of age.

But it was Geoffrey Fisher, not George Bell or Cyril Garbett, who went to Canterbury. The general view was that Bell's forthrightness in condemning the war strategy of the Government did not commend him to the Prime Minister and was most unpopular at the Palace. As Alan Don, Dean of Westminster, confided to his diary: 'George has been both courageous and indiscreet in his speeches about the war ... He has paid the penalty of his conscientious opposition to the more fire-eating patriots in the House of Lords'. Bell himself was not surprised at being passed over and wrote to his brothers: 'I have no illusions about the Church's attitude to me – he [Churchill] is the last person to put me in any position of greater influence'.

This does not mean that these were, necessarily, the only reasons for his exclusion from Canterbury. Dr Jasper, in his perceptive biography of Bishop Bell, has suggested others; and William Temple certainly thought of Fisher as his successor and frequently said to his wife that he must retire from Lambeth in time to give 'Geoffrey a go'. The passing over of Dr Bell, however, does raise questions as to the limitations at that time involved in the process of nomination to office by the Crown on the advice of the Prime Minister.

We shall see later that this was a matter which was of increasing concern to some leading churchmen and was discussed by more than one Commission. Geoffrey Fisher firmly believed that the role of the Prime Minister was neither in practice nor theologically an improper one. It had worked well, so he claimed, though he recognised that it had been abused in the past by being manipulated for political ends. Indeed, way back in the 18th century the Duke of Newcastle had used episcopal appointments in the interest of the Whig party – but this was unlikely to return.

Geoffrey Fisher has given us an interesting account of his lunch with Winston Churchill at Number 10 Downing Street not long after his appointment, an encounter which recalls that of Archbishop Tait, in similar circumstances, with Benjamin Disraeli. Both Prime Ministers were innocent of any intimate knowledge of ecclesiastical affairs or persons. In the course of their conversation Churchill displayed a little 'upmanship' by asking what the Archbishop elect thought of Renan's *Vie de Jésus*, and affecting some surprise on being told that he had never read it. As they parted Geoffrey Fisher suspected that the Prime

Minister had already sized him up as 'an obviously second best who would perhaps do'.

While at London Geoffrey Fisher had not become a national figure, so much so that to the mass of the British public he came to Canterbury as one relatively unknown. Hence coverage in the popular press was restrained; and the National Clergy Association complained that such comment confined itself to saying that he was a competent organiser. *The Times* newspaper, however, gave him a most enthusiastic and warm write-up, concluding with these words: 'If energy, wisdom, and courage are today among the qualities most desirable in an Archbishop of Canterbury, they will be found characteristic of him who, strengthened by the prayers and good wishes of Christendom all the world over, will shortly be enthroned in the seat of St Augustine'.

On 2 January 1945, Dr Fisher, Bishop of London, was nominated by the Prime Minister to the Crown for election by the Dean and Chapter of Canterbury as Primate of All England. The ancient legal procedure then began to unwind itself. The election duly took place in the crypt of the Cathedral on 22 January where, just over a week later, this election was confirmed by a Commission of Bishops presided over by the Archbishop of the Northern Province. Geoffrey Fisher was now legally Archbishop and therefore in possession of the rights and dignities of his office, though the enthronement did not take place until 19 April 1945. This delay was due to a breakdown in the heating system in the Cathedral which led the *Church Times* to ask whether there was any such facility available when St Anselm was enthroned. This significant occasion was a splendid affair, that is so far as the exigencies of war and security would allow. The day chosen, the Feast of St Alphege, seemed specially appropriate since he was martyred by the Danes in AD 1106, his altar tomb being in Canterbury Cathedral until destroyed at the time of the Reformation. The Dean and Chapter of Canterbury – Hewlett Johnson was the Dean – were determined to gather together as representative a congregation as could be, ecumenically world-wide and equally comprehensive in respect of the civic authorities. The choice was indeed imaginative including members of staff who had worked at Lambeth, four maids from the Old Palace in Canterbury and six representatives from Repton. Alan Don, newly appointed Dean of Westminster and every inch a Scotsman, was insistent that the Moderator of the General Assembly of the Church of Scotland – the Established Church – should not be 'lumped together with the Moderator of the Free Church Federal Council'. Geoffrey Fisher himself was particularly anxious that the Presiding Bishop of the Protestant Episcopal Church of America should attend in person – which he did. It was an augury of a close and significant relationship which was to follow across the years.

So this solemn service, a nice blend of the traditional and more recent innovations, got under way as the Primate of All England was inducted, installed and enthroned in the Office of Archbishop of Canterbury by Archdeacon Alec Sargent. If he showed little visible signs of emotion when seated in St Augustine's chair, it was yet for him a solemn moment long to be remembered. His sermon was one of hope but not of facile optimism. He frankly recognised that the times were indeed critical and out of joint. 'The Church and the Nation stand together under God in their respective duties. The Church has much to put in order if it is faithfully to serve the Nation; the Nation has much to learn and to unlearn if it is to heed what God says to it through His Church. For many years past the two have been drawing apart. There is the possibility, the fear, that this alienation may continue to increase. There is also before us the possibility, even the hope, certainly a challenge, that they should come together again in a Christian faith which is not ashamed to be definite, explicit and binding.'

It was significant that Geoffrey Fisher gave prominence to the secular power in this way. For many in the vast congregation thoughts of a former occasion must have thrust themselves up into a poignant remembrance. The Archbishop spoke for them, as well as for himself, when he appropriately concluded his address with these words:

'Another enthronement, scarcely three years ago, is in the minds of us all and the sense of our impoverishment broods heavily upon us. William Temple, whose ardent spirit and creative mind ever joined truth to action, set the course for the Church and for many outside it and fired us with his own enthusiasm. Bereft of him we must go forward in his courageous faith'. "Our primary need", he told us three years ago, "is for minds nurtured by the truth of God, hearts open to the love of God" . . . to this work we dedicate ourselves.'

This was, and understandably, a sermon devoted to general principles, rather than explicit application to immediate affairs. Pleasing to many was his associating the whole Anglican Communion and the Free Churches with the sentiments that he expressed.

Earlier in this biography we were given an intimate glimspe of Geoffrey Fisher's harrowing emotions when he was offered, and finally accepted, the Bishopric of London. Now during the interregnum at London both Cosmo Lang and the Archbishop of York gave it as their firm opinion that if he were offered the primatial see of Canterbury it was his bounden duty to accept. However, though Geoffrey Fisher seems to have experienced none of the traumas of 1939, he yet wrote to Garbett expressing his 'sheer repugnance' in attempting to cope with a 'terrifying task' far 'beyond his compass'.

Geoffrey Fisher had now been a Bishop for some thirteen years and as a result had grown in confidence. Thus he reassured himself, maybe a little jauntily, with these words: 'I followed William Temple in 1914 as Headmaster of Repton. If I could do it then, I can do it now'.

As to his reception by his fellow bishops we cannot tell since their letters no longer exist. To one uniquely interested, the appointment gave intense pleasure and satisfaction – Frances Temple, the former Archbishop's widow. Writing to Geoffrey Fisher from the Old Palace on 4 January 1944 she expressed herself simply: 'In fact if any other decision had been taken I could hardly have borne it. You are the one among the bishops who most reminds me of William in *character* and it seems to me that it is character and personality that will matter most during these next years'.

One of the first tasks which fell to Geoffrey and Rosamond Fisher – it must have reminded them of moving into Fulham in 1939 – was to establish themselves in the Palace of Lambeth. This was not easy for it had been extremely ravaged by the war, and the Temples, who had no family, were living in the basement, using Archbishop Davidson's bedroom as a drawing room. It was all very much 'hugger-mugger' and though there was ample room it was totally unsuitable for discharging the responsibilities of the Archbishop's office. It was obvious that the Fishers had to make up their minds, and quickly, as to what to do with Lambeth – and also with the Old Palace at Canterbury, 'a lovely house under the shadow of the Cathedral'. Sir Philip Baker-Wilbraham of the Ecclesiastical Commissioners advised that Lambeth Palace must be restored but at the same time the Old Palace should be disposed of. The Archbishop immediately concurred with the former proposal but effectively demurred to the latter which would have put him back to pre-Frederick Temple days. He was, after all, a Diocesan Bishop snatching every moment of precious time available to exercise this particular ministry. To be visible in Canterbury as a local resident seemed to be essential.

But what about Lambeth Palace? The Palace was ancient but restored way back in 1830, when it was converted into a Victorian residence possessing a very lovely drawing room and an extremely large study. As to the latter's capaciousness Cosmo Lang used to say that when people came to see him they realised that the Church of England was a very great institution. Of this prelatical observation Geoffrey Fisher commented: 'I don't feel that a palatial room adds anything to the dignity of the Church and I should be miserable working in that vast room'. He did not have to.

Geoffrey Fisher decided, in principle, that part of this large building must be allocated to the family and not 'muddled up' with official rooms. Hence a new Lambeth Palace emerged out of the destruction of the old, shaped for its primary purpose. The complete work of restoration at Lambeth, undertaken by the firm of Seely and Paget which included the library and chapel, took many years to complete though the Archbishop and Mrs Fisher moved from Fulham to Lambeth on Monday 19 February 1945.

The Archbishop took an enormous interest in every detail of the work and kept in close touch with the architects, Paul Paget and Lord Mottistone to whom he referred as his apostles and who became great friends.

From the word go Geoffrey Fisher recognised the potentialities of Lambeth Palace, not only *vis-à-vis* the Church of England but in relation to the Anglican Communion a a whole. From this derived the setting up of the hostel in the 1950s which became so vital a part of the Lambeth scene and hospitality. Miss Forman, Mrs Fisher's sister, was appointed warden and was made responsible for all the domestic side of the Palace. There can be no doubt that this hostel was a great success ministering to a real need in bringing together bishops and clergy from all over the Anglican Communion, as well as providing somewhere to stay in London at a reasonable cost.

The Archbishop made a point when possible to meet all those who stayed there and he worshipped with them in the chapel. Another valuable use of the hostel was as a meeting place for groups of one kind or another. Wives were also welcome to stay there by which many friendships were formed. Miss Peggy Forman herself was indefatigable and an enormous help to the Fishers.

CHAPTER 13

The Cathedral Church of Christ

LIVING within the precincts at Canterbury as near neighbours were members of the Dean and Chapter, the minor canons, and the musical foundation prominent amongst whom was the organist. Archiepiscopal relations with these were indeed important.

We now turn to consider Geoffrey taking up his task as the Diocesan Bishop of Canterbury. The internal politics of Deans and Chapters, particularly in relation to their Bishop, do not easily permit of any objective or straightforward analysis. Obviously they vary according to the persons involved, the constitution of the Cathedral, past history and the overall religious climate of the day. Talented men come to cathedrals as canons, having held earlier in their lives responsible positions often in a parish. Now they may no longer enjoy a former independence. Corporate decisions obtain and the frustration to which this can lead may encourage members of Chapter to entertain the illusion that they could manage the show much better on their own. Sometimes – it is a cynical reflection – corporate differences with the Bishop, their Father in God, can serve to unite the Chapter in a common hostility.

The Dean who presided over the Chapter at Canterbury was the Very Reverend Hewlett Johnson, whose name became almost a household word and remained so during the whole of Geoffrey Fisher's achiepiscopate. He began life as an engineer and is said to have worked at the bench with Mr Charles Chaplin. The conflict between the two, however, was not in any sense personal. Often after a service, the Dean would be seen respectfully escorting the Archbishop to his residence. When a chorister asked if they were talking about Communism, the reply came from the Headmaster of the Choir School: 'No, about their children'. Indeed, the Dean speaks of Dr Fisher as a 'very kind man personally', though they were diametrically opposed in their outlook on politics. In reverse the Archbishop describes the Dean as 'charming, gracious and friendly once he was off his main subject of socialism and Russia'. Geoffrey Fisher, however, felt bound to say, rightly or wrongly, that he was quite 'ineffective' in running the Cathedral. If the latter pejorative judgement is more or less true, it may be accounted for by his many and long absences abroad which must have drained much of his energy and left him unaware of what was happening at home. Since the Dean became so continuing an anxiety for the

Archbishop, we shall refer to their mutual relations at greater length in the next chapter.

A Dean needs to be around the campus and, like the Deity, 'about in the quad'. Members of the Chapter were by no means unfriendly to the Dean though somewhat embarrassed at times.

What happened, we may ask, in the Cathedral when the Dean was on one of his long absences abroad? Geoffrey Fisher's view was that Canon Shirley, Headmaster of the King's School, stepped into the breach and dominated the Chapter. He was undoubtedly shrewd, a man of great talent and force of character who in the interests of a good cause could become quite ruthless. Many alleged that his main loyalty was to the School, and that this led to a sustained concern to add to its plant by acquiring property in the precincts which belonged to the Dean and Chapter. Shirley, who could display great charm, had the ability and the nerve to act decisively, particularly in getting rid of personnel when they ceased to be useful to him and the School.

It is said that when an eminent ecclesiastic – none more so – was told of Canon Shirley's death he paused thoughtfully before remarking: 'This persuades me, more than ever, that there must be an intermediate state'. This was, indeed, a perceptive assessment. Certainly his services to King's School at a critical period in its long history were incalculable.

Canon Alec Sargent, Archdeacon of Canterbury, was an historian who knew much of the antiquities of the City. He was kind, with great charm, and generally helpful, though the Archbishop was of opinion that as an old King's man his natural inclination was to back Shirley when the chips were down and the School was involved.

Julian Bickersteth, who, according to the Archbishop was a 'dear man and a saint', had spent earlier years as Headmaster of St Peter's School in Adelaide where he ran into difficulties for 'pushing confession beyond the point that they would stand for'. Though liking him as a person, Geoffrey Fisher questioned his judgement.

There are many situations endemic in the day-to-day life of a Cathedral which can cause heat and frustration between Bishop and Chapter such as those unfamiliar with ecclesiastical institutions find it difficult to take seriously. Among these is the order of precedence in processions, which, perhaps, has as its only minimal advantage – if you can but get it right – that it removes embarrassment and inhibits presumption. Suffragan Bishops, because of a certain ambiguity of status, neither 'fish, flesh, fowl nor good red herring', were particularly vulnerable in becoming at Canterbury focal points of controversy. One illustration which involved the Archbishop must suffice.

On Christmas Day 1950, Geoffrey Fisher asked the Bishop of Dover to walk in his archiepiscopal procession in the Cathedral. It was, perhaps to be expected, that this would give offence to the Chapter, so much so that the Archbishop, while standing his ground, wrote an apologetic letter some time later to the Dean in which he explained that he had no intention of violating the statutes or upsetting members of the Chapter. The fact was, of course, that while the latter saw a Suffragan Bishop as an Honorary Canon of the Cathedral, the Archbishop understood him as engaged in episcopal functions as a member of his own *familia*.

The Archbishop's letter was considered by Chapter and a courteous reply was sent from the Dean though the Archbishop's argument was not conceded. The Statutes, he contended, had been meticulously examined but they specifically precluded the interpretation which the Archbishop had put on them. They made a clear 'historic and logical distinction' between services which came within the authority of the Archbishop and those under the Dean and Chapter. The Archbishop, after receiving this letter, still maintained that the Statutes left him free to come to the Cathedral with such attendants waiting upon him as he might choose.

Thus this dispute rumbled on leading to many letters; to much toing and froing between the Archbishop and Chapter; to disputes as to who, when the Archbishop was absent, pronounced the blessing and was given 'the highest place of dignity'. Geoffrey Fisher at times felt himself in the unhappy predicament of being uncomfortably positioned between Scylla and Charybdis, pressured by the Suffragan Bishops on the one hand and the intransigence of the Dean and Chapter on the other. Cutting away the refinements, the controversy could be reduced to a dispute as to the categories of special worshipful occasions held in the Cathedral. The Chapter believed there were two, the Archbishop three.

Many objective observers who have lived their lives outside Cathedral precincts may well see such a *contretemps* as a veritable storm in a minuscule teacup, a terrible waste of time and a diversion of energies which could have been better directed elsewhere. However, this is not the whole truth. Behind the heartache and the irritation, the combatants felt, or affected to feel, that certain important principles were at stake relating to the built-in rights of the Dean and Chapter, together with the status and powers of the Archbishop in his own Cathedral. What is quite clear is that the Statutes permitted different interpretations particularly where emotion tended to cloud judgement. Also even the lawyers could not definitively agree. The pity is that Archbishop and Chapter could not themselves come to an agreement satisfying to both parties, perhaps over a bottle of wine together in a domestic and relaxed atmosphere.

There were other areas in the corporate life of the Cathedral where there were occasional differences. For example, having his archiepiscopal residence in the precincts, meant that Geoffrey Fisher was bound to pick up gossip as to what was happening around him. Sometimes he was approached to intervene in Cathedral affairs, but wisely recognised that to do so where Chapter decisions were concerned would obviously appear as an unconstitutional interference. On the whole the Archbishop managed to avoid this though it was not always easy. Thus, the departure of highly talented men from the Cathedral, as for example, Dr Gerald Knight, Organist and Master of the Choristers; the incomparable liturgiologist Joseph Poole, Precentor; and Clive Pare, Headmaster of the Choir School, led to much gossipy speculation. The Archbishop was known not to regard this near mass exodus with favour. How far it was wise to engage himself, even remotely, in matters of this kind, is a moot point. Certainly his presence on the campus meant that he was no remote figure which did not help him, try as he might, to remain neutral where domestic matters were concerned and interested parties consulted him. Thus the Archbishop himself believed that had he not, *inter alia*, let his views be known, a quite remarkable lady, Miss Babington, in charge of the Friends of the Cathedral, would have disappeared from the scene earlier than in fact she did.

We have seen how determined Geoffrey Fisher was to retain a family house in Canterbury. This made it possible for Rosamond Fisher to entertain widely and with genuine warmth. The usual practice was for the Archbishop to spend weekends in Canterbury, this giving him the opportunity of knowing local personnel and getting into the parishes. Because of the limited time available to him for this purpose, he was seldom seen at the ordinary statutory services in the Cathedral. The exceptions, of course, were the great festivals, when he would preach at matins and celebrate at the Sung Eucharist.

As to the domestic life of the Cathedral, an ex-choir boy writes: 'Christmas was the time when the choristers came most into contact with the Fishers. The Archbishop and Mrs Fisher were friendly with Clive Pare and took a great interest in the boys. Clive used to say that they knew the Fishers better than they did the Dean and Chapter. Rosamond Fisher, in particular, was astonishingly good at learning and remembering their names. Every year there were two visits to the Old Palace. 'On Christmas Eve, after supper', so our old chorister goes on, 'we would go to selected houses in the Precincts; to the Deanery – but never to the Shirleys' – and always to the Old Palace. We knew nearly all the six sons and would find the Fisher family at the dinner table, Rosamond in a long dress. Then two or three days after Christmas we would go round again for a party. Charles, one of the sons, arranged the games and we rushed about happily in the huge house. Fisher would attend the tea and wear a paper hat, etc., but later he would disappear.

One Easter Eve I met Mrs Fisher in the town. She asked me and another boy to tea. It was boiled eggs. After a while Dr Fisher came in wearing pyjamas and dressing gown. "I was so depressed by Oxford sinking in the Boat Race", he explained, "I went to bed".'

CHAPTER 14

The Very Reverend The Dean of Canterbury

GEOFFREY Fisher never doubted that Hewlett Johnson was, according to his own lights, a good, gracious and indeed a holy man. It was his political affiliations with countries east of the Iron Curtain which caused him perturbation and embarrassment. Nor did Geoffrey Fisher doubt that the Dean was doctrinally orthodox and a firm defender of the Faith. That he held the two together bemused the Archbishop but he did not question the Dean's honesty of purpose. It needs to be remembered, of course, that the background of this account of the relations between Archbishop and Dean was the Cold War, the Berlin Airlift and the Mindszenty Trials.

An augury of their future relationship can be glimpsed from the Dean's enthusiastic letter of greeting to the new Archbishop as he went to Lambeth. He had himself recently returned from Moscow and while there assisted at the consecration of the Catholicos of Armenia and also been presented with a beautiful crucifix by Patriarch Alexis of Moscow at a Victory Day Service. Would Archbishop Fisher, he asked, give him permission to wear this emblem?

The Archbishop responded to this letter in the warmest terms granting the asked for permission. 'What an exhilarating time you have had. I followed your movements in the Press with admiration for your enthusiasm and endurance, and what a varied collection of people you made contact with.'

It was a honeymoon period which was not destined to last long. Very soon the Archbishop received a letter from eighty residents in Blackpool protesting against a proposed decanal visit to their City on behalf of the Anglo-Soviet Friendship League. In their opinion he would be better engaged in the work for which he was ordained. The Archbishop's chaplain replied shortly but courteously pointing out that the Archbishop was not responsible for the Dean's engagements. Quite clearly the Archbishop had no authority over Dr Johnson but of this he found it difficult to convince the public at large. The constitution of the Church of England is not easily understood and distinctions between Dean and Archbishop when both have the same Canterbury designation fly above the heads of the ordinary citizen – or indeed commissar. Frequent were the occasions when Geoffrey Fisher did his best to persuade the uninitiated that the two offices were most certainly not one and indivisible, but often to no effect.

In the summer of 1947 Herbert Waddams of the Council on Foreign Relations called in at the Foreign Office to see Mr Sargent on behalf of the Archbishop, to inform him of the Dean's intention to visit the Balkans, and asking whether there were any arguments the Archbishop might use to dissuade him from undertaking such a journey. The question was not new to the Foreign Office for recently they had discussed the advisability of a bishop of the Established Church visiting Bulgaria or Rumania and had come to the conclusion that it was not helpful. Undoubtedly political capital was made out of such visits and it might be, said Sargent, that the British Government would soon release 'horrifying facts about the Bulgarian regime'.

The Archbishop now approached the Dean, tactfully saying that he had already made contact with the Foreign Office and had been told that it was 'very undesirable that any English ecclesiastics should visit these countries'.

The Dean replied to the Archbishop in a letter of inordinate length but of great restraint. He remained convinced, even after reading the Archbishop's epistle with the most 'earnest consideration,' that it was only by 'the widest charity and understanding' that it was possible to break down class and social barriers, national fears and suspicions between countries. In all humbleness he suggested that diplomacy as understood by the Foreign Office was not the appropriate guide for Christian reconciliation.

Matters came to a head again in 1949 when Hewlett Johnson went to the United States at a time when anti-Communist feeling had become almost paranoiac in that country. The result was to increase the number of protests coming to Lambeth. The Dean's tour of Hollywood attracted the comment that he was the most theatrical personality who had been there since Bernard Shaw. If this were true, then certainly the Dean was in good company.

Typical of a vast correspondence concerning the Dean which came into Lambeth during Geoffrey Fisher's archiepiscopate was a letter from an irate Colonel Fletcher, outraged by the Dean's American tour. It was simply inconceivable to him why the Archbishop did not remove him from office. Had he not taught them at Marlborough to be disciplined and courageous?

'You and your churches are empty', he wrote, 'and are treated with mild contempt by thousands because you are not prepared to take action.' If he were not a time-serving prelate he would order the Dean to go, and if he refused, he should go himself.

An increasing shoal of criticism from all and sundry induced the Archbishop, in self-defence, to draw up an official disclaimer of the Dean's views. In courtesy he passed this on to the Dean evoking the comment that it tallied with what he himself had stated publicly to the press in Britain, America and Canada.

There was, in fact, nothing effective that the Archbishop could really do except perhaps to keep a cool head while others were losing theirs and to dissociate himself from the Dean's views.

The Dean's visit to Canada, which was given extensive press coverage, followed the same pattern as his previous tour of Australia. One thing is certain, namely that the innumerable letters which flowed into Lambeth from Archbishops, Bishops and lay people, were both time-consuming to read and wearisome to answer. Some were not so easily dealt with and raised problems. For example, T. S. Eliot had arranged to give the annual Oration for the Friends of the Cathedral in 1951 but he now wrote saying that he must withdraw from this engagement since the Dean would be giving the vote of thanks. The Archbishop's response, unwisely so it transpired, was to ask the Dean to absent himself on this occasion. However, when this matter came before the Chapter its members would contemplate no such absentee-ism. Thus the Archbishop was forced to eat humble pie and to let T. S. Eliot know that his request could not be granted.

A not dissimilar situation developed in respect of the Dean in his chairmanship of King's School, Canterbury. This escalated into a crisis, when in 1955 the Russians invaded Hungary and Britain sent troops into Egypt. The Dean took the view that whereas the Russians were 'invited' to go into Hungary by its legitimate government, the British invasion of the Suez had no such justification. This aroused a veritable storm of protest and as a result a group of members of the King's School Governing Body called vociferously for the Dean's resignation from his chairmanship which he held *ex officio* as Dean of Canterbury. Canon Shirley reacted by declaring the Deanery out of bounds to the boys of the School. The Dean's position – he meant it as an eirenical gesture – was that he could not resign the chairmanship since, *inter alia*, it would be prejudicial to the office which he held. He did, however, agree to confer with the Archbishop who was the School's Visitor. The latter made the proposal that, on certain public occasions, he as Visitor should act for the Dean thus preserving the rights of the latter's Office and this the Dean accepted. However, Hewlett by 1961 was back again chairing meetings of the Governing Body. He was indeed a survivor!

Many ordinary people's attitude to this continuing *contretemps* was one of a 'gut reaction' which convinced them, against the evidence, that there must be a legal means of removing the Dean from his Office. However, Geoffrey Fisher was emphatic that there was no such way. Waldron Smithers, a Member of Parliament, believed that he could be legally dealt with through the allegiance which he owed to the Crown as spelled out in the 39 Articles of Religion in the Book of Common Prayer. This, of course, was not true and the Archbishop was quick to point this out.

Anti-Dean of Canterbury sentiment reached a grand climax, with severe international repercussions, when he visited China and subsequently declared in a speech to the British-China Friendship Association, that he had collected an 'exhaustive and scientific assemblage of evidence', personally verified *in situ*, that the American Forces had dropped germ bombs on Chinese territory. Lord Allen let the Archbishop know that it was his intention in the House of Lords to ask whether there was not a legal way of taking action against the Dean. It was, of course, a *cause célèbre* which the daily press understandably enjoyed and exploited. The *Daily Sketch* highlighted it under the heading 'Dupe in the Deanery'; and *The Manchester Guardian* 'The Credulous Traveller'.

On 15 July 1952, in an emotionally charged Upper House, this matter came up for their Lordships' consideration. The Archbishop regarded it as his responsibility to introduce an objective and reasoned approach into a debate which could well lack these steadying ingredients. What, he asked, within terms of the law, was the nature of the charges brought against the Dean? No accusation had been laid against him on the grounds that he held certain political views which were contrary to Christian doctrine. Nor was he yet a danger to public safety though he might be a thorn in the flesh to all of them. However both Church and State had stood up to a great many other victims of unreason, self-delusion and blind partisanship and had come through them successfully. 'I think we can put up with the Dean,' he concluded, 'if only the Privy Council would lose interest in him others would do likewise.' Lord Attlee, with his usual prudence – he was a master of the low profile – in the course of the debate was emphatic in declaring the unwisdom of Parliament trying to take any action in a matter of this kind.

For politeness' sake, Geoffrey Fisher wrote to the Dean apologising for not sending him in advance, as he had intended, the script of his speech.

The Dean's reaction was to give vent to long pent-up feelings, which, for once, burst through the restraints of his customary courtesy. 'Let me observe,' so he began a letter to the Archbishop, 'that it is Your Grace's political opinions which prevent cordial relations with the Churches of the East, prevent constant visitations and friendly contacts.' There were occasions, as time went on, when the Archbishop himself tended to lose his usual calm. Thus his testy reply to the Dean's *cri de coeur* was somewhat acid. Had the Dean but taken his, the Archbishop's, words seriously he would have given up political propagada – or resigned his Deanery.

It is not surprising that this serious controversy should begin to grow more intense and to disturb the peace even of the City of Canterbury itself. Actions by the Dean, perhaps insignificant in themselves, added fuel to an ever increasing fire. Thus he could hardly have been surprised that its citizens did not take kindly to his allowing the local Communists to hold a meeting in the Deanery. This led to a storm of protest, some of it levelled against the Archbishop himself for his apparent complacency. The Archbishop, however, wisely endeavoured to play it down: '. . . if the Church took to excommunicating people whose political views were regrettable, the results would be disastrous and freedom of speech impaired'.

The local Member of Parliament, Mr John White, grew steadily more uneasy and attacked the Dean publicly in an address given in Slater's Hall in Canterbury, concentrating on his allegations against the American Government in respect of germ warfare. Two days later, in the Cathedral, the Dean occupied the pulpit for some forty minutes as he replied to the charges made against himself. One of the letters which arrived at Lambeth from a businessman in Coventry deserves a passing reference. A great deal of trade, he alleged, had been lost by the Dean's activities and by prelates and clergy whose own Church and district were neglected, resulting in much wickedness and vice. Yet they still concerned themselves with foreign missions rather than in doing their work at home. How could we expect natives, he asked, some two or three generations removed from cannibalism, to be equal to our civilisation of over 1000 years? Must we not expect thinking business-men to complain: Why does the Church advocate race equality? Should it not keep out of politics and mind its own very serious business at home?

This letter is almost a classic of its kind but does not stand alone. Perhaps the tragedy is that the writer was expressing, in sincerity, a view which many of his fellow citizens shared – at least subliminally.

Letter writing was almost second nature to Geoffrey Fisher and often he sent personal replies when many would have thought a formal acknowledgement from one of his chaplains was more than adequate. In his personal letters he could be surprisingly frank even to strangers. For example, in response to a correspondent who stated baldly that the Dean must be either completely ignorant or a deliberate liar, he replied that human nature was not quite as simple as that. Indeed there were all kinds of self-delusions in us all. The Dean, he insisted, had never subscribed to atheistic Marxism: nor had he ever joined the Communist Party. 'Difficult though it may be for us to understand, he does sincerely and genuinely believe the Christian Gospel.'

Particular incidents connected with the activities of the Dean of Canterbury continued to irritate, not least one of his most ham-fisted indiscretions which it was not easy for him to live down. On Easter Day 1956, the Archbishop while processing out of the Cathedral after

Evensong ran into the non-attending Dean escorting Malenkov on a conducted tour around the church. To be fair to the Dean he had warned Dr Fisher that he would be receiving the Soviet statesman in the Deanery at 2.15 pm, but that he would not be introducing him to the Archbishop. An apology for this omission was probably supererogatory. Unfortunately, the Russian party turned up late which led to the collision with the evening congregation. The Archbishop, somewhat exasperated, expressed surprise that no apology had yet been offered him. 'You are the Dean of Canterbury Cathedral,' he wrote, 'the Mother Church of the Anglican Communion', and to bring this man and all that he stood for to Canterbury on Easter Day was provocative in the extreme.

In so far as Geoffrey Fisher was resolute in not encouraging any witch-hunt or legislation against the Dean he did well; also in his believing that there was a value in the maintenance of freedom of speech and belief. Far better to have an institution which errs on the side of toleration rather than one in which liberty is denied and the price of its expression is exclusion from office or even gaol. Geoffrey Fisher, to his credit, was able to separate views which he did not share from the integrity of the man who held them.

The Church of England, it may well be argued, would be the poorer without adherents of the Dean's calibre and courage, willing to authenticate themselves at the cost of unpopularity and misunderstanding. The really sad fact about the Dean is that his very extremism and at times gullibility, prevented his being the reconciler which he undoubtedly wished to be.

CHAPTER 15

The Diocese

BOTH in Chester and London Geoffrey Fisher was a conscientious and hard-working diocesan Bishop who saw his priority as getting to know his people, particularly the clergy, and encouraging in them a Christian commitment which should permeate all areas of life, personal as well as collective. It was this basic approach that he took with him to Canterbury. Here, however, he was to face a problem, ever present in his ministry but now heightened. The most precious commodity for him was time and he was always conscious at Canterbury how limited were the clock hours available for the exclusive use of the Diocese. To a former chaplain he wrote some three years after he went to Lambeth: 'As for me I stagger from one thing to another after the fashion which you know only too well from personal experience. Surprise at the number of things I do . . . alarm and regret at the number of things I leave undone.' It needs to be remembered, of course, that Geoffrey Fisher inherited the two Suffragan Bishops of Croydon and Dover; to which a third Bishop of Maidstone, Stanley Betts, was added in 1956. Without them, and a sensible delegation of responsibility to them, the administration and oversight of the diocese would have been grossly inadequate. However, only a man so physically fit and so highly organised could have achieved so much in the diocese as Geoffrey Fisher undoubtedly accomplished.

Before embarking on his Diocesan ministry and while as yet only Archbishop-designate Geoffrey Fisher let his general approach and priorities be known. In his first letter to his new Diocese as Archbishop-designate he wrote: 'I can say that my greatest happiness will be in the diocesan family and in visits to its parishes. I have hardly ever come back from a parish without feeling renewed in spirit by the faith and fellowship of my brethren in Christ. London has indeed won my deep affection, but one thing it could not give me as Chester did – the joy of visits to country towns and country villages. That joy I look forward to recovering again.'

As soon as possible after his enthronement in May 1945 he announced that his 'real desire' was to find opportunities of meeting the clergy and their flock, though he added that this was bound to be 'slow work'. To this end he mapped out a programme of what he hoped to achieve before the end of the year, to implement which he would venture to invite himself to various parishes, beginning with those central ones which had a natural priority. For the rest he would wish to go chiefly to those which his predecessor had not got round to. His parochial calls were always an 'event' when he certainly came alive as friend and pastor in this brief encounter. I quote, as a typical example, his visiting the parish of St John's Church, Folkestone. The Church, which seated some 600 people, was crowded and chairs were put in the nave. After the service he chatted in a natural and friendly way to members of the congregation as they proceeded to the Church Hall. Here he spoke freely to the Mayor, Aldermen and Councillors, members of St John's Ambulance and the Parochial Church Council and other organisations. Then it was back to the vicarage for lunch where he put a young and somewhat overawed wife immediately at her ease. When he discovered that his hostess hailed from Yorkshire and her husband from London he remarked: 'One of you comes from the North, the other from the South. I have the advantage over both of you because I come from the Midlands and we Midlanders have all the virtues of those in the North and South and none of the vices.' The incumbent's wife was born and bred a Quaker which encouraged the Archbishop to ask numerous questions pertaining to Quaker beliefs and practices. They chatted easily until Archbishop and parish priest went into the study. Told by the vicar that through lack of space he must get rid of some of his classical books the archbishop immediately interjected: 'Why on earth keep these two volumes of Plautus?' Noticing a large building on the other side of the vicarage he asked what it was and on being told it was the Royal Victoria Hospital he requested to be taken round the wards where he spent well over an hour. He was highly amused with Victoria, a young Nigerian nurse, who, when asked what Church she belonged to, replied 'CMS'. It was all 'unhurried visiting' the vicar comments and it greatly endeared him to everybody.

The Archbishop's regret was that he could not be as peripatetic about his diocese as he would have wished. The multiplicity of his responsibilities and commitments as Primate of All England and head of the Anglican Communion inevitably entailed that during certain periods over the years his diocese had to take second place. Such was the case in the summer of 1948 because of the Lambeth Conference, followed almost immediately by the Assembly in Amsterdam of the World Council of Churches. He writes with genuine feeling in his Diocesan Notes of the very great loss this enforced absenteeism was to him. Still he treasured the memory of a very happy five days shortly after Easter during which time he visited seven parishes from Deal and Ramsgate on one side of the Diocese to Upchurch, Lower Halstow and Frittenden on the other. 'How can it not be refreshing and inspiring for me?' he asked, 'when I can thus come into close touch with the beauty and interest of our Kentish churches.' In spite of many difficulties and demands on his time he managed to conduct a third of the total confirmations in the diocese leaving the rest to his suffragan bishops.

In his early years in the Canterbury Diocese the Archbishop tried to concentrate very largely on the individual parish, but after some six years he was reminded – it had been his regular practice, both in Chester and London – by the 'friendly representations of the Tait Missioner' of a 'duty which was also a desire'. This was to visit the Rural Deaneries which consisted of a group of parishes in a particular area. Hence on 9 February 1950 he made contact with the Rural Deans letting them know that it was his intention in March and April to visit each Chapter and in order to facilitate this he sent a schedule of dates which he himself could manage and which he asked them if possible to approve. 'For the rest', he wrote, 'I hope that in Chapter the clergy will feel free to question or even to heckle me in anything that they would like me to know. At the same time I shall hope to have the chance of a few words with each member of the Chapter while I am there.'

Having thus prepared the way, in April 1950, he made what he described as a 'lightning tour' of the Ruri-Decanal Chapters. He admitted to finding it strenuous but enjoyable and rewarding. No two Chapters were quite alike in their 'general feeling' or in the subjects which they wished to discuss. All were 'interesting and friendly'. He urged upon them the necessity from time to time to go into retreat and suggested they should agree on a book or books which each priest should study 'to bring them back to the spiritual basis of their ministry and their people'.

Most of the Archbishop's visits to the Deaneries were outstanding successes but this was not always the case as he frankly admitted. For example he did not feel he went down very well at Croydon early in 1951 and he wrote calling the attention of the Suffragan Bishop to this failure. His words show a real capacity to be self-critical: 'I'm afraid I rather failed to do my stuff on Monday with this Chapter and I am all the more conscious of the fact because the Sutton Deanery on Tuesday was so good. It was partly my fault. I was rather tired after Sunday and I really had not thought in the least what was going to happen or what I was going to say. Partly the conditions were difficult; the Parish Hall is not an attractive place, the numbers were larger and so arranged that it was almost impossible to get a feeling of informality. At Maidstone the numbers were smaller and the clergy were all around me in a big room in the vicarage. As a result we all became very matey and discussed lots of things together.'

As in Chester the Archbishop always gave support and helped to inspire parochial missions within Rural Deaneries. Thus when one was planned for Sandwich he wrote a commendatory letter to each parish, in addition to three others intended for regular churchgoers, for those 'loosely attached' and for those who did not take Christ seriously.

An innovation, very congenial to his temperament, were Conferences designed to help him in getting to know his clergy and give assistance to them in their ministry. The first took place at Dymchurch in a Butlin's Holiday Camp on 7–11 May 1951. To encourage and make it possible for parish clergy to attend and to regard the Conference as a high priority, he urged the laity to accept gladly the absence of their priests over a period of five days. Also, he urged all churchpeople to unite in prayer that God would grant a renewal of the Holy Spirit to the clergy who attended showing each of them how to be more faithful and effective in preaching Christ as Lord. Two hundred and eighty clergymen responded to the Archbishop's call and the Canterbury Diocesan flag hung proudly from a tall mast throughout the Conference. The staff of the Holiday Camp began their season a week earlier to provide the necessary plant, feeding and amenities. It was Geoffrey Fisher's wish that the clergy should be encouraged to do some serious thinking. Thus the morning was devoted to two lectures given by Canon Hugh Herklots, prominent in the Student Christian Movement, whose theme was the command of Jesus to watch, to love and to rejoice; by Roger Lloyd, historian of the Church of England and Canon of Winchester, on 'The Anglican tradition in modern Britain'. In the afternoon there were more informal talks given by Frank Bennett, Rector of Wigan, his general approach being 'hard hitting, lit up by an extraordinary agile wit'. The evening was devoted to the Archbishop's Hour during which he revelled in answering questions thrown to him at random. It was all a very lively affair.

The Archbishop himself felt that this first and experimental conference had gone well and that it helped to make the clergy feel that they were much more of a family by getting to know each other and their Bishop better. His hope was that this stimulus would overflow into the parishes and so quicken their corporate life. At the final meal the Archbishop thanked the waitresses for the way in which they had looked after the clergy. Certainly during the course of the conference their first and somewhat frigid attitude had undergone a distinct thaw. 'I guarantee,' he said to them, 'that before you came to this conference most of you would have run a mile to get away from a parson. But now we shan't be able to keep you away from them.'

The general consensus, by no means confined to the Archbishop and his immediate staff, was that this conference had proved sufficiently successful to encourage the planning of a second. In fact three such conferences in all were laid on during his archiepiscopate.

If parochial 'get-togethers', conferences and meetings of Ruri-Decanal Chapters had their place as embodying a rising tide of local interest, it was in the Diocesan Conference that both clergy and laity were brought together for serious discussion and decision making. Geoffrey Fisher always entertained a 'high view' of the status and significance of this body, not only because it gave the Bishop the opportunity of sharing problems and exchanging ideas with leading parishioners all over the diocese but also because he could refer to areas of the Church and the Nation's corporate life wider than ecclesiastical boundaries.

Early in 1950 he set out clearly, in an address to Convocation, the importance which he attached to these assemblies. Such synods, he said, should become a normal ingredient of diocesan life. They should be concerned not so much with the details of administration but with 'mutual consultation on principles concerning faith, worship, moral discipline and pastoral offices'. The difficulty, he felt, was to determine precisely what 'regular' meant in this context. If it only meant 'when the Bishop happens to think he would like one', then its meetings would certainly in fact be pretty irregular. The Synod must meet at least once every year. Only by regularly coming together could it assist by mutual consultation the Bishop in his administration of the diocese, and the clergy in carrying out their duties. Also it might be that matters under discussion, in particular in Convocation and the Church Assembly, should be locally debated.

A reading of the reports of the Canterbury Diocesan Conference which met regularly twice a year during Geoffrey Fisher's archiepiscopate show them to be lively, dealing with significant business. The intention, of course, was that those at the Conference should go back and report to their parishes. Unlike some of his episcopal colleagues, the Archbishop enjoyed chairing these occasions and this helped him to do it well and to jolly others along. His flashes of humour usually went down well.

The domestic and administrative affairs of the Diocese were inevitably for the Archbishop a constant interest. After his Enthronement one of his first tasks was to meet the Board of Finance, the Standing Committee of the Conference, the Education Committee and the Greater Chapter. Having done this he had a session with the Committee for Diocesan Re-organisation.

Canterbury was fortunate in having access to excellent financial expertise though this did not mean that the Archbishop forbore to examine carefully and make his views known on the Annual Budget. He realised only too well that such budgets reflected diocesan priorities and not only in spending. One of the subjects he persistently kept before Diocesan Conference was the incomes of the clergy, and he was pleased to write in the November issue of the Canterbury Notes for 1947 that whereas when he first came to the diocese and brought this matter up there were 117 parishes below the minimum stipend of £500 per annum, this number had now fallen to under 50. It would not have done so without constant prodding by Geoffrey Fisher. The Annual Budget was a family affair and he hoped its demands would be met ungrudgingly. In this respect, Geoffrey Fisher had no inhibitions about raising money provided that it was used *ad gloriam Dei*, that is to minister to real human needs. His knowledgeable interest in all the structures and plant of the diocese was certainly an incentive to lay people and clergy, immediately involved, to regard what they were doing as supremely important.

CHAPTER 16

Peace and its problems in Europe

(i)

GEOFFREY Fisher was enthroned as Archbishop of Canterbury some four months before the end of the war in Europe. In Britain there was a quiet determination among responsible people to build a better and more just social order. Thus the Labour Party, swept into power by the Forces' vote, and welded into a disciplined body under the restrained yet effective leadership of Clement Attlee, set out to achieve a society based on Keynesian economics in a welfare state inspired by Beveridge. It was certainly a bold ambition but the times were by no means unpropitious since no longer was Britain solely preoccupied with winning the war. The Christian Church, with its incarnational Gospel, could not be indifferent to this new world, painfully emerging out of the ruins of the old.

The Archbishop's early months at Lambeth coincided with the Allies increasing their grip upon a Germany in ruins and with its people demoralised. He was indeed sensitive to their terrible plight, but believed it would be wrong to allow this to deflect the Allies from their first duty which was to break the German military machine. Maybe the very extremity of suffering involved in this process was necessary if the German people were to learn to 'hate and abjure that militarism which for so long they have idolized and idealized'.

Suffering at this terrible level was, of course, by no means confined to ex-enemies. Northern Holland, to mention but one country, was experiencing the slow starvation of its people which 'exceeds in horror, the horrors of the war'.

The Archbishop had himself, by reason of his chairmanship of the Joint Standing Committee, given much thought to the character of the peace which should follow the war, and was well versed in Papal pronouncements on the basic principles which ought to inform it. At the time of the San Francisco Conference he issued a statement jointly with Dr Garbett, Archbishop of York, stressing the importance of the decisions which were to be made, particularly concerning 'the structure of the World Organisation which is to preserve peace and control international relations in the post-war world'. It was the bounden duty of Christians to support these deliberations by earnest and constant prayer.

In assessing the peace settlement which eventually emerged Geoffrey Fisher adopted a realistic position, namely that 'there was no solution which could adequately meet all the rights and wrongs of the case'. On the whole he believed that at Yalta 'the claims both of justice and expediency were satisfied,' though Poland constituted 'the most difficult example of the abiding problem of how to apply to human affairs in their disorder the principles of freedom and justice'.

Geoffrey Fisher was deeply distressed at the considerable anti-German sentiment – Vansittartism as it was called – which he saw around him, though he did not believe it was so extensive as did Kurt Hahn, Headmaster of Gordonstoun, with whom he entered into a long correspondence, and whom he greatly admired.

In response to this mood Geoffrey Fisher, on 24 May 1945, declared publicly that the victors must not allow themselves to be unjust to their former enemies. This speech evoked a bitter *riposte* from Brussels, reported in the continental edition of *The Daily Mail*: 'Humain pour les Allemands, oui, de pardon non jamais'. Meanwhile the Archbishop's postbag was full to overflowing. One letter which must have moved him came from a major stationed at the Second Army Head-quarters and written upon his first entering Belsen. His simple, objective account bears witness to a tragedy beyond human comprehension: 'After a short time we came to a pile of dead female bodies, 80 yards by 30 yards, and about 3 feet high. There must have been at least 500 lying there, thrown on top of one another, so thin and so emaciated it was difficult to believe they had ever been people at all. Many of them were covered in horrible sores. The sight was something I am quite unable to describe and the smell was its equal. And yet even here there were people sitting down cooking a potato on a fire or lying in the sun.' The Major could find solace only in the thought that what he had seen made his military service 'worthwhile'.

The Archbishop was never in any doubt as to what the final end of British-German relations must be and he expressed this well in a letter written in June 1945: 'We should entirely agree that our governing purpose must be the reconciliation of our enemies and the redemption of evil-doers. We must never allow ourselves to be indifferent to the shattered, perplexed, despairing, guilty or half-guilty millions of our foes or to our own blindness and guilt in allowing the evil in Germany to grow without at a much earlier stage taking violent action to arrest it.'

Post-war statesmen did not enter the new age sustained by any Utopian dreams. Hence the newly constituted United Nations was more realistically conceived than its ill-fated predecessor the League of Nations. Winston Churchill was apprehensive of dangers looming ahead which he believed could only be avoided by imaginative thinking and bold planning. So it was that, frustrated and smarting under his electoral defeat, he was moved by a new vision to match the hour –

that of a United Europe. Hence he galvanised himself into action and founded a society, transcending the political divide, to promote this end, and in doing so to draw inspiration from that 'spiritual unity' once characteristic of Christendom. The Archbishop gave this his full support, being strongly of the opinion that artificially contrived schemes for unity failed to move people and that it was better to build on the already existing community of Western Europe. Thus he supported a motion in the House of Lords which declared its 'readiness to welcome the progressive establishment of a United Europe in which the true spiritual values of its past culture will be preserved, developed and expressed in such communion again as may prove to be acceptable and desirable'. Writing to the Archbishop, Winston Churchill expressed the concern which he personally felt: 'It is my deep conviction, as I think you know, that if we are to avoid the catastrophe of a third world war we must somehow contribute to bring order out of the chaos in Europe, break down national hatreds and suspicions and foster by every means in our power the essentials of unity and the practice of co-operation. To attain this end we must arouse the fervour of a crusade'. Hence his concern to win the support of the churches throughout Europe. The Archbishop rallied to his cause, secured the scholarly Dean of St Paul's as a signatory to the appeal, and presided over a crowded meeting in the Albert Hall on 14 May 1947, when he commended in strong terms the 'Crusade'. Five Anglican bishops were present.

Inevitably, however, the time came when it was necessary to work out in practical terms exactly what a United Europe implied. Here insular Britain began to drag her feet and Churchill, back in 10 Downing Street, found his energies and interests directed elsewhere. However, this movement for a United Europe cannot be entirely written off. It was not without its influence on the formation of the European Economic Community; on the assembling of the Hague Conference in 1948; and in prompting Schumann's pan-European policy. At least Geoffrey Fisher gave it his warm support, thus helping to identify the *Ecclesia Anglicana* with its overriding purpose.

If there were urgent social and personal problems in the United Kingdom such as those resulting from demobilisation, these were as nothing compared with those on the Continent after a war of unparalleled destruction and intense social unsettlement. As hostilities ceased a primary duty rested upon Christian leaders in Britain as they looked across the Channel to their separated brethren in Germany to discover what their real situation was; to re-open relations with them; and to bring them hope in their desperation. They had indeed been through the vale of suffering and many had come out of it broken, dispirited and guilt-ridden. Individual Christians in Germany had indeed resisted

Hitler and, like Dietrich Bonhoeffer, some had paid the price with their lives. Others had openly conformed, secretly hoping that the war would bring about the Führer's downfall; a number had gone along with the regime, preferring not to know its terrors.

The more responsible Christians in Britain saw the role of the reformed Churches in Germany as central to the re-integration of that country into the international community of Western Europe. However, if initiatives were to be taken in the United Kingdom it was imperative that their efforts should have the full support of the military commander in the British zone. He was none other than Field Marshal Montgomery, a somewhat eccentric, dedicated, evangelical churchman wedded to muscular Christianity. It was equally important that financial help should be forthcoming from the British Government. Fortunately the Field Marshal had let the Archbishop know early that it was his 'firm conviction that in the reconstruction and redemption of Germany, the churches of that country must play a significant part'. Thus encouraged, Archbishop Fisher wrote a long letter to the Field Marshal in the summer of 1945 thanking him for this expression of his views and making a few points of his own. He had been conferring with a group of Christian leaders and they had all accepted that there must be an 'agreed policy' on which right relations with German Christians could be based. Also the chaplains on the ground were repeatedly asking the Archbishop how they ought to behave towards German pastors, and whether there was any official attitude to which they should conform. Both the Church of England and the British Council of Churches needed guidance if they were to promote reconciliation with their Christian brethren in Germany.

Clearly what was required were directions from the Field Marshal as to official policy which needed to be co-ordinated with the Americans and the French, and, if possible, with the Russians. In addition, the Archbishop suggested that some knowledgeable person such as the bilingual Padre Tindall who knew the German Church before the War, should make a survey of the existing situation and advise concerning policy. If this were agreed he could be attached to the Field Marshal's office for a month or so. To this request Montgomery responded positively and made Tindall a staff chaplain at the same time briefing him to survey at first hand the general position; to discuss it with German pastors; and prepare a report for the guidance of the Army chaplains and those responsible for directing them. The report duly appeared and a copy was sent to Lambeth. It was perceptive and proved valuable in laying down guidelines. From this the Archbishop now produced a memorandum of his own. In it he admitted that whereas the Roman Catholic Church had, on the whole, been anti-Nazi, the Lutheran and Reformed Churches were more ambivalent in part because of their high doctrine of the State. Some of those who, during the war, took this view were now preaching repentance but it was important that they should not be regarded as merely agents of the victors.

Of course it was understandable, after a long, grim and bitter war ending with obliteration bombing and unconditional surrender, that the pace of restoring relations between victor and vanquished should be slow. However, Geoffrey Fisher expressed himself 'thankful beyond words that the way is now opening up for the resumption of personal contact between the Churches of this country and Christian people in Germany'.

One of the main obstacles to progress was the division of Germany into zones with differing sovereign states administering them. Thus Pastor Asmussen complained to the Archbishop that conditions in the French Zone, because of strong anti-German feeling, were 'particularly distressing', a complaint which the Archbishop passed on to Pastor Boegner. 'In every country', the Archbishop contended, 'the Church must live and bear witness to what our Lord said of sin, righteousness and judgement. Within the defeated country conversions and renewal can only come in German hearts. All that we can do, humbly and without any self-righteousness, is to give the encouragement of fellowship in the Gospel and the Truth of Christ. It is everything that once more we can address one another.'

Field Marshal Montgomery, as he surveyed this mixed scene, was inclined to take a very practical view. They must do everything, he urged the Archbishop, to rebut in the youth of Germany 'idleness, boredom and fear of the future'. Trade unions should be revived together with other organisations such as Boy Scouts and those dealing with youth work generally. 'The best antidote to bad ideas', he commented cryptically, 'is to possess good ones.'

Geoffrey Fisher realised that the support of the British Government was vital if chasms of misunderstanding in Germany were to be effectively bridged. To promote this eirenic work he wrote to the Secretary of State for War acquainting him with Professor Tindall's report, and offering the following comments culled from it: (1) the German Churches greatly need a breath of 'outside air'; (2) there was a number of German leaders – Bishop Wurm of Stuttgart was a conspicuous example – with whom the West could work in restoring 'authentic Christianity'; (3) the German Churches would welcome conferring with Churches beyond their own shores; (4) the religious dimension was not adequately provided for by the relevant section of the Education Branch of the British Commission: better still would be a specifically constituted Church Affairs Board'.

In the light of such general observations the Archbishop made four positive requests of the Secretary of State for War namely that: (1) representatives of the British Council of Churches and the Christian Reconstruction in Europe Committee be sent out to Germany for discussion with its Church leaders; (2) personnel from the German Churches be authorised to accept invitations to attend conferences abroad and facilities provided for them to do this; (3) the British Control Commission be encouraged to press for arrangements to enable German churchmen in different zones to meet one another; (4) a church leader of high standing be nominated immediately as adviser to a separate Church Affairs Section on policy matters affecting the German Evangelical Churches.

The Secretary of State for War, in acknowledging this letter, (15 September) assured the Archbishop that he was as anxious as anyone to do all he could to help the Church to restore true religion in that country. Hence the Archbishop's proposals would be 'carefully and sympathetically examined'. Lack of transport facilities in Germany made it difficult to arrange visits of English churchmen or to provide facilities for Germans to leave their homeland.

The Archbishop was undoubtedly disappointed with this somewhat negative response but expressed the hope that the difficulties to which the Secretary of State for War had referred would soon be overcome. However, as to one of his proposals, namely that which related to visits by Church leaders from England to Germany, he must represent with some asperity, that there would be grounds for very 'great indignation and protest' if a facility granted to the Archbishop of Westminster were not at once granted to him to lay on a visit to the 'no less important Reformed Church of that country of long standing'.

In September 1945 Geoffrey Fisher called a small representative group to Lambeth which included the Chaplain-General, the Dean of St Paul's, Gordon Rupp, Professor Tindall and Oliver Tomkins. The purpose was to discuss the general problems inherent in resuming relations with the German churches. In the course of these discussions Gordon Rupp – he was a leading authority in England on Lutheranism – questioned the validity of such a concept as 'corporate repentance'; and was equally sceptical as to the oft-repeated criticism that the Lutheran Church as a body was 'hand in glove with the State no matter what this entailed'. His view was that Nazism could have been got rid of only by armed rebellion but few at the time would have supported so radical a solution. Nothing particularly significant seems to have emerged from this Lambeth meeting and Oliver Tomkins confessed that none of the group was 'proud' of his performance.

Geoffrey Fisher did not, as the months went by, cease both to pressurise the British Government to do something more about the dire plight of Europe and to awaken a public and Christian conscience concerning it. Early in December 1945 he took part in a debate in the House of Lords concerning the desperate plight of the displaced Poles in Germany, in the course of which he asked for monthly reports on the general situation *vis-à-vis* these unhappy people. At the same time Geoffrey Fisher invited the Archbishop of Westminster to Lambeth in order to associate him and the two Moderators of the General Assembly of the Church of Scotland and of the Free Church Federal Council in sending Christmas greetings to fellow Christians round the world, 'rejoicing with those delivered from suffering, sorrowing with all who still suffer and praying that the Prince of Peace may draw us ever more closely together in hope, faith and love'.

Another complicating factor at the time, making relief work the more difficult, was the uncertainty caused in Germany by the transition from direct military surveillance to the increasing civilian control of the Control Commission. Even the Archbishop was forced to admit that in many respects he was 'in the dark' as to where authority in particular areas actually lay. These were indeed critical days, a watershed in the immediate history of post-war Germany. Particularly significant was the Stuttgart Conference when the famous declaration was drawn up, largely by Pastor Niemöller, in which Christian Germans acknowledged a 'solidarity of guilt' but looked forward in hope to a future reconciliation. This assembly would certainly not have achieved what it did were it not for the eirenic presence of Bishop George Bell who embodied in himself the best of all that this Conference stood for. As to the general conditions in Germany he reported to Geoffrey Fisher that the towns were terribly devastated, Berlin being 'an inferno in ruins' – a sight incredible unless one had seen it with one's own eyes. Bishop Bell took with him to Stuttgart a personal letter from the Archbishop of Canterbury to Bishop Wurm to whom it must have come as a beacon of hope. There were deep spiritual problems ahead for the German Church, so Geoffrey Fisher foretold, but 'the great thing is that once more we can be in touch with each other in the fellowship of our faith in Jesus Christ Our Lord and find in mutual prayer and discussion how to walk together again in the service of his purposes'. He realised only too well that the Confessional Church had endured a period of isolation, but now this was over and he viewed with the greatest expectancy the steps which, under the leadership of Bishop Wurm, the German Church was taking to recreate itself.

On 27 November 1945 the Archbishop of Canterbury broadcast to the German people thus being the first English churchman to do so since the fighting had ceased. He began by recalling what disasters false leaders had brought on their country, at the same time stressing that Britain was anxious to relieve their suffering and hasten 'the time when in the comity of nations Germany can again have its place'. He then urged them to make their own distinctive and positive contribution to a national revival. Particularly he appealed to the youth of Germany, conscious as they must be of the 'spiritual vacuum' around them, to return to Christian faith and allegiance, in order that they might, with churches of other nations, co-operate in rebuilding a Christian order of society.

As the Archbishop surveyed the contemporary scene, so he was the more convinced that Christian faith alone in Germany could minister to the needs of its disillusioned citizens. Thus when later in the year he sent a message to the National Union of Czechoslovak Students, celebrating International Students Day after six years during which freedom was 'perverted and suppressed,' he urged them 'to commit themselves to truth as a solemn vocation, to serve their own people, serve the fellowship of peoples, serve God.'

The early post-war years in Germany, with so many signs of physical destruction on all sides, and characterised by a mood often of gloom and depression, were indeed critical. There were at least some in the Forces who felt that to offset this pessimism some dramatic, symbolic gesture was needed to inspire a vision and to kindle hope. Such was a proposal which emanated from no less a person than the General Officer commanding the British troops in Berlin. The idea was that the Army should build in a shattered Berlin a Church of Witness to Christ as the way of peace. This proposal found its way to Montgomery who asked that it be sent on to the Archbishop via the Chaplain-General. The latter envisaged a central dome from which there would branch out chapels of remembrance. A plaque, in all the languages of Europe, would testify that this Church was erected not as a memorial of war but as a directive to the way of peace. It was not surprising that Geoffrey Fisher and the Archbishop of York came to the conclusion that the project was not viable and with this decision the Chaplain-General reluctantly agreed. Thus it was shelved and no more was heard of it.

If conditions in Germany were grim for their own nationals they were by no means easy for the occupying forces of the victors. So much was this the case that responsible citizens in Britain were uneasy at what they heard, rightly or wrongly, as to the morals of the troops, the more so when it became Government policy to send over to the Continent young conscripts of eighteen in order to make possible the return of those who had served during the war years.

Hence the Blackburn Diocesan Council for Religious Education, with its Bishop in the chair, passed a resolution deploring the state of affairs, particularly calling attention to the incidence of venereal disease. Finally, of course, it was the Government which must be held responsible for what was happening among the British troops in Germany, and early in 1947 Geoffrey Fisher headed a deputation to Bellinger, Secretary of State for War, comprising representatives of the trade unions, industry and the Headmasters' Conference. Their main and pressing concern was the young conscript. In a subsequent correspondence the Archbishop expressed his satisfaction to Mr Bellinger with the marriage course which he described as 'triumphantly satisfactory', though he reminded the Minister that venereal disease remained a problem giving cause for widespread alarm.

Conditions such as were alleged to obtain in Germany do not suddenly mend, and on 23 October 1947 the Archbishop called together to Lambeth a 'high-level' group which included the Bishops of London and Chichester, the Moderator of the Free Church Federal Council, Tom Craske, Education Secretary of the Church Assembly, and Sir Frank Willis, Secretary of the Young Men's Christian Association. The purpose was to confer on 'matters relating to the Forces in Germany and the German situation generally'. The discussion was wide-ranging, covering many areas of deep concern. The Moderator stressed 'the fierce temptations' to which young men in the Forces were exposed – sex and the black market. He urged strongly, in supporting the Archbishop, that eighteen-year-old conscripts should not be sent abroad and if they were they should be treated as training cadets. The Bishop of Chichester was convinced that people in England remained quite unaware of the really grim conditions in Germany. Sir Frank Willis, drawing upon a wide experience of the work of the Young Men's Christian Association, paid tribute to the co-operation of Field Marshal Montgomery, Commander-in-Chief, in helping their relief efforts. Sir Frank believed that the high rate of venereal disease was largely due to drink.

The outcome of this meeting was an interview between the Archbishop and Mr Shinwell, then Secretary of State for War, when the former explained carefully to the Minister the factual situation in Germany as he understood it.

The subject of the young conscripts suddenly erupted into a matter of public controversy when it was proposed in the House of Commons that the period of conscription be extended from 12 to 18 months, so as to make possible the increasing demobilisation of troops in the occupying zone. A strong, if predictable, opponent of the use of conscription in this way was Dr Charles Raven, pacifist chairman of Christian International Service. As head of a Cambridge college he could call upon a wide experience of young students.

Geoffrey Fisher maintained that there had been great changes for the better as was clearly shown in a recent report by a Free Church delegation. Dr Raven, on the other hand, alleged that years at Cambridge had proved to him beyond doubt that sending out an ordinary youngster at the age of eighteen into occupied Germany was just 'devilry and absolutely corrupting'. So this controversy ended with an agreement to differ.

Relations between the British Occupying Forces in Germany and the indigenous population were bound to be both uneasy and difficult once hostilities ceased and victor and vanquished confronted one another. The military authorities, in order to bypass some of the resulting problems, decided on an official policy of non-fraternisation. This expedient had a mixed reception both in England and on the Continent, many entertaining severe scruples as to its morality and Christian validation. Particularly was this the case among the chaplains who at ground level had to implement the policy. Even as early as 1945 thirteen chaplains who attended a refresher course at Poperinghe took the opportunity of passing a resolution raising critical questions which they dispatched to Lambeth. Two chaplains dissented totally from the policy, protesting that non-fraternisation was 'wholly inconsistent with the Christian approach to the problem'. The Chaplain-General had meanwhile been going the rounds of some five conferences, all of which expressed a degree of unease as to their relations with German pastors and the ethics of non-fraternisation, though he himself was in favour of it but only for a very limited period.

Amongst those in England who protested against non-fraternisation was the distinguished vicar of St George's Church, Cannon Street, Fr John Groser, a cultured and dedicated left-winger. 'Without exception,' so he informed the Archbishop, 'every letter I receive from Christians in the Army, as in the new civil department, contains a protest about it asking me if something can be done by the Church at home.' Guy Clutton Brock, formerly of Oxford House till appointed in charge of one of the religious sections of the United Nations Relief and Rehabilitation Administration, felt so strongly that he contemplated resignation over the issue. *The Times* newspaper contained an article urging the lifting of the ban.

The Archbishop well realised that Groser's was a significant letter and that he was voicing the sentiments of a large number of responsible people. In reply he stressed that immediately after the cessation of hostilities it was certainly right to start with non-fraternisation; nor did it conflict with any Christian principles, since the goal was the re-education of Germany. Suddenly to lift the ban would lead to a 'great deal of fraternisation of the worst kind'. There should be freedom of intercourse between English chaplains and German pastors and he was at present 'deep in negotiations about this'.

The Archbishop's answer was certainly a substantial one: but the sheer logic of events and the assertion of a natural humanity meant that non-fraternisation soon became a thing of the past without any formal or official condemnation of it on moral grounds.

(ii)

So far as concerned the building up of the waste places in a shattered Europe on the verge of total collapse this was the prime responsibility of the United Nations Relief and Rehabilitation Administration (UNRRA) which was dependent upon money donated by governments and voluntary agencies. Inevitably some were critical of the way UNRRA discharged its duties and Geoffrey Fisher was forced to admit that sometimes plans, carefully worked out on the drawing board, had not in practice been well implemented. This was serious, since there were certain disaster areas where the provision of relief needed to be immediate. Such were, for example, northern Holland and Poland. The future status of the latter depended on political decisions already prejudiced against her by the growing cleavage between Russia and the West.

There were, co-operating with UNRRA, such agencies as the Department of Reconstruction, Inter-Church Aid, and Christian Reconstruction in Europe, these being under the aegis of the newly constituted World Council of Churches (WCC). National committees set up by the various member Churches of WCC raised money and the Anglican Church Assembly voted substantial sums towards the United Kingdom's national appeal for one million pounds.

One of the first and most urgent problems to be tackled in Europe was quite literally the threat of widespread famine. The Continent was in a state of chaos; transport facilities were scarce; industrial production at a low ebb, even to non-existence in certain areas. Geoffrey Fisher was constant in urging charitable giving, though he felt that corporately the Church of England, in its recent grant, had done its best. He spoke strongly on this matter in the House of Lords, so much so that, at the request of Victor Gollancz, his speech was published. Basically he believed it was a matter for governments which meant that it was the task of the Churches to keep the British Government active in discharging this obvious duty. Such was the case with the plight of refugees in East Germany, Hungary and Austria. The food situation there was critical and as a consequence disease was rampant and spreading fast. In this crisis, the Reverend Archie Craig, a distinguished member of the Church of Scotland and of the British Council of Churches, exhorted the Archbishop to use all his authority and agents of propaganda to demand that the Government should act. His cry did not fall on deaf ears and the Archbishop arranged for an ecumenical group to wait upon Prime Minister Attlee, and to confer with him as to conditions generally in Europe and what ought to be done about them. At the same time Bishop Bell himself reminded the Prime Minister that the Potsdam Conference had agreed that any transfer of population should be humane, and that further expulsions of Germans from the East should be suspended pending an enquiry by the Allied Commission. He was horrified by what he had seen in Stuttgart, and wrote an impassioned letter to Lambeth stressing that it would be an enormous help in dealing with this terrible situation if the Archbishop were to appeal publicly for a cut in the bread ration to save those starving in Europe. Such a sacrificial policy would serve to emphasise the urgency of the crisis. All the clergy must be made aware of this terrible tragedy. 'In the face of such a catastrophe the degree of need should be the criterion of giving.'

Prompted by his *cri de coeur* the Archbishop immediately issued a statement which was published both in *The Times* and *The Manchester Guardian*, calling attention in the most forthright terms to the 'horror' of world-wide famine such as threatened the very existence of millions of the earth's inhabitants. Only massive international action could hope to remedy this grievous ill and here Britain had a special responsibility for India and the British zone in Germany. If governments were effectively to handle this global problem then they must be reinforced by a vigorous public opinion. 'There have certainly been some suggestions', the Archbishop observed, 'that we should deny ourselves any increase of rations and sacrifice some part of our very large reserves of food. The Government is, I think, afraid of offending public opinion by saying too much of the extremities of famine which threaten, or by asking too much of us. I am confident that I speak for all Christian people, and I think I speak for public opinion in general, when I say to the Government: "Tell the facts, give us an official statement month by month, that we may know how things are going; do not apologize for asking us to save, to accept restrictions, to make sacrifices; ask and we will willingly support you. Under God we are one family of men and women".'

This strong appeal to the Government Geoffrey Fisher followed up with an address delivered at his own Diocesan Conference which was reproduced in his Canterbury Notes for May 1946. It told the same story and threw down the same challenge.

As time went on, and the situation itself seemed to worsen the Archbishop grew more critical of British policy and confessed to Sir Richard Acland, founder of the ephemeral Commonwealth Party and a great moralist in politics, that 'the Government itself is not guiltless,' though he added with muted approval that it was 'at last moving'. Churchmen, by and large, kept up the pressure and at the November session of the Church Assembly two resolutions were passed urging more concentrated efforts to deal with the existing food shortage on the Continent. In sending these resolutions to the Prime Minister the Archbishop presumed to say that it did not help – indeed it was a grave 'psychological blunder' – that on the very day when the newspaper reported a desperate dearth of provisions in Germany, an increased allowance of food for Britain over Christmas was announced. Clement Attlee acknowledged this letter only formally.

There was, of course, a sense in which, faced with a challenge so global in its outreach, no one could conscientiously be satisfied that all which the situation demanded was in fact being met. Only a united effort comparable with that expended during the Second World War could prove to be adequate; but the Allies were too exhausted and lacked the dynamic will to measure up to so extensive and novel a challenge. It was understandable that both the British and the World Council of Churches should regard the Archbishop, because of his unique office, as their most powerful advocate in approaching the British Government. He did not fail them, though sometimes, maybe, the World Council tended to exaggerate the extent of his influence. However, when Cockburn of the WCC telephoned him from Geneva complaining that the International Red Cross was seriously handicapped in bringing out internees simply because of a lack of petrol to transport them, the Archbishop was able straightaway, by forcefully putting this matter before Sir James Gregg at the War Office, to solve this problem.

The plight of the refugees continued to be a severe one made worse by ideological divisions in Europe between East and West. As late as two years after the fighting had ceased Archbishop Fisher entered into a correspondence with Mr Ernest Bevin, then Foreign Secretary, explaining that he regularly received a large number of letters on behalf of these 'unhappy people', particularly refugees domiciled in Italy. In particular he urged that control over the latter should not pass into the hands of the Italian Government. In reply the Foreign Secretary made the usual comment, not necessarily untrue, that the Government was doing its best; indeed there were 21,000 Yugoslavs for whom the British Government had accepted responsibility and of whom 11,000 were already in Britain and 10,000 held by the Allied Commission. The suffering of these victims of war was felt by the Archbishop to be sufficiently critical for him to head a further delegation to the Prime Minister which included Cardinal Griffin, Lord Beveridge and Sir Stafford Heathcote Smith, the last two representing the Refugees Defence Committee. The Archbishop expressed deep concern for all displaced persons, particularly since the Italians lacked the necessary power to exercise control, in addition to which many of their own nationals were in the hands of the Yugoslavs. Cardinal Griffin urged the Government to do all that it could while the opportunity remained.

It has to be said again that the supreme tragedy in trying to do justice, and to act humanely to those suffering from the cruel aftermath of war, was the increasing polarisation of Europe into East and West, seen in the Russian attempt at a 'take-over' in Berlin and the resulting airlift. The result, inevitably, was mutual suspicion between the major powers and the consequent introduction of political, rather than humanitarian, considerations into the treatment of refugees and displaced persons. One such defenceless group consisted of some 150 Latvians interned in Sweden and destined to be handed over to the Russians, whose plight was brought to the attention of the Archbishop by Duncan-Jones, Dean of Chichester and chairman of the Continental Committee for Refugees. Their only 'crime' was forcibly to have been conscripted into the German armies. The Church of Sweden, having been unable to persuade its own Government to do anything for them, now sought the help of the Church of England. The Archbishop personally saw its pastor, Slokenburg, whom wisely he admonished not to assume too easily that the Archbishop's intervention would prove successful. Another group consisted of loyal Austrians, also recruited against their will into Hitler's armies, and consequently now interned in Germany. In respect of both of these groups Geoffrey Fisher personally saw Sir Alexander Cadogan at the Foreign Office, particularizing in detail their plight. Tactfully, he emphasised how greatly he was aware of the difficulties besetting the Government as it tried to enforce the Geneva Convention under which no displaced person, unless he was a war criminal, should be repatriated against his will. The British and American Governments had sought to conform to this requirement and it would be tragic, he said, if the Swedish Government did not do likewise.

Among the myriads of refugees there were some individuals who for one reason or another – a few may have been collaborators – had been caught and were to be compulsorily extradited. In a veritable ocean of suffering and distress the claims of a single human being for justice might well be regarded as unimportant. There were those, however, who championed their cause and approached the Archbishop of Canterbury in the hope that he would be able to help them. It is to his credit that when he thought it right, he did so, investigating each case with meticulous care and interceding with the Government in the process. One example may be quoted as typical of many others.

Dr Najadanna, so Bishop Buxton informed Geoffrey Fisher, had been vetted and passed by all the relevant authorities, in spite of which he was due to be deported, contrary to the protection which the Geneva Convention granted to such persons. The Archbishop was himself a little sceptical as to the rights and wrongs of this intricate case, but took it up seriously. This meant much labour, with letters to and from

Sergeant at the Foreign Office. The result was that after a thorough re-investigation it was decided that though Najadanna was at heart hostile to the Allies he was an intellectual rather than a political collaborator. Hence, he was unlikely to get a fair trial if deported and the British Government, therefore, refused to hand him over. Sergeant, in a letter to the Archbishop, thanked him for his considerable help commenting that such borderline cases were the ones which required the most thorough scrutiny and the delay had enabled this one to be resolved in his favour. Geoffrey Fisher, on his part, responded generously: 'May I say how greatly I appreciate the immense care that has been given to the consideration of his case and how thankful I am at the result'.

Archbishop Fisher fulfilled a long entertained ambition when in November 1948 he first visited Germany after the war and met many of the people with whom he had corresponded over the years. His journey was not so much a fact finding one – though there was this aspect about it – as a goodwill mission which enabled him to give encouragement, express thanks to the occupying Forces, and to make warm personal contacts. Though essentially in Germany to meet British personnel he yet found time to converse with German pastors and to sample, if only briefly, the life of their communities.

The Archbishop's programme, as was usually the case, was a crowded one and included addresses; discussions with CCG officers; meetings with chaplains; a visit to the new building of the World Council of Churches; sessions with German Church leaders and clergy; tours of welfare centres and refugee camps; calling in on Army and RAF units; visits to theological colleges, youth centres and camps for displaced persons; lunch with the Bishop of Hamburg and a tour of that devastated city; attending civic receptions; broadcasting; conferring with regional commissioners; interviews with the German press – and so one might go on!

This summary shows clearly the Archbishop's determination 'to see something of the queer life going on around him'. The address which he gave to the rank and file of Army personnel was unusual and perhaps because of this was listened to attentively. His desire, he said, was to re-inforce their morale by indicating what an important and historic role they were being called upon to discharge. It was their mission to 'carry with them the good name of the British people and that is the thing of which we are all proud'. Also they were in part responsible for what Europe would be like in thirty, fifty or a hundred years hence, since there was no doubt that Germany would once again be a 'great nation'. At Hamburg the Archbishop preached to an Anglo-German congregation who were, he said, one in their belief in the Kingdom which Christ had inaugurated. To General Sir Brian Robertson, Military Governor and Commander-in-Chief, he regretted his inability to get to Berlin but was particularly gratified at what seemed 'a real revival of a helpful and constructive attitude to life' on the part of young Germans. General Robertson took the opportunity of raising with the Archbishop the need to co-ordinate under the Bishop of Croydon the chaplaincy work done by the Army and the Royal Air Force. This was a complicated domestic matter with a great deal of *amour propre* involved. The Archbishop's response was a mediating one. The CCG chaplains must remain under the jurisdiction of the Bishop of London but there was no reason why, for practical purposes, at least in Germany, they should not be treated as 'one team' under the Bishop of Croydon, Cuthbert Bardsley.

Some of Geoffrey Fisher's comments as he moved from place to place, annotating his typescript itinerary, indicate a vivid interest in all that he saw, such as to make him so delightful a guest to entertain. He soaked up information like a piece of blotting paper storing it in his mind for future reference. For example, he remembered later how at lunch some German leaders urged the need for currency reform and their fears of an anti-Christian 'welfare socialism' taking over. Occasionally he found much bitterness among German industrialists who alleged that British business interests were seeking to re-establish themselves at the expense of giving a fair opportunity to German commerce. Particularly he was concerned to hold out the right hand of fellowship to bemused German Christians. He was as desirous to meet the ordinary soldier or airman as he was the heads of the 'establishment'; and he was able to leave behind him an abiding impression in what was indeed a very brief encounter. Thus Brigadier the Lord Ballantrae who was in command of the first Battalion of the Black Watch stationed in Duesberg, a grim place in the Ruhr, discovered for himself 'how easy he was, spreading goodwill all round Germany like a bore-wave during his progress'. The visit well lived up to his expectations and they then spent a couple of hours talking about people, and places – and the Church of Scotland.

It is never easy to assess whether a tour of this kind was, or was not, a success. What we do know is that many who looked forward eagerly to it were high in the Archbishop's praise. Thus Sir Ian Robertson wrote enthusiastically that 'all the reports he had heard gave glowing accounts of its success'. 'There is no doubt', he commented, 'that by his visit he had done a big thing for the whole British community in Germany and for the work which we are striving to do among the Germans.' With this verdict Major-General Bishop concurred: 'Many distinguished people', he wrote, 'have visited us but we have never before enjoyed a visit so much, nor received such great inspiration.' His letter of thanks to the Archbishop concludes: 'I hope that we may live by the high example which you have set us'.

The Archbishop took with him on this visit Herbert Waddams, by no means an uncritical admirer of the Primate of All England. When he returned to Lambeth he drew up his own 'Notes on a visit to Germany 9 December 1948'. His final paragraph may be quoted: 'The whole visit was a tremendous strain, even to me who had no speeches to make and who did not have to spend so much time making light conversation with other people. But the Archbishop maintained his serenity throughout and his friendly interest in everybody and everything never flagged. I am sure that all those with whom he came in contact thought the same.'

CHAPTER 17

The World Council of Churches and Evanston

(i)

THE story of the Ecumenical Movement is a stirring one, marked by the great conferences of Mission at Edinburgh, Jerusalem and Madras; of Life and Work at Stockholm and Oxford; of Faith and Order at Lausanne and Edinburgh – all these leading to William Temple proposing in the Church Assembly in 1938 that the Archbishops of York and Canterbury be empowered to send representatives to a provisional conference, the intention of which was to set up a World Council of Churches. This resolution was carried, though there was a small minority who opposed it on the grounds that it would proliferate pontifical pronouncements committing all member Churches. In the summer of 1941 and in spite of the critical war situation, the previous resolution was definitively confirmed.

William Temple's death on 24 October 1944 took nearly everyone, except intimates, by complete surprise. No man is indispensable, but this cruel loss was a grievous blow. However, what William Temple had achieved in this field owed little to his being Archbishop of Canterbury, though holding this august office added authority and prestige to his labours. Basically it was his own stature, abilities and dedication to a World Church which moved others to work with, and to follow him.

It cannot be said that Geoffrey Fisher had as yet shown more than a minimal interest in the world-wide ecumenical movement, though William Temple had secured his nomination, while at London, to the chairmanship of the Executive Committee of the British Council of Churches. However, though he never set his sights on being another William Temple nor could claim such single-minded dedication to this cause, he recognised that the very nature of his new role required associating himself actively, and through him the Church of England, with the ecumenical movement.

No one was more aware of his inexperience in this field than Geoffrey Fisher himself. Temple's death left a vacancy on the Provisional Committee of the World Council and when Dr Marc Boegner, Dr Alphons Koechlin and Dr Visser't Hooft, its secretary, went to Lambeth and invited him to become a member of this Committee he replied simply that as yet he knew little about the workings of WCC but wished to emulate his predecessor. He was, therefore, willing to accept the nomination. Dr Visser't Hooft comments on this interview: 'The unreserved support which he gave from this time forward to WCC was a great help in the decisive period until the Second Assembly'.

The new Archbishop's lack of experience in the ecumenical field and yet the high expectancy entertained of an Archbishop of Canterbury in this area constituted in some respects an embarrassment to himself and to others. The immediate and inevitable effect of the Archbishop's membership of the Provisional Committee was to enlarge the range of his interests and help to give him a world-wide perspective such as later was of great help to him as the Senior Bishop of the Anglican Communion. John R. Mott, the great American Methodist who, perhaps more than any other single person except William Temple, witnessed and worked for a World Church across the years, was quick to recognise the significance of Geoffrey Fisher's enhanced status. In an encouraging letter to the new Primate he acknowledged the debt he personally owed to the 'wise counsel and influential support' of Dr Fisher's three immediate predecessors at Lambeth. At the same time he expressed his deep satisfaction at the Archbishop's agreeing to serve on the Provisional Committee. In a very personal reply Geoffrey Fisher recalled how 'enthralled' he had been as an undergraduate to talk briefly with John R. Mott after his giving an address in the Examination School at Oxford. Though it was an 'ill thing' to be unexpectedly called to follow William Temple he could only hope to be faithful to his example. At least he himself could claim to quote his own words that 'The ecumenical movement is as dear to my heart as it was to his'.

The Archbishop's personal situation was now changed from that of a detached observer to that of an active involvement in the affairs of the World Council. This was early seen when Stephen Neill, Assistant to the Archbishop, was approached by Dr Visser't Hooft to join the staff of the World Council as Co-Director of its Study Department. In advising him to accept Geoffrey Fisher commented that the ecumenical movement was of 'supreme moment' and that Anglicans had a vital part to play in its promotion. It was, therefore, important to have a member of the Church of England 'at the heart of it' in Geneva during the run-up to the Assembly at Amsterdam when the WCC was to be formally inaugurated. The Archbishop also wrote to Oliver Tomkins, General Secretary of the Faith and Order Committee of the World Council, since he was anxious that Neill should go to Geneva as soon as possible to gain experience there and make himself known. It was his intention to invite Neill to attend the Lambeth Conference as an observer though not as a member.

The inauguration of the World Council of Churches was in every sense a unique event in the history of Western Christendom. Nothing comparable had been attempted before and it was therefore generally agreed that meticulous planning for the great day was essential. One question loomed large, namely who, in addition to representatives of Member Churches, should be invited and in what capacity. It was recognised from the outset that the Roman Catholic Church would not officially join the Council since membership would have been seen as violating deeply cherished principles concerning the nature of the Church. Geoffrey Fisher was surprised, however, to find in a conversation with Sir Francis Osborne, British Minister at the Vatican, that he knew nothing at all about the WCC nor had he ever heard of it. The Archbishop, with his usual thoroughness, asked Oliver Tomkins to fill up this gap and he himself further wrote a supporting letter. Thus informed Sir Francis Osborne promised to pass on to his Holiness at his next audience some factual information about the Council and was convinced that he would be 'greatly interested'. Nothing concrete, of course, came from this assurance as officialdom in the Roman Catholic Church was not yet open to the 'winds of change', nor had any contact yet been made informally with the Vatican. However, this did not prevent some members of the World Council speculating as to how this *impasse* in the representation of Roman Catholics at the Council could be overcome. Many expedients were suggested for securing such a representation, in which Cardinal de Jong, Archbishop of Utrecht, was involved.

Geoffrey Fisher was clear from the beginning that there ought to be Roman Catholic observers at Amsterdam, but that it would be much better for these to be chosen by the Pope himself. His reasons for this are set out clearly in a letter to Boegner written on 28 April 1948. 'To take only those we select is a hole-and-corner affair, better than nothing. To have officially appointed observers from Rome is an outward gesture of recognition warmly to be welcomed. We want Rome to observe us but we can't claim to order what spectacles they shall observe us through.' Indeed, if the Cardinal Archbishop of Utrecht were to send in a list consisting of some of the 'bitterest enemies of the Ecumenical Movement', surely we should not complain but welcome the chance of influencing them to a better frame of mind. Dr Visser't Hooft sadly reflected that if the Roman Catholics refused to send observers then it would prove that the remarkable literature expressing a strong ecumenical spirit emanating from certain Roman Catholic authors in recent years was 'out of tune with the official policy of the Roman Catholic hierarchy'. Yet the leaders of the WCC remained reluctant to acquiesce in a complete absence of Roman Catholics from the Assembly and a last effort to overcome this was made at a meeting of the Provisional Committee. The idea was mooted that the WCC should take an initiative by inviting a few Roman Catholics to attend the Assembly quite informally and unofficially. Finally, however, protracted negotiations ended by getting nowhere, and thus no Roman Catholics attended the first General Assembly of the World Council of Churches. Geoffrey Fisher was certainly disappointed though not surprised for he never really thought that a Roman Catholic presence at the Assembly was viable although many individual Roman Catholics would have wished to be there.

In contrast to those who elected not to attend there were those who sought, uninvited, to come in on the act and thus involve themselves in the affairs of the nascent World Council. Such was an American, Myron Taylor, a well-meaning but somewhat naive layman who had a finger in numerous pies. Following alleged instructions from the White House, he asked Geoffrey Fisher whether President Truman might send his own personal representative to Amsterdam. He also expressed his surprise that no Mohammedan was invited which he regarded as 'very narrow'; he also deplored any invitations being sent to Churches under Russian influence. But Geoffrey Fisher was adamant that to invite observers from governments would lead them 'into all sorts of trouble', and Visser't Hooft was appalled at Myron Taylor's 'monumental ignorance'. He did, by sheer importunity, secure an interview with the Archbishop at Lambeth, but the latter took the wise precaution of having with him the Archbishop of York, the Bishop of Chichester and Bishop Sherrill of the Protestant Episcopal Church of America. They firmly rejected Myron Taylor's scheme to persuade the Pope and the WCC to issue a statement reiterating President Truman's ideas in general. Disillusioned, he rationalised his lack of success as follows: 'Though he had endeavoured to bring together the leaders of the Churches they had been unable to say with one voice that Christ was their Master and the source of their strength against the hosts of irreligion which would bring the world to final disaster'.

The difficulties, as we have seen, in the way of Roman Catholics attending the Assembly at Amsterdam in any capacity finally proved insuperable. The situation *vis-à-vis* Russian Christians was even more complicated, since the political divide between East and West constituted a hostile environment in which to bring Churches so divided together. Moreover the Orthodox Russian Church was itself fragmented, some of its leaders having fled to the West, the result of which was the setting up of an émigré Church. Clearly relations between the two sections of the Orthodox Russian Church were non-co-operative. Geoffrey Fisher and Visser't Hooft, reflecting the common mind of the World Council, felt they must take stock of, and not ignore, this divisive situation. In particular they must consider to what extent the attendance of the Russian Orthodox Church at Amsterdam would bring with it 'dangerous political implications'. The World Council

Geoffrey Fisher with his parents and family as a small boy.

At Prep School – Lindley Lodge (GF: top row, fourth from left).

Geoffrey Fisher with his family (standing behind parents).

Member of Exeter College, Oxford rowing eight (GF: third from left).

Headmaster of Repton – Speech Day, 1928

Engagement to Rosamond
Forman.

With Harry, eldest son
(later Sir Henry Fisher).

Rosamond Fisher with her
three eldest sons, Harry,
Frank and Charles.

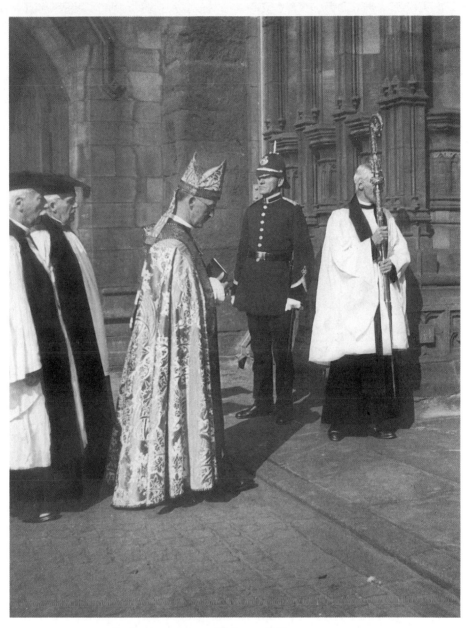

Enthronement as Bishop of Chester, 1932.

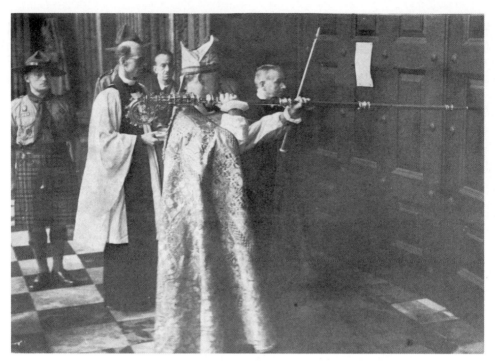

Enthronement as Bishop of London in St Paul's Cathedral, 1939.

Meeting with Cardinal Hinsley and Archbishop William Temple,
London, 1941.

Enthronement as Archbishop of Canterbury, 1945.

Family group at the Old Palace, Canterbury.

With Bishop Krutitsky of the Russian Orthodox Church and Archbishop Garbett, 1945.

With Archbishop Damaskinos of the Greek Orthodox Church.

was in fact being ushered into existence at the very time that the Great Powers were drifting apart in mutual hostility. The descent of the Iron Curtain, if it sealed off the East of Europe from the West and vice versa, brought with it many severe problems which could not but have repercussions upon the Churches, not least upon ecumenical relations. In his famous Fulton speech, Winston Churchill suggested that the Allies, having successfully defeated the Nazis, were now confronted with an even more dangerous enemy in a Russia dedicated to militant and ideological communism. To grow to maturity in this kind of environment was bound to present the World Council with serious problems even if at the same time this sad situation testified to the need for Christians to get together world-wide. Geoffrey Fisher was certainly concerned that the Churches should bridge and transcend these divisions wherever possible. Thus in 1945, soon after the end of the war, he entertained at Lambeth Metropolitan Nickolae and told him something of the proposed formation of the World Council. This purely personal and informal discussion was followed up by Dr Fisher dispatching a letter to the Metropolitan on 14 May 1946 telling him of a meeting of the Provisional Committee in February at Geneva. On the same day the Archbishop wrote to the Soviet Ambassador in London putting him fully into the picture. Already, he wrote, some nineteen Christian bodies had accepted membership which included several Provinces of the Anglican Communion as well as some Orthodox Churches. Protestant and Reformed Churches had also joined but it was important to keep the ecclesiastical balance right. To help ensure this, so he informed the Soviet Ambassador, invitations had been sent to the Patriarch of Moscow and the Patriarchs of the other autocephalous Eastern Orthodox Churches. He was acquainting the Metropolitan with these developments, he wrote, in the hope that the Soviet Ambassador would co-operate by forwarding his letter to ensure its safe delivery. No one expected, given the contemporary ideological climate, that the securing of a Russian presence would prove easy. It certainly did not, and at the beginning of December Visser't Hooft was unable to report to the Archbishop any real progress. To offset this, however, it was hoped that two delegates from Moscow would make a special study in both Paris and Geneva of the proposed World Council but this did not prove easy because of the difficulties in obtaining visas. It was clear that the authorities in Moscow were disinclined to speed up negotiations.

Geoffrey Fisher consistently wished that the Russian Orthodox Church should send official delegates to Amsterdam. Invitations were sent and it may be thought significant that the questions which these prompted in the Russians were largely that of an ecclesiastical character. They included: what other Orthodox Churches had accepted invitations; what subjects were to be discussed? How, in particular, would the Orthodox be deployed? If they came, would they be given a fair share in the programme and could they be assured that no émigré Russians would be present? Were there minimum and maximum plans for Russian involvement?

Geoffrey Fisher left it to Visser't Hooft, as General Secretary, to answer these queries, making it clear to the Patriarch of Moscow that if the Russian Church participated it would certainly have its fair share in the programme. Also there would be no publicity until Moscow had given its approval. That there was a widespread, if somewhat submerged, feeling that this first meeting of a newly-established international Christian organisation was significant is certainly borne out in the curiosity and interest shown by the Russian Government, maybe sparked off by the letter from the Archbishop. On 24 March 1948 a diplomat from the Soviet Embassy had a long conversation at Lambeth with the Archbishop in the company of Herbert Waddams which largely consisted of questions from the Russian and answers by the Archbishop. For example, he wished to know the membership of the Provisional Committee and indeed of the World Council as a whole; what other Committees there were; and who composed them? What did the Council endeavour to do; and how was it financed? Waddams then took over and dealt with these later enquiries at considerable length subsequently following this up by an even fuller documentation. The diplomat, warming to his subject, fired a few further questions concerning the Church of Scotland and the Free Church Federal Council; also what particular political party did the WCC 'lean to'?

If the Russian Orthodox Church remained critical and did not feel able to join, this was not the case with the Greek Orthodox Churches. True there were difficulties and hesitations but under the persuasion of Archbishop Germanos who had been on the WCC Provisional Committe from 1938 to 1948 and was President 1948–52 – coupled with a personal visit by Visser't Hooft to Greece – these hesitations were overcome.

So it was that the inauguration of the World Council took place against the backcloth of a threatening and divisive world situation. Hence the Amsterdam Assembly decided that one of the Presidents should be an Asian with the result that Professor J. C. Chao was appointed a sixth member.

After one year in office he complained to the Council of its condemnation of North Korea as an aggressor; and questioned the motives of the appeal issued from the Stockholm Peace Conference. The Professor's words were pungent: 'It placed me in a very strange position as a patriotic Chinese. I must protest against the Toronto message – this set out to allay fears that the WCC might become a super-church – which sounds so much like Wall Street'. He went on to say that he felt complete freedom to affirm his faith in, and his loyalty to, Christ his Lord and Saviour. In this situation Professor Chao decided to retire from the Praesidium, a step which some described as 'courageous, wise and Christian'.

If churchmen in Communist countries tended to be critical of the WCC Visser't Hooft was able to assure the Archbishop that so far as Greek-speaking Orthodox were concerned the position was encouraging. It was clear that the Patriarch wished to establish co-operative relations with the World Council and was looking forward to receiving a delegation from it early in 1947.

The resignation was a forceful reminder that the WCC was a world organisation and the world was very much divided. The near absolutism of international politics made it much harder to regard differences of view simply as diversities which could easily be contained by a reasonable give and take. Qualifications for membership of the WCC also were liable to give rise to controversy as was brought out in a conversation into which Archbishop Fisher entered with a professor of the Postgraduate Department of the University of Pretoria. The professor explained that he had taken this initiative in the hope that they might explore together possibilities as to whether the Dutch Reformed Church could safely join the World Council without compromising its own principles. He further explained carefully that the Dutch Reformed Church comprised three different denominations, close to each other theologically but with certain confessional differences. Thus he made the following points:

(1) In the Council's formularies there was no reference to the Doctrine of the Trinity. Was the intention behind this to exclude Trinitarianism? (2) If this were the case then it might be that the Dutch Reformed Church would not feel at home in the World Council.

To this the Archbishop retorted: 'No! Nor does any other Church. That is precisely why we belong. If we all felt at home with one another there would not be a WCC but an Ecumenical General Council as in the Early Church.' The Orthodox on occasion were not at all happy, nor were some Anglicans. The same might be true of other Churches. The whole point, he maintained, was that 'we recognise that we all share in a faith in Jesus Christ which both means a certain degree of unity, and demands in seeking fellowship that Our Lord may lead us into the real unity that He desires. The fact that the Dutch Reformed Church would not feel at home is the strongest argument for its joining.'

These somewhat paradoxical comments can probably be best interpreted as emphasising a liberal approach to doctrinal matters.

However, the professor was not yet content to leave matters in this somewhat enigmatic situation and he went on to probe further. Would the Dutch Reformed Church, he asked, find itself in a minority and regularly outvoted? To this the Archbishop replied: 'Yes, it might be but the WCC does not commit any Church. Even a minority of one might be useful in compelling the Churches to ponder over the truth which they proclaimed.' Would not, so the professor pushed him further – and as events were to prove it was an important question – the Dutch Reformed Church 'arrive under suspicion and be resented because of its attitude to the natives in South Africa?' So far from apologising for its policy to the blacks, the Dutch Church claimed to have done a great deal to improve their lot. The Archbishop replied that as in the case of Professor Hromadka, who held office in the Communist Government of Czechoslovakia, the Dutch Reformed Church would be listened to with sympathy. Its presence on the Council was urgently needed.

Geoffrey Fisher was careful not to say anything to suggest that he approved the policy of apartheid: only that holding such a view did not preclude membership of the World Council of Churches. The Dutch Reformed Church did in fact join.

It was perhaps inevitable in view of the wide range of churchmanship and denominations on the World Council that problems presented themselves when they came together in corporate acts of worship. The growing sense of unity, in the eyes of many, demanded free and unfettered worship in which all fully participated. Others felt it to be morally wrong to anticipate what would be appropriate when their union, the one with the other, was more complete. Until that day came, 'Open Communions' – this was a Eucharist at which all attending were invited to receive the Sacrament – seemed improper, almost hypocritical. To express this more simply, the problem arose from the theological conviction that it was irregular for an Episcopalian to receive Communion from a Church whose ministry was defective either in that it had no valid bishops – or no bishops at all. Most Free Churchmen welcomed 'Open Communions' in principle, whereas many Anglicans and the Orthodox Churches generally opposed them. Geoffrey Fisher was not an absolutist in this matter and had he been a free agent, which he was not, he would have opted on the side of an extensive liberality. But he could not ignore the fact that he was Archbishop of Canterbury and that if 'Open Communions' were to become a normality then this should be recognised and sanctioned by the Anglican Churches as a whole. Thus in October 1946 he wrote to the Archbishop of Sydney in whose Cathedral an 'Open Communion' had been held, warning him that there would be no such joint Communion at the World Council of Churches Conferences, either in Geneva or Britain. The particular celebration at Oxford when the Archbishop of Canterbury invited all present to communicate was a unique ecumenical occasion and not such as to create a precedent for the future. However, this particular occasion illustrated that whatever his personal view – and it was a liberal one – he did not, as Primate of All England, necessarily oppose every particular instance of an 'Open Communion'.

This matter of corporate worship raised questions involving the individual conscience, denominational loyalty and the enabling powers of the World Council itself. It came up again later in connection with the Training Centre. What happened there, so the Archbishop felt, was especially significant since, as he wrote to Oliver Tomkins who inclined to take an extremely liberal view, the Centre must be like Caesar's wife 'above reproach'. 'You can imagine the disservice which would be done in the Church of England to the Ecumenical Movement', he warned, 'if rumours came back home of what some people [regard] as irregularities and betrayals occurring at the Ecumenical Centre.' Thus, in this sensitive situation he was inclined to take a view 'stricter' than the 'freer' attitude laid down in Resolution 42 of the 1930 Lambeth Conference. As Primate of All England he felt he must be faithful to its regulations where Church of England clergy were concerned; hence he could not give permission for members of the *Ecclesia Anglicana* to receive the sacrament in Protestant, non-episcopal churches as part of a normal practice. There was nothing to inhibit them attending such services but they should not participate by receiving the sacrament. However, he was prepared to make a distinction between an 'Open Communion' for an *ad hoc* group meeting to promote reunion; and at normal annual meetings of the World Council of Churches.

At Amsterdam (to anticipate) on this uniquely great occasion which formally inaugurated the World Council there was in fact an 'Open Communion' when the celebrant was the Bishop of Chichester. Even this did not escape criticism from High Anglicans, their cause being championed by Michael Bruce, the parish priest of Chiddingfold, who complained to the Archbishop of this 'irregularity'. Geoffrey Fisher replied by setting out in detail the Anglican position, though admitting that this particular celebration at Amsterdam did not formally or fully comply with it. With some asperity the Archbishop commented to the Bishop of Chichester that it was a pity Michael Bruce seemed to think that 'the whole theological salvation of the Church of England rested on his shoulders'.

In its early years, before its formal inauguration, the World Council was obviously feeling its way, establishing codes of practice and discovering its vocation of the moment. Here Geoffrey Fisher was on the side of caution as became evident in his reaction to Visser't Hooft's suggestion that the World Council of Churches should send a Christmas message to the world. Such an action, the Archbishop warned the General Secretary, was fraught with difficulties, 'inappropriate', and should therefore only be sparingly resorted to. His last words distilled in a cable were certainly cryptic: 'Regard precedent of hortatory Christmas Message as dangerous, especially without previous consultation with signatories. Suggest sensible Message from Provisional Committee to Heads of Member Churches'.

As the date for the inauguration of the Assembly drew nearer, particular problems needed to be settled. One was quite simply how were the various Churches to be represented? Here Archbishop Fisher, and this proved a common view, believed that this must be left to the participating Churches themselves within the numbers allocated to them. So far as concerned the Church of England this was not easy and led to some embarrassment. Bishop Bell and Oliver Tomkins sent a tentative list to Lambeth which included Canon John Collins of St Paul's Cathedral and Professor Donald MacKinnon, a theologian of exceptional if somewhat erratic brilliance. The Archbishop of York, Cyril Garbett, felt that the choice of representatives should not be entrusted to the Church Assembly and that it would be better, at least on this first occasion, to leave the selection to the two Archbishops. He himself would wish R. R. Williams, Principal of St John's College at Durham and Herbert Waddams to be included. As for himself, he was doubtful whether he ought to go to Amsterdam since, as he put it, 'this is one of the new Movements from which men of my age ought to stand aside so as to give an opportunity to the younger men'. Geoffrey Fisher held the view strongly, as against Bishop Bell, that to bypass the Church Assembly was unconstitutional. He wished both Archbishops to be delegates but to have behind them the authority of the Church Assembly, though he believed elections for the two Primates to be out of place. Thus he inclined to the view that they should be authorised to attend by virtue of their office.

Another question which was bound to arise was the relationship between the member Churches and the World Council as a whole, a matter made the more complicated in that the National Councils preceded the inauguration of their 'big brother'. It was a matter of *solvitur in ambulando* since clearly there were no precedents to turn to for guidance. The Archbishop was convinced – he was always organisationally minded – and so informed the Bishop of Chichester, that there must be a continuing body whose responsibility it was to keep the Church of England in touch with the affairs of the World Council of Churches. To this end he advised that the Church Assembly should set up a group of some twenty people, half of whom would be nominated by the Standing Committee. These suggestions of the Archbishop, though not carried out quite in this form, show clearly that he was concerned to take the World Council of Churches seriously.

They show also that he was well aware that its very existence introduced another dimension into the life and witness of its member Churches.

So the long awaited and carefully prepared General Assembly of the World Council of Churches met in Amsterdam on 22 August–4 September 1948. There were gathered together over 2,000 representatives from 147 Protestant and Orthodox Churches drawn from 44 countries. On the day previous to its coming together Visser't Hooft received a letter from the Cardinal Archbishop of Utrecht enclosing a document which was to be read in its Churches. This stated that the absence of a Roman Catholic presence at the Assembly was due exclusively to dogmatic theological grounds but the Vatican, in spite of this, urged congregations to pray for the newly-founded World Council. This was an appreciated gesture.

The procession at the beginning of the Conference was impressive though there were no trumpets, no fanfares, no uniforms. Indeed maybe it gained much from this low profile since all present felt that they were making history. Present in the spirit if not visible in the flesh, were surely a vast company who had laboured hard to prepare for this day but were not destined to see its consummation. The theme of the Conference was 'Man's Disorder and God's Design', this being handled under three main headings: The Universal Church in God's Design; The Church and the Disorder of Society; The Church and International Disorder.

All the lecturers were distinguished in their own particular fields and some at least, within a theological context, were household names – churchmen such as Reinhold Niebuhr, Emil Brunner, J. H. Oldham, Karl Barth and Josef Hromadka. It was a solid diet, but it matched the mood of the Assembly which was seriously endeavouring to see a divided world within a more ultimate perspective of a Christian hope. The calibre of the lecturers, speaking from within their differing traditions, eschewed the superficiality encapsulated in the misleading slogan 'Christ or Communism'. Present throughout were Christian leaders from whose vision of a World Church, incarnated in a visible society, the World Council of Churches had sprung.

Central to this unique conference was the inauguration ceremony itself. Marc Boegner, President of the Protestant Federation of France – it was particularly appropriate that he should be entrusted with this task – proposed a formal resolution to bring into being the World Council of Churches. It was, as expected, passed *nemine contradicente*. The Archbishop of Canterbury, who was in the Chair, then called for brief period of silence after which he led the Assembly in thanking God for having brought them to this hour. He long remembered this historic occasion and in retirement wrote: 'Some chairmen would have become emotional in their prayers, their thanksgiving, their sung Te Deums. Being myself a very restrained person I had to say something . . . but it was all on a very quiet and deep but not ostentatious note.'

At the end of the Assembly it fell once more to Geoffrey Fisher to thank all those who, behind the scenes, no matter in what capacity, had made this Assembly possible. This was the kind of exercise which the Archbishop enjoyed and did well. He usually took the opportunity of introducing a lighter touch in order to stifle a deeper emotion. On this occasion he coined the phrase which went down well: 'They also serve who only duplicate'.

One practical decision was made at Amsterdam which, according to his taped autobiography, was suggested by Geoffrey Fisher himself and which did much across subsequent years to associate the Council with a world-wide membership. This proposal was as follows.

It was natural that with the establishment of a formal constitution for the World Council the character of its leadership should be seriously discussed. During the course of the Assembly, Newton Flew came to see the Archbishop saying that great difficulty was being experienced about the future Presidency of the Council. Had William Temple not died, he would doubtless have been asked to accept the role of Chairman or President for life. However, now things had changed and though he, Geoffrey Fisher, had followed Temple on the Provisional Committee it was not felt appropriate that he should go on as a permanent chairman. The Archbishop replied immediately: 'Indeed it isn't'. The ice thus being broken they then went on to discuss this matter with great frankness. The result may be summarised in the Archbishop's own words: 'I think the best thing is to have different parts of the world, that is five different communities all represented on the body of Presidents, not Chairmen but Presidents, and in turn presiding'. This proposal was approved and a group Presidency set up, Visser't Hooft's designation of it as the Praesidium being accepted, which, as Geoffrey Fisher dryly observed, had a 'good Germanic flavour' about it.

It had, of course, been self-evident for some time that no one person could step into William Temple's shoes. His identity with the World Council was complete and he had been with it from the word go, indeed even before this when a World Council was but a dream. However, so long as Geoffrey Fisher was a member of the Praesidium – that was from 1948 to 1954 the year of the Second Assembly in Evanston – he felt a particular responsibility resting upon himself. Of course, the time which he could allocate to the affairs of the World Council was in the nature of the case limited, and it was difficult for him even to attend meetings of the Provisional Commitee. Thus, when asked to write an article on the WCC for a magazine *The Living*

Church, he expressed his dilemma as follows: 'There is no lack of will to do what you ask but it is the literal truth to say that I cannot conceivably find time to do it. Each day I barely manage to be ready for the duties of that day and the number of things requiring time and consideration, which I have to put off, constantly grows. Some of these are urgent and even they have to wait for weeks until I can deal with them. It would be mere folly to say that I could produce anything of the kind you want.'

One wonders whether sometimes he recalled the words of his early mentor, Frank Fletcher: 'Delegate, delegate!'

In spite of the difficulties, in which very busy men always find themselves, Visser't Hooft was concerned that the Praesidium should be something more than a purely formal and honorific body. Thus in September 1951 he suggested to Geoffrey Fisher that the Presidents should meet together for three days in February of the following year, *not* he was anxious to point out, to consider matters of administration, 'but rather to discuss in an unhurried manner some of the great issues of the Christian agenda and the world situation generally'. In particular, he wished to highlight: (1) the difficulties and often ambiguous nature of the relations with Christian Churches behind the Iron Curtain, and the right approach to the confrontation between East and West; (2) the new mood arising within the Roman Catholic Church particularly in relation to the most recent utterances of the Vatican, and the extraordinary amount of unrest in that Communion. He suggested that those attending this small 'get-together' should be the Bishop of Chichester (he was now chairman of the Central Committee), Dr Fry and, of course, the indefatigable Dr Mott.

Before the Praesidium came together, the executive committee of the WCC met in Paris and on 1 February issued a statement underlining that the chief task of the WCC was to maintain and develop the fellowship already existing between the Christian Churches as they worked out side by side the implications of the Lordship of Christ. Also, the Committee took note of the contemporary situation – the terrible suffering of the Korean people; the deterioration in the international situation; the explosive character of the world scene; and the fact that seven hundred million people formerly dependent on an imperial power were now independent.

So the Praesidium, hosted by Geoffrey Fisher, duly met at Lambeth on 2, 3 and 4 February 1951. They ranged widely in their discussion on the contemporary scene – the role and function of the Praesidium; the distinction between speaking collectively for WCC or on behalf of one Church only; relations with Churches behind the Iron Curtain; the correct attitude to the Vatican, and the possibility of an audience with the Pope and the Apostolic Delegate; the stance of the World Council of Churches in time of war; the staffing of the Council; the Church in China; and religious freedom. This was indeed a daunting agenda and quite clearly could not have been tackled in real depth. Also the meeting was confidential to those participating, and no official report was issued though there seems to have been general agreement that it was 'a most useful occasion'. What the agenda itself showed, however, was important – namely that it really was a *World* Council and that its writ was a comprehensive one. In all these complex matters there was no one political stance adopted by the World Council as the withdrawal of Professor Chao from the Praesidium made only too evident. Politics, because of differing national loyalties and the emergence of a widely dispersed Marxist Communism on a world stage, introduced a particularly divisive factor not always too easy to transcend, bypass or contain.

Geoffrey Fisher long remembered as outstanding personalities Dibelius, Bishop of Berlin, 'most notable and remarkable' for what he had achieved just by quiet, courageous faithfulness to the Church; the more ebullient and unrestrained Niemüller; also the American Franklin Fry, chairman of the Central Committee with his statesmanlike qualities from which the Council greatly benefited and also for his puckish sense of humour which alleviated the tension in many a difficulty. As for his own personal experience of this first WCC Assembly Geoffrey Fisher recalled modestly: 'I listened, I only spoke where there was some point which I felt it was important to keep under control, lest it should be pushed too far. Whenever I did that, I was pretty sure that Sherrill would sometimes speak on some practical issue and I was almost always ready to support him, and I think that the World Council had got a certain respect for the quiet part that Sherrill and I took in the background, not one of the leaders but helping to keep the thing running.' This is indeed a modest claim.

The Archbishop was himself convinced that Amsterdam marked a real milestone in the long pilgrimage of Christian history. Speaking in London over the Columbia Broadcasting network he claimed that: 'The abiding significance of Amsterdam is this – that it inaugurates a Council of Christians which will, please God, continue and will continually draw [Churches] together into fuller understanding and co-operation'.

(ii)
Evanston

The Assembly at Amsterdam was felt at the time to be uniquely significant but it could not be expected that the second at Evanston, in the United States of America, in 1954 could make quite the same impact. Also the political life of the United States was suffering from the excesses of McCarthyism which was undermining the democratic process in America. The Central Committee, meeting at Toronto in 1950, decided that since the world was 'full of false hopes, of fear and of despair' the main theme of the next Assembly should be 'Jesus Christ as Lord is the only hope of both the Church and the World'.

Geoffrey Fisher was, naturally, concerned to secure the best possible representation from England at Evanston, and he circularized the Bishops of the two Provinces of Canterbury and York asking for their nominations to match an equal number put forward by the Church Assembly. For the purpose of financial economy and convenience it was wisely accepted that the eighteen delegates to Evanston would also attend the Anglican Church Congress which was to follow at Minneapolis.

During this pre-Assembly phase, Geoffrey Fisher was in close touch with Dr Visser't Hooft with whom he had a long conversation on 25 June 1953 on matters relevant to the future of the World Council. As was usually the case with the Archbishop, talk centred around practical considerations. He was anxious, for example, that Max Warren should be present at Evanston which would serve to promote a close link between the International Missionary Council and the WCC. Geoffrey Fisher and Dr Visser't Hooft discussed frankly some of the difficulties in having a plurality of Presidents – and the latter put it to the Archbishop that if all the Presidents retired together there might well be a move to return to a single Presidency, in which case there would be everything to be said for asking Bishop Bell to accept this significant role. 'I am wholly in favour of this,' Geoffrey Fisher concurred, 'I think it would be admirable and it would relieve him of the constant burden of the Central Committee and Executive Committee.'

Dr Visser't Hooft was equally concerned – beyond the requirements of courtesy – that if Geoffrey Fisher were himself to retire from office he would still be able to keep closely in touch with the concerns of the World Council, maybe as a member of the Central Committee. The Archbishop saw the point but questioned whether he ought to accept such an invitation, particularly as the Church of England was allowed only three members, and his own routine workload was already excessive. As it was, the WCC sensibly decided to retain the Praesidium.

Other subjects which came up for discussion via the General Secretary and the Archbishop were the future of Stephen Neill; and the fact that the Church of India, Burma and Ceylon had accepted, under certain conditions, the ministry of bishops and priests consecrated or ordained by the Church of South India.

The proximity of the Second General Assembly encouraged Herbert Waddams of the Council on Foreign Relations to speculate upon the future, in particular the relationship of the Church of England to the World Council. Most important in his view was to plan what happened during the intervals between Assemblies. At the moment the implementation of decisions was carried out by the permanent staff at Geneva in co-operation with the Central and Executive Committees, reinforced by occasional informal consultations. A weakness here was there being no members of the Church of England on the regular staff at Geneva, though Oliver Tomkins was influential as a member of the Faith and Order Commission and David Say as Secretary of the British Council of Churches. In practice the *Ecclesia Anglicana* made its contribution through outstanding personalities who at the same time held office as, for example, George Bell and to a lesser extent Geoffrey Fisher, the former as chairman of the Central Committee.

A conclusion drawn by Herbert Waddams was that more permanent structural links needed to be forged between Lambeth and the World Council – links which did not depend on accidental circumstances. The Archbishop should be kept in contact with all important developments through a member of his own staff permanently charged with this duty. In his view this person should be the General Secretary of the Council on Foreign Relations who was already fully cognisant of the ecumenical scene. Indeed he should be sent to Evanston as the Archbishop's delegate and not only as an observer.

As so often happened with Waddams' suggestions, Geoffrey Fisher admitted to seeing their relevance but believed there were other considerations to bear in mind, these being such as the legitimate claims of the Northern Province. Thus the question of an adequate representation of the Church of England at Evanston remained a pressing problem. It was one on which Bishop Bell had strong opinions since he was convinced that the Church of England delegates ought to be chosen at as high and distinguished a level as possible. As things appeared at the moment, however, the representation was 'most undistinguished'. To give it more clout he suggested the names of Henry Willink and John Redcliffe Maud, Secretary to the Ministry of Fuel and Power. Bell was also of opinion that the last place should be allocated to Waddams rather than to any representative of the British Council of Churches. Geoffrey Fisher could not agree and protested to the Archbishop of York that he did not feel, as George Bell seemed to do, that the 'whole future of the Church of England really depended on Waddams being a delegate and not a consultant'. 'I have stuck to my guns', he added.

Bishop Bell, however, was a determined man and did not find it easy to take this decision passively, as a letter dated 3 October makes evident. 'I am afraid I *am* greatly disappointed,' he protested, 'and even discouraged on account of your omission of Waddams ... I thought he was entirely safe.' As a result of the Archbishop's decision Waddams now had no chance of getting on to the Central Committee of the

World Council. 'What worries me', the Bishop complained, 'is the almost complete lack of any organisation for getting the World Council into the mind of the Church of England.' It was the very thing that Waddams could achieve. As a consultant, however, he would have litle status. Bell's forthright letter could have given the Archbishop little joy.

Geoffrey Fisher was undoubtedly concerned to ensure that the Evanston Assembly was carefully prepared and this meant looking objectively at the costs involved, since he was unhappy at the preponderance of American money which went into financing various operations of the World Council. As it was, eighty eight per cent of the total budget needed for expenses and travel to Evanston was provided by the Protestant Episcopal Church of that country. Geoffrey Fisher felt that the time had come for the WCC to deal realistically with this situation and see that the cost of Assemblies and other meetings was widely shared. He believed that this had become possible now that Canada was in a position to bear more of the load. The Archbishop drew up two memoranda, and attempted an approximate budget with an allocation for travel expenses. It was an exercise which gave him a great deal of private pleasure.

The Second Assembly at Evanston proved no anti-climax to the first, as might well have happened. This was in part due to the careful planning of Visser't Hooft, to the warm hospitality of the Americans, and the great sense of purpose which prevailed generally. The official report of the conference states that whereas in 1948 at Amsterdam the overriding task had been to create the World Council of Churches, at Evanston it was to 'examine the unity given to the Churches in the past six years and to explore those areas in which disunity was most apparent and in which unity was most effective'; and this it had to do against the background of the polarisation of East and West. Here theological differences were faced up to and explored in greater depth than in 1948.

Geoffrey Fisher was unwell at the first session and Bishop Bell deputised for him, but he soon recovered and chaired a special plenary session on 25 August, the eleventh day of the Conference. He also had the responsibility of welcoming and responding to the President of the United States, Dwight Eisenhower, who urged the Assembly to lead the way by inviting every single person in every single country of the world who believed in the power of prayer to the Supreme Being, to join in a mighty simultaneous act of faith. Geoffrey Fisher began his speech by admitting that it was difficult for an Englishman to confine himself to his brief when he had the opportunity to 'speak of the time when the President headed the grand alliance of their two countries on the battlefields of Europe'. The respective roles of the United States

Government, he reminded his audience, and that of the World Council of Churches were different. 'Neither sovereignty is absolute. Each exists not in its own right but by God's appointment and subject to his divine will to carry forward his purpose for the children of men. It was the sovereign responsibility of the Church to proclaim, according to the will and mind of Christ, that faith, that vision of truth, without which men perish, life loses its flavour, and nations work their own suicide. It is the sovereign responsibility of the secular authority within its own sphere to be the guardian of those gifts of God to men wherein consists their human dignity and their divine vocation.'

The corporate worship at Evanston for the most part inevitably reflected both the divisions of Christendom as well as its 'togetherness'. Dr Ernest Payne, preaching at the Sunday celebration of the Eucharist, referred realistically to this ambiguity in these words: 'We cannot but be aware that so long as we cannot be together at the Lord's table we have gone only a small part of the way towards our appointed goal'.

Geoffrey Fisher was not one hundred per cent physically fit during part of the Assembly but recovered his customary good health and won the following tribute from Dr Payne: 'To his matchless blend of dignity and cordiality he adds a sense of humour and a democratic touch that win him friends among delegates of all nations'.

Nothing could have been more regrettable, as suggested earlier, than the division between East and West, which bedevilled the early years of the World Council of Churches and certainly complicated, if indeed it did not frustrate, its ecumenical role. However, in 1955, as leaders of the WCC assembled in Geneva, there were signs on the Eastern political horizon which encouraged observers to be more optimistic than they had been of late in relation to the solving of some of the world's problems. The most recent approach by the World Council of Churches to the Moscow Patriarchate had met with a not discouraging response, with the result that the Central Committee decided in 1956 to accept an invitation to meet in Hungary the following year. Dr Visser't Hooft believed that there was a genuine desire on the part of the Churches in Hungary to enter into fellowship with their fellow European Christians. It was Geoffrey Fisher's firm intention to attend but as he sought advice on this decision – probably from the Foreign Office – he became increasingly uneasy as to whether he ought to make the journey since the leaders of the Protestant Church in Hungary were closely identified with the Communist Government. However, he was hopeful that the Bishop of Chichester would be willing to accept the invitation, which in fact he did. The Reverend David Say, who was present throughout and sent in a report of its proceedings to Lambeth, gave it as his opinion that a WCC presence was 'a good thing' and 'not so embarrassing as first thought', except perhaps at the official banquet.

Sherrill, of the Protestant Episcopal Church of America, took the opportunity of expressing to the Archbishop the hope that the political situation in Hungary would improve. Visser't Hooft's verdict was that the journey to Hungary was 'meaningful' and the delegation had been 'well received' in that country. It is ironic to record that the Russian armies entered Budapest on 4 November 1956 and the Hungarian Churches were thereby precluded from putting out further feelers to the West at least for the time being.

Geoffrey Fisher ceased to be a member of the Praesidium after the Second Assembly in 1954 though he remained became a member of the Central Committee till 1961. The Function and Structure Committee proposed during the General Assembly at Evanston that retiring Presidents should not immediately be eligible for re-election. This limitation would make possible a wider spread of Presidents elected from different geographical regions and political systems. This proposal was strongly opposed by William Wand, Bishop of London, and a vigorous debate took place which made it clear that a large majority was in favour of the proposition brought up by the Function and Structure Committee. The Archbishop had, wisely, let it be known that he was in no sense whatever 'worried' about this change and the principle was accordingly established. It was felt appropriate that Geoffrey Fisher should, personally and on behalf of other retiring Presidents, make a speech to the Assembly which he did, illuminating it with his customary humour. 'We have been elected to do nothing,' he said, 'and we have done it well!' Of this open confession Visser't Hooft commented: 'His own contribution to the life of the Council spoke louder than this witticism'. Certainly Visser't Hooft consistently emphasized the significance of the role which members of the Praesidium played, individually as well as corporately. When Geoffrey Fisher himself reflected, modestly, on his own contribution to the WCC he saw it as one of assisting it to pursue a steady course; to see that its organisation and way of doing things was sound and practical; and that the Church of England should take it seriously and be equipped to give it full support.

The strong desire by the Bishop of London to retain a built in status as President for the Archbishop of Canterbury generated a great deal of heat, and was bitterly opposed by many though it was swept under the carpet in the official report. Canon Max Warren, who attended the Conference, confesses that he felt the Bishop's speech to be 'inopportune and unimaginative'. It was 'monstrous' that the 'contribution of our Communion to the World Council of Churches should be affected by whether or not the Archbishop is one of its Presidents. He further confessed to having felt ashamed during the debate of being an Anglican, though he appreciated David Say, later Bishop of Rochester, who reminded delegates that the WCC contained 163 Churches, drawn from 48 countries. 'We are moving away from the day when the Ecumenical movement depended on great personalities.'

There will be occasions in this biography in relation to particular issues, such as the imposition of apartheid in South Africa, when Geoffrey Fisher will appear within the context of the World Council. However, there was one matter in its ongoing life where Geoffrey Fisher saw what was happening with increasing apprehension. It is to this that we now briefly turn. It has to do with Christian reunion.

It was Geoffrey Fisher's basic belief that schemes for reunion should be undertaken and sponsored by the Churches concerned negotiating individually or corporately the one with the other. It was not, for example, up to the Faith and Order commission, which after a long and independent existence had merged itself into the World Council of Churches, to take initiatives. What it should do was to provide a supportive 'technical' or theological service for the Churches concerned. In other words there were severe limitations which the Faith and Order Commission ought to impose upon itself. This controversial matter was debated during a meeting of the British Council of Churches at Birmingham in 1956 when an address was given by Dr Robert Nelson who expressed the hope that the Archbishop did not see the work of the Faith and Order Commission as 'extraneous' to the Churches. Indeed, it existed only to serve them in their 'common quest for the manifestation of Christian unity'.

The Archbishop, thus challenged, poured out his feelings into the experienced ear of Oliver Tomkins. 'That the Commission should take cognisance of Church Union Schemes was one thing,' he affirmed, 'but in doing this it must not run any risk of appearing to be a pressure group of any kind encouraging any one Church in one direction or another.' In the Archbishop's eyes the Commission was abandoning its traditional role of being the 'handmaid' of the Church in relation to Christian unity but was striking out on its own. 'We all know the tendency of any organised body to seek its own aggrandisement.' It seemed to be less resistant than it should be to the danger of shifting from church to movement, 'from handmaid to training centre, from being at the call of the Churches to calling the Churches to follow it'.

Such language may seem extreme but it did in fact genuinely express the strength of the Archbishop's feelings at the time. It was a tragic mistake, so the Archbishop believed, when the independence of the Faith and Order Commission was broken as a result of its incorporation into the World Council of Churches. This meant that it ceased to be an objective theological advisory body handling problems of faith in relation to contemporary situations but was absorbed into the general policy making of the WCC. He had struggled hard to prevent this, as had Sherrill, but was unsuccessful. In its independent status the Commission did invaluable work and when its members were considering the theology of the Churches they were able to do so without any sense of responsibility to anybody but themselves. Geoffrey Fisher believed that this new status was evident in a change of tone and emphasis at the Third Assembly in New Delhi at the time of his retirement. The WCC had ceased to be, or gave the appearance of having ceased to be, an advisory body in relation to member Churches: rather it tended to be telling them what to do rather than to discover how it could help them. Such reflections – they were written in Geoffrey Fisher's retirement – may suggest an old man's nostalgia for an earlier period in the history of the WCC when it was more open and less rigid. He was not, however, a lone voice, and maybe what is happening today (1990s) to the WCC is not entirely unrelated to Geoffrey Fisher's critical thinking.

CHAPTER 18

The Lambeth Staff

A Prime Minister of the United Kingdom in entering upon his onerous office does not lack support. Not only has he a Cabinet, largely of his own choosing, but also a professional Civil Service to help and lean on which continues independently of changes in Government. True opinions may well differ as to how far this élite body limits the Prime Minister's freedom of action. What is certain is that it exists to provide an ongoing service and to implement governmental policy. The Archbishop of Canterbury in his equally onerous office has no such advantages. The revival of sitting Convocations in the 1850s; the advent of ten-yearly Lambeth Conferences beginning in the 1860s; the growth of self-consciousness within the worldwide Anglican Communion; the inauguration of the Church Assembly and its various specialised boards; and the setting up of the British and World Council of Churches – all these added new dimensions to the outreach of the office of Primate of All England. Archbishop Edward Benson (1829–1896) was, perhaps, the first to recognise the need for more expert help and guidance if he were to discharge the multitudinous duties which necessarily came his way; but his efforts to secure some form of 'Cardinalate' from the Canons of Westminster proved in vain. Thus he was forced to confess that he had often 'neither the time nor the energy left to deliberate widely and closely about the Church's needs'.

Archbishop Davidson admitted that his task of 'holding the Church together' was an impossible one but disclaimed any need for a central staff. Cosmo Lang, his successor, contended that the predicament of the Archbishop might be met by making more use of the various Church societies which had of late sprung up. William Temple admitted that there was a real need to equip Lambeth for the twentieth century, but died before he could do anything about it. Whether his personal way of managing things would have inhibited his taking remedial action is a moot point. On 25 February 1945, F. A. Iremonger, William Temple's biographer, maintained in the pulpit of St Mary's Church, Oxford, that what the Archbishop needed was a headquarters with an appropriate staff if the Church were to deal effectively with the great problems then confronting it.

It was not, however, only high level counsel which the Archbishop needed. There was also the sheer volume of work which through the daily post now came flooding into Lambeth and which just had to be dealt with. This had grown over the years and could strain almost to breaking point the domestic set up which was not really designed to cope with such a work load.

Two more comments may be offered on the general situation. First, that any radical change to bring the system up to date would mean the expenditure of more money, and it was never easy to extract from the Church Assembly or the Commissioners extra supplies of this precious commodity. Second, there was a strong prejudice against professional- ising Lambeth overmuch and building up a centralized bureaucracy. That the system was able to cope was largely due to the loyalty and high commitment of those responsible for making it work.

It was into this situation that Geoffrey Fisher came as 'number one' to Lambeth in 1945. Two things he brought with him – a reputation for tidy administration which he regarded, not as an ability to be ashamed of, but as one demanding sensitivity to people and a pastoral approach. Also he had an enormous capacity for hard work, even on occasions doing 'chore' things which he could easily have delegated to others but which gave him satisfaction. Geoffrey Fisher was a compul- sive letter writer and Herbert Waddams who was seconded to Lambeth from the Church of England Council on Foreign Relations for some eighteen months and, therefore, observed the Archbishop's work rate at first hand, gives the following vivid impression of what it entailed: 'Owing to the fact that the Archbishop is an immensely fast worker, and happens to delight in mastering all the details of almost all the problems which come before him, he is able to grapple with his work. But it means that every minute of every day is taken up with dealing with business. It can be said without any hesitation that anyone less quick in mental agility, or less ready to spend every hour at the work, or less enamoured of work, or less interested in administration and detail – anyone without any of these characteristics would find it impossible to deal with all the work which the Archbishop handles.'

As to this heavy load there appeared to some people one obvious solution, namely relieving the Archbishop of Canterbury of any dioce- san responsibility altogether. This, however, Geoffrey Fisher would not contemplate. 'To leave the Archbishop without a Diocese', he wrote, 'would put him in a false position and would in fact deprive him of almost all the simple pastoral contacts which are his chief means of refreshment of spirit. If once he can get a really competent and adequate staff, I don't think he would find any difficulty in coping with the Canterbury end.' This shedding of the Diocese of Canterbury was to be raised in many contexts, mainly in terms of the demands made by the Anglican Communion of which the Archbishop was the titular and prestigious head.

At the top of the structural pyramid which Geoffrey Fisher inherited was the Senior Chaplain – there were four of them during the years 1945–1961 and five Resident or Domestic Chaplains (See Appendix V). There were in all four secretaries, all women. The senior dealt generally with the Archbishop's filing; wrote letters for and received instructions from him. For most of Geoffrey Fisher's time at Lambeth she was the excellent and efficient Miss Priscilla Lethbridge who became a friend of the family. She also dealt with 'Fixed Days', the House of Lords rota and other 'appropriate matters'. 'I could not manage without her' so Geoffrey Fisher testified. There were three other secretaries, one for the Senior Chaplain who handled general affairs as required by the Archbishop; another for the Domestic Chaplain who was responsible for the diocesan correspondence; and a third Anne Roynon, who worked mainly for Mrs Fisher in her Church and public activities.

In addition, Geoffrey Fisher inherited a Mr Clements who straddled all departments but whose supreme value, so the Archbishop confessed, was his readiness to have letters dictated to him 'at any time of the day or night, weekdays or Sundays'. Clements' willingness to accommodate himself to the Archbishop's schedule of work was invaluable since, to quote again his own words, 'very often I cannot begin to dictate my letters until 5.00 in the evening, or on Saturday evening, and very often I have to clear off a whole batch of them by dictating for one hour or two on Sunday. In due course, after Clements retired, the Archbishop took to using a dictaphone deployed even during his holiday, although he maintained that he much preferred to dictate letters personally to his secretary. It was a system which worked well as long as, in the Archbishop's words, 'everybody does anything that needs to be done at any time for anybody'. Lambeth was undoubtedly under-staffed and its personnel fully stretched to deal with Geoffrey Fisher's enormous and ceaseless output of letters and memoranda as well as speeches and sermons. It was only a spirit of give and take, going along with good personal relations which made it possible for business to be conducted efficiently and smoothly. Here the warm manner in which the Archbishop and Mrs Fisher thought of their staff as members of an extended family, sharing its domesticity and corporate life, made a difference – as did the Archbishop's humour which bubbled over from time to time.

Opening the enormous post in the morning was no casual or perfunctory affair, rather a ritual performance. It was the Archbishop's invariable custom to do this in the presence of his chaplains – and, after his appointment, with Robert Beloe, the Lay Secretary. At this daily session all topics arising out of the correspondence – and some which did not – were freely discussed. Like Dr Johnson, Geoffrey Fisher loved to have his 'talk out' but he also welcomed a frank comeback from members of his staff. Sometimes, if convinced, he would change his mind or defer sending a letter for further reflection. A case in point was one which he wrote to Kruschev which was later rejected. On one envelope there was scribbled 'Dragon Consumed'.

Significant of his pastoral concern was the Archbishop instituting, after the restoration of the chapel, a corporate Communion for all members of the staff without distinction of grade or status. The Archbishop would himself celebrate and afterwards everyone break-fasted together in the large dining-room, Mrs Fisher making sure that the personnel around the table were well and truly mixed up. A charlady might be sitting next to the Archbishop. This helped to create a very real sense of belonging to a community.

There were some however, and this included the Archbishop himself, who did not regard the Lambeth Palace 'set-up' as adequate for the fifties and sixties. Prominent among these was Herbert Waddams who drew up a frank and confidential *aide-memoire* calling attention to what he regarded as a chronic weakness – the absence of any co-ordinating chief of staff. It was essential in his opinion that so over-worked a team, with separate but interrelated responsibilities, should be subject to one co-ordinating authority. Thus the senior chaplain should be a chief of staff who transcended the departments and had control over the whole office. The four secretaries should be exclusively occupied with Lambeth business, the two principals being highly trained, one handling the ecclesiastical, the other the lay side. These should be present at every discussion relevant to their departments and which concerned the Archbishop. Perhaps there should be a separate secretary for Mrs Fisher? In line with these proposals Waddams suggested that new members of staff should be told their hours of duty; their holidays, which should include one Saturday off a month; also when they would be required to follow the Archbishop to Canterbury. There should be a proper scale of salaries with provision for pensions. Fully-trained secretaries ought to be trusted, indeed expected, to write their own short letters. Something should be done to secure for them increasing scope as they acquired greater experience since, in his view, the present situation must cause frustration for senior professional women. By such a rationalization he believed the Archbishop would be relieved of extensive chores, this being 'absolutely essential' if he were to be released for more creative work.

In general, the overall aim of these proposals was to shift the burden of routine matters away from the Archbishop on to the re-arranged staff, leaving the Archbishop to spend more time on matters of policy.

The Archbishop had great respect for Waddams' intelligence and was certainly sensitive, in general, to the force of these suggestions. In fact, he had encouraged Waddams to give his attention to these matters.

Indeed when Canon Waddams in 1959 left England for a post in Canada, Geoffrey Fisher wrote to him confessing his feelings at this 'devastating loss, to me, to us, and to Lambeth'. He wished it had been possible for him to stay, and so long as he was Archbishop he would be 'keeping a weather eye open with a view to bring him back'. However, he saw a potential threat in the creation of a Major Domo, a chief of staff, at the proposed level. Thus he peppered Waddams' document with pithy comments, mostly pejorative, including many a 'No! No!'. As for a chief of staff he ought not, as Archbishop, to put all his eggs into one basket; and anyhow there were 'not many clergymen available of the calibre of Mervyn Haigh or George Bell'. What Geoffrey Fisher himself felt he needed was twofold – a high level senior chaplain and an equally high level lay secretary and press officer. As to the first, he set out, with resolution, to find him.

This did not prove easy and he defined what he was looking for in these terms: '. . . administrative competence, sound and critical judgement, an interest in the public affairs of the Church, with a statesmanlike approach to them and the power to make wide contacts easily and faithfully'.

This was an ambitious remit and those to whom he made preliminary feelers declined. Among such was Noel Davey, Secretary of the Society for Promoting Christian Knowledge, who advised that what the Archbishop needed was not inspiration but organisation. To this remark Geoffrey Fisher replied: 'It is queer how nobody believes me when I say what I really want. I do not want organisation, I can do that perfectly well myself. It is wisdom and theology and what you call inspiration. However, I must look elsewhere for it.'

The Archbishop remained convinced that he would be doing 'an illservice' to himself and the Church of England if he were to put in a lightweight as senior chaplain. In all he considered some thirteen possibilities, and got so far as offering the post to the Venerable Percy Harthill, Archdeacon of Stoke on Trent, who courteously declined partly on the grounds of his pacifism. Finally, in 1951, after having consulted widely he appointed Dr Eric Jay, Dean of Nassau and Rector of Christ Church Cathedral. An extract from the letter despatched to the Dean is worth quoting. 'On your side it suffices to know that you have the job of keeping the Archbishop on the right lines, releasing him of as much work as he will let you take over, and telling him what you think, however little he likes it. On my side I want somebody of ability who knows the Church and has a wise judgement and a charitable spirit.' Dr Jay long outstayed his probationary year and served at Lambeth until 1958, when he left to become Principal of the Theological College in Montreal. He was a man of wide experience having been a chaplain in the RAF Volunteer Reserve during the war, holding various benefices and a lectureship at King's College, London. It was a wise appointment and worked well.

As to a lay secretary, ten years' experience at Lambeth convinced the Archbishop of the need for such a member of staff who would handle what may be loosely described as secular business. For example, episcopal representation in the House of Lords was somewhat haphazard and needed proper organisation. In 1957 Geoffrey Fisher corresponded with Lord Silsoe, First Church Estates Commissioner, concerning the provision of a salary for such a post. Consistently Geoffrey Fisher took the view that it was wrong for the Church to try to get full-time professional help on the cheap.

Geoffrey Fisher's long letter to Lord Silsoe accepting the financial arrangement is revealing, particularly in his comments on the working habits of three of his predecessors – and his modest assessment of his own powers. 'The time is drawing nearer', he wrote, 'when the Office will pass from me to somebody else. Without going into details I may summarise an historical process thus. Davidson had ample time with his two chaplains and two secretaries to do his work with extraordinary thoroughness, and at the same time to spend many hours in the House of Lords and in the Athenaeum. Lang still covered the whole of that ground, though the pressure was greater, but being a bachelor and a very quick worker and looking for no leisure for his own enjoyment, he kept pace; even so he took at least three months' holiday as Davidson had done, and was away from Lambeth altogether from the end of July to the end of October. William Temple never had his heart in administrative work; he always did it with the utmost care, but it took a lot out of him. He would have gone on doing all the work which only he could do as a theological, ecclesiastical and social thinker. He must have broken under the double strain later if not when he did.' As for his own abilities they were more akin to those of a 'cab horse'. 'I can stand great strain', he writes, 'and can go on putting one foot in front of the other *ad infinitum*; thus I have been able to keep pace more or less with the volume of necessary work which, in fact, has grown in my time immensely. I do not think any successor of mine would, or could, or ought to try to do all that I have done in addition to contributions of his own which he will certainly wish to make. In other words, I stand at a watershed of history in this matter. All my successors will need and must have a really first class lay secretary to cover a field which is outside the field at present covered by my two chaplains.' Also, he adds, a lay secretary could fittingly make it one of his tasks to act as a liaison officer between the newly created Boards and the Archbishop.

In supposing that the appointment of a lay secretary must await the coming of his successor Geoffrey Fisher was unduly pessimistic. Lord Silsoe believed he had found the right man in Robert Beloe who had already, at a high level, proved himself in public service. He was then Chief Education Officer for Surrey, and had done more than any other person to implement Butler's Education Act of 1944 which opened up maintained schools to talent. He also pioneered the first comprehensives.

Thus it was that Beloe secured the appointment as the Archbishop's first Lay Secretary, giving up to do so an important educational post while in the full flood of his powers, much to the surprise of his professional colleagues. Not surprisingly, after so many years without one, Geoffrey Fisher did not quite know how best to use Robert Beloe. Indeed he and his secretary were at first given office accommodation tucked away in Morton's Tower remote from the vital nerve centre of the Palace where the Chaplains, Priscilla Lethbridge and the Archbishop worked. Beloe soon realised that he could not do his job subject to such enforced isolation. Geoffrey Fisher when approached saw the point immediately and Beloe was given an office in the Palace and the whole situation was changed overnight. Thus he set about his task with tact, carving out specific areas where his wide experience and undoubted gifts were used to the full. The Archbishop found in him an acute professional mind and someone who, like himself, recognised the virtue of good, well-ordered administration. Not least of his services to the Church of England was his taking over responsibility for episcopal representation in the House of Lords. This enabled the bishops to speak out of a greater knowledge though Beloe fully recognised their individual responsibilities. In practice this meant that some member of the episcopate was always present and primed when a significant theme was under discussion. Perhaps the greatest tribute to Beloe was that a Lay Secretary is now regarded as a necessity. Fears that the Archbishop might not be willing 'to do any real delegating' proved groundless. Robert Beloe was left free to do an excellent job without frustration but fully in co-operation with the Archbishop and others on the staff. His efficiency won respect and he became an effective liaison officer between Church House, Millbank and Lambeth. This was particularly necessary *vis-à-vis* the Church Commissioners who had for too long distanced themselves from the internal politics of the Church of England.

Thus without any revolutionary or radical change Geoffrey Fisher left to his successor a far better equipped, business-like and efficient Lambeth staff than he had inherited from his predecessor. Though he did not go all the way with Herbert Waddams, fearing, rightly or wrongly, that his own status and ultimate control would tend to be weakened, the Archbishop in principle, saw the cogency of his suggestions. The 'Clements' with all their enthusiasm and devotion gave way to a more clearly articulated system, and an informed lay opinion became more significant at Lambeth. What can be said without exaggeration is that Geoffrey Fisher's own example of a concentrated application to his desk meant much and his sense of humour lightened many a heavy load.

But this story is not complete and will be told in a subsequent chapter. A fully-professional and competent press officer had been increasingly felt an overriding need. At long last he arrived in the person of Robert Hornby who completely transformed relations with the Media. The sad fact is that so far as Geoffrey Fisher was concerned he appeared so late in the day; but at least he came in time to handle a critical and complex situation when the Archbishop visited Pope John XXIII in Rome in 1960.

Perhaps we may notice here briefly that when Sir Henry Dashwood, his legal official – a great pluralist – disgorged his many offices, the Archbishop was firm and friendly in bringing this about though he was vigilant in not building up again a comparable empire.

CHAPTER 19

Clerical Stipends

BASIC to the life, the witness and the Christian commitment of the Church of England are its parish priests. They are in the front line and are still for the most part engaged in a full-time ministry, residing with their families among the people they serve, and provided with an income by the Church for doing so. This system goes back to a remote past, indeed to the days before the Norman Conquest when the Germanic tribes from Europe settled in England mostly in small townships. Chaucer's 'Poor Parson of a Town' and Oliver Goldsmith's rural clergyman 'passing rich with Forty pounds a year' are heirs to the same inheritance and have their counterparts today even though society around them has radically changed. There are some 13,155 parishes throughout the length and breadth of the land and some 10,608 priests working in them. It is still true that every inch of English soil, unless it is situated within a 'Peculiar', as for example are the Precincts of Westminster Abbey, is within the boundaries of a parish. To maintain such a ministry, numerically large, is vastly expensive, its requirements far exceeding the ancient endowments provided for this purpose and now administered through the Church Commissioners.

In 1948, at a time when licences were needed for house building, Geoffrey Fisher wrote to Aneurin Bevan, then a Minister at the Home Office, in connection with parsonage houses. The Archbishop fully recognised the need to build cottages for agricultural labourers, but claimed, that the provison of a parsonage house was just as important. 'The incumbent of a country parish is, or ought to be, a key worker therein. It is a mere truth that in many country villages all the social life of the parish, the provision of social events, the care and training of the children, and the like, centres around the church and looks for its leadership to the vicar.' Mr Bevan's response was co-operative but in being so he pointed out that the obtaining of a licence must depend on (1) the new building being necessary for adequate religious facilities (2) the local authority supported the application; (3) the project fitting into the local housing programme.

When Geoffrey Fisher went to Canterbury in 1945 the financing of the parochial ministry had reached a point of near-crisis. There were several reasons for this predicament. A steady and relentless increase in the rate of inflation as the century went on had progressively made life more difficult for those who lived on fixed incomes. Also, the Church had lost a great deal of its capital resources through such legislation as the Tithes Act of 1936 and was to be further denuded by the Transport Bill of 1948. Then, again, the number of incumbents with private means had steadily decreased, though the commitments of the Church had grown.

Geoffrey Fisher was indeed vividly aware of this financial situation which was steadily eroding the incomes of the parish clergy and had tried to do something about it when he was at Chester. Though never himself a parish priest he was heir to a long line of country parsons and throughout his life was convinced of the unique significance of their ministry. Also he realised that a Church which recruited married clergy must accept its financial implications. The situation had gone steadily from bad to worse since Geoffrey Fisher had first encountered it before the war. It could not, therefore, have come as a surprise that he had not been long at Lambeth before the severe straits of the clergy and their struggle to survive, came before the Church Assembly. This resulted from a resolution introduced by Lady Bridgeman on 15 November 1946, the chief speaker being the Senior Commissioner, Sir Philip Baker Wilbraham, who was uniquely in a position to know what the problem was at firsthand since the Commissioners were the chief providers. Sir Philip painted a grim and almost frightening picture. In a mood of stark realism he stressed the losses of capital resources through Acts of Parliament, already referred to, the effect of these being exacerbated by the government's policy of cheap money. Indeed, 'Every factor of the last ten years', so Sir Philip maintained, 'has been against us'. Then came his 'crunch' conclusion introduced almost dramatically. If this crisis were to be successfully overcome it was useless to look to the Commissioners for more money from sources already stretched to the limit. Any re-distribution of existing resources would only create other problems. Nor would a centrally-sponsored appeal measure up to the solving of so severe a problem. 'The only remedy', he affirmed, 'is to bring home to parishioners in every walk of life, that the greater share of responsibility for supporting the ministry must pass more and more to the Church people of the parishes. Nothing but new money is going to help.' To accept this responsibility meant a radical psychological change since for centuries most incumbents had never looked to their congregations to provide for them financially. Historically, indeed, in rural parishes, it was the bucolic parishioners themselves who expected to be at the receiving end of any *largesse* that was going around.

The ball was now being placed firmly in the court of the Church Assembly and through it to the laity in the parishes. After this debate, characterized by a sense of urgency, Geoffrey Fisher acted promptly, organizing a meeting in Lambeth Palace at which there were present representatives of the Ecclesiastical Commissioners, Queen Anne's Bounty (it had not yet amalgamated), the Central Board of Finance, two Church Assembly committees dealing with cognate matters, and the Chairmen of the Houses of Clergy and Laity. This mixed body got down to business, so much so that on Tuesday 11 February 1947 the Archbishop reported back their findings to the Church Assembly. He introduced the subject by a brief historical survey, letting members of the Assembly know exactly how the present crisis had come about, and repeating what had already been said by the Commission as to the need for new money. There should be more flexibility, the Archbishop maintained, in combining benefices by pluralities, and in the grouping of parishes as social needs changed. He then spelt out the figures item by item which told their own ominous story. So seriously did the Archbishop regard the financial consequences of the Transport Bill – the Church would lose £41,000 per annum – that in January 1947 he led a delegation consisting of leading churchmen, Anglican, Free Church, Presbyterian, together with a member of the Jewish Community, to wait upon Hugh Dalton, Chancellor of the Exchequer, and, incidentally, the son of a Canon of St George's, Windsor. The Archbishop urged that the Transport Bill should at least be modified, particularly in view of the fact that the losses imposed by it on the Church would follow close upon a serious diminution of income resulting from the surrender of investments in the railways for gilt-edged compensation stock. But though he listened with close attention, replied predictably that it was not possible for him to make exceptions in the interests of particular charities.

To return to the meeting of the Church Assembly, Geoffrey Fisher went on to state what his and the Commissioners' ambition was in spite of the severity of this contemporary challenge. 'It was that every office, beneficed or unbeneficed, which the diocese recognises as requisite, shall carry with it at least the minimum stipend which the diocese adopts for that office.' The Archbishop concluded with words of reassurance and encouragement: 'I hope that what I have said will convey at least this – that there is a most genuine concern for [the clergy's] condition and difficulties often intolerable; that those in positions of central authority feel that concern most profoundly; that a real and concerted effort has been made to see how their situation may be mended'.

This statement which led to the immediate goal that every beneficed clergymen should be guaranteed a minimum income of £500 per annum became known as 'the Archbishop's Challenge'. To secure its implementation the House of Laity appointed a Continuing Committee which reported back what it had done to the Archbishop, in May 1951. He was indeed impressed with the success of its efforts so far, and this enabled him to go back to the Church Assembly and give a further report in November 1951, subsequently printed under the heading: *A Task for the Laity*. In this exposition he went further, and suggested that the minimum stipend in future be calculated on a net basis. In pledging himself to this figure he assured the Assembly that he had the full support of the bishops whom he had consulted. To give publicity to his *Task for the Laity*, in view of its importance nation-wide, Geoffrey Fisher held a press conference at Lambeth in which he explained succinctly what the Church of England was doing to cope with a difficult financial situation, and what this sad situation meant in human terms.

Central to this endeavour to improve the lot of the parochial clergy was, of course, the Ecclesiastical Commission, a statutory body set up by Parliament in the thirties of the last century to administer, for the benefit of the Church, the vast estates, many of them capitalized, vested in it. On its willing co-operation any attempt to relieve the plight of the clergy must depend. The First Church Estates Commissioner was appointed by the Crown, and was an ex-officio member of the Church Assembly. Geoffrey Fisher welcomed this since he was anxious to make the Commissioners as sensitive as possible to the needs of the Church, and for the Church to become aware of the difficulties which often confronted the Commissioners. The Commissioners were often the subject of criticism, and it was Geoffrey Fisher's policy to make their image more acceptable to the rank and file of English churchpeople, and to promote mutual understanding between the two. Hence the Archbishop took the opportunity in the course of his Report to the Assembly to express appreciation for the efforts of the Commissioners in this field. Particularly, he called attention to its policy of increasing de-centralization which made administration more personal *vis-à-vis* the diocese, and the diocese therefore more co-operative. Under Scheme K the Commissioners pledged themselves to supplement parochial giving at a cost *in toto* of a quarter million pounds annually.

The Archbishop brought his Report to an end by making two practical suggestions. The first task, to be tackled by the dioceses individually, was to enquire parish by parish what the precise financial situation in respect of stipends was. If any were found to be below the prescribed standard they must consider how the gap could be bridged. Secondly, full use should be made of the Diocesan Conference to secure its enthusiastic support for the Archbishop's Appeal and to encourage initiatives flowing from it. A laymen's committee should be set up, with a Diocesan Secretary serving it. It was, maybe, with a degree of pride if not of self-satisfaction – for there was still much to do – that the Archbishop ended his Report with these words: 'I am, I think, content to leave this matter for the present jointly to the care of the Church

Commissioners, in consultation with Diocesan Secretaries, to the Continuation Committee of the House of Laity of the Church Assembly – and above all, to each diocese and to the laity.'

Before his own Diocesan Conference met in June 1952, the Archbishop was busily preparing the ground. He circularized every incumbent in the diocese asking for his views as to how this challenge could most usefully be met. Having secured and sifted their answers, he referred them back to every parochial church council, putting to them the blunt question as to what they intended to do about it and equally about the urgent demand to secure money for the training of a sufficient number of ordinands. 'The successful accomplishment of these tasks is a vital necessity', he told the diocese and, 'if we were to fail in them it would in the end destroy the Church.'

Geoffrey Fisher left the June meeting of the Diocesan Conference 1952 greatly enheartened and confident that the financial obligations to which members had committed themselves would be accepted 'boldly, even cheerfully'; indeed, so far as his personal observations had gone in not a few dioceses the financial burden was being tackled in good heart. As the value of money continued to fall, so Church people, he counselled, must give more of it to maintain the same level of work and ministry. Stipends were certainly now increasing and the Archbishop looked forward to raising the minimum 'as soon as possible'.

The Archbishop felt strongly, and never failed to reiterate this conviction, that raising money to promote adequate incomes for the clergy should be regarded as exclusively a lay responsibility. There was something improper, he thought, certainly embarrassing, for clergy to go around cap in hand begging financial support for themselves, particularly as there were so many good causes – training of ordinands, for example – competing for help.

Yet if lay people were to rally their forces in respect of clerical stipends, so Geoffrey Fisher believed almost passionately, then they must be fully informed of what the present factual situation was, what had brought it about and what they should do to remedy it. Here he proved to be right.

The increasing escalation in clerical stipends, however, did not only derive from increased giving in the parishes. Sir Philip Baker Wilbraham, it will be remembered, on the first occasion he addressed the Church Assembly of which he was a member, emphasised that there was no possibility of extra money coming from the Commissioners. However, and fortunately, he proved to be wrong. There was, providentially, another way by which the Church Commissioners (as they were called after the merger of the Ecclesiastical Commission with Queen Anne's Bounty) could increase their parochial contributions and

to this we briefly turn. Given the vast resources of the Church
Commissioners, the way in which they invested their money was of
high importance. Indeed the Archbishop blamed incumbents who
refused their consent to allow beneficial changes in their present
parochial investments. For some time he himself had come to feel that
the annual yield from the capital investments held by the Church
Commissioners could and ought to be increased. Geoffrey Fisher
continued uneasy, and did not become less so when he received a letter
from R. A. Butler, then Chancellor of the Exchequer, suggesting that
Stock Exchange investments and real property held by the Church
Commissioners should be dealt with separately and maybe a small
committee might be set up to advise. As a result of this letter, Geoffrey
Fisher consulted the Archbishop of York and the Bishop of London
who both agreed that a new policy of investment by the Church
Commissioners was necessary. Malcolm Trustram Eve, later Lord
Silsoe, who, along with his office as First Church Estates Com-
missioner, was chairman of the Estates and Finance Committee, which
had the responsibility of managing the Commissioners' estates and
investments, had extensive experience as chairman of the War Damage
Commission in which capacity he had dealings with Geoffrey Fisher.
On taking over at the Commissioners from Sir Philip Baker Wilbraham,
Trustram Eve wrote to the Archbishop in these terms: 'In starting as
First Estates Commissioner I want to have some long-distance aim in
mind about stipends and pensions of the clergy'. He had gone into the
figures, a difficult exercise, and had convinced himself that their present
level of payment was quite 'derisory'. In a document which he
subsequently drew up, giving it the title somewhat facetiously 'The
Hopes of Eve', he expressed the view that he should start by setting
himself a 'target figure'. His suggestion was that the basic rate for
unbeneficed clergy should be £400 per annum; for beneficed clergy
£550 plus a free house; also that there should be an incremental scale
for the unbeneficed from £400 to £500; for beneficed clergy from £600
to £800. Also he had in mind special allowances for exceptional
responsibilities and a general allowance up to £250. Geoffrey Fisher
was indeed encouraged by this document and the initiative that
Trustram Eve had taken which was 'entirely along the right lines and
directed towards the right goal'. He felt that it might be helpful to
distinguish between 'small' and 'standard' parishes, the former being
below 2,000, the latter above.

Perhaps the significance of Trustram Eve's letter lay in his thinking
'big'. Geoffrey Fisher was delighted that he should show, thus early,
his interest in the affairs of the Church, in particular the priority of the
stipends of the clergy. Certainly his desire to do better for the parish
clergy has, over the years, been progressively implemented: though not

his desire, in line with his commercial experience, to introduce differentials.

In another area, however, Trustram Eve worked to good effect. It was his view that the investment policy of the Church Commissioners was totally out of date, being too cautious, and he proceeded to act, with the full support and encouragement of the Archbishop, on this assumption. Together they transformed the financial position of the parish clergy by making it possible for them to survive in an inflationary age. One wonders precisely what would have happened to the parish clergy had there not been a radical change in the Church Commissioners' investment policy.

A transformation in the level of clerical incomes was certainly effected, but there could be no question of this remuneration being large enough to encourage any luxurious living as Geoffrey Fisher was quick to point out to a clergyman who asked for a grant to enable his children to go to boarding school. The Church was not on a commercial basis with its customers but in the relation of members of a family. 'The clergy can only be paid what the laity provide.'

In his retirement and looking back on the Archiepiscopate in terms of positive achievements he lists, as one of the best things he ever did, 'the saving of the clergy not merely from poverty but from destitution leading up to the present situation (1965) with a minimum stipend of something like £1,000 a year and a house – and a far better pension scheme for them and their widows'.

It may not be out of place, in a chapter devoted to clerical stipends to conclude with a brief reference to the amalgamation of Queen Anne's Bounty and the Ecclesiastical Commission in the fifties of this century. The former derived from Queen Anne in 1704, surrendering the revenues of the first fruits and tenths vested in the Crown to augment the incomes of small impoverished parishes. The latter, the Ecclesiastical Commission, goes back to legislation in the thirties of the last century which reallocated more equitably the Church's financial resources, part of which money went to benefices. Thus two agencies existed side by side until they were brought together on 1 April 1948. This amalgamation was indeed a tricky exercise with a great deal of *amour propre* involved; and it is extremely doubtful whether it would have been accomplished relatively smoothly were it not for the tact, the patience and the negotiating skill of Geoffrey Fisher. It would have been easy for those administering Queen Anne's Bounty to regard this union as a criticism of its work, but this would have been quite unfair since it was discharging its remit well. However it was clearly more efficient administratively and financially for the two to merge, and this was precisely what happened. The new creation was given the title 'The Church Commissioners'.

CHAPTER 20

Revision of Canon Law

WHEN Geoffrey Fisher arrived unexpectedly at Lambeth in 1945 he came to the conclusion that an overriding priority was to restore liturgical order and discipline into the worshipful life of the established Church. Disorder, so he believed, existed to such an extent that it had led to irregularities and confusion in the use of the Book of Common Prayer, much to the irritation of lay worshippers. To quote his own words: 'Because I had the instincts of a headmaster I knew that [coping with this] was absolutely essential for the well-ordering of the Church of England. The lack of order had been quite dreadful.'

This was no new problem in the national Church and had been experienced in a most extreme form way back in the days of Bishop Bancroft (1544–1610) – later Archbishop – when the puritans were seeking to mould the newly-established *Ecclesia Anglicana* according to their own theological convictions. Bancroft set out to offset this by codifying and issuing in Convocation a set of 'Constitutions and Canons Ecclesiastical' drawn from various 'Articles, Injunctions and synodical Acts promulgated in the reigns of Edward VI and Elizabeth I'. These Canons were given their *imprimatur* by King James I as Supreme Governor of the Church of England though they were never authorised by Act of Parliament. In fact they were almost a dead letter even from the word go.

Similarly, though Church and State had ceased to be integrated the one with the other, Geoffrey Fisher felt there was a need, and his days at London reinforced this conviction, to establish a more coherent pattern of law and order in the Church of England, not least in the use of the Book of Common Prayer and in relation to marriage. He believed that if the clergy were to conform to certain standards they should, in the interests of everyone, know clearly what those standards were. Also these must be felt by the bulk of the clergy and lay people to be reasonable and not oppressive. To secure this the Archbishop recognised that the approval of the clergy must be sought through Convocation, and the laity *via* the Church Assembly, the latter being a comparatively recent innovation. The difficulty here was that the Church of England did not represent a homogenous society since by a quirk of history (or was it by divine Providence?) it included, because it was the church of the nation, a variety of theological and worshipful attitudes which had lived within it since the Reformation, though at times their adherents were uncomfortable bedfellows. Also the national

Church was, in law, tied to the State which meant in practice the need to take account of Parliament when contemplating any significant change in the general pattern of its life and worship. Certainly the 1604 Canons presupposed a different kind of society, religious and culturally, from that of contemporary Britain. This had long been recognised. In mid-Victorian England, a Dean of Ely, who had served on a Royal Commission confessed his complete ignorance as to what constituted lawful authority or where it lay; and Lord Justice Vaisey asserted that what the words of the 1604 Canons meant in this context was as obscure to himself as to anybody else. Randall Davidson, in lighter vein, when talking of lawful authority and asked where it lay, replied quite simply 'in me'.

The revision of Canon Law was a mammoth task but it was one which Geoffrey Fisher found singularly congenial. Maybe he recalled happy far-off days when he was drawing up the rule book at Repton! Indeed he describes it as 'the most absorbing and all-embracing topic' of his whole archiepiscopate!

This exercise, however, must not for a single moment be thought of as solely the brainchild of Geoffrey Fisher. It most certainly was not! This task had been considered by Convocation over many years, so much so that a commission was set up under the chairmanship of Archbishop Garbett in 1939 to take under review 'the whole question of the revision and codification of the Canon Law.' The war years intervened but at its close the talks were taken up again which led Bishop Bell, sceptical of the whole project, to protest to Garbett that he did not think it was in accordance with the 'history and genius of the Church of England'. Dr Fisher thought otherwise, and a report duly appeared in 1947 containing the bare bones of a proposed revised set of canons.

So it was that the Canterbury and York Convocations, in the summer of 1947, decided to proceed with the revision of Canon Law thus implementing the Report of the Commission published in the same year. At the time a steering committee was set up which included four bishops, one of them being the efficient Dr Wand, Bishop of London, and four members of the Lower Houses.

This decision to go forward did not commend itself universally to all sections of the Church of England, though it commanded a substantial majority in Convocation. Bitter protests came in to Lambeth from societies, parishes and individuals, for the most part from the more evangelical and protestant wings of the Church of England. The National Union of Protestants, *inter alia*, sent a public letter to the Archbishops, Bishops, Proctors and Members of Convocation, urging them to abandon revision altogether, and content themselves only with essential amendments as proposed by the Union. Prominent among individual critics was Joynson Hicks whose emotional speech in the House of Commons was largely responsible for securing the rejection of the Deposited Book in 1928. The author of the Preface in Crockford's Clerical Directory, the anonymity of which every reader tries to break, was equally sceptical affirming that 'to frame laws governing too many activities of the clergy and too many aspects of church life and practice is rather a symptom of moral and spiritual weakness than of vigorous life'.

The criticisms which came in to Lambeth at least served to reinforce the Archbishop's clear conviction that it was important the revision should win the support of lay people. Traditionally Canon law revision was a matter only for the clergy in Convocation and not for the more recently established Church Assembly. It was Geoffrey Fisher's conviction, and rightly so, that this enterprise must be the concern of the whole Church and that the laity represented in the Church Assembly must therefore be consulted.

Once the process began it soon became clear that the revision of canon law was no easy exercise, and was made more difficult because the *Ecclesia Anglicana* was not, in law, a voluntary society but an established Church. True it had acquired the power, through what were known as Measures, to initiate its own legislation under the Enabling Act of 1929: but these, to have the force of law, needed the formal approval of Parliament. Also such proposed legislation was vetted by an expert ecclesiastical committee lest any of its enactments should be prejudicial to the rights of His Majesty's subjects. This meant that every clause in every canon must be scrutinized with thoroughness by the Crown lawyers. Thus the revision proved a long and tedious business though it was well on the road to completion at the time of Dr Fisher's retirement in 1961.

In order to avoid any kind of misunderstanding Geoffrey Fisher, in his presidential address to the full Synod on 15 January, stated clearly the procedure to be followed. Each canon would come before the Convocations of Canterbury and York, first to the Upper House and then sent down, with amendments if any, to the Lower. If either House so wished, a particular canon could be referred to a joint session of both Houses. Though there was no constitutional obligation for the laity to be consulted yet the Archbishop pledged 'without hesitation' that the Convocation would give the most careful consideration to any advice offered, or amendments proposed by the laity. As to their legal authorisation some canons might require a Royal Licence, some a Measure, and one or two an Act of Parliament. The Archbishop wisely, as an additional safeguard, appointed his own legal committee, consisting of Lord Justice Vaisey and Lord Denning, together with Chancellors Wigglesworth and Ashworth. From the beginning the committee laid it down as absolutely essential that every canon must be 'accepted unanimously within the Church' before any steps were taken to secure for them legal validation, either by way of a Measure or Act of Parliament. True there might be an 'irreconcilable minority' who would oppose particular canons, and in such a case it would be wise at least to pause before going further. By the time the committee had examined 134 canons it decided that 20 of this number could be passed by Measure, and a further seven required an Act of Parliament.

Geoffrey Fisher realised from the beginning that with an established Church the revision of its Canon Law could not be a private and domestic affair only. Hence he prepared a memorandum for the Lord Chancellor, the Prime Minister and the Home Secretary, prior to the Convocations really getting under way, setting out the case for Revision. In this document he explained that the Church had initially to decide whether to apply to the Crown for Letters of Business. On the advice of his Legal Secretary, H. T. A. Dashwood, he decided to make no such application, but for Convocation to proceed on its own authority leaving an approach to the Crown till later. Therefore, he recognised that it was incumbent on him to inform the Establishment what precisely the Church intended to do; how it was to do this; and why it was necessary to be done.

The Lord Chancellor, William Jowett, replied in a somewhat enigmatic way but allowed that so far the Archbishop 'had not put a foot wrong' and that the successful accomplishment of what he intended would be an 'immense spiritual gain'. The Prime Minister, Clement Attlee, saw the Archbishop personally and by letter assured him that he was 'perfectly in order in carrying on [this] revision of the canons'. No letter from the Home Secretary seems to have survived.

All was now geared for action. By January 1949 the Convocations began work in earnest as also did the steering committee. Some tension between the Canterbury and York Convocations was perhaps inevitable at times the latter being determined 'not to be treated as a junior partner'. This led to a 'mild revolt' since a great deal of its time, arising out of the revision, was now being spent on Canterbury business.

On 3 July 1951, Archbishop Fisher wrote again to the Prime Minister, giving it as his opinion that the process had now reached the stage when it would be helpful to have an 'informal talk with someone in the Government'. He would prefer not to delay such consultation until the Convocations and Church Assembly had finished their task, since informal early advice would be invaluable and avoid later difficulties. However, he was not asking at this stage for any 'formal and official all-clear'.

The Prime Minister replied saying that the best way of meeting the Archbishop's request was for him to appoint a small committee headed by Sir Thomas Barnes, the Solicitor-General. Geoffrey Fisher at once agreed to pass on the proposed canons to this committee as they were progressively ground out 'from the mill of the two Convocations', and before they went up to the House of Lords. Also he was prepared at any time for joint meetings to be held between Barnes and his own steering committee.

Sir Thomas took up this burden with commendable zeal and his association with this task certainly gave confidence to the 'revisionists', and helped them to avoid many pitfalls in such an intricate and sensitive operation. During the discussions between the two committees Sir Thomas Barnes repeatedly expressed a concern for the laity reminding the revisers that anything which might seem to prejudice the rights of citizens must have Parliamentary authority. To clarify this important matter the two Primates had an interview with the Solicitor-General on 12 February 1952 when it became clear that they must differentiate between those canons which (a) related to purely spiritual concerns; (b) merely reaffirmed existing statute law; (c) only bound the clergy; (d) did not bind anyone but only embodied the doctrine or custom of the Church.

The Archbishop's comment on this meeting perhaps deserves quotation: 'Ellis had rather thought that the canons were to declare the mind of the Church rather than to make a law for the Church. I said that the clergy ought to be bound by canons; that was what canonical obedience means. Consistory courts ought to be able to impose penalties, even deprivation for breaches of canons.'

It was clear to Geoffrey Fisher, and here most of the legalists agreed with him, that if a mandate were sought from Parliament for all the canons it would make that Assembly 'arbiters of things which hitherto they had no concern with whatever'. Thus Geoffrey Fisher summed up the situation as follows: 'Convocation made canons and Convocation alone would annul them'.

The place of laity in the revision continued to be a matter of debate and heart-searching. Many evangelical clergymen still looked to Parliament as the final safeguard of their rights and privileges. To allay their fears, a resolution proposed by Dr Addleshaw, Canon of York, passed through the full synod and ran as follows: 'That in the opinion of this Convocation the laity of the province should be consulted through elected representatives, on any canon or resolution of Convocation; touching the doctrines, discipline or worship of the Church'.

However, at no point in this long and protracted exercise was there a time when all were satisfied that the procedure to implement the canons was entirely adequate. Among doubters was Sir Patrick Spens, sometime Chief Justice of India, who remained unconvinced. His firm conviction was that some of the proposed canons did conflict with current legislation, and the effect of this might be to place the Crown 'in a most invidious and undesirable position', thereby exposing the Sovereign to public criticism.

One canon which led to great difficulty for the Archbishop was that which sought to dissuade a Church of England priest from taking advantage of the discretion granted under the Herbert Act of 1937, which allowed him to marry or refuse to marry a divorced person in his church – in spite of the common law – whose previous partner was still alive. To persevere with such a canon, so Sir Thomas must have warned him, would inevitably mean that the Home Secretary could not submit such a canon to the Queen, since it would be illegal, under Section 3 of the Clergy Act of 1533, as 'repugnant' to the civil law. Also it might bring her as Supreme Governor into public controversy. Quintin Hogg, then a Member of Parliament for St Marylebone, wrote to the Archbishop in February 1954 complaining that one of the objections to the canon lay in its seeking to impose, by a majority vote in Convocation, a standard of behaviour on certain members of the Church of England to which it was known they did not subscribe. There was in fact no way out of this dilemma, and the small group which the Archbishop set up to discuss this vexed question reported that it could not advise any attempt to change the civil law at present. There was thus no alternative but to jettison the canon altogether. The Archbishop referred to the withdrawal of this clause as 'generally accepted as altogether wise and in the best interest of the Church's witness to Our Lord's teaching'. This certainly makes a virtue of necessity, but it does not conceal the fact that a canon of this kind, no matter how much the Church might have tried to persist with it, would never have become law.

An attempt to put into action the absolute confidentiality of the 'seal' of the confession met a similar fate and for not totally dissimilar reasons.

There was still a minority which was not very happy with the general approach, inherent in this revision. Thus a weighty *critique* came from the pen of Dr Walter Matthews who claimed that it ran counter to the comprehensiveness of the Church of England. 'The attempt to regulate all the activities of the clergy,' he warned, 'and to cover every aspect of life may easily lead to a restriction of the pastoral freedom of the parish clergy'. This could affect their whole status as clergy and ministers.

Another canon (number 17), intended to end years of debate by detailing the vestments which could be worn in church by the minister, became a matter of prolonged controversy. The bishops, and not least the Archbishop, realised that in this particular field emotions and prejudices ran high, and a clause was inserted to the effect that the wearing of the permitted vestment left the doctrine of the Church of

England entirely unchanged. In particular it was complained that the biblical principles of the Reformation were being undermined and that the general tendency of the canons was to increase the powers of the bishop.

Such criticisms showed clearly that there were minority interests in the Church of England which felt that their deeply-held convictions went by default. One correspondent, Malcolm McQueen, drew attention to the fact that doctrinal agreement in the Church of England was unobtainable, and this was the reason why some of the clergy, 'both left and right of centre', regarded the present pressure of canon law revision, in particular that which concerns 'lawful authority, as a party move designed to squeeze the evangelical and Catholic wings into a straight-jacket'. 'Where Evangelicals differ', he went on, 'from Your Grace is in your suggestion that because a majority vote either in Convocation or the Church Assembly goes against them, they should therefore accept the situation as the mind of the Church, and, as we are often told, the mind of the Holy Spirit. Are we really to accede to the doctrine that majorities are always right?'

One thing is certain and it is that, whatever we think of these criticisms, Geoffrey Fisher had no desire to single out evangelicals for severe treatment.

It was incumbent on Geoffrey Fisher to reply to such attacks coming from diverse quarters and this he did in an address to Convocation in May 1957 as well as in numerous private letters and interviews. The burden of his defence was that the so-called laws were but 'norms' to which members of the family were expected loyally to conform.

As to complaints concerning how the canons might be deployed he replied firmly: 'They cannot be used by anybody for any intentions of their own beyond what they say'. Bishops had no intention of running about seeking whom they could bring charges against; 'that was not their habit'.

Geoffrey Fisher had always recognised, and frequently referred to the fact, that changes in the canons would require new ecclesiastical courts to enforce them. In 1956 there were four courts and five *quasi* courts for each diocese, and six courts for each Province. The final court of appeal in all cases was the Judicial Committee of the Privy Council, which gave great offence to many who felt that a secular and state-appointed body should not be involved in determining doctrine in the Church of England. The proliferation of courts also fell under severe criticism.

To deal generally with this situation Geoffrey Fisher and the Archbishop of York set up a commission which reported in 1956. It suggested a radical reform, namely a drastic reduction in the number of courts. So far as clergy were concerned it proposed making a distinction between 'conduct' cases – immorality, neglect of duty – and 'reserved' cases which included doctrine and worship. The former would go to the diocesan court with appeal to the provincial; the latter to a new court of Ecclesiastical Causes, its personnel to consist of bishops and three laymen distinguished in the law. The Judicial Committee of the Privy Council would no longer be involved as the court of appeal. Immediately on receiving the Commission's report Geoffrey Fisher sent it, with comments, to Sir Thomas Barnes and to the Lord Chancellor, Viscount Kilmuir, who had taken over from Lord Simmonds. This gave Geoffrey Fisher a further opportunity of explaining at length what Canon Law revision, 'a task long overdue', was all about. However, there was no point now in going forward, so the Archbishop realised, without first finding out whether the Government would look favourably on the specific proposals in the Report; but it was not until 1963 by which time the Archbishop had been retired for two years, that the Ecclesiastical Jurisdiction Measure became law. In the course of its progress certain amendments were made, as for example restoring the Judicial Committee of the Privy Council for appeals in 'conduct cases', though not every one approved the proposals. Thus Canon Welsby writes: 'Unfortunately in dismantling the previous complicated and cumbersome machinery, it was replaced by procedures hardly less so'.

But to return. On 10 January 1957 Harold Macmillan 'emerged' to follow Anthony Eden as Prime Minister and in due course the Archbishop informed him, together with Hugh Gaitskell, Leader of the Opposition, of the precise situation in respect of the revision of Canon Law. Macmillan responded by making the suggestion that Sir Hubert Ashton, Second Church Estates Commissioner, His Honour Judge Hobson, a lawyer of wide experience, and Mr Enoch Powell, Member of Parliament, should advise the Archbishops though in a purely unofficial capacity.

Discussion on the concept of 'lawful authority' and the membership of the final court of appeal brought with it personal tensions leading to Bishop Wand's resigning from the Commission. The Archbishop was inevitably drawn in, and tried to pour oil on troubled waters by suggesting that the revised canons were not fixed for all time like the laws of the Medes and Persians, but would need to be kept under constant review.

As time went on opposition did not die down, nor did time devoted to it in Convocation and the Church Assembly grow less. Even in the later fifties the end of the revising process did not yet seem in sight. What was most galling for Geoffrey Fisher was the growing disillusion of his episcopal colleagues with this long drawn-out enterprise. This all came to the boil at a residential conference, called together by the bishops themselves at Westcott House in Cambridge in June 1959. As the cut and thrust of debate on this occasion went on, so Geoffrey Fisher began to feel that he had a 'sort of little rebellion' on his hands. According to notes drawn up by his chaplain, not a single bishop expressed an enthusiastic, one hundred per cent support for the revision. In this respect Michael Ramsey, Archbishop of York, was foremost in maintaining that the revision was undertaken in preference to more needed reform, only because the Report, commissioned by the Church Assembly, happened to be on the table. He believed that they must now decide rapidly which canons to pass and which should be shelved or postponed. The Bishop of Peterborough was even more radical, asserting that the revision had caused a great deal of episcopal frustration and had exposed the bishops to ridicule. His solution was to put the whole thing into cold storage. The Bishop of Guildford suggested postponement for five years; the Bishop of Winchester a severe process of pruning. The Archbishop in reply gave a broad survey concentrating upon the general situation which had made a new set of canons necessary.

What is unfortunately true is that the exorbitant demand on precious time for the revision in Convocation and the Church Assembly did much to sour personal relations between the Archbishop and the Bench during his last two or three years in office. Indeed he himself admitted that from time to time he had to 'keep pushing the bishops on'; and urge them 'not to get despondent or bored'. It was 'vital' that the revision should be carried through successfully.

To the Archbishop's tidy mind the case for revision seemed self-evident. All it was seeking to do was simply to register the responsible and reasonable consensus view as to how the Church of England should organise its collective life. Those who differed from this consensus at either end of the ecclesiastical spectrum must not be allowed 'to rock the boat'. Equally self-evident was it that Convocation and the Church Assembly were the only two corporate bodies which had the constitutional authority to proclaim what that majority view was. From this basic position Geoffrey Fisher never swerved, nor did he warm to any suggestion that the time spent on the revision was ill spent. Quite the reverse! In his taped autobiography written a few years after his retirement he claimed that this exercise was one of the greatest achievements of his archiepiscopate. At least it may be said on Geoffrey Fisher's behalf that the fears of those who predicted that the canons would change the whole character of the Church of England, weaken the biblical authority of the faith, undermine the status of the parish priest, overwhelm the bishops with countless permissive requests – these forebodings have not been realised. The fact is that the revised canons have not loomed large in the immediate or the subliminal consciousness of members of the Church of England as a whole. Newly ordained clergy are largely unaware of them.

Does this mean that the enterprise was, or was not, worthwhile; or, as Walter Matthews suggested, that 'there was nothing so wrong that a few episcopal letters might not have put right'. Any answer to a hypothetical question of this kind must in the nature of the case be largely speculative and subjective. Certainly, though this has little or no popular appeal, the revision did lead to a tidying up of ancient statutory legislation which bears upon the relationship of the *Ecclesia Anglicana* to the State, and this was worthwhile. Such was the view of Sir Harold Kent, Procurator General and Treasury solicitor.

Also it might be claimed that there was some value in replacing out-of-date and irrelevant canons by new ones. But whether such benefits merited such a lavish expenditure of time who can tell? In addition there were those who did not think that the immediate post-war years were the right time to embark upon it but here the argument could work both ways.

Canon Paul Welsby, a Church historian, has drawn attention to the fact that in his Presidential address to Convocation in May 1947, the very day on which the revision of canon law began in earnest, Geoffrey Fisher first referred to such great issues as keeping internal peace and reviving British industry. He then went on to say that the country needed all it possessed of political wisdom to cope with such problems and it was the first duty of Christians to measure up to the challenge. 'It is very doubtful', so Canon Welsby comments, 'whether many people were able to see how the revision of Canon Law would contribute significantly to this task.'

One thing, however, can be said for certain, namely that had it not been for Geoffrey Fisher's absolute dedication and dynamic energy, the revision of canon law on so comprehensive a scale might well have faltered and failed.

CHAPTER 21

Bishops, the Establishment and Crown Appointments

(i)

A BISHOP in Anglo-Saxon days was an important man. He sat in the county court; attended its national counterpart the witenagemot; often owned extensive estates; and was frequently with the King at Court. Hence nominations to the episcopate could be politically significant and remained so throughout the Middle Ages. The procedure was for bishops, under the final jurisdiction of the papacy in Rome, to be elected by the cathedral chapter of the diocese in which they were to serve. In practice the monarch frequently made a deal with the Pope who brought pressure to bear on the chapter, thereby enabling the Crown to get the man it wanted. Under the parliamentary legislation of Henry VIII the King as Supreme Governor of the *Ecclesia Anglicana* replaced the Pope, but formal election of bishops by cathedral chapters continued though the latter were required, under the Act of Praemunire, to elect the royal nominee. As the monarchy lost power, so it was in fact the Prime Minister who finally decided upon the royal nominee. However, since the head of the government was increasingly caught up in his political preoccupations, and was conscious of his own lack of knowledge in this field, so twentieth century Prime Ministers needed advice. That excellent person Mandell Creighton, Bishop of London, was often approached to give advice: Lloyd George sought it from the not so well informed Dr Ernest Pearce, Bishop of Worcester.

A new development in the process of nominating bishops came with the institutionalization of this somewhat informal advice by the appointment of a permanent civil servant as Patronage Secretary. This led to the distancing of the Prime Minister from preliminary consultations thereby increasing the influence of the Archbishop of Canterbury.

From 1945 to 1961, through his unique office as Archbishop of Canterbury, Geoffrey Fisher was destined to leave his stamp upon the episcopate of the Church of England. It is this that will now concern us.

During this period he had to deal with four Prime Ministers – Winston Churchill (1944–1945); Clement Attlee (1945–1951); Winston Churchill (1951–1955); Anthony Eden (1955–1956); and Harold Macmillan (1957–1963). These Prime Ministers were served by three Patronage Secretaries – Anthony Bevir, David Stephens and John

Hewitt. It is therefore appropriate, at this point, to say something of Geoffrey Fisher's relations with these civil servants, since he was constantly in touch with them. We shall refer to Prime Ministers in the context of particular appointments.

Geoffrey Fisher was fortunate to inherit Anthony Bevir, whom Attlee described as 'a walking Crockford'. He was an eminently clubbable man who kept his ear pretty close to the ground. Though entirely opposed to the setting up of formal committees with which the Prime Minister was expected to confer, his practice was to visit widely and to make innumerable personal contacts, not least with lay people. His responsibility was more or less as wide as the Crown's Patronage, and this included the Archbishops, forty-one diocesan bishops, thirty deans and some two hundred clergy in Crown livings.

The part that Bevir was called upon to play became the more significant because both Prime Minister Attlee and Archbishop Fisher had entered newly into office and, what is more, found awaiting them many bishoprics to be filled. Geoffrey Fisher writes that his discussions with Bevir were 'very full' but that he could be 'terribly long-winded' – a favourite expression of the Archbishop's. Bevir, unlike some of his successors, was careful never to press his own opinions or force a name upon the Archbishop. Thus, when seeing the Prime Minister, he would never go outside the names put forward and approved by Lambeth. Geoffrey Fisher used to claim that he could not remember a time when his first choice was not accepted. In saying this his memory was certainly playing him false. Indeed, there were occasions when he himself, in the light of experience, was sufficiently artful to put forward a first choice whom he knew to be unacceptable to the Prime Minister in order to make certain of securing his own choice whom he had placed second.

The Archbishop did not have the same confidence in Bevir's successor, David Stephens, though they were loyal to each other in public. Geoffrey Fisher suspected him of 'a certain independence of thought', so much so that he never quite knew whether the information that David Stephens gave him emanated from the Prime Minister or was his own private opinion. Matters were brought to a head in May 1956 in connection with an appointment to the bishopric of Ely. The Archbishop saw Stephens and discussed various possibilities, finally letting him know that his first choice was John Moorman, Principal of Chichester Theological College, who was also approved by the Archbishop of York. There it rested until some weeks later Stephens reported that, during the interval, he had found out that the Prime Minister would be happy with an alternative choice. This news took the Archbishop completely by surprise, but so far had the affair now gone that the Prime Minister was only waiting for a letter from the

Archbishop before nominating Noel Hudson. Geoffrey Fisher realistically recognised that he had lost out, and the Bishop of Newcastle's appointment to Ely went forward. In a memorandum drawn up at the time Geoffrey Fisher recorded that he regarded this as a complete rupture of the whole system. 'I have always maintained in public', he went on, 'that the system works well because there was complete freedom of discussion between the PM and the Archbishop of Canterbury, and over the Northern Province with the Archbishop of York.' If Stephens wished to continue in a confidential relationship with the Archbishop, then he must never advise the Prime Minister on a particular appointment until he knew the Archbishop's mind.

The Archbishop of Canterbury was not alone in thinking that David Stephens, maybe from the best of motives, had exceeded his brief. Michael Ramsey of York entertained the same view and believed that Geoffrey Fisher ought to do something about it. The Archbishop confessed that he found his relationship with Stephens 'always a tricky one'. In due course, Geoffrey Fisher informed David Stephens that he must refrain from acting upon his own personal judgement or initiative. His task was to be a piece of 'blotting paper,' a bit of the 'under-counter machinery'. Fortunately, so the Archbishop wrote to Michael Ramsey, David Stephens 'took all this in good part'.

One has sympathy with both parties though doubtless Dr Fisher was right in insisting on Stephens confining himself to exploratory work. On the other hand, it is not always easy to decide where precisely to draw the line.

When Geoffrey Fisher went to Lambeth he found awaiting him a backlog of episcopal appointments. Not surprisingly he ran into difficulties in part because the former personal way of doing things was now giving place to another which had not yet fully established itself. The Archbishop was unfortunate in that the first major ecclesiastical appointment with which he had to deal was that of his own successor to London. There was, in the eyes of many churchmen, and indeed of lay people, one person, namely George Bell, whose claims were outstanding and who might well have gone to Canterbury. Now there seemed an opportunity to make amends and to place this distinguished ecclesiastic in a bishopric which, in terms of influence, was second only to Canterbury. Bishop Bell himself certainly expected that this appointment might be offered him. The percipient Dr Garbett, however, doubted whether Bevir would even mention his name to the Prime Minister so intense was Churchill's animus against him. Yet Bell, he thought, ought to be pressed upon him if the Church were to have any voice in this key appointment.

Faced with this awkward, indeed embarrassing, situation Geoffrey Fisher drew up a memorandum: 'A Successor for London, January

1945'. As to the diocese: (a) the work involved was heavy but there were three excellent Suffragans; (b) it made a great difference to the Archbishop of Canterbury if the Bishop of London was 'a man of sound judgement to whom he can look for counsel and advice'; (c) the diocese presented a special problem of Church order and discipline; (d) a Bishop of London occupied a prominent position relative to the City, the House of Lords and public life generally.

The Archbishop then dealt directly with the claims of Bishop Bell who he emphasized must certainly be considered. The first three considerations he would undoubtedly fulfil admirably. In many ways he was obviously the right man but two things had to be borne in mind. In the early days of the war, he incurred great criticism for some of his utterances especially in relation to night bombing over Germany. In this he was greatly misunderstood. Also he was passionately concerned with the necessity to enter into fellowship with former enemy Christians on the Continent. His appointment might evoke a measure of popular criticism, but this would be forgotten when the war ended: indeed the remarkable position that he held among Christians in Sweden, Norway and Germany might be of the greatest value. He himself, as Archbishop, would find his help and wisdom invaluable over 'nine-tenths of the field'.

Geoffrey Fisher, in this extensive memorandum, then went on to consider other names which had been put forward. These he dismissed except for Bishop Woodward of Bristol, who had undoubted gifts having proved himself earlier in life a popular and successful incumbent of the parish of St John's, Smith Square, in London. The Archbishop of York, Geoffrey Fisher concluded, had seen his memorandum and approved the views expressed in it.

This document was duly sent to Winston Churchill who, in acknowledging it on 14 March, observed only that one candidate who was sixty-seven seemed too old. Could he be sent a further name before coming to a final decision?

It seemed clear from this letter that the Prime Minister once again had rejected Bishop Bell on the grounds of his being politically unacceptable, a decision which Dr Fisher inadvisedly conveyed verbally to the Bishop of Chichester at a chance meeting in the County Office. Two days later – and who can sit in judgement upon him – Bell gave vent to his long pent-up emotions in an explosive letter expressing anger and surprise that, to quote his own words, 'when the Church is being tested in a severe way – as well as criticized – although you as Archbishop are convinced in your own mind that a particular person is the best person from the point of view of the Church for this difficult and responsible office of the Bishop of London, you should not let the case go without a vigorous effort to give effect to your convictions because of a political objection raised by the Prime Minister and Buckingham Palace'.

This letter cut the Archbishop to the quick. He now bitterly regretted that he gave way to 'the impulse of a moment' rather than keep silent. Honesty, however, compelled the Archbishop to say to Dr Bell, galling though it was, that his was not the only name put forward to the Prime Minister.

In his distress Geoffrey Fisher now wrote to Cosmo Lang receiving a reply dated 5 April. Lang had always said that the right man for London was George Bell, though he was well aware of the Prime Minister's built-in objection on political grounds, mistaken though this objection was. Thus he believed it was useless to urge Bell's claims.

Winston Churchill having, as it were, cleared Bell out of the way, seemed now to be veering toward Woodward in spite of his age. However, this tangled web of negotiation was by no means yet over. There were interviews between the Archbishop of York and Sir Anthony Bevir duly reported to Lambeth, and it was at one of these, greatly to Dr Garbett's surprise, that he learnt the Prime Minister was thinking of nominating to London, as a younger man, William Wand, Bishop of Bath and Wells. The Archbishop of York could only retort that to do this would be to act contrary to the specific advice given him by both Archbishops.

And so it went on, and still, after a vacancy of five months no announcement of a bishop for London had been made. A frustrated and angry Geoffrey Fisher now sent off a very forthright letter to 10 Downing Street. While appreciating that the Prime Minister had many responsibilities, he stressed 'the paralysing effect of having no one who can take final decisions or direct diocesan policy'. Might he suggest, with respect, that it would not be improper for him to accept the recommendations which the two Archbishops had consistently made.

The Prime Minister without any apology for the inconvenience he had caused asked for more time to complete his enquiries. And so it was that Dr Wand went to London – and made a good Bishop! Sir Anthony Bevir was careful to let the Archbishop know that the decision had finally been taken when he personally was out of London!

Fairness to the Prime Minister makes it necessary to add that, in asserting his right to put one of his own choosing to the Crown, he was acting strictly within his constitutional powers. Whether such a system ought to obtain was, of course, another matter. Many will have doubts. The consequence was that the Prime Minister, in responding to what he may have regarded as the popular gut reaction of many an Englishman, had denied the established Church, in the office of Bishop of London, at a testing period in its history, the one distinguished churchman of an international reputation recommended by both Archbishops.

When Geoffrey Fisher came to Lambeth there was, as we have seen, an extensive backlog of vacant bishoprics, this being largely due to bishops now retiring who had prolonged their stay in office over the 'duration'. However, before these dioceses could receive their new bishops a general election on 5 July 1945, when the predominant national mood was for change, swept Winston Churchill out of office and the Labour Party into Government with Clement Attlee as Prime Minister.

Clement Attlee, so does Geoffrey Fisher describe him, was 'extremely shrewd'. A churchman by family tradition if not a regular attender, he had enough knowledge, on occasions, to be critical of archiepiscopal advice. He freely accepted that appointments to office in the Church in the gift of the Crown were a constitutional responsibility that he must take seriously. If a Prime Minister were to plead that he was far too busy to apply his mind to these things then, so Clement Attlee affirmed to a Crown Appointments Commission, this was a clear indication that he had not yet learnt how to delegate. Apart from his official adviser, the Patronage Secretary, Attlee had others whom he could call upon informally, such for example as Jowett who became Lord Chancellor, and Sir Stafford Cripps, a member of the Labour Cabinet. Also Attlee had views of his own as to the kind of clergyman who would make a good diocesan bishop. Thus he was convinced that scholars and theologians made better deans than bishops and that he ought to look for potential episcopal material to the parishes rather than to the universities. He felt also that there was a tendency to appoint too many from public schools, and always he had a leaning towards younger men and the more 'adventurous' among them.

At the end of July 1945, the Archbishop had a long conversation with Anthony Bevir during which he put forward a number of names largely emanating from William Temple admitting, as he did so, that he viewed some of these without conviction. This was a view which Attlee shared and conveyed frankly to the Archbishop in a long letter perhaps unique of its kind as coming from a Prime Minister to an Archbishop of Canterbury. He had certainly investigated all the names on the list, he wrote, but they seemed to him all of a piece and were, with few exceptions, elderly. Also though they were 'obviously men of considerable qualities and attainments, they would appear to be suitable for routine appointments, but not to have outstanding qualities of leadership with the ability to arouse enthusiasm'. They resembled good staff officers and technicians rather than commanders in the field. The material fight against fascists and communists was won: it was now time to win the spiritual battle. He feared that a younger generation would be disappointed at these first episcopal appointments after the war. 'The times in which we live', he concluded, 'seem to me to call for boldness and the crusading spirit. I should like to see them exhibited in the forthcoming appointments to the bench.'

This was not an easy letter to answer, particularly as Geoffrey Fisher had himself regarded the list from Temple as an unexciting one, though the best to hand. But, he asked the Prime Minister, was the analogy of the commanders in the field a fair one? Was not that of chief of staff better? Dick Sheppard and Studdert Kennedy certainly 'inspired enthusiasm' but it would have been quite disastrous to make them bishops.

Clement Attlee was not reassured and he informed the Archbishop that he had commended McGowan – one of his 'younger men' – for Wakefield. Meanwhile he stood his ground.

This initial exchange of letters between Archbishop and Prime Minister indicated that the latter as head of His Majesty's Government expected a real dialogue with the Primate of All England on this matter of Crown preferment. Indeed the Archbishop was the first to admit that there were occasions when Clement Attlee came up with a name that he himself had not thought of. Sometimes it happened in reverse. A case in point – a very sad one – was that of a distinguished scholar who had spent long years in a deanery, thereby incurring a well-deserved reputation for being difficult. The Archbishop, supported by his brother of York, pressed him hard upon Attlee for the Diocese of Bath and Wells, then for Lincoln. However, the Prime Minister was adamant that extreme 'drawbacks of temperament' made him unsuitable – and to this he stuck in spite of strong protests by the historian G. M. Trevelyan.

Perhaps the very objectivity of the Prime Minister made possible at times a more informed judgement. Yet this could happen in reverse. Thus Geoffrey Fisher was anxious that F. A. Cockin, a Canon of St Paul's Cathedral, with wide experience in education, should go to Bristol but the Prime Minister believed that at 67 he was too old. The Archbishop decided to contest this rigorously. It disturbed him, he wrote to Downing Street on 22 March 1946, that in dismissing him he had said nothing about his considerable merits, only his age. To apply this yardstick as a general principle in Church appointments would be 'quite disastrous'. The Prime Minister sensibly gave way.

Both Archbishop and Prime Minister in the early years of their co-operation were certainly hard-pressed since six diocesan appointments were made in 1946. Whatever the judgement on the end result, it can hardly be claimed that the whole process was carried through 'decently and in order'. There were constant delays; uncertainties; many changes of plan; and very little co-ordination by those involved. The days, of course, had very properly gone when matters of this kind could be settled in the Athenaeum or at Lambeth over the dinner table.

However, bishop-making certainly began to go more smoothly as Archbishop and Prime Minister got to know each other and the latter's initial enthusiasm began to be tempered with a greater realism. Thus, when on 14 January 1949 Geoffrey Fisher saw the Prime Minister with a list of names, some of whom had been put forward by deans and chapters, all five were accepted without comment. The fact was that Attlee, unlike Gladstone, was unable to back up his general judgement with any intimate knowledge of the ecclesiastical field.

It would be tedious to comment upon all episcopal appointments with which the Archbishop had to deal during his years at Lambeth. It may be helpful, however, to refer briefly to those which have some special interest.

Chelmsford became vacant in November 1950 on the retirement of Henry Wilson, a strong evangelical churchman. Early in the year the Bishop wrote to Lambeth saying that the diocese needed a new approach under another leader if its ever-growing problems were really to be tackled. The Archbishop in his reply expressed his doubt as to whether any of the men mentioned by the Bishop had the ability and depth to lead a diocese. In response to this briefing the Prime Minister also put forward a name on which the Archbishop commented that he would be very happy to see him in some very important and prominent parish, but not in a bishopric until he had quite clearly proved himself. The choice finally fell on Faulkner Allison, who was of the same evangelical persuasion as his predecessor.

Phillip Loyd, Bishop of St Albans, resigned in the same year. The Archbishop proceeded on his usual enquiries, and soon found out that many clergy in the diocese felt that the Dean of the Cathedral, a man of great force of character about whom different opinions were held, would constitute a serious problem for any incoming diocesan. Nor were the parish clergy alone in thinking this. Certainly the Dean had shown commendable courage and independence some years earlier when, after Hiroshima and Nagasaki, he refused to hold a conventional victory service of thanksgiving in the Cathedral. Some ten names came to Lambeth and Geoffrey Fisher made extensive enquiries prior to opting for Gresford Jones, Suffragan Bishop of Willesden, whom he had come to know well during his years at Fulham. As it was, the Prime Minister accepted the Archbishop's choice and nominated him to the Crown.

In 1952 the distinguished scholar, Bishop Alwyn Williams, formerly Headmaster of Winchester and Dean of Christ Church, Oxford, was translated to Winchester, thus vacating Durham, a key diocese in the northern Province. Amongst the eight persons considered for this office, five were already diocesan bishops. Both the outgoing Bishop, together with the Dean and Chapter of Durham, placed Michael Ramsey, Regius Professor of Divinity at Cambridge, at the top of their list, the former describing him as a good scholar with an original mind, though, maybe a 'little weak in administrative gifts or sufficient practical commonsense for a diocese like Durham'. No one could gainsay Ramsey's considerable and unusual talents. Geoffrey Fisher, who had been his headmaster at Repton, gave him his full support. If he had any reservation it was as to whether his greatest contribution to the Church for the next five years ought not to be one of theological scholarship, particularly as he had only been two years in his present post. Also he was a little concerned as to how he would fare administratively in charge of a diocese. Thus he wrote to the Prime Minister in these terms: 'I have known him intimately since he was a pupil of mine. He is outstanding both for his theological ability, and for his personal saintliness of character. If he was to be offered Durham I should not question it.' So it was that Michael Ramsey embarked upon an episcopate in the North.

Finding the right bishop for St Edmundsbury and Ipswich in 1956 gave rise to difficulties. Geoffrey Fisher had no doubt, in principle, as to the kind of man needed and wrote to the Prime Minister a perceptive letter, revealing, incidentally, as much about his own priorities as about the diocese and its retiring bishop. The Archbishop was convinced that it suffered from what he called 'over-efficient administration' and, therefore, above all needed a pastoral bishop 'who will commend himself to the squires and the county people and spend his whole time going among them and getting to know them'. Thus his mind turned first to a number of priests, all of them pastorally orientated. Their successive refusals led to long delay, so much so that the local member of Parliament, who had represented Bury St Edmunds for over twenty years, wrote protesting strongly to the Archbishop. The Lord Lieutenant also said it was imperative that an appointment should be announced soon. Thus on 29 March 1954 the Archbishop made contact with the Prime Minister suggesting two priests both with parish experience. The result was that A. H. Morris, Bishop of Pontefract, whom Geoffrey Fisher described 'as good as gold', was nominated Bishop of St Edmundsbury and Ipswich on 4 May 1954. It would be difficult to conceive of two men more contrasted than he and his predecessor, but this was intended.

The Diocese of Oxford, with Christ Church Cathedral right in the heart of the University and constitutionally integrated with the College, gave the Archbishop much to ponder over when Bishop Kirk, theologian and canonist, died on 5 June 1954. John Lowe, Dean of Christ Church, a commonsensical Canadian, furnished him with some very forthright views: 'The Diocese', he wrote, 'is in a serious mess administratively and financially ... the fact is that (and no doubt largely due to his state of health) burning pastoral problems have been neglected and there has been an administrative stand-still.' The diocese had gained the reputation for being 'in the pocket of a party'. Not much attention, he asserted, needed to be given to the demands of the University. The Dean then mentioned a certain number of names some, in his opinion, suitable, others unsuitable. In his final letter to the Prime Minister Geoffrey Fisher put forward two names intimating his preference. The Archbishop's advice was followed and Harry Carpenter, Warden of Keble, was nominated on 17 December 1954.

On 15 August 1955 Geoffrey Fisher wrote one of his occasional long letters to the Prime Minister, then Anthony Eden, who had been three months in office and, therefore, so Geoffrey Fisher felt, needed to be introduced into some of the intricacies and hazards of bishop-making. In this letter he surveyed the whole field as it was at the moment, calling particular attention to vacancies at Worcester and Bradford, listing bishops who might benefit from a translation – Attlee never really liked translations! – and clergy of episcopal calibre who merited consideration – and others who did not, and why!

Anthony Eden was not so knowledgeable as, for example, Clement Attlee came to be, but he was keen to learn. A meeting between the two was arranged for 24 September 1955, but at the last moment this was cancelled for fear lest the Press should exploit the occasion as connected with Princess Margaret and her relations with Group Captain Townsend which was hot news at the time.

Two important appointments now commanded the attention of both Prime Minister and Archbishop through the unexpected resignation of William Wand of London after some ten years in office, together with the approaching retirement of Dr Garbett. Geoffrey Fisher always regarded London as a uniquely significant see, and a far better school for grooming a future Archbishop of Canterbury than York. In August the Archbishop got into touch with the Prime Minister confessing that he did not see any obvious person as a Metropolitan for the northern Province, and then with disarming frankness listing candidly, for Eden's benefit, some of the possibilities, three of whom he described as 'utterly wise but too self-effacing'; 'not well balanced and with a judgement not altogether to be trusted'; 'the greatest of all the present bishops in experience, wisdom and prestige'. The Archbishop also made a surprising, indeed curious suggestion, namely that perhaps Bishop Wand might be prepared to undertake this high office at York 'as a public service, while younger men have time to develop'. Fisher then gave a commendatory write-up of Michael Ramsey as the best theologian on the Bench, a first-rate scholar and a 'character' too. He was clearly marked out for an archiepiscopal office; but it might be good for him if he could be left at Durham a little longer. As to the bishopric of London, its holder needed 'real strength and distinction'. He then named some possible candidates, commenting upon each one as he went along in these terms – 'over-weighted at London'; 'fails too much to win full confidence as a spiritual leader, perhaps because of an element of self-importance'; 'discipline over his clergy who fall into moral disasters of one kind or another weak and indulgent'; 'quiet, pastoral, personal' but could he project himself adequately into the turmoil of the See of London? The retiring Bishop, William Wand, came down firmly on the side of Michael Ramsey as his successor, a suggestion to which Geoffrey Fisher now reacted 'very favourably' since he would probably be the next Archbishop of Canterbury.

In October Dr Fisher had a further long conversation with the Prime Minister, as a result of which he duly reported to the Archbishop of York that he doubted whether Downing Street would agree to Michael Ramsey's nomination to London. This news evoked from Garbett the sad comment: 'Of course I should like him to succeed me here (i.e. York). He has all the gifts, and far more than I have ever had, but if he came here for a few years, objections might be made against another translation from York to Canterbury. As it was he supported his going to London. Maybe, significant of a niggling sense of guilt for not earlier pressing harder, was a letter written on 4 November by Garbett to Lambeth: 'I have had a brainwave, though possibly you may think it a weakening of the brain due to age and illness'. It was to translate George Bell, aged 72, from Chichester to London.

The Archbishop of Canterbury brought this suggestion immediately, and with enthusiasm, to the Prime Minister, assuring him that if this were acted upon it would in no sense be a 'stop-gap', owing to the 'quite exceptional prestige which he [Bell] enjoys in the Church at home and all over the world'. However, Anthony Eden made it plain that he was not to be wooed in this direction any more than was Churchill. Geoffrey Fisher was now getting increasingly weary of the delay and urged upon the Prime Minister the need for the appointment to be made soon. In response to this pressure Anthony Eden now decided to break new ground with a somewhat novel suggestion, namely to consider for London either the Bishop of Edinburgh or the Archbishop of Perth in Australia. As these protracted negotiations seemed to be getting nowhere, Geoffrey Fisher's mind inevitably returned to Michael Ramsey for London. 'Personally' – and he now addressed himself directly to the Bishop of Durham which he had not done hitherto – 'I think it would be the best thing for you also. There is no doubt, God willing, you will spend many of your days as an Archbishop; it would give you unqualified preparation for that office to meet the manifold experiences which fall to the Bishop of London.' With his characteristic sense of duty Michel Ramsey replied that he would leave his future to others. The result was, and the decision seems to have been taken by the Prime Minister personally, that Michael Ramsey went to York and not to London.

This left two vacancies – Durham and London. The Archbishop now proceeded to put forward four names in respect of the former, two of whom declined, one of these having developed the habit of saying '*nolo episcopari*' almost as a routine operation. It came as no surprise, however, when Maurice Harland, Bishop of Lincoln, went to Durham, but the same cannot be said of the announcement on 10 January 1956 that Montgomery Campbell, Bishop of Guildford, was going to London. No one could dispute his intimate knowledge of the great metropolis; his pastoral concern; his shrewd commonsense; his complete lack of 'side' and his inimitable if mordant wit. This was undoubtedly a purely personal appointment by Geoffrey Fisher, for the Archbishop and Montgomery Campbell were close friends. But he was already approaching his seventies and, to quote his own words: 'Such powers as I have are fading fast with advancing years,' to which he added modestly that he 'never had the qualities.' To friends he remarked with typical self-depreciation that they had 'scraped the barrel bare' before finding him at the bottom. Certainly he was no innovator, though his clergy liked him. We may be fairly safe in supposing that, to the Archbishop, this was a holding operation.

There were occasions when Geoffrey Fisher, to meet what he felt a greater need, incurred criticism for moving clergy too rapidly from one post to another. An extreme instance was that of Bishop Stopford's nomination to the bishopric of Peterborough on 15 June 1956, in spite of his having been consecrated Bishop of Fulham as recently as 11 June 1955. George Bell, understandably in view of his concern for the Anglican Church in Europe, took grave exception to this hasty translation and protested vigorously against it. It would, he alleged, create an unhappy impression with regard to the Church of England's attitude to foreign chaplaincies and indeed to Britain's embassies. He therefore urged the Bishop of Fulham to decline the invitation, which would have the added advantage of saving the Archbishop himself from 'a major blunder'.

Bell's was no lone voice. The Bishop of Bristol also wrote to Stopford in similar terms complaining that to treat Europe in this way must expose Geoffrey Fisher to serious criticism. His private view was that this appointment was another example of the Archbishop's 'hand to mouth policy of recent years'. A somewhat facetious letter came to the Bishop-Designate from Anreas Rinkel, the old Catholic Archbishop of Utrecht expressing a modicum of surprise. But Geoffrey Fisher could not be persuaded to change his mind. To Robert Stopford he confessed that he would have wished to keep him 'a little longer' at Fulham but 'it can't be . . . The Church must have you at Peterborough. You must go there for the good of the Church.' So Robert Stopford went!

This was not the only case when Geoffrey Fisher erred in this way and his reply to Bell's criticisms was not very convincing and must have left him as bemused as before. He had tried to avoid this nomination but it proved quite impossible to exclude Stopford's claims.

In the course of 1957 Dr Simpson, Bishop of Southwark, intimated to the Archbishop his intention of resigning his See, upon which the Archbishop commended to the Crown, Mervyn Stockwood, vicar of the University Church in Cambridge. 'If he makes his mistakes', he commented, 'it is a very good place for him to make them in'. Negative commendation this may be, but sometimes to make mistakes is the road to maturity! In passing his name on to the Prime Minister, David Stephens agreed that Mervyn Stockwood was now at the height of his powers though from the political point of view a somewhat controversial character. Macmillan, heir to the nineteenth century liberal tradition at its best, appointed Mervyn Stockwood to Southwark and took a personal, if somewhat facetious, pride in so doing. Geoffrey Fisher wrote a truly archiepiscopal letter to the new recruit to the Bench: 'I do not know what fortunes await you as a Bishop. Of one thing I am pretty certain and that is that daily throughout your career your conviction will grow that the Holy Spirit had put you in this Office and that if anything goes wrong it is not a misreading of His will, but human failings in carrying it out.'

In July, F. A. Cockin resigned from the See of Bristol and Geoffrey Fisher sent to the Prime Minister as his only serious candidate the name of Oliver Tomkins, a great personal friend, and Warden of Lincoln Theological College, who had been involved intimately with the World Council of Churches at the time of its inception. The Prime Minister, with whom the Archbishop's relations were not universally friendly, in accepting this nomination protested that in principle he should be given more than one name; and in a similar situation later he claimed that such treatment was not consonant with the 'contract that you gave me for the appearance of a choice of some kind'. Recalling these incidents in July 1963, after his retirement, to the Church and State Commission Dr Fisher claimed that he had consulted widely but could not find anybody who was nearly as suitable. Indeed he was at the time experiencing increasing difficulty in finding people who really had the qualities needed for episcopal office. To David Stephens he complained: 'we have drained the reservoir dry at the moment'.

In such an institution as the Church of England bishop-making was bound to be a continuing as well as important preoccupation for any Archbishop of Canterbury; he could not escape from it. In 1959 several appointments required to be made, including the dioceses of Derby, Norwich and Truro. As to the first, Geoffrey Allen, Principal of Ripon Hall and formerly Bishop in Egypt, was pressed upon Geoffrey Fisher by the Prime Minister who probably felt, as did many Prime Ministers, that they ought to have a particular concern for those who had served the Church overseas. As to Norwich, vacant through the retirement of Dr Herbert and distinguished by its association with the Royal Family through Sandringham, the Archbishop circulated all his episcopal colleagues asking to be sent names of suitable persons for 'the rather feudal and slow-going people of Norfolk'. The result was the nomination of the excellent Launcelot Fleming.

In the case of Truro, Geoffrey Fisher was spurred into activity by a letter from its retiring bishop, Dr Morgan, who admitted realistically that he was beginning to slow down. 'Oh dear, oh dear', came the immediate reply. 'Every time there is a vacant bishopric we find it harder to get the right man.' Here he suggested the nomination of John Key, Bishop of Sherborne, who, passed over for Norwich, became a worthy bishop of Truro.

There certainly seemed to be signs that after some fifteen years selecting bishops Geoffrey Fisher was running a little out of steam if not growing somewhat weary. Though his stint was moving towards its close, he had yet two more diocesan appointments awaiting him before his retirement – Bath and Wells, and Blackburn. In conveying to the Prime Minister news of the impending vacancy in the former diocese the Archbishop commented that the diocese was situated in a lovely part of the world and that he himself would be 'very happy' to become its bishop! As it was he put forward the name of E. B. Henderson, Suffragan Bishop of Tewkesbury, who was duly appointed.

Blackburn, however, was to prove more difficult. Michael Ramsey, in his capacity as Archbishop of York, suggested four names. One of these was Ambrose Reeves, formerly Bishop of Johannesburg, who had distinguished himself in South Africa by his courageous, sustained and forthright opposition to the evil policy of apartheid. The Archbishop of Canterbury's letter to the Prime Minister, in response to this particular proposal, is sufficiently important to merit a mention.

He began by suggesting that the Prime Minister must decide 'whether it is politic at such a moment to put in an English diocese a Bishop around whom so many storms had arisen through his championing the cause of the indigenous African population'. He believed, however that Ambrose Reeves was genuinely concerned to promote reconciliation between black and white. In spite of this a very strongly critical view was entertained of him. If he were to be offered a diocese in England then Blackburn would be singularly appropriate. The letter concluded by suggesting three other names.

To many this letter will make rather unhappy reading, and some may question whether, if the Prime Minister were to exclude Ambrose Reeves on grounds of political expediency, it was up to the Archbishop to provide the ammunition to do so. As it was Bishop Claxton, and not Ambrose Reeves, went to Blackburn.

By and large, on his own admission, the Archbishop did not concern himself with appointments to deaneries and canonries, though in the latter part of his archiepiscopate he was frequently consulted about them by the Crown. One appointment to the Cathedral Church of the Diocese of London particularly engaged the Archbishop's attention in the summer of 1948. This began with a letter from Sir Anthony Bevir, acquainting him of Prime Minister Attlee's intention of appointing John Collins, founder of Christian Action and Dean of Oriel College, Oxford, to a canonry at St Paul's. He was impressed by the reports which he had received of his energy, administrative ability and scholarship. Such an appointment would give the chapter 'a man of character and active mind'. In arriving at this conclusion he, the Prime Minister, had examined the field but had found no one 'likely to prove so suitable'.

This was certainly not the view taken by Archbishop Fisher and on 15 June he wrote to Bevir stressing that 'he had a good deal of hesitation', shared by Wand, Bishop of London, concerning John Collins. They doubted whether he would prove an easy member of the Chapter, and might spend himself in interests of his own outside the Cathedral.

Here, however, fortunately, the Archbishop did not have his own way. On 25 June 1948 Clement Attlee informed him that he had considered the whole matter carefully, and was 'still inclined to prefer Collins' of whose character and ability he had 'personal experience'. He then added, somewhat surprisingly, that he was consulting the Palace about him. After doing so, the appointment went forward and St Paul's received one of its most distinguished Canons who, like Bell, came to enjoy, and deservedly so, a world-wide reputation for his fight against apartheid at a time when many churchmen bent over backwards to excuse it.

In 1955 another appointment to St Paul's caused comment of a different kind. As the result of a suggestion by Joost de Blank, then Bishop of Stepney, the name of the retiring Bishop of London, William Wand, came up for consideration in connection with his holding a canonry at this Cathedral. Anthony Bevir first introduced this possibility in a letter written to the Dean of St Paul's describing it as 'unprecedented'. If it were seriously contemplated it would be necessary to consult the new Bishop of London, as well as the Archbishop of Canterbury. When Geoffrey Fisher was first made privy to this proposal he was, and understandably, opposed to it. However, the Dean wrote saying that he himself was 'cordially' in favour. His preaching, he believed, would be good for the Cathedral and he was confident that the Bishop would work 'happily and loyally' with the rest of the Chapter, and 'scrupulously confine himself to the Cathedral'. Thus reassured the Archbishop gave his blessing to this unusual appointment, adding that he thought it unfair to ask the view of the new Bishop of London since he would be bound to say 'yes'. In fact it worked at one level well, since Dr Wand was scrupulous in not acting the bishop, and was a regular attender at services.

(ii)

As to suffragan Bishops the procedure was for the Diocesan to choose his own man since the appointment, in a sense, was personal to himself; but also, at the same time, to consult the Metropolitan of the Province, thus introducing into the process of selection a more objective reference. In addition the custom had grown up, in respect of the nominations of this category of bishops, for two names to be sent by the Archbishop to the Prime Minister, it being understood, without exception, that the first would be chosen. By this means, at least formally if fictionally, the Crown was provided with a choice and the royal prerogative thus respected. Geoffrey Fisher believed that it was prudent for the diocese to be consulted informally since, in many cases, its board of finance provided the stipend for the incoming bishop.

During Dr Fisher's tenure of office at Lambeth some twenty-six suffragan Bishops were appointed, of whom quite a few later became diocesans. Dr Fisher saw consultation with himself as an essential ingredient, and not something to be regarded as a mere formality. On one occasion, quite irregularly, when Geoffrey Fisher could not agree with the choice of the diocesan bishop, he sought to persuade the Prime Minister to pass on to the Crown the name of the second nominee. The Prime Minister replied that 'the custom of taking the first name automatically was so strong that he did not think it right to break it'.

The nomination of John Robinson, Dean of Clare College, Cambridge, by Mervyn Stockwood, Simpson's successor, to the suffragan see of Woolwich, led to an interesting correspondence in which the Bishop of the diocese, the Master of Clare College, and the Archbishop of York, all participated.

Mervyn Stockwood was determined to get the man of his own choosing, who he believed was uniquely fitted to pioneer a part-time clerical ministry and also to bring a greater theological emphasis to bear on the life of the diocese. On the other hand the Archbishop of

York and the Master of Clare believed that John Robinson should stay in Cambridge to continue his studies there. Geoffrey Fisher shared this view but did not wish to stand in the way of the Bishop of the diocese and passed his name on to the Prime Minister. So it was that *Honest to God* came to have an episcopal author, which certainly added to its interest and its sales.

The fiction of the second name and the comments made upon known 'non-starters' could lead to almost Gilbertian situations. At the request of the Bishop of Gloucester in 1955, in connection with the appointment of a suffragan as Bishop of Tewkesbury, the Archbishop enlightened him as to the usual procedure. The number two, he stressed, was never taken and he need not, therefore, be even told that his name was going forward to the Prime Minister unless the bishop wished to do so. On the other hand he must be a person whose record for the post sounds credible, on paper, to the Prime Minister. One therefore must not treat the second name too 'light-heartedly'.

The status of suffragan bishops was a matter which concerned Geoffrey Fisher greatly. Of course their general happiness and fulfilment depended largely on easy relations with the Diocesan who had appointed them to their office. They possessed no legally defined area of jurisdiction and when the bishop who nominated them either retired, was translated or died, life for the suffragan bishop could be difficult. But for the theologically-minded suffragans more important was the real nature of their function. Here bishops held different views. Ought not, some asked, every bishop in the exercise of his ministry to have grouped around him, integrated with his 'familia', his fellow presbyters and the laity. Cut off from these was he not maimed, an isolated figure, almost a Melchisedec without ancestry, unable to realize or fulfil his true episcopate? In June 1959, Geoffrey Fisher drew up a paper: 'The Place of Suffragan Bishops in the Synodical Government of the Church'. It was not a document which could claim to have theological depth. This was not its intention nor, probably, was Geoffrey Fisher particularly interested in this aspect of a complex problem. Rather he was particularly concerned to solve certain practical problems. Formerly suffragan bishops had, for the most part, held the office of archdeacon together with a benefice which had the effect of integrating them with the diocesan structure. Now, since the Church Commissioners had provided them with independent stipends, this was no longer the case. As a consequence they ceased to sit in Convocation or the Church Assembly, a deprivation which led to frustration. This could be remedied, so Geoffrey Fisher suggested, by their being summoned to one of these bodies as a recognised group, even if they were not given full voting rights.

During Geoffrey Fisher's sixteen years at Lambeth over fifty diocesan bishops were appointed in the Provinces of Canterbury and York. We have endeavoured to give a somewhat selective survey, taken from Geoffrey Fisher's correspondence at Lambeth, which illustrates how the nomination of bishops worked in practice independently of any theory or *rationale* as to the essence of episcopacy as such. The appointment system had never been devised formally around a table but had evolved over the years. However, in the twentieth century this customary procedure was beginning to have its critics. Unease at the way episcopal appointments were made was voiced even before the Second World War, and in June 1939 the Church Assembly resolved: 'That while valuing the establishment of the Church of England as an expression of the Nation's recognition of religion, the Church of England nevertheless is of the opinion that the present form impedes the fulfilment of the responsibilities of the Church as a spiritual society' – a declaration which aroused the intense ire of Professor Norman Sykes. However, before the year ended, Britain was again at war and national energies were directed towards winning it. In the two decades following the cessation of hostilities knowledgeable churchmen, both clerical and lay, took up again the long-deferred debate. In 1946, Lord Justice Vaisey, a keen member of the Church of England, called together an informal but distinguished group consisting, *inter alia*, of the Dean of Winchester (Selwyn); Professor Mortimer (later to become Bishop of Exeter); Dr Jalland (an ecclesiastical historian); and Professor Jacob of Manchester University. The task its members set themselves was to review the whole structure of the appointment system. By November 1946 they had made sufficient progress to send in a report to Lambeth. Central to their criticisms of the existing procedure was the method by which the selective process was effected and particularly the dominance of the State in the final decision-making. Thus they proposed to offset this imbalance by requiring the Prime Minister to put his nominee before the Chapter of the Diocese concerned, which would then be free to accept or reject him. If it chose the latter, the Prime Minister would need to think again and come back with a further name or names. They also suggested that the penalties of praemunire should be abolished as also the Crown's entitlement to appoint by letters patent. However, the group would wish to retain the confirmation of episcopal election, and also the unfettered right of the Archbishop of Canterbury to refuse to consecrate if in conscience he felt unable to do so. This initial report concluded with the sensible submission that the group would not wish to continue to meet 'unless some measure of support and sympathy' for their doing so was forthcoming from both Archbishops.

After conferring with Cyril Garbett the Archbishop replied with a not discouraging letter but felt it incumbent to say that so long as the establishment of the Church of England obtained, the proposals put forward by Vaisey's group were extremely difficult to implement since by giving a virtual veto to the cathedral chapter they invaded the prerogative of the Crown. Indeed, it was doubtful whether the Supreme Governor could, or ought, to allow himself to be placed in this position. All that the Church could hope for was to build up customary procedures which would enable its voice to be heard more effectively than at present in the preliminary stages.

Vaisey acknowledged this letter, promising to share it with his colleagues but the papers at Lambeth are silent as to any further developments. The probability is that the group met no more and was disbanded, deterred by obvious legal difficulties inherent in the establishment. Geoffrey Fisher was not, however, ungrateful for the initiative which Lord Justice Vaisey had taken.

This matter of the royal prerogative was to loom large in any advice given to the Archbishop by the Crown lawyers. Thus Sir Harold Kent, HM Procurator-General and Treasury Solicitor, advised the Archbishop that many of the reforms being mooted could not be achieved by an ecclesiastical measure or parliamentary legislation since they might prove damaging to the interests of the Crown. The price of securing them could well entail another Royal Commission leading to disestablishment, and this at all costs the Archbishop wished to avoid.

What Geoffrey Fisher at that time feared did in part happen for the Moberly Commission on Crown Appointments, set up in 1949, reported back in 1952. This Commission in itself sparked off a general discussion as to how far the present system was right in principle or worked well in practice.

It was to be expected that in any such discussion it was episcopal appointments which would take pride of place, whether in Convocation or the Church Assembly or at Bishops' Meetings. Many were the letters on this subject which the Archbishop received, and on which he commented freely. For example, to Lord Selborne he wrote agreeing that nominations to the Crown should remain with the Prime Minister, but that the role of the Archbishop should be strengthened. He did not agree, however, that the Church as such should have a power of veto, since it might prejudice the free and informal talks in which Archbishop and Prime Minister engaged. To Sir Ernest Barker, who had written an article on episcopal appointments in *The Frontier*, the Archbishop admitted, though most reluctantly, that he might accept an advisory committee if only 'to allay the suspicions of some stupid people' who believe that an Archbishop 'always chooses wrongly if left to himself'. Geoffrey Fisher did not believe that any occupant of Lambeth would use his powers to advance his own political interests, though he fully recognised that this had been the case in the past. There could be situations, he acknowledged, if rarely, when the Archbishop would prefer not to have the invidious responsibility of choosing between the names which had come up to the Prime Minister. Where the Archbishop agreed with some critics – perhaps he remembered the strictures of Clement Attlee – was in the need to cast the net more widely when it came to choosing the personnel of the Bench. Within three years of his going to Lambeth he circularized, with the approval of Dr Garbett, all the diocesan bishops asking them to send in names of any priests known to themselves, inside or outside their diocese, whom they thought should be considered for episcopal office. The replies back to Lambeth certainly proved useful and some of those suggested actually went on to become bishops either at home or overseas. However, lists grow out of date and some four years later – and indeed from time to time throughout his Archiepiscopate – Geoffrey Fisher repeated the same request, asking the bishops whether they would think a diocese in England or overseas the more suitable. However, to the Howicke Commission, which met after his retirement, he confessed that the hopes which he entertained from these efforts were not realised, since many of the names which came in he knew already. Also the bishops were obviously diffident and he found they responded more readily to the direct question: 'Is X the right man for this particular diocese rather than who is the right man?' 'You have to do the spade work yourself' was his realistic conclusion. Maybe Geoffrey Fisher's own estimate on the value of these lists of episcopal possibilities was a little too pessimistic. Certainly John Hewitt, giving evidence before the same Commission, claimed that they were a step in the right direction. The Archbishop consistently maintained that people were wrong in supposing that there was an abundant supply of clergymen with the gifts necessary in a bishop, that is of winning confidence in the diocese and the Church as a whole. Facetiously he remarked that the days were gone when in the process of selection one could or ought to say: 'Well, here are all these professors and editors of Greek plays, and so forth – which of them shall we choose?' It could be that the First World War, in eliminating a whole generation, was in a measure responsible for the paucity in episcopal material.

Others, who took this view believed that this shortage of supply, in so far as it existed, was due to the lack of effective lay participation in selection and, paradoxically, the excessive power of the Prime Minister. The Archbishop did not share this opinion, maintaining that the system of private consultation which had developed across the years was adequate to ensure that the best interests of the Church were fully safeguarded. Thus though he himself originally supported a proposal for the setting up by the Church Assembly of an Ecclesiastical Advisory Committee consisting of three bishops, three non-episcopal clergy and three laymen, he withdrew from this position at the Moberly Commission though he did not totally reject it.

Basically in this area – it was by no means always the case – Geoffrey Fisher took a conservative view being chary of disturbing long-established custom unless there were overriding reasons for so doing. In support of this approach he regarded it as significant that successive commissions over the previous twenty-five years had decided that the system of appointment by the Crown on the nomination of the Prime Minister should remain. Consistently, as we have seen, Geoffrey Fisher contended that consultation with the Prime Minister had proved of great assistance to successive archbishops since Downing Street had sources of information not always available to Lambeth. 'After all,' he commented, 'no man is Prime Minister of this country without a great deal of exercise of judgement on persons and facts, and his judgement may, between three equally good people, be a relevant factor which I do not wish to denigrate at all.' Where some complained of 'mystique' and an impenetrable private huddle, Geoffrey Fisher saw a much needed confidentiality, which annoyed him when broken.

It will be seen that the Archbishop's attitude was in the main pragmatic. For him the question 'does it work?' – it is, incidentally, sometimes difficult to know precisely what this means or what the yardstick is – took precedence over nice theological arguments as to the nature of the Church and the secularity of the State. The relationship between the two societies would vary according to time, place and circumstance. However, he was certainly not averse to all change on principle, far from it. The *congé d'élire* (freedom to elect) was a 'nonsense' and the Act of Praemunire which visited summary punishment upon recalcitrant chapters who refused to vote for the Crown's nominee must not continue in its present form; also the Royal Warrant with its 'pains and penalties' clauses should be got rid of altogether. However, he did not believe, as did Vaisey's group, that there ought to be, as recommended in 1939, some institutionalized, built-in, mandatory system which ensured the interest of the Church in a wider consultative process. Geoffrey Fisher did not see things this way.

Convinced believer in the establishment as he was and remained, he yet held 'that one basic principle is beyond dispute, that the Church has from Christ full responsibility for the appointing of its own bishops to be chief pastors for the edifying and self-government of the Church of Christ'. If not free to do this the Church would need to take stock of its situation and if it could no longer freely authenticate its own life, then 'Establishment would have to go'. As it was the existing political climate did not, in his opinion, require this. However, there were some churchmen, in reverse, who regarded the existing system not as giving excessive powers to the State through the Prime Minister but to the

Church through the Archbishop, particularly when he was dealing with non-knowledgeable, non-interested heads of Government. Thus Dr Alec Vidler, Dean of King's College, Cambridge, suspected that the Prime Minister could be used as a smokescreen to mask what was in fact exclusively archiepiscopal nomination. Hence he deplored Dr Fisher's statement to the Crown Appointments Commission that he had, in practice, a veto on appointments. Doubtless Alec Vidler's was a minority view particularly offensive to High Church Anglicans though the number of those who shared it was not inconsiderable. It was also probably true that the Archbishop, to allay fears of Erastianism and State domination, tended to overplay his own hand.,

Can it be fairly claimed that the undoubtedly powerful influence exercised by Geoffrey Fisher on the appointment of bishops was on the whole salutary so far as the life and witness of the Church of England was concerned? This is a question, of course, to which there can, in the nature of the case, be no definitive answer. Indeed the criteria of judgement are ill-defined even as to what constitutes a good bishop. Certainly Dr Bell thought that the Archbishop was over-cautious; that he tended to fight shy of unusual and exceptional men for fear that they might 'rock the boat'. This preference for mediocrity, so he believed, was likely to have deleterious effects on the vitality of the Church of England in the next twenty years. But was Dr Bell right? Many will have their doubts. As to the quality of the bishops it needs to be remembered that quite a few distinguished men – Max Warren, for example, and I could quote others – whom he pressed to become bishops resolutely declined.

Certainly the Archbishop did not see himself as opting for solid worth at the expense of unusual priests with exceptional gifts, if he could find them.

It is also true that during the sixteen years of Geoffrey Fisher's archiepiscopate the process of consultation had been extended and institutionalized. The way was in fact being prepared for Mr Callaghan who, when Prime Minister (1976–1979), by a gentleman's agreement with the Archbishop of Canterbury promised in his episcopal nominations to the Crown to limit his choice to one of two names submitted to him by the Church's own Board. This was in fact a radical change for it meant the initiative now lay with the Church and the power exercised by the Prime Minister was made subservient to it. However, the Establishment, if eroded, yet remained.

(iii)

There were over seventy diocesan bishops holding office during Geoffrey Fisher's reign at Lambeth most of whom he had a hand in appointing. It was as natural as inevitable that he should regard himself as standing in a special relationship with them. Many were the occasions when he visited their dioceses maybe for some special domestic event; for a national commemoration; or, more rarely, for a consecration. Frequently they would seek his advice and he supported them in illness. The bishops were brought corporately together into the Upper Houses of the Convocations of Canterbury and York; also into the Church Assembly. In addition, the bishops of both Provinces had their regular meetings at Lambeth chaired by the Archbishop – of which more later.

Particularly important for any Primate of All England was his relationship with his fellow Metropolitan of York; not least how effectively they worked together, and respected each other. When Geoffrey Fisher took over at Lambeth, Cyril Garbett had been some three years in this office and was firmly entrenched. The two were, in fact, close personal friends and Geoffrey Fisher regularly consulted him and greatly admired his judgement. So close was their intimacy that Garbett had his own private room at Lambeth where he always stayed when in London – he was unmarried – thus enabling them easily and regularly to confer on matters of mutual concern. A familiar sight was to see him arriving at the Palace laden with a case full of papers.

It was important that relations between Canterbury and York should be right not least because each headed his own Convocation, and it could be difficult if tensions between them got out of hand. Interesting in this context is a handwritten letter with which the Primate of All England greeted his brother Primate's eightieth birthday. 'I am in the Cotswolds for a few days' relief', he wrote, 'and from here send this salutation. The right word to describe what I feel towards you is, I think *homage*, the kind of devotion one feels for one of royal stature – this is what you are in the Church, with all that royalty stands for – authority, influence, leadership and popular trust, and the power to uplift and inspire. With ever deeper emotion, I thank you for your goodness to me for these last ten years, so patient with my impetuosities and delays, and so affectionate and wise in your co-operation.' This is no formal tribute and though obviously designed to please, it rings true, suggesting that within their relationship there was a dimension of respect leading almost to reverence. Garbett was not an easy man to get to know intimately but Geoffrey Fisher seems to have succeeded in 'crossing the divide'. On his part, the Archbishop of York was one of Dr Fisher's most consistent supporters. Thus, when the *Sunday Express* in November 1955 indulged in one of its customary anti-Church of England vendettas, majoring on the Archbishop, he comforted him with the words: 'There has been no time when your prestige was higher and your influence been greater, both in Church and Nation, than at the present time'.

Geoffrey Fisher visited the Archbishop of York during his final illness and at his memorial service recalled 'the strength of his aquiline features and manner of speech; the strength of his opinions tenaciously held and trenchantly expressed; the strength to carry other people's burdens, and always in the thick of the fight for righteousness and against the evils which he so detested – a glorious example, in its very highest, of the spiritual grace and genius of the Church of England'.

The choice of the Bishop of Durham, Michael Ramsey, as Cyril Garbett's successor was almost inevitable and indeed widely welcomed. However, for Geoffrey Fisher, Michael Ramsey at York with all his virtues and personal sanctity was not so congenial as the presence there of his predecessor. They were in many ways two different people in churchmanship, in temperament and interests. Thus, not surprisingly, relations between them were often, particularly in the latter years, edgy and uneasy, and were not helped by the fact that Michael Ramsey was at Repton when the Archbishop was his headmaster.

Geoffrey Fisher represented a middle-of-the-road position within the *Ecclesia Anglicana*, and sought to encourage the evangelicals to play their full part in the life of the Church. He did not believe in organic re-union, certainly not in any foreseeable future, nor did he hold ultimate, ontological convictions as to the *esse* of the historic episcopate in the same way as did his brother of York. Michael Ramsey entertained a 'high' view of the episcopal office, and opposed any attempt to compromise its apostolic integrity even in the supposed interest of a more rapid re-union. Geoffrey Fisher was ebullient, a 'workamaniac', extremely forthcoming with a genuine if extrovert interest in other people. Michael Ramsey, on the other hand, was shy, gauche, bereft of small talk and finding it difficult at times to communicate though this did not mean he lacked concern for people. He could be admirably relaxed with young theological students when they were peppering him with questions. He never ceased himself to be a student; had spiritual depth; great inner resources, and pronounced moral courage. It is perhaps sad that Michael Ramsey's holding such time-consuming ecclesiastical offices precluded the possibility of his writing the really 'big book' of which he was most certainly capable. Geoffrey Fisher, on the other hand, was highly intelligent but on his own admission lacked the instincts of the scholar, being more interested in people than in ideas and suspicious of 'nit-picking theologians'. One often gets the impression, maybe quite falsely, that with their differing gifts each felt a measure of inferiority if only subliminally in the presence of the other. In lighter vein we may hazard the opinion that if these two men were rolled into one the result might well be the emergence of the complete Archbishop of Canterbury; alas! the Deity does not seem to contrive things this way.

It is inevitable, human nature being what it is, that an archbishop should tend to gravitate to one bishop rather than another. For Mervyn Haigh, Bishop of Winchester, Geoffrey Fisher entertained a great admiration; thought highly of his talents, and consulted him frequently. This was particularly the case in connection with the Lambeth Conference of 1948. Some bishops became personal friends as for example Cuthbert Bardsley (Coventry), Vernon Smith (Leicester), David Say (Rochester), Donald Coggan, who finally followed him to Canterbury, Montgomery Campbell (London) and Oliver Tomkins (Bristol). Maybe a word should be said of Geoffrey Fisher's relationship with Robert Stopford who held a multiplicity of posts in education; as Bishop of Fulham, Peterborough and London. As his biographer writes it was a relationship crucial to his advancement. 'He was very much Fisher's man, and was prepared to accept the role which Fisher wanted him to enact.' However, Stopford was basically a shy man, and his relationship to Geoffrey Fisher seems to lack warmth and was confined to ecclesiastical affairs. Many have said that it was Geoffrey Fisher's wish that he should follow him to Canterbury, but there seems little evidence to support this. Usually those who worked closely with him became friends. This does not seem the case with Stopford.

Geoffrey Fisher, though some of the bishops questioned this, believed that certain committees or boards set up by the Church Assembly should have episcopal chairmen. With these, of course, the Archbishop was at times in close contact. The Archbishop's own ecumenical committee thus saw much of him.

Though it was not one of his major interests, the Archbishop corresponded regularly with Bishop Colin Dunlop of Jarrow, Chairman of the Liturgical Commission. Left to himself Geoffrey Fisher would probably have been content with the 1662 and 1928 Liturgy subject to a few minimal changes. In this respect he regarded himself as taking a commonsensical, almost layman's, point of view. Thus when Colin Dunlop informed him that his Commission had spent several hours discussing theologically the difference in the Communion Rite between the Offertory and the Eucharistic oblation, but had arrived at no definitive answer, he replied trenchantly, expressing no surprise at this failure. 'How many discussions end in that way', he commented. 'All I would suggest is this. I hope as you get on with your work you won't spend too much time discussing questions which if I dare say so, do not really admit of any final answer and [should] not really be asked at all. I have noticed in many different ways how much time and energy the Church, or its theologians, spend in trying to find inconclusive answers to questions where the answer cannot be objective, and can only depend upon how people tend to feel.'

Sometimes when he visited a cathedral he came away in a somewhat critical mood. Such was the case at Southwark where the Provost was George Reindorp, later Bishop of Guildford and then of Salisbury. It was his conviction that the service for the consecration of bishops, when many lay people, not zealous churchgoers were present, was far too long. He, therefore, shortened the singing of the litany in procession. The Archbishop was certainly not pleased particularly since he feared lest the Provost's shortening should prove the thin edge of the proverbial wedge. As he put it, he did not believe that the extreme length of the service ought to be deplored. 'For my own part', he informed the Provost, 'I find that the flow and rhythm and progress of the service is so superb that it carries me along with it without any sense of tedium or distraction at all.' He had also heard with great regret, that the Provost and Bishop had 'played about' with the ordination service. In general he believed the services in the Book of Common Prayer 'stand beyond criticism'. New ways of 'disordering [were] always dangerous and encouraged that very lawlessness' which he deplored. Thus he was not prepared, he wrote, 'to authorize any shortening of the liturgy at all'.

On many occasions irregularities were brought to the Archbishop's notice in which case he would complain to the bishop concerned. Hence he expressed his displeasure to Dr Robert Mortimer, Bishop of Exeter, for wearing white gloves – or were they red? – at a service in the Cathedral; also when Princess Margaret distributed bibles at an Ordination of priests in Southwark Cathedral. At other times he would be called in for advice and arbitration when difficulties were dividing a cathedral community as, for example, at Coventry and Guildford.

The correspondence between Mervyn Stockwood, Bishop of Southwark, and Geoffrey Fisher is always interesting, indeed entertaining, showing that in spite of their being mutually critical at times, at one level they understood each other. On first going to his diocese the Archbishop gave him two objectives: (1) 'to bridge the gap between the Church and the vast untouched masses of people in his diocese'; (2) 'to introduce liturgical order'. The Archbishop later admitted that the Bishop had 'jumped into these tasks with both feet'. Letters of advice flowed from Lambeth to Southwark in response to many enquiries. What ought he to do, Mervyn asked, with those who refuse to receive the cup at services of holy communion? The response was immediate; 'it is a piece of bad manners and before long they will grow tired of it. But meanwhile we should not (and cannot) *force* them to communicate in both kinds. The congregation must endure them just as they have to endure their [other] stupidities.'

Certainly in these early days Mervyn Stockwood had his teething troubles and was appreciative of the help the Archbishop gave him. 'I do want you to know', he wrote, 'how much I treasure your wonderful friendship since my consecration. As you know better than anybody, life has not been easy during the past six months but it has made all the difference to know that you have been at my side to advise and encourage and to be a friend. For that and much more – I am deeply grateful.' This is no formal letter, and it pointed to a mutually trustful relationship. 'I have enjoyed you and hope always to enjoy you because after my own heart you courageously take and give both advice and rebuke!' – so Geoffrey Fisher responded.

Geoffrey Fisher's correspondence at Lambeth makes it clear, as we might expect, that he acted in the capacity of a pastor to many a bishop in his hour of need. We take one letter almost at random, when Henry Skelton, Bishop of Lincoln, was struck down with a severe coronary thrombosis. 'The great thing for the moment is that you have come through this danger. Your only job at present is to be quiet and content in bed and during the months of rest that must follow not allowing yourself to fret or be impatient. The Bishop of Dorchester had exactly the same attack and treatment. When I saw him the other day – and his looks bore him out – he said that he had never been better in his life. So, just wait for returning strength – and *enjoy* the rest and let it do its full work in you. There is no need for you to look further ahead – but let me say this much. I have every reason to suppose that you can and ought to take up your work at Lincoln again – at first going slow, no doubt, and for all I know never going *quite* so fast as you used to. But that is what I hope and expect – and what I am sure the diocese hopes and expects.'

This is indeed an encouraging letter – but the bishop finally had no option but to retire.

Geoffrey Fisher often said, in differing contexts, that the Church of England did not know how best to use its bishops, a criticism which he believed to be equally true of the Roman Catholic Church. Hence the Archbishop's relations corporately with the episcopate are for many reasons important. By and large, on major issues, Geoffrey Fisher wished the bishops to stand together once Convocation or the Church Assembly had come to a decision. 'To go it alone' was not to be encouraged though respect must be shown to the individual conscience. Important in the collective life of the episcopate were the long-established Bishops' Meetings held at Lambeth which go back at least to the seventeenth century and were held regularly three or four times a year. These were private and confidential and access to whatever minutes were kept was strictly forbidden to the outsider. This confidentiality was at times attacked and often resented. Thus the Reverend C. E. Douglas referred to 'secret meetings behind locked doors'. Such an innuendo, so Geoffrey Fisher maintained, was singularly inept since all that the bishops discussed must come before Convocation or the

Church Assembly if decision making proved necessary. However, in the face of this criticism, the Archbishop called a small group of clergy to Lambeth and read to them the agendas for the last two meetings which in their content certainly did not suggest a cloak-and-dagger conspiracy of silence. Of course, each archbishop had his own way of doing things and this was reflected in his handling of these regular 'get-togethers'. At least one member of the Bench, the Bishop of Sheffield, felt that they took on a different character with the advent of Geoffrey Fisher. Under both Lang and Temple such occasions tended to be 'informal and brotherly' whereas Dr Fisher used them, with some success, as a means of 'closing episcopal ranks on some controversial issues'. At Bishops' Meetings, so Oliver Tomkins writes, a somewhat antiquated decorum obtained. Gaiters were *de riguer* and Mervyn Stockwood's lack of them was not approved. 'If I take the trouble to dress properly, I expect the same of you'. The Bishops addressed each other like Shakespearean characters such as 'Rochester, what do you think?'

The change of mood, or shall we say the different approach, which according to Leslie Hunter characterized the Bishops' Meetings when Geoffrey Fisher took over, does not mean that the Archbishop's relations with his episcopal colleagues were other than cordial, particularly in the early and middle years of his archiepiscopate. They appreciated his sense of purpose, general liveliness and highly developed sense of humour. Of course, as with most corporate bodies meeting regularly, feelings and tempers could run high. Thus Dr Ralph Taylor, Bishop of Sodor and Man, complained bitterly to the Archbishop that when he spoke on the subject of 'a theological college for women' he was all the time 'interrupted and heckled'. After expressing his 'deep distress', the Archbishop replied that bishops were quite frequently interrupted and perhaps there was too much of it. Indeed, he regarded himself 'as guilty as anybody else'. This, however, was by no means the only complaint. In July 1952 the Bishop of Chichester complained to Geoffrey Fisher that the agendas for the Bishops' Meetings were too full, and that so many administrative matters were included that there was little time to discuss important questions of Church policy. Such views, it may be noticed, had been expressed at a Bishops' Meeting as early as 1944 when Temple was in charge. Spencer Leeson of Peterborough believed that the effect and influence for good of these Bishops' Meetings could be strengthened if they started with half an hour in Lambeth Parish Church. Also items on the agenda should be cut down and resolutions only included in the minutes. Regular reports should be shortened and time provided at each meeting for a number of topics of current and general spiritual importance; more members should be encouraged to speak.

As the years went by and the Church Assembly became more structured, many diocesan bishops began to feel they were undertaking more and more ploys, thereby neglecting their real responsibilities as Fathers in God. Also many felt that Geoffrey Fisher was becoming more dictatorial and argumentative. These and other kindred matters were brought before a Bishops' Meeting in January 1956 at which two papers were read by the Bishops of Sheffield and Gloucester. Put simply, the gravamen of their grievances was that they were kept far too busy, often with small and insignificant matters, and wished to shed part of this load.

The bishops now followed up this initiative by arranging a residential episcopal conference, to which there were also invited six Welsh and two Scottish bishops, at Westcott House, Cambridge, in June 1959. The Archbishop of Canterbury was present, though he found it difficult to fit this 'new type of meeting' into his diary and was consequently forced to be away in London one evening. A number of papers were given including 'The Determining of Priorities in Church of England Policy' (the Bishop of Manchester); 'The Future of the Anglican Communion and the Role of the Lambeth Conference Within It' (the Bishop of Chichester); and 'The Church's Approach to Industry' (the Archbishop of York and the Bishop of Sheffield).

The Conference proved to be a remarkable occasion as is made evident in the notes drawn up by Geoffrey Fisher himself and his chaplain. They record that the Archbishop was 'very restrained' at the outset, but later became voluble. The discussion roamed widely, the bishops taking full advantage of this unique opportunity to give vent to their long pent-up frustrations. They were clearly apprehensive of the growth of the Boards set up by the Church Assembly and their increasing dominance in deciding policy, which had the effect of weakening the status of Convocation. Reflections around these themes served to open the floodgates and various expedients were suggested to lighten the episcopal load such as more delegation; that institutions of incumbents be confined to the cathedral leaving archdeacons to hold their inductions in the parishes; that bishops should have ten weeks' annual leave; that all diocesans should have a full-time chaplain; that they accept fewer invitations to preach sermons or chair conferences. At a point Michael Ramsey, who in his inimitable way dominated the discussion with a minimum of talk, complained that they had wandered away from the original reason for being at Westcott. What the bishops really wanted was to distance themselves from the administrative machinery at the centre, thus enabling them to exercise an effective leadership in their own diocese. For example, the 'committee capacity' of the York Convocation had been strained to near breaking-point. Leonard Wilson, the saintly Bishop of Birmingham, complained that many of them had gained the impression that they were not expected to enter into discussions at Bishops' Meetings; while the lively and newly-appointed Bishop of Southwark added that it seemed not the done thing to contradict the chairman.

In reply to this orgy of criticisms the Archbishop insisted that he welcomed free and frank discussion of contemporary issues. He much regretted that of late too much time had been devoted to emphasizing worship at the expense of morals, and on the Church rather than on the Gospel — an observation that was by no means acceptable to Michael Ramsey — and he said so!

Deep down, the Archbishop must have found this 'mini-rebellion' gravely disturbing, and he could not have been happy at the evident fear of some bishops that the Church was in process of being too highly organised with too many regulations and rigid structures. Clearly there was a mood of frustration increased by the bishops being 'together in one place'.

The remaining months of Geoffrey Fisher's archiepiscopate were never more busy — with visits to Africa and the Far East, not to mention his pilgrimage to Jerusalem, Istanbul and Rome. If any radical steps needed to be taken by the Archbishop it was too late for him to do much about it. Nor must we take these complaints at face value. What they may well register, however, was that the time was drawing ever nearer when Geoffrey Fisher ought to lay aside his monumental labours.

CHAPTER 22

The Coronation of Queen Elizabeth II

ON the morning of 6 February 1952, Geoffrey Fisher was confined to bed with bronchitis, a rare experience for him, though he was able, assisted by his chaplains, to deal with his correspondence in the usual way. At 9.15 am a telephone message came through from Major Edward Ford, the King's Private Secretary, informing him that George VI had died at Sandringham during the night. The new Queen, Princess Elizabeth, with her husband the Prince Philip, Duke of Edinburgh, were at that moment in Kenya on their way to Australia and New Zealand.

The death of the King, if not its suddenness, could not have taken the Archbishop completely by surprise, for he was one of the few who knew how serious his physical condition had been for some time. As far back as December 1948, the King was afflicted with a 'tiresome' illness and wrote somewhat sadly to the Archbishop: 'I do need to let up from work for a time, I feel. These last twelve years have been a trial for all of us, and I have had my full share of anxieties. But I have derived comfort from the many letters I have received from all kinds of people sending me their sympathy and not a few containing cures for all diseases excepting my own.' He was, in fact, suffering from a form of thrombosis and early arterial sclerosis.

The King had been operated on in March 1949, the Archbishop being assured at the time by Sir Alan Lascelles, his Private Secretary, that the surgery, in itself, had undoubtedly been successful. His health, however, continued to give cause for anxiety and when a further operation for cancer became necessary in September 1951 the Queen and her children received the Sacrament together from the Archbishop in Lambeth Palace Chapel. This enabled her, she wrote, 'to face that nightmare day with a renewed and strengthened faith.' Sunday 2 December 1951 was decreed a Day of National Prayer, when services of thanksgiving were held up and down the country for the King's recovery. George VI, for a short time, felt himself to be making progress and so apprised the Archbishop. 'Your prayers and those of countless others helped me so much at the time of anxiety concerning myself, and they have surely been answered in a most wonderful way. I am feeling much better and a stay here in the Norfolk air will, I am sure, do me all the good in the world.' His last public appearance was at an Installation of the Knights of the Bath in Westminster Abbey. On

31 January 1952 he seemed well enough to wave goodbye to Princess Elizabeth and the Duke of Edinburgh as they left London Airport for their protracted tour overseas. On 6 February he died.

As soon as the Archbishop heard the sad news his first care was to convey his grief and sympathy to Queen Elizabeth, and to various members of the Royal Family including Queen Mary to whom, understandably, it came as a shattering blow. The Archbishop also rang up Dr Percy Herbert, Bishop of Norwich and Clerk of the Closet, asking him to minister pastorally at Sandringham to the Queen Mother and to act for him in anything relating to the funeral.

On the morning of the King's death the Executive Committee of the World Council of Churches was meeting in Lambeth Palace when the news was brought to its members; the deliberations were immediately interrupted and the Bishop of Chichester conducted a service in the chapel. The Archbishop meanwhile telephoned a message for the Nation to the Press Association and the religious papers.

Over the years a ritual pattern following the death of a sovereign had been established and it was felt to be important that this should be meticulously observed. Fortunately a file for the death of King George V had been deposited at Lambeth and it was a matter of devouring its contents and securing their implementation. The Archbishop of Canterbury was required by an Order in Council to draw up a special form of service for use in the parishes. Meanwhile, the Deans of St Paul's and Westminster invited him to preach on the following Sunday but his doctor, Wilfrid Dykes Bower, advised that in view of his indisposition he should certainly not accept.

Confined as he thus was to his room it was necessary to secure deputies to act for him at the various formalities consequent upon a monarch's death. Thus the Archbishop of York and the Bishop of London were both present at a special meeting of the Privy Council for drawing up the time-honoured proclamation. The Bishop of Chichester undertook to conduct prayers in the House of Lords.

Lambeth, as might be expected, was inundated with enquiries from diocesan bishops as to how, *inter alia*, they should amend the State Prayers. Many overseas Churches of the Anglican Communion, as well as Orthodox and others, requested that their message of sympathy should be forwarded to the Queen and the Queen Mother. In the late afternoon of 7 February the young Queen Elizabeth and the Duke of Edinburgh arrived back at London Airport. The Archbishop's illness prevented, much to his regret, his being present to welcome the new monarch as she stepped on English soil for the first time as sovereign.

The overriding priority was now to organise the Lying-in-State. Here the Archbishop was fortunate since he had available a detailed account, drawn up by Alan Don, when Archbishop Lang's Chaplain, of the ceremonial used for George V some sixteen years earlier in Westminster Hall, and also for his funeral in St George's Chapel, Windsor. The policy was to follow this customary procedure, though if this were done too slavishly the Archbishop feared lest an unhappy controversy might follow. The reasons for this may be briefly stated.

George VI was, of course, not only King of England but also of the United Kingdom; this meant that Scottish sentiment, which found a voice in the Established Church of that land, was sensitive to what it properly regarded as its rights and privileges. The theft of the Stone of Scone from the Abbey on Christmas Eve 1951 had not lessened that feeling.

The Archbishop of Canterbury was well aware of this delicate situation and had he not been, Alan Don, a dour Scotsman from Dundee and Dean of Westminster, would most certainly have reminded him. Thus when the Moderator of the General Assembly of the Church of Scotland wrote asking that he might be allowed to attend the royal interment at Windsor, the Archbishop supported this request and at the same time asked the authorities that a similar invitation be sent to the Moderator of the Free Church Federal Council. It needs to be said that the Archbishop would have approved treating the Roman Catholic Archbishop of Wesminster in the same way had he not known that the Cardinal would have declined such an invitation. So it was that only the Moderators were present.

Thus the solemn ritual now began to unfold itself. The Archbishop was unable to officiate at the ceremony which preceded the Lying-in State in Westminster Hall; but he was fit enough to make the journey to Windsor for the King's funeral. The ritual pattern of the King's passing was now complete as the Lord Chamberlain broke his wand of office over his Sovereign's grave. The Archbishop also gave an address to a packed congregation in St Paul's Cathedral on 17 February when, referring to the service in St George's Chapel, he expressed himself with an unusual eloquence. A few lines which refer to the service at Windsor may be quoted:

'The Nation, the Commonwealth, the World, with measured tread and muffled drums and solemn hearts brought to the Chapel the mortal remains of the King, and all that still belonged to this world, and stopped there away from the world on which the battle had been fought, into the profound and powerful peace of the House of God . . . The trumpets of faith were resounding all about us, touching with that comfort human sorrow and translating time's utterances into eternal truths.'

Few denied that, called unexpectedly to a high and unique office in critical days, George VI had overcome a natural diffidence and served his people extremely well.

There was a long-established and amply documented procedure for the organisation of a coronation which was almost immediately set in motion. What was known as the Coronation Commission was now called together with the Duke of Edinburgh as its chairman, this being a prelude to the Privy Council appointing a Coronation Committee which would nominate its own executive. The overall responsibility for the ceremony fell by tradition to the Duke of Norfolk, the Earl Marshal, while responsibility for drawing up the Rite fell to the Archbishop of Canterbury. Obviously, in the smooth-running of the extensive preparations much depended upon the ease and manner in which these two worked with each other. One limitation was, from the outset, imposed upon the general planning. In 1936 it would have been thought almost indecent to talk about money. In 1952 it was recognised that regard must be had for financial considerations.

A few words about the Coronation Rite itself may be helpful at this point as an introduction to the significant role which the Archbishop played in determining its precise structure, and the manner in which it was to be carried out.

Over many centuries Primates of All England had established a customary right to officiate and preside over the supreme act of crowning and anointing the Sovereign. In its origin the Coronation Rite goes back to distant days when the Germanic ruler upon his election was raised on a shield by the chief men of the tribe. The Church brought its distinctive theological framework to bear upon this ancient ritual. The ceremony was, therefore, religious in character yet at the same time a political act. In earlier days these were one and indivisible. In England, the Order, probably an adaptation of that used at Frankish imperial coronations, can be traced back to King Edgar in 973. It reached its most elaborate expression in the *Liber Regalis* of Edward II, (1308). The fundamental structure was threefold and has so continued to this day: (1) the promises taken by the Monarch and his acclamation by the people; (2) his Consecration and Anointing, an ingredient introduced by the Church; (3) his Vesting, Crowning and Enthronement, followed by the Homage and his receiving the Sacrament.

The ceremony was framed within the Eucharist and it was thus built into the verities of Christian faith, vividly portrayed in pageantry and a rich symbolism. It realistically required the Baronage, which constituted centres of power and authority, to exercise these in the interests of a unifying national purpose embodied in the will of the Sovereign. Conversely, it required the Monarch, in return for such obedience, to protect his people and safeguard their feudal liberties.

The task of drawing up the order of service rested with the Archbishop – as a very junior bishop he was present at the coronation of George VI – but he fully recognised that to discharge this duty he needed help. Thus, following precedent, he promptly set up his own advisory committee which consisted of four liturgical and historical scholars together with Dr Alan Don. None of these by temperament was radical or revolutionary. Professor Ratcliffe, in his letter of acceptance to serve on the committee, made it plain that he believed passionately that though there was room for minor adaptations, the general character of the Rite should not be tampered with. It was integrated with the Established Church and it must retain its English character at all costs. However, the Dean of Westminster had one advantage over his more academic colleagues, namely a direct knowledge of the Coronation in 1937 through his being senior chaplain to Archbishop Lang. The committee, according to its lights, served the Archbishop well and he deployed their talents to the full. If it were intended that there should be a modernization of the Rite, Geoffrey Fisher would have needed to choose a different type of committee altogether. However, the temptation to be conservative did not necessarily reflect the predominant mood among the more thoughtful elements of the Nation. The Rite was self-evidently medieval and as such its feudal ethos was felt by some no longer to correspond with the social and political realities of post-war Britain. Not surprisingly, therefore, many responsible people thought drastic changes were necessary if the Coronation Rite were to communicate any meaning to a largely industrialized and secular society. Also there were problems created by its exclusively Anglican character which inevitably led many to ask whether other Christian denominations ought not to participate, and beyond this what about the other Faiths within a newly emerging Commonwealth?

Such concern and questioning found public expression in a leading article which appeared in *The Times* newspaper on 5 May 1952. Without mincing his words, the writer demanded a complete revision of the whole Coronation order of service in the light of developing needs and contemporary attitudes. 'With so long a time for preparation', the writer commented, 'it is to be hoped that the Ecclesiastical Authorities will at last undertake the thorough revision of the Rite itself.'

The Times leader writer was not the only one to call for a serious reappraisal. Canon Raven, formerly Regius Professor of Divinity at Cambridge, reported to Lambeth on his return from Canada in the summer of 1952, that from conversations he had there he felt strongly that something less archaic and domestic should now be drawn up. 'I found out', he went on, 'the opinion strongly stated that on the last occasion the pageantry was wholly out of date and lacking in any sort of relevance to the world today. I promised to pass on to you these

comments at the risk of seeming impertinent. There is a great opportunity that you can take. It may be impossible to avoid a mere repetition
of the tradition. But at least it is worth passing on to you the result of
several talks.'

The Archbishop was not over-pleased with such views so frankly
expressed. Was not Canon Raven's point, he wrote in reply, equivalent
to saying that Westminster Abbey was too domestic and austere. True,
there might be an additional way of recognising the Dominions and
the Commonwealth, though he would not readily be a party to
dismantling the structure of the ancient Rite, however out-of-date its
pageantry might be.

To this *riposte* Raven retorted that such Canadian criticism as he
had heard was primarily directed to the fact that the bishops of most
English sees and the ancient peerage were summoned with particular
privileges, while the oldest of Canadian bishoprics and chief leaders in
the Nation were given no part in the service. Maybe he ought himself
to ventilate the whole matter in *The Times*.

Commonwealth involvement was indeed a matter of deep concern
to many. A correspondent, Kenneth de Courcy, suggested that the only
way of securing it was through the Anglican Church, widely distributed
as it was throughout the Commonwealth. Here, the Archbishop
pointed out that at the Coronation he presided as Primate of All
England, but this capacity gave him no right to summon to Westminster
Abbey from overseas bishops of the Anglican Communion none of
whose Churches was established or came under his authority.

de Courcy's somewhat peeved reaction to the Archbishop's muted
response was to complain that 'The whole trend is to do very little if
anything about the Coronation, and to postpone these larger issues to
the next one which normally will be at least fifty years off'.

Sir Olaf Caroe, a distinguished Civil Servant, with long experience
of high office in India, was equally anxious that new constitutional
developments in the Commonwealth should be reflected in the form of
the Coronation service. Indeed, there were now seven independent
member States and his view was that it might be possible for their
Governor-Generals to be given an active part when the Queen dis-
carded St Edward's crown for the Imperial one or, failing this, to revive
the ancient ceremony in Westminster Hall.

These proposals were taken up enthusiastically by Dr Bell, Bishop
of Chichester, who regarded them as 'enormously important', though
he was not so foolish as to believe that they were new to the
Archbishop. The present Coronation, he believed, would be decisive
for history. The Archbishop's response to Bell was essentially realistic.
If the Commonwealth were included in the Homage both India and
South Africa would certainly refuse to attend. What he had done was

to make two references in the service to all the Queen's realms and territories; and had personally, though not officially, invited the Primates of every province in the Anglican Communion within the Commonwealth.

To another correspondent he admitted that the inter-faith character of the Commonwealth did in fact constitute a real problem *vis-à-vis* an exclusively Christian Coronation service. It was for this reason that suggestions were being put forward to revive Westminster Hall as a *locus* for additional ceremonies not felt to be proper in the Abbey itself. The Archbishop, however, claimed this would lead to a transference of interest from the Coronation in the Abbey to the Commonwealth in Westminster Hall. That venue would then be more and more put forward as the rallying point to which all the people of the Commonwealth could come without any real religious difficulty, and our Mohammedan friends and our Hindu friends would less and less wish to attend the Christian ceremony in the Abbey. Indeed Roman Catholics would say: Why should we attend this non-significant ceremony when we have a secularly significant ceremony in Westminster Hall? At the present time, he wrote emphatically, the Coronation in the Abbey, 'is all or nothing. It is the spiritual significance of the religious act or it is nothing at all.'

Though this was not known to the general public, suggestions to modernize the service had support in the highest circles. On 16 June 1952 Geoffrey Fisher records in his coronation diary: 'I had some talk with the Duke of Edinburgh; he wanted to know how some features relevant to the world today could be introduced. He accepted that they could not be introduced into the Rite itself within the Communion Office.' The Archbishop suggested that possibly at the Recognition the Archbishop instead of asking the same question four times, should direct himself to a different group, as, for example, Sirs of the Dominions, Sirs of the Colonial Empire, etc. The Archbishop comments that the Duke was attracted by this suggestion. Indeed he did not give the matter up and some five months later when the Archbishop had a long interview with the Queen he returned to this theme and promised that he would explore these matters, though not optimistic of a favourable outcome.

In theory and on paper Commonwealth participation seemed feasible enough but in fact it proved quite impracticable as the Commonwealth Office was not slow to point out. To prosecute it seriously would entail approaching each individual country with the interminable delays which this would necessarily entail. After all, the Queen's constitutional position was not, as in the case of her great great grandmother, that of 'Empress' but more simply 'Head' of a Commonwealth of independent nations, some of them republics. Whatever hopes might have been entertained of securing their involvement were given a final quietus by the decisive intervention of Lord Swinton, Secretary of State for the Colonies. It was quite 'hopeless', he argued, to get Commonwealth countries to accept the proposed changes. Nehru was already making renewed difficulties, having withdrawn permission for the High Commissioner in London to carry a standard or for his own carriage to have an escort. Nehru went so far as to intimate that he himself might not join the procession at all. Nothing should be done which could lead to criticism in his country. Pakistan was on the eve of declaring itself a republic. The feeling of the Dominions as a whole could be expressed in these words: 'For Heaven's sake don't go and create new problems when we have such difficulty in coming to agreement round the table about the style and titles and other things'.

The last to be heard of proposals for extending the Homage came at a meeting of the Coronation Committee of the Privy Council held on 16 February 1953 when Clement Attlee, supported by Herbert Morrison and Chuter Ede, asked that the Speaker of the House of Commons should do homage after the peers as a representative of 'the common man'. However, the request was dismissed on the grounds that it was now too late to consult all member states of the Commonwealth. Mr Attlee was neither satisfied nor pleased at this summary answer, nor was he convinced that the time needed to consult the Commonwealth presented such formidable difficulties. This was the first opportunity, he complained somewhat peevishly, which he had to raise the matter formally, a criticism to which the Archbishop replied that he and members of the Coronation Committee had been asked to revise the Coronation Rite way back in June, but no approach for a change had been made to him by any member of the Committee.

There was one further ingredient in the coronation service which was calculated to arouse passions if it were disturbed, though this did not deter the Bishop of Monmouth in April 1953 preaching a sermon in which he attacked the traditional oath taken by the Sovereign in which she promised to protect the Protestant faith. Such phraseology, he maintained, was not so much inadequate as incorrect. This led to a mild flurry in the ecclesiastical dovecotes and a long correspondence in *The Spectator* and the *Church Times*, the chief participants being the Bishop himself and Norman Sykes. Finally, the Archbishop requested the bishop to desist from further controversy. The simple fact was, of course, that the omission of the term 'Protestant' would have caused even greater controversy than its inclusion. One trembles to think of possible repercussions in Northern Ireland!

So it came about that changes were not made in the Recognition, Homage or The Oath. The Commonwealth countries were given no particular role and there was no additional ceremony in Westminster

Hall. The failure to effect any of these proposals long rankled even after the Coronation had come and gone. The *Manchester Guardian*, on 22 December 1953, condemned the Archbishop for not being more imaginative or open to suggestion and, in particular, commented unfavourably on an article of his in the *Round Table* in which he had given his account of the impracticability of bringing about Commonwealth participation. 'As its Head', he asserted 'the Queen's position was "inescapably secular".'

Obviously there was a general disinclination to make changes on the part of both churchmen and laity involved in its presentation. Moreover, the Archbishop's own Committee were, in the main, concerned with securing a correct liturgical sequence and respect for historical precedent rather than with meeting the demands of a new social, religious and economic order. Maybe in the same way as Charles II's Coronation after years of unsettlement invited those present to look back nostalgically to the past, so a not dissimilar sentiment obtained in 1953.

The drawing up of the Coronation Rite did not occasion much difficulty once it was decided not to tackle the problem of its modernisation and in the early stages Geoffrey Fisher let the Committee get on with its work unhindered. On 7 October 1952 its members met the Archbishop at Lambeth and spent 'a very happy and astonishingly successful' evening with him. Between 5.00 pm and dinner they went through all matters of substance concerning the Rite, leaving the minor ones – these were largely linguistic – to be settled later in the warm after-glow of a good meal. The Archbishop was then left to draw up a first draft which he submitted to the Queen in November after which the draft came back to the Committee.

One question was bound to arise: What part, if any, should be allotted to the Duke of Edinburgh, the more so as the Queen had specifically asked that he should be given one. The Archbishop felt this need equally strongly. But here precedents were few and it seemed as if only some minor adjustments could be devised to meet the Queen's request. Such were, for example, walking next behind the Queen at the processional entry; sitting on a fald stool on the right of the Sovereign in the sanctuary; joining her as she received Communion. At this point Geoffrey Fisher volunteered that he was entirely willing to forgo his claim, in favour of the Duke, to do his homage before anybody else 'even if it meant the Church consenting to act second to a layman'. In fact, in making this gesture, Geoffrey Fisher was following a precedent set by Archbishop Tenison in 1713 when George, Prince of Denmark and husband of Queen Anne, was granted the same privilege.

Other minor adjustments were made in the interests of what was regarded as a more correct or orderly procedure none of which would strike the uninformed layman as particularly significant even if he were percipient enough to be conscious of them. Here the Archbishop's concentration upon details was seen at its best. For example the Queen was not to follow her forebear, Queen Victoria, in disrobing in St Edward's Chapel prior to putting on the Colobium Sindonis. The Archbishop himself drew up meticulous instructions as to how the revised sequence was to be worked out, and saw personally that the participants were thoroughly rehearsed. He also showed a great interest in the royal robes, and supervised the unpacking of the chests laid up after the Coronation of the late King. It then suddenly dawned on those concerned that not all were suitable, since George VI was a man and Queen Elizabeth a woman!

A traditional feature of the Coronation was the music. Not surprisingly, composers over the centuries regarded such royal occasions as an opportunity to embellish and enrich the ceremony with fine music, splendidly performed. Geoffrey Fisher invited William McKie, Organist and Master of the Choristers at Westminster Abbey to accept under his overall supervision, responsibility for the Coronation music as its Director. According to tradition the Master of the Queen's Music was associated with the Director in the discharge of his duties, though the final voice, so the Archbishop was careful to point out, lay with the Abbey organist. William McKie accepted the invitation with a fitting sense of the honour paid him. A highly-strung, sensitive musician, in his way a perfectionist, who hailed from that centre of Australian musical talent Melbourne, he also possessed an exceptional flair for tidy administration. Dr McKie's first step was to consult with Sir Adrian Boult as well as Sir William Walton and at the same time to appoint a small committee of advisers consisting of Sir Ernest Bullock, a former organist at the Abbey and with experience of the last Coronation; Sir William Harris of St George's Chapel, Windsor; Dr Stanley Roper of the Chapels Royal; and Dr John Dykes Bower of St Paul's Cathedral.

The Archbishop could not, and did not, claim any particular musical expertise. He did feel, however, and maybe fairly, that he could judge the mood of the average Englishman whose experience in this field was limited. Thus he was sympathetic to the suggestion that the congregation should have its part to play in a familiar hymn, 'All people that on earth do dwell' for which Vaughan Williams wrote a new arrangement and fanfare. The music was distinguished by a number of new works by contemporary composers which, *inter alia*, included an introit, 'Behold O God our Defender' by Herbert Howells; a homage anthem 'O Lord our Governor' by Healey Willan; 'O taste and see how gracious the Lord is' by Vaughan Williams; a *Te Deum* which concluded the Coronation ceremony by Sir William Walton.

William McKie and his committee got down to their task with a will matched by an equally commendable speed, so much so that by the end of October when he met the Archbishop at Lambeth he was able to present him with a completed programme. This was accepted on the spot.

Dr William McKie and the Archbishop found co-operation easy, since both knew where they stood with each other and mutual respect was maintained throughout. The Archbishop wisely left the musicians to carry on without interference. It says much for the Archbishop and William McKie that everything went so smoothly, particularly since there were three choirs working together – the Abbey, St George's, Windsor and the Chapel Royal. To secure effective co-operation between such a diversity of musical talent is never easy. When all was over the Archbishop was able with a good conscience, to give generous praise to all concerned.

Every great national and royal occasion, especially one which straddles the two worlds of Church and State, raises the thorny question of who should be invited to attend. Some people, in the nature of the case, must be present but there are always a number who are borderline cases though they do not necessarily see themselves as falling into this category. Coronations are no exception to this almost universal rule.

This problem rose in an acute form in 1953 in relation to a person who so far from being a suppliant soliciting favours might well earlier have been seated in the Coronation Chair. On 6 November 1952 the Queen, while entertaining the Archbishop to lunch in Buckingham Palace, took the initiative in asking him what his reaction would be if the Duke of Windsor were to request that he might attend. The question was by no means academic since the Queen had been given to understand that he was coming over to England during the next month when the matter might be raised. The Archbishop's immediate view – and in this the Queen saw eye to eye with him – was that such attendance would be wholly and entirely undesirable. The Duke's presence would create a difficult situation for many people and if he did not see that for himself then he ought to be told it.

The Archbishop did not let it rest there, but regarded the possibility of a visit of this kind with such seriousness that he saw Alan Lascelles, the Queen's Secretary, who was of the same mind but doubted whether he himself could do anything effectively to dissuade him. However, Lascelles did write to the Duke's lawyers, a step which Geoffrey Fisher regarded as eminently proper and in line with the attitude of the Prime Minister. He believed that this action by the Queen's Secretary would ensure the removal of the danger and so it proved. Thus the Duke of Windsor was spared the experience which some have claimed, though almost certainly falsely, came the way of the Young Pretender who surreptitiously attended the Coronation of King George III.

If the Duke of Windsor wished to attend but could not, there were others who might have been in the Abbey but chose not to be. The reference is, in particular, to Cardinal Griffin and members of the Roman Catholic hierarchy. The facts are as follows:

On 28 October 1952 the Archbishop sent to the Cardinal a somewhat embarrassed letter. He had been asked to deal, so he explained, with the allocation of invitations to various religious bodies. In 1937 four invitations were earmarked for Roman Catholics in the United Kingdom and two for Northern Ireland. None, however, was taken up. The same provision was to be made again but what would be the Cardinal's response? The latter replied on 24 November that he found it difficult to be definite since he was not sure of the nature of the invitation. If they were addressed personally to himself and other Roman Catholic bishops they would have to be declined. If, however, they were addressed to the Catholic authorities in such a way that the latter were free to nominate representative Catholic laymen, he thought undoubtedly they would be accepted. The Archbishop, not unexpectedly, replied to the Cardinal that the precedent set in 1937 would be followed. The result inevitably was that no Roman Catholic bishops attended.

There was also some talk of Mr Frank Buchman of Moral Rearmament fame receiving an invitation. Here Geoffrey Fisher was adamant that if an American unconnected with the United States Government or the Diplomatic Corps were invited it should be Dr Sherrill, Presiding Bishop of the Protestant Episcopal Church of America.

Perhaps the most important decision which Geoffrey Fisher and the Coronation Committee were called upon to make, certainly so far as the general public was concerned, centred around the question – should the Coronation be televised and if so how much of it? The decision adopted at the Coronation in 1937 was simple, no television – it was in its infancy – but permission was given for the filming of the whole ceremony. The initial mood of the Earl Marshal and the rest of the Committee except for Sir George Bellew, Garter King of Arms, was to prohibit television of any kind on the grounds of the obtrusiveness of the equipment and the disturbing effects of the high level of light required, particularly when this was focussed on the Queen. In taking this decision, the Committee at the outset was largely unaware of the technical progress which had been made over the last few years and which reduced the level of light required. Outside commercial interests also began to make their voices heard by bringing pressure to bear upon the Earl Marshal who more and more leant upon the Archbishop for decision-making in this sensitive area. Geoffrey Fisher had originally associated himself with the Committee in imposing a complete ban but he was beginning to veer away from this decision though still regarding certain aspects of the Coronation service as too intimate for public viewing. Here he believed that a distinction ought to be drawn between 'live television' and film. Still there was a subliminal feeling, not amenable to argument, that there was something almost improper in exhibiting worshippers engaged in prayer; also that loyal subjects should be in their parish church while the Coronation was going on.

Members of the Corporation, however, saw the Coronation as a unique opportunity to display their skills and they began, forthwith, to apply a relentless, almost ruthless pressure upon the Committee. Its first breakthrough, though minimal, was permission to televise the procession on entry as it moved eastwards to the choir screen and later westwards on going out. But the BBC was by no means satisfied with so meagre an offering. Sir William Haley intervened personally to say that the Corporation could meet all reasonable objections, and that this was too important a national event to be submitted to an emasculated presentation. On 1 August he pleaded his case with the Archbishop supplementing what the Director-General had said, but in spite of this it seemed still as if the Coronation Committee would budge no further. There now came into the lists a formidable figure in the person of the Prime Minister – Winston Churchill. He immediately summoned an informal meeting at which there were present himself and the Archbishop, Sir Alan Lascelles and Sir Harold Emmerson, Permanent Secretary to the Ministry of Works. It was obvious from the beginning that the Prime Minister had made up his mind that there must be full television. The Archbishop took the opportunity of explaining carefully the reasons for his own and the Committee's scruples to such an exposure, not least the spiritual aspects of the occasion. The Prime Minster, according to Geoffrey Fisher, found all this too subtle and sophisticated but stuck even more forcefully to the view that there must be uninhibited television. And so it was that in 1952 it was publicly announced that there would be full television coverage, east as well as west of the choir screen. Only the Anointing and the reception of the Sacrament would be private. The Archbishop was still concerned lest the young Queen should be disturbed by excessive light, but as the result of a test in the Abbey the Queen expressed her complete satisfaction.

Concerning sound radio suffice to say that the Archbishop was in favour of covering the whole of the ceremony, though even here Dr Garbett of York was totally opposed to including the Anointing and the Communion.

The general view after the Coronation, in spite of these initial misgivings, was that television, radio and film added considerably to its impact in enabling members of the public, many of them unchurched, to identify themselves personally with the spirit of this unique and historic ceremony. The *New Statesman*'s witticism testified to this judgement: 'Dimbleby Ill; Coronation Postponed'. Certainly his commentary was a major factor in the remarkable success of the broadcast. For many 1953 was indeed the year of the televised Coronation.

The Archbishop's attitude was one of *solvitur in ambulando*. With a natural prejudice against the media he endeavoured to steer a middle course, realizing progressively both the benefits and hazards. Certainly without the decisive intervention of the Prime Minister and the persistence of the BBC, who would not take 'no' for an answer, the television coverage would not have been so lavish and satisfying as it, fortunately, was.

As 2 June came nearer so Geoffrey Fisher's thoughts centred more and more upon the young Queen. She was then twenty-seven years of age, eight years older than was her great great grandmother, Victoria, when she came to her crowning. The custom that monarchs could turn to Archbishops of Canterbury for spiritual and pastoral help goes back centuries, indeed at least to the time of William the Conqueror who sought counsel from Lanfranc. How far they availed themselves of this help depended on the personalities of both. Geoffrey Fisher certainly felt that he had thrust into his hands a solemn duty as Archbishop to use the opportunity thus given him to the full. The Queen was young and was still mourning the premature loss of a much-loved father. Her crowning could be for her the most religiously significant experience bearing upon her life-long vocation as sovereign. The intricate and elaborate nature of the Coronation ritual meant of necessity that the Archbishop must see a great deal of the Queen during the early and formative months of her reign.

With the Coronation imminent, almost at the eleventh hour, the Archbishop decided to produce a small Book of Devotions which the Queen could use daily during the last month. Increasing work forced him to recognize that to accomplish this project he needed help. Thus he turned to two ladies, heading up two very different communities – Miss Margaret Potts of St Julian's and Mother Clare of St Andrew's. The letters which he wrote to them on 31 March 1953 described precisely what was in his mind: namely that it was his duty to prepare the Queen for her Coronation. She was a person well able to prepare herself; but his desire was to provide her, and those dearest to her, with some simple aid to their own self-preparation. What he wanted from these two ladies was a set of short devotions to be used from 1 May to 2 June. Both accepted with alacrity though a little frightened at the prospect. Both, to their credit, sent in their scripts within a fortnight. 'It has been a terrible rush,' the Archbishop confessed to Noel Davey of the Society for Promoting Christian Knowledge, 'with a little more time we could have improved it so immensely.'

The book was all accomplished in a rush: 'begun, continued and ended within a month'. Indeed Geoffrey Fisher was forced to give up part of a much needed pre-Coronation holiday in order to complete it.

Perhaps Archbishop Fisher was apologizing over-much. Certain classes of work are better done under pressure as many authors and musical composers can testify. Noel Davey, originally sceptical of the project, described certain sections of the devotions as 'quite excellent' and others as 'magnificent'. Copies were produced, some seventeen in all, beautifully but simply bound in leather. The Queen Mother, in thanking the Archbishop for her copy, described it as 'quite perfect, so helpful and lovely and simple,' enabling her to be associated with the Queen as she prepared herself for 'this very tremendous day in her young life.' She concluded her letter: 'It was such a delight to see you at Windsor, you always do me good'.

The Archbishop and Mrs Fisher spent a happy weekend with the Queen at Windsor on 27 April when they talked together and he reminded her that Archbishop Lang, on the Sunday prior to her father's Coronation, had gone to the Palace to conduct a short service. He offered to do the same and she gladly accepted. There were further opportunities for private talks as the day drew closer. One such conversation on 15 May he remembered vividly. It was at a rehearsal and the Queen was sitting in the Coronation Chair undisturbed. The Archbishop went up to her and they had a long conversation. 'She was quite on her own,' he writes, 'with a look of real happiness on her face and spoke enthusiastically of the little book saying that she was using it morning by morning in company with her family. She welcomed the suggestion of a private rehearsal for the actual crowning.' The Archbishop, in making this suggestion, probably had in mind Cosmo Lang's near disaster with the crown at the previous Coronation in 1937. Speaking generally of the Queen's demeanour during the final rehearsal he wrote at the time: 'She was at her absolute best, sincere, gay, happy, intensely interested, asking all the right questions about her movements and carrying them out very naturally and impressively'.

There can be no doubt that the frequent rehearsals, at which the Queen was usually represented by the Duchess of Norfolk, contributed greatly to the success of 'the day'. Maybe Archbishop Fisher was aware of the laconic comment of the Dean of Westminster after the Coronation of Queen Victoria: 'there almost certainly ought to have been a rehearsal'. Geoffrey Fisher was gratified with the smoothness and rapidity with which the rehearsals were run through, though sometimes small details needed prolonged attention. For example, it took many attempts to get the timing right for the Queen's bowing to the altar as she entered through the choir. The Archbishop was particularly impressed with the Duchess of Norfolk of whom he could not speak too highly. He describes her as a superb stand-in for the Queen, very cool and collected and picking up very quickly what she had to do.

The Archbishop and Earl Marshal worked in complete harmony which was indeed fortunate. With two such strong personalities there could easily have been endless friction wherever their spheres of interest and influence overlapped. That this did not happen was a great tribute to both. With Sir George Bellew, an interesting personality, the Archbishop admitted that he fought frequently but always ended up on friendly terms. 'If he told me that I did not know how to run the show, I told him that he knew nothing about ceremonial in an ecclesiastical setting.' On at least one occasion when the Archbishop had fought him stoutly, he admitted that Garter King of Arms had been entirely right and he had been entirely wrong. At the final rehearsal all was peace and harmony between the two.

A candid critic, the Groom of the Robes, gave it as his opinion that when the Archbishop was present he 'realized for the first time the meaning of the phrase "the Church Militant".' However, on most occasions when tempers were frayed, as they were bound to be from time to time, Geoffrey Fisher's sense of fun and unfailing good humour helped him and others through.

On Sunday 31 May on the very eve of the Coronation the Archbishop preached to a large congregation in Canterbury Cathedral when Parry's 'I was Glad' as well as William Walton's *Te Deum* were sung. On returning to London he went straight to Buckingham Palace threading his way through the crowds to do so. During an hour's stay, as the Queen and the Duke knelt, so the Archbishop said a few prayers and gave them his blessing. They talked together of the spiritual associations of the Coronation and appropriately, the royal couple signed the Archbishop's copy of the Queen's little book. Recalling the visit the Archbishop wrote 'There was really a feeling of mutual trust free of all kind of constraint, and I felt that the Queen and I were entirely in step for the Coronation itself'. It was gratifying for the Archbishop to hear from several sources that on the day before the Coronation the Queen said that she had absolute confidence in the Archbishop and was reassured by the thought of him being present with her throughout the service. The Archbishop's last and final commitment, prior to 'the day' was to conduct the devotions and to preach at a broadcast service in St Paul's Cathedral. He also wrote an article for the *Radio Times* explaining the Rite in simple terms.

Queen Victoria records in her diary that she rose early on the day of her Coronation to a cloudless summer sky and brilliant sunshine. No such meteorological greeting welcomed her great-great-granddaughter on 2 June 1953. The morning turned out cloudy and cold, threatening rain which descended later in the morning. At Lambeth Palace the household were up early, not least Mr Pennock, the faithful chauffeur to the Fisher family. Their guests included Mrs Temple, wife of the former Archbishop. At 9.25 am the Archbishop said matins in the Palace Chapel, including a special prayer for the Queen. He then robed and travelled by car with a motor-cycle escort to the Abbey accompanied by Canon Ian White-Thompson and his two chaplains, Eric Jay and John Long. The scene in Parliament Square, where the stands were filled to capacity and pennants were flying, gave the appearance of a medieval tournament.

As the Archbishop stepped out of his car at the annexe which had been specially constructed at the west end of the Abbey nave he was given a cheer by those sitting in the Colonial Office stand. He with his party found that the Dean and Chapter of Westminster in their blue copes embellished by lions and unicorns were already carrying the royal regalia in procession to St Edward's Chapel. At about 10.15 am the Royal Family entered the Abbey followed by the Queen Mother, who was to add another intimate association with the Collegiate Church of St Peter in Westminster to the many that she had acquired throughout the years. Calm and very self-possessed, the Archbishop had still three last-minute commissions to discharge: namely, to tell the Bishop of London that he would be carrying the paten on a cushion as seeming more fitting than in his hands; to prompt the Maids of Honour to make a curtsey at the appropriate place in the Creed; to inform the two supporting Bishops, Durham and Bath and Wells, that they must allow the Queen and her train bearers to precede them out of St Edward's Chapel after the disrobing.

At 11.00 am the Queen and the Duke of Edinburgh arrived in the Golden Coach and the procession moved off at 11.07 am. The long-awaited and carefully prepared ceremony had begun, the Westminster Scholars being the first to greet the sovereign with the traditional *Vivat! Vivat! Regina Elizabetha*! Progressively and solemnly, without hitches, the majestic ritual unfolded itself as it moved easily from Recognition to Anointing. Investiture to Crowning: Homage to Eucharist. There was a feeling in the congregation that history was being re-enacted and made contemporary, finding its point and purpose in the dedication of a young sovereign to an age-long, awesome responsibility – and all this within a church which had seen the centuries slip by as succeeding monarchs came within its walls for their hallowing.

By 1.55 pm this august ceremony had receded into an irretrievable past. As the great procession withdrew through the choir and nave westwards, the Queen walked slowly, wearing the Imperial Crown and carrying the sceptre and orb. With the Duke of Edinburgh she lingered for a time in the annexe spending some fifteen minutes alone with the Archbishop.

For Geoffrey Fisher the day was not yet over. At 6.30 pm he was at the Pathé studio in Oxford Street with the Duke of Norfolk, viewing the films which had been taken earlier. They were shown shots by cameras from different vantage points throughout the Abbey. The only cuts which the Archbishop and Earl Marshal requested were those of the Queen and Duke of Edinburgh receiving the Sacrament and the two close-ups of the Queen and the Queen Mother which they thought too long.

After the viewing it was back to Lambeth for the Archbishop where he spent some time with his guests, on the roof of the east wing of the Palace, watching the display of fireworks. Doubtless when the Primate of All England finally retired for the night he slept well.

All had certainly gone according to plan and the advantage of having thoroughly rehearsed the ceremony was evident throughout. However, in so lengthy and elaborate a ritual it was inevitable that some errors should creep in, though unobserved by the majority of the congregation. The Queen made her one and only mistake when she forgot the carefully rehearsed curtsey during her processional entry. The Archbishop later commented: 'I was trying hard to will her to remember but failed. Neither of the supporting bishops liked to prompt her, not quite knowing whether she had forgotten until it was too late to take action.'

The Queen, however, was not the only one to slip up. The Archbishop himself did likewise. This happened when the complicated ritual had reached the point when the sword was being redeemed and returned to the altar. The Archbishop took this as his cue for receiving the armills. There was an embarrassing pause until he suddenly realised his mistake and threw up his arms in distress – an involuntary gesture betokening 'what have I done?' but which Garter described as a 'charming little blessing that you gave the Queen while the sword was being redeemed'.

The Queen was aware of his blunder and told him in the annexe that she did her best to stop him coming out and was willing him hard not to do so. The Archbishop commented ruefully that they were 'all square'.

The Archbishop confessed later that for him the placing of the crown on the Queen's head was a particularly anxious moment since it must remain in this position for the rest of the ceremony. At rehearsals he was able to benefit from the advice of the Duchess of Norfolk who used to say: 'A little more forward, a little further down at the back'.

The Earl Marshal was in no sense an aggressive personality but he could, very properly, be firm on occasions. Thus he issued a strict order that everything on 2 June should be exactly as it was at the final rehearsal. There must be no last minute *ad hoc* deviations even if these were thought to be improvements. This sensible order, however, was not fully observed. Here, surprisingly, the Dean of Westminster slipped up and made two errors. First, he was not wearing his particular cope as agreed, and secondly, he replaced the small basin used at rehearsals to receive the oblations by an enormous alms dish – 'a monstrous object' so the Archbishop complained, the result being that when he turned to the Queen the sheer size of the receptacle prevented him getting close to her so that she had to stretch out to the middle of the dish in order to deposit her offering.

The Archbishop was kept busy immediately after the Coronation by giving a number of addresses to various groups and interests. For example, on 5 June he preached at a New Zealand Service of Thanksgiving in St Paul's Cathedral in which he spoke of being caught up under the spell of that tremendous event which every 'train of thought or conversation came back to'. Two days later he addressed a Commonwealth gathering in the Abbey and gave there the first of a series of addresses under the general theme 'Forward from the Coronation'.

It was to be expected that the Archbishop would receive a large number of appreciative letters from the United Kingdom and overseas. A few representative ones may be quoted, that from Sir Ian Jacob, Director-General of the BBC, having a special interest in view of the protracted doubts and difficulties connected with television. He began by complimenting the Archbishop personally on his splendid performance in an august role. 'The full effect,' he went on, 'spiritual as much as ceremonial, was perfectly conveyed and must have had a profound impression on everyone.' A letter which undoubtedly gave Geoffrey Fisher peculiar pleasure came from the Bishop of Chichester who earlier had been somewhat critical: 'The last Coronation, 1937, was moving and religious but this excelled it in both qualities'. Dr Ratcliffe, a member of the small committee set up by the Archbishop and who saw things through the eyes of an academic liturgiologist historically orientated, was equally enthusastic. 'It was the best Coronation,' he affirmed, 'from the point of view of the Rite.' The Archbishop had nobly fulfilled his part and his voice was magnificent. As to the Queen 'no one who saw the service on television could now think of her out of the context of her Consecration and Coronation'. J. R. Phillip, Procurator of the Church of Scotland, spoke of the Archbishop's voice as the voice of a friend which brought him a special message.

Henry Fisher, the Archbishop's eldest son, expressed the family's satisfaction, which must have been full to overflowing. Without reserve he paid tribute to the consummate skill and artistry with which his father had conducted the whole ceremony and the great pleasure it had given him. The prophet is not always without honour in his own country!

One letter, written on 20 June 1953, had unique authority and significance; it came from the Queen and read as follows:

> 'A moment's pause during these hectic days gives me the opportunity of trying to express my sincere thanks to you for all your help and support both before and during the Coronation Service. I find it very difficult to put into words just what it meant to me but your continual encouragement and explanation made the tremendous significance of the service and the strain of that long day so much easier to face. In particular, both Philip and I would like to thank you for your prayers for us on the evening of Trinity Sunday – they gave us both much needed strength and calmness. The little Book of Devotions for the month before June 2nd, which you so kindly wrote for us was greatly valued and we are all most grateful to you for enabling us to all join together in thoughts and prayers all leading up to the day itself. This letter is very badly expressed but I do hope you will realise how ever grateful I shall always be to you.
>
> Yours very sincerely,
> Elizabeth R.'

The Press is always unpredictable and often its more sophisticated elements find pleasure in running counter to popular opinion. On this occasion, however, former criticisms were muted and on the whole the papers were generous in their praise. We confine ourselves to quoting from a *Times* leader which when read now in the nineties seems almost prophetic, striking as it did a solemn and serious note against the background of a general euphoria. It took as its heading 'AND AFTER?' 'The Empire', it remarked, 'has now gone to be replaced by a feeling of Commonwealth and community'. The pageantry of the Coronation was 'both the inward and outward expression of the greatest coming together of free peoples, freely associated, that the world has ever seen'. But it needed to be said that the British people had had a holiday from reality long enough. The time had now come for Britain 'to find anew her place in the world, earning it not merely by her past example but by her present exertions'. The grim fact was that 'Britain's economy still swayed on a knife edge' and that 'her people, a good people grown careless, had the power to find a contemporary role given the will'.

There had been much talk, prior to the Coronation of the Committee meeting again to review the situation in the light of 2 June 1953, particularly as to how far criticisms that the ritual was archaic were valid. However, the excitement and congratulations which followed the Coronation, together with the hope that the next such occasion would be some fifty years ahead, discouraged any enthusiasm to embark upon such a review. It was rightly felt that conditions would probably be so different at the end of the century that any forward planning so early would consume time to no purpose. One area the Archbishop did comment upon, however, largely as the result of an initiative from the conscientious Dr William McKie. Music did not raise political or constitutional issues! What William McKie did was to ask certain questions which Geoffrey Fisher answered as follows: in general he did not think, as some had complained, that the music was excessive since only 'grand music was adequate to the greatness of the occasion or of the ceremony'. Maybe some of the music was a little over-elaborate and here he instanced the 'Veni Creator.' He believed that the 'run-up' to the enthroning would have been enhanced by drums and a brief fanfare. Once the Homage was over the excitement had passed; hence the singing of 'All People That On Earth Do Dwell' enabled members of the congregation to express themselves. A possible mistake, the Archbishop felt, was the placing of the *Te Deum* right at the end of the ceremony which came as an anti-climax and was, in fact, a re-duplication of the Church's creed; he would replace it by a grand singing of the much shorter 150th Psalm, after which the orchestra could play until the Queen appeared for her final exit.

There can be no doubt that in the opinion of the public the Archbishop had done well. What the average citizen could not know were the infinite pains, interest and enthusiasm with which he had approached and prepared himself for the ceremony. He was not a highly artistic man and his attitude to aesthetics, indeed to liturgy, was basically commonsensical and pragmatic. His was an Englishman's approach to pageantry, as was his deep conviction that the traditional Rite could still be given meaning to the secularized millions of Britain and beyond. Doubtless there was something about a young and beautiful Queen which moved him emotionally, as was the case with Victoria and the phlegmatic Lord Melbourne, thus encouraging him to use to the full all the opportunities, pastoral and otherwise, which the Coronation provided for an Archbishop. He possessed a finely modulated speaking voice which he made the most of and which gave the ceremony a strong sense of purpose and a momentum which was maintained throughout. It might well be claimed that he should have been more persistent in trying to bring the Rite up to date and, thereby, more expressive of post-war political and economic realities. After all, the Homage, in the character of those who paid it, was an irrelevant anachronism and frustrated the very point and purpose of the original political intention of the Rite. The Lector Theologiae at Westminster Abbey in his report suggested that maybe the prestigious nobility doing their homage should have been replaced by the Press barons, the Trade unions, the Confederation of British Industry, where effective power lies. But radical change would have proved difficult constitutionally and the Archbishop only half believed in the need to secure it. The Earl Marshal, who was ultimately in charge, did not wish it and the young Queen and her husband, though certainly in favour of modernization, did not know how in practice to bring it about. The Commonwealth countries saw the Coronation as essentially a United Kingdom affair. So the conservatives prevailed, understandably maybe, since after a long war unparalleled in human history, Britain as a whole was content to fall back on a tradition which had been built up over centuries, had served her well and was reminiscent of a past neither forgotten nor inglorious. Perhaps the dignity of the ritual, the capacity of its symbols to utter those thoughts which break through language and escape even these recalled the most hardened, if only subliminally, to their vestigial roots.

As to the long-term effects of the Coronation on the Nation after the captains and kings had departed who can tell? Here one cannot argue from cause to effect. So far as the immediate impact was concerned, thanks to radio and television, it was not inconsiderable. Perhaps it may be claimed that in the case of the young Queen the solemnity of the Coronation service itself, as well as the pastoral ministrations of the Archbishop have not been without their effect across the years. Very wisely Geoffrey Fisher resisted the attempts made to institute an annual service or some other form of celebration to commemorate the Coronation. Such, he realized, would not carry conviction and would soon become a somewhat pathetic anti-climax, indeed an increasing embarrassment. At this point, maybe, we can allow the Archbishop to speak for himself and to have the last word. 'I have a feeling that the religious significance of the Coronation has been much more generally appreciated than at the last Coronation, and I think the Queen's request for the prayers of everybody in her Christmas broadcast made a very deep impression from what I hear. I should judge that markedly in some stands, and quite definitely in all, the service was followed closely and for the most part in silence with people standing for the hymn and singing it, and the absolute silence of the excellent broadcast during the Communion was observed. If this was indeed so its spiritual value must have been very great.'

One incident connected with the Coronation which nearly led Geoffrey Fisher into an embarrassing public controversy has been left to the end of the chapter since its impact came later. It relates to a blunder which the Archbishop made on the day of the last rehearsal.

A question agitating many people's minds at the time of the Coronation was whether the Moderator of the General Assembly of the Church of Scotland which, like the *Ecclesia Anglicana*, is an established Church though non-espiscopal, should be allocated any part in the Coronation Rite. Dr Alan Don, Dean of Westminster, was most anxious that he should and finally it was agreed that the Moderator should participate in presenting the Scriptures to the Queen saying the words devised by Henry Compton, Bishop of London, for the Coronation of 1689. Certainly this was a triumph of reason and equity over passion and prejudice. Dr Fisher, however, remained unhappy, particularly since he knew that the Moderator would be seated during the service near the High Altar between the Archbishop of York on his right and the Bishop of London on his left. This would mean that when he, Geoffrey Fisher, and Dr Don distributed the bread and the wine during the Eucharist they would have to pass him by since he was not to receive the Sacrament. So emotionally disturbed was Geoffrey Fisher by this seemingly deliberate exclusion of the Moderator that on the very day of the final rehearsal, as the procession was about to move, the conscience-striken Archbishop explained to the Moderator that it was unthinkable he could ignore him in this way. So to prevent this he would ask him to extend his clasped hands and then, as a sign of fellowship, he, the Archbishop, would lay his own hands on the Moderator's as a symbolic gesture. On 'the day', overcome with emotion, as he came to the Moderator, he conformed to the private arrangement which had been agreed but added the words: 'Feed on him in thy heart by faith with thanksgiving'. Alas! the Archbishop had entirely forgotten to advise the Dean of Westminster of this change of plan with the result that the latter, taken completely by surprise and thinking the Moderator had received the sacramental bread, offered him the wine which he courteously declined. This incident aroused little comment at the time for a strict confidentiality was maintained among the few who knew of it. However, some time later a zealous Presbyterian minister came to hear of it and determined to find out the facts. It seemed, therefore, as if this embarrassing story might 'break'. Dr Pitt Watson, the Moderator at the time of the Coronation, corresponded with Geoffrey Fisher who completely accepted his version of events as to what actually happened. Fortunately no public controversy developed, but Geoffrey Fisher, though the motivation was excellent, certainly made an error of judgement.

In retrospect it must be deplored that the Moderator was not invited to receive the Sacrament. Though a few purists might have objected, the vast majority of people would have felt it to be singularly appropriate. As it was the Archbishop, unfortunately, got the worst of both worlds; but if ever there was a case of *corruptio optimi pessima* this was surely such an occasion.

CHAPTER 23

The Archbishop and the Royal Family

THE custom had long been established that the Archbishop of Canterbury stood in a special relationship with the sovereign and the members of the royal family, a relationship not necessarily shared by any particular diocesan bishop. He was indeed the first subject of the realm and as such took precedence over every other. Yet this relationship was not built into the law of the land, though the custom that he should crown the sovereign was so strong as to be almost a constitutional requirement. Also, his status *vis-à-vis* conducting royal baptisms, even if it were not quite so firm, was a strong one. Often the Archbishop saw himself as a personal adviser to the sovereign, but here much depended on the temperaments of the monarch and the Archbishop. Also how they related to each other. Lanfranc, we know, in early days was a constant adviser of William the Conqueror. However, King James I certainly did not look to George Abbott, his Archbishop, for counsel or advice. On the contrary, he secured his suspension from office. Queen Anne was equally averse to Archbishop Tenison, and looked elsewhere for counsel and support. Queen Victoria found a faithful friend in Wellesley, her Dean of Windsor, and cold-shouldered the occupant of Lambeth. On the other hand, Davidson was intimate with George V. Temple was not long enough at Lambeth to establish the same familiarity, nor was he the kind of person who would find it easy to do so.

Geoffrey Fisher, by his easygoing friendliness and exuberance, overcame a natural shyness in both George VI and Queen Elizabeth, making for a more easy relationship. He also believed in the monarchy, regarding it as occupying a significant place in the life of the nation. He saw the royal family as needing to mirror all that was best in British society. Hence, he regarded it as his duty, when asked, to acquaint the sovereign with the feelings of the Church or the nation, if only a minority opinion, when any particular action of one of its members attracted a great deal of public criticism. This did not always make him popular but to him it was a duty from which he seldom shrank, though he did it with a measure of tact and restraint. Also, it was customary for the Queen's private secretary, without inhibiting the complete freedom of the sovereign, to take the initiative in consulting the Archbishop on matters affecting the monarchy. Geoffrey Fisher was not a High Churchman and the religious approach of the royal family, broad and in the eighteenth century sense of the word 'non-enthusi-astic', was one which he both understood and to which he responded. His concern was that its members should be, and should be seen to be, regular worshippers in the Established Church at least once on Sun-days, and regular, but not necessarily weekly, receivers of the Sacrament.

Such general statements will now be spelt out in particular instances.

Geoffrey Fisher had many opportunities, through marriages, births and deaths, of entering into natural relationships with members of the royal family at what were numinous moments in life when there are deep stirrings of the human spirit. The Archbishop was in many respects ideally suited to bring support in such situations and to use his pastoral gifts to good advantage. Such, for example, were the marriage of Princess Elizabeth to the Duke of Edinburgh in 1947; Prince Charles's baptism in 1948 and Princess Anne's in 1950; King George's funeral in 1952 and Queen Mary's in 1953; the Coronation of Queen Elizabeth II in June of the same year; the marriage of Princess Margaret to Mr Anthony Armstrong-Jones in 1960, and the baptism of Prince Andrew in 1960.

Reflecting on these events many years later, Geoffrey Fisher records: 'On two occasions I met the whole Royal Family and in the most solemn and intimate way. The first was when I took a little service in Marlborough House, the morning after Queen Mary died; they came together in the Drawing Room and I said a few prayers and read from the Bible. This is the kind of thing one never forgets. Whether I did it properly or well I haven't the slightest idea. But at least it was done, and it was a bond between us. The other such occasion was in the chapel of Marlborough House, before the funeral of Queen Mary, when they were all present and I spoke a few words to them and celebrated the Holy Communion with them. There were, of course, many wonderful occasions when I was associated with the Royal Family. The glorious Silver Wedding celebration in St Paul's of King George VI and the present Queen Mother was most moving. I had always been overwhelmed by the vastness and grandeur of St Paul's. But on that occasion I felt that St Paul's was as intimate as a domestic chapel with the beloved King George and his wife, the Queen, present as was their family. One could not but feel sympathetic, domestic affection carrying us up to the Almighty God.'

Often on a royal occasion the Archbishop was entrusted with the most difficult task of giving the address. The temptation at ceremonies of this kind is to be overfulsome at the expense of truth, or in reaction against this to be pedestrianly factual and dull. Indeed, the Archbishop did not always entirely avoid this.

Geoffrey Fisher's attitude certainly to the younger members of the royal family was uniformly protective. An early example of this came when Princess Elizabeth was touring Canada in 1946. On 27 February a correspondent wrote to Lambeth from Toronto urging the Archbishop to use his influence with Her Royal Highness in view of criticisms made, quite unfairly, that she was frequenting nightclubs. Mr Vernon admitted that, as was equally the case in America, the Canadian press was 'flamboyant' and had given these visits 'stupid and unwanted publicity'. Such headlines were common as: 'Princess Hits the Highspots'; 'In the Footsteps of Windsor'. In a poll, Mr Vernon added, taken in a train travelling from Montreal to Toronto, out of some 372 passengers, 287 'strongly disapproved of the Princess's activities'. The Archbishop immediately wrote to Sir Alan Lascelles, private secretary to the Princess, stressing that Mr Vernon 'appears to write in a proper spirit with a desire to be helpful'. Could he suggest how he ought to reply and was there any means of restraining a 'mischievous press'. Sir Alan, in a somewhat curt reply, commented that Mr Vernon would have done better not to have written to the Archbishop at all and that there was no means of influencing the Press. The only way to prevent hostile comment on her 'innocent activities' would be for Her Royal Highness to discontinue such visits to places where people danced. His advice, since the Archbishop sought it, was merely to send Mr Vernon 'a polite acknowledgement in the third person'.

The Archbishop did not in fact reply in this minimal form but contented himself with writing: 'There is nothing in any degree undesirable about it and the Royal House in all ways is giving an excellent and good example of home life at its best. It is indeed regrettable if the Press in your country and the USA gives any other impression'.

This complaint from Canada verged on the ridiculous. Others had more substance, even if they represented an unreasonable minority view. In May 1948, G. H. Crossland of the Methodist Church Union wrote to Lambeth complaining that Princess Elizabeth and the Duke of Edinburgh had, with their hosts, attended the races in Paris on Whit Sunday, thus contributing to the 'secularisation of the Lord's Day' and creating an 'unfortunate precedent'. 'Would it not be possible ', he enquired, 'for you to convey to them the profound regret and sorrow of many Christian people at the Race attendance . . . I trust Your Grace would find some suitable way of making known an opinion which I am sure is shared by many fellow Christians in the Church of England.'

The Archbishop replied that it was easy to understand his feelings, and that he would bear them in mind though it was not so simple a matter since 'Christian opinion would certainly not be united on one side or the other'. Crossland was not the only voice of complaint. The

General Secretary of the World Evangelical Alliance expressed his 'shocked feelings' and said that he had received many long-distance telephone calls to this effect. H. B. Grace urged the Archbishop to emulate honest Hugh Latimer, and W. E. Farndale, President of the Methodist Conference, voiced his 'serious concern'.

There can be little doubt that Geoffrey Fisher personally shared some of the scruples of his correspondent – he himself was strongly opposed to any form of gambling. However, his earlier exchange of letters with Lascelles did not encourage him to embark on any practical action even if it were possible. He did, however, write to Farndale saying that if the opportunity arose he would report his feelings, but he added a cautionary note to the effect that he was 'not prepared to say that [he] will make an opportunity since in the Church of England there are diverse opinions and certainly not enough feeling to justify [him] in making representations of Church of England opinion.'

The last word, not unexpectedly, came from the Lord's Day Observance Council which at its June meeting desired its Secretary to express surprise and disappointment that as the exalted head of the national Church His Grace has made no public reference whatever on this matter. His 'silence' was regrettable. The Archbishop was learning, but he was right in saying to his critics that any public statement on this matter issued by him would certainly not have universal approval in the Church of England.

On 18 April 1947, he sent Princess Elizabeth a message on behalf of the bishops, clergy and people of the Church of England expressing loyal and loving greetings with congratulations and good wishes on her twenty-first birthday. 'May God who has so enriched her life ever bless and enrich it all her days.'

On 8 July 1948, the King acquainted the Archbishop privately of the betrothal of Princess Elizabeth to Lieutenant Philip Mountbatten. The marriage of the heir presumptive to the throne was, of course, an important national event; but one practical matter was of concern to the Archbishop, namely the status of the bridegroom, who was born in Greece and remained a member of the Orthodox Church. Dr Fisher wrote to the King on 14 July suggesting that Philip be received into the Church of England, and having secured royal approval for this step he saw Philip on 21 September. The Archbishop also, for fear that the authorities of the Greek Church might suggest two marriage ceremonies, talked to his 'own beloved' Archbishop Germanos, the representative in London of the Oecumenical Patriach, 'a great man'. He saw the point and raised no objection to Philip's joining the Church of England.

The Archbishop felt it was better not to emphasise over-much Philip Mountbatten's Greek Orthodox ancestry, and for this reason he hesitated to suggest that Germanos should be robed and seated in the sanctuary when the marriage was solemnised in the Abbey. Would not an honourable seat in the choir be the appropriate way of dealing with Germanos. The Dean of Westminster, who was responsible for the seating, agreed.

However, rumours circulated, probably groundless, but disseminated by the Reverend C. E. Douglas, a member of the Church Assembly who had made for himself a 'corner' in relationships between the Orthodox Churches and the Church of England. He was given to understand that the Lieutenant himself did not see the necessity for the steps proposed. Douglas's own view was that such a formal reception was not required and that the precedents set by Prince Albert, Queen Alexandra and the Duchess of Kent, could be followed. In other words, admission to the Holy Communion, together with his British citizenship and obvious willingness to undertake the duties of membership in the Church of England, were adequate. Indeed, Philip might enrol himself on a parochial register.

Douglas, however, was with the Archbishop in strongly opposing any idea of a second marriage ceremony but would wish that Germanos should attend the wedding in the Abbey, say a prayer and give a blessing at the end. This did not in fact happen.

So Prince Philip's reception into the Church of England went foward and took place in the temporary chapel at Lambeth on St Michael and All Angels Day in September 1947. At an informal tea party afterwards, Princess Elizabeth being present, the Lieutenant playfully remarked: 'Couldn't you marry us this afternoon, Archbishop? It would save such a lot of fuss'. The suggestion was not followed up! Hence, on 15 November, the Archbishop went to Buckingham Palace to go through the marriage service with the bride and bridegroom. He also had a private talk with the latter who was relieved to hear that Dr Fisher would not be wearing a train such as had caused difficulty to the Archbishop of York when presenting a loyal address at the Palace. As early as 31 July, in an interview with the King, the Archbishop of Canterbury was asked to invite his fellow Primate of York to give the address. The latter's response to this request in a letter to Geoffrey Fisher is certainly frank: 'I am rather dismayed at the thought of giving the Address. As an unmarried man, I always have an inferiority complex about this. I expect I shall ask you and Mrs Fisher to prepare it for me'.

The custom was, *vis-à-vis* a royal marriage at this level, for a loyal address to go to the Palace from the Convocation of Canterbury. The Archbishop asked Dr S. C. Carpenter, Dean of Exeter, to undertake this ploy but his effort was described by Dr Walter Matthews as 'impertinent' and the Archbishop rejected it on the grounds that it 'was not really suitable'. Certainly the opening words were not promising:

'When a young maiden gives her hand in marriage to a man and consents to join her life with him it means that she emerges from the privacy of home and family and stands, it may be for the first time, in the public eye'. It saved the Archbishop a great deal of embarrassment when he decided to write the address himself, though he wisely let the Bishop of Winchester and the Dean of St Paul's see the finished product for their approval.

As the day of the wedding drew nearer, the Archbishop visited the Palace to view the presents, and was invited to a reception, 'quite Victorian in its beauty and splendour' when Mrs Fisher, somewhat shyly sporting a tiara, was relieved when she found a large number of ladies similarly adorned.

And so, the traumas behind the scenes being now disposed of, 20 November, the day of the marriage, came. To help the ordinary listener on the radio to understand the significance of the broadcast service and the vows taken, the Archbishop drew up an 'Introduction' which concluded: 'Whether used in Westminster Abbey or in a simple parish church unmistakeably it declares the dignity of Christian marriage and surrounds it with the loving purpose and continuing grace of Christ'.

A detailed account of the ceremony was drawn up by Mrs Fisher who sat at the east end of the choir. The Abbey, she wrote, was its 'usual splendid self, its traditions, royal associations coming alive and showing off to best advantage the colour, commitment and pageantry of the occasion'. The Archbishop's procession was headed by the Moderator of the General Assembly of the Church of Scotland – he had no speaking part – and was followed by the Bishops of London and Norwich. As to the bride, when she passed through the choir to the sacrarium, Mrs Fisher commented: 'She looked absolutely lovely coming up the aisle and though her dress was in fact made of satin, the general effect of her whole outfit was a diaphanous one with her lovely train of silk tulle and her veil. She looked very calm as she walked up the aisle and two little pages were enchanting with their solemn responsible faces'. After the service was over, the royal family, with the Archbishop and the Dean of Westminster, withdrew to St Edward's Chapel for the signing of the register. The King was 'deeply moved and on the verge of tears', remarking to the Archbishop: 'It is a far more moving thing to give away your daughter than to be married yourself'.

The Archbishop and Mrs Fisher went afterwards to the Palace for the wedding breakfast at which he said grace, having mingled while waiting for the cars with the Attlees, the Churchills and General Smuts. It gave the Archbishop great satisfaction some months later when the Italian Ambassador on calling in at Lambeth told him that he found the royal wedding simple and moving, a contrast from the 'more flamboyant Roman Catholic worship'. Doubtless the simplicity to which the Ambassador referred was in part due to the dignified, restrained and yet personal way the Archbishop conducted the ceremony.

We have already noticed that it fell to the Archbishop to baptize the infants of many members of the royal family. This on occasions led to some personal embarrassment. Thus the birth of Charles (Prince of Wales), which Geoffrey Fisher greeted with an appropriate telegram to the Queen, led to his receiving a request from the Baptismal Reform Movement in the form of a telegram from the vicar of St Augustine's church, Bermondsey, which ran as follows: 'With great respect suggest use influence towards Public Baptism of Royal baby, per Lambeth recommendation. Secondary consideration provide opportunities for public rejoicing. Royal Family set example of public worship. Public Baptism of great value'. Geoffrey Fisher's reply to the telegram and to a similar letter from H. G. Blomfield was terse and forthright. It was 'impossible to suggest any departure from the tradition that the Royal babies are baptised in one of the Private Chapels of the King'. These precedents could not be violated in this way. As it happens, many baptisms take place in school chapels and elsewhere, as for example in St Stephen's chapel in the House of Commons. There would be grave inconveniences if the royal baptisms were held in Westminster Abbey which would lead to great crowds and the presence of the police. There *was* in fact a congregation at the Palace as representative as in a parish church.

Another similar protest came from the Bishop of Bradford, representing the northern branch of the Baptismal Reform Movement. It ran as follows: 'We, the undersigned humbly suggest to Your Grace that if you are able to exercise any influence in this matter, the Baptism of the Royal infant should be administered publicly. We believe that such an event would provide great opportunities for National rejoicing. It would also set the example of compliance with the rubric in the Prayer Book of 1662'. This telegram got the same treatment. Maybe from a purely practical point of view the Archbishop was right, but a little more sensitivity to what the Baptismal Reform Movement was about might have been helpful.

Modern royalty, indeed like their medieval predecessors, tend to be constantly on the move. Their travels are of national interest and a careful watch was kept on them where they went, whom they saw and what they did. When there were criticisms and a religious interest seemed to be involved, the complainant often would write to Lambeth (as we have already seen) hoping that the Archbishop would take up his cause, and do so more effectively than if he had undertaken this himself.

In 1949, it was announced that Princess Margaret was to visit the

Vatican. At least two people, a Methodist superintendent in Tonbridge and a lady in Colindale, protested against this as causing 'grave disquiet' and urged the Archbishop to prevent it. Geoffrey Fisher did not necessarily wish to associate himself with this criticism nor did he even know whether in fact the visit was to take place. (*The Times* newspaper had said nothing about it). He thought it his duty, however, to acquaint Sir Alan Lascelles that letters were beginning to come to him and 'no doubt a good many people will be disturbed by such a visit'. To this letter Lascelles replied admitting that the Palace was getting 'plenty of letters from all the usual people about the possibility of Princess Margaret paying a courtesy call on the Pope when she is in Rome'. He went on: 'Any suggestion that any member of the Royal Family is taking notice of His Holiness invariably produces a similar crop. I never do any more than acknowledge them politely and, if the writers become too importunate, I send them to the Home Secretary. Such critics forget that the Pope is a Head of a sovereign state and that the Queen is diplomatically represented at the Vatican and as a consequence little acts of politeness are well nigh inevitable'. The Princess' he reaffirmed, 'will probably visit the Vatican' – which she did. Doubtless extreme Protestant opinion felt it keenly, though more liberal people welcomed it.

A more serious controversy developed over Princess Elizabeth's proposed visit to the Buddhist Temple of the Tooth in Kandy, Ceylon. The Archbishop was first made aware of this possibility by a notice in *The Sunday Times* to the effect that the Princess and the Duke of Edinburgh were to make an offertory of gold sovereigns on this occasion. The suggestion that she should do this in the Temple came from the Governor-General who saw it as a perfectly normal act of courtesy when distinguished people visited Kandy. The Archbishop was clearly worried as to the possible repercussions of this eirenic gesture. 'I felt myself,' so he wrote to Sir Martin Charteris, the Princess's private secretary, 'there was need for some caution here. If it were supposed in Ceylon' he continued, 'or indeed elsewhere, that in some form or manner the Princess was paying homage to the Buddha in his Temple, it might seriously discourage and injure Singhalese Christians who have come out of Buddhism into Christianity. To visit the Temple is one thing: to make an offertory apparently to the Buddha is another thing and might be regarded as injurious to the Christian Church in Ceylon It would be rather like going to India and making an offering in a Mosque'. Such views were shared by the Bishop of Colombo. Perhaps the best solution would be for the Princess and the Duke simply to make a charitable gift to a society for the relief of Buddhists.

Martin Charteris was not anxious to accommodate himself entirely to the Archbishop's views, though the Bishop of Gloucester, among others, supported them. As her private secretary Charteris explained, what the Princess and Duke were doing was merely customary, though he recognised the need for some caution. The Princess herself felt it right to follow the advice of the Governor-General of Ceylon. 'Since her actions are always scrutinized and commented upon the Princess feels that her failure to do so might cause offence to the Buddhist subjects of the King of Ceylon and elsewhere'. The Archbishop, meanwhile, remained in touch with the Bishop of Colombo.

As it was, the death of King George VI and the accession of Princess Elizabeth to the Throne led to the visit being called off for the time being.

However, it proved to be merely a postponement, for early in 1953 plans were renewed for the Queen to go to Ceylon. Not surprisingly, the same problems as in 1951 arose again, made somewhat more acute, as she herself realised, by her now being Queen and recently crowned in Westminster Abbey. The matter was one on which the Queen, very properly in view of her constitutional position, sought advice from her Prime Minister who was now Winston Churchill and it was left to him to confer with the Archbishop. The latter's alarm was now heightened by a rumour that the visit to the Temple was to take place on Good Friday. The Archbishop immediately got in touch with Lascelles, the Queen's secretary, letting him know that the Bishop of Colombo was still worried and would prefer the visit to the Temple not to take place: 'If in spite of all it is felt that she must go to the Temple of the Tooth, I hope that it might not be on her programme but that, as sometimes happens, it might be said to be on the spur of the moment although carefully planned beforehand, and quietly and not in State, she slips off and sees the Temple'. The Tooth itself in this case should not be on display. Sir Michael Adeane, who had now become the Queen's private secretary, wrote reassuringly to the Archbishop saying that he himself would be with the Queen, and that she would probably not be going to the Temple at all. Meanwhile, protests continued to come in to Lambeth in the main from evangelicals, lay and clerical, who lavishly illustrated their case from biblical texts such as: 'He that sacrificeth unto any God, save unto the Lord only, he shall be utterly destroyed'.

The discussion had now reached Cabinet level and Winston Churchill did his best to mollify the Archbishop by explaining a little more fully the general background of what was intended, pointing out that he himself had written to Sir John Kotelawala, the new Prime Minister of Ceylon. This was important because constitutionally in relation to the Commonwealth he was the person to advise the Queen in respect of his own country. The Prime Minister was reassuring in that, so he wrote, it was traditional for a royal procession of elephants and for Engish royalty, following the practise of the ancient Kings of Kandy to witness it from the Octagon of the Temple of the Tooth, this being reached via a corridor through the Temple. The Prime Minister went on to say that he would be distressed if the Queen did not see the Buddha's Tooth since such an omission would serve to mar the whole visit to Ceylon. The requirement to remove one's shoes was merely an act of courtesy and there would be no offertory. The Queen's own attitude, Winston Churchill informed the Archbishop, was that she had no objection to the visit to the Temple, provided no religious ceremony was involved. Also, as Queen of Ceylon, she was reluctant to reject the advice of the Prime Minister of that country. For these reasons, the Cabinet's advice to the Queen was that she should go forward with the visit, though it was realised that this would be criticized by churchmen in both Ceylon and Britain. The Queen was fully aware of the great difference in her position on Church matters now that she had ascended the Throne. 'Nevertheless,' Sir Michael went on, 'she said to me this morning that she felt that if going into a temple for a non-religious ceremony, in order to satisfy the wishes of many millions of her Buddhist subjects was going to afford offence to the Christians, it was a sad commentary on their trust in her Christian faith, which she herself considered to be above question'. The Cabinet's recommendations would, Sir Michael added, weigh heavily with the Queen and if she accepted the invitation it would be 'to maintain the structure of the British Commonwealth in the form it is at present'. The Queen was convinced that the Prime Minister of Ceylon would be 'ready to defend and explain her action to the Church Authorities, or to any other section of the British Public which might criticise it' – particularly to the Archbishop of Canterbury. The latter was informed privately of the Queen's approach to the visit, and responded by saying that much would depend on the attitude of the Press, and he therefore urged Sir Michael Adeane to see that it was presented by the media in a 'calm and objective way' without suggesting that the Queen was doing some kind of 'homage to the Buddhist religion'. It was clearly recognised at the Palace and particularly by the Queen that the Archbishop must be kept in close touch with developments at Whitehall, Colombo and London.

The Queen had now made her final decision to go on with the visit to Kandy, and the Archbishop fully concurred. Sir Edward Ford, an Assistant Private Secretary to the Queen, informed the Archbishop that the Queen was pleased and relieved to hear of his full support for the decision, which she had made. Edward Ford added that he was sure the Archbishop would expect the Queen to pay the usual courtesies which would be expected of a Mohammedan in Westminster Abbey. The Archbishop replied that he was 'entirely happy', provided that: (a)

the Queen was visiting the Temple primarily to watch the traditional
procession of elephants; (b) she removed her shoes to conform to the
local custom; (c) there was no religious ceremony of any kind and no
offertory.

The Archbishop also took the precaution to prevent, so far as was
possible hostile comment by getting in touch with the editors of the
Church of England Newspaper, *The Guardian* and the *Church Times*,
explaining what was to happen and suggesting how they might handle
it. He also wrote to *The Times*.

Thus the visit to the Temple of the Tooth went forward without
incident or hostile press coverage, though evangelicals were not
pleased.

It cannot be claimed that Geoffrey Fisher was an enthusiastic
supporter of this enterprise. The dialogue of faiths had not yet got
under way. Also he was particularly under pressure from the Bishop of
Colombo; and the missionary societies, evangelically geared, found it
hard to understand the why and the wherefore of this visit. However,
the Archbishop realised that the visit derived from the initiative of the
Prime Minister in Ceylon; and was welcomed by the British Government and the Palace. Once the decision was made that it should go
forward the Archbishop did everything in his power to minimize
friction and to dampen down possible controversy. The Queen
throughout showed surprising poise and maturity for one who had so
recently come to the Throne. She was indeed sensitive to the Commonwealth dimension in the process of decision-making, an augury of the
steady and continuing support which she was to give over the years to
this association of autonomous states.

It is often the case that Archbishops of Canterbury meet up at public
dinners with individual members of the royal family. Such happened in
July 1949, when Geoffrey Fisher sat next to Princess Marie Louise
when they reminisced about Winnington Ingram, Bishop of London,
whom both had known well. The result was that the Archbishop sent
her the Bishop's biography. It did not conceal, so he commented, his
'weaknesses in administration and the like but it does make evident the
astonishing power of his personal faith and love which made him such
a unique and magnetic person'. In the course of their conversation at
dinner, the Princess confessed that no clergyman had ever called on
her, and that if she were dying she would not know whom to send for.
With his customary efficiency the Archbishop later found out that the
church concerned was Grosvenor Chapel, which induced him to write
to its minister, the Reverend H. G. Whiteman, at Liddon House, asking
him to call and get to know her. 'She is a good and spirited old lady',
he commented, 'who has always been a faithful Christian, and in the
past has done a good deal of social work in a Christian spirit'. The

Reverend H. G. Whiteman, unfortunately if understandably, regarded the Archbishop's letter as an implied criticism, and he pointed out that the Princess had not in fact been to the Chapel since he had arrived there nor was her name given to him by his predecessor. True, some time ago he heard that she wanted to see him but this was so indirect that he thought it an intrusion to follow it up. He promised, however, to see that this 'omission' was now repaired.

The royal family often became subject to irresponsible gossip of such a kind as to percolate through to Lambeth. Typical was a correspondent who wrote saying that she constantly heard from Roman Catholics, one a priest, that King Edward VII was received into that Church on his deathbed. The Archbishop, ludicrous though this story might appear, felt it his duty to pass it on to Sir Alan Lascelles. Lascelles replied that though he himself had never heard this particular story, his colleagues told him that this was one of the 'hardy annuals'. 'For your private information,' he added, 'the King has personally assured me that the story is entirely without foundation; and I feel that if there had been even a shadow of such foundation, I should have heard of it from my sister, Blanche Lloyd, who was lady-in-waiting as a Maid of Honour to Queen Alexandra at the time of the King's death.' One explanation of this story might be that Lord Halifax once publicly referred to Edward VII as a 'staunch member of the Catholic church', from which, he commented, the "uneducated" might infer a member of the Church of Rome.

Royalty today, with modern means of transport, are more peripatetic than ever before. Such movement often leads to enquiries reaching Lambeth. Thus when in 1952 the Princess Royal was planning to visit Barbados, the Bishop of Trinidad enquired of the Archbishop what preferences did she entertain in her church-going habits. He could minister to all kinds, he wrote. 'It would be most unfortunate,' he pointed out, 'if in so religious a part of the world as the West Indies – or, perhaps more accurately, so church-going a part of the world – there should be any slip-up.' The Archbishop consulted Dr Garbett of York, and also wrote to the Princess Royal herself, as a result of which he suggested to the Bishop that she would prefer an early said celebration on Sundays with matins later.

In October 1954, the Queen Mother was due to visit Guildford, and her private secretary asked the Archbishop whether there ought to be a service on that occasion. He replied that usually his answer to such a question, when doubtful, was 'no': but in this case it was 'unhesitatingly yes'.

Some royal visits in which the Archbishop was engaged were indeed happy and relaxed, and presented few problems. Such was the case when the Queen visited the Archbishop's old school, Marlborough, of which he was Visitor, in October 1955. Michael Adeane described it as 'one of the pleasantest and happiest evenings of the year'; and Arthur Penn wrote enthusiastically that 'the combination of an exceptional occasion and of a delightful informality produced a pleasure which is not often found and those of us who had the good fortune to be present will long bear it in our hearts and minds'.

Later in the year 1955, the Archbishop's advice was sought in connection with the Queen's departure for Nigeria. Here, for the benefit of her private secretary, he set out in some detail the background of church life in that country situated as it was in the proposed Province of West Africa, with its four dioceses, three of which had African bishops. Dr Fisher also got in touch with the Archbishop there, suggesting he should give the Blessing at the service in Lagos Cathedral but that he should tactfully make it clear to his bishops that his presence was a duty owed to the Queen. All went well and Michael Adeane thanked the Archbishop for his 'valuable advice'.

Some occasions could well prove sensitive and among such was the proposed visit of the Queen in 1960 to address the General Assembly of the Church of Scotland. On this matter the Archbishop wrote at length to Sir Austin Strutt. Some old controversies, he reflected, never seemed to die and this was true north of the Border where the publication of the Anglican-Presbyterian Report had stirred up 'flames of controversy once more'. If it were known that he, the Archbishop, had advised the Queen against such a visit to the General Assembly to celebrate Knox and the Scottish Reformation, it would be 'another knife with which to stab the Church of England'. Doubtless some members of the *Ecclesia Anglicana* would take 'an ill view' of such a visit by the Queen but he himself did not. The Church of Scotland was the established Church of that country. In many ways the Queen, as Supreme Governor of the Church of England by undertaking this journey was recognising the position of the Church of Scotland, honouring it with her personal presence. Indeed, it was through his initiative that the Church of Scotland was given 'a little place' in the Coronation Service. This was accepted gratefully by 'the best members' of the Church of Scotland, though the Nationalists complained that it was a very little share. If he thought that the Queen's appearance at the General Assembly was 'likely to start a series of increasing demands upon her' he should be against it. In an accompanying private letter, he pointed out that the Queen had not yet visited the Church Assembly! It only remains to add that the visit to the General Assembly went well.

The Archbishop felt that among his responsibilities he was called upon to entertain a concern for the provisions made for the worshipful life of the Queen as the Supreme Governor of the Church of England.

For example, he corresponded on this matter concerning the facilities on HMS *Gothic* on which she was travelling to Australia.

Events connected with the royal family and their entourage have always attracted public interest though the content of the reportage is too often frivolous. No such criticism can be lodged at the door of the vicar of Kidlington, who sent a letter to the Archbishop on 26 September 1953. This concerned the religious ministrations provided for the domestic staff of the royal family at Buckingham Palace, Windsor, Sandringham and Balmoral, the royal residences. There were in fact, he stated, no facilities for Holy Communion on Sunday mornings nor any service laid on for the children. The Archbishop was disturbed at this news, and wrote to the Reverend Maurice Foxell, Sub-Dean of the Chapels Royal, who confirmed that this was the case. There was in fact no chapel in Buckingham Palace since it was destroyed in the last war. Under George V there were daily prayers at 9.00 am, when the Court was in residence, as also there was a monthly Holy Communion. This gave the Chaplain a pastoral opportunity: with the closure of the Chapel this had come to an end. Foxell himself asked Sir Piers Leigh, Master of the Household, for the allocation of a room till the Chapel was restored, but was told that there was not a 'convenient room available'. He had mentioned this both to the Queen and the Duke of Edinburgh, but though he was sure they were 'favourable' nothing had happened, and consequently he did not feel he could do any more.

So the problem thus described remained, but the Archbishop felt he could not leave it as it was, and he wrote personally to the Queen pointing out to her that the chaplains had a responsibility in relation to the staff at Buckingham Palace but during the 'whole time' of his archiepiscopate there had been no opportunity for members of staff to attend Holy Communion except on their weekends off. He would wish to raise two matters: (1) that duties could be so arranged as to make attendance at Holy Communion possible; (2) that there should be a chapel at least in Buckingham Palace.

Until this could be laid on there should be a small room adapted for such a purpose. This would give Maurice Foxell a chance of getting to know the personnel. 'Again, Madam,' he concluded, 'all I ask is whether I might explore the matter further with Sir Piers Leigh or whomsoever you might appoint during your absence'. The Archbishop followed this matter up with a confidential talk to the Queen Mother on 30 October. She thought that something could be done while the Queen was away in Australia and she would discuss this with her. At her last party before she departed to the Antipodes, Her Majesty referred to this matter in conversation with the Archbishop in a spirit of 'great sympathy and understanding'. It remains only to say that something was done and, *inter alia*, the chapel, as a result, was itself finally restored.

The Archbishop felt strongly that the spiritual life of members of the royal family mattered, not only to themselves but to the nation. Thus on 6 April 1950, in wishing Queen Mary 'every joy and peace and spiritual comfort at the great Easter Festival of Our Risen Lord,' he added these words: '. . . if at any time I can be of service to Your Majesty by coming to Marlborough House to take a brief service to celebrate Holy Communion, to save your going out of doors, I am at your command'.

When the Queen returned in 1954 from a long tour of the Commonwealth, the Archbishop was among those who believed that she should be given a royal homecoming. He was, however, a little 'narked' that Winston Churchill, then Prime Minister, without any reference to Lambeth should jump the gun and publicly urge that church bells be rung. This led to a missive to Lord Salisbury suggesting the Prime Minister and Archbishop should confer, but nothing came of this. Geoffrey Fisher was opposed to overdoing things and he did not believe the Queen would appreciate a service in St Paul's Cathedral. He drew up a statement which survives in his own handwriting in Lambeth Palace Library: 'In London we are able to give visible expression to our rejoicing at the Queen's safe return, greeting her as she sets foot again on English soil at Westminster, cheering her through the streets back to Buckingham Palace – the church bells from their ancient towers proclaiming for all of us the Nation's welcome and every one of us is saying again and again – 'how lovely to have you back again'. And then we say a very affectionate and admiring 'well done'. For there never has been such a Queen's tour in distance covered, in countries visited, in the number of people met, greeted, conquered and inspired, nor in the ceaseless demands made upon the Queen herself. By universal consent she has done it marvellously – flawlessly and joyfully – bringing everywhere new power to [old] loyalties, new unity to the family of the Commonwealth, a new lovely fragrance to the lives of all who came in reach of her. Not for nothing was she anointed, consecrated, crowned in the Abbey a year ago. God is in all this and His hand is upon her. When all is said, we say from our hearts, 'thank God for her – and God bless her'.

Read years afterwards and more calmly these sentiments strike one as exaggerated and fulsome; yet they reflect a contemporary mood not least engendered by a young Queen in the aftermath of her Coronation.

If Winston Churchill had upset the Archbishop by his somewhat cavalier treatment of the Church and its bells, Geoffrey Fisher was equally disappointed that he, as Archbishop, was not among those who were to be invited to greet the Queen on her return at Westminster

Pier. He admitted that according to strict protocol an Archbishop was not usually present on such occasions but, as he told Lord Scarbrough, such an exclusion was 'pointedly wrong on this special occasion'. 'The Church crowned the Queen not long before she started,' he wrote, 'the splendour and deeply spiritual meaning of her Coronation preceded and went with her. Almost everywhere she attended Anglican cathedral services all round the world. Anglican Primates and Archbishops were included in those who welcomed her. At Malta, by way of contrast, the Roman Catholic Archbishop will take a very prominent part among those who will welcome her to Malta. And yet when she gets home again, stands on English soil, the Archbishop of Canterbury is not there and the Church is not represented'.

The argument which Geoffrey Fisher here put forward and which he claimed constituted an unanswerable case for a change in protocol, at least on this occasion, was conceded, though Lord Scarbrough warned the Archbishop not to 'think it appropriate that the Archbishop of Canterbury is automatically present'.

From time to time the Archbishop saw the Queen, not so much on matters of business or specific issues, but to talk freely with her. These sessions were so informal as not to leave any official record behind them. However, on one occasion at least the Archbishop recorded an account of a conversation held on 29 October 1958 which lasted about an hour. In his recollections of this audience, he described it as of 'a most cheerful, easy and far-ranging character'.

The Queen began by mentioning Guildford Cathedral and her embarrassment because she wished to be present at the institution of the new Dean but the date, tentatively fixed, was alas! 1 June 1960 – Derby Day! Here the Archbishop tactfully replied that he 'would quietly persuade the Bishop that the Tuesday would be a more convenient day for him (ie the Archbishop) and then he would write to Michael Adeane begging to correct his previous letter as it now appeared that the Tuesday would suit the Diocese better than the Wednesday.

The Archbishop now referred to her 'magnificent bearing' at the Opening of Parliament and 'not least, on the way she had delivered her speech, saying "Gov-ern-ment" rather than "Guvment". She confessed to having rejected some phrases in the script as unspeakable and got them altered though she had to accept some dreadful jargon such as 'specific statutory proposals'.

Of this interview, the Archbishop writes: 'She was in very good form, laughing at my jokes and laughing at a large number of her own'. What he could not say, though certainly true, was that it was he made it easy for a charming yet naturally shy person to respond positively in this uninhibited way.

The interest of the public, or perhaps more accurately, the interest of the Press in 'titivating' the public did not only focus on the immediate circle of the royal family but on more distant connections not least on their marriages, particularly when there were unusual features about them.

Such was the marriage of Lady Anson, daughter of Queen Elizabeth's brother, to Prince George of Denmark which was due to take place in the private chapel of Glamis Castle on 16 September 1950, the ceremony to be conducted by a Danish pastor. The Prince and the Princess Axel of Denmark and the Crown Prince of Norway were to stay at Balmoral. Sir Alan Lascelles had early taken the Archbishop into his confidence about the ceremony since one of the parties was a divorcee. King George VI had declared his intention of not attending and this was conveyed to the Archbishop. The Queen, however, was so intimately involved family-wise as 'to make her non-attendance impossible'.

It was inevitable that the marriage should incur criticism, particularly in some Church circles. Thus Harold Riley, Secretary of the Church Union, wrote to the Archbishop that in view of the circumstances it was 'very unfortunate that there will be an appearance of public approval on the part of their Majesties for remarriage after divorce'. 'It would seem a pity', he went on, 'that they should not be made aware of the distress which their action will cause to many. And if Your Grace is able to make any representations in the matter I should like you to know that you would be representing the opinion of many devout Church people.' To this letter the Archbishop replied that it was 'never safe' to trust Press reports. He had in fact made his views known to the Queen and no minister of either the Church of Scotland or the Church of England would officiate. Great family pressure had been brought to bear upon the Queen. On the same day as he sent off his letter to Riley he also wrote to the Queen. This letter deserves quotation at length:

To Her Majesty, the Queen, Madam: 'May I crave pardon if I am speaking out of my place; nothing but a sense of necessity would make me write about what I may refer to as the Glamis Wedding. Madam, may I say how deeply I sympathise with you on being faced with an intolerably difficult decision, with the most profound family affections and loyalties telling so compellingly on the one side. Sir Alan Lascelles has told me, by the King's instructions, what the situation is. The Church of England is in no way compromised since the Officiating Minister will not be a Minister of the Church of England or of the Church of Scotland or of the Episcopal Church in Scotland, and the King will not be present. That, if necessary, I can state publicly. To Your Majesty's presence at the Wedding, I should of course make no public reproach whatsoever; and I hope no one else will. As I said before, I acutely realise the tremendous pressure upon you of family ties. But Madam, I feel it to be my duty humbly to submit to you certain considerations, even though I am confident they have not been absent from your mind. I can put them very shortly. If in spite of all the pressure of natural affections upon you you did not attend the Wedding, it would, as hardly anything else could, strengthen the hands of all who are struggling to preserve Christian standards of marriage. If you attend it (and even more if Princess Margaret is with you) it will terribly weaken that cause; and, Madam, the more fatally, if I may dare to say it, because you have so gloriously led us all in proclaiming Christian principles of marriage. I so deeply appreciate your dilemma; but one cannot speak about it in public, and part of the cancer destroying the stability of marriage in people's minds, is that each family when the trouble comes into the family circle, so naturally makes allowance and by doing so weakens the Christian witness. With humble respect I do really tremble to think of the effect which your presence there would have on the Mothers' Union and on all who are trying to uphold Christian standards of marriage – and of how enemies of those standards will take advantage of it. Madam, I must write because your influence in this matter is unique. I must say so much to ease my own conscience. But I write with the deepest respect and with the utmost sympathy for you in this predicament'.

The Archbishop kept the Primus of the Scottish Episcopal Church and the Archbishop of York informed of developments, stressing the agonising dilemma of the Queen. It is clear from his letter to her that he was doubtful whether it would prove effective. As the day of the wedding drew nearer many telephone calls were exchanged between those involved. The Bishop of St Andrews seems to have thought that he would be conducting the ceremony but apparently was unaware of the particular background to the marriage – which he finally learned of from the newspapers.

To make confusion worse confounded, it was rumoured that a Canon Horison, in the same state of ignorance, believed himself to be taking the wedding. Lascelles rang Lambeth to say that the Queen was most grateful for the Archbishop's letter of sympathy, understanding and forcefulness and was 'still in a quandary'. Princess Alice, Duchess of Gloucester, was 'greatly distressed' at the prospect of the wedding and herself sought help and advice from Archbishop Fisher. 'What ordinary people do is their own concern up to a point, but what the King and Queen and Royal Family do is a matter of concern, and I dread the harm done and the repercussions if the King and Queen and their daughter countenance this marriage of a divorced person' – so he wrote to Princess Alice.

It was all an anxious and exhausting time. Sir Alan Lascelles felt it most keenly and unburdened himself to the Archbishop. Quite obviously communication between the various parties was poor and Sir Alan partly blamed Canon Horison and the Danish Embassy for some of the 'leakages'. The Queen, he confided to Geoffrey Fisher, was 'distressed' that he, the Archbishop, should be equally so. 'You and I have a good deal to put up with in all this. Luckily we are both broad-shouldered'.

For the more popular Press, 'The Glamis Wedding' provided appetizing copy. *The Sunday Express* on 17 September 1950, carried an article by John Gordon under the heading: 'The Archbishop and the Queen' in the course of which he wrote: 'Not so long ago an Archbishop of Canterbury helped to push a British King off the Throne. Yesterday another Archbishop of Canterbury subjected the Queen to an intolerable humiliation'. A correspondent to the same newspaper regretted that Dr Fisher had not lived in the time of Henry VIII. 'There would then be one vacancy for an Archbishop', so he commented.

One cannot but feel sorry for all concerned, particularly in respect of the conflict of loyalties by which most of them were torn. The Archbishop had long taken the view that the Church of England must show its disapproval of divorce by refusing to marry a divorcee in a Church building and had seen this as an essential witness. He entertained a 'high' view of the monarchy and the importance of the example that it set. Its members should be beyond reproach. In this case, he went further, taking the view that the mere presence of royalty at the marriage of a divorcee would be seen as a tacit or implied approval of what had taken place. Here, it might well be argued, that the Archbishop committed himself to a too extreme attitude, particularly in view of the highly-charged emotional situation in which the Queen found herself. Also attendance at a wedding might not necessarily be taken as approving all the circumstances attaching to it.

The marriage duly went forward and the Queen attended it.

The Glamis Wedding was exceptional in its repercussions though earlier in the year there had been a marriage which Geoffrey Fisher feared might lead to publicity based on a misunderstanding. This was the Rhodes-Elphinstone wedding, the latter being a connection of the royal family. This marriage had behind it a divorce in the form of a legal decree of nullity which Dennis Rhodes had successfully sought. The decree of nullity was another way of saying that there never had been a valid legal marriage from the beginning. The Archbishop consulted his legal secretary, H. T. A. Dashwood, and as a result of his advice very properly issued a special licence for the marriage to take place. Fortunately, in this case, Press publicity was at a very much lower level.

Geoffrey Fisher was in no way involved in the abdication of King

Edward VIII so that he escaped the vilification which the ecclesiastics who were then concerned drew upon themselves. The subsequent history of the Duke of Windsor after his leaving England if, as seems likely, it was one of domestic felicity with Mrs Simpson, yet presented problems in denying him what we now call 'job satisfaction'.

For a time the Duke of Windsor was Governor of the Bahamas in which capacity he felt keenly his alienation from the Church of England and its sacraments. The Bishop of Nassau, in response to an enquiry from Lambeth early in 1946, wrote to the Archbishop conveying his own somewhat sombre reflections. The Duke and Duchess when in Nassau attended worship in Christ Church Cathedral about once a month and on special occasions such as Good Friday. They slipped in quietly, sitting inconspicuously at the back of the church. They were generous in their financial support of the charitable works undertaken by the congregation. They never attended the celebration of Holy Communion in the Cathedral though they would, in other churches, at a late sung mass when only the celebrant received the sacrament. Their object was not to make themselves conspicuous. Fortunately for the present Bishop, so he told Archbishop Fisher, the ecclesiastical status of the Duke and Duchess was determined by his predecessor, Bishop John Douglas, namely that they could be church members but not communicants receiving the sacraments. Dr Fisher preferred to leave matters as they were, though his chaplain let the Bishop of Nassau know that if there were any change in their status the Archbishop would wish to be 'reassured' that the Duke had 'a real desire' to receive the sacrament and was duly penitent.

It is a pity that this matter was not taken up but left in this bleak ambiguity. If it had been, maybe this picture of the Duke in exile would not seem so pathetic.

It has often been said of members of the royal family in the United Kingdom that if they did not exist someone would need to invent them. To journalists and those addicted to gossip, they are invaluable and many are the apocryphal stories which circulate about them. In 1957, Geoffrey Fisher was apprised of a booklet written by Father R. C. Fuller, a Roman Catholic priest, in which he related that Queen Mary used a church of that persuasion engaging in the harmless exercise of putting flowers on a statue of Our Lady. The Archbishop made enquiries of Lady Cynthia Colville, her aide, as to whether there was any truth in this story. She denied it, adding that it was a perfect example of 'wishful thinking'. The Queen Mother, she said, never went on mysterious journeys.

Geoffrey Fisher took action by writing to Cardinal Godfrey at Westminster Cathedral asking him to withdraw this untrue statement from the booklet which he willingly agreed to do in the next issue.

For good measure the Archbishop also paid a call on Pope Hennessy, Queen Mary's biographer, introducing himself jocularly as 'sometimes Enemy Number One of the Roman Catholic Church'. Pope Hennessy in a subsequent letter to the Archbishop remarked that the Roman Church might well have reminded the Queen Mother of the Florentine churches where she was taken to mass by her parents in the years 1883-1885 where they almost certainly went for the music.

Archbishops of Canterbury in their dealing with royalty frequently prove to be accident-prone, sometimes in the very nature of the case, at other times as the result of an irresponsible Press which affected to see the role of the Primate of all England as an ecclesiastical policeman, whose concern was to inhibit members of the Royal Family from what, left to themselves, they would wish to do. Archbishop Lang had strong opinions about this, and the above is perhaps not an unfair or inaccurate account of what happened in the *cause célèbre* of Princess Margaret to which we now turn.

As the Princess grew up, Geoffrey Fisher saw her frequently, admiring her many-sided gifts and interests. As he looked back on these days in retirement, he recalled her as 'always friendly, always intelligent and always entertaining'. She was also a conscientious and regular churchgoer, attending the Lent courses regularly at St Paul's, Knightsbridge when the Reverend E. B. Henderson (later Bishop of Bath and Wells) was vicar, often accompanied by her cousin, Elizabeth Elphinstone. She was helped spiritually by Mother Mary Clare.

The crisis with which Archbishop Fisher became associated began when it was widely reported that Princess Margaret was intending to marry Group Captain Peter Townsend, who, prior to leaving the Queen Mother's household to become an air attaché in Brussels, had been the innocent party in divorce proceedings. Speculation as to Princess Margaret's intentions increased, and her secretary felt it necessary to appeal to the Press, with 'its customary courtesy and co-operation', to respect her privacy. On 28 October 1955 there appeared the announcement that: 'Princess Margaret had gone to Lambeth Palace yesterday afternoon and was received by the Archbishop of Canterbury. She stayed nearly an hour'.

While Princess Margaret was making up her mind on this major issue which must affect the whole pattern of her future life, the popular Press – and not only they – seized the opportunity to make its view heard. *The Daily Mirror*, for example, (26 October), pontificated with magisterial authority: 'The time has come for plain speaking', it protested; and then went on to condemn 'this cruel plan' to persuade the Princess, 'against her will', to break off the relationship. *The Times* newspaper (26 October) weighed up the pros and cons solemnly: 'If the Princess finally decides, with all the anxious deliberations that clearly she has given to her problem, that she is unable to make the sacrifice involved in her continued dedication to her inherited past, then she has a right to lay down a burden that is too heavy for her. It would, however, involve withdrawal not merely from her formal rights in the succession established by law, together with such official duties as sometimes fall to her under the Regency Acts, but abandonment of her place in the Royal Family as a group fulfilling innumerable symbolic and representative duties'. However, on 1 November, a formal statement was issued announcing that the Princess had decided not to marry the Group Captain. In arriving at this decision she was 'mindful of the Church's teaching that Christian marriage is indissoluble'. She had acted alone on the grounds of conscience and she thanked those who had prayed for her and the help given throughout by Group Captain Townsend.

It was difficult for many, particularly those who were ill-disposed to the Church, to accept what in fact was true, namely that on her last visit to Lambeth the Archbishop had not attempted to persuade the Princess to break off the engagement. Press, radio and television coverage was, as might have been expected, extensive, the strain on the Archbishop being equally heavy, and beginning to tell on him. Thus it was unfortunate that in an interview with Richard Dimbleby the Archbishop remonstrated testily that he did not care 'two hoots' what people might be saying and that much of it represented a 'popular wave of stupid emotionalism'. Such language evoked a further extreme reaction which, paradoxically, went far to justify the somewhat intemperate words which the Archbishop had himself used.

The Daily Mirror (3 and 5 November) commented that Princess Margaret's decision must not be allowed 'to wreck two lives,' protesting that there was 'a rising tide of anger' and the time had now come for the Church of England to be disestablished. *The News Chronicle* declared that the national church should look again at the whole question of divorce and remarriage. Even the *San Francisco News*, emanating from that delectable cable car city on the West Coast of America, expressed blank astonishment at the whole business. 'We Americans never will understand British royalty. Let's admit it. It all started with George III, the foolish King who lost this fabulous Colony'. When the Archbishop, some time later, travelling on the *Edinburgh Castle* held a Press conference in Cape Town, he was inundated with questions about Princess Margaret to all of which – it was certainly out of character – he replied: 'No comment'. He did deny firmly, however, that all England was discussing the 'plight' of the Princess.

Lord Boothby, with monumental inaccuracy, came up with a story reproduced in *The Spectator*, that when Princess Margaret visited the Archbishop at Lambeth she was taken into his study, surrounded by open books on his desk, these being there to assist him from the Church's point of view in arguing the case with her, chapter and verse. The Princess asked him to put away the books so Lord Boothby informs us. The Archbishop was emphatic that this story was completely without foundation. He had no books with him whatever, and, he went on: 'I received her as I would anybody else in the quietness of my study . . . She did say straightaway what her decision had been, and I received it, of course, with gratitude and thanksgiving to Almighty God. And that's all there was about that'. As to the charge that he had brought an unfair influence to bear upon her decision-making, this was a 'complete fabrication'. Lady Fisher in a private letter to the Dean of Westminster also confirmed that Princess Margaret came to Lambeth Palace to inform the Archbishop of the decision, which she herself had already made. Princess Margaret, she said, was a well-informed Christian who had regularly attended the Lent lectures held annually at Lambeth Palace, a feature of Mrs Fisher's hospitality. 'Certainly she did not need the Archbishop to tell her about what the Church's attitude to marriage and divorce was'.

This *contretemps* had everything in it to bring out a latent anti-Church feeling not least in the Beaverbrook press. By associating this *odium ecclesiasticum* with the public's genuine sympathy for a distressed young lady, the popular Press had a national scapegoat, thereby meeting a subliminal human need.

It must not be thought for a moment that only critical letters came to Lambeth. A file in the library is headed: 'Letters of Appreciation Following Princess Margaret's Statement and the Archbishop's TV Interview'. The retired Bishop of Kentucky complimented Geoffrey Fisher on the 'firmness, the love and downright commonsense with which he had handled the delicate and troublesome business of the possible marriage of the Princess to a divorced man'.

The news of the engagement of Princess Margaret to Mr Anthony Armstrong-Jones, an event which when announced came as a complete surprise to the public and even the Press, gave great pleasure and satisfaction to the Archbishop of Canterbury. As usual he saw both the bride and bridegroom together and carefully prepared them for the wedding ceremony.

Though unknown to people by and large, a mild controversy as to what was to happen at the service in the Abbey developed between the Archbishop and Eric Abbott, the eirenic Dean of Westminster, who was for many years a close friend of Princess Margaret. Westminster Abbey is a Royal Peculiar and takes pride in its exemption from any form of episcopal jurisdiction, coming as it does directly under the Queen as Visitor. This means that the Dean is Ordinary, and thus responsible for the form and content of its services. On 10 March 1960 the Archbishop wrote to the Dean saying that Princess Margaret agreed that if he were to read a lesson from the pulpit where the sermon was usually preached, it would look as if he had 'dodged' giving one. Would the Dean himself undertake the Address, this being limited to some five minutes, and could he secure the approval of the Princess who was known to be against having a sermon. The Dean replied that it was wrong of him to 'press Princess Margaret beyond a certain point and that for the Archbishop to say prayers at this stage of the service was against precedent'. The Archbishop found it hard to accept this ruling, and explained to the Dean that the five parts of the Marriage Rite were a unity and this must be preserved in respect of those taking part in the service. As to precedents, he never felt bound by them but judged each case on its own merits. The Dean, supported by Chapter, was adamant and stood his ground.

There was another matter to which the Archbishop felt he must call the Dean's attention. The rubrics which related to the ceremonial had been changed from those drawn up for the Queen's wedding some years earlier. Thus he believed the collective description 'visiting Prelates' was wholly inadequate and that the particular names should be listed. In particular he himself was not simply a 'visiting Prelate' but was in the Abbey on the express command of the Sovereign. In order to add force to what was a reasonable request the Archbishop sought to enlist the support of Lord Nugent but ended his letter to him on a lighter note: 'My dear Nugent, having tried quite unsuccessfully to keep you in order for many years, I am delighted of a chance of having another go at you before you relinquish your present office.' Nugent agreed with the Archbishop that the proper names should be included. In this matter concerning the order of service and its precise form the Dean of Westminster constitutionally had the last word. It is to his credit that without weakening his own position he met the Archbishop's reasonable request. How such a style in respect of individual names crept into the order of service must remain a mystery, except to those who knew the story from the inside.

These and like things are *trivia*, but it must be taken as significant that at St Paul's Cathedral, Canterbury and the Abbey, the Archbishop had brushes with the respective Deans and Chapters over matters ceremonial of this kind. Such was by no means unique to Geoffrey Fisher. Perhaps it was the spot which defiles the robe, the wart on Cromwell's face. True it is that the Abbey has had no difficulties with Dr Fisher's three successors and one may suspect the same is true of Canterbury and St Paul's.

There was a large attendance in the Abbey for the wedding of Princess Margaret with Mr Anthony Armstrong-Jones, when 'official people', ministers and ambassadors were there in full force. All the members of the royal family were present including the Queen of Denmark and the bride came in on the arm of the Duke of Edinburgh. Mrs Fisher, who sat next to Oliver Messel, uncle of the bridegroom, perpetuated her memories of this occasion in a detailed and delightful account. The Dean of Westminster read the introduction and the Archbishop of Canterbury conducted the marriage ceremony, the former's mild controversy now forgotten. There was one minor hitch when Princess Margaret, in an excess of enthusiasm, instead of following the Archbishop leapt in with 'for richer for poorer'. Mrs Fisher's comment was that she had been rehearsed 'a bit too thoroughly'.

After this august ceremony, the reception in Buckingham Palace, to which the Fishers were invited, was a more relaxed affair. Mrs Fisher observed that as the bride and bridegroom went off on their honeymoon the children, led by Prince Charles, picked up the rose petals and pelted the guests. Some fell on the Queen until the Duke rasped out 'Stop that at once. You can throw them at each other if you want to'. They did and the Prince stuffed some petals into the mouth of one of the little bridesmaids. She was so pleased that she asked him to do it again and went off chewing them.

This was the last occasion when Dr Fisher participated in a royal ceremony as Primate of All England. He always did well, conducting such services with dignity, ease and sincerity. It is important that an Archbishop should be able to give to great worshipful events a special 'flavour', and see them as having a representational significance.

Before this chapter is brought to a close it may not be inappropriate to catch a glimpse of the Archbishop and Mrs Fisher entertaining the royal family in their own home, on an occasion which they thought sufficiently significant to merit such company.

Among the many buildings which suffered extensively during the war was Lambeth Palace, particularly grievous being the destruction of its chapel. Its restoration was a matter of deep concern to the Archbishop and the architects Lord Mottistone and Paul Paget were commissioned to undertake it. They were confronted with many problems, architectural, aesthetic and functional. When the work was on the eve of completion, Mrs Fisher began to make plans for a celebration artfully using the occasion to hasten certain other works of restoration on the house, such as the papering of the drawing room, and giving it a fitted carpet, curtains and new covers. The polished corridor and dining room were similarly treated for the first time since the war. There were present on this historic evening the Queen, the Duke of Edinburgh, the Queen Mother and Princess Margaret, together with the Diocesan Bishops and representatives of the wider Anglican Communion. Mrs Fisher went to great pains to secure beautiful flower arrangements and Gerald Knight, Director of the Royal School of Church Music, was responsible for the music. A first-class choir was recruited to sing in the west gallery of the chapel.

The Archbishop decided that the great day, which was fixed for 19 October 1955, should be preceded by a more domestic occasion. Thus on the 18th all the Lambeth Palace family, past and present, including ex-secretaries, gardeners, caretakers, and domestic staff, assembled for a special evensong when Mrs Fisher played the organ. The Archbishop gave an impromptu address, taking as his theme the long history of the chapel and those who had worshipped in it. Three of the Fisher sons were present.

So the day of the Queen's visit came. Presentations were made in the drawing room and at a point during the dinner in the guard room – we are quoting from Mrs Fisher – 'Geoff made a short, witty speech after we'd drunk the Queen's health, and after saying there weren't going to be any speeches!' He recalled the first Elizabeth's three days and nights spent in Lambeth Palace which one historian described as 'both costly and embarrassing'. 'I thought I'd better bring that in, Ma'am, in case you were contemplating doing the same thing'. Everyone roared with laughter and the Duke, like a flash, said: 'Oh yes, I've brought my suitcase with me,' and the Queen Mother added: 'Mine's coming later, but I have my toothbrush in my bag!' The party finally resorted to the Great Hall where a small orchestra of recorders, harpsichords, with some strings played Elizabethan music, some of it taken from manuscripts in the library. The royal guests stayed until 11.00 pm and as they stood at the top of the stairs before departing and the bishops were hurrying along the gallery, the Duke asked whether there was any collective noun for the episcopate, putting forward a 'surplus' or 'surplice' of bishops. The Queen thought a 'drift' would be better. The Archbishop liked neither of these so they compromised on a 'dignity' of bishops. The royal family certainly enjoyed themselves as may be seen from the warmth of their farewell and the thank-you letters which followed. The Duke promised as they left: 'We'll be back soon!', and the Queen Mother said of the 'dignity' of bishops standing around: 'I'd like to take some of them home with me' – she didn't particularize whom – 'they are such dears, I can't bear to leave them'.

It had indeed been a happy and relaxed evening, planned yet informal and spiced with much wit and humour. Above all the occasion was of historic significance, being the first occasion since the reign of Queen Elizabeth I that a monarch of England had worshipped and dined with her bishops in Lambeth Palace. The service itself, which took the form of evensong, in its simplicity and solemnity, expressed the deep feelings of all present. The Archbishop of York read the first lesson and the Archbishop of Wales the second, while the Primus of the Scottish

Episcopal Church said the prayers. It was fitting that the Chapel, founded in 1197 by Archbishop Hubert Walter, should be rededicated by his successor.

As for Geoffrey Fisher's relations with the members of the royal family, perhaps the Duke of Edinburgh may be allowed to have the last word in a quotation from a letter which he sent to the Archbishop at the time of his retirement: 'I suppose we shall not be seeing quite as much of you as in the past but you will always have a special place in our regard and affection, not so much as Archbishop but literally as our Parish Priest! You have done all those particularly personal things for us and our family which are normally done in the parish and I like to think this has given us a very special relationship; none of your successors will ever have quite the same jobs to do for us. I hope you may have many useful and fruitful years ahead of you'.

Some three weeks later Lord and Lady Fisher were received at Buckingham Palace in order that the Queen, to use Edward Ford's words, might be able 'to thank you personally for all that you have done for her and her family since you have been Archbishop of Canterbury'.

CHAPTER 24

The Rise of Christianity and *Lady Chatterley's Lover*

GEOFFREY Fisher was neither a philosopher who speculated over-much on the imponderables of human existence nor a theologian, exploring in depth the mysteries of faith. Rather it was the effect on human behaviour, individual and corporate, of a commitment to Christ as Lord, which concerned him most.

However, in his capacity as Primate of All England, he could not withdraw from public theological controversy not least that which referred to the content and character of Christian faith. The most prominent involvement of this kind during his Archiepiscopate was that which he had with Dr E. W. Barnes who was a mathematician of distinction at Cambridge, a Canon of Westminster – where he alleged spent the happiest years of his life – and Master of the Temple, prior to his becoming Bishop of Birmingham. Dr Barnes was an active exponent of biological evolution and equally a strong opponent of high sacramental claims. In commending his views he displayed the spirit of a crusader being passionately convinced that it was the refusal of the Church to take modern science seriously which prevented many thoughtful laymen committing themselves, with intellectual integrity, to Christian faith. On 20 October 1927, he wrote a letter to *The Times* inviting the then Archbishop of Canterbury, Randall Davidson, 'to consider what steps can be taken to help those of us who are giving of our best to fit the Church to be in the future the spiritual guide of an educated nation'. Thus Dr Barnes saw himself as an evangelist, concerned to preach a gospel which did not affront the human reason. His efforts to realise this ambition led to the most serious and certainly the most explosive theological controversy during Dr Fisher's time at Lambeth. This resulted from the publication, in 1947, of his book *The Rise of Christianity*. It has to be admitted that though the motivation behind this work was excellent, namely to commend Christian faith to thoughtful and may be sceptical laymen, this was, perhaps, not one of the Bishop's best performances. Intended to be a factual study of the early history of the Church, Dr Barnes had not researched sufficiently widely nor mastered his material adequately to sustain his main thesis. Even his transparent honesty could not disguise the fact that into an allegedly objective historical thesis he had fallen to the temptation of interjecting too many *a priori* categories which conditioned his inter-pretation. The Archbishop of Canterbury was immediately inundated with an avalanche of protests and it was impossible for him, even if he had so wished, to ignore the inevitable controversy. Rightly or wrongly, fortunately or unfortunately, the office of Archbishop of Canterbury precluded the possibility of a silent neutrality.

The Bishop, with his customary courtesy, sent the Archbishop a copy of his book which the latter acknowledged on 13 May 1947. He accepted the Bishop's view, that an independent scholar should not feel bound to reach 'conclusions prescribed by the Christian Communion to which he belonged'. Yet the Bishop must remember that he held high office in the Church of England and that the thesis he was putting forward rejected Christ's pre-existence; and also his showing himself alive after his crucifixion. Thus he was fundamentally departing from the doctrines held by the Communion to which he belonged. He did not question the right of an individual person to hold such views but the question was how far these were compatible with his office as a bishop. 'The Church of England', he stressed, 'by its liberal tradition gives a great deal of freedom to its members but there is a point at which a limit is reached as to what is tolerable and that point is reached earlier in the case of a bishop, who is specially charged with the responsibility of guarding the tradition of the Church'. 'Quite honestly', he went on, 'I think that the holding of your opinions and the holding of your office are incompatible, and for myself I believe you ought in conscience to feel the same'. The effect of his 'wild negations' was to undermine so much of the gospel narrative.

Having discharged his conscience in this respect the Archbishop was careful to add: 'Finally let me repeat . . . all that you have said in your book has been said with great sincerity and a complete devotion to truth as you see it. About that there is no question'. In reply to this letter Dr Barnes admitted that to receive it came as a 'great disappointment', particularly in view of his anxiety that increasing numbers of young people, whose inclinations veered to Christian faith, felt that they could not reconcile it with the assured results of modern science. If the Archbishop had time to read some of the key paragraphs in his work he might agree that he, the Bishop, had not strayed into any 'fundamental departures' from the Faith; nor could he accept that it was impossible for him to retain the office of a bishop which he had held for nearly twenty-three years.

The claim that a more vigorous standard of orthodoxy was required in bishops because of their particular responsibility to safeguard doctrine was not one which was universally held, though William Temple, when Archbishop of York, went out of his way in a foreword to the Report: *Doctrine in the Church of England*, published in 1938, to affirm that in view of his episcopal office he would wish it to be known that he accepted the Virgin Birth as historic fact.

Among the first things that the Archbishop did when the controversy broke out was to consult with the Archbishop of York and the Bishops of Chichester and Winchester. They all agreed that it was 'impossible to exaggerate the gravity' of the situation, and that though there were 'strong reasons for taking no formal action' the results of doing nothing could be 'even more severe'. Also Roman Catholic controversialists would make the most of this unhappy Anglican debate. But given this dilemma what could helpfully be done? Here opinions understandably differed. Dr Leonard Hodgson, a sensitive and liberal Regius Professor of Theology at Oxford, maintained that a healthy body ought to be able to carry 'a few poisoned parts', and any judicial procedure or heresy trial was out of the question. It would be better for the bishops to give a positive declaration of the content of the Christian faith in the Upper House of Convocation rather than a 'negative disowning or condemnation'.

There seemed to be general episcopal agreement that whatever steps were taken there must be no resort to law. Writing to the Bishop of London, Geoffrey Fisher emphasized that trials in the past had proved disastrous, but this did not mean that there was nothing that could be done. Perhaps the Upper House of Convocation might handle the charge of heresy leaving it to the Archbishop to deal personally with Dr Barnes, *inter alia* by not inviting him to Bishops' Meetings or to the Lambeth Conference.

Dr Fisher was concerned, as we have seen, not to impugn the character or sincerity of the Bishop in any way. 'He has a charming, saintly, Quakerish faith,' he wrote, 'but he also has a very stupid (*sic*) mind and the lust for being a martyr. It is open to him – indeed he has said it to me already more or less – to claim that the book while being an objective historical statement of the beginning of Christianity does not necessarily represent all that he believes'.

The bishops and leading churchmen, were by no means unanimous as to what action, if any, ought to be taken. The Bishop of London, High-Churchman as he was, would have preferred the whole matter to be allowed to lapse into a 'decent obscurity'. The Bishop of Oxford, Dr Kirk, was also for ignoring it. The Bishops of Durham and Southwell were equally opposed to any public action and believed that the Bishop of Birmingham could be safely left to the theologians. Dr Alec Vidler was convinced that the best way of responding to *The Rise of Christianity* was to encourage the work of the best contemporary scholars, men such as Manson and Dodd who would be better occupied combating the errors of the present generation rather than of the last. On the other hand there were those who consistently held that it was not a matter of justice being done but of its being seen to be done. The Archbishop of York, for example, felt from the word go, as did Selwyn,

Dean of Winchester, that some public act was required, particularly in view of a 'wide indignation at the prospect of Bishop Barnes retaining his episcopal office'.

An obvious time to discuss the book in the first instance – it had the advantage of complete confidentiality – was at one of the regular Bishops' Meetings. When it was decided to do this Geoffrey Fisher had the embarrassing task of asking Dr Barnes to absent himself from the next session. If any action were planned then he promised to inform the Bishop as to its character. The Bishop of Birmingham's reply, though he recognised he must accept the Archbishop's ruling, was precisely what might have been reasonably expected, namely that it seemed odd he should be absent when his own book was being discussed. However, he took the opportunity of reiterating that a careful reading would make it clear that he retained all the essentials of Christian faith. He called attention to the fact that *Essays and Reviews* in its time was felt to be a radical statement of the Christian position and as such condemned, but was now 'accepted by all'.

So the controversy continued. The Modern Churchmen's Union, to the surprise of many, gave the book a devastating review in its Journal, though Canon Richardson, Principal of Ripon Hall, inserted a favourable notice in a Birmingham Bulletin. Canon Charles Raven, a considerable theologian, writing, it must be said, cautiously, gave the work a sympathetic review much to the annoyance of the orthodox Canon Smyth, a church historian of considerable merit. Professor Norman Sykes, who had written authoritatively on the 18th century Church, correcting many false assumptions, advised strongly against any Synodical censure which could well have a boomerang effect – and certainly increase the sale of the book!

However, such liberal approaches had no effect upon the reactions of many ordinary lay Christians who had little doubt as to what ought to be done. Thus the Reverend W. Bathurst, a parish priest, reported from his rural rectory that a member of his congregation asked why it was that a bishop could deny or emasculate almost all the great Christian doctrines, and nothing apparently was to be done about it. To this critical comment the Archbishop replied that until the Church had its own courts there were no means of taking action that did not involve appeal to the Privy Council which would be highly undesirable. He then added, for the Rector's benefit, some wise words, namely that the proper reply was through scholarship. Nor, in fairness to the Bishop, ought it to be assumed that a 'detached book of historical investigation' exhausted the sum total of the Bishop's own beliefs. For himself he must make it plain that did he, the Archbishop, profess the views expressed in the book he would not continue to hold the office of a bishop.

It was not easy for Geoffrey Fisher, on whom the burden of responsibility must finally rest, to make up his mind as to the right course of action. However, slowly, he came to the view, and in this he had the strong support of the Archbishop of York – indeed, he was pressurized by him – that it was a matter of choosing the lesser of two evils. Thus he decided to make a statement in full Synod of the Canterbury Convocation at its next meeting. By doing things this way he would prevent a debate taking place either in the Upper or Lower House meeting separately. His hopes were twofold – first that his words would defuse the situation, thereby preventing action by those flexing their muscles for a fight; second that he would encourage the clergy to feel that official cognizance at the highest level had been taken of what the Bishop had written. Geoffrey Fisher was convinced throughout that unless he did something, clergy in Birmingham and members of the Church Union would act unilaterally in condemnation.

The drawing-up of the statement presented certain difficulties not least because Geoffrey Fisher was facing 'the impossible task' of finding any time in which to prepare it. Indeed, he was forced to write his first draft, which he circularized widely among the bishops, during the night of 29–30 September on his return from Germany. The reception of this attempt was mixed. The Bishop of Chichester was still not happy, believing that an 'open letter' would be better than a statement given to Convocation by its President. If this suggestion of his, however, was not taken up then the address should be shorter rather than longer. The Bishop of London remained 'extremely uneasy', but the Bishop of Barking found it 'balanced, fair-minded and charitable'.

On the day before the statement was read in Convocation the Archbishop courteously wrote to the Bishop of Birmingham. He had thought long and consulted others, he explained to the Bishop, as to what action, if any, he should take. It was now clear that he must 'go public' and therefore he enclosed a copy of what he intended to say. Only by making such a statement himself was it possible to avoid motions being debated in the Lower House. So it was that on Wednesday 15 October, the Archbishop, after referring briefly to the sad economic plight of the country and Princess Elizabeth's marriage, addressed both Houses of Convocation on the Bishop's *The Rise of Christianity*.

Undoubtedly, he began, the publication of this book had caused both 'distress and indignation' to Church people, in respect of which two considerations must be borne in mind. The Church must always regard 'with patience and sympathy, though obviously not always with agreement, honest men who with knowledge both of the Christian faith and of the advance of secular knowledge try to harmonize their different approaches to truth'. This was the Bishop's intention. Secondly, it was impossible 'not to appreciate the profound sincerity and devotion with which the Bishop regards, and has always regarded, the Person of Our Lord'. The Bishop accepts as 'authoritative dogma' that the activity of God in the material world 'is in accordance with uniform laws which express the invariable character of His control of phenomena'. However this was strongly denied by other scholars who were concerned with the philosophical presuppositions of Christian doctrine. The reader on his part must be on his guard against the Bishop's assumption that anything in the New Testament which did not commend itself to the Bishop's own spiritual perception could not be true. The intelligent reader must also watch carefully how the Bishop deals with biblical evidence. Many eminent New Testament scholars who have carefully studied this particular field do not assent to the Bishop's conclusions.

The Archbishop then followed up these critical remarks by dealing with the nub of the practical problem as he saw it. 'A Bishop from the nature of his office, by reason of his responsibilities to the Church and to its ministry is, I think, called upon to judge himself and to be judged by stricter standards than may be allowed to others. So long as he retains that office he must satisfy himself that he is adequately and faithfully expressing, in his teaching, the general doctrine of the Church and its scriptural basis which he is pledged by his office to defend and promote. The Bishop of Birmingham may be satisfied that his teaching conforms to these requirements. I would have no trial in this matter, but I must say, for my part, that I am not so satisfied. If his views were mine I should not feel that I could still hold episcopal office in the Church.'

The Archbishop brought his address to an end with these words: 'I trust that what I have said, with the full sense of the responsibility of my office, may serve to minimize the harm, and give to members of the Church such reassurance as they may need'.

This was a most carefully prepared statement. The Archbishop did not say categorically, indeed he studiously avoided saying this publicly throughout the controversy as a whole, that the Bishop of Birmingham *ought* to resign; only that he himself would do so in similar circumstances. An obvious answer to such a statement might well be that the Bishop was not the Archbishop and could not necessarily either be expected or required to behave as if he were.

As we have seen, by making his statement in the full House of Convocation, and using a presidential address for this purpose, the Archbishop precluded debate and therefore denied to the Bishop the right to reply. Geoffrey Fisher's hope, however, was that as a result of his words members of the Church of England would feel that justice had been seen to be done, and traditional faith vindicated as a viable intellectual option. He had further made it clear that there was to be no official action taken against the Bishop by due process of law.

The controversy, outside Convocation, was not yet over. That, of course, was too much to hope for and maybe would not necessarily have been a good thing. The *Sunday Pictorial* serialised parts of *The Rise of Christianity* and invited Dr Blunt, Bishop of Bradford, to write a series of articles on the book's general theme. His basic contention in these somewhat caustic articles centred around the criticism that Dr Barnes was 'still wallowing in the trough of scientific theory, fashionable fifty years ago, that the universe is a rigidly closed system of physical causation, which spiritual forces cannot affect'. Also, he maintained, Dr Barnes 'seems entirely inhibited against any philosophical idea'.

This 'spill-over' of the *contretemps* into the popular Press served only to confirm Geoffrey Fisher in his view that there was an 'element in the popular Press which is deplorable, and that protests by Church leaders against this had little effect'. Nor was this controversy confined to England for the Bishop of Ballarat circulated a protest against Bishop Barnes throughout Australia. Roscow Shedden, Assistant Bishop in the Diocese of Oxford and vicar of Wantage, confessed his disappointment in an 'open letter' to his diocesan Bishop, deploring that nothing more was now to be done after the Archbishop had spoken in Convocation. The Presbyterian Church of Scotland, he pointed out, would deal with the matter by setting up a Commission of Enquiry which could, if this body so decided, lead to a prosecution for heresy. In reply to this letter Geoffrey Fisher urged Bishop Shedden to re-consider his views, largely because there was no way of proceeding against Dr Barnes which precluded appeal to a purely secular court. Dr C. E. M. Joad, who incurred severe displeasure from professional philosophers by making their arcane expertise intelligible to the thoughtful layman, attacked the Bishop of Birmingham in the *Sunday Dispatch*, while Canon Bezzant deplored that the Archbishop should suggest a double standard in respect of orthodoxy, one for a bishop another for an ordinary priest. He conceded, however, that there could have been no more liberal and statesman-like handling of a most difficult problem than was given in the Archbishop's speech in Convocation. The Archbishop of York, however, was not able to prevent this matter appearing on the agenda of the Lower House of the Northern Convocation which passed a Resolution condemning the book.

As the months went by and the immediate shock of *The Rise of Christianity* receded, so some responsible people began to have second thoughts on the matter generally. Dr Cockin, Bishop of Bristol, expressed his anxiety lest the condemnation of Barnes would be taken as 'another example of orthodoxy drowning an honest man'. The only appropriate way of dealing with the book's 'manifold defects' was by scholarly exposition. The Church of England, unlike the Church of Rome, allowed a real measure of freedom of expression, and 'trusts to truth to prevail over error as the result of open discussion'. In contrast, Father Raynes of Mirfield was for rallying overseas bishops to demand firmer action against Barnes, which drew forth from Geoffrey Fisher the somewhat caustic *riposte* namely that it would be better if Father Raynes 'had a little more confidence in the people on the bridge'.

On Sunday 23 May 1948 the Bishop of Birmingham preached a sermon in St George's Church, Edinburgh – it was Trinity Sunday – the invitation to do so being a recognition of the kindness shown by the City of Birmingham to the Scottish munition girls stationed there during the War. The Scottish Church Union sent a protest to Lambeth and the Bishop of Edinburgh complained that this preachment would make more difficult relations between the Episcopal and the established Church of Scotland.

Bishop Barnes wisely took protests and criticisms in his stride and maintained a dignified calm throughout what must have been some-what of a trying ordeal. Indeed, towards the end of the year, he sent to Lambeth a report on the 'Forward Movement', drawn up by a group which for three years had been active in preparing a scheme for the provision, in the Birmingham diocese, of new parishes as well as the building of church halls and parsonages. Not unnaturally, there was a great desire 'on the part of everyone' that the Archbishop would himself attend to mark this event, giving the address and that Mrs Fisher would accompany him. The Archbishop gave a perhaps predict-able reply, namely that apart from the fact that he was otherwise engaged on that day he must in honesty say that he would not feel free to accept the invitation. To do so would run counter to his speech in Convocation.

The controversy, if it had not yet quite burnt itself out as these affairs usually do, ceased to be headline news, but there were still eddies in the current. For example, Dr Loyd, Bishop of St Albans, the most eirenic of prelates, after consulting Lambeth declined to vote for Dr Barnes' re-election to the Council of King's College, London. On his part the Bishop of Birmingham did not allow himself to be muzzled by this sustained hostility and in February 1949 he preached in his Cathedral Church giving it as his opinion that 'without theological changes the Church would perish'; and that liberals were ploughing at the moment 'a hard furrow'. The Archbishop apprehensively asked to see the script but no exchange of letters, fortunately, seems to have followed.

In 1949 Geoffrey Fisher had a further *contretemps* with the Bishop of Birmingham, the alleged circumstances of which were as follows.

On 19 May, Dr Selwyn, the ultra-orthodox, theologically-minded but awkward Dean of Winchester, acquainted the Archbishop that he intended to raise at the October meeting of Convocation the case of a candidate for ordination as a deacon who was recently, after a careful examination by the Bishop of Southwark, rejected as unsuitable for ordination on doctrinal grounds – a judgement which, he understood, was confirmed by the Archbishop of the Province. However, some three months later this rejected ordinand was made a deacon by the Bishop of Birmingham.

The Archbishop on receipt of the Dean's letter now made his own enquiries from Dr Simpson, Bishop of Southwark, from the Archdeacon of Birmingham and, of course, from Dr Barnes himself. From the feelers that he thus put out, Geoffrey Fisher established that the facts were certainly not as the Dean had led him to suppose. Indeed they were far different. The requirements of the Ordinal had been meticulously observed, and the Bishop himself had taken great pains to enquire of Dr Simpson whether he wished to raise any objections to Mr Smith's ordination by himself. Great care was also taken to confirm that the Theological College report was satisfactory and also that the ordinand's papers in the General Ordination Examination were up to standard. The Bishop of Birmingham concluded his report to Lambeth as follows:

> Because the Bishop of Southwark's Chaplains were doubtful as to his orthodoxy I myself interviewed him for one hour and a half and was satisfied by his doctrinal position.

The last sentence here was hardly calculated to satisfy the Archbishop but it was quite clear that the Dean of Winchester's account of the facts was certainly a garbled *ex parte* version of what had actually taken place. Having found out the true situation Geoffrey Fisher was certainly wise, whatever his private feelings may have been, in letting matters rest.

After nearly thirty years of an episcopate distinguished by great moral courage, by a passion to follow whither truth leads, and an evangelistic zeal to commend Christian faith to those who found a rigid orthodoxy unacceptable, Bishop Barnes retired in 1953.

Geoffrey Fisher found himself in a difficult position in his dealings with Dr Barnes. He respected the Bishop's integrity and did not wish to impair freedom of speech. However, it was his conscientious opinion that the Bishop had undermined fundamental Christian doctrines, whereas in his position as Bishop, and not least himself as Archbishop, were both required to maintain them. There can be little doubt that if the Archbishop had not spoken out in Convocation there would have been extensive debates in the Lower House of Canterbury on *The Rise of*

Christianity, characterised, doubtless, by much emotion and primitive witch-hunting. The Archbishop and Bishop treated each other publicly with respect and courtesy but temperamentally they were not in tune, and interpreted their respective roles somewhat differently. It has often been asked whether, if Geoffrey Fisher had handled the matter more personally – the same has been said in respect of his dealings with Hewlett Johnson, Dean of Canterbury – the result might have been different. The fact is that Geoffrey Fisher did engage in a long private discussion with Dr Barnes but basically both stood their ground. Dr Barnes defended his book and insisted that he wrote it for the benefit of thoughtful churchmen and lay people. In particular, when Geoffrey Fisher asked him whether the Resurrection event was no more than an 'impression, a spiritual awareness in the minds of the Disciples', Barnes replied: 'Yes, something like that'.

It is understandable that Sir John Barnes in his excellent biography of his father should suggest that the Bishop felt himself to be badly treated by the Archbishop. Certainly it was indefensible for the bishops corporately to contemplate discussing the matter for the first time at an episcopal meeting without the Bishop himself being present. This would seem to be opposed to any concept of natural justice. Maybe, in the light of hindsight, it might have been better if the Archbishop had firmly resisted the pressure brought to bear upon him and let matters take their course hoping that in the meantime tempers would cool. But had he adopted this course others would not have abandoned their plea for action simply because the Archbishop was inactive. History is not like this. However few will deny that if words needed to be spoken the Archbishop's were on the whole as courteous and as generous as they could be given the circumstances.

It is, I think, worth noting that Barnes' theological views in relation to Christian doctrine and the ministry of Jesus – not his more wild speculations as to Christian origins in *The Rise of Christianity* – found a place in the report 'Doctrine in the Church of England' published in 1938. Certainly for many young people at the time – including the author of this biography – Dr Barnes' fearless thinking helped them to cling to their Christian faith without compromising their consciences or intellectual integrity.

If the Archbishop found himself at the centre of a controversial storm arising out of Dr Barnes' *The Rise of Christianity* it is equally true that he became involved in the consequences of John Robinson, Suffragan Bishop of Woolwich, giving evidence on behalf of the publishers in the case concerning D. H. Lawrence's *Lady Chatterley's Lover*. The point at issue was whether the book constituted an obscene publication according to the law: if so its publication was illegal. The trial became a *cause célèbre* and Lambeth was overwhelmed with letters and telephone calls protesting against the Bishop. The Archbishop, who admitted that he had not read the book and had no intention of doing so, condemned the Bishop on practical grounds in relation to his episcopal office. 'The distress you have caused to many Christian people,' he told him, 'is so great that I think I must say something in public.' This he did at his Diocesan Conference, having first sent the script to the Bishop. He accepted that John Robinson had a full right to appear as a witness on the purely legal issue involved, but his episcopal status led to 'great confusion [since] everything he said as a Bishop would be interpreted as pastoral'. For the Christian, adultery 'whether in fact or lustful longing, is always a sin'. The Bishop was mistaken in believing that he could take part in this trial without becoming 'a stumbling block and a cause of offence to many ordinary Christians'.

The Archbishop was not alone in the attitude that he took. The *Church Times* condemned *Lady Chatterley's Lover* as also did Monsignor Gordon Wheeler, Administrator of Westminster Cathedral. Not so Miss Valerie Pitt, a member of the General Synod and a University don who asked Geoffrey Fisher bluntly whether it was right for her to introduce students to any literature in which characters commit adultery. Martin Jarrett-Kerr of the Community of the Resurrection dispatched a very long letter to Lambeth. 'I start from the assumption' he began, 'that we live in a post-Christian era; that the Church is, for 80 per cent of the population a curious and a quaint survival, as interesting and as irrelevant as most of the specimens in the local museum. Lawrence's awareness of the cultural death threatening modern man; his extraordinary power to locate the root corruption in human relations, all bear the mark of a great original genius.' To his critics Geoffrey Fisher denied that he himself had made any judgement whatever on D. H. Lawrence's written works. Indeed the Church would be 'grossly mistaken' to attempt to do so. He himself was in favour of freedom and against censorship. His concern was pastoral in relation to a suffragan bishop. John Robinson remained firm and did not recant though expressing his deep regret for any embarrassment he had caused the Archbishop and pain to others. However, now that the dust has had time to settle John Robinson may well be thought by many to have come out of this *cause célèbre* very courageously – and very well!

PART FOUR:

ECUMENICITY AND REUNION

'Thank God for the benefits
of plurality' – G.F.

CHAPTER 25

The Free Churches and the Methodists

No sooner had Geoffrey Fisher come to Lambeth in 1945 than he took up the cause of ecumenicity with enthusiasm and felt that he might properly begin with the situation in Britain. The war was over and in some ways, if not in all, the times were propitious. The Lambeth Quadrilateral of 1920 appealed to all who believed in Christ as their Lord, and were baptized into the name of the Holy Trinity, to draw nearer to each other. The bishops confessed frankly their collective guilt which had frustrated the activity of the Holy Spirit in His reconciling work. The Lambeth Fathers therefore called for new efforts aimed to promote the restoration of unity. This stirring message was transmitted by Randall Davidson, Archbishop of Canterbury, to the different Churches in Britain and Overseas.

The Free Churches were not slow in responding to this appeal and as a result there appeared in April 1921 *The Free Churches and the Lambeth Conference Appeal* issued by the Federal Council of the Evangelical Churches in England. This made it evident that they were willing to enter into a dialogue with the Church of England. As a consequence, representatives of both the Council and the *Ecclesia Anglicana* met spasmodically over the following years, the results of their labours being published, on the eve of the outbreak of the Second World War, in three documents designated: *Outline of a Re-Union Scheme; The Practice of Inter-Communion*; and *1662 and Today*. The dialogue was now effectively on, and its opportunities as well as its difficulties were writ large in *A Reply of the Free Church Federal Council* issued in 1941.

The literature around ecumenicism thus began to grow, and among those who studied this increasing documentation with meticulous care, none was more concerned than Geoffrey Fisher, newly arrived at Lambeth. He thus, as a deliberate act of policy, determined to make ecumenicity a high priority and to use the prestige of his unique office to promote this end. His first act was to ask whether the Free Churches would be prepared to re-open former discussion, halted by the war, an invitation which they gladly accepted. At the same time the Archbishop took the initiative in setting up two committees representing respectively the more Catholic and Evangelical wings of the Church of England. In respect of the first he liaised with Gregory Dix, a monk from Nashdom, whose *Shape of the Liturgy* had left a permanent impression upon many a parish priest. Michael Ramsey, Professor of Divinity at the University of Durham, agreed to chair this Committee. The membership included Dr R. C. Mortimer, Regius Professor of Moral and Pastoral Theology at Oxford, and T. S. Eliot. The other group was chaired by Dr Donald Coggan, Principal of the London College of Divinity, and amongst its members were Henry Chadwick, Chaplain of Queen's College, Cambridge, and inevitably, M. A. C. Warren, General Secretary of the Church Missionary Society. The quality of the personnel in this latter committee shows that there had been a lively response among evangelical clergy to Geoffrey Fisher's call, when Bishop of London, to equip themselves for service in the wider Church.

There were those, it must be confessed, who, arguing from past experience, took a pessimistic view as to the immediate prospects for these renewed conversations. They urged that all schemes for re-union should be postponed until further study, theological reflection and prayer 'should lead to a recovered apprehension of the balance of Christian truth'. This advice, in the judgement of the new Archbishop, was a counsel of despair. What the times demanded was a new and more imaginative practical approach to the elusive goal of re-union. This he himself attempted to provide without waiting for either of his two committees to report back. The occasion was a University sermon delivered at Cambridge on 23 November 1946 and later published under the title: *A Step Forward in Church Relations*. This discourse certainly deserves the description given to it by the church historian Roger Lloyd – 'a red letter day in the development of modern ecumenicism'. What Geoffrey Fisher had in mind may perhaps be better left to his own words: 'My Cambridge sermon had nobody's sanction but my own. I consulted nobody about it beforehand. It was borne in upon me from experience of reunion schemes in the United States and Canada; and I felt the attempt to get, in this country, organised schemes was hopeless. I wanted to break the deadlock, since politicians, secular and ecclesiastical, fall into the error of thinking in terms of the past and of "cut and dried principles". They seemed unable to realise that "life and thought are fluid and the Holy Spirit means them to be fluid".'

In essentials the Archbishop proposed that the Free Churches should consider – it became a key phrase – 'taking episcopacy into their own systems,' a daring approach to the ecumenical problem since it was the unique claims for episcopacy which had hitherto proved a stumbling block on the road to re-union. We quote the Archbishop's own words: 'There is a suggestion which I should like in all humility to make to my brethren of other denominations. We do not desire a federation: that does not restore the circulation . . . we are not yet ready for organic or constitutional union. But there can be a process of assimilation, of growing alike. What we need is that while the folds remain distinct, there should be a movement towards a free and unfettered exchange of life in worship and sacrament between them, as there is already of prayer and thought and Christian fellowship . . . My longing is not yet that we should be *united* with other Churches in this country, but that we should grow to full *communion with them.*'

Having thus prepared the ground, Geoffrey Fisher went on to make practical and positive proposals which may again be best set out in his own words: 'The non-episcopal churches have accepted the principle that episcopacy must exist along with other elements in a re-united church. For reasons obvious enough in church history they fear what may be made of episcopacy. But they accept the fact of it. If they do so for a re-united church, why not also, and earlier, for the process of assimilation as a step towards full communion? It may well be argued that in a re-united Church they could guard themselves in the constitution against abuses of episcopacy. But they could do so far more effectively by taking it into their own system.'

This sermon, if it disturbed some High Anglicans, certainly made a vivid impression in Free Church circles. It should be noticed that the Archbishop never advocated, even later as an ideal, a merger of all denominations into one centralised and unified Church. Rather he envisaged a Church of England making certain adjustments in its inner structure to ensure greater lay participation; and at the same time for Presbyterian and Free Churches, including Methodists, to incorporate episcopacy in one form or another into their own systems. A rigid uniformity could not be entertained for a single moment, since there was a diverse Reformation inheritance to take account of.

That Geoffrey Fisher, at Cambridge, should have made his case with persuasive charm and tolerance impressed his congregation greatly. One Free Churchman present wrote ecstatically: 'He was so simple and unaffected in his style, so brotherly and cordial in his attitude that he won all our hearts. His good humour too was most cultivated.'

However, charm and an obvious eirenic concern did not prevent critics raising, as they saw it, more ultimate theological questions. There seemed to be loose ends, they complained, not congenial to logical minds geared to a more formal and structured approach. On his part the Archbishop saw his address not as an exact blueprint of the shape of things to come but rather as the intimation of a direction towards which to move.

Not surprisingly, reactions to the Archbishop's address varied, largely in response to already existing, built-in convictions. We quote a few typical examples.

Gregory Dix was profoundly unhappy with its general ethos, and protested to Lambeth that his own group's endeavour to tackle the questions which the Archbishop had set them seemed now to be of only secondary importance. To quote modern jargon, the Archbishop had 'moved the goal posts!' Given Gregory Dix's basic attitude to matters ecumenical this protest was not unreasonable. The Archbishop was content to reply that within a re-united Church there need not be complete uniformity, or indeed loss of identity. Methodists and others 'would no doubt be able to retain some of their customs and some degree of autonomy'. Such be believed to have been historically the pattern in the early church.

Hensley Henson, in retirement but in his day a consistent theological radical, confessed to having read the sermon with 'profound interest and sympathy'; but, he asked pointedly, was the episcopal 'polity' which Free Churchmen were invited to incorporate into their systems that of Charles Gore who held that episcopacy was 'an essential part of the economy of redemption' or that of Lightfoot who did not? If the Archbishop had in mind the former there was no basis for negotiations with Free Churchmen; if the latter then it was for the Church of England honestly to admit that non-episcopal ministries of the Word and Sacrament 'may be spiritually valid ministries within the Covenant,' and therefore 'ought to be accepted and thankfully used by Churchmen'.

In response to this searching enquiry Geoffrey Fisher contended that episcopacy had basically to do with function. Whatever the system, there must be an office with authority to ordain ministers; to exercise pastoral oversight; and to safeguard Christian doctrine. 'More than this is not required . . . so long as there is the office with its functions anybody is free to theorise about it.'

Bishop Hensley's point was also put to Geoffrey Fisher by Benjamin Perkins, General Secretary of the Methodist Church's Department for Chapel Affairs, who conceded that his fellow Methodists were prepared to accept episcopacy, but not with the high theological implications often associated with it.

A number of bishops wrote to Lambeth expressing themselves 'puzzled' as to what precisely it meant to 'take episcopacy into the system', and urging the Archbishop to discuss the matter at a Bishops' Meeting. Dr Charles Raven – he and Geoffrey Fisher by no means always saw eye to eye – thanked him with a 'full heart' though warning him that 'a few stupid letters from Anglo Catholics of no prominence' would wing their way in to Lambeth Palace. Hence an ordinary parish priest accused the Archbishop of 'throwing a bombshell into the works, and stirring up a controversy that may well split the Church of England in twain.' To the Bishop of Peterborough the Archbishop wrote that his sermon presupposed two stages – an interchange of ministry at presbytery level; and the acceptance by the Free Churches of the fact and the function of the episcopal office. This entailed the existence 'for some generations of two parallel episcopal churches with full inter-communion but not a merging'. Dr Leslie Weatherhead, preaching at Friends' House, proclaimed that he would join the Church of England tomorrow were it not for matters of belief such as the 39 Articles; and the link with the state.

The ecclesiastical press was divided – the *Church Times* referred with surprise to his 'unexpected remarks' and the Archbishop's pre-sumption in offering 'guidance'. The *British Weekly* interpreted the Archbishop as 'thinking aloud'. Fortunately, it commented somewhat sardonically, 'Anglicans are used to the shocks of private episcopal utterances'.

There can be no doubt that Geoffrey Fisher's Cambridge sermon had a considerable effect upon his contemporaries, and Roger Lloyd, to quote him again, is not going too far when he writes: 'it did take the ecumenical movement out of the deep-freeze and got inter-Church discussions going again'. It was, he further claimed, 'one of the most effective of modern sermons'.

Not only did this address in fact renew and re-invigorate re-union hopes but it also affected Geoffrey Fisher personally in his capacity as Archbishop. He had declared his hand thus early, and it was clear – even if sometimes he speculatively envisaged 'organic union' as a very distant 'far-off divine event' – that such a concept did not really fit into his practical scheme for a re-united Church. Thus the general reaction to his sermon was such as to encourage Geoffrey Fisher not to let it remain a purely theoretical exercise to swell future ecumenical archives, but as a spur to action in the not too distant future. After so long a hold-up he wanted something done, and a former momentum not only recovered but accelerated.

Hence on 27 November 1946 he invited to Lambeth a group which included, *inter alia*, the Moderator of the Free Church Federal Council together with its secretary; also the Bishop of Derby, chairman of his own recently constituted ecumenical committee. This coming together was quite informal, the intention being to prime the Moderator so that he could introduce this subject the more knowledgeably at the next meeting of his Council. The Archbishop reminded those present of the general background which prompted his sermon, and his conviction that a radically new approach was needed more acceptable to Free Churchmen since former negotiations had proved fruitless.

The discussion turned to points of difference between them during which the Bishop of Derby made it clear that certain aspects of episcopacy must be preserved – for example, those which concerned the ordination of priests, pastoral oversight and their guardianship of

Christian doctrine. The Archbishop then endeavoured to explain more precisely what he meant by 'receiving each other's ministries'. The Church of England, for example, by its increasing deployment of lay people had been progressively recovering elements associated traditionally with Free Churchmen and Presbyterians. This process should be reciprocal, though the giving and receiving of episcopacy would come late in the day. Meanwhile ministries now held in separation should be regarded as valid if not complete.

On the day following this meeting Dr Howard Roberts wrote enthusiastically to the Archbishop, expressing his gratitude for the warmth of welcome; for his frankness in answering questions; and his 'sympathetic understanding of their difficulties and reservations'. 'If I may say so,' he went on, 'I am persuaded that you have opened a way for an unprecedented advance in the cause of re-union. I should like you to know that some of us who are outside the Anglican Communion share your concern about the spiritual values enshrined in the historic episcopate and . . . we look to the day of further communion.'

As Geoffrey Fisher now saw it, the immediate task was to search for a basis upon which the separated Churches, without losing their identity, could overcome their scruples by drawing closer to the Church of England – and vice versa. Yet if this were to happen, even if it was a matter of hastening slowly, some definite and practical steps needed to be taken.

A further meeting, with the same personnel, now took place at which the important decision was taken that future discussions would be held not with the Free Church Federal Council, as such, but with representatives of the individual denominations. The Archbishop then urged the various Churches, as a priority, to resume the long-suspended conversations, and if they did so 'not to be concerned with the defence of their own position' but with reaching out so far as they could to find a synthesis of what might be called Catholic and Protestant approaches.

It is now time to return to the two committees, the one High Anglican, the other more evangelical, which Geoffrey Fisher had himself brought into being. The remit to both was the same, namely to examine the present deadlock and to come up with suggestions as to how it could be overcome. They should in the process of doing this ask themselves: (1) What is the underlying cause, philosophical and theological, of the conflict or contrast between the Catholic and Protestant tradition? (2) What are the fundamental points of doctrine around which these crystalise? (3) Is a synthesis of these differences possible? (4) If not, can the traditions co-exist within one ecclesiastical body and, if so, under what conditions?

Both of these groups produced printed reports, the first designated *Catholicity, a Study of the Conflict of Christian Traditions in the West,* the second *The Fullness of Christ, the Churches' Growth into Catholicity.*

The former document was edited by Michael Ramsey which led to an uneasy exchange of letters between him and the Archbishop. Geoffrey Fisher thought that some reference ought to be made to the careful preparatory work undertaken by the Faith and Order Committee; also he regretted a reference to the South Indian Re-Union Scheme which accused its supporters of regarding the apostolate of a bishop as 'a thing indifferent'. This statement, so the Archbishop complained, was simply 'untrue', and as a consequence Michael Ramsey agreed to delete the offending passage. At the latter's request Dr Fisher wrote a foreword, which led to a further 'brush' between the Archbishop and Professor Ramsey concerning the opening paragraph which he (Ramsey) had read with 'surprise and pain'. 'Your Grace views us,' he protested, 'as a set of people who have consistently criticized and now at last have been persuaded to do something constructive.' Also he was not happy with the Archbishop's version as to how the work of his group originated, and he therefore requested that the paragraph referring to this be deleted. To this the Archbishop concurred, though, in order to put the record right he insisted that the setting up of the group had arisen from conversation between himself and Gregory Dix.

Geoffrey Fisher's foreword admirably expressed his point of view and an extract, which could not have been entirely welcome to either Michael Ramsey or Gregory Dix, may be quoted: 'That unity which must be reborn will include something of all the patterns, not in their falsities and negations, but in those elements of devotion and convictions, of dogma and discipline which they contain'.

There is a genuine difference of emphasis here, between such as Gregory Dix, as well as Michael Ramsey, and the Archbishop. Geoffrey Fisher believed the Free Churchmen were firm in their intention to retain their own 'distinctive witness which meant that the concept of uniformity could not be realistically entertained for a single moment'. But there were difficulties which a non-Anglican put as follows: 'If a traditional episcopacy was modified and in the process diluted to accommodate non-conformity, many of the Archbishop's own community would find this unacceptable'. The fact, of course, was that the comprehensiveness of the Church of England, so highly prized by its supporters, presented some difficulties when it came to discussing matters ecumenical.

Geoffrey Fisher was certainly encouraged by the Free Churches accepting his invitation to resume conversations, not least because they continued purposefully over the next five years. He himself took a great personal interest and was present at some of their key meetings, hoping thereby to keep up the momentum. Perhaps we can highlight one such early meeting held at Lambeth on 23 May 1947 to which Baptists, Methodists, Congregationalists, Independents, the Wesleyan Reform Union, the Churches of Christ and the Countess of Huntingdon's Connexion were all invited. Also in attendance was the Reverend J. H. Wishart representing the General Assembly of the Presbyterian Church of Scotland.

The intention of this meeting was to explore again the possibility of progressively implementing the Archbishop's Cambridge sermon. There were, so the Archbishop pointed out, four stages on the way to full Communion – of course this was not the same as organic union – which he briefly outlined: (1) the recognition by each Communion of their catholicity; (2) the admission by each Church of members of other Communions to participate in its sacraments; (3) the recognition that progress towards inter-communion did not require the acceptance of all the doctrinal statements, or the sacramental and liturgical practices characteristic of the others, though each believes the others to hold the essentials of Christian faith; (4) the interchange of ministries, as contemplated in his sermon, was not to be regarded as 'fictitious'. After making these points the Archbishop withdrew. He had certainly given them enough to think about!

Dr Fisher's own ecumenical concern did not, however, lead him to approve all the activities arising from some spontaneous initiatives. For example, a united service of Holy Communion was planned for 24 September 1947 at St Germain's Church in Birmingham at which Methodists, Baptists and Congregationalists were to take part and the vicar of the parish was to celebrate assisted by three ministers. As soon as Geoffrey Fisher was informed of this proposal he wrote to the incumbent concerned – he did not approach the Bishop – calling attention to its irregularity, in that it did not conform so far as Anglicans were concerned, with resolutions passed in Convocation; also it betrayed a misunderstanding of his Cambridge sermon. In taking this stand, the Archbishop was conscious that publicity given to schemes for promoting re-union was causing a measure of concern among some conservative evangelical members of the Church of England, as for example such as Lord Templewood, an extreme Protestant evangelical who had been deeply involved, as a member of Parliament, in the rejection of the Deposited Prayer Book in 1928. The noble Lord himself believed that there was 'grave anxiety amongst many of the most loyal Anglicans that any abandonment of its historical position would impede the Church's work'.

The nexus of the Church of England with the State, the product of a long history, continued for many conscientious Free Churchmen to be a hindrance on the way to re-union. Thus Dr Aubrey, chairman of the

Baptist Union, told the Archbishop that he was not happy about an established Church, and that this applied equally to many of his brethen. Geoffrey Fisher never accepted the charges, sometimes levelled against him, that re-union, as he understood it, would inevitably lead either to an artificial federalism or, more probably, to anarchy and lawlessness. To one such critic, the incumbent of New Basford, Birmingham, the Reverend W. T. P. Wheeler, he wrote an interesting letter from which the following is an extract: 'All my efforts for some time past have been towards getting a full degree of an unrestricted inter-communion between the Church of England and other denominations, as for example with Methodists in England or Presbyterians in Scotland. Personally I look forward to a long, long period in which there are churches acceptable to one another and enjoying the full degree of inter-communion but completely autonomous. To have one vast centrally organised Church would be merely to guarantee that either heresy or at least folly, would dominate the whole situation. All over the world centralized government ends in that direction. But if you have separate churches in close harmony and in full inter-communion then each can have its special ethos and direction and freedom is preserved. Indeed it would be very much like what you find in the early Church at Corinth, and the Church at Athens, and the Church in Jerusalem and in Rome.'

Not all, perhaps, would accept the historical parallel with the primitive church. This letter shows how far, thus early, he was at variance with those who saw organic unity as the one thing needful and the only goal for re-union worthy of pursuing.

Geoffrey Fisher was constantly reflecting in a purely practical way around the general theme of church relations. Hence as a result of what he called his 'holiday essay' – he often came up with something when off work – he asked Dr Baker, Methodist Secretary of the Free Church Federal Council, whether it might help in promoting co-operative relations with the Church of England and Methodism if existing administrative units such as the diocese, archdeaconry and rural deaneries in the Church of England had their Free Church counterparts? Why not begin by investigating possibilities in Kent, Surrey and Sussex, he asked. Dr Baker responded promptly agreeing that the idea was an excellent one, and in fact the Archbishop's senior chaplain, Freddie Temple and his lay secretary, Robert Beloe, did confer with the Free Churches on this suggestion, but nothing seems to have come from this enquiry.

We now return to the conversations with the Evangelical Free Churches of England re-opened at the instigation of the Archbishop, and concerning which the Lambeth Fathers in 1948 expressed the hope that 'these conversations thus happily begun may, by the blessing of

God, lead to fruitful results'. It had been left to each Free Church to take up with the Archbishop the offer of conversations if it so wished. The Methodist Church, perhaps understandably since it was derivative from Anglicanism, and had not left the Church of England on any great Reformation principle, nor drawn up a formal confession of faith, was among the first to respond positively to this offer. Hence at its annual Conference in 1953, encouraged by those who had taken part in the discussions which led to the appearance of *Church Relations in England* (1950) a resolution put forward by its Faith and Order Committee was passed, namely, that 'the Methodist Church would be prepared to proceed to a further stage in the promotion of inter-communion with the Church of England, provided that it was given assurances: (a) that the Church of England acknowledged that their divisions were within the Christian body; (b) that the same liberty of interpretation as to the nature of episcopacy and of priesthood would be accorded to the Methodist Church as already prevailed in the Church of England; (c) that the Methodist Church would be free to maintain relations of inter-communion and fellowship with other non-episcopal churches which it now enjoyed.'

With certain reservations and strongly urged to do so by the Archbishop of Canterbury, the Convocations of Canterbury and York in 1955 approved these proposals, and the Lambeth Fathers in 1958 added their blessing, though stressing that organic union was accepted as the ultimate aim, and that this aim be kept firmly in view after the establishment of inter-communion.

This absolute insistence on organic union, with inter-communion but a step along the road towards it, could not have been welcome to Geoffrey Fisher – but the story of the fate of this attempt at Anglican/Methodist inter-communion must be left to a final chapter 'Ecumenicity in Retirement'.

CHAPTER 26

The Church of Scotland

(i)

GEOFFREY Fisher's relations with the established Church of Scotland were inevitably conditioned by a history going back to the 16th century, that is to John Knox and the Reformation of which he was the spearhead. In 1560 the Church of Scotland was set up on Presbyterian lines, complete with a Confession of Faith and Worship linked to the Anglo-German Book of Common Prayer. Basically they proclaimed Christ as Lord over all. But Presbyterianism had to fight hard to maintain itself, which meant a ruthless struggle against the Stuart monarchy whose policy was succinctly summed up in: 'No Bishop, No King'. In 1638 the General Assembly succeeded in sweeping episcopacy aside while the execution of Charles I led to the Westminster Assembly, which authorized the Directory of Public Worship and the Shorter Catechism of the Presbyterian Church. The struggle was not yet over, but the bloodless Revolution of 1688, which brought to England as its monarch Calvinist William III, led to the final establishment of Presbyterianism in Scotland as the national religion. The 19th century was its golden period, when this Reformation Church came of age.

The effect of this ongoing saga was to make the Kirk a great national institution, so much so that the monarch is a Presbyterian when north of the Border, and an Episcopalian south of it. Allegiance to it was more than a purely religious commitment, since it drew upon a deep Scottish sentiment. Geoffrey Fisher was to find that negotiations with the Kirk proved a more sensitive exercise than with the Free Churchmen in England, though in neither case did the negotiations end in success.

One ingredient of Church life in Scotland proved an embarrassment to Geoffrey Fisher in his efforts to draw closer to the Scottish Kirk. This may be briefly stated.

When the Presbyterians took over under William, their victory was not one hundred per cent complete. There was a small minority of Anglican clergy, who, in spite of being 'rabbled' out of their livings, refused to renounce their episcopal orders. Through the initiative of Archbishop Tenison, a strong Whig, they were allowed to continue to exercise their ministry within an Episcopal Church of Scotland in full communion with the Church of England – that is provided they took the oaths to William and Mary. Thus their Church, under its

Primus, became an outpost of an episcopalian empire north of the Border.

We have already seen how the Lambeth Bishops in 1920 issued an appeal to all Christian people to draw ever closer together. The momentum thus generated led to conversations between the Church of England and the Church of Scotland which continued fitfully through the years, though the Second World War led to their interruption. Geoffrey Fisher's epoch-making Cambridge sermon gave him the opportunity to write to Dr Baillie, Moderator of the General Assembly of the Church of Scotland, asking whether past talks could be reopened on the understanding that the Primus of the Episcopal Church of Scotland be associated with them.

Dr Baillie's initial reaction was very much to the point but certainly not encouraging. 'I am afraid my judgement is', he confessed frankly, 'that there is not the slightest prospect of our Church today taking steps to appoint bishops in order that the Church of England should agree to inter-communion with us'. The situation might be different if such appointments were seen as part of a wider corporate union. Enlarging on this theme Dr Baillie went on to make the following points: (1) Any Christian was welcome at Presbyterian altars. (2) Hence the Archbishop's Cambridge proposals were seen as one-sided. (3) The sentiment in Scotland against the name and office of bishop was still very powerful. (4) The Cambridge proposals, if implemented, must affect Presbyterians throughout the Commonwealth. (5) As for the the Primus of the Episcopal Church of Scotland his presence at the discussion might well constitute an embarrassment.

In response to this somewhat daunting reply the Archbishop endeavoured to enlighten the Moderator as to what his Cambridge proposals precisely entailed, proposals, he reminded Dr Baillie, analogous to the Canadian model. They required that ministers of each Church should receive ordination from the other. Organic union was a long way off and could only be achieved, if at all, after an extensive period of inter-communion.

Matters seem to have lain fallow for a time until in March 1949 the Archbishop wrote to the Moderator suggesting that in the light of his Cambridge sermon he wished to reopen conversations with his ecumenical committee, which was already engaged in holding talks with Free Churchmen.

At this stage Geoffrey Fisher recognised that he must keep the Primus of the Episcopal Church in touch with events. Indeed he had insisted from the word go that the Episcopal Church should be represented at any of the conversations; but in precisely what capacity? In acquainting the Primus with the willingness of the Presbyterian Inter-Church Relations Committee to lift the ban and renew conversations he added that it had no objection to representatives from the Scottish Episcopal Church being present at the talks but not, it insisted, as participants but as observers.

Things were now beginning to move, and the General Assembly accepted the advice of its Committee, it being understood that Geoffrey Fisher's sermon should constitute the agenda. There was to be no repeat of the abortive conversations of the thirties. Six members of the Church of Scotland were nominated to represent the Kirk which included Professors Manson and Baillie. It only remained for Dr Taylor to inform Geoffrey Fisher, which he did on Good Friday 1949, that his committee 'cordially agreed' that talks should be resumed. The Archbishop now nominated his team – the Bishops of Derby, Durham and Manchester, Professor Ramsey, Canon Greenslade, and the Reverend F. J. Taylor, the Rector of Christ Church, Claughton. Thus the Archbishop was able to announce in Convocation that talks with the Church of Scotland were to be reopened.

However the Primus and his bishops were far from happy and to Geoffrey Fisher they constituted an embarrassment, giving the impression of an Anglican Church at odds within itself. To remove any doubt as to their feelings the Primus sent a strong letter to the Archbishop. 'You know we are very touchy on these matters,' he wrote, 'and very jealous of our position and our dignity as representing the Anglican section of the Episcopal Church of the world in a Presbyterian country. Some of us felt we had been rather slighted by this idea of observers.' Also he felt that the General Assembly of the Church of Scotland had rather 'queered the pitch of the Conversations' since they were clearly not prepared to discuss the union issue within the context of the Cambridge sermon. 'We know it all so well up here' he commented ruefully.

The Archbishop was not pleased with this outburst and in a lengthy letter written on 20 June 1949 he enlightened the Primus further concerning the character of the conversations. They were basically between the Presbyterian nominees and his own committee. To make these talks tripartite by formally bringing in the Episcopal Church would at this stage alter its whole character and balance. Central to the present discussions was the Cambridge sermon; hence the approach was 'tentative, exploratory and informal'. Maybe it might prove possible for the Episcopal Church of Scotland to have observers who were free to make general comments. In this case the Archbishop would be prepared to nominate them if the Primus wished. This, in fact, happened. For them to be called 'consultants' would not be acceptable.

The situation for all concerned was a difficult one, the Scottish Episcopalians feeling 'considerable disquiet' being convinced that the

English bishops were not really sensitive to their unique position. Certainly so far as Geoffrey Fisher and the Derby Committee were concerned, they were more preoccupied with their own relations to the Church of Scotland than with the nice scruples entertained by the Episcopalians. The Primus believed that he and his colleagues should be treated exactly as were members of the Church of England.

The controversy *vis-à-vis* the Scottish Episcopalian Church dragged on with the result that Dr Baillie took advantage of a meeting of the British Council of Churches to suggest to the Archbishop that to offset the presence of the Scottish Episcopalians, representatives from the Scottish Presbyterian Church in England, should be invited to attend the discussions.

Against this background and the fact that commending episcopacy to the Scots in any form was not easy, the talks did not get off to a very good start, and in 1952 they were suspended.

Geoffrey Fisher was indeed disappointed, and to break the *impasse* he proposed to the Moderator of the General Assembly that the Bishop of Derby and Professor Manson should confer together with a view to agreeing the circumstances under which the talks might be resumed. This intervention proved successful, and the Archbishop was sufficiently encouraged to feel able to say that the resumed talks 'were going ahead like smoke'.

One significant change, hitherto hotly contested but now voluntarily conceded by the Church of Scotland, was a permission for the Episcopalians to be made full participants. This was 'splendid' Geoffrey Fisher commented, though he expressed the hope that the numbers involved would not become 'too large'.

It was within the context of this new optimism that it was first mooted that the Archbishop might pay a visit to the General Assembly. Thus forewarned Geoffrey Fisher had no difficulty in accepting the formal invitation, confessing later that in doing so he consulted no one. Certainly he was creating a precedent which aroused considerable interest. Some one thousand five hundred Commissioners were present to give him a 'cordial reception' and to applaud him 'warmly'. His opening gambit was much appreciated and probably set even the more serious at their ease. 'Here in this Assembly Hall is an even worse den of theological lions, hungry, voracious and slightly carnivorous' – to which an elder Commissioner from below the press benches was heard grumpily to exclaim: 'what the deuce is he doing here anyhow?' Many were grateful for his statesman-like review following up his Cambridge sermon of the subtly changing influence which had brought nearer improved Christian relations. 'Much of the mood of the occasion', writes one who was present, 'was set by Dr Fisher himself. His address was light-hearted as well as serious.' So it was that Geoffrey Fisher returned to Lambeth well satisfied with his visit which he described as 'very happy and encouraging'. The fact that the two Churches could discuss 'in such friendship and mutual sympathy their relations with each other was in itself significant'.

The Archbishop was intensely concerned to keep up the momentum and to this end he invited the participants to Lambeth Palace for some four days. Expressing their appreciation Dr Whitehorne later wrote: 'There could not have been a happier meeting place for the conversations last week than Lambeth Palace, and I want to thank you for your hospitable kindness in making us your friends, and for your personal presence with us in the midst of an unexpectedly busy week. In all these and similar comings and goings between the Churches, it is always a stimulus to me to know of your own earnest desire that we should grow together.' It was during this session at Lambeth that the possibility of a draft report was first considered.

Thus the conversations went on and sufficient progress was made for there to be issued in 1958 a document: 'Relations between the Church of England and the Church of Scotland – a Joint Report'. That it should have proved possible to issue such a document was indeed a great achievement, and Geoffrey Fisher by his personal influence and tact could justly claim to be in a large measure responsible.

Drawing upon the Archbishop's Cambridge sermon the Report suggested a practical way forward by a process of 'cross-fertilisation' or to use Dr Fisher's favourite word 'assimilation'. The great obstacles which lay in between their present situation and that of inter-communion were frankly admitted – obstacles rooted in a long religious, political and cultural history which would not go away at will, and affected both Church and State. Not to be daunted, however, the authors of the Report believed that some further progress, if only as a first interim step, could be made. For example clergy and ministers might exchange pulpits and members of one church receive the Sacrament at the others. Consideration could be given to the introduction of 'bishops in presbytery' into the Church of Scotland. In reverse, episcopacy in the Church of England could develop a more corporate and conciliar character; and moves towards establishing a ministry of elders could be initiated. The overriding intention was for this to find a permanent place within the government and pastoral life of the *Ecclesia Anglicana*.

These proposals represent a brave attempt to move ahead in a progressive, practical and concrete way, and thus to restore the wholeness and balance of a fully authenticated Church.

It was now necessary for the Report to go before the Canterbury and York Convocations in England and the General Assembly in Scotland. The former expressed their 'satisfaction' with the proposals in principle, and resolved that the Archbishops be asked to set up a joint study group to explore both them and the relevant Lambeth Resolutions. On this group representative observers from the Episcopal Church of Scotland and the Presbyterian Church in England were to be included. The Bishop of Exeter was appointed chairman.

Everything however depended on the reception of these proposals north of the border where it soon became apparent that their general tenor was too much for a grass-roots, vestigial national sentiment. Thus the Scottish edition of the *Daily Express* irresponsibly described the Report as 'an English plot to ensnare the Scots'. The proprietor of this newspaper was Lord Beaverbrook, who entertained a deep animosity against the Church of England, going back to the Abdication of Edward VIII and Archbishop Lang's alleged involvement in it. Such ridiculous language, of course, must not be taken seriously but that it could be employed at all says much. Episcopacy north of the border had only too clearly left behind it the deep impress of a persecutor frustrating the national will. Many, if not a majority of theologically minded members of the General Assembly, had little doubt as to what they termed "the Bishops" Book.' Its general purport, they claimed, was 'a denial of the Catholicity of the Church of Scotland and of the validity and regularity of its ministry within the Church Catholic'.

The immediate run up to the debate in the General Assembly was indeed for the Archbishop a time of great anxiety, stress and strain. The *denouement* could represent the shipwreck of all his hopes. On 17 May *The Times* newspaper devoted a leader to the conversations and their future prospects. The writer stressed that the Church of Scotland was a 'proud system'; hence the need, if disunity were to be overcome, for humility in any approach to her. The leader writer also questioned the wisdom of the Church of England in its insistence on episcopacy which might suggest that Presbyterian orders were regarded as invalid. The Archbishop's instant reaction was to profess: 'I thankfully acknowledge the Church of Scotland, as equally with my own church, or the Church of Rome or the Orthodox Churches as part of Christ's Church militant here on earth'.

At this critical time Geoffrey Fisher was fortunate in being kept in touch with what was happening in Edinburgh and its general mood by Dr A. Craig who in a long career held *inter alia* the offices of Moderator of the Free Church Federal Council, General Secretary of the British Council of Churches, as well as Moderator of the General Assembly of the Church of Scotland. His wide experience, ecumenical concerns and shrewd judgement were invaluable to Geoffrey Fisher in assessing events north of the border. Archie Craig confessed early in May that he did not know what finally would happen in the General Assembly. 'The present feeling', he commented, 'of our people is hostile to the central proposals of the Report as they stand, and insufficiently aware

– and sometimes lamentably ignorant – of their theological grounding.'
On the other hand, he went on, a good number of people have been
telling him that 'they will be astounded if any move to throw out the
Report neck and crop will succeed. They think that a solid mass of
opinion, hitherto silent, will be in favour of keeping the door open . . .
in the first instance among ourselves and, when the time is ripe, to
renewed conversations'.

To Archie Craig, Geoffrey Fisher was able to speak his mind freely.
Thus in giving his views on the validity of Presbyterian orders he
confessed that 'validity' was 'a perfectly stupid phrase and means
nothing'. Enlarging on this theme he added: 'I simply do not know
how to measure validity as God measures it!' The only sense in which
he could understand the term was 'not according to the rules of the
Church of England'.

At the end of May 1958, the long-awaited debate, which some
dreaded, took place in the General Assembly. Archie Craig proved to
be right, and Geoffrey Fisher wrote from Lambeth to him on 31 May.
'What a field day you had in the General Assembly and how thankful I
am that, under your wise guidance, the Assembly agreed to a further
year's study of the Report.' It was a typical ecclesiastical compromise
but in this case a compromise which to such as Geoffrey Fisher, who
wished the Joint Report well, a near victory. The danger had been that
in the expected heated atmosphere it could have been rejected lock,
stock and barrel.

Perhaps a few quotations may give a 'feel' of the debate. George
McLeod, founder of the Iona Community, indulged his customary force
and eloquence urging the Assembly to be 'patient about bishops and
impatient about bombs' – he was well known for his pacifism! Bishops,
he pointed out during the debate, were by no means the preserve of the
Church of England and he urged his fellow Presbyters to give up fighting
yesterday's war. In a personal letter to the Archbishop he gave it as his
opinion that the Assembly 'recovered its dignity in the debate which was
at a high level and ended in the right decision'. Up till then the debate
had been 'deplorable'. Dr Baillie sadly reflected that the proposals were
a hundred years ahead of the views of the vast majority of ministers. He
only wished they could recognise that Anglicanism was more than the
Church of England. Craig summed up the impact of the Joint Report by
maintaining that even amongst those anxious for unity what 'stuck in
their throats' were the implications about episcopacy concealed in such
a phrase as 'taking it into their system'.

It will come as no surprise that amongst the most severe critics of
proceedings in the General Assembly was the Primus who observed
somewhat cynically how 'wide of the mark the Moderator had proved
in the optimism which he had expressed earlier when they met in

Lambeth Palace'. As to the debate in the Assembly, so he observed to Geoffrey Fisher, 'ignorance and misinterpretation were in ample supply' though he was pleased that for the most part his 'own folk kept their mouths shut and their pens idle'. Those who did express themselves 'pleaded' that the Report be 'given a chance'. What distressed him was the 'outrageous attitude to bishops' and the 'bitter spirit in which it was expressed'.

The final upshot of the debates, and decision-making, in the English Convocations and in the Scottish Assembly was that these two established churches set up their own internal committees – the Church of Scotland to embark upon a year's study, the Committee to consist of ministers and members of the laity including some women; the Church of England to establish a Joint Committe of the two Provincial Convocations under the chairmanship of the Bishop of Exeter. The possibility was envisaged that the latter would be joined by nominees from the Episcopal Churches of Scotland, Wales and Ireland. However, so far as Geoffrey Fisher was concerned, before these two bodies reported back, he himself had retired.

It had long been recognized that the conversations between the two established Churches had far more than a purely domestic interest. Both Anglicanism and Presbyterianism were world-wide Communions. Hence it was both understandable and expected that the Joint Report would be discussed at the Lambeth Conference of 1958 when the following four resolutions were passed: (1) The Report was welcomed as a 'signal illustration of a move in the relations between the two Churches'. (2) It should be carefully studied by the Inter-Church Relations Committee of the Church of Scotland; and also (3) by the Anglican Churches in general particularly where Anglicans and Presbyterians lived together side by side. (4) It noted with 'satisfaction and thankfulness' the remarkable measure of concentrated agreement which the theologians had reached; and asked that consideration might be given to Anglican and Presbyterian traditions drawing more closely together by 'mutual assimilation of their respective Church Orders'.

There was nothing remarkable in these recommendations, though the last one must have given great satisfaction to Archbishop Fisher. What the deliberations of the Lambeth Conference did, however, was to encourage both Churches to go forward, this being reflected in the October meeting of the Canterbury Convocation when resolutions were passed, conveyed to the Moderator by the Archbishop, calling for further conversations.

(ii)

There now happened what can only be described as a great misfortune so far as it concerned the delicate and unfinished negotiations between the two established Churches. 1560 was a significant year in the history of the Reformation in Scotland, and the Kirk decided to mark it with thanksgiving and commemorations. To this end it invited Churches both near and far, including Anglican Churches throughout the world, to join with them in these celebrations. An invitation, therefore, came to Geoffrey Fisher, as head of the Anglican Communion, to participate. The Archbishop saw himself in a difficult position, particularly in respect of the reaction to the invitation among members of the Church of England in the United Kingdom. Nothing he felt must be allowed to frustrate the progress of the ecumenical conversations. His immediate reply was to remind the Moderator that it was not customary for the Anglican Church to send delegations to celebrate movements such as the Reformation in general, though it had done so in relation to specific events. In particular the Archbishop was anxious that the Primus of the Church of Scotland, whatever he said, should respond courteously to the Moderator's formal invitation. The Primus replied that he appreciated the kindness of the invitation, but could not accept since 1560 was associated with too much that his Church deplored and believed to be desperately wrong. Thus to join in thanksgivings would 'lack reality'. He did, however, not wish the absence of the Episcopal Church in any way to interfere with the celebrations. This was not a reply of which Geoffrey Fisher fully approved, any more than he did a reference to the celebrations in the Primus's diocesan magazine which he described as 'foolish'. Whereas, so said the Primus, Protestants looked back to the Reformation, Anglicans looked back to the Fathers. (In the margin of this letter, Geoffrey Fisher scribbled 'Why not both?')

However, Geoffrey Fisher was preoccupied as to how he, as Archbishop of Canterbury, ought to respond to the Moderator's invitation. Anxious as he was to please the Moderator and thereby not to prejudice the talks, he yet did not wish to distance himself from the Anglican Episcopal Church in Scotland, Wales and Ireland. Thus he decided that whatever he did he would not send a bishop to the celebrations to represent him, and this he made clear in a friendly letter to the principal clerk, in spite of his earnest desire to do all in his power to increase friendship and fellowship between the two established Churches.

It is quite clear that Geoffrey Fisher began to grow somewhat weary of this new controversy and the part that the Primus was playing in it. On 31 July he addressed to him an interesting and perceptive letter. He admitted that the invitations did present problems, as well south as north of the border. The Congregationalists wanted to remember the Evictions; the Anglicans the 1662 Book of Common Prayer. The Roman Catholics staged pilgrimages all across London to memorialize Smithfield martyrs put to death under Elizabeth. He himself was tempted to stage counter-demonstrations for martyrs under Mary –

but, he commented, 'how hateful counter-demonstrations would be'. 'I have sometimes said to myself,' so he ruminated, 'how glorious it would be to combine in a great memorial for those who lost their lives fighting for or against the Reformation. Some day we shall get to see it, but it may be still a long way out of sight.' (Here the Archbishop proved to be wrong for such a memorial now exists in Westminster Abbey.) He admitted to being conscious that the Episcopal Church in Scotland was in a minority and there could be occasions when the Church of England might have to move in advance of its wishes.

As to the Primus it was his view that Geoffrey Fisher took the matter of the invitations far too seriously. As he wrote to Lambeth: 'They choose to throw a party, we don't want to go. Why should we if we find it will be quite unreal and very uncomfortable. It has nothing or very little to do with unity.' On the other hand the Bishop of Chelmsford commented to the Archbishop that the Primus was 'quite unbalanced' in his attitude to the Church of Scotland.

To be fair to the Primus we need to remember that he was the Metropolitan of a Church the sole *raison d'être* of whose very existence in Scotland, apart from a quirk of history, lay in its episcopal character. Inroads against this must threaten its survival. Hence in his view relations between the Anglican Episcopal Churches of England, Scotland, Ireland and Wales took precedence over relations betwen two Churches distinguished in the main only by their establishment status. Archbishop Fisher was not impressed with such an argument, commenting: 'The fact is, I think, that the Primus had rather lost control of himself over the whole business of Scottish relations'.

Dr Fisher was still preoccupied with the invitations sent by the Kirk to the Anglican Churches since the collective refusal by those in the United Kingdom had a 'very ill reception' when reported to the British Council of Churches at its Nottingham Meeting. There now came the news that the Queen herself had accepted an invitation to be present at the celebrations in Edinburgh, a fact which, as the Archbishop told the Primus, made it more difficult for him 'to try and hold a position which he already knew to be untenable'.

The Queen's electing to go north of the border encouraged the Archbishop to hope that the Episcopal Church might be prepared to reconsider its position. He was, however, soon to discover that this was far from the case. 'The Queen has made things very difficult and why she should choose to underline the business so heavily I cannot imagine' – so the Primus complained to Lambeth. 'It would look too much like snobbery', for him to attend in these circumstances.

All attempts – and the Archbishop made many – to persuade the Scottish Episcopal Church to change its mind were thus doomed to failure. However he stuck to his original intention and invited the Dean of St Paul's – after his first choice, Professor Norman Sykes was stricken down with a mortal illness – to be present at the celebrations as his representative. The Primus now reiterated his acute displeasure, and protested that whatever the Archbishop might say 'nothing alters the fact that the Archbishop of Canterbury is represented in a celebration which the Bishops of the Province do not feel able to support; ... I wish English folk would realise that the Border is a reality and not a mere figure of speech or a line on a map; the whole outlook and ethos is different. One might just as well treat Americans as Englishmen.'

Geoffrey Fisher felt that the time had now come to give the Primus a piece of his mind which he did in a letter without inhibitions – but he never sent it! The gist of the letter is contained in one sentence: 'From my own personal knowledge I am quite certain that some of the difficulties in Scotland have been created by the Episcopal Church of Scotland ... you unfortunately from the very first made it a matter to be judged by Christian doctrines without regard to good manners.' In a subsequent letter to the Primus the Archbishop could not resist the temptation of giving a lecture in these magisterial words: 'The Church of Scotland, the Scottish Episcopal Church and the Church of England are all brethren in Christ. They recognise each other as being within the broad embrace of the Church of God. Furthermore, both for good or ill, all came through the period of the Reformation as heirs, if not equally, of it. After long estrangement, the three Churches are actively seeking through official discussions and through many personal friendships, to draw together in mingled thanksgiving and penitence of the past and in strong hope for the future.'

In August 1960, the Archbishop took part in a service in St Giles, Edinburgh without any 'by your leave' from the Bishop of the Diocese. 'I would not have thought' the Archbishop commented to the Primus, 'that you and your bishops would really wish to limit or control me in the exercise of my own judgement.'

The choice of Walter Matthews as the Archbishop's representative at the celebrations in Edinburgh proved a most happy one. He received communion with some 1,200 others at a service in St Giles, following his 'own inclinations'. He reported back to Geoffrey Fisher that there were 'hard feelings about the Episcopal Church of Scotland and its attitude'.

It has been mentioned earlier that the Queen herself, whose constitutional position was that of an Episcopalian south of the border, and a Presbyterian north of it, had declared her intention to visit the General Assembly in Edinburgh during the celebrations. This visit gave the Archbishop of Canterbury intense satisfaction, and he expressed this afterwards in the following letter to Her Majesty:

'Madam,

May I first say how glad I was that Your Majesty visited the General Assembly of the Church of Scotland and how grateful I was for the address which you there delivered. I am afraid that the Episcopal Church took the whole celebrations amiss and refused in a somewhat discourteous way to send a representative. To spare their ungenerous feelings I did not send a Bishop. But in spite of all their protestations and out of courtesy and good will towards the Church of Scotland I was happy to send the Dean of St Paul's to represent me. May I say that Your Majesty perceived just the one thing about the Reformation which needed to be said and in the acceptance of which all Christians could unite.' (The reference is to the Bible).

Maybe one of the reasons for writing was to explain to the Queen why it was that at a ceremony in Scotland which she thought it right to attend, the Archbishop was a conspicuous absentee.

It is perhaps appropriate to leave the Archbishop's relations with the Church of Scotland and the conversations between the two Churches at this point. When the Report on them finally emerged Geoffrey Fisher was living in retirement in Dorset. Looked at from the perspective of thirty years later this chapter makes depressing reading. However, the initiative taken by the Archbishop was by no means sterile, even if the talks seem to have brought with them little practical results. What is true is that many Church leaders north and south of the border got to know each other at first hand, and thus to become a little more sensitive to, and knowledgeable of, their differing points of view. Once again, *inter alia* it was on the rock of episcopacy that the conversations shipwrecked. The Kirk did not really wish to assimilate episcopacy. Anglican Orthodoxy, on the other hand, required it and the general mood at the time was veering towards organic unity. Geoffrey Fisher believed that it was possible to overcome this dilemma by respecting the integrity of both Churches as they grew closer together, but to most dogmatic theologians at both ends of the ecclesiastical spectrum, the endeavour to bypass tough theological problems in the way he proposed was then just not 'on'. It is significant that there has been no real progress in the last quarter of a century with Anglican/Presbyterian relations. It could be that at the end of the day Geoffrey Fisher may well prove to have been right.

CHAPTER 27

The United Church of South India

THE two preceding chapters which related to conversations between Anglican, Methodist and Presbyterian theologians derived from an initiative taken personally by the Archbishop of Canterbury on behalf of the Church of England. This is not the case in respect of the United Church of South India. Indeed the initiative here came from Christians of different denominations living in the subcontinent of India. However, the results of this initiative could not but be of concern to the Church of England and the Anglican Communion as a whole, particularly since they had to ask themselves what their relationship with this new Church should be – a Church which, incidentally, included some of their former members.

It is to this that we now turn.

(i)

Amongst the most interesting of re-union schemes affecting the Church of England and the world-wide Anglican Communion perhaps pride of place may be given to that which was initiated in South India. It was at the time unique, bold, imaginative and pioneering. The overall intention was to cut through or bypass such major difficulties all too often experienced in any attempts at re-union, difficulties created by emphasizing the unique status of episcopacy as the very *esse* of the Church.

The scheme made provision for two parallel ministries, Anglican and Episcopal, Free Church and non-Episcopal, to exist together side by side in the one Church though after the date of its inauguration all incoming clergy would henceforth be ordained by bishops. This scheme had been a long time in the process of gestation. Indeed its origins go back to the end of the First World War when Christians living in a culture and a country not their own, and surrounded by an indigenous population largely Hindu, came together to take stock of their overall situation. Regretfully, they were forced to confess that being divided in their worship into separate denominational groups – Anglican, Presbyterian, Congregationalist and Methodist, each with its own ministers, plant and establishment – had been nurtured in the religious struggles of Europe. Viewed from so vast a distance and so different a culture, they seemed strangely irrelevant to their present needs. Also it was wasteful of resources and distorted their gospel of unity in Christ. So keenly did certain clergy and ministers belonging to the Anglican and South India United Church feel this separation from one another that they met and declared their conviction that it was the will of God that their respective Churches should unite. 'We find ourselves weak', they said, 'and relatively impotent by our unhappy divisions, which they did not desire to perpetuate'. The Synod and General Assembly of their respective denominations gave their warm approval to this radical affirmation; and in 1925 the Methodists decided to throw in their lot with them.

A Joint Committee was set up which came together regularly and to such effect that by 1944 the three denominations agreed to go forward and implement a scheme for a United Church. The Anglican Province of India, Burma and Ceylon gladly released four of its dioceses thus making them free to enter the new Church. At the same time its Metropolitan circularized all his fellow Archbishops through-out the Anglican Communion asking whether in view of this secession they would remain in communion with his Province, and enter into full communion with the Church of South India once it was in-augurated?

As well as writing to fellow Metropolitans he also sent a personal letter to the Archbishops of Canterbury (Temple) and York (Garbett). The result was a meeting of the Southern and Northern Convocations in July 1943 when the two Primates affirmed their belief that the Church of England would not break off communion with the Church of India, Burma and Ceylon simply because of its willingness to release four dioceses for membership of the new Church. However, for the time being, the Church of England would only enter into a restricted communion with the Church of South India, thereby following the decision of the Lambeth Conference way back in 1930.

The debate in the Convocation proved, for many, a frustrating experience particularly to those opposed strongly to the re-union scheme, and who believed that the Church of England should officially distance itself from it. Prominent among these were Gregory Dix of Nashdom Abbey, a distinguished theologian, and Father Raymond Raynes of Mirfield, a monk of deep spirituality who felt passionately that to enter into communion of any kind with the Church of South India would betray the faith as set out in the Book of Common Prayer. Raynes was not a member of Convocation, and thus was unable to speak his mind in that Assembly, to remedy which he wrote an open letter to the Archbishop of Canterbury condemning the scheme's concept of episcopacy as 'so vague and unsatisfactory as to cast doubt upon the whole intention of the Church of England in its consecration of bishops. He therefore asked the Archbishop to enlighten their consciences, and to restore to them that trust and affection which they would like to entertain for their Fathers in God.' The controversy thus

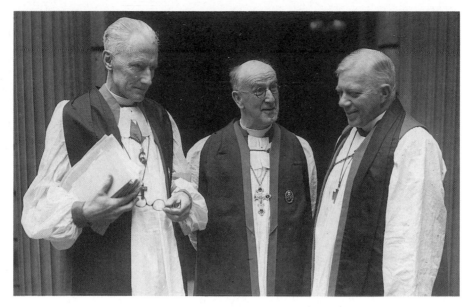

With the Bishop of Winchester (Mervyn Haigh) and the Bishop of Chichester
(George Bell).

The Fishers relaxing during Canadian Tour, 1946.

With H.R.H. Princess Elizabeth in the Canterbury Precincts, 1947.

Wedding of H.R.H. Princess Elizabeth, 1947.

With his chaplain, the Reverend J. S. Long, in the garden of
Lambeth Palace, 1950.

On deck *en route* to
Australia and New
Zealand, 1950.

The Archbishop with the
Archbishop of Brisbane
(R. C. Halse) during his
tour of Australia and New
Zealand.

The Archbishop places St Edward's Crown on the Queen's head.

With pages at the Coronation, 1953.

The Archbishop wearing the Coronation Cope and Mitre given him by the Japanese Church.

The Archbishop in his Canterbury study.

The Archbishop and Mrs Fisher with some of their grandchildren.

begun grew in momentum as the heads of the religious houses rallied to Father Raynes' support and even threatened schism.

It was at this stage in the developing controversy that Archbishop Temple died in October 1944, leaving the handling of this sensitive situation to Geoffrey Fisher, his successor in Saint Augustine's Chair. Though in the main approving William Temple's overall policy, the new Archbishop was yet critical of his seeming reluctance to take Convocation into his confidence and to keep its members fully informed. Indeed the last session had left opponents with the impression that the debate had been somewhat stage-managed by the two Primates. Geoffrey Fisher was as convinced as his predecessor that the re-union scheme should go forward with the blessing of the Church of England even though he was not entirely happy with its approach to ministry. He further recognised, as did Temple, that the young Church must go outside the Anglican Communion for the time being. It was a difficult time for the rank and file of the Church of England bishops, some of whom sympathized with the critical approach of the heads of the religious houses, though equally critical of the extreme lengths to which they seemed willing to push their opposition. Among these was Leslie Owen, Bishop of Lincoln, who assumed the difficult role of mediator between Father Raynes and Lambeth. From his own enquiries the bishop reported to Dr Fisher that the threat to secede was no idle one, since for many this was a matter of conscience, though he himself was more convinced than ever that he must remain, in the last resort, loyal to the Church of England. The immediate priority, so he advised the Archbishop, was another meeting of Convocation and the sooner the better.

During these anxious days Geoffrey Fisher kept in close touch with Dr Cyril Garbett who presided over the northern Convocation and who was certainly exercised in his mind as to the possible consequences which might flow from the implementation of the re-union scheme. There was much in it which he 'heartily disliked' but, so he reflected, maybe in 'twenty or thirty years time the position may have changed and Catholic principles in it may have prevailed'. They must do everything in their power to prevent any kind of secession which would have disastrous effects upon the Eastern Churches.

The pressure on Archbishop Fisher to make a statement in Convocation was now increasing particularly as it was felt in many circles, not least by the Archbishop himself, that the previous Convocation debate was somewhat perfunctory. Tomkinson, vicar of All Saints, Margaret Street, a church which had, in the 19th century, spearheaded the Oxford Movement, urged the Archbishop to say something 'loudly and clearly SOON' (*sic*) in order to allay mounting fears, and to prevent the possible departure from the Church of England of some of its younger clergy. 'The Church is in peril', he warned – a *cri de coeur* to which Geoffrey Fisher retorted somewhat drily that Tomkinson was not the first person to remind him that 'trouble was brewing over the South India Scheme'. The mass of Church of England clergy felt somewhat bemused, and were not at all sure whether they understood what the Church of South India scheme was really about. It was, therefore, imperative that the Archbishop should relieve them of their uncertainties, and this meant that his statement to Convocation must be carefully drawn up to meet this felt need. He therefore submitted his script to Dr Kirk, a legalist and Bishop of Oxford, who commented that he was glad the Archbishop felt unhappy with parts of Temple's statement; also that he had very properly stressed the provisional nature of some of its proposals.

On 15 May 1945 the Archbishop delivered his long awaited statement in the full Synod of the Convocation of Canterbury. It was certainly one of his best performances not least because he set himself a limited objective and achieved it. His concern was not so much to evaluate the scheme in itself as to let people know precisely what its terms were. This he did systematically and without adornment. Thus he outlined with great care the juxtaposition of two ministries, Episcopal and non-Episcopal, in the one Church until such time as only the former would obtain. He also pointed out that after some thirty years following its inauguration there would be a general review of the situation as it had developed.

Nicholas Mosley in his *The Life of Raymond Raynes* comments: 'Dr Fisher made a speech in Convocation which by a clarity of exposition that no one else had yet achieved quietened both sets of extremists. He defined ambiguous terms such as "inter-Communion" and "partial-Communion" and was explicit that the Church of England would not be in full communion with the new Church but that he hoped it would be one day.'

The Archbishop's statement to Convocation ended with these impressive words: 'Inevitably I have had to speak mostly of limitations, restrictions and safeguards. There is another approach to the matter of which I have said nothing, one which should engage our utmost sympathy and prayers and hopes. For this enterprise, born of much faith and prayer and charity, rests on the belief and hope that divided Churches will in the living unity of a corporate life achieve a unity of faith, order, worship and witness true to the traditions of the Universal Church, in which each contributing Church will find enrichment and fulfilment in the Body of Christ. If that aspect of the matter has been absent from what I have said, as not being apposite to my particular purpose, it is certainly present in the minds of us all.'

The day of the inauguration of the new Church was fixed for 27

September and this led to a mild agitation for a further meeting of Convocation before this took place. The Archbishop – and this was equally true of his brother of York – was anxious to avoid a further debate at least for the present, considering it likely to fuel once more opposition to the scheme rather than to help it on its way. Both Primates agreed that it would suffice for a brief announcement of its inception to be made in the northern and southern Convocations. It was significant, however, that the Archbishop of Canterbury sent to the Press at this time a resolution passed by the Archbishops and Bishops of England and Wales assuring their fellow Anglicans, who had gone forth from their Communion to join the new Church of South India, of their prayers and continuing fellowship with them. They expressed their earnest hope that God would use them and their fellows in the Church of South India.

(ii)

So far as concerned the Church of England, CSI was launched on its way. However, this by no means led to the end of controversy and it is to this that we now turn.

The Church of South India, by its own decision and knowing that it would go outside the Anglican fold, was also no longer in unrestricted Communion with the Church of England. This raised an important question as to how far grants given by SPG to the four dioceses now ceasing to be within the Province of India, Burma and Ceylon, could any longer legally be paid over to the new United Church. Independently of any restrictions thus imposed by law, there were High Churchmen on the Catholic wing of the *Ecclesia Anglicana* who wished, for the time being at least, to freeze any financial aid. This could well prove disastrous since the four Anglican dioceses had never been self-supporting. Thus it was important to find out precisely what the legal situation was *vis-à-vis*, for example, the Colonial Bishopric and the Church Endowment Funds. Legal advice was sought and as a result an assurance was given that the Bishop of Madras could certainly use the latter fund for the United Church of South India. A similar opinion was given in respect of the Central Bishopric Fund so long as these monies were deployed for the stipends of clergy.

A great deal of support in manpower and money traditionally came to South India from the great missionary societies. Fortunately, though not unexpectedly, the evangelical Church Missionary Society let it be known immediately that it would continue to support its work in South India. This was not the case, however, with the more High Anglican Society for the Propagation of the Gospel. Here views were divided, and the issue came to a crisis so far as clerical incomes were concerned. The majority report of the SPG standing committee sought a compromise by making the stipends of those clergy who were serving under Bishops in South India dependent upon their satisfying an outside authority on their doctrinal orthodoxy. This expedient was described by Geoffrey Fisher as a 'serious embarrassment', 'not workable', and 'terribly ungenerous'. He thus protested vigorously to Bishop Roberts, the secretary, against this act of discrimination, urging him to see that the SPG continued to give help to such missionary dioceses and institutions as they at present supported. There was a serious danger, he warned, of the SPG making itself 'narrower in outlook' than was the Church of which it claimed to be an agent. The SPG standing committee met again on receipt of this protest, but the result was disappointing to the Archbishop who was convinced that the Church of South India would not be prepared to negotiate with the Society on the basis that its missionaries be segregated as an identifiable unit. If the SPG were to insist on this then its subscribers should be allowed to divert their subscription direct to the missionaries involved. In this case the President and Vice-Presidents could sponsor a Fund to this end and invite subscriptions to it.

Geoffrey Fisher felt this matter deeply, and told Michael Bruce, a parish priest strongly opposed to the South India Scheme, that in their concern for Catholic Order 'they will end up by putting themselves out of reach of it'. To the Bishop of Salisbury, Geoffrey Fisher confessed that he was dong his best 'to save SPG from its own follies but it is very difficult'. Equally to the Bishop of Derby, chairman of his Ecumenical Committee, he expressed his intention to fight the battle not on the 'merits of the Scheme' but as a matter of 'conscience'. Most interested, of course, in this unhappy squabble was the Metropolitan of India who saw at first hand the consequences of restricting grants for work in the field. Geoffrey Fisher kept him in very close touch with what was happening and sent him a detailed letter on 15 July 1947. In this he referred to the 'alarums and excursions' in the SPG over South India; and his own success in securing that any subscriber to SPG could ask that his subscription should go to a separate account and thence through the Society to the support of former SPG workers. This compromise was reached 'without the sense of victory or defeat but with general goodwill'. He expressed his own satisfaction at this change of heart particularly as he saw it in the light of a 'first step towards curbing those in the country who are devoting themselves to denigrating the Scheme'.

It was a grief to many that difficulties with the SPG over the Special Fund lingered so long. True, SPG had gone a long way to accommodating itself to a new situation in South India but niggling points of controversy remained. The Archbishop of York, with his accustomed sanity, felt that the issue should be rationally discussed at a Bishops'

Meeting since it would be a 'scandal if the new Church was penalised financially'. Both the Bishop of Madras and the Moderator of the Church in South India reported to Lambeth the urgent need to provide financial support for those workers, hitherto in receipt of SPG funds, but who were now in a measure deprived of them. Unless considerable sums were made available quickly educational institutions would be forced to close. This diminution in grants was the more critical since the cost of living had suffered a four-fold increase. The Archbishop of Canterbury, thus prompted, took the initiative in bringing this matter before his episcopal colleagues, the result of which was that four diocesans urged the SPG to continue their financial aid in full at least till the end of 1948.

A controversy so long drawn out, and only partially resolved, led almost inevitably to tempers rising. It seemed curiously odd to some people that deep theological convictions as to the nature of episcopacy could possibly end up by depriving a young Church of the support necessary to discharge its fundamental mission. On the other hand it seemed equally curious, though to a smaller number, that fundamental, theological convictions could be so easily jettisoned. Rawlinson, Bishop of Derby, was numbered among the former category and was irritated by the attitude of the SPG so much so as to bring the matter up at his Diocesan Conference. The Archbishop of Canterbury was equally critical of the SPG, but did not believe that a public controversy around this issue would do any good to anybody. Hence he dropped the Bishop of Derby a polite hint that he should 'lay off' the SPG for the time being, at least while negotiations with the Society were still going on.

While awaiting a solution Geoffrey Fisher suggested to Bishop Wand of London, whose churchmanship was sympathetic to the SPG, that he gather together a few like-minded bishops with the intention of taking this matter up with the Society; but nothing seems to have resulted from this suggestion any more than did similar requests that the same bishop might issue an appeal, or alert the Press to the plight of some of the clergy in South India. However, the *Church of England Newspaper* and the *Record* agreed to make an effort to raise money.

It would be as embarrassing as tedious to dwell on the 'falling out of faithful friends' to which this controversy unfortunately led. The Bishop of Derby protested to Lambeth that 'promises and fair words have been officially uttered by our Communion to South India but in the sphere of deeds as contrasted with words, what has happened is that officially help has been cut off'. Particularly upsetting to the Bishop was his seeming rift with Geoffrey Fisher. 'You and I', he lamented, 'have been so close to one another in outlook and policy as well as friendship that any of the least clouding of our relationship I find most distressing.' It was typical of the Archbishop that he assured the Bishop there was nothing personal about this. It was all a matter of tactics not policy, since both he and the Bishop condemned the attitude of the Society for the Propagation of the Gospel and the Mothers' Union.

Not surprisingly, this controversy concerning relations with the United Church of South India had repercussions in Britain north of the Border. Thus the Primus of the Episcopal Church of Scotland got into touch with Lambeth since, as he put it, the *raison d'être*, the very existence and lifeblood of his Church, depended on a high view of episcopacy as the very *esse* of Catholic Order. He therefore regarded any recognition of the Church of South India as threatening the whole status of the Episcopal Church of Scotland, indeed its right to exist at all.

However, the Episcopal Church of Scotland, having privately conveyed to the Archbishop its view on the Church of South India, left it for further comment to the Lambeth Conference.

It was of course inevitable that the 1948 Lambeth Conference should discuss the United Church of South India which had been inaugurated in the previous year. Indeed, it was given a restrained prominence in the introductory Encyclical which the Archbishop himself signed and which he had a significant part in drawing up. The Encyclical recorded that the Church of South India had been a 'chief concern' by reason of the fact that under its terms 'for the first time since the great division of Christendom at the Reformation, an Act of Union has taken place in which episcopal and non-episcopal traditions have been united in a more comprehensive expression of the Universal Church'. 'The Conference', it went on, 'gives thanks to God for the measure of unity thus locally achieved. At the same time it records that some features of the Constitution of the Church of South India give rise to uncertainty or grave misgivings in the minds of many, and hopes that such action may be taken as to lead to the day when the present measure of mutual recognition and inter-communion may become full Communion between the Church of South India and the Churches of the Anglican Communion. We have pledged ourselves to do all in our power, by consultation, work and prayer to bring about that end.'

The Encyclical admitted frankly that there was a 'divergence of opinion' as to the status of bishops and clergy consecrated or ordained at or since the inauguration. The Lambeth bishops, however, with the full support of Geoffrey Fisher, did not wish to condemn outright or declare invalid their Orders; nor did they wish to deny to anyone liberty of conscience.

Complaints did in fact come in to Lambeth from time to time illustrating a degree of frustration on the part of some priests of the

Church of South India (CSI). A letter from the Bishop of Madras deplored the fact that Anglican priests could not celebrate or receive Communion in Free Churches. In spite of his strong feelings the Archbishop begged him to conform to the Lambeth position though he admitted that it would demand an 'enormous act of self-sacrifice and spiritual deprivation to do this'. In similar vein in January 1958 Geoffrey Fisher wrote to Bishop Newbigin of the United Church of South India informing him that he ought to confine himself to celebrating at Church of England altars in Britain, and this only on the understanding that he did not celebrate in future in the Free Churches. At the same time he told him that it would not be possible for bishops of the CSI to attend the Lambeth Conference of 1958. If he were to invite them he would need also to treat in the same way, for example, the Church in the Philippines, which had close associations with the Episcopal Church of America, as well as the Spanish Reformed Churches.

Once launched, it was not surprising that the *Church Times* arrogated to itself the responsibility of being a High Church Anglican watchdog monitoring the CSI's progress. The Archbishop could not refrain from suggesting to the editor that 'one of the most difficult operations is to pass from the defensive to the co-operative'. He hoped, however, that the *Church Times* would be willing to do just this.

As the years went on, and CSI was beginning to have a history, Geoffrey Fisher believed that it was high time, in the light of the experience so far gained, for a fresh appraisal of its status to be made. This would consider Anglican relations to it in the round, and also how its priests and personnel would fare when they travelled abroad. It had always been recognised, since the Lambeth Conference of 1930, that CSI would go outside the Anglican Communion and become a separate Province of what the Archbishop described as 'the Church Universal'. Yet many people, so the Archbishop observed, still regarded the united Church of South India as 'tied up' with the Church of England, though this was certainly not the view of the Bishop of Madras, who writing to Geoffrey Fisher expressed himself as follows: 'I am not an Anglican Bishop. I do not regard myself as having any Anglican status nor do I receive it'. Rather he saw himself as thoroughly integrated with CSI. What he found somewhat ironic was that whereas the United Church was in full Communion with Presbyterians, Congregationalists and Methodists throughout the world, Episcopal Churches still hung back from a full recognition.

One of the questions which arose and on which there were differences of opinion was how ex-Anglican priests within CSI should be treated personally when abroad. Geoffrey Fisher was of opinion that there was an analogy here with priests of the Church of Finland, who in coming to England would not expect to celebrate Holy Communion according to the rite of the *Ecclesia Anglicana*.

Behind these discussions as to how an ex-Anglican priest working in the Church of South India should exercise his ministry when away from home there lay the more final question as to the relationship of CSI with the Anglican Communion as a whole. Here Geoffrey Fisher, in spite of criticisms which he entertained *vis-à-vis* the CSI Ordinal, (see pp. 000) was yet convinced that the time had come for the Church of England to face up to the question of whether it would now accept into its fellowship, as occasion demanded, clergy ordained since the union of the Church of South India. Indeed to the Archbishop of Melbourne he confided: 'I am prepared to agree, though I do not do it in public, that the existing regulations of Convocation cannot gainsay the fact that their ordination is valid and may be recognised by a Bishop if he wants to. What we all hope is that now there may be full recognition given to such ordination by an Act of Convocation'. It has not yet come!

(iii)

It is certainly significant that in order to bring to birth the United Church of South India, the Anglican Province of India, Burma and Ceylon willingly co-operated by releasing to the new Church some four of its existing dioceses. The fact is that reunion was very much in the air in the sub-continent, and quite clearly the situation which had led to the inauguration of CSI was not by any means unique to Southern India. The same ecclesiastical pluralism existed elsewhere in the sub-continent and it was therefore to be expected that a not totally dissimilar initiative should be taken in respect of Ceylon, North India and Burma. The Archbishop of Canterbury was co-operative from the beginning as was seen when the Bishop of Colombo in January 1949 asked his advice as to how he could proceed to advance a United Church in his diocese. The Archbishop duly informed him of the correct procedure which required that as soon as the scheme had been drawn up the Bishop should confer with his diocese. If it approved the scheme then he should lay it before the General Council of the Church of India, Burma and Ceylon. When this hurdle was successfully surmounted he must then circularize the Metropolitans of the Anglican Communion including, of course, the Archbishop of Canterbury.

It could not have come as a surprise to many people that as soon as the scheme became public the *Church Times* published a critique stressing that this new effort at re-union was more comprehensive in character than that of South India in that it catered for 39,000 Anglicans, 21,000 Methodists, 5,500 Baptists, 4,250 Presbyterians and 2,000 of the Church of South India. In particular, the *Church Times* was critical of the manner in which the various denominations offered and received each other's Orders. Their own ministries, so the *Church Times* argued, were imperfect and limited in authority by the very reason of their separation the one from the other. They were therefore unable to confer validity upon their respective Orders by a cross-fertilisation of this kind. The Lambeth Conference of 1958 took a different view, and stated it as follows: 'The rite is intended to convey everything of value in the Anglican ministry including the tradition of episcopal ordination. Whilst no judgement was passed on the reality to supply whatever each might need . . . we may surely trust that God will answer the prayers of his people and provide for the resultant Churches a ministry possessed of all the richness of inheritance which the uniting Churches previously treasured in separation.' The Archbishop now got into touch with the Metropolitan of India pointing out that there were substantial differences between the Ceylon and the South India scheme, since the former set up a unified ministry from the word go. Thus there would be no progressive realisation of a full ministry to be realised only across the years. The question arose, so the Archbishop wrote, as to whether the Anglican Communion could go straight into full Communion with the new Church. The best way, he suggested, to answer this question was to consult the Anglican Communion, and the Provinces within it, through the new consultative body which had been set up. At some time the Church of England would have to make up its mind and pass an opinion on this key question. Geoffrey Fisher then indulged in an interesting *cri de coeur*. 'I do not want to get involved', he wrote, 'in the same confusion that arose over CSI when William Temple, after consulting Convocation but not in its name, laid down an interim policy. Whatever in due course is done about Ceylon ought to be done officially by Convocation. If and when you want official advice from the Church of England I shall, therefore, bring it before Convocation.' What he hoped to do was to get CSI out of the way before considering the Ceylon scheme. As he saw it, apart from merely minor points, the main question in relation to Ceylon simply was – does the proposed form of ordination make the Church fully episcopal? Perhaps, he reflected, it was not so far removed from what he himself had adumbrated in his Cambridge sermon. The Archbishop made it clear to the Metropolitan that he was not opposed to the Church of England being in full Communion with an episcopal Church which was itself in full Communion with one which was non-episcopal. Indeed there was a precedent for this in Sweden's relations with Norway whose bishops were not in the Apostolic succession. The Bishop of Derby, 'as an individual theologian' expressed himself 'attracted' by the Ceylon scheme for unification through a service, 'the precise significance of which is left to be determined by God'.

The general atmosphere in India and its environs was now one of change and the Lambeth Conference of 1958 when asked to give advice on further plans for re-union in Ceylon, North India and Pakistan reported that all three schemes showed 'clear evidence of the guidance of the Holy Spirit' which marked a 'great and significant step towards the recovery of the Church Universal'. They believed it was possible for the Church of Sri Lanka to be from the outset in full Communion with Provinces of the Anglican Communion. With some modifications the Churches of North India and Pakistan could have the same expectations. They prayed that these unions might go forward.

In January 1959 the Archbishop held a meeting at Lambeth in connection with the re-union scheme for North India which, as was the case with the Lambeth Fathers, had won his enthusiastic support. Indeed he called it a 'marvel of grace' and commended it in these words: 'In the Church of God there is Ordination and there is, also in some Churches, Episcopal Ordination. In the plan each Church offers to God and to one another the Ordination that it has in the rite of Unification. The rite most properly does not ask God to define to us precisely what he gives to each.'

However, as we have already seen, this was not everyone's view. The Church Union entertained strong objections, and five members of the Derby Committee drew up a minority report against it. To the Bishop of Lahore the Archbishop wrote of his battle 'to defend the Lambeth Conference Report against some very important, influential theologians and liturgical experts here at home who regard the whole North India plan as anathema'. Among such was Eric Mascal, lecturer in the philosophy of religion at Oxford, whom Geoffrey Fisher accused, in a letter to the Metropolitan of India, of 'sniping' at it the whole time. Stephen Neill felt that 'when the verbiage has been pared away the answer of Lambeth is negative. This is not Episcopal Ordination. If this is so, Episcopal Ordination is no longer necessary as a pre-requisite to full Communion between Anglican and non-Anglican Churches.' The Bishop of Exeter described the North India scheme as a 'blind alley' to which the Archbishop retorted that it was a better scheme than that of the Church of South India, and asked whether it could not be seen as 'blazing a trail far better than CSI; and one which might rapidly lead to re-union in other parts of the world'. As to Dr Ratcliffe, a conservative liturgiologist critical of the scheme, the Archbishop summarily dismissed him as 'a pure liturgiologist, bound hand and foot to a verbalism of past liturgies'.

However, Geoffrey Fisher could not but recognise that the theological opposition was indeed an influential one. Among its members none was more respected for his learning, ecumenical spirit and liberal catholic position than Michael Ramsey, Archbishop of York, who drew up for the benefit of his fellow Metropolitan: 'A Note on the Plan for a United Church in North India and Pakistan'. His comments may be briefly summarised as follows:

(1) The authors of the Plan wish a united Ministry of Bishops and Presbyters, this to be brought about in a service in which God is asked to effect this coming together.

(2) They desire to avoid the necessity of particularizing what has happened since God does all.

(3) Anglicans are asked to understand it as an ordination but does its content permit of this interpretation?

(4) Several aspects of this procedure suggest the answer 'no', not least because it must be limited in scope and authority by lacking the seal of the whole Church. Will people recognise that genuine orders in the historic succession have been conferred?

To these scruples Geoffrey Fisher replied that Michael Ramsey had failed to recognise the distinction between the generic term 'ordination' applied to all ministers brought together into the United Church and the specific term 'Episcopal Ordination'. The Bishops at the Lambeth Conference were satisfied that episcopal orders as well as the orders of other Churches were being offered for acceptance to God who granted what was needed for their fulness. In this respect there was no progressive entry into an episcopal ministry over the years. It was there made available for all from the beginning.

The Lambeth Fathers ended their Report on these re-union schemes thus: 'We pray that these Unions may go forward.' They did – and with Geoffrey Fisher's blessing. Perhaps he could claim at least *pars minima fui* if not *pars magna fui*.

CHAPTER 28

Roman Catholics and Catholicism

(i)

IT would be difficult to imagine a more convinced and built-in member of the Church of England by heredity, nurture and temperament than Geoffrey Fisher. Scion of a long line of country incumbents, the parish church of Higham on the Hill and its local school exercised an influence which the two Methodist chapels could not rival. Marlborough, his public school, was a Church of England foundation and Exeter College to which he went, though no longer a preserve of the Established Church, had its chaplain and regular rhythm of Anglican services. Repton School did indeed contain a few Catholics and some from the Free Churches, but the assumption was in chapel and classroom that the school lived its life within the liberal ethos and self-assurance of the national Church. Geoffrey Fisher believed in the clerical headmaster, and confessed that he personally could not adequately fulfil his duties were he not an ordained priest. Along with this loyalty and the assumptions which went with it, the Archbishop admits, when looking back on his life, that he grew up with an inbred opposition to anything that smelt of Rome. 'I objected to their doctrine; I objected to their methods of reasoning, basing their arguments on non-existent evidence.'

Roman Catholics when Geoffrey Fisher was a boy were still, in a measure, sealed off, socially as well as theologically, from the rest of the nation. Years later Father Corbishly, a Jesuit priest, confessed that until he went up to Oxford he had spent his days almost exclusively among Roman Catholics in Liverpool, socially, culturally and religiously, though 'ghetto' would perhaps be too strong a word.

For Geoffrey Fisher it was only during the war years that things began to change and among his first acts on becoming Archbishop was to call together to Lambeth members of the Joint Committee of the Life and Liberty Weeks and the Sword of the Spirit, reminding them that they had for some years worked together, but that it was no longer possible for him to continue as their chairman. Wasn't it possible, he asked, for an Ecumenical Committee, which included Roman Catholics and straddled the divide between the various Churches and denominations to be set up as its successor? The matter was discussed and the Roman Catholic representative, Bishop Craven, replied that he thought this was perfectly posssible, and that he would request Cardinal Griffin to promote it; but in fact there was no comeback. This was a great disappointment to Geoffrey Fisher, but repeated efforts on his part to establish such a committee proved abortive through the unwillingness of the Cardinal Archbishop to co-operate. Things might have been different had Cardinal Hinsley, who sanctioned the original wartime venture, still been in office. For Geoffrey Fisher, at least, the experience of this Committee had been a liberal education. This did not mean that his built-in suspicion of Roman Catholics suddenly disappeared; rather that personal relations engendered by working together began, if only tentatively, to break down barriers. The end of hostilities, by removing the crisis which had brought these churchmen together ecumenically, undoubtedly slowed down the momentum, and encouraged a retreat into denominational loyalties. However, the Archbishop and the new Cardinal met each other over tea at Lambeth on 30 May 1946, when they had a frank discussion of affairs of mutual concern such as the work of the Sword of the Spirit, religious freedom, Spain and Russia. The Archbishop took the opportunity of putting to the Cardinal that what would really help co-operation in Britain would be an agreement that at joint meetings there should be silence followed by all saying together the Lord's Prayer. Without this there was no evidence at all that they were meeting as Christians. This, however, the Cardinal would not concede.

There were, unfortunately, many situations which could easily lead to bad temper and an unwillingness to witness together. Such inhibiting occasions were most likely to arise when Roman Catholics were invited to co-operate with the Established Church of England when the latter was discharging a national role. A typical case occurred in 1949 when Father Groser, a popular East End incumbent, got into touch with the Archbishop on the question of civic services, particularly as they concerned Roman Catholic mayors who declined to attend an Anglican parish church for such a purpose. The result was a letter to the Cardinal Archbishop of Westminster from Lambeth asking for his views. The Cardinal replied pointing out that as early as 1924 the Roman Catholic hierarchy put on record that they were 'gravely concerned' at the serious departure from prescribed practice, when Catholic mayors attended non-Roman Catholic services, a policy which was reaffirmed on 25 October 1938. In response to this reply the Archbishop restated his own position, namely that on a National Day of Prayer, the mayor as a representative of the monarch should go with the corporation to the parish church though he, the Archbishop, entirely recognised that no one should be expected to act against his conscience. To ensure this the Roman Catholic mayor ought to nominate a deputy to act for him. What he should not do was to attend another church of his own persuasion and invite members of the corporation to go with him. The advantage of an ecclesiastical establishment was precisely that it overcame the difficulty which could confront, for example, a Jewish mayor or one who was a member of a Christian Science Church.

Geoffrey Fisher was unwilling to let matters rest there and through the initiative of Lord Salisbury he had a long conversation with the Cardinal in Archbishop's House, Westminster, when he deplored the crumbling moral fabric of Europe, and the consequent need for the churches to work together to offset it. Cardinal Griffin agreed that co-operation could be secured in the moral and political fields, but in the religious areas never 'and that must be treated, as things stand, as final'. Geoffrey Fisher, however, was still reluctant to leave matters there. Thus he also solicited the help of the Roman Catholic Bishop Myers in the hope that he would commend to the Cardinal the desirability of his having informal meetings from time to time with the Archbishop of Canterbury and one or two Free Churchmen; but there was no positive response to these initiatives. Later in September 1946 the Archbishop tackled the Cardinal again informally at a party as to joint meetings – but heard no more.

There can be no doubt that Geoffrey Fisher found it more difficult to establish co-operative relations with Cardinal Griffin than with his predecessor, Cardinal Hinsley. Writing to Lord Salisbury he admitted this frankly in these words: 'Whatever the Cardinal may say, it is a fact that since Cardinal Hinsley died the Romans have become much more difficult to co-operate with'. Archbishop Matthew suggested that any future conversation between the Cardinal and the Archbishop should be held on neutral ground and not at Lambeth as on the last occasion.

In fairness to Cardinal Griffin, perhaps it ought to be said that for the Head of the Roman Catholic hierarchy to confer regularly with the Archbishop of Canterbury and one or two Free Churchmen must have seemed in the mid-forties a dangerous departure from normal practice. Often what irritated, and led to a high degree of heat may seem to us trivial, but it did not appear so to many at the time. A further example of this in another area was the difficulty in agreeing an acceptable order of signatures when it was a matter of sending a joint letter to *The Times* on some national issue. It was the contention of the Cardinal that his name must appear immediately after that of the Archbishop of Canterbury, as was the case, so he maintained, in the time of Cardinal Hinsley. Such a claim did not commend itself to the Moderator of the General Assembly of the Church of Scotland, another established church. This vexed question again arose when a joint letter was proposed in connection with the Peace Conference in San Francisco. Geoffrey Fisher wrote to the Cardinal suggesting that the order of signatures should read Cantuar, Ebor, the Cardinal, the Church of Scotland and the Moderator of the Free Church Federal Council only to be met by a peremptory reply from Dr Griffin that he would only sign if his signature came immediately after that of the Archbishop. Anxious to be conciliatory, Geoffrey Fisher complied, whereupon the Archbishop of York withdrew his name rather than sign below the Cardinal's. Equally severe was a letter to Lambeth from Daniel Lamont, Convener of the Committee in the General Administration of the Church of Scotland, complaining that the new order had given general dissatisfaction in Scotland and had as a consequence been referred to his Committee. 'In point of fact,' he wrote, 'our Moderator has precedence over any representative of the Roman Catholic Church.' To ignore this was 'most undesirable and must not be repeated'.

Geoffrey Fisher's acknowledgement of this letter was, and could only be, an abject apology made necessary, he asserted, by his having mis-read the order of precedence on an earlier document. As for the future he proposed the following: the Archbishops of Canterbury and York; the Moderator of the General Assembly of the Church of Scotland; the Archbishop of Westminster; and the Moderator of the Free Church Federal Council. Clearly, he reiterated, the Established Churches must come first. If it were a matter of either the Roman Catholic Church or the Church of Scotland he would opt for the latter, and make public the reason for this choice.

In taking this line Geoffrey Fisher would not have had the support of High Church Anglican opinion and certainly not of the Episcopal Church of Scotland.

So this unhappy exchange of letters continued though Cardinal Griffin believed it would be a 'mistake' to make it a matter of public controversy, particularly since the practice of joint letters was only of recent origin.

To dilate further on this frustrating aspect of ecumenical relations would indeed be tedious. What bemused the Cardinal, and understandably so, was why it should be necessary for the Church of England to be represented by two signatures, Canterbury and York, while everybody else had but one. Here the Archbishop endeavoured to enlighten the Cardinal with a little objective Church history, explaining that in domestic matters in England it was customary for the two Primates of the northern and southern Province to act together – but he remained unconvinced. Cardinal Griffin's reaction to this epistle was simply to re-state the position which he had consistently held from the beginning. There this matter rested for some time and subterfuges such as printing the signatures of these ecclesiatical leaders in parallel columns side by side did not commend themselves. The end result of this *contretemps* was that the Cardinal's signature no longer appeared. And there the matter rested for the time being.

We have stressed, and rightly, that Geoffrey Fisher was conciliatory by temperament, but for many years he was convinced that the Roman

Catholics must be watched carefully lest they should increasingly infiltrate the national life, particularly where the *media* were concerned. From information that he received privately, the Archbishop gained the impression that Roman Catholic influence was excessive at *The Times* in Printing House Square. His suspicions were not lessened when on the retirement of its Editor, Barrington-Ward, his successor was an Irishman, a graduate of Trinity College, Dublin, and a Roman Catholic if not a practising one. The responsibility for the paper's policy lay, of course, with the Editor, though if the management dissented from his policy it could remove him. It was one of the Archbishop's firm convictions that Fleet Street 'had always been full of Irishmen, many of whom were Roman Catholics'. On 31 October 1949 an article appeared in *The Times* under the heading 'Catholicism Today', which began with a reference to the world-wide character of the Roman Communion, stressing its near four hundred million members and 369 archiepiscopal sees. The author went on to discuss Roman Catholic doctrines, admitting that it was not easy here to distinguish between the essential and non-essential. However, he prophesied that in the foreseeable future non-Roman Christians would submit to the Papal See.

The article sparked off a considerable correspondence, later published, Roman Catholics being the main contributors. Geoffrey Fisher was uncertain as to whether there ought to be any official Anglican response and he got into touch with some of the bishops to this end; but they did not, as a whole, encourage any such reply. However, one did come from the Archbishop's senior chaplain, Dr Eric Jay, under the paradoxical title: *Infallible Fallacies*. This booklet is pungent, snappily written, neither bad-tempered nor aggressive. The Roman Catholic Archbishop of Liverpool, Dr Heenan, later to become Archbishop of Westminster, described it as 'fascinating', but 'full of mistakes'. Dr Fisher extolled it as giving an effective answer to Roman Catholic claims being 'courteous, quickly read and cheap'.

The letters which came in to *The Times* from Roman Catholics revealed two quite different approaches. There were those which expressed, without qualification, the most extreme claims. Thus G. A. Beck, Coadjutor Bishop of Brent, stated starkly that every jot and tittle of Roman Catholic doctrine must be accepted on the authority of the one God who reveals it through his Church. It thus followed that there could be no praying together, since there was ultimately no common mind. To Roman Catholics, nurtured strictly in this tradition, Anglican Bishops were simply laymen. Other Roman Catholics, however, adopted a more liberal approach, which Geoffrey Fisher characterised as stressing 'the rightness and necessity of establishing what may be called civilised relations with those who differ from them so that in an atmosphere of Christian charity differences may be explored and, where common action is possible, it may be taken'. Typical was a letter from Ampleforth Abbey, nursery of Catholic learning (and having an interesting link with Westminster Abbey, a former Benedictine monastery) which claimed that the breakaway at the Reformation was due to the Papacy at the time having become 'in some respects an unlovely thing'. Hence only love would bring back the separated Churches.

In a memorandum he drew up at the time the Archbishop repeated his view, sadly, that the momentum of the outreach towards one another generated by the war years had slowed down, but this 'had not been due to a change of feeling on the part of the Church of England or Free Churches but to what appears to us to have been a deliberate withdrawal by the authorities of the Church of Rome in this country. Our wish remains for such co-operation as is possible upon the basis of such principles as are held in common. Effective relations must mean, at the least, saying the Lord's Prayer together.'

As is not unusual after the Editor of *The Times* has given a particular correspondence a good run, it was brought to a close with a somewhat magisterial leading article. This appeared on 29 November and the Archbishop digested it late at night, on the eve of his departure for Malta, which might well mean, so he confessed, that his immediate comments thrown off in 'extreme haste' were perhaps written in 'unwisdom'.

The leading article was the product of an extreme Anglo-Catholic who went so far as to claim that the Roman Catholic Church was 'the only Communion commanded and empowered by God that it might proclaim certain specific sacramental teaching and discipline'.

After the correspondence and leading article, the Archbishop went so far as to protest 'vigorously' to some of the directors of the paper claiming that many people think that Roman Catholics have captured *The Times*.

In raising this issue the Archbishop was not alone. Sir Campbell Stewart called at Lambeth on 8 December to share his concern, and to deplore the influence which he believed the Roman Catholics were bringing to bear on the paper's policy. He strongly advised the Archbishop to have it out with the proprietor Lord Astor, confronting him personally. This he did and they met at Lambeth when Geoffrey Fisher frankly made the following points: (1) Protestants were realistically not expecting that 'one generous gesture from the Holy See would lead to reunion'; (2) The leader in *The Times* which had occasioned such controversy confined itself to an expression of Roman claims in an extreme form, whereas 'the real significance of the correspondence shows that there was a division of opinion amongst Roman Catholics themselves'; (3) The leader called on the Churches in England, other than the Roman Catholics, to 'remove the impression that they did not desire unity with the zeal they had a few years ago'. The reality was, in fact, precisely the opposite in that it was the Roman Catholic Church which had withdrawn from such co-operation.

Unfortunately, we have only Geoffrey Fisher's account of this interview and the effect of his strictures upon the recipient. He admitted, however, that Lord Astor gave an assurance that the Editor, whom he knew 'very well', would not abuse his position. Geoffrey Fisher allowed that it was a 'friendly discussion' though Lord Astor would not accept the main charge but defended his colleagues.

This correspondence in *The Times* certainly went some way to provoking a near witch-hunt which was neither reasonable nor healthy. There was talk of Roman Catholic infiltration into the Foreign Office and the Royal Air Force. Thus an RAF chaplain had written some years earlier to Dr Eric Jay, senior chaplain at Lambeth, alleging that three or four specialists in the Medical Services of the Forces were Roman Catholics. 'I am afraid, there is every evidence of a Popish plot in the Services,' he claimed, 'and we ought to be awake in time. Unfortunately, those who ought to be coping with this were too blundering and clumsy to deal with this sort of thing.' Dr Eric Jay took this letter sufficiently seriously to write to the RAF Chaplain-in-Chief on 26 March 1953, stating that there seemed no doubt whatever that the RAF Medical School was 'top heavy with Roman Catholics' and that there was cause for anxiety. Wisely, Dr Jay went on to say that he did not believe these men were given their appointments by reason of their being Roman Catholics but because they seemed right for the job. Thus Dr Jay was opposed to the Archbishop making any formal approach to Lord Portal, Marshal of the Royal Air Force, since, in his opinion, 'no good would come of it, and interdenominational relations within the RAF which were at present extremely happy might well be spoilt'. The best plan was to let things take their normal course particularly as in due time the flow of Irish doctors would be nothing like so great as it used to be. With this advice the Archbishop concurred.

The promotion of closer relations between the various Christian Churches was not easy and there were many setbacks on the way. Paradoxically the very frustrations were an indication that Christians of differing denominations were becoming increasingly aware of each other and this was certainly true of Rome. On 20 December 1949, Pope Pius XII, who was elevated to the Pontificate at the beginning of the Second World War, issued to local ordinands: 'Instructions on the Oecumenical Movement'. Geoffrey Fisher welcomed this as 'timely and appropriate', showing a concern for inter-church relations. He was grateful that the pronouncement approved, for the first time, ecumenical meetings for the purpose of common action 'in defence of the fundamental principles of Christianity', and their beginning with the Lord's Prayer. However, as Archbishop, he must express his disappointment at 'the conditions laid down by the Pope for Roman Catholics taking part with Christians of other denominations in discussing matters of faith and morals'. They could be held only with the approval of a 'competent, ecclesiastical authority'. In practice, so he maintained, this would tend to discourage and not encourage such gatherings. What was most desirable was that theologians of different Church traditions should discuss together the grounds of their beliefs, and their general method of approach to doctrinal questions. He recognised that the Vatican would rightly require that Roman Catholics should 'faithfully state Roman Catholic doctrine, as members of the Church of England should truly represent theirs'.

The Archbishop's statement concluded on a positive note, namely his welcoming 'that in these important matters, the Roman Church is willing, however cautiously, to contemplate joint discussions'.

If this Papal pronouncement looked back – Geoffrey Fisher maintained it did – to the Joint Ecumenical Committee which met in England during the War; certainly it may equally claim to have anticipated ARCIC – the Anglican Roman Catholic International Commission.

Within a year of the Pope's producing his statement, there were rumours that a Papal pronouncement was imminent defining the doctrine of the Assumption of the Blessed Virgin Mary, this being the first dogma to be proclaimed since 1870, and the first concerning the Holy Family since 1874. It asserted that Our Lady, at the end of her life was, in body and soul, 'assumed into Heavenly Glory'. Unknown in the early days of the Church, it was declared by Pope Benedict XIV a 'probable opinion'. As early as 14 June 1950, Geoffrey Fisher wrote to the Archbishop of York suggesting that the Church of England ought not to be taken by surprise, but should be ready with its own statement when the day of its promulgation came. To this suggestion the Archbishop of the northern Province concurred adding that it was rumoured that *Munificentissimus Dei* would be promulgated on 15 August 1950. To this end, Geoffrey Fisher consulted leading Anglican churchmen particularly since the proposed Papal announcement must be of concern to non-Roman Christians. From such replies the Archbishops drew up an Anglican response. Dr Bouquet, a distinguished scholar, informed the Archbishop that though His Holiness had been widely advised to abandon this doctrinal statement, yet he stood in such awe of the American Cardinals that he was likely to go forward with the pronouncement.

As it became clear that the Pope was still delaying his pronouncement, so the two Primates of the northern and southern Provinces decided to make their own statement public perhaps in the hope that it might restrain His Holiness from going forward. This they did by issuing it from Lambeth Palace through the Press Bureau of the Church of England on 17 August 1950. The Archbishops began by saying that the effect of the intended Papal pronouncement, assuming it were authoritatively proclaimed, would be to make the doctrine of Our Lady's Assumption 'a necessary part of the Christian Revelation and will henceforth require Roman Catholics to believe it to be true'. On behalf of the Church of England they wished to state 'publicly' that it did not and could not, hold this doctrine as a necessary part of Christian faith, unsupported as it was, by any scriptural evidence. So the joint statement concludes: 'We profoundly regret that the Roman Catholic Church has chosen by this act to increase dogmatic differences in Christendom, and has thereby gravely injured the growth of under-standing between Christians, based on a common possession of the fundamental truths of the Gospel'.

It will be noticed that the *rationale* for the Church of England presuming to intervene in the affairs of another Church was not based only on the truth question involved, but on a unilateral action proposed by the Papacy which could well prejudice further inter-Church rela-tions. The statement was essentially a Church of England document, and it is interesting to notice that in response to an enquiry from Geoffrey Fisher, Dr H. Watkins-Jones, Convener of the Methodist Faith and Order Committee, gave it as his opinion that perhaps some reply ought to be considered though he recognised the right of the Roman Catholics to do as they pleased in a matter of this kind. Perhaps this was because the Methodists felt themselves more distanced from the Papal Church and its affairs. The Papal pronouncement *Munificen-tissimus Dei* duly appeared on 1 November some two and a half months after the statement of the Archbishops of Canterbury and York.

The tendency of Roman Catholics in England no longer to see themselves as basically an expatriate Irish community and as a conse-quence to integrate themselves more into their immediate social environment led, indirectly, to a particular situation which gave Geoffrey Fisher a measure of anxiety.

The reference is to mixed marriages, that is a marriage between a Roman and an Anglican. For both communities this could become a problem, and certainly it was inevitable that the Archbishop of Canterbury should often become intimately involved in the heartache to which it could lead. Many indeed were the parents and parish priests who wrote to Lambeth for help and guidance. In response to many such demands the Archbishop drew up a document headed: 'Advice to

Anglicans on Mixed Marriages Between Members of the Church of England and the Church of Rome'.

It was his duty, he wrote, to give advice and to do this in such a way, as far as possible, to be helpful to the Roman Catholics concerned as well as to the Anglicans. His personal experience was that after patient 'explanations' it was often possible to reach a conclusion which satisfied consciences on both sides. Thus it was better to think in personal terms of *this man* and *this woman* brought up in 'a moral and spiritual atmosphere partly similar and partly startlingly different'. When an Anglican and a Roman Catholic began to fall in love they should consider where they were going. The Roman Catholic Church openly discouraged mixed marriages; the Church of England did not encourage them because of the difficulties involved. However, he had designed this pamphlet for those who had more or less committed themselves to such a marriage. His hope was that both parties would regard a religious ceremony as essential; but it was precisely here that 'a mountain of difficulties began to appear before them'. The Roman Catholic priest would require four things of the non-Roman partner: (1) the signing of a document to ensure that all children of the marriage were brought up as Roman Catholics; (2) a promise that he/she would not interfere 'with the religious beliefs of the Roman Catholic partner'; (3) a requirement by the Roman Catholic to do his or her best to induce the other partner to join the Church of Rome; (4) the Roman priest must obtain official permission to conduct the ceremony.

Each of these conditions, the Archbishop contended, needed careful examination, since the Anglican was being asked to 'renounce the greatest and most responsible part of the duties which God lays upon him'. The Roman Catholic Church 'with a good conscience' could not require this.

Of course in a mixed marriage the question as to which Faith children were to be brought up in was bound to arise. There was, however, so the Archbishop recognised, a real difficulty here since the religious belief of a Roman Catholic demanded total obedience to the Church in its separation from the life of the Church of England. Thus any criticism of the Church of Rome by an Anglican partner would be regarded as 'interference'. The really Christian task, so the Archbishop advised, was for them both 'to see their differences of Church allegiance as transcended in their discipleship of Christ and even a source of strength in it'. For the Anglican this would be an easy thing at least to attempt but for the Roman Catholic it was from the beginning forbidden to attempt such a thing.

One particular example of Geoffrey Fisher's general reaction to these requirements may be quoted – it could be paralleled by very many others – which shows the problem in bold relief since the father of the bride was the incumbent of a parish in the Church of England, and the time of the marriage happened to coincide with the pronouncement by the Roman Catholic hierarchy against mixed marriages. Perplexed as to what his course ought to be – the girl was under 20 – the parish priest wrote to Lambeth setting out the circumstances at some length, and making it clear that the young man and his family were convinced Roman Catholics. Would it be possible, he asked, for the Roman Catholic authorities to allow the marriage to take place in his parish church, since to deny this seemed like surrendering the position of the Anglican Church in the eyes of his parishioners. Would a working compromise be for there to be two services, one in each Church? His concern, of course, was that the happiness of the young couple should not be 'spoilt' by an *impasse* created by differing ecclesiastical loyalties.

The Archbishop replied expressing his regret at the girl's predicament, and giving the conditions which would be imposed, were his daughter to marry a Roman Catholic. He then proceeded to offer some advice, on the assumption that the bride wished to maintain her own personal integrity and freedom as a good Anglican. (1) She would refuse to sign the document consenting to the bringing up of her children as Roman Catholics. (2) She must accept that her husband will be expected to do his best to convert her to the Church of Rome. (3) She should ask her fiancé to be married in the Church of England, though he will be told by his Church not to do this. (4) On his refusal it would be proper for her, under protest, to consent to be married in his Church thereby witnessing to a charity such as, in obedience to his Church, the bridegroom was precluded from showing.

The young man, on being apprised of Dr Fisher's letter, responded by saying that he felt sure the Archbishop would not wish him to be disloyal to the fundamental principles of his faith, even for the sake of his marriage. The bride's father confessed himself 'in a pretty hopeless position against the full authority of the Roman Catholic Church and a discipline which really amounts to tyranny extended even to Anglicans who marry Roman Catholics'. Could not the matter be taken up officially by the Church of England?

To this request, all the Archbishop could suggest was that the daughter might refuse to accept the conditions required by the Roman Catholic Church. Of course she must have 'complete freedom' in making her decision, but in so doing 'she cannot avoid responsibility for them'. Both the Church of Rome and the Church of England, he concluded, 'place fundamental principles far above the claims of marriage itself'.

This, however, was not the end of the story. The young man decided not to sign the document which required him to seek his wife's conversion and as a consequence he was married in the Anglican parish church. Unhappily the result was that subsequently the husband began to feel keenly that in the eyes of his Church he had sinned. He, therefore, never discussed religion, abandoned going to mass and the wife ceased to attend the Anglican Church.

For all concerned the consequences were tragic, due in part to institutionalized religion authenticating its own norms at the expense of the welfare and fulfilment of two young people. They were indeed the victims of a long ecclesiastical history, not of their own choosing. The cold logic of *Apostolicae Curae*, was unassailable. The position *vis-à vis* mixed marriages could only be changed within the pattern of a theological shift, more developed ecumenical relations, and greater psychological awareness. It was not the Archbishop's fault that the advice which he felt it right to give seems from the brief glimpse that we have of this young couple not to have worked out well. In this clash of Churches and principles no one could win. Perhaps the Archbishop was just as much a victim of the system as the bride and groom.

Mixed marriages were not the only area where there were clashes between the Church of Rome and the Church of England. There were Anglicans who felt worried at some Roman Catholic activities of a missionary character. Here Bishop Bell of Chichester was one of the most vigilant, asking the Archbishop at the end of 1948 to put 'Roman Catholic propaganda' on the agenda for a Bishops' Meeting. As an illustration of what he had in mind he wrote: 'There is a real danger now of the Roman Catholics establishing themselves as the Church which has a privileged position in hospitals, being the only Church according to present arrangements which is to have a chapel reserved for its own use'. In this area of controversy Bishop Bell believed that the Society for Promoting Christian Knowledge needed 'stirring up' so as to be more energetic in publishing literature opposing Roman claims. The Archbishop dutifully wrote to Noel Davey, its Editor, commending the Bishops' suggestion. The Archbishop of York, with whom Geoffrey Fisher shared this problem, was pleased to be able to report that both SPCK and the Church Information Board had produced much good and popular literature opposing Roman Catholic claims though he was unhappy with religious propaganda against them at a time when they were being persecuted in Central Europe. At times, it must be confessed, Anglican reaction was undoubtedly too sensitive, almost ridiculous if not paranoiac. A case in point was the *furore* which developed when the Archbishop was persuaded to protest to Lord Latham of the London Passenger Transport Board against an advertisement prominently displayed on a Number 7 bus and bearing the words 'The Catholic Church 2000 Years Old'. The result was an emphatic 'no' from Lord Latham to any request for its removal. Perhaps a greater injection of humour and a more relaxed mood would have gone a long way to minimize irritation and relax tension – but the time for this was not quite yet.

As the Roman Catholic Church slowly edged itself out of its isolation so, paradoxically, did occasions for friction between it and the Church of England tend to increase. A separated community has few external relations. Lions do not fight whales. We quote another and typical example of irritation.

By an Act of Parliament, passed in 1851, the Roman Catholic Church was debarred from giving to its bishops territorial titles within the United Kingdom. (This prohibition was removed in 1870.) In July 1953 Herbert Waddams, for the benefit of the Archbishop, drew up a paper *Roman Catholic Bishops' Territorial Titles* in which he maintained that this permission was being used to 'the descredit of the Church of England'. A particular instance of this 'impudence' was the creation of a so-called titular Abbot of Westminster claiming a spiritual apostolic succession from the pre-Reformation Benedictine Abbey. Waddams interpreted this as a sign of continuing warfare waged against the Church of England; though he did not think any official action should be taken. It has to be said that Waddams took too seriously what is regarded today as a pleasing historic link between the Abbey and the Benedictine Community at Ampleforth.

Titles ascribed to Roman Catholic bishops were a subject to which the Archbishop gave a concentrated attention, and his observant eye noticed a letter published in *The Times* signed 'Edmund, Bishop of Nottingham', upon which he immediately wrote to the Editor pointing out that Christian names, followed by geographical titles, were right only for the Established Church. He also drew up a memorandum in which he claimed that it was against the law of the land for Roman Catholics to use a nomenclature of this kind, since only the Sovereign could bestow ecclesiastical titles of honour and dignity.

At the summer session on 4 July 1955 of the Convocation of the southern Province, Canon Kemp, a legalist, claimed that the Roman Catholic Church practised an ecclesiastical apartheid 'as rigid and menacing as any political Iron Curtain'. Commenting on this accusation gave the Archbishop an opportunity to indulge a favourite *cri de coeur*: 'Therein' he proclaimed, 'lies, perhaps, the greatest existing hindrance to the advancement of the Kingdom of God amongst men'. The Roman Catholic Church forbids any kind or degree of ecclesiastical partnership between itself and the other Churches of Christendom, even the elementary partnership of praying together to our common Lord for grace to grow in partnership. Seeing this great evil in their system, and knowing from history how constantly it threatens all ecclesiastical bodies, 'we must be very careful', he warned, 'to avoid it among ourselves'.

The wisdom of this attack, clearly begotten of frustration and delivered *extempore* – the Archbishop earlier in the day had condemned South Africa's policy of apartheid in his Presidential address – was questioned by many outside as well as within the Roman Catholic Church. The *Catholic Herald*, described the speech as an 'unhappy attack showing a misconception of Christian faith, Catholic teaching and Catholic behaviour'. Lord Pakenham, a prominent left-wing Roman Catholic layman, confessed that he was 'inexpresibly saddened'. Herbert Waddams, with his wide contacts on the Continent, was also deeply distressed and drew up 'notes for the Archbishop', expressing his feelings of dismay. The address could well have repercussions upon Roman Catholics abroad, he argued. 'Those with whom I am in touch,' Waddams wrote, 'may say to themselves that it is useless to make any attempt to build bridges seriously if the Archbishop of Canterbury castigates the RCs in such terms.' It would be better in the future, Waddams advised, if Dr Fisher put his criticisms in a more positive context in order to 'encourage a change of view'. The reverberations of Geoffrey Fisher's remarks lingered long and in October at a meeting of the Committee of the Council on Foreign Relations the view was expressed that the Archbishop's strictures on co-operation were too general – an observation to which he retorted that the Pope on 6 August had urged the 145 million Christians in Russia and the Middle East to return to Rome. However, it must have disturbed the Archbishop greatly when Bishop Michael Ramsey of Durham joined the critics in a personal letter as follows: 'While I am writing, I feel I must say how deeply I regretted Your Grace's remarks about the Roman Church as reported. A number of members of York Convocation spoke to me about this, all in terms of regret. I thought that the analogy used was really unfair. As for the "worst hindrance to the Kingdom of God", Almightly God alone can assess what are the worst setbacks to his purpose in our sinful world. Forgive me for writing as I do, but what I have said is very much an understatement of what I feel.'

The Archbishop of Canterbury's reply, after a facetious introduction – 'I am used to getting more kicks than halfpence, but perhaps yours should be assessed at half-a-crown' – went on to suggest that Michael Ramsey was unaware, during the years after Cardinal Hinsley's death, of the breaking off, one after another, of every responsible link between the Church of Rome and other Churches in the country. It was no exaggeration to call it a policy of ecclesiastical apartheid, and it was accompanied by ceaseless hostility against the Church of England. This meant that Christian people were diverted from their proper work of preaching the Kingdom by the constant necessity of defences of all kinds against assaults from the Church of Rome. The Archbishop of

York, Dr Garbett, agreed that it was really impossible to go on ignoring the temper of mind with which the official Church of Rome treated the Church of England.

This reference by Geoffrey Fisher to the Archbishop of York calls attention to the fact that the latter was one hundred per cent behind his fellow Primate in these strictures. Indeed, the latter's letter of approval is forthright. 'I am so glad you said what you did,' he wrote, 'I am sure the time has come when we must no longer be content with a defensive attitude. I believe our own people would be greatly encouraged if they feel we are prepared to be militant against Rome.'

However, the letters that came to Lambeth were, by and large, critical of Dr Fisher's public attack. Judge Charles Abbott wrote in from the Federation of Malaysia expressing his 'deep shock', adding, 'I cannot but think that your expressions must have caused some grief to Her Majesty the Queen because these expressions have outraged the faith of her loyal and devoted Roman Catholic subjects'. *Le Monde* reported the Archbishop's words as an outrage which led Geoffrey Fisher, on receiving a letter of protest from Pastor Marc Boegner of Paris, to assure him that he was only referring in his Address to Catholics in England – an important limitation which perhaps earlier he should have made crystal clear.

The relationship between the monarchy in Britain and its Roman Catholic subjects, so far as one can discover it, had not, in the fifties, changed much in the course of the years. There was an established practice for Buckingham Palace to consult with Lambeth on any matters concerning Roman Catholics, rather than to deal, in the first instance, with the Cardinal Archbishop of Westminster. By and large successive Sovereigns in the twentieth century have been true to their inheritance as Supreme Governors of the Church of England in safeguarding the rights of the Establishment to represent the religious life of the nation. This practice could not but have the effect of making many Roman Catholics feel out in the cold, and not fully integrated with the nation. An illustration of this sense of isolation may be seen when Herbert Waddams had an interview with a French priest, Hero de Cheux, who expressed the view that it would be a good thing 'if the Queen were to take an opportunity of expressing her support for the Ecumenical Movement, and in the course of so doing explicitly mention the Church of Rome'. The Bishop of Chichester also reported to the Archbishop that he had had a conversation with de Cheux, who spoke in favour of such 'a friendly strategy'. It would prove valuable, particularly as the Vatican 'seems to have got hold of the idea that Roman Catholics in England were treated in unfriendly ways'. When asked what he would expect the Queen to say, the Bishop volunteered the following; 'As Defender of the Faith, I want to pay solemn homage to all my Commonwealth subjects, who, throughout the world, live their lives invincibly attached to the fundamental values and the essential truths of Christianity, and I want to assure all of them, Anglicans, Catholics, etc, without any exception, of my constant and affectionate solicitude'. The Archbishop was not convinced of the wisdom of such a proposal, and confessed to George Bell that he had thought about this very carefully and the longer he did so the less he liked it. It would be thought 'terribly artificial', and would have no particular effect upon the Vatican. Hence he had little confidence in recommending this suggestion to Lascelles, the Queen's private secretary.

Thus no approach was made to the Palace, and one suspects that anyhow it would have been unsuccessful.

Sometimes eirenic attempts to bridge the gulf between Anglicans and Roman Catholics could begin well, miscarry, and turn sour. Such happened on the death of Cardinal Griffin in 1956, when the relationship of the Queen to her Roman Catholic subjects again became a matter of controversy. Geoffrey Fisher's contacts with him had never been easy, but 'forgetting those things which are behind', he sent the following telegram to the Roman Catholic hierarchy. 'Please accept deepest sympathy from myself and the Church of England upon loss of your leader so steadfast through tribulation.' This was a human gesture which doubtless meant much, and it is a pity it could not be left there. However, the *Catholic Times* deplored the fact that the Queen was not represented at his funeral, particularly as there were 30 million Catholics throughout the Commonwealth, and the Cardinal of Westminster was 'still regarded as the outstanding person in that great body of subjects giving allegiance to the Crown'. The same view was expressed by Dr Heenan. The fact was that the Queen, in this matter, rightly or wrongly, acted in accordance with past precedents. Geoffrey Fisher's reaction to these Roman Catholic criticisms was immediate and angry. Hence he wrote a draft, intemperate letter to Dr Alan Don, Dean of Westminster, suggesting a reply from him in a letter to *The Times*, stressing: (1) it was not for Roman Catholics to tell the Queen how she ought to behave; (2) neither Cardinal Griffin nor any episcopal member of the Roman Catholic hierarchy was present in the Abbey at the Queen's Coronation, though the Cardinal had been invited; (3) the hierarchy was not officially represented in the Abbey at the memorial services for either Archbishops Temple or Lang.

It is quite inconceivable that the Archbishop really intended to send this particular letter. Doubtless it served as a relief to his own feelings of frustration, since he could never have expected so courteous a person as Dr Alan Don to fire the gun which he, the Archbishop, had loaded. That this is a fair picture of the Archbishop's motivation he himself confirmed in a letter to the Dean dated 15 September: 'I wrote to you merely to get it off my chest. Indignation has to have some vent; but the matter is forgotten and it would certainly be altogether unsuitable to start a correspondence in *The Times* about it so now please leave the matter alone.'

During the interregnum at Westminster Cathedral following the death of Cardinal Griffin an unfortunate *contretemps* occurred over a meeting organised at the Albert Hall in connection with the Russian 'take-over' of Hungary and the resulting massacres. The Archbishop agreed to say prayers at the end of the meeting but was distressed to find that this led to controversy. Among those invited was Dr Heenan, then Roman Catholic Archbishop of Liverpool. But the Roman Catholic authorities made it clear that if the Archbishop of Canterbury said prayers then Dr Heenan would not come. However, in the end he came but left before the meeting closed, many probably assuming him to have caught the last train to Liverpool!

Such frequent 'hiccoughs' in the mutual relations of Anglicans and Roman Catholics at the highest level were a considerable strain on the Archbishop of Canterbury, and were equally frustrating to a growing number of sincere Christians on both sides of the divide. On 18 November 1955 Douglas Woodruff, Editor of the *Tablet* – best of all religious weeklies – whom Dr Fisher had come to know when chairman of the wartime Joint Committee, lamented that the earlier flowering of their ecumenical relations had now withered away. In saying this he expressed surprise that Geoffrey Fisher, as Archbishop, should wish to 'foster' as he undoubtedly did a sense of 'fellowship' with Roman Catholics since his Office required him to 'criticize and reprobate what [he] was bound to consider a less pure and worthy form of the Christian religion'. Was it not true, he asked, that the Archbishop, because of his Office, was bound to exercise the role of a 'watchdog'? To this somewhat cynical observation the Archbishop of Canterbury replied that it was his duty to seek as co-operative relations as possible, recognising each other as disciples of Christ. To be on visiting terms in each other's houses seemed to him as 'simple an act of Christian courtesy and hospitality as can be found'.

Knowing Douglas Woodruff well the Archbishop, in January 1957, on his own initiative, decided to resume this correspondence assuring him that he saw the existence of separated Churches as the 'fundamental evil' in the same way as did the Pope. The Church of England deplored such divisions because they frustrated the purposes of Christ. However he could not accept the Roman Catholic solution – absorption. What the Archbishop wished was for a group of Anglicans and Roman Catholics to meet in order to discuss 'day-to-day causes of friction' and misunderstandings in a friendly atmosphere with a view to their mitigation. Nothing positive, however, came from this approach. It was the Archbishop's constant complaint – he aired it in a speech at Lichfield in 1957 – that the Roman Catholic hierarchy in England was less co-operative than their counterparts on the Continent. To offset this attitude the Archbishop came to the dangerous conclusion that it might be better to deal direct with the Apostolic Delegate in Britain, representing the Pope, than with the hierarchy in Westminster and Liverpool – particularly when matters affected the British Government. 'Hitherto,' as he himself put it, 'when points of conflict have arisen between us and the Roman Catholic Church in religious matters and in the secular life of the community, we have fought our own battles with the Roman authorities, but if the Pope is diplomatically represented in England we should require the Government to take up diplomatic cudgels for us when matters of dispute arise. In this case it would be brought up in the House of Lords.' It is difficult to believe that Dr Fisher was really serious in making this suggestion. The Apostolic Delegate had, of course, no jurisdiction over the Roman Catholic hierarchy in England, and therefore, so comments Geoffrey Fisher, 'they take little notice of him'. But there could be a real and helpful liaison between the Archbishop and the Apostolic Delegate which might lead to helpful discussion between them on certain issues. The Pope, of course, was free to act through the Cardinal Archbishop but he could equally use the Apostolic Delegate. Maybe, so Geoffrey Fisher further speculated, this might well prove the way to develop a real and abiding link betwen the Vatican and Lambeth. To ensure this it would help if Apostolic Delegates were appointed who were knowledgeable about the Church of England and had a real sympathy for it. The sad fact was that the present Apostolic Delegate, Monsignor O'Hara, 'if not anti-Church of England was so ignorant of it as to be in effect hostile'.

The latter pejorative reference witnesses to a brush which the Archbishop had with the Apostolic Delegate in the summer of 1959. This rose out of an article published in the *Daily Express* on birth control and family planning written by Mervyn Stockwood, Bishop of Southwark. This piece of journalism evoked a severe rebuke from the Apostolic Delegate in a letter to the Bishop dated 21 June. 'I find it extremely difficult to believe', he wrote, 'that you could be associated with a movement which outraged the Christian conscience, not only of my co-religionists but of so many sterling men and women, the backbone of England in the Anglican Communion.' When apprised of this letter the Archbishop was not pleased, being aggrieved that one of his own diocesan bishops should be attacked by one who had no *locus standi* in a matter of this kind, the more so as he himself and Anglican bishops at the Lambeth Conference of 1958 took the view that the practice of birth control could be a 'positive Christian duty'. His immediate reaction was to write a severe but short letter to the Apostolic Delegate, which clearly stated that the rebuke was 'uncalled for', and that the rules of diplomatic courtesy had been violated in relation to someone not under his jurisdiction. The Apostolic Delegate pointed out that his correspondence with Mervyn Stockwood, was in no sense official, and he fully realised that those outside the faith and worship of his Church were also outside his jurisdiction.

It has to be said that the status of the Apostolic Delegate as the Pope's man in England was, in some respects, unclear. Many years earlier the Duke of Norfolk proposed that he should be elevated to the Diplomatic Corps as Nuncio, thus bringing the United Kingdom in line with other sovereign states which had ambassadors at the Vatican. Such a proposal was mooted again in 1959, and could not but interest the Archbishop of Canterbury. Discussing this matter with Lord Salisbury, he called attention to a real difficulty as he saw it, in that whenever a Nuncio did anything outrageous or unfriendly to this country 'he [the Archbishop] might think it right to bring this matter up in the House of Lords, as with any other temporal state'. However nothing came of this – fortunately!

By calling attention, some may feel overmuch, to the frustration felt by the Archbishop of Canterbury in particular and many Anglicans in general, at their relations with Roman Catholics it is important not to create the impression that there was no co-operation between them. On 23 April 1957 for example, the Cardinal Archbishop of Westminster joined with the Primate of All England on a delegation led by Lord Beveridge to the Prime Minister on the plight of displaced persons in Europe, a matter concerning which the Archbishop had corresponded with the Foreign Secretary and which he had raised in the Church Assembly. Also Cardinal and Archbishop, together with the Moderator of the General Assembly of the Church of Scotland, co-operated in an endeavour to restore compulsory church parades. Their plea proved unsuccessful since the proposal was stopped at Cabinet level by Emmanuel Shinwell, Secretary of State for War. It was certainly a good thing in the way of building bridges, that the Archbishop was represented at the enthronement of the Archbishop of Paris. Such an 'act of courtesy', he was assured, had helped 'to dispose men's minds in France and Britain 'both to the political and cultural unity which was scandalously overdue, and the spiritual unity whose absence is our common shame'. On occasions lack of co-operation was due, not to a spirit of exclusiveness, but a genuine difference of view on a moral problem. Such was the case when Lord Amulree, a doctor of medicine, introduced a Bill in the House of Lords which would have the effect of exonerating a medical practitioner if he conducted an abortion in order to preserve the life and well-being of the mother. This was a matter on which Cardinal Griffin and his Church took an absolutist view and he expressed the hope to the Archbishop that he would support him in securing the rejection of the Bill in the House. Geoffrey Fisher consulted Bishop Kirk of Oxford and the Archbishop of York, the latter taking the view that an absolute rejection of abortion in all circumstances was 'an inhuman doctrine'. Geoffrey Fisher also could not adopt the Cardinal's position though he told him that he would probably vote against Lord Amulree's Bill for other reasons, but this never was put to the test for the Bill was withdrawn.

In the year 1958 Cardinal Pacelli, Pope Pius XII, who had held the Pontificate since 2 March 1939, died at the age of 82. At the time of his election he was Papal Secretary – a rare thing – and his appointment was a recognition of the need for an experienced politician and diplomat to guide the Church through the great dangers that threatened. His Holiness was destined to endure the hazards of a world war when his position in the Papal State in Rome, located in Mussolini's Italy then allied to Hitler's Germany, was fraught with danger and difficulty. The ambiguities of his position, which made a consistent policy difficult, await a more informed verdict of his pontificate in the light of greater factual evidence. His death was followed by an incident which could have led to an irrational display of anti-Roman Catholic sentiment, trivial though the incident was. On the day of Pope Pius' requiem, the Archbishop of Canterbury learnt, *via* his postbag, that at an ancient castle under the care of the Ministry of Works, a flag was flown at half-mast. The Pope was, of course, a territorial Sovereign but why, asked the Archbishop's correspondent, was the flag not flown on the day of his death rather than on the day of the requiem? The Archbishop made enquiries through Herbert Waddams, who ferreted out the information that it was so decreed by an Order from the Queen upon the advice of the Lord Chamberlain. The Archbishop, wisely, took the matter no further and did not send off the letter he had written to R. A. Butler.

(ii)

Pope Pius XII's successor in 1958 was John XXIII who was 77 years of age. He was of peasant origin from Northern Italy, and had a wide diplomatic experience behind him as well as being Patriarch of Venice. To Anglicans this election seemed an obvious 'stop-gap' appointment until a younger and more energetic candidate emerged. Never was a greater misjudgement made!

On Pope John's election Geoffrey Fisher immediately sent a telegram of good wishes and fraternal greetings, the first of its kind ever to go from Lambeth to the Vatican on such an occasion. Within a few days there came back the reply: 'Vatican City, Doctor Fisher, Lambeth Palace, London. Sovereign Pontiff, bidding me acknowledge receipt of your thoughtful message of greetings and good wishes, directs me to give expression of his sincere appreciation and gratitude for your courteous gesture, Tardini, Secretary of State'. Herbert Waddams commented: 'If only it had been addressed to the Archbishop of Canterbury and not to Dr Fisher it would have been perfect! However, it is a very valuable and friendly gesture. I feel tempted to exploit it by releasing it to the Press, but that would really spoil the flavour of it.' Geoffrey Fisher was to meet up again with Cardinal Tardini some three years later! The Archbishop gave further evidence of his ecumenical spirit towards Roman Catholics at this time by dedicating a stone tablet honouring eighteen Carthusian monks martyred under Henry VIII. The memorial bore these words: 'Remember before God the monks and lay brothers of the Carthusian House of Salutation who worshipped at this altar, and for conscience' sake endured torment and death'. The *Catholic Leader* described the Archbishop's act as 'promoting tolerance and love between Catholics and Protestants'.

It was a great disappointment when Cardinal Godfrey, Griffin's successor, declined an invitation sent by Geoffrey Fisher to attend a social event in connection with the 1958 Lambeth Conference. In expressing thanks for the invitation he asserted, that, for himself or a deputy to participate in any events connected with the Conference 'would undoubtedly be misunderstood', both by his own and the Archbishop's people. The Archbishop, on his part, found it difficult to understand such an attitude, traditional though it might have been some two decades earlier, and lamented that it seemed 'impossible for us as two Christian brethren to exhibit the normal courtesies which should obtain between civilised men'. Sadly, he commented, it was 'difficult for us to escape from our history'. Thus the Reverend John Satterthwaite, on a two-day visit to Belgium at the end of January 1958, found Catholics there who strongly disapproved of the Cardinal's refusal to attend a social function, Moeller being particularly 'indignant'. On reporting back to Lambeth he told Geoffrey Fisher that continental Catholics looked forward to better things under Godfrey's successor, whom they hoped might be Dr Heenan, Archbishop of Liverpool.

Geoffrey Fisher, in spite of this seeming rebuff, was ill at ease in leaving matters as they were, and he drew up a draft letter to the Cardinal which reflected on his own views and hopes at the time. He began by making it clear that his purpose in writing was merely to 'ventilate a subject rather than to ask either for his advice or action'. So far as the Church of England was concerned, relations with Roman Catholics on the Continent, and with learned societies at home, were 'friendly and encouraging', but when it came to formal and official relations betwen the hierarchy in England and themselves it was 'distant, unfriendly and from time to time hostile'. The Roman Catholics 'take every opportunity of advancing their own interests, whether openly or secretly; and they do not pretend to regard our interests or to seek any form of common interest'. This was no new thing since 'history makes it intelligible that in this country the Roman Church should play the part of an injured and struggling minority'. The result was that Roman Catholics visiting the United Kingdom from overseas were aware of 'aggressiveness,' sometimes 'transgressing the limits of charity and courtesy'. He often wondered whether this applied equally to members of other Churches in the Anglican Communion and he had contemplated trying to find out. There is no evidence that this draft letter was in fact sent to Cardinal Godfrey.

To everyone's surprise, except perhaps to a small intimate circle of friends, Pope John XXIII was bent on asserting a highly individual pontificate. Sensitive to the winds of change, himself not 'a curial man', he felt convinced, under the constraint of the Holy Spirit, that a special vocation was imposed upon him to breathe into the Church the breath of a new and liberating life. He was naturally conscious of having but a short time in which to do this, and at the commencement of his Pontificate, he issued the following encyclical: 'We open our hearts and our arms to all those who are separated from the Apostolic See, where Peter himself and his successors "even unto the consummation of the world" fulfils the command, given him by Christ, "to bind and to loose all things on this earth and to feed the flocks of the Lord".'

Though the language here is traditional yet it breathes a new spirit. In line with this 'leaping over the wall' was the Pope's setting up an Ecumenical Secretariat under Cardinal Bea to study Christian unity. The World Council of Churches, of which Geoffrey Fisher was a former President, was quick to respond to the new spirit. Indeed Dr Visser 't Hooft, its General Secretary, wrote to the Archbishop on 27 January 1959 suggesting that the Pope's action had a special significance for the World Council. The new Pope seemed convinced that all Christians had a common task, but whether 'he will be able to convince the Curia is another matter'. At least there was now a chance of a general improvement in the relations between Roman Catholics and other Christians. Yet it was important, so Visser 't Hooft concluded, 'that the World Council of Churches guarded itself against excessive hopes, while recognising that real progress could only lie in a truly universal pan-Christian Council'.

The Archbishop hardly needed this warning since he had suffered far too many disappointments in the ecumenical field to indulge naively in wishful thinking. Also, in spite of many encouraging reports, the new

Pope was to him an unknown quantity. It was more a matter of 'by their fruits shall ye know them'.

In the expectation that there would be progress in the area of ecumenical relations, Geoffrey Fisher re-opened a correspondence with Lord Pakenham, a liberal-minded yet staunch Roman Catholic layman, reminding him that for some years he himself had been trying to get a small semi-official liaison committee *vis-à-vis* the Church of England and the Roman Catholic Church in this country, where points of friction which daily arose between them could be examined with a view to making the co-existence of the two communities less painful and un-Christian. Yet all his efforts had been 'fruitless', but he intended to go on occasionally inviting discussion with people like Lord Pakenham. Geoffrey Fisher still needed convincing that the undoubted signs of possible improved relations emanating from the Vatican were not simply straws in the wind. Thus to the Bishop of Peterborough he urged caution. The Pope's first encyclical, though 'full of human kindness' was unyielding when it came to Papal claims, calling on non-Romans to 'return to Mother'.

Geoffrey Fisher, however, in his caution had misinterpreted the new mood as the Reverend John Satterthwaite pointed out to the Archbishop. In any efforts to co-operate more effectively with Rome it was imperative, so Satterthwaite advised, to deal directly with Cardinal Bea. 'The new Pope', he explained 'regards re-union as his spiritual mission and he hopes for greater personal contact with his separated brethren.' In words which were later to acquire an increased significance he went on: '. . . if ever you [i.e. the Archbishop] would consent to visit Rome, Pope John would be delighted to welcome you and a visit could be arranged with the utmost discretion. Arrangements should be handled direct through Cardinal Tardini.' Dickinson and Satterthwaite, on the eve of their spending a fortnight in Rome in order to explain the *ethos* of the Church of England to members of the Major Orders, asked the Archbishop whether he had any comments to make concerning this proposed visit, to which he responded by saying that they might take the following message direct to the Pope:

(1) That the Archbishop thanked him most sincerely for the cordial letter which he sent through Cardinal Tardini in response to a welcoming one from himself. (2) That a conference to increase understanding and co-operation would be very acceptable to the Church of England 'at any level' providing it was quite clear that conditions were entirely open and with complete freedom of expression; (3) If in connection with an Ecumenical Council the Pope wished to invite, *inter alia*, the Church of England, to an open top-level conference, this would be responded to with alacrity provided once again the conditions and agenda were all 'open and non-tendentious.' (4) Conver-

sations were in fact going on between little groups of Anglicans and Romans on the Continent and here in England which was good; but if the Pope were to feel there was room for a 'more settled group recognized and encouraged by authority he would be wholly in favour'. Such a group could discuss theological and practical questions – the sort of Roman/Anglican equivalent of the World Council of Churches Faith and Order Commission but on a very small domestic scale meeting probably on the Continent and not in England. The group should be given no publicity. However what it did would be reported directly to the Vatican and to Lambeth. (5) The real difficulty here was the non-existence of a 'liaison group' in England, though he himself had tried to get one going and had discussed it with Lord Pakenham and Pope Henessy. (6) Perhaps the position and status of the Apostolic Delegate might be discussed with His Holiness, this being a matter concerning which the Archbishop was himself becoming increasingly pre-occupied.

Geoffrey Fisher was the kind of person who took his interests and concerns with him even on holiday, though not with the agonising introspection which, so we are told, was customary with Pope Paul VI. In August 1959 he went on holiday to Scotland and while there, he took the opportunity to draw up a longish document 'The Problem of Church Unity: a Reasonable and Pastoral Approach by the Archbishop of Canterbury'. The Roman Catholic Church was not included in this survey though it began with a quotation from Bishop Christopher Wordsworth: '. . . the Church of England became Protestant at the Reformation in order that she might be more truly and purely Catholic'. It was no part of her policy, he asserted, for Protestants generally to align themselves against Rome. 'I am most anxious', he wrote, 'to promote closer relations with our brethren in the Roman Catholic Church. I have personal friends among the Romans, both in this country and on the Continent. When I preach for Father Brandeth in Paris for his patronal festival in April I have specially asked that I might have an opportunity of calling upon the Cardinal Archbishop and of visiting the Vistinée Centre.'

Meanwhile the new Pontiff was quick to use his high and unique office to promote ecumenicity – but this we must leave to a subsequent chapter.

(iii)

Tensions between Anglicans and Roman Catholics did not only exist within England. They certainly were a feature of life in Malta.

This island, set in the Mediterranean, the vast majority of whose citizens are Roman Catholics, was seized by the British in 1800 and became a Colony in 1847. Under its Constitution of 1947 the rights of religious minorities were guaranteed by law. However it was not easy in practice to secure their implementation, and it was a constant complaint of the Archbishop that Anglican clergy in Malta found it difficult to fulfil their ministry, as was seen in their conducting mixed marriages. Also there was opposition to their wearing their clerical robes in public. Here Geoffrey Fisher's view was simple and clear-cut. All citizens should be free to execute their legal rights, and he looked to the British Government, that was to the Colonial Secretary, Lennox Boyd, to secure this. Hence numerous letters from Lambeth found their way to the Colonial Office. So strongly did Geoffrey Fisher regard this matter that he brought it before the British Council of Churches in April 1956 whose members entertained equally strong feelings. It was a question of civil liberty.

Lennox Boyd, however, found himself in a difficult position. He could not dispute the fact that the freedoms which the Archbishop claimed were guaranteed by law, and that in this respect his case was unanswerable. Yet he believed that there were other factors in the total situation which needed to be taken into account – as in Cyprus. Malta was a naval and military base, and he saw its retention as essential to the security of the free world. To implement the full rights of religious minorities would create general unsettlement in the island, and prove prejudicial to its use as a NATO base. Thus though Geoffrey Fisher pleaded, time and time again, for the Colonial Secretary to declare publicly his intention simply to enforce the law, he did not comply. If he were to do this, he maintained in justification, he would face a political crisis. 'All parties', he wrote to Geoffrey Fisher, 'would combine in a violent and passionate opposition.' Hence the Archbishop bombarded the Minister with protests, but to no effect, in many an exchange of views enlivened at times with a measure of badinage. 'I fear I am becoming more of a nuisance to you than Grivas or Makarios – and I am harder to get away from', so wrote the Archbishop. (The reference is to the deportation of Makarios). To this Lennox Boyd replied: 'I only wish that other Primates to whom you refer in your post script were as understanding as you are. You need have no fear that I have a place reserved for you in the Seychelles. But where eventually are you sending me?'

Such occasional flippancy, however, did not conceal the serious issues at stake as may be seen in the following profession of faith by the Archbishop: 'There are some things which conscience compels me to do: to defend religious freedom anywhere in the world is required of me by my conscience, and is required of me in Malta'.

But this quandary ceased to be a British responsibility when Malta became independent on 31 May 1964.

* * *

On the island of Malta it was understandable, if highly regrettable, that it was decided at the end of the war to build two memorials one for Roman Catholics, the other for non-Catholics, in honour of members of the services and the Merchant Navy who took part in the defence of the island. The latter shrine at St Paul's Valetta was dedicated by the Archbishop of Canterbury on 30 November 1949, when he spent many busy days on the island. However when the Imperial War Graves Commission decided to establish a cemetery on the island it determined to cut through these difficulties by seeing that it was for all the fallen, irrespective of any religious or national affiliations. To many this seemed a praiseworthy object: but its implementation was by no means easy. Indeed without the persistence of the Commission – and of Geoffrey Fisher – it might well have foundered. It was further agreed that Anglicans, Roman Catholics and the Free Churches as well as representatives of Islam should take part in the dedication ceremony; but what was to be its shape and who was to do what? Here Geoffrey Fisher was presented with a problem, namely how to satisfy Cardinal Matthew on the one hand and the Anglican and Free Church chaplains on the other. On more than one occasion it seemed likely that negotiations would break down, and that one party would walk out. Chalmers – and no man was more eirenic – who represented the War Graves Commission was often in despair and Cardinal Matthew near to tears. Reflecting on these somewhat unhappy negotiations the Archbishop regretted that they had been bedevilled from the start. 'The only good thing about them', he cynically observed, 'is that all concerned in one way or another contributed to the bedevilment and therefore can regard one another with sympathy.' Still, at long last, they arrived at a working agreement.

The same difficulties were experienced at the dedication of the Alamein memorial when the Archbishop, who was away in America, returned to find that 'the Roman Catholics had stolen a march on the others' by announcing their intention to hold a requiem mass separate from the joint ceremony but within the site. On hearing this Victor Pike, the Chaplain General, was furious and communicated his anger to Cuthbert Bardsley, the Archbishop's Episcopal Representative to the Forces. Also General Hall, commanding in Egypt, protested firmly that unless present arrangements were radically changed his troops would not be attending. A similar message came from the Anglican Bishop in Egypt. There was, as a peripheral complication, profound annoyance north of the Border because the Service Paper listed the Church of Scotland under 'Free Churches'. The Archbishop saw Cardinal Matthew privately and then summoned Chalmers with Alastair Laing – Ceremonial Officer of the War Graves Commission – together with Cuthbert Bardsley, Victor Pike and the Chaplain-in-Chief for the Royal

Air Force to meet him at Lambeth. The Archbishop, according to Chalmers, delivered 'a truly wonderful rocket' to the War Graves Commission for failing to consult adequately before the event. 'It was', he went on, 'very much like a visit to the headmaster's study.' But the *impasse* continued, and Matthew told the Commission that the Roman Catholics were unable to participate. It was now left to the Archbishop to tackle the Cardinal who after two long hours was unyielding and rose to depart. However Geoffrey Fisher pushed him back roughly in his seat saying: 'No you don't. We've got to get a better ending than this!' Finally the Archbishop won the battle when Cardinal Matthew agreed with his suggestion that the Roman Catholics should not take part in the short official service of dedication, but that after Field Marshal Montgomery had been conducted around the Memorial, a Catholic mass should be celebrated.

Looking back on these days Geoffrey Fisher maintained that the Alamein Dedication was 'one of the nastiest things' he ever had to deal with. Chambers who witnessed Geoffrey Fisher in action admired his patience, his negotiating skills as well as his genuine desire to promote reconciliation. He long remembered the last act of this drama which took place in Canterbury. It coincided with the announcement on the placards that Len Hutton, the Yorkshire professional, was to captain the English cricket eleven. He ruefully drew the conclusion that it was easier to break new ground on the sports field than in the area of ecumenical relations, where Roman Catholics were concerned.

PART FIVE:

THE ARCHBISHOP, THE NATION
AND SOCIETY

CHAPTER 29

The Nuclear Bomb

IT has been suggested in the course of this biography that Geoffrey Fisher had a deep personal faith in Christ as Lord. In him this did not lead to metaphysical speculation as to the 'why and wherefore' of human existence, rather what concerned him most was the expression of this commitment in daily living, in the life of the individual and society collectively. Hence his practical concern with ethics and morality – and with history. This did not mean that like F. D. Maurice he endeavoured to draw up a consistent social philosophy. He was far happier when addressing himself to business men, schoolteachers, trade unions and the like, drawing out what was implicit in their own skills and discipline.

The intention in this section on the Church and Society is to 'sample' some of his practical concerns. True, selection in this field is arbitrary not because of the scarcity of the material but its plenty. Perhaps he comes near to exemplifying what some have described as 'holy wordliness' – the interpenetration of the sacred by the secular.

We begin with Geoffrey Fisher's handling of a moral challenge unique in history – the nuclear bomb.

Geoffrey Fisher had been in his high office only a matter of months before he was confronted with an event unparalleled in the history of mankind. On 1 June 1945, in the midst of the American-Japanese War, wantonly provoked by the attack on Pearl Harbour, the American Committee as it was termed, in consultation with the Scientific Panel, made the three following momentous decisions: (1) that an atom bomb should be dropped on Japan as soon as possible; (2) that it be used against a target, military and civilian; (3) that no prior warning should be given. The result of this decision was the releasing on 5 August of a nuclear bomb on Hiroshima with the intention of destroying the city in one stroke. The attempt was successful. The Americans estimated that 78,150 of the city's population, men, women and children were killed in scenes of indescrible terror. Three days later Nagasaki experienced a like fate, though the total casualties were marginally less. The Japanese government, on the express command of the Emperor, capitulated. Except to the British Prime Minister, Clement Attlee, who was given advance notice by the President of the United States, this awesome event came as a complete surprise. The vast mass of United Kingdom citizens, not least those who 'profess and call themselves

Christians', heard the news with a feeling of numbness which clouded any spontaneous celebration of victory. There was a sense that mankind had tasted the bitter fruits of the tree of knowledge; had stared into the abyss; and that unless a fallible humanity could resist the temptations which such a new accession of power had thrust into its hands, the prospect of human survival on this planet would be bleak.

Not unnaturally the Archbishop of Canterbury, often regarded as keeper of the national conscience, was inundated with telephone calls and letters of protest from those who, in anger and disillusion, pleaded with him to dissociate the Church of England altogether from what they regarded as an act of unparalleled shame. Indeed the Archbishop was a sitting target for those who in their bemusement did not know where else to look for guidance. Could the terms of the just war be stretched so far as to include near genocide as the lesser of two evils? So numerous were the phone calls flooding into Lambeth that the Archbishop was forced to go into hiding. Certainly Geoffrey Fisher fully recognised the gravity of the moral dilemma facing Christians, though when it came to apportioning blame he did not rush into condemnation. Most of the letter-writers to Lambeth suffered no such inhibition, not least many who were parish priests, and, as a consequence, had their magazine articles to write and sermons of thanksgiving to preach. Thus The Right Reverend J. C. Mann, formerly Bishop of Kyambu, recalled in a letter to the Archbishop that in the autumn of 1937 when Japan began the systematic bombing of Chinese cities, Archbishop Cosmo Lang headed the signatories to a letter in *The Times* which condemned this deliberate attack on civilians rejecting any argument to justify it on the grounds of military expediency. The Reverend John Collins, then a chaplain in the Royal Air Force, protested against the cynical disregard of previous claims that the Western democracies 'stood against barbarism'. Why, he asked, had there been no official protest from the Church against America for being the first to use this indiscriminate weapon?' Could not the Archbishop issue a considered statement? To be living at this moment, as he was in an officers' mess, was an embarrassing experience, making one almost physically sick. All pretence to be fighting to preserve a decent way of life had been thrown overboard.

Geoffrey Fisher's immediate reaction to the dropping of the bomb was one of horror, shock and surprise, though at the time he knew little or nothing as to its long term effects through radiation. What the Archbishop did know was that he could not keep silent since he held an office which required him to speak. The area of public concern was far too extensive for the atom bomb to be accepted as just one more weapon, if more powerful, in the military armoury. Geoffrey Fisher let his response to this unique situation *inter alia* be known in numerous letters; in a debate in the House of Lords; in the *Sun* newspaper; in the September issue of the Canterbury Gazette – which was later published as a separate pamphlet. Though his general approach in these differing contexts varied, according to those to whom it was addressed, the burden of what he said was ultimately the same. One of the inhibitions preventing him from fully identifying himself with certain sections of Christian opinion was his conscientious conviction that he could not, without any reservation, condemn the American government though he passionately hoped that 'the sheer horror of this weapon will strengthen the general will to outlaw not only it but all that it stands for'. It was this attempt to be objective which some of his critics found exasperating, and which, for example, drew forth from Murray Rogers of the Church Missionary Society these bitter words: 'Thousands of British people, Christians and non-Christians, know in their hearts that we have done an utterly wrong thing, and feel utterly ashamed of it.'

We turn now to consider Geoffrey Fisher's reply to his critics most of whom could not have been happy with the opening words of his statement in his diocesan letter of September 1945 – indeed they leave a nasty taste in the mouth: 'Of the victory which God has granted to us and our Allies, I will say no more here. We have celebrated it with humble gratitude and reserve.' They should be grateful he went on that the Americans had discovered the 'method' before the Germans. True, opinions differed as to whether the bomb ought to have been used at all. Some have argued that its use had saved more human lives than it dreadfully destroyed by bringing the war to a sudden end. The argument against its deployment, he maintained, was on two different levels – that it had given Japan an excuse for saying that she had not really been defeated at all; and that it showed mankind ever accommodating its conscience to more deadly and inhuman forms of warfare, abandoning one restraint after another. The question now was this. Having looked into the abyss could humanity extricate itself? Certainly not if there were another major war, nor if every nation secretly sought to exploit nuclear energy for destructive military purposes. As to the future the role of the United Nations was all important. 'The way of deliverance is the Charter of the United Nations. Every nation which signs it must live by it, and between them there must be no military secrets'.

The Archbishop's speech in the House of Lords basically struck a similar note. He went out of his way, however, not to condemn those who devoted their lives to exploring the mysteries of the universe around them. It was not their fault if such discoveries were abused. 'I give all honour to the scientists who have discovered the power', he said. 'Let it never be said that this disgraces the scientists.'

The Archbishop took the initiative in appointing a strong representative committee, sponsored by the British Council of Churches, which included Bishop George Bell and Donald McKinnon, at that time Lecturer in Philosophy at Balliol College, Oxford. Its report, however, though it illuminated the many-sided nature of the ethical problem did little to suggest its resolution.

The atom bomb was soon replaced by the hydrogen variety and Geoffrey Fisher in his Canterbury Diocesan Notes took a grimly realistic view, maintaining that it would be almost impossible for a responsible statesman to forbid scientists to pursue the production of this bomb. To do so would be to put their own people at a disadvantage as compared with others who knew, or might know in the future, how to make this hideous engine of destruction. The moral justification of the arms race had begun. True, he added, nations ought to agree not to use atomic weapons at all but they did not trust one another sufficiently to do this. Hence the need for effective inspection and control. In the meantime the Archbishop prophesied that 'the production of atom and hydrogen bombs and of every other monstrously evil weapon will go ahead, leaving us as our only security that if any nation wishes to begin the use of them it would be deterred by the knowledge that it could hardly avoid a destruction of itself as ghastly as that which it sought to inflict'.

The basic fact, Archbishop Fisher predicted, was that in spite of high-sounding phrases and repeated appeals by religious leaders, the weaponry of the Great Powers, in particular Russia, America and Britain, grew ever more lethal and fearsome. Thus within a month of the end of the War rocket bombs were being tested in Central Australia, this once again swelling the Lambeth post bag. Hence, on 10 October 1946, the Archbishop wrote a careful letter to the Secretary of State, pointing out that the area chosen for these tests was set aside as a native reserve for aborigines, and if they went forward the inhabitants would have to be removed elsewhere. He enclosed a letter of protest from the Australian International Missionary Council to which the Secretary of State replied in a typical diplomatic letter assuring the Archbishop that he would 'bear in mind' his representations. As might have been foreseen the tests went forward.

It was understandable that members of the peace movement should tend to take the view that the Church was not as active in this area as it ought to be – indeed grossly inactive. Thus Mrs Noel Baker, a person in her own right and wife of a distinguished parliamentarian, complained bitterly to the Archbishop that when her husband asked a question in the House of Commons on the nuclear deterrent not a single leader of the Church mentioned the evils of the atomic bomb apart from Dr Soper in the House of Lords. In reply the Archbishop made his customary response, namely that the Church should not issue sudden *ad hoc* pronouncements on every issue which progressively arose. However, it had already spoken its mind over the years on this grave issue, and had condemned the spiritual evil and physical terrors of atom and hydrogen bombs. It was up to the statesmen to devise the political steps necessary to control and get rid of them. He had himself put down a motion for this to be discussed in the June meeting of the Canterbury Convocation.

It is only fair to the Archbishop to say that he was often misrepresented in the media as a result of the various statements that he made on the nuclear issue. An extreme case of this occurred on the BBC in December 1955, on the popular programme 'Any Questions'. One of the questions put to the panel ran as follows: 'What were the reactions of the team when the Archbishop of Canterbury declared that Communism must be subdued even to the extent of using the H-bomb?' All the members proceeded to castigate the Archbishop, Wedgwood Benn in particular. Fortunately the Chairman, the astute Freddie Grisewood, interjected saying that the Archbishop had not in fact used the particular phrase attributed to him, but had only referred to the H-bomb as being a deterrent. Geoffrey Fisher immediately wrote to Sir Ian Jacob, chairman of the BBC Board of Governors, protesting that the participants made him assert precisely the opposite of what he had in fact said on the occasion from which the quotation was taken. The programme, he complained, was 'completely inaccurate and dreadfully misleading'. Thus he must insist on an apology which was duly forthcoming. Indeed Sir Ian ate very humble pie.

However, the Archbishop continued to incur criticism because, though a churchman, he committed himself to the view that in a fallen world the H-bomb was necessary as a deterrent. At the same time he denied that the Church put its trust in fear. It was states which made war.

Yet as the years went on, Dr Fisher began to entertain increasing doubts as to how long the deterrent would continue to deter; also he was not happy as to the ethical implications of its justification. He therefore took the initiative in writing to Sir Anthony Eden, then Prime Minister, expressing his own disquiet and informing Sir Anthony that there was 'a growing opinion among the Churches that the British and American Governments must take a fresh initiative *now* in the field of atomic warfare and disarmament if the situation is to be kept under any kind of moral control'. It was possible, he went on, to make a case for the possession of the bomb as a deterrent in line with what the Prime Minister himself had maintained. Yet since a final act of suicide was unthinkable the present situation could lead to local wars with impunity. Thus the moral case for the bomb 'daily decreases'. Hence he urged as a practical policy that Britain should work for a general reduction in armaments; for the prohibition of certain classes of weapons; for the establishment of effective inspection and control even though these may not be completely foolproof; to limit proliferation by making a distinction between strategic and tactical weapons.

This was, perhaps, an unusual letter for an Archbishop of Canterbury to write to a Prime Minister, and probably owed much to Admiral Sir Anthony Buzzard who, for many worried churchmen, had become somewhat of a nuclear guru.

The Prime Minister certainly took this letter seriously, and in his reply set out at length the Government's policy in this field. He rejected the view that the H-bomb was losing its deterrent power when both sides possessed it in quantity. The Government started from the premise that the West 'will never be the aggressor', a position recently reaffirmed in the Declaration from Washington. The best hope for preserving the peace was for the West to remain 'the strongest-armed'. However, the frustration of many sincere churchmen – and this included the Archbishop himself – remained, the more so since it seemed that the nuclear deterrent had come to stay. The Archbishop, meanwhile, consistently did what he could to encourage those individuals and institutions who were seeking to build up a more peaceful world. Thus he wrote to Clement Davies, Leader of the Liberal Party, concerning the Association of Parliamentarians for World Government, applauding his efforts though confessing sadly 'that no machinery worth anything can be constructed until its principal partners are willing to trust one another'.

It has to be confessed that there was at least one occasion in respect of nuclear weapons when the Archbishop expressed himself so ambiguously as to leave his listeners puzzled, even shocked. Such was the case when in answer to a question by a university student in Africa he remarked that it might be within the Providence of God that humanity should destroy itself. This utterance led, and very understandably, to howls of protest. The Archbishop strongly denied that he ever meant by the use of such a phrase to imply that God intended to bring about humanity's final destruction in this way. His language here must be condemned since the term 'Providence' implies to the ordinary believer God's merciful ordering of the affairs of this world to advance his Kingdom of love and fulfilment. To use the designation 'Providence' in exclusively judgemental and pejorative terms is dangerously misleading.

It is to the credit of Geoffrey Fisher that in his general approach to the agonising dilemma presented by nuclear weapons he recognised from the outset that different views could responsibly be held; and that he himself must protect the right of Anglicans to express them. To a critic of Bishop Bell in 1947 he responded as follows: 'You also refer to the Bishop's unpatriotic pronouncements during the war. With some of those pronouncements I disagreed myself but they were no more unpatriotic than he is. May I put it like this: a vast number of people, including many scientists, felt that the dropping of the atomic bomb raised acute moral problems and many people felt compelled to condemn the action on Christian grounds. The Bishop of Chichester and others felt that the introduction of mass bombing of industrial targets, with inevitable indiscriminate attacks on civilians, also raised acute moral problems. The Bishop [Bell] felt they were mostly indefensible and had the courage to say so, although he knew that he differed not only from general opinion but also from many churchmen. His action was not in any kind of way lack of patriotism, but an immense desire that war should not degrade our moral standards.'

The Archbishop, before his retirement in 1961, had an unfortunate brush with the Prime Minister, Harold Macmillan, over this general issue. This arose when Dr Fisher presided over a meeting of the British Council of Churches which had spent the final morning discussing a report drawn up by the International Affairs Department on Disarmament. In its dying moments, Archbishop Fisher, off the cuff, expressed surprise that so far there had been no official response by the Government to a recent 'remarkable' statement by the Russian leader Khrushchev pleading for total disarmament with full international control. Indeed, so commented the Archbishop, that was what they had all been praying for over a period of years, and Mr Khrushchev 'could not more effectively have read the New Testament'.

These observations of the Archbishop, widely reported in the Press, certainly added to his postbag with, in the main, critical letters. One lady commented: 'How Khrushchev must be laughing'! More important was a letter from the Prime Minister himself who made it abundantly clear that he was anything but pleased with these *ad hoc* remarks of the Archbishop. He must, so he wrote, express surprise that the Primate of All England made no reference to a similar utterance by the British Foreign Secretary, Mr Selwyn Lloyd, which contained proposals which were 'detailed, progressive and likely to be effective. Perhaps he had not heard of this!' Equally he might not be aware of the use which communist newspapers were making of his statement. 'I do not mind this so much in this country', he added, 'but throughout the Commonwealth and in every uncommitted country it will be used as the basis for unscrupulous propaganda.'

The Archbishop responded by saying that hitherto the Russians had blocked the way to any form of international control in relation to disarmament. Now Khrushchev had opened the matter up in a way which the Prime Minister had always said was the nub of the problem – international control. All that he, Geoffrey Fisher, had done at the

Conference of the British Council of Churches was to stimulate his audience to form a judgement about what Khrushchev had said. If the Press were saying, to quote Geoffrey Fisher's own words, 'that I have called Khrushchev's objective good Christianity I don't object to that ... If they are reproaching the West for being less welcoming than I was, I think the West deserves it'. The reportage of his remarks in the United States and Britain, he complained, was 'not only damning with faint praise but plain damning'. He had again looked at *The Times* treatment of Khrushchev's speech and could only say of it that it shows 'no spark of generosity or even common sense'.

There is, of course, a background to this correspondence between the Archbishop and the Prime Minister. The former had always been uneasy at the assumption that the nuclear deterrent could be a permanent ingredient in the military armoury of the West. He consistently maintained that the only reason for still possessing the bomb was to use it as a means of bargaining it away. Khrushchev's unexpected initiative seemed to offer a faint hope that this might become a reality.

What this *contretemps* further illustrates is that the relationship between the Prime Minister and the Archbishop was often an 'edgy' one; and the former was not happy with what he regarded as the latter's intrusion into the political sphere.

Before leaving the nuclear deterrent perhaps we may offer two brief comments. The Archbishop's approach to the problem shows again his reluctance to resort 'to absolute judgements'. He is pragmatic and responsive to Niebuhr's ethical thesis of the 'lesser of two evils'. Geoffrey Fisher emphasized, time and time again, the supreme significance of the United Nations in keeping the peace. He believed in it; supported it consistently; and used his influence as Archbishop to this end.

CHAPTER 30

Marriage, Divorce and the Family

WE have frequently noticed that Geoffrey Fisher was more concerned with the application of Christian insights to ordinary, everyday living than, as he saw it, with the splitting of nice theological hairs. He believed that a religious stance must have its effect upon the behaviour of both individuals and communities and it was, therefore, the responsibility of the Church to spell out what this meant in practical terms. Nowhere was this more needed than in the sanctities of home and family particularly within the institution of marriage. The protection of its integrity was, therefore, important not only to the Christian but to society as a whole, to its stability and general well-being. He had already shown this interest and concern when he was Bishop of Chester. Already there was in germ 'his marriage discipline'.

The canon law of the medieval Church laid it down that the marriage bond, when properly entered into, was indissoluble. However, two classes of divorce were permitted known as (a) *a vinculo* – a decree of nullity which was equivalent to saying that there had never been, from the beginning, a valid marriage; (b) *e mensa et thoro*, the equivalent of what we should now call a legal separation.

At the time of the Reformation in England papal jurisdiction ceased, and the ecclesiastical courts which gave decrees of nullity and separation went with it. Insofar as the authority hitherto vested ultimately in the Pope remained, it was transferred to the Sovereign, the Supreme Governor of the Church of England. Thus until the Divorce Act of 1853 there were no means of securing a divorce in England, *a vinculo*, except by act of Parliament.

When Geoffrey Fisher was appointed Archbishop, he became Primate of a Church unique among the non-Roman churches of Europe in that it retained the vestiges of a medieval past without effective ecclesiastical courts to moderate its absolutism. Moreover he entered into office at a time when many responsible people, and this included not only churchmen, were becoming increasingly alarmed at the steady increase in marriage breakdowns leading to legal divorce. The figures speak for themselves. Before the First World War 800 petitions for divorce were filed. After the Second World War (1945) the number had risen to 25,000 and by the following year to 40,000. This increase continued throughout the many years of Geoffrey Fisher's archiepiscopate.

One of the effects of this enormous increase in divorce litigation was its soaring beyond the capacity of the divorce judges expeditiously to cope with it. Long delays became the order of the day. The congestion grew so serious that the Archbishop was given to understand that the Lord Chancellor (Lord Simon) intended to bring a Bill before Parliament allowing registrars to preside over undefended cases. If this were the case, so the Archbishop informed the Lord Chancellor, the Church would certainly wish to oppose it with all its might. To this forthright protest the Lord Chancellor replied that the Bill was only under consideration and he invited the Archbishop to discuss the whole matter with himself personally. Geoffrey Fisher did so and suggested that in such undefended cases divorce should not be granted until after six years of marriage; also that only a judge of the High Court should pronounce a decree absolute. The Lord Chancellor followed this up by sending to Lambeth the substance of the proposed Bill which the Archbishop passed on for comment to Lord Denning and Mr Justice Collins, neither of whom was convinced of its wisdom. Both of them expressed their admiration for the Primate's 'quick and sure grasp of the problem', and agreed with him that these cases should be kept, if possible, in the High Court.

The office of Lord Chancellor was now taken over by Lord Jowett, upon a change of government, and he went out of his way to win the Archbishop's general support, believing it eminently desirable that they should keep in close touch with each other.

Geoffrey Fisher, gratified that the Government was seeking to improve the Bill, gave evidence in the summer of 1946 before a committee under the chairmanship of Lord Denning, at which he stressed the need to provide means for assisting reconciliation between the parties before they resorted to divorce. Such a severing of the marriage bond, so the Archbishop insisted, was not a purely private, individual affair to be determined on points of law only, but rather 'a social matter threatening family and social stability'. It was typical of Geoffrey Fisher that prior to appearing before the commission he carefully prepared his brief, drawing up five pages of 'Notes and Evidence'.

The Archbishop was anxious, by imposing a stamp duty, to improve the image of civil marriages, thereby redeeming them from being 'a dingy casual occasion'. To reinforce this intention he got into touch with the Bishop of Birmingham as well as the incumbents of Portsea and Leeds asking specific questions as to how civil marriages were conducted in their areas. He also set up a small committee on which five bishops served, London being chairman, which reported back that the conditions prevailing in register offices 'left a lot to be desired'.

The Archbishop expressed his concern, and referred to this during a debate in the House of Lords that neither on the application form nor during the ceremony itself were the parties informed that in England the law assumed a life-long union between husband and wife. This was a matter he regarded as sufficiently serious to take up at length with the Lord Chancellor. To secure this insertion did not prove easy and the Registrar-General replied that he must have time to consider it.

The Archbishop was surely right in regarding what happened in register offices as important, not least because the number of people resorting to civil marriages was increasing and the official policy of the Church of England in refusing church weddings to divorcees, whose former spouses were still alive, was adding to its number. Hence Geoffrey Fisher's concern that such marriages should not be regarded as easy options, less binding on the consciences of the contracting parties.

However, some critics were uneasy cncerning the effects of Anglican doctrine on relations between Church and State. Hence, in 1907 – followed by subsequent legislation – Parliament passed an Act legalising marriages between a man and his deceased wife's sister – a union hitherto prohibited in the Table of Affinity in the 1662 Book of Common Prayer which had statutory authority. A further extension of this permission was attempted in January 1949 when Lord Jowett informed Geoffrey Fisher that a Bill was to come before Parliament enabling a man to marry his divorced wife's sister – as though the wife were dead – and a woman to marry a divorced husband's brother. Marriage, however, was excluded if there had been a divorce arising out of the adultery of the husband, or conversely of the wife. Geoffrey Fisher admitted that his natural instinct was to oppose the Bill on the grounds that there was not much public demand for it; but beyond this he believed that it was a further attack on the integrity of home and family. In taking this view the Archbishop was supported by Garbett, Archbishop of York, and Kirk, Bishop of Oxford. Denning, in sympathizing with the Archbishop, was forced to confess that the anomalies of the law as they existed at the moment were indefensible. When the Bill came up for its second reading in the House of Lords the Archbishop opposed it and his opposition, along with others, led the government to block it.

The medieval Church, while maintaining in principle the indissolubility of marriage, yet softened, in practice, this rigorism through resort to decrees of nullity. Geoffrey Fisher was himself opposed to any reintroduction of ecclesiastical courts to pronounce such decrees, though this did not prevent him at times speculating about this possibility. Most unwisely, so it proved, the Archbishop used the opportunity given at a dinner of the Medical-Legal Society to refer to decrees of nullity in relation to the consummation of a marriage when contraceptives were used. As light relief – he was a guest speaker – he threw off the remark that 'our Judges have not the slightest idea of what the law of nullity really is'. 'Indeed,' he went on, 'Lord Merriman had overlooked the fact that under the Herbert Act of 1937 an additional reason for nullity was wilful refusal to consummate the marriage.' *The Times* newspaper reported the Archbishop's speech on the following day. Such critical and highly damaging remarks uttered by the Primate of All England and directed against the leader of a closely-knit profession which prided itself on its talents and integrity, were not likely to pass unnoticed, nor did they. For Lord Merriman – he was President of the Probate, Admiralty and Divorce Divisions – the opportunity to reply presented itself in Edinburgh at a dinner of the Scottish Law Agents where, maybe, attacks on Archbishops could claim venerable historical precedents. He denied forcefully that the judges were ignorant of the law relating to nullity and warned against the 'astonishing suggestion' of the Church setting up its own courts to pronounce decrees of nullity. Lord Merriman, at the same time, despatched a letter to Lambeth running to some seven pages, in which he did not pull his punches. He thought some of the Archbishop's gibes were 'rather cheap' and he regretted that at least he did not give him credit for knowing elementary points of law in connection with his own jurisdiction. Perhaps, so he commented, 'the reformed branch of the Catholic Church established by law in this Kingdom might make it a matter of conscience to inculcate respect for the rule of law from which it derived its establishment, instead of holding up His Majesty's Judges to public ridicule.'

Lord Merriman could hardly have expressed himself with greater force or clarity. Nor was he alone in giving vent to his indignation direct to the Archbishop. William Jowett, the Lord Chancellor, wrote on 30 January expressing his 'great distress', reminding the Archbishop that nothing he might say in public on a topic which so clearly concerned the Church could be regarded as casual. The divergence between the law of the Church and the law of the land should give them both 'grave anxiety'.

Many distinguished people began to enter the lists and gave the Archbishop the advantage of their frank admonition and advice, amongst them being Dr Marie Stopes, the gynaecologist and Mr Quintin Hogg, Member of Parliament and later Lord Hailsham. Geoffrey Fisher realised that it was to Lord Merriman that he must direct his reply. This he did on 13 February 1950, offering a most sincere if embarrassed apology, admitting that he should not have used an after-dinner speech in so casual a way. He assured him, however, that the Church did not intend to set up its own courts.

Lord Merriman was essentially too good-natured a man to nourish a grievance and he acknowledged this letter in the friendliest manner.

It was a favourite theory of his, he wrote, that 'most of the important things in life happen in consequence of friendly encounters on social occasions'.

The background to this unfortunate personal *contretemps* was an increasing concern, entertained by some churchmen, regarding the status of marriage in relation to the law, a concern which led the Government to set up a Royal Commission on Marriage and Divorce. It was understandable that this should be of interest to the ecclesiastical authorities and that Geoffrey Fisher should seek Church representation upon it. The Lord Chancellor, in consultation with Mr Morrison, the Home Secretary, was not discouraging and let the Archbishop know that he would do his best to see that this happened. However, in spite of these hopeful words, and much to the Archbishop's disappointment, there was no Anglican representation on the Commission which was presided over by Lord Morton of Heryton. Nor did any minister of religion sit on it either. This meant that Geoffrey Fisher had to exercise influence in other ways which he did by keeping in close touch with its chairman, and seeing him from time to time. At one such interview which took place in July, 1953, the Archbishop expressed his alarm at what he described as the 'startling suggestion' that those who were married at a Christian service 'till death do us part' should be denied access to the divorce courts. If there were a cold 'logic' about this prohibition in that it 'takes the Churches at their word', yet they could not accept it. 'I maintained that in principle', so Geoffrey Fisher wrote in recalling this interview, 'the Church would not grant that Parliament may deny to all its members a civil liberty granted to other citizens.' Lord Morton saw the point; but it is difficult to believe that any such proposal could have been seriously intended. The Archbishop also encouraged the Church of England Moral Welfare Council to lay before the Commission 'a perfectly clear statement of the Church's attitude to marriage and divorce'.

On the eve of the publication of the Royal Commission's report in January 1956, Sir William Haley, editor of *The Times*, came to see the Archbishop to discuss with him the Church's attitude in general, particularly as he confessed to being shocked by the number of clergymen who had written supporting the idea of Princess Margaret's marriage with Group Captain Townsend. Did this mean, he asked, that there were wide differences of opinion within the Church itself? In reply the Archbishop gave him a brief history of the present situation leading to the concordat which had been agreed when a proposed canon ran into difficulty concerning the re-marriage of a divorced person in church while a previous partner was living. However, he fully recognised that the Church had a pastoral responsibility to divorcees and those whose marriages had broken down; but he did not recommend any change in the civil law at the moment. The Church had contemplated fighting this battle but had realistically come to the conclusion that it was a lost cause so far as Parliament was concerned.

In 1959, a strong lobby determined to reintroduce the Bill which had miscarried on its first appearance some ten years previously. Michael Ramsey, Archbishop of York, got in touch with Lambeth deploring its re-appearance and urged Geoffrey Fisher to re-affirm the 'cogent' reasons he had already given for opposing it. Geoffrey Fisher wrote a personal letter to Lord Kilmuir, advising him that he would speak against the Bill in the Lords, which, if it were to become law, would necessitate the withdrawal of a draft canon with a consequent and unfortunate 'row' in Convocation. 'It had always been my hope', the Archbishop commented, 'that over these extremely difficult questions of marriage legislation, the Law of the State and the Law of the Church would always be the same though the Herbert Act had already made one small break.' Lord Mancroft's Bill, he pointed out, could be amended simply by adding a clause to the effect that 'the Act shall not be taken to restrain the Church of England or any other religious body from forbidding by Canon or other regulation for their own members such marriages as are by this Bill made lawful'. However, it was not to prove so simple and Lord Kilmuir replied firmly that the Government did not intend to block the Bill as it had done in 1949 nor did he think that Geoffrey Fisher's amendment which created two categories of citizens would help; indeed it would be bitterly resented.

The Archbishop duly spoke when the Divorced Wife's Sister Bill came before the Lords in March 1959. He found that the general atmosphere had somewhat changed since the last debate, in part due to the Royal Commission having reported in favour of the principle which the Bill enshrined. In opening his speech he stressed that he spoke entirely as a member of the public interested in the general well-being of all citizens. Lord Mancroft claimed that the law as it stood was 'anomalous, cruel, illogical and unnecessary'.

However, the Archbishop's strictures were in vain, Lord Denning claiming that the arguments in favour of the Bill were 'overwhelming'. Not surprisingly it was successfully carried through the Upper House.

Geoffrey Fisher did not get a very good press for his intervention in this debate. The *Daily Herald* comments: 'We say UTTER NON-SENSE', and went on to refer to the Archbishop as 'one of the most antiquated thinkers in Britain'.

We have seen that the Archbishop entertained a sustained hostility against anything which he thought weakened or threatened the stability of family life. In his judgement the rapid increase in the number of divorces did precisely this, though he did not condemn all incidences of divorce out of hand; or maintain that re-marriage after divorce was in all circumstances wrong. Thus he never committed himself theologically to the absolute indissolubility of the marriage bond. It was his view that there were, in practice, situations in which divorce constituted the lesser of two evils – in other words that though resort to it must of necessity represent a failure in human relations it was better to recognise this when all attempts at reconciliation had failed.

We now turn to consider the Archbishop's attitude pastorally to marriage breakdown in terms of the policy and practice of the Church of England as laid down in Convocation – and which he strongly approved. This may, perhaps, be best stated in general terms before we illustrate briefly how it worked in practice.

Late in 1954 and again early in 1955 Geoffrey Fisher called a conference, which met at Lambeth, to discuss two fundamental questions: (1) What was the best policy for the Church of England in the present marriage situation? (2) How could this be put into effect? Those present included Bishops and Proctors of the provinces of Canterbury and York; representatives of different brands of churchmanship; members of the House of Commons, and lawyers. Though differences of opinion were apparent throughout, Geoffrey Fisher worked hard for, and to a degree obtained, a general consensus which considering the wide diversity of attitudes was a singular achievement. The report, drawn up at the Conference, was sent to the Canon Law Steering Committee of the two Convocations and to a joint committee of the Canterbury Convocation which was considering the pastoral care of divorced people.

The report begins by calling attention to the dilemma of a double responsibility which the Church must discharge – 'a strict and uncompromising witness to Christ's teaching on marriage' and yet, at the same time, bringing a pastoral ministry to bear on those whose marriages were in the process of breaking up, or had already broken up. Such unfortunate people should be as much the special care of the parish priest as the 'sick and afflicted'. If help were brought early he might be able to prevent the collapse of the original marriage, but when reconciliation finally proved impossible he must recognise that there might be grounds for a divorce.

As to Christ's teaching he clearly laid down that marriage was a lifelong union of a man to a woman to the exclusion of all others, but Christ, so the Archbishop maintained, was not a 'legislator' if by that is meant telling the Church for all time how to deal with 'marriage discipline'. Here the Church was left free, in response to the guidance of the Holy Spirit, to find its own way according to His will.

Members of the Conference were of the view that the Church should maintain its own position as set out in the draft canons and in resolutions of the Convocations. On the other hand the clergy should show 'a charitable understanding' of their fellow priests who, in a 'good conscience', felt it right to marry divorced persons in church. The provisions for 'discipline' in respect of divorcees should be included in resolutions of Convocation. As to those who had contracted marriages while a former partner was living their 'communicant status' must be referred to the Bishop who, when he was satisfied that their receiving the sacrament would not give 'grave offence' or be to the 'hurt of their own souls', could authorise their re-admission to the sacrament.

The Archbishop approved this *via media* believing it to be a truly consensus view though it was not *in toto* acceptable to everybody. These regulations were authorised by the Canterbury Convocation in 1957 and by that of York a year later. His own words of commendation may be quoted: 'In any matter of controversy the first duty of a Christian is to analyse the facts, all of them, so far as he can dispassionately. Thereby he will certainly protect himself against various emotions which too easily obscure or disturb the right proportions of a matter.'

The service of blessing, as it came to be known, which was used in Church over divorced husbands and wives, was regarded by the Archbishop as having great pastoral significance, though it was seldom, if ever, at that time used by High Churchmen who believed in the absolute indissolubility of the marriage bond. In giving permission in his own diocese for such services, the Archbishop usually attached certain conditions though some of the latter were relaxed as time went on. The service should be pastoral and private with only intimate friends present. Sometimes the Archbishop would enclose his own suggested order which began with a restrained and not embarrassing statement as to why a legal marriage could not take place in church, to be followed by the priest saying: 'Knowing the purposes for which God ordained matrimony, you seek His grace and blessing that you may live together in faithfulness to one another, reverently, discreetly, soberly, in prosperity and adversity, all the days of your life. For that grace and blessing we herewith join our prayers to yours. But first, I call upon you, to certify before God your pledge of fidelity to one another.' The couple were then asked, in the light of their being made legally man and wife at the register office, to pledge themselves, as in the 1928 Prayer Book 'to love, comfort and honour one another till death us do part', to which each replied 'I will'. After prayers, which included where appropriate one for child bearing, there was a blessing.

This Order needs to be read against the climate prevailing at the time and the opposition of some clergy against the use of any such service at all.

The Church's marriage discipline remained a sensitive subject, the more so because instances of divorce increased within the Church's membership and some critics tended to see the discipline as frustrating the Church's evangelistic mission. The Mothers' Union was, in general, strongly in favour of taking a firm line.

Church courts continued to remain a sore point with Geoffrey Fisher from the time when, as early as 1947, he had written to Harold Macmillan, then Chancellor of the Exchequer, protesting that he disliked the idea of such courts intensely though the Church might be driven to consider this course, but only subsequent to proceedings in a competent secular court.

The application of the Church's marriage discipline to individual cases led to a considerable correspondence for the Archbishop as incumbents in the diocese of Canterbury, chaplains in the Forces and bishops sought his advice and sometimes a ruling. Indeed among the Archbishop's personal papers at Lambeth are six files containing requests or making general enquiries, these being indexed alphabetically – a rich mine for the social historian to explore! In responding, the Archbishop laid himself open to being misunderstood by well-intentioned laymen, since he was usually – but by no means always – forced to make decisions without direct personal acquaintance with those upon whom he was sitting in judgement. It was for this reason that some of the clergy believed that matters of this kind should be left to the man on the spot – the parish priest. On the other hand, given the time available to him, it is quite remarkable how many people Geoffrey Fisher managed to see personally.

Hard cases may make bad law, but against the background of the unsettlement caused by the war many of the stories which came into Lambeth were heart-rending. Most letters related to re-marriage in church or, on occasions, re-admission to Holy Communion. Some times, but very rarely, the Archbishop might appear unduly severe, as in the case of a certain mayor upon whom he imposed a ban of three years' exclusion from the sacrament, even though his chaplain would have readmitted him 'immediately'. The mayor was, so his chaplain affirmed, a man of 'deep spirituality'.

It would be quite unfair to suppose that the Archbishop, in dealing with individual people, showed any lack of compassion; quite the reverse. But it was his considered view that the Church must witness to the life-long character of marriage and that any weakening of this resolve would lead to an increase in the number of marriage break-downs. Thus he urged many a petitioner to see his exclusion from re-marriage in church in these terms, that is as a vicarious witness, if painful, to Christian standards. In this endeavour he was seldom successful. The *via media*, as we have seen, was the service of blessing and here the Archbishop could be, and was, generous in his offer to help, provided that past failure was acknowledged and there was a real determination to achieve, in a second marriage, what had been lacking in the first.

The Archbishop's concern is shown in his desire to help those whose marriages were exposed to exceptional strain at the end of the war. Welcome as demobilisation was it brought its own hazards with it. Amongst these were severe problems of readjustment when husbands, long absent, returned to their wives almost as strangers. Some women had made other attachments and if their marital relationships were to be restored they needed to be recreated. Geoffrey Fisher, newly come to Canterbury, was acutely aware of these problems, and in June wrote to Major-General Gower, Director of the Men's Welfare Services intimating his intention to invite to Lambeth a dozen or so people to discuss this immediate problem. Meanwhile it might also be arranged for servicemen and their wives to meet one another before demobilization and be advised of some of the pitfalls which might well confront them. The Conference duly met, and the Archbishop decided to make the whole subject public by devoting his address at the Canterbury Diocesan Conference on 16 July 1945 to this urgent matter. His practical suggestion was to set up panels of clergy, doctors and lawyers to advise in their respective spheres; and to co-ordinate the work now being done by separate agencies. He further advocated that this experiment should be financed by public money, but not thereby be subject to public control. In addition whatever Government came into power there should be a 'ruthless housing policy'. These suggestions as the Archbishop intended, were given wide publicity in the Press and sparked off a public debate: but little, in terms of practical results, seems to have flowed from them. Not many such panels along the lines suggested were in fact set up, nor were they equipped to discharge the administrative responsibility involved. However, it did at least show the Archbishop's deep desire to get something done.

As to priests who had themselves re-married after divorce, as distinct from those who were content simply to sue for divorce, he believed they could not minister happily in an ordinary parish to people who must be urged to take their vows with full intention never to break them.

It was Geoffrey Fisher's constant desire to do all that he could to minimize the incidence of divorce, not least through supporting agencies which had reconciliation as their chief aim. He had long been interested in the Marriage Guidance Council and as Bishop of London, when it drew up ten working objectives, he went through them taking exception only to one as repugnant to the Christian conscience. When he moved to Canterbury he accepted the office of President and did not regard this as only a sinecure. He believed that, on the whole, the Council was working on 'the right lines', though it made no claim to be specifically Christian. There were, on occasions, tensions within the Council due to its mixed membership, and for this reason, as President, he spent much time trying to keep the balance right though it was not easy. 'People who specialise', he remarked, 'on this kind of work are very liable to overweight technique . . . They often draw attention to books which for the ordinary person are certainly inscrutable and not very suitable even for the specialists.' These are wise words!

There were other problems of a different order confronting the welfare of the family which for Geoffrey Fisher were a matter of serious concern. These arose from the increasing application of scientific technology to ever wider areas of human experience. The resulting situation was admirably described by the Archbishop himself in a speech which he delivered at a conference of the Student Christian Movement in Westminster in January 1948. Mankind, he said, was becoming increasingly master of natural processes so much so that he could now do things hitherto impossible. 'He can blast the world to pieces. He can destroy the natural fertility of the soil. He can inseminate artificially, and in theory produce all the children of a nation from one father.' Man was no longer a slave of nature but had assumed a responsibility over it and he was now being driven to answer the question 'By what moral and spiritual principle shall man's power over nature be directed?'

One result of this increasing control was the capacity for the male sperm to be artificially inseminated into the female womb and there fertilized. The Archbishop saw the dangers inherent in these new medical techniques, and though resort to artificial insemination was not so extensive in Britain as in America it was yet growing. What ought to be a Christian response to this completely new situation? Requests for guidance came to Lambeth from individual parishes and *inter alia* from such societies as the Mothers' Union. Thus the Archbishop secured a discussion of this matter at a Bishops' Meeting and in 1948 appointed a commission which reported back in the same year. The general drift of their deliberations formed the substance of a speech delivered by the Archbishop in the House of Lords on 16 March 1949 which was widely publicized. Artificial insemination by the husband, he contended, was tolerable, but by any other donor 'was wrong in principle and contrary to all Christian standards'. In maintaining that artificial insemination by the husband (AIH) was justifiable in the right circumstances but that artificial insemination by any other donor (AID) was not, he felt himself to be speaking for the vast bulk of opinion within the Church of England and indeed Christian opinion more generally. AID, apart from its moral aspect, presented many legal problems in relation to paternity and hence inheritance. Thus 'it astounded and perturbed' him that the Medical Defence Union should have given advice to medical practitioners on how to protect themselves professionally against adverse legal consequences. The practice of AID was adultery and 'directly opposed to a universal social interest'.

This address in the Lords led to many congratulatory letters, including one from Dr Scott Lidgett; also to an interesting correspondence between the Archbishop and Dr Forbes, Secretary of the Medical Defence Union, the latter disagreeing with Geoffrey Fisher in his assertion that the doctors were deliberately inviting parents to commit perjury since the baby could be registered simply as illegitimate. It was a matter of some satisfaction to the Archbishop that, concerning AID, the Pope, advised by his canonists, took the same view as himself though in relation to insemination within wedlock (AIH) the Pope was 'a great deal less clear and had, as usual, hedged the matter around and split hairs'. It was, in Geoffrey Fisher's view, the duty of the parish clergy to be fully informed on these matters so as to give knowledgeable advice.

Artificial insemination was a highly delicate, intimate matter and the Archbishop felt aggrieved when the British Broadcasting Corporation laid on a discussion on this theme, one of the speakers being a clergyman of known radical views. It was, he maintained, unfortunate that there was no one present who could have given the Church's point of view as, for example, a member of the Moral Welfare Council – or indeed himself!

It has often been noticed that the Archbishop of Canterbury, because of his office, was seen by many as a guardian, and at times a censor of public morals. It was a role which on occasions he was prepared to assume, on others not. Thus he received many letters in connection with the sale of contraceptives in slot machines. Among such correspondents were Sir Basil Henriques, a distinguished Jewish layman; Dr Graham Little and Sir Ernest Barker. The Archbishop admitted that he was 'deeply and actively concerned' and no words were 'too strong' in which to express his disapproval. He got into touch with the Home Secretary who arranged, through a bye-law, to prohibit such sales in the future, though it was still possible for a child of any age to purchase them over the counter since the shopkeeper could not legally refuse. He urged that this be dealt with through legislation.

On one theme the Archbishop spoke more than once – the need for a wise and informed use of family planning. Thus to clear up misunderstandings on this matter he devoted a letter in the Canterbury Dioscesan Notes to this important subject. He made two points: by family planning was meant a recognition by parents that they bore a direct responsibility for a conscious choice in regard to the size and spacing of their family; secondly, there was room for legitimate differences as to the methods which might be properly employed in planning the family. The Roman Catholic Church allowed only abstinence and the 'safe period', but there were other methods, available through scientific skill, to inhibit nature and these could be rightly used within marriage. Parents should be wise in their planning so as to prevent unfair burdens being placed upon mothers, children or indeed society. The use of contraceptives outside marriage was always sinful.

It was a matter of great satisfaction to the Archbishop that the Anglican Church at the Lambeth Conference of 1948 spoke out clearly on a proper and Christian use of contraception. Perhaps reference may be made in this context to a case which came before the courts early in 1948 in which the Archbishop was involved. In this litigation a complainant petitioned for a divorce on the grounds that the marriage had not been consummated by the refusal of one party to abandon contraception. Geoffrey Fisher felt it proper to issue a statement arguing that the marriage had been consummated since the procreation of children was not its only purpose. However, to prevent procreation in this way against the will of one party to the marriage was a 'grave sin'. The court upheld the Archbishop's view on this matter.

When the Wolfenden Report on homosexuality appeared in 1957 Geoffrey Fisher studied it carefully and endeavoured to assess it in the October number of his Canterbury Notes. He was glad that a clear distinction had been made between a sin and a crime. All practising homosexuals sin against God but this does not mean that the law at every point should take cognisance of what they do. There was 'a realm which is not the law's business, a sacred area of privacy where people make their choices and decisions, fashion their characters; asserting their own essential rights and liberties into which the law generally speaking must not intrude'. True it is not easy to draw a line between what is a private sin only and what is an offence against public order and the general good. If the law can do anything, without undue interference, to strengthen the moral stamina of the people, it ought to do so. A crime, however, is a different matter, being a sin against society and social order of such a kind that the law ought to take note of it.

Whatever one may think of the practical conclusions to which Geoffrey Fisher arrived in respect of homosexuality this article in his Canterbury Notes is an excellent piece of work. His general approach shows, for his day, a breadth of view, a liberal approach, and respect for the individual within society. One wonders whether if Geoffrey

Fisher were to engage in a similar *critique* today, he would want to 'liberalise' his approach in 1957.

Perhaps it ought to be added that in ethical matters of this kind the Archbishop could – and very sensibly did – seek invaluable advice from Canon Gordon Dunstan, Clerical Secretary of the Church of England Council for Social Work. It was in part his thinking which lay behind the concept of marriage, written into law, which changes the emphasis in divorce legislation away from a redress of grievances through the matrimonial offence to asking the question whether the marriage had broken down beyond reasonable hope of recovery. Canon Dunstan also acted as secretary to a high level group, convened by the Archbishop and under the chairmanship of Max Warren, to consider 'The Family in Contemporary Society'. The Archbishop showed a great interest in its deliberations and its report may well claim to be amongst the most significant and relevant of its kind produced under the *aegis* of the Church of England. In retirement Geoffrey Fisher thanked Canon Gordon Dunstan for his support in these words: 'You cannot know how much deep spiritual encouragement you have given me during these years of doctrinal confusion and conflict by your occasional hints of sympathetic understanding'.

CHAPTER 31

Parliament, Politics and Prime Ministers

THE Archbishop of Canterbury was a member of the House of Lords, a privilege and responsibility which he enjoyed *ex officio* with the Archbishop of York, the Bishops of London, Durham and Winchester, and a number of other bishops in order of seniority. This representation of bishops in the Upper House has a long history behind it going back to medieval and, in embryo, Anglo-Saxon days. In the 18th century the bishops constituted a solid phalanx of support for Whig governments, and manipulation of episcopal appointments by such an expert in this exercise as the Duke of Newcastle enabled the government to depend upon the bishops in time of need. Amongst 19th century Primates of All England it was Archbishop Tait who commanded greatest respect in the House of Lords. This did not happen by accident for Tait deliberately mastered the technique of how to speak in such an assembly in addition to which he constantly attended to get the 'feel' of the House. Often he went into the Press Gallery of the Commons.

This reference to Tait is important, since it illustrates almost dramatically the difference between then and the situation when Geoffrey Fisher took over. No sucessor to Tait has tried to measure up to his example since, quite literally, he could not afford the time to do so. Yet Geoffrey Fisher still believed that there was a value in having an effective episcopal representation in the House of Lords from the national Church and that the opportunity to do this should be used purposefully and not squandered.

It was not unexpected, however, that when the Labour Party came into power in 1945 after the war, the spirit which animated it was one of reform and re-appraisal of ancient institutions. To set out to restructure the House of Lords or indeed to abolish it altogether was no novelty but had been frequently mooted. True, the status and constitutional significance of the Upper House was radically affected by the Parliament Act of 1910 passed in the first year of the reign of King George V. Henceforward the House of Lords could delay legislation passed in the House of Commons but if the Lower House persisted it could finally get its own way. Periodically, however, there were rumblings that something more was needed to democratize the Upper Chamber thus making it relevant to a contemporary society. For example, many thought that the representation of hereditary peers and bishops was either anomalous, excessive or both. So the Labour

Government began to flex its muscles and some four years after taking office Prime Minister Attlee took an initiative by inviting the Archbishop to consider how the bishops ought to fare in a reformed Upper Chamber. The two met and Geoffrey Fisher agreed that the episcopal representation in the House of Lords could be reduced, but that the two Primates and the senior bishops should retain their seats. This prompted the Prime Minister to ask whether a small number of bishops should be nominated by the Crown as life peers for the period of their episcopal office; and also ought the monopoly of the Church of England to be broken by offering some peerages to leaders of other Churches. Mr Attlee, who obviously had given much thought to this matter, also wondered whether there ought to be a chaplain to say prayers in the House of Lords as in the Commons, to which Geoffrey Fisher responded immediately: 'Why not the Dean of Westminster?' The Archbishop consulted his fellow Primate of York, who in his turn saw Lord Salisbury. They were doubtful as to the Prime Minister's suggestion for life peers and would prefer election by their fellow bishops as happened with Scottish peers who were in the Upper House. It became clear that the Labour Party, in so far as Attlee had conferred with some of its members, did not favour any representation in the House of Lords by the Roman Catholics through its Cardinal or the Jewish Community through the Chief Rabbi. The upshot of these consultations was a letter to the Prime Minister from the Archbishop in which he confirmed that those he had consulted were in general agreement with the proposals in respect of a reformed House of Lords so far as bishops were concerned. They approved that: (1) the two Archbishops, together with the Bishops of London, Durham and Winchester should without question, retain their seats *ex officio*; (2) five other diocesan bishops should sit in the Lords; (3) these should not have their place in the Upper House merely on the grounds of seniority, but in terms of the likelihood of their making a useful contribution. Amongst these there should be younger bishops: (4) these five should be elected by their fellow bishops; (5) if election was not viable then there should be a convention, embodied in an exchange of letters between the Prime Minister and the Archbishop of Canterbury.

The Archbishop confessed that he was glad the Prime Minister did not contemplate other religious denominations being given statutory representation in the Upper House on the same footing as the five senior Sees. 'Any move of that sort', he commented, 'would raise extreme difficulties.' Indeed annual office holders such as the Moderators of the General Assembly of the Church of Scotland and the Free Church Federal Council should not enjoy a built-in status. Hence it was better to use life peerages. This correspondence certainly seemed encouraging but nothing came of it. Though there was general agreement in the Labour Party, and indeed beyond it, that something ought to be done about the Upper House there was no agreement as to how this could best be brought about. Schemes got bogged down between those who contended that the Lords ought to be abolished 'root and branch'; those who recognised the need for a second chamber but thought that some kind of electoral system ought to be embodied *vis-à-vis* its membership; and those who opted for the most minimal changes on the grounds that, surprisingly, it worked.

An attempt to re-activate a proposal of this kind was made in March 1953 which does not seem to have got above ground. However, the Earl of Glasgow wrote to the Archbishop asking what were his views as to the Church of Scotland being represented in the House of Lords. His reply is revealing, namely that he believed it would be a great mistake if representatives of other Churches in the United Kingdom were in the Lords: but he could see the logic for a claim on behalf of the Established Church of Scotland. 'But this is not a logical world', the Archbishop went on, 'and if that claim were put forward I am perfectly certain that, quite apart from the Roman Catholics, the Free Churches would certainly demand that they should have representatives as well, and it would be almost impossible to resist.' Where, he asked do you draw the line? What about the Unitarians and the Moral Re-armers? However, once again, nothing transpired from this private approach to the Archbishop. Thus the Church of England retained its monopoly.

There was another group, very extensive, who felt that they deserved and ought to have an adequate representation in the Upper House. These were women, but a Bill to do something about them was rejected on three successive occasions. Thus thwarted, those who had sponsored it decided to proceed by petition and as a result the Archbishop was asked by Lady Ravensdale, a daughter of the formidable Marquess Curzon and herself sharing his aristocratic mien, to be a signatory. Though indeed sympathetic to the general aims of the petition, he declined on the grounds that it was not customary for an Archbishop to sign such documents.

Perhaps it ought to be said that the creation of life peerages has done something, if not everything, to ease the problem. If there seemed a possibility that episcopal representation in the House of Lords might at some time be reduced, there was yet another section of the community who, along with peers, lunatics, prisoners in gaol and undischarged bankrupts, were excluded as a class from the House of Commons. The reference is to ordained priests of the Church of England. This exclusion has an ancient history. Originally Parliament was, to a great extent, a fiscal assembly upon which the monarchy largely depended to raise the finance necessary to govern the country and to fight its wars. The clergy, however, were taxed separately in their own Convocation until Archbishop Sheldon (1598–1677) by a private arrangement with the Earl of Clarendon agreed, that this anomaly should cease. However, the exclusion from sitting in the House of Commons remained.

In 1948, when the Representation of the People's Act was published, two members of Parliament, John Parker and Ivor Bulmer-Thomas, the latter a distinguished churchman and a member of the Church Assembly, put down an amendment providing that the clergy should in future be entitled to sit in the House of Commons. When Sir Philip Baker-Wilbraham, Dean of the Arches, heard of this move, he asked the Archbishop to request Ivor Bulmer-Thomas to withdraw his support to the amendment. This the Archbishop did on 5 May 1948. In his letter requesting this the Archbishop stressed that before taking such a step much careful thought was needed. His, the Archbishop's, immediate reaction was against the suggestion and indeed there was a strong climate of opinion opposed to it. 'Our clergy', he wrote, 'do not identify themselves with the practical working of political parties and I fear only the worst sort of clergymen would ever think of entering Parliament. In any case it really does conflict with their ordination vows to give their full-time service to the Church.' In a courteous reply Bulmer-Thomas admitted that he was hesitant to sign the amendment and had he known the Archbishop was opposed to it he would not have given it his support.

Geoffrey Fisher believed that the bishops still had a useful role to play in the House of Lords though to secure this their attendance needed to be more systematically organised. Indeed not infrequently he received bitter complaints at the absence or inadequacy of episcopal participation when some major national issue was being discussed. However, he was well aware, from his own personal experience at Chester and London, that there were severe difficulties in the way of an effective representation of bishops in the Upper House. Members of the Bench were far too busy; and the pressure on them grew ever greater, so much so that regular attendance was simply out of the question. This unsatisfactory situation was not finally tackled, in spite of the Archbishop's staff doing their best, until Robert Beloe took over at Lambeth as Lay Secretary in 1959 and gave it his zealous attention. It meant, first of all, keeping abreast of the Parliamentary timetable, in particular knowing when certain bills were to be introduced or particular subjects discussed. It entailed further discussion as to which bishop was best equipped to handle a specialised theme and seeing that he was properly briefed in order to do so. Geoffrey Fisher had no desire to iron out differences on the Bench or for all the bishops to speak with one voice. Indeed, he relates with approval that in the debate on the proposed Federation of Northern and Southern Rhodesia and Nyasaland, he spoke in its favour and Bishop Bell spoke against. (The latter incidentally proved to be right). In particular it was one of Robert Beloe's responsibilities to ensure that the Archbishop was present, and prepared to speak in the House when certain key matters were coming up which demanded something authoritative from the Bench, such as, for example, the moral and social health of the nation; the future of a Commonwealth country when its freedom seemed to be at stake; or some critical matter of foreign policy. Reference to such occasions are to be found throughout this biography in the relevant chapters. It may help, however, to indicate the breadth of the Archbishop's social and political concerns if we list some of the subjects debated in the House of Lords during his archiepiscopate and in which he participated. They include: the atom bomb; conditions in central Europe; the transference of populations from Poland, Czechoslovakia, Austria and Hungary; the situation in Italy; the work of the United Nations; genocide; marriage failure and reconciliation; legitimacy and artificial insemination; a fixed date for Easter; education; foreign policy; iron and steel industrial re-organisation; Russia; charitable trusts; flood disaster in East England; Television Bill; Uganda; Kenya; Cyprus; death penalty; Small Lotteries Bill; The Middle East; Egypt, Israel and the Suez crisis; Oxford traffic; Homicide Bill; Ghana; artificial insemination of married women; homosexuality; Street Offences Bill; Legitimacy Bill; betting and gambling; newspapers; Christian unity.

The Archbishop always, and very properly, felt himself bound to be true to his own conscience, and in so doing he never hesitated to speak or vote for or against the Government whichever seemed to him to be right. When attacked by Lord Hailsham for opposing the Government at the time of the invasion of Egypt he justified his attitude as follows: 'It is the statesman's duty to start from Caesar's end and to fulfil his trust for the temporal welfare of his people, praying (as you movingly said in the House of Lords) that in so doing he may render as much obedience to the perfect will of God as the conditions of a sinful world admit. It is my duty as a Christian leader to begin from God's end as revealed to us in Jesus Christ and to try faithfully and humbly to relate what I can perceive of His perfect will to our temporal affairs. That must be my special contribution . . . It is not surprising if starting from different ends (though with a common desire and sincerity) we do not come to an exact agreement.' Either might be wrong, he added. Not everyone, I suspect, would accept this, perhaps, too simplistic analysis. As to the effectiveness of his own performances in the House of Lords Geoffrey Fisher in retirement writes: 'I can say straight off that I was never at ease in the House of Lords, except when I was actually speaking, and then I was only at ease because I had got what I wanted to say written in front of me, and if not quite reading it, delivering it from my paper. I always felt that it was a very, very critical audience; that you couldn't just be easy and make jokes – you'd be quoted and replied to.'

Sometimes the Archbishop took a more positive view as to his own achievements and makes the claim: 'I think I was genuinely listened to in the House of Lords with interest and respect, partly because they never quite knew what line I was going to take – they knew it wouldn't be merely the pompous, flat, normal ecclesiastical line, and I think I made them think a bit.' One testimonial to his efforts in the Lords, which he prized highly, came from Lord Winterton who having for some years earlier been the 'Father' of the Lower House, played an almost similar role in the Upper Chamber. Though he rarely agreed with the stance of the Archbishop he yet reckoned that he was the 'clearest and most concise speaker in the House of Lords and there was never any doubt about what he was meaning to say'. Certainly one of the Archbishop's great assets was his willingness to inform himself and seek help, when it was needed, from sources qualified to give it. The House of Lords, by universal assent, was (and is) not an easy body to address since its collective expertise is considerable. A shoddy, ill-prepared performance by an Archbishop of Canterbury would not only let himself down but depreciate the currency of his office. The Archbishop undoubtedly had an excellent speaking voice, an economical and direct use of the English language and a very logical mind. If he avoided flights of oratory he must have known that such effusions did not particularly commend themselves to the House. One important fact he had to bear in mind was that, too often, whatever he said people would take to be, rightly or wrongly, the authentic voice of the Church of England. He was for them its mouthpiece. Sometimes, without overdoing it – often a temptation with him but usually held in check – he could introduce a lighter touch.

It is inevitable that an Archbishop of Canterbury should be brought into direct contact with the Prime Minister as Head of Government – after all he had appointed him! The days, however, had long gone since they dined in each other's houses and met regularly at the Athenaeum. Even had these days in a measure lingered, Geoffrey Fisher would not have taken much advantage of them not being a particularly clubbable man. His visits to the Athenaeum were rare.

The Archbishop's first Prime Minister was Sir Winston Churchill. Their relations were never close or intimate and the Archbishop must have recognised that his appointment to Lambeth by Churchill was not so much a vote of confidence in him as a vote of no confidence in Bishop Bell – or anyone else. Geoffrey Fisher recalled in these words his first interview with the Prime Minister after becoming Primate:

'Winston Churchill appointed me and I always had very pleasant relations with him, but he obviously really had no interests in common with me and as I said in my little country church (Trent) on his death, he had no very real religion but it was a religion of Englishmen. He had a very real belief in providence but it was God as the God with a special care for the values of the British people. There was nothing obscure about this: it was utterly right, but not at all linked on to the particular religion which bears the name of the Christian faith.'

This testimony suggests a fairly formal relationship and this was almost certainly what it was. Churchill as a historian appreciated the ancient character of the office which Geoffrey Fisher held and its unique place in British history over the centuries but the lack of any real interest by Churchill in the Church of England led to terrible delays in appointments, evoking strongly complaining letters from the Archbishop. They moved in different worlds as was evident in their life-styles and though the twain had of necessity to meet there was no effective cross-fertilization of minds. This did not prevent, however, at least on Geoffrey Fisher's part, exchanges of courtesy. Thus when in 1951 Winston Churchill was recalled to office after his electoral defeat following the Second World War Geoffrey Fisher sent him a letter of congratulations and welcome. 'May I be allowed', he wrote, 'to send a brief message of goodwill to you as you resume chief responsibility for our national affairs, remembering as I do the immense and intractable tasks which confront you, the Nation and the world.' It was impossible to exaggerate, 'how much depends upon the course set for us in the next few years by the government and upon the response which it wins from the people ... may God's blessing be with you and your colleagues to give you wisdom and courage and good success'.

With Clement Attlee, Churchill's successor as Prime Minister in 1945, the Archbishop's relationship was quite different. Though not himself a regular churchgoer – his sister, Mary Attlee, was a missionary in Africa and Mrs Attlee's father a convinced evangelical churchman who conducted open-air services on Hampstead Heath – Geoffrey Fisher admired Attlee's quiet and meticulous efficiency; his deliberate low profile and complete lack of ostentation. Neither affected to indulge any patrician upmanship and their manner of life had much in common. Also without taking sides in the party political game the Archbishop felt himself in general sympathy with the kind of non-doctrinaire, liberal, pragmatic socialism for which Attlee stood and which he sought to implement in the Welfare State during the years immediately after the war. Though the Archbishop was far more ebullient and outgoing they shared a middle-class, public school background. They met fairly frequently and discussed matters of personal and national concern face to face. Geoffrey Fisher writes of him in his 'taped autobiography': 'Attlee was a splendid person to work with. When things occurred he preferred me to go and talk with him directly and that I liked. Everything was dealt with speedily, properly, completely, and I knew exactly where I was with him.' It was a case of 'two of a kind'.

Winston Churchill returned to 10 Downing Street in 1951 to be followed by Sir Anthony Eden five years later. Archbishop Fisher's first encounter, not long after he had gone to Lambeth, with Sir Anthony Eden, was when the latter held the office of Foreign Secretary. Geoffrey Fisher wrote to him explaining that from time to time various matters came to him which were of interest to the Government and concerning which, therefore, he ought to confer with the Foreign Secretary. Among such were, for example, an ecclesiastical scheme in relation to the Falkland Islands; and a proposed division of the Diocese of Egypt and the Sudan. Also he wished, according to a now established custom, to introduce a new Bishop of Gibraltar to the Foreign Secretary, particularly since his diocese ranged from Spain along the southern shore of the Mediterranean, to Turkey, Bulgaria and Romania.

When Sir Anthony Eden became Prime Minister – having waited in the wings far too long owing to Winston Churchill's reluctance to resign – Geoffrey Fisher shared, with many, a national mood of optimism and hope at his taking over. He was known to be liberal in outlook, a good Commonwealth man – not quite so good a European – and a convinced internationalist. What the public did not know was that Eden was already physically unwell and that 'hope deferred' if it had not made the heart grow sick at least had sapped the cutting edge of his judgement and weakened his will. Geoffrey Fisher greeted his arrival with a letter to Downing Street, part of which bears quotation: 'May I now venture to send you a word of greeting and God speed as with your substantial majority you now turn once more to the duties of a new Parliament. I would assure you of my earnest prayer that you may be guided in all the heavy and ceaseless burdens of your office. I count it a great thing that, at this critical moment in history, one with your own great gifts and fine spirit of national unity and progress should be in this responsible office. I just wanted to send you this word of greeting and goodwill.'

However, Anthony Eden's stay in No 10 Downing Street was destined to be relatively brief. Disaster overtook him in the notorious invasion of Egypt in 1956 when, in collusion with the Israelis and the French, military action was taken allegedly to keep the peace but in fact to 'topple' President Nasser who had closed the Suez Canal. No event more brought out the Archbishop's righteous indignation than this irresponsible attack on Egypt. He regarded it as a total denial of Britain's solemn obligations under the Charter of the United Nations.

It fell to the hapless Lord Kilmuir, the Lord Chancellor, to defend the policy of Sir Anthony's Government in the House of Lords and consequently to be at the receiving end of the Archbishop's wrath. Kilmuir's contention was that Britain had gone into Egypt as a fire engine might go to put out a blaze. As he was developing this theme the Archbishop interjected and it is at this point that we can turn to Hansard to take up the story. Its significance may I hope pardon its length.

> '*The Lord Archbishop of Canterbury*: My Lords, the noble and learned Viscount referred to the attacking power against which we have to exercise self-defence. Who is the attacking power?
> *The Lord Chancellor*: My Lords, I said that self-defence extended to the protection of nationals on someone else's territory. In that case we have the right to intervene and use force in that territory to protect our nationals. Then the second point arises – I hope I made this clear; I intended to put it entirely fairly – first we make a peaceful landing; then, if the power into whose territory we are going says that they will resist with all their force, the force which we have the right to use is automatically extended to that sufficient to repulse the force threatened.
> *The Lord Archbishop of Canterbury*: Which is the attacking power in this case?
> *The Lord Chancellor*: In the case I have mentioned the person who threatens to use force in answer to a proferred peaceful intervention.
> *The Lord Archbishop of Canterbury*: Here is the Canal: here are our Nationals; here is our property. There is an attack upon them which you have to resist, who is making the attack?
> *The Lord Chancellor*: I see now. The Most Reverend Primate is asking me a question of fact.
>
> *The Lord Archbishop of Canterbury*: Yes.
> *The Lord Chancellor*: Then I will deal with that. The threat of force is made by the person who refuses to stop the hostile operations that are threatening the people and the installations. I really must be allowed to continue, perhaps after just one more interruption.
> *The Lord Archbishop of Canterbury*: Who is the attacking power in this case?
> *The Lord Chancellor*: I should have thought the Most Reverend Primate might have guessed for himself. It is obviously Egypt who has refused to stop.
> *The Lord Archbishop of Canterbury*: This is terribly important and perhaps I might ask the Lord Chancellor this. Where does the operational force originate? I should have thought that the attacking force, whether you like it or not, was Israel. Is that not so?
> *The Lord Chancellor*: Yes. I explained the law, and I was going to proceed to the facts but in applying that to this case, our Nationals, our ships and the Canal itself are in danger from the conflict between Israel and Egypt. We then, with, I believe, complete moral propriety and rightness, asked them both to stop the conflict which is threatening our

Nationals, our ships and the Canal. The Most Reverend Primate really must not interrupt again.

Several Noble Lords: Order, order!

The Lord Chancellor: The Israelis agreed to stop hostilities and to retire, but Egypt refused and indicated that they would use force to prevent the steps which we proposed for a peaceful stoppage of the fighting. That is the sense in which I used it. Perhaps now the Most Reverend Primate will allow me to continue my speech.

The Archbishop of Canterbury: May I say this? I entirely accept every-thing that the Lord Chancellor has said. I was not criticising it or attacking it. I was merely asking a question: Where did the force originate? That, he says, is Israel; and that is all I want to establish.

A Noble Lord: No; he did not say that.

The Lord Chancellor: The Most Reverend Primate has, I am sure, entirely unintentionally, sought to confuse two situations. There is the first when Israel crossed the border. Then there is the second situation, which I have been at some pains to explain, when the Egyptians refused our peaceful measures. I hope that I have now made that clear.

The Lord Archbishop of Canterbury: I merely said that there are two statements, one and two. You omitted one, I have now inserted one.

The Lord Chancellor: I am always happy to have the co-operation of the Most Reverend Primate in making a speech. I have always said, both in public and privately, that he is one of the best speakers in London, and I am sure that any speech of mine will be greatly improved by his interruptions.'

No one, I suspect, reading today the Lord Chancellor's replies to the Archbishop's questions, would assume, what in fact was the case, that Great Britain, France and Israel had connived together to launch this invasion.

This encounter with Lord Kilmuir lived long in Geoffrey Fisher's memory, not least the comment of Lord Jowett, a former school-mate at Marlborough, and later himself Lord Chancellor. As they left the chamber after the debate, he remarked: 'Well, Fisher, that's one of the best pieces of cross-examination I've ever heard'. The Archbishop, however, had to admit that it was 'pretty brutal'.

This was, perhaps, one of the fiercest attacks on a minister of the Crown ever made in the House of Lords by an Archbishop of Canterbury. It arose from the strength of his feelings and a sense of betrayal. 'I felt', he wrote later 'that they (the British Government) had not only lost a terribly good opportunity of doing the right thing, they had done a ghastly wrong thing.' Geoffrey Fisher was a strong supporter of the United Nations and felt that the intervention of the British Government over Suez was retrogressive and in opposition to the new and hopeful winds of change that were then blowing through the corridors of power. Ever since the end of the Second world War, so he believed, there had once more been kindled an ambition to put an end to force as an instrument of international politics. The United Nations was struggling to become the means of reconciling quarrels but on this occasion Great Britain 'had ignored the United Nations and used force against Egypt ... it seemed to me absolutely frightful'.

The Archbishop himself took part in the debate over the Suez crisis in which he had earlier intervened so decisively. As often happens when great issues of principle are at stake there were many impressive speeches, some contending strongly that the whole issue certainly should have been referred to the United Nations, others that in so critical an emergency it was proper to take immediate and unilateral action. The Archbishop argued strongly that there was no such emergency – indeed quite the reverse – since the Canal was blocked and could not suddenly be re-opened. The right course was to go to the United Nations. The Archbishop suspected, and here he was at one with Her Majesty's Opposition, that the Government might resort again to the use of force and he expressed these fears in a letter to *The Times* on 17 September 1956.

It must be admitted that Geoffrey Fisher later came to regret the virulence in which he attacked the Lord Chancellor though he remained one hundred per cent condemnatory of the Government's policy. Writing to Lord Hailsham, who had reprimanded him on this score, he confessed his sorrow in having intervened in the way that he did. However, he was right to expose the policy of the Government, insisting that the Nation and Commonwealth were 'deeply disturbed and many Christians were unhappy about the manner in which the British Government had discharged its obligations to the United Nations'. His only concern personally was to be a 'peace-maker', pledged to a 'more excellent way'.

At the beginning of 1957, after the shipwreck of Eden's foreign policy in the Suez Canal, Harold Macmillan 'emerged' as Prime Minister, perhaps the last of the patricians, having bypassed and beaten at the post both R. A. Butler and Hailsham. Liberal, cultivated, one of the more progressive Tories, and a 'character', he had served an apprenticeship as Chancellor of the Exchequer in which office many thought that he had done well. Unfortunately, in this capacity, he fell foul of the Archbishop of Canterbury over his Premium Bonds. These were intended to give a boost to the national economy without apparent hurt, since the investor risked only the income on his capital, the latter remaining inviolate.

To the Archbishop this was in fact nothing less than a refined form of gambling, and gambling was a practice against which he had always taken a firm line – even to raffles. The debate on Premium Bonds duly came up in the House of Lords. The Archbishop, as we have seen, could be forthright at times and this was one such occasion. He described the Bill to legalise Premium Bonds as 'squalid' though, as he cynically put it, he was sure the Chancellor of the Exchequer would get his own way. His objection to the Bill fundamentally was that it gave Governmental backing to an irresponsible transfer of wealth – wealth which had not been earned by any contribution to the welfare of society. Also it was not the way for a nation to get out of financial difficulty.

This forthright archiepiscopal condemnation drew forth a protest from Lord Hailsham though he had given no prior notice of his intention to do so. For this grievous omission he made an ample apology expressing the hope that His Grace would 'view with compassion the melancholy spectacle of a penitent Viscount approaching the chair of St Augustine on hands and knees, clad in sackcloth, with ashes on his head and penitential palms in his hands'. To this pleasantry Geoffrey Fisher responded with the olive branch: 'it was worth the error to have an apology in such magnificent words'.

This unhappy clash, however, did not prevent the Archbishop from writing a letter of encouragement to Harold Macmillan as he went to 10 Downing Street. 'I intrude for a moment', he wrote, 'to assure you that my prayers and the prayers of the Church will prevent and follow you as you take up the supreme responsibility at a supremely difficult time. The country, I believe, knows that above all it needs an astringent call to the only things which ever unite people – strict moral discipline and subordination of the sectional to an accepted national purpose. It is terribly hard to get such a call across amid the lunacies and lies of political conflicts. I pray that you and your colleagues may be rightly guided to find the way by God's Providence and your dependence on Him.' In his reply the Prime Minister volunteered that he would welcome an early opportunity of having a talk with the Archbishop, which he did on 25 January 1957. So far as the Archbishop could recall it later in his retirement, this interview lasted half an hour and was most disappointing. 'What astonished me was that he directed it . . . throughout to his time at Oxford as an undergraduate.' He was nostalgic to a degree and confessed to being at that time interested in theology.

This story is revealing and the assumption can only be that the Prime Minister was determined at all costs not to talk about current political issues with the Archbishop or to find what his mind on them was. A more fruitful interview however, though its scope was minimal, took place when the Archbishop, as chairman of the Trustees of the British Museum, went to Downing Street in order to press upon the Prime Minister the absolute necessity of getting on with the new building programme. The scheme had been approved in principle and the property had been bought, but there was no architect, no plan and nothing was moving. With his usual thoroughness the Archbishop sent in advance a memorandum which he had drawn up on this scheme for the benefit of the Prime Minister, the Minister of Works and the Chancellor of the Exchequer. The Prime Minister's opening gambit, as Geoffrey Fisher recalled it, was as follows: 'Archbishop, isn't it true that the British Museum has to receive a copy of every work published?' After a reply in the affirmative he went on: 'Well, I'm a book-seller and I think that is the most awful nonsense and waste of time and it ought to be altered'. The Archbishop instantly retorted that the Trustees would 'strongly resist any attempt to remove this privilege'.

The Prime Minister then turned to discuss with the Archbishop the constitution and the general set-up of the British Museum. It was a matter on which he had very strong feelings. The three *ex officio* members of the committee which controlled its affairs were the Archbishop as the Principal Trustee, the Lord Chancellor and the Speaker of the House of Commons. For the Archbishop this was an exacting commitment since he was already over-busy; but he gave himself to it without stint and regularly chaired its meetings. An additional difficulty, not unpredictable, was endeavouring to persuade the Treasury to release adequate funds.

Thus the Archbishop thought that a new way of handling its business should be considered. In this respect he and the Prime Minister were of a common mind though the Archbishop came away from the interview half convinced, though almost certainly wrongly, that the Prime Minister wished to replace him by somebody else. Indeed on his retirement, Lord Crawford complimented the Archbishop on being an excellent chairman and giving everybody full opportunity of having his say. In fact the Archbishop greatly enjoyed his Museum connection as it called upon his administrative skills.

The most serious clash in which Archbishop and Prime Minister engaged arose out of a remark by the latter at a public meeting, when he reassured his audience with the words: 'You've never had it so good'. The Archbishop was shocked and in an address in Croydon Parish Church on 11 January 1960 he referred to this utterance as follows: 'The Church today lives perhaps in a time of England's greatest peril. We have fought for freedom, we have suffered and sacrificed for freedom. But having won freedom our peril now is that we may forget what it is for, and, becoming tolerant, we may become traitors to truth. There is a dreadful current phrase – it is indeed dreadful – "We've never had it so good". Whenever I hear it I say to myself in the words of Our Lord "How hardly shall they that have riches enter into the Kingdom of Heaven"? R. A. Butler rallied to the defence of the Prime Minister in a speech in his constituency at Saffron

Walden. Would his Grace the Archbishop of Canterbury, he asked, prefer the Prime Minister to say 'you've never had it so bad'?

More important than these comments was a magisterial and very long reply by the Prime Minister himself to the Archbishop, which merits a short quotation. 'I observe that preaching at Croydon Parish Church you commented on a phrase which I once used about conditions in Britain – 'They've never had it so good'. Of course I have always added to this that we must try to keep it good and that this requires both a moral and intellectual steadfastness. I also share your view as a churchman that the material condition of a people must by no means be the only criterion. Unless it has the spiritual values it will fail. Nevertheless, it is the function of Governments to try and improve material conditions and I have always thought that the Church supported us in this effort. The attack on poverty, the attempts to clear the slums, to deal with low wages, to remove unemployment, all these were always impressed upon me by your great predecessor, Dr Temple, as truly Christian duties.'

It was of course imperative for Geoffrey Fisher to respond to the Prime Minister and this he did in a short letter dated 28 January 1960: 'The parentage of slogans', he began, 'is quickly forgotten.' He himself was unaware that the slogan had any political implications whatsoever, or that it presupposed a general judgement on the contemporary political situation. However he still believed that the quotation was 'often used to justify a smug contentment which ignores the perils of our own situation'.

This was indeed a most unfortunate controversy, and Geoffrey Fisher's reply not very adequate. There can be no question but that he had a point, and one can well understand his reaction to the kind of complacency which the phrase seemed to suggest. That the Prime Minister should have taken Geoffrey Fisher's words so seriously may well reflect something about the relationship between the two. Perhaps some may feel that both protagonists were ultimately right but that Macmillan came better out of the immediate argument.

CHAPTER 32

The Media – Press, Radio and Television

(i)

The Press

GEOFFREY Fisher recognised the need for the Church of England to communicate with the general public and he saw this as integral to the proclamation of the Gospel. He further realised that this could only be achieved by careful planning. It would not happen by accident. On the other hand an official ecclesiastical press establishment could never alter the simple fact that so far as concerned journalists they would always wish to go for news to the fountain head, that is to Lambeth. It was here in his early years that the Archbishop ran into difficulty.

In the middle years of the 19th century it was hardly felt necessary to stimulate the Church to communicate effectively with the public. Among the 'top' newspapers religious controversy was still hot news and the correspondence column in *The Times*, with its magisterial leading articles, was read with avidity. Even printed sermons attracted a readership! This interest, however, had passed its peak as the Victorian era gave way to the Edwardian but the Church was slow to realize that it must take a more positive attitude where the dissemination of news about itself was concerned. It first began to attempt this when before the outbreak of the Second World War it set up a Church Information Board which remained active throughout the subsequent hostilities. Its function was to answer questions put to it and to send out news items relevant to the Church's involvement in, and attitude towards, a nation at war. In peacetime more than 1,000 enquiries were dealt with each year at the bureau and even during the war years they ran into hundreds. Significant in this respect, since it stressed the need to take the *media* seriously, was the report: *Towards the Conversion of England*. Equally this was the case with the *Commission on Evangelism* which met under the chairmanship of Bishop Chavasse of Rochester. These advocated a large publicity campaign deploying, where possible, the use of press, radio and television. These proposals were referred to the Publicity Commission on which there served Sir Kenneth Grubb and Paul Williams. The Government also set up the Ministry of Information to handle the dissemination of news during the war years on which, representing the Church of England, was the Reverend Ronald Williams, later Bishop of Leicester. It has to be admitted that when Dr Fisher first arrived at Lambeth relations with the Press did not present themselves as a high priority. Indeed Geoffrey

Fisher tells us that among the first things he did was to cancel his predecessor's subscription to a press cutting agency. 'To look at them,' he commented, 'would only cause me annoyance and irritation and anger and do no good: so I abjured them and I am glad.' He was later to learn how mistaken he was!

But Dr Fisher was to learn the hard way as is evidenced in a document he wrote *Publicity, 1947*. In this he welcomed the proposal: that the Society for Promoting Christian Knowledge should become the Church's publishing agent, along with the appointment of a new officer in charge of publicity answerable to the Church Assembly. His salary, the Archbishop suggested, ought to be commensurate with his wide-ranging responsibilities and his professional status.

The Archbishop was only too conscious of the financial implications of these proposals and the built-in reluctance of the Church Assembly to provide adequate funds for what some members saw, rightly or wrongly, as a growing bureaucracy.

Thus, Geoffrey Fisher, in spite of sustained efforts – he even offered office accommodation gratis at Lambeth – was forced reluctantly to accept that money to implement what he wished was not forthcoming. The Archbishop was by no means the only person who regretted the cautious, if not hostile, attitude of the Church Assembly, and its reluctance to furnish the Church with a plant which was 'well organised and efficient'. To try to secure this on the cheap was counter-productive. The result was that, for the time being at least, the present unsatisfactory situation, with no experienced press relations officer at Lambeth, continued.

We have suggested earlier that so far as the popular papers were concerned it was the Archbishop to whom journalists wished to put their enquiries rather than to a commission or official bureau. This placed the Archbishop in an invidious position such as could lead to near disaster. Too often the image which was uncritically presented by the Press to the public was exclusively that of a moral censor of the nation. Archbishop Fisher, on his own admission, certainly ran into difficulties with Fleet Street during his early days at Lambeth. There was a particular reason for this. Often, during the evenings, the Archbishop might be alone in the Palace, his chaplains having gone home, and would as a consequence himself answer the telephone. By temperament naturally open and talkative he was sometimes, as they say, 'taken for a ride', which subsequently led to irritation and embarrassment.

The Reverent Cyril Armitage, Rector of St Bride's, who was sensitive to the heartbeat of the press, was convinced from his own observations and that of others who were habitués of the Press Club, that the image which most journalists had of the Archbishop was a 'quite one-sided one'. They knew him only in his official capacity and as a critic of their activities; they were, unfortunately, entirely unaware of another Geoffrey Fisher, human and approachable. He was, therefore, anxious that Dr Fisher should come along informally with no set agenda, perhaps quite unannounced, to the Press Club as his personal guest.

Dr Fisher responded enthusiastically but felt that an 'ad hoc' visit, as the Rector of St Bride's contemplated, was not really appropriate and that it would be better if he responded to a formal invitation. Armitage was delighted with this acceptance and expressed the hope that it would dispel for ever the image which the Archbishop had unhappily acquired. An objective but by no means unfavourable account of this Press Club encounter appeared in *The Observer* part of which well deserves a mention. The Archbishop, it reports, gave a 'brilliant performance of how to deal with questions of every imaginable kind. Far abler than most politicians, even of the first rank, he showed not only the worldly wisdom of a Prince of the Church but also the wit, charm and "know-how" of the successful public school headmaster'. Clearly Dr Fisher was not to be taken lightly; but a note of criticism, implying that he was too slick and polished then creeps in. 'He knows just how to give adroit answers that snuff out his questioner.'

Cyril Armitage, as befitted his temperament, gives a more dramatic and less favourable account of what happened. After forty minutes or so answering questions, he as an Anglican felt immensely proud of the Archbishop. Then, to quote the *ipsissima verba* of the Rector, there was a pause while he put elbows on the table, looked round the room at every face there, and remarked: 'Well, the headmaster is waiting, has the sixth form nothing more to say?' 'The legend of the headmaster had been well and truly launched' – so the Rector comments.

Too much ought not to be made of this latter incident, and one suspects that had the journalists looked more closely at the Archbishop they would have detected a twinkle in his eye. However, there were certainly occasions when Geoffrey Fisher could appear too self-assured and maybe this was one of them. Some journalists present remembered, in contrast, how Pope John XXIII, when first confronted by the Press remarked: 'I am sorry if I am a little awkward. I am a simple man.'

Archbishop Fisher, it must be admitted, was for most of his life critical of the general tenor of the media, in particular Fleet Street. In a letter to Bernard Pawley, then Rector of Elland and later to advise the Archbishop on Roman Catholic affairs, Geoffrey Fisher gave vent to his feelings in these words:

'It is a good thing for people to distrust what they see in the press and still more to distrust entirely the headline. It is, I am afraid, true that they are quite unscrupulous in turning things to suit themselves . . . I say the press, but it is only some papers which greatly offend in this way. I do not think a frontal attack on the press would do much good, but if some opportunity of talking to editors presents itself I shall use it.'

This attack on a section of the Press – it was, of course, written in a private letter – was by no means entirely off the mark, if exaggerated. Thus in February 1954 the industry decided to put its own house in order and a Press Council to maintain professional standards was set up to which appeal could be made by ordinary members of the public who felt themselves aggrieved. The Archbishop immediately wrote warmly to its secretary, A. P. Robbins, and as an example of the need for it instanced recent articles concerning three people who had been released from prison. His words are worth quoting:

'Anything that frustrates the bringing back into good citizenship the life of these unfortunate people is to be deplored, and I have no doubt that publicity often destroys the very work which the prisons themselves and the community are trying to do for these women and girls.'

This letter was certainly taken seriously as was also the archiepiscopal protest against the exploitation of condemned murderers awaiting execution as, in particular, Mrs Ruth Ellis.

Though the Archbishop often appeared before the public as a critic of the media he yet, as he became increasingly knowledgeable, endeavoured to be more objective. This may be seen in an address given to the Press Gallery Luncheon Club which was both frank and in a sense helpful though it most certainly did not escape criticism. In the course of his talk he complained that some sections of the Press deliberately set out to undermine the authority of the Church, largely because the latter took a particular stand, for example, on divorce.

Such charges, publicly uttered and widely reported, could not be expected to pass unnoticed. *The Manchester Guardian* and the *Daily Express* replied vigorously to these accusations. Also Brian Roberts, Chief of the Executive Committee of the Clerical Institute of Journalists, felt it incumbent on him to write to *The Times*. The Archbishop's criticisms, he observed somewhat acidly, displayed a 'fundamentally erroneous view of the functions of the Press in a free society'. Its duty was not to campaign for any cause but 'to hold up a mirror to the whole range of human activity, to reflect not only the values but the frailties of man'.

For a person so obviously moralistically orientated it was not easy for such as Dr Fisher to respond wholeheartedly to the principles which informed Brian Roberts' comment. In a sense both of them, from their different angles, were saying something important for there can be no pure objectivity in the selection and handling of news items. Value judgements must inevitably creep in. To make his point the more clear the Archbishop, in a personal reply to Brian Roberts, listed a number of specific instances of what he deplored. These included a report in the *News Chronicle* of a marriage in Lambeth Chapel which called attention to his having kissed two of the bridesmaids!

Mr Roberts came back at the Archbishop admitting that, of course, there were black sheep in every fold and sad lapses from good taste obviously occurred, but restraint could go too far. For example, the conspiracy of silence in which the Press co-operated before the Abdication of Edward VIII proved, in its effects, unfortunate since it contributed to making the sudden crisis, when it broke, much more difficult to handle.

The Press Council was not unaware that there was substance in some of the charges which the Archbishop and others levelled against certain sections of the news media. Thus its General Council issued a statement at the end of March 1960 in which it confessed, in relation to the exploitation of sex, that three Sunday newspapers had allowed their reporting to be 'debased to a level which is a disgrace to British journalism'.

The Archbishop's views on some newspapers and journalists were certainly shared by many ordinary and unpretentious members of the public. In a debate in the House of Lords, Geoffrey Fisher spoke at some length, having carefully prepared his brief with the assistance of Colonel Hornby whom he had recently appointed Press Officer. The general tenor of what he said was appreciative, generous yet critical. Thus he was careful to point out that he entertained a high regard for Fleet Street and the members of the journalistic profession, most of whom were 'friendly, alert, right-minded, sensible and competent people'.

Yet often the Press was guilty of serious offences against the ordinary canons of good judgement which gave proprietors 'a reputation for insincerity, indifference to truth, irresponsibility – and worse, which it in no way deserved'. Fairness made him say that where these appeared to exist often they were due to the 'merciless demands of speed and circulation in a highly competitive field'. What mattered was that those engaged in the media should consider how abuses were to be prevented. Certainly they could not be eliminated by tampering with the freedom of the Press thereby denying to journalists the right to speak freely of religion and of truth, the hallmarks of a civilised society. Maybe every profession needs the equivalent of the doctors' Hippocratic oath. The owners of newspapers should voluntarily accept right standards, though finally immediate responsibility must rest with the editors.

The Archbishop was gratified in that this speech in the Lords was given – it was by no means always the case – a very appreciative reception; and this was equally true of the subsequent press coverage. Indeed *The Yorkshire Post* suggested that the debate in the Lords might do some good, mainly because of the Archbishop's fair-minded and illuminating contribution. *The Daily Sketch* headed its report: 'The Best Press – says the Archbishop' and the *Daily Express* commented: 'Freedom's The Hallmark says Dr Fisher.' H. S. Taylor, churchwarden of St Bride's, Fleet Street, and a lifelong working journalist, recorded that the Archbishop 'focused on a limited area and made a most impressive contribution'.

The reference in the Archbishop's speech to the role of the editors seemed likely to lead to some practical results. Linton Andrews of *The Yorkshire Post* followed it up by suggesting that editors should seek by discussion among themselves to develop an accepted 'wisdom of journalistic morals and manners'. Dr Fisher took the initiative by inviting a number of London editors to Lambeth to dine together and to converse with one another. He did this, he explained, because unless he himself acted nothing was likely to happen. The silence of the records which remain at Lambeth does not encourage us to believe that much came of this archiepiscopal initiative.

The irritation which on occasion the Press evoked in Dr Fisher, and to which, maybe, he too often gave public expression, was in itself a negative recognition of the power and influence of this media. The most persuasive influence in helping the Archbishop to adopt a different approach was Colonel Robert Hornby whom be appointed his Press Officer in 1960. The Colonel had extensive experience of the Press at first hand and in this area was a professional of high skill. His first act was to lay on a monthly analysis of the Press coverage of Church affairs, the cuttings being divided into three categories – fair, neutral and adverse. The Archbishop was the first to admit how valuable this categorisation was and in an appreciative letter he wrote: 'It is a great comfort to me that this kind of analysis of Press notices is going on all the time and I shall rest secure in the knowledge that when anything *ought* to be brought to my notice it certainly would be.'

It was his new Press Officer who helped to make the Archbishop understand that relations with journalists should not be seen negatively in terms of keeping an eye on them. Rather the Church must ask itself what image it wished to project to the nation and how this could be best secured.

Geoffrey Fisher was not only concerned with the daily press. He was particularly vigilant where one ecclesiastical paper was concerned – namely the *Church Times*, which he regarded as too exclusively linked up with one wing of the Church of England. 'While nobody would wish the *Church Times* to alter its general ecclesiastical allegiance', so the Archbishop wrote to a member of the Board of Management, that he 'often desired that on the one side it should be less petulant and partisan and on the other side that it should attempt what it does not often attempt now, to give a less limited picture of the various activities and movements, official and unofficial, of the Church of England.' In this exchange of letters the Archbishop sought to suggest a working compromise between the responsibility of the *Church Times* to the Church of England as a whole and to the High Church Anglican tradition within it. This problem was never resolved to Geoffrey Fisher's (or to others) satisfaction, hence the many letters he sent to succeeding editors. Typical among these was his serious complaint at the handling in July 1948 of the Lambeth Conference when 320 bishops from all over the world assembled in St Paul's Cathedral in a great service. The *Church Times*, he complained, 'totally and absolutely ignored it.' This he considered an insult to all concerned, not least to the Presiding Bishop of the Protestant Episcopal Church in the United States.

The Archbishop and the new editor, Miss Rosamond Essex, a daughter of the manse, had a long session together at Lambeth when they discussed their mutual concerns with complete freedom and the Archbishop described her as 'very honest, serious and reliable'. She volunteered that she wished to make the *Church Times* 'sane and really approximate to central' particularly in relation to the united Church of South India.

The exigencies of space do not make possible reference to many letters which, periodically, passed from Lambeth to the editorial desk of the *Church Times* – and vice versa. These are often psychologically revealing. 'You kindly allow me now and again to call you to account for your actions', he wrote to Miss Essex in avuncular mood, eliciting the charming reply: 'The *Church Times* always receives Your Grace's animadversions with respect'. *Amour-propre* was sometimes involved. Thus Mr Palmer and Miss Essex protested against the exclusion of the religious press – the secular press was there in full force – when the Royal Family went to Lambeth Palace for the re-dedication of the ancient Chapel, blitzed during the war. Understandably they were not mollified by the somewhat lame excuse namely that Dr Jay, the Archbishop's senior chaplain, was present representing the Press.

Yet these occasional tensions were all forgotten (perhaps not quite!) when the *Church Times* celebrated its 5,000th issue and the Archbishop sent it the following congratulatory message: 'The *Church Times* deals with the most indispensable and most dangerous of all commodities – words. No doubt over all its 5,000 issues much has been said well and not a little said, whether in manner or substance less well. All of us who have to deal professionally with words will sympathise with and applaud the *Church Times*. Certainly as I have come to observe the pages, I have been delighted to see much growth in the wisdom, maturity and grace of its utterances and reporting. It plays an indispensable part in the public life of the Church of England and I send this message of gratitude and confident expectation of good things to come which is not the least part of the gratitude.'

Perhaps these congratulations gained from the fact that a soft note of critical realism has crept in.

The *Church Times* was not the only religious weekly produced for the Church of England readers. The ethos of another church paper, *The Guardian*,* was liberal and middle of the road – and perhaps that was why it went out of business! In 1951 things came to a crisis financially and *The Guardian* died, testifying thereby that liberalism within the Church of England was not organised into a party with a defined clientèle.

As to the evangelical *Church of England Newspaper* the editor, during Geoffrey Fisher's stay at Lambeth, was the forceful and dynamic Reverend Clifford Rhodes who was an extreme radical and for a time Secretary of the Modern Churchmen's Union. Relations between Archbishop Fisher and the Editor were never easy and the former regarded the CEN as often 'perverse and misleading'.

(ii)
Radio and Television

Although Archbishop Fisher confessed on more than one occasion that he, personally, had little time to give to radio or television he could by no means be indifferent to these new and important media. Quite the reverse. Not only did he himself give numerous broadcasts, but he was concerned with the general deployment of this means of communication, in particular how the Church itself should use it. One of the side-effects of radio and television has been uniquely to bring the Archbishop into millions of homes as never before. The Primate of All England, hitherto a somewhat shadowy figure for most citizens, was now recognisable in the flesh and seen, for better or for worse, as a spokesman for the Church of England.

The facilities of radio and television were readily available to Geoffrey Fisher and there were certain fixed points in the year of which he took advantage as, for example, to give New Year and Easter messages for listeners both in the United Kingdom and overseas. These, though 'burdensome' – yet less so when they were delivered from his own home – he thought had a 'real advantage'. Royal occasions, not least the Coronation and interviews such as those with Richard Dimbleby brought him before the British public. At the same time he recognised that too frequent exposure could lead to diminishing

* Not to be confused with *The Manchester Guardian* now known as *The Guardian*.

returns. 'Give me excess of it, that, surfeiting, The appetite may sicken, and so die.'

The Archbishop developed a fairly clear idea as to how one in his office ought to conduct himself on the media and the limitation which this imposed upon him. In a letter to Mackowsky of the BBC he thus set out his own priorities: 'As Archbishop I am in a queer position: it is in general my duty to speak for the Church or at least to the best of my ability to express the mind of the Church. If I speak on television, I should inevitably be speaking in some sense *ex cathedra* and yet under conditions which could reduce anything I said to the level of ordinary discussion with pros and cons and making out a better case or a worse case. I fear that I could only appear in a television programme of any kind if it was a quite clear matter of standing both outside and above the ordinary run of controversial discussions in which I was fully and officially declaring the mind of the Church on some important topic.'

The Archbishop was not a charismatic character who compelled attention nor did he wish to be such; but he usually expressed himself well and spoke good sense whether it was acceptable or not. His general appearance on television was businesslike and his voice first class. On occasions he could be unpredictable and a little unnerving to an interviewer as, for example, to Kenneth Harris in the following exchange concerning the Archbishop on holiday: KH:'What do you like doing?' GF:'I was asked that in Scotland last year and I said, "nothing".' KH:'Really, what do you do, fishing?' GF:'No.' KH:'What do you do then, shooting?' GF:'No.' KH:'What *do* you do?' GF:'Nothing. The great joy is I don't have to talk to anybody.'

In contrast with the irritation which he sometimes felt when dealing with the Press the Archbishop thought that on the whole the BBC was doing a good job. This may be seen in his response to a letter sent to him by Captain C. H. Roleston, General Secretary of the Listeners' Association, who enclosed a far from objective document: *The case against the BBC*. In this polemic it was maintained that the Corporation had pursued a constant policy of advocating Communism and of trying to disrupt the life of this country. The Association thus sought support from the Archbishop for calling upon the Government to set up a commission of enquiry. In spite of the extremism of the Association's views Geoffrey Fisher felt that he must take the request seriously which he did in a fairly lengthy reply. The BBC, he told the Captain, does try to discharge fairly a very difficult role. Indeed he had as often heard it accused of being unduly conservative as of being favourable to the left. Equally he had met people who accused the Corporation of giving too much prominence to Christianity and others who protested that it gave far too little. Thus he could not possibly sign any resolution urging the Government to set up a commission of enquiry.

Archbishop Fisher was always careful, no matter by whom pressurized, not to associate his office with complaints unless he felt he could conscientiously do so. Thus when Alexander Comfort, a well-known humanist, gave a series of talks on the theme: 'The Pattern of the Future' and Sir Waldron Smithers MP sent to Lambeth a violent protest — 'You are the Head of the Church Militant and it is about time that someone took these Communists by the scruff of the neck and drove them with scourges out of the temple', his reply was to the point. After admitting that he had heard none of the talks, he enlightened Waldron Smithers as to BBC policy of which he approved. 'There is, as you know,' he wrote, 'a large body of opinion in the Universities and elsewhere which does find Christian doctrine unacceptable on the grounds of reason. The BBC's policy is that this body of opinion should have a right to express itself through the BBC, and so long as it is reasonably done I do not think that we can quarrel with this decision.'

On this position, restrained but coming down on the side of a tolerating liberty, Geoffrey Fisher stood his ground firmly. He took the same line with protesters to talks by Mrs Margaret Knight, the humanist.

Geoffrey Fisher received at Lambeth an avalanche of complaints that Roman Catholics were getting more than their fair share of available broadcasting time. Dr Fisher believed in 'a just balance between the denominations' and wisely sent such complaints to Francis House, Head of Religious Broadcasting. House very sensibly responded by giving Dr Fisher a purely objective statement which effectively disposed of the charges simply by showing that they were not true. There was, so he reassured Lambeth, no change in policy at all in favour of Roman Catholics.

House was indeed wise in letting the facts speak for themselves. It is somewhat ironic that not a few members of the Roman Catholic community entertained a diametrically contrary view complaining that in their allocation they got rather a raw deal, a view which the hierarchy put forcefully to the Beveridge Committee on Broadcasting set up in 1950. This area was a sensitive one though on the whole Dr Fisher believed allocations to the respective denominations to be equitable.

The overall approval of the way in which the BBC discharged its duties did not prevent Geoffrey Fisher bringing to the notice of its authorities either his own criticisms or those of others sent to him. He was himself particularly distressed when the commentator at Queen Mary's funeral in March 1953 used the phrase 'Queen Mary will go on her last journey to Westminster Hall'. Such a form of words, and there were others like it, struck him as wholly out of place in identifying the deceased with her mortal remains. Language like this was 'quite intolerable to a Christian and equally absurd to those who don't believe'. Hence he took the matter up with the chairman of the BBC who agreed that the language was 'offensive' and 'due to thoughtlessness'.

Radio and television were new media and though there were some 'naturals' who took to them like a duck to water these were few and far between. Most people needed to learn how best to use these new facilities. Geoffrey Fisher was amongst those who believed that if clergy were to be effective they needed training. To do something about this Roy McKay, when Head of Religious Broadcasting, saw the Archbishop in November 1956 pointing out that this new medium could be of great service to the Church but so far nothing had been done actively to promote this. On the other hand the Roman Catholics had already set up a training centre for this purpose.

How to use radio and television to this end provoked considerable discussion. Many people tended to believe that the general tone of broadcasting was more important in this context than what went over in the specifically Christian slots. On the whole the Archbishop felt that the BBC did well though on occasions he could be critical of the religious programmes both as to content but more frequently to the personnel who put them over. Sometimes he thought that both BBC and ITV abused their independence in their choice of broadcasters. Writing to the Reverend F. R. Coleman, General Secretary of the Church Union, he instanced F. A. Cockin, Bishop of Bristol, and William Greer, Bishop of Manchester, as 'excellent' broadcasters but complained of others as 'agnostic' or 'rendered unsuitable by their mannerisms or sheer ignorance'. These were *ad hoc* remarks in a private letter but they do reflect a measure of unease and remind us a little of the phrase he too often used of 'rocking the boat'. To parade doubts and hesitations on a Christian programme publicly to so vast an audience was, he thought, probably not good. It was better to occupy a liberal central ground.

In February 1958 Captain Brownrigg of Associated Rediffusion suggested that broadcasting needed a Christian bias and to ensure this he approached the Reverend Mervyn Charles-Edwards, a well known vicar of St Martin-in-the-Fields, later Bishop of Worcester, to become adviser to the company. He accepted but recognised that someone with more time to undertake this responsibility was needed. Would it be possible, he asked the Archbishop, for an incumbent and his church to be set aside for this purpose? The Archbishop brought this important matter before the Bishops' Meeting. Also he drew up a memorandum on 'Television Training', suggesting an arrangement by which clergymen wishing to appear on TV in general programmes could get some kind of official approval of their competence. In addition ought the

Church to start some training centre for TV and radio to which clergy could go?

Many people were beginning to think this way, and Howard Thomas, Managing Director of ABC Television, informed the Archbishop that he was in process of preparing a scheme for training clergy and he, therefore, asked the Archbishop to give it his blessing by appointing two representatives to assist with this project, along with nominees from other denominations. Dr Fisher replied complimenting him on an excellent scheme and the 'admirable purpose of his arrangements'. Cockin, chairman of CRAC was equally impressed remarking that the independent companies seemed to show more initiative than the BBC, probably because they were not so restricted financially. However, not much seems to have come from this particular initiative though, maybe, it helped to inspire the Church of England Broadcasting and Television Training Council.

If the Archbishop sometimes complained to the BBC it was fair game when this, on occasions, happened in reverse and some remark emanating from Lambeth was felt to be prejudicial to the Corporation. This happened in connection with the work of the BBC's School Broadcasting Council which hoped to pioneer the resources of this new medium to supplement teaching in the classroom. In March 1952, Dr Fisher was reported in *The Times* as being critical of this new development on the grounds that it was 'anti-social', and particularly likely to come in between the teacher and the pupils. So seriously did the BBC take this somewhat mild expression of opinion that Sir William Haley, the Director-General, got into touch with the Archbishop stressing that it was just because of this danger that the BBC had made it plain that everything it did in school broadcasting must be carefully considered and guided by its School Broadcasting Council.

It is necessary at this point to refer to the constitutional status of the British Broadcasting Corporation which by Act of Parliament replaced the British Broadcasting Company. Subject to this Act, and within its terms, the British Broadcasting Corporation was an independent body charged with the responsibility of putting on programmes, determining their character and participants. To give advice in this delicate and sensitive area the Governors had earlier set up a Central Religious Advisory Committee (CRAC) the membership of which was drawn from the various denominations. This Committee had no mandatory authority but, as its designation suggests, was advisory to the professional full-time staff in the Religious Broadcasting Department to whom it was a useful sounding-board, though its members often served to cancel each other out when it came to making positive recommendations – a situation, one suspects, not entirely unwelcome to the professionals on the BBC staff. It should be noticed that all those, clerical and lay, working in the Religious Broadcasting Department were employed directly by the BBC Governors.

This statutory independence was cherished by the BBC and not least by those who served in the Religious Department. Geoffrey Fisher, though he never admitted this in public, was not happy with, and often found frustrating, the 'island' status or independence of the BBC. His only way of dealing with this situation was to cultivate co-operative relations with the Director-General and the Head of Religious Broadcasting. Here his influence must in part depend on his own tact, restraint and sensitivity to the constitutional position; also on the respective character and temperament of the Director-General and the Head of Religious Broadcasting.

Many were the letters exchanged between the Director-General and Lambeth, the general tenor of which strikes one as co-operative on both sides. The Archbishop realised that the office of Director-General was a difficult assignment and that he, no more than himself as Archbishop, had a free hand. What can be said is that a letter from Lambeth was always taken seriously at Broadcasting House.

Perhaps from the Archbishop's point of view the more immediately important was the Head of Religious Broadcasting Department. The most effective way of exerting influence, except when the Archbishop felt a matter to be so important that he must go immediately to the Director-General, was to keep in close personal contact with this 'number one', who was not expected to be a charismatic character or even a compulsive broadcaster. Indeed the policy of the BBC, after its experience of W. H. Elliot who became almost an unofficial radio padre in pre-war days, was not to repeat this situation. True, an attempt was made to do so but the experiment did not last long. The Head of Religious Broadcasting Department of the BBC was expected to be the kind of person who could survey the field of religious broadcasting as a whole, be ecumenical in his outlook, be in touch with national religious opinion and be capable of heading up a team and keeping it happy. Of the two Heads of Religious Broadcasting during his archiepiscopate it was, perhaps, Francis House who had closest links with the Archbishop. For the BBC it remained a permanent problem how to handle 'hot' controversial religious issues especially those domestic to the Church of England. Thus in February 1949 Francis House sought the Archbishop's advice concerning the *contretemps* which centred around Bishop Barnes of Birmingham and his book *The Rise of Christianity*. The situation was complicated but the Archbishop was confident that Francis House would wish to 'represent different points of view'.

The Festival of Britain in 1951 was a great opportunity for radio and television to boost a national morale which had slumped somewhat since the end of the War. On 16 February Francis House wrote to the Archbishop outlining his plans for the first Sunday of the Festival. Geoffrey Fisher's response was immediate, namely that the programme as suggested was 'quite impossible' since the middle of the morning was to be occupied with a high mass in Westminster Cathedral, while immediately preceding this service the Archbishop of Canterbury and the Moderators of the Church of Scotland and the Free Church Federal Council were to participate in an act of worship lasting three-quarters of an hour. The main service ought, in the Archbishop's view, to be broadcast from an Anglican cathedral with a suitable sermon, while the Church of Scotland should have a service on its own, and the Roman Catholics should fit into this arrangement.

Francis House's rejoinder was an apology for not giving the Archbishop a complete picture of the programme, having confined himself to what was to take place on the first Sunday. In fact on 3 May there was to be an opening service in St Paul's Cathedral, as well as Anglican services of dedication in the Festival Hall, and a sung celebration of Holy Communion from John Keble Church, Mill Hill.

The Archbishop's reply to this mollifyng letter is interesting enough to be quoted more or less in full: 'I am sorry to be a nuisance and to add difficulties to your job which is difficult enough anyhow. Your approach is quite legitimate but I am bound to consider my own approach. One cannot expect the ordinary person "to look before and after" to see whether in the general layout the balance is preserved. Sunday stands on its own feet . . . in fact a considerable number of people, I am sure, will simply jump to the conclusion that Rome has been given a show of her own while the Church of England, the Church of Scotland and the Free Churches have a combined show . . . Of course I ought not to be telling you how to arrange your programmes'. Fortunately they knew and understood each other well and House was sensitive to the Archbishop's point of view and conformed to his wishes.

On 30 September 1953 the Reverend Francis House, who in all served the BBC as Director of Religious Broadcasting for some ten years, had a long talk with the Archbishop at Lambeth as to his own future, since he intended to quit the BBC in 1955 (he did in fact become Associate General Secretry of the World Council of Churches). They then turned to discuss his successor at the BBC though the Archbishop admitted that ideally he would have wished House to stay longer. As to the new appointment thus made necessary it is clear that Sir Ian Jacob, the Director-General, while quite prepared to seek the Archbishop's advice, would not allow the nomination to be taken over by Lambeth. The appointment was the responsibility of the BBC Governors and he intended that this should effectively be the case. Consultation and conferring, yes: nomination, no!

On 5 January 1954 Sir Ian Jacob informed the Archbishop that as soon as they had made up their own mind as to the kind of person and qualifications they were looking for he would welcome the opportunity of discussing the whole matter with the Archbishop. Sir Ian went on to say that House's view was that his successor ought to be a 'policy' rather than a 'programme' man. Also churchpeople needed to reckon with the advent of competitive television.

The effect of this letter was to encourage the Archbishop immediately to consult widely. The Bishop of Bristol, chairman of CRAC, came up with a list of some nine possibilities which, added to lists drawn up by Dr Fisher and Sir Ian Jacob, came to no less than the astronomical number of some fifty-three names. On 16 March 1954, Archbishop Fisher met Sir Ian in company with Mr Grisewood of the Corporation. They got down to business straightaway ending up with a short list of four, the order of preference being an archdeacon, a London parish priest, the warden of a college, and the secretary of a church council. On 22 July, the Archbishop wrote a long letter to Sir Ian giving his own personal estimate of the four names put forward, all of whom he described as in the 'alpha class'. So the process went on, Sir Ian interviewing and reporting back to Lambeth with some shrewd comments. One candidate he found 'impressive, in fact too much so'. Another was the 'wrong sort of person' for this particular post and, therefore likely to prove 'a fish out of water'. The other two, in turn, were offered the post but both declined it, one in spite of considerable pressure from the Archbishop.

These refusals meant that they were back to square one so that the whole process of decision making had to begin all over again. The Archbishop now came up with the name of a distinguished incumbent in Bristol of left wing views who, he wrote to Sir Ian, was 'head and shoulders above anybody who has yet been mentioned'. However, Sir Ian elected to play for safety – the vicar was a controversial character – and the Governors decided to look elsewhere. The Archbishop was not pleased and described this decision regarding the rejected candidate as 'pusillanimous and stupid'. At the same time he protested to Sir Ian that he would not be able to find as good a man in his place and he would like to have a word about his being an 'individualist'.

It seemed as if this process of selection and rejection was to go on interminably but finally there was appointed one whose name had hitherto not been mentioned, namely Roy McKay, chaplain of Canford School and earlier a parish priest of considerable experience in three livings. This proved an excellent choice and he held the post from 1955 to 1963. There is here a paucity of manuscript evidence but it seems reasonably certain that the choice did not come up initially through Geoffrey Fisher but was suggestd by Dr Bell, Bishop of Chichester.

With Sir Hugh Carleton Green, Director of News and Current Affairs (1958–1959) and Director-General (1960–1969) Geoffrey Fisher's relations were not so easy as with Sir Ian Jacob, though by the time that Sir Hugh was firmly in the saddle Dr Fisher had retired. On Sir Hugh taking up his office the Archbishop sent him good wishes 'in what is one of the most difficult posts . . . that anyone can hold'. He urged the Director-General – the time of the evening news bulletin had been changed from 9 pm to 10 pm – to preserve one quarter of an hour for 'objective news coverage' without any editorial comment – perhaps in the nature of the case, an impossible ambition. He also took the opportunity of informing Sir Hugh of the existence of the Church of England's two councils for radio and television.

Mention has been made earlier of the setting up of Independent Television and we now turn to consider the circumstances attending its birth. Dr Fisher's interest in the media inevitably led to his becoming deeply involved in the controversy which the advent of ITV brought with it.

The case for a second channel drew support from two quarters: first from those who recognised that television could be exploited commercially, and secondly from those who deplored a monopoly and wished to increase the area of choice.

Archbishop Fisher held strong views on this proposed innovation, largely because he feared the possible consequences flowing from the manner in which the project was to be financed. These views he expressed in two debates in the House of Lords; in a statement to the British Council of Churches; and in a letter to Earl de la Warr, the Postmaster-General. The effect of the Government's proposals as first adumbrated to establish a second channel, so the Archbishop warned, would be to create a university, a new educational institution 'far more pervasive and potent' than either Oxford or Cambridge or any modern university. 'It will pursue students into their own homes, into their own domestic circles, and there present them, with all the art it can command, with lectures, demonstrations, entertainments and the whole curriculum of the University.' This it would do audibly and visually to students numbering millions from youth to old age. He was fully aware that the *riposte* might be that the new television authority was to concern itself only with entertainment, but entertainment was in part at least educational and necessarily so. He was not opposed to an alternative channel in principle but questioned how far advertisers, whose interest was in selling a commodity, would bring undue influence to bear upon the character and selection of programmes themselves. In particular, though by no means exclusively, he had in his mind religious programmes. In this respect he was not happy with the Government's intentions as first set out in a White Paper and now embodied in what he described as a 'bad Bill'. The Archbishop's hope, therefore, was to secure a better Act of Parliament by amending the present one in such a way as to be acceptable both to the Government and to its critics. In this respect Dr Fisher's basic position was that all television output should be financed from one common pool fed primarily by licence fees; secondly, but only if it should prove necessary, by money from advertisers. Once in the pool it should be divided by a fixed proportion between the BBC and the commercial providers. He had encountered no argument so far against this except that the BBC did not like any alternative programme not under its own control.

There were other facets of the Bill which caused the Archbishop anxiety. As to the proposed new Authority which, as well as owning the physical apparatus, would shoulder the responsibilities for the overall censorship of programmes, this disturbed him, not least because censorship was the 'most futile and ineffective of all possible duties'. If the controllers of advertisements became a separate department, acting on behalf of both Corporations, then there would seem to be no reason why the new Corporation should not share the proceeds and be the providers of alternative programmes.

These suggestions are interesting as showing the Archbishop's mind at the time but they were not to be realized in full, particularly in respect of a cross-fertilization of the two Corporations. However there was doubt in many circles as to whether the Bill, in its present form, would get through Parliament. Lady Rhys Williams, a strong Liberal and a BBC Governor whom the Archbishop consulted, was in favour of some form of compromise.

During these months Geoffrey Fisher was in close touch with Earl de la Warr, the Postmaster-General, securing his support for extending the writ of CRAC to include the new Corporation, and expressing his conviction that with mutual give and take the Bill could be negotiated through both Houses of Parliament. On 22 January 1954, the Archbishop had an interview with Lord Duncannon and Norman Collins – later to be Director of ATV Network Ltd – who questioned the Archbishop as to his view on the BBC policy of not building up a single, dynamic, outstanding religious personality. His reply was guarded. It was up to CRAC to advise but he himself was 'dead against setting up an English version of Bishop Sheen such as the Radio Doctor'.

The politicians who were sponsoring the Bill fully appreciated that it must be of infinite concern to the Churches. Thus on 2 March the Postmaster General discussed the matter with a Committee chaired by the Bishop of London. The Archbishop sat in on this meeting but seems, non-characteristically, to have been tantalizingly silent, maybe because he himself had drawn up a memorandum for the benefit of the

British Council of Churches suggesting the kinds of questions that it ought to ask of the Postmaster-General. In this document he urged that the Authority should have the sole right to lay on religious programmes.

When the definitive text of the proposed Television Bill was finally released, the British Council of Churches, after long discussion, publicized its views in July 1954. By so doing it made clear that in its judgement the introduction of commercial television would be an unwise policy fraught with graver risks than were justified. It urged the Government to bring forward proposals which could command general support.

The Archbishop, as might have been expected, went through the text of the Television Bill with the proverbial toothcomb, suggesting a number of amendments along the lines indicated earlier in this chapter. Once again he protested against programme contractors having power to lay on a religious slot. If this were allowed it would put CRAC in a near impossible position, for example if a particular company were dominated by say the Seventh Day Adventists. He pleaded that the Bill be strengthened in this respect, since he remained entirely unconvinced that the present policy of the Government would not in practice leave the decisive influence in programme planning with the advertisers. Ought not, he asked, the programme companies to be forbidden to put on any religious programmes and should not these be confined to the Authority as the Church of Scotland wished. CRAC must be given the opportunity of seeing all such programmes before they were sent out, particularly as he could find nothing in the Bill which prevented any religious body from buying time from a programme contractor. The Postmaster-General, on the other hand, claimed that it would be better if CRAC dealt only with the Authority on questions of principle and long-term planning of religious broadcasts.

In the final debate in the House of Lords the Archbishop spoke for about half an hour and was supported among others by Lords Waverley and Beveridge. He began by expressing his appreciation of what the Government had already done to improve the Bill; but he still regarded it as a bad Bill, and he hoped it would be withdrawn and reconsidered. If this were not done and the Bill went through a Second Reading, then he hoped it would be amended so as to make the new Authority master in its own house. It was nonsense to call it an Independent Authority when in fact it was 'bound hand and foot far more than the BBC is, to the Government, to the contractors and to the advertisers'. Let there be, he urged, one Authority 'really independent and really responsible'. What he personally hoped for was that it be entrusted with the great task of providing by itself or through the companies all religious programmes.

It was, perhaps, one of Geoffrey Fisher's most effective speeches. He was forceful, destructive in his analysis of the shortcomings of the Bill yet constructive in suggesting amendments to put them right, spicing what he said with a somewhat mordant wit. Lord Reith, formerly number one of the original British Broadcasting Company who immediately followed him began his oration: 'My Lords I have never heard the most Reverend Prelate in the pulpit but I must say I should not like to be a malefactor under the lash of his Reverence'. Nor did the Archbishop confine himself to speaking formally for, in the course of the debate, he interjected some fifteen times. One amendment which was passed through the Lords must have given Geoffrey Fisher great satisfaction. Under its terms in addition to the £2 million loan, a further sum not exceeding £750,000 a year from the licence revenue was to be placed at the disposal of the controlling body, thus securing for the new Authority independent financial resources as Geoffrey Fisher himself had suggested. Though this was acceptd by the Lords it found little favour with those who wanted the new Authority to be dependent solely on its capacity to pay its own way by attracting investment.

Thus finally independent commercial television made its appearance. Though its constitution was not wholly what the Archbishop wanted, yet it conformed in certain respects to his basic criteria and safeguards. He had never objected to a second channel as such; only to 'the deleterious effects' which might result from commercial operators, unfettered, seeking to sell their commodities by having an effective say in the selection of programmes. They did not in this respect, get what they wanted.

The effect, in the long term, of commercial television lies outside the scope of this biography. Though it might be claimed that the introduction of competition between the two Authorities has not raised the standard of either, certainly Geoffrey Fisher's worst fears were not realised partly through the amendments which he helped to secure.

CHAPTER 33

Education

(i)

GEOFFREY Fisher spent many years full time in the independent sector as a member of the teaching staff at Marlborough and as Headmaster of Repton. However he had become, across the years, intimately involved with the maintained sector through his ongoing concern, both as Bishop and Archbishop, with Church schools. Geoffrey Fisher believed passionately – it was part of his early personal inheritance – that the Church of England must not walk out of the educational field, even if this meant making gigantic financial efforts to remain in it.

The *annus mirabilis*, education-wise, in the twentieth century was undoubtedly 1944 when R. A. Butler, a cultivated and dedicated liberal, piloted a Bill through Parliament. The background inspiring his reforming zeal was in the main three fold: (1) The distressing evidence of chronic deprivation revealed only too clearly in many of the children evacuated to the countryside from their run-down city conurbations. (2) The grim fact that the degradation of Hitler's Germany, of Mussolini's Italy and Franco's Spain had been nurtured in a supposedly Christian Europe. (3) A determination that no longer should the nation's education be bedevilled, and reform frustrated, by internecine strife between the various Christian denominations. Hence R. A. Butler – his great ally was William Temple, Archbishop of Canterbury – committed himself to passing through Parliament new legislation which was destined to shape the pattern of the national education for young people in the post-war years till well on in the century. He determined not to wait for the end of hostilities before embarking upon this great enterprise. Thus there appeared in 1943 a White Paper *Educational Reconstruction* which indulged a *critique* of what was wrong and what the Government intended to do to put this right. William Temple, the Archbishop of Canterbury, immediately welcomed the document as providing for the Church ' a glorious opportunity'. *The Times* newspaper wrote dramatically that 'the time for a settlement is now or never'. It was for this reason that Butler, in preparing the White Paper, had discussed what was to be its contents with a wide spread of Christian opinion, Anglican, Free Church and Roman Catholic.

It was at this stage in the preparatory process that Geoffrey Fisher, then Bishop of London, was brought into these consultations. It was still no easy thing, but not so difficult as in former years, to secure a religious consensus since built-in attitudes arising from deep convictions tend to persist. However recalling these days Geoffrey Fisher wrote: '. . . though most of the discussions which the delegates from the Protestant Churches had with Mr Butler related to the theological content of an agreed syllabus their aims were educational and not ecclesiastical'. In company with most Anglicans, Geoffrey Fisher was a firm supporter of compulsory religious instruction with a conscience clause to make withdrawal possible. What he deplored was the sad fact that, and he never ceased to try do to something about this, there was a shortage of teachers fully qualified to give such instruction though he hoped that after the war this situation might be mended.

During his years at London, as we have seen, Geoffrey Fisher's main preoccupation educationally was to provide some form of instruction for young people who for one reason or another were not evacuated – or were evacuated but periodically returned home. He secured the co-operation of the London County Council in providing materials for the opening of premises, church halls among them, and encouraging clergy themselves to set up schools and teach in them.

But blitz and bombs did not prevent, indeed they stimulated, serious discussion in Convocation, the Church Assembly and the National Society, on the educational shape of things to come. The Free Churches also explored the same area. An *Appeal* issued by the Archbishops emphasised the importance of Christian faith in the education of the nation's children. Here it was important, so Geoffrey Fisher stressed, that all co-operate – parents, teachers and the public. He admitted regretfully that still at times the echoes of the old controversial spirit of suspicion and antagonism obtained though, so he wrote confidently in his Diocesan Gazette: 'Our faces are set away from it'. The chief merit about the 1944 proposals, so he argued, was that they had the united support of the Anglican Church together with the Free Churches and, it might be, of the Roman Catholics. 'There must be trust on both sides, trust by the Nation that the Church will declare honestly all that it can read of the will and mind of Christ; trust by the Church that the Nation will try earnestly to translate that will into its laws, administration, custom and spirit; and will welcome and not resent it if the Church criticises what seems to be contrary to that will.'

However, it was to be expected that some Roman Catholics, together with a few Anglicans and Free Churchmen, 'moved by conscience', might attack the general approach of the White Paper which made Geoffrey Fisher anxious lest once again an Education Bill should become a battleground for denominational strife. 'If that happened,' he warned, 'it would be a disaster for education and a disaster for religion.' Fortunately, Butler had done his preparatory work of consultation far too thoroughly, wooed too many interests, explained and illustrated his case too well for minority protests to be effective.

Particularly important, indeed supremely so in this respect, was the Minister's decision to retain the Dual System – a cross-fertilization of Church and State. Had he not done this he might possibly have found himself back in the denominational *impasse*. Essentially Butler himself was thinking in terms of what Christians of all denominations together could positively contribute to English education.

It came as a great shock to educationalists generally when Archbishop Temple died unexpectedly in October 1944. Maybe it was fortunate that he was followed by Geoffrey Fisher who was already involved with R. A. Butler in his reforms.

Often it is the case that there is one spot that defiles the robe, and it is not surprising, therefore, that one clause in the proposed Bill caused a great deal of perturbation and anger among members of the Church of England, and understandably so. It was 'Regulation No. 23', the effect of which was to extend to secondary schools the prohibition which already existed in primary schools, in respect of ordained ministers of the Church of England teaching in them full time.

Geoffrey Fisher, supported by the National Society and the Bishop of Chichester brought this matter with great energy and determination before R. A. Butler and set out clearly the Church of England's grounds for legitimate complaint: (1) There were many excellent clergy teaching in grammar schools. They should be encouraged to continue. (2) It was not unusual for head teachers to get ordained while holding office. Would they be expected to resign? (3) This regulation would widen the gap between the independent and state schools. (4) To talk of clerical domination was now meaningless.

However, R. A. Butler would not be moved – apart from emphasising that he had discretionary reserve powers – probably because of strong opposition from the National Union of Teachers.

The importance of Butler's 1944 Education Act can hardly be exaggerated. Indeed it laid down a normative pattern for English schools until the introduction of the comprehensives and the abolition of the direct grant. Butler must be given the main credit for conceiving and pioneering a system which, as never before, opened up the universities – not least by extending the school age to 16 – to boys and girls of academic talent independent of their social status. Also he saw religion as having a central and not a peripheral place in promoting humane values and responsible citizenship. Even Winston Churchill went public at the time with the cryptic observation that religion was 'the fundamental element in school life'.

Geoffrey Fisher was grateful for the opportunities and the challenge which the Act provided. For the first time in the history of English education religious instruction and an act of worship were made compulsory. Indeed it was the only subject that was!

The Archbishop now proceeded to use his unique office, and the leadership which it implied, to see that the Church of England took maximum advantage of the benefits which the new Act brought to it. Some of these benefits had to be paid for in hard cash, since the implementation of the Act required some schools to be enlarged, others to be modernized, and new ones to be built in order to cope with the increased intake. The Archbishop was indeed the right man to keep the Anglican Church fully alive to its additional financial responsibilities, and the need to equip itself to face them. This policy may be seen particularly at work in relation to voluntary aided and controlled schools created by the Act. Here it has to be said that a measure of animus was generated against the Roman Catholics in that, though they accepted State money for their voluntary aided schools, they yet believed that the State should entirely fund their own maintained denominational institutions. To concede this, so Geoffrey Fisher asserted, would at 'one blow' destroy the settlement in Butler's Education Act and would 'reawaken all the old ecclesiastical squabbles'. Yet the Archbishop admitted that some Anglicans were unhappy that the State should subsidise inter-denominational teaching one hundred per cent and denominational only fifty, a view with which the Bishop of Peterborough, Chairman of the National Society, had some sympathy. However, Geoffrey Fisher took a more realistic approach, namely that if the Church were to ask one hundred per cent for denominational schools they might go altogether. The great thing was to take full advantage of what the Government generously offered.

It was a consistent policy with Geoffrey Fisher, going back to Chester days, to encourage and, when this failed, cajole parishes into keeping their Church schools which, under the Act, had become voluntary aided status, and in which they would be able to offer their denominational religious teaching. The state funded such schools except that the managers had to find fifty per cent for capital expenditure on buildings (later progressively lowered). Unfortunately one of the penalties of the Church of England being early in the educational field was that many of its schools were old, dilapidated and urgently in need of renovation. For many small parishes this was a daunting prospect in spite of the generosity of the State subsidy. The result was that many incumbents and school managers saw the retention of aided status as an unrealizable ambition. Hence, they gave up the unequal struggle and the schools became fully maintained. However, and this was a main plank in Geoffrey Fisher's platform, aided status was not the only option. It was possible for the managers to apply for controlled status which was a half-way house between voluntary, aided and fully maintained.

Thus as soon as the 1944 Education Act became law Geoffrey Fisher personally circularized all diocesan bishops concerning its scope and precise terms. In doing this his great concern was to encourage school managers who just could not raise the money for aided status not to throw in their hand but to apply to be 'controlled'. Controlled status, he pointed out, brought many solid benefits, not least of which were the use of its buildings by the parish and, at the request of parents, provision for religious instruction according to the Church of England. The parish priest was a foundation member of the management committee. His responsibility was to see that no school should ever be closed without the full agreement of the local authority.

Geoffrey Fisher realised that in the resolution of this problem the incumbent was all important. Thus he exhorted the clergy of his diocese in his monthly Gazette for August 1949 to act purposefully in this situation and he sent a personal letter to all incumbents. His efforts were by no means unsuccessful and within a short space of time it was estimated that out of 144 diocesan schools 105 had applied for controlled status.

(ii)

The 1944 Act undoubtedly led to a quickened interest in the prestigious National Society which had been founded in the thirties of the previous century to handle governmental grants for the building of Church schools. In this, and other contexts, it had done much good work and enjoyed a high reputation arising from the dedication of those who served it.

Geoffrey Fisher had close relations with the National Society while Bishop of London, a difficult period indeed for education in London. His first formal introduction to the Society after he became Archbishop, was when he addressed its annual meeting in June 1945. He began by asking what were the true characteristics of the Christian educator and here he suggested that he was a seeker after knowledge and a worshipper. There was a time when the Christian tended to 'pick up' the verities of his faith 'casually', but in their present situation this was no longer adequate. There was abroad 'a widespread implicit atheism', the only defence against such unfaith being a well-grounded theological commitment. 'It is our duty', he affirmed, 'to make the word theology and what it stands for as familiar and as little frightening as the word science.' He then reminded members that in 1934 the Society was given a new charter under which it was required to cater for the educational needs of all ages. He indicated what this entailed and expressed his belief that the 1944 Education Act represented an invitation to the Church to enter into a creative partnership with the State to further the cause of Christian education. As to schools, 'aided' and 'controlled', both offered positive advantages to the Church. The Archbishop's words did not fall on deaf ears!

Opportunities, however, are challenges and the new educational climate, engendered by Butler's Act, demanded much in effort and response. For well over a century the National Society existed on its own, answerable to no one but itself. As a result of prolonged discussion and encouraged by the Archbishop, a commission met under the chairmanship of Lord Selborne which led to the setting up of the Church of England Council for Education, under which there were separate departments dealing with various aspects, such as schools; youth; adults; and training colleges. This attempt organisationally to bring the Church up to date gained wide support. The new Council was answerable to the Church Assembly and the long-established National Society was expected to liaise with it. Not surprisingly members of the latter were bemused as to what this meant in practice, the more so as there was no formal working agreement as to the allocation of respective powers.

It was, of course, inevitable that in the resulting debate, domestic to the Church, Archbishop Fisher should be brought prominently into it. He was in fact torn two ways. On the one hand, he fully recognised the great work of the National Society across the century at a critical and pioneering period in the Church's involvement with education. On the other hand he was in favour of the Church Assembly establishing itself as a central authority co-ordinating the Church's overall ministry. Thus he was not entirely happy with a Society being entirely out on a limb, seemingly 'entire of itself'. Hence he wrote as follows to Spencer Leeson, Bishop of Peterborough, formerly headmaster of Winchester and now chairman of the National Society: 'The short history of this matter is, I suppose, as follows. In the old days the National Society was the sole Church of England Society concerning itself with education and was, therefore, of immense power. Then other areas of concern grew up like children's education, youth, adults and so forth. The new Charter was a valiant effort to bring this all under the National Society umbrella and it failed because the subscribers to the Natonal Society insisted on keeping their control of elections to the Standing Committee and so it came about that the Selborne Commission, which the National Society had a hand in setting up, decided that there should be new and separate organs of the Church Assembly. The National Society is left, therefore, no longer with any official position except as a general handmaid to the Education Council.'

It was to be expected that the increasingly significant Church Assembly (which was to culminate in its becoming the General Synod) should spawn new structures answerable to itself. Therefore, if the National Society were to continue to discharge its traditional role then some new *modus vivendi*, at the purely practical level, with the Church Assembly would have to be established. Education, so far as the

Church of England was concerned, involved so many areas that, along with the growing specialization, a synoptic approach needed to be taken. Such indeed was the view of the Durham Report which embodied the findings of a commission meeting under the chairmanship of Bishop Ramsey.

The mood of the National Society was one of frustration and uncertainty, so much so that the Reverend E. F. Hall, its Secretary, at one time contemplated resignation, a prospect which the Bishop of Peterborough informed the Archbishop he viewed with considerable alarm. Geoffrey Fisher sought out the Secretary and found him depressed and anxious. The present trend, he alleged, was moving along the lines of restricting the scope of the National Society to its original function of looking after Church schools. His natural inclination was to resign his post and go back to Devon.

A solution, however, was worked out and approved by the Church Assembly under which two councils with executive powers were to be set up to deal with the religious education of children outside as well as inside school. The National Society would affiliate these councils to itself while at the same time they would be linked up to the new Central Council. By this compromise the Society would be left responsible for school and children's work generally and all that went along with these.

Hall remained unconvinced that this was the right solution since it seemed to him as if the National Society was being gradually, if politely, run down. He was not alone in thinking this way. Hugh Lyon, a former headmaster of Rugby School, who had been approached in connection with becoming chairman of the National Society, was of the same opinion and proposed that the Gordian knot be untied by the abolition of the Schools Council altogether. If this were done the Standing Committee of the National Society could be re-constituted to include diocesan representatives and then be invited by the Church Assembly to take over the work of the now disbanded Council. In commenting on this suggestion the Archbishop told the Bishop of Peterborough that the National Society was 'apparently getting into a bit of a mess' but that he hoped at all costs they would avoid another Selborne Committee.

The Archbishop was still in a quandary, deeply conscious of the great contribution which the National Society had made across the years yet, at the same time, concerned that there should be greater co-ordination of the Church's work and witness through a central body, namely the Church Assembly. To liquidate the National Society would almost certainly arouse a *furore* and indeed need an Act of Parliament to bring it about. In this critical situation the Archbishop had an interview with the Reverend H. Pink, then Chairman of the National

Society, following this up by a formal letter to avoid any misunderstanding. The National Society, he wrote, still had an existence of its own, discharging a particular educational responsibility; yet it could not disregard the fact that the Council of Education was now in existence with supporting committees including one for schools directly responsible to the Church Assembly. Hitherto, when the National Society spoke out of its long history this was interpreted throughout the country as the authoritative voice of the Church of England; but now the Society ought not to take any decisive action without reaching agreement with the Schools Council. Ultimately only the Church Assembly could speak officially on behalf of the Church of England in matters of education.

Geoffrey Fisher must have realised that if this were the situation then an independent autonomous National Society could not survive. Perhaps Hugh Lyon was right in maintaining that, in view of this relegation of the Society to a subordinate position, it might be kinder to bring it to an end altogether.

However the English have a happy knack of blundering through in spite of a defiance of formal logic. A solution was found and Geoffrey Fisher helped to bring this about which may be summarized in the words of the *Church of England Year Book*. 'The work of the Board of Education in connection with Schools is carried out in close association with the National Society ... The two bodies have the same Chairman, General Secretary and administrative officers.' As to the National Society, so it goes on, it 'works in close association with the Board of Education and greatly values its independent status which enables it to take initiatives in developing new work in response to opportunities as they arise'.

The wording of these statements when carefully examined points to the difficulties of arriving at a working compromise. However there seems to be a general agreement that this *via media* works well.

(iii)

It may be that among Church of England bishops of his day Geoffrey Fisher was one of the few who had attended a maintained village school. True he left it at a tender age but continued to have a link with the maintained sector through his concern for Church schools. For many years, as we have seen, he was headmaster of Repton School and throughout life, in spite of the tremendous demands made on his time, he kept up his links with the independent sector. Indeed he became for a short time not only Chairman of the Governing Body of his old school but also of the Governing Bodies Association. In addition he was visitor of a number of educational and academic institutions including All Souls College, Oxford. Holding such a plurality of offices swelled to overflowing his already mountainous post-bag. Also as well as specific commitments his advice was frequently sought, largely because he was felt to have both experience and influence. How he found time to do this one may well wonder but then as a contemporary said of him, he was a 'workamaniac' with a passion for tidy administration. It is understandable that Geoffrey Fisher should retain an abiding affection for Repton though it may be questioned whether he ought to have combined the Primacy of All England with the chairmanship of its Governing Body. One may well have a modicum of sympathy with a Repton headmaster who somewhat ruefully confided to a visitor: 'It's no joke having as your chairman a former headmaster who happens to be Archbishop of Canterbury'. His interest in the school was real and not nominal, displaying itself in a variety of ways which the exigencies of space do not allow us to enumerate. Suffice that when the school decided to review its overall financial position in 1951 Geoffrey Fisher supported the economic ethics of a loveable Dickensian character. 'It is a fixed principle of mine', the Archbishop emphasised, 'never to spend money until you have it to spend.' 'I shall be much happier', he went on, 'if any addition to the salary scale could have been conceived in the light of the accounts for 1952–3.' In the meantime he himself drew up a list of salaries which he admitted were 'far less lavish' but were within the budget.

The summary dismissal of one headmaster led to an enormous correspondence, including a circular letter issued by the Headmasters' Conference advising its members not to apply for the vacant post. A meeting was summoned to Lambeth when, thanks to the Archbishop, this complex matter was sorted out, R. A. Butler assuring Geoffrey Fisher that by his intervention he had 'helped a worthwhile school get back on an even keel'.

Many were the governing bodies who sought his advice particularly when appointing a new headmaster. Geoffrey Fisher was always chary of lending his name to commend a particular academic institution but he made an exception for one school because of its highly distinctive ethos. His words here are not without interest: 'The Outward Bound School at Abergavenny,' he wrote, 'has made a remarkable and distinguished contribution to the service of youth. The School aims at developing simultaneously, the spirit of innovation and initiative with appreciation of the qualities required for co-operation and citizenship, for a strong and disciplined character, and as the basis of all else a firm hold on the Christian religion. These aims it carries out most effectively as is shown by the tributes made by the boys who pass through the School. This School fully deserves encouragement and extension.'

If Geoffrey Fisher had a foot in both camps, the independent and the maintained, he was yet vividly aware that between the two there was a great gulf fixed. This was more pronounced in boys' than in girls' schools, due in part to the latter in its Association of Head Teachers including representatives of both sectors. Nor were these barriers effectively broken down through the institution of direct grant schools, which brought together fee-paying and non-fee-paying pupils.

But the absolutism of this chasm was tending to be questioned as the Second World War ended, for reasons both ideological and practical. Educational change was in the air and many responsible people began to question whether the quality of the State system did not suffer as a result of many responsible parents preferring to educate their children outside it. Also others asked whether it was not socially divisive to segregate young people in this way, thus giving birth to an élitist educational apartheid. Thus the Fleming Committee, in responding to the winds of change, recommended that twenty-five per cent of places at independent schools should be taken up by the Ministry of Education for scholars from the maintained sector. As a result six hundred such places were put into a pool but few were taken up. Local Education Authorities were not prepared to lose some of their academically brightest scholars in this manner – or find the money.

As Chairman of the Governing Bodies Association and in view of the Church of England's links with a number of public schools it became inevitable that Geoffrey Fisher should be aware of, and become involved in, this by now continuing debate. Lord Pakenham, a dedicated Roman Catholic and equally devoted to the Socialist cause, got in touch with the Archbishop in February 1953 intimating that he might be putting down a motion in the Upper House for discussion, in which case he would call attention to the problems associated with public schools. The Archbishop replied that he himself was concerned with, *inter alia*, the financial problems to which the continuance of many such institutions were subject as a result of inflation.

He was equally concerned with the implementation of the positive suggestions put forward by the Fleming Committee which was set up by R. A. Butler when President of the Board of Education and on which Geoffrey Fischer served. The Committee reported back in 1944 recommending that independent schools should open themselves to all pupils who would benefit from the education offered irrespective of the income of the parents. However, neither the education authorities nor the schools themselves showed much enthusiasm to put the scheme into practice. Indeed, the proposals of the Fleming Report rapidly became a dead letter.

Meanwhile Geoffrey Fisher got together a few people to draw up a document as to how public schools saw their future in relation to the state system. He himself was at one with those who felt that some initiatives must now be taken by the independent schools themselves, not simply to safeguard their own interests but to give a reasonable account of themselves and how they could extend more widely the service that they gave to the nation. Sir Robert Birley, then headmaster of Eton, added to the discussion by drawing up a paper liberal in character which, however, Geoffrey Fisher described as somewhat 'bitty', and as a result produced one of his own. In this he was largely concerned with principles, raising the question as to what, in particular, constituted a public school since they were different in their origins and indeed often in their outlook and ethos. Here he stressed the importance of the boarding facilities which most public schools, unlike those in the maintained sector, provided and how such a provision could be extended to cater for a variety of needs and family back-grounds. He believed that the ultimate problem for public schools, beyond finance, was educational, and it was in this respect that he contended that the only justification for privilege was its return in service to the community.

The growing together and cross-fertilization of maintained and independent schools was easier to approve in principle than in practice. It was not a cause which Geoffrey Fisher could possibly find time to champion publicly though he would have certainly welcomed any enlargement of its scope. What he would not accept was the complete abolition and expropriation of the independent sector. He, as we have seen, regretted that the Fleming Report in its proposals for a state intake had proved a damp squib. However, Geoffrey Fisher had far too many preoccupations to lead a crusade, though he certainly wished to bridge the gulf which separated the two sectors. They have remained in existence to this day – and maybe are likely to continue so in any foreseeable future.

(iv)

Though Geoffrey Fisher was always a little sceptical of what he would call the 'theoretician' this did not prevent him from reflecting seriously on matters of national concern and asking more than superficial questions about them. Not least among such subjects was the education given in schools and colleges.

In general he felt bound to confess that the whole process had ceased to exercise a co-ordinating influence conditioning the quest for knowl-edge. Indeed it had tended to become more a divisive than a unifying intellectual force. True, of course, teaching must provide all pupils, male and female, with tools – 'tools of all shapes and sizes for the work of the world, some simple tools, easy to handle, some fine, delicate, complicated, all of them useful or capable of being useful for the well-being of mankind'. But the fact was that, overall, education had lost its 'shape and structure', and had become fragmented, 'a multitude of isolated subjects, each claiming for itself independence and autonomy'. The specialist had taken over and 'the field of the knowable' has so vastly increased that no one can really master more than a few 'inches' of it. Contact between students over the whole area is equally lost. What mattered in practice was how these tools, these powers of control over the environment were exercised; the ends that they served. Yet such overriding questions inescapably presupposed or depended upon a more ultimate and personal enquiry: 'what am I here for; to what, to whom am I responsible? Am I responsible to myself alone, to a confused mass of transient generations of meaningless men, or to God who put sense into the nonsense which man makes of the world?'

Thus education was finally linked up with the quest for meaning and here the Archbishop deplored what he regarded as a growing secularization, the result being that 'we are becoming not better, but worse educated . . . scales of interpretation use false weights and balances and out of it all comes nothing of faith or practice worth living by'. His fear in the field of education was that the burdens of administration and the very techniques of teaching would overshadow the ends they exist to serve until they ministered to the bodies of their pupils and to their minds more than to their souls. 'The result was that today no basic truths were being presented to the young by their social environment' which lacked any discipline of mind and spirit capable of purging them of error and sin. Hence many pupils are 'greatly distracted, overwrought, overstrained by the pace of the world today; terribly involved in the secondary features of modern life, in the things less essential or not essential at all, the things which embarrassed and devalued life.' Hence his fear for the future, paradoxically, was that 'one system of moral or political ideology should be impressed on the mind of every teacher and pupil by the radio, the television, the controlled press and the constant screening of people to purge them of "unpermitted thoughts".' Here, it must be allowed, Geoffrey Fisher was calling attention to a situation which confronts modern man and must make him pause and reflect. The Archbishop's answer to this severe dilemma was a serious, informed presentation of, and commitment to, a liberal Christian faith which emphasizes the place of reason and endeavours to see life steadily and to see it whole.

PART SIX:

THE WORLD-WIDE ANGLICAN COMMUNION

CHAPTER 34

Visits to Canada and America, 1946

THE Anglican Communion, in some respects like the British Empire, came into existence almost by inadvertence. The Archbishop of Canterbury is its prestigious and titular head – Geoffrey Fisher on occasions called himself 'President' – and though this brings with it considerable influence it yet gives him no built-in constitutional authority over churches which have become autonomous. From time to time there have been murmurings that the head of the Anglican Communion should be someone free of Provincial and Diocesan responsibilities and no longer necessarily a British citizen. This matter was privately, off the record, discussed by a small unofficial group at the Evanston Congress; but the historic tradition, centred in Canterbury, has survived, though for how much longer who knows?

During Geoffrey Fisher's tenure of office there existed within the Anglican Communion some sixteen autonomous churches or Provinces which he described as a 'great family of churches within the Holy Catholic Church which has its own special task and responsibility'. He believed passionately in its role and saw it as having a specific contribution to make to the Church, not least in its comprehensiveness which included within itself Evangelicals and Anglo-Catholics as well as liberals and modernists. Thus he writes: 'The real strength and glory and special responsibility of the Anglican Churches is that they hold these in one fellowship without resort either to schism or suppression. They need each other for their own correction.' For this reason the Archbishop believed that Anglicans were in a unique position to perform a service to the whole church and prepare the way for a fuller inter-communion. It was world-wide and in this respect the designation 'Anglican' was already a 'misnomer' since there were now indigenous Churches not only in former British Dominions but *inter alia* in China and Japan.

In the interest of the Anglican Communion Geoffrey Fisher travelled extensively; wrote innumerable letters, pastoral and otherwise to its bishops; entertained them at Lambeth; and, not least, gave thought and energy to building up an infra-structure so that member churches could act together during the period when the ten-yearly Conferences were not in session. Nor must we forget that he encouraged many dioceses to group themselves into Provinces when, on their own, they lacked confidence to do so.

It is to these extensive labours that we now turn.

(i)
Canada 1946

Of all the Archbishops up to his day Geoffrey Fisher was by far the most peripatetic. One reason for this is self-evident, namely the development of air travel which made vast distances seem almost on the doorstep. No comparable facilities existed for his predecessors.

Air travel, in annihilating distance, had the effect of bringing together peoples, religions and cultures which had hitherto been shut off the one from the other. Thus members of the widely dispersed churches of the Anglican Communion which had sprung up either through the emigration of British citizens to other lands or to missionary enterprise still retained a vestigial sentiment for Canterbury and all that it stood for. This was fostered by their being brought together to Lambeth every ten years these churches being in various stages along the road to full autonomy. The link with the Mother Church was therefore significant as was the position of the Queen to the Commonwealth.

Geoffrey Fisher's first visit overseas, after going to Lambeth, was to Canada and the United States of America, the primary purpose of which was to encourage, now that the war was over, the Bishops in these countries to attend the Lambeth Conference due to meet in 1948. For the hitherto untravelled Archbishop it was an entirely novel experience and maybe he was not without some apprehension as to how he would fare, when with his wife, Rosamond, they travelled aboard the *Mauretania* leaving England on 25 August 1946. A fellow passenger was the distinguished soldier, Field Marshal Montgomery, whom Dr Fisher found an entertaining companion. One day he rasped out: 'Archbishop, I want to hear how you run the Church of England. Will you come to tea with Mrs Fisher in my cabin?' The Fishers duly accepted the invitation and, tea finished, the reverse of what the Archbishop anticipated happened since Monty himself took over, 'I will tell you how to run the Church of England – you need more discipline'. It was fitting that the Archbishop should remind the Field Marshal that it was not so easy to order clergymen about as it was an army.

This Canadian visit was particularly important for Geoffrey Fisher since it was the first of a series of tours throughout the world wide Anglican Communion. In this respect Canada was to lay down the pattern of things to come – preaching in cathedrals; conferring with clergy; giving addresses at official luncheons and dinners; meeting representatives of Governmental and civic authorities; and sampling the general life of the country and often the beauty of its landscape. In one sense Canada was a more straightforward introduction to what was a new experience since as one of the older Commonwealth countries there was still a strong British sentiment. The Archbishop, in his own person, was a vivid and emotional reminder of the rock whence many of its citizens had been hewn. Mrs Fisher, when she accompanied the Archbishop on these arduous tours, participated in them to the full, often speaking to groups of women and discharging her own commitments. One Canadian paper described her as 'a tall pleasant looking woman and a person in her own right'. She was indeed more than adequate to any occasion.

The Archbishop and Mrs Fisher on arrival in Halifax, the capital of Nova Scotia, where they stayed at Bishops Lodge, were entertained at a civic reception being presented with a silver salver and a box of chocolates! Later in the day the Archbishop met a number of local clergy.

Launched on his way the Archbishop went on to Quebec, the cultural capital of French Canada and the seat of a strong separatist movement. His initial reaction was to feel how strange it all seemed – 'an outlandish, entirely non-English place'. Together with Field Marshal Montgomery he was entertained at an official lunch given by the French-speaking Governor. It was not until he preached in the cathedral, a wooden building, that he began to feel at home as he heard the men and boys practising Anglican chants as in any parish church at home. The day concluded with his speaking to, and answering questions from, a conference of visiting and local clergy. He admitted, in discussion, that he saw no sign of a mass religious revival in the near future. However, he thought intellectuals as well as those connected with the arts were in fact returning to Christian faith which might have an influence on a less cultured generation some thirty or forty years hence.

The Archbishop gained in confidence once he began to do things. Much depended on his own and his wife's personality and general approach. Important in the assessment made of Dr Fisher was, of course, the verdict of the Press and in this respect the auguries remained good throughout the tour. In a leader in one of Canada's oldest newspapers he was given a warm write-up: 'It will be difficult,' it ran, 'to over-estimate the significance of this visit of Archbishop Fisher to members of the Church of England in Canada who see in him the spiritual head of the whole Anglican Communion. If local skies are not always blue at this season of the year local hearts are ever warm and local hospitality is invariably open-handed.'

The Archbishop arrived on 28 August in Ottawa, Canada's capital city, distinguished for its Parliament, Cathedral and University. The warm greetings of the Mayor who had waited long hours to receive him amply atoned for the inclemency of the weather. The welcoming party included Sir Alexander Clutterbuck, the United Kingdom's High Commissioner, who was joined by his wife and with whom the Fishers stayed. It was evident, so one of the receiving party remarked, that the Archbishop had been a schoolmaster so much at home was he in conversation with six youths who took the initiative in speaking to him. The Press had done its homework well, managing to ferret out that while Bishop of Chester he had performed on a barrel organ in the streets of the city for a sponsored charity and with his six sons, plus a little clerical help, had played football against the choirboys. It all added up to suggesting that he was a relaxed and companionable human being.

Toronto, capital of the province of Ontario and a great industrial, commercial and educational centre, proved equally hospitable with an afternoon reception in Trinity College and an evening dinner party. In the course of his sermon in Toronto Cathedral he gave it as his firm opinion that he saw 'no insoluble barriers between a Union of Protestant Churches'. Undoubtedly, this went down well and he made a significant impression on this great city. The evening paper, *Saturday Night*, described him as 'a tireless champion for justice, a fearless enemy of slums, overcrowding and unemployment'. As he moved freely about Canada and was submitted to a veritable barrage of questions, he had no inhibitions about handling contemporary and controversial issues. It was a matter of satisfaction to him that though his official relations with Roman Catholics in Canada were more or less non-existent, the Mayors of Halifax, Quebec and Montreal 'went out of their way to greet their guest'. When he spoke to the Manitoba Luncheon Club in Winnipeg, a record number of over five hundred persons turned up to hear him. Universities and colleges in Halifax, Toronto, Winnipeg and British Columbia awarded him honorary degrees.

Geoffrey Fisher arrived in Winnipeg on Tuesday 3 October, a date carefully chosen to make it possible for him to attend and preach at a Synod service the next morning. This gave him the opportunity of addressing the episcopate of the Anglican Church in Canada and of stressing its historic place within the Anglican Communion. In the afternoon he attended a meeting of the Synod, preaching again in the evening at a Service of Witness. On his last day he broadcast to the Nation giving impressions of his visit and expressing his gratitude for the welcome which he had received. This address, though it could not be couched in the same language today, conjured up a vivid impression of a Britain at war; a London blitzed; and Canadian troops waiting for D-Day. He concluded with these words: 'Along with our convictions go the binding ties of traditions and memories and affections which link Canada and Great Britain. They are reborn in every generation. Our young men came here to be trained in the RAF and you have many thousands of English brides. Your young manhood came to us, lived among us, and from our shores went into action. Common convictions, common memories well tested make us friends. God bless you!'

One great advantage attaching to a tour of this kind was that it gave the Archbishop the opportunity of getting to know ecclesiastical personnel in a free and informal way, most of whom he would meet us again in many contexts in the years to come. As an example of this we may instance Bishop G.P. Kingston whom he first encountered in Hamilton and who later became Primate of All Canada. They went by rail together on the long journey from Hamilton to Quebec and then on through a very stormy night to Ottawa, so stormy that the train was delayed. Such travel provided an opportunity for ample conversation and a real cross fertilisation of minds.

Many were the people who thanked him personally for all that he had done while in Canada and for what he had come to mean to them. Indeed, Archibald Fleming, Bishop of the Arctic, wrote letting him know that in his view the Archbishop had made 'a greater contribution to international goodwill than did our war hero General Montgomery, in spite of all the flag waving'. After he had left Canada for America the General Synod of the Canadian Church formally passed a Resolution of which the following is an extract: 'We tender our respects to the present holder of the Mother See of our Anglican Communion, a prelate no less illustrious than any of his predecessors, a man full of humanity, deep piety, and clear vision, one who in a few short days has endeared himself to all by his charming personality and generous friendship.'

It is too often given, in formal Resolutions, to rush to superlatives, but this tribute has a genuine ring about it. Its *ipsissima verba* were brought over in person to Lambeth by Dr A. R. Beverley, Bishop of Toronto.

The Archbishop had successfully negotiated the challenge and the hazards of a busy fortnight, showing astonishing physical energy, thereby making himself available to all and sundry. Such a beginning which won universal esteem held out great promise for the future.

(ii)

America 1946

From Winnipeg after his concentrated visit to Canada Geoffrey Fisher flew to Philadelphia, the capital of Pennsylvania, a port of entry and famous for its historical association wiith the Liberty Bell and Independence Hall. There the Fishers stayed with the Houstons in their very luxurious house ten miles out of the city, a 'grand old Philadelphian family'. So lavish and generous was the hospitality that Geoffrey Fisher disciplined himself to exercise restraint in expressing a wish lest it should be immediately attended to. He also learnt never to mention Roosevelt to a convinced Republican, certainly not to such as old Houston who at any reference to his name resorted to a vituperation reminiscent to Geoffrey Fisher of the denunciation of Lloyd George by blimpish conservatives. The Archbishop drew the conclusion that in the eyes of his hosts Roosevelt had betrayed his class by introducing the dreadful socialist ideals of the New Deal. A further inference, no matter how unpalatable to Geoffrey Fisher, was the discovery that many members of the American Episcopal Church were deeply entrenched in the politics of the Republican Party. It seems extremely unlikely that Mr Houston would have approved the admiring sentiments expressed by Geoffrey Fisher in a cablegram to the Presiding Bishop of the Protestant Episcopal Church of the United States upon the death of President Roosevelt. 'We praise God for his life', he wrote, 'grieve for his death and pray that the Christian principles for which he strove with rock-like fidelity may prevail among men.'

America was a new experience for the Archbishop and though he did not get to know the more seamy side of its life, he immediately warmed to the exuberance, the vitality and sometimes the brashness of its people enriched by a social, ethnic and cultural mix.

In Philadelphia his first task was to address a Scottish contingent belonging to the Brotherhood of St Andrew, but he was soon whisked off by train to New York where he gave a half hour address at a lunch, the hosts being the World Council of Churches and the theme 'Ecumenical Faith and Order'. Then it was back to Philadelphia for the Convention of the Episcopal Church which was attended by some one hundred and fifty bishops from all over the United States. It gave him a unique opportunity – this was the main reason for his visit – both to commend as a 'must' their participation in the forthcoming Lambeth Conference and to lecture at length on the significance of the Anglican Communion. So impressed was one diocesan bishop that he was heard to exclaim: 'Say, this sounds something we ought to come to, is that so?' The Archbishop did not find it difficult to answer in the affirmative! By the extensive personal contacts which he cultivated at the Convention he made it possible for the Lambeth Conference in 1948 to be 'a re-union of friends rather than a concourse of strangers!'

Geoffrey Fisher's address to the Joint Convention was carefully prepared as equally it had been at Winnipeg. The intention was to bring to a focus what he wished to say to the Episcopal Church of America as he himself took over at Lambeth. The text was later produced in the Advent edition of the *Anglican* in 1946. It deserves a liberal quotation.

The Archbishop began by suggesting that the 'sorry state' of the world was the inevitable result of 'abolishing' God and making man 'the measure of all things'. It was against this background that he turned to consider the role of the Anglican Communion. The major priority was as rapidly as possible to fashion its own internal organs of self-government which would give it greater authority. The Archbishop was careful to point out that there was an element in the Anglican tradition 'not easy to give a name to which acts as a watchdog and brings into our tradition a special element of intellectual integrity, of sobriety and moderation of judgement, of moral earnestness, an element which is as aware of what we do not know as of what we do, which does not wish to go beyond the evidence but to judge all things with large and reasonable charity'.

He then went on to observe that the same diversities which were being experienced in America had existed in England during the last century – Evangelical, Tractarian, Anglo-Catholic and Modernist. Since central authority was weak on the spiritual side and complicated on the legal, there was little central control exercised over these differing manifestations of the one spirit. Perhaps that had been in the end a good thing since thereby each had made its distinctive contribution, gone its own way and revealed its own limitations. As to contemporary ecumenical relations he referred to, and worked out, the implications of his Cambridge Sermon.

Another significant occasion took place on 9 September when the Archbishop was the guest at a lunch held in New York under the auspices of the World Council of Churches. This gave him an opportunity to suggest what the Council might become but was not yet, an utterance which the veteran Dr Mott, its secretary, declared to be a 'sufficient justification in itself for the voyage across the Atlantic'. Referring to the Roman Catholic Communion the Archbishop said: 'Between us and them there remains very largely an iron curtain. Sometimes it rusts through but then it gets patched up again from the other side.' Many Roman Catholics were interested and anxious to enter into co-operative relations but they were prevented from going further by the 'highest circles'.

On 19 September the Archbishop preached in Washington Cathedral and was determined to use the opportunity to leave behind him in the New World a truly ecumenical message. He expressed his satisfaction that in the Cathedral there were representatives of various denominations other than his own. In the past Christian bodies used to 'fight and snarl' at each other, now they recognise that their very divisions are held within God's household'. The general temper had changed between Churches and of great significance was it that in humility and friendship Christians were seeking 'the way by which Christ would remove those things that divide us and which are not of his truth'. In respect of Britain and the United States they shared a common literature, a common law, common political ideals and common religious and moral values. 'Unless we stand together,' he concluded, 'the vision of one world can became a delusion and a snare to entrap civilisation itself.'

This address was followed in the evening by one of his most acceptable and light-hearted speeches. This was at a reception and dinner, jointly sponsored by Washington Cathedral and the Washington branch of the English Speaking Union. Summarising his visit after having set foot on its shores for the first time a month previously, he thus described it: 'I have delivered speeches, addresses, sermons and the like at the rate of 1.95 *per diem*. I would not actually guarantee that figure but it is near enough. I have shaken hands with more people than I could possibly have counted and I have addressed multitudes.' He was deeply grateful, he went on, for the astonishing welcome given him and their respect for his ancient office. Indeed, to quote again his own words, 'I was asked so often what was the cute idea about my leggings that I felt compelled before I left New York, in a public speech, to explain why I wear leggings. Washington, no doubt, is better educated'. In the same light-hearted vein he confided to them that some persons in Philadelphia – they were not numerically large enough to be called a party – wished to nominate him as the next President of the United States, a piece of political intelligence which he thought ought to be known in Washington. However he had given the matter most careful consideration and he was sure they would be sorry to hear that he had decided not to run.

As for himself, the Archbishop went on: 'I am no pessimist, I do not believe that the world is to be blown to pieces by atomic bombs or by warring nations. It is going to take all the patience and all the faith that any of us have to see us through these difficult years ahead, but my faith does not falter that we shall find our way through'.

One of Geoffrey Fisher's most enjoyable and satisfying days while in America was spent in Princeton, perhaps the most English of all American universities, where he warmed to its most attractive campus, to its high reputation for scholarship, to its river, rowing and pioneering football. No visit by an English churchman could have been more opportune since the University of Princeton was celebrating the bicentenary of its foundation. The Archbishop stayed with the President and delivered the first Commemoration Sermon. He confessed to feeling somewhat unnerved when told that he was following William Temple as guest preacher – unnerved lest his effort should seem somewhat of an anti-climax. However, President Dodds was emphatic that this had not been the case. Indeed had he coached Dr Fisher for a week he could not have shown more sensitivity to Princeton's problems!

The Archbishop's sermon, even if it might appear to be bringing coals to Newcastle, was directed towards the basic ends of a University. 'Historical conditions change', he said, 'but the function of the University remains constant – to pursue knowledge, to apprehend truth, to relate appearance to reality, and one reality to another... Each generation tends to think that truth originates with itself and is impatient with the past. A university is the denial of any such self-centred pride. It holds in its keeping the forgotten and the unpopular truth until once more it is needed. It tempers the excesses of today's impetuous thought with the patiently acquired and long tested perspectives of the past. It is the faithful steward bringing out of its treasure house things new and old.' The Archbishop concluded his discourse by a reference to contemporary humanism, condemning the fallacy, propounded at the lower levels, that whatever technology can do is right to be done. The danger inherent in a 'standardised range of social amenities' was that it might imperil man's spiritual freedom.

Not all Geoffrey Fisher's short and first visit to the United States was pitched at so high a level. His stay, as he departed from New York, had its exciting and exhilarating, even hysterical moments. The Governor, Mr John Dewey, placed his car at Dr Fisher's disposal and on one occasion he was driven through the streets to the accompaniment of police motor cyclists, the shriek of their sirens being at a maximum. As to the speed this was judged to have been so great as to have exceeded that of Archbishop Garbett in Chicago! The result was that he left America proudly taking with him an official document which read: 'To whom it may concern. On September 15th, 1946, while visiting the City of New York, His Grace the Archbishop of Canterbury and his wife, Mrs Fisher, while under motor-cycle escort of the Police Department of this city traveled (*sic*) at the speed of 80 miles per hour.' Mrs Fisher was obviously a glutton for punishment.

The Rector of Trinity, New York, summarised more than his own impressions of this visit to the United States in these words: 'It is certain that no one else in so brief a time could have so strengthened all our ties with the Anglican Communion'.

Not the least of the tangible results flowing from it was the presence at the Lambeth Conference of 1948 of some sixty six Anglican Bishops. In general the effects of his visit was that he left the shores of the United States no longer an impersonal figure whose only image was that of a headmaster.

CHAPTER 35

The Lambeth Conference, 1948

CONSISTENTLY throughout his archiepiscopate, Geoffrey Fisher regarded the interest of the Anglican Communion as a high priority on his agenda; but to give so geographically dispersed a community an identity and a sense of belonging was by no means easy. It was in order to do just this that Archbishop Longley, way back in 1867, called all Anglican Bishops to his private residence at Lambeth Palace. It was indeed a bow at a venture but it paid off. One hundred and forty-four bishops were invited and just over one half responded. The Lambeth Conferences had been well and truly launched. The Anglican Communion was in part if not wholly the by-product and legacy of an expanding British Empire. As Christians within the United Kingdom developed a missionary ardour, so the Society for the Propagation of the Gospel, the Church Missionary Society and the Universities Mission to Central Africa, began the task of near-global conversion. Archbishop Tait in the latter decades of the ninetenth century interpreted his Christian faith in triumphalist terms and saw its expression, with its derivative of scientific technology, as part of God's providential ordering of his universe. Attendance at these conferences which met every ten years steadily grew in numbers. The last to assemble before Geoffrey Fisher went to Lambeth was held in 1930 and was presided over by Cosmo Lang. His patrician style of chairmanship did not endear him to those accustomed to a more democratic and informal style. A contemporary church historian writes: 'The Americans and most of the Canadians did not find it a very happy experience, feeling that it was managed too exclusively by English Bishops'. This view was underlined, somewhat bitterly, by Bishop Hensley Henson: 'These four men, Lang, Temple, Palmer and Headlam, were the most potent figures in the Conference and the fact is not *solely* due to their official positions and personal ability though, of course, these are very considerable. The habit of personal association and the common loyalty to institutions – in their case Balliol and All Souls – have counted for much.'

The 1930 Conference, however, if disappointing at a purely personal level, was by no means entirely sterile. The Report, a long one, on the Doctrine of Man strove valiantly amongst other things to reconcile religion and science and in the opinion of some percipient readers not entirely unsuccessfully. The section on the Unity of the Church, drawn up by a large committee, bore the vivid impress of its chairman,

William Temple, who saw to it that there was consultation with the Free Churches and the Orthodox. So far as the South India Scheme was concerned, though the Conference was sensitive to its objectives, it decided that the proposed United Church should not at its inception be in full communion with Anglican Churches; but should be seen as a province of the Church Universal. Such a social problem as birth control was given a muted if reluctant approval. Maybe conditions in India saw to this.

It needs to be remembered, of course, that these Conferences were not, like Parliament, legislative bodies possessing authority to bind member churches. They could suggest, woo, persuade even cajole, but they could not lay down the law. It was left to the separate churches to accept, reject or modify their findings. If they opted for the first, as was usually the case, implementation was through their own constitutional procedures.

No one, of course, suspected in 1930 that it would be nearly twenty years before the next Lambeth Conference could assemble. The Second World War (1939–1945), made a Conference in 1940, as intended, quite out of the question. However, before dispersing in 1930, members had agreed the subject for the next Conference – 'The Doctrine of Man'.

When Geoffrey Fisher became Archbishop he determined that a Lambeth Conference must be called as soon as was practically possible. There were many difficulties in the way – transport, money and the willingness of the Bishops of the New World to come. He decided, after discussion with many overseas Bishops, not least with the Presiding Bishop of the Protestant Episcopal Church of America, that 1948 was the earliest practical date. 'It was vital in my mind', so Geoffrey Fisher writes, 'for the Anglican Communion, after this long interval, to come together to re-discover themselves as an Anglican family and fellowship. And here, above all, I thought of the American Bishops'. In spite of their reactions to '1930' Geoffrey Fisher never doubted that the American Bishops would in fact respond to an invitation from himself but, more important, would they be in good heart when they came? If the general ethos of 1948 were to be a repeat performance of 1930 then 1948 might well prove the last occasion that the Conference assembled. The Archbishop determined it should be otherwise. He was fortunate in that he had come to know well Henry Sherrill, the Presiding Bishop of the Protestant Episcopal Church of the United States of America. There were many problems to which Geoffrey Fisher needed to address himself in connection with the Conference of 1948. First of all where should it take place? Here the tradition was firmly established that they met at Lambeth but the Palace at the conclusion of the war was partly in ruins and quite unfit, as it was, to receive bishops from all over the world. However, undaunted, he was determined to hold it in his own home.

'The Lambeth Conference', he wrote, 'had always been held in Lambeth Palace itself and this was, in a very real sense, an essential thing, because the Lambeth Conference started as a little domestic affair, the Archbishops of Canterbury calling a few bishops from overseas, for the membership then was small.' Geoffrey Fisher was concerned to maintain this informal character and not break with tradition. This meant that the Conference must be held in the Library which entailed its complete restoration. The Archbishop was able to secure a licence from the Ministry of Works and he commissioned the architects, Mottistone & Paget, to get on with it. By dint of great efforts on everyone's part the operation was completed in time for the Conference to meet and assemble there.

Equally important, of course, was the Agenda. This was a sensitive question since the social and political climate had changed radically since the Conference last met. Indeed the new world that had emerged was conditioned by the aftermath of war. Painfully the United Nations had been brought to birth; and the World Council of Churches inaugurated; Europe was divided into East and West; Marxism being propagated as more than an economic or political option. After much discussion, however, it was decided to adopt *in toto* the agenda as agreed in 1930 for the Conference due to be held eighteen years later. Its main themes were:

(1) The Christian Doctrine of Man. (2) The Church and the Modern World. (3) The Unity of the Church. (4) The Anglican Communion. (5a) The Church's Discipline in Marriage. (5b) Baptism and Confirmation. (5c) Proposed Chinese Canon on Ordination of a Deaconess to the Priesthood.

The plan was, during the first week, for the various Committees handling the major themes to be appointed and for the Reports on them to be considered in the last fortnight. The Archbishop was conscious that dealing with such a wide-ranging collection of subjects must mean working under pressure but here he believed, maybe a little optimistically, that, 'the fact that it's got to be done very quickly means that everybody is on the spot the whole time, trying to bring everything to a conclusion'.

There was another matter on which Geoffrey Fisher had very strong opinions but on which Dr Eric Mascall, a distinguished philosophical theologian from Christ Church, Oxford, saw things differently. Mascall believed, and he was not alone in this, that in view of the multitudinous responsibilities and preoccupations of diocesan bishops, they ought to have the assistance of a group of resident theologians to give advice when needed. Geoffrey Fisher took precisely the opposite line. Here, perhaps, it is best to let him speak for himself: 'They (i.e. the Bishops) don't come unprepared at all. What it means is that they have to bring to a decisive point all their experience through the years in administering their own Dioceses . . . and by themselves, speak together and try to keep some common counsel for the future of the Church.'

These are forthright words and very revealing of the Archbishop's personal approach. There is more to be said for them than many will probably allow. Certainly, F.D. Maurice believed that the most sensitive theology is linked to reflection upon ordinary, necessary, everyday human experience and that the 'systematiser' is of 'the devil.' On the other hand it does not follow that those who 'do' theology lack practical experience of its application. As it was the theologians had to wait till 1968, when Michael Ramsey was in charge, to gain admittance.

For Geoffrey Fisher chairing such an assembly was a challenging experience and he was only too well aware of how much depended on him personally. In his opening speech he begged the indulgence of the bishops for any mistakes he might make as a newcomer, not only in the Chair but generally during the Conference. However, so comments one of the American Bishops, 'he gave us very little occasion to grant it. If he did make any mistakes in procedure those of us who were as new as himself – and that was the great majority – did not notice them, but we did notice the masterly blend of geniality, resource and firmness with which he guided the Conference through all its phases.'

So far as the day-to-day running of the Conference was concerned, Geoffrey Fisher was fortunate in being able to call upon the services of Mervyn Haigh, Bishop of Winchester, as Secretary. He went to great pains to get to know everyone, superintending with tact and thoroughness the work of the Committees. Among his responsibilities was the important duty of producing the final Report, agreeing it with members of the Conference (and the Archbishop!) and seeing it though the Press. As the Conference drew to a close the pressure on him increased and it was only the Archbishop's encouragement and stimulus which enabled him to achieve the near impossible in producing the Report on time. Indeed, at the end of this purely practical exercise it was the Archbishop who almost took over. One asset Mervyn Haigh undoubtedly possessed – the ability to write good, stylistic English prose.

No Conference constituted of such a wide spread of membership could be expected to avoid some difficulties and not to experience a few traumas. An example may be seen in the work of the first Committee dealing with the Christian Doctrine of Man. Its Secretary was Bishop N.B. Nash of Massachusetts and amongst its members – they acted as chairmen – were Dr F.R. Barry, Bishop of Southwell, author of *The Relevance of Christianity*, a book which made a great impact in its day; and Dr Wand, Bishop of London. The intention was that the Report on the Christian Doctrine of Man should be divided into two – the first section theological in its approach, the second, chaired by Bishop Barry, contemporary and dealing with the Christian in modern society.

Unfortunately, the two groups did not 'gell', and indeed almost seemed to be at war with each other. In near despair, Bishop Nash came to the Archbishop, who called all the participants together, and gave it as his opinion that there must be two Reports, not one, and that in between them should be inserted the Report of the Second Committee. The Bishop of London certainly did not like it, but Geoffrey Fisher insisted.

In the Archbishop's opinion among the most important concerns which fell under review at the Conference was that on Christian Unity, in particular that novel and imaginative attempt to achieve re-union in the United Church of South India.

In contrast, perhaps, with such high 'theologising', it is encouraging to find, unobtrusively tucked away in the same section under the heading 'Friendship between Christians', the following:

> The Conference recognises that work of great value for the cause of reunion has been accomplished by the cultivation of personal friendships between Christians of different denominations; it believes that such friendships assist the growth of mutual understanding and of intercession; and it encourages members of the Anglican Communion to cultivate such friendships.

One suspects that Geoffrey Fisher had a hand in drawing up this simple testimony embodied in Resolution 77. Ecumenicity is not only fostered by formal discussions in the studies of academics! Special mention, perhaps, ought to be made of the section 'The Church and War', which is serious, honest, anything but complacent, and by implication rebuts the falsity of the simplistic 'Christ or communism'. Geoffrey Fisher constantly sought to place a proper emphasis on being practical and down-to-earth. Two examples of this approach may perhaps be quoted.

The first relates to the 'Seven Rules for Churchmen' in which Dr Fisher and the Archbishop of York were particularly involved. The purpose of these rules was to encourage a disciplined pattern of life in the ordinary Christian's home – daily private prayer; Bible reading; Sunday church attendance; receiving the Sacrament regularly; personal service to Church, neighbourhood and community; and supporting the work of the Church overseas.

To some these guide lines may appear somewhat jejune and propositional, but to many their very definite character has proved helpful.

The second was the drawing up of the Anglican Cycle of Prayer in which each day of the year is allocated to a particular Province. This is still used regularly and has enabled Anglicans throughout the world to pray more thoughtfully and, as a by-product, to become more vividly aware of the extent, character and problems confronting the world-wide church today. Prayer may well be 'the soul's sincere desire uttered or unexpressed' but Geoffrey Fisher believed that many people benefit from positive suggestions: also in praying *with* the Church on the same day.

Dr Johnson pontificated with pride: 'When a man is tired of London he is tired of life'. The Fishers were concerned that those who came from such vast distances to Lambeth should sample its life and its unique history and culture. On 13 July the Bishops were received by King George VI in Buckingham Palace; and on the following day they lunched at the Mansion House as the guests of the Lord Mayor of London. In the afternoon the Church Missionary Society entertained them at its headquarters in Salisbury Square.

Mrs Frances Temple, widow of the former Archbishop of Canterbury, was in charge of the hospitality and in spite of the difficulties imposed by rationing she did extremely well. So far as concerned the general atmosphere which obtained throughout, the consensus view was that unlike 1930 it was all that could be desired. Mrs Fisher was a great asset and her generous hospitality together with the kindly feminine touch which she herself brought to bear on every occasion when needed added enormously to the happiness and contentment of all.

Any estimate of a Lambeth Conference must accept that the Archbishop who presides is all important, much more so than would be the case with a run-of-the-mill 'get together'. Invitations go out in his name; until 1968 the Conference took place in his own home; his personality, general approach, attitude to people and way of doing things subtly overflow and pervade the general atmosphere from beginning to end.

Perhaps the first most important thing about the Lambeth Conference of 1948 was that it happened, and thanks to the Archbishop's drive, as soon after the war as was humanly possible and practical. By this he ensured that the series would continue. Undoubtedly he gave the Conference a highly personal flavour and a sense that the Anglican Communion really was an extended family bound closely together in its allegiance to a common Lord, and that this family had a vital contribution to make in the post-war world. Also the Archbishop's exuberance and inbuilt optimism, if it had its dangers in encouraging complacency was more than atoned for in the sense of purpose which it helped to engender, transfigured by the 'sure and certain hope' of

Christian faith. The Lambeth Conferences right from the word go were multi-coloured, multi-ethnic, multi-cultural – and this added much in interest and was in itself a liberal education.

Maybe the Official Year Book of the Church of England issued in 1949, if a little too euphoric, is worth quoting in this context:

'Many Bishops attending the Conference felt that they had re-discovered how much they shared in common and how great was their unity of mind and spirit. In the opinion of the senior Bishops there was no question, as compared with the Lambeth Conference of 1930 (when so many of the English and American Bishops seemed to have different interests) that on this occasion they had all been considering much the same issues and were better informed in advance on the range of subjects coming before the Conference. Even when there was agreement to differ on some aspects of the South India scheme, the differences seemed less important owing to the area of agreement and the growth of a world-wide ecumenical outlook. The Bishops went away immensely encouraged and feeling they were backed by world-wide prayer and understanding.'

It was to be expected that Henry Sherrill would be lavish in his praise. 'Everywhere I go I hear such enthusiastic comments from our Bishops as to Lambeth and you. It is impossible to over-state what the Conference meant to all of us Americans'.

Surely the presiding Bishop of the United States would not have written to Cosmo Lang in quite such terms in 1930!

A more explicit testimony to the Archbishop was paid to him by Claude Blagden, Bishop of Peterborough. 'The present Archbishop who had never been at a Lambeth Conference before, and now found himself presiding over this as host won the hearts of all our visitors making them feel that there was nothing cold or clammy in the welcome which England gave them, and keeping the Conference alive with his vigour and energy and unfailing humour. This, the foreigner felt was one of those with whom you could do business who spoke the same tongue and followed the same lines as yourself.'

It would have been almost unnatural if the Lambeth Conference escaped criticism of any kind. Perhaps the most weighty came in an editorial in *Theology* published in November 1948. The membership of the Conference, so the editor alleged, could not be justified on 'the grounds either of episcopalian tradition or of sound reason'. Out of the 326 bishops attending, 240 were diocesans leaving 86 who had no jurisdiction as suffragans, assistants or coadjutors.

On what principle were these latter invited? Bishop Gore, so the Editor observed, declined an invitation to attend the 1920 Conference because 'the possession of diocesan responsibility – he had resigned the Bishopric of Oxford – was indispensable to taking a proper part in the counsels of the Conference.' The editor of *Theology* also deplored the staggering preponderance of English bishops. Of the 86 present without jurisdiction, 63 came from the Provinces of Canterbury and York, which outnumbered the entire representation of the Protestant Episcopal Church in the United States of America. In fact, the English contingent *in toto* constituted one third of the total attendance – and the diocese of Oxford itself contributed five bishops!

A further criticism was more theologically orientated. Ought not a bishop, the Editor asked, to be surrounded by his Presbyters and Laity? Without them was not his episcopate maimed and defective? Yet, in spite of this, there was no mention in the 1948 Report of any presbyter-counsellors being included. 'It is a serious question,' he writes, 'whether these facts concerning the composition of the Conference on the one hand and the absence of the "inferior clergy" and theological experts on the other, may not tend gravely to weaken the moral authority of the Conference's findings and recommendations and to defeat the Anglican endeavour to commend constitutional episcopacy to the Churches.'

These were not criticisms which Geoffrey Fisher took very seriously though as we have seen the accusation concerning the absence of theologians from the scene riled him and he replied vigorously to it.

Roger Lloyd, in *The Church of England, 1900–1965* writing in 1967, believed, though he did not blame them for this, that the Lambeth Fathers were naively optimistic in supposing that for those with eyes to see there were signs that the tide of unfaith was beginning turn. The Bishops were not alone in this, but it certainly did not mean that they were unaware of the world they were living in, nor of the dreadful danger of nuclear war with the destruction of civilisation itself. Geoffrey Fisher did not believe that a religious revival was imminent though taking a longer view he thought that the Christian Church might win the intellectual argument.

The Lambeth Conference of 1948 deserves remembrance by reason of its bold planning for the future. In this policy, Geoffrey Fisher was personally involved and it owed much to his initiatives. It was often said, sometimes with pejorative implications, that Geoffrey Fisher was a first-class administrator more at home with running institutions than with proliferating ideas to inform them. The Anglican Communion certainly owed much to his organising skill and his looking critically at its structures in a global context. One thing struck him forcefully at this, his first, Lambeth. It was the lack of continuity and the tendency for everything to go into cold storage for a ten-year period between the Conferences in spite of the existence of the Lambeth Consultative Body set up earlier. What was needed, to quote modern jargon, was an infrastructure, a means of enabling this global community to continue to be active once the Lambeth Fathers had packed their bags and gone home, many of them to meet together no more. A changing personnel of this kind was in itself inimical to the development of a real corporate sense, or the sustaining of a continuing policy.

From such thinking there came two new institutions approved enthusiastically, namely the Anglican Advisory Council for Missionary Strategy and the Anglican Congress to which 'bishops, clergy and laity from all over the world came together to discuss, listen to papers, to worship together and above all to get to know each other'. It first met in Minneapolis in 1954 – a Congress to which we shall refer later.

The Anglican Advisory Council for Missionary Strategy was the product of a deep feeling, to quote Geoffrey Fisher's own words, 'that in this developing world, there ought to be somebody with an eye upon the whole Anglican Communion, its development . . . and its strategic problems, thereby to secure that the weaker elements received encouragement from the stronger, the poorer from the richer.' The Advisory Council, in order to promote its global role, also recognised the need to appoint regional representatives but the Council unfortunately had neither the means generally or the money to realise this objective. In spite of its grand sounding name, Geoffrey Fisher used to say that the Council was in reality one person, his own close friend, the grossly overworked Canon McLeod Campbell, who had given himself to Christian Mission over the years. All McLeod Campbell could hope to do was to keep things ticking over until a proper staff could be recruited. Meanwhile both Geoffrey Fisher and Henry Sherrill became involved in the Council's affairs. The World Anglican Congress duly held its first meeting at Minneapolis in August 1954, the theme being 'The Call of God and the Mission of the Anglican Communion'. The Archbishop became deeply immersed in its preparation and confessed that he had never been 'more driven'. Indeed he went in the previous year to spend a 'holiday' with the Presiding Bishop of the Protestant Episcopal Church of America to discuss its preparations. As usually happened he got caught up in many chores in which the selection of representatives and finance loomed large. In respect of the latter he maintained, realistically if reluctantly, that 'the Americans alone had the resources of money to make the thing work' and he was deeply impressed with their generosity. Still, Geoffrey Fisher was never happy with this financial dependence upon the United States and he did his best to supplement the $15,000 provided for him by Henry Sherrill. Thus he circularised every bishop of the Anglican Communion and also approached the major Missionary Societies though he was reluctant to divert resources away from direct giving for work in the field. The situation in which many African bishops found themselves was epitomised in a letter from the Bishop of Nyasaland excusing his absence from the Congress. The diocese, he wrote, was poor and if he went to Minneapolis the Africans would say: 'It is just as we thought; in spite of all his talk about shortage of money when the bishop wants to do something himself, the money is there'.

The run-up to Minneapolis meant the dispatch of innumerable letters, some to secure group leaders and secretaries. Perhaps his most difficult task – people are often touchy on such points – was to determine some order of precedence, a matter which the Archbishop had dealt with successfully at the Lambeth Conference of 1948, except that the Church of Ireland felt that it ought to have come before the Church of Wales!

The Archbishop preached at the opening service of the Congress introducing his theme in a more philosophical vein than usual. Christian truth, he emphasised, is not only apprehended by the reason, but is more a moral than an intellectual possession. 'The truth of life is to be found in action and in the power of what Christ does in us.' He concluded with a visionary intimation of a 'greater Church into which we may bring our gifts and lay them at His feet, along with Churches of other traditions, a truer society in which the justice of God has overridden the inequalities of nature and history!'

The Minneapolis Congress was, like Melchizedek, without ancestry that is, it was the first of its kind. To quote Geoffrey Fisher: 'There was really nothing for it by way of business because there was nothing to record'. There were no minutes, and he himself included on the agenda a meeting of the Anglican Advisory Committee on Missionary Strategy. In addition he 'invented' two further significant pieces of business, one relating to a proposed college, the other to the Jerusalem Bishopric.

A missionary theological college, St Augustine's, situated in Canterbury, had been forced to close thus leaving its excellent premises vacant. The intention now was to use these buildings to introduce clergy from all over the world into the basic principles of the Anglican Communion. Once learnt, students could take them back to their own countries. Hence the College might serve as a breeding ground for future leaders of the Church overseas. The project began well, the first Warden being Canon France, to be followed in 1951 by Kenneth Sansbury who had experience of the Anglican Church in Tokyo. Geoffrey Fisher describes him as having 'a feeling for people of other national backgrounds' and having helped many priests from overseas – some American and Canadian, others from Africa and the Far East. The Archbishop was later gratified to discover, on his extensive travels, how many clergy holding positions of great responsibility had passed through the College.

Another responsibility laid on the Anglican Communion at Minneapolis concerned the Jerusalem Bishopric. Geoffrey Fisher always recognised the importance of a significant Anglican presence in the Holy City and to mark this he elevated the Bishopric into a Metropolitan See, thus putting it on a level with the heads of Orthodox and Roman Catholic Churches.

Both of these projects were, alas, handicapped by inadequate funding, so much so that to deal with this obstinate problem – and here Geoffrey Fisher must be given a great deal of the credit – the Congress decided to support both of these good causes by levying a common charge on member churches according to their ability and willingness to pay. This decision was more than a matter of finance, since it helped to foster a sense of corporate responsibility. However, in spite of all his efforts and the College meeting a real need, St Augustine's ran into great difficulties and was finally closed. For the Archbishop this was a bitter disappointment.

CHAPTER 36

The Archbishop and Canada, 1954

WITHIN some eight years of his first visit Geoffrey Fisher was back again in Canada, after having attended the meetings of the Anglican Congress at Minneapolis (4–13 August) and the Second World Assembly of the World Council of Churches in Evanston, Illinois where he met many Canadians. On Tuesday 31 August the Archbishop, Mrs Fisher and one of their sons left Chicago at 1.00 pm passing through Winnipeg and arriving at Regina in the Diocese of Qu'Appelle on 1 September. Also this return visit was to last longer, but was restricted to Western Canada. There was thus much more time for private talk and for sampling a little of Canada's spectacular natural beauty. His method of transport was as varied as the sights he saw. He travelled many miles on the Canadian Pacific Railway, as well as moving from place to place by car, by air – and even by cruiser. During his stay he followed the pattern set on his previous visit. He attended a State banquet hosted by the Governor; opened the Wallace Gardens; dedicated a window in memory of Bishop Winnington Ingram at Christ Church Cathedral, Victoria; and laid the cornerstone of Edmonton's new Cathedral.

The Archbishop reckoned that in the course of his travels in Canada he had covered seven thousand miles in thirty days, slept in twenty-two beds and delivered forty-four sermons and speeches. In most of his more serious addresses he handled the theme of the significant place held by the Anglican Communion in the contemporary ecclesiastical world. In Victoria on 7 September he declared that 'a sort of Commonwealth of churches and not organic unity is the aim of Protestants'. Indeed any premature establishment of the latter would be 'the worst thing for Christendom'. Recalling later his stay in the Province of Victoria, he felt that most significant were his many informal discussions concerning the spiritual life, and inter-communion between the churches. At a more popular level he never forgot that his was in part a goodwill mission and that much depended upon how he reacted to ordinary people and identified himself with them in their situation. The accustomed press conferences he took in his stride and spoke at them easily, freely and informally.

Certain impressions which remained deeply embedded in his mind were not necessarily spectacular but personal to himself. For example he recalled a landslide in Saskatoon which motivated the driver on the Canadian Pacific Railway to go 'like smoke' to get him back in time to address a meeting in Winnipeg. A ride of this kind appealed immensely to the perpetual schoolboy which on occasion welled up inside him. Having safely reached journey's end in time, he went to some pains to thank and congratulate the driver. Another memory was of his being confronted by a journalist in Winnipeg who asked for the script of his address. The Archbishop had to admit that he spoke from notes and therefore could not oblige. The reply came that this was very unfair to journalists for if he could not provide the script then they were sunk. When the Archbishop breathed the word 'shorthand' he was told that there wasn't a reporter around who could use it.

At certain moments on this Canadian tour Geoffrey Fisher confessed to have been greatly moved. Such was the case when visiting a school of which an old Reptonian was headmaster; also when he flew up to Peace River – 'the furthest north I got' – with nothing further until one arrived at the Pole. Yet in spite of this the local people came to shake his hand from two hundred miles around, by car and by any form of transport they could lay their hands on. He held a service and Mrs Fisher conducted a Mothers' Union meeting.

One incident in his Canadian tour is worth a brief mention since it illustrates admirably Geoffrey Fisher's interest in and concern for young people. On a day in August as he walked out of Toronto Cathedral he ran into two young people whom he greeted with the words: 'Two comical Englishmen'. He found out that they had just emigrated and were feeling homesick. They chatted and the Archbishop gave them his card, urging them to let him know how they settled in. He returned to England to a very heavy work load but they were often in his thoughts. Hearing nothing he did his homework, wrote a dozen letters, and managed to ferret out the addresses of their parents, and through them opened up a correspondence with the boys. The last letter which survives at Lambeth from the Archbishop, written two days before Christmas in 1954, is high testimony to a pastoral concern. We quote it *in toto*:

> My dear John and Don, the Christmas card of a large and elaborate kind reached me with its message that it came from 'two comical Englishmen'. You cannot think how delighted I was to receive it. First because it showed me you had not forgotten our little meeting in Toronto last August; secondly because it indicated to me that all was well with you; and thirdly what you have sent is admirable. We can, as you know, make it up in a little stable with the picture of the Wise Men, and the cattle and the manger and the Blessed Virgin Mary and the child; and it is specially suitable as I have got several grandchildren staying in the house with me who will be delighted by it.'

This second tour of Canada concluded on 27 September on which day he went across the unguarded frontier to New York, received an honorary degree and sailed home on the *Queen Elizabeth*. Once on board to quote his own words: 'I did nothing'.

Dr H. E. Sexton, Bishop of British Colombia, was lavish in his praise. 'Your visit', he wrote, 'has inspired us all, and infused new life into our parishes, and as regards Commonwealth relations a Royal tour could not have been more effective.'

Reflecting on his extensive tour Geoffrey Fisher writes: 'If by virtue of my office I brought to these churches a renewed sense of the fellowship and scope of the Anglican Churches throughout the world, I came back myself with a renewed gratitude for what Our Lord has entrusted to us in the Anglican tradition and a deepened sense of its power and its responsibilities . . . Indeed, there was no lack anywhere of those who had deeply treasured ties with England or who had a deep and understanding regard for us.'

Such nostalgia moved him but no Archbishop did more than he, throughout the Anglican Communion, to promote independence, and the responsibility which went along with it.

The personal contacts which the Archbishop made in Canada in 1946; his emphasis on reunion where Protestants were concerned; the presence of Canadian Bishops at the Lambeth Conference in 1948 – these all encouraged the Reverend J.R.P. Sclater, Moderator of the United Church of Canada and the chairman of the National Commission on Reunion, to approach the Archbishop by letter in the summer of 1954 and also to follow this up by seeing him at Lambeth. His concern was to promote the cause of ecumenicity and, in particular, to further the reunion of churches in Canada itself. During his interview he told Dr Fisher that members of the United Church were willing to commit themselves to a 'serious attempt to work for the adoption of episcopacy in a constitutional form'. The Archbishop carefully explained that if a church adopted episcopacy this should be actively expressed through an exchange of ministries; and that it was better first attempted when there were practical reasons for so doing. The Archbishop realised the sensitive nature of the subject and that therefore he must tread warily and on no account usurp the role of the Canadian Primate or give the appearance of interfering. Being Senior Bishop of the Anglican Communion gave him no such authority. Hence he wrote immediately to the Primate of All Canada acquainting him with what had happened and commenting that in the process of achieving full Communion there must be tolerance of some anomalies which could mean members of either Communion jurisdiction-wise being Episcopal as well as Presbyterian. These anomalies, he thought, must not be allowed to last too long. He had told Sclater not to communicate his views to anyone without the Primate of Canada's explicit permission.

The reaction of the Primate, if not hostile, was hardly encouraging. He was obviously not happy that Sclater should have gone direct to the Archbishop without any authorisation from his own Reunion Committee to which he was sending a copy of the Archbishop's letter. Nothing more seems to have transpired from Sclater's approach to Lambeth arising from the unilateral action which he had taken. Clearly the Primate of All Canada resented being by-passed in this way.

There were, however, occasions when the Primate himself sought Dr Fisher's advice. One such matter of this kind, discussed with the Archbishop during the Lambeth Conference, was the status and character of the Canadian primacy.

This was the kind of enquiry which Geoffrey Fisher revelled in and he entered into an extensive correspondence on this subject. He made various suggestions, in particular that the Primate should always be Archbishop of the Province of Ontario but without a Diocese. However he could not persuade Dr Barfoot when he became Primate to take this step. The present climate, so he told Geoffrey Fisher, was unfavourable to teasing out this matter and he himself did not favour the Ontario solution. Both Houses of Bishops in Rupertsland and Ontario had declared it to be unwise for the present to have a fixed Primatial See. At this point the Archbishop of Canterbury's involvement ceases.

Geoffrey Fisher's relations with the Canadian Church were not, of course, confined to constitution making as the correspondence at Lambeth makes plain. Thus earlier in May 1948 the Primate of Canada sought his help as to the possibility of recruiting from England clergy for the Church in Canada. The Archbishop conferred with Dr Garbett of York but was forced to confess that in spite of their sympathy they did not think it would be wise to encourage such an appeal at the moment. Hardly any ordinands were recruited during the war years and many clergymen were still serving as chaplains in Germany.

In 1947 when the great flood disaster in East Anglia brought with it considerable loss of life and much destruction of property, the Canadian Church rallied nobly to Britain's aid and the Archbishop of Canterbury co-operated with the Primate of All Canada in the not very easy task of sorting out priorities and distributing the money. Additional finance, channelled through the British Council of Churches and intended for hard-hit dioceses in Britain, constituted an even more difficult problem, not least because the appeal was finally over-subscribed and the Archbishop could not therefore use it for its intended purpose. As it was, and after much correspondence (undertaken by himself) he finally donated this surplus for the repair of historic churches. In these protracted negotiations, the Archbishop showed his usual meticulous care, grasp of detail and tact, though one wonders whether the stooge work would not have been better done by somebody else!

The Archbishop did not lack proofs, if he needed them, that the Canadians were a generous people who looked beyond their own frontiers to a world in desperate need. This was clearly indicated in the relief which they sent to Korea. Also in August 1955 the Archbishop put the chronic needs of Central Africa to the Archbishop of Rupertsland particularly in Rhodesia, Nyasaland, Uganda and Kenya, all of them within the British Commonwealth and at 'an extraordinarily important stage of their historical development'. He outlined in some detail their problems and suggested that a gift of some £10,000–£15,000 would be of 'untold value'. The Archbishop did not ask in vain.

CHAPTER 37

The Lambeth Conference, 1958

By the time Geoffrey Fisher summoned the Lambeth Conference of 1958 he had been some fourteen years in office as Archbishop; had presided over the inauguration of the World Council of Churches in 1948; and the meeting of the Anglican Congress at Minneapolis in 1954. The 1948 Lambeth Conference, in the nature of the case, was hastily prepared, and many of the bishops who met again had been isolated by the war years. In 1958 things were different. The Advisory and Consultative Council had met regularly; Geoffrey Fisher had not only travelled far and wide to countries including Australia and New Zealand but had entered into an extensive correspondence with Anglican bishops the world over. Also, there had been many signs of great activity within the Church of England itself. Following Geoffrey Fisher's ecumenical sermon at Cambridge, negotiations had taken place between the *Ecclesia Anglicana* and other Churches. A new mood of self criticism possessed the churches. They had a gospel but this itself was on trial. Triumphalism had gone.

Geoffrey Fisher chose as his Episcopal Secretary for the 1958 Conference Robert Stopford, Bishop of Peterborough, whose meticulous and painstaking, if somewhat unimaginative style, ideally suited him for this important role, in which application to details took precedence for the time being over creative thinking. He found it easy to work to a system. His assistant was Dr Eric Jay, who had been by now the Archbishop's senior chaplain for some seven years; was widely knowledgeable of the Anglican Communion and greatly respected within it. The two of them together enabled the Archbishop to keep closely in touch with what was happening at the Conference day by day. The 'run-up' was in part marred by the unhappy controversy over the invitation to attend the Conference sent to Archbishop Makarios, the Cypriot religious as well as national leader. This was particularly unfortunate since it attracted the wrong kind of publicity at the outset – but more of this later.

The Bishops who had attended the Conference in 1948 found awaiting them a very different Lambeth Palace. Gone were the pitiable stacks of books damaged by fire and water, which were now lining the walls of the Great Hall and handsomely bound by modern craftsmen. The Chapel was restored to its former beauty. The 14th-century Guard Room was set aside as the Bishops' rest room. Impressive portraits of successive archbishops going back to the Reformation adorned once more its walls and also straddled the Long Gallery.

This 'new look' made possible a comfortable and a more lavish hospitality. Some of the Bishops, including the Archbishop of York, the Bishop of Peterborough, the Metropolitan of India and the Presiding Bishop of Japan stayed throughout in the Palace. A dozen or so Bishops, some with their wives, spent successively two nights in the Palace as guests of their hosts. Choosing these was a sensitive undertaking, demanding consummate tact, so much so that Geoffrey Fisher decided to handle it in terms of three categories – Bishops from missionary dioceses who were still under the personal jurisdiction of the Primate of All England; Bishops from far off, isolated dioceses; and those in the younger dioceses of the Anglican Communion. Lunch and tea were served in a large marquee on the lawn for all attending the Conference. Miss Lister, who with Mrs Fisher headed the Hospitality Committee, set up an enquiry office in the Palace which was greatly appreciated. Both the Archbishop and his wife went out of their way to make the bishops feel at home in somewhat exceptional surroundings, even to providing a measure of musical entertainment. As Mrs Fisher put it, somewhat light-heartedly, their ambition was to ensure that bishops and their wives need not have a dull moment during the evenings and, in particular over the weekends. A group of women, including some from Westminster Abbey as before, introduced these episcopal wives to London's historic buildings – and its theatres. At the weekends the Archbishop and Mrs Fisher entertained some twenty guests at the Old Palace in Canterbury, the effect of which was to relieve the pressure on the staff at Lambeth. As in 1948, Church House, so near to Lambeth, was used as a club. The social side of the visit, by general acclaim, was indeed well and imaginatively handled.

It is important to stress that this lighter side of the Conference was not seen as a peripheral exercise unrelated to the main purpose of this world assembly. By creating the friendly atmosphere of a home – for this is what Lambeth Palace was to the Archbishop – the hope was to encourage the bishops and their wives to think of the Anglican Communion itself within this family context.

The lectures and discussions in themselves could not do this – particularly as the women were excluded from them. (Maybe the day is not far distant when this will change!) Only direct personal encounter could secure this and indeed on occasions having fun together.

In many respects Geoffrey Fisher learnt from criticisms which came up at the previous Conference, for example the preponderance of English bishops. Thus from the Provinces of Canterbury and York only six suffragans, assistants or former bishops – Dr Bell was *sui generis* – were invited and this was felt to be about right. As a result the grand total was some twenty fewer. To the regret of everyone no bishop from mainland China was present, a sad reminder of the politically divisive situation in that country. A notable absentee from the Conference was any representative of the Spanish Episcopal Church in Madrid, which in itself was, paradoxically, a tribute to the significance in which this Assembly was held by General Franco.

The Conference began on Thursday 3 July with the traditional ceremony in Canterbury Cathedral. The Archbishop sat in St Augustine's Chair, where he received representatives of other Communions – Baptists, Congregationalists, Lutherans, the Eastern Churches and the Old Catholics – and following these the bishops of the world-wide Anglican Communion. It took some twenty minutes for the procession to move through the nave. *The Times* correspondent, in comparing the robes of the Russian Prelates with the sombre habits of the Lutherans, likened the latter to figures in a Rembrandt painting. For the first time the service was televised and the Archbishop preached the sermon.

On Saturday 5 July the delegates from the Scandinavian Church, the German Evangelical Church, The Church of Scotland and The Free Church Federal Council were received by the Archbishop. It was significant of the Lambeth Conference having come of age that the Queen, Queen Elizabeth the Queen Mother, and members of the Government received the Bishops in the course of the Conference.

On 4 July, the Bishops got down to business, light relief being provided by a young man, dressed as a bishop and with his girl friend standing up in the Great Hall and giving those assembled the benefit of an impromptu sermon before being unceremoniously ushered out. It transpired that they were members of the League of Empire Loyalists.

No emphasis on the significance of the warm hospitality offered to the Bishops should be allowed to minimise the importance of the formal agenda, with its lectures and group discussions together with its daily worship. These were, of course, central to the Bishops coming together and it was decided to follow the same general pattern as in 1948. With so many Bishops attending the smaller group was essential, not only for convenience, but to use to the best advantage particular gifts and specialised experience – and maybe to overcome a natural shyness. The separate Committees, under the over-riding theme 'Reconciliation', dealt with the following subjects:

1. The Scriptures: Their Authority and Message. 2. Church Unity and the Church Universal. 3. Progress in the Anglican Communion, (a) Missionary Appeal and Strategy, (b) The Book of Common Prayer, (c) Ministries and Manpower. 4. The Reconciling of Conflicts between and within Nations. 5. The Family in Contemporary Society.

It is not, of course, the purpose of this chapter to give a detailed account of these deliberations or offer a *critique* of its various reports.

Our concern is with Geoffrey Fisher and his personal contribution to, and involvement in, the whole exercise.

Church unity once again loomed large in the thoughts and priorities of the Bishops and Geoffrey Fisher was particularly interested in the Resolution which endeavoured to define the various kinds of mutual relationships into which Churches could enter. It stressed in particular, the difference between inter and full communion, as well as organic unity, a subject to which the Archbishop had given a great deal of thought and had indeed gone into print. To understand the nature of these distinctions would, so it seemed to Geoffrey Fisher's tidy mind, remove a great deal of muddled and confused thinking. He further thought that his own Cambridge Sermon would help in this process, particularly since, in his judgement, some 'have often gone astray by losing sight of it'. It was a great satisfaction to the Archbishop that the Conference felt able to thank God for the grace which He had bestowed upon the bishops, presbyters and people of the Church of South India in these past ten years and the response to that grace shown in the growth of missionary zeal. However – the continued exclusion of non-episcopally ordained ministers from Anglican altars and the denial of full communion showed there was a long way to go yet.

The Archbishop long remembered an incident arising out of the lengthy discussions of the Committee on 'Church Unity and the Church Universal' when it seemed to have come to a deadlock. In its extremity a member came to see the Archbishop in the evening saying that they were absolutely stuck *vis-à-vis* the precise form for the Service of Reconciliation satisfactory to both Anglicans and Presbyterians. The Archbishop rose early and was in his study at 5.30 am seeing himself, to quote his own words, as a Trade Union leader 'bringing two sides together'. His redrafting proved acceptable and is to be found in the Report, Section 2.36.

The work of the various Conference Committees was inevitably unequal. It was generally felt that the section on 'The reconciling of conflicts between and within Nations' was somewhat ordinary and commonplace – a view held by Geoffrey Fisher himself – at least in that it made little impression and 'had no particular effect'. Perhaps it was an area where novelty was not to be expected. It evoked from Geoffrey Fisher the comment: 'The more I feel you can only talk about, deal with, and pray for persons, rather than abstract things like peace, or settlements or anything else. It all depends on the leaders, on their personality, and the kind of people they get to follow them . . . it's a question of personal morality, if you like to use that word, and personal wisdom which in the end settles it.'

One section of the Report came to be recognised as of outstanding quality, namely that which dealt with 'The Family in Contemporary Society'. The discussion here gained much from its being brought within the world-wide context of the Anglican Communion. This was an area which greatly concerned Geoffrey Fisher and to which he had given much attention. Indeed on the eve of the 1958 Lambeth Conference there appeared the Report 'The Family in Contemporary Society', drafted by Professor Gordon Dunstan and issued by the Church of England's Board for Social Responsibility. This excellent piece of work, the result of extensive research, broke new ground. To it, the deliberations of the Conference owed much. The Chairman of this Committee was Stephen Bayne, Bishop of Olympia, who brought a deep pastoral concern and a wide experience of life generally to bear upon its deliberations. The intention of the Lambeth Fathers was to encourage responsible parenthood through family planning and using contraceptives in the process. The Report put before Christian people a sacramental attitude to sex within the state of matrimony. In the following unambiguous words the Anglican Communion crossed the Rubicon which separated it from the Roman obedience. 'It is utterly wrong to urge that unless children are specifically desired sexual intercourse is of the nature of sin. It is also wrong to say that such intercourse ought not to be engaged in except with the willing intention to procreate children.' Thus marriage is placed in the wider context of God's purpose in creation in which sexual satisfaction has a proper place. Some American bishops argued that this section remained one of the finest treatises available on the ideals of Christian marriage and served as the basis for the Bishops' reply to the Papal Encyclical on birth control. Geoffrey Fisher, in this respect, contrasted the conclusions of the 1958 Lambeth Conference with the Pope's 'pathetic wrestling' with this problem which need not be a problem at all. The Anglican Church had without doubt travelled far since in 1920 it had declared: 'We utter an emphatic warning against the unnatural means for the avoidance of conception, together with the grave dangers – physical, moral and religious – thereby incurred and against the evils with which the extension of such use threatens the race.'

Perhaps the appropriate comment is that the Anglican Church finds no difficulty in admitting that it is on occasions wrong! It has no built in infallibilities. 'Thank God for the benefit of plurality, whether between Communions, or Churches or Christians' – so comments Dr Fisher!

The Conference did not, however, weaken what was known as the Anglican marriage discipline, namely that no divorced person should be married in Church during the lifetime of the former partner and that the readmission of such people to Holy Communion required the permission of the Bishop. A heightened emphasis, however, was placed on a pastoral ministry to the divorced. What was new at the Conference, was a frank admission of the nature of sexuality, its God-given origins, its sacramental character – yet its temptations and possible abuse.

Another Committee which was headed by Michael Ramsey dealt with the Scriptures, their Authority and Message. Included amongst its members were Dr Philip Carrington, Archbishop of Quebec and Metropolitan of Canada – scholar and historian – and Dr A.T.P. Williams, Bishop of Winchester, who for some ten years had been heavily involved in the production of the New English Bible. The general approach of the group was liberal, the theological thinking profound as might be expected from its leadership.

Lambeth Conferences meet every ten years and the work involved in their organisation is tremendous. It was clearly an advantage in the case of Geoffrey Fisher that he presided over two such occasions, this being unique. However, there was a problem involved in ten-yearly meetings and this was felt early. An Advisory Council on Missionary Strategy was appointed in 1948 but the immediate results were disappointing, Bishop Bayne complaining that it had not yet implemented the 1948 Resolution that each church should appoint regional officers to ensure a liaison between different parts of the Anglican Communion.

For this neglect, to which we have already referred, Geoffrey Fisher blamed the situation confronting Canon McLeod Campbell, who held the office of Secretary of the Advisory Council, on a lack of staff, lack of money, and lack of time. There seemed little point in making decisions every ten years if there was no effective means of implementing them.

It was out of this situation that Geoffrey Fisher and others became convinced that the Lambeth Conference needed an Executive Officer whose task it would be to travel globally, thereby giving an identity to what could too easily lack shape and 'cohesion'. In a world of 'competing systems, rival philosophies and expanding frontiers of knowledge' the Anglican Communion must be held together.

Thus it was that the 1958 Lambeth Conference decided to appoint a full-time secretary for the Advisory Council on Missionary Strategy and it was left to the Archbishop of Canterbury with the approval of the Consultatative Council to appoint him. The remit to this officer was to collect and disseminate information; to keep open the lines of communication; and make contact where necessary with responsible authorities ecclesiastical or civic. At the same time the intention was to strengthen the Advisory Council by the Archbishop of Canterbury becoming its *ex officio* Chairman.

Inevitably, everything depended upon the character and ability of the first secretary to the Advisory Council, and how far he was capable of using the opportunities which opened up before him. In practice the appointment was made by the Archbishop of Canterbury for which he incurred a degree of criticism not in respect of the person nominated, but in the way in which it was done. There seemed at first two possibilities – Ambrose Reeves of Johannesburg and Stephen Bayne whose reputation had grown steadily as a result of his chairing the Committee dealing with Home and Family. Ambrose Reeves, however, declined the offer and it was Stephen Bayne, Bishop of Olympia, who on 19 April 1959 was appointed to the surprise of many and not without criticism, which was certainly not helpful to Bayne as he began his Herculean task. An American Bishop wrote of this nomination: 'Bayne got off to a bad start because Archbishop Fisher wrote letters to many of us asking for nominations, then before we could reply he announced the appointment of Bayne – which particularly upset the Canadian Bishops'.

It was unfortunate that the Archbishop should have acted in what appeared to many so arbitrary a manner, but this, it must be admitted, was in line with a tendency which became more evident as Geoffrey Fisher approached his retirement. However, he sought to placate criticism by the form of the public announcement of Bayne's appointment which stated that it had been decided upon by the Metropolitans of the Anglican Communion. His chief duty was to act as 'controller' of the Anglican Advisory Council on Missionary Strategy.

The unfortunate repercussions following Bishop Bayne's nomination made him understandably worried as to the nature of his relations with the Archbishop and how far he would be left free to get on with the job. Wisely he let the Archbishop know of his anxieties and received the following reply written on 13 March 1959: 'You mention your own strong feeling that there ought to be a certain degree of looseness in the new post making it clear that this is not an English invention nor merely an extension of my office. With that I wholly agree. I might have been guilty of describing it as a kind of auxiliary office to me . . . I really never meant that but I did realise that I should be unloading many things on to you to my own great relief which at present I carry about entirely on my own shoulders. But, of course, in this office you are entirely your own master, responsible to the Anglican Council on Missionary Strategy for any tasks that you take on at their request, and responsible to the Consultative Body of the Lambeth Conference for any assignments you take on at their request – which means in effect at my request – so there we are.'

Stephen Bayne's appointment was, it is generally admitted, an inspired choice and for this Geoffrey Fisher must be given a measure of praise. Bayne was a thinker who asked questions; reflected around the contemporary scene; and was thoroughly committed to a global role for the Anglican Communion. Also he had energy, sensitivity to people – and that indispensable adjunct, a sense of humour. In his report to Geoffrey Fisher, which related to the last full year of the Archbishop's tenure of office at Lambeth, he was able to say that he had travelled over 130,000 miles during which time he visited most of the far-flung member Churches. Certainly this went a long way to justify Geoffrey Fisher's contention that what was required was not another committee but a person. Supported by the Archbishop, Stephen Bayne continued with his efforts to secure an Anglican representative in Rome, and having sorted out with Geoffrey Fisher the nature of the office, he was happy himself to be appointed to it thus representing in the Eternal City the 'President' of the Lambeth Conference rather than 'the Primate of All England'. Finance was a real problem and Geoffrey Fisher was helpful and well understood the extent of the need.

Correspondence between Archbishop and Executive Officer was frank and informal and Geoffrey Fisher believed that Bayne brought to his new office 'a magnificent spiritual vision, and determination of all kinds'.

Geoffrey Fisher was not a man who easily displayed emotion in public nor did he do so at his last Lambeth Conference in 1958. Rather at the end of the last session he introduced a lighter note. Montgomery Campbell, renowned for his somewhat mordant wit and brevity of speech, had been silent thoughout the whole proceedings. The Archbishop, in commenting upon this asked him whether he might wish to give them the benefit of his wisdom though late in the day. Slowly drawing himself up to his full height – he was well over six feet – he replied tersely 'No' and promptly sat down.

The Primate of All England recalls the very moment of the parting of the ways as follows: 'We all knew each other; trusted each other; there was the fellowship feeling from the very beginning; the whole thing went magnificently; and all I can do now is to say that never in my life have I been so moved as at the closing Service in Westminster Abbey'. Henry Sherrill was the obvious preacher and he did not conceal his deep feelings on this memorable occasion. After the act of worship the Bishops went in procession from the Abbey to the Chapter House and the Archbishop bade farewell to all the Bishops of the Anglican Communion in words of gratitude, love and affection, reminding them that most of those present would never meet again in this world. Memories of the past, unusual with him, came flooding back into his consciousness and it was only with difficulty that he prevented himself from breaking down. He was particularly moved to see standing in front of him R. H. Owen, Archbishop of New Zealand, whom he had known at Oxford and who had been headmaster of Uppingham while he was at Repton. As they departed he said: 'We have in the last five weeks been living close to the kingdom of heaven' and then his voice faltered. He ended hurriedly and turned to go out. He had burst into tears.

PART SEVEN:

ARCHIEPISCOPAL TOURS AND THE SETTING UP
OF PROVINCES

CHAPTER 38

Australia

(i)

AT the Lambeth Conference of 1948 the Archbishop was pressed by the bishops of Australia and New Zealand to visit their countries, an invitation which he felt he must accept. He immediately began to make plans for the journey and on 7 May 1949 informed the King of his intended travels, calling attention to the fact that the Diocese of Canterbury in New Zealand was celebrating its centenary during the following year. Sir Alan Lascelles, the King's Private Secretary, in reply asked what was the normal procedure in regard to necessary business when the Archbishop was out of the country for any length of time. Did he nominate someone to act for him or did his responsibilities automatically devolve upon the Archbishop of York? The answer was that in relation to Canterbury diocesan business, the Archbishop had already set up a Commission, consisting of the Suffragan Bishops of Dover and Croydon with full power of attorney. As to matters concerning both Provinces, in certain areas this would fall to the Bishop of London as Dean of the Province.

Meanwhile the Primate of All England had been corresponding with the Archbishops of Sydney and of New Zealand as to the most appropriate time for the visit during 1950, the latter months from his point of view being preferable.

Finding the fares for extensive tours of this kind was often a problem. Fortunately the British Council agreed to meet the cost of his travel to and from New Zealand and to make the necessary arrangements. Also it assured the Archbishop that he could expect to receive a great welcome and that his visit would contribute towards strengthening the bonds of goodwill and understanding within the British Commonwealth.

So it was that on 22 September 1950 the Archbishop and Mrs Fisher, accompanied by the Reverend Clive Parc, headmaster of Canterbury Choir School, embarked on the *Dominion Monarch*. After calling in at Las Palmas where he celebrated Communion, the ship berthed for twelve hours at Cape Town which gave Geoffrey Fisher the opportunity of meeting its Archbishop and his own brother Leonard, Bishop of Natal. He and Rosamond went ashore, shook hands with all and sundry and enjoyed Bishopscourt, an old Colonial house built in the Dutch style and with a trout stream running through the garden. They were both made vividly, indeed painfully, aware on the *Dominion*

Monarch of the fragmentation of the various Christian churches. Thus the Anglicans received their Communion in the lounge, and the Roman Catholics a few feet away in the drawing room. Mrs Fisher was shocked. 'I have never felt so much before how shameful our disunity is', she commented.

On 17 October at 9.00am the *Dominion Monarch* berthed at Fremantle, arriving there so late that the original programme, which allocated the Archbishop three days in Western Australia, had to be curtailed into forty hectic hours. He was welcomed by Dr R.W.H. Moline, Archbishop of Perth and formerly Vicar of St Paul's, Knightsbridge, and by the Mayor. They then drove in brilliant sunshine to Perth, capital of Western Australia, a city which so immediately captivated the impressionable Archbishop that he later confessed to finding it 'in some ways the most attractive of all Australian cities'. Its beautiful situation on the Swan River and its pronounced English character made an immediate appeal. The Cathedral was small and unfinished, like many in Australia, but he yet described it as 'lovely'.

The Archbishop, though it was his first visit, did not come to Australia as to a *terra incognita*. He had already met many of its bishops headed by Dr H.W.K. Mowll, Archbishop of Sydney, at the Lambeth Conference. Also the Archbishop had the benefit of some perceptive comments recorded by Bishop Bell of Chichester who had himself visited that great country not long before. It was, so the Bishop suggested, the enormous size which made a 'sense of belonging the more difficult, increased by a lack of corporate leadership'. The method of episcopal appointment, which gave too large a voice to the Diocese, encouraged an introverted rather than an outward looking Church. Theologically the Australian Church was weak which might perhaps be overcome by the export for five-year periods of English scholars. Also not enough significance was given to women in the life of the Church as a whole – a situation which Mrs Fisher was acutely to feel.

Once in Australia, the Archbishop was certainly thrown in at the deep end. After calling in at Perth on the University and St George's Anglican College, he was received at Government House by Sir James and Lady Mitchell. Early in the afternoon he addressed 1,500 schoolchildren during a short service in St George's Cathedral. In the evening he spoke at a meeting organised by the World Council of Churches, followed by a 'hilarious supper' attended by Church leaders. St Luke's Day began with his preaching and celebrating at a sung Eucharist in the Cathedral. Among a diversity of functions was a reception laid on by the Mayor who described the Archbishop as 'some boy' – 'an indication,' writes the Archbishop of Perth, 'of the kind of personal relations already established between our guests and their new friends'. Geoffrey Fisher then went on, preceded by a mounted escort, which gave him great delight, to lunch at Parliament House. Present on this occasion were members of the English cricket eleven on the eve of their tour. The Archbishop of Perth, who was a fellow guest, recalls this reception in these words: 'They (the Test team) supplied an opportunity of which the Archbishop was not slow to avail himself in his reply to addresses of welcome from the Premier and the Leader of the Opposition. Both speakers claimed that Australians were deeply religious, although they might not always show it by their church attendance. The Archbishop in reply spoke of his own great passion for cricket, although he admitted that he had not played it or followed it since leaving school, indeed seldom if ever watched it. When the Archbishop had finished a fellow guest exclaimed 'well bowled', and so, comments Geoffrey Fisher, 'all laughed to their hearts' content'.

After this reception which preceded lunch at Parliament House, a garden party at the Deanery provided an opportunity for clergy and their wives to meet the Archbishop who later addressed some of the clergy.

The Perth visit ended with Festal Evensong at which the Archbishop addressed a packed congregation. A fanfare of trumpets sounded as he entered the Cathedral led by his chaplain carrying the Cross of Canterbury. At the conclusion of the service the clergy formed a guard of honour and the worshippers gathered to wave farewell as the Archbishop, Mrs Fisher and his chaplain started on their sixty mile drive to Northam.

This introduction to Western Australia set the pattern of the shape of things to come. During the next fortnight the Archbishop moved steadily across Australia, his main ports of call being Kalgoorlie, Adelaide, Bathurst, Geelong, Melbourne, Grafton, Canberra, Newcastle and finally Sydney. In all he visited some sixteen out of twenty-five dioceses. There were frequent whistle stops along the railroad when he greeted and talked to isolated communities. The usual 'drill', as he and Mrs Fisher moved from State to State, was for the Archbishop to preach in the Cathedral, to be entertained by Governmental and Civic Authorities, and for him to address and converse with church people, clerical and lay; also he was able to meet many Free Churchmen and to make contact with other groups of various kinds, some educational.

The Archbishop was glad, at the beginning of his tour, to travel by train across the vast and semi-inhabited Nullarbor Plain – 'those endless miles of pure desert which took us three days and three nights, with nothing but little shrub bushes interspersed with small settlements'. He long remembered the intense heat of Kalgoorlie, an isolated, derelict ghost town which had once been a thriving centre for traffic in gold. There he met three incumbents, who represented, with their wives, the total work force of the diocese. The Mayor, a good Methodist, turned out in his full robes to greet them while the Archbishop chatted freely to settlers and their families whose responsible task it was to keep the railroad in constant repair. Young people instinctively responded to Geoffrey Fisher, whether it were a matter of five small children with whom he chatted after an open-air Eucharist in Adelaide, or older boys and girls in schools and at youth rallies. He was expert at giving short, impromptu, 'off-the-cuff' talks. Not surprisingly he met the Flying Doctor and was deeply impressed with what he described as a 'wonderful service'. From Fort Augustus where he arrived on the day of Princess Anne's Baptism he cabled his congratulations direct to Princess Elizabeth. At Adelaide the Archbishop broadcast to the whole Australian people and enjoyed meeting the reception committee which included the Prime Minister of South Australia, Mr T. Playford, a Baptist and an 'excellent and upright man'. He also addressed six hundred business and professional men, receiving sustained applause. On his departure the Bishop said to him: 'You have won the affection of clergy and laity and most of all the people'.

Melbourne, in Victoria, looms large in the consciousness of all Australians and wins a grudging respect even in Sydney. The city bears evidence of a 19th century past, not least in its elegant buildings which won the enthusiastic admiration of Sir John Betjeman; also it is distinguished by a strong musical and cultural tradition. The Archbishop arrived there on 29 October and left some four days later. They were certainly crowded days for both the Archbishop and Mrs Fisher. He began with two broadcast sermons in the Cathedral, followed by an address to the clergy in the Chapter House; then on to visit two schools and Melbourne University where he was received by the Vice-Chancellor. A civic reception in the Town Hall followed, preceding lunch at Government House and a garden party hosted by the World Council of Churches and attended by clergy of all denominations.

And so their progress went on steadily and, for him and Mrs Fisher, happily. They stayed, among other places, at Brisbane, the capital of Queensland, a high-spot of the tour where he gave a memorable address on the welfare state stressing its dangers but also its splendid opportunities. From Brisbane it was on to Armidale, an educational centre; to Grafton, renowned for its annual Jacaranda Festival; to Newcastle, rapidly flexing its industrial muscle and the Anglican Theological College where he met clergy and their wives; finally to Hobart, capital of Tasmania, and a preachment in the Cathedral.

His visit to Canberra, established in 1912 as the capital and seat of the Federal Government, could not but be significant. It was appropriate that he should here be honoured by being the guest of the Governor-General. He described the city as a 'curious place in process of development, its ground plan being more evident from the air'. The Archbishop was particularly impressed with the remarkable memorial to commemorate the dead of the First World War. Mrs Fisher was entertained by the Governor-General's daughter and lunched with Mrs Menzies prior to her husband, the Prime Minister – an Anglophile and an enthusiastic cricketer – hosting a reception in the evening.

Geoffrey Fisher was now approaching the climax of his Australian tour and not even a car crash *en route* in which the Archbishop of Sydney and Mrs Fisher were involved – the car was a total write-off – was allowed to dampen the general enthusiasm. So it was that late in the afternoon they entered Sydney with its beaches full of sunshine; its famous Sydney Harbour Bridge and its American culture. His description of his entry into the city conjures up a lively scene. He and Mrs Fisher were escorted in an open car, preceded by prancing horses which made a magnificent cavalcade, while those hanging out of the windows of Sydney's skyscrapers threw down their tickertape. 'It was indeed a good show', so he commented. Even a threatened railway strike failed to dampen the general enthusiasm or prevent the crowds swarming around his car. 'It was one of the proudest moments of my life', Rosamond Fisher wrote later. 'The streets were thickly lined with people. We had to wave back to them and I tried to be like the Queen.'

Dr and Mrs Fisher were certainly given V.I.P. treatment. The Prime Minister was there as well as the Mayor and, *mirabile dictu*, representative Roman Catholics. The Fishers stayed with the Archbishop of Sydney, Dr Mowll, who was an old boy of King's School, Canterbury. His hospitality was kindness itself and no difference of churchmanship – he gave his support to the schismatic Church of England in South Africa much to Geoffrey Fisher's chagrin – was allowed to interfere with the warmth of their personal relations. This does credit to both men for Geoffrey Fisher deplored the fact that the Church in Sydney 'was almost entirely rock-bottom Irish Protestant – terribly so, and convinced of the rightness of what it says'. He believed that it was this extreme Evangelical churchmanship which had the paradoxical effect of provoking an equally extreme Anglo-Catholicism, especially in the Dioceses of Rockingham, Brisbane and Adelaide.

The first official calls that the Archbishop paid were to the Governor and the Prime Minister. There was the inevitable Press conference as at the beginning of his tour; the consecration by the Primate of All England of a new memorial chapel in Moore's Theological College; a dinner party at Bishopscourt; a sermon in the Cathedral; a speech in a cinema in Wollongong, a reception by the Lord Mayor at which the Archbishop addressed an audience of over 2,500 people in the Town Hall. Particularly significant was 21 November which he spent with the Governor and Lady Northcott and dined with members of the Government of New South Wales.

The last two days were largely concerned with ecclesiastical matters and it was in this context that Geoffrey Fisher determined to use his influence as the senior bishop of the Anglican Communion. He met, informally, a number of bishops and on the morning of 23 November, preached at a service attended by members of the General Synod. Then came the great moment, the climax of his visit to Australia when he addressed its members in the afternoon, handling the sensitive theme of the constitutional position of the Church of England in Australia, a matter to which we shall turn in the second half of this chapter.

It was a disappointment to Geoffrey Fisher that while in Sydney the Roman Catholics, to quote his own words, took great care not to come near him, unlike the Roman Catholic Bishop of Brisbane, 'a grand man' who made a point of conversing with him at a reception. On Friday 24 November, the Archbishop drove from Government House to the Cathedral where he bade his hosts and Australia farewell. It was the conclusion of a historic and memorable visit, unique, at that time, for an Archbishop of Canterbury.

It is customary to thank distinguished visitors somewhat effusively when their tour is over. Good manners at least require this. Some of the tributes which came the way of Geoffrey Fisher, however, suggest more than a polite acknowledgement for services rendered. The Archbishop of Perth, for example, when Geoffrey Fisher left his first port of call, talked of his 'taking the place by storm'. A letter from South Australia may, perhaps, be quoted in full as indicative of other tributes of a similar nature:

> The visit of the Archbishop has helped us a lot. It was the talk of the city. The addresses he gave were, of course, able and authoritative on every occasion and commanded great attention from Civic and Parliamentary quarters as well as from professional men and business people, nonconformist leaders and all the rank and file. His Grace was in a happy mood . . . The visit has done much to break down any stiffness between the Church and nonconformity.

Robert Menzies also expressed his great satisfaction in a letter to *The Times* in which he wrote 'It deserves to be widely known that the Archbishop's visit stirred men's hearts and minds all over Australia. He spoke as did his gracious wife to very many thousands but his appeal was always to the individual's duty in a cynical and distracted world. His language was elevated and simple, his message subtle and robust. At the very moment of my departure from England I am moved to pay this small tribute, politician and Presbyterian as I am, to a great man.'

Following in the footsteps of Geoffrey Fisher throughout Australia was A.P. Herbert who confessed that it was as if he were in the 'wake of a battleship' so great was the impact the Archbishop had made.

(ii)

A Constitution

The Church of England in Australia, such was the legal designation, derived from United Kingdom emigration to that country. Consequently links with 'home' and the Mother Church, in spite of geographical distance, were inevitably close and ministered to an understandable nostalgia. Many of its clergy and bishops in the early days were trained in England. In South Africa this link proved so strong that it was one of the psychological causes which brought the schismatic Church of England in South Africa into being – a church which in spite of all the Archbishop's pressure and persuasion he could not encourage to return to the Anglican Episcopal Church of the Province. The Australian situation was not entirely dissimilar though it never led to such an extreme result even if in one part of Australia a breakaway separatism seemed a real possibility. Certainly the Anglican Church there experienced tensions between different brands of churchmanship which in England went right back to the days of the Reformation. In the home country, however, this diversity was held together, if uneasily at times, by a common membership in an established national church. Overseas this situation could not obtain in the same way, not least because emigration to Australia, as the 20th century advanced, ceased to be almost exclusively British but increasingly multi-national. Thus the links with Great Britain, though they continued strong, were weakened and it became clear to the more percipient members of the Church of England in Australia that they must move towards an indigenous Church preserving an historical inheritance but authenticating its own life. It therefore came as a surprise to some in Australia to learn from a sermon preached by the Archbishop of Canterbury in Westminster Abbey in August 1947 that he believed this time had come and that advantage should be taken of it. The Church in Australia, he said, enjoys complete spiritual autonomy and is free to revise its formularies and to determine its law of worship in accordance with its own desires. Little did the Archbishop then know that the legal reality was, in fact, far otherwise as he himself discovered when Bishop Batty of Newcastle (Australia) acquainted him with a judgement given by Mr Justice Roper, Chief Judge in Equity, in New South Wales, in 1948. The circumstances surrounding this ruling may be briefly stated.

Twenty-three laymen in the Diocese of Bathurst brought a case against their Bishop on the grounds that he had authorised the use of an Order of Holy Communion – it came from what was known as the Red Book – which did not tally with that in the Book of Common Prayer. The legal question involved concerned whether such an action by the Bishop was a breach of the trust under which Church property belonging to the Diocese of Bathurst was held. Mr Justice Roper concluded: 'The Church of England came out to New South Wales as part of the established Church of England and nothing has taken place subsequently which had destroyed that relationship'.

In view of this judgement, so the Bishop of Newcastle informed Archbishop Fisher, the position which he, the Archbishop had set out in his sermon was unhappily not the case.

The effect of this judgement, if it were good in law, implied clearly that liturgical freedom in the Anglican Church of Australia was severely limited since it was tied to the Church of England. A court ruling fraught with such momentous consequences could not be ignored. In strict legal terms, the price of deviation from the Book of Common Prayer could entail loss of ecclesiastical properties. So seriously did Geoffrey Fisher view this situation that he got into touch with one of the few remaining informed canonists in England, Bishop Kirk of Oxford, who gave it as his opinion that it would be unwise for the Bishop of Bathurst to appeal against the ruling to the Privy Council. If, on the other hand, he simply disregarded the judgement the practical outcome might be to reinforce the need for a new Constitution for the Church of England in Australia.

The Archbishop now called a group together to confer with him at Lambeth consisting of Bishop Batty of Newcastle in Australia, Dr Don, Dean of Westminster, plus a few ecclesiastical lawyers. Their collective wisdom was that the Bishop of Bathurst was 'batting on a sticky wicket' and it was not surprising that the decision of the Court in Australia had gone against him. The result of this informal conference was that the Archbishop counselled the Bishop of Bathurst not to appeal against the judgement. He did advise, however, that he make application for a legal modification of the four Injunctions which tied the Church of Australia too closely to the Mother Church of England.

The Archbishop realised, of course, from the beginning that the issue at stake was a far wider one than simply the withdrawing of the 'Red Book' which the Bishop of Bathurst had in fact already decided to do. Underlying this disturbing situation was a problem fundamental to the future status and character of the Anglican Church in Australia. Of this the Archbishop was necessarily reminded by the fact that the Church of England was in process of revising its own Canon Law which led to his receiving a cablegram from Australia, signed by Archdeacon Begbie and others, which stated that a large body of clergy and laity in the Diocese of Sydney were deeply concerned by the Canon

Law proposals, so much so that they asked that their further consideration be delayed. The Archbishop confessed to Batty that his immediate reaction was to reply; 'Mind your own business. If we wish to revise our Canon Law, it is no concern of yours.' 'Then I paused,' he went on, 'remembering the queer relation in which the Church in Australia stands to English Ecclesiastical Law.' Thus he asked Bishop Batty for a 'clear statement' of precisely how far relationships between the Churches were in any way governed by the Canons of the Church of England. Batty's reply was not unexpected. It was that opinions differed. He then indulged in a private *cri de coeur*. For over thirty years he had been striving to secure a self-governing Constitution for the Church of England in Australia but his efforts again and again had been frustrated by the opposition of the Protestant wing in the Sydney Diocese.

The Archbishop now felt himself able to reply to Archdeacon Begbie. There was no hurry in this matter, he explained, since the proposed Canons had yet to obtain the assent of the Laity in the Church Assembly. However, it would be improper for him to interfere with 'the very complicated Church Law in Australia,' though he, personally, found it difficult to believe that the proposed Canon could bind the Church in that country. The result of this correspondence was to lead to private and confidential talks at the Lambeth Conference in 1948 which bore fruit when the Archbishop some two years later was himself in Australia. The logic here was irrefutable, namely that the solution to a very real problem lay outside England.

During the weeks that followed Geoffrey Fisher's arrival in Australia he was able to discover for himself the reaction of churchmen on the spot to the constitutional position which they had inherited. He found that most of them, outside Sydney, believed that the Anglican Church in Australia must assert its own autonomy and that this could best be done by drawing up a new Constitution for the whole Church. It was not, however, until he got to Sydney at the end of his tour that the Archbishop, as we have seen, addressed himself publicly to this constitutional problem within the Australian Church. The opportunity to use to the full the moral authority of his unique office presented itself when he acepted an invitation to address the House of Bishops and the General Synod.

He first dealt with the episcopal and hence diocesan requirements of the Australian Church and did so by raising a number of questions. For example, could Kalgoorlie be maintained as a separate diocese with only three priests? Ought not such small numbers to be put under Suffragans to the Archbishop but without all the paraphernalia of the customary diocesan establishment? Ought the normal Anglican rule which requires a Metropolitan to have a minimum of four dioceses under his jurisdiction to be dispensed with? Should each State have its own Archbishop, though this could lead to his isolation?

The answer to such questions might, he suggested, encourage the view that the Australian Church ought to be strengthened at the centre so as to bring more support to the Provinces. To this end why not an Archbishop of Australia with a small Diocese say at Canberra which would release him from the workload of a large Diocese or Province yet at the same time free him from the Sydney-Melbourne tension created by a rival churchmanship? If it were asked whether such an Archbishop would have anything to do the answer must be 'Yes', since without him there would never be a Church of Australia, only Provincial Churches loosely connected. Such an Archbishop would greatly increase internal cohesion, would represent the Church as a whole, and be a channel through which the world-wide concerns of the Anglican Communion could be made known to individual dioceses.

Such general reflections led him to the inescapable conclusion, that the Church of England in Australia must equip itself with a viable Constitution. 'It would be fatal if the Church in Australia declared that it could not get a Constitution; they must make another attempt. I am told that at the coming Synod it is to be suggested that the attempt should be abandoned; to do so would be a scandal. Give Sydney every safeguard . . . but get a Constitution. Fear must be replaced by trust.'

As to the designation 'the Church of England in Australia' he could well understand its sentimental appeal but it was 'incorrect and misleading.' The whole purpose of the proposed new Constitution must be to establish the Church in Australia as an autonomous member of the Anglican Communion. Why not 'the Church of Australia in Communion with the Church of England' – or more simply 'the Church of Australia?' The latter won the day.

The Archbishop's contribution, however, did not end with his departure from Australia. Before leaving he promised N.G. Hilliard, Bishop Co-adjutor of Sydney, in what he described as 'a lighthearted mood' that he himself would have a 'shot' at drawing up a Constitution, but never anticipated that in fact he would get round to it. But Dr Fisher was as good as his jocular word and spent his return journey to England from New Zealand doing precisely this. It was, for him, a congenial task and one in which he became more expert as the years went by. Such Constitutions were usually divided into two sections, the first designated 'Fundamental Declarations' which defined what the Church essentially was; the second how this particular Church should govern itself. Here, for Australia, the Archbishop in his document provided a General Synod for the whole Church comprising Bishops, Clergy and Laity voting together except when a separate vote was called for. In this respect his proposal differed from the Australian Draft Constitution under which voting was in separate Houses and no Resolution could be carried without the concurrence of the House of Bishops. 'In England,' Geoffrey Fisher commented, 'we are not so episcopal as that.' In sending his Draft to the Bishop of Newcastle the Archbishop admitted that he had little detailed knowledge of the Australian Church and that the Bishop might therefore well dismiss his effort as irrelevant. Dr Batty replied thanking the Archbishop for the help that he was giving them 'to wrestle with our constitutional problems'. In general the Archbishop's view was that the official Draft was far too complicated, and would, in respect of its numerous Canons, benefit from radical and judicial pruning going along with simplification. Also the Australian Draft tended to provide excessive and often unnecessary safeguards against the most unlikely contingencies almost to the point of absurdity. Realistically he saw the General Synod as competent to deal with everything but since doctrine, ceremonial and forms of worship were to many Church people a matter of conscience, an 'escape clause' for dioceses, at the expense of formal logic should be inserted. His words, as follows in his 'Observations', are both wise and liberal:

'Properly speaking a Canon should apply to every Diocese. But I recognise that by the way in which the Church in Australia has grown up that cannot yet be. Therefore full liberty should be given to a Diocese to contract out of any Canon so far as its own internal life of faith, ceremonial, discipline, etc, is concerned.'

The Archbishop's Draft, plus his comments on it, could not have reached the Bishop of Newcastle at a more opportune moment. Indeed, the Constitution Committee of the General Synod had just met and it was clear to its members that the indigenous Australian Draft would not secure the required approval by the Dioceses, certainly if the Amendments put forward by Sydney were included. As the Bishop saw it there were now only two possibilities: (1) To recommend individual provincial action whilst strengthening the General Synod; (2) To endeavour through mutual concessions to produce a Constitution which all could agree while giving to any 'apprehensive' Dioceses 'the right to contract out of any provision of the Constitution.'

In fact the latter was a concession which the Archbishop, if with reluctance, had himself adumbrated some months earlier when he addressed the General Synod. This provision was also in his own Draft. Taking a realistic view this accommodation was preferable to the whole project foundering.

Dr Batty kept the Archbishop fully informed, at the same time seeking his advice during the protracted negotiations which dragged on over the next five years. Fortunately, we need not, in this biography of Geoffrey Fisher, enter into these intricacies in detail; suffice to call attention to salient points in so far as they affected the Archbishop.

One thorny problem was the Appellate Tribunal which, under the terms of the Australian Draft, was required to consult the House of Bishops before making a definitive judgement or giving an opinion on matters of doctrine. But how would the Diocese of Sydney react to these proposals, particularly since it was 'adamant' that the last word on doctrine should rest with the Tribunal on which laymen were in the majority? 'This is one of the main rocks,' Batty reported back to Lambeth, 'on which the Constitutional hopes have been shattered more than once in the past.' As for himself, he felt he could salve his own conscience by arguing that the Appellate Tribunal was appointed by the General Synod which thus had a delegated episcopal authority behind it. Geoffrey Fisher accepted this compromise – as we have seen he suggested it – though he made two further proposals either of which would ensure a majority of clergy on the tribunal while providing for a very fair expression of lay opinion.

Getting the Constitution accepted was certainly a long haul but there was a general feeling among responsible Australian churchmen that it was now or never. Two factors were significant throughout in keeping things moving – Geoffrey Fisher's constant revisions and in the process making more simple his own Draft; and the sustained activity of Dr Batty, the most outstanding member of the Synod in this context.

Thus the Continuation Committee, having finalised its Draft, largely based on the Archbishop's, secured approval for it by the Convention in 1955 and in the same year by the General Synod.

It was now a matter of getting the Constitution approved by the Dioceses. Here Dr Batty was doubtful whether it would be successful in evangelical Sydney and in expressing his fears to the Archbishop intimated that other dioceses would go on with the Constitution regardless. The advice from Lambeth was peremptory: 'Go ahead without any doubt or hesitation,' in the hope that 'wiser counsels will prevail.' Fortunately they did!

David Gainsey, Secretary of the Continuation Committee, generously acknowledged the debt they owed the Archbishop who when they seemed to have reached an *impasse* pleaded successfully with the General Synod in 1950, and with several of the leaders of the various groups, to tackle the job afresh.

The Continuation Committee in its report to the General Synod in 1955 publicly reported that it had been 'assisted in its work by the Archbishop of Canterbury who had submitted to the Committee a revised and simplified Constitution which he had personally prepared'.

The fact that Geoffrey Fisher was able to intervene so decisively derived from a variety of causes. First he brought to bear upon the debate the prestige and the moral authority of the Primate of All England and Senior Bishop of the Anglican Communion. Secondly, he could view the controversy and its proper resolution more objectively than many who had lived, uncomfortably, with it in Australia for many years. Not even the most zealous Evangelical churchman in the Diocese of Sydney could accuse the Archbishop of being an extreme Anglo-Catholic either by upbringing or conviction! He stood on the middle ground between high churchmen on the one hand, and low evangelicals on the other. Thirdly, the creation of autonomous churches was a cause to which the Archbishop had devoted much time and thought, believing it to be essential if the Anglican Communion were effectively to face the challenges of the future. Fourthly, Archbishop Fisher, by his outgoing personality, had won golden opinions while traversing Australia. This made a great difference as it always does in negotiations.

When the Archbishop reflected upon his visit to Australia some years later he gave it as his opinion that perhaps the most important contribution which he had made to the Church in Australia was his championing publicly the cause of a new Constitution which led to one integrated Church. 'I am inclined to think,' we quote his own words, 'that it was the best thing I did in the Antipodes. The Australians took it extremely well and were really rather exhilarated by having a number of blows straight from the shoulder.'

On their return home, the Archbishop and Mrs Fisher were given an official welcome in the Central Hall, Westminster laid on by Dr Garbett, when kind and appreciative things were said about their visit to Australia and new Zealand which followed it.

It may not be inappropriate to notice here how important was the contribution which Mrs Fisher made to the success of this and other tours, overcoming an initial terror of air flights to do so. She entered into them with great enthusiasm, was garlanded with flowers wherever she went and proved a shrewd observer of the human scene. On many occasions she and the Archbishop separated so that they might undertake their individual ploys.

At times she could be somewhat critical of what she saw. Her one disappointment in Australia – it was but the spot which defiled the robe – was the dominance of the male in many areas of civic and religious life. Few women held prominent posts in the Church, and she was quietly amused if disapproving, to find that at many large receptions the women would congregate together at one end talking about domestic affairs while the men discussed business and farming at the other. Mrs Fisher's interest in animals, in the landscape, in vegetation and the flowers, particularly at Grafton, was pronounced.

CHAPTER 39

New Zealand

AT the Lambeth Conference of 1948 Geoffrey Fisher met and got to know some six bishops from the Province of New Zealand, which included the Primate, Archbishop C. West-Watson, the Bishop of Nelson, P. W. Stephenson, the Bishop of Auckland, W.J. Simkin and the Suffragan Bishop of Aotearoa, F.A. Bennett. New Zealand was on the eve of celebrating an anniversary than which there was none more significant in the course of its ongoing history. On 17 December, 1850 four emigrant ships from Britain had landed at Lyttleton near Christchurch. Not surprisingly it was at the 1948 Lambeth Conference that the idea was conceived of an archiepiscopal visit to New Zealand to coincide with the celebration of this historic event.

New Zealand owed much to the Church of England and to that remarkable man George Augustus Selwyn (1809–1878) who was consecrated Bishop of New Zealand in 1841. Almost alone he organised a scheme for the self-government of his diocese and visited England in 1854 to secure the necessary legal authorisation. He also arranged for the Church in New Zealand to manage its own affairs by means of a General Synod consisting of the Bishop, Presbyters and Laity which first met in 1859. Without doubt, Selwyn's pioneering work had an influence far beyond New Zealand, and was not without its effect upon the calling of the first Lambeth Conference by Archbishop Longley on 25 September, 1867 which the Bishop himself attended. The suggestion made by the Archbishop of New Zealand that the Primate of All England, accompanied by Mrs Fisher, should visit that country in 1950 was a prospect which Geoffrey Fisher received with the greatest pleasure and satisfaction. He, therefore, set about preparations for the tour with his usual care. Among his papers at Lambeth is a memorandum in which an anonymous writer gives his reflections upon New Zealand and its general ambience. Its general level of culture and education, he wrote, was not high though its people were generous, courageous yet materialistic. At weekends everything shuts down and horse racing takes over; nearly every one bets. Also the New Zealand Government, through its Public Relations Board, was most helpful in providing notes on the various personnel – governmental and civic – whom the Archbishop would be meeting in the course of his travels. When he, with his accustomed emphasis on the practical, asked a clerical New Zealander what clothes he should wear he received the

Assembly of the World Council of Churches, Evanston, USA 1954: The Archbishop of Canterbury and the Right Reverend Henry Sherrill, Presiding Bishop of the Episcopal Church of USA.

The Archbishop and Mrs Fisher with their staff at Lambeth Palace, July 1955.

Rededication of Lambeth Palace Chapel after its restoration in the presence of the Queen, the Royal Family and the Bishops of the Church of England, 19 October 1955.

Greeting African and Indian Ladies in Mbale, Uganda, 1955.

Consecration of four African Bishops in Uganda, Namirembe Cathedral,
May 1955.

Mrs Fisher greeting
Kikuyu women at
Fort Hall, Kenya.

The Archbishop greeting a Sister in East Africa, 1955.

Inauguration of the Province of
Central Africa in Salisbury
Cathedral, Southern Rhodesia, 8
May 1955.

Sharing a joke with the
Archbishop of Cape Town
(G. H. Clayton), the Archbishop
of Central Africa (E. F. Paget
and the Bishop of Matabeleland
(W. J. Hughes), after the
inauguration of the Province of
Central Africa.

The Archbishop talking to two Nuns.

The Archbishop in Nigeria, 1960.

The Archbishop with the Patriarch of the Armenians in Turkey, 1960.

The Archbishop in Istanbul greeted by the Oecumenical Patriarch, 1960.

Surveying the Holy Land, 1960.

reply 'A pair of shorts and an open neck shirt', 'This is just what I would like to wear', he protested, 'but they won't let me.'

The Archbishop and Mrs Fisher, after their most successful tour of Australia, left from the docks at Sydney to board the *Monowre* en route for New Zealand. They were deeply moved as the Australian Bishops dressed in their cassocks, sang lustily: 'For they are jolly good fellows'. The two of them were escorted on to the bridge by the Captain as they sailed out of 'this lovely harbour' under the great bridge. Rosamond Fisher relates that they now 'thankfully relaxed and slept for most of the three days' voyage', until they sighted the northern tip of New Zealand on the evening of 27 November and arrived at Auckland on the following morning. As they neared the dockside they glimpsed the Bishop and Archdeacon of Auckland waiting to greet them and as soon as the gangway was down they came aboard accompanied by the Mayor and representatives of the Governor-General and the Prime Minister. A group of children sang a heart-warming welcome. Once disembarked and greeted by bishops, clergy and laity, the Archbishop could not but recall that it was from this very spot that George Augustus Selwyn set out to fulfil the explicit charge given him by Archbishop Longley namely to use his See 'as a fountain diffusing the stream of salvation over the islands and coasts of the Pacific'.

The itinerary for Geoffrey Fisher's journey began in Auckland in North Island and ended up at Christchurch, South Island, the route being *via* Hamilton, Rotorua and Napier. This meant that for the next month both the Archbishop and Mrs Fisher travelled New Zealand almost non-stop, fulfilling engagements so numerous as to make severe physical demands upon them. But to both it was *labor amoris*. All we can hope to do is to highlight some of its key events and to suggest the general atmosphere which obtained wherever they went. Central, of course, as it was the reason for the visit, were the Centenary Celebrations at Christchurch. Of all his tours this one, perhaps, aroused the greatest enthusiasm, largely because British sentiment was stronger in New Zealand than in other Commonwealth countries. Certainly New Zealand was the most English, still bearing the impress of the pioneering initiatives of Bishop Selwyn which led to the Church of England playing a strongly formative part in building up the life and loyalties of the nation. Indeed the 1850 settlers left their native land blessed on their way by Archbishop Sumner at a service in St Paul's Cathedral.

When Rosamond Fisher travelled with the Archbishop on these exhausting tours she played a full part in them. Never was this more the case than in New Zealand, where the Mothers' Union was traditionally strong. She spoke to numerous such gatherings and encouraged in her hearers a sense of pride in belonging to a society widely distributed throughout the Anglican world. The shape and pattern of the visit were very similar to that in Australia though geographically on a reduced scale. On the eve of their final departure Mrs Fisher drew up a list of the people they had met and come to know. It is certainly comprehensive – Maori Mothers' Union members; bishops, clergy and their wives; Mayors, Mayoresses and councillors; Prime Ministers, the Governor-General; captains and crews of ships, drivers of government cars and escort policemen; school teachers and their pupils. Even in these brief encounters Geoffrey and Rosamond Fisher were adept in making effective relations. It was indeed more than a shake of the hand. Rosamond Fisher, commenting on the above list, said that all were 'kind friends who made our visit so memorable and so happy'. The fact is, of course, that both Geoffrey Fisher and Rosamond really were interested in people.

It was typical of the pace and tempo of the Archbishop's whole itinerary that on the very first day, having arrived in Auckland early in the morning, almost immediately he was in the Cathedral Church of St Mary attending a liturgical welcome. Dean Monteath long remembered seeing the Archbishop's eyes, during the service, 'scanning the mellow timbers of the building, and the stained glass of the sanctuary'. In the afterrnoon the Dean came across him again, alone in the Cathedral walking up and down or just quietly sitting: 'I always imagined a wooden church as a temporary construction', he remarked, 'but here you have a Cathedral of great beauty which looks as if it could last for centuries'.

It was in Auckland that the Archbishop made his first personal contact with the Maoris whose community numbered about 115,000. True the Archbishop had been earlier briefed by the Archbishop of New Zealand who expressed his concern for the future status of these indigenous inhabitants. For many years there had been a Maori suffragan bishop, the greatly beloved Bishop Augustus Bennett of Aotearoa, though there had been difficulties which led some to doubt whether it would be wise to appoint a Maori successor. Yet if this innovation were abandoned, the Maoris might be tempted to form a Maori Church. As it was a Maori priest, Metana Panapa, was appointed Bennett's successor and was consecrated a bishop on 29 August 1951.

Dr Fisher, in response to the Archbishop's letter, confessed that he was ignorant of the problems of the South Pacific; but one of the bonuses of being at Lambeth was that it compelled him to acquire much information which it was 'good to know'. Geoffrey Fisher was now to meet the Maoris face to face at Queen Victoria School where its girls gave him the warmest of traditional welcomes. He, on his part, was soon at home among them and was seen, in characteristic guise, walking through the grounds his arms around a girl on either side. His visit to St Stephen's Boys School for Maoris was an equal success and the Dean of Auckland writes: 'It was my job to see that he kept to his programme, but this was quite impossible. This school is renowned for its rugby football – need I say more! He was virtually mobbed by teams of boys discussing their favourite topics, and was in his most exultant mood, enjoying every moment and giving out so much.' The boys treated the Archbishop and Mrs Fisher to some of their more fearsome war dances, their eyes rolling wildly. The leader reappeared a little later, this time in a red cassock and white surplice!

The next day the Archbishop was the celebrant in the Cathedral at a Mothers' Union Festival when members from all over the diocese, including a large proportion of Maoris were present. The Cathedral was full to overflowing and hundreds were standing outside, joining heartily in the congregational singing. Another, if small incident, may be quoted, typifying his immediate impact upon the young. The choir boys were captivated by him and on the eve of his leaving they dashed to a nearby shop, pooled their resources, bought a box of chocolates and gave it to him with a little speech by the senior boy. He opened the box as they drove off offering the contents around and telling the boys how much this simple gesture meant to him.

Space does not permit our dilating on the Archbishop's steady progress from North to South Island. At Hamiliton after an act of worship, the Archbishop was reported missing but was finally found in the belfry where a new peal had just been installed. The Archbishop and Mrs Fisher were indeed thrilled by the spectacular scenery around them, particularly as they threaded their way along the 200 miles of mountain roads soaring to near 3,000 feet and then dropping down into a deep rift which led to Napier. To construct such a pass, so the deeply impressed Mrs Fisher commented, was a veritable triumph of engineering. Napier was of particular interest to the Archbishop since way back in 1930 an earthquake destroyed the Cathedral and as a consequence they were still worshipping in a wooden building. On the next day they left for Wellington diverting to visit Wanganui another great public school. 'Windy Wellington' lived up to its 'weather reputation' but in spite of Mrs Fisher not feeling well she addressed a meeting of some 3,000 people which included a large contingent from the Mothers' Union. The crossing to South Island could be quite nerve-racking, since it entailed going through a narrow pass which Geoffrey and Rosamond Fisher successfully negotiated at three in the morning. In Nelson they stayed at Bishopsdale, the loveliest of all episcopal houses, which was set on a hillside enriched by a wonderful display of trees, shrubs and flowers. The final destination for the Archbishop was

Christchurch and apart from a short stop for a picnic lunch they were hard at it from early morning to the evening, Mrs Fisher feeling that the countryside often reminded her of Wales and Scotland. Some areas had obviously been devastated by bush fires, evidence of which were thousands and thousands of dead trees gruesome in their suggesting serried ranks of skeletons.

At long last, across the Canterbury plain – 'as flat as the flattest parts of Lincolnshire' – they came to the hallowed site to which England, a hundred years earlier, had dispatched settlers in four sailing ships. It was hence appropriate that the lay celebrations should take the form of a dramatic re-enactment of the landing at Lyttleton which lies over the Cashmere Hills, ten miles from Christchurch itself. Mrs Fisher writes: 'The actors fully and very correctly dressed and equipped with old-fashioned luggage came ashore in long boats where they were greeted by speeches of welcome. The drama took place on a raised stage and microphones enabled the vast assembly to hear the spoken words. Everything was done in style and 1,500 people sat down in a dockside shed at a banquet where addresses were given by the Governor-General, the Prime Minister and the Archbishop of Canterbury.'

The historic day started early when Geoffrey Fisher celebrated Holy Communion in a packed Cathedral and recorded peals of the bells of Westminster Abbey, St Paul's Cathedral and Christ Church, Oxford rang forth. This was followed by the great Thanksgiving Service which was indeed the culmination of months of careful preparation. Provision was made for the congregation to overflow into the square outside which, with its central space and three streets leading to it, resembled a large open-air Cathedral. An indication of the number of worshippers can be seen in that some 29,000 service papers were distributed. Every available inch of space was deployed even to using offices and shop windows around the Square. The Cathedral Choir led the singing inside the Church, while a large voluntary choir performed outside. Before the Sermon, the Governor-General Lord Freyberg, and his wife, together with Mrs Fisher, were escorted to the platform at the West End of the Cathedral to be joined, in procession, by the Archbishop of New Zealand and his Bishops, followed by the Archbishop of Canterbury. The Governor-General appropriately read a message from His Majesty, King George VI. It was indeed a stirring sight that confronted Geoffrey Fisher as he climbed on to the platform and embarked upon his sermon preaching on the familiar text: 'For he looked for a city that hath foundations, whose builder and maker is God'. As befitted so valedictory an occasion he first paid tribute to the vision of the Founding Fathers Bishop Selwyn, Edward Gibbon Wakefield and John Robert Godley – the 'planners' who had, in days gone by, made this celebration possible. He commended the Church of England for its courageous championship of a humane colonising policy based on Christian principles; and he made a special mention of all that successive Governments had done for New Zealand over the past one hundred years. The early settlers had indeed handed on to posterity a true and unselfish tradition. He concluded with these words: 'So I greet you on this glorious day when here, citizens with a wonderful tradition, members of the great family of the British Commonwealth, bound by splendid ties of loyalty to the King and to one another, look back upon the achievements of those who made this heritage for you; praise God for it, and looking to the future we look not afraid, not fearful, prepared to give whatever may be demanded of us, as these pioneers did, in building a true community among men.'

The enthusiasm and emotion which accompanied this commemoration were intense. Never before had the Archbishop preached to some thirty thousand people physically gathered together 'with one accord in one place'. Nostalgia for a distant homeland had, doubtless, much to do with this collective response though Dr Fisher's words invited the congregation to look to the future. However, they were still able to respond with fervour to 'O faith of England taught of old' and to be stirred by the trumpeters who in their red coats, blue breeches, white stockings, and silver-buckled shoes sounded a fanfare specially written for the occasion. Appropriately the service was ecumenical, the Moderator of the Presbyterian Assembly of New Zealand and the President of the Methodist Conference attending. Alas the Roman Catholics were conspicuous only by their absence.

The crowded month spent in New Zealand was now rapidly drawing to a close. The Archbishop and Mrs Fisher, with the chaplain, went off to Dunedin, where a corporate communion was celebrated followed by a large meeting of the Mothers' Union with the Dominion and Diocesan Presidents present. Fittingly at the close, a group of Maori mothers sang their farewell on which Mrs Fisher – perhaps to conceal or express the depth of her feelings – commented that it had become well known in England in Gracie Fields' version 'Now is the hour when we must say goodbye'. The result was that all joined spontaneously to sing it in English. It only remained for the Archbishop and Mrs Fisher, on the following morning, to drive, in a temperature over 90 degrees Fahrenheit, to enjoy their first brief 'holiday', ascending into the mountains to get at least a glimpse of the snow covered 'Alps'. The day, Mrs Fisher writes, was 'crystal clear' and they saw Mount Cook and Mount Tasman 'in all their loveliness'. The next morning they left Lyttleton early in the steamer for Wellington which they reached at 6 pm and were 'quickly transferred' without fuss to their home for the coming month.

It had been a gruelling four weeks but to the Fishers it was deeply satisfying and rewarding. They could not but be moved to represent the world-wide Anglican Church on a uniquely historic occasion and in an office which ante-dated that of the British Monarchy. Travelling so many miles by car and not by air, made *ad hoc* contacts possible including visits to the outback where they met many lonely and scattered families. Mrs Fisher sympathised with the women whose husbands were far away rounding up the cattle. Often a reception could be so uninhibited that the Primate of All England was literally smothered by those who wished to shake his hand: at least once the Archbishop had to be rescued by the police!

However, Geoffrey Fisher's appeal was not only to a nostalgic British sentiment. During his month in New Zealand he addressed all kinds of people on all sorts of occasions and on a diversity of subjects – clergy and laity, specialised groups of men and women, academics, Rotarians, the list is almost endless. The themes which he handled were on the whole simple, serious, and he believed significant. Looked at from the vantage ground of the last decade of the twentieth century they may seem traditional and simplistic. The keynote of the first address he gave in New Zealand was the dire need for everyone to stand firm in the faith over against the materialism rife in contemporary society. 'The State and the secular life come first today', he said at a civic reception in Wellington 'but this was not always so.' A corrective to this over-emphasis was to give priority to regular Sunday worship, an old-fashioned practice, maybe, but still relevant. Thus he deprecated the way in which the car took families at weekends into the open countryside all the hours of daylight, thus making them unmindful of their religious obligations. Tramping the hills was no alternative to church-going.

There was little new or original in this address – but it was said with conviction and couched in a direct language which the ordinary person could understand. Perhaps he was a little influenced by the five duties of a churchgoer drawn up at the Lambeth Conference! By no means, however, did he suggest that religion should be kept out of politics. Indeed he urged Christians 'to get into world affairs and set standards'. They should show the reality of their faith by Christian service in public life. This was important since, though the Archbishop was a great supporter of the Welfare State, he believed that it demanded of every citizen a higher standard of morality for it to work fairly and efficiently. If this was not forthcoming then the Welfare State could be abused. It needed honest work and self-sacrifice.

Just before Geoffrey Fisher left New Zealand, an extra meeting at short notice was added to the Archbishop's programme by the National Council of Churches. It took place on Friday 13 December and the

Archbishop was given as his subject recent developments in the Inter-Church field. Many thought that this talk to a more specialist audience was one of his most valuable discourses. The Archbishop reviewed the growth of ecumenicism from the time of the Amsterdam Assembly suggesting his own views as to what the next step should be. He looked forward to the time when all Churches, without losing their distinctive features, should contain the essential characteristics of Catholicity, including episcopal, presbyterial and congregational elements.

The Principal of College House, Martin Sullivan, later Dean of St Paul's Cathedral, as he reflected upon the Archbishop's visit suggested that he left behind him, as a result of his many addresses and press conferences, two simple truths relating to the meaning of Anglican Churchmanship, namely: to the need for every citizen to accept increasing personal responsibility through honest work and self-sacrifice; to be true to the vision of a community devoted to a Christ-like ideal necessary to give direction in a new Country.

More important even than the impact of his teaching, however, was the impression left behind of his own personality. Here the Principal of College House comments: 'It was obvious that for him people mattered and mattered greatly. Wherever he went, he found himself surrounded by men and women. His approach to each one of them was direct and personal. In every place he would be seen, standing arm in arm with someone across a lawn, up and down a veranda or around a building. He seemed to have that vitality and freshness which speaks of an inward peace.'

CHAPTER 40

West Africa

(i)

DURING his tenure of office at Lambeth Geoffrey Fisher made four journeys to Africa for the purpose of inaugurating autonomous Provinces within the world-wide Anglican Communion. In general terms, though not in every particular, these Constitutions were modelled on that of the already existing Province of South Africa. This meant that each had, as a focal point of unity, a Metropolitan-Archbishop who presided over the General Synod on which each Diocese was represented.

In the eyes of many Europeans, until experience taught them otherwise, Africa all too easily and uncritically presented itself as a largely homogeneous black continent in which numbers of whites and Asians had settled. This did not correspond with the facts for the black population was distributed among people of different ethnic origins and tribal patterns as well as religious and cultural backgrounds. Colonisation by the Great Powers had been piecemeal; and the approach to their responsibilities, not least to their final departure from the scene, was varied. Thus in the general acquisitive scramble for territory in Africa by the West, the boundaries of the African States then set up were contrived and artificial. White supremacy was superimposed upon vast areas richly diverse; and often in this process tribal identities and the cohesion which went with them were obliterated. Into the vestigial remains of this wide-ranging pluralism came the Anglican Church ministering at first to white settlers living abroad, but inevitably at length leaping over the wall into missionary activity as did most other churches and denominations. The *Ecclesia Anglicana* brought with it an administrative hierarchical system which went back to Augustine's mission of AD 597 – and came to include bishops, deans and chapters, archdeacons, rural deans and parish clergy. In England, and this was pragmatically the result of a long history in which the English nation began as the child of the Church, there was a close interlocking legal nexus with the State under the Royal Supremacy. The latter, the Establishment, was, of course, non-exportable and could not therefore obtain throughout the Anglican Communion overseas.

Geoffrey Fisher was destined to play a leading role in bringing to birth constitutionally autonomous ecclesiastical Provinces throughout Africa. These led, in the course of time, to indigenous churches as the dominating influence of a white leadership, out of all proportion to its numbers, delined. Thus Max Warren, the General Secretary of the Church Missionary Society, after quoting Karl Marx's dictum that capitalism and colonialism by their very nature dig their own graves, went on to add: 'It was part of Geoffrey Fisher's far-sighted and practical statesmanship that he saw the same was true of missionary and ecclesiasticial paternalism. The steady and deliberate diminution of the Metropolitan authority of Canterbury was the sequel to this awareness.'

Geoffrey Fisher consistently gave close and time-consuming personal attention to drawing up the Provincial Constitutions for West, Central and East Africa. He also drew up Constitutions for many Dioceses. The Archbishop, as we have seen, inherited a special Committee to advise him in this important but intricate area, its chairman being Bishop Palmer formerly of Bombay. The Archbishop was not at first made aware of the existence of the Committee, so much so that when confronted on going to Lambeth with the need of a Constitution for Mombasa he undertook this task himself. However, the drawing up of a Constitution was to him no wearisome labour but a task congenial to his temperament. Hence, he tended to take this exercise more and more into his own hands. Indeed he once confessed: 'If I had another career, I might have become a perfectly competent parliamentary draughtsman'.

It should be noticed that when Geoffrey Fisher went to Lambeth there was still a large number of what were described as 'Overseas Bishops of the Canterbury Jurisdiction'. This, on occasions, could lead to such absurd situations as the Archbishop, thousands of miles away from the scene of the 'crime', being required to sift a mass of evidence and decide, for example, whether a Ugandan priest had illegally sold rice from his own front door. Increasingly Geoffrey Fisher came to the conclusion that, if only in terms of sheer practicality, the Anglican Church in Africa must grow up and authenticate its own life.

Though directly admiring the pioneering work of different missionary societies Geoffrey Fisher yet deplored some of its side-effects. For example the Church Missionary Society tended to be loyal to the Evangelical tradition of Charles Simeon; the Universities Mission to Central Africa to the High Church tradition of the Oxford Movement exemplified in such as Charles Gore. Geoffrey Fisher felt a deep sense of remorse that such pluralism should introduce divisions in Africa arising from varieties of churchmanship which had their roots and relevance far away in the chequered religious history of Western Europe. There ought to be in Africa, he was convinced, a recognisable uniformity in church life sufficient at least for an Anglican when moving from one part of that great Continent to another to feel himself as belonging to the same Church. Thus not least among the advantages of Provincial status was its overcoming a sense of isolation in smaller and distant areas, while providing in its General Synod a final authority for faith and order. It was, moreover, a safeguard against remote dioceses becoming monolithic and introspective both in churchmanship and theological stance; also against eccentric schemes for reunion.

However it was one thing to recognise the need for Provinces, quite another to set them up in practice, so great were the difficulties necessarily involved. These may be briefly listed and will be illustrated existentially throughout this chapter.

First there was a natural conservatism resistant to change and apprehensive of the unknown, such as the shedding of jurisdiction from Canterbury might seem to bring with it. Here sentiment loomed large and many dioceses were reluctant to break this traditional link. Particularly was this the case with some older bishops, who shrank from cultivating a wider allegiance and looked primarily to the missionary society which supported their work. Secondly, difficulties often presented themselves in determining what dioceses should go into which newly constituted Province – and what dioceses should be left out! This was not always easy to resolve. Sometimes, it is true, history or geography could help to decide it, but not always. More serious were political, cultural and tribal factors, particularly since many black Africans had a built-in distrust of the white settler and warmed more easily to a remote Archbishop not on the spot.

During his stay at Lambeth, and not least as a result of his leadership, persistence and drive, four Provinces were set up in Africa: West Africa (1951); Central Africa (1955); East Africa (1960); Uganda (1960). In no case was this an easy or straightforward exercise though the extent of the difficulties varied in each instance. The setting up of these Provinces entailed a vast correspondence, much exhausting travel, countless interviews with bishops, clergy, Government personnel both black and white. In a personal message to the Western Equatorial African Church Magazine, Geoffrey Fisher wrote: 'One of the privileges which as the Archbishop of Canterbury I can set against the heavy duties of my office is that of being in constant touch with Provinces and Dioceses of the Anglican Communion all over the world, having a share in their faith and their fortunes . . . further I have close links with all your Bishops; with all but one I shared the vivid fellowship of the recent Lambeth Conference . . . and I am constantly having the delight of meeting West African Christians here in London from Nigeria and elsewhere.'

(ii)

We now turn from these general observations to examine how the Archbishop of Canterbury used his metropolitical status as Primate of

All England, to establish Provinces in Africa in relation to Churches under his jurisdiction. We begin with West Africa which brought together the Dioceses of Lagos, Sierra Leone, Accra, the Niger, Gambia and the Rio Pongas. This did not prove easy and many responsible church people, black and white, were apprehensive of the consequences which might flow from it, not least from the withdrawal of the Archbishop of Canterbury's personal jurisdiction.

The possibility of such a Province had been mooted for several years and as early as 1944, at the request of William Temple, then Archbishop of Canterbury, the bishops of West Africa met in conference at Accra for this purpose. However, the Archbishop's sudden death delayed but did not hinder the project from going forward. Geoffrey Fisher had not been long at Lambeth before he received the text of a proposed Constitution which he referred to Bishop Palmer. By 1946 the Bishop and his colleagues, having worked upon the script, were in a position to let Dr Fisher have a first draft based on the South African model. It was important that any terms of such Constitutions should be right and that they should not lay up problems for future generations. Here, Dr Fisher was helpful being well aware of possible dangers and of his responsibility to prevent them. As he pointed out to Sherwood Jones, Bishop of Lagos, '. . . it is essential that the constitutional Foundations shall be well and truly laid. The legal pitfalls are very considerable as has recently been shown in Australia . . . It is my bounden duty to see that every care is taken to secure a workable and fool-proof Constitution for the Province which will not land it subsequently in legal difficulties with the Diocese.'

The practical problem was not only one of getting the right balance in the Constitution but of persuading those who were hesitant to go forward. One such was Canon Howells who saw the Archbishop at Lambeth on 30 April 1947. The Church in West Africa, he explained to Dr Fisher, was at the moment so exclusively English that no African priest was allowed to preach or minister in it. The Africans had little understanding of what Provincial status meant and anyhow resented such a change being imposed upon them from above. Not least they deplored the implication, as they saw it, that the Archbishop of Canterbury wished to rid himself of responsibility for them. The Archbishop, however, was not convinced that such inhibitions should hinder a steady progess towards Provincial status. Such a step was under consideration long before he went to Lambeth and it was only after the Diocesan Synods had approved that he decided to go forward. But Canon Howells persisted in urging caution. Let things develop naturally was his advice. The Archbishop made the gesture of promising to re-open the whole matter when the bishops of West Africa met together at Lambeth in 1948.

Perhaps Canon Howells' anxieties were excessive since there was a built-in safeguard against undue haste as each diocese had to be dealt with separately and this was time-consuming. What the Archbishop was not prepared to contemplate was the launching of a new Province with only two dioceses (as, for example, the Niger and Lagos). In spite of the fears of some, the more optimistic were strongly in favour of going forward hoping that the whole enterprise might be carried through by 1949. To this end the Archbishop received a formal request from the Bishop of Lagos to launch the new Province during that year. However, this timetable proved quite impracticable since there were many thorny problems still unresolved. Prominent amongst these, as we have suggested, was the fear by some of losing the protecting umbrella of the Archbishop of Canterbury's jurisdiction. In compensation Samuel Phillips, Assistant Bishop of Lagos, was in favour of an Archbishop's Committee to undertake the nomination of Diocesan Bishops. It was Geoffrey Fisher himself, however, who insisted that such an expedient would frustrate the proper functioning of responsible synodical government. However, nothing came of this proposal.

It had become Anglican practice that there should be a minimum of four dioceses to constitute a Province. The need to obtain their multiple agreement was in itself an inhibiting factor to making rapid progess. Particularly was this the case with the Diocese of Accra where the general situation was one of disorder and frustration. This was largely due, so was the common opinion, to the age and incapacity of the Bishop who influenced his Diocesan Synod to oppose the proposed Provincial Constitution on the grounds that once inaugurated, it would encourage unwise ecumenical schemes for reunion. Geoffrey Fisher expressed his surprise at such opposition since, as he told the Bishop of Accra, this was at variance with the views received from the Bishops of Lagos, Sierra Leone and Gambia. The Archbishop's strong view was that the existence of a Province of West Africa would in itself be a safeguard against any eccentric attempts at reunion. One thing, alas, was essential namely that the octogenarian Bishop should go. To assist this, the Archbishop, after making contact with his brother, wrote to the Bishop a very strong but understanding letter urging his resignation. This he peremptorily refused, thus frustrating the hopes of the indigenous clergy, though under this pressure he at last agreed to approve the new Provincial Constitution. It was not, however, until April 1951, after Geoffrey Fisher determined to extract a formal resignation (with another letter to his brother) that he retired.

The quality as well as the general attitude of the episcopate in West Africa was important if the setting up of a new Province was to be initiated with a good send-off. In many respects, unfortunately, the very virtue of the older type of missionary bishop, paternalistic and necessary in earlier days, was a handicap in facing up to a radically emerging challenge.

In 1945 Bishop Lasbury of Nigeria intimated his intention to resign. After an abortive effort was made to secure as his successor 'an outstanding evangelical' clergyman from the Diocese of Southwark, the Archbishop nominated Cecil Patterson who for three years had been Assistant Bishop on the Niger and was to become Archbishop and Metropolitan of West Africa in 1961. Although experienced in the life of the Church in that area – he had served there since 1934 – the new Bishop soon ran into difficulties largely due to the general spirit of the Diocese in being conservative and hostile to change. The Archbishop of Canterbury was sensitive to his problems and did his best to rally him in an understanding letter. 'I know,' he wrote, 'that natural sentiment constantly makes it difficult for people to accept happily disturbances of the arrangements to which they are accustomed . . . it is no disrespect for the past when new arrangements have to be made; indeed it is often the faithful work of the past which makes this necessary.'

In fairness to Bishop Patterson it has to be admitted that the large geographical extent of the Diocese on the Niger, the home of the 'wonderfully organised and cohesive' Ibo people, had long been felt to constitute certain problems in relation to the inauguration of the Province of Western Africa. Bishop Patterson took the view that Nigeria should be divided into a number of dioceses, thereby justifying its becoming a Province in its own right. The Archbishop questioned the wisdom of this solution and for three reasons – that Nigeria was not strong enough to support a Province on its own; the absence of Nigeria from the proposed Province would weaken it; that if Nigeria was left on its own it might be tempted to enter, unilaterally, into reunion schemes and in so doing go outside the Anglican Communion.

It would be tedious to particularise the difficulties experienced by the various dioceses on the way to their entering into one Province. However, the Constitution having, in principle, been approved it was now up to the Archbishop to put it before his own Committee which he did early in 1949. His members worked hard on it till in May the Archbishop was able to send a memorandum explaining its terms to the Bishops concerned – Niger, Lagos, Accra and Gambia with the Rio Pongas.

The Archbishop was not yet 'home and dry'. The Bishop of Lagos criticised the Draft on the grounds that the latest revision differed seriously from that first put forward. 'Very true,' replied the Archbishop, but there had been many consultations since then involving Lambeth and West African Bishops. Where changes had been made it was on the whole with their consent. It had certainly been a long haul before the Constitution was finally approved. Under its terms the only remaining legal nexus with the historic See of Canterbury lay in the Archbishop being the final court of appeal.

The time had now come to plan the inauguration ceremony. Thus in the early autumn of 1950, three Bishops – John Daly of Gambia and the Rio Pongas, Leslie Vining of Lagos and John Horstead of Sierra Leone – called at Lambeth Palace to confer with the Archbishop on the 'run up' to this great occasion. After a lengthy discussion and when they had reached the point of agreeing that it should take place in 1951 Geoffrey Fisher, to the astonishment of the other three, suddenly interjected: 'Let me get my diary and see when I can come'. Bishop Horstead later commented: 'The idea of the Archbishop of Canterbury coming in person to West Africa had never entered our heads. Such a visit would make history for never before had the Primate travelled to inaugurate in person a new Province of the Anglican Communion.'

The next question to answer was where the inauguration should take place, a matter not so easily resolved as it would be in England. It was at first difficult to choose between Lagos and Accra but they finally opted for Sierra Leone in spite of the fact that it was a poor and small Diocese – and that in April water in Freetown was in short supply! It was, however, the cradle where the Anglican Church was born and this sentimental association decided the choice.

As a last duty before he left England on 10 April 1951 the Archbishop sent a somewhat hesitant and half-apologetic letter to King George VI informing him that he was leaving for Freetown in the colony of Sierra Leone on a work of 'great importance in the life of the Anglican Communion in West Africa'. He then went on to explain, in some detail, the character of the occasion and how this great step forward to independence came at a time when there were also changes in secular government in that region. 'I reproach myself,' he wrote, 'for not having written earlier to give Your Majesty this information in which case I should also have asked whether Your Majesty could possibly give me some very brief message to the Church in West Africa which I could read at the service of inaugurating the Province on Tuesday next, 17 April. I dare hardly ask or expect that such a message might be sent to me by cable and, if so, it must be my own fault for missing an opportunity which I am sure Your Majesty would have wished to take of wishing Godspeed to the Church in West Africa on this important occasion.' This letter is surely a classic of its kind but the King does not seem to have responded to it probably for fear of creating a precedent. Maybe it would have been an excellent precedent to make!

When the Archbishop arrived at the Government Wharf in Freetown he was greeted by the Mayor and a Service of Thanksgiving was held in St George's Cathedral. There then followed a week of great exertion, which may be briefly summarised – attendance at a garden party in the grounds of the Annie Walech Memorial School; participation in the consecration of Roderick Coote as Bishop of Gambia and the Rio Pongas; a tour of the colony's villages and churches; a conference with Diocesan representatives; addressing the Synod; a reception by a United Christian Council of Welcome; a journey to Bo with the Governor, and a visit to Fourah Bay.

The highlight of the visit and, of course, its primary purpose, was the service which inaugurated the new Province of West Africa in St George's Cathedral, Freetown, early in the morning of 17 April. It began with a fine fanfare of trumpets, and a solemn procession into the Cathedral led by six African Diocesans and four Assistant Bishops. The service took the form of a sung Eucharist with a full choir and was, as might have been expected, very English in the rite used (1662); also in the hymns chosen, the robes worn and words spoken. What was not so English was the large congregation's exuberant, uninhibited singing, colourful dress and rapt attention which gave the occasion a truly African flavour. The climax came when the Bishops signed the Preamble and Articles of the Constitution, after which the Archbishop formally released them from his Primatial Jurisdiction.

The Archbishop preached the sermon addressing the congregation simply, and with great moral force. He took as his text – a favourite with him – 'Jerusalem which is above is free which is the Mother of us all'. His theme centred around the privilege yet responsibilities associated with freedom. On the dark side it could bring an abuse of power which 'marks one of the great tragedies of history' as could be seen in 'the dreadful evil of slavery, an evil almost as old as mankind, but for a season vilely exploited and multiplied for gain and introduced as a leprosy into the record of the British people'. It would be all too easy for West Africa to succumb to the temptation of taking over from Europe 'precisely our bad things, our insoluble problems, our deadly materialism, our poverty of spirit, or indeed to learn from totalitarian countries the utterly false creeds which seek to build freedom by violence, to create liberty by bondage and to exalt the spirit of man by denying his significance'. Ultimately the future of West Africa depended 'less upon governments than upon people, their education in wisdom and capacity to learn from experience'. He concluded his address with these words: 'In all the travail of these times and of the times to come may the whole church and the Church of West Africa be strong to deliver men from every bondage into the freedom of Jerusalem which is above and is the Mother of us all'. This address said what he was to say, with local variants, on many future occasions.

After the service the prime duty of the new Province was to elect their first Metropolitan which it proceeded to do in the person of Bishop L.G. Vining of Lagos.

Archbishop Fisher returned to England bringing back with him many vivid impressions of his short but significant visit. Perhaps one of his greatest satisfactions, in retrospect, was to be told that when some two years later he placed the crown on the Queen's head at her Coronation, the boys from Bishopscourt School who were following the ceremony intently on their television screen greeted him with a loud 'Pa Canter'.

CHAPTER 41

Central Africa

THE desire and need for a provincial organisation was not of course envisaged as being confined to West Africa. Such a structure had now become normative for an autonomous church within the Anglican Communion. The only question in determining the appropriate time to achieve this was how far there existed substantial local support including financial, necessary to sustain a Province once created. There must be firm roots from which it could grow.

The experience of having helped to plan and to launch one Province stood the Archbishop in good stead when he turned to achieving the same goal in Central Africa. In this case, however, the Archbishop was to face far greater problems and difficulties. The setting up of a Province in West Africa, as we have seen, coincided with a time of political change in Nigeria and the Gold Coast. This was equally true, indeed more so, in respect of Central Africa since the new province was to include Northern and Southern Rhodesia with Nyasaland; and it was these very territories which the British Government intended to bring together into a political Federation. This policy was to prove a confusing and at times a complicating factor.

True the establishment of a Province had been under consideration for some time quite independently of any Government policy as to the future constitutional position in this part of Africa. However it was difficult, certainly in the eyes of the black population, to separate the one from the other, particularly against the background of a highly charged political situation. For this reason Wilfred Parker, the Bishop of Pretoria (previously of Nyasaland) advised the Archbishop to make this distinction clear from the outset.

In drawing up its Provincial Constitution Geoffrey Fisher had sought advice from the Reverend John McLeod Campbell, Secretary to the Tropical African Territorial Council and formerly Principal of Trinity College, Kandy, in Ceylon. As well as conferring with the Council, the Archbishop also, in September 1951, got into touch with the Right Reverend W. Parker, Bishop of Pretoria, asking his view concerning a Province of Central Africa. His attitude was that no real danger would result from imposing a Province against the wishes of some Africans since there was majority support in the dioceses for such a scheme. In finding out the reaction of their bishops it would be helpful, right from the start – thus removing groundless fears – if the Archbishop made a radical distinction between ecclesiastical and political unification. They had no necessary connection the one with the other. The hope now was that the Province would be established by the end of 1952.

Meanwhile the Archbishop himself drew up a memorandum on the Church in Central Africa. From the general tenor of this document it was apparent that he had been made aware that the setting up of a Provincial structure in Central Africa presented unique problems and was likely to prove politically explosive.

The public *rationale* advanced for the policy of Federation was basically economic since Nyasaland was a poor country, mainly agricultural with much unemployment and in serious financial straits: Northern Rhodesia was dependent upon the wealth derived from its copper belt and would benefit from developing secondary industries; Southern Rhodesia had the most balanced economy but suffered from a shortage of labour. Many Africans, however, were highly suspicious since they had always opposed closer links with Southern Rhodesia because of its 'native policy' of white domination. True the Government had committed itself to holding a referendum in the three territories, but it was widely rumoured that if the majority of the indigenous African population said 'no' to Federation it would be imposed upon them willy-nilly. The Archbishop was determined to find out for himself the pros and cons of the Government's case for Federation and in particular whether it really was, as alleged, in the interests of the whole population black as well as white. To this end in September 1952, he drew up a questionnaire which he dispatched to the bishops immediately involved. In this he asked: (1) Is Federation 'wise and good' and how will it affect the Africans even if it is imposed upon them against their will? (2) Is the present scheme the only one which can secure a measure of agreement? (3) Can it be held on Christian grounds that Federation is a means of resisting the racial influences which are spreading from South Africa northwards? (4) What is African opinion on Federation and what proportion of Africans has an opinion? (5) How far are such opinions founded on knowledge? (6) Can such suspicions as exist against Federation be justified? Ought the whole project to be resisted in the interests of the Africans?

The replies of the three Bishops betrayed clearly their own reservations. The Bishop of Nyasaland believed that the Africans should be persuaded to accept Federation though it must not finally be forced upon them regardless. The Bishop of Southern Rhodesia was on the whole in favour of going forward. His colleague of Northern Rhodesia confessed that this was a very emotional issue. The African leaders were working for black domination but if they were not to secure this, Federation was probably for them the next best solution in serving to offset the subtle infiltration of racism from South Africa. He agreed, however, that Federation should not be forced on the blacks. On the whole their verdict was that Federation could be in the interest of all concerned. The Archbishop of Cape Town was firmly of the opinion that plans for a new Province ought to be provisional until the referendum on the principle of Federation had taken place. The Roman Catholic Archbishop, David Matthew, who had experience of Africa at first hand, maintained: (1) Federation was probably in the long term interest of the Africans, though it was doubtful whether they would accept this. (2) Many whites in Southern Rhodesia were bitterly opposed to it as being weighted on the side of the African population.

Geoffrey Fisher's own enquiries, together with his reading of official Government handouts led him to form a favourable view on Federation as 'likely to be acceptable and beneficial to both races'. It was the economic argument which he found decisive.

Yet though supporting Federation, the Archbishop believed that the British Government had done little actively to commend it in the tribal areas, nor had it given any guidance to the District Commissioners who were the men on the spot and in a position to be helpful. This, Dr Fisher complained, was to be regretted since Federation could have significant consequences for the whole future life of the Africans. A vital condition for success was mutual trust between the races, the Africans needing to accept that Europeans were living alongside of them and the Europeans correspondingly to overcome their suspicion of the Africans. Yet he stuck to his conviction that Federation if only it could be sensibly and fairly implemented – which he sometimes doubted – would prove in everyone's interests. This basic approach he set out at length in a letter to *The Times* newspaper dated 17 October 1952 in which he condemned Sir Geoffrey Huggins, the Governor of Northern Rhodesia, for having said of the African Affairs Board, set up under the terms of the proposed Act of Federation to safeguard the rights of the Africans, that it could do no harm – to the whites, of course – and if it served no useful purpose it could later be got rid of. In spite of such an indiscretion, however, the Archbishop, in the main, felt he must accept the good faith of the Government as explicitly set forth in the White Paper, namely that the intention in planning the Federation was: 'the advancement of the Africans in partnership with the Europeans.' However, he remained sceptical of the motives of some of the latter's leaders. Yet in spite of such qualified support Geoffrey Fisher did not hesitate to condemn what he regarded as the 'somewhat steam-roller approach' exemplified by the new Minister of State for Colonial Affairs, Lennox Boyd, whom he described as 'not playing fair'. Indeed 'to hold a referendum but in advance to let it be known that Federation would go forward whatever its results must provoke suspicion'. The African, the Archbishop commented, 'does not appreciate the subtleties of party politics'.

Lord Alport, chairman of the Joint East and Central African Board, took advantage of the Archbishop's letter to *The Times* to write to Lambeth critically expressing a strongly pro-white point of view. There was an increasing antagonism, he wrote, on the part of the Africans towards the Christian faith, the result being that missionaries in East Africa had seen the work of a lifetime destroyed. For this calamity the Churches themselves must be blamed for bringing to an end any hope of future development. This was not a letter which pleased the Archbishop and he hotly contested the implied charges against the Churches; but Lord Alport remained obdurate.

The difficulty in coming to a firm decision *vis-à-vis* the Province was, therefore, the uncertainty as to what was likely to be the fate of Federation itself. Geoffrey Fisher, understandably, grew impatient at the delay thus caused particularly as the final decision was left, by the other Bishops, to himself and the Archbishop of Cape Town. To clarify his own mind at this stage he drew up another paper on the immediate situation. This indicates clearly that he continued to believe, in spite of the Metropolitan of South Africa, that the bulk of Africans and Europeans were anxious that the Province should now be established. Hence in January 1953 Geoffrey Fisher took the plunge in suggesting to the Archbishop of Cape Town that he now 'consider seriously the month of August 1953 for the inauguration ceremony.' Alas! This bold attempt to hurry things up ran into almost immediate difficulty. Opposition to Federation was all the time growing, supported by a vociferous political lobby. The British Council of Churches at a meeting in Belfast issued a firm statement on the need to secure African support. 'The achievement of partnership,' so it asserted, 'will not be followed by brushing aside the fears of Africans as completely ill-founded or as the creation of a politically minded minority . . . They value freedom above economic or administrative advantage.'

Geoffrey Fisher, as we have seen, had more or less persuaded himself into the opposite conclusion and could, on occasions, express this in an extreme form. Writing to Philip Eastman of the Quakers on 19 January he declared his belief that Federation, on almost any terms that the Conference is likely to agree to, 'is the one hope for the Africans themselves'. 'I am convinced', he went on, 'that once established, it would be a growing point for the kind of partnership that has been fought for, with the added influence of Northern Rhodesia and Nyasaland. If it is rejected it will be a victory, not for the Africans at all, but for the reactionary Europeans in Southern Rhodesia. I very much doubt whether the Moderator of the Church of Scotland would agree with me in all this.' These were very strong and challenging words, and never was the Archbishop to be proved more wrong!

Geoffrey Fisher now decided to take advantage of the Constitutional Conference meeting in London to invite two of its number – Sir Godfrey Huggins, Governor of Northern, and Sir Roy Welenski, Governor of Southern, Rhodesia destined to become the first Prime Minister of the ill-fated Federation – to give their views on the inauguration of a Province as distinct from that of a Federation. They both encouraged him to go forward with it; promised their 'strong support', and urged a public statement which made it 'crystal-clear' that there was no connection between the inauguration of a Province and the setting up of a Federation.

Among ecclesiastical personnel, doubts began to return as to the right course of action. This was made plain in the Archbishop of Cape Town's reply to Geoffrey Fisher's letter asking him to consider August as the most suitable month for the inauguration. In this epistle he placed great emphasis on the following points: (1) The formation of a Province was not a matter of religious principle, but of 'administrative convenience'. (2) It was a 'fallacy' to suppose that the Church could be entirely indifferent to political boundaries. (3) If political Federation was implemented then so should the ecclesiastical Province. (4) If Federation failed it would be a mistake to create a Province during the present year. 'These are very definite opinions,' he wrote, 'and I cannot pretend to be in favour of something which I think is likely to be a serious handicap to the work of the Church.'

To move on happily to provincial status in the face of this metropolitical letter was not easy and Geoffrey Fisher immediately sent copies of it to the Central African Bishops who were due to meet. As a result the Bishop of Nyasaland confessed to having reservations and the Vicar-General of Southern Rhodesia wrote to the Archbishop urging that the inauguration of the Province should be deferred at least until the fate of the Federation was known. The Bishops of Mashonaland, Nyasaland and Northern Rhodesia duly met on February 18–19. Their report, immediately dispatched to Lambeth, was not encouraging. The opposition to Federation by the Africans, they confirmed, was general in all three territories, but most apparent in Nyasaland while increasing steadily in Northern Rhodesia.

Public interest in Britain was aroused not, of course, on the issue of provincial status but concerning political Federation. Miss Perham, a sturdy and informed defender of human rights for the African people, wrote to *The Times* on 25 February stressing that even if they were not fully politically mature this did not mean that power over them should be transferred to a group of people who, however high their individual merit, together represented a small racial minority of employers and large land owners. The Africa Bureau issued a Press statement against Federation and the Reverend Michael Scott saw the Archbishop with a request for a National Day of Prayer.

In these circumstances the Archbishop joined with the Moderator of the General Assembly of the Church of Scotland and the Moderator of the Free Chuch Federal Council, in sending a further letter to *The Times*. Its main point was to emphasise that unless some gesture of a true and genuine acceptance of partnership was apparent it was unreasonable to impose Federation.

This letter drew from Lord Swinton of the Royal Commonwealth Office a strong statement reaffirming Government policy. What so many well disposed but 'woolly-minded' people did not recognise, he wrote, was that the greatest hope for any enlightened and constructive approach to African problems and the greatest impetus towards a liberal policy 'was the federation of the Territories. The one thing that would play straight into the hands of the extremists on both sides would be the defeat of the federal proposals'. The Archbishop penned a very careful reply in which he agreed that a 'fair hearing' should be given to them.

Lord Swinton was not alone in adding to the Archbishop's postbag. The Bishop of Mashonaland, the Dean of Manchester, the United Nations Association, the Quakers at Friends' House – these all pleaded for a liberal approach and for respecting black African opinion.

The Archbishop of Canterbury was, understandably, becoming more frustrated and perplexed as the arguments went to and fro, and he admitted to the Bishop of Mashonaland that he found this whole business of when to launch the Province 'more and more complex and difficult and Federation no less vexing'. Doubtless it was with relief that he received from the Central African Bishops the awaited letter on 11 March 1953 asking him to postpone the date of the inauguration of the new Province until 1954 or 1955. The African Congress, they said, was everywhere active against it and there was widespread unrest; in addition there was as yet no existing House of Laity in the Synod. Thus advised by those most intimately involved the Archbishop acted promptly. On 4 April, and without consulting further he issued a Press statement from Lambeth postponing the inauguration of the Province definitively until 1954–5 in order 'to avoid confusion between the proposal for political Federation in Central Africa and a scheme for a new ecclesiastical Province of the Anglican Communion covering the same area'. It was at least a relief to the Archbishop to have got such a notice in the public Press! Everyone now awaited the result of the referendum, and a debate took place in the House of Lords when the Archbishop expressed with force and clarity his views as outlined in the course of this chapter. On 9 April 1953 the referendum took place and the die was cast in favour of Federation. This verdict led to the Central African Bishops meeting on 2 July at Bulawayo with their former doubts for the time being, at least, resolved. Their hope now was that within a year of the setting up of the Federation – it was established on 1 August 1953 – the Government would have dispelled the fears of the blacks in Nyasaland and in this expectancy they petitioned the Archbishop to consider inaugurating the Province in October or November 1954. These dates, however, proved impossible but the Archbishop saw the need to avoid too long a delay and finally fixed it for 9 May 1955.

The Archbishop remained deeply concerned that the Federation, which he had backed from the beginning, should fulfil the high expectations of those who sincerely believed that this unification could have a great future in promoting the interests of all citizens. Thus when Lord Llewellyn left to take up the post of the First Governor of the Federation, the Archbishop wished him Godspeed; 'I am one of those who believes,' he wrote, 'that the possibility of good outweighs the possibility of evil as a result of Federation. But it will require the most wise guidance by everybody concerned in these early formative years. And I do pray that God will help and guide you with all the patience and wisdom and charity that you will need. It will be a great thing if you have the privilege of seeing this new experiment through its early years to a successful conclusion.' The first Parliament of the newly Federated territories met on 3 February 1954 but the high hopes which Geoffrey Fisher, *inter alios*, entertained were not to be realized. After the Monkton Report in 1960 the African leaders in Nyasaland and Northern Rhodesia were granted the right to secede which proved a prelude to the Federation being brought to an end at the close of 1963 by which time Geoffrey Fisher had retired.

It remained now for the Archbishop to make preparations for his visit to Central Africa for the Inauguration Service of the Province on 9 May 1955. Many letters went to and fro between Lambeth, the Central African Bishops and Geoffrey Clayton, the Archbishop of Cape Town, both in respect of Geoffrey Fisher's itinerary when he arrived, and practical questions in relation to the Service of Inauguration. There was, for example, the question of what robes he should wear and here his suggestion for cope and mitre was freely accepted. Then there was the more important but controversial question as to what Rite should be used for the Eucharist. The Dean of Salisbury, the newly appointed ffrench Beytagh, assumed it would be that which was customary in Africa but this was met by a firm archiepiscopal refusal. Dr Fisher made it clear that he would wish to use the Liturgy of the Church of England, namely 1662. The Archbishop's decision was by no means universally welcomed and the Central African Bishops, directly involved, took the matter up with him. There were only two Liturgies in use, they explained, one being that of the Province of South Africa, the other that used by the Diocese of Matabeleland. Both of these had synodical sanction and confusion would result if there were any departure from them.

The Archbishop replied that so far as vestments were concerned he would happily conform to the customary usage, though in giving his consent he could not resist the comment – it was an oft-repeated criticism – that 'a lot of bishops in cope and mitre only emphasises to my mind that a mitre is an astonishingly ugly and sometimes repellent head dress and that only the orthodox have succeeded in devising a comely ecclesiastical head dress'. Here, maybe, Geoffrey Fisher was expressing more than a minority view! The Rite was a different matter and the Archbishop went on: 'Your point about Liturgy is much more difficult. Is there not something improper in asking the Archbishop of Canterbury (especially when he visits two Dioceses still under his jurisdiction and two Dioceses in which the Book of Common Prayer is still, I believe, an alternative use) to abandon the official Liturgy of the Church he represents for a local variant of it? After all, one of the essential purposes of my visit is to demonstrate the link with the See of Canterbury and the Church of England and I certainly do not do that by following a local Liturgy.'

The Bishops concerned found this hard to bear and urged the Archbishop to change his mind, but in vain.

Other matters concerning the service in the Cathedral were also raised. What about incense? Here the Archbishop had to confess that he just couldn't 'cope'; it wasn't his kind of ceremonial but so long as its use did not interfere with himself he would raise no objections.

And so it was that the Archbishop with Mrs Fisher, at long last left London Airport *en route* for Central Africa finding time, however, before the Inauguration, to stay with his brother Leonard, Bishop of Natal. As on his other tours in the capacity of Senior Bishop of the Anglican Communion he was overwhelmed with engagements and sight-seeing, the latter including a visit to the awesome Victoria Falls.

The Service of Inauguration – which took place in Salisbury Cathedral at 9.30 am – was a truly great and triumphant occasion. One who was present comments as follows:

'It is difficult to portray in words an adequate picture of the Mass of the Inauguration of the Province; perhaps the best idea of its dignity and impressiveness can be given by the fact that two or three Europeans in Salisbury talking to me about it afterwards compared it with the Coronation. There took part in it, the two Archbishops, the four Central Africa Bishops, Bishop Robert Taylor of Pretoria, the Bishop of St John's, the Bishop of Accra and Bishop Eric Hamilton, and the

Dean of Windsor who was representing the Central Office of the U.M.C.A. The service itself was most beautifully ordered and the ceremony of the actual Inauguration of the Province took place after the Creed and was followed by the sermon preached by the Archbishop of Cape Town. At the conclusion of the Mass the Archbishop of Canterbury laid the foundation stone of the Bell Tower to be erected to house a peal recently given by an anonymous donor to the cathedral. Then the four Bishops of the new Province withdrew to the Lady Chapel and after prayer elected Edward Paget, Bishop of Mashonaland, to be the first Archbishop of Central Africa.'

The use of the 1662 Rite did, as anticipated, unfortunately cause a little irritation, though perhaps, it ought to be added, that the Rite then used in Africa (and still) owes as little to truly indigenous African sentiment as did the Liturgy which the Archbishop employed. It was in the presentation and performance that they were reminded of the rock whence they were hewn.

At the Evensong which followed, the four Bishops presented the new Metropolitan to the Archbishops of Canterbury and Cape Town. The two Archbishops then presented him to the congregation, and Geoffrey Fisher installed him in his throne. A priest, together with a Lay Representative from each of the four Dioceses, professed the allegiance of both clergy and laity to their new Archbishop. The sermon was then preached by the Archbishop of Canterbury, a solemn *Te Deum* was sung and the Archbishop of Central Africa pronounced the Blessing. In his sermon Geoffrey Fisher stressed that the real danger confronting them was not race and colour but differences of wealth, cultural background and levels of social experience.

On the next day the Provincial Synod met for the first time under the Presidency of the Archbishop of Central Africa when the Archbishops of Canterbury and Cape Town briefly addressed those assembled. A day later the newly installed Metropolitan, along with the Bishops of the Province, said goodbye to the Primate of All England and Mrs Fisher at Salisbury Airport where they later heard the news of the arrival of their fifth grandchild – a girl. Perhaps this new birth mirrored, in the hope and expectancy which it engendered, the spirit in which this newly fledged Province entered its wider world.

The Archbishop, however, did not return immediately to Britain after the Inauguration of the Central African Province but went on to Salisbury and visited Fort Hall in Kenya, where he laid the foundation stone in the church to be built in memory of the African martyrs killed by the Mau Mau.

Perhaps a few words should be added in general on the Archbishop's visit to Central Africa. The secular authorities recognised that this was no ordinary visitor and as a consequence he stayed at Government

House in Lusaka, Zambia and Salisbury where dinners and garden parties were laid on in his honour; he visited Mission stations, schools and colleges; enjoyed the company of many at civic lunches and dinners; inspected a copper mine; had tea with chiefs and representative Africans; visited an African compound; saw the grave of Rhodes at Matapo; delivered mid-day addresses; was entertained by High Commissioners; laid the foundation stone for a new church at Umvukwes – and, of course, met numerous Anglican clergy, indigenous as well as British.

It was certainly a significant visit, and came at a time – it was soon to pass – when some colonies still basked in the sunset of an Empire's afterglow. The Archbishop was a symbolic figure. Thus Frank Thorne, Bishop of Nyasaland, could with sincerity, write that for the Africans, as appeared in all the speeches of welcome to the Archbishop, what delighted them most was that it had been granted to them to see with their own eyes 'Geoffrey our Bishop' for whom they had prayed by name Sunday by Sunday for so many years – and to find him a real Father in God, full of joy and love. Equally satisfying was the almost fairy tale improbability of it all. 'I remember,' Bishop Frank Thorne wrote, 'that it suddenly came upon us, the Archbishop, Mrs Fisher and myself, that evening on the journey by Lake Mowdis how unlikely it was that the Archbishop of Canterbury should be sitting in a motorboat on a lake in Central Africa, and yet there it was really happening, history in the making.'

One is conscious here, not only of a sincere tribute to Archbishop Fisher but of a substantial nostalgia for a past inheritance, felt poignantly by an English African Bishop whose Church had just left its historic moorings in Canterbury for wider and as yet uncharted seas within the Anglican Communion.

A visit of this kind could not be expected to pass off unaffected by the social and political climate of the day, not least when those 'winds of change', referred to later by Harold Macmillan, Prime Minister of Great Britain, were beginning to gather momentum. There would indeed have been something lacking in such a tour if the rough places suddenly became plain. It was during this visit at St Michael College in Blantyre that in a discussion with students the Archbishop used the unfortunate and ambiguous phrase that 'all men are equal in the love of God but not in the sight of God'. It would be impossible to imagine a form of words more calculated to be misunderstood in so highly charged a political atmosphere. Nor is it easy to understand precisely what this comment means – or was intended to mean. If it merely implies that God loves everybody but is aware that the intellectual quotient of some is higher than others it is so trite as to be hardly worth saying.

The Archbishop himself experienced at first hand the practical workings of the colour bar and he certainly did not like it. Thus a reception in his honour had to be held in a private house because the white settlers refused the facilities of a local club as they did not want Africans 'plunging about their gardens'. 'This was just a reminder', so Geoffrey Fisher commented, 'of the schizophrenia present among the white population.'

The Archbishop and Mrs Fisher left Central Africa on a high note. On the eve of their departure at a garden party an African presented the Archbishop with an ivory elephant as a token of appreciation. 'We give you ivory,' he said, 'because that is what we give to our chiefs and you are the biggest Christian in the Church.' Immediately there came the reply: 'My wife has just reminded me that the elephant never forgets. I shall never forget you!'

Perhaps Bishop Green Wilkinson of Northern Rhodesia may be allowed to have the last word: 'I know that all who met you,' he wrote to the Archbishop, 'caught a new joy in life from you and that your words and presence will have a lasting influence for good upon the country.'

CHAPTER 42

East Africa

(i)
The Diocese of Masasi

THE setting up of Provinces in the vast African Continent was by the end of Geoffrey Fisher's archiepiscopate almost complete. The system was certainly proving its worth and providing help, encouragement and companionship to Bishops whose tasks were never easy but always challenging. The Province of East Africa with its twelve dioceses was long in the process of gestation – but it finally came and did so in time to make a significant episcopal appointment possible. The facts are not without interest and may be briefly stated.

In the year 1960 the diocese of Masasi became vacant. Maybe Geoffrey Fisher recalled that some fifteen years earlier he had suggested as a briefing for a new Bishop that he should: (1) be fit to rule; (2) be capable of delegating; (3) be able to act wisely in relation to secular government; (4) be familiar with the liturgy of Swahili as approved by Archbishop Randall Davidson.

It was therefore, in 1960, a matter of finding the right man. Among the many names mentioned, that of Trevor Huddleston was put forward by a fellow member of the Community of the Resurrection. In this he was supported by the Archbishop of York, Lord Howick and Richard Wood, MP. Huddleston both enjoyed and deserved a high reputaion for fearlessly championing the rights of the indigenous Africans. Canon Broomfield – he was a commissary for Masasi – supported him though admitting to Archbishop Fisher that he did not always see eye to eye with him. The general view in 1960 was that whoever the incoming bishop, he must be able to win the confidence and affection of both Africans and Europeans. Also he must be universally recognised as a 'big man'.

Within this context Canon Broomfield believed that there was no indigenous African qualified at the moment to take over. He accepted that Trevor Huddleston had made many 'grievous mistakes' and he would not therefore recommend him for a bishopric in South Africa, Kenya or in the Federation. However, he yet believed he would be right for Masasi. Geoffrey Fisher followed up this letter by writing to the Bishops of Mombasa, Central Tanganyika, South West Tanganyika and Zanzibar all of whom let it be known that they approved of Trevor Huddleston particularly as Masasi would be joining the new Province of East Africa. His name was also put forward by the U.M.C.A. The

Archbishop now asked the bishops whether they would wish Trevor Huddleston to be sounded out? Undoubtedly he had 'devotion, prophetic powers, and outstanding ability ... (if) not always wise or statesmanlike' in his advocacy of the cause of the native Africans in South Africa. A fortnight later the Archbishop followed up this letter with another which must have come as a surprise, perhaps a shock, to the episcopal recipients. It ran as follows: 'I write a confidential letter to you and your fellow diocesan bishops about the appointment of a bishop to the diocese of Masasi. I feel bound to say now (though with a heavy heart) that I should find myself unable to nominate him [Huddleston] to the Bishopric even if all of you wanted me to do so. He is a friend and a devoted person, and he has mobilised a great many people to pray for South Africa in this crisis, but he has identified himself with political objectives namely to turn the present South African Government out of office.' Hence he, the Archbishop, personally could not accept responsibility (as Metropolitan) for Huddleston's appointment to the Bishopric of Masasi.

There then follows what may appear a quite remarkable *volte-face* since he goes on: 'That does not mean that the bishops must not appoint him. It does mean, I fear, that if you want him for Masasi you must advise me to leave the See vacant till the Province is in being and you must then yourselves appoint and consecrate him'.

On 30 April the Bishop of Mombasa – the future Metropolitan of the new Province, with its eleven dioceses – wrote to the Archbishop saying they would follow this procedure. So far Trevor Huddleston had not been officially approached; but things now began to move. Canon G. W. Broomfield wrote informing the Archbishop that the Bishops of East Africa were now seriously considering appointing Trevor Huddleston who had assured him that he would not interfere in East Africa in a way that was 'necessary in South Africa'. The Canon appreciated the Archbishop's view but the Bishops hoped that he would give his blessing to this appointment. 'I do feel very strongly,' he concluded, 'having held various posts in Africa, that Trevor Huddleston's appointment would prove of great value to the Church in East Africa'.

Geoffrey Fisher realised that the time had now come for himself to communicate direct with Trevor Huddleston and to assure him that if East Africa wanted him then he would wish him to know that he had the Archbishop's full support. 'You must not worry about the past', he wrote warmly and reassuringly, 'the slate has been wiped clean.'

So the Provincial Constitution with its eleven dioceses was allowed to operate and on 22 June 1960, Huddleston wrote a long letter to Geoffrey Fisher giving his spiritual autobiography – 'the rock whence he was hewn'. Thus it was that the consecration of the new bishop took place in the Church of St Nicholas, Dar-es-Salaam on 30 November 1960. The Archbishop of Canterbury was in Jerusalem at the beginning of his last and most spectacular tour but he did not neglect to send a cable to the new Bishop wishing him well. This evoked the following reply. 'Your cable to me on my consecration on St Andrew's Day was just one more reminder of your very great goodness. I cannot imagine how, in the midst of such a tremendously busy and exciting pilgrimage you could have found time to think of me. The fact that you did so means far more than I can express. Certainly that visit of yours and the Roman one, have been a wonderful encouragement to all Christians every-where. And you must feel very happy at the welcome you received. Still it cannot have been without real cost, physically and mentally and spiritually to yourself'. The Bishop concluded his letter, 'Yours ever affectionately and gratefully'.

This correspondence, and indeed the consecration itself does credit both to the Bishop and Archbishop – and shows what a generous, honest and loving person Geoffrey Fisher was.

(ii)

This chapter would not be complete without a brief reference to a most unhappy situation in which Geoffrey Fisher became involved. The reference is to the curious and violent phenomenon known as Mau Mau.

To find out more accurately what this was the Church Missionary Society, early in 1953, sent out to Kenya the experienced Canon Bewes who had spent some twenty years in the Kikuyu Reserve. Geoffrey Fisher seized this opportunity to express his sympathy and pay tribute to fellow Christians in that troubled land. The Canon went there more in the capacity of a friend than grand inquisitor, visiting many of the affected areas. He found that most Africans condemned Mau Mau's atrocities but felt themselves to suffer nagging land hunger, as well as from a 'social slights' and educational deprivation. The economic fact was that Kenya needed to increase the fertility of its soil and to attract capital to bolster up its economy. There was tension everywhere and the general mood was one of bitterness. At a Press Conference, attended by some members of the House of Commons, Canon Bewes on his return from Kenya gave specific instances of police brutality. The Archbishop of Canterbury also testified to receiving many letters to this same effect so much so that he asked for an interview with Oliver Lyttelton, Secretary of State for the Commonwealth which took place on 11 February, Canon Bewes also being present. According to Geoffrey Fisher's account in a letter to Dr Bell of Chichester, the Commonwealth Secretary began by being 'very off hand and uncom-municative' until he convinced him that they were there to be helpful to the Government and not attack it. He then at once changed his attitude and became 'very understanding, very ready to help and extremely anxious that everything should be done to cope with irregularities and scandals in Kenya'. One fortunate result of this interview was Canon Bewes being consulted from time to time by the Commonwealth Office.

The Archbishop was always somewhat critical of Oliver Lyttelton but had a high regard for the Governor of Kenya, Sir Evelyn Baring, 'a keen and devoted Christian'. He, Geoffrey Fisher, was quite convinced that there had been 'frightful misbehaviour of one kind and another', both by the police and the military as was evidenced at the court martial of a British officer for 'ruthlessly shooting down Kikuyu citizens'. *The Times* newspaper devoted a leading article to this sorry happening under the heading 'A National Conscience'. The Warden of Student Movement House, Miss Mary Trevelyan, asked the Archbishop to make his voice heard in denunciation. 'Please assure your people', came the reply that, 'the whole Christian Church is united against any violation of the true spiritual status and freedom of the Africans'. Again and again the Church had made its position utterly clear, and had 'called upon people in multi-racial societies to work on a basis of Christian love and respect for a true parternship'. Indeed so grave was the situation that the leading Christian Churches had issued a statement making plain their 'abhorrence' of much which was taking place. However, Leonard Beecher, the Bishop of Mombasa, following the customary line of African bishops, counselled the Archbishop to leave protest to members of the indigenous church.

The Archbishop now had an interview lasting some one and a half hours with Sir Evelyn Baring who commented frankly on these ghastly events. The regular army, he said was very good; the Kenya regiment was 'pretty good'; the Police Force not frightfully good; the Kenya Poka Reserve, consisting in the main of local settlers, a real problem, and his intention was to get rid of three hundred of them. Mau Mau, he pointed out, was not new but had existed as a secret society for some years and was a strange amalgam of nationalism and witchcraft fanned by modern techniques of propaganda. Jomo Kenyatta in his opinion was 'very able and very evil having learnt the tricks of the trade in Moscow'. On the whole the attitude of the Europeans in the face of it was 'liberal'.

Geoffrey Fisher wisely kept in touch with the Church Missionary Society through such knowledgeable people as Max Warren, until 1959 when Mau Mau had ceased.

In the light of Jomo Kenyatta's career subsequent to his release from internment and when, as an elder statesman, he became President of Kenya, one wonders whether Sir Evelyn would have reaffirmed the same judgement had he made it later.

CHAPTER 43

Kabaka Mutesa II and the Buganda

GEOFFREY Fisher had now inaugurated two Anglican provinces in West and Central Africa. It was his firm intention to do the same in Uganda. However before we turn our attention to his efforts in this field it is necessary to consider political and constitutional difficulties in Uganda which became for the Archbishop a pressing preoccupation.

The Archbishop soon learned that being Metropolitan of the Anglican Church in Uganda was no sinecure. As such he could not avoid becoming involved in its domestic affairs through matters which came to him on appeal. For example, when a priest authorised laymen to conduct their own agape on his station, the matter ended up at Lambeth. Equally when the Archbishop appointed native-born Canon Bulaya, warmly commended by His Highness the Omukama, as assistant bishop in Uganda, it subsequently got bogged down in tribal and personal animosities and Geoffrey Fisher was called in to arbitrate.

The Right Reverend Cyril Stuart, Bishop of Uganda who was consecrated way back in 1934, was understandably greatly disturbed at conditions generally in his diocese and was seriously contemplating resignation. Fortunately in spite of geographical distance he found at Lambeth a shoulder to weep on. In 1948 a petition signed by many Ugandans, accused the Bishop, in collusion with the Government of the Protectorate, of alienating from the Church its lands and mineral rights. 'I always get a bit muddled over land matters', so he confessed to the Archbishop. These worries certainly undermined the Bishop's health and Geoffrey Fisher described his condition as 'oscillating badly between elation and extreme depression.'

In May 1948, to add to the Bishop's anxieties, riots broke out in Kampala resulting in much loss of life and over a million pounds worth of property destroyed. While fires were still burning around him and he was protected from danger by his African clergy, he despatched to Lambeth a full report of these violent events. A new factor, no less unsettling because it was personal and tribal, was now introduced into this already unstable situation. This concerned the Kabaka who was the equivalent of a reigning monarch with an aura attracting a reverential loyalty from his half a million subjects who constituted the most advanced tribe, not only in Uganda but throughout East Africa. In commending him to the Archbishop, the Bishop of Uganda wrote: 'He is a very nice lad (aged 19) with perfect manners and a sense of humour. You would like him.' The Kabaka, who had spent two years at Magdalene College in Cambridge, contracted a Christian morganatic marriage to a girl of his own choosing, but some three months later he 'fell head over heels in love' with a married woman whom he took into his compound. The Bishop was put into an embarrassing position and unburdened himself to the Archbishop. The Kabaka's bad example, so he wrote, 'would be noted all over East Africa where monogamy was frequently under attack and not only from the more conservative elements but also from the progressive'.

The Archbishop replied with an understanding and helpful letter agreeing that the situation was 'terribly wounding' for the Bishop and asking him to pass on to the Kabaka his own deep concern. The situation did not mend but seemed to go from bad to worse. The Bishop reported to Lambeth that he had had a long conversation with 'the lad' whom he found friendly and 'glad to talk it out'. What the Bishop dreaded was the Kabaka being led to repudiate the Christian Church as a 'foreign institution', and as a consequence being dominated by the 'bad lots and intriguers' who surrounded him in the Palace.

This domestic unsettlement did not go away in spite of the Bishop's endeavours to mend the situation in a three hour session with the Kabaka who however remained determined to make 'the other woman' his Queen. Confessing that he felt 'tired over the whole thing', the Bishop in a long letter to Lambeth sought the Archbishop's advice. Geoffrey Fisher's immediate reaction was that he himself ought not to interfere in a matter of this private nature but on hearing that the Kabaka was coming over to England he urged him to be accompanied by his wife – 'a duty' he owed to himself, to her, to his friends in England and to Britain. Being together again might restore the relationship of trust in which the marriage had been born. 'My dear Kabaka,' the Archbishop went on, 'may I in all sincerity and friendship add another word. You have a great position; your own Nation and people and country are at a critical stage in their development as they come into this new and difficult world. An immense responsibility rests upon you as their leader; if you betray the trust you betray them and their future.'

This letter concluded with the Archbishop inviting him to stay with him in Canterbury.

The Kabaka responded positively to this request and brought his wife with him. The Archbishop found her 'perfectly charming' but the Kabaka somewhat 'elusive' and 'difficult to get into close touch with' though he proved 'a very pleasant guest'. He had a few words with him at Canterbury expressing his concern but as the Archbishop wrote to the Bishop of Uganda 'it may not have done much good but I am pretty sure it was better than talking to him at length on his matrimonial affairs'.

It is no criticism of the Archbishop to suggest that in this approach to the Kabaka he did not take full account of the fact that the Kabaka was being judged by conformity to a pattern of marriage alien to the *mores* of his Ugandan tribal inheritance.

The time had now come to consider seriously whether Bishop Stuart, submitted as he now was to exceptional strain, ought at his own suggestion, to be allowed to retire. The Ugandan Advisory Council met and while all seven Africans 'begged' the present Bishop to continue in office, three Europeans took a contrary view. Wisely Geoffrey Fisher sought advice from the knowledgeable Max Warren who came up with four names; but it was not till four years later that Leslie Brown, Principal of Kerala United Theological Seminary, Trivandrum, was consecrated Bishop of Uganda in Southwark Cathedral on 6 January 1953. He was certainly a man of wide experience and had served in East Africa and in the United Church of South India. He was deservedly described by Dr Coggan, Michael Ramsey's successor at Lambeth, as 'a great man'.

The appointment was doubly important in view of Geoffrey Fisher's intention to create in the future two Anglican Provinces in East Africa. It is difficult to imagine a more daunting prospect than that which faced Leslie Brown as he took over in Uganda in 1953. The matrimonial situation of the Kabaka had not righted itself and when the new Bishop called on him, soon after his arrival, he found him hoping that his wife would divorce him thus leaving him free to marry her sister. The Bishop, at this first interview, gained the impression that the Kabaka had no desire 'to put things right'; so much so that he, as Bishop, felt it proper to warn him that if the situation degenerated it might lead to excommunication.

Meanwhile Bishops in Uganda were hoping that the Archbishop might take an initiative with Buckingham Palace in securing the Kabaka's attendance at the Coronation. He did in fact see the Lord Chamberlain and the Kabaka was duly present on this memorable occasion.

The Kabaka's visit to this country gave the Archbishop an opportunity to see him immediately on his arrival and also among the crowds at a Buckingham Palace garden party. They were disappointing encounters and the Kabaka himself admitted that his actions were 'bad, bad for himself, and bad for his people'.

The Kabaka, however, continued to be the subject of controversy not only because of his private life, but as the rallying ground of a strong tribal sentiment which feared lest Uganda should have imposed upon it, as in Central Africa, a form of Federation under which Uganda in general and the Buganda in particular would cease to be an African state but become multi-racial. This latter fear was a real one, for Oliver Lyttelton, the Colonial Secretary, had himself, at a public dinner, indiscreetly referred to the possibility of an East African Federation.

The Kabaka was indeed in a difficult position and the Attorney-General warned him that if he persisted in publicly disagreeing with the Government's policy then he would be breaking the agreement signed with Britain way back in the year 1900. To this the Kabaka replied that it was intolerable for him to acquiesce in a policy which he believed to be against the best interests of his own people. The result of this seeming defiance was his deportation to Britain on the orders of Her Majesty's Government. Bishop Leslie Brown believed, and so told the Archbishop, that the real responsibility for this unhappy turn of events lay with the Colonial Secretary and his 'incredibly foolish speech' at an East African dinner advocating the possibility of a federation. 'Almost overnight,' the Bishop wrote to Lambeth, 'the Kabaka, as a result of his deportation, leaped into popularity.' The only way now open for Lyttelton was resignation since he would never be trusted again. Sir Andrew Cohen, the Governor, was on the contrary growing in popularity.

The effect of this deportation was to fan even higher the fires of Ugandan discontent. The Kabaka, in his anxiety, got into touch with the Archbishop who responded with practical advice. Whatever the rights or wrongs on either side he would be wise, at least for the time being, to accept his deportation, though it was important that he should express 'the fundamental fears' of his people against a multi-racial state, fears which the British Government should be pressed to remove.

The Archbishop now agreed to receive at Lambeth a Bugandan delegation which had come to join the Kabaka. The resulting discussion which went on for some one and a half hours centred around the position of the Kabaka, his 'hankering after abdication' and his desire to live in England. The Archbishop believed that the delegation was ready to work out a reasonable solution and he expressed the hope that the British Government would equally contribute to bringing this about. As Oliver Lyttelton was due to see the delegation later, the Archbishop sent him a report on his own interview with its members stressing his conviction that these representatives of the Lukiko, the Legislative Council, were 'sincere and honest folk'.

The removal of the Kabaka from the political scene in his own country continued to aggravate his supporters and those who had not hitherto been among their number. Thus the Omukana of Toro, his cousin, urged the Archbishop to take up the cudgels on his behalf with the British Government. The Archbishop replied cautiously to this approach confessing his great concern but pointing out that he had to be 'extremely careful in all political matters not to interfere beyond [his] proper sphere'. The clash between the Kabaka and the Government, which had led to the former's exile, was a political one and for the time being needed to be accepted. As to the question of a Federation of East African territories, the British Government had now definitively removed any fears that this might happen; and he would himself do all that he could to preserve Uganda as an African state and to make this 'clear to the world'. 'We of England,' he informed the Omukana 'must for some time be trustees while Africans as a whole develop in education and political experience but we must hold Uganda in trust so that nothing shall be done to prejudice its future as an African state with a Government predominantly African.'

The Archbishop now got into touch with Oliver Lyttelton and after admitting that the Kabaka had 'inflamed all these fears and suspicions,' urged him to allay genuine Ugandan anxieties since 'if we were in their position we should feel all their fears and resent any attempts to treat them lightly.' The Buganda must be reassured on these points.

The Archbishop's general concern was to lower the temperature and to move forward one step at a time, within the options that were practically viable. Hence he deplored what he called a 'crassly stupid speech about Federation' given by the recently retired, if well meaning, Bishop Stuart in which he protested that the Kabaka was merely 'voicing the opinions of all his peoples and to deport him therefore was a blunder. Mr Lyttelton, by his "incredible folly" had bitterly disappointed these loyal people.' As if this speech were not in itself enough the former Bishop of Uganda followed it up by letters to the *Church of England Newspaper* and the *The Observer* as well as a Ugandan local newspaper. The letter to the *The Observer* contained these words – deleted, fortunately by the Editor – 'Unless I am wrong there will be bloodshed in the whole of Africa and Mr Lyttelton will be responsible. If Mr Lyttleton was employed by the Russians he could not have served them better.' The Archbishop felt that he could not remain inactive when a Bishop of the Church of England had evoked a well-merited Government rebuke and he addressed to him the following stern words: 'I must let you know how deeply I deplore that you should have written in this strain. I am afraid these words as printed must have done untold harm out there. I know how deeply you feel all this – more deeply, of course, than any of us here can – but it is my duty to tell you that in my judgement you have spoken most inadvisedly. I am sure you will agree and now wish some of your words were unsaid but unfortunately the repercussions caused by them cannot be undone.'

The unhappy Bishop was indeed contrite and within a matter of hours he admitted that his letter was 'unwise', a copy of which apology the Archbishop sent to Hopkinson at the Colonial Office.

The Archbishop now found himself caught up in a controversy fraught with serious consequences, which it was not easy for him to sort out. Max Warren advised him to see the Bugandan Delegation again, particularly as he deplored the moral offences of the Kabaka being used by the British Government for what were in fact purely political ends. The Archbishop responded positively to this suggestion and held a further session with the Delegation of six led by Mugwanya, the Chief Justice, whose clearly defined purpose was to secure the return of the Kabaka, in a 'friendly and helpful atmosphere'. In the course of the discussion, and having touched on the Kabaka's domestic situation, Geoffrey Fisher advised that if the Kabaka were not to return the reasons must be purely political. They should explore together what an African state for Uganda really entailed.

The Archbishop's general approach during this interview with the Bugandan Delegation was undoubtedly courteous, helpful and co-operative. One of its members told Lord Listowel, who was later to become Governor-General of Ghana, confessed how much encouragement he and his colleagues had received from the sympathetic way in which the Archbishop had discussed their difficulties. At the end of the meeting the Delegation asked the Archbishop to seek another interview for them with the Colonial Secretary to which he consented provided they agreed not to introduce for discussion the Kabaka's immediate return.

The Archbishop was as good as his word, but Oliver Lyttelton refused a second session with the Delegation on the grounds that decisions in relation to the Kabaka had already been finalised, and anyhow its membership did not represent all Ugandan opinion. This negative response gave no satisfaction to the Archbishop and he replied in a very tough letter of over three hundred words, admitting to his disappointment that the Colonial Secretary did not allow him, the Archbishop, to help him in his task. 'I have always found', he wrote, 'that it is far better to talk to the people with whom one has a difference [rather] than to refuse to see them and I still think it would do a great deal of good . . . if you agreed to have an informal, general conversation with the Delegation.'

Dr Fisher was indeed anxious to do the right thing even if his personal experience of East Africa at first hand was slender. Fortunately he had access to a considerable knowledge acquired by churchmen and missionaries working in Uganda over the years. This point may be illustrated by a perceptive letter, based on his personal knowledge, from the Reverend John Taylor, C.M.S. ex-missionary at Bishop Tucker Memorial College, Mukono (later Bishop of Winchester) sent to Max Warren and forwarded by him to Lambeth. 'At present,' Taylor wrote, 'it seems to me that what has happened is one more example of our failure as Europeans to recognize the deep differences between African cultural patterns and our own.' The Kabaka was still a figure of 'great emotional significance in the lives of almost all Bugandan women and girls going back to the time when every woman was at the disposal of the Kabaka'. He was 'a great husband figure' and his absence weakened the stability of Christian marriage as even a Mothers' Union speaker was prepared to allow. 'The crucial question is the real nature of the Kabaka's demand for Bugandan independence from the rest of the Protectorate.'

Such an unusual letter was not likely to commend itself overmuch to the Colonial Secretary or more generally to members of the Colonial Office. Its contents moved in a world to which by nurture and training as civil servants they were strangers. However the Archbishop's sustained pressure did lead to the Delegation, before it went home, having further interviews with the Secretary of State for the Colonies.

Behind the flurry of letters, meetings and interviews there was, as we have seen, a very real constitutional issue which was put succinctly by the Archbishop as follows: How does the office of Kabaka fit into the proposed democratic reforms incorporated into a new Constitution? Would he be a Constitutional monarch or an agent of the Protectorate? More ultimately, how did the existing *mores* and culture of Uganda in general and Buganda in particular, square with a democratic Western pattern? Miss Margery Perham, a stout defender of the rights of the Africans, wrote to the Archbishop stressing that an acceptable constitutional compromise had yet to be worked out for an ancient kingdom, 'a precious expression of African pride and tradition in a dangerous, changing world'.

There existed a strong and increasing lobby in England which was profoundly disturbed by the Government's policy and, in particular, the attitude of the Colonial Office. More than once Geoffrey Fisher described Oliver Lyttelton as 'not as tactful as he ought to be' and 'very clumsy in his handling of these things'. He therefore assured Lord Listowel that he would be prepared to join a deputation to make submissions to the Colonial Secretary.

The Archbishop was always open to meet personally those involved in African affairs and in February 1954 the Archbishop saw the Governor, Sir Andrew Cohen, whose decision it was in the first instance to recommend the deportation of the Kabaka. The Archbishop was distressed to find the Governor in a very bad way as if he were in imminent danger of a nervous breakdown. However, the Governor appreciated this opportunity of discussing his own position and informed Geoffrey Fisher he had now himself addressed the Lukiko agreeing in principle to appoint an investigating committee.

On the eve of its return to Uganda the Archbishop entertained members of the Delegation to dinner at Lambeth – a 'friendly gesture', so he told Max Warren, 'rather than a discussion on politics'. Max Warren was delighted at the laying on of this hospitality and assured the Archbishop that this gesture would be remembered as one of the 'highlights' of their entire visit to England. Just before the Delegation finally left, Geoffrey Fisher wrote in warm terms to Kaluli Sempe addressing him 'My dear friend' and going on: 'What joy it has been to meet you . . . your friendship which showed itself in the fact that we could talk openly to one another without fear of misunderstanding meant a great deal to me and I shall long treasure the memory of it'.

What had been happening in Uganda was felt by Geoffrey Fisher to be sufficiently significant for him, on 16 November 1950, to address the Church Assembly on this theme making his own views clearly known yet emphasising the complexity of the general situation. It was a matter of reconciling opposed interests arising within a context both political and personal. One aspect of this whole affair undoubtedly distressed the Archbishop greatly – his inability to get alongside the Kabaka and be of any real help to him. Perhaps he was not far wide of the mark when he wrote: 'I cannot help feeling that he is a little afraid of having to stand the kind of interrogation which privately I should put him through'.

Anger at the Kabaka's deportation was by no means confined to England. Thus Frederick Willis, Bishop of Delhi, reminded the Archbishop that for thirty-six generations Buganda had never been without its Kabaka. He therefore suggested that when the Queen went out to visit that country she should reinstate him as an act of clemency, a request which Dr Fisher passed on to the Colonial office but which was, not unexpectedly, turned down.

The Government now decided to send out Professor Sir Keith Hancock, Director of the Institute of Commonwealth Studies, to investigate conditions in Uganda and to explore the possibility of drawing up a Constitution. The Archbishop thoroughly approved this initiative and felt it now unwise for him to make any public comments until Sir Keith had completed his task.

At long last, on 15 May 1954, the Archbishop and the Kabaka met in the company of the Ugandan Mulieri. It was indeed a free and frank exchange of views, Geoffrey Fisher wisely letting the Kabaka give vent to his feelings, which he did by complaining about the attitude of the Church in Uganda and his 'bitter disappointment that the new Bishop had not taken sides in the matter and given a lead'. Here the Archbishop was able to explain that Bishop Brown knew nothing of his deportation until it had taken place. Mulieri enlarged on the present sorry state of affairs in his country – British goods being boycotted, and little children collecting money to promote the Kabaka's return.

There was much criticism, in general terms, of the Governor who they feared might hinder Sir Keith doing anything effective about an African state. The Archbishop reminded them that the Governor was suffering from severe strain but that this ought not to prevent the Committee pushing on with its work.

If Sir Keith's report settled the constitutional problem of the Kabak-aship and the status of the Kabaka, then, so the Archbishop claimed, it would not be unreasonable to urge the Government to reconsider his position.

Geoffrey Fisher now pinned all his hopes on a successful outcome to Sir Keith Hancock's constitutional mission. Thus on the very day on which he had seen off Mulieri, he congratulated Sir Andrew Cohen on having secured so distinguished a man as Sir Keith to investigate the Constitutional position; also he assured the Governor he would do everything possible to persuade the Buganda to cease its agitation for the Kabaka's return until Hancock's report came out. He added: 'I put this strongly because I feel strongly, and I do earnestly pray that you will be able to see your way to accepting in full what the Professor [Hancock] has said to you.' Sir Andrew's immediate reaction was to assure the Archbishop that he was doing all he could to make things 'easy' for Hancock; but his difficulty lay in his having to take part in the political game, 'as well as being umpire and policeman to keep the crowd in order'.

The last sentence was ominous. The pent-up emotions of anger and frustration in Uganda had now spilled over once more into violence and rioting – a clear indication that the Africans had, unfortunately, lost confidence in the Governor. A telegram reporting these events and appealing for British justice to prevail almost inevitably came through to the Archbishop at Lambeth. On 31 May the Governor decreed a State of Emergency in the Province of Buganda and on the same day, so he reported to Geoffrey Fisher, he had banned three of the most extreme newspapers since they were threats to law and order.

The general situation was now so serious that the Secretary of State for the Colonies, whose record could hardly be described as brilliant, was replaced by Mr Lennox Boyd. On 22 October he had an interview with the Archbishop remarking, at the outset, that he understood Dr Fisher from time to time brought various matters to the notice of the Colonial Secretary. Thus encouraged, Geoffrey Fisher, sent a long letter of some 1,700 words to the new Colonial Secretary, in the course of which he pulled no punches. Its contents may be briefly summarized. He pleaded earnestly for the absolute necessity of the Kabaka's return without which, he warned, the constitutional propos-als would founder and be 'a running sore of division and discontent', thus bedevilling future progress. All Africa was watching Uganda which was the one African state 'pure and simple' in East Africa and to Africans, therefore 'a touchstone of judgement'. Nor should the character of the Kabaka weigh in this matter. The Kabaka was, in fact, caught up in a conflict of loyalties between what he owed to the Governor on the one hand and on the other to the Lukiko. Such a situation was 'full of obscurities and pitfalls'. The Kabaka's restoration would deeply satisfy his own people and help a settlement. 'Who', the Archbishop asked, 'would gain *anything* by excluding him any longer?' Hence he urged the Government to change its mind thus giving the Kabaka the opportunity of redeeming the situation. Geoffrey Fisher, however, advised caution, suggesting that the Colonial Secretary did nothing till Professor Hancock had reported. He also proposed that he, the Archbishop, should bring a few people, knowledgeable about Uganda, to see him.

And so the drama of events gathered momentum, reaching a climax when on 5 November 1954, Mr J. B. Griffin, Chief Justice of Uganda, gave judgement in a case brought to test the validity of the British Government's withdrawal of recognition from Kabaka Mutesa II. The verdict was that in authorising his deportation the British Government had exceeded its powers under Article VI of the Uganda Agreement. It was therefore null and void. The Government wisely recognised that it must give way though it imposed certain conditions on the Kabaka's return. The House of Lords debated the new situation on 16 November on which occasion the Archbishop spoke with great force and frankness. 'Christian opinion', he said, 'had been deeply and anxiously exercised over this unhappy matter ever since the Kabaka was deported. Mistakes had been made on both sides but he now hoped that all would work together so that within a reasonable time, the Constitution being agreed, the Kabaka would return.' The Archbishop expressed the hope that the exemplary patience of the Lukiko and of the people of Uganda would continue.

To the Kabaka the Archbishop now sent a generous letter, expressing his 'great relief and satisfaction' when he heard the news of the Court's decision. It was an answer to prayer. Nothing could be better, he commented, than the Kabaka's own statement in *The Times* which he had read that morning expressing the hope that all the people of Buganda would steadfastly go ahead along the way now open: he earnestly hoped that before the end of the next year he might be returned once more to his own people. Would the Kabaka, he asked, like to come and spend Christmas with the Fisher family at Canterbury? The answer was that he must spend Christmas with any of his subjects who might be in London. However, the *amende honorable* came when a delightful Christmas greeting from the Kabaka arrived at the Palace in Canterbury. To Mulieri, whom Geoffrey Fisher had come to know well and greatly to admire, he wrote a very friendly, even affectionate, letter and received an equally warm reply.

Things in Uganda were now moving to a triumphal climax. On 9 May 1955, the great Lukiko of Uganda accepted, subject to certain amendments, Sir Keith Hancock's constitutional reforms – a compromise solution – 'everybody concerned [trying] to see the point of view of others'. At the same time the Lukiko also condemned a multi-racial Government for Uganda. On 16 July, the last obstacle to the Kabaka's return was removed when the Lukiko accepted the agreement negotiated by the Delegation in London with Mr Lennox Boyd. The Bishop of Uganda advised the Archbishop that the Bugandan Government was anxious to express in the presence of the Lukiko its gratitude for the help that the Christian Churches in general and the Archbishop in particular had given to their country. As soon as the Governor was acquainted with this intention he summoned the Bishop to him in an angry mood expressing grave concern 'as he considers this will have considerable political repercussions, not least at a time when there is renewed activity between the Government and the Lukiko about the return of the Kabaka'. The British Government, however, was easily placated, urging only that the occasion be as 'informal' as possible. Thus the Archbishop had the rare privilege of receiving in a crowded Lukiko the thanks of the Bugandan people for all that Christians in Britain, and particularly he himself, had done for their people. Geoffrey Fisher replied that he had been interested in their country since a boy and was sensitive to its immediate problems, while accepting that the objective must be an independent sovereign state for its people. The Assembly ended with traditional songs, everyone voicing their thanks for the Archbishop's words of advice and encouragement. His visit had done much to revive good relations between the Buganda and Britain. Dr Fisher was also the recipient of gifts and appreciative letters. *The Times* reported that his speech was punctuated by loud applause; that he won 'golden opinions' from all; and the whole ceremony was for him 'a marked personal triumph'.

The time had now come when the Archbishop felt able to send the following letter to the Kabaka which he did with genuine feeling: 'May I write to express my heartfelt thanksgiving to God that the way is now open to an agreed solution of these Constitutional problems and that you can look to a speedy return to your throne and people. You know how earnestly I have been concerned from the beginning and have prayed that on every side goodwill and mutual understanding would prevail. The details of the settlement are, of course, important but far more important is the triumph of mutual friendship and trust between all concerned. I have admired intensely the wisdom and patience of the members of the Delegation which I met here, and of the Lukiko and others whom I met in Uganda. I think a great deal is owed to the obvious desire of the Colonial Secretary to reach a fair settlement but the heaviest burden of anxiety has rested upon you, and your patient understanding has contributed more than anything to this result. I thank God for it.'

Lennox Boyd received from the Archbishop his due praise. 'There were a thousand pitfalls,' he wrote, 'but all through I have had a conviction that an agreed solution would be possible. That rested chiefly in my knowledge that you were determined to do everything in your power to secure it.' Geoffrey Fisher's relations with Lennox Boyd had been excellent throughout. With Mulieri, Geoffrey Fisher felt that he enjoyed a very special relationship which he greatly prized, so much so that when he failed to secure election to the Lukiko he sent him a letter of genuine sympathy. 'It struck me', the Archbishop wrote, 'you might be feeling a little downhearted. It is only too common in this life for those who played a formative part in difficult times to find that when the solution has come . . . their services are not needed further.' Even with the Governor, Sir Andrew Cohen, the Archbishop decided to bury the hatchet and he sent and received a kind letter.

The long period of waiting and frustration was now approaching its end and the Kabaka returned in triumph to his native land in the summer of 1955, the Archbishop being given a glowing report of this eagerly awaited event by the Bishop of Uganda. 'There were large cheering crowds all the way from Entebbe Airport as Mutesa II entered the Cathedral of Kampala on a National Day.' 'I believe', he wrote to the Archbishop, 'a great number of Bugandans realised something of the debt they owe to [your] fatherly counsel and support.' The Bishop of Uganda himself preached the sermon.

Most Ugandans must have thought, as equally they hoped, that this homecoming represented the end of the Kabaka's and the Buganda's constitutional problems. Alas! This proved far from the case, since there were many loose ends in the constitutional settlement still to tie up. This meant that the Kabaka was often away in London, so much so that in September 1960 the Archbishop received an anxious call from Kampala asking for the return of the Kabaka with full powers. This agitation arose out of Buganda's continuing fear of a unitary Government for the whole protectorate which would have the effect of placing power in the hands of young politicians from other tribes. The Bugandans wished for a more decentralised government, thus preserving the sovereignty of the Kabaka who, of course, could not expect to rule the whole of a pluralist tribal state. Thus they now wished to break the agreement made when the Kabaka now returned from exile. On the other hand the Bugandans were concerned to stress that the realisation of their hopes was not meant to be a breach of friendship with Britain but merely protective against their being swamped and thus losing their identity. The Governor of Uganda was very well aware of this fear and complained to the Archbishop that it led the Kabaka and his advisers – 'a poorer lot than ever' – to refuse to co-operate in plans for constitutional advance in Uganda with early independence. 'What they fail to see', he commented, was 'that there will have to be some settlement or accommodation between Buganda and the rest of the Protectorate which outnumbers them three to one; and that this would best take place while the British are still here.' In the Governor's view a secession with as a consequence isolation was 'geographically and physically impossible'.

Geoffrey Fisher was himself placed in a difficult position since he was the recipient of conflicting requests. In addition Katakirro asked his help in securing the emending of recent legislation designed to deal with the intimidation and violence in Uganda during the period of the registration of votes for the forthcoming elections. The Archbishop's response to this appeal was, perhaps, predictable, namely that it was the unhappy duty of a Government to maintain 'public order' which could mean its assuming reserve powers though it must exercise them with care and restraint. He deplored the Kabaka's ministers not agreeing with the constitutional proposals put forward by the Commission chaired by the Earl of Munster.

The fears of the Bugandans for themselves and the Kabakaship under the new Constitutional proposals were too deep-seated to be easily removed and the consequence was that they appealed to the Colonial Secretary for permission to secede – a request which, not surprisingly, was refused. The Archbishop now felt that he should acquaint the Colonial Secretary with the substance of a letter he had received from the Bishop of Namirembe – formerly Bishop of Uganda – to the effect that if a certain form of Federal Government were granted, guaranteeing independence for the Buganda and its institutions, then it must be required to withdraw its refusal to co-operate with the rest of the Protectorate. Hence the Archbishop reminded the Colonial Secretary that in Nigeria its 'salvation' was only found by creating a loose Confederation which satisfied the Princes in North Africa. Hence, it was easy to understand why the Kabaka and his Government felt that something similar might be secured for them.

The Secretary of State now made it public that so far as Her Majesty's Government was concerned there was no question of any part of the Protectorate seceding so long as Britain had authority. At the same time he informed the Archbishop that he believed it wrong to suppose as did Bishop Leslie Brown that Buganda's future could be assured within a federal system; nor for that matter would the Kabaka himself subscribe to the kind of settlement which had obtained in

Northern Nigeria. He went on, somewhat paradoxically, to add that he had not absolutely ruled out some form of a federal system and had set up in 1960 a Uganda Relationship Commission to consider a suitable Government for Uganda though unfortunately the Kabaka would not co-operate. The Secretary of State advised the Kabaka that he must make concessions to his neighbours, particularly since, even if they rejected them, it would strengthen his negotiating position. Finally, the Secretary appealed to the Archbishop in view of his 'unique authority' to write to the Kabaka in an effort to convince him that responsible people in Britain were worried at his position.

The Archbishop certainly contemplated writing to the Kabaka; indeed he drew up a draft letter, but on reflection felt it unwise to send it. Whether he could have been of any help in this situation is doubtful. However, he kept in close touch with Leslie Brown, and other responsible leaders in Uganda. As a result the Archbishop was convinced more than ever that a spirit of trust and mutual confidence between the Protectorate and all the local Governments was imperative.

So concerned was Dr Fisher with the future of Uganda that he despatched an epistle to Katakirro reflecting at length on the general position in mid-November 1960. Undoubtedly the neighbours of the Buganda entertained grave fears lest the preservation of its freedom should threaten their own. The Christian way to solve such problems, maintained the Archbishop, was one of reconciliation. Thus the new Constitution should be one that all people could accept though the Governor had not yet been able to secure this. The fact was that some authority must be placed over the Kabaka if Buganda was to become part of a unified and greater State. On the other hand the majesty and mystique of the Kabaka within Uganda must be preserved.

The British Government, however, found the Kabaka's ministers uncooperative, even obstructive, while the ministers on their part regarded the British Government as equally intransigent. The Archbishop was sensitive to the Government's dilemma in that having given the Buganda an assurance that its special position would be respected it had also commited itself to the outcome of the deliberations of the Relationship Commission. (It almost recalls the ambiguities of the Balfour Declaration!) He himself could only make one suggestion, namely that the Government should give an assurance that if no acceptable constitutional device could be found then provision must be made to respect the internal stability of Buganda together with the special Royal Prerogative and position which belonged to the Kabaka. But how?

Fortunately the Archbishop benefitted at this time from the advice of his new Lay Secretary, Robert Beloe, who had an interview with the Head of the East Africa Department of the Colonial Office whose members may be resented what they regarded as excessive interference from Lambeth.

Geoffrey Fisher now felt it politic to protest that he no longer desired to get involved in the political aspects of Uganda's problems, particularly since he did not wish to link them up in any way with the establishment of two Provinces in East Africa. 'I know,' to quote his own words to Leslie Brown, 'how dangerous it is for me to interfere at all.' However, in view of the historic role which the Church Missionary Society and UMCA had played in Uganda, this restraint if carried to excess was not in practice possible – nor was it in fact congenial to the Archbishop's temperament. Thus he wrote to the Governor, on 21 November 1960, suggesting that the members of the Relationship Commission should visit Buganda in order to become sensitive to its traditions. At the same time he sent a letter to Lennox Boyd sounding a cautionary note. 'I am terribly afraid that we are failing to spot the grain of truth which lies in the chaff of the Kabaka's mind.' The latter and his ministers, he complained, had done everything wrong, but they had a real fear that 'behind their backs or over their heads, by one device or another, they would lose for ever that degree of pride and self-respect which in a real sense the British Government promised to preserve to them'. This was his and indeed their worry.

Geoffrey Fisher could not see any easy way out of this *impasse* – the constitutional need for a united Uganda possessing a strong central government yet at the same time a near autonomous Buganda retaining its traditional Kabakaship. Indeed, he well understood the point of the Colonial Secretary's remarks: 'I have to try and walk a tightrope'.

The spate of letters continued between the Archbishop – in spite of his attempts to withdraw – the Secretary of State for the Colonies, the Governor of Uganda and Earl Munster, chairman of the Relationship Commission, whose courage in taking over this responsibility Geoffrey Fisher greatly admired. As to the latter, the Archbishop advised him to consult Leslie Brown whose views coincided largely with his own, namely that it was necessary to help the Kabaka and his ministers to save face. Thus prompted, the chairman of the Commission conversed with Leslie Brown and also saw the Kabaka twice, assuring him that the Government intended to maintain the Kabakaship.

In the heat of this seemingly never-ending controversy centred around apparently irreconcilable interests Geoffrey Fisher sent a letter to the Kabaka saying that he had given Katakirro sound but unpalatable advice. 'I have recently', he went on, 'been giving equally sound, and, I suspect, equally unpalatable advice to leading Statesmen in Rhodesia and the Federation. In every country of Africa, the problem is different; but in all of them the way to a solution is, I am sure, the same – to put rights and laws to protect them into the second place (or even lower) and to put first duties – duties to a whole country and to *all* its citizens, however unequally yoked together they might be, duties to the principle of good neighbourliness revealed to us by Our Lord Jesus Christ and made possible for us by the Grace of the Holy Spirit. Again I send my affectionate greetings and good wishes to you and yours.'

In principle it may well be that this homily was unexceptionable but it leaves, at the practical level, much ill-defined as to its specific application to particular political situations.

The Kabaka was, of course, a sitting target for advice, sought and unsought, and the Governor of Uganda suggested that the Archbishop should add one more to the many letters he had sent him. On 1 January 1961 the Lukiko met and declared for secession. The Archbishop reacted immediately, expressing to the Kabaka his own great regret at this momentous step. 'It seemed to us,' he wrote, 'you had been doing your utmost to restrain them from such a reckless decision but in vain. It is indeed heartrending for us all. What now?'

It was indeed a case of 'What now?' but the sands of time were running out so far as the Archbishop himself was concerned. On 31 May 1961 he ceased to be Archbishop and Primate of All England so that political affairs in Uganda which preoccupied him during his archiepiscopate ceased to be his personal and official concern. Suffice here to say that in March 1962 Buganda, and three of the four districts of the Western Region, achieved a special relationship with the central government. On 9 October 1963 the Kabaka of Buganda was elected President. However Buganda, in company with the three other kingdoms, found itself in an impossible constitutional position wholly incompatible with Uganda functioning as a fully sovereign state. When Milton Obote became head of Government, the Kabaka was expelled from his Palace and fled to England never to return to his native land. He died a victim to his own royal destiny.

Political affairs in Uganda demanded much, some may think a disproportionate amount of Geoffrey Fisher's time, but he felt it right, in view of the close relationship of Anglican missionary societies with this country, to give lavishly of his energies to its problems. Quite clearly Robert Beloe his Lay Secretary tried in a measure to restrain him. Perhaps we should notice, in bringing this chapter to a close, that Geoffrey Fisher became involved in a controversy centring around three deportations, namely those of the Kabaka, Archbishop Makarios and Seretse Khama, heir to the Chieftainship of the Bamangwalta tribe in Bechuanaland. The latter's 'offence' was to have married Ruth, a white English girl – quite illegally they were refused a church wedding – and the result was his being suspended from his office and exiled for five years by the Labour Government, which the Conservative Government that followed made permanent. Progressive opinion in England was aroused and its exponents suspected the sinister hand of the South African Government, wedded to apartheid, in these events. A meeting of protest addressed by Seretse Khama took place at the Caxton Hall in London, and the British Council of Churches held a private session chaired by the Archbishop with 'no holds barred'. During the course of its deliberations Geoffrey Fisher volunteered to lead a delegation to the Government containing members who 'might wish to say what he himelf might not be prepared to say.' Carefully he prepared a statement and took with him a representative group which included Dr Norman Goodall, Sir Kenneth Grubb and the Reverend K. K. Orchard. The Archbishop closely interrogated the Government as to whether deporting Seretse Khama was really necessary; and he repeated the fears *vis-à-vis* South Africa.

The result of this and other pressures was the return to his country and to his traditional office of Seretse Khama. There was indeed a further consequence – the progressive setting up there of a fully democratic society.

The lavish quotation of letters from Geoffrey Fisher which this chapter contains illustrates at the practical level the extent of his commitment to the people of Uganda and their future.

CHAPTER 44

Uganda

WE have deliberately dealt at some length with the close involvement of Geoffrey Fisher in the political struggle in Uganda centring around the young Kabaka and his desire to preserve a truly African state within the Protectorate. The fact that the Archbishop of Canterbury felt it right to be so involved bears witness to the strongly formative influence which the Church of England had exercised educationally, and as a consequence politically, on the indigenous population through the labours of the Church Missionary Society, the Universities' Mission to Central Africa, and the London Missionary Society. Indeed many of the young leaders who came to the fore in the struggle for independence had been educated in their schools.

So far as Geoffrey Fisher was concerned we have seen that he planned to set up two or three ecclesiastical Provinces in Uganda and East Africa though it would be difficult to imagine a more difficult time to attempt to do this. Indeed Leslie Brown wrote to the Archbishop on 6 April 1954; 'It is impossible for anyone outside the country to realise the tension and the mistrust between Africans and Europeans – this is not overt but is daily becoming more offensive – almost anything done by Europeans is regarded with suspicion. There are influences which are trying to persuade our Church people that white domination is such an integral part of our Church system that they must leave the Church.'

Undeterred Geoffrey Fisher drew up a confidential memorandum for the perusal of the bishops detailing how he saw the situation and pointing out some of the pitfalls in the way of implementing his plans. Choosing which particular diocese should go into which Province demanded the skill of a chess player purposefully moving his pieces on the board. In a Continent such as Africa tribal and territorial boundaries were not always clearly defined. One of the purposes of a Province, of course, was to achieve a greater co-ordination; to get rid of the frustrations of bishops being answerable to a metropolitan distant in Lambeth; to make it easier to create new dioceses when the need arose. In April 1954 the Archbishop saw the Bishop of Mombasa and later had a long session at Lambeth with the Bishop of Central Tanganyika, the latter having many years of diocesan experience behind him in Africa. Archbishop and Bishop agreed that Uganda ought to become a separate Province as also should Tanganyika and Kenya, though the last of these did not yet contain the four Dioceses usually regarded as the minimum to constitute an Anglican Province. These three Provinces could thus make up the Church of East Africa, subject to the metropolitical jurisdiction of the Archbishop of Canterbury, that is until an Archbishop for East Africa was appointed. Such a grouping would require a change in Diocesan relationships with the missionary societies, not least in the area of finance. In particular, the Diocese of Tanganyika would need reassurance that it was not be be put under the control of Dioceses associated with the Universities' Mission to Central Africa. Geoffrey Fisher had early come to the conclusion that in the new Province Leslie Brown should be the first Metropolitan and that he should preside over two English and two or three African Bishops. It was imperative that at this stage in its development the new Metropolitan should be supported by some really first-class Archdeacons, Diocesan Secretaries and the like, especially in his own Archdiocese.

As 1960 came ever nearer and there were rumours that Geoffrey Fisher's retirement was imminent, the Bishop of Uganda urged him: '*Please don't* retire until you have launched us on our way'. Uganda was still in a state of unsettlement, and its diocesan secretary, Kenneth Sharpe, informed the Archbishop on 2 February 1960 that there was serious rioting, and also disquiet among the clergy concerning their basic stipends. Still, as a diocesan officer he had no wish to hold up the Inauguration of the Province on this score. The Archbishop was equally determined that the setting up of the Province should be no longer delayed. To this end he discussed its constitution with interested parties remarking shrewdly that 'Constitutions are made to fit facts and not vice-versa'. His decision was that the Bishops Suffragan should have the status of Diocesan Bishops in the Provincial Synod along with the Bishop on the Upper Nile.

There still remained those who felt that the institution of a Province was premature but the Archbishop's reasons for pushing forward rapidly were not entirely personal as he explained to the Bishop on the Upper Nile. Though for many reasons he argued one might wish that developments of a Provincial kind could have waited perhaps for another decade, the risks of moving too slowly were great. It was essential to provide from the Church at home many well-equipped clergy and laity, 'happy to be Assistants and not Overseers; but able to fortify the infant Province and its Dioceses in administrative skills and in practical theology'. The Bishop of Uganda, so he explained to his fellow Bishop on the Upper Nile, had put before the Archbishop certain plans which he had approved for a re-distribution of dioceses. As to the province, 'I eagerly hope', Geoffrey Fisher wrote, 'that I may have the privilege in person of handing over my jurisdiction and of inaugurating the Province in the early part of the year.' So it was that on 1 July

Uganda

1960, the Diocese on the Upper Nile with Metropolitical approval from Canterbury was divided into a number of Dioceses. The next decision to be taken was the location of the Metropolitan's Cathedral. The Dioceses themselves opted for Kampala, a choice which Geoffrey Fisher approved since it would be 'at the centre of affairs in the anxious days when the politics and internal unity of the country are so much disturbed'. He also approved the choice of Leslie Brown as Metropolitan, though he knew this would come as a great disappointment to the Bishop on the Upper Nile, who had given long and faithful service. Thus he wrote him an understanding letter explaining that it was a difficult choice to make and that he would have been 'happy' with him but political developments meant that the new Metropolitan must be based in Kampala. Doubtless this explanation eased some of the pain of being passed over.

So it was that, on 16 April 1960 the Province of Uganda, Rwanda and Burundi with its eleven dioceses was set up, Leslie Brown having been translated to the Bishopric of Nambirembe as the Archbishop had wished. This was a great achievement against the background of racial strife and political division. Certainly Geoffrey Fisher was able to say with pardonable pride – 'Pars Magna Fui.

Perhaps it may not be inappropriate to draw this section on West, Central and East Africa to a close with a brief reference to his tours there in general.

There can be no question that Geoffrey Fisher enjoyed every moment of his many journeys to Africa, physically strenuous as they undoubtedly were; this was in no small measure due to the openness, exuberance and spontaneity of the black population. One of his chaplains writes that to catch a glimpse of him 'waving, shaking hands and talking to a crowd of Kikuyus who could not understand a word of his English' was to become aware of a group radiantly happy, and an Archbishop surmounting the barriers of language and race'.

As the day of his retirement drew closer so the Archbishop became vividly aware of 'unfinished business', tasks waiting to be done. One event which he anticipated with pleasure was the celebration of Nigeria's independence fixed for 2 October 1960 in the Church of Christ at Lagos. Though it was difficult for him to fit this into his schedule – it meant postponing the Michaelmas Ordination – he knew he must accept the invitation. As he wrote at the time: 'what happens in Africa over the next fifty years matters for the future happiness and welfare of mankind more than anything else.'

The celebrations lasted from Friday 23 September when the Archbishop and Mrs Fisher arrived at Kano Airport until they left for England on 2 October the day of the thanksgiving service. Amongst the distinguished guests was Princess Alexandra.

The Archbishop's hosts at Bishops Court were the Deputy Governor, the Bishop of Lagos and Mrs Howells. Seldom did the Primate of all England spend a more hectic week; or enjoyed a more varied programme which included a Tattoo on the race course; a Firework Display; and a large Nigerian Exhibition.

CHAPTER 45

South Africa

THE first Province of the Anglican Church to be established in Africa, not surprisingly had its Metropolitical See in Cape Town. Indeed, as we have seen its Constitution served as a model for those which came afterwards.

We turn now to Geoffrey Fisher's involvement, as Archbishop of Canterbury, with the Church of this Province at a time when social *mores* were beginning to change and black consciousness was emerging as a strong political force. Field Marshal Smuts was still Prime Minister when Geoffrey Fisher went to Lambeth but in 1948 the Nationalist leader, Dr D. F. Malan, was returned to power after a General Election in which the blacks and coloureds were excluded from the voting register. Malan was a man of high intelligence who had gained a doctorate for a thesis on the philosopher Berkeley, but politically he was wedded to white supremacy not as a transitional stage on the way to the building up of 'One People', but as unalterably required by a divine decree and written into law. In holding this quasi-theological view he was but obedient to the official teaching of the Dutch Reformed Church of which he was a zealous member, a Church rooted in Calvinism, nurtured on the traditions of the Great Trek, and consisting of some two and a half million adherents. From this *milieu* there grew the policy of apartheid, euphemistically described as 'separate development'.

The inferior status of the non-whites which this enshrined could only be maintained by mandatory controls over large areas of personal life imposed by a ruthless police force administering savage punishments to secure their enforcement. Hence South Africa was brought into line with the totalitarian régimes of Europe. So far as this affected race relations apartheid had, at that time, but not in earlier days, the more or less full support of the Dutch Reformed Church to which most members of the Nationalist Government belonged. The position of the Anglican Church, with its 1,400,000 members, one million of them being blacks or coloureds, threw up increasing problems with corresponding challenges. Much depended on the quality, wisdom and courage of its leaders. Dr Russell Darbyshire, Archbishop of Cape Town, who had been ill for some time, died in 1948 on the eve of the Lambeth conference. His successor was Geoffrey Clayton who had already shown his worth as Bishop of Johannesburg. Clayton, an old

'Rugbeian', was an accomplished theologian who had spent many years as a Cambridge don, and served as a parish priest in Chesterfield. Naturally shy and withdrawn he yet possessed great moral courage when tested and his opposition to the policy of apartheid, based on deeply held doctrinal principles, remained unwavering. Though he never sought a head-on collision with the Government, he did not shrink from it when, in his judgement, loyalty to the Gospel made it necessary. Geoffrey Fisher soon recognised his merit, and depended largely upon him for advice as to how Lambeth and the Church of England generally could best assist the Church of the Province in its struggle with the State. Numerous letters passed between Canterbury and Cape Town as well as to South African bishops generally.

It was inevitable that Archbishop Fisher should be consulted over appointments to the Anglican Church of South Africa, particularly in the case of its Bishops since it was still the case that these were recruited in part from England. One, in particular, who sought his advice before making a decision and for whom it proved fraught with significance personally and for the Church of the Province, was Ambrose Reeves. A high churchman of very definite views, he believed passionately that Christians in response to their incarnational faith, must respond to the social and political challenges of their day. The Bishopric of Johannesburg became vacant in 1948 through the translation of Dr Clayton to Cape Town. Ambrose Reeves was at that time Vicar of St Nicholas Church in Liverpool where he had spent some six exciting years, making his presence felt and bringing a Christian witness to bear on various aspects of the city's life. Privately advised that he was being seriously considered for the vacant bishopric, the most important diocese in the Province of South Africa, he wrote for advice to Archbishop Fisher, receiving a reply dated 15 February 1949.

Church life in the Johannesburg Diocese was strong and active but, so the Archbishop warned, faced with immense difficulties arising from the situation of the indigenous population. Maybe Ambrose Reeves had read Alan Paton's moving novel *Cry the Beloved Country* – it was recommended to him by Geoffrey Fisher – which exposed the cruelty inherent in the Government policy. Thus one of the Bishop's first duties would be to lead effectively a 'Crusade against the evil side of the colour problem'. If he were prepared to do this he should let his name go forward. He did and never was archiepiscopal advice more seriously taken or more literally, indeed sacrificially, lived out.

In this short letter Dr Fisher used the word 'problem'. Certainly the Church of the Province of South Africa was beset with them. To condemn apartheid in formal pronouncements was one thing, but how to respond to it in practice, in its many ramifications, was another. The situation was made the more difficult for both bishops and parish priests in that they could not always rely on the support of the white members of their own congregations. Geoffrey Fisher's personal concern was for the Church of England to offer such help and encouragement as the Church of the Province would welcome and find useful. He was not always sure what this implied but as will be seen, he came for the most part to rely on the advice of the Archbishop of Cape Town so long as this office was held by Dr Clayton.

The policy of the South African Government had wide repercussions in many areas of life. Thus early in 1949 a small group led by the Reverend Michael Scott, a member of the Christian Council of South Africa, having already written to the Queen, the Prime Minister and Dr Malan, sought to enlist the Archbishop's support to prevent the Union Government taking over the mandated territories of South West Africa. Michael Scott also got into touch with Bishop Roberts, Secretary of the Society for the Propagation of the Gospel, who passed on this enquiry to Lambeth conscious that 'uninvited interference from outside might do more harm than good'. Geoffrey Fisher felt himself equally sceptical and in no position to give the Bishop authoritative guidance. Hence he himself got into touch with Archbishop Clayton asking precisely how he, the Archbishop and his fellow Bishops in England, could come behind the Church of the Province on this particular issue, and more widely on race relations in general, particularly at a time when the South African Government was stepping up the pressure against the black population. Clayton's reply, which he often repeated in subsequent correspondence with Lambeth, was that initiatives taken in England and directed against the South African Government were liable to prove counter-productive, since their immediate effect was to unite some people behind official policy who might otherwise have questioned or even opposed it. It would be more helpful to encourage English churchmen to support the South African Bishops in their testing situation. Dr Clayton's *ipsissima verba* are worth quoting: 'We believe that the Church of the Province of South Africa must fight its own battles, and must fight them in South Africa. We believe that anything that looks like an appeal on our part to the Church of England would be a grave mistake and would weaken rather than strengthen our hands here and we are in no way conscious of any failure to back us on the part of the Church of England, but we believe that a debate in the Church Assembly and a resolution of the Church Assembly would do us more harm than good. What is important for us here is that we shall be increasingly regarded as a South African Church, not an exotic church with its real home in England.' This advice from Cape Town, so strongly expressed, was sincerely given and it came from one whose consistent anti-apartheid stance could not be questioned. Even Ambrose Reeves, some few years later, let Archbishop Fisher know that he shared the same basic approach. However this view was by no means universal in the Anglican Church of South Africa.

Following the advice of Archbishop Clayton, Geoffrey Fisher declined, at Michael Scott's request, to approach Mr Attlee, then Prime Minister, and Dr Malan, with a view to the racial issue in South Africa being discussed at the Commonwealth Conference. Meanwhile, as Ambrose Reeves put it, the pathological interest in racial characteristics continued to dominate the Union. A young educated South African thus expresed the frustrated feelings of his generation: 'They cannot recognise us as a real brother in Christ because they fear us too much as a potential brother-in-law.'

Not everyone in or outside South Africa, however, was convinced that the Church of England need play so restricted a role as the Archbishop of Cape Town thought proper to assign to it. There were those such as Michael Scott, Trevor Huddleston, Provincial in South Africa of the Community of the Resurrection, and John Collins, a Canon of St Paul's Cathedral which gave him access to a uniquely powerful pulpit in London, who believed that the conscience of Britain ought to be aroused and that it should make itself heard in South Africa in no uncertain terms. It was understandable that such men should feel a strong sense of frustration at what they regarded as the apathy of the Church of England due, in part, to its 'organisational structure' depriving it of a measure of independence.

The future of the mandated territories of Bechuanaland, Swaziland and Busutoland remained a problem which the Churches, in the light of their Gospel, could not ignore and to which the Archbishop of Canterbury, because of his unique status, could not be indifferent. Any occupation and assertion of sovereignty over them by the South African Government would clearly be illegal and a violation of the United Nations Charter. The current racial policies of the Union made the matter one of added urgency since informed public opinion in Britain, stimulated by comment and rumour, grew increasingly uneasy, typical of which unease was a letter from Shaun Heron, Editor of the *British Weekly*, to Archbishop Fisher expressing his fears that these territories might be handed over to the South African Government. Certainly the Basuto negotiations had ended without any firm assurances that such fears were groundless.

The Archbishop's reply was meant to be reassuring. The British Government had no intention, he said, of dealing in this way with the High Commission Territories. However, to provoke a 'mature row' over this possibility would not help since its effect might be to drive Dr Malan on to 'stupidity and obstinacy'. He, as Archbishop, had associated himself wholeheartedly with a resolution recently passed in the

British Council of Churches which reaffirmed its conviction that no transfer of these territories to the Union Government could be made without the full consent of the people concerned. Such a transference, if it took place, 'would deeply wound the conscience of Christians and of the civilised world'.

Geoffrey Fisher was kept reasonably well informed of what was happening in South Africa by a steady stream of letters from Anglican Bishops in the Province. From Ambrose Reeves, whose energy and clear-cut Christian convictions he admired, he heard often. Johannesburg was in many respects a barometer, registering the political and social climate of urban South Africa at its most explosive. Hence its Bishop was caught up willy-nilly in these stresses and strains. His letters to Lambeth, therefore, have a particular interest. In January 1951 he sent to Dr Fisher a resumé of conditions generally in his Diocese. He was initiating conversations between the Dutch Reformed and English speaking churches, 'very preliminary', he commented, 'and conducted both in Afrikaans and English'. He himself at the moment was actively engaged in a diocesan mission to the Europeans and also endeavouring to increase the church's evangelistic activity. There had been disturbances in the city and 'unpleasant happenings' in his own house on New Year's Day. 'We were awakened', he writes, 'at 5.30 am by one of the servants telling us that the house was on fire. Fortunately we were able to get it under control by the time the fire engines arrived, although not before the fire had done considerable damage and the smoke so penetrated into the rooms that we are now in the throes of redecorating.

The maintenance of apartheid meant of necessity, as opposition against it grew, increasing control and more extensive oppressive legislation. The Bantu Education Act of 1953 put every African student under the control of the Government and the education provided in academic institutions was designed to fit the pupils for the inferior and subservient roles which they were destined to play. The Criminal Law Amendment Act provided severe punishments for incitement to break the law even by means of peaceful protest. It also gave authority to the Governor General to proclaim a state of emergency under which legal enactments could be suspended; also the Government was given power to legislate by decree. Trevor Huddleston, Provincial of the Community of the Resurrection in South Africa, 1949–1956, wrote to Canon Collins protesting that if these enactments were passed he and other colleagues would face arrest and imprisonment. He therefore urged him to build up publicity in England so that if this were to happen the British public would at least know what was going on and why. This appeal led to an exchange of letters between the Archbishops of Canterbury and Cape Town, also between Canon Collins and the

Bishop of Johannesburg, as to the part which the Church of England ought properly and helpfully to play. Dr Clayton still stuck firmly to his view that Trevor Huddleston was wrong in 'trying to galvanise the resistance movement into action', particularly while a General Election was being held in South Africa. However, he was the first to recognise the need for the Church of the Province to resist oppression and to accept the full weight of responsibility devolving upon himself. He had now firmly come to the conclusion that a severe protest must be made to the Union Government against its racial policy as embodied in the recent legislation; and that as President of the Christian Council of South Africa it was particularly incumbent upon him to make his voice heard. He therefore drew up a massive indictment which he sent to the Prime Minister, the Minister of Justice and also to Geoffrey Fisher. In this document he condemned the Public Safety Bill as a 'dangerous extension of the principle of Government by regulation'. As to the Criminal Law Amendment Bill he was adamant: 'We desire to say that the Christian Church can never undertake to maintain silence in the face of laws which seem to infringe Christian principles'. If they were commanded to do so they could only say with the Apostles that they 'must obey God rather than men'. The sentences imposed under the Acts, he complained, were uniformly too severe and he urged the Government, after the General Election, 'to call into consultation representatives of the non-Europeans in this country'.

As the general situation in South Africa steadily worsened, so Geoffrey Fisher felt he must not keep silent and in April 1953 he delivered a very outspoken address condemning apartheid at a meeting of the British Council of Churches in Birmingham. His remarks were widely reported in Britain and in South Africa where they were received with great hostility by the Nationalist press. *The Burger*, a leading Cape Town newspaper, carried an article suggesting that as the Archbishop was the 'Head' of the Coronation ceremony the Prime Minister of the Union would be justified in cancelling his acceptance of the invitation to attend. The Archbishop of Cape Town in a letter to Lambeth commented with what proved to be prophetic insight that he believed the Union would not stay long in the Commonwealth since the acting Prime Minister wanted a republic outside it. They were in for a difficult time in the Union, and he only wished he had more confidence in his own judgement as to what ought to be done. Recently the Dutch Reformed Church Missionary Council had invited the Anglican with the Protestant Churches to a conference but had stipulated that none but whites should attend. His own view was that they could not accept on these terms. Theirs was not a white but a multi-racial church.

There can be no doubt that the Archbishop of Canterbury's Birmingham address was being taken seriously at governmental levels in South Africa. At the request of the Prime Minister, Dr Malan, the High Commissioner in London called upon Lord Swinton at the Commonwealth Relations Office to lodge a formal protest, expressing 'great indignation'. The speech was particularly unfortunate, he complained, at a time when Dr Malan was being urged by his own supporters and the press generally not to attend the Coronation. It would now make it much more difficult for him to 'argue for his own strong views to remain in the Commonwealth'. Lord Swinton immediately got into touch with the Archbishop, passing on the grave news of the High Commssioner's strictures and elaborating on them in the process. There were two points in particular, he noted, to which Dr Malan took grave exception. The first was the references to 'sub-human living conditions in Johannesburg'. True, there were bad slums around the city but ought not the Archbishop, in fairness, to have said something about the slum clearance schemes? Secondly, Dr Malan strongly objected to apartheid, which he preferred to call 'separate development', being described as 'slavery'. Unfortunately the Archbishop's words were given additional weight from the fact that many South African citizens misunderstood the nature of his office and ascribed to his utterances governmental significance.

A complaint of this kind coming from the head of a Commonwealth country needed to be taken seriously. For this reason it is worth quoting the Archbishop's reply to Lord Swinton. 'I very rarely make comments on South African affairs beyond supporting all that our Bishops in South Africa so admirably say, and the High Commissioner apparently had himself noted that I try to restrain others from making heated comments. At the same time I cannot always keep silence; and from time to time I am bound to declare what is the prevailing Christian opinion on world or Commonwealth affairs in which Christian opinions are involved. I enclose a copy of what I said in Birmingham, and you will observe that I reviewed Africa as a whole and it would have been quite impossible to make no reference at all to South Africa. If you will read what I said I think you will agree that it was fair comment even if forcefully expressed. I did not describe apartheid as slavery pure and simple, but as 'a sort of slavery', and of course any political system which permanently keeps the majority of the inhabitants of the country in an inferior condition can properly be so described. Apparently Dr Malan takes my mention of the living conditions in Johannesburg as an attack upon himself. I never mentioned him nor did I attribute the blame for it to anybody. . . . There is no doubt that the conditions there are properly described as a social disease. It really is not my fault if people in South Africa misunderstand my position and are stupid enough to suppose that when I speak on matters of public interest I speak for the Government. It is time they learned that while the Archbishop holds a high place by virtue of his office he speaks so far as possible in the name of the Church and of Christian opinion and not in the name of the Government.'

Reference has already been made to Bishop Ambrose Reeves of Johannesburg and his forthright opposition to the Bantu Education Act, even to the extent of closing Church schools rather than comply with its terms. This certainly showed the strength of his will as well as making him subject to attack bordering on persecution. So acutely did some of his friends feel his exposed position that one of them, Miss Mary Trevelyan, called the attention of the Archbishop to the desperate plight of the Bishop and his family, what with the arrest of his black clergy, the tapping of his telephone, and the opening of his letters. In spite of this he continued undeterred his protests against the banning of black students from the University of Salisbury. But in Miss Trevelyan's opinion he had had enough and should be brought back to England – a view with which the Archbishop of Cape Town when asked his opinion by Dr Fisher, strongly disagreed since it would be understood as a victory for the South African Government.

If the Archbishop of Canterbury's public pronouncements about South Africa were on the whole restrained, he yet used his pen and on occasion broke loose from Dr Clayton's guidelines. Such happened on his receiving a copy of *Dagbrak* a paper produced in Johannesburg containing an article on 'separate development' by Mr O. Patrer Machers. The Archbishop was stimulated to reply and writing to the Editor he drew a contrast between the terms of the Central African Federation which placed the African on the lowest rung of the ladder, but made it possible for him through a 'proper progress in a multi-racial community to enter into a steady growth in partnership'. Under apartheid there was for the natives no ladder at all.

In the House of Lords the Archbishop also forcefully expressed the same view when he stated baldly that as South Africa developed, the balance of power, sooner or later, would shift from the Europeans to the non-Europeans. Since civilisation had become the common property of them both, this was to be 'wholly accepted as a right thing'.

We have referred on more than one occasion to the Bantu Education Act which was now beginning to bite. This piece of legislation grievously affected the Church of England which through the mission-ary societies had established many church schools in the Union over the years. Thus Father Raynes of the Community of the Resurrection gloomily predicted, on his return from South Africa, that within two years nearly all denominational schools would be lost. Dr Fisher was foremost in condemning this piece of legislation seeing its ruthless efficiency as the inevitable consequence of imposing the policy of apartheid.

On 19 October 1954, the Archbishop addressed both Houses of Convocation on this issue. All the protests being voiced in South Africa, he claimed, pointed to the relentless pursuit of a policy towards the native population which was condemned by almost all Church opinion, outside the Dutch Reformed Church, as unchristian in principle as it was bound, in the long run, to prove catastrophic in practice. He then proceeded to list the evils of government policy such as bringing native education under the Minister of Native Affairs; the steps taken to ensure that the education given to natives should be strictly limited to what the government thought to be good for them; the expropriation of natives from the Western areas of Johannesburg; the confining of the tenure of Church properties to a year at a time. All these, he claimed, were 'such as to encourage or tend to encourage deterioration in the relationship between the natives and the Government'. This was totalitarianism and differed not at all from the suppression of freedom and Church life in Communist countries. It was 'strange', he reflected, that the South African Government 'does not begin to suspect its own wisdom when it finds itself imitating the methods of Communist government and control'.

The Observer in reporting the Archbishop's speech in a leader 'A case for action', asked pointedly whether it was true that all Britain could do was to give moral support to offset these evils.

The British Council of Churches followed this up by urging the Archbishop of Canterbury and Christian leaders generally to get together to see what practical steps ought to be taken. Geoffrey Fisher thus prompted, called a representative group to Lambeth and as a result the Reverend Fenton Morley and the Reverend Derrick Greeves, one an Anglican the other a Methodist, were sent to South Africa to sound out opinion on the spot. The Archbishop also wrote to Dr Clayton asking for guidance and adding: 'We are utterly dependent upon you and your advice'. The advice from Cape Town duly arrived and reflected the decisions taken at a meeting of the Provincial Synod, namely that it was not practicable to continue the church schools on the basis of voluntary contributions once they were deprived of financial support from the government. Thus it was better – here the Bishop of Johannesburg dissented – to opt for the lesser of two evils and to lease the school buildings to the State, otherwise there would be no education offered to the Africans at all. Meanwhile, ways should be explored to enlist voluntary teachers' help for at least some of the pupils.

The report from Fenton Morley and Derrick Greeves did not differ materially from that already given by the Archbishop of Cape Town. It stated that the Bishops of the Province did not wish for a dramatic appeal in England to save the schools though the Roman Catholics hoped to keep theirs going on a reduced subsidy. More generally, the report noted that apart from the Dutch Reformed Church, all condemned the Bantu Education Act. The right practical response to apartheid was difficult to determine and in the sad circumstances in which they found themselves some Africans would welcome separate development if it were fair and total.

It was galling for liberal-minded Christians in England to acquiesce in the virtual liquidation of the Anglican schools. Many wrote to Lambeth urging positive action to prevent such closures and John Collins advised that the present intention of Christian Action, in co-operation with the Society for the Propagation of the Gospel, and others, was to launch an appeal. Geoffrey Fisher, in response to this information, got into touch with Dr Bell, Bishop of Chichester, asking him to co-ordinate such financial efforts though it must be understood that this did not imply an officially sponsored Church of England appeal.

The Bishop of Johannesburg's absolutist policy by no means commended itself to many churchmen either in South Africa or England. Thus he wrote a detailed letter to Lambeth in which he justified his position on the grounds that it was divisive 'to assign a place of permanent inferiority to the African', thus violating 'the principle of true education'. 'It is my conviction,' he wrote, 'that if a proposed system of education is morally indefensible, the Church has no right to assist the authorities in carrying out their plans, however remotely or indirectly.'

Ambrose Reeves thus made a strong case and it sprang from a deep conviction. Geoffrey Fisher respected and understood his desire to have nothing to do with Government policy. What swayed the Archbishop, however, was his belief that withdrawal of the schools from all educational use was mistaken in that it would lead to a terrible deprivation for African children.

Concern with events in South Africa was by no means confined to the United Kingdom since the Church of that Province was a member of the world-wide Anglican Communion and also of the World Council of Churches. Hence the Bishop of Michigan, A. H. Crowley, enquired of the Archbishop in January 1954 what really was the cause of the present unrest in South Africa. Geoffrey Fisher replied by sending him a brief sketch of the historical and sociological background which underlay the current problems. Europeans were now outnumbered by nine to two, thus presenting them, as a minority, with a challenge to preserve their distinctive culture. 'The maintenance of white supremacy depended, paradoxically, on the employment of black labour. History had thrown up a further cleavage between the Dutch-speaking Boers and the English-speaking British.

Geoffrey Fisher's oppostion to apartheid was forthright but this by no means exempted him from criticism, not least from loyal members of the *Ecclesia Anglicana*. Typical was a letter from a Colonel Grant who accused the Archbishop of being lukewarm where apartheid was concerned when compared with such as Trevor Huddleston. To his critics, Dr Fisher protested in reply that he did not differ in any way from them as to the evils of apartheid but only on the means by which the Church of England could most effectively combat it. All agreed that there was something seriously wrong in South Africa as he himself had discovered in 1955 when *en route* for the Rhodesias. However, seeking to persuade an opposition to change its views was by no means the same as being indifferent to the issues involved. So far as apartheid was concerned, the Church of England had condemned it time and time again and he himself had joined in such condemnations. Indeed the World Council of Churches had declared against it at its meeting in Evanston.

Lying behind such a letter as that of Colonel Grant's was a feeling of impotence, experienced by many, as the grip of apartheid was being intensified in South Africa. With this there necessarily went the apparatus of a police state. Were there no political steps which could be taken against it?

Symptomatic of this unease was a letter written by the Bishop of Grahamstown early in 1957, protesting bitterly to Lambeth against newly proposed legislation under which it would be unlawful to hold any acts of worship in an urban area for a racially mixed congregation unless the Church was situated in a native location. Also prohibited were meetings of blacks in such an area without the permission of the Minister for Native Affairs. Here, so the Bishop alleged, was a projected invasion of the rights of the Church in respect of the freedom of her people to worship. All synods were inter-racial and they alone could elect bishops. The situation was indeed serious since such a law directly prevented the Church from discharging her proper function.

The South African bishops felt that they could not remain passive under this attack and a small episcopal committee comprising Grahamstown, Pretoria, Johannesburg and Natal met and reported unanimously that if this legislation became law the Church of the Province must not obey it. Not only would they – so Archbishop Clayton reported to Dr Fisher – be forced into this position but they would be unwilling to ask for any permissions from the Minister for Native Affairs since this would, in effect, be tantamount to admitting his right to say 'no'. Inevitably, therefore, all the Bishops, including himself, would become liable to arrest and imprisonment. 'I am not in the least anxious to go to prison,' he commented ruefully to the Archbishop, 'but I do not see how it is to be avoided'. The Government, by such an enactment, could bring all missionary work to a standstill; tear up leases; and prevent clergy coming over from England. 'I am sufficiently cowardly', he concluded, 'to wish that the Bishops had accepted my resignation. But I must try to carry on'.

The Archbishop of Cape Town enclosed, for Geoffrey Fisher's benefit, a letter he had sent to Dr Malan, the Prime Minister, in which he set out precisely what the effects of the Bill would be on the Church of the Province in relation to religious freedom. He did not mince his words: 'We recognise the great gravity of disobedience to the law of the land. We believe that obedience to secular authority, even in matters about which we differ in opinion, is a command laid upon us by God. But we are commanded to render unto Caesar the things which be Caesar's and unto God the things that are God's. There are, therefore, some matters which are God's and not Caesar's'.

Such a worsening situation was a grievous anxiety to so sensitive a man as Geoffrey Clayton whose health for some time had been in decline. Perhaps it came as no surprise to his friends that on the very day that he dispatched his letter to Lambeth, and thus prior to the Archbishop's receiving it, he died. Geoffrey Fisher received the following telegram: 'Our well beloved Archbishop of Cape Town died suddenly and peacefully today Thursday, Roy Cowdray'. Geoffrey Fisher wired back immediately: 'Heartfelt sympathy with Diocese and Province at loss of a great Christian, a powerful leader, and a wise statesman. The Church of England joins in your mourning and in rejoicing for what God has done through him.'

It was a sad blow for the Province to be deprived at so critical a time, of a leader in whom his episcopal colleagues had confidence. In a crisis situation, though never provocatively seeking confrontation, he had not hesitated to remain firm and resolute. Geoffrey Fisher was determined that due honours should be paid him at a memorial service in England, and confessed to Kenneth Slack, Secretary of the British Council of Churches, that he was tempted to make the occasion 'an organised demonstration against the policy of the South African Government'. At the same time he wrote to the Bishop of Grahamstown asking whether he himself as Archbishop of Canterbury, or the Church of England as a whole, could be of any help to the Church of the Province in its present travail. 'It is', he wrote, 'incredibly stupid as well as evil of them now to take this step of interfering with religious liberty and freedom but there it is.'

Without apparently waiting for a reply from the Bishop of Grahamstown the Archbishop decided, on his own responsibility, to write directly to Dr Malan's successor, Mr J. G. Strijdom, Prime Minister of

South Africa, this initiative leading to a correspondence, maybe unique of its kind, between a Primate of All England and the head of a Commonwealth country. So exceptional an exchange of letters merits more than a perfunctory reference. The first from Geoffrey Fisher dated 17 March 1957 began with an expression of his great shock at the death of Dr Clayton which, to quote his own words, 'makes me wonder in great perplexity and humility whether there is anything I can do which will not do more harm than good.' However he was now writing in a spirit of prayer and fear hoping that the Prime Minister would read his letter with patience and regard it as no more than 'an attempt of one Christian to speak to another'.

They differed profoundly on the subject of apartheid which he did not wish, in itself, to discuss but he could not refrain from urging him not to extend it to the point where 'absolutely fundamental truths of society are being violated,and the consciences of millions of fellow Christians were terribly wounded'. Into this category there fell the Native Laws Amendment Bill, and the separate Univerities Bill, the first erecting a barrier against freedom of worship and assembly; the latter 'eating at the roots of educational freedom'. He ended with a personal appeal. 'If you could but remove these two threats no real harm would be done to anything but governmental reputation for rigid consistency. On the contrary all over the world you would win for your country a new respect.'

We can admire the Archbishop for writing – even if he were a little naive in entertaining any hope of success.

The South African Prime Minister was not long in sending a predictable reply. The Native Laws Amendment Bill, he argued, followed the general principles of apartheid and was in line with former legislation by Parliament when Generals Hertzog and Smuts were in power. The opposition's campaign of misrepresentation was orchestrated by propagandists who 'seldom if ever see the outside or inside of a Church and in some instances are utterly opposed to our Christian religion'.

Geoffrey Fisher was by his own confession naturally argumentative and he now came back to the South African Prime Minister in a lengthy reply. In this he asked pointedly why there should be special legislation to deal with possible infringements of public order which, surely, were already dealt with by the ordinary laws of the land. He also expressed great surprise that Mr Strijdom had said nothing whatever about his own, i.e. the Archbishop's strictures on the denial of academic freedom which meant that his own government 'finds itself in the same category as the Nazis in Germany or the Communists in Russia'. For full measure the Archbishop sent him copies of Resolutions passed in the Convocations of Canterbury and York.

The Prime Minister of South Africa had by now had enough and he brought the correspondence to a close by alleging that he and the Archbishop differed so fundamentally on the matters under discussion that to continue the correspondence could serve no good purpose. 'A personal discussion might bring about more clarity but that, at the present moment, is of course, impossible.'

Meanwhile the South African bishops on 14 July 1957 sent a pastoral letter to their clergy suggesting how they might react to the new Acts. In brief they counselled a responsible disobedience and encouraged them with the thought that they were not without allies. Indeed, a sympathetic public opinion was springing up in many places as indicative of which was a communication to Lambeth from the American Commission of Public Affairs, the membership of which included Eleanor Roosevelt, Bishop James Pike and Martin Luther King. They urged the Archbishop to sponsor an international committee to protest against putting 156 opponents of apartheid on trial. To this appeal Geoffrey Fisher replied that for an American committee to organise a universal protest might prove disastrous since it could be argued that the United States had a not dissimilar problem in its midst which it had so far failed effectively to solve.

(ii)

One urgent and most important practical task awaiting the Church of the Province of South Africa arising out of the death of Dr Clayton was the election of a new Archbishop of Cape Town. As an autonomous Chuch, the responsibility for the appointment lay exclusively with the Church of the Province through its accustomed constitutional procedures. As so often happened the Archbishop of Canterbury as the senior Bishop of the Anglican Communion and also knowing the field, particularly in England, was consulted and a list of five English priests was sent to him for comment, none of whom, however, struck him as 'completely convincing'. He himself wrote to five Bishops – York, London, Durham, Chichester, Edinburgh – asking for their comments and suggestions. The number of names which hurricaned into Lambeth was extensive as were the comments made upon them by Geoffrey Fisher. The Bishop of Edinburgh was resolutely opposed to looking outside the province of South Africa – a very understandable view.

Early in May 1957 the Archbishop, with a degree of surprise received a letter from Joost de Blank, Bishop of Stepney and the son of Dutch parents, conveying the information that he had been elected Archbishop of Cape Town by the Local Assembly and that this had been unanimously endorsed by the House of Bishops. He confided to the Archbishop that he had no desire whatever to leave his work in London and that he had a mother of 87 who lived with him. The Archbishop had not, in fact, supported his candidature but presented with a *fait accompli*, he replied that as a general rule an aged mother should not be 'a deciding factor in a matter of this kind' and that if he himself were in a similar situation he would feel it his bounden duty to accept. Thus encouraged, Bishop Joost de Blank accepted this advice which had reinforced his own view. On hearing of this decision, the Archbishop promptly followed this up with a more weighty letter which began: 'Now may I pray for you all those powers of wise judgement and quiet courage which the Church in South Africa so needs in these testing days. The situation will not alarm you. The Christian need never be alarmed by anything in this sinful world and indeed the conflict stimulates. The burden we bear is first to know what we ought to do after the mind of Our Lord and then to find the right way of doing it . . . there are 100 inviting wrong ways of doing it calling to us! Again 'burden' is not the right word. It is an absorbing occupation of all our faculties and certainly *you* will find happiness and strength in that.'

The new Archbishop had undoubted gifts and, as they say, had charisma, being prone to dramatise his own personal situation and not averse to 'encounter politics' when he thought great issues were at stake. He was the stuff of which martyrs were made and perhaps would have found it a tragic fulfilment had this been his destiny. To Stepney as its Suffragan Bishop he had brought colour, sparkle and leadership.

Such was the man who was called upon to occupy Bishopscourt in Cape Town. He could not have gone there at a more critical time and it was not long before he introduced a greater dynamic and, to use Dr Fisher's words to Ambrose Reeves, a more 'crusading' spirit into the life and witness of the Church in South Africa. Nowhere was this more evident than in relation to opposing apartheid. Letters of protest continued to flow into Lambeth, many from South African churchmen who felt themselves impotent to do much by way of remedy. To one protester the Archbishop expressed his sorrow at 'the suffering caused by the heartless application of a senseless policy of apartheid' which the Church of England regards as 'non-christian in principle'.

Indigenous African opposition now began to be more organised and on 21 March 1960 there suddenly erupted a human tragedy which has cut deeply into black consciousness. During daylight hours resentment against the Pass Laws, harassment by the police and constant interference with freedom of movement found expression in a large demonstration at Sharpeville, an African location outside Vereeniging in the Transvaal. What began as a peaceful protest might have continued as such had not the police panicked leaving 69 people dead and 178 wounded, of whom 40 were women and children. A similar disturbance, though with far fewer casualties, took place at a township near Cape Town. Race relations were destined never to be quite the same again after Sharpeville. World opinion was shocked and found little for its comfort in Dr Verwoerd's words in Parliament: 'These riots are periodic phenomena. They have nothing to do with reference books.' The Archbishop of Canterbury wrote immediately for more information to Ambrose Reeves who replied that, in future, methods of crowd control must be worked out which did not involve so terrible a threat to human life; also that a distinction must be made between an army and a police force. Contributing to what happened at Sharpeville, he maintained, was an entire lack of consultation between the Government and the African leaders, evidence of which was the official description of events on 21 March as an organised 'revolt'. There were, in fact, some 5,000 and not 25,000 Africans outside the police station where they had gathered to discuss passes. Nor had the crowd any intention of being violent as could be seen in the fact that the Africans brought their wives and children with them.

Feeling in Britain ran high and manifested itself in a request from the new Archbishop of Cape Town for Geoffrey Fisher to call on all Anglicans in Britain and throughout the world to pray for South Africa on the 50th anniversary of the founding of the Union. The House of Lords responded to the general mood by holding a debate on 31 March in which Geoffrey Fisher participated.

From South Africa there now came a strong if depressing letter from the Venerable C. T. Wood, Archdeacon of Cape Town, writing as the mouthpiece of the Metropolitan of the Province. The Churches, he wrote to Lambeth, were now virtually silenced under the emergency regulation of 30 March. In these grave circumstances it was evident that the Archbishop of Cape Town was understandably prepared to depart from the low profile and guidelines which Archbishop Clayton had recommended. In his opinion it would greatly strengthen their witness should the Archbishop feel able to give some words of encouragement to those who were determined, however difficult it might be, to be loyal to the implications of their faith at this time. The Archdeacon was particularly distressed, *inter alia*, by the detention of Chief Luthuli and Dr Z. K. Malthens, and he much hoped that the Archbishop would do what he could on their behalf with all the 'great emphasis' at his command. Events now were moving at such a pace that unless a halt could be called to the ruthlessness of the present methods of restoring order much resentment and bitterness would follow. The Overseas Christian Council also took the view that unless the Archbishop of Canterbury made some public pronouncement on this great issue the impression would be created that the Churches did not corporately disapprove of apartheid.

The Archbishop, however, was in a quandary, believing that the Churches had made their attitude to apartheid perfectly clear on more than one occasion, hence his reluctance to go it alone in a personal statement. He would prefer a text drawn up by the Overseas Council which he could submit to the Archbishop of York for his and his own approval. To quote his chaplain Dr Eric Jay: The Archbishop 'has an inherent dislike of writing an official pronouncement and would be glad for someone else to do this for him'. Even Bishop Gresford Jones, who was intimate with the Archbishop, failed to persuade his lay secretary to overcome Geoffrey Fisher's scruples. Not surprisingly both the British and World Council of Churches had been inundated with telegrams of protest. The Archdeacon of Cape Town, on behalf of his Metropolitan, argued the case for a strong public anti-apartheid policy. Equally the British Council of Churches was anxious to pass a resolution declaring 'solidarity with the robust witness' of the Churches of South Africa. Representatives of the Dutch Reformed Church, on the other hand, appealed to the members of the World Council to be on their guard against the 'slanted picture of South Africa presented by the world press over a long period'. They admitted, however, that their Reformed Church had its shortcomings.

The Archdeacon of Cape Town reminded the Archbishop that way back in 1954 the World Council of Churches had stated that 'if it were to become clear that the application of such a policy of separation was inevitably accompanied by injustice and humiliation then it should stand condemned in the eyes of all'; also later it affirmed that 'segregation in all its forms is contrary to the Gospel and incompatible with the Christian doctrine of man and with the nature of the Church of Christ. It therefore urged the Church within its membership to renounce all forms of segregation or discrimination and to work for the same cause within society. No words could have been more categorical both in language and content or thrown down a greater challenge.

Into this highly charged, post-Sharpeville, situation there was now introduced a new factor in the dynamic, thrustful leadership of the recently appointed Archbishop of Cape Town. On the very day that the World Council of Churches met, Dr Joost de Blank issued a statement calling on all Churches repesented on this body to dissociate themselves from the Dutch Reformed Churches until they repudiated compulsory apartheid which had been condemned by the World Council of Churches at Evanston and by the Lambeth Conference in 1958. Unless the Dutch Reformed Churches repudiated apartheid the Anglican Church of the Province, he decreed, could no longer be linked up with them in the World Council and it hoped that other Churches would do the same.

This announcement came as a veritable bomb-shell though it is probably not true that it was wrung from Dr Joost de Blank at an interview with the *New York Herald* 'on the spur of the moment'. The World Council of Churches immediately realised that it must take this new situation seriously since it not only had relevance in the area of race relations but also affected relations between its member churches. Thus it sent a representative, Dr Bellhurst, to South Africa for a 10-day visit to determine the underlying causes of 'disturbances' there, and to explain to the Archbishop of Cape Town that threats of expulsion or withdrawal from the World Council of Churches 'would not help to create the atmosphere in which constructive action could be taken'.

Archbishop Joost de Blank emphatically did not see things this way and he instructed his Archdeacon to repeat authoritatively that unless the Dutch Reformed Churches changed their attitude to apartheid and condemned the Government for its ruthless action at Sharpeville the Church of the Province could no longer remain fellow members with them in the World Council of Churches. In taking this extreme line Joost de Blank had the support of Ambrose Reeves.

The Archbishop of Cape Town's threatened withdrawal of his Province elicited a letter to Geoffrey Fisher written on 14 April upon Dr Visser't Hooft acquainting him with the general position. He deeply deplored Joost de Blank's gesture, he wrote, particularly at a time when some members of the Dutch Reformed Church had lost confidence in the South African Government. The proposed withdrawal could only worsen the general atmosphere, putting member churches into an impossible position while undermining the very concept of a World Council of Churches. As evidence of this, its constitution made no provision for expulsion.

The Archbishop of Canterbury found himself in complete agreement with Visser't Hooft and in equal disagreement with his fellow Metropolitan of Cape Town. His immediate reaction was to send a cable to Joost de Blank asking whether the reported statement was true, namely that the Anglican Province in South Africa could not remain in the World Council linked with the Dutch Reformed Churches unless they repudiated compulsory apartheid. Moreover, he asked, was this his personal opinion or an official policy agreed by the Bishops. From Cape Town there came the reply: 'Agreed by emergency meeting Episcopal Standing Committee but first call from World Council fact-finding Commission for public repudiation of compulsory apartheid in Church and State essential for combined co-operation.'

Archbishop Joost de Blank had certainly set the cat among the pigeons and the result was a great stir and fluttering in ecclesiastical dovecotes. Many in England took the view that though the Church of the Province was suffering grievously a decision of such wide-ranging implications ought not to have been taken unilaterally and without prior discussion. Thus Michael Ramsey, Archbishop of York, commented to Geoffrey Fisher: 'You do not cure one form of apartheid by inventing another form'.

The eirenic and most popular Bishop Lakdasa de Mel, destined in 1962 to become Metropolitan of the Church of India, Pakistan, Burma and Ceylon urged restraint on both sides. 'We must gently reason with the Archbishop of Cape Town and the Bishop of Johannesburg' he suggested, a view shared by Henry Sherrill, Presiding Bishop of the Episcopal Church of America. Geoffrey Fisher, in reply to a critical correspondent complaining of the passivity of the Church's protest in various fields, contended that it was not called upon to take political action. Hence it had done nothing practical to bring its influence to bear upon the purely political situation either in Russia or in Hungary.

The Archbishop of Cape Town was in no mood to be deterred from what he personally felt to be right by the critical comments of others. What he regarded as absolutely essential was a categorical repudiation of apartheid by all those who profess and call themselves Christians; and nothing, he believed, could witness so strongly to this as the severance of all ties with the erring Dutch Reformed Churches. Only so could the indigenous African, who saw too much around him of a church wedded to white domination, be convinced that the Anglican Church 'meant business'. Dr Joost de Blank was certainly not without his supporters in England. A group of young priests, headed by Paul Oestreicher, decided to give up a part of their income to be used at Dr Fisher's discretion for the Church of the Province, for which purpose they asked him to undertake the circularisation of letters soliciting funds. He responded by describing this gesture as 'a striking token of moral enthusiasm and idealism' but declined the suggestion that he should act as a postman.

It was against the background of this worsening political and racial situation that Harold Macmillan, Prime Minister of Great Britain, visited South Africa and was invited to address a joint meeting of both Houses of Parliament. He could not know that the continuance of South Africa as a member state of the Commonwealth hung in the balance. No one expected him to refer to ecclesiastical matters or particular legislative acts which had caused so much distress and controversy. However the Prime Minister on his arrival had a long talk with the Archbishop of Cape Town at a High Commissioner's garden party. This time, the occasion and the setting for his address were as historic as were the words in which with tact, firmness and courtesy he commended the cause of a truly liberal society. With great courage – he was a guest speaker in a foreign if Commonwealth country – he said: 'I hope you don't mind my saying frankly that there are some aspects of your policies which make it impossible for us to give South Africa our support and encouragement without being false to our own deep convictions about the political destinies of free men'. One pregnant and germinal phrase he left behind him – 'the winds of change' – which still reverberates in the continent of Africa and not only there. Dr Verwoerd was not pleased. The Archbishop of Canterbury, however, was among the many who were greatly impressed by the Prime Minister's speech. Thus, later, in his presidential address to both Houses of the Southern Convocation on 10 May he quoted from it lavishly calling particular attention to Macmillan's extension of 'mind your own business', to include 'but mind how it affects my business too'. As an illustration, so the Archbishop commented, the South African Government by its own policies imposed burdens on the hearts and consciences of other member states of the Commonwealth offensive to Christian faith and to a common humanity.

It was inevitable, in view of the stand taken by the Anglican Church of the Province of South Africa under the leadership of its new Archbishop' that the World Council of Churches should be concerned about the effects of Joost de Blank's policy upon the relations between member churches. Hence it decided to send a carefully drawn up letter to the eight Churches in South Africa belonging to the World Council which, of course, included the Dutch Reformed Church. The letter began by reminding them that a key function of WCC was to remove a sense of isolation among its members since it was 'of the genius of the ecumenical movement that fellowship is maintained even when disagreement concerns profound and urgent matters'. It was, therefore, unfortunate that the ecumenical community, as a whole, was largely ignorant of what was happening in South Africa. To help overcome this the World Council of Churches produced a short history of the development of apartheid in South Africa from the time when the Dutch Reformed Church taught that discriminating between races in the life of the Church was unscriptural till today when it was held by the majority that such distinctions were in conformity with God's plan and purpose.

In order to prevent a voluntary withdrawal of the Dutch Reformed Church or, in reverse, the withdrawal of the Church of the Province of South Africa from the World Council of Churches, Visser't Hooft made contact with the Archbishop of Cape Town inviting him to a consultation with representatives of the Dutch Reformed Churches. Joost de Blank was sceptical as to the value of such a meeting and would himself have preferred a purely fact-finding commission but agreed to consult his fellow bishops as to their participation. It was 'a delicate matter' and he was grateful to the World Council for its initiative. 'But peace,' he insisted, 'even in the Church cannot be purchased at the cost of righteousness.'

The Archbishop of Canterbury was kept in close touch with these developments and towards the end of May he received a communication from Joost de Blank telling him that the reaction of the Christian Churches of South Africa was one of dissatisfaction with WCC's attitude towards the Dutch Reformed Church – an attitude which some suspected might be influenced by Visser't Hooft himself being Dutch. Dr Joost de Blank confessed that he was disturbed at the African Christian Council being bypassed by the World Council and he must emphasise that the Dutch Reformed Communion was more than a Church. Indeed it was near to becoming a political party, engaged in machinations and manipulating educational agencies. Meanwhile, the misery in Africa and the estrangement of the Africans from the Church would continue until Christians disassociated themselves from apartheid in a manner which was public and irrevocable.

Geoffrey Fisher was most anxious to heal the festering wounds which injured relations between the Anglican and Dutch Reformed Churches in South Africa and was prepared to use the prestige of his office to this end. Thus he summoned to Lambeth an ecumenical gathering, the deliberations of which may be summarised by quoting from the private journal of the Venerable C. T. Wood, Archdeacon of Cape Town, which gives an impression of the occasion from his point of view.

After listing those present – the Archbishop of Canterbury, Dr Stephen Bayne, the Bishop of Johannesburg, Dr Billhurst of the WCC, Alan Booth, a Methodist and himself – the Archdeacon goes on: 'It was a further attempt to disentangle the tensions between the Church of the Province, the WCC and the Dutch Reformed Church. I found I had to stand up to the Archbishop but had great encouragement from Stephen Bayne who alone appreciates the stand that we are taking and the dilemma that we are in. Dr Billhurst had paid a visit to South Africa and had made proposals which I felt the Archbishop of Cape Town would not find acceptable. It was decided that Stephen Bayne should fly to Cape Town. I am sure this will be of great help and will relieve me of a very great responsibility'.

This meeting left the participants frustrated with each other and it is clear from this account that the Archdeacon of Cape Town rightly or wrongly felt that neither the World Council of Churches nor the Archbishop of Canterbury were fully sensitive to the nature of the harsh tensions and traumas now being experienced by church people in South Africa. They were more concerned, in his view, to keep everyone together, particularly the whites, than to face up to the ultimate challenge which apartheid constituted to the Christian Gospel.

In the discussion Ambrose Reeves occupied a more middle ground and the Archbishop of Canterbury thanked him, to quote his own words: 'with all my heart for the help you gave me'.

The Archbishop, immediately after the meeting, addressed a very frank letter to the Archdeacon of Cape Town who together with Ambrose Reeves was suspicious of the role being played by Visser't Hooft, Secretary of the World Council of Churches. If this were merited it was certainly mutual since, as Dr Fisher pointed out, Visser't Hooft regarded Joost de Blank as a complicating ingredient in a delicate situation. The Archbishop's advice to Dr Joost de Blank was to accept the policy decision of the General Consultative Council of the Anglican Communion although unfortunately this body would not be meeting to consider policy until March or April 1961. Meanwhile some relationship betwen the Dutch Reformed Church and the Archbishop of Cape Town needed to be re-established. It was better, so Geoffrey Fisher thought, for the World Council of Churches to keep out of the *contretemps* and to leave matters with Stephen Bayne who, he suggested, should attend the Bishops meeting in South Africa on 20 January. Copies of this correspondence were sent to the Archbishops of Cape Town and York, also to the Bishop of Johannesburg.

Dr Fisher was now convinced, and in fact always had been, that the first and overriding priority was to lower the temperature of the personal relations between Cape Town and the Dutch Reformed Church. This was made the more difficult, so he believed, by Joost de Blank's erratic judgement, and he accused him to Visser't Hooft of denying to the Dutch Reformed Church any genuine Christian concern at all; also that he entirely distrusted the World Council and its emissaries. These are strong words but to be fair to both Archbishops of Canterbury and Cape Town it must be admitted that temperamentally they were anti-pathetic. The one saw, unfairly, the charisma of the egocentric prophet; the other, equally unfairly, the unimaginative, rule-obsessed headmaster.

About this time there arrived on the Archbishop's desk at Lambeth a dramatic sermon to mark the jubilee of the Union of South Africa which Joost de Blank had preached in the cathedral in Cape Town on 29 May 1960. He began with references to biblical jubilees and then called attention to the contrast between these and the present occasion. 'Instead of proclaiming liberty we maintain a state of emergency. Instead of returning every man to his possessions, we know of at least 1,600 people who are detained in prisons, apart from the refugees who have fled abroad for sanctuary. Instead of returning every man to his family, we still continue with a system of migratory labour that deliberately breaks up families, that keeps man from wife and parents from children.' In his letter to Lambeth enclosing this sermon, Archbishop Joost de Blank accused the Dutch Reformed Church of 'playing a hypocritical game', and engaging in their official magazine *Die Kerkbode* in a personal attack upon himself. This was the third such affront and until this latest one was disowned he could see no prospect of worthwhile consultation between the Church of the Province and the Dutch Reformed Church.

The *impasse* now seemed unbridgeable, the more so as the Archbishop of Cape Town had, unfortunately some may think, made the dispute intensely personal, maintaining that it would be 'healthier all round if things were brought to a head'. 'Until there is a change of heart in the D.R.C.' he explained, 'the Church of the Province of South Africa cannot be associated with them.' The Provincial Synod was due to meet later in the year and already resolutions were being prepared calling upon the Church of the Province to withdraw from the World Council.

The exchange of letters between Lambeth and Cape Town inexorably went on and the one just referred to led to a long and instantaneous *riposte* from Archbishop Fisher. In this he suggested that the tone of Joost de Blank's letter gave the impression that he was beginning to feel the strain to which he was being subjected. He then went on to spell out his own position in what was clearly a developing crisis. Particularly he wished to assure the Archbishop of Cape Town that he entertained a deep concern for him personally, precariously positioned, as he was, within a triangle – 'You, the Dutch Reformed Church and the World Council of Churches.' To be frank, he said, he must deplore that Joost had openly brought the World Council of Churches into the conflict and he suggested that he drop altogether the whole question concerning membership of the WCC which could only cause bitterness of spirit throughout the Anglican Communion.

The Archbishop of Canterbury now pinned his hopes, slender as they might appear, on the success of Stephen Bayne's meeting with the South African bishops; though he feared that any *modus vivendi* would shipwreck on the intransigence of Joost de Blank. Was the latter's attitude, he asked himself, due to the fact that 'under the great spiritual and nervous strain upon him, a weakness of self projection which was natural to him has been intensely aggravated'. If he declined to be present at the meeting, then the member churches should proceed without him.

Perhaps Geoffrey Fisher was himself feeling the strain and this may account for his seeming to bypass Joost de Blank by sending direct to Visser't Hooft his own proposed resolution in which after tactfully paying tribute to the Archbishop of Cape Town for his leadership in bringing the policy of apartheid before WCC he expressed the desire that this episcopal discussion might bring forth 'light and hope to the Christian community in South Africa'.

Archbishop Joost de Blank, in spite of appeals to do so, remained unwilling to accommodate himself to the views of Dr Fisher or of Visser't Hooft. 'I confess in perfect frankness,' he wrote, 'I regret that you have not yet seen that apartheid as practised in South Africa is anti-Christian. The Americans have discovered that even such good sentiments as "separate but equal development" prove to be a hollow fraud neither separate nor equal.'

This letter got Geoffrey Fisher 'on the raw' and he replied to the main charge provoked by the distinction he had made between apartheid 'in principle' and 'in practice'. 'You think that I have not yet seen that apartheid as practised in South Africa is anti-Christian. But I have always seen that and have always been concerned that it is diabolically anti-Christian. In almost my first public utterance years ago I denounced apartheid as slavery.'

The effect of this epistle was to move Archbishop Joost de Blank – he was basically a most kind emotional and warm-hearted person – to a generous reply. He was, he told Archbishop Fisher, consistently gratified for all his public utterances on the subject of apartheid. 'I want to assure you,' he went on, 'how indebted the Church of the Province is to you for your valiant championship of our cause.' He would be delighted if he and Mrs Fisher were to stay with him at Bishopscourt where they could be 'undisturbed for as long as they liked!'

Perhaps it was a pity that Archbishop Fisher could not sufficiently forget 'the care of all the Churches' to accept this invitation.

A sign, however, that Archbishop Joost de Blank, without weakening his own deep convictions, was seeking some kind of *modus vivendi* became evident in a letter which he drew up for dispatch to all the Primates of the Anglican Communion. It stated simply that the Church of the Province of South Africa had disagreements with the Dutch Reformed Church over its official support of the Government's policy of apartheid. At his request the World Council of Churches had intervened and was calling a conference. At least this was a clear indication that Joost de Blank now accepted that WCC had a role.

Meanwhile as the Church of the Province of South Africa continued to experience extreme tensions so Geoffrey Fisher's mind went back to the letters he had exchanged with Prime Minister Strijdom. Now, however, a successor, Dr H. F. Verwoerd, had been some three years in office. Would it be worth while for him, as Archbishop of Canterbury, to make another approach? In asking this question he was well aware that Alan Paton had described Verwoerd as 'the architect of separate development'; which meant that any appeal to Mr Verwoerd must accept his being wedded to this philosophy. Certainly Geoffrey Fisher toyed with this idea sufficiently seriously to draw up in full a draft letter, which however on second thoughts he never sent. This very long letter, dated 7 June 1960 illustrates the Archbishop's profound disappointment at the obvious failure of any attempt from outside, or protest from within South Africa, to prevent the ruthless implementation of the evil policy of apartheid.

The Archbishop, in his draft letter, began by saying that he was addressing Dr Verwoerd as Christian to Christian. He himself had made clear on many occasions his hostility to apartheid. But, bypassing this radical disagreement: could not Dr Verwoerd accept that in its application there had been 'harshness and rigidity' such as could reasonably be held to give offence? Could he not, therefore, convene a group of people from the world of business, the universities, and social welfare, etc, to draw up a list of grievances which could be tackled forthwith as a gesture coming from the Government by which to win confidence inside and outside South Africa?

It is a sad letter in its *naiveté* and non-realism – but it does witness to the Archbishop's intense desire to get some movement in South Africa towards better things if only minimal. However to secure these he concedes far too much; and the very thought of Dr Verwoerd calling a conference along the lines suggested is surely fanciful.

Geoffrey Fisher, following the example of his predecessors at Lambeth, always regarded his office as the Senior Bishop of the Anglican Communion as imposing upon him a special responsibility for the welfare of Anglican bishops working overseas, some of whom like his brother Leonard, were English. Quite a few returned home on the completion of their service in South Africa either to retire or in the hopes of securing another post in their native land. It was this excessively strong English sentiment which worried Dr Clayton and made him doubly concerned to Africanise the Church of the Province both in its ethos and personnel. One bishop who, as we have seen earlier, experienced a testing time in the Province was Ambrose Reeves of Johannesburg. To the difficulties confronting him in his episcopal office there was added the deep sorrow of the tragic death of a greatly loved son.

On 1 April 1960, Ambrose Reeves was warned by three knowledgeable friends that he was on a Government 'hit list' for imminent arrest consequent upon his bitter protests at the time of the Sharpeville shootings. Following this advice he withdrew from South Africa and entered Swaziland before, on 21 April, flying to London. Geoffrey Fisher and Dr Michael Ramsey, Archbishop of York, both felt that the Bishop had endured enough and that it was fair for him to return to a post in England. The latter wished to see him as Bishop of Blackburn, though he recognised that the Prime Minister might be deterrred from such an appointment through fear of prejudicing Commonwealth relations with South Africa. Archbishop Joost de Blank welcomed this proposal though confessing that he would be 'quite bereft as a result'. Geoffrey Fisher informed Visser't Hooft of this possibility; but it was not to be. Charles Claxton in fact went to Blackburn and Ambrose Reeves returned to Johannesburg on 10 September. Two days later, by an illegal order of the South African Government, he was deported and arrived back in England on the same day. The Archbishop of Canterbury was himself in Africa to inaugurate the Eastern Province of the African Church, and in an address which he delivered on Tuesday 13 September he took as his theme 'Nothing to Fear'. As a Metropolitan and holding a unique position in the Anglican Communion he felt he had the solemn duty of speaking to them, being distressed and sad at recent events in the Union, in particular the 'vicious activity' directed against the Bishop of Johannesburg.

Bishop Stephen Bayne held strongly to the conviction that the deportation of a Bishop in this way was a matter of grievous concern to the Anglican Church as a whole. Hence, he took the initiative in drawing up a draft statement to be issued jointly by the Primates of all the Provinces but he was unable to persuade Geoffrey Fisher to approve such a step though he agreed with its sentiments.

Writing later, Geoffrey Fisher expressed his reactions as follows: 'I am afraid we disagreed. I told him that the Provinces of the Anglican Communion have never yet united in any statement on any subject, and I think it would be embarrassing and dangerous if we took such action in this particular conflict in South Africa, the more so as the Archbishop of Cape Town is not free from making blunders affecting the Anglican Communion or in his dealings with the World Council of Churches.'

Such a negative response from Lambeth certainly surprised Stephen Bayne who admitted to being 'taken aback' at the Archbishop's 'queer view of things'. However, he loyally accepted this decision, merely remarking that the Archbishop was the 'boss' and that was the end of the matter.

Stephen Bayne was not the only one who thought that a tough line ought to be taken over Ambrose Reeve's deportation. John Robinson, Suffragan Bishop of Southwark and holding the office of chairman of the Cambridge African Council, issued to the local press in South East London an article condemning the South African Government. The Archbishop, as in the case of Stephen Bayne, was not pleased and he despatched a letter to the Bishop which began: 'Will you allow my age and office to give you a hint in the hope that it may be helpful.' His basic contention was that a diocesan bishop was free to make statements on any subject but for a junior suffragan to do this at such a time was 'unwise and misleading'. He was convinced that in England, to quote his own words 'We Bishops ought never in public to tell the Prime Minister what he ought to do. He carries responsibilities where we do not'.

Perhaps we may comment that if Geoffrey Fisher conformed to this self denying ordinance in public he certainly did not in private as this biography amply illustrates. For good measure the Archbishop gave John Robinson further words of advice: 'If reporters begin to think you are the kind of person they can get statements from more easily than from other Bishops, you are laying yourself open to many temptations'.

The referendum as to whether South Africa should remain in the Commonwealth or become a Republic – the blacks and coloureds were, of course, excluded from voting though the result of the poll affected them intimately – took place on 5 October 1960. The verdict was an overwhelming vote for secession. Geoffrey Fisher's comment to Joost de Blank was short and very much to the point: 'The faint hope that the referendum might go the other way came to nothing, which means, I suppose, that the present tyranny will get no better for a long time to come.' Here he was right, though the subsequent withdrawal from the Commonwealth saved the British Government a great deal of embarrassment.

Archbishop Fisher began to wonder whether the Conference arranged by the World Council of Churches due to take place in South Africa on 8 November could now be held in the Republic, though to do so might give participants 'a feel of this country'. On the other hand such a venue would mean Ambrose Reeve's exclusion, 'a miserable thing.' He accordingly sought a consultation with the High Commissioner in London: but Ambrose Reeves did not attend.

With this sad assessment of the effects of the withdrawal the Archbishop of Cape Town entirely concurred. There would be even less chance now of 'a change of heart or mind on the part of the Government'. Once again Joost de Blank invited the Archbishop and Mrs Fisher to stay with him at Bishopscourt, but Stephen Bayne advised him that to accept at the moment would 'do harm'.

There were two concerns or preoccupations which were never far from Geoffrey Fisher's thoughts – finding a suitable post for Ambrose Reeves, and the results of the forthcoming consultation of the eight South African Churches under the aegis of WCC.

As to Ambrose Reeves, the Archbishop of Cape Town had no doubt that he would never be allowed to return to South Africa. Hence, he was 'sadly convinced' that the Bishop must at some time or another resign his See which meant that a fitting post must be found for him in

England. Writing early in November Geoffrey Fisher was forced to confess that so far as his efforts to this end were concerned they had 'completely failed'.

The long awaited consultation of delegates from the eight member Churches of the World Council of Churches in South Africa met at Cottesloe on 15 December 1960. Also present were representatives of the WCC and Bishop Lakdasa de Mel, Metropolitan of the Church of India, Pakistan, Burma and Ceylon, who was there representing the Anglican Communion. As a result of their deliberations a long statement of some 25,000 words was drawn up. This recognised the diverse racial roots in South Africa as 'indigenous', and defended the rights of the non-whites to own land, to participate directly in Government, and to worship in any church they wished. It affirmed that there were no scriptural grounds for the prohibition of mixed marriages, although due consideration should be given to certain social factors which might make such marriages 'inadvisable'. The members of the Dutch Reformed Church disassociated themselves from this statement, declaring that they 'reject integration in any form as a solution to the problem'.

The Conference, in spite of all the preceding controversy, was in many respects a triumph for the Archbishop of Cape Town. He was tactfully advised by Archbishop de Mel to cultivate 'a low profile' and he loyally adhered to this advice throughout. At the end of the Conference, however, when prayers were being said, Joost de Blank stood up with a paper in his hands, speaking humbly and simply and expressing a desire for better relations with the Dutch Reformed Church. To the members of his own communion he admitted frankly that he had obviously been mistaken in some of the statements which he had made though he thought that the Church had not always made its position sufficiently clear. For this he apologised and asked forgiveness. Dr Vandemoore, on behalf of the Dutch Reformed Church, responded equally generously. Bishop Lakdasa de Mel whispered to Joost de Blank at the conclusion of the Conference: 'Nobly done, Your Grace.'

The statement which emerged from the Conference was wholly to the liking of the Archbishop of Cape Town and he could not have asked for more though it inevitably pushed the Dutch Reformed Church further out on a limb in relation to fellow Christians in South Africa. Still it was something that they had all met together and entered into a frank exchange of views. The World Council of Churches, in its own Report, claimed that one of the benefits flowing from the Conference was a new spirit created between the Cape and Transvaal churches on the one hand and the English speaking churches on the other. This was probably true and Joost de Blank by his dramatic intervention, so much in character, should be given his due praise. Tribute must also be paid to the Dutch Reformed Church in sitting through a conference and taking part in it when so much that they heard ran diametrically counter to their deeply held convictions.

The ultimate tragedy was inherent in two Churches, one espousing a religio-political view which it believed to be biblical and which the South African Government translated into action greatly to the injury of its black and coloured citizens; and the other Church regarding this political philosophy as anathema and a radical betrayal of Christian faith. It was not easy to see, since the political and social structure of the nation was 'legally' determined by one party over against the other, how the two could easily agree to differ. This was no academic encounter of two rival theological views but a confrontation which affected family life, economic ambitions, civic and national status.

The problems which dominate this chapter in Archbishop Fisher's biography are not alas! 'old unhappy, far off things and battles long ago'. Yet as these words are being written there is more occasion for hope than there has been since apartheid was first inflicted on the black population of South Africa many years ago. May this hope fulfil its promise.

PART EIGHT:

THE MIDDLE EAST

CHAPTER 46

The Holy Land

It may seem surprising that the biography of a mid-twentieth century Archbishop of Canterbury should contain a chapter on the Holy Land. Certainly no archiepiscopal biography, subsequent to Geoffrey Fisher's, will need to handle this complex, tragic and as yet unfinished theme. The reasons for the necessity of this inclusion deserve a brief mention.

At the end of the First World War the Holy Land was placed under British administration by a League of Nations Mandate which imposed on the UK the obligation 'to place the country under such political, administrative conditions as will secure the establishment of the Jewish National home while at the same time safeguarding the civil and religious rights of all the inhabitants of Jerusalem'. It was a near impossible remit from the beginning with constant tensions between Jews and Palestinians, but it was raised to another dimension by the Second World War, by the horrors of the Holocaust and the desperate plight of thousands of Jewish refugees marooned in Europe.

The sixteen years of Geoffrey Fisher's archiepiscopate covered a period of internecine strife in the Holy Land, spilling over into bloodshed leading to violence and civil war. The immediate background of this significant period in contemporary history was the terrible plight of those Jews who had survived the horrors of the Holocaust only to find themselves stateless with no home to go to.

The British Government not surprisingly fell under attack from both sides, not least from Jews living in America. It may well be that British policy in relation to Jewish refugees was unimaginative, harsh and ill-conceived even though its motivation – not to upset Arab susceptibilities – was understandable. Such a policy, vacillating and often not well informed, was a target for constant protest and recrimination. Not surprisingly, addresses and appeals for help were sent in abundance to Lambeth, their authors fondly believing that an Archbishop of Canterbury could influence decision-making in high places. However Geoffrey Fisher, to his credit, took such appeals seriously, replied to them conscientiously and endeavoured to be of help even if, on occasion, he was a little out of his depth and the British Government non-co-operative.

The end of the War in Europe in May 1945 by no means brought immediate release to those Jews still living or 'partly living' in Germany, who had miraculously survived the terrible scourge of Hitler. They desperately needed help and a haven to provide which the quota system had been set up. This, however, was not being implemented and the change to a Labour Government in Britain did little to humanise current policy. President Truman, under Zionist pressure, wrote personally to Clement Attlee urging that 100,000 Jewish refugees be admitted to Palestine forthwith. There was no response to this appeal and both Jews and Arabs, in frustration and mutual animosity, began to resort to violence against each other. Both parties, from time to time, appealed to the Archbishop for help, forgetting in doing so that the British Government's control over the Middle East was being steadily eroded. Evidence of the strength of Arab feeling was forcefully brought home to Geoffrey Fisher by a cablegram from the chairman of the Palestinian Arab Party on 24 September 1945. This communication reiterated basic Arab demands including one that Jewish immigration into the Holy Land must cease. It also demanded the ending of the British Mandate to be followed by the formation of an Arab independent, democratic Government bound to Great Britain by a treaty of alliance and friendship. The cablegram further insisted that the Arabs could not accept any solution that did not implement these basic demands.

Meanwhile the Middle East conditions were rapidly deteriorating. The Anglican Bishop in Jerusalem, Weston Stewart, saw it as his duty to keep Lambeth informed as to what was happening around him, being convinced that the deplorable events in the Holy Land were largely due to the 'ambiguous, if not self-contradictory, nature of the Mandate under which Britain administered Palestine'. 'I have no solution to offer,' he wrote candidly, 'save the development and growth of the Christian element in this country ... there are many in administrative and political positions who realise themselves that the true answer lies in bringing the Christian faith to both parties.' Candour compels the comment that even if desirable and not just a pious, non-realistic fancy, this missionising could not be conceived as an immediate even a long term solution.

There was throughout this period increasing concern at the apparent bankruptcy of British policy, bedevilled still by the ambiguities of the Balfour Declaration, and a loss of credibility, due to the U.K. issuing a statement that a solution must be found since Britain could no longer bear, unilaterally, the full weight of the burden of government imposed upon it under the Mandate. The Archbishop felt it proper to take notice of the situation in the Holy Land in the December edition (1945) of his Canterbury Diocesan Gazette. In this he suggested that the recent Government declaration was especially important because 'it concerns the fortunes of those sorely tried Jews of Europe who have survived the deliberate attempt by the Nazis to exterminate their race, an attempt which brought vile treatment and death to many millions of Jews'. Christians could not fail to be concerned with what was happening in the Middle East, and the statement by the Government was welcome in making it clear that a solution of the Jewish problem could not be found only, or even mainly, in Palestine.

For various reasons, however, Jewish concern at this time centred mainly around the desperate plight of the Jews still in captivity and the determination of their fellows to rescue them at all costs. Hence the Chief Rabbi of Great Britain, the greatly respected Dr Hertz, sent a telegram on 2 July 1946 both to the Archbishop and Dr Aubrey, President of the Baptist Union of Great Britain, protesting against the Government's wholesale arrest of their leaders in Palestine and the terrible plight of the Jews in Europe, frustrated as they undoubtedly were by the restrictions on emigration imposed by the United Kingdom. The arrests recently carried out on the Sabbath were 'a deliberate insult'. 'All responsible Jews,' he reiterated, 'condemned acts of violence no matter from what quarter'. The British Government was attempting to force back the hand of Providence, 'but as with Cyrus, it would but set Israel upon the march towards that ultimate restoration of Israel foretold by our prophets'.

These bitter words must be read within the context of the grave situation at the time. Certainly the British Government was in an almost impossible position being subject to attack from all quarters. Immediately upon receiving his telegram Dr Aubrey wrote to the Archbishop with some strong comments. 'I find no enthusiasm,' he protested, 'among Free Churchmen, among whom there is no trace of anti-semitism, for the idea of giving control of Palestine to the Jews and dispossessing the people who have been in effective possession for over a thousand years.' Dr Aubrey admitted, however, that Christians had 'a real duty' both to Jews on the Continent and to Arabs already in Palestine.

The Board of Deputies of British Jewry also issued a statement (30 June 1946) appealing to the whole British people to insist that the Government's policy be reversed – a statement which, not unexpectedly, found its way to Lambeth. Dr Fisher was painfully aware of the agonizing feelings of British Jews and therefore of the difficult position of the Chief Rabbi. To establish better personal relations he invited him to Lambeth thus enabling him to recognise at first hand how real, as distinct from nominal, was Dr Fisher's interest in Palestinian affairs. The result was that when the Chief Rabbi visited Jerusalem in the summer of 1946 he felt free to report back to Lambeth his immediate impressions, namely that something must be done to prevent the drift to an 'irremediable state'.

The role of the Archbishop was a difficult one as he sought to be objective and to work for a just solution in the interests of all concerned. The fact was, however, that his influence on Government policy was minimal. In such an exposed position he was bound on occasions to be a target for scurrilous abuse, as for example, in a pamphlet, issued by the 'Honour the Martyrs of Israel Associations', which attacked him for saying that there were 'some good Germans' – a statement which had the effect of 'condoning murderers of Jewish babies'. The sender of the pamphlet, Dr Bernstein, demanded a reply since 'your silence will be regarded by us as the best proof that the welfare of the murderers and of the Aryan beasts is nearer to your heart than the sufferings of the innocent, helpless victims'. The Archbishop, however, refused to be drawn and contented himself with a comment that the pamphlet was an 'altogether deplorable document'. Maybe, but even more so were the circumstances which evoked it!

Jews who were themselves at a safe distance from Europe and the Middle East felt it, and rightly so, incumbent upon them to champion the cause of their less fortunate brethren. Thus, the Jewish community in Sydney, Australia, were active in espousing the cause of a Palestinian homeland. Greatly influenced by this community was the Anglican Bishop of Sydney who wrote at considerable length to Lambeth expressing strongly pro-Jewish sentiments.

Geoffrey Fisher, provoked by this episcopal letter, reacted by giving his own version of Palestinian affairs in some detail. He could not, he explained, subscribe to the Jewish case when stated in so extreme a form. Justice must be done to all the inhabitants but this could not be effected by making the Arabs 'subject' to the Jewish race. To prevent this from happening meant promoting an elementary justice quite apart from the political need to establish friendly relations with the Arabs thus preventing their looking towards Russia. For himself, he had now come to favour a federal solution and he repeated his view that the admission of a hundred thousand Jews into Palestine would not really solve the problem of the refugees. There were six hundred thousand still in Europe and the Arabs feared that once a hundred thousand had entered Palestine the demand would be for another such intake. Those being admitted were not the old and the infirm but 'young men, many of them trained in brutal methods so common recently in Europe'. In his opinion President Truman had 'bedevilled' the whole situation, particularly when he refused to co-operate with Britain in implementing a federal solution. A recent visit to America had convinced the Archbishop that Truman's actions were dictated by political considerations intended to woo the Jewish vote in the November elections.

This letter makes it clear that Geoffrey Fisher was greatly influenced by the reports which he received from the Anglican Church in Jerusalem. Hence the Bishop of Sydney could only express his bemusement that 'each group looking at the same problem sees an entirely different picture'. To recognise this is often the beginning if not the end of wisdom!

The complicated issue of the respective rights of the Jews and Arabs in Palestine continued to be a major pre-occupation for Dr Fisher and he went public on this issue at his Diocesan Conference in July 1946 and in a letter despatched to *The Times* newspaper. The immediate cause for doing so was a dramatic action by the British Government in putting the leader of the Jewish Agency, together with some two thousand others, into detention camps, the ostensible purpose being to offset the increasing terrorism.

The gist of both letter and address which W. W. Simpson, Secretary of the Council of Christians and Jews, described as 'most helpful', was to ask whether, in view of the current stockpiling of arms, this recent public action undertaken by the British Government was necessary in the interests of public order as the Prime Minister claimed. His own conviction remained that while suggestions that Britain had acted from any feeling of anti-semitism, 'a devilish poison', were false yet justice demanded that the Government should publicly produce the evidence on which it had acted. However as to the future there seemed two options!

First, there was the scheme put forward by the Anglo-American Committee published on 6 April 1946 and which had been described as 'showing a remarkable insight into the whole problem'. It proposed that the British trusteeship should be continued until it was possible for a single Government to take over. This would entail neither a Jewish nor Arab state. Geoffrey Fisher's view was that though a 'most desirable solution', it would prove difficult to achieve since it required full co-operation between this country and America over a long period of time, both in carrying so heavy a burden and in promoting the success of the scheme. In fact these proposals proved unacceptable to both Jews and Arabs and were killed stone dead by Mr Attlee within forty-eight hours of their publication.

The second approach, so the Archbishop continued, was that put forward by the Peel Commission which had advocated partition into two provinces under a Supreme Council consisting of Jews and Arabs. Such a proposal, the Archbishop commented, had its own problems even if of a different kind but was easier to make work. On the whole the Archbishop preferred the latter, but stressed that whichever were adopted it was imperative there be a clear and public declaration of an agreed policy.

The Archbishop then turned to ask whether either of these sets of proposals could deal effectively with the fate of myriads of Jewish refugees at loose in Europe. He thought not, since their most grievous and immediate problem was not directly related to the long term future of Palestine. 'It is a dangerous mistake,' he concluded, 'to concentrate too much on what Palestine might do. The real problem which must not be shirked and for which Palestine certainly cannot be the solution is that of the half million and more Jews and all the other displaced persons in Germany where their race had suffered the vilest, most horrible, and most terribly effective persecution and slaughter in all its long history of persecution.' The real need was a United Nations solution which would encourage member states to offer asylum.

The Archbishop's obvious personal concern for Palestine, his recognition of the British Government's responsibility for its welfare so long as the Mandate remained legally operational – these, as well as the Anglican Church's presence in Jerusalem – encouraged many Christians to write to Lambeth with their own varied policies and comments. Perhaps the most interesting letter came from Kenneth Cragg, Warden of St Justin's House, Beirut, than whom none was more knowledgeable concerning the Middle East in relation to Islam. He maintained that the time was long overdue for a statement by Christian leaders laying down the principles which ought to form the basis of a settlement in Palestine. This was particularly needed in view of the 'moral wrong' of the Balfour Declaration.

Kenneth Cragg's observations undoubtedly got the Archbishop 'on the raw'. 'The Churches', he protested somewhat sharply, 'would do no good to anybody by re-opening the discussion on the morality or immorality of the Balfour Declaration. Too much has happened since then. A truly just solution must be, *inter alia*, fair to the Jews who rightly or wrongly have been allowed to establish themselves in Palestine.' To this *riposte* Cragg replied by what he must have regarded as a piece of astringent if cynical realism, namely that no solution to the problem would prove possible unless imposed by overwhelming military force.

Terrorism, to which both Jew and Arab had now resorted, not least the outrage committed in St David's Hotel by the Stern Gang in which one hundred people were killed, half being British officers, brought its reaction in an orgy of emotion and unreason. Typical was an Anglican parish priest who wrote to the Archbishop expressing violent anti-semitic feeling, and declaring that the Jews were the enemies of Britain as were the Germans during the last war. 'Indeed,' he asked, 'what right had the Jews to be in Palestine at all? Jerusalem should be constituted "a place of repentance".' The Archbishop's reply to this intemperate and ill-informed letter is worth quotation. It was not a matter of being pro-Jewish, he pointed out, but of 'fighting racial prejudice and passion where it exists. . . . The Balfour Declaration may have been a mistake. The Mandate under which we govern Palestine may have been wrong. Certainly both created expectation among the Jews impossible to fulfil without injury to the Arabs. As things have come to be, I have thought for some time that some form of partition is the only solution. . . . The one crime that a Christian may not commit is to allow his spirit to be infected by racial hatreds which are not only contrary to the spirit of the Gospel but, as you can see for yourself, have bred poisonous consequences whenever they have prevailed.'

This private letter, probably penned in haste, is revealing as to the rightness of his principles but maybe to the sketchiness of his historical perspective. Meanwhile the terrible plight of the Jewish refugees continued to agitate the minds of responsible politicians and the mass of compassionate human beings. This was no new post-war problem. Towards the end of 1940 some three and a half thousand Jews had managed to escape from Hitler's hell to Palestine in three unseaworthy ships, only to be immediately interned with a view to their deportations elsewhere. Such was the result of a British policy which 'locked up the Holy Land to access'. Of these beleaguered people two hundred were later drowned as the result of an explosion in the ship *Patria*; while one thousand five hundred men and women were shipped off to Mauritius where, so writes a correspondent to Lambeth, the 'misery and suffering of these innocent people was appalling'. To make a bad situation worse once they got to Mauritius there they stuck. In March 1944, Dr Norman McLean, Moderator of the General Assembly of the Church of Scotland, vented his wrath to the Archbishop in these bitter words: 'Something very serious has happened to humanity. In 1772 Lord Mansfield decided that a slave became free the instant he stepped ashore in England. No slave ever fled from such terrors as these refugees fled from but no part of the world would receive them.'

Dr McLean's was not, of course, a lone voice. Far from it. From Sydney, Australia, a memorandum on the Mauritius internees was sent to Lambeth sponsored by The United Emergency Committee for European Jewry. With it went a letter of commendation from the Right Reverend C. Vernon Pilcher, Bishop Coadjutor of Sydney, urging the Archbishop to take the matter up in the House of Lords. Geoffrey Fisher, in reply, confessed that the document was a 'profoundly disturbing one,' though he did not know how much the situation had changed recently or what precise action he himself could take. However he would make enquiries as to any practical line of action. 'It is really dreadful,' confessed the Archbishop, 'to read letters of this kind coming from innocent people who find themselves in the charge of the Government.'

Geoffrey Fisher was as good as his word and addressed himself to Oliver Stanley, Secretary of State for the Colonies, calling his attention to the 'very distressing' condition under which these internees were living in Mauritius and illustrating their plight with quotations from some 'heart rending' letters. He would be grateful if the Secretary of State could give some assurance that whatever the conditions were in the past, they were now satisfactory and 'not such as to impose any hardships upon these unfortunate people'. The Minister's reply suggests a measure of official complacency which the facts do not seem to warrant. He could assure the Archbishop that the Government and people of Mauritius had done their utmost to make life pleasant for these unfortunate refugees. Their general health was 'satisfactory' and they were granted as much personal liberty as could be conceded to those living in such communal circumstances. The truth was that after four years on the island most of them were thoroughly dissatisfied and anxious to secure their release. However, they were now due to go to Palestine, though the Minister could not say when, owing to the exigencies of shipping.

Geoffrey Fisher acknowledged the letter through his chaplain saying briefly, perhaps ambiguously, that he 'fully understood the position in Mauritius.' It is not surprising that against the background of what was then happening in Palestine a mood of pessimism and near hopelesness should prevail, so complex and highly charged emotionally was the situation. Archdeacon MacInnes, who was to become Bishop in Jerusalem, telephoned the Archbishop, with the full support of Sir Andrew Cunningham, High Commissioner in Palestine – but unsuccessfully – asking him to promote a National Day of Prayer such as had been organised during the dark days of the war.

British statesmanship was certainly not seen at its best or most fruitful in Palestine at this time. To rally an informed public opinion the Council of Christians and Jews had been formed in 1942 to rebut any form of anti-semitism, its Presidents being the Archbishop of Canterbury, the Chief Rabbi, the Moderator of the General Assembly of the Church of Scotland, the Cardinal Archbishop of Westminster and the Moderator of the Free Church Federal Council. It is significant that they passed a resolution condemning *inter alia* all forms of terrorism, wherever and by whom perpetrated. If a moderate Jewish opinion could thus manifest itself in England, its expression was by no means accepted universally. Indeed it led to the Archbishop becoming the target for bitter attacks on British policies in a telegram sent to Lambeth Palace from the Committee of Palestine. Its extremism testifies to the depth of Jewish feeling as the following extract illustrates: 'I read with astonishment your resolution which was adopted at the Annual Meeting of the Conference (*sic*) of Christians and Jews in London condemning what you call Jewish terrorism in Palestine. What impudence! When the Jew dies in the gas chambers you profoundly eulogise him and when he dies fighting for what is his by the law of

God and Man you call him terrorist ... There was not a nation or people that received its independence from the British yoke without resorting to arms.' Such sentiments, couched in so extreme a language, did not commend Zionism to the Archbishop though he fully recognised that they did not characterise Jewry as a whole and that collectively the Jewish community had 'sustained ills darker than death or night'.

In August 1947 when he was, unfortunately, unable to attend, Parliament debated at length the general situation in Palestine. The Archbishop was convinced that the voice of the Church should be heard and he thus arranged for the Bishop of Derby to make the following two points in the course of the debate: that if the agitation to promote the extreme claims of Zionism were removed, Jews and Arabs could happily, and to their mutual advantage, live together; that any form of anti-semitism in Britain must be stamped out.

The first of these two points was, of course, a gross over-simplification; but it had become clear that British political initiatives, and the will to maintain them, had now spent their force. On 31 January 1947 Winston Churchill, the Leader of the Opposition, demanded in the House of Commons that Britain should give up the Mandate since there seemed no cogent reason for any longer maintaining a British presence in Palestine. This view prevailed and on 25 February 1948 the British Administration withdrew on the orders of the Government in London, its members abandoning their posts and leaving their office files behind them. They thus left both Jews and Arabs without any guidance or support.

This act of self-abnegation brought to an end one of the least happy chapters in British history. Its immediate consequence was that the power vacuum thus created was filled by the United Nations which offered the Israelis a State within the boundaries it prescribed. They accepted with alacrity and the State of Israel was proclaimed on 14 May 1948. The Palestinians, however declined a similar offer refusing to contemplate any form of partition which required a Palestinian state to live alongside a Jewish one. The Bishop of the Anglican Church in Jerusalem and the Moderator of the General Assembly of the Church of Scotland, in the light of these momentous events, presented a memorandum to the United Nations Special Committee on Palestine, in which they stressed that there were two matters on which Christian opinion would need to be satisfied: the protection of the Holy Places and the guarantee of religious liberty. As to the first, this did not only relate to Jerusalem since the whole land was sacred. As to the second, this had wide ramifications, particularly in respect of the right to missionise. Here, emphasis should be placed on the highest good of Palestine and the world rather than the strategic or economic interests of any one power. This meant bearing in mind the unique status and character of the Holy Land as the cradle of three great world religions.

So far as concerned the realisation of these *desiderata*, the authors of this memorandum emphasised that though this complex problem had now become the responsibility of the United Nations yet so long as the current intransigence obtained between Jew and Arab it was impossible to satisfy both communities. Geoffrey Fisher commented cynically that it was no solution if as Britain withdrew, the Government of Palestine should rest in the hands of Bolivia, Czechoslovakia, Denmark, Panama and the Philippines. 'You cannot feel much sense of security,' he wrote, 'in their competence to manage this extraordinarily difficult business of transferring authority to a Jewish and an Arab state!'

What precisely to do about Jerusalem was fraught with additional difficulties. Under the latest proposals Jerusalem and some of the surrounding villages were to be placed under an international Trustee-ship Council which was to guarantee fundamental freedoms, though there was no specific mention of the right to convert. Access to the Holy Places was to be safeguarded by the Governor of Palestine. The Archbishop's comments on these proposals were to the point, namely that the proof of this pudding would lie in the eating. 'It is indeed a terribly anxious time for you,' so he wrote to the Bishop in Jerusalem. 'None of us can feel at all happy about the working out of the business though we must pray that fears may be liars. You have all my sympathy.' To allay such fears the Archbishops of Canterbury and York made their views public in a letter to *The Times* newspaper which appeared on 27 February 1948. It began with an assumption which was later to prove somewhat wishful in its thinking, namely that whatever the future of the rest of Palestine might be it must be agreed that the City of Jerusalem, with its surrounding towns and villages, should lie outside any Jewish or Arab State and be administered under a Trusteeship Council. Was it even now too late, the Archbishops asked, for the parties to the conflict 'to determine that the area be kept inviolate until handed over to the Trusteeship Council'. To achieve this must depend on the co-operation within Palestine of its political and religious leaders. An exchange of letters between the Archbishop and Viscount Astor gives a fair picture of Geoffrey Fisher's views, feelings and anxieties at this volatile and explosive time. 'It is difficult indeed,' he wrote, 'to know what people of goodwill or what the Christian Church can do in the face of the deplorable situation in Palestine. If I may dare to say so, the USA Government has for some time past invited the disaster which is now threatening by its action. It is, as you say, in a jam and so is UNO. For myself I have always distrusted partition and thought there ought to be a unified Government with

Jewish and Arab cantons under it. The Jews naturally and ardently desire something they can call a State so that it can secure for them direct representation at UNO.'

As a result of these recent events law and order further deteriorated as warfare between Jews and Arabs increased in violence and extent. Meanwhile the Arab Legion was working havoc in the Holy City. In these circumstances, the British Government informed the Bishop in Jerusalem, Weston Stewart, that it was issuing instructions advising all British subjects to leave Palestine as soon as possible. The Bishop, faced with a critically dangerous situation, turned to Lambeth for counsel giving his personal opinion that it would be 'utterly wrong' for the Anglican Church including himself as its Bishop, to quit. True some clergy and teachers were departing and he might have to house the remaining staff within the Cathedral compound, in which case an office would be established in trans-Jordan under Archdeacon MacInnes. Particularly what concerned him were those Jewish Christians whose lives were becoming increasingly difficult. This constituted an additional reason for his staying put since he was contemplating instituting for them, under the Red Cross, an international asylum. 'May I therefore ask your approval,' the Bishop enquired of Geoffrey Fisher, 'and your blessing to my staying on with my wife, who has already been evacuated from Iraq in 1941, and from Palestine in 1947, and with a Palestine staff? We feel that while the other patriarchs and bishoprics remain it would be nothing less than a disaster that our Church should abandon its Palestinian flock, however intransigent, to their fate.' Perhaps later, he added, he might even have an opportunity to act as a mediator! The Archbishop immediately sent a cable giving his warm approval on 16 April following it up the same day with a letter confirming this permission with the 'gravest sense of responsibility and concern'.

So it was that Archbishop and Bishop kept in close touch during these fateful days. A further report from Jerusalem written on 26 April got through to Lambeth. The British Community, it said, was dwindling but the Bishop was hoping that St George's Cathedral and its precincts would be included in an international reserve. Where possible, he was evacuating the threatened Jewish Christians. Meanwhile, preparation for war went on, in spite of appeals for a truce and even as he wrote this report, numbers of unauthorised people were digging trenches on the school playground and no one could stop them. 'I am afraid' he commented, 'it is true we have reached a point where no *foreign* voice will be listened to unless there is overwhelming force behind it.' Conditions inside Jerusalem, as this correspondence indicates, were now desperate. World Jewry became restive and the result was three cables dispatched to Lambeth. The first came from the Union

of the All Orthodox Rabbis in America and Canada. It read as follows;
'We believe even at this late hour action of His Majesty's Government
can be decisive to effect immediate cessation of bloodshed. Implore
Your Grace to use utmost influence with His Majesty's Government in
this direction which is our bounden duty before God and man.
Preservation of the Holy City will earn Great Britain everlasting
gratitude of all humanity and world Jewry.' The second was sent by
the New York Board of Rabbis urging that the Archbishop 'intercede
for the prompt withdrawal from Jerusalem of the Arab Legion,
organised, led and financed by the British Government'. The third from
Paris ended with the cryptic yet poignant words: 'Save Jerusalem from
destruction'.

Responsible Jews in England felt that they could not stand idly by
while the fate of their kith and kin hung in the balance. Keith Joseph,
a Fellow of All Souls College, Oxford, and an Alderman of the City of
London, sent the Archbishop a series of penetrating questions to which
he himself gave short, pithy answers. 'Is the trans-Jordan Arab Legion
attacking Jerusalem? Yes. Are any British active list officers serving
with it? Yes. Is the attack made with British supplies handed over in
advance before the Mandate ended? Question of opinion. Could Mr
Bevin, the Foreign Secretary, call the Arab Legion off its Jerusalem
attack? According to my information, yes.'

The Archbishop's position was by no means an easy one. He doubted
whether he was in a position to do anything effective, quite apart from
the inadequacy of his information though he still had sources of news
from Jerusalem, particularly through the Bishop. It was 'difficult to
intervene,' he told Keith Joseph, 'at any rate until the situation became
a little clearer'. A wrong done by one side, so he ruefully commented,
'produces a wrong done by the other side and so it goes on'.

So deeply did these events prey upon the Archbishop's mind that he
addressed Convocation almost on the spur of the moment on 28 May
1948, acquainting its members with what was happening in general
and, in particular, the violent scenes throughout Palestine, not least in
the Holy City. Also, on the same day, he sent off two telegrams to Mr
Trygve Lie, Secretary-General of the United Nations, one on behalf of
the World Council of Churches, the other from the bishops and clergy
of the Province of Canterbury. In these he stressed that the WCC
would strongly support any steps to achieve a truce in Palestine and
that Christian opinion throughout the world was deeply stirred by the
horror of the fighting in the Holy Land.

Disturbing cables now began to arrive at Lambeth. One such was
from the Jewish community in New York affirming that international
correspondents of unquestioned veracity had confirmed that the shell-
ing of Jerusalem was being undertaken by British guns made available

by British finance to the Arab Legion, the intention being that King Abdullah under British influence should become King of Jerusalem.

On 16 November 1948 the Archbishop once more wrote to *The Times* protesting against what he regarded as ever increasing Jewish claims. He feared, in particular, that the Jews would possess themselves of the Old City as well as the New. It was, in his opinion, 'necessary to reassert in the plainest terms that Jerusalem New and Old – for the two could not be separated – with the Holy Places must remain under international control. The City is holy ground for three great religions. It cannot be allowed to pass into the hands of the Jews alone.' Therefore he invited world Jewry in Britain and in the United States of America to declare that they would accept the authority of the United Nations in dealing with this issue. Not unexpectedly, the Archbishop received a reply from Israel Brodie, the Chief Rabbi in the United Kingdom, its tone being moderate as befitted so humane a person. The Archbishop, he pointed out, had raised three questions, on each of which he would wish to comment. (1) The Israeli Government had made it plain that it accepted UN regulations *vis-á-vis* its territory; (2) Dr Weizmann, President of the New State of Israel, had always made it clear that Israel laid no claims to the New City of Jerusalem or to the control of the Holy Places; (3) No one, he was sure, British or American, would expect Israel to accept individual agreements before the UN had formulated its final overall policy. For himself he would co-operate with the Archbishop in any real effort to secure peace.

The controversy and the violence meanwhile unhappily continued. The Acting Representative of the Provisional Government in Palestine himself wrote to *The Times* on 28 November reporting that the Jewish Agency accepted internationalisation in principle but it could not ignore the events of a year ago when the Arab Legion began its onslaught on Jerusalem in defiance of the United Nations. The result was that the Legion captured the Old City and destroyed the Jewish quarter. Only the resistance of the Jews prevented its complete capture, and thousands of Jews were as a consequence isolated in Jerusalem. James Parkes, who devoted a life-time to an understanding of the Palestinian situation within the context of an ongoing Jewish presence in the Holy Land now drew up a carefully prepared and practical paper which he dispatched to Lambeth. The problem of internationalising the administration in Jerusalem, as in the proposals put forward by the United Nations, was that it made no provision for the control of communications or of the water supply. Since the second half of the 19th century the Jews had constituted a majority of the population in the Holy City, and it was understandable, therefore, that they should wish to control one of the four roads which led into Israel.

So it was that the internationalisation of Jerusalem, desirable in theory, was not easy to achieve in practice, even though the Bishop in Jerusalem, writing to the Archbishop in March 1949, maintained that many Arab and non-Arab Christians wanted it. To this end the Bishop himself submitted a Paper to the United Nations Conciliation Commission which was charged with drawing up a settlement. The Pope in his Good Friday address added the weight of his unique office in urging an international regime for Jerusalem, its environs and for the protection of the Holy Places.

At this time of crisis Geoffrey Fisher became engaged in a correspondence with a Miss Warburton who had behind her considerable experience in the Middle East and whom he encouraged by assuring her that it was always interesting 'to get any new suggestions that might help to solve the Jerusalem deadlock'. She had in fact recently been in the Holy City where she discussed the general situation with Norman Goodall, Archdeacon MacInnes and Dr O. F. Nolde, Director of the Commission of the Churches on International Affairs. Her view was that the Israeli Government could never abandon the New City apart from a small sector. Hence the only practical solution was that the Jews should remain there, and the Arabs in the Old City, though the control of it should be internationalised. Indeed, as to the latter, it was quite 'unthinkable' that Christians and Muslims would ever allow the Old City to become a purely Jewish possession. How mistaken you can be!

Amongst many proposals which were being bandied about at the time was one which could claim a special authority, namely that put forward to the United Nations by its own Conciliation Commission. In essence, this suggested that the area in Jerusalem which was to be placed under international control should be divided into two municipal zones: Jewish and Arab, the line of demarcation to be that of the present armistice. The Archbishop, however, believed this solution to bristle with difficulties and if implemented likely to increase rather than diminish strife and uncertainty. The plan would only succeed, so the Archbishop felt strongly, if it had the goodwill of both parties which it clearly had not. The Arabs did not welcome it and spokesmen on behalf of the Israeli Government rejected it outright.

Holding such critical views of the *quasi* official plan proposed by the Conciliation Commission of the United Nations, the Archbishop now took the unprecedented step of putting forward a plan of his own. In the process of drawing this up he consulted widely, including Dr O. F. Nolde, who immediately advised him to confer with Malik, chairman of the Lebanese Delegation to the United Nations. He did so, giving him an outline of his own proposals and receiving a reply when as Geoffrey Fisher himself confessed 'his own mind was very full of the problem and anxiously seeking to find some way by which the existing deadlock might be broken and some room for manoeuvre found'. Malik's general reaction to the proposals was not unfavourable since at least, if implemented, they would protect Jerusalem from further damage. He welcomed 'a responsible and authoritative case for the internationalisation of the Holy City,' but believed that the real difficulty with its implementation was less with Israel and Jordan than with the United States' reluctance to bring these two together. Geoffrey Fisher also corresponded with the Israeli Legation in London and received an interesting letter from one of its spokesmen, who gave the scheme a somewhat mixed reception. On the one hand, he wrote, he was 'happy' that their minds 'travelled along together so much of the road'. They both, to quote his own words 'fervently wished to see a part of Jerusalem becoming once more the symbol of a "real City of Peace" within which Christians, Jews and Muslims may meet together in unity and from which the shining light of goodwill may be shed forth upon the world'. On the other hand, candour compelled him to add that the steps which the Archbishop proposed in order to secure this great blessing represented 'far too ideal a solution'. Internationalisation depended for its successful working on the goodwill of ordinary citizens and their willingness, on either side of the border, to abandon a previous allegiance and 'to settle down peaceably together to make a new life as citizens of the world'. After all the bloodshed and political passion it was just too much to ask. Yet this did not mean giving up all hope of creating there, where the Holy Places were situated, 'the nucleus, small but vital, of an international community of religions, of scholars, of those interested in religious thought, in culture, and in philosophy'.

The Archbishop of Canterbury having thus conferred widely, not least with his brother Primate of York, was not deterred and his Memorandum was presented to the United Nations, under the aegis of the World Council of Churches in December 1949. Initially, as we have seen, Geoffrey Fisher had been sparked off to engage upon this exercise by the inadequacies, as he saw them, of other plans, in particular that put forward by the United Nations Conciliation Commission. To this plan of the UN he referred critically in his own document particularly in relation to the character of the international *enclave*, which was to be divided into two municipal zones – Jewish and Palestinian. It was essential that the extent of these areas should be final and definitive, but this one derives 'from military operations and is not the product of reasoned thought'. Archbishop Fisher's solution was to establish an international *enclave* right in the heart of Jerusalem in which Jew and Arab would have equal rights and in which there would be no municipal zones but one administrative authority under the trusteeship of the United Nations. This area would include the Old

City with the Holy Places, the business and shopping centres, Mount Scopius, the Hebrew University and the Mount of Olives. The Jews would be confined to their possession of the New City and there should be a measure of internationalisation in Nazareth and other holy places outside Jerusalem. His scheme would place the Hebrew University and the Mount of Olives in the international instead of in the Arab municipal zone as proposed by the Commission; while the area south of Terra Sancta College, formerly within the Arab residential area, would be absorbed into the *enclave* and not belong to the Israelis. The latter, however, would be allowed to return to the former Jewish quarter in the Old City.

Though this plan of the Archbishop's was submitted to the United Nations through the good offices of the World Council of Churches it was essentially a private document for discussion by the Political Committee. In drawing it up Geoffrey Fisher was captivated by the vision of a Jerusalem which would take its rightful place as a spiritual, global centre and in which 'Jew, Moslem, and Christian should play their full part in making it a living city and in which adherents of all three faiths would take their share in building up its cultural life'. Jews and Arabs had it in their power to make a decision which would 'ennoble the spirit of mankind. History rarely offers such opportunities but if they are not taken they are lost for ever.'

Geoffrey Fisher seldom assumed the prophetic mantle. Here he indeed did and it was now a matter of awaiting reactions to the initiative which he had taken. At least he could find some encouragement from the fact that *The Times* newspaper thought the memorandum sufficiently significant to quote from it liberally and the *Jewish Chronicle* reproduced it in full. However, comments which came to the Archbishop from Jerusalem *via* the Anglican Bishop were not so favourable, a fact which the Bishop tactfully ascribed to an inadequate understanding of what the proposals really implied. The Arabs wrote them off as implying 'Jewish Jerusalem for the Jews; Arab Jerusalem for internationalisation'. In respect of this latter accusation, the Bishop in Jerusalem confessed himself somewhat bemused, even apprehensive, writing to the Archbishop: 'Undoubtedly your proposals do admit of this interpretation and I am probably myself at fault in that I did not foresee it and warn you'. He had heard that the British Consul-General, Sir Hugh Dawe, who had the full text, was very disturbed and was sure that the British Government would be considerably embarrassed by it. Sir Hugh further believed that the Government did not regard internationalisation as possible, and that in the end, if set up, it would 'let the Christians down'. Particularly the Archbishop ought first to have consulted the Foreign Office before releasing his own opinions, to which strictures the Bishop in Jerusalem retorted, with some asperity, that the Government might equally have consulted the Archbishop. The Bishop also told Sir Hugh it was important that those in Jerusalem should be disabused of any idea that the Primate intended to concede everything to the Jews and nothing to the Arabs.

That the Archbishop's memorandum did in fact embarrass the Government there can be little doubt. Burrows, a member of the Foreign Office, frankly told Waddams he had received a telegram from the British Council for Foreign Relations Delegation at the United Nations expressing dismay at the wide circulation of the memorandum which certainly appeared to give a great deal to the Jews at the expense of the Arabs – and this in spite of the fact that the latter's support was essential to the working out of any settlement. The Jews on the other hand saw it as supporting claims to internationalise the Old City. It might be that the United Kingdom delegation must in conscience oppose it.

Waddams, however, rallied to the Archbishop's defence. His effort to bring peace to so disturbed a country was wholly justified. His clear, analytical mind often enabled him to see things objectively which few others could.

Geoffrey Fisher, it must be admitted, had not yet personally visited the Holy Land and therefore could not really be sensitive at first hand to its religious climate and political *ethos*. Passions were running high, divisions were profound, so much so that no solution, no matter how intrinsically reasonable, could hope to gain a general assent. Only a United Nations peace-keeping force, backing up what UN decided, could hope to be effective but this was significantly lacking. It was the failure of the two main contestants to agree a compromise which made successive schemes, though impressive on the drawing board, fail abysmally in practice. Dr Fisher saw himself as occupying the middle ground and may well, cynically, have been reinforced in this view by the fact that both parties to the dispute opposed his solution.

The General Assembly of the United Nations, though it did not accept the proposals set out in the Archbishop's memorandum, yet decided for the internationalisation of Jerusalem. The Primate of All England, however, sadly confessed in his Canterbury *Diocesan Notes* that it was widely believed that it would prove impracticable to carry this decision into effect since the Israeli State was determined to make it unworkable. Also, it seemed that the Jewish and Arab authorities were proposing to agree between themselves the demarcation line across which they would confront each other.

Perhaps it is not surprising that Geoffrey Fisher began to doubt the wisdom, realistically, of his intervention though he reassured himself with the thought that at least his memorandum had not done any real harm or 'made a bad situation worse'. Nor did he accept the criticism of James Parkes who in confessing his regret that the Archbishop had written his memorandum, maintained that it could not stand up to close scrutiny either on grounds of impartiality or realism. Geoffrey Fisher always denied, and strongly, that his proposals were in any way designed to be pro-Jewish. True, they entailed giving to the Jews a part of Jerusalem but they also required their giving up a great deal which they already occupied and surrendering any hopes of possessing the Old City. Cardinal Godfrey, Archbishop of Westminster, when asked for a Roman Catholic opinion by the knowledgeable Max Warren, perhaps wisely evaded the question by simply remarking that there was no change in the attitude of the Holy See since the promulgation of the Encyclicals *Multiplicatis* and *Redemptori Nostris*.

It was now becoming every day more clear, as the Archbishop had foreseen, that the establishment of an international *enclave* in Jerusalem was 'as good as dead', although the General Assembly of the United Nations decided as late as mid-December 1950 in its favour. The Israelis were making the New City the seat of their Government and it seemed as if the Old City would remain in the hands of the Arabs. The latter fact did not alter Geoffrey Fisher's conviction that it was 'hard to believe that the ultimate aim of the Jews will not be to possess themselves of the Old City also, and indeed some of them expressly say so'.

The Archbishop never abandoned his belief that the partial internationalisation of Jerusalem was the right course to take and in his more optimistic moments managed to persuade himself that this was gaining support at the United Nations.

Finally – perhaps this adverb should be used only in a relative sense – the settlement arrived at was neither the internationalisation which the Archbishop desired nor the partition which he was regretfully prepared to accept. The Israelis, as we have seen, seized the opportunity presented to them of establishing an independent state; but the Palestinians declined to do likewise since they were not prepared to achieve statehood alongside of Israel. Perhaps the emotional atmosphere was too highly charged, against the background of a mutual hostility, to permit of a solution which could at the time have brought about a fair compromise with an equal justice for both. By the time of the Six Days War and the settlement, to which it led by *force majeure*, even if not internationally recognised, Geoffrey Fisher had been in retirement for some six years. That he had applied himself seriously to the problem of Palestine there can be no doubt; and that in the process he upset the British Government by following an independent line was equally true. Maybe he was a little out of his depth and shared the prejudices of many Englishmen. In fairness to Geoffrey Fisher perhaps it should be said that the time had not yet come when an Archbishop of Canterbury would give himself to exploring 'a theology of the land'.

CHAPTER 47

The Jerusalem Bishopric

GEOFFREY Fisher was of necessity involved in Palestinian politics through the Anglican Bishopric in Jerusalem. This was established by Archbishop Howley, with the backing of Queen Victoria, way back in 1841, as a joint venture with the German Lutheran Church and the King of Prussia. This project was opposed by the Tractarians – indeed Newman said that it finally 'shattered' his faith in the Church of England – and later ran into considerable difficulty. Indeed for some five years the diocese was without a bishop until the succession was restored by Archbishop Benson after the Prussian Lutheran Church had withdrawn its support. Since 1886 the see was maintained by Anglicans alone and had acquired an extended jurisdiction stretching far beyond the confines of Jerusalem. Included, particularly in the Holy City, were many Arabs, and though successive bishops tried to hold the balance between them and the non-Arab Christians this mixed clientèle had the effect of making the Anglican Church in Jerusalem particularly sensitive to Arab opinion. Here politics and religion were inextricably inter-woven.

In 1943, Weston Stewart, Bishop in Jerusalem, stayed at Fulham Palace with the Bishop of London who had a traditional historic interest in the Anglican Church overseas. They discussed problems relating to the Jerusalem bishopric. Geoffrey Fisher could not have suspected that within a matter of two years he would himself become Archbishop of Canterbury, and thus intimately involved with the subjects of their conversation.

One of the continuing questions in relation to Jerusalem, going back many years, was that of the Christian Arabs of whom there were in all, so it was then estimated, some 8,000, ministered to by 12 clergy under the Council of the Arab Evangelical Episcopal Church. Their history encouraged them to cherish, and wish to maintain, their independence, the more so as many of them were left, by the violence of near civil war, homeless and in a desperate plight. This feeling after an identity, linked with maintaining an independent status, was fostered over the years by the Constitution which had been granted to them in 1905 by the Church Missionary Society.

Under a religious community ordinance, issued by the Turkish Palestinian Government, Muslim, Jewish and Christian communities were given legal recognition with the right to hold religious courts dealing with their own internal matters of personal status. However, the Anglican Church was not regarded, in its own right, as a recognised community under the ordinance though in practice the Turkish administration treated Protestants collectively as such. Gordon Brown, Bishop in Jerusalem, had preferred to leave well alone and not to disturb the status quo, but since 1927 those urging that a constitution should be given to the Council and Congregation of the Jerusalem Bishopric became more vocal. Hence, the Bishop in Jerusalem submitted, but unsuccessfully, a petition to Archbishop Lang in 1933 arguing the case for such legal recognition; but the latter was more interested at the time in securing an overall constitution for the Anglican Bishopric which would include the Arabic Councils and Congregations.

The situation, however, did not remain static and in due course this proposal was referred to the Archbishop's Advisory Committee which dealt with such questions, the most prominent on this body being Bishop Palmer who had been involved in a correspondence with members of the Jerusalem Bishopric over many years. Thus on 24 May 1945, the Bishop in Jerusalem wrote to Geoffrey Fisher enclosing a revised version of the existing Arab regulations. He confessed that he was not 'entirely happy' with it, but since these were regulations drawn up by the Church Missionary Society some years earlier they had not a free hand. At least the revised draft was less separatist than the previous one.

The Archbishop passed on the letter with the proposed regulations to his Advisory Committee which took a favourable view of the new proposals and advised that the Archbishop give them a 'hearty general approval'. In taking this attitude, its members recognised that the Bishop in Jerusalem was the best judge of the appropriate timing, namely whether such a registration of the Palestinian Arabic Evangelical Episcopal Community (PAEEC) ought to precede or follow the contemplated overall re-organisation of the Bishopric.

The Archbishop accepted the new regulations with only a few amendments, these being designed to offset any tendency to achieve a near total autonomy. Such archiepiscopal emendations received the full approval of Bishop Palmer who commented that they constituted 'just one of the things that you can say and which the Arab community will probably take from you'.

On one matter of fact, however – an important one – Bishop Palmer corrected the Archbishop. Weston Stewart, he pointed out, was not Bishop 'of' Jerusalem, that is of any geographical area where he customarily ministered to all persons under his jurisdiction. This distinction needed to be made clear since 'of' might be resented by the Roman Catholic Bishops, as well as by the Patriarch of the Orthodox

Church. Bishop Weston Stewart was, therefore, Bishop 'in' Jerusalem. Geoffrey Fisher saw the point and acted upon it.

The Archbishop now brought the correspondence concerning the proposed change in status to a close by summarising his own position in a lengthy epistle to the Bishop in Jerusalem. He reiterated that there were clauses in the regulations which, if he were starting afresh, he would wish to put differently, but bearing in mind past controversies the proposed regulations marked a great advance. If they still left an 'unwarranted' degree of independence to the Arabic-speaking community its past record gave confidence that this freedom would not be abused. He was satisfied that these regulations were in harmony with church doctrine and order. Thus reassured, he was certain that it was right 'to satisfy the natural desire of the Arabic-speaking community to be registered as a religious body and to seek a legal recognition on the basis of the proposed regulations'. Indeed, the Archbishop was prepared to go further in regarding it as 'highly desirable that the whole Anglican body in Palestine should be so registered'. Finally he congratulated Bishop Weston Stewart on having brought matters so far towards a fruitful solution and expressed his own appreciation for the care, labour and wisdom with which he had dealt with such an 'intricate matter'.

What this correspondence shows is that though the Archbishop of Canterbury could not possibly know the situation in Palestine at first hand, yet it was valuable for the Bishop on the spot to have available at Lambeth one who had sound common sense, and was still, at this time, constitutionally involved as the Metropolitan. Clearly the future of the Arab Church could not be dealt with independently of the project of a constitution for the Anglican Church in the Middle East as a whole. The solution of the problem was not made easier by the background of political unrest and the fact that two of the parishes of the Arabic Council were situated in the State of Israel and others in Islamic territory.

The Bishop in Jerusalem, in order to get things moving with the more ambitious project, went over to Lambeth to discuss matters with the Archbishop bringing with him a draft Ordinance drawn up by the Bishop's Attorney-General, which gave the Arab Council community status within the extensive orbit of the Anglican Communion. However this proposal was promptly rejected by the Arab Council since its members had long entertained the ambition, as an indigenous religious community, of going back to the days of the pre-Mandate Turkish régime thereby securing such recognition without reference to any 'foreign connection'.

Such a claim the Bishop admitted might well seem 'trifling' to the Archbishop, but it was very 'real' to the Arab congregation. Across the

years its members had developed a strong racial and cultural consciousness. They placed great emphasis on being 'self-governing' and 'self-
supporting'; an attitude derivative from the policy of the Church
Missionary Society in its early days. 'I feel', the Bishop commented,
'they had a basically wrong idea of the Church, an idea that is Turkish,
racial and defeatist but the responsibility for this lay at the door of
Britain who had failed to teach them a true one. Perhaps the English
Church had gone too far in encouraging a degree of separatism among
Arab Anglicans, the reason for this being fear of schism had it done
otherwise.'

The precise relationship of the Arabic Council with the Bishop in
Jerusalem thus continued to be a severe problem particularly since the
Council was determined to remain both Arab and Anglican. But this,
its congregation believed, could only fully be secured if they had their
own Bishop in which case, they claimed, all their problems would
disappear.

As he pondered over these complex possibilities Geoffrey Fisher put
his thoughts on paper in a memorandum dated 25 September 1947.
'While perfectly willing to accept a special relationship with the Bishop
and allegiance to the Book of Common Prayer', so the Archbishop
began, 'the Arabic Congregation yet wanted a spiritual status, uncomplicated by any reference to the Church of England.' The Archbishop's
solution of this dilemma was to substitute for 'The Bishop of the
Church of England' the form: 'The Bishop in Communion with the
Church of England Resident in Jerusalem'. This had the advantage of
enabling the Archbishop to appoint an American or Canadian Bishop,
thus making it clear that the Bishop in Jerusalem represented the whole
body of the Anglican Communion. However, as to whether such a
concession would mollify Arab feeling the Archbishop confessed that
he could not tell.

The above reference to the possibility of an American Bishop may
serve to emphasise another dimension of the problem. The Archbishop
was by no means unaware that Palestine and the Middle East generally,
were of interest to the Protestant Episcopal Church of America; and
bearing this in mind he conferred frequently with his close friend,
Henry Sherrill, its Presiding Bishop. These discussions were wide-
ranging, including in their purview the dioceses of Egypt and Iran as
well as Jerusalem.

Yet in spite of proposals, conferring and memoranda, the problem
of the Arab Council and its demands remained unsolved. Hence in
December 1954 Geoffrey Fisher had a talk at Lambeth with its leading
churchman, Canon Najib Ataliah Cuba'in which proved frank and
friendly. The Archbishop seized the opportunity in this conversation to
assure the Canon that there was no intention of weakening his

community, quite the reverse. He further expressed his satisfaction that the Arab Council was on the eve of accepting the regulations and agreed that there ought then to be a diocesan constitution. Yet he must say that to have an Arab Bishop for so small a church – it had some 8,000 members with 12 clergy – was contrary to Catholic Order. On this matter the Archbishop's views were to change under the pressure of events.

The Archbishop confessed later that due to his own tiredness he himself was not at his best in this interview and the discussion was consequently 'superficial'. He yet felt it had value in helping him to establish a personal relationship.

Reporting this conversation to Bishop Weston Stewart, Geoffrey Fisher emphasised that he was by no means lacking sympathy with Canon Cuba'in – indeed, his own sister had ministered to Arabs in the Holy Land – but as to an Arab Bishop or Assistant Bishop this could not happen until there was a proper constitutional relationship between the Arab Episcopal Council and the Anglican Diocese. One could not simply ignore either the small numbers involved or the principle that the Bishop had jurisdiction over all Anglicans in his diocese. Thus Anglicans in Weston Stewart's area of Jerusalem, whether Arab or whatever their race or nationality, came under his care and jurisdiction. Thus when he, (Geoffrey Fisher) as Metropolitan, nominated Bishops overseas, they became not Bishops in the Church of England but in the Church of God exercising authority within the Anglican Communion. He was conscious that Bishop Weston Stewart had devised a number of regulations but had been unable to secure agreement on them. He must therefore ask the Bishop to take the matter up again with the Arab Christians in which case he would hope to send three advisers to Jerusalem to confer with the Arab Episcopal Council and report back to him. It must be understood that his decision as Metropolitan was final. Failing this he would invite the Arab Council to appoint three representatives, with Weston Stewart, to meet him at Lambeth.

The time had certainly now come to finalise the revised draft of the original constitution given them by the Church Missionary Society which was far from being truly episcopal. Nobody, he wrote reassuringly, would want to deprive the Arab Church unnecessarily of powers of self-government, but in a diocesan constitution it must be made absolutely clear that powers belong finally to the Diocese as a whole, governed by its Bishop with the co-operation of clergy and laity. Yet an effort ought to be made, within this context, to provide special arrangements to meet the particular needs of the Arab community. In spite of the Archbishop's eirenic words the problem of reconciling the two interests was certainly no easy one. He did not lack advisers but their advice varied from person to person.

Meanwhile the three English clergymen, nominated by the Archbishop, began talks with their opposite numbers on the Arab Church Council. Many letters, friendly in tone, passed between Lambeth and Jerusalem, Canon Cuba'in acknowledging that he was 'heartened and encouraged by them'. The Bishop in Jerusalem, however, felt that he must not encourage excessive or immediate expectations. Thus he told the Canon that he could not for the present contemplate an Arab Bishop as his successor or the nomination of an Arab 'parallel' Father in God. All must now wait for the appearance of the constitution but, to repeat, this was complicated by the overall problem of meeting the demands of the Arab Church Council and at the same time serving the best interests of the Anglican Communion in the Middle East as a whole.

On 24 June 1955 Geoffrey Fisher dispatched his revised draft of a constitution to the Bishop in Jerusalem. In an accompanying letter he made it clear – it was an oft-repeated theme – that there could not be any idea of an Arab Bishop until a proper constitutional relationship had been established between the Arab Evangelical Episcopal Community and the Anglican Communion. Here it needed to be realistically recognised that when this happened no Church in Palestine, historically derived from the Church of England, could any longer regard itself as still linked up constitutionally with this established national church. Rather it had become part of the world-wide Anglican Communion. It was now up to the Arab Episcopal Community itself to tackle the question of the diocesan constitution and agree it with the relevant authorities. If finally there was no such agreement then this thorny problem should be taken up again by the representatives of each party. Later in the year Geoffrey Fisher got into touch with the Reverend C. S. Milford of the Church Missionary Society, stressing his deep concern to bring the Arab Evangelical Episcopal Community into a right relationship with the Diocese and repeating his conviction that the Church Missionary Society had probably started things off on the wrong foot when it gave the Arab Community its own Charter.

The position of the Archbishop, distant in Lambeth yet caught up in the passions and politics of the Middle East, was by no means an enviable one. The Arabic Church was but one among many of his preoccupations. Thus he was concerned with the promotion of Islamic studies; the provision of an Assistant Bishop for the oil fields; the general position of chaplains in Iran already finding life there near impossible; the appointing of a successor to Bishop Weston Stewart who had declared his firm intention to resign.

Geoffrey Fisher increasingly came to the conclusion that the diverse problems confronting the Anglican Church in the Middle East could not be tackled piecemeal. There was need for an overall strategy, so much so that when considering the appointment of a new Bishop in

Jerusalem he must ask himself to what kind of office, and how extensive would be his responsibilities? For example, would his writ be confined to Palestine? As a result of a conversation on 17 October 1955 with Bishop Stewart (with whom he was on very co-operative terms) he drew up a further document on the Jerusalem bishopric in which he endeavoured to survey the field as a whole. For the Arab Evangelical Episcopal Council – 'the local problem' he called it – he felt he had a very special responsibility. 'I cannot disown this community,' he wrote, 'on the grounds, as some say, that it ought not to be there. It wants to remain with us and we have a duty to it increased by the harsh treatment of recent years which has left so many Arabs homeless and without a country.' Yet the Archbishop could not ignore the fact that the 'independent leanings' of the Arab community if pushed too far would serve to make the realisation of his more ambitious plans for the Middle East almost impossible.

The Arab Church was determined to sustain the pressure and on 7 August 1956 it dispatched a letter to Lambeth which was friendly but made it quite clear, once again, that they wanted an indigenous, episcopal Church, at the heart of the extensive diocesan structure which was now envisaged.

Geoffrey Fisher had now, at least in his own eyes, firmly committed himself to the creation of a Middle Eastern Province which he believed had many advantages, not least that of 'easing' problems associated with the existence of an indigenous Arab Church. The Province was to include dioceses in Jerusalem, Egypt, the Sudan and Iran which it was hoped would lead to a closer integration between them. The Archbishop now embarked on an extensive process of consultation with the above dioceses and with all the Metropolitans of the Anglican Communion except those of China and Japan. To all he sent a copy of the proposed constitution asking for comments. Among the replies there were no bishops who totally disagreed with its terms though the Archbishops of the West Indies and Cape Town expressed some dismay at the powers retained by the Archbishop of Canterbury. Dr Norman Goodall who was on the staff of the World Council of Churches also feared that linking Egypt, Jerusalem and Iran with Canterbury was 'a serious political impediment'.

There was now a great deal of conferring and a further circularisation of the Bishop by which time the Archbishop's proposals were fully if privately launched. It was indeed, however, unfortunate that the background to these negotiations was the Suez invasion, when Israel in alliance with Britain and France attacked Egypt. Canon E. M. Bickersteth, formerly secretary of the Jerusalem and East Mission, felt that the tragic escapade made it even more important to go forward with the implementation of the new Province.

The imminent resignation of Bishop Stewart not surprisingly led to much speculation concerning his successor as well as to the nature of the office to which he was to be appointed. Equally understandably, the vacancy led to redoubled efforts by the Arab Council while there was time to secure a bishop of their own 'kith and kin'. Requests to this end were sent to the Reverend C. S. Milford, Secretary of the Church Missionary Society for the West Asia Mission, who passed them on to Lambeth only to receive the reply that the time had not yet come. Indeed it was still not easy to determine the best way forward with so many apparently conflicting interests involved. Certainly it is not difficult to sympathise with the frustration of Canon Cuba'in. As to Geoffrey Fisher he, on occasions, indulged a fanciful reverie as follows: 'Perhaps, the solution might mean something really drastic like setting up an Archbishop or Patriarch of the Anglican Communion in Jerusalem, with Arab Bishops in all these countries and a European Bishop to look after the oil fields and the like, the Patriarch becoming just like an Eastern Patriarch, the spider in the middle of the web.'

The problem of Canon Cuba'in remained but Geoffrey Fisher realised that if the Canon's wishes were to be implemented this might defeat the whole object so close to his heart of establishing a Province for Jerusalem and the whole of the Middle East.

It was now up to Dr Fisher to bring to a head his scheme and to implement the constitution which the four Bishops immediately concerned and the Anglican Metropolitans had approved. There remained the task of sharing the document with the British and Jordanian Governments as well as persuading the Arab Church that this was the best possible course open to them and to everyone else.

No one could doubt, for a moment, the significance, short and long term, of the choice that was to be made of the new Metropolitan. The Archbishop believed that he knew the man uniquely fitted for this appointment. Hence on 6 January 1957 he wrote to Canon Max Warren, General Secretary of the Church Missionary Society, a man of long experience and great wisdom, inviting him to accept the nomination. After indicating the nature of the commitment involved the Archbishop expressed himself as follows: 'I come to the point and with deep emotion to put it bluntly and squarely, would you consent to become the first Archbishop of the Province or the last Bishop in Jerusalem as the case may be? – an absolutely key appointment.' The reply to this *cri de coeur* was unequivocal and it came almost immediately in a somewhat shattering letter. The whole scenario in the Middle East, Max Warren observed, had radically changed since the Archbishop had summoned a group of them to Lambeth for discussion last summer. The anti-Western revolt had now reached a new level. Britain was discredited and other Governments were becoming involved as well as Jordan, namely the United States, in 'an area where on Islamic grounds alone, there is no recognition of a distinction between Church and State'. Thus any such development, i.e. the creation of a new Province would automatically be considered a device by which British imperialism could infiltrate the Middle East once more. The proposed Province, would straddle twelve sovereign States as well as Aden and the Persian sheikhdoms. Most of the Moslems would regard the new Archbishop as in fact a diplomat. If these difficulties could be overcome the Province might well be inaugurated before Bishop Stewart left, coinciding with setting up the Diocese of Oman. If the new Province were brought into existence it should be effected jointly through the Archbishop of Canterbury in association with the Metropolitan of India and the Provincial Bishops of China and Japan. As for himself personally, he suffered from three serious disqualifications from holding the office which the Archbishop had suggested to him. He did not speak Arabic or French; he knew 'nothing whatever of Orthodoxy and was an Anglican evangelical'; thirdly his domestic situation was that he had an old mother of 89; finally he felt no inward call '*testimonium internum spiritus*'.

This was, to say the least, a most discouraging letter raising wider issues than the person of the new Metropolitan. Perhaps it was unfortunate that Geoffrey Fisher had not before discussed the general situation with Dr Warren though the latter was one of a group which met earlier at Lambeth. The effect of Max Warren's letter was almost immediate – the abandonment, at least for the present, of any provincial scheme. After consultation with Bickersteth Dr Fisher offered the bishopric to Archdeacon MacInnes to whom he wrote remarking that there was everything to be said for his appointment. The Archdeacon accepted and the appointment was made public. The fact that this notice appeared just over a month from the date of Max Warren's declining suggests that the Archbishop had already made up his mind that if Warren failed him he would then opt for MacInnes.

The bald announcement of the latter's nomination, however, did not answer the question as to what precisely the character of the bishopric was to be, not least in relation to the possible creation of an archiepiscopal See in the future. It could, therefore, have come as no surprise to Geoffrey Fisher when Canon Cuba'in asked him to receive at Lambeth a delegation from Jordan, Lebanon, and Israel plus himself, to discuss matters generally. The Archbishop gladly concurred and the delegation, headed by the Canon, was duly received at Lambeth when a frank exchange of views took place. Writing on his return to Jerusalem, Canon Cuba'in thanked the Archbishop for the spirit in which he had conducted the discussion, this being 'a great inspiration' to all of them. Back home a few members seem to have been somewhat indiscreet with the result that the British Consul General in Jerusalem alerted the Foreign Office that there were new plans for the bishopric and that these 'differed in some important details from what was originally envisaged'. Herbert Waddams warned the Archbishop that the Foreign Office might seek information from the 'man on the spot' and it might not welcome the new plans. Certainly, it should be now consulted.

Another interested party, as well as the British Government, in any appointment to the Anglican bishopric in Jerusalem, both as to the person nominated and the nature, if changed, of his office, must of course, be the Orthodox Patriarch, inheritor of a long tradition in the Holy City. Once more, Waddams, after conferring with Bishop Stewart and Max Warren, got into touch with the Archbishop and suggested that the following words be inserted in whatever Articles were drawn up in constituting the new bishopric or archbishopric: 'The foregoing provisions in no way change the traditional recognition by the Archbishop of Canterbury of the Orthodox Patriarch of Jerusalem as the rightful Bishop of the Holy City nor do they imply any claim on the part of the Anglican Bishop named to intrude into the territorial jurisdiction of the Bishops, Archbishops and Metropolitan, and Patriarchs of the Holy Orthodox Church in question.'

It was not to be expected that the Arab Council when they heard of this *caveat*, would receive the news with equanimity. In fact, they took 'violent exception' to it. 'It seems to deprive us and our Bishop of any right to exist', they commented, and certainly it could be understood in such a way. The Archbishop, however, made some slight amendments to meet the scruples of the Arab Council and added the words that 'Anglican representatives in the Middle East with all other Christian people would endeavour to increase mutual understanding and co-operation in the Church of God.'

There were still many problems as yet unresolved and Bishop Weston Stewart confessed that he was not clear as to the future status of St George's Cathedral or of Jerusalem itself. There was now a great deal of 'toing and froing', hesitations and differences of view as to the precise way ahead. Waddams admitted to being anxious over the territorial rather than the diocesan status of the Arab Bishop if appointed. Would it not be better, he asked, if he were bishop of a rite, namely the Anglican Arabic Rite which would mean that his writ could also include Israel.

The Archbishop, after lengthy discussions with MacInnes, Canon Edward Bickersteth, the Bishop in Egypt and Herbert Waddams, radically revised the constitution, sending on 25 June notice of the proposed changes to the Bishops concerned, including of course Cuba'in. The Archbishop now admitted that the creation of a Province was 'too ambitious' and 'unsuitable'. An immediate and overriding priority, therefore, was to encourage a sense of fellowship among the

Bishops of the Middle East, particularly since they represented a small Anglican community and were all facing the same problems of nationalism and a resurgent Islam. Fortunately they possessed full freedom to advance or retreat *vis-á-vis* self-government as circumstances required. However, the Archbishop had not totally abandoned his more ambitious scheme but for the moment he decided on a half-way house, namely to set up an episcopal synod as the 'right instrument of Government' under the Archbishop in Jerusalem as Metropolitan. He himself produced Articles for its proper functioning which he dispatched to his Chancellor H.T.A. Dashwood. Of these final plans he commented for the benefit of his legal official: 'All that happens is that I create a Committee of Bishops who would not, of course, elect their Archbishop.' Dashwood agreed that what the Archbishop proposed was perfectly in order. Having thus been given the legal 'all clear', the Archbishop was now in a position to issue an encyclical in which he announced that the style of the Metropolitan in Jerusalem should henceforth be 'the Archbishop in Jerusalem in communion with the See of Canterbury in the Collegiate Church of St George the Martyr in Jerusalem'. He was to exercise episcopal supervision over Anglican congregations resident in the Middle East.

When the Arab Council met it was only too evident that its deliberations were influenced by the contemporary political and military situation which was tearing Palestine apart. Indeed there was talk of boycotting the new Archbishop's enthronement which if persisted in, so Geoffrey Fisher warned, 'would gain nothing'. The atmosphere was 'very near to boiling point' intensified by 'wild things being said'. Fortunately no such threat was carried out and on Friday 30 August 1957 Canon A. C. MacInnes was enthroned as Archbishop in Jerusalem in the Collegiate Church of St George. The service was printed in English and Arabic and the institution was carried out by Canon Cuba'in. Present in the sanctuary was a remarkable assembly of representatives of the various churches; remarkable both in its number and ecumenical 'spread'. Some six hundred people flocked into the cathedral which number included the Governor of Jordan.

The story of the Anglican Church in Jerusalem however was not yet complete, for Archbishop Fisher had approved after much hesitation the creation of a diocese of Jordan, Syria and the Lebanon. Its constitution was to be a simple one, though there was a feeling, particularly in American churches, that a bishop having episcopal jurisdiction over Anglican congregations in Jordan should have some oversight in Jerusalem so long as part of the Holy City was under the sovereignty of the State of Jordan. The setting up of this new diocese had the advantage of enabling Geoffrey Fisher, at long last, to overcome former scruples in having an Arab bishop.

So it was that at the first meeting of the new episcopal synod of the Anglican Church in the Middle East, with the full approval of the Archbishop of Canterbury, the diocese of Jordan, Lebanon, and Syria was established and on 6 January 1958 Najib Atalah Cuba'in was consecrated its Bishop. This was indeed a happy and inevitable choice for he was a good man and a faithful pastor. If on occasions he could appear over-sensitive he was but reflecting the mood of his own people.

This was indeed the day which the Arab Christian Community had passionately worked for and Geoffrey Fisher sent off a telegram of greetings and congratulations from Lambeth. Archbishop MacInnes provided the Archbishop with an account of what happened in Jerusalem – a good augury for the shape of things to come. Dr Fisher must also have been gratified that the first letter Bishop Cuba'in wrote after the ceremony was to Lambeth acknowledging the 'loving concern and attention and care' Geoffrey Fisher had manifested to bring this new diocese into being. 'May I say,' he added, 'that we as a new and inexperienced Diocese look forward to your advice and guidance.' He anticipated with pleasure seeing the Archbishop when he came with his wife to London for the Lambeth Conference. In acknowledging these kind sentiments the Archbishop – it was typical – advised that the Bishop's first task was to bring into existence a Diocesan Board of Finance, properly registered and recognised by civil law, with the Bishop as its President. After this there must be a representative Diocesan Council with which he could confer. To be of help he was sending him some notes on diocesan organisation.

What Geoffrey Fisher wished for and hoped to achieve in respect of a Province was not fully realised during his own archiepiscopate. However, he did secure for the Archbishop in Jerusalem, through the Synod, a closer relationship between himself and the Bishops in the Middle East. What this chapter well illustrates are some of the difficulties, the pitfalls and the challenges which could face the Anglican Communion when confronting explosive situations in a world politically and religiously divided.

CHAPTER 48

Egypt

WE now turn to the Archbishop's relations with Egypt, which began almost as soon as he went to Lambeth in 1945. The Bishop was Dr Llewellyn Gwynne who had given almost a life-time's service to the Anglican Church in the Middle East. The occasion of his getting into touch with Lambeth arose from the alleged intention of the Egyptian Government to limit the traditional freedoms of the Jewish and Christian communities. This was to be effected by a Bill which specifically discriminated against foreign residents and raised the whole question of their expatriate status. Hitherto for centuries Christians in Egypt and other Islamic countries had enjoyed the right *inter alia* to adjudicate their marriage concerns in their own courts.

So seriously did the Bishop in Egypt take the threat of this proposed legislation that, at the request of the United Council of Churches in Egypt, on which Roman Catholics were represented, he despatched to Lambeth a memorandum expressing grave concern, and asking that the Archbishop should himself approach the Foreign Office in London to sort this matter out; though he feared that any such appeal would be referred back to the British Embassy in Cairo, in which case the reply almost inevitably would be that this was a purely domestic affair so far as Egypt was concerned.

The promulgation of such restrictive legislation bore witness to a rising tide of nationalism and a strong anti-Western sentiment which was beginning to be rampant in the Middle East. It is quite clear that the legislation was felt keenly by Dr Gwynne not least because he had been in Egypt so long that he found it difficult to adapt himself to the emergence of an unfamiliar world.

Geoffrey Fisher, who was not yet very knowledgeable concerning delicate political problems in this part of the world, wisely consulted Max Warren, at that time secretary of the Joint Committee on Religious Liberty, who advised him to tread warily. There were, he pointed out, religious minorities all over the world and the present Egyptian crisis should be understood as but one manifestation of a more global situation. Also, the Bishop in Egypt should take into account the 'notorious sensitivity of our Foreign Office to all questions dealing with Islamic countries'.

The Archbishop, thus made conscious of his lack of knowledge in this area, brought together to Lambeth a small group on 30 October

1945 with a view to organising a collective approach to the British Government. However, nothing definite seems to have resulted from this initiative and the Foreign Secretary, as expected, did nothing.

Not all the problems confronting the Anglican Church in Egypt, however, concerned relationships with that country's Government. One, much nearer home, had to do with the Church's internal life and structure. The setting up of precise diocesan boundaries could constitute, as we have seen earlier, intricate problems, difficult to resolve since there were so many factors to take into account in the process of making a judgement. At the end of William Temple's archiepiscopate a scheme was contemplated to split the existing Diocese of Egypt into two by hiving off the Sudan. The reasons for this proposal were in part the vast distances involved for a single bishop; also political and cultural considerations. The scheme got to the stage where Alfred Gelsthorpe, Assistant Bishop in Egypt, was being thought of as the first Bishop of this new independent Diocese. However, the unexpected death of Archbishop Temple created a new situation and Geoffrey Fisher, though convinced that the decision was a wise one, felt he must not take for granted the approval of the 82-year-old Bishop Gwynne. The latter, however, was happy to support the nomination of his assistant bishop, Alfred Gelsthorpe, than whom no one had more first-hand experience of North-East Africa. Mr Eden, the Foreign Secretary, advised only that the ecclesiastical authorities should inform the Governor-General of the Sudan.

Considering the future of the Diocese of Egypt particularly in relation to its forming part of a Province, led to a great deal of anxious thought not least since in time past the diocese had been integrated into the widely dispersed Jerusalem bishopric. There was in fact one practical problem which the creation of a new Diocese in the Sudan highlighted and that was finance. Dealing with this resistant problem might appear somewhat of a pedestrian chore but it was not so to Geoffrey Fisher who always took seriously, and sometimes one suspects derived much satisfaction in totting up the figures and drawing from them a workable budget. In the present case the money problem was complicated by Bishop Gwynne being already engaged in an Appeal for £40,000; also by the need to increase considerably the stipends of the clergy in both dioceses. The English community in Egypt was small and the Church Board of Finance was experiencing difficulty even in meeting its existing commitments. The Archbishop certainly did his best by writing numerous time-consuming letters in support of raising this money.

It was not only finance, however, which caused problems. The unique constitutional authority of the Archbishop's office in relation to dioceses not yet within a Province, meant that Lambeth was the final authority in matters appertaining to the proper ordering of the Diocese in Egypt. Complaints of various kinds thus came to the Archbishop, most serious of which was a communication, dated 20 May 1945, from a group of worshippers at the Cathedral, calling urgent attention to its present plight. The writers admitted that 'true Christianity' did not naturally thrive in such a city as Cairo which made it the more unfortunate that the English community had been pastorally neglected for many years, so much so that barely twenty per cent ever came to the Cathedral except for marriages and funerals. 'All young Clergy', the complainants alleged, 'have left or are leaving Egypt since from the Archdeacon downwards they are regarded as children to be directed or quashed by their chief as the mood demands but never allowed a free hand in their work'. The Bishop, 'however charming to meet at luncheons and dinner parties where he is a great success as a raconteur of stories of life in the Sudan, is really beyond the work of the pulpit'. On Sunday 6 May when everyone was looking forward with thankfulness to approaching peace he gave one of his usual diatribes on the characters of Hitler and Mussolini.

This is a sad letter, sad because it bears witness to a very old man who lived irrevocably in the past. That Bishop Gwynne had done good work in Egypt and sacrificially given himself to the best interests, as he saw them, of the British community, there can be no doubt. But apart from his great age and declining powers, it was clear that his paternalistic approach was no longer acceptable. Events had caught up with him. By general assent, and reports of visitors to Cairo, it was only too evident that Bishop Gwynne should go.

So it fell to Geoffrey Fisher, not for the first or last time, to urge a Bishop's retirement in order to promote the welfare of his flock. In his letter requesting him to resign he wrote, kindly but firmly, that in the general interests of the diocese, now and in the near future, the bishop ought to lay aside his duties. The reply – we quote his own words – does Bishop Gwynne great credit: 'If you are asking me to resign, you only do what I asked you to do – for a man of nearly 83 is no judge of his own limitations. I only hope I have done no harm to our beloved Diocese by staying too long.'

The Diocese in Egypt – if the Sudan were severed it would, of course, be smaller – still included Abyssinia and the coast along the Red Sea. Also Cairo was an important centre of the Moslem world. In considering Gwynne's successor Geoffrey Fisher consulted widely including, of course, Max Warren and the Church Missionary Society. He conferred further with the English diocesan bishops and some four names were discussed but none of these, not even the well-favoured Johnston, Archdeacon of Cairo, was offered the appointment. In spite of Geoffrey Fisher's initial feeling that Egypt needed someone who had first-hand knowledge of the Middle East he finally offered the diocese to Geoffrey

Allen, Archdeacon of Birmingham, an appointment of which Dr Barnes, his bishop, did not entirely approve as his curt note to Geoffrey Fisher makes plain: 'I do not want selfishly to keep Allen here . . . but frankly I think he would be wasted in Egypt'. However, the appointment went forward and Geoffrey Allen was consecrated Bishop in Egypt in Southwark Cathedral on 25 January 1947.

Whether Bishop Barnes' use of the word 'wasted' is appropriate in this context is a moot point. It is certainly doubtful, whether Allen's undoubted gifts suited the requirements of this particular diocese where he stayed for some five years, leaving to become Principal of the Theological College at Ripon Hall. Many members of the British community thought that the Archbishop should have offered the post to Archdeacon Johnstone, who already had proved his worth in the unusual conditions of modern Egypt. Maybe the Archdeacon himself, in spite of his modesty, thought the same! Geoffrey Fisher, conscious of an understandably disappointed candidate – he was not always over-sensitive to situations of this kind – sent him a frank but comforting letter, explaining that his name had been carefully considered but that he felt the diocese now needed 'special gifts of youth' – Geoffrey Allen was then in his middle forties! – as well as of scholarship and leadership. Also Allen had served in China. He hoped that he and the new Bishop would work 'happily' together. The Archbishop received a charming reply, assuring him that he would co-operate to the full with his new Diocesan. One basic conviction Geoffrey Allen shared with the Archbishop, namely that in ministering to scattered British Christians overseas, the various Christian denominations should work together. In his eyes such co-operation was 'visibly illustrating the principle of Christian unity'. In this respect Geoffrey Allen's ecumenicity was enthusiastic and impeccable.

There were at times, for an overseas Bishop, knotty problems concerning which he would wish to consult Lambeth. One such presented itself in the early months of 1949 when Bishop Allen received from a Greek Orthodox priest a request to be received into the Anglican Church. The reply from Lambeth was an emphatic 'no', not on strictly theological grounds but empirically on the probable consequences flowing from such an action. It was particularly important, so Dr Fisher wrote to the Bishop, that in 'the Middle East,' to quote his own words, ' nothing should be done to offend the Greek Church, the more so as the Patriarch of Alexandria, as I judge from some correspondence I have had with him, is in something of a critical and suspicious mood with regard to the Church of England'. His advice, therefore, was not to respond positively to this request.

The Archbishop gave much thought, and indeed received much counsel, as to the whole future of the Bishopric in Egypt; and was aware of talk that Iran should take over the Dioceses of Aden, Ethiopia and Eritrea. Bishop Gelsthorpe was in favour of an enlarged Diocese of the Sudan and persuaded the Archbishop into this view. Writing to A. R. Beverley, Bishop of Toronto, on this complex problem, Geoffrey Fisher confessed that there were so many possibilities that at the end of the day he felt the solution must be an ecumenical one. True the time was not yet appropriate but it might help if a group of bishops were called together to explore this possibility.

Geoffrey Fisher was constantly being made aware, even after the departure of Bishop Gwynne, that there were problems in Egypt facing the Anglican Church. The English community was dwindling and the commercial interest which they represented was equally declining. The expense of maintaining the Cathedral, acute in the days of the former bishop, did not grow less. Hence, in considering this overall situation one solution put forward with powerful advocacy was to link up Egypt with the Diocese of Jerusalem which would be in fact to restore a situation which obtained before the First World War. The Egyptian Government, so it was understood, would raise no objection provided that the 'headquarters' of the new See were not located in the state of Israel. There was quite clearly no absolutely right way of determining diocesan boundaries nor the relation of one to the other in the Middle East. The criteria were far too complex, the general situation too volatile, the future too unpredictable, to make this possible. There still remained a vestigial conviction that wherever English people were gathered there the National Church should be present to minister to them, in spite of vast distances, meagreness of numbers and financial exigencies. Along with this went a desire to keep the flag flying. Geoffrey Fisher's oft-repeated cry for an ecumenical solution to this undoubted problem though so obviously right was theologically premature. In practice it was more feasible to turn to the American Protestant Episcopal Church for help, though this had its drawbacks.

In July 1951 a group of Mediterranean bishops, through Geoffrey Fisher's initiative, met him at an important 'get-together' in Lambeth. They divided their time between the practical and the theological – if it is legitimate to make such a distinction. As to the practical, pending a future political settlement, the area of the Gaza Strip, they maintained should be put under the jurisdiction of the Bishop in Jerusalem with additional help being provided by the Bishop in Egypt. This was important since this terrain, populated by Arab refugees, was cut off from the State of Jordan. The Church Missionary Society's hospital at Gaza was the only mission still active. As far as Iran was concerned the Bishops agreed that the Christian Church there was in a precarious position but it was important for it to retain a presence.

In 1952 on the eve of his retirement, Geoffrey Allen drew up his own memorandum in which he argued strongly a basically financial case for Egypt going back to Jerusalem. He began by accepting that they were approaching the permanent end to effective British influence in Egypt. The diocese was unwieldy, stretching from Eritrea to Ethiopia. Certainly the latter could be better looked after from Khartoum or Mombasa; and as to Aden it could be transferred to Khartoum. The best way of doing this would be to announce that Egypt was to be incorporated into a Province centred upon Jerusalem pending an Anglican strategy for the Middle East as a whole. The British Ambassador, who was consulted, gave it as his opinion that he could see no difficulty in these proposals. In some respects they were not unlike those adumbrated by Geoffrey Fisher himself.

Max Warren, however, after a conversation with Bishop Allen, felt he could not support these radical re-arrangements and gave the Archbishop his reasons for rejecting them. If the state of Egypt were to acquire a real and effective independence, this could halt the present reduction of British personnel. Cairo was the intellectual capital of the Moslem world which meant that Christian scholars, perhaps encouraged by a scholar-bishop, ought to be there also. He did not believe that occasional visits to Egypt from Jerusalem by the bishop or his suffragan, or the provost or archdeacon, would prove adequate to maintain a real and living contact. He recognised that the Bishop in Egypt's ideas were largely based on considerations of finance but this factor must be considered within the priorities of an Anglican strategy for the Middle East as a whole. Geoffrey Fisher also conferred with Edward Bickersteth, Honorary Canon of St George's Cathedral in Jerusalem, with McLeod Campbell, and the Archbishop of York, who all took the view that it would be a 'gravely retrograde step not to have a Bishop in Egypt particularly because of Anglican relations with the Coptic Church'. In reporting this view to Bishop Allen, Geoffrey Fisher suggested that the Bishop should discuss this matter with his own Council, though not making any public announcement prior to his impending resignation. Geoffrey Allen duly followed this advice and found that his Diocesan Council, as might have been anticipated, wished for the continuance of the Bishopric in Egypt. This view was supported by the English Chaplaincy Board, though it added that it could give no guarantee of finding the extra finance which the maintenance of the Bishopric would entail. Bishop William Cash of Worcester was also in favour of preserving things as they were. The Bishop in Jerusalem made it abundantly clear that he was not at all willing to accept the responsibility of receiving Egypt, indeed were he to do so he would need extra episcopal assistance. At the moment he was already seeking help from one or more American clergy to minister in Haifa, Beirut, Jerusalem and the Persian Gulf.

It was clear to Bishop Allen that his proposals were unlikely to go forward, at least for the present, but in recognising this he wrote a further interesting letter to the Archbishop which in the light of subsequent history seems almost prophetic. Fundamentally he contended that the Church was shortsighted in refusing to face up to contemporary realities. Egypt, he again asserted, was no longer a dominant sphere of British interest and it was doubtful whether the United Kingdom was any longer a central power in the general politics of the Middle East. For example, British Overseas Airways was now directing its flights over other areas and the Middle East Office was moving some of its work from Cairo to Beirut. The little Arabic Church and a falling number of British residents just could not support the Bishopric. It was important, in this context, not to rely on the advice of those who think 'in terms of pre-war patterns or nostalgic longings for its return'.

Geoffrey Fisher always kept his eyes open to what was happening around him, even to reading countless memoranda. One day, in February 1951, his attention was drawn to a note in Geoffrey Allen's Diocesan Review reporting that in the previous December the Church Council had met for the first time under its new constitution. The Archbishop immediately wrote to the Bishop pointing out that he could not remember having seen a final draft of this document. Could a copy be sent to him? The Bishop replied that he had deliberately not troubled the Archbishop since the revision involved no change in the material ecclesiastical position of the diocese. It did, however, draw closer together the English and Arab-speaking members, long overdue, by giving direct representation to Egyptian clergy in outlying churches on the same basis as English chaplains. The Bishop enclosed a copy of the new constitution to which the Archbishop responded by approving it, agreeing that its terms 'set out the position very clearly and satisfactorily and meet, I imagine, all your demands'.

Archdeacon Johnstone, who originally had been passed over for Geoffrey Allen, was appointed his successor as Bishop in Egypt much to the satisfaction of British residents. The Bishop met the Archbishop at Lambeth and frankly discussed the Anglican Church in the light of the recent Suez disaster. His views on the future of the Diocese were far different from those of his immediate predecessor. As to the financial position there now seemed every hope that the diocese could become solvent. The Egyptian clergy, *mirabile dictu*, had remained loyal during the recent disturbances which encouraged the Bishop since it seemed to indicate that they could still sustain an indigenous church in this unsettled country. Relations with the Coptic Church were friendly though the tendency during the late troubles had been for them to keep clear of the Anglican Church for fear of compromising themselves politically with the Egyptian Government. It was clear that the Bishop was very much aware of what it meant for Christians to be living in the midst of an Islamic community; and that he himself was quite 'terrified' of stirring up Moslem hostility though rumours that the Egyptian Government intended to coerce Christians into an Islamic allegiance were groundless. In his view Egypt was a 'focal point' in Anglican relations with the Moslem world, and in this respect he believed that there was a very real function indeed for the Church of England in that country. Thus he hoped that the diocese would continue its separate existence: and if an agreement were to be made between the two Governments he was sure that the future could be faced with confidence.

Right relations with Moslems were increasingly regarded as of supreme importance but they were not made easier when the Anglican Church saw itself, and was so seen by others, as a Missionary Society wedded to conversion. Indeed not a few Anglican Christians had come from Islam. To many a devout Englishman, stimulated by an irresponsible press, Colonel Nasser, President of Egypt, appeared as the arch-enemy of Britain. So much was this the case that Dr Charles Malik, Foreign Minister in the Lebanon, and later a member of the World Council of Churches Central Committee, called upon the Archbishop at Lambeth. The ensuing conversation is interesting in the light of subsequent events and the abuse heaped upon Nasser, not least by Anthony Eden. Geoffrey Fisher asked him frankly what he thought of the President and he received the following illuminating reply that 'he was a simple man, quite uneducated, puritanical and motivated by Egyptian nationalism; the raising of the standard of living of the masses; deep resentment of France and Britain; and faith in the army. All his reactions could be boiled down to one of these. He disliked everything European, and fundamentally wanted to put the clock back in Egypt one hundred years before European influence came there.'

This is certainly not an unattractive portrait and carries conviction, though far removed from the stereotype caricature customarily served up for home consumption in the British press. It was essential, Malik maintained, for Britain, together with America, to work out a common policy. The prospects for Christianity in Egypt, he thought, were 'gloomy' and after Suez near impossible.

The Anglican Church was thus destined to live its life in a post-colonial era with a resurgent Islam and a West dependent on Middle Eastern oil if it were to maintain its high standard of living.

It is now appropriate, against the background of this general situation, to return to the 'get-together' at Lambeth of the Archbishop with members of the episcopate in this part of the world. He found the bishops only too conscious of their exposed position, exacerbated, so they believed, by a lack of governmental support from Britain of which they complained bitterly. Clearly the claims of Christian faith, in their view, were taken far less seriously than they used to be; but it was still important that in any public statements sent from Britain overseas Christian standards and values should be both emphasised and maintained. By so doing Britain would gain respect in her dealings with other Churches and, not least, *vis-à-vis* other faiths. They therefore asked the Archbishop to call the attention of the Foreign Office to their concern in general. Fortunately, so they allowed, very few Government officials overseas were 'openly hostile' to the Church; indeed many were its keen supporters. 'Yet,' so the bishops maintained, 'it is not so easy to feel satisfaction that officials generally give the kind of positive support to the Christian traditions of their country which the best of them would regard as necessary.' There was a time when Government officials and their subordinates were strict about Sunday observances but this was 'very much less common now'. Attendance at Sunday worship strengthened the witness of the Church in alien cultures and increased respect, particularly among Moslems. Indeed attendance at Sunday worship might well be regarded as a 'public duty' resting upon British officials overseas. There was no harm in remembering that the Church of England was an Established Church and that the Queen was the 'Supreme Governor'. Moslems were very much more influenced by a sincere practice of Christianity than by what they considered as insincere attempts to placate them.

The bishops then turned to the British Council and here they condemned its 'ludicrous attempt' to disassociate itself from a specifically Christian approach and the 'stupidities' of some junior officials in doing this. As to the British Broadcasting Corporation the bishops drew special attention to the readings from the Koran which had caused a great deal of offence to Christians living abroad. This was seen as cutting the ground from under their feet. It was not the business of the BBC to propagate the Moslem religion.

This is a remarkable document – and it is for this reason that it has been quoted at some length – representing the views of Anglican bishops, at grass roots level, working overseas in the Middle East. However, one can but suspect that they largely derived from nostalgia for a vanished age when the position of the British Raj was far different and the place of the Christian faith more significant. Also the bishops met prior to the inter-faith dialogue being considered a serious pursuit. Rather it was seen as in itself inimical to Christian evangelism.

It was left to Sir Anthony Eden to acknowledge this somewhat critical letter which he did by admitting that he found himself in general agreement with the terms of the memorandum since personal standards ought to be high. However, he felt he should to sound a note of warning. It might be that certain moral qualities were more often found in believing and practising Christians than elsewhere but he could not make this the test in selecting staff. As to personal behaviour he believed the bishops were 'unduly pessimistic'. 'Doubtless there are', he wrote, 'in any community weaker brethren; there are also men of upright character and complete integrity who are not members of the Church of England or, indeed, of any Church.' But he did not consider it to be within the option of the Foreign Service to proselytise. True, it was difficult to draw a proper line between tolerance and respect for the deeply-held belief of Moslems and others and 'falling over backwards to please them'. Perhaps it was relevant to notice that the Commonwealth was not only a Christian association of peoples but in large measure also an Islamic association. He would 'strongly deprecate any behaviour by members of the Foreign Service calculated to give religious offence to Moslems'.

It may be thought that Anthony Eden realistically got the better of this argument; and that the Archbishop was probably unwise to respond in so forthright a manner to the understandable mood of the Mediterranean bishops, many of whom were painfully aware of a declining British influence in the Middle East. Also the whole concept of mission was in process of change and was beginning to be understood in the somewhat different terms of dialogue.

CHAPTER 49

Cyprus

THE period of Geoffrey Fisher's archiepiscopate coincided with the British Government's increasing disengagement from many of its overseas commitments, the *tempo* varying according to time, place and circumstance. Britain became less and less an imperial power as former colonies achieved independence within a newly-emerging Commonwealth. This process of disengagement meant withdrawing from territories hitherto regarded as strategically important. This was true of Cyprus, the possession of which was once thought necessary to keep the highway of the Mediterranean open to British shipping.

Cyprus contained a mixed population, some eighty per cent of which belonged to the Greek Orthodox Church and looked to Greece for support; the remaining twenty per cent were Islamic and turned to Turkey as their natural ally and protector. This somewhat uneasy situation, embodying a confrontation of religions, cultures and races, was only too prone to escalate into violence. Since 1878 the island had been administered by the British Colonial Office and under Article 33 of the governing regulations the archbishopric must always be held by a Cypriot. Ordinance 34, however, gave the Governor a veto on the election of the Archbishop, an imposition which the Orthodox Church could not accept and which led to complaints going to the Colonial Office.

This veto was felt keenly by the Orthodox Church since it was traditionally subject to no external authority, its freedom from the Patriarch of Antioch being decreed as early as AD 431. Both the Patriarch of Alexandria as well as the Anglican Bishop in Jerusalem wrote to Geoffrey Fisher as soon as he went to Lambeth maintaining that the veto must go since its removal was 'long overdue'. The Archbishop immediately got into touch with the Secretary of State for the Colonies informing him that he had received 'a most moving letter' from Bishop Leontios of Paphos imploring him to do all in his power to recover an independent 'Spiritual Head' for the Greek Cypriot Church. Geoffrey Fisher was successful, in co-operation with Germanos, in reaching a 'gentlemen's agreement' by which the veto was abolished but it was agreed that no one 'utterly unacceptable' to the British Government would be elected to the office of Archbishop of Cyprus. This was a good beginning for Geoffrey Fisher.

The general state of affairs in Cyprus at the time that Geoffrey Fisher went to Lambeth was one of unsettlement and disturbance. This was due to a complex of causes derivative, in part, from the war and the privations which Cypriots had then endured; also to the high expectations which the war encouraged but which were not yet fulfilled. The Orthodox Church of Cyprus embodied and expressed the national aspirations of the Cypriot people which found its popular platform in *Enosis* – Union with Greece. Oliver Tomkins, then General Secretary of the World Council of Churches, prophesied in March 1947 that when a new Archbishop (and Synod) were elected, *Enosis* would constitute a major pre-occupation with the Cypriot Church.

It was inevitable that aggrieved Cypriots, feeling themselves or their Church victimised, should turn to Geoffrey Fisher as a person of great influence, for redress. Thus on 18 December 1945, Creech Jones, the Minister, with Lord Winster, visited the Archbishop at Lambeth when in discussion they made the following points: (1) The Church in Cyprus was going all out for *Enosis* which was a legitimate stance even if it were 'stupid' to want to unite with Greece at such a time of internal upheaval; (2) Could the Archbishop of Canterbury use his influence to encourage moderates in the Orthodox Cypriot Church to confine the agitation for *Enosis* within the law?; (3) Maybe the appeal of *Enosis* derived from a concern by the Orthodox Cypriot Church to maintain its own autonomy even if politically the island were to lose out. As so often Geoffrey Fisher consulted Herbert Waddams after this interview and received from him some practical advice, in particular that at all costs he must avoid giving the appearance that, as Archbishop, he was merely an instrument of governmental policy. Such would be damaging to his ecclesiastical prestige and influence.

Meanwhile a new Archbishop and Ethnarch of Cyprus was elected, the choice falling upon Makarios III, Bishop of Kition, who had studied earlier in Boston on a scholarship awarded by the World Council of Churches. An impressive person in appearance and style; a patriot (as Ethnarch) and Churchman (as Archbishop) he regarded the two roles as one and indivisible; it was unfortunate for him that the Colonial Office tended to see in him only a locus for violence and terrorism, almost certainly unjustly.

No ecclesiastic could have entered upon his responsibilities at a more difficult time. He was immediately confronted with an island caught up in the ambiguities of politics; in the strong appeal of *Enosis*; in the problem of the Turkish minority; and in the determination of the British Government at all costs to maintain Cyprus as a military base under the control of the Governor and Military Commander, Sir John Harding.

Makarios was not unknown to the Archbishop since they met on two occasions at Lambeth when they discussed matters generally. In

June 1955, the Archbishop wrote to him in connection with the increasing violence in the island. He expressed anxiety lest the absence of any clear statement from the Church authorities and particularly from himself as their undisputed leader might incline people to suppose that the Church was in fact supporting such outrages as had occurred. The Archbishop thus asked Makarios to give a lead by repudiating violence, to which request he received the following reply: 'I am profoundly grieved by the course events have taken in Cyprus in the last few days. Unfortunately, the serious situation which has been created here cannot be remedied by suggestions or advisory circulars.' No official condemnation by himself would find at present the desired response but would involve the risk of exposing him 'rather unprofitably'.

Referring to this reply in a debate in the House of Lords, the Archbishop commented that Makarios spoke not as a churchman called to uphold a religious principle but as a politician calculating risks and chances. One cannot but wonder whether Archbishop Fisher here was not making too easy and facile a distinction, hardly relevant in Cyprus at the time. Be this as it may, Sir John Harding had now convinced himself that Makarios so far from restraining was himself inciting violence, and after conferring with Lennox Boyd, the Colonial Secretary, and securing his approval, he dramatically deported Makarios in March 1956 to the Seychelles in the Indian Ocean. The grounds were that he had been 'deeply implicated in the campaign of terrorism' launched by Eoka, the militant wing of *Enosis*. This action came as a bombshell and introduced into an already highly charged situation a further explosion of greater intensity – and with devastating repercussions. To the Orthodox Church this was an act of sacrilege, wholly without justification, indeed a crude assertion of imperial power at its worst. The Archbishop of Canterbury was not consulted and, therefore, the news of it came unheralded as a bolt from the blue.

The newly constituted World Council of Churches which had long been concerned to bridge the gulf between the Orthodox Churches of the East and the Churches of the West was inundated at its headquarters in Geneva with cables, telegrams and letters expressing both rage and protest. The General Secretary of WCC, Visser't Hooft, on returning to Geneva 'in hopeful mood' in March 1956, having just visited Australia and New Zealand, found the office in a mood of crisis. 'The Greek Churches were reacting in the sharpest possible ways, and demanding that the World Council take immediate action.' Visser't Hooft immediately recognised the severity of the situation thus created and took the view that if the World Council were to keep silent at this moment, the solidarity between East and West which had been a keynote of the Ecumenical Movement would be shown to be 'verbal rather than real'. The customary procedure in a sudden crisis of this kind was for the chairman, vice-chairman and the General Secretary to put out a statement, but the chairman Dr Fry, was travelling in Russia and unavailable. In these somewhat exceptional circumstances Visser't Hooft decided, to quote his own words, that the General Secretary 'must put his own neck out'. He himself, therefore, issued a statement to the Press in which he made the following points: (1) That the statement was the personal view of the General Secretary; (2) That this act against the Head of an ancient Church was very deeply resented throughout the Eastern Orthodox world and that it endangered the efforts of the World Council to bring 'Eastern' and 'Western' Churches together; (3) That Christians of other Churches should express their deep sympathy with the Orthodox Church; (4) That the World Council of Churches Commission on International Affairs had already expressed in 1954 its recognition of the right and fitness of the people of Cyprus for self-determination; (5) That the deportation of Archbishop Makarios was not in line with the best traditions of British statesmanship.

The statement made by the General Secretary was well received by the Orthodox Churches, but how would it appear to British eyes? He was not long kept in doubt for on 15 March 1956 the matter was debated in the House of Lords.

Lord Winster, on behalf of the Government, stressed that the stability of Cyprus was a high priority not only for Britain but for the Grand Alliance as a whole. The Archbishop, in his speech, occupied a middle ground and sought to help the House as a whole to an understanding of the unique position which Archbishop Makarios held in Cyprus where he discharged a double role, one as Archbishop of the Orthodox Church, the other as the Ethnarch. To remove the Archbishop in this way was to injure the integrity of an ancient Church, thus preventing its living out its canonical and full life. Whatever Archbishop Makarios did, he did equally as a churchman and as politician. The tradition in Cyprus in this respect was different from that which obtained in Britain; hence the need for both Churches to understand each other. 'The British Government, therefore,' he said, 'must do a hard thing and recognise that whatever his political activities, Archbishop Makarios remains the Head of an independent Church, a religious and Christian leader, whose presence is indispensable to the proper functioning of that Church.' Yet he believed that Archbishop Makarios had put himself in the wrong by seeming to condone violence, and he concluded by making three practical suggestions on which he hoped the Governments of Greece, Turkey and Britain might all agree: (1) To appoint a competent person or persons to draw up a constitution for Cyprus which could then be discussed with Makarios; (2) For the three powers to appeal, along with the deported Archbishop, for an end to terrorism; (3) For Makarios to be assured that his exile was only temporary.

This was possibly one of the most effective speeches which the Archbishop ever delivered in the House of Lords. It was restrained but definite in its practical suggestions; it was critical of both the British Government and the Cypriots, though constructive; and it was concerned to promote reconciliation by interpreting the minds and the hopes of those bogged down in this unfortunate dispute.

After the debate, in private conversation, a noble Lord accused the Archbishop of having taken his stand firmly on both sides of the fence. 'Of course,' he replied, '[that] was my intention. You can't begin to reconcile people unless you can stand in with both of them enough to gain their confidence. I did not spare Makarios nor did I acquit the British Government.' *The Times* newspaper, in its edition of Friday 16 March, described the Archbishop's speech as 'of a quality and content which placed it in a class apart from anything which the Commons offered yesterday'.

Publicly, and in private, Geoffrey Fisher condemned the General Secretary of the World Council of Churches for his unilateral action. Something of the headmaster of former days was displayed when on 16 March a severe letter was despatched from Lambeth to Geneva which the recipient himself described as a 'rap on my knuckles', and the 'strongest reprimand I had ever had from a Head of a Church in the Council'.

Geoffrey Fisher pointed out to the General Secretary that he was precluded by his office from writing in a purely personal capacity and the effect of his having done so meant that Lambeth had received numerous telegrams which forced him to explain his own position. 'It is really intolerable', he commented, 'that I should be compelled also to justify my position to you as Secretary of the World Council of Churches.' There was, in his opinion, no need for an instant reply on the merits of the case. To Kenneth Slack, Secretary of the British Council of Churches, Archbishop Fisher admitted that his was a 'rather explosive letter' to send to Geneva. Visser't Hooft, on receiving this archiepiscopal reprimand, responded immediately by firmly, but politely standing his ground. According to extant correspondence, Visser't Hooft – it was a rare privilege – seems to have had the last word with the Archbishop in this *contretemps*. 'The raspberry is swallowed', he wrote, 'the bath is taken. Some day I hope we can have a post-mortem on this.' It does not seem that they did!

Perhaps it is understandable that some felt Geoffrey Fisher to have acted unnecessarily severely with the General Secretary, particularly since Dr Payne, a member of the World Council's Central Committee, and later a President, raised no objection to his issuing a statement.

Bishop Bell also felt that Visser't Hooft was certainly right in what he did, indeed could hardly have done otherwise – and so he informed the Archbishop.

Following Visser't Hooft's statement numerous communications came to Lambeth, one from Field Marshal Sir John Harding who was unhappy at the approach of the Archbishop and testified to this unease at a Press conference. In particular he was opposed to the suggestion of any immediate renewal of negotiations with Makarios. As a result, Geoffrey Fisher took the initiative in sending Sir John Harding a copy of his speech in the Lords so that he might read precisely what he had actually said and the context of his saying it. The Archbishop felt it appropriate to add a personal note to one who was carrying so heavy a load in Cyprus. 'May I say, finally, how deeply I sympathise with you in your hateful tasks (i.e. restoring law and order) and how much I admire the way in which you have tackled it all through.'

Cyprus, and what to do about it, had now developed into an international problem which meant that Britain, had she wished, could neither sweep it under the carpet nor treat it as a purely domestic affair. Turkey, Greece, the people of Cyprus and, of course, the Orthodox Churches were all intimately involved. On 27 March 1956, a report by Sir Kenneth Grubb and Dr O. Frederick Nolde, Chairman and Director of the Commission of the Churches on International Affairs, appeared reaffirming that (a) the United Kingdom should formally acknowledge the right of Cyprus to self-determination, and that (b) Cyprus on its part should accept an interim period for progress till self-determination was finally achieved.

One of the problems confronting Lambeth (and indeed the British Government) was the difficulty in getting at the real facts in view of the conflicting evidence which came out of the island. Thus the Archdeacon of Cyprus confessed that the link between the Orthodox Church, *Enosis*, and terrorism was very difficult to disentangle.

Letters came into Lambeth from near and far. Thus Archbishop Michael of the Greek Archdiocese of North and South America wrote on behalf of their 'Spiritual Leader', Archbishop Makarios, expressing appreciation of Lambeth's sensitivity to the 'shock and distress felt by our Church due to the drastic action of the British authorities and our failure to understand the policy behind the deportation'. Equally unsettling was a letter from the Canadian Council of Churches supporting Geoffrey Fisher's proposals for negotiation. The Council made three concrete suggestions designed to promote reconciliation and a permanent settlement: (a) That the British Government appoint an expert to draw up a constitution; (b) That the Greek and Turkish Governments be invited to join Britain in an appeal for the end of violence; (c) That Archbishop Makarios be released as soon as possible.

It became evident that the British Government was under general attack even by her friends, the gravamen of the charge brought against her being that apart from the radical step of deporting Archbishop Makarios she had done little in the way of implementing any coherent policy. The oft-repeated utterance that there could be no negotiations until violence ended and order was restored seemed singularly negative and sterile. For this reason the Archbishop while asking Satterthwaite, at that time Assistant General Secretary of the Church of England Council on Foreign Relations, to find out what concrete evidence there was for linking up Makarios with terrorism, sent to Lennox Boyd, the Colonial Secretary, an extract from Hansard which contained his speech in the Lords.

On 29 March Geoffrey Fisher sent off his first letter of any real substance to the Colonial Secretary in which he questioned whether he was right in talking of drawing up a constitution on the spot. His own suggestion was that an independent person (or persons) should undertake this, and that the finished product be negotiated with Makarios who would be required to dissociate himself from violence. Not content with his letter the Archbishop followed it up with another on 4 April 1956, striking a note of urgency. In the eyes of Greeks all over the world Britain had done a wrong thing in deporting Makarios and it was not possible to convince them otherwise by merely denying that it was so. The Colonial Secretary must give a clear indication that the British Government was intending at the earliest possible moment to heal the breach by some constructive act. 'The one fatal thing', he warned, 'is to leave the wound to fester and so grow gangrenous. You cannot yourself provide the dressing and the bandage for in the eyes of the Orthodox you inflicted the wound.'

This was strong meat but Lennox Boyd again repeated in the House of Commons that there was no question of any negotiations until law and order were restored.

So this somewhat ding-dong battle between the Archbishop and those who felt like him, and the Colonial Secretary continued. On 19 April the Archbishop was back at it again in a strong letter. 'I wonder,' he asked, 'whether you realise what has been done by Christian people to save the Government from unrestrained indignation and denunciation by a vast number of non-politically minded people.' He himself had kept on saying 'Keep quiet, the Government must be meditating some constructive step', but then the Prime Minister dashed all these hopes by repeating that the condition of any progress was the cessation of violence.

No one could have tried harder to keep the Colonial Secretary in touch with ecclesiastical opinion generally than Geoffrey Fisher. However, there were a few, and Kenneth Grubb was one of them, who believed that churchmen might be more likely to get a constructive policy by 'not prodding too much'.

On 23 April, St George's Day, the Archbishop resorted to his customary procedure of drawing up an *aide-memoire*, in this case very largely confined to reporting a telephone call from Lennox Boyd. It was not a happy or helpful exchange of views. The Colonial Secretary began by saying that Field Marshal Harding was sending him a full account of the events leading up to the deportation and reiterating how impossible Makarios was. The Archbishop had replied – on the 'phone – that this did not so much interest him as the 'dreadful failure of any action since then'. What he wanted was for negotiations to be started. If there could be conversations with Bulganin and Khrushchev, surely there was no 'insuperable obstacle' to negotiating with Makarios!

The half-yearly meeting of the British Council of Churches took place on 24–25 April when it was inevitable that Cyprus would loom large on its agenda. Geoffrey Fisher himself addressed the conference, his speech being in the main an attack, serious yet having its lighter moments, on Government policy. 'Perhaps I ought to be allowed by way of what Aristotle would call a "catharsis" or "purgation" to express a little indignation of my own, not now against anything that anyone in Cyprus or regarding Cyprus has done, but quite simply against our own Government for apparently, and as far as we are allowed to know, doing nothing constructive at all.' He himself had made suggestions six weeks ago which were welcomed by moderates in Cyprus but they were followed by complete inaction on the part of the Government.

The British Council of Churches, at this half-yearly meeting, proceeded to pass four resolutions as follows: (1) That it regretted the prevalent terrorism; (2) That it recognised the great concern of the Greek Cypriots; (3) That it commended Archbishop Fisher's proposals for immediate negotiations; (4) That it intended to maintain fellowship between Christians in Britain and those in Cyprus, Greece and Turkey.

Not unexpectedly, Lennox Boyd did not take kindly to the Archbishop's plain speaking at the BCC Conference. 'You told me', he complained 'that you were going to criticise the Government over the Cyprus policy and I told you how unfair that was: it was, however, natural for you to make your own speech.' He further accused the Archbishop of a strange inability to recognise the existence of Cabinet Government. The policy on Cyprus, directed against 'the murderous activities of the Greek Orthodox Church', was not personal to himself but approved by the Government whose collective responsibility it was.

On the whole – it by no means always happened – Archbishop Fisher was given a good press for his address to the British Council of Churches. The *Manchester Guardian* (25 April 1956) reported it under the heading 'Primate Condemns British Policy in Cyprus'. *The Times* newspaper used the caption: 'Archbishop of Canterbury's Indignation on Cyprus,' and the *Church Times* (27 April) the more explicit heading: 'Primate's Reproof of Inaction by British Government'. The *Sunday Express*, however, struck a different note in its heading: 'Head of Church and Head of State in Bitter Row over Policy to meet Cyprus Terror. Cabinet to rap Primate'.

That the Archbishop's criticisms of Government policy were taken seriously is indicated by a letter from Field Marshal Sir John Harding to Lambeth. The contents are interesting, not least in setting out at length the basis of the policy which the Field Marshal was implementing. It was his 'firm conviction' that in the present international scene 'the full use of the whole island' for military purposes was indispensable to the maintenance of British influence in the Middle East and the security of the free world. He did not believe that reconciliation could be achieved by any negotiations with Makarios whose objective was none other than to promote *Enosis*, i.e. union with Greece.

Against the background of this heated controversy, it was encouraging for the Archbishop to receive a letter from Sir Charles Peake at the British Embassy in Athens saying how much he had admired his recent utterances in the House of Lords and elsewhere, and re-affirming his belief that it would be difficult to find anyone other than Makarios with whom 'to do business in the future'.

So far in the course of his correspondence, though he was there in the background, Geoffrey Fisher had made little direct contact with the Prime Minister himself, largely because Cyprus was the great preoccupation of Lennox Boyd, the Colonial Secretary. Now, however, on 4 May Anthony Eden wrote to the Archbishop expressing frankly his views as to recent events and the Archbishop's role in them. What had distressed and disturbed him, so he complained, was that the Archbishop should have so much misunderstood the Government's policies. He equally wished for a negotiated constitution but law and order needed to come first. 'I would like to assure you', he concluded, 'that I am always at your disposal if you would like to have a talk before making a speech on this terribly thorny subject. If you had been able to do this on the present occasion I feel pretty sure that we could have avoided these misunderstandings, which I regret as much as you do.' The Archbishop, in reply, pointed out to Anthony Eden that he had in fact written to Lennox Boyd asking if there were anything in particular he might say.

This temperate letter, from the Prime Minister, obviously intended to be eirenic though it may conceal a measure of irritation, does not seem to have impressed the Archbishop over much. Three days after receiving it he wrote to Sir Charles Peake that it was saddening that in spite of the lessons of the past, the Government seemed quite incapable of 'seeing beyond the ends of their noses'.

That Cyprus constituted a great pre-occupation for the Archbishop at this time can be seen from his having interviews with Mr Noel Baker; Archbishop Athenagoras, the Bishop of Melita, the Oecumenical Patriarch's representative in Geneva; Sir Paul Pavlidis; and Visser 't Hooft. By these numerous contacts he believed himself to have won the confidence of the Greek Cypriots and was much gratified by a telegram from the Bishop of Kition, Locum Tenens of the Archbishopric of Cyprus, which read: 'We desire to express the gratitude of the Church and people of Cyprus for your proposals and speeches on the question of Cyprus in the House of Lords, and we cherish the hope that Your Grace and the Church of England will continue your insistence for a just and Christian solution to the Cyprus question'.

To this message the Archbishop replied with disarming frankness in these words: 'I am rather embarrassed by the way in which they (Cypriot leaders) look to me as, so to speak, the only saviour of the situation in sight. I have to be careful as you can understand to make suggestions to the Government in the most acceptable form. It is easy to cause them offence, and indeed I have already done so to some extent.'

That there were serious differences between the Archbishop and the Government as to the way ahead was, of course, by now public property. Maybe this was in the back of his mind when Canon Giles, Chaplain General to the Forces, wrote to the Archbishop reporting on conditions in Cyprus and affirming that the troops, and indeed the civilians there, were behind Sir John Harding in making the restoration of law and order a 'prerequisite for any negotiations'. In reply to the Chaplain General, the Archbishop did not mince his words in condemning Government policy as 'sheer folly and worse'. 'Their failure,' he wrote, 'was in psychology and elementary Christian common sense; and our troops in Cyprus have to bear the consequences.'

Geoffrey Fisher was beginning painfully to realise that though the Cyprus situation was 'deteriorating daily', any intervention by himself could be counter-productive. Thus when the British Council of Churches sought an interview with the Colonial Secretary, the Archbishop suggested that the deputation be led by Pitt-Watson, a former Moderator of the General Assembly of the Church of Scotland, since his (the Archbishop's) presence on it would antagonise the Government. He had been 'warned off' their territory or what they regarded as theirs. However, after much travail of spirit, things began to take on a more promising appearance, when the Government announced that it had entrusted the drawing-up of a constitution for Cyprus to Lord Radcliffe whom it appointed in 1956 Constitutional Commissioner for

Cyprus. He came with a rich experience behind him as Director of the Ministry of Information during the War, and as a member of the Punjab and Bengal Boundary Commission. Geoffrey Fisher was delighted, and could not refrain from saying to Pavlidis that this step was the first proposal he had made in his speech in the House of Lords. However deep emotions resulting from the killings and the deportation had cut too deeply to permit of a sudden healing. At first, Lord Radcliffe was cold-shouldered by many Cypriot leaders and as a consequence the Archbishop got into touch with the Bishop of Kition imploring him 'to speak freely' to the noble lord. Proceeding by majority vote had already been conceded, as had respect for the Turkish minority. 'All of you in Cyprus should now speak to Lord Radcliffe without prejudice', he counselled, 'saying what is in your minds.' Geoffrey Fisher also wrote to Lord Radcliffe wishing him well and evoking the reply that he was aware of the Archbishop's 'keen interest' and would visit him at Lambeth. On 25 July, some six weeks after his previous speech, the Archbishop was again on his feet in the Upper House of Parliament, concentrating on the theme of reconciliation, within the context of Lord Radcliffe's visit to the island. It was now necessary to drop controversial matters, and to avoid explosive terms such as 'self-determination'. Also it would help if everyone refrained from harping upon 'terrorism'. What they must concentrate upon was 'an instrument of self-government' to bring Archbishop Makarios back into the picture for the negotiations on the constitution. He regretted Governmental statements that violence must end before negotiations could begin. He looked forward to a liberal constitution providing for an elective majority government with safeguards for minorities.

However, all was not yet to move forward so easily as Geoffrey Fisher passionately hoped. Pavlidis spoke for more than himself when he wrote, in disillusioned mood, to the Archbishop at the end of July that he and his fellow-countrymen had lost faith in the intentions of the British Government and consequently saw little advantage in talking to Lord Radcliffe. 'It was indeed unfortunate', he wrote, 'that the latter had arrived so late on the scene and they relied on the Archbishop to bring peace to this unfortunate island through a solution that would put an end to executions, would bring Archbishop Makarios back to the negotiating table; and would be acceptable to the population.'

An anxious spectator of the scene in Cyprus was Visser't Hooft who feared its general repercussions upon the Ecumenical Movement and in particular its effect upon the relations of the Eastern Orthodox Churches with those of the West. In September 1956 he shared his feelings with the Archbishop. There was now talk of the Greek

Government moving the Patriarchate from Turkish Istanbul to the Greek Mount Athos. If this were done it would 'create an earthquake in Orthodoxy' as well as widen the gulf between the Greek and the Western Churches generally. Sensibly Geoffrey Fisher had from the beginning taken the view that he must keep Visser't Hooft informed of the state of affairs in Cyprus, though reminding him at the same time that the World Council of Churches had no 'official position' in this matter and that its task, in the main, was to 'redress the emotional overtones' which too often had bedevilled the whole crisis. Geoffrey Fisher now suggested to the Colonial Secretary that the proposed new constitution might well provide the last hope and it should be accompanied by a new offer of a truce to the terrorists.

So far as the Colonial Office was concerned if there seemed to be occasional movement it was too often offset by a corresponding reaction to immobility. Thus Lennox Boyd felt himself unable to go along with a renewal of the truce offered to the terrorists as the Archbishop suggested in his previous letter, partly because the Government must be on its guard against the tactical moves of Grivas in his promotion of Eoka. Also to negotiate with Makarios 'unrepentant and unshriven' would encourage the Greeks 'to shrug off their part of the responsibility for a solution of the international problem which was in part of their own making'. Hence he would prefer the Archbishop not to take any initiatives in suggesting talks between Cypriots and Greeks with Archbishop Makarios present. To this Geoffrey Fisher agreed. The suggestion was now put forward by the Greek Prime Minister, Karamanlis, and, it would seem, by General Eisenhower, that Makarios should return as Archbishop but not as Ethnarch, a proposal which Geoffrey Fisher was rightly quick to reject as 'not feasible', since it was quite impossible for him to detach himself altogether from his political leadership.

Against this frustrating background, the Archbishop on 10 December 1956 had a long session, at their request, with Lennox Boyd and Sir John Harding, a session which he confessed, if not productive, was 'friendly throughout'. As a lead-in Geoffrey Fisher put to them the heart-searching question, namely, was the situation in Cyprus getting worse? If that were the case how did they intend to launch the constitution?

After a preliminary skirmish the Field Marshal admitted, in respect of the first question that the situation was deteriorating and the delay in agreeing the constitution had increased this. Also he had been given inadequate military equipment to secure law and order but in spite of this he had 'slogged away' at suppressing terrorism – but had done little else. It was clear, so Geoffrey Fisher recorded in a private memorandum, that Lennox Boyd – and this, certainly, was not to his discredit – was emotionally disturbed at the deaths of British soldiers. Lord Radcliffe's constitution would become law, so the Archbishop was informed, through an Order in Council but once promulgated no further emendations could be made. But what about Makarios, Geoffrey Fisher asked? 'I argued', he records, 'that they should ask the Greek Government to sound Makarios before its publication. This they resisted fiercely saying that the Turks would "go through the roof" if Makarios were made partner to the negotiations.' Clearly, neither Lennox Boyd nor Sir John were prepared to make any approach to Makarios beforehand. The procedure to be followed was an announcement in the House of Commons that a copy of the constitution had been sent to Archbishop Makarios in the Seychelles and to the Cypriot leaders. Would they, Dr Fisher then asked, be allowed to confer? At this point Lennox Boyd and Field Marshal Harding looked at each other but there was no positive response. His own impression was that they were 'terrified' of the Turks and seemed to dismiss Makarios as 'irrelevant'. Nor had they thought in terms of world opinion. Recalling this interview a week later the Archbishop told Kenneth Slack that Lennox Boyd 'talked far too much and it was difficult to pin him down'. However, he felt that he did get home to them that if their new proposals were to have any possible chance of success they must arrange for direct consultation between the Cypriot leaders and Makarios.

A week after this interview, indeed on Christmas Day, Lennox Boyd wrote to the Archbishop in his own handwriting letting him know that he was off to Greece and Turkey to discuss the constitution with their two Governments.

So the days went by with an unhappy and frustrated Archbishop regretful, almost resentful, at the lack of progress. He took comfort, however, from the thought that something might happen when in 1957 Sir Anthony Eden, for health reasons, gave way to Mr Harold Macmillan as Prime Minister. The Archbishop did not defer long before writing to the new occupant of Number 10 Downing Street expressing his concern and 'increasing alarm at the general situation in Cyprus'. In his view it was now dominated by the Turks who were talking in ruthless terms of the Greeks and Cypriots. The constitutional problem was the most important and he would suggest that Sir John Harding should now be replaced by a civil administrator, aided by a competent soldier. The coming of a new Prime Minister provided the opportunity for a fresh start. Perhaps he himself (Geoffrey Fisher) might usefully act as a mediator between the Prime Minister and Archbishop Makarios?

It cannot be said that Mr Macmillan responded to this offer with any enthusiasm, nor did he accept the Archbishop's analysis of the present situation. The Turks, he said, had in fact accepted self-determination for both communities.

In April 1957 Cyprus came up again for discussion in the House of Lords. The Archbishop confessed during the debate that he did not see himself in the position of a judge but as a reconciler, particularly in view of the close link between the Church of England and the Greek Orthodox Church. It was right to expect four things: (1) that Makarios act with restraint; (2) that international matters concerning Cyprus be referred to NATO – the North Atlantic Treaty Organisation; (3) that progress be made in implementing Lord Radcliffe's constitution; (4) that resort to partition should be seen as a 'final and total failure'. Lord Radcliffe's proposed constitution – a valiant effort to be fair to the various groups involved – was at last completed with the result that Archbishop Fisher wrote immediately to Makarios urging him to accept it as a basis for discussion, and giving him the reason why he believed the recommendations to be 'wise and fair'. He therefore invited the Cypriot Archbishop to give him his own reactions.

Geoffrey Fisher had consistently recognised the unique status of Makarios in Cypriot life, politically as well as religiously, and had made himself unpopular by maintaining to the British Government that he must not be ignored nor treated other than in his double capacity. However, it seems that even Geoffrey Fisher – there were press reports that Makarios had rejected Lord Radcliffe's proposals – was growing a little disillusioned with the Ethnarch. To Bishop Parfitt of Madagascar he wrote of Makarios in near desperation as follows: 'He is so vain in his fanaticism that I think he welcomes publicity and then misuses it to the utmost. It is a tragedy that he should now be throwing away the future peace and wellbeing of his own island and of his own people, but there it is.' Whatever views might be taken of Makarios by non-Cypriots – he was released from the Seychelles in March 1957 – his popularity with his own people remained unabated. Thus Mr Phedias Doukaris, of the Ethnarchy of Cyprus, encouraged by Geoffrey Fisher's speech in the House of Lords, waited on him at Canterbury asking him four questions: (1) when could discussions start with Archbishop Makarios?; (2) what was the next step?; (3) could Makarios come to London?; (4) would self-determination be now pursued?

Geoffrey Fisher replied to these key questions by saying that this depended on Archbishop Makarios's own approach and his not repeating his former mistakes. At the moment the Turkish voice carried more weight. Self-determination would not be secured by force and in any negotiations NATO and Turkey must be taken into account.

The Archbishop felt that the time had now come, without fear or favour, to let Makarios have his own reaction to the latter's reported rejection of Lord Radcliffe's constitution. This he did on 18 June 1957, prefacing his remarks with the assurance that he was 'anxious to do anything within his power to help towards a final settlement of the Cyprus situation'. It was for this reason that he had urged him to accept the constitution as a basis for discussion. If ever self-determination were to be seriously considered then it must be based on the constitution which Lord Radcliffe had produced. Hence, he invited Makarios to give his view on the constitution since it was only in the popular press that he recently learnt of his turning it down. 'I must not hide my opinion from you', he wrote, 'that your action in this respect was not wise . . . naturally it is not for me to do more than give the advice of a friend, but I shall be doing less than my duty if I do not tell you that help from friends in England can only be based on full and frank exchange of information.'

In thus writing, Geoffrey Fisher realistically recognised that a *sine qua non* of success in these difficult deliberations must be a co-operative Makarios, such was his high standing among his own people. Hence in January 1958 he drew up a draft letter which contained a passionate personal appeal to him to eschew any resort to violence which only led to 'more violence, more deaths, more wounds, more suffering'. Could he not now 'make an act of pure Christian witness?'; and give the utmost possible help to the new Governor, Sir Hugh Foot, who was 'determined to reach the best possible solution which will enable peace and security to return'. However, this letter was not sent to Makarios on the advice of the cautious Waddams.

On 28 February 1958, Mr Doukaris of the Cyprus Ethnarchy, just back from Athens, called in at Lambeth conveying a message from Archbishop Makarios which made two points: (1) he was alarmed at the British Government's statement concerning a possible partition and the setting up of a Turkish section; (2) he was convinced that the only way forward was direct negotiations between the British Government and representatives of the people of Cyprus, but not bringing in either Turkey or Greece. To this Geoffrey Fisher retorted that there could be no settlement which did not involve Turkey with its NATO associations and Greece, though the Cypriots could expect a large measure of self-government.

The Archbishop of Canterbury was not the only member of the episcopate of the Church of England concerned with the situation in Cyprus. On 1 March 1958 that doughty champion of human rights, Bishop Bell, had an hour's conversation with the King of the Hellenes and Queen Frederika in the royal palace at Athens and later sent a report on this encounter to Lambeth. England, the King felt, had constantly failed to 'deal rightly' with Cyprus. Self-government without self-determination was bound to breed mistrust.

Geoffrey Fisher, according to long and established custom, now sent an invitation to Makarios, as head of an ancient Orthodox Church, to attend the Lambeth Conference of 1958 as an observer. There was nothing exceptional in this since Makarios's predecessors had received a like courtesy and to exclude him would, therefore, appear as an act of discrimination on purely political grounds. Before doing so the Archbishop sent Waddams to the Foreign Office letting it know his intention. On first hearing this news and lest he might be a 'little unbalanced in this matter' Lennox Boyd consulted two very senior civil servants on whose judgement he felt he could reply. One replied: 'Words fail me' and the other: 'If this could be published in the General Assembly now meeting in Edinburgh the proposal for Bishops in Presbytery would have shorter shrift than it seems likely to receive'. In a letter of protest sent to the Archbishop by the Colonial Secretary on 22 May he wrote sharply that it was difficult to believe that the Archbishop of Canterbury 'could be blind to the sort of misrepresentation to which the marked paragraph of his letter is liable'.

Such a direct challenge to the Archbishop's authority in an area domestic to the Anglican Communion could not, so Geoffrey Fisher thought, be allowed to pass unchallenged. What was important, he wrote was not the terms of the invitation but the invitation itself. If the Government had not wished him to send one, there was plenty of time to tell him in which case he would have refrained from doing so. (Waddams thought this admission a great mistake.) Both Sir William Hayter of the Foreign Office, and Sir Hugh Foot confirmed that they understood this was a purely ecclesiastical matter. Fortunately the Prime Minister, as befitted his liberal temperament, was more restrained in his reaction to the invitation than the Colonial Secretary, and assured the Archbishop that he acquitted him of any charge of deliberately causing him embarrassment. He also appreciated that the Foreign Office had early knowledge of the invitation.

Informed and responsible opinion within the Church of England was certainly behind the Archbishop in this matter. The Church of England Council on Foreign Relations issued a statement coming down firmly in support of the Archbishop.

This, alas, was the kind of controversy in which the press feel free to indulge a subliminal anti-clericalism. Criticism of Geoffrey Fisher in certain sections was certainly hostile in the extreme. The *Sunday Times*, asserted that he had 'seriously disturbed many Christian men and women in the country'; and *The Times* that he had 'deeply embarrassed and displeased the Government'. Among the popular Press, the *Daily Express* launched a bitter invective against the Archbishop. So severe were some of the attacks that Geoffrey Fisher seriously contemplated holding his own Press conference to rebut them but Waddams wisely persuaded him against this on the grounds that it was no good trying to get the truth published in certain sections of the press. Geoffrey Fisher, however, felt very keenly the attacks upon him, which induced him to make a statement in the Church Assembly outlining the course of events. Meanwhile, Archbishop Makarios sent a letter to Lambeth intimating diplomatically that other duties made it impossible for him to be present at the Conference – a reply which gave Geoffrey Fisher 'great relief' as well as saving the Orthodox Archbishop from personal embarrassment.

Sometimes Geoffrey Fisher was accident-prone, very largely because he could do things on the spur of the moment and was an open not a subtle personality. Nothing could have proved more unfortunate at so sensitive a time than the Archbishop's appearance 'live' on a popular programme when in response to a question, he described Makarios as a 'low character'. Archbishop Athenagoras, a friend of the Archbishop, immediately rang up Lambeth in a state of great indignation accusing Geoffrey Fisher of uttering a 'public insult'. Dr Fisher realised the possible serious consequences of this incident and consulted John Satterthwaite. The result was the dispatch of the following telegram which shows evident signs of great embarrassment: 'Archbishop Makarios ecclesiastical office highly honoured by me. My remark especially precluded reflections on his personal character. Criticism confined strictly to certain political aspects. Sincerely regret use of unpremeditated phrase liable to give offence. Earnestly pray that ecclesiastical brotherhood may remain unimpaired'. The telegram was also issued to the Press.

The World Council of Churches, against the background of its ecumenical commitment, by no means lost interest in Cyprus and its politico-ecclesiastical affairs. In January 1959 it sent a delegation to the island which was disturbed to find the Orthodox Church there devoting so much of its energies to the realisation of its political goals. Visser't Hooft explained to Geoffrey Fisher that the World Council of Churches' visit was fraternal in character; and he stressed the significance of the return of Makarios as the only man who could give effective leadership.

Long-drawn-out political controversies, affecting intimately the life of nations, tend to end suddenly only to be resurrected after their solutions cease to satisfy. It was much like this with Cyprus. Finally, in February 1959 an agreement was concluded by Greece, Turkey and the United Kingdom under which Cyprus was to become independent, though the UK retained sovereignty over the areas containing the military bases. Against the background of these momentous events the hitherto unexpected happened and Archbishop Makarios was received by Geoffrey Fisher in Lambeth Palace where they talked intimately with each other for nearly an hour.

The Press release simply describes them as discussing the welfare of the Church of Christ and its furtherance of the Kingdom of God. For both of them – Makarios was unaccompanied apart from security guards – it must have been an occasion full of memories of past days and of expectations, *dei gratia*, to be realised in the future. Geoffrey Fisher writes that before he had time to address him Makarios took the initiative saying 'we must not look back'. The Archbishop responded by assuring him that he was pleased to have this opportunity of a personal, private and informal talk. He reminded him that the Prime Minister had said that all were victorious; but Makarios thought it equally appropriate to say that all had been defeated since everyone had to make great sacrifices, but that was as it should be. Geoffrey Fisher then asked Makarios whether he was satisfied about the future. This led him to say that he would return to Cyprus full of hope that this island would be a 'model' for the world based on justice. He confessed frankly that he had misgivings as to whether the constitution would work, and was not happy with the arrangements for setting up a military headquarters, with Greeks, Turks, British and Cypriot soldiers scattered about the island to implement the tripartite agreement. He thought it might do more harm than good, a view which, privately, Geoffrey Fisher himself thought possible. When asked about his own personal position, Makarios replied that his great ambition was to get out of politics altogether and to devote himself to the Church and its needs but this would not be possible immediately. Geoffrey Fisher agreed that inevitably Makarios must be the first President – he was elected to this office on 14 December 1959 – though he hoped it would be more on the French than on the American model. In March 1961 Cyprus joined the Commonwealth. Archbishop Fisher spoke of the Suez crisis and the shame that many in Britain had felt at this crude reassertion of imperialism, though fortunately the Government had realised its mistake and had finally handed the matter over to the United Nations. He also hoped that Makarios would be able to give the Church in Cyprus a 'spring clean' and he pledged the willingness of the Church of England to help this process in any way open to it. In particular Geoffrey Fisher raised the possibility of renewing the 1931 Anglican/Orthodox Conversations and was pleased when Makarios replied that he would be only too happy to co-operate.

Archbishop Fisher ended his long account of this interview with these words: 'He looked tired: he looked as though he had taken this matter, which was both a beating and a victory, in a really constructive spirit. He was not as he had been before, smooth and in his shell: one got the feeling that one was talking to a man who was thinking and open to listening.'

There were still matters, however, relating to the negotiations which had yet to be finalised and freely accepted, but the constitutional politicians had now taken over and Geoffrey Fisher admitted that he was 'only a spectator of the present negotiations'.

To the Colonial Secretary he observed that there was a real danger from 'niggling processes of bargaining when an open uncalculating gesture of generosity would transform the problem'. John Profumo of the Foreign Office and later Secretary of State for War, complained to Archbishop Fisher that eight square miles was not enough for 'necessary military installations and facilities'.

Makarios's own position, in the process of his taking over, was certainly no easy one opposed as he was by the Communists and having his difficulties with Grivas. It was understandable that the discussion over the bases, which Makarios maintained should be placed under Cypriot control, was protracted and therefore deeply worrying to Geoffrey Fisher. When a *Times* leader accused Makarios of 'obstinacy' the Archbishop of Canterbury commented to the Colonial Secretary that maybe the delay might be 'equally due to our obstinacy'. The British Government, in his view, had no moral right to cling to the bases at all. The Archbishop was to have one more opportunity of participating in a debate in the House of Lords (2 June) when he reiterated that the leading political figure in Cyprus, Makarios, was himself the Head of a Church with which the *Ecclesia Anglicana* had ecumenical relations. This did not mean that he himself approved all Makarios's attitudes but as Primate of All England he must be concerned 'to preserve to the utmost of his power friendly relations with the Cypriot Church and its Archbishop'. He went a long way towards doing this.

Many were the telegrams of mutual congratulations which were exchanged on Independence Day. Undoubtedly that which gave Geoffrey Fisher greatest satisfaction came from Archbishop Makarios himself: 'Deeply moved by your kind message on the occasion of proclamation of Cyprus Republic. I convey to you cordial thanks for your interest in Cyprus which I greatly appreciated and send to you my best and brotherly wishes.'

Geoffrey Fisher ceased to be Archbishop of Canterbury in 1961 and died before the Greek-inspired coup on 15 July 1974 which deposed Archbishop Makarios. This was followed by Turkey invading the island which led eventually to partition.

PART NINE:

THE FAR EAST

CHAPTER 50

Pakistan, India and Hong Kong

GEOFFREY Fisher had travelled far and wide throughout the Anglican Communion and as the time for his retirement drew ever nearer he was made sadly aware that there were still some Churches which he had not yet come to know at first hand. Chief among these were those situated in the Far East. Thus when Dr Yashiro, the Presiding Bishop of the Anglican Church in Japan, invited the Archbishop to fulfil a long deferred ambition to visit him, as Primate of All England and senior bishop of the Anglican Communion, he accepted with alacrity, not least because there were other Churches he could call in upon while out East.

Politically the sub-continent of India was now partitioned into two sovereign, independent states both within the Commonwealth – India largely Hindu though seeing itself as religiously neutral; Pakistan mainly Moslem and proud of its Islamic inheritance. (The cost of this partition was civil war and the loss of half a million lives.) Hong Kong remained a Crown Colony but was separated by only a chain of hills from the People's Republic of Communist China. Japan was painfully yet successfully lifting itself out of the miasma of defeat after the terrible events of Hiroshima and Nagasaki. With American aid it was now seeking to achieve a democratic, industrial and capitalist society. Korea was divided by the boundary of the 38th parallel across which Communist and non-Communist forces glared at each other in an uneasy peace.

The dominant mood in the Far East was one of strong antipathy to colonial rule linked to a longing among ordinary people for a better and more fulfilled life, freed from disease, hunger and squalid deprivation. Over-population, untapped natural resources, exacerbated by droves of political refugees – these constituted an ever-present and seemingly insoluble problem. It was against the background of this challenging situation and in a mixed religious environment that the Christian Church had to live its life and witness to its faith. The Archbishop had long committed himself to the view that the Anglican Church, wherever it existed geographically, so far as practically possible must be indigenous in its leadership and in its cultural and religious expression even if it would continue for some years to need help from the West, particularly from America.

Geoffrey Fisher had welcomed the fact of India's independence though grieved at its attendant circumstances. During the war years the leaders were imprisoned but as soon as hostilities ceased they emerged to continue the struggle. The situation for the Anglican Church was difficult and the Bishop of Lahore wrote a pathetic letter to Geoffrey Fisher telling of the murders, arson and looting going on around him. The Archbishop was foremost in heading an appeal for aid, so desperately needed, commending it in a letter to *The Times* newspaper, and lunching with Lady Mountbatten to find out more fully the grim facts of the situation.

When at the end of 1946 Pandit Nehru came to England for negotiations with the British Government, the Archbishop invited him, to meet a few friends at the Savoy Hotel which unfortunately proved impossible. However he sent a letter to Nehru – also to Jinnah – which deserves quotation: 'I would like to let you know how earnestly Christian people in this country are praying for you and all concerned in the present discussions. Upon all of you rest the making of a decision fraught with life or death not only for India but for the world.' He then went on: 'Great differences can only be healed by trust and by all not only giving trust but showing themselves to be deserving of trust . . . All this may mean compromise, but in truth compromise is not merely a political device but an expression of that trust of which I spoke.'

As a prelude to his Far Eastern tour, Geoffrey Fisher corresponded both with the Foreign Office and Lennox Boyd, the Minister for the Commonwealth, advising them of his plans and seeking their help in informing Ambassadors and in securing visas. This help was gladly given.

(i)
Pakistan

The Archbishop and Mrs Fisher accompanied by Canon Sansbury, left London Airport on Palm Sunday in 1959 and after a comfortable flight, though held up for some hours in Rome, arrived in Karachi at 2.30 am the next morning. In spite of the lateness of the hour they were met by the Deputy High Commissioner, the Assistant Bishop of Karachi and a hundred members of the local Christian community who loaded them with the traditional garlands of flowers. Early in the morning the Archbishop preached in Holy Trinity Church, destined to become the cathedral of the new diocese of Karachi. During the course of his sermon he contrasted the arduous journeys of St Paul with the speed and comfort of his own travels. The Church of England, he said, had sought to give to her daughter churches what she had long prized in her own inheritance. It was now up to them to find a way to express the same eternal gospel, in terms of their own culture, remembering that simplicity was central to the whole Anglican tradition.

Geoffrey and Rosamond Fisher then called on the President of Pakistan. It was the season of Ramadan when Moslems fast from sunrise to sunset and this prevented his being able to entertain them at an official lunch. They found Government House, from within, as impressive as were its beautifully tended gardens from without. They noted the President's western appearance, being attracted by his friendly manner. Mrs Fisher was delighted to learn that her brother had been his Commanding Officer when the President served in the Forces of the Crown many years earlier.

The Archbishop's party left Karachi in a Viscount for Lahore, passing over the Great Sindi Desert and catching glimpses of vast irrigational schemes, a legacy of Imperial rule. Much in Lahore fascinated the Archbishop and Mrs Fisher, not least the kaleidoscopic methods of transport in its thronged streets in which camels condescended to pull vehicles of all sorts, shapes and sizes; donkeys, in lower profile, doing their stint in pairs; and erratic cyclists vying with each other to make this crowded city, as Mrs Fisher put it, 'more terrifying than London'.

On the next day the Archbishop and Mrs Fisher were showered with rose petals as they walked to the Cathedral of the Resurrection along a red carpet covered with a white drugget. On this occasion the Archbishop administered the Sacrament to over three hundred people after which he and Rosamond lingered chatting easily and informally to all and sundry among the Church members. The Archbishop got the impression that they were an alive community and growing rapidly. Also recruitment of ordinands was on the increase and missionaries from Australia and New Zealand were serving happily under Pakistani priests. The Archbishop went on to the United Theological Seminary at Guj Ranwala where he spoke to the students on Church unity, suggesting what they themselves might do to promote it. In the afternoon they met the Governor of West Pakistan who was a graduate of St John's College, Cambridge, and especially interested in the prime need for a more widely distributed irrigational system, having chaired, at one stage in his career, an agricultural commission. A rally followed in the cathedral grounds when the Archbishop shook hundreds of hands and was greeted enthusiastically as 'Archbishop of Canterbury Zindabad!' which inspired him to reply: 'Pakistan Zindabad; Lahore Zindabad!' In his sermon he spoke enthusiastically of what he had seen of their Church life but confessed to being made forcefully aware of the tremendous problems facing Pakistan as, for example, the divide between East and West; the teeming mass of refugees; the disputes with India over Karachi; and, not least, sheer downright poverty. He was heartened, however, by their bishops' determination, in spite of these difficulties and challenges to lead a Church 'intent on mission'.

Of the visit to Pakistan, Canon Sansbury, who saw it at first hand, writes: 'The Archbishop's apostolic love and care for all the Churches, his unaffected friendliness and his concern for individuals won a natural response of sympathy and affection'. One priest commented: 'This is an historic occasion to have an Archbishop of Canterbury visiting Pakistan. We shall remember it for many years.' 'No', replied a layman standing near by, 'we shall remember it all our lives.'

Reflecting later in St Margaret's Church, Westminster, on his stay in Pakistan the Archbishop said: 'I found a military dictatorship (Ayub Khan) in office which had only one interest, a moral interest, to abolish corruption, to tackle problems in honesty and do the works of justice. Its spiritual purpose was appreciated and was bearing fruit'. Was this an over-optimistic, or indeed a true if simplistic diagnosis?

(ii)
India

The Archbishop and Mrs Fisher arrived at Dumdum Airport, Calcutta, the capital of West Bengal, at 11.00 am on Maundy Thursday where they were met by Bishop A. N. Mukerjee the Metropolitan of India, Pakistan, Burma and Ceylon, and the Deputy High Commissioner accompanied by their wives. Calcutta with its teeming six million inhabitants, its sacred river the Ganges swollen with the rains at the time of the Archbishop's visit, and unique in India, impressed the Archbishop as a city of vivid contrasts. There were fine, broad avenues and narrow streets; modern air-conditioned offices cheek by jowl with ramshackle huts; high-powered American limousines competing with bullock carts, rickshaws and wayward cyclists. Calcutta, a port and commercial centre, formerly the seat of the Imperial Government, was still the administrative centre of West Bengal. The city had a residential British population of some eight thousand, in the midst of whom there was located the Cathedral of the Metropolitical Province of India, Pakistan, Burma and Ceylon. As they drove from the airport to the city the Archbishop looked out upon a scene of devastating poverty such as he had never witnessed before. He long remembered the impact made upon him and later recalled it in these words: 'there were the pavements on each side . . . covered with men, women and children whose only home was on the pavements. They lived there, they were born there and they died there – it was a ghastly thought and goodness knows how it could ever be tackled or cleansed.' Mrs Fisher wrote to her children that 'Calcutta interested us greatly, the *hordes* of people walking aimlessly about – the cows strolling or lying where they will – the little children behind, sluicing water over themselves from street pumps'. Both the Archbishop and Mrs Fisher expressed surprise that

Calcutta had retained so many monuments erected during the days of the British Raj, not least the huge memorial to Queen Victoria, flanked by that almost legendary figure, her Viceroy, Lord Curzon, bowing respectfully before her. 'Some nations', the Archbishop commented, 'would have pulled down all the statues of British soldiers and administrators. Not India. There they stand, evidence that India can appreciate history and can accept with generous appreciation legacies of the British rule, and then can still trust Britons who go in humility to serve India before themselves.' Exaggerated testimony, maybe, but not entirely undeserved.

The Archbishop, on the first afternoon, began with the inevitable Press conference, followed by a courtesy call on the Governor of West Bengal – a most remarkable woman, daughter of a former poetess, one of Gandhi's disciples and fellow writers. She spoke at length to the Archbishop of the refugee problem which had then grown to the almost astronomical proportion of over four millions. He lunched with his 'dear friend', the Metropolitan of India, though he did not regard him as a particularly inspiring leader. He was received by the High Commissioner whom he had met many years earlier in Germany just after the end of the war: he also called on the Chief Minister, Dr B. C. Roy.

The Archbishop and Mrs Fisher were certainly kept busy. A visit to St John's and the old mission church dating back to the days of Warren Hastings filled Mrs Fisher with compassion for a somewhat 'pitiful group of Anglo-Indians, painfully learning how to integrate themselves with the new India'. On Good Friday the Archbishop testified to his ecumenical spirit by attending a service in the Armenian Church and giving what an admirer described as a 'superb address', which, in its emphasis on reconciliation, may have helped that community to resolve some of its internal difficulties.

On the next day the Archbishop and Mrs Fisher moved in an environment where signs of Britain's imperial past, with its inevitable Christian mission, were very much in evidence. There the young people laid on a special event for the Fishers' benefit. Mrs Fisher writes: 'we started by going to a rally of representative children from two diocesan schools. It was held in the grounds of the larger. This was a country estate formerly belonging to a merchant of the East India Company. Many schools cater for Anglo-Indian children and some of them are quite fair-haired and blue-eyed. They are very poor, many of them, and the diocese gives bursaries to enable them to be educated.' The rally concluded with the usual tea and presents. Later in the afternoon they were entertained at a civic reception by the Mayor, Alderman and Councillors of Calcutta. As the Archbishop entered the council chamber he had the unusual experience of being accosted by a

European who whispered in his ear that apart from the Mayor himself, the Council was 'as corrupt as could be'. The Archbishop was somewhat taken aback since he was due to make a complimentary speech and such information disturbed him as to its truth or falsity. As it was he managed to reconcile integrity and courtesy without offence. 'Two hundred years ago', he began, 'England was riddled with corruption but now, thank God, we've improved, and now the standard of public life is high.' Mrs Fisher was still apprehensive as to possible repercussions in the Press on what she felt was quite a 'dangerous topic', particularly as the Archbishop spoke 'freely' and was a guest. She was relieved when some councillors expressed their keen appreciation of the Archbishop's address.

In spite of a stomach infection due to the heat, Geoffrey Fisher carried out his full programme on Easter Sunday, preaching and celebrating Holy Communion in Bishop's College, and following this up by delivering a sermon in the cathedral to a packed congregation, for whose benefit it was translated, phrase by phrase, by a Bengali 'with a vigour and a fire and an impressiveness', so the Archbishop commented, 'which my little effort by itself did not possess'. In the evening he relaxed in the company of a few devoted Old Reptonians! This kind of 'get-together' had now established itself as a normal, almost ritual performance while he was on his travels. Monday 30 March proved to be almost the busiest during his stay in Calcutta. It included celebrating in St Paul's Cathedral early in the morning; attending a display of Indian dancing; visiting a number of churches; lunching with the Deputy High Commissioner; enjoying himself and entertaining others at a garden party in the grounds of the Cathedral – all this ending with evensong enlivened by massed bands, and a Hammond organ!

The following day the Archbishop and Mrs Fisher were at Barrackpore formerly a great Army headquarters and still a transit camp for the Gurkhas. After presiding at the Eucharist in the Cathedral of St Bartholomew, where he dedicated a stone seat sent over from Canterbury, he addressed the diocesan clergy at Bishop's House and called in on the Oxford Mission. Wednesday, their last day, was a relaxed one and they had time to embark upon a trip on the river – 'a most delightful and interesting experience, going about four miles up and then back'. They were intrigued with the bathers ceremonially cleansing themselves in the sacred waters – and the many temples that they passed *en route*.

It had been a strenuous time in an India where never far below the surface were signs of a political situation which was to affect the future of the Congress Party following upon the death of Nehru. It was the refugee problem, however, which caused Geoffrey Fisher most anxiety and great distress. 'The problem has to be seen to be believed', he wrote, 'and only a part can be seen. But it is appalling enough. How can they be provided with homes, work, food, a purpose in life? With many other problems pressing, not least China across the Border and in Tibet, how is India to provide work where there is none, or homes where there are none, or a purpose when the community has no purpose for you. No one can avoid this ghastly problem in Calcutta, and any answer must be slow and partial.'

The Archbishop was objective enough to suspect that the future of Christianity in India, though Hindus recognised its contribution to the spiritual life of the nation as a whole, must be regarded as uncertain. Whenever he had the opportunity,the Archbishop spoke to the leaders of other denominations concerning the Anglican attitude to reunion, thus going some way to placate the ill-will occasioned by decisions at the Lambeth Conference concerning the scheme for North India. Perhaps, more immediately important, the Archbishop's visit had encouraged, by his personal warmth and obvious sense of fellowship with them, Christians in India who, with their compatriots, were finding life by no means easy in a changing world. Undoubtedly there was a 'growing prejudice' in Indian Government circles against foreign missions which manifested itself in preventing clergy from proselytizing in the bazaars which had been their custom. The result was that both Bishop Roberts of the Society for the Propagation of the Gospel and the Bishop of Calcutta proposed that Geoffrey Fisher should lodge a formal complaint to Pandit Nehru, Prime Minister of India. However, the Archbishop and the Metropolitan of India were strongly opposed to such an action, particularly as missionaries were still perfectly free to go into the schools and to undertake other duties for which the indigenous native clergy were not yet equipped. Indeed to quote from a letter of the Metropolitan to Lambeth: 'the English missionaries get on perfectly all right as it is' and an approach to the Minister might lead to their being 'limited far more than they are now'. Geoffrey Fisher concurred and no action was taken. He was usually on the side of restraint – and leaving well alone.

It must have come as a great satisfaction to Geoffrey Fisher on his return to England to receive a long letter from Malcolm McDonald paying tribute in particular to the significance of his visit to India. The following extract deserves quotation: 'Your visit to India and all you said and did during that hot and humid week, gave immense pleasure and satisfaction to so many people both Christian and non-Christian. You have greatly helped us in our task of maintaining and developing friendships and understanding between the United Kingdom and India – and in maintaining our Faith'.

(iii)
Hong Kong

On 1 April the Archbishop and Mrs Fisher left Calcutta for Hong Kong. On their arrival they were given a warm welcome by a large party of clergy including Bishop Hall and, after a Press conference, they left for the episcopal house some ten miles distant in the hills where they found the scenery spectacular and deeply satisfying. On the next day the Archbishop was kept busy calling on the Governor, spending the morning with churchmen and visiting St John's College. In the evening the Fishers were entertained to dinner in Government House – all 'very formal and correct'. 'Really it is incredible', commented Mrs Fisher, 'that men can still be found who are so pukka. This one is an extreme case but he is a very good Governor.'

In Hong Kong the Archbishop preached at the cathedral in the morning and later at a diocesan service. It was clear from the text of these sermons that Geoffrey Fisher, once again, was appalled by the social conditions which he saw around him. 'Here in Hong Kong and elsewhere in Asia', he reflected sadly, 'the pressing problem is not to distribute the world's goods evenly, but to get enough of them to meet a human situation nearly out of control.. . . Elsewhere the standard of living is seen by comparison to be fat and prosperous and well liking.' However, he did not allow this preoccupation to prevent his visit being one of real joy and in his cathedral sermon he assured his congregation that he had been caught up into the shared glory of their faith and fellowship. Embarking upon more controversial ground he referred to the poverty of Christian witness, consequent upon 'taking an un-Christian part in national ambitions and rivalries and hostilities'. Also he deplored 'internal ecclesiastical conflicts in which Christians allow their own passions to break the unity of the Holy Spirit and the bond of God's peace'. But, in reverse, Christians in every continent were now being drawn together in a movement towards reconciliation to which the World Council of Churches was bearing a 'potent witness'. 'So my brethren', he concluded, 'I greet you. Our conditions of life, our experiences, our background of historical circumstances are utterly different. But we can talk in our language of worship; we can sing the same spiritual songs; we can for a very brief moment love one another because we all love the brotherhood and honour all men.'

The Archbishop was, on the whole, greatly impressed with what he saw during his short stay in Hong Kong, some may suspect excessively so since his assessment was based on too small a sample of its collective and total life. He found in its people much that was 'vivid (and) colourful' a 'happy life everywhere', indeed an example of colonization at its best 'in which two communities, Chinese and British, were living their own lives but each respecting and trusting the other'. He admired the tremendous effort which the Government was making to deal effectively with the 'incredible problem of over-population in a confined space in contrast with what was being attempted in Calcutta. True, there were shacks on the pavements and hillsides in Hong Kong, but these were offset by the construction of great blocks of flats.' The future prospects seemed brighter.

Church life in Hong Kong, its vitality and energy – he always admired these – particularly the social and evangelistic work undertaken by many priests made a lasting impression. It was a matter of great regret for him that he could not visit the Anglican Church in China on the mainland. However, he assured Bishop Chen of Shanghai of his concern for them and that the Church in China would be much in his thoughts and prayers on his return.

The Reverend Freddie Temple – he was Dean of St John's Cathedral at the time – accompanied the Archbishop on this visit and referred to it as 'a wonderful four days which has done us all a great deal of good and given us all new heart and encouragement'. One keen young wife commented that it was a 'draught of good, clean, fresh water on a hot day'. Doubtless the Archbishop spent most of his available time talking with Bishop Hall but evidence for the content of their conversations is lacking. By and large his main concern was to show the flag, to make the Bishop, his clergy and faithful laity feel the reality of membership in the world-wide Anglican Communion, a fellowship enriched by their corporate prayers and worship. No one was better equipped to do this than the Archbishop.

CHAPTER 51

China

(i)

WHAT was happening religiously in China during the early forties of this present century constituted for Christians, and not least for Anglicans, a serious challenge to which it was not easy to see how best to respond. One obstacle to providing effective help for fellow Anglican Christians was the difficulty of finding out precisely what the situation there was. Apart from occasional letters smuggled out or scrappy information leaking through from visitors ignorance prevailed.

When Geoffrey Fisher became Archbishop in 1945 the Church in China for some eight years had been submitted to ordeal by war and the havoc that goes along with it. All but two Anglican dioceses had been disrupted by enemy invasion; half of its bishops, together with clergy and leading laymen, were in Japanese hands, their colleges and schools being converted into institutions to house refugees. Congregations were scattered, hospitals and churches destroyed. In order to begin the work of reconstruction once Japan had surrendered after the twin horrors of Hiroshima and Nagasaki it was desperately important that money should be raised in the United Kingdom and practical means be found to transfer it to China. Thus in March 1945 Geoffrey Fisher wrote to McLeod Campbell explaining that he himself and the Archbishop of York could not back an appeal until they had consulted and secured the support of the Missionary Council. Also a *sine qua non* of successful fund-raising must be the setting up of an effective appeal committee with a responsible and representative membership to see the whole thing through.

Preparations for raising £100,000 moved steadily forward and on 8 October 1945, the Archbishop held a Press Conference in Lambeth Palace at which the appeal, a comprehensive one directed towards a general restoration of the Anglican Church in China after years of a destructive war, was finally launched. It included such diverse objectives as the maintenance of the clergy; renovation of church property; initiating new work along the Burma Road; building a central headquarters for the Church which now comprised some thirteen widely dispersed dioceses. The chairman of the appeal was Bishop Mann formerly of Kyambu in Japan.

At the end of 1945, Dr A. T. Scott, Chairman of the House of Bishops in China, who with other bishops had just emerged from two and a half years of internment at Weesham, wrote a newsy letter to the Archbishop in response to an anxious enquiry from Lambeth concerning the appeal and the Lambeth Conference of 1948. It was difficult, the Bishop said, to get money into China and he had therefore passed on the Archbishop's letter to Bishop Tsen of Honan.

As to the Presiding Bishop's experience of internment, it was his constant practice to make light of it, though Geoffrey Fisher was not taken in by this subterfuge, believing his imprisonment to have been 'unpleasant and irksome to body and soul'. In the same mood of understatement when the Society for the Propagation of the Gospel congratulated the Bishop on surviving his 'unspeakable ordeal' he felt it proper to inform his fellow bishops that 'the confinement within the compound walls and in crowded cells, the absence of news, and occasional shortage of food – these were far outweighed by many blessings namely freedom of worship (we had daily services all the two and a half years); friendly and useful contacts with Roman Catholics and many Protestants, and others who went "nowhere"; plenty of work for all, everything down to the most menial jobs being done by internees; games, concerts, lectures, plays (secular and religious); a good library; and a wonderful hospital created out of chaos'.

Another correspondent to Lambeth, Alec Maxwell, Assistant Bishop in West Szechwan, thanked the Archbishop for his Cambridge sermon and went on to suggest that the conditions of stress and strain under which they had lived in China for some years had brought with them a growth in ecumenical understanding though he suspected that on occasions they might have been somewhat 'disloyal' to the Church of England; but then, exceptional conditions of living had led to exceptional and new attitudes.

There was one problem, however, thrown up by the war, which was causing grave concern both within and outside the Anglican Church in China and to which Bishop Scott called the new Archbishop's attention in a letter dated 31 December 1945. This related to the ordination of a woman priest by Bishop Hall of Hong Kong, a matter which will be dealt with in the second half of this chapter. Suffice at the moment that though the resulting controversy was a worrying preoccupation, taking up a great deal of Geoffrey Fisher's time, there were many other pressing issues in relation to China which equally concerned him.

The Chinese Church was painfully, yet in hope, trying to recreate its indigenous life but in doing this felt dependent upon help from outside. The Archbishop of Canterbury recognised that times were exceptional and though, with the establishment of an autonomous Anglican Church in China, jurisdiction over it had passed out of his hands, yet he continued to take a lively interest in its affairs. Basically he did this by maintaining, where possible, a correspondence with its bishops, some of whom, from time to time, journeyed to England where they were warmly received and entertained at Lambeth. As the senior bishop of the Anglican Communion he had a world-wide, if ill-defined remit, and in respect of the bishops in China he did not forget that some of them had gone out there from England and that a special responsibility devolved upon him to support and sustain them in their labours and often hardships. For example, in November 1946 he assured Bishop Wellington of Shantung that he was well aware of his 'difficult conditions, grievous trials [and] faithful witness'. The presiding bishop (Dr Scott) presented Geoffrey Fisher, on behalf of his episcopal colleagues, with the cross which had given him comfort during his years of internment. The Archbishop acknowledged this rare gift in these words: 'The cross will ever remain with me to remind me of the Church in China as it rises from the darkness through which it has passed to face with courage and faith the days of reconstruction and new advance'. In addition to his personal correspondence the Archbishop kept abreast of affairs in China, so far as they came his way, by regularly reading the official proceedings of its diocesan and provincial synods. However, it could not be denied that the background against which the Anglican Church in China struggled to re-create its corporate existence was grim. There were, at one time, three warring factions – the invading Japanese, the Nationalist Army of Chiang Kai-Shek and the Communist forces of Mao Tse-Tung. The withdrawal of the Japanese consequent upon their involvement in the war with America after Pearl Harbour left the other two combatants to fight it out in a ruthless civil war. The genius of Mao led him to avoid the towns and deploy his army in the countryside. His Long March is an epic which, no matter what assessment history may make of its architect, will never cease to be told so long as human valour is held in veneration. After General Chiang Kai-Shek was forced to give up the unequal struggle and withdraw with his followers to Taiwan, Mao firmly established himself and initiated moderate social reforms. On 1 October 1949 the Chinese People's Republic was proclaimed. With a population of some 970 million Mao's Government claimed sovereignty over one-fifth of the world's population.

The new régime, firmly wedded to its own version of Marxism and now in control, inevitably made life more difficult for Christians, not least for the bishops of the Anglican Communion. During the course of 1950 members of the episcopate shared their anxieties with the Archbishop as they faced so uncertain a future. The conviction was growing among them that the English bishops had no place in the new Communist China and that they could best serve the interests of the Anglican Church there, and particularly their Chinese brother bishops, by withdrawing. Thus Bishop Curtis described to the Archbishop the contemporary situation, as he found it, in these words: 'We foreign bishops are dropping out at an accelerated pace. The new authorities do not wish to have foreigners at the head of any institution which wishes to register as a "Peoples Organisation". We are having very difficult times under the new régime, not from any persecution – we are all entirely free to carry on all our work as before and the behaviour of their soldiers has been exemplary right through in these parts. But taxes are absolutely enormous and look like making our school work quite impossible.' He was aware, however, that though the general situation in his area was only moderately hostile other bishops elsewhere fared far worse.

Reports which came to Geoffrey Fisher certainly bore this out. As a consequence, the seventy-year-old Bishop of Peking felt that he ought to resign since present conditions, he was sure, called for a Chinese episcopate. It was almost impossible for him as a foreigner to get permission to travel, with the result that he had long been unable to visit the country parishes in his diocese. Also he felt himself increasingly out of touch with the 'present trend of events and opinions in China'. The Bishop of Shantung painted an even more gloomy picture, clouded by his own experience. He had been released from a prisoner of war camp five years ago since when he had been unable to carry out any episcopal duties. He was prohibited from travelling, but had to confess that his presence 'up-country' was not desired by the Chinese clergy. To be non-Chinese was in itself a handicap.

It says much for the English bishops in China that they were able to read the signs of the times with a perceptive objectivity but without bitterness. Thus the Bishop of Eastern Szechwan gave it as his opinion that as there had been great changes since the setting up of the People's Republic so there must be great changes in the Church 'to match them'. True, freedom of religion was guaranteed under the new constitution but leadership would inevitably rest in Chinese hands. Personally, he was looking forward to this. This episcopal assessment was confirmed in an article in *The Information Service* for Saturday, 8 April 1950, published weekly by the Department of Research and Education of the Federal Council of Churches of Christ in America – a publication sent regularly to the Archbishop. This particular number stated succinctly that in the emerging China two things were certain: (1) The new Government had come to stay; (2) There was no future for the Kuomintang since the Christian Church was under grave suspicion on account of its reputed connection with the twin evils of imperialism and capitalism. Also, Chinese Christians felt 'a sub-conscious resentment' that so much Christian work depended on foreign aid. In prewar days, there were 5,000 missionaries in China; since the war the peak figure was 3,500 and now it had fallen to below 2,000. Clearly the older paternalistic missionary era was drawing to a close which meant that its modern counterpart must be seen to be a servant and not an overlord of his people.

An indication of the truth implicit in this American article was the consecration of five Chinese bishops during the first six months of 1950. Geoffrey Fisher, from his own extensive postbag, as well as from conversations with bishops from China, was certainly made aware of the significance of what was happening and the consequent overriding need for a fully indigenous Chinese clergy. However, as Marxists increasingly and successfully propagated their gospel and gained control over the media so it was getting more difficult to obtain authentic news, particularly after the death of Bishop Lindel Tsen on his way back from the Lambeth Conference. Also Geoffrey Fisher recognised the need to be guarded in his correspondence. 'The storm is not yet over; it seems to be wise not to have the letter published anywhere' – such comments sent to Lambeth told their own story. Thus writing to Bishop Chang, of Fukien, Chairman of the House of Bishops, Geoffrey Fisher fully agreed that in a new situation 'it was absolutely right' that European bishops should resign to make way for Chinese members of the Church. The fear at Lambeth lest letters from England should compromise the Chinese bishops was a very real one and inhibited a frank exchange of views. Thus the Bishop of Fukien in writing to the Archbishop on 8 November 1951 telling him of the centenary celebrations of missionary enterprise in his diocese, informed him that no one from overseas would be invited to attend though it would have been 'a great thrill' to have had the successor of St Augustine, Cranmer and Laud amongst them. The Archbishop responded by assuring the Bishop that he had the Church in China and the people of China constantly in his thoughts as they lived through these days of confusion and experiment. On occasions Geoffrey Fisher was able to get news more directly as, for example, when David Paton, who had earlier been an assistant curate at St Stephen's Church in Hong Kong, visited that city in 1951. On his return he reported that he found Bishop R. O. Hall 'stale' and 'having lost his *élan*', though in his judgement he ought not to move at the moment since 'it would shut the chink now open between Hong Kong and the Church in China'. David Paton was in fact drawing attention to a very real problem now confronting the diocese of Hong Kong. A 'chink' there might be but it was more or less shut off from the Chinese mainland and hence from any province of the Anglican Church. It was indeed 'out on a limb' and in such circumstances Geoffrey Fisher seriously considered that the diocese of Hong Kong might voluntarily return to the jurisdiction of Canterbury. David Paton's thinking also led him this way, so much so that if there were to be a change of bishops he suggested as a suitable successor

The Archbishop with the Apostolic Delegate and His Beatitude the Latin Patriarch in Jerusalem.

The Archbishop with the Archbishop in Jerusalem
(The Most Reverend A. C. MacInnes.)

'This is no Christian camel'

The Archbishop on his way to the Vatican for his historic meeting with Pope John XXIII, 2 December 1960. (*No photographs were allowed within the Vatican*).

With children in the Piazza Navona, Rome, 1960.

The Archbishop in Lambeth Palace Chapel.

The Archbishop and Mrs Fisher relaxing at Lambeth, 1960.

With the gardeners and chauffeur, May 1961, on leaving Lambeth.

The Fishers in retirement with the Archbishop of York and Mrs Coggan at Bishopthorpe.

Combined Golden Wedding and 80th Birthday celebration at
Trent 5 May 1967.

Country walk at Trent.

Lady Fisher, in the presence of the Dean of Westminster and Sir Henry Fisher, on 13 October 1977, unveiling a plaque in Westminster Abbey commemorating all those who, Protestant and Roman Catholic, at the time of the Reformation surrendered their lives for Christ and conscience sake. The suggestion for such a memorial came from Geoffrey Fisher, Archbishop of Canterbury 1945–1961.

George She who had an English wife. As so often happened, Geoffrey Fisher put his reflections on this possible return of Hong Kong to Canterbury into a memorandum: 'I would make it clear', he wrote, 'that I should endeavour, as far as possible, to be in fact to them what the House of Bishops in China would have been, and to allow them to operate according to the Chinese Church Constitution. The thing would only become acute if the election of a new Bishop arose, but then they would certainly have to seek my consent as their re-adopted Metropolitan'.

In the archives at Lambeth there is an envelope marked: 'Strictly Confidential' which contains the translation of a letter dated 13 May 1951, sent by Bishop Mo Yung In to the Reverend Chung Yang Leafi, Secretary of the Standing Committee of the Chinese Church. It relates to an interview between the writer and Law Wak, a Government official responsible for Church affairs in Canton. The general tenor of the letter was that Bishop Hall, though 'among Westerns the most open-minded man', yet suffered from the fact that 'there are still [a] great many things which he does not understand of the People's Government'. Hence he should tender his resignation to the House of Bishops of the Province of China. More generally, the Church in mainland China should break off all relations with the diocese of Hong Kong; and the cost of 'running the Church' should be cut down to a minimum and new sources of income found as an alternative to foreign aid. As to future theological training this must depend on the policy of the Government Education Department.

In forwarding this letter to the Archbishop, Bishop Hall commented that he himself inferred from it that the Government of the People's Republic though 'determined' was prepared to be 'reasonable' in making known its requirements in respect of private societies permitted to operate in China.

The Standing Committee of the Church of Hong Kong met to take stock of its new predicament and made certain decisions. It agreed to petition the Chinese House of Bishops that Kwan Jung, minus Hong Kong and Macao, should be created a new diocese of South China. The Standing Committee also expressed its willingness to become a detached diocese, conforming to the worship of Chung Hua Sheng Kung Hui (CHSKH) – the government-sponsored state church – and for Bishop Hall to tender his resignation as an active member of the House of Bishops.

The Archbishop felt genuine sympathy for Bishop Hall who, despite their recent disagreement over the ordination of a woman priest, had given years of dedicated service to the diocese of Hong Kong during a most traumatic period in its ongoing life. 'I repeat', Geoffrey Fisher wrote to the bishop, 'how profoundly I sympathise with you in your difficult situation, increasingly cut off from the other bishops of the Church in China by your own desire not to cause them embarrassment; indeed the whole situation must be full of difficulties but it is everything that you should be there in Hong Kong with your own deep spiritual witness.'

The Archbishop took the opportunity in this letter to revert to the idea of Hong Kong becoming a detached diocese. If this were its expressed wish then he suggested that it should find 'temporary shelter' under the jurisdiction of the Primate of All England. Certainly, he wrote, it was against Anglican tradition that there should be any diocese without a Metropolitan. Geoffrey Fisher, at the end of this letter, gave expression to one of his rare moods of near pessimism: 'How full the world is of bitter things and how heavy the burden which rests upon faithful souls. God keep you all.'

Bishop Hall appreciated the Archbishop's kindness in offering this accommodating 'return' but remained uneasy as to its possible outcome. 'Of course', he wrote, 'take me under your wing' yet he could not forget his 'Chinese colleagues, clerical and lay [who] had been so happy and proud of their provincial life and responsibility. To return to some form of colonisation must be very sad and bitter to them; and also might prove seriously embarrassing should they be handed over on a plate – with Hong Kong – to the People's Government of China.' Bishop Hall was not happy that the second strongest Chinese Church was without a Chinese bishop; whereas the Congregational, Methodist and Baptist Churches all had indigenous ministers.

On 13 June 1951, the House of Bishops and the Standing Committee of CHSKH met in Shanghai and though only Bishops from Shanghai were present, passed a resolution which completely severed the bishopric of Hong Kong and Macao from the General Synod of CHSKH, though it would be expected voluntarily to conform to its doctrines and canons. This meant that the old Victorian diocese of Hong Kong was now divided and its Western areas, administered by the British, formed into the new Hong Kong diocese. The increasing Government pressure being put on CHSKH can be seen in that the House of Bishops laid it down that in future they would have nothing to do with foreign missions and that they would cancel their membership of the 'reactionary' World Council of Churches – a withdrawal in which, so Bishop Hall assured the Archbishop, he had not been involved. This was indeed a radical change and the Archbishop called the attention of Bishop Roberts, Secretary of the Society for the Propagation of the Gospel, to its wide ramifications. No longer was Hong Kong a missionary diocese but a Chinese diocese separated from its mother Church and looking to Dr Fisher as chairman of the Lambeth Conference to safeguard its interests for the time being.

It was clear to Geoffrey Fisher that the Anglican Church in China was painfully adjusting itself, as a condition of survival, to pressures being put upon it by Mao's People's Republic. This meant ridding itself of foreign links, missionary and clerical, and conforming to a state-inspired anti-Americanism which was rife, its nationals being accused of using the Christian Churches as instruments of aggression in Korea. Speaking at a public meeting Bishop Chen proclaimed: 'From now on not only should we make better efforts to develop the independence and reform campaign but all the poisonous influence of the Americans should be thoroughly eliminated from our thoughts'.

How far this extreme anti-Western attitude on the part of the Chinese Church was a genuine posture or was prudently paraded for the sake of self-preservation it is hard to say. Possibly a mixture of both. Miss Purchas of Shanghai, calling on the Archbishop at Lambeth, told him that clergy there had 'unwillingly' cut themselves off from the West. Hence, she urged: 'Please do not believe all that you hear or read about us. Please trust us. Do not defend us – he who is defended is doomed.' 'Christians', she said, 'are doing their best to keep training going. The demand for the compulsory union of denominations is commended less vigorously than it used to be.' In certain areas pressure upon the Church had increased but no 'straight issue' leading to confrontation had yet arisen. Some felt that the Church should go underground but this was impossible since 'the organisation forces everything to the top and only the police can operate underground'. What she realistically admitted was that the Chinese Church had relied too extensively on American money.

The sustained effort, under pressure, to make the Church in China more exclusively Chinese, which in principle, if not in the manner of its practical application, was not unacceptable, on occasions had its lighter side. In August 1951 Bishop Hall in a brief letter wrote asking Geoffrey Fisher whether he had already acquired a Chinese name. To remedy this, if the answer were 'no', he had been given 'Feysshi Der' which was pronounced 'Feyshoo-Duck' meaning 'spiritual comfort' and 'virtue'. We can but hope that 'a rose by any other name would smell as sweet'.

As we have seen, the withdrawal constitutionally of the diocese of Hong Kong from the Church of mainland China was itself a reaction from increasing nationalist pressure. Hence in August 1951 the 20th Synod of the Diocese of Hong Kong followed up the Archbishop's own suggestion and petitioned him to act in the present circumstances as their Metropolitan. The Archbishop, in this 'emergency', regarded acceptance of this request as 'regrettable but inevitable'. 'In accepting these duties', he wrote to Hall, 'I regard myself as a trustee for the Church of Chung Hua Sheng Kung Hui and in exercising my political functions I shall always be guided, as far as conditions permit, by the Canons and Constitution of the Church.'

If Geoffrey Fisher through this constitutional change was more closely associated with the affairs of the Anglican Church in Hong Kong the drift, in respect of the Church on the mainland, was all the other way. The bishops were increasingly home-bred and worked with conviction to set up an indigenous Church no longer dependent for its resources on external support. Though opposed to Communism as an ideology such cries as 'liberation from the West' stirred in them an emotional response – and understandably so. Typical of this latter mood was a 'Denunciation Meeting of Christians' held in Foochow on 28 July 1951 at which Bishop Chang denounced the wicked use of the diocese of Fukien for over a century as a locus for imperial aggression on China. When informed of the Assembly by Canon Max Warren, the Archbishop confessed that this report made 'very sad reading' but he ascribed no blame to the Bishop. 'I would say', he explained, 'that a bishop is justified in throwing tons of bricks *at us* if thereby he can keep the Church in the faith and himself in faithful service to it.' 'To disown and in part condemn the Western world even beyond its merits is a small price to pay', he wrote to the Reverend K. Ting, who contemplated returning to China – a brave and strong decision.

More and more the Church on the mainland was being cut off and it was left to such as Bishop Hall and the very occasional visitor to provide the Archbishop with any information concerning it. In 1952, Hall came over to London and spent some time with Geoffrey Fisher at Lambeth. They agreed that it was most unwise to use Hong Kong 'as a listening post through which to get news from the Church in China'. On the other hand, the Church in Hong Kong, because of its unique position, was in fact inevitably looking outward to the Chinese diaspora in the Pacific. The Bishop discussed the constitutional position of his Church and the possibility of founding a university in the city of Hong Kong.

The Archbishop welcomed any scrap of information that came his way. Such was the case when the Very Reverend Alexander Trivett, formerly Dean of Holy Trinity Church, Shanghai, let the Archbishop know that Bishop Francis Carey was still confined in that city though his loneliness had been lightened by 'a most charming letter' from none other than Geoffrey Cantuar. David Paton wrote to the Archbishop ruefully: 'Prayer is now the only, as it has always been, and the best way in which we can help other Chinese fellow Christians'.

It was now difficult for a visitor from the West to get physically into China except, for example, as a member of a trade delegation. One priest, however, a West Indian, Dr Marcus James, did make the journey and drew up a full and informative report for the benefit of the

Archbishop. He had seen the Presiding Bishop Chin as well as Bishops Lin, Mao and Tim. He discovered that the silence of the bishops in answering letters was due to their correspondence being opened. Thus if any of the writers were to confess publicly that that they were not free to travel to Minneapolis for the meeting of the Anglican Congress they would incur the displeasure of the Government. Hence they preferred not to receive letters. The authorities of the People's Republic were as strongly opposed to Christianity as ever though at the moment the situation was somewhat easier, perhaps because they wanted to woo the Buddhists and Islam. The basic structure of the episcopate and the diocese was still intact; but Bishop Chen of Hankow was interned, having been a supporter of General Chiang Kai-Shek. At the moment no pressure was being brought to bear upon the bishops to join the United States-sponsored Church which had really not effectively got off the ground as had its counterpart in Japan.

The years were now moving on to 1958 when the next Lambeth Conference was due to meet, thus providing a great interest for the world-wide Anglican Communion. The Archbishop felt, of necessity, that he must tread warily so far as the Church in China was concerned, though he got through a personal message to Bishop Robin Chen sounding him out as to its representation if any. Not surprisingly the Bishop's initial reaction was defensive but he confessed his willingness to consider the matter carefully. Obviously the Church of China was not yet sure of itself. A letter to Max Warren from the Reverend Harry Wittenbach put the matter succinctly: 'It has had to repudiate the West', it ran, 'and every bishop has had to convince the Government that he is free of the taint of Western imperialism as it exercised its insidious influence through Western missionaries'. Thus if the bishops were to respond to the Archbishop's invitation to Lambeth they might well find themselves once more under severe state pressure. On the other hand it could be that the Government of the People's Republic might itself wish some of the bishops to make the visit to the West for the experience thus gained. Canon Max Warren was equally insistent on the need for restraint so far as publicity for the Conference was concerned.

Though 'treading warily' the Archbishop did take certain initiatives *vis-à-vis* China from time to time. For example, he endeavoured, by writing direct to Bishop Chen, to get a list of dioceses and their bishops in order to update an intercession leaflet for use by Anglican cathedrals. Bishop Chen did himself come over to England in the summer of 1956 and Geoffrey Fisher described his visit 'as a great success' though he declined at the outset to accept an invitation to stay in Lambeth Palace. Perhaps the designation of the venue ruled it out. Also the Archbishop received at Lambeth the Reverend Shen Fann whose father had some years earlier presented Geoffrey Fisher with a fine copy of the Scriptures in Chinese. They discussed the Lambeth Conference, the Archbishop being encouraged to believe that some of the Chinese bishops might be present. He was sorry to be told, though he could not have been surprised, that the Chinese Fund, raised by the Canadians, could not be used now in the present political climate.

As the date of the 1958 Lambeth Conference drew nearer the question exercising the Archbishop's mind and to which there seemed to be no immediate answer, was whether any Chinese bishops would be attending at all. As late as the early summer of 1958 he was given to understand that some five intended to make the journey: then in July that none would be coming. Unfortunately the issue had become clouded and complicated when American and British troops invaded Lebanon with the result that Bishop Chen, Chairman of the House of Bishops, sent a cablegram stating categorically that he could not come, news which the Archbishop received with a 'heavy heart'. In his cablegram the Bishop asked, in relation to what was happening in the Middle East, that his condemnation of British and American aggression should be circulated to the bishops attending. Also that the Chinese bishops should be sent 'full information concerning the discussions of the Conference on this proposal'. It was a request to which the Archbishop felt he could not give his consent. 'The Conference', he explained, 'does not take into account current incidents of international politics nor pronounce upon them', though it was concerned with the broad issues of spiritual significance underlying the tensions and conflicts, national, racial and credal. There was here a clear conflict of views and interests. Whether the Chinese bishops ever intended seriously to attend the Lambeth Conference, or whether if they so intended they would have been free to come, must remain a matter of doubt. It could well be that their general attitude veered to the belief that it was unwise for them to do so in view of the political situation then obtaining in China. The eruption in the Middle East with American and British involvement clinched matters so that no Chinese bishop from the mainland was present, nor was any reference made to their absence for fear of embarrassing them. Bishop Hall alone attended and served on a sub-committee. For Geoffrey Fisher, the non-appearance of the Chinese bishops was a bitter disappointment though it could not have come as a surprise. Indeed, as a result of his long experience of the Church in China though unable to step on to the soil of the mainland, Bishop Hall was able to make shrewd judgements on the future of the Church in Hong Kong. His view, often strongly expressed, was that Churches tied to the Church of England, but situated in another country and operating under a Trust Deed, could continue to preserve that status only so long as the ecclesiastical, indeed political, environment was favourable. The time would inevitably come when the Trust Deed needed revision in order to make a *modus vivendi* possible. He often asked himself what this meant in respect of Hong Kong.

It was with this situation of uncertainty in Hong Kong still unresolved, that Geoffrey Fisher retired from his Office as Archbishop of Canterbury in 1961.

(ii)

A Woman Priest

There was one problem, thrown up by the exigencies of war, which caused grave concern within the Anglican Church in China and to which Bishop Scott, Chairman of the House of Bishops, referred in a letter, dated 31 December 1944, to Geoffrey Fisher then on the eve of being appointed Archbishop of Canterbury. This concerned the ordination of a woman priest by Bishop Hall of Hong Kong. Such a step could not but command the attention of an Archbishop, no matter what were his personal views on the general issue itself. Also, it must be of interest to the Anglican Communion as a whole. Doubtless at the time there were some who saw the ensuing controversy as consuming energies which were better directed to what Geoffrey Fisher called the 'terrific task of reconstruction'. Perhaps the two issues were not entirely unrelated. The story lying behind this *cause célèbre* goes back to the archiepiscopate of William Temple and undoubtedly clouded the last months of his life.

In 1942 Bishop Hall of Hong Kong licensed Sister Tsi, who had successfully passed through the ordination course common to the Chinese clergy as a whole, to be in sole charge of a congregation of 150 people who received the Sacrament of Holy Communion monthly from an assistant bishop. However, when Hong Kong fell to invading forces neither he nor any other priest could get to them. On 4 June 1943, the Bishop of Hong Kong wrote to William Temple what the latter felt to be a most disturbing letter which included these words: 'In order that a congregation of 150 folk may have the Sacraments I have given her [Sister Tsi] permission to celebrate the Lord's Supper'. He then went on to say that could he have reached her physically he would have ordained her a priest rather than have given her permission to celebrate the Eucharist since the latter was 'more contrary to the tradition and meaning of the ordained ministry than to ordain a woman'. He would be reporting this to their General Synod and he hoped the next meeting of the Lambeth Conference would allow such ordinations where there was a shortage of priests. William Temple found the implications of this letter devastating. But Bishop Hall was not content to let the matter rest there though Archbishop Temple advised him, later in the year, that it was better in an emergency like this to let Sister Tsi celebrate Communion rather than for her to be ordained a priest which would give her a permanent status. In spite of this archiepiscopal admonition, Bishop Hall ordained Sister (Litimoi) Tsi a priest on St Paul's Day 1944 and licensed her to minister to the beleaguered congregation. 'I have had an amazing feeling of quiet conviction about all this', he told William Temple in a letter written on the very day after the ordination, 'as if it were how God wanted it to happen rather than a formal representation first which would result in women who claimed the right to be priests pressing [for] ordination even when there was no real need of them.' The practical effect of his action was that one more congregation would receive Communion which, when the route was open, necessitated a priest travelling monthly a distance equivalent to that from London to York. The step he had taken had nothing to do with the equality of women but with the needs of his own diocese, nor did he expect anyone else to recognise her orders at present. 'I resisted the temptation to give her the name of Cordelia' – so he concluded his letter.

China was more remote physically and psychologically in those days than it is now, but the news of what had happened could not be kept private to that country even though isolated by war. Prestige, Editor of the *Church Times* read of it in *The Reaper*, a bi-monthly leaflet issued by the New Zealand Board, and immediately wrote to William Temple simply asking whether the report was true. William Temple was in a difficult position. He certainly disapproved of what had happened but his more speculative mind inclined him to ask theological questions as to the rightness or the wrongness in itself of a woman's ordination. This is clearly seen in the extremely long letter in which he replied to Prestige. He was awaiting the arrival in England of a Chinese bishop, he said, to whom he would give a message that 'they [the Chinese bishops] should make some statement to the effect that the action taken by Bishop Hall was of a purely emergency character and that they were referring it to the Lambeth Conference in order that some guidance might be offered to all Provinces on the whole subject'. He enlarged, for the benefit of Prestige, on the 'most grave pastoral emergency which induced the Bishop to act as he did' and confessed that if he could find 'any shadow of theological ground for the ordination of women' he would be enormously 'comforted'. In writing these words it may be that Temple remembered, way back in 1920, that he had stated in the York Convocation that while entirely opposed to the ordination of women, he was aware that the reasons he was able to give for his position seemed to him not nearly strong enough to support the vigour of his opposition.

Once the news became public there were many who complained to

Lambeth of the Bishop's action. Alec Vidler, Dean of King's College, Cambridge, for example, maintained that there could be no assurance that the ministerial actions of a 'deaconess' were actions of the Church. The Lambeth Conference of 1920 had decreed that the Order of Deaconesses was the one and only Order of the Ministry so far as women were concerned. The Council for the Defence of Church Principles issued a disclaimer simply because it was not possible for women to become priests since they were 'incapable of being the subject of the Sacrament of ordination to the priesthood by reason of their position in the divine economy'. Perhaps to be expected was a letter of a different purport supporting the Bishop from the Society for the Equal Ministry of Men and Women in the Church.

It was at this point that Archbishop Temple's bad health led to Geoffrey Fisher becoming increasingly involved in this growing controversy. Archbishop Temple had drawn up a lengthy letter for despatch to the Bishop of Hong King which Dr Fisher brought before the bishops where it had a somewhat critical reception on the grounds that it was too complex. Dr Bell, Bishop of Chichester, believed that William Temple was 'multiplying difficulties for himself' if he began 'starting hares of a theological or semi-theological kind'. On the contrary, the letter to go to Bishop Hall should be 'quite brief and to the point', condemning unilateral action of this kind. Geoffrey Fisher strongly concurred with these sentiments. He believed it was the irregularity of the ordination which automatically condemned it and made it therefore unnecessary to delve into nice theological arguments. His opinion was that Temple's letter presented too many 'targets' and for an official letter was much too concerned with explaining why no notice of this ordination had been taken earlier.

In spite of his illness Archbishop Temple was prepared to follow up the suggestions put to him by the bishops. Thus he shortened his original letter to Hall and included in the revised draft the phrase: 'High authorities have declared that a woman is incapable of receiving the Grace of Orders'. William Temple, however, remained unhappy with what he had himself written, having a nagging feeling that it showed a too negative approach, so much so that he was toying with the idea of sending, with the shortened official letter expressing the mind of the English bishops, another and more private one of his own. With this suggestion Geoffrey Fisher, on behalf of the bishops, concurred, though not it would seem with enthusiasm, adding the further request that the official letter should include the phrase: *'Ultra Vires'*. Meanwhile the controversy in England was beginning to grow as more people came to know of the ordination and publicity correspondingly increased. But on the very day when Geoffrey Fisher wrote to the Archbishop urging him to include in his official letter to Hall the words: 'I must say that this ordination cannot be recognised as such in the Church of England', William Temple died.

Archbishop Temple's death meant that Geoffrey Fisher, who had presided over the Southern Convocation during William Temple's illness – he did not become Archbishop of Canterbury till January 1945 – now took the lead in handling the negotiations consequent upon Bishop Hall's action. His approach to the problem was less theologically orientated than that of his predecessor being based on the undoubted fact that the ordination of a woman was without parallel or precedent. It was a radical innovation and one which the Anglican Communion as a whole, in his belief, could not tolerate. In a letter, undated but almost certainly written soon after William Temple's death, he accepted that Hong Kong was not subject to the jurisdiction of Canterbury but to the Chinese Synod, although the appointment of the Bishop rested with him until he surrendered it. His own hope was that the Chinese bishops would repudiate Bishop Hall's action, and that the Bishop himself would withdraw his permission to deaconess Tsi to celebrate and would not carry out his threat of resignation. The controversy had still a long way to go as letters were exchanged, interviews held and Synods met.

In July 1945, Dr Fisher had a long conversation with Bishop Hall at Lambeth. From the Archbishop's point of view it was a frustrating experience. The Bishop said that his intention was to abide by the decision of the Chinese House of Bishops but re-affirmed that, if it went against him, he would resign. The Archbishop deplored this as in fact holding a pistol to the heads of the members of the House of Bishops. His proper course, he told him firmly, was 'to suspend this woman from all priestly functions pending a decision by the House of Bishops'. He pointed out the extreme difficulty of leaving the deaconess to officiate until the House made up its mind. If the decision were she might not officiate then this would lead to the resignation of Bishop Hall: if it compromised with a half 'yes' this would 'shatter the Anglican Communion'. The English Provinces and South Africa 'would not stand for it'. If, on the other hand, the Chinese Church decided to refer the whole matter to the Lambeth Conference he was sure it would turn down any compromise solution. He reminded Hall, once again, and forcefully, that on his own responsibility he had done something which had never been attempted before in any Episcopal Church.

The Archbishop at first encouraged himself with the belief that Hall was impressed with some of his arguments: but this optimism was dispelled when he 'let slip', on leaving, that apart from the needs of the present emergency he thought that women clergy would prove to be necessary in the Church of China. Thus Geoffrey Fisher was forced to recognise that Bishop Hall remained unmoved, turning a 'deaf ear' to his appeal. 'He is perfectly certain that he is right', he commented to Bishop Scott some months later, 'although he did not attempt to meet the arguments I put to him hoping the House of Bishops would approve or not disown his action.'

Geoffrey Fisher remained deeply exercised in his mind after this meeting and was in no way convinced that the Bishop would inhibit Sister Litimoi before the Chinese Synod met. On 3 August 1945 he wrote to the Bishop in pessimistic vein. If he declined to follow his, the Archbishop's, advice then Geoffrey Fisher asked him to set out a 'considered statement for not doing so'. 'It is not really a question of respect for my office', he wrote, 'but of clear thinking.' He outlined once more the situation as he saw it, concluding that it was most desirable for the good of the Church that he should be able to follow his advice.

Bishop Hall did not lack fellow bishops in China – some four or five – who advised him immediately to suspend the former deaconess but these appeals were without avail. At the end of September he sent a letter to the Archbishop which deserves liberal quotation: 'I write with intense personal regret', he began, 'to say that I am unable to accept your advice. I have only one reason. I acted in obedience to our Lord's Commission. I do not believe He wishes me to undo what I have done. That is my reaction to you as Chairman of the Anglican Communion who have shown me such consideration and kindness, [but] I must try and say a little more.' It was basically a pastoral situation out of which this ordination arose. 'Ecclesiastically I know – again to quote Archbishop Temple – my action was *Ultra Vires*. Spiritually I know it was not. I beg you, my dear Archbishop, to have no anxiety about the future – or that our handling of this matter in the Chung Hua Sheng Kung Hui [the Synod] and bringing it to Lambeth will do harm to the Church of God. What is wrongly done will perish; what is truly done can only strengthen Christ's Church.'

Bishop Hall was in fact lifting the whole issue out of the area where the cut and thrust of argument and precedents have relevance. It was not a view, in relation to this particular matter, that Archbishop Fisher felt he could subscribe to nor was he moved by an implied reference to Gamaliel's counsel to the Jewish Sanhedrin. With somewhat cold logic the Archbishop repeated, in a subsequent letter written on 12 October 1945, what he had already said to the Bishop personally, namely that it was essentially a matter of Church order and discipline. 'The question is whether a person appointed to an ecclesiastical office has a right, on his own authority, to go beyond the powers which the Church gives him.' He agreed with William Temple that in the circumstances the Bishop would have done better to have licensed the deaconess to celebrate Holy Communion during an interim period.

Archbishop Fisher was indeed conscious that in his involvement with this ecclesiastical controversy he must not give the impression of interfering in the internal affairs of an autonomous Church. In a long communication to Dr Scott, Chairman, he emphasised that he had never in any respect wished to give the appearance of such interference but he had been told by Bishop Tsu that the Chinese Church regarded its responsibilities more widely than to its own territory. This was particularly the case, Geoffrey Fisher commented, where unilateral action was likely to 'imperil the unity of the Anglican Communion'. He admitted that 'some would hold that a woman is incapable of receiving the character of priesthood' but here he remarked peremptorarily: 'I do not want to go into arguments about all that'. In relation to the next meeting of the Synod he warned its Chairman that if it were to approve Bishop Hall's action, then he had no doubt but that some Provinces of the Anglican Communion would question whether they could remain in communion with it. What then, asked the Archbishop, ought the bishops of the Chinese Church to do, a question to which he had no difficulty in replying that they should recognise that: (1) an approval of Bishop Hall's action would be 'an overwhelming disaster' to the Anglican Communion; (2) to defer a decision till the next Lambeth Conference would leave Deaconess Tsi exercising priestly functions; (3) to repudiate what the Bishop had done must be followed by a prohibition of her acting as a priest or being regarded as such.

In taking this firm line, the Archbishop was anxious that Bishop Scott should not think he was insensitive or pursuing a personal vendetta against Bishop Hall. 'It grieves me greatly', he wrote to him, 'to advise you to take this course, but I am perfectly sure it is right . . . Bishop Hall is so good and so glorious that to rebuke him in this way is beyond words grievous. But it seems to me to be the duty of your House to say to him: "You are wrong . . . such a breach of Catholic precedent [is] only to be contemplated if the whole Church were able to agree upon it".' The least the Synod could do, so he concluded, would be to refer the matter to the Lambeth Conference but at the same time immediately to suspend the deaconess from all priestly functions.

How far Geoffrey Fisher's (and William Temple's) firm line contributed to the final result can only be surmised. Certainly Geoffrey Fisher must have been gratified that when the Chinese Synod finally met in Shanghai in March 1946 the following agreed statement was passed and made public:

> 'That this house regrets the uncanonical action of the Bishop of Hong Kong in ordaining Deaconess Tsi to the Priesthood; and having understood that Deaconess Tsi has already placed in his hands her resignation from her priestly ministry this House requests the Bishop of Hong Kong

to accept it. The Bishop of Hong Kong has acted in accordance with this Resolution.'

On 15 April 1946 this statement was published by the Press Bureau of the Church of England, particular reference being made to the 'wider setting' in which this statement should be regarded. The Archbishop expressed his satisfaction in an appreciative letter to the Chairman of the Synod.

This Resolution, thus disposed of, the Chinese Synod later went on to discuss the ordination of women in a more general context. Here the Archbishop was not so well pleased with the motion which it now proposed to submit to the next Lambeth Conference in 1948. It ran as follows:

> 'For the period of twenty years from the adoption of this Canon by General Synod a Deaconess may be ordained to the Priesthood provided that:
> (1) She has the same theological, spiritual and pastoral qualifications as are required of a Deacon before ordination to the Priesthood;
> (2) She is a full 30 years old and unmarried and intends to remain unmarried and undertakes, should she later find herself called to the vocation of marriage, to return her licence to the Bishop;
> (3) That this Canon lapses unless re-enacted at the expiration of twenty years from its adoption by General Synod though women ordained under it shall continue their ministry for the rest of their lifetime.'

This resolution must have made it easier for Bishop Hall to accept the condemnation of his own action. In essence it asked that there be granted, within the Anglican Communion and subject to certain safeguards, liberty to experiment with the ordination of women to the priesthood for some twenty years. The Resolution also recognised that the issue of the ordination of women was of concern to the Anglican Church as a whole. At the same time it resolved 'That the Bishops from China who attend the Lambeth Conference be asked to present the different views of the Chinese Church on this matter for reference'.

These Resolutions, however, with their experimental period, by no means commended themselves to Geoffrey Fisher who protested against them to Bishop Scott. They rested on no principle, he complained. 'The thing is to be done or not done. It cannot be played with for twenty years.' Here, however, Bishop Scott stood firm. It was perfectly proper, he replied, for his Synod to submit for discussion to the next Lambeth Conference the general question of the ordination of women. It would be equally proper for the Conference, if it wished, 'to quash the problem at the start.'

All now awaited the outcome of the deliberations at the Lambeth Conference. Eleven Chinese bishops made the long journey and benefitted greatly from this experience in view of their years of isolation. A committee of some fourteen members, under the chairmanship of Alwyn Williams, Bishop of Durham, was set up to consider and report on the Resolutions referred to it by the Chinese Synod. Its personnel included Dr Lindel Tsen, chairman of the House of Bishops, R. O. Hall (inevitably), two other bishops from China, three English bishops and others from the widely dispersed Anglican Communion. Three out of the four bishops from China argued strongly that since the Anglican tradition was based on the autonomy of the member Churches it was, therefore, in order for the Chinese bishops to submit their Resolution and in so doing not to entail 'any breach of fellowship'. The committee, however, while recognising the unusual situation prevailing in China and also the high standing there of women, felt obliged to commend the rejection of the proposed Resolution. It felt that it was of so radical an order as to merit the fullest possible consideration of the Anglican Communion as a whole, relating as it did to the Ordinal of the Book of Common Prayer; and Resolution 67 of the Lambeth Conference. The Conference, in Resolutions 113–116, accepted after debate the recommendations of their sub-committee.

The story of the ordination of Deaconess Tsi, set within the context of catastrophic political, cultural and economic events in the Far East and their repercussions on Christian Churches in China, is not without relevance, the more so today because the ordination of women has become a contemporary debate within the Anglican Communion and some of its autonomous Churches have already resorted to it. No one, not even his opponents, ever denied or doubted the integrity of Ronald Hall who gave the best years of his life to China.

In relation to Deaconess Tsi (Litimöi), Bishop Hall might well claim that so far from weaving fancies, his action in this instance derived solely out of the exigencies of hard facts. Though he disclaimed any particular interest in campaigning for the ordination of women as such, his actions spoke louder than words. In fact he was, of course, affirming that women were capable of receiving the grace of orders though he never argued this case any more than did Archbishop Fisher in reverse. Indeed the latter deliberately eschewed involving himself in this theological debate. It was the irregularity of it all; the flying in the face of tradition unilaterally; the consequential possibility of schism which disturbed him – and this at a time when the Church in China was vulnerable and painfully emerging out of persecution and isolation. The Archbishop was also concerned with the effect of this ordination upon the Roman Catholic and Orthodox Churches. Bishop Hall, also, adopting a pragmatic approach, took as his overriding yardstick the desperate need to meet an existing problem. He fully allowed that the issue was not finally only domestic to China but it was the immediate deprivation of a congregation of the Sacrament of Holy Communion which weighed most heavily upon him – and his deep conviction that in what he had done he was responding to the Lord's will.

It is to the credit of both Archbishop and Bishop that neither allowed this controversy to interfere with their personal relationship which remained good. The ordination of women is now increasingly resorted to within the Anglican Communion independently of any utilitarian justification in terms of the need for additional clergy. Perhaps, in this general context Bishop Hall may be remembered with honour, though he did not live long enough to attend a service in Westminster Abbey, on 21 January 1984, in the presence of the Reverend Tsi when corporate thanks were offered for the long years of her priestly ministry. A message was then read expressing these sentiments from Dr Runcie, Archbishop of Canterbury.

It may not be inappropriate as this chapter is brought to a close to refer briefly to Geoffrey Fisher's reaction to the decision made in 1959 by the Protestant Church of Sweden to ordain women priests. His own reactions he communicated in letters to the Most Reverend Gunnar Hultgren, Archbishop of Uppsala and Dr Sven Evander, a theologian. Though he regarded this step as 'in the highest degree irregular whether it is lawful or not', he yet saw it as an action which 'will be regarded in the Church of England as falling within these matters of doctrine on which our two churches may hold different opinions without injuring their fellowship'. Each church here should respect the other's independence. This was not quite his view way back in 1945!

As to the theological issue involved, the Archbishop recognised that many regarded such an ordination as 'contrary to Holy Scripture', and hence invalid because 'they lacked approval from the whole Church'. However he concluded a letter to Dr Sven Evander with these words: 'Stephen Langton, I think it was, told me that he couldn't find any theological reason against the ordination of women at all. This is a point which it would be very good to get clarified a little bit; the trouble so often is that people resist a new movement, partly for right motives, and partly wrong, and those who get the wrong ideas do damage to their own cause, and to the cause of the rest of us . . . I am always a little unhappy when those who disagree with me get up and say that it is utterly contrary to Scripture and therefore to God's words.'

CHAPTER 52

Japan and Korea

(i)

IT was now time for Geoffrey Fisher to move on to Japan, but this was by no means his first experience of the Christian Church in that country though it was his first visit in person. It is to this that we now turn.

Geoffrey Fisher had been but a few months in office when the 'atomisation' of Hiroshima and Nagasaki brought the war in the Far East to a sudden and awesome end. It was only when hostilities ceased that Christians in the West were able to take stock of what had been happening to their fellow Anglicans in the years following Pearl Harbour. It was a story not entirely dissimilar to that of China under the People's Republic.

In the spring of 1940, as the result of a rising tide of nationalism generated by the war, the Japanese Diet passed legislation controlling all religious bodies, specifying Shinto, Buddhism and Christianity as three recognised religions, though the third represented only one half per cent of the total population. The intention of the Government was to concentrate Christian organisations into approved groups to further which, through Government pressure, an Amalgamated Church was formed of non-Roman Catholic Christians and coercion was brought to bear upon the Anglican Church, the Nippon Sei Ko Kai, to join this schismatic body. At the same time the legal status of NSKK was abolished.

The Bishops of the Anglican Church were divided as to what course they should follow. The majority was against joining the Amalgamated Church, but a minority genuinely felt that to do so might be the only way of preserving Anglicanism since it was unlikely that it would ever be revived in its pure form. (The assumption was, of course, that Japan would win the war.) To secure recognition, Churches needed to recast their rules and regulations into a prescribed form before submitting them to the Bureau of Religion for the approval of the Minister of Education. To comply with this requirement a special Committee of the Nippon Sei Ko Kai was set up. In October 1941 various denominations staged a rally celebrating their readiness to unite and a Japanese Church known as Kyodan was established into which there went about one-third of the former Anglican Church membership, including some of the most able clergy and their congregations. This meant that over two hundred churches refused to merge their existence into the new pan-Protestant State-sponsored body. The question, when peace finally came and Geoffrey Fisher went to Lambeth, was whether and on what condition, these 'defectors' should be allowed to re-enter the NSKK. It was a very emotional question.

The NSKK was undoubtedly weak in leadership, the strongest and by far the most distinguished among the surviving bishops being Yashiro of Kobe. The more percipient and far-seeing among the bishops were for making re-entry as easy as possible and thus to heal the schism. The situation, however, was made the more difficult in that on 24 August 1943, the Bishops who had joined the Kyodan, that is the Amalgamated Church, had consecrated some seven bishops which was a clear breach of the constitution and canons of the NSKK.

This was not the only problem confronting the Anglican Church in Japan at the end of the war. There was a desperate shortage of money, serious if the ministrations of the clergy were to be maintained, and the work of reconstruction to go forward.

When Geoffrey Fisher became Archbishop he obviously knew little of conditions inside Japan, in common with most of his fellow bishops. The first news that came to him from that quarter emanated from St J. Tucker, Presiding Bishop of the Protestant Episcopal Church of America, who wrote to Lambeth in December 1945, recording his general impressions namely that the Anglican Church was weak in leadership in spite of which, however, it was imperative that it should re-assert its independence. For the time being it was impossible to send missionaries to evangelise in Japan. Hence it was better to inject teachers and set up theological schools which was what the Japanese Christians themselves wished. The American Church was already in process of sending a delegation to Japan, China and the Philippines.

Clearly it was necessary to break down the barriers erected by the war and re-open channels of communication between the Japanese Church and their fellow Christians in the West. Norman Brinstead, Anglican Bishop of the Philippine Islands, arrived in Tokyo on 14 November 1945, and a report of this visit was sent to Geoffrey Fisher. The Bishop assured the Japanese that the Church in America had 'no desire to take back any of the authority transferred to NSKK but was anxious to help and advise'. It expected the Church in Japan to regain its unity by healing the breach created by the schism.

The process of re-establishing the NSKK now began in real earnest. The National Convention met in Tokyo on 13 December 1945 and decided that the Church should revert to its former constitution and canons. At the same time it unanimously passed a resolution conveying 'affectionate greetings to the Church of England, desiring that their fellowship might be deepened in the mind of Christ'.

To this eirenic gesture the Archbishop of Canterbury, intent upon renewing fellowship between the Church of England and the Church of Japan both of which had been through 'the furnace of great trials', responded with equal generosity. He was now beginning to hear what was happening to his fellow bishops in the Far East and their great desire, as rapidly as possible, to restore mutual relations. He himself was hoping soon to send two representatives to Japan.

More information had begun to arrive in Lambeth from people who had been to Japan and from the Special Committee of the Missionary Council which was busily engaged collecting news of all kinds. It was reassuring for the Archbishop to receive information from Dr Horton dated 15 February 1946 in which he confessed to finding the Japanese friendly to the West, so strong was the reaction from the militarism which had brought its people to such a terrifying disaster.

Remembering his promise to the Presiding Bishop of the Japanese Church, Geoffrey Fisher chose Bishops Heaslett and Mann to join an Anglican delegation of goodwill. To facilitate this visit, which finally embarked on 1 May 1946, the Archbishop wrote to Mr Ernest Bevin asking him to make it easy for the two bishops to undertake the journey thus early after the war. The Americans, he explained, were already trying to bridge the gulf created by the hostilities between their two countries. 'It is, I think', he wrote, 'really undesirable if all the Christian contacts made in the formative period are with the Americans.' Mr Bevin proved co-operative and arranged for the United States Military Mission to give permits to the two bishops. Arrived in Tokyo, Bishop Heaslett kept Dr Fisher informed generally of the Church situation there. The task of the delegation was to greet personally members of the Japanese Church, to make some appraisal of their present state, and to discuss how the Anglican Church could help in the work of reconstruction. As to the latter, the delegation came to the conclusion that it could best serve by sending out to Japan priests of experience. The members of the delegation seem to have acquitted themselves well and the Presiding Bishop thanked Geoffrey Fisher for the 'fatherly kindness' of the two English members of the Commission.

The greatest problem confronting the Japanese bishops was still how to deal with the schismatics, concerning whom the Presiding Bishop wrote to Lambeth. 'We must be fair', he asserted, 'and must try to win them back to the Church with love.' Within some months of writing this letter the Presiding Bishop had died and Geoffrey Fisher sent a telegram of sympathy to Tomuda Sugati, a former Alumnus of Trinity College, Dublin, and Acting Presiding Bishop. 'It is a great grief', he wrote, 'that so soon after an emergence from the furnace of War the Church should lose such a beloved and trusted leader. In all the letters that I have exchanged with him his constant faith in Christ, his devotion to the Church and his loving fellowship with the Church of England shone out.'

The Lambeth Conference of 1948 was a significant event for the Japanese Church since for years it had been separated from the rest of the Anglican Communion. There were bitter memories of Pearl Harbour on the one side and of Hiroshima and Nagasaki on the other. Also changes of personnel added further complication to years of isolation. Three bishops in the end made the journey to Lambeth led by the new Presiding Bishop, M. H. Yashiro, than whom no one was more fitted both by temperament and by conviction to initiate and sustain the process of reconciliation. He was determined that the predicament of the Japanese Anglican Church should be discussed at length during the course of the Conference. The party left Japan, with the personal good wishes of the Emperor, the Prime Minister and General Mac-Arthur. The Australian and New Zealand bishops contributed financially towards the general expenses of the visit. Their presence was genuinely welcomed and Bishop Yashiro spent time privately with the Archbishop on his arrival which both described as being 'altogether delightful'. As an indication of the depth of their emotion, the Japanese bishops presented the Primate of All England with a cope and mitre, both of outstanding beauty and fine examples of local craft skills. Not all English nationals, it must be frankly confessed, as Geoffrey Fisher's post bag illustrates were enthusiastic at erstwhile enemies being treated as friends and 'brothers beloved'. A lady from near Derby, expressed her 'disgust' at the prospect of Japanese bishops being received so kindly in England. The Archbishop replied admitting that 'terrible atrocities' had been committed by wartime Japan but that, in contrast, Christians in that country had displayed great 'heroism'.

During the course of the Conference the Archbishop arranged, in response to a specific request from Bishop Yashiro, for a sub-committee of nine bishops under the chairmanship of the Bishop of Peterborough, to go into the whole matter of the 'status' of certain Japanese bishops. As a result of their recommendations, resolutions were passed approving and welcoming the 'expressed intention of the NSKK to receive back the six bishops into its fellowship and to entrust them with episcopal functions and jurisdiction'.

The Lambeth Conference proved a great inspiration for the three Japanese bishops who had been cut off from the Anglican Communion for so long. Indeed the Presiding Bishop wrote from Chicago on his way home to thank the Archbishop of Canterbury for his consistent kindness. The Archbishop in acknowledging this letter wrote: 'You may be assured that you made a great impression upon all our people who heard you speak.' They were very valued members of the Conference; and he himself personally greatly appreciated their 'friendship'.

As a result of the Lambeth Conference and the many private

conversations in which the Archbishop engaged, he drew up a memorandum on the Church of England and its relations with the NSKK in
which he made plain his desire one day to attend a meeting of their
General Synod. He also envisaged a committee being set up in England
for Japanese affairs so that when Bishop Yashiro sought advice he
could be referred to such a body. The Archbishop recorded in his
memorandum that the NSKK would welcome a supply of English
clergy prepared to do duty there for, say, some three years.

It could not reasonably be expected, after the mutual recriminations
and the divisions created by war, that everything would move easily
and steadily forward to reconciliation, peace and harmony within the
Anglican Church in Japan. There were constant rumours that those
who returned from their sojourn in the 'United Church' were 'frowned
upon' by their brother loyalists though the Archbishop was assured to
the contrary by Bishop A. T. Takasi when he was on a visit to London.
If it were true, however, this was certainly not due to any lack of
warmth on the part of Yashiro the Presiding Bishop. Indeed the
Archbishop expressed deep appreciation of the way in which he had
implemented the reconciling Resolutions 89–91 of the Lambeth Conference. He for his part was convinced that 'the bishops who had
entered this Amalgamated Church and consecrated bishops therein,
though mistaken as to the manner and method to be pursued, were
themselves trying, in what they thought to be the only way available,
to perpetuate the episcopal tradition of the Anglican Church'. He was
thankful that out of the turmoil of divided councils had come 'full
reconciliation'.

The Archbishop made a special point of keeping up with the Church
in Japan through a fairly regular corrrespondence with its bishops and
by seeing those who visited London. In the early years after the war
there were many in China, maybe as a reaction to American occupation, who were communist, but Bishop Yanagihara of Osaka assured
the Archbishop that this would not be the case in Japan and he proved
to be right. In November 1950 the Bishop was able to report to
Lambeth that the number of communicants in his diocese had reached
eighty-eight per cent of its pre-war number and its financial giving
stood at sixty-four per cent. In the previous April the Synod had
adopted an evangelistic programme which its members believed doubly
important in view of the 'communisation' of China.

The Church of England had long enjoyed a historic link with the
Church in Japan, though its numerical outreach was not extensive. It
was inevitable, however, that at the end of the war, the prestige and
the money of the Protestant Episcopal Church of America should carry
with it greater influencc. Expressive of this was the large American
Episcopal community looked after by various chaplains of the United

States Army and also by an American Anglican Bishop in Tokyo, who wisely anticipating the time when USA troops would be withdrawn wished to build a permanent church in Tokyo for all Anglicans. In contrast the solitary church belonging to the Church of England in Tokyo was burnt down during the war and there seemed little prospect of its being replaced as a permanent building.

The Archbishop, on being consulted about this situation, began by coming down firmly in favour of a church in Tokyo to meet the needs of all Anglican communities. This 'should be encouraged and carried forward to completion' since it was a matter of 'real importance' that there should be in Tokyo one Church 'where both American and English Episcopalians can find their own services in their own language'. However, in its implementation certain points should be borne in mind which he set out carefully under seven headings all suggesting how this church should be jointly brought into being and jointly run. Both the Book of Common Prayer and the Episcopal Prayer Book would be used and he declared himself ready to discuss this whole matter at length with Bishops Sherrill and Yashiro.

A scheme in principle along these lines was debated at the Lambeth Conference of 1958 and successfully went forward.

The rapidity of the recovery of the NSKK, when seen within the context of contemporary events, was remarkable. For this Bishops Yashiro and Sherrill, with the Archbishop, merit high praise. There were occasions, however, when the legacy of war made for complications and this happened in 1957, and arose out of the proposal to conduct an H-bomb test in the Christmas Islands. Not surprisingly, in view of the terrifying experience which the people in Japan had undergone, this test was strongly opposed throughout Japan and Bishop Yashiro shared this view to the full. The Archbishop was highly sensitive to the Bishop's strong feelings and the two kept very closely in touch, the former seeing to it that the Archbishop was made aware of the sustained protests in Japan. Commenting to the Reverend R. J. Hammer, Professor at the NSKK Central Theological College in Tokyo, the Archbishop wrote: 'I am happy to say that I agree with everything that he [Bishop Yashiro] said and I thought that the line he took and the reasons with which he supported it were absolutely right'. He particularly admired 'the quiet courage and determination and cheerfulness with which he took up his position in faith and stuck to it'. It was not, of course, easy for Bishop Yashiro to authenticate his reactions and those of the Japanese people. He did, however, suggest to Geoffrey Fisher, that the matter might be discussed at the Lambeth Conference, though in no sense did he wish the Church to be a tool of the State.

Condemnation of the tests and protests did not only arise in Japan. When the Bishop of Chichester – Geoffrey Fisher thought 'unwisely' –

moved a resolution in the British Council of Churches deploring the Government's action the vote was more or less equally divided for and against. 'Many of us felt we did not have the knowledge, technical and strategic, on which to make a decision. Our hearts were all for the motion but heads felt uninformed', so commented the Archbishop. Perhaps on a matter so fraught with ethical and theological implications the Council ought to have made itself better informed!

It was not only official bodies and leaders of Churches who discussed this terrible dilemma. The Archbishop received a protest from the Young People's Association of St Paul's Church in Niigatu describing the tests as 'contrary to the wishes of Christian people everywhere'.

The position of the Archbishop was not one which he found easy to authenticate. To quote his own words he 'fully understood that he, [Bishop Yashiro] and the Japanese people in general were strongly opposed to the nuclear tests'; and he had encouraged the Bishop to communicate these views, on behalf of his Church and people, to those in the seats of power. What he felt he could not do was to adopt the position which the Bishop of Chichester held, namely that the British Government should abandon these tests altogether. What he could do, however, was to let the Government know how strong were the feelings of responsible people in Japan against the tests. His position illustrates again how national loyalties and attitudes often divide Churches as effectively as do doctrinal differences, in fact more so. What must be said of Geoffrey Fisher is that his personal interest and caring concern for the Japanese bishops encouraged and sustained the Anglican Church in Japan at a time when it was trying desperately hard to restore its life in a disillusioned and war-shattered land.

(ii)

It had long been the Archbishop's wish personally to visit Japan and in 1959 he at last achieved this ambition. Bishop Yashiro, the Presiding Bishop, after long years had become a close personal friend. It was natural that Archbishop Fisher should desire to see him in his own country and the opportunity presented itself when the cathedral of St Michael, Kobe, was due to be consecrated during the centenary year of the Japanese Church. Bishop Yashiro was most anxious to bring the tour off, so much so that he managed to involve the Japanese Government to the extent of contributing towards its cost.

On 6 April the Archbishop and Rosamond Fisher arrived, for a fortnight's visit, at Haneda Airport outside Tokyo, after a flight which was delayed by fear that a terrorist bomb might be on board. Fortunately this proved to be a false alarm. The Archbishop and Mrs Fisher were received by Sir Oscar Morland, the newly appointed British Ambassador, and by their host, Bishop Yashiro. This was followed by a reception of a different kind when Geoffrey Fisher faced two hundred voluble newsmen. As the Archbishop, in relaxed mood and with a twinkle in his eye rose to speak, he addressed the gathering: 'Mr President, Governor, ladies and gentlemen and the intolerable company of photographers'. Fortunately this went down well! When asked what he most wished to see in Japan he replied without hesitation: 'Bishop Yashiro'.

The Archbishop and Mrs Fisher, accompanied by the British Ambassador, were then driven to the Imperial Hotel where they became the first persons to occupy the Royal Suite which they found grand if very American. Their immediate reactions to Tokyo itself, though not to its inhabitants, were unfavourable. 'A most undistinguished city', so Mrs Fisher described it, 'with slums as bad as South London.' On the first morning Geoffrey and Rosamond Fisher were taken, through streets gaily decorated for an imminent Royal wedding, to the Imperial Palace for an audience with Emperor Hirohito and Empress Nagubo. Mrs Fisher duly reported the experience to her family. 'This was a very formal affair and I put on my best blue and grey hat to fit it. The Emperor talks most of the time with his eyes shut, but she is very sweet and gentle and lovely and reminded me of the Queen Mother. I had to talk to her first while Father spoke to the Emperor – and later we changed over. She was fairly easy so we could carry on and develop a theme once she had started it, but he was far more sticky and shy. We stayed about half an hour.' It was obviously neither a lengthy nor an easy interview and does not seem to have got very far – nor, probably, was it intended to do so! It was a courtesy call and as such certainly reflected the significance of the Archbishop's tour of Japan in official circles.

If the Emperor of Japan had lost his quasi divine status members of the royal family had not forfeited their popular appeal. At a subsequent Press Conference, on 13 April, the Archbishop was asked what his impressions were of the recent royal wedding. He replied that he was out of the city on the day but was sure that it had given general happiness. He himself had written a letter of congratulations to the royal couple. The Archbishop was also asked his views on such subjects as family planning, over-population and Christian unity, to all of which he gave predictable answers though maybe not quite so predictable to his listeners. Also, who was his favourite poet, to which he replied frankly that he was not particularly fond of poetry but that when he was young, Browning had pride of place.

We return now to his second day in Tokyo which was certainly fully deployed. It saw him with Princess Chicheta, widow of the Emperor's younger brother, at the British Japan Society; at Festal Evensong in the Athletic Centre in Tokyo – a kind of Empress Hall – which was attended by over nine thousand people and marked the opening of the Centenary Celebrations. It was fitting that the Archbishop of Canterbury should appear resplendent in the cope and mitre given him by the Japanese Church and which he had deliberately worn at the Coronation of Queen Elizabeth as a symbol of the healing of the pains and divisions of the war years. In the evening he went to a dinner hosted by the National Council of the Japanese Anglican Church which was followed by a mass meeting.

For the ensuing fortnight the Archbishop and Mrs Fisher journeyed in and out of Tokyo, to Kanbo, Osaka, Kobe, Kyoto, Yokohama and Naru. During this period he preached seven sermons and gave innumerable addresses as well as extempore talks.

Most colourful and significant amongst official entertainments was his dining as the guest of Mr Kishe at the State Banquet. Interesting also was his reception by a number of local authorities and the Japan British Society. It was, of course, natural that many diocesan and missionary societies at work in Japan should invite him to meet their personnel. Such a crowded schedule gave the Archbishop the opportunity to present a recognisable face to members of the world-wide Anglican Communion greatly to their pleasure and his own satisfaction.

A memorable event, not without its traumas, took place in St Paul's University founded and endowed by the American Episcopal Church and the only Christian institution of its kind in Japan. It had some seven thousand students and educated them from primary school upwards. The Archbishop expected himself to be receiving an honorary degree of a Doctor of Divinity and it was not until he went on to the platform that he suddenly saw from the programme that he was to be awarded a Doctorate in Civil Law. Recalling this incident some years afterwards, he wrote: 'I hurriedly had to adjust what I wanted to say; there came into my mind something that I had said somewhere else, perhaps in the United States for a D.C.L. where I had talked about the majesty of the law and Richard Hooker, a 17th century English divine. Mrs Fisher gave it as her opinion that he had met this unexpected challenge 'brilliantly'.

The most ambitious address that the Archbishop delivered while in Japan, however, was a public lecture at the Mainichi International Salon, on 'The basic needs of civilisation'. It was the kind of broad theme, not academic or philosophical, but practical and ethical in dealing with which he felt most at home. A brief summary of the substance of what he said is not out of place since it touched on certain aspects of life which were relevant to contemporary Japan.

The paradox inherent in the modern world, so Geoffrey Fisher asserted, was that the increased productivity necessary to maintain its standard of living at a certain level made technological demands on the shape of society which could threaten or destroy 'free, personal, human living'. Also for the world to become a truly civilised society there must be a revival of respect for authority, whether exercised by parents, rulers – or indeed the police. (There had been of late much trouble with student demonstrations.) Life was being made the more psychologically disturbing by the fact that hanging over this generation there was the ghastly menace of nuclear war. This must mean that the nations which possessed such weaponry should 'grow out of them as soon as possible'. The United Nations Organisation was brought into existence that the world might learn a more excellent way and already it was doing 'superb work'. With surprising candour, since he was in a foreign country, he confessed that his own country 'shocked the world two or three years ago by slipping backward for a grim moment in using military force'. (The reference was to the British invasion of Suez in October 1956.) Turning to more intimate and personal areas of human relations he concluded that for a healthy civilisation it was essential that sexual satisfaction should be kept 'within the circle of the family and domestic relationships where they belong'. He then pleaded for greater international co-operation in the economic spheres and pursuing this theme he condemned British business for the way in which it had endeavoured to keep rival Japanese firms out of United Kingdom markets. This attempted exclusion was a good example of how easily civilised ways of living together were 'imperilled'. Finally, all peoples and nations would be judged by what they coveted and prized most. He left his audience with these words: 'The greatest of all the needs of civilisation is the need for a common spiritual coinage, a spiritual gold standard, proof against all inflation and deflation. Man can only find such a standard outside and above all men and sovereign over all men, in religion and God.'

This lecture was not, nor was it intended to be, highly original or speculative. It represented the candid reflections of a mind more concerned with the practicalities of living and the maintenance of a civilised order, as he understood it, rather than with theoretical problems unrelated to day-to-day experience and which had their reality – so he saw it – only in the study. The lecture was well-received and given wide publicity in the Press.

The climax of the Archbishop's visit, as it was his primary purpose in making the journey, was the consecration of the new cathedral at Kobe on 14 April. The building itself was simple, austere and in the modern idiom, being situated in a strategic position on one of the city's new highways. It was built in two storeys, the church above, the 'plant' below. Mrs Fisher described it as 'very nice, light and open'. Some fifteen hundred people gathered there on this occasion, most of them sitting on the floor, though chairs were provided for the Westerners. Bishop Yashiro presided and the service took the traditional form of prayers in the baptistry, on the chancel steps and in the sanctuary. The Archbishop – this had been a closely guarded secret – presented to the Bishop a paten and chalice from England for use in the cathedral, together with a pastoral staff for Bishop Yashiro. It fell to the Archbishop to give the address for which he took as his text – not for the first time – 'But Jerusalem, which is above, is free; which is the Mother of us all'. Christians, he said, live in more than one world, their chief home being neither in Japan nor in England, but in the Kingdom. Yet for the time being, they inhabited the unregenerate world of human passions, fear, pride, malice and envy. Nevertheless this world was God's world and because of this there was much that was good and lovely in it, though mankind spoils it by 'the imaginations of their hearts and the inventions of their hands'.

Another significant event took place on the day following, namely the dedication by Geoffrey Fisher of the ever-expanding University of St Andrew's at Osaka. At the time of his visit it possessed one faculty but there were plans to enlarge the curriculum and at the same time to add to the buildings. The Governor of the Hyogo Prefecture and the Mayor of Osaka entertained the Archbishop to lunch at the International Fair Hotel thus expressing the goodwill of both Government and Civic authorities.

The Fishers were indeed easy guests to entertain. They appreciated the beauty of Kyoto and its environs; the loveliness and sensitive displays of Japanese flowers; the awesome majesty of its mountains; the religious inheritance embodied in its temples. 'Today was a sightseeing day', Mrs Fisher wrote to her family, 'and we drove to the holiest and oldest Buddhist shrine in the land. The Abbot met us and took us into his home where we had ceremonial tea, green and thick (Father upset his – an awful gaffe, I think!) and sweet jelly and ordinary green tea. Incense burned on braziers and all round the room. He was a dear old man (80) and seemed holy. They are real monks, celibate and under a strict rule. The Temple or Shrine has many buildings all of wood and 1,200 years old.'

It is difficult to believe that either Geoffrey or Rosamond would have reacted so positively in Reptonian days to a Buddhist temple! They had travelled far since then – and not only geographically.

Japanese cooking intrigued them and not least the implements with which to eat what was provided. We quote from the Archbishop: 'Afterwards our hosts took us to a special restaurant and there we had a lovely meal; I noticed as we began that there was a considerable gap between me and my neighbour on my right hand and left, but as the meal went on and my neighbour on my left and I began to talk, I noticed that there was another young lady on my right and these were Geisha girls, part of the entertainment, and we had a most entertaining time talking to them. One of them said to me "How old do you think I am?" . . . I looked and my neighbour on the other side looked and I said "Well I should think under 99" at which they both laughed; it was the only way I could get out of a very tricky situation.'

A particular treat which came at the end of the Japanese visit was an evening at the Kalaka Theatre. 'This is their ancient traditional theatre form', Mrs Fisher wrote afterwards, '. . . the whole thing is tremendously stylised and exaggerated. There is a long row of men immobile, all across the back of the stage who either play three stringed guitars or funny toneless drums, or sing in a most peculiar and tuneless way.'

(iii)
Korea

Before finally leaving the Far East it was arranged for the Archbishop and Mrs Fisher to undertake a hurried visit to Korea. In spite of aircraft trouble and a near abortive flight, they managed to fulfil this engagement. On Monday 20 April they left Tokyo in an American aeroplane for Seoul, Korea's capital city. On arrival they were received by a guard of honour recruited from the three services which gave them a salute of 14 guns! Many distinguished Koreans and a number of diplomats were lined up to greet them and the Archbishop stood at the saluting base while the band played the two national anthems. All this was a prelude to his getting into a jeep and inspecting the guard. This may all seem singularly out of character for an Archbishop but Mrs Fisher commented that it was 'the grandest reception they had had'.

The Anglican Diocese of Korea – a country which for 500 years was a vassal state of China – began with Charles John Cooper who was consecrated Bishop on All Saints' Day, 1889. This infant Church from then on owed much to a remarkable series of bishops, so much so that in spite of untold difficulties, political and racial, there were at work in Korea by 1939 nineteen Korean priests and a number of sisters belonging to the Society of the Holy Spirit. Anti-British feeling, however, steadily grew with the outbreak of World War Two which threatened the very existence of the ten thousand Christians. In 1950 Bishop Cooper, two British priests and a sister were arrested by the Communists. Only the Bishop survived the dreadful death march and, in general, the hunger and cold of internment. In 1953 he returned to build up the Korean Church once more.

It was against this background that Geoffrey Fisher came to Korea in 1959 to be welcomed by Bishop Daly, Cooper's successor, whom he had already met in West Africa. His arrival was opportune for the Lambeth Conference in 1958 had stressed the need for indigenous clergy and the Archbishop was able to find out how far the Anglican Church was achieving this ambition – which it certainly was. The Archbishop in his brief visit backed up Bishop Daly's policy of self-government, self-support and self-propagation. Equally, perhaps more important, was the help and encouragement that the Archbishop personally brought with him. They lunched together with the Chaplain of the United States Forces. This was followed by Evensong in the cathedral attended by members of various Christian denominations including Roman Catholics. On the following morning, after a Sung Eucharist, also in the cathedral, the Archbishop discussed matters of common concern with the clergy and doubtless learned much of conditions generally in Korea. After this the Archbishop and Mrs Fisher were received by the President, a statesman with an international reputation, and his wife Mrs Syngman Rhee. They then left for Geoffrey Fisher to be awarded an honorary degree by a large Methodist University at a ceremony in the open air. Immediately following this he laid a foundation stone in Bede's House. In the evening they met the President again when he entertained them to dinner and both of them gratefully accepted his permission, indeed advice, to use a knife and fork. It is a pity that we have no record of the conversation which must have accompanied the meal.

The next three days were equally busy ones for the distinguished visitors, not least interesting among many engagements being a few hours spent at the Eighth Army Retreat Centre. Rosamond Fisher made time, as she often did on her travels, to spend a morning with the Seoul Branch of the Mother's Union. She found a lively group, anxious to look beyond their own immediate frontiers, and busily engaged in building a hall towards which they each contributed a shilling a month! Doubtless Rosamond Fisher's visit came as an inspiration, as a letter of thanks to her indicates. 'It is a great honour to have you with us this morning. We are especially happy that you have come to Korea in this beautiful springtime. We thank God and praise Him for your safe arrival after so long a voyage. We pray that God will bless you and your family, give you good health and lead you safely to your journey's end.' They admitted to not having taken as much responsibility for the life of the Church community as they should: but now that the war was over they intended to do more in the future. 'We are conscious of the world-wide fellowship', they said, 'and we are making enquiries as to how we will be able to join with them in a fuller membership.' We can be sure that Rosamond Fisher responded to the following request: 'We will appreciate any advice or words of wisdom that you could give us that would improve our Mothers' Union of the Seoul Anglican Church.'

At the end of this visit they left for Tokyo, the guard of honour again turning out and repeating the previous musical repertoire with the addition of 'Auld Lang Syne'. However, there were no guns because those who were due to fire them failed to turn up!

Once back in Tokyo a dinner party was laid on for them at the British Embassy and early on the following morning they were at the airport to fly to Hokkaido. However, it had blown a gale during the night and the rain was still teeming down with the result that their aircraft was one and a half hours late in arriving in Tokyo. The pilot, undeterred, set off but after two and a half hours in the air he announced that he could not land at Hokkaido because of a typhoon and hence he must return to Tokyo. Back again he set off once more at 2.30 pm for the same destination only to meet a like fate as before. Hope deferred can indeed make the heart grow sick and when the steward at Tokyo announced that there would be one further attempt to get to Hokkaido even the Fishers felt that they had had enough and returned to the British Embassy.

On the Saturday they finally left Tokyo for Hong Kong *en route* for London. Their departure led to a moving send-off. Many friends came from Kobe and Osaka and Bishop Yashiro knelt to receive his blessing as the Archbishop stepped into the aeroplane. It was a truly apostolic scene and one is reminded of St Paul's departure from Ephesus.

The touchdown in Hong Kong was intended to last only some forty-five minutes which the Archbishop and Mrs Fisher spent with Bishop Hall and Dean Freddie Temple before they entered their aircraft again to depart. However, there was one final hitch before they were safely homeward bound, since as they entered the aircraft the pilot non-chalantly announced that he was unable to start the engine! Those on board were now advised to disembark which it was well that they did since they had to wait another twenty-four hours before they finally got away. The Fishers spent the time profitably with the Dean and Mrs Temple. So at long last they began their thirty-hour flight, touching down at Bangkok, Calcutta, Delhi, Karachi, Beirut and Frankfurt before they landed at Heathrow. Mrs Fisher long remembered the lovely cloud effects on the homeward journey, the glimpse of glory that was Greece set in the blueness of the Aegean Sea; and Cyprus, on which St Paul landed and which had acquired associations for the Archbishop of another order.

The visit to Japan which had thus concluded, was generally and rightly accounted a great success. It was not such as to lead to deep theological discussions at formal conferences; rather it was in essence, as so many of his journeys were, a goodwill mission. Geoffrey Fisher was in fact the first Primate of All England to step on to Japanese soil. His visit there had particular significance, not only as a pioneering exercise which later Archbishops were to follow, but as a means of helping to reconcile those Christian leaders who had opposed the Government policy for a state-dominated united Church and others who, with equal integrity, had seen it as their duty to join.

The Archbishop found much to admire in Japanese life and in its people. He expressed his satisfaction that though deriving from missionary efforts emanating from Britain, America and Canada, NSKK was yet a Church 'indigenous and autonomous . . . gifted and devout'. Inevitably it had problems in its attitude, for example, to over-population. Here the Lambeth Conference offered guidelines for a Christian approach to birth control. Legislation to permit abortion, the Archbishop described as a 'sad and shameful thing'. As to the Japanese people he found them 'so industrious, so ingenious and hard-working' – virtues congenial to his own temperament. Yet he realistically recognised that this very energy brought with it great problems which were also being experienced in the West where along with the benefits flowing from scientific technology there went much that was destructive and corroding. This seeming paradox was indeed recognised by the perceptive Japanese themselves but in this area, so the Archbishop believed, the West had failed them. If Japan had its 'lovely good' and 'forbidding evil' equally, Europe and America had its 'utilitarian good' and its 'alluring and vulgar evil'. Yet both communites were lovable and they must learn from each other 'only the good'. In seeking this an indigenous Japanese Church ought to be able to help and to guide.

Once home the Archbishop felt it incumbent on him to give an account of his stewardship while abroad. He did this in a sermon preached in St Margaret's Church, Westminster; as well as in an address to Convocation; and in his Diocesan Notes from which we have already quoted.

As to his own reflections in general on his tour we cannot do better than quote his own words: 'If I regarded only the human and political problems of these countries (Pakistan, India, Japan and Korea) I should indeed be alarmed and fearful. If I regarded only the material resources of the Anglican Churches in these countries, I should indeed feel overwhelmed with their inadequacy. But in fact I have come back immensely encouraged and inspired in my faith in God, and my faith in the Church, in my faith in the Anglican Communion, in my faith in the Kingdom of God. The strength of the flock is not in its size or its resources but in its Shepherd.'

It was indeed within the context of the Anglican Communion that the Archbishop, by and large, saw the significance of his extensive tours. He believed that the growth of its autonomous Churches, each authenticating its own life and culture yet held together in a loose federation, gave it a contemporary and much needed role. Geoffrey

Fisher saw the structure and pattern of the Anglican Communion as an intimation of what a United Church might and ought to be.

Reference has already been made to Bishop Yashiro as a close personal friend of the Archbishop. It must have been a peculiar satisfaction to Geoffrey Fisher when he received an affectionate letter at Lambeth written by the Bishop on 13 April 1960, recalling that just over a year ago he had been welcoming the Archbishop to Osaka. It would please the Archbishop to know, Dr Yashiro wrote, that in the font which His Grace had blessed he had baptised sixty-nine persons on Easter Day and since then some thirty-eight. He proceeded to regale the Archbishop with some family news and concluded by saying that he was in process of drawing up a memorial album on the Fishers' visit.

The intimacy of the relations between these two Church leaders brings the Anglican Communion alive in terms of personal friendship and of Christian commitment, transcending yet including race and nation.

CHAPTER 53

Singapore and a Pacific Province

(i)

AFTER the defeat and collapse of Japan following Hiroshima and Nagasaki, Britain became aware of what many of its nationals, not least Christians, had suffered through imprisonment, forced labour, torture and death. It was imperative, therefore, that not only physical but spiritual help should be brought to them. For many Churchmen it was not possible immediately to resume their former duties. In the process of renewal and reconstruction a heavy responsibility inevitably rested upon the Archbishop of Canterbury. It is this which will constitute the main concern of this chapter.

News of what was happening at the end of hostilities in the Far East came early to the Archbishop as the result of a letter from a naval Chaplain written on 9 October 1945, by the Reverend C. R. Luckraft, who had recently been in Singapore to participate in a victory parade. While there, he had met the Right Reverend Leonard Wilson whose epic courage and Christian bearing under torture and imprisonment made him a legend even in his own lifetime. Daily services, Luckraft reported to the Archbishop, had been gallantly maintained in the Cathedral at Singapore by Chinese and Malaysian priests, and occasionally by a Japanese. Two matters were, understandably, worrying Bishop Wilson – namely how soon would he rejoin his family in England, and his regret that though help was being brought to them by many agencies they had heard nothing from the Church of England at home. However this was no fault of the Archbishop.

On 8 August 1945, Geoffrey Fisher had written to Lord Mountbatten, Chief of Combined Operations, requesting that as soon as the Bishop of Singapore was liberated a message of welcome should be delivered to him. Unfortunately however it never arrived. Hence the Archbishop followed it up with another, from which we quote: 'You have been constantly in my thoughts. From many quarters I have received most moving testimonies to your fortitude under extreme tortures and to the wonderful impression which your Christian witness and courage has made not only in Singapore but throughout Malaya . . . No words of mine can be adequate but I do want you to know that we at home immensely appreciate, at its full worth, all that you have suffered and done: . . . but there must come a reaction and I am thankful that you are taking two or three months rest with your family in Australia. In due course, we shall be able to welcome you here in London.'

King George VI himself expressed an interest in and admiration for the Bishop's Christian fortitude and the Archbishop provided him with details of this modern epic. Geoffrey Fisher, at a public dinner, also devoted his 'postprandial oratory' to this theme, receiving a nice compliment from the King's Private Secretary for an address which he described as 'one of the best that I have ever listened to'.

Geoffrey Fisher felt keenly his responsibility for providing a future for the Bishops who had suffered so much, though he was insistent that they should be thoroughly rested before they resumed their ministry. However, he doubted whether some of them would wish to return to their former dioceses. The general unsettlement of the time with its complex political and social changes, and the newness of personnel after a long war, brought to the fore the future of the Anglican Communion in the Far East. Also questions were being asked as to how far missionary and educational activities fitted into a pluralistic world.

Geoffrey Fisher, as we have seen, made it a keystone of his strategy in relation to the Anglican Communion to further the setting up of autonomous provinces and recruiting indigenous clergy. In line with this general policy he met the Bishop of Singapore in London on 6 May 1946, when he expressed the view that the time had come for him to move on from Singapore. In fact he was nominated to the deanery of Manchester in 1948 and later became Bishop of Birmingham.

Understandably, in view of the importance of Singapore in the Far East, there was much speculation as to the kind of person in general, and who in particular, should be his successor. Thus Malcolm Mac-Donald, Secretary of State for the Colonies, showed his interest by passing on his own observations to the Archbishop. Particularly he stressed the multi-racial character of Malaysia; also the religious mix, Buddhist, Christian, Confucian, Hindu and Islamic. Such diversity constituted a problem since it was not easy 'to join these together in a common spirit.' Hence it would be 'extremely unfortunate' if the Bishop's successor were 'rather narrow'.

Various names were put forward until finally Henry Baines, Rector of Rugby, a friend of the Fisher family who had been a missionary in Hong Kong, was chosen. He was not long in office before he experienced at first hand the truth of MacDonald's comments. In February 1951, he reported to Lambeth that the Moslems had rioted in Singapore which led to much stone-throwing targeted at the Cathedral. There was a general feeling of insecurity expressive of the problems generated by the 'momentous experiment' of seeking to build a nation out of so heterogeneous religious and cultural ingredients. To work within such a *milieu*, so the Bishop maintained, needed 'at the top' effective leadership. Personally he had received nothing but kindness from the Governor.

One of the problems which loomed large in the process of diocese or province-making was the seemingly innocuous one of nomenclature. Here it was not the case that 'a rose by any other name would smell as sweet'. On one occasion at least, Geoffrey Fisher, on his own initiative and without consulting the Government, proposed to change the title of the Diocese of Borneo. The *riposte* was such as not to encourage him to do this again.

On the whole the Bishop of Singapore believed that there was little precedent in the Far East for naming a diocese after its Cathedral city. In respect of Singapore the Archbishop approached Sir Alec Douglas Home, Secretary of State for Commonwealth Relations, who gave it as his opinion – since the Bishop might have jurisdiction over Thailand, Vietnam, Laos, Cambodia, Sumatra and Java; and since also the Government of the Federation was not happy with the use of the term Malaya – that the title should be 'South East Asia'. The Archbishop, however, thought this was far 'too pretentious' and the Bishop of Singapore regarded it as 'quite intolerable'. He himself favoured 'Malaya and Singapore' but no change was in fact made.

In spite of his four years as a Chaplain at the Cathedral of St John in Hong Kong, it was for Henry Baines a great leap to leave Rugby for the distant and unique Singapore. He, therefore, always remained grateful to the Archbishop for his continued support and on St Peter's Day, 1959, the tenth anniversary of his consecration, he expressed appreciation in these words: 'I am always helped by remembering your own constant kindness and leadership before and since my consecration; and am always grateful for this'. In this year he was offered the Deanery of Carlisle. However, he decided that he ought not to accept at a time when the long negotiations for provincial status seemed to be on the verge of completion. This and other matters meant that letters between Bishop and Archbishop were constant. The Bishop was indeed pleased when the Reverend Freddie Temple, a nephew of Geoffrey Fisher's predecessor, who had been Dean of Hong Kong, became Senior Chaplain at Lambeth particularly since he would be in a position to keep the Archbishop in touch with Eastern affairs.

Though the Bishop declined to go to Carlisle in 1959, at the end of the same year he accepted nomination to the Bishopric of Wellington in New Zealand. Geoffrey Fisher received this news with very mixed feelings as is evident in the following extract from a letter sent to Baines while he was in process of making up his mind: 'This is a tremendous decision for you to make; I have no doubt about the answer, nor in your own heart have you . . . The one grief is that it lays aside the possibility of your resuming life in the English scene. So many people have been looking forward to the day when you would take your honoured place amongst us once more . . . you know that

Rosamond and I will feel very aggrieved, but on the other hand here is a work for which, if I may say so, I think you are particularly suited.' As to what would await him in New Zealand he went on: 'I have seen something of the Diocese of Wellington. Owen, the present Bishop, has not the quality of mind, affection and support, of seeing visions, and applying himself to carrying them out. You will come to a Diocese feeling a great sense of starvation and you will bring just what is needed to feed the hungry sheep.' Also he would step into a lovely country, a lovely place, a lovely life. The building of Wellington Cathedral was a great enterprise but alas! Archbishop Owen had never taken it seriously and others had to 'drive him at the point of a bayonet' to do anything about it.

Henry Baines' departure for New Zealand led to great heart searchings and a degree of emotional upset when it came to choosing his successor. Had it been left to the departing Bishop he would undoubtedly not have appointed a European since to do so would stamp the Church as an alien ingredient at a time of rising nationalism throughout Malaya. Such would also serve, so he counselled Geoffrey Fisher, to identify the Church with the *Ancien Régime* and in the process mean a great loss of face for the native-born Assistant Bishop, Roland Koh.

The interval between Baines leaving and the consecration of his successor in November 1961, was occupied with an extensive correspondence which illustrates some of the problems and frustrations involved in nominating overseas bishops by the Archbishop from Lambeth.

The exchange of letters began when the Archbishop wrote to Baines, still Bishop of Singapore on 2 February 1960 laying down the pattern which ought to be followed in respect of the choice of his successor. First, it was the task of the Representative Committee of Singapore to acquaint him, the Archbishop, with the needs and wishes of the Diocese but not to convene the Synod to discuss it since 'a public debate would do more harm than good'. Three members of the committee were potential candidates, and he therefore suggested that they ought to withdraw from the committee. Bishop Koh, he pointed out, did not in fact have to resign as Assistant Bishop simply because Henry Baines was departing. The Archbishop confessed that he did not relish the proposal that each member of the Synod should be invited to suggest a name!

To this letter Bishop Baines replied that Roland Koh was 'full of energy and purposeful drive' and was undoubtedly of mature judgement though he, the Bishop, had not always agreed with him. If he sometimes upset the European Administrators with what they considered 'ill-conceived proposals', he was basically 'a simple and honest disciple of our Lord'. Some English people may have got the impression of 'superficiality', but his pastoral ministry was in fact 'enthusiastic and thorough'. It would certainly be a mistake to have another Englishman; and here it was significant that the Roman Catholics had appointed two Asian priests in Penang and Kuala Lumpur. Geoffrey Fisher, however, was not convinced and on 20 April 1960, wrote to Bishop Hall of Hong Kong asking whether, since Koh was not yet ready, in his judgement, to take over, he would himself be prepared to go to Singapore, this initiative having the support of Bishop Bayne, the Executive Officer of the Anglican Communion and the Reverend Freddie Temple. The Archbishop explained that in his opinion the relationship between the senior clergy in the diocese had deteriorated. Bishop Hall, in reply, now came up with an alternative proposal, namely that Roland Koh be appointed Bishop with two Assistant Bishops, one Indian the other American or English.

As to himself, the Bishop of Hong Kong seems to have been somewhat in a quandary, but on 8 June after further hesitation he 'finally and absolutely' said 'no'. His wife, so he confided to the Archbishop, was most unhappy at the prospect of such a move.

The run up to the Singapore appointments and the preparations for a Province entailed a great deal of activity behind the scenes. Thus the Archbishop was somewhat alarmed to hear of an unofficial meeting concerning the proposed Province attended by the Bishops of Rangoon, Borneo and Hong Kong together with Roland Koh. Somewhat peeved, he felt it necessary to remind the Bishops that though it was proper for them to discuss matters concerning their future as freely as they wished – it being clear that there was a general desire for 'some constitutional step forward' – yet he must remind them that progress in this field depended upon himself as Metropolitan; and the initiative must come from him. Hence the Memorandum that he himself had circulated. 'If you will forgive a gentle criticism,' he wrote to Bishop Hall, 'it has not helped me all through this time that when I have written confidential letters to you about Singapore, you have asked other people what they thought about them. My letters were confidential to you personally and no one else.'

Contrary to so much advice Geoffrey Fisher had now firmly made up his mind that the next Bishop of Singapore must be an Englishman and that Bishop Koh could not, as yet, 'attempt the larger duties' since, the planning for provincial status could not be left out of account nor the general situation in South East Asia. He therefore asked the Bishops, including those of Rangoon, Singapore and Hong Kong, to advise him 'authoritatively about the steps to be taken in constitutional development'. There must, he felt certain, be a Council covering the whole area, and the Chinese dimension in South East Asia, which received financial support from the United States, must be taken into account.

As for himself he welcomed the suggestion that Bishop Koh should be a Coadjutor Bishop though without any guaranteed right of succession. In his own mind it was the question of finance which constituted a fundamental problem. He was at the moment toying with the idea of Kenneth Sansbury, Warden of St Augustine's College, Canterbury, becoming the next Bishop of Singapore. Unfortunately as in all appointments, the longer the delay the more gossip, responsible and irresponsible, begins to circulate. Thus a local paper let it be known publicly that they would welcome an Asian bishop and Synod formally submitted to Geoffrey Fisher the two names of Bishop Koh and the Archdeacon of Singapore. The Archbishop then decided to take Bishop Koh into his confidence – this was indeed delicate and embarrassing – and to let him know candidly how his own mind was working, particularly in relation to 'far-reaching problems'. 'I have to consider primarily', he wrote, 'the interest of the Dioceses of S. and M. but they are so bound up with the general welfare of the whole Church in South East Asia that I am compelled to take a wider view, and in particular to have in mind my own responsibilities as Metropolitan towards Borneo, Hong Kong, Korea and indirectly Rangoon. A Province might relieve me of these responsibilities but for the present I have to bear them. I have come to the conclusion that for the sake of your own Diocese and all the other Dioceses, I must try to appoint to Singapore some person of exceptional experience and aptitudes to whom I can look to be my special adviser and counsellor on all that concerns South East Asia as well as on the special concerns of Singapore and Malaya.' His own choice was for Canon Sansbury, in earlier years Chaplain to the British Embassy in Tokyo. He realised of course that he must 'strengthen and establish' Koh's position.

Koh, on receipt of this letter which from his own point of view must have seemed very disappointing, assured the Archbishop of his co-operation though he went on: 'It is easy to forget that Singapore and Malaya are no longer British. They are now independent and have their own special laws, with the consequence that all those coming to Singapore and Malaya from outside must get Professional Visit Permits valid for twelve months. It is not possible, therefore, immediately to qualify for citizenship and this inevitably reduces any feeling of identification with local people.' Bishop Baines was fortunate in being a Singapore citizen and was allowed to vote in a General Election. Sansbury could be neither and had no local language. Nor would he be able to spare any time for extra-diocesan work. As far as he, Koh, was concerned, he admitted frankly that he could no longer hold down his two posts of Assistant Bishop and Vicar of St Mary's Church, Kuala Lumpur, though he would be happy with either of them – but not both. His own advice to the Archbishop was that Canon Sansbury should be made the Archbishop's Commissary but not yet put in charge of a diocese. He must have time to consider the prospect of becoming a 'Prophet, Adviser and Counsellor'. Things should be left as they were until the Synod met in April or May when it should be asked: does it want to split the Diocese into two or to continue as at present? As for himself he wanted no new appointment at the moment.

For the Archbishop this must have been a somewhat disturbing letter, posing many problems. In September a further communication expressing doubts came to Lambeth from a responsible source urging the Archbishop to see that Sansbury was given instructions to delegate at least part of the diocesan work for some three to five years. Also, the announcement of his appointment must at the same time contain a reference to the commissioning of Bishop Koh as Assistant Bishop with special relation to work in Malaya. It would be difficult publicly to explain the significance of the designation 'Coadjutor Bishop'. Fortunately this terminology was dropped.

The Archbishop sent copies of the above two letters to Sansbury who confessed to finding them 'not very reassuring' and Koh's letter 'frankly hostile once you get through the oriental verbiage'. He had hoped for a more 'welcoming spirit'. The writer of the second letter obviously believed that Roland Koh had the qualities necessary in a diocesan bishop which made him, Sansbury, suspect that his first few months would be 'very difficult'. Hence, he must ask the Archbishop for some delay in his giving a definitive acceptance. Geoffrey Fisher's response to these understandable scruples was to reply immediately and firmly. The nomination was his responsibility, he pointed out, and his choice of Sansbury was 'a deliberate judgement'. It would be a 'serious mistake' to appoint Koh to the Diocese, and even Bishop Baines, who originally had opted for a non-European now believed that any temporary difficulties arising out of Sansbury's appointment would be easily overcome. Two days later Sansbury wrote with a final acceptance which was immediately announced in the Press. The Archbishop now wrote to Koh – there was a little wishful thinking about this – saying that he deeply appreciated 'the humble, delicate and loving spirit' in which he had written to Lambeth and agreed that he must be relieved from the office of parish priest. He had written definitively to the Bishops of Hong Kong, Borneo, Korea and Rangoon letting them know of the appointment of Canon Sansbury. The latter now got in touch with Bishop Koh in terms which he hoped might prove reassuring. He had accepted the Archbishop's nomination, he explained, only after his 'pressing invitation' and in doing so had Koh's position very much in his mind. He intended a 'full sharing' and agreed that the designation 'Coadjutor' must be dropped.

However, this complicated matter was by no means over. Koh cabled the Archbishop requesting him to postpone the announcement of the nomination, following this up with a letter. The proposed announcement, he alleged, gave no reason for the delay and this had rendered it impossible for him to remain in the Diocese since the Press would conclude that the Archbishop had no confidence in him. He therefore suggested the addition of these words to the formal notice in the Press: 'In turn Canon Sansbury, with the approval of the Archbishop, has decided to appoint Bishop Koh, Assistant Bishop of the Diocese, to be his Commissary in Malaya, Thailand and Indo-China. This appointment places Bishop Koh in full charge of Anglican work in these territories. Further, it is the wish of Canon Sansbury to elevate St Mary's church in Kuala Lumpur to be the Cathedral Church in the Federation of Malaya with Bishop Koh as Provost.' The Archbishop wrote back to Bishop Koh that he could not possibly concede these additions because it would mean a change in diocesan affairs before Canon Sansbury even arrived on the scene: However he had telegraphed the Bishop saying that the Church Information Office would issue the following slightly amended version: 'In order to fulfil wider responsibilities in South East Asia the Bishop Designate, with the full approval of the Archbishop of Canterbury, proposes to grant Bishop Koh an extended commission in the Diocese of Singapore and Malaya giving him a greater share of episcopal responsibility.' Cables went back and forth and it was with profound relief that the Archbishop was able to write to Roland Koh on 1 November 1960 in these terms: 'Your letter gives me an assurance that you feel settled in mind and ready to look forward with eagerness to your joint work with Canon Sansbury.'

So it happened that Kenneth Sansbury was consecrated Bishop of Singapore in Canterbury Cathedral, on 6 January 1961, Bishops Bayne and Wilson attending. There does not appear to have been any member of the episcopate from South East Asia in the congregation. Bishop Roland Peck-Chiang Koh, who had been consecrated Assistant Bishop of Singapore in the same Cathedral on 11 June 1958 by the Archbishop of Canterbury, was now nominated Suffragan Bishop in Kuala Lampur in 1961 and some four years later was translated to the Bishopric of Jesselton.

This somewhat lengthy documentation admirably illustrates the difficulties confronting an Archbishop in making appointments at a distance. It shows the need for an autonomous Province so that episcopal nominations could arise from within the dioceses involved. It also indicated the need as soon as practical to have an indigenous clergy, made the more necessary and urgent by rising nationalism, and the setting up of independent nation-states in the Far East which tended to provoke anti-western colonial sentiment. The result was that English bishops and English priests became increasingly unacceptable, irrespective of their individual merit. No one can deny that Kenneth Sansbury, during his five years in Singapore, before leaving to become Secretary of the British Council of Churches, brought high talent and absolute dedication to his pastoral ministry. His tact in dealing with Roland Koh was also exemplary; and he did well even though he was an Englishman.

(ii)

Provinces in the Pacific and South East Asia

The concern to establish Provinces in missionary dioceses went back many years and grew out of the logic of facts. As early as 1920 and 1930 two Lambeth Conferences agreed that each diocese should as soon as possible find its place as a constituent member in a neighbouring Province. The problem here was that not always did a neighbouring province exist nor did all dioceses have a formally agreed Constitution. During the Lambeth Conference of 1948 an informal get-together of Pacific Bishops met at which the Archbishop was asked to appoint a commission to determine areas of episcopal administration throughout the Pacific. In response to this request he consulted the Metropolitan of Sydney and the Presiding Bishop of the Protestant Episcopal Church of America the result of which was that he drew up a paper 'A Question of a Province'. This carefully reasoned document was read to a meeting of the Anglican Communion Advisory Council on Missionary Strategy under the chairmanship of the Archbishop of Sydney. This representative gathering unanimously came to the following conclusions which were implemented: (1) that the time had not yet come for the formal constitution of a Province or Provinces. (2) that the principle of regional groups was acceptable given the following conditions: (a) that two councils be formed for the Episcopal Church in South East Asia (Singapore, Borneo, Hong Kong and Rangoon) and in the South Pacific (New Guinea, Melanesia, Polynesia); (b) that each council should meet at least every two years and jointly every five years; (c) that it elect a President to serve for five years.

In this process of decision-making and accepting the principle of *solvitur in ambulando* Geoffrey Fisher might well be satisfied with the initiatives he had taken. He had definite ideas as to the structural organisation suitable for the Anglican Communion and in his own position as Archbishop of Canterbury he was able to exercise a considerable influence. It was an area in which his judgement was usually sound.

CHAPTER 54

The Western Hemisphere

(i)

Brazil, Argentina and the Falkland Islands

In this biography we have dealt at some length with the many worldwide journeys that Geoffrey Fisher made as Senior Bishop of the Anglican Communion. These tours were indeed important, not only in themselves but because they laid down the pattern which subsequent Archbishops have felt it appropriate and right to follow. Hence the Primate of All England is now expected 'to put a girdle round about the earth' and not, like a colourful Stuart monarch, vow never to go on his travels again. He is expected to be peripatetic.

There were regions of the world's surface, however, which he was destined never to visit in person but for which he had a built-in responsibility and felt a concern. The reference is to such territories in the Western Hemisphere as, for example, Brazil, Argentina, the Falkland Islands, Jamaica, Bermuda – to mention but a few. Dotted about this vast area were many British expatriates, particularly in South America where many had large business interests. The established Church of England with its Bishops and parochial clergy was there to minister to them pastorally.

Geoffrey Fisher had not been long at Canterbury when, at the instigation of Bishop Weller, he announced that the two dioceses of Argentina and East South America with the Falkland Islands were to be combined. Shortly afterwards Bishop Weller resigned.

The appointment of his successor gives an interesting impression of one aspect of an ex-patriate community living abroad.

There was an obvious and talented candidate for the vacancy namely Bishop D. L. Evans of Brazil. Geoffrey Fisher, as a result of extensive enquiries, was firmly convinced that he had the right qualities. Already he had shown himself capable of running a diocese; he had a thorough working knowledge of both Spanish and Portuguese; and above all he was a 'likeable' personality. This was not, it must be said, how some members of the Standing Committee who were involved in the appointment regarded him. They affected to deplore, so they described it, his lack of what 'a public school and a university gives'. Geoffrey Fisher was not pleased and he wrote to the Archdeacon of the Diocese deploring this prejudice against Evans asserting strongly that whether true or false, it must not be allowed to outweigh his other considerable merits.

There seems no question but that the Archbishop's assessment of the situation was a true one and that Bishop Evans being turned down by the Standing Committee on a majority vote was due to his not being 'out of the top drawer'. As a member of the Standing Committee put it to Bishop Weller as they walked out of the meeting: 'We are really snobs, aren't we?' It is to the credit of the Archbishop, as a Memorandum he drew up at the time makes evident, that he refused to accept as final the judgement of the Standing Committee and asked it to reconsider the whole matter. At the same time he told Bishop Weller that he could only pass over Bishop Evans if he were thoroughly convinced that the opposition to him was so intense as to frustrate his subsequent ministry in the diocese. At the same time he went back to the two Archdeacons of the diocese who were reassuring in advising him to ignore altogether the opposition. When the Standing Committee finally met five members voted against Evans, two were for him and three abstained. The Archbishop after contemplating but rejecting co-opting to the Committee consulted representatives of other dioceses. Finally he managed to persuade the Standing Committee, in order to bypass its own divisions, to leave the appointment of the new bishop entirely to himself without even a recommendation.

So it was that on 16 April Geoffrey Fisher wrote to Evans offering him the Bishopric. His words, in doing this, testify to the 'in-fighting' which had preceded his nomination. 'I am happy to write to you', he began, 'with the invitation that you should allow me to appoint you as Bishop of the newly united Diocese with its long title covering South America and the Falkland Islands. I am sorry that I had to delay so long but it seemed to be necessary to make quite sure of my ground and to be satisfied that if you were appointed you would have the goodwill and the support of the Diocese . . . What matters above all is that you should bring to the oversight of the Diocese not only ability but the true spirit of pastoral devotion as its Father in God. These I am sure that you do bring'. The Archbishop with his usual commonsensical approach turned then to discuss briefly finance while at the same time advising the Bishop to satisfy the South American Missionary Society of his fidelity to its traditions.

In response to this letter Bishop Evans replied immediately with a cablegram: 'Humbly accept – S.A.M.S. have every assurance required – letter following'.

It remained only for the Archbishop to confer with the Presiding Bishop of the Protestant Episcopal Church of the United States of America over the adjustments to some diocesan boundaries which this union of two dioceses would entail.

The story of this appointment, which worked well, has more than a local interest. It shows only too clearly how sometimes seemingly democratic procedures can be manipulated by a small caucus to get its own way for inadequate reasons based largely on prejudice. It would have been easy for Geoffrey Fisher, separated by thousands of miles of ocean, to let the ban on Evans stand. Only a high sense of duty, persistence and a willingness to spend time informing himself, prevented this happening. It also indicates that on some occasions the exercise of the Archbishop's metropolitical authority served as a protection against local prejudice.

The Lambeth sources are silent as to the subsequent ministry of Bishop Evans – no news in this area is usually good news – until June 1959 when two interested laymen came to see the Archbishop at Lambeth concerning his salary. They explained carefully how the Bishop's income was made up, stressing that there was no endowment or allowances for a house, transport or car. They asked the Archbishop whether he could help to raise the annual stipend to one thousand pounds. In the course of their conversation the question was raised, though without success, as to the possibility of the Foreign Office being encouraged to contribute. The Archbishop decided to share this problem with Bishop Bayne, the Executive Officer of the Anglican Communion, asking him to take under review this whole problem in so far as it related to South America. He also made approaches to the South American Missionary Society for help and was not entirely unsuccessful.

A more serious problem, however, confronted the Archbishop in his dealing with the *Ecclesia Anglicana* in South America which was not simply domestic to the Church of England. This arose out of the following situation. The Church of England began its ministry in South America as early as 1819 when a British Chaplaincy was established in Rio de Janeiro, this being the first non-Roman Church to be active in that country. Its intention was simply to serve a British clientèle, temporarily or permanently domiciled in South America. By the time that Geoffrey Fisher became Archbishop the number of British residents was around nineteen thousand and they were ministered to by a few clergy supplemented by British Chaplains in Central and Northern Brazil. The Protestant Episcopal Church of America did not begin to take an official interest in that country until 1889 and, unlike the Church of England, it was almost from the word go a missionary church dedicated to evangelism. In 1900 the district where it operated was accepted as a Missionary Diocese of the Protestant Episcopal Church in America.

Thus there were two Anglican Churches in Brazil, the Church of England under Bishop Evans and the American Episcopal Church under Bishop Melcher. Not suprisingly this led to complications which were brought to the notice of the Archbishop of Canterbury, particularly as it was a governing principle of the Anglican Communion that only one Church should be active in any given geographical area. For two Anglican Bishops to exist side by side under different Metopolitans, and in possible competition the one with the other, seemed to be improper. Perhaps in Brazil the problem was not quite so clear cut since, as Bishop Evans maintained, the Church of England dealt only with British citizens located around Rio and extending to the coast; whereas the American Church was active in three dioceses positioned in the south east corner of that vast country. Hence, so he contended, in fact there was no overlapping of jurisdictions, the Church of England Bishop going to the north, the American to the south. Only in Rio did they meet where the Church of England Archdeacon resided.

The presence of the two Churches operating in the same country, no matter how much or how little there was of overlap, appeared to Henry Sherrill, Presiding Bishop of the Protestant Episcopal Church of America, to present real problems. In July 1951 while in England, staying at Lambeth, he raised the question in general terms stressing particularly the 'awkward position' of the Episcopal Church in that while the Church of England Chaplaincy possessed a very fine church in Rio de Janeiro the Americans, had no church in that city at all. This rankled and the result was many aggrieved letters from Bishop Melcher to Evans with some bad temper on both sides. Both Archbishop and Presiding Bishop were anxious that this unhappy situation should not escalate particularly, as the latter put it, they were 'such good friends that the frankest statements can be written back and forth without misunderstanding'. So it was that Sherrill later wrote to Geoffrey Fisher in a reconciling mood: 'I am not inclined to raise the question about Brazil, or in fact in any other place. Let us continue as we are in friendship and in trust, and these organisational matters in time will take care of themselves'. And so for a few years they did, the Episcopal Church of America being content to work under the present conditions until 'such time as a change of jurisdiction could be effected with a readiness of acceptance that is not yet apparent'.

In fact, however, the problem resolutely refused to go away, being made more difficult by personal antipathies 'on the ground'. Thus within four years Fisher and Sherrill found it necessary to work out a *modus vivendi* to ease such stress and strain. This was successfully achieved and came into force on 1 October 1955. They believed that their solution of the problem respected the integrity of both Churches by making special provisions for the episcopal care of particular groups thereby successfully preventing the overlapping which had caused friction. The Archbishop wisely sent all the documentation to Sir Henry Dashwood, his legal adviser, who saw no objection to the scheme which, in his opinion, conformed to the basic principles of the Anglican

Communion. However, he shrewdly cautioned that in practice everything would depend on the common sense and the goodwill of those
who worked it. Sir Henry proved to be right for there were certainly
teething troubles in the early days due, so Geoffrey Fisher contended,
to the terms not being properly understood. However for the rest of
the Archbishop's stay at Lambeth the *modus vivendi* of 1955 stuck.
Geoffrey Fisher, greatly helped by the sensible attitude of his friend
Sherrill, had shown a realistic and balanced approach to a problem
bristling with difficulties – and had solved it in the interest of all
concerned.

(ii)
Jamaica

Amongst the many West Indian islands Jamaica, with a population of
well over two million, with its fine capital, Kingston, its cricket prowess
and membership of the British Commonwealth, could claim a real
distinction. In 1951 a severe and devastating hurricane hit the island
and the Bishop of Jamaica immediately invited Geoffrey Fisher to fly
out to the stricken island for some ten days. The request was an
indication of the esteem in which he and his office were held but
reluctantly, at such short notice and with four important engagements
during the coming week, he was forced to decline. This however was
no solitary cry for help since his advice was often sought by the Bishop
on Church matters of pressing concern. Thus he was consulted over
the difficulty in finding the right man as Chaplain of the University;
also on the tensions created by the Church in not applying to divorcees
the marriage discipline accepted throughout the Anglican Communion.

Far more painful, distressing and embarrassing, was a controversy
which developed around the Right Reverend Basil Dale, Bishop of
Jamaica, who had been consecrated to this see in 1950. He was a
greatly experienced, sensitive priest who had held many responsible
posts including that of a missionary to British Honduras. In Jamaica
he became increasingly, almost obsessively, frustrated by a growing
conviction that a strong anti-white attitude on the part of the black
population was directed to ridding all whites from any positions of
'prominence or influence' in the Islands.

Thus rumours circulated that Europeans had been ousted from the
Jamaican Christian Council. 'Any stick will do with which to beat
the white man' – such it was alleged constituted the attitude of
the indigenous blacks. Geoffrey Fisher, while accepting that there was
an 'undercurrent of racism' in Jamaica, was yet convinced that the
Bishop had grossly and irresponsibly exaggerated the extent of it, a
view also held by Hugh Foot, the Governor. Into this most unhappy
situation there was now introduced a further complication when

Bishop Dale left the Island for Britain and declared his intention of resigning forthwith. This was for the Archbishop, a shattering blow and he had a long discussion with the Bishop at Lambeth, telling him that if only he would stand firm all would be well. Thus he advised him to go back at once to Jamaica. 'It is your duty to be there' he said, and 'you can then reconsider and tell me if you still feel you ought to resign'. If he chose the latter then he must do it 'with dignity'. Meanwhile Geoffrey Fisher was energetically trying to find a new post for him in England which led to his writing to four diocesan Bishops asking whether they could provide a benefice for him or alternatively some episcopal work. Two bishops responded positively but Dale declined to accept their offers. Finally he did resign from the bishopric of Jamaica and became in 1955 Rector of Haslemere in Surrey which he held till 1962. He also combined with this the post of an assistant bishop in the Guildford Diocese till 1967.

There can be no doubt that this whole business was most worrying to Geoffrey Fisher and its resolution owed much to his continuing concern to be both understanding yet firm. Without him the finding of an alternative ministry could have proved difficult indeed.

(iii)
Bermuda

Bermuda, one of a group of 360 islands only twenty of which are inhabited, has a population of over eighty thousand. Hamilton, its capital city, is a favourite winter resort for wealthy Americans taking full advantage of tax concessions.

In 1946, the Right Reverend Hefer Brown, the Anglican Bishop of Bermuda, aged 81, wrote to Lambeth asking whether he ought to resign or would it be proper for him to stay a little longer while he looked round for a house. In response to this enquiry Geoffrey Fisher invited the opinion of a group of people including the Governor of the Islands. As a result he replied to the Bishop that he could 'with a clear conscience' postpone his retirement knowing that it was the general wish of his people to retain him for a time as their Bishop. Also this delay would give a breathing space for planning the future of the diocese in the light of the coming of a successor. A delegation from the diocese which visited Geoffrey Fisher stressed that they did not wish to go into a Canadian Province but would prefer their Bishop to be a suffragan of Canterbury. Perhaps he might spend a short time each year in England. To this suggestion the Archbishop replied firmly that this was not possible.

In the course of the discussion it became evident to the Archbishop that the Canon Residentiary at the Cathedral had really nothing to do since the Bishop himself ran the Cathedral. On the other hand if the

Canon took this over there would be little left for the Bishop! The Delegation was particularly suspicious of the Americans, being strongly English in its sentiment. Not unexpectedly there was much talk on the problems confronting those ministering to mixed black and white congregations.

The Archbishop also had the advantage of a long talk with Lord Rowallen, later Chief Scout, on the overall condition of the Church in the West Indies. The general picture he painted was by no means a favourable one. British people, he asserted, regarded the bishops in general as 'deplorably bad and defeatist'. The dioceses were, apart from Jamaica, Anglo-Catholic; and the Romans were 'extremely punishing'.

Hefer Brown, encouraged by Archbishop Fisher, stayed in office for another two years which meant that a successor needed to be appointed in 1948. The Archbishop was anxious to find out precisely what part personally he himself had to play in this decision-making, particularly since he felt disinclined to accept the suggestion that he should put three names forward out of which the Synod would choose one. What he had realistically to accept was that the appointment did not rest exclusively in his own hands as Primate of all England. His private view was that it would be better, after consultation, if he himself were to nominate a priest of his own choosing. This, however, was not agreeable to the Synod. Many possibilities were considered, until the post was offered to, and accepted by, Dr Jago, formerly Chaplain-in-Chief of the Royal Air Force.

So far as the health of the Diocese in the West Indies was concerned – and elsewhere – much depended on the character and capacity of the Bishop, particularly in his relations with the Governor; also how he handled the colour question which could manifest itself in a variety of forms. Thus Miss Ethel Whitehorn while in Bermuda found segregation practised even within the Cathedral itself. In evidence of this, so she told the Archbishop, a coloured friend of hers was forbidden to sit in the area reserved for whites. She had protested to Bishop Jago but he replied that they were dependent on their American Trustees and these simply would not attend unless segregation was practised. Not content with making her complaint to the Archbishop, Miss Whitehorn followed this up with a letter to *The Observer*. Dr Jay, the Senior Chaplain of Lambeth, a priest of enlightened liberal views who had himself served in Bermuda, undertook a reply to this complaint on behalf of the Archbishop. However, thus prompted, the Archbishop himself took this matter up direct with Jago and asked him categorically whether any colour bar was being practised in respect of admission to the Cathedral; also, and in particular, was there any discrimination at the altar? He replied that there was no colour bar whatever at services nor was any form of apartheid resorted to at Communion. On the contrary, 'there are in fact instances of white persons of standing in the community electing to kneel side by side with their coloured brethren at the altar and in some parish churches this is on the increase. However, there were still parishes where long established families were still communicated first.'

The West Indies was in fact passing through a period of social and political change which came to a head in an extreme form in Guyana where in 1953 the United Kingdom Government sent in the troops and suspended the Constitution. There was, to quote from a letter of the Archbishop of the West Indies to Lambeth, 'an insidious rise of the People's Progressive Party which was largely Communist'. Freedom of speech was being suppressed and things were moving towards a totalitarian state in the face of which the opposition was 'ineffective and could do little'. In these circumstances, he claimed, the armed intervention by the British Government was timely. Fortunately the Governor, Sir Alfred Savage, was excellent and the Archbishop was himself optimistic that they would be able to weather the storm and build up the Island's life again.

The Archbishop of the West Indies was not the only Bishop who endeavoured to keep Geoffrey Fisher in touch with what was happening in this part of the world. His advice was often sought in many a context. When compared with these great ethnic, sociological and political problems ecclesiastical controversies concerning the use of the Book of Common Prayer might seem very 'small beer' and thus unimportant. Yet Geoffrey Fisher could not ignore the fact that visitors from Britain to Bermuda, more usually of the evangelical persuasion, brought their critical comments to Lambeth. His response varied from saying that, understandably, they were conscious of the contrast between what they were used to at home and what they found in the island. They must remember that what they found there was what those in Bermuda wanted. However he felt it proper to pass such complaints on to the Archbishop of the West Indies. Indeed he himself contemplated sending a letter from Lambeth around the Anglican Provinces calling attention to the situation but concluded that this would probably do more harm than good.

With Bishop Jago – he was one of a diminishing number of Overseas Bishops of the Canterbury Jurisdiction – Geoffrey Fisher was able to form a relaxed and friendly relationship, made easier by the fact that the two had come to know each other well when Jago was Chaplain-in-Chief to the Royal Air Force. At Christmastide 1949 the Bishop sent greetings to Lambeth enclosing a photograph of himself amidst his clergy. In acknowledging this gift Geoffrey Fisher commented that he could see that the Bishop was 'in good trim' and considering what some groups of clergymen looked like when exposed to the camera, Jago's 'little team give a very good impression indeed'. They struck him as an 'excellent lot of men'. A further quotation from this archiepiscopal letter shows both Geoffrey Fisher's concern for, and the support he could give to, a distant bishop. 'I do not doubt' he wrote, 'that you feel rather far away from home and a little isolated but as your letter shows, you have plenty to occupy you, not only your own flock, but the tourist harvests and excursions from America.' Indeed had Jago put a foot wrong when taking over the diocese it would have soon percolated through to Lambeth. As it was, the only news that had reached him was that he had made a 'first class impression on his arrival'. 'I have no doubt that they are as happy with you as you are with them' – so he concluded.

In 1956 Geoffrey Fisher was busy collecting names for a new Bishop of Bermuda on the resignation of Dr Jago. During the vacancy the Archbishop was approached as to whether he would appoint a temporary visiting Bishop to hold the fort but he firmly declined on the grounds that this might give the impression of a long vacancy. It was better to appoint a successor without delay. There was, in addition, a particular reason why there should not be a protracted interregnum, namely that a new Roman Catholic Bishop was in process of being nominated – a much less complicated and time-consuming operation in a more authoritarian church!

Under the existing Constitution it fell to the Synod to take the necessary steps for electing a successor, as a prelude to which the Archbishop provided three names for consideration and nomination. It was not a way of doing things which Geoffrey Fisher approved and he protested to Canon Marriott that he found it most unsatisfactory: 'I really feel that this is not a proper request to make of the Archbishop!'. If they had this degree of trust, the Synod should ask him to propose one name to go before the Committee. Should this proposal be accepted he would comply – but he could not anyhow limit himself to choosing a man under 50!

Perhaps we may note that this electoral procedure certainly caused confusion, so much so that an appointment to the Bishopric of Bermuda, subsequent to Geoffrey Fisher's retirement, had to be quashed to everybody's embarrassment after it had been publicly announced because the procedure was not correctly followed.

After much conferring the Reverend A. L. E. Williams, Vicar of St Peter with St Swithin, Bournemouth, with a long and varied track record behind him, was appointed and held this office till 1962 by which time Geoffrey Fisher himself had retired. Bishop Williams, after a few years found himself at odds with the Governor and made a strong complaint to the Archbishop who felt the criticisms to be sufficiently important to merit his passing them on to the Colonial Secretary, Ian Mcleod, '. . . if there is criticism from so responsible a quarter, I thought you ought to know it', so he wrote.

More than once an approach came from the Diocese to Lambeth to the effect that Bermuda should enter the Province of Canterbury. The Archbishop explained to those who put the request that overseas dioceses under his final jurisdiction were in fact not attached to any Province. To make the latter possible would require the most complicated legislation as it would effect the Constitution of the Upper and Lower Houses of Convocation. The lawyers would say that such a transference was impossible. Even if it could be achieved the result would be 'fictitious'. Nor could he approve as a long term solution any expedient to prevent Bermuda becoming integrated into the Province of the West Indies.

This brief and highly selective picture of the Anglican Church in the Western Hemisphere may serve, it is hoped, to pinpoint an area of concern in which the Archbishop was necessarily involved and which he took most seriously. It meant much letter-writing, many interviews, resort to ecclesiastical lawyers – and seeing from time to time his friend Henry Sherrill.

PART TEN:

A HISTORIC JOURNEY

CHAPTER 55

The Preparation

THERE can be no doubt that Geoffrey Fisher saw his historic journey to Jerusalem, Istanbul (Constantinople) and Rome in November/December 1960 as the culmination of his archiepiscopate and richly symbolic. He took a pride in the *Ecclesia Anglicana* and believed that as Primate of All England, Archbishop of Canterbury and titular head of the world-wide Anglican Communion, he held a uniquely historic office. Nor did he ever forget that this Church was both Catholic and Reformed thus straddling the divisions which on the Continent had generated separated Communions.

In his taped autobiography Geoffrey Fisher tells us that the inspiration to undertake this journey came to him in a 'flash'. We quote his own words: 'I was in my study; I remember I was walking to and fro thinking about something, and suddenly there came as an inspiration, Jerusalem, Istanbul, Rome. And it lay in my mind. I told it to the Secretary for the Council on Foreign Relations (Satterthwaite) and nobody else. A moment came when I had several Bishops in my study, and we talked about things concerning Rome, and I mentioned this idea, and they all took it. But it only came to me like that because a lot of things had preceded the coming of the "flash".'

The reference here to a 'lot of things' calls attention to the fact that central to the whole purpose of this ecumenical journey was its consummation in Rome.

The planning of the visit to Jerusalem presented few difficulties. Archbishop MacInnes was *in situ* and thus able to advise and make all the necessary arrangements both before and throughout Dr Fisher's stay in Palestine.

As to Istanbul the Archbishop had for many years developed a marked interest in the Orthodox Church, not least because of the 'immense friendship, goodness of heart and devotedness' of Archbishop Germanos whom he came to know well as the representative in London of the Oecumenical Patriarch. Indeed, Geoffrey Fisher would sometimes attend services in his Church which came to have, surprisingly for him, 'a strange attraction', though its music was 'wild and foreign'. His relations with the Orthodox Church were further strengthened when the Patriarch of all the Russias stayed with him at Lambeth. Equally the Archbishop's membership of the Praesidium of the World Council of Churches brought him from time to time in close contact with many Eastern churchmen. Thus as soon as it became known that a visit to this Eastern Rome was to take place, Visser't Hooft informed the Archbishop that he would find the Patriarch in need of consolation in view of the seeming collapse of his imaginative plan for holding a pan-Orthodox assembly in Rhodes.

Jerusalem, Istanbul, Rome – these three seemed to Dr Fisher unique centres for an archiepiscopal, ecumenical pilgrimage. However, and not surprisingly, it was Rome which aroused the greatest public interest and which was to present the most severe difficulties.

There was one reason, in particular, which encouraged Archbishop Fisher to look more hopefully to Rome than otherwise might have been the case. His Holiness Pope John XXIII's humility, warmth and ecumenical zeal soon became increasingly evident in spite of some opposition to his initiatives by the Curia.

The Holy Father – time was not on his side – did not long delay in publicly declaring his hand. On 25 January 1959 he announced that he would be summoning an Ecumenical Council charged with the task 'to seek for the unity which is longed for by Christians in all parts of the world', and to which he was considering inviting representatives of the 'Separated Churches' as observers. Matters were not to work out quite in this way but the whole spirit which Pope John engendered was far removed from that of an earlier encyclical issued by his predecessor in 1946 under which all discussions with non-Catholics were forbidden. In spite of this, however, some contacts with Anglicans were maintained, for example with Bishop Bell, though these were not given much publicity.

Thus the advent of Pope John XXIII early led to a process of loosening up. Evidence of this was seen in that Anglicans travelling to Rome were received at the Vatican and observers from the World Council of Churches were invited to Vatican II. Amongst such visitors welcomed by the Pope was Mervyn Stockwood, Bishop of Southwark, who was said to have exclaimed to his interpreter after his audience that he really must persuade the Archbishop of Canterbury to pay such a visit! The Archbishop however needed neither persuasion nor prompting. Indeed at this very time he was pre-occupied with securing greater co-operation with the Church of Rome. Thus he called together to Lambeth the Archbishop of York, two diocesan bishops, Bishop Bayne, the Executive Director of the Anglican Communion and John Satterthwaite, General Secretary of the Church of England Council on Foreign Relations. The resulting discussion was a protracted one during which the following points were made: (1) That they really did not know precisely what the Pope had in mind to further the cause of unity. Certainly he had already shown himself 'friendly and forthcoming' but did this new mood extend beyond 'return to us'? (2) Already there was an internal struggle within the Roman Catholic Church between those who wished to go forward and those who did not; (3) If feelers were put out to Rome this must not be allowed to drive a wedge between the Orthodox and the Anglicans.

In these circumstances the group collectively asked what ought the Anglican Church to do? To this practical question the consensus view was that nothing in the nature of a general approach to the Romans should yet be attempted but that there ought to be an Anglican liaison officer in Rome in addition to the chaplains of the English and American Churches. In Geoffrey Fisher's summary of this meeting he writes: 'I ventilated the possibility of a journey in November to Jerusalem; Istanbul (as guest of the Oecumenical Patriarch); Rome (to visit the Pope). All were excited at the prospect and encouraged me to go on with it'.

On 4 June 1959 it was announced from the Vatican that the Pope had set up a Secritariat for promoting Christian unity to be presided over by Cardinal Bea, known to be intimate with the Pope as a confidential adviser. In July, Monsignor Willebrands, himself committed to an outgoing catholicism, came over to London and met the Reverend John Satterthwaite who confided to him the Archbishop's desire to visit Rome as part of a wider ecumenical pilgrimage. This intention was passed on by Cardinal Bea direct to the Pope and a welcoming response was dispatched to Lambeth by the Cardinal's Secretary of State. Things were beginning to warm up. In the month of August Geoffrey Fisher attended a meeting of the World Council of Churches at St Andrews in Scotland to which Willebrands had been invited as informally representing the Roman Church. His presence increased the circulation of rumours that Geoffrey Fisher might be visiting Rome. Hence to prevent misunderstandings the Cardinal felt that a clear and sober statement to the Press needed to be made if there were plans for such a visit to the Vatican in the near future.

Those who hoped that until a formal notice had been issued the matter should be treated as confidential were to be bitterly disappointed. Willebrands' informal conversations with Dr Fisher at St Andrews led to speculation that it was he himself who had suggested the visit with the full knowledge and approval of the Pope. If this were true, so Willebrands complained to Satterthwaite, this could be rightly regarded as an 'abuse of the glorious hospitality of the World Council of Churches ... as if I had used this hospitality for my own pre-arranged purposes. Could not this falsehood,' he asked, 'be categorically denied?'

It was now obviously necessary, in order to prevent further irresponsible gossip – assuming that the visit was to take place – that its date should be 'finalised' and then made public. The Pope let it be known informally, both to Willebrands and Bea, that he would gladly receive the Archbishop at the Vatican. It remained only for Willebrands to put this into a letter to Satterthwaite which he did on 27 October 1960. 'We are now happy', he wrote, 'to give you the answer of the Holy Father regarding the visit of His Grace the Archbishop of Canterbury that His Holiness will be most happy to receive His Grace during the indicated time. The Holy Father mentioned, of course, that the visit would be of a private nature and be considered as a customary visit.' A Press release was now drawn up and agreed, Willebrands suggesting a form of words to be issued before 1 November. It stated simply that in the course of his travels the Archbishop would pay a courtesy visit on His Holiness Pope John XXIII.

Thus this proposed meeting of Pope and Archbishop now became public and back in Rome Willebrands wrote a further letter to Satterthwaite on 5 November, deploring the rather short and matter of fact notice of this exceptional event in the official Vatican paper which described the Primate of All England simply as Dr Fisher. Willebrands declared his intention to Satterthwaite of controlling official Press announcements in the future, though this was to prove easier said than done. Also he gave an assurance that the Holy Father would show the Archbishop 'great respect and friendliness'.

Cardinal Bea now suggested that the audience be fixed for 2 December and this was accepted by Lambeth, the Archbishop formally communicating this information to the Apostolic Delegate in the United Kingdom and to Cardinal Heenan, Archbishop of Liverpool. (There was a vacancy at Archbishop's House, Westminster.) He also advised the Metropolitans and Bishops of the Anglican Communion together with the leaders of the Free Churches in Great Britain. As the news of the pilgrimage circulated the general reaction was favourable with but a few exceptions to which reference will be made later. Certainly congratulatory letters poured into Lambeth. Mervyn Stockwood, Bishop of Southwark, who saw himself as having blazed a trail, wrote to Geoffrey Fisher confessing that he was well aware of the 'difficulties, the false hopes and the unkind criticism' which the Archbishop would experience, adding: 'But thank God you are pointing the way by holding out the hand of reconciliation'. The Bishop of Gloucester, in extolling the visit, admitted that he had not found it easy to be 'wholehearted' in his support of the Ecumenical Movement so long as it was 'directed mainly towards the Protestant Churches'. This new initiative would put a 'different colour on the whole thing'. Bishop Bayne, Chief Executive Officer of the Anglican Communion, eschewed using the terminology 'pilgrimage' but conceived the visit in a way most normal people would see it, namely as 'a generous and imaginative breaking of a deadlock in the Christian brotherhood'. Indeed, most people would 'thank God that at last one central figure in Christendom has the heart and the will to make the first move'.

Amongst prominent Free Churchmen who applauded the Archbishop's initiative were Harold Roberts, Hugh Martin, Ernest Payne, Eric Fenn, Aubrey Vere and William Tindal. The Bishop of Argyll and the Isles of the Episcopal Church of Scotland described it, in his usual colourful style, as 'a very interesting and worthwhile safari'.

As already suggested there were those who felt unable to take so optimistic a view of the possible consequences of this visit. The Archbishop of Utrecht expressed his doubts as to whether the Vatican would for a moment withdraw its pronouncement on infallibility and complained that Rome had been 'for us Old Catholics for centuries an angry stepmother'. In response to these doubts the Archbishop explained that his visit was not designed to seek a compromise on doctrinal or ecclesiastical order 'but simply to create a situation of mutual friendship'. In reply to the Archbishop of Perth's enquiry as to whether he would broach the thorny question of joint prayers he replied that he did hope his visit might help to 'unfreeze these Romans in England who are the most repellent and icy of all'.

Typical of an extreme Protestant view and of the man, was a news-heading in the *Ulster Clarion* edited by the Reverend Ian Paisley: 'Nearer my Pope to thee, nearer to Thee'.

Perhaps it was to be expected that news of the intended pilgrimage to Rome would cause a groundswell of Protestant feeling which led to the Queen being approached to prevent it. This request was taken sufficiently seriously for the Queen's Private Secretary, Sir Martin Charteris, to telephone Lambeth saying that he was advised by the Home Office that the Queen 'even if she wanted to had no power to prevent the Archbishop visiting the Pope'. The research here apparently went back to 1955 when Sir Arthur Strutt drew up a memorandum to this effect in connection with a proposed tour abroad by the Dean of Canterbury.

The Archbishop, however, felt it both right and courteous, to convey to the Queen, the Supreme Governor of the Church of England – and before the news became public – precisely what he had in mind. This he did in a letter dated 18 October in which he explained the nature of the visit and the significance of its threefold character. The Oecumenical Patriarch in Istanbul, he pointed out, was the head of all the Orthodox Churches though each one was autonomous. Recently the Patriarch had experienced difficulties in preventing the Patriarch of the Russian Church in Moscow from 'stealing something of his pre-eminence and prestige'. His visit to Rome, he explained, was 'revolutionary'. No Archbishop of Canterbury had visited Rome since Cardinal Pole in the sixteenth century and no Archbishop could have 'reached out across the schism in this way till now'. 'That I can do it,' he went on, 'is due entirely to the fact that the Pope, many in the Vatican, and Continental Roman Catholics (but conspicuously *not* the hierarchy here in England) have of late changed their attitude to us so resolutely. They are showing great interest in the World Council of Churches and the ecumenical movement generally!' He then went on to suggest to the Queen the significance of the Pope's 'Great Council' to be held in 1962; and the possibility of a more liberal attitude to non-Roman churches. It was against this background that he had conceived the idea of visiting Rome. '. . . some people or organisations in England will suspect the worst and will denounce my visit as being in one way a surrender to the Church of Rome.' He admitted that he himself strongly rejected Rome's uncatholic dogmas and had resented and resisted 'the many falsities and cruelties involved in their attitude to us and other Christian Bodies'.

The Queen replied in an encouraging letter which ran as follows: 'What a tremendous tour you are undertaking – the Jerusalem visit sounds most interesting and also Istanbul where I am sure that your visit will help to create confidence. If you do go to Rome would it be the first time that the Archbishop of Canterbury has visited the Pope? There seems to be a strongly deep-rooted distrust of the Roman Church in this country and I hope you won't get as many angry, pleading, hurt, or merely how *could* you do such a thing, letters as I got last year before I went to the Vatican! It was quite a worry at the time'.

There were others, as well as the Queen, who needed to be informed definitively and personally of the Archbishop's imminent travels. In his negotiations to arrange the itinerary the Archbishop had, through the Council on Foreign Relations, been in touch with the Foreign Office, securing its approval and co-operation at every stage. He followed this up, on 19 October, by bringing the Prime Minister, Mr Harold Macmillan fully into the picture and enclosing a copy of his letter to the Queen. The Prime Minister responded by suggesting that they ought to confer together upon such great questions which, though rooted in the past, could yet well influence the future. It is unlikely that two such busy people ever found time to meet in this context of ideas and beliefs. Perhaps this was a pity!

No account of the 'run-up' to the pilgrimage would be complete without some reference to reactions among Roman Catholics in England. Though Geoffrey Fisher was unaware of it, since this was deliberately concealed from him, an influential group of members of that community, as soon as they heard of the possibility of such a visit, did everything they could to promote it on the assumption that the Roman Catholic hierarchy in England would do their best to frustrate it. This support group which consisted basically of Mr John Todhunter, a prominent Roman Catholic layman, Canon Rea and Dom Bennett Innes, a Downside Benedictine, discreetly circularised a short paper suggesting that a number of priests, in the confidence of Archbishop Heenan, should be brought together to offset any activity from a hostile quarter. This private document was sent to the Anglican Bishops of London and Chelmsford as well as to Monsignor Cardinale in Rome who showed it personally to Pope John XXIII. In order to avoid being counter-productive it was agreed that whatever the group did should be carried out with restraint and that meanwhile no provocative action from the Roman end should be embarked upon. Thus Todhunter was distressed when he learnt that John Satterthwaite, with the best of intentions, had suggested that Dickinson, a Cambridge Don, soon to visit Rome, should propose as soon as he got there that discussions take place between Roman and Anglican theologians. Todhunter saw the red light when it suddenly struck him that if this proposal were put to His Holiness Pope John XXIII he would inevitably consult the Westminster hierarchy with the result that control of this operation would pass from the Vatican to Archbishop's House when fatal delays and difficulties would arise.

Conversations of so significant a kind could hardly be kept private nor were they. The fact that confidentiality was inevitably breached meant that so strong an advocate of talks as Cardinal Bea had at times to issue a word of re-assurance to the more cautious. Thus he proclaimed publicly that the Roman Church could not compromise on matters of doctrine though it could do so 'in spheres of liturgy, organisation and discipline'. It is not easy to see how such distinctions can be drawn though doubtless the Archbishop was grateful for the Cardinal's willingness to make them, at least for the time being.

Todhunter and his group continued to fear any precipitous action by those supporting the Archbishop's visit. Thus they were apprehensive when a Roman Catholic Benedictine, backed up by some Anglicans, suggested that Geoffrey Fisher should take an initiative in thanking the Pope for his ecumenical zeal. Equally the Archbishop declined Oliver Tomkins' request, made again with the best intentions, to issue a statement encouraging the setting up of a group of theologians to consider points at issue between the two Communions. What Todhunter dreaded, was that this should encourage Cardinal Tardini, in charge of the Press Office at the Vatican, to make contact with those members of the Roman Catholic hierarchy in England who opposed the visit. Here Todhunter and Geoffrey Fisher were fortunate in that Cardinal Heenan, Archbishop of Liverpool and later to become Archbishop of Westminster, gave the visit his enthusiastic backing, this attitude being at variance with that of the majority of the hierarchy. It certainly helped the project when Heenan was appointed to the newly established Secretariat for Christian Unity, which required many trips to Rome, enabling him to commend the visit to the Pope. The climax came, much to Todhunter's satisfaction, when the Roman hierarchy met and Archbishop Heenan communicated to them a message from the Pope 'in a totally different tone'. 'So that is how', Todhunter commented triumphantly, 'the citadel of English Roman Catholic Apartheid fell to Pope John on Wednesday 12 April 1960, all quietly and agreeably'. Later in the summer, Cardinal Bea held a conference for bishops and clergy at which he expressed himself in similar terms.

Mention has been made of Cardinal Heenan whose support was significant in overcoming Roman Catholic opposition to the visit. Certainly his relations with Geoffrey Fisher were excellent. Another ally, also on the Secretariat for Christian Unity, was Father Corr, described by the Archbishop as a 'nice friendly man'. On one occasion he sought the Archbishop's advice as to how the Pope could set about securing non-Roman observers at Vatican II. Geoffrey Fisher suggested that so far as the non-Episcopal Churches were concerned, an approach should be made to the World Council of Churches with a view to getting the attendance of some ten or twelve representatives. As to Episcopal Churches perhaps the Oecumenical Patriarch and he himself should be invited to nominate six observers. The Archbishop on his part used this opportunity to bring up the question of the relations between himself and the Roman Catholic hierarchy in England and expressed disappointment at his own failure to follow up the beginnings in co-operation forged during the exigencies of the last war. To help improve this unhappy situation it was agreed that he and the Archbishop of York should bring together, with Archbishop Heenan, a few people on either side to discuss the way forward. (Geoffrey Fisher's retirement not long afterwards prevented his arranging such a discussion.)

Recalling these conversations concerning Vatican II, many years later, Geoffrey Fisher commented: 'What a revolution that I, as Archbishop of Canterbury, should be discussing with a man who would go straight to the Council of Cardinal Bea's Secretariat where ideas would be ventilated which afterwards might be translated into direct relationship between Rome and ourselves'.

CHAPTER 56

Jerusalem

AT 10.30 a.m. on 22 November 1960, Geoffrey Fisher, accompanied by his Senior Chaplain, the Reverend Frederick Temple, a nephew of Archbishop William Temple, and John Satterthwaite, Secretary of the Church of England Council on Foreign Relations walked out of Lambeth Palace to embark upon a truly historic journey. Some two hours later they left London Airport *en route* for Jerusalem. The 'plane touched down at Frankfurt-on-Main, arriving at Beirut that same evening. As the aircraft approached the brilliantly lit city the Archbishop was able to glimpse the hills of Lebanon. He was met by the British Ambassador, Sir Philip Moore Crossthwaite, a diplomat of wide experience in the Middle East, whom the Archbishop found 'kindly and welcoming'. He was also received by the Reverend J. Grimstead, the Resident Anglican Chaplain. The Archbishop spent the night at the Embassy, having as a fellow guest Stephen Spender who was on his way to 'an obscure conference on Tolstoy'. Conversation seems to have flowed easily, evidence for which is their late going to bed. In spite of this nocturnal session the Archbishop left early, departing from Beirut at 8.20 a.m. and arriving in Tel Aviv, where he was met by the Governor, the Mayor, the Archbishop in Jerusalem, the Bishop in Jordan, Libya and Syria (Cuba' in) and representatives of the Orthodox Churches. The Archbishop was now to experience, for the first time, the fascinating drive up to Jerusalem which for him had the interest of novelty but whose biblical sites had been familiar to him, in imagination at least, since early childhood.

The first day in Jerusalem (23 November) set the pattern for the crowded schedule which was to follow since the City contained so much that was sacred and significant to a devout Christian. There were many religious sites to view, churches to pray in and representative people, lay and ecclesiastical, to meet. Also there was a political dimension which the Archbishop could not ignore and where he knew he must tread warily. The division between Arab and Jew made it the more necessary, in his contacts with the Anglican Church, to recognise that the majority of its members were Arab and that these embodied an indigenous Palestinian Christianity. Also the American dimension needed to be taken into account.

It was appropriate that on his arrival in Jerusalem Geoffrey Fisher should first visit Archbishop MacInnes' Cathedral Church of St George where he was greeted by the singing of a *Te Deum* at a 'little Service'. Having gladly discharged this act of courtesy, he drove to the Mount of Olives situated on the range of hills east of Jerusalem and separated from the Temple Mountain by the Kedron Valley. He then walked around the traditional site of Bethphage where the disciples found the donkey on which Christ rode into Jerusalem on the Jericho Road. Nearby was Gethsemane where He prayed in great agony. After lunch with Bishop Cuba'in and making a few personal calls he travelled the five miles to Bethlehem, a busy, thriving town of some 15,000 inhabitants where he was received by the Mayor at Rachel's tomb and looked out on to the Shepherds' fields. He prayed in the Basilica of the Church of the Nativity, said to be founded by Constantine and restored by Justinian. Inside it were grottoes having legendary associations with the birth of Jesus. After viewing these it was back to St George's for a tea party with the Cathedral staff and, later, dinner with the Cuba'ins.

Thursday 24 November was for the Archbishop a never-to-be forgotten day. It began early with a call upon the newly appointed American Chaplain – it was Thanksgiving Day – and his celebrating Holy Communion. As to what followed the Archbishop writes in his private diary: '... it is really impossible to describe or even to remember the impression of this day – moving beyond belief not merely and chiefly because of the historic scenes of Our Lord's Passion but because of these events recalled in the midst of people of all sorts and myself'. The Archbishop found the Acting Governor 'friendly' and he much appreciated the privilege of driving right into the Temple area where he was met by the Guardian, Sheik Mustafu Ansari who surprised him by being dressed in ordinary weekday clothes and looking more like a guide than a dignitary. Geoffrey Fisher's own interest and enthusiasm about everything he saw made him a most acceptable sightseer and maybe he recalled that over a decade ago he was busily engaged in studying maps of the Holy City while preparing his own abortive scheme for dividing Palestine between Jews and Arabs. The Dome of the Rock built by Abul-El-Meleck on the site of the Temple in AD 688 after the Arab Conquest, was judged by the Archbishop 'very fine'. He entered the holy shrine in a spirit of reverence putting on the large slippers as a mark of respect – and, as he said, to protect the carpets! Here he was received at the door by the cousins of the Sheik whose family was the traditional guardian of the Temple area.

However, the high spot of this tour of Jerusalem was undoubtedly reached when the Archbishop threaded his way along the *Via Dolorosa*. Though his own account of this experience is somewhat disjointed and repetitive – it was written literally within hours of its happening – it yet deserves quotation: 'The Stations of the Cross are really ecclesiastical inventions, the supposed events being placed at convenient places in streets leading from the Praetorium down to the Typaec Valley in the City and then up steps to the Church of the Holy Sepulchre. Looking at the people in their cave-like shops I did realise how Our Lord must have walked through its narrow crowded streets of people doing their ordinary work and very likely paying little heed to the procession. So up and up to the forecourt of the Church of the Holy Sepulchre. As I approached the doorway the Latin organ played "God Save the Queen" (What of the Papal edict excommunicating Elizabeth!) and the Armenian bells clanged. I cannot describe the Church. I hardly saw it. I remember the first place [where] I knelt – a stone on which Our Lord's Body was supposed to have rested from Calvary on one side to the Sepulchre on the other . . . why can I not recall this? Because throughout in a strange way I became not only passive but feeling a kind of victim with Our Lord. For from the moment I entered the Church I was engulfed in a great crowd of Orthodox and Franciscans who surrounded me and, so to speak, pushed and hustled me on all sides. Moreover, my arm on the left side was held by sometimes two, sometimes three Top Orthodox, while my right hand was upheld by the Chief Franciscans, a devoted disciple of mine, Paulos keeping tight hold most of the way; and an Armenian sometimes holding [me] too. There were many steps down to St Helena's Chapel and up and down everywhere. I hardly walked; I hardly had a chance to stumble, since I was almost propelled by others, Franciscans and Armenians, who *cared* for me and *loved* me as they bore me round. At a place I would kneel and *feel* Our Lord looking on [at this] strange mixture of past and present: then borne on again. And so to speak I was pulled this way and that and felt lovingly at their mercy. And I felt that somehow like this Our Lord was pulled and hustled and felt at the mercy of his voluntary guardians. More than that I cannot recall. At intervals the Bells would clang again. The whole thing was an astonishing flowing of every kind of an excited emotion round and over ME – not as a person, but as a kind of central point of their triumphal "showing forth"'.

However, there was a sombre side to this experience. Thus early in his visit the Archbishop was made vividly aware that 'the divisions of the denominations are intense: their territories are marked out; they watch like cats lest anyone gains an inch not his! Yet, paradoxically, they were already fused together in One, as they maintained themselves against one another'.

For the Archbishop, in this city of many Churches, an important part of his mission was to introduce himself to the Patriarchs and to extend to them fraternal greetings. First to be called upon was the Greek Patriarch who received him in his residence at the threshold of his audience chamber. After a short speech of welcome to the Primate of All England, His Beatitude pronounced a blessing and presented the Primate with a silver salver. As to what these two ecclesiastics said to each other as they sipped their coffee was probably not so significant as the mere fact that they were there together in one place. Indeed, Geoffrey Fisher later confessed that he could not remember a word of their conversation!

His next port of call was, very properly, the Latin Patriarch, 'a friendly man', when the same procedure was followed as also was the case with the Armenian Patriarch and the Brotherhood of St James. To each of them the Archbishop gave an inscribed copy of the Book of Common Prayer.

These were all courtesy calls, the basic intention being for the Archbishop to introduce himself and to greet as an Anglican the heads of the various Churches. Brief speeches were delivered, he himself in his diary confessing that he used the opportunity to 'hint at some home truths'. His session with the Franciscan Custodian and his Brethren seems to have been more informal and relaxed making possible a true meeting of minds. 'Here was I', he writes, 'sitting in the seat of honour in an assembly of Franciscans. Their Chief was abounding in friendship saying 'there is no barrier between us but language', to which Geoffrey Fisher retorted that when people can laugh together, 'all barriers are overcome!' Maybe such language on both sides was extravagant due to the excitement and unique character of the occasion but at least it represented a desire to break down barriers which had survived far too long. In the same ecumenical spirit, the Archbishop was presented, as he left the Franciscans, with a scroll and the Custodian, on the authority of the Pope, decorated him with the Medal for Pilgrims. The monks crowded round him, many of them kneeling and kissing his ring. Father O'Donovan, who served in the Jerusalem diocese, exclaimed: 'after this I can believe anything', adding that he was 'aghast at the attitude of the English R.C.s when this is possible'.

In the afternoon of this second day the Archbishop had a most important engagement fraught with a unique significance. This was a 'get together' with Bishop Cuba'in and others of his diocese. Geoffrey Fisher had seen the Bishop many times at Lambeth; had corresponded regularly with him; and had already enjoyed his hospitality in Jerusalem. This was a more formal occasion however which included discussion on subjects of mutual concern. Geoffrey Fisher certainly used this valuable opportunity to the full. Following his customary practice he shook hands with the whole company and entered into a long conversation with two lawyers, taking satisfaction in thinking that he had 'helped to solve their doubts' – probably concerning some legal aspects of the recently negotiated diocesan constitution. Bishop Cuba'in welcomed the Archbishop warmly after which the latter responded with a few words addressed to the whole gathering. It had always been Geoffrey Fisher's wish, he said, that members of this Arab Congregation should feel themselves engrafted into the world-wide Anglican Communion without losing their distinctive 'Arabness' which necessarily involved a link with the Archbishop in Jerusalem as Metropolitan and also with Lambeth. The Archbishop began by giving a short history of the Jerusalem bishopric going back many years prior to the creation of the new diocese of which Cuba'in was its first Bishop.

The domestic character of this occasion was well represented when an Arab lady stepped forward and presented him with a Latin New Testament and also with a silver knife to be given to Mrs Fisher. This led the Archbishop to explain why, to their mutual regret, she was unable to be with him.

It was by now mid-afternoon and the Archbishop had been on the 'go' since early morning. He now indulged himself in the luxury of fifteen minutes' sleep, after which he was off again at 3.30 pm to view more closely Gethsemane and experience its poignant associations. He was moved by the Franciscan garden with the old olive trees and entered into the new Church in the Rock. After this, he was 'armed' by the Greeks into their Church, the Franciscans staying outside, leaving the Archbishop to thread his way down a long staircase to the vault of the Virgin's tomb. Now it was the turn for the Franciscans to take over again which they did by escorting him to a small chapel dedicated to the Disciples praying on the lake. Once he had emerged safely into the open air the double escort resumed their joint protective role.

From this world of Christian tradition and pious fancy, Geoffrey Fisher was brought back into the twentieth century by a visit to the Rockefeller Museum, a building which greatly impressed him and where he was taken to see its treasures which included fragments of the Dead Sea Scrolls. After a brief rest – like Winston Churchill this always restored him to full vigour – he was off to an 'At Home' with the Consul-General where he met a large number of people, amongst whom were representatives from the Commonwealth; members of the United Nations' peace-keeping force; personnel from UNRRA; the Director of a Cheshire Home; and many journalists. Doubtless it was with a degree of private satisfaction that he later entrusted to the confidentiality of his diary that many of those present were amazed at his physical resilience. Indeed a member of the Press gave it as his opinion that though he had accompanied a number of royal tours none was so hectic as this one. His general assessment was one of astonishment at its success and the 'enthusiasm with which everything had gone'. Finally in bringing this eventful day to a close he went back to base for dinner with Archbishop MacInnes, two of his fellow guests being the British Consul and his wife. Fortunately, perhaps, he was back in his bedroom by 10.40 pm, when he wrote up his diary, switched off the light at 12.10 am and 'slept well'.

Friday 25 November was again 'fairly non-stop'. It began with a question-session laid on by a BBC team who were annoyed with ITV for stealing a march on them by getting in first. The interrogation was, as might be expected, somewhat as follows: (1) What places had impressed him most, to which he replied: 'The Temple area with the City crowding in on one side, the Mount of Olives raising itself on the other'. (2) What were the prospects for Christian Unity? Here he confessed to being greatly encouraged by what he had witnessed in Jerusalem. True there were divisions among the Churches but all were clearly comprehended in a brotherhood, if not a theological unity.

Later the Archbishop set out for Ramallah, a considerable town beyond the airport, the journey being through what he describes as an 'exciting' countryside. He found there a small church which the congregration had now outgrown and as a consequence migrated into the hospitable house of the Parson. The Women's organisation gave the Archbishop a most beautifully worked piece of material for Mrs Fisher. His impressions on leaving Ramallah are recorded in his private diary: 'We went to and fro among the hills. I could not take my eyes off them. Along this desolate [countryside] is the Valley of Adders and no wonder! Some [land] seemed too rocky for cultivation but most were terraced to the last inch with stone walls with olive trees here and there.' Geoffrey Fisher's attitude, by and large, to biblical sites was one of a reverent agnosticism though at Jacob's Well near to Mount Girazim he knelt down at the little stone altar and drank its fresh water, almost persuaded that he was on the actual site where Jesus met the Samaritan woman. He was welcomed by a Greek Orthodox churchman and concluded his stay with coffee at the Priests' House where he was hospitably received. Then on to Nablus, a largish town which had been rebuilt after an earthquake. Here he looked in on the hospital where he was regaled with affectionate memories of Sister Katie. Then between two mountains up to Sobaste Hill Top, the Old Samarian capital of the Northern Kingdom till 722 BC when it fell before the Assyrians. To 'placate' the Press he was photographed against the background of a cactus tree and a patient donkey. An ambitious attempt to induce a passing camel to be one of the company proved quite a different matter. 'It held its head high and looked with contempt on us all, with me holding it by a head rope. Then the owner made it get down, unbelievably clumsy, front first and then knees, joints of back legs and so to earth! I put my hand on its head a bit afraid it might bite, and I said: "It is no Christian camel". Then I tried again. It fought and gave in and just snorted scornfully. I did not know that its owner was telling me not to put my hand on its head as it would bite; it looked a surly brute.'

From the Hill Top they proceeded to the assembly point where the Archbishop was again submitted to ordeal by photographs but this time in the company of a troop of Arab Boy Scouts. Then he witnessed some spectacular dancing and had coffee with the old men of the village. For lunch the Archbishop was conducted to a private house belonging to a cultivated Arab family with a 'charming daughter'. To please his guests the host had invited a large number to share the repast with him including a group of Orthodox churchmen. The table 'groaned and there were two huge dishes with half a sheep on them'. Geoffrey Fisher, however, consumed rice, yoghurt, sweetcorn and fruit, thus playing the part of a good food reformer. He left a little more knowledgeable as to what Our Lord referred to at the Last Supper in the phrase 'dippeth his hand with me in the dish'.

After lunch the party went off to a synagogue which consisted of a plain room with a curtain concealing the ark. He met its leading men including the aged Rabbi in charge. There were three chairs on two of which were deposited the Scrolls of the Samaritan Pentateuch. As a great privilege there lay exposed the oldest Scroll of all taken that morning from a safe, and written, so he was told 'ten years after the death of Moses'. Later Geoffrey Fisher spoke to boys from a technical school and discussed their education with them. He could not but wonder what these boys made of their traditional faith. In taking his leave and expressing his thanks, the Archbishop assured them that their small community would never be forgotten so long as the story of the Good Samaritan continued to be told.

It was not to be wondered at that Dr Fisher 'slept a bit' on his way back to Jerusalem before looking in on the Order of St John's Hospital and arriving back in time for the Mayor's Reception. At this function he shook hands with multitudes of people, including the Apostolic Delegate who turned up to meet the Archbishop for the first time. The Mayor made a speech and Geoffrey Fisher replied 'on the spur of the moment' taking as his theme 'freedom'. Jerusalem, he said, was a witness to unity since it was home to three faiths and also endeavoured to harmonise the civic with the religious life. After this he managed to secure two hours' sleep before a dinner in the precincts of St George's. Geoffrey Fisher was always a good conversationalist not least because he was genuinely interested in the people to whom he was talking and this broke down barriers. He exchanged views with Sir Patrick Hancock, British Ambassador to Israel and his wife. Another lady, a Roman Catholic, he found over-talkative which tempted him light-heartedly to enlighten her about 'the other side of the Church of Rome'. Later in the evening Sir Patrick Hancock spoke frankly to the Archbishop about Israel. It was remarkable what it had done to bring together so miscellaneous an assortment of Jews from many lands. It had done this partly through religion (though there was little real Judaism); partly through military service – and a common fear of Egypt. The fact was that both Israel and Jordan depended on each other for their freedom against Nasser and should be open allies. The very top men knew this; but no one dare say it. The Arabs were too fanatically anti-Jew and were for getting their old lands back.

Saturday 26 November, which the Archbishop spent in Jerusalem, was used by him as, in a sense, a mopping-up operation. At his special request he was taken early at 7.30 am by Archbishop MacInnes to the Church of the Holy Sepulchre so that he might experience it in greater quiet and absorb its atmosphere in a way which had been quite impossible on his former visit. Having done this he called on the Mayor, Teddy Kollek, a 'very good, humble man', to thank him for the party on the previous night. He told the Archbishop that the civic authority was in process of a large-scale tree planting operation on the Mount of Olives analagous to the one million trees which had been planted in Jordan. Geoffrey Fisher then viewed the excavations on the site of the Pool of Bethesda, consisting of two great cisterns where Christ healed the lame man. The White Father who was escorting him explained that it might well be that the 'troubling of the water' occurred when it was transferred from one cistern to the other. Being pressed for time on this, his last day, he went immediately off to Jericho. The drive there 'beggaring description', to quote his own words, took him through desperately arid mountains and steep valleys of friable lime-stone along a tortuous road ever mounting higher and higher. So up and up they went, then down and down into the great Rift Valley which reminded the Archbishop of Kenya. Dr MacInnes repeated what was almost his theme song that though the world knew what the Jews had done to develop Israel few knew of the achievements of the Arabs. A main purpose for the Archbishop undertaking this journey was to see the excavations at Jericho. He found that Joshua's walls had disappeared by human destruction and erosion. There were strata reaching to Abraham's period in 2,000 BC, and more to the seventh and eighth millenium. A vivid contrast followed when Geoffrey Fisher inspected two refugee camps run by the Young Men's Christian Association which had trained some 100,000 boys and girls in particu-lar skills. And so, finally, once more back to Jerusalem for a reception in MacInnes' Hall at 4.30 pm. The guest list was impressive and included the Apostolic Delegate, the various Patriarchs, and the Fran-ciscan Custodians. MacInnes delivered a brief word of welcome and the Archbishop was equally brief in reply. Then all assembled came up, headed by two old blind ladies who had known Sister Katie, and he shook them all by hand. The 'very nice Mayor' of Bethlehem was also among these.

Very understandably Geoffrey Fisher was keyed up to a high state of excitement, indeed satisfaction, at the spontaneous and warm tributes paid him. Alas! news came through from London arising out of a local Arab report that the Archbishop at the Mayor's reception on the previous evening had blamed English statesmen for the Palestinian 'mess'. For the moment the Archbishop was overwhelmed with grief and sadly wrote in his private diary: 'It shook me a bit. From the height of happiness it pushed me down to a sort of gloom that I had done everything wrong and anyhow what was the good of it all?' However the Archbishop felt that he could not let such a grave and embarrassing accusation go unanswered and he denied it in these words: '. . . in the distress of the Holy Land, I did not conceal that my country had had a share in bringing it about but I blamed none, for all had acted in the highest purpose and good conscience'. 'History', he concluded ruefully, 'is a hard master.'

This incident is personally revealing in that it illustrates how sensitive, deep down, Geoffrey Fisher really was, though he usually affected to take everything in his stride.

The truth is that it was unfortunate the British reporters had left the reception before the Archbishop spoke which meant that the English newspapers were dependent on foreign journalists. Geoffrey Fisher, fortunately, was not without supporters. Redfern of the *Sunday Express*, and Taylor of Reuters were deeply disturbed at what they regarded as a deplorable attack on the Archbishop. As a consequence they rang up London to the effect that the local paper was completely unfair and the Archbishop had categorically denied it.

At each 'port of call' – Jerusalem, Istanbul and Rome – Geoffrey Fisher preached a sermon carefully prepared, well expressed and of contemporary significance, these being later published under the general heading 'Feeling Our Way'. Collectively they bear witness to a deep conviction. 'Wherever I went' he writes, 'I found myself met with and embraced by that very spirit of unity which I was seeking to explore'.

His sermon in the Collegiate Church of St George the Martyr, Jerusalem on Wednesday 27 November was realistic, encouraging and helpful. Recognising that they were living in a world of competition, rivalry and a cold war dividing man from man, race from race, and creed from creed, yet at the same time there was 'blowing through the churches, not a wind of change but a great wind of fellowship in Christ'. As for himself he confessed: 'I feel, we feel, a renewal of faith, hope and charity'.

On 28 November after celebrating Communion in St George's

Cathedral, Geoffrey Fisher gave an interview to Jordan Broadcasting, the questions being as he put it 'straightforward'. He then gave time to Archbishop MacInnes, discussing with him the problems of Persia and the appointment of a new Bishop; whether Dr Cragg would prove the right man to take episcopal charge of Egypt; and how a stipend could be found for this particular appointment. He discussed the scheme to institute a college at St George's, primarily for Anglican theologians, a project which Geoffrey Fisher commended because 'it is really something we owe not only to ourselves but to the other communities'. He preached during Matins, his own verdict on this effort being that it was 'good stuff' and, though long, went down quite well. This over, he immediately crossed into Israel and called on the Mayor. Farewells followed after which he visited a religious centre and was received by a Rabbinate judge. This was indeed a cordial visit.

It is quite clear from his diary that Archbishop Fisher regarded his stay in Jerusalem as specially important, both to himself and to the church as a whole. He found encouragement in the rapturous and uninhibited welcome with which he had been universally received. He was convinced, to quote his own words, that 'the Holy Spirit is using my tour to draw men together by cords of love . . . I claim nothing, I have nothing'. He believed that there was an upsurge of the spirit and as a result 'everyone feels a move to some greater unity and sees in my visit a symbol of an *impulse* and a prayer for closer unity between the Churches'.

In the course of his travels Geoffrey Fisher picked up a great deal of political and informal gossip. Thus while one evening having supper in Jerusalem with the Governor who had formerly been Ambassador in London, the latter proved extremely explicit, giving it as his opinion that if the ultimate choice had to be made Jordan would side with Israel *against* Nasser. To his diary Geoffrey Fisher sadly confided: 'The conflict is unending – without a glimmer of reconciliation anywhere. The Arabs cry *Justice* against the Jew; the Jew, what I have I keep and see what I can make of it'.

The Archbishop could not but be concerned with the general situation of Christians, most of them Arabs, living in Jerusalem even if his conclusions were somewhat paradoxical. He was shocked by the denominational jealousy which obtained between the various Churches where the possession and stewardship of the Holy Places were concerned. Committed to what used to be the average Englishman's dedication to a work ethic, and his own life-style across the years, he tended to believe that the 'venom' and mutual recrimination between the various Churches, only too evident, derived largely from members not having enough to occupy their minds.

Above and beyond political and religious division, Geoffrey Fisher undoubtedly found his first and brief encounter with the Holy Land a soul-searching experience. His own religious faith was ultimately a simple commitment to Christ as Lord, a faith which sustained him across the years. As it was within this context that his visit to Palestine came alive and was lifted, at times, into an almost mystical identity with his Saviour. Thus he confesses that in the Church of the Holy Sepulchre, after having traversed the *Via Dolorosa* he was 'in prayer rather than praying', feeling that Christ who had suffered all the contradictions of sinners was with him. He was 'almost in tears of spiritual exaltation' when he travelled northward within Israel and was fascinated with the physical terrain which had been the scene of Christ's ministry. It was thoughts of Jesus which were uppermost in his mind. Here he was conscious of 'Our Lord walking from village to village and to Jacob's well; people gathering round him and his talking to them of God's kingdom'. Most of Jesus' life was spent in this countryside working there, teaching, and at last in Jerusalem 'arguing and dying'. It was only in his personal, private diary that Geoffrey Fisher unburdened himself in this intimate way.

CHAPTER 57

Istanbul

THE Archbishop reported early at Jerusalem Airport for his flight to Beirut, timed to depart at 9.30 a.m. He was accompanied by Archbishop MacInnes and Bishop Cuba'in who, with a group of social workers, were off to attend a conference. During the brief flight of just over an hour Dr Fisher was able to look down upon the Plain of Jezreel, the Sea of Galilee and Mount Hermon, the latter rearing its snow-capped peak to some 9,000 feet. There was a special reason why the Archbishop was anxious to visit the Lebanon even if only briefly. The Greek Orthodox Bishop there, Sabiti, whom he had entertained at Lambeth during the summer, was eager to return the generous hospitality he had received during his visit to London, which included an audience with the Queen. Not surprisingly, therefore, the Metropolitan was awaiting him at the airport in the company of churchmen representing various Christian denominations. Present also were the Chef de Protocol of the Ministry for Foreign Affairs and Mr Crossthwaite, Consul-General of the British Embassy. The Archbishop drove with the Metropolitan to his residence, where he was given the honour of sitting enthroned in the great Council Chamber. There followed a 'sumptuous' lunch attended by some twenty guests. After a brief rest the Archbishop called on the Maronite Patriarch at his Monastery of Bkerke which was half an hour's drive from the city of Beirut. Here he was cordially received and photographs were taken prominently figuring the Archbishop. On his drive back he called in at the Residence of the Armenian Patriarch and later attended a reception given by the combined Councils of St George's Church. As important, though not so spectacular as some other contacts which he made, was the Archbishop's meeting over tea with Bishop Cuba'in and the Beirut Church Council. The Archbishop complimented them on having 'made good' and discussed with them their need for a church, a hall, a site and a parsonage.

To finish off this hurried visit, a large dinner party was laid on in the Archbishop's Palace at which some 110 people were present. Dr Fisher was not, by natural inclination, a 'dressy' man but on this occasion he sported his Armenian Cross and Franciscan Medal, in addition to the Royal Victorian Chain and the GCVO Star. The British Ambassador was pleased at this display but thought it unfortunate that conspicuous by his absence was the Sunni Mufti of the Lebanon who did not even send another in his place, apparently on the grounds that wine was to be served. The non-Christian communities were represented, therefore, only by one of the two Druse Shiahs. On the other hand the Christians were there in full force, the Armenian Catholicos attending in person and sitting at the table on the Archbishop's right. This gave the latter the opportunity, in the course of a protracted meal, to advise the Catholicos to secure an agreement with the Supreme Catholicos along the lines of the constitutional relationship which obtained between Canterbury and York. Geoffrey Fisher comments that he 'took it well' and gave him an icon at the end of the dinner. It was not until 12.30 a.m. that the Archbishop was able to get to bed. He tells us that he slept well though, not surprisingly, he woke up in the course of the night when he took a 'little digestive pill'.

Diplomats, by the very nature of their profession, tend to be somewhat over-anxious, anticipating difficulties. However Crossthwaite was agreeably surprised with how well the banquet had gone. 'It was indeed a happy occasion', so he reported home to London. 'The atmosphere was noticeably more cordial than the high standard of Arab hospitality alone would have required'. 'I have since met', he went on, 'many of those who were present and they all agreed on this and on the genuine pleasure caused by Dr Fisher's visit here and his interest in promoting closer relations between the two Churches.' Indeed though the visit was a brief one, Crossthwaite believed that the Archbishop's appearance in Beirut had done a vast deal for Great Britain's stock in Lebanon.

At Beirut airport there was a moving series of goodbyes for the departing Archbishop. Metropolitan Suiliel, in his barely understandable French, asked that his respects be conveyed to the Queen, the Duke of Edinburgh and Mrs Fisher. There then followed warm farewells to Archbishop MacInnes and Bishop Cuba'in after which at 6.05 a.m., in brilliant sunshine, the Archbishop became airborne, arriving some two and a half hours later in Istanbul, where he found that the sunshine had given way to cloudy, coldish weather, 'very English'. He was met by a reception committee consisting of the Metropolitans of Philadelphia, Intros, Sardis and Tenedos. Geoffrey Fisher soon felt that the last of these was the most liberal, due he suspected, to his having been in charge, at an earlier stage in his ministry, of the Orthodox community in Leeds and Manchester. Also waiting to greet the Archbishop was a group of Anglican clergymen. While in Istanbul, Geoffrey Fisher was the guest of his Holiness the Most Reverend Athenagoras, Oecumenical Patriarch of Constantinople, though he was put up at the Hilton Hotel.

It was to be expected, though it came as somewhat of a shock to the Archbishop personally, that he should be made immediately aware of a totally different atmosphere and not only in the weather. In Jerusalem he had felt that 'the Church and the Churches were the important features and the rest 'nowhere'. He had been fêted and surrounded by admiring monks and excited onlookers. Now in Constantinople he suddenly found himself in 'an impersonal, large city, where no one is noticed or matters – a Turkish, Moslem city at that'. Maybe this contrasting experience was salutary in reminding the Archbishop that in spite of its Christian foundation by Constantine in AD 326, and the recognition of its Patriarch as Supreme in the East vying with the Pontiff in Rome, Constantinople was a Turkish city and had been so since 1453. True, under the Treaty of Lausanne, drawn up in 1918, its Government was required to safeguard the rights of Christians who resided there, in return for which concessions the Patriarch of the city was required to reside in Turkey. Saint Sophia from being a Christian church had become a mosque until it was finally converted into a museum. In British diplomatic circles some were uneasy at the timing of the Archbishop's visit to Istanbul the reasons for which G.C. Wetheridge, the British Consul-General, set out in a dispatch to the Foreign Office in London. The trials of the members of the former régime were certain to be still in session to which the Oecumenical Patriarch was to be called as a witness concerning the anti-Greek riots in September 1955.

Geoffrey Fisher's visit to Istanbul began in the Patriarchal Cathedral of St George when he blessed the people and was presented with a cross. He was then escorted to the study of His All Holiness the Oecumenical Patriarch of Constantinople, a most impressive figure, some six feet three inches in height, with a long, flowing white beard and a benign countenance. The two were not unknown to each other having met years before in America. His All Holiness now introduced the Archbishop to the members of the synod after which he attended an all-male lunch at the residence of the Consul-General, a keen Christian and lay reader. The United Kingdom Ambassador flew in from Ankara when the two engaged in a wide-ranging conversation which included an exchange of views on the Nuremburg Trials and whether it was better for justice to be seen to be done than for lynch law to have taken over. The Archbishop's party was then conducted to Hagia Sophia, where they saw the well-known mosaic pavement. The Archbishop was pleased to meet the Armenian Patriarch who had incurred criticism earlier in the year when he was indiscreet enough to write to Mr Mendoris, the Greek Prime Minister, applauding his drastic measures against rioting students. Archbishop Fisher was regaled with gossip by the Armenian Patriarch concerning Pope John who years previously had been Apostolic Delegate in Istanbul. It was in this city, that the future Pontiff had 'learned his friendly commonsense relations to Orthodox and Anglican'. He was 'no diplomat', just a 'humble, simple, loving person', and with 'no kind of inhibition'. The Patriarch was sure that the Archbishop and the Pope 'would get on like wildfire'. The Pope wanted nothing more than to be relieved of his high office and to return to his Piedmontese village home!

The evening was devoted to a supper laid on by the Anglican Community at which the Archbishop met a number of people, including women, whom he would not otherwise have encountered. They embarked upon what Dr Fisher described as 'a real go on unity', during which time he had an opportunity of discussing general matters with the Apostolic Delegate as well as with the Bishop of Tenedos. The exact nature of this conversation the Archbishop does not reveal, his comment being tantalisingly brief, namely that whatever he said they had 'swallowed it'.

The next day, 30 November, even the indefatigable Geoffrey Fisher found 'a sort of endurance test'. It began with his attending 'a nice little celebration' at 8 am in the Chapel of St Helena, situated in the grounds of the Consul-General's residence, at which fifteen communicants were present. Some two hours later he sampled the Liturgy of St Andrew which, he found 'impressive', though his Protestant eyes saw it as 'crying out for Reformation', not least because of the time 'wasted' by members of the Holy Synod in their genuflecting repeatedly three times to each other. Perhaps his judgement was conditioned somewhat by his being required to stand for a stretch of three hours! The Oecumenical Patriarch, clad in his red and gold vestments, a jewelled crown on his head, presented the Archbishop, who was wearing his Coronation cope, after which he was kissed and embraced by all present, an ordeal to which he had valiantly accustomed himself across the years. His All Holiness read a speech of welcome to which the Archbishop replied. The two churchmen embraced one another, after which the Patriarch hung an icon round the Archbishop's neck. He also presented a cross to his chaplain. Most of the congregation then filed past to greet the Primate of All England and when he finally left the church he was given a spontaneous ovation. This was the prelude to a 'banquet lunch' at the Patriarchate when, in return, the Archbishop himself distributed gifts to His Holiness which included the customary silver salver.

For Geoffrey Fisher his address delivered in Christ Church, Istanbul, earlier in the day was indeed important as he had long been interested in and concerned for the Greek Orthodox Church in spite of a somewhat English attitude to its liturgy. His basic message on this occasion was expressed in these words: 'Every Church must look beyond itself to the family of Churches as in Apostolic times the Church in Jerusalem looked out, first as leader and then as a fellow

member only, to the Churches in Asia, in Egypt, in Greece and in time
to Rome'. As to contemporary ecumenicism he distilled his own feelings
thus: 'May I draw a distinction here which I find useful between Unity
and Union in the Church and between the Churches. Union for me
stands for something formal, functional, reasoned and ratified. Such
unions have a great importance, a truly sacramental importance
whether in the union of the marriage bond or the union of the churches
in one communion. It is to that kind of Union, a formulated Union, a
concordat between Churches which nevertheless still remain separately
identifiable and responsible, that the Churches are slowly beginning to
reach out'.

The climax to the Istanbul visit was now reached when the Archbishop and the Oecumenical Patriarch – only John Satterthwate was
present – engaged in a long discussion, theologically orientated. This
was indeed a significant conversation and the Archbishop had been
primed in advance by Visser't Hooft, as to how it might be used to the
best advantage. The Patriarch, he counselled, needed 'consolation and
encouragement', since recently his 'imaginative plan for a pan-Orthodox
meeting in Rhodes seem to have collapsed'. True he was now thinking
in terms of a revised date in the spring but this again was unlikely to
take place since Greece was preoccupied with internal difficulties. In
this unhopeful situation it was important that the Patriarch should not
abandon his ecumenical plans but persist in promoting them.

Having acted on this advice the Archbishop's conversation with the
Patriarch then centred around the validity of Anglican Orders and
hence inter-communion. Here the Metropolitan of the Orthodox
Church believed that the latter could follow given a mutually recognised Baptism, Orders and Eucharist. The two also briefly turned their
attention to the contemporary political situation. Geoffrey Fisher
summed up his impressions of the Patriarch and their discussions in
these words: '. . . a very happy and useful conversation. He is really
grateful for the encouragement given by me. He wants a rapid advance
of Churches into a unity of convenience. He regards me as having set
the pace. He told me to tell the Pope – "He Must Act!".' The Patriarch
also confided to the Archbishop that he hoped to be in London in the
following year.

In the evening Dr Fisher presided over a confirmation service at the
Anglican Church of St George after which his last engagement was to
attend a supper party, the host being the Holy Synod and the guests
including the Consul-Generals of the United States and Lebanon; also
Mr Crossthwaite. There were, of course, the customary speeches
concluding with the Archbishop presenting to Patriarch Athenagoras a
Lambeth cross together with the traditional silver salver on which were
inscribed the arms of Canterbury.

There can be no doubt that the Patriarch was deeply appreciative of Geoffrey Fisher's visit. At a time of political unrest in the Middle East it did something to advance his prestige in the eyes of his own communion – and more widely. By encouraging the Patriarch to champion the cause of the World Council of Churches, in respect of which some of his Metropolitans entertained grave suspicions, Geoffrey Fisher helped to bridge the gulf between East and West, thus relieving a sense of isolation. The Archbishop did well in urging the need for the Greek Orthodox Church to confer with Anglicans and to exchange theological students. It is perhaps significant that the Governor of Istanbul told Crossthwaite that he was impressed by the Archbishop's kindliness and dignity.

It cannot be said, however, that members of the Turkish press showed much interest in the presence among them of the Primate of All England. True, some photographs appeared but by and large publicity was at the level of highlighting the fact that the Archbishop had married members of the royal family! Compared with the near hysteria of Jerusalem, the brief stay in Istanbul was pitched in a more minor key. There were no applauding or jostling crowds; no long car rides into the countryside; no legacy of a British past involvement. This does not mean that the visit lacked historic significance. Not for a moment. It meant much that an Archbishop of Canterbury brought, personally, greetings to an ancient Church living within an Islamic country yet preserving across the centuries traditions of an Eastern Rome. This was in itself an ecumenical gesture of high importance. Certainly Metropolitan Athenagoras welcomed him most warmly.

CHAPTER 58

Rome

EVERYTHING was now set for what most people regarded as the crowning moment of the Pilgrimage and certainly its most dramatic, namely Geoffrey Fisher's meeting with His Holiness Pope John XXIII. At 10.40 am, 1 December 1960, after a brief Press conference, the Archbishop was airborne for Rome. Once settled in the 'plane Geoffrey Fisher sorted out his papers, re-read the script of his Rome sermon and was so preoccupied that he took only a fleeting glance at the beauties of the Aegean and the rich associations of Attica. The 'plane touched down for an hour at Athens where he was greeted by the British Ambassador, together with representatives of the Anglican Church and an Orthodox Greek Bishop.

If the Archbishop during his flight reflected upon the reception which was to await him in Rome he must have been aware that it would not be entirely welcoming. Robert Hornby, his newly appointed Press Secretary, had gone ahead to the Eternal City to prepare the ground, particularly in the area of publicity. He was not there long before he became conscious, to quote his own words, of 'the risks that the Archbishop ran and the courage [needed] to make the visit . . . The odds were against him'. Pope John himself and Cardinal Bea certainly wanted it to be a success but Cardinal Tardini, in charge of the Secretariat, and others in the Curia emphatically did not see things this way. Colonel Hornby had brought with him a knowledgeable Reuter's correspondent with many contacts in Rome and was told by Sir Peter Scarlett, Her Majesty's Minister to the Holy See, that Cardinal Tardini had put a press 'blackout' on the visit and was insisting that the Archbishop should be described simply as 'Dr Fisher'. The Press Club in Rome was denied to him. So seriously did the Archbishop's Press Secretary see this situation that he called on the Head of Police concerned with information and pointed out to him the dire consequences of attempts, under pressure from Tardini, to prevent any form of publicity – namely the bad atmosphere this would create; the distortion of such news as leaked out; and an unfavourable world reaction.

Fortunately however, for Hornby, the press outside Italy was getting interested and this was less controllable by the Curia. Also, and perhaps more importantly, Sir Peter Scarlett, and Sir Ashley Clarke, British Ambassador in Rome, both committed Anglicans, were determined to do all that they could to make the visit a success. In addition, and equally so motivated, there were Roman Catholics having direct access to the Pope, such as Cardinal Willebrands and the Reverend Gerard Corr, OSB, the latter being one of the two English members of the Secretariat who had called on the Archbishop at Lambeth on the eve of his setting out on his travels.

The Primate of All England landed in Rome at 1.50 pm and was received by Sir Ashley Clarke, Sir Peter Scarlett and Canon D. J. N. Wanstall, Chaplain to the British Embassy and Vicar of All Saints Church in Rome. The Archbishop, defying the ban, spoke to the Press and answered questions in a frank and uninhibited manner. The result was that Italian television 'startled' the Vatican Secretariat by quoting the Archbishop as saying that his visit was 'official' – in other words that he came to Rome as Archbishop of Canterbury and not informally as a private person.

Geoffrey Fisher left immediately for the British Embassy where he was introduced to Brian McDermott, a lay Roman Catholic who had resided in Rome for many years and was First Secretary in the British Legation to the Holy See. Geoffrey Fisher had brought with him a statement which had been agreed with Cardinal Bea earlier at Lambeth and which he had extensively revised in the Hilton Hotel on the night before his departure from Istanbul. The intention was that this document should be issued to the Press as a joint statement after his audience with the Pope.

However, this document proved to be a major bone of contention and Hornby spent three days in negotiating it. There were difficulties as to the style in which the Archbishop should be designated as well as the nature of the visit. To anticipate events the statement was still not yet definitively agreed on the morning of 2 December when Geoffrey Fisher was on his way to the Vatican.

But to return. On his arrival in Rome the Archbishop handed this document to McDermott who took it to the office of the Vatican. Meanwhile Dr Fisher had tea with Sir Ashley and then attended a reception in the vestry of All Saints' Church at which there were present members of the Council of the Italian Evangelical Church. The Archbishop confessed later that it gave him great satisfaction, before he saw the Pope, to have made contact with those who were 'nearest to us as members of the Reformed Churches'. He then, at Evensong, preached a carefully prepared sermon which a journalist from the World Service of the BBC described as 'most impressive' and Sir Peter Scarlett as 'of great brilliance'. The Archbishop began by speaking generously of the debt which the Anglican Church owed to Rome; and then went on to develop a theme which some might have thought 'diametrically opposed' to the teaching of that Church. It was a theme which he had already elaborated in Jerusalem and Istanbul namely that within the unity of the Church as the Body of Christ there must continue to be distinct Churches with their individual domestic life and who witnessed 'faithfully' to their own particular inheritance. Full organic unity was in the future, perhaps never to be attained. At this point in his address he distinguished between what he described as an Imperial Church and a Commonwealth of Churches which he believed to have obtained in the early days of Christianity. For the Churches to come closer together must presuppose unity of discipleship and mutual love.

This address is important since it shows quite clearly that there was a profound difference between the Archbishop's view on 're-union' and that entertained, in equal good faith, by the Pope in his Encyclical *Ad Petram Cathedram* of 29 June 1959, which was, doubtless, issued to reassure Roman Catholics at a time when His Holiness and other members of his flock were looking beyond their own frontiers. For John XXIII and all previous Popes, so runs the Encyclical, the Roman Catholic Church could never be just one of a plurality of Churches nor be seen as incomplete or imperfect until at some distant date, all Christ's sheep were incorporated into the one fold. The Church of Rome was already 'here and now, the mystical Body of Christ, complete in all its parts'. (It needs, perhaps to be said that Geoffrey Fisher's views on re-union were by no means shared by all Anglican theologians). This basic difference early began to manifest itself when it came to securing agreement on the terms of the joint Press communiqué. Indeed some days before Geoffrey Fisher arrived in Rome the Secretariat had drawn up its own statement which made it evident that ecclesiastical or doctrinal matters were not on the agenda. The Archbishop's draft on the other hand, clearly implied that ecclesiastical matters could well, in a general way, be discussed with His Holiness.

The Service at St George's being over, the Archbishop went to the Legation where he and his immediate party were entertained to dinner by Sir Peter and his wife, Lady Scarlett, the latter being described by Geoffrey Fisher as a 'fierce anti-Roman who believed in showing the flag'. After dinner McDermott returned with the bald announcement that the Archbishop's draft 'would not do'. The Vatican, which meant in fact Tardini's office, objected to it on many grounds, not least to the use of such words as 'they discussed' or the designation 'the Churches of the East'. Language of this kind implied something more than a courtesy visit and might be thought to contravene the Pope's *Ad Petram Cathedram*.

Nor was it only the joint statement which was turned down for McDermott confirmed that none of its Legation might lunch with the Archbishop on the morrow; that no official photographs of Geoffrey

Fisher with the Pope could be taken; and that he was not to be allowed to meet Cardinal Bea. This was, of course, all Tardini's doing – but here he was not destined to get his own way. After receiving McDermott's disturbing news which raised matters of principle in relation to the whole character of the audience, an 'endless discussion' took place around the dining-room table. Geoffrey Fisher realised that something must be done – and done quickly. He decided that the only way out of the *impasse* was for him to abandon the idea of a joint statement and to replace it by an exclusively Anglican one. This he promised to produce by 8.30 on the following morning. Geoffrey Fisher was as good as his word. He worked on it till 12.15 after which he took twenty-five drops of Chloroden and went to bed. He was up again at 5.00 am, re-read his draft, did not like it, wrote another and returned to bed. At breakfast, Freddie Temple, Satterthwaite and Sir Peter approved the revised script before it was dispatched to the Vatican.

The great day, so long awaited, Friday 2 December, had now come and it began with the Archbishop celebrating the Eucharist in the Armenian Church and inviting the congregation of some three hundred communicants to pray that his audience with the Pope might further the work of the Spirit 'through and in the Church'. But there were still important matters unresolved and Sir Peter Scarlett was early at the Vatican seeking to finalise the statement. In his villa, Geoffrey Fisher, Freddie Temple, Robert Beloe and Colonel Hornby were anxiously awaiting his return. At 10.30 am he came back with the shattering news that he had been unsuccessful. Dr Fisher's immediate and frustrated reaction was to say to his Senior Chaplain: 'Get the cars; it looks as though we shall have to leave without seeing the Pope'. Sir Peter, recognising the seriousness of the crisis, galvanised himself once more into action and returned to the Vatican hoping at the eleventh hour to retrieve the situation and recognising that Geoffrey Fisher's threat to depart might prove the most powerful weapon in his armoury. At the same time Tardini was still seeking to change the wording of the communiqué and applying pressure upon the Editor of the *Osservatore Romano*, the official organ of the Vatican, to control its reportage.

Geoffrey Fisher, however, come what may, determined to go forward and later in the morning, wearing his bishop's purple cassock, also his Canterbury cap, and taking with him Freddie Temple, Brian McDermott and John Satterthwaite, set out by car for the Vatican. One cannot but wonder whether, in spite of his severe and immediate anxieties, Geoffrey Fisher gave a passing thought to Thomas Arundel, Archbishop of Canterbury, who in 1397 made the same journey to win the support, in the midst of his troubles, of Pope Benedict IX.

It became increasingly evident to Geoffrey Fisher as he entered the

Vatican that he was being given special honours. The Swiss Guards, for example, who were at that time in Retreat, were present in full force resplendent in their traditional uniforms; red carpets, reserved for VIPs, were there in profusion. The Archbishop was received at the steps of the palace by the Chamberlain of Sword and Cape who a fortnight earlier had escorted the British Prime Minister into the papal presence.

It is a moot point as to how far Geoffrey Fisher, as he went into the Pope's presence, was aware that Cardinal Ottaviani had insisted on replacing Mgr Cardinale as interpreter by Mgr Samori whose doctrine was sound but whose acquaintance with the English language was slight. This, so Sir Ashley Clarke alleges, 'reduced the degree of communication between the two protagonists'.

The Archbishop was alone with the Pope for almost an hour (together with Samori) and for the last five minutes the two chaplains were taken in and presented to His Holiness. Official sources concerning what was said, from the Roman Catholic end, are not available. However, Geoffrey Fisher has left behind him two accounts, the first dictated by him to John Satterthwaite within twenty minutes of the audience and the second in his taped autobiography written in his retirement some years later.

As the earliest of the two must be regarded as the more authoritative, and since it has never been published it seems proper to quote it at some length:

> 'The Pope came to the Library door to meet the Archbp. and the two shook each other warmly by the hand. The Archbp. said, "We are making history Your Holiness", to which the Pope agreed. The Pope pointed to the big globe and began talking quickly about Eisenhower's visit, and explained how he had been able to send a message through him to the Turkish Prime Minister. He mentioned the necessity of keeping in touch, especially where difficulties occurred.
>
> 'The Archbp. then said that he had just come from Istanbul and spoke of his great admiration for the Oecumenical Patriarch. He gave the Pope the Patriarchical message, viz that His All H. wished to do everything in his power to better relations between the Churches and that he would welcome an opportunity of meeting the Pope (on neutral ground).
>
> 'At the first mention of the Orthodox Patriarch the Pope beamed and shook his own imaginary whiskers and laughed. The Pope mentioned that he had known and liked the Anglican Chaplain during his time in Istanbul, but could not remember his name.
>
> 'The Archbp. said that whilst he had been in Istanbul he had been received most warmly by the inter-Nuncio – Mgr. Francesco Lordani – who lived in the same house which the Pope shared when Apostolic Delegate in Istanbul. The Archbp. passed on Mgr. Lordani's message that he preferred being a simple Parish Priest and did not care for the life of diplomacy.

'Jerusalem was next discussed and the Archbp. said how moved he had been by the warmth of his reception from every section of the Church. He confessed to being particularly moved by the friendship of the Franciscans – who were obviously hoping for some result from the Archbishop's visit.

'This led to the Pope expressing his great yearning for the unity of all Xtian brethren. The Pope said that he desired unity quite simply in the words of St. John's Gospel – chapter 17 "That they may be one, even as we are one, I in them and thou in me, that they may be made perfect in me".

'At this point the Holy Father gave the Archbp. a folder containing copies of his Addresses last Aug[ust] to the Directors of Catholic Action. Monsignor Samori then read a paragraph from page 3.

'The Archbp. spoke afterwards about the need for friendship and understanding between Christians of every denomination and said that in England there was a great lack of contact between R.C.s and Anglicans. The Pope never followed this up directly but referred to Cardinal Bea and outlined his hopes of better understanding now that the Secretariat for Unity had been established. The Archbp. congratulated the Pope on this machinery [*sic*] and said that he himself looked upon it as one of the best actions of the Pope since he took office as a regular means of communications . . . The Pope accepted the Archbp.'s praise of Cardinal Bea and said that he knew he was the right man for the post. The Holy Father went on to say that he had in fact arranged for the Archbp. to meet Cardinal Bea that afternoon. The forthcoming Vatican Council was then discussed at some length and the Pope emphasised that it would be concerned with the R.C. Church first and foremost as R.C.s must order their own affairs first. He said too that there were many things which would benefit by reform. The Archbp. said he appreciated that the Vatican Council intended to have the R.C. Church as its prime concern, but he went on to remind the Pope that non-R.C.s were already interested in what was being done. The Pope said that in due course he expected that they would be able to take up matters regarding other Churches and [he] read an extract (from page 5) of his special Address to the Council.

'At this point, when the Pope spoke of his concern for the Separated Eastern Churches and for the Protestant Churches, the Archbp. inserted a plea for Anglicans too as falling in neither of these categories and the Pope readily accepted the distinction of Anglicans having a different position from Protestant bodies generally.

'The Pope then went on to speak of our distant forebears and said what joy it was that he as successor of St. Peter should be brought into contact with the Church of St. Augustine. The thought of this alone had given him great happiness. The Archbp. said he was profoundly thankful that such a visit and contacts were possible. He pointed out that no-one could return to the past and that it is useless merely looking backwards. What is necessary is that we all advance – that in going forward *together* we will never remain quite the same as we were before. The Archbp. said that this was why he was so thankful to hear of the existence of Cardinal Bea's Council.

'The Pope then mentioned the Malines Conversations and said that he had been interested in Anglicanism from that time. The Archbp. said that, because of the times, the conversations then were surrounded by secrecy and suspicion – made even more difficult by the antagonism of Roman Catholics in England. He pointed out that no direct contact between Archbishop Davidson and the Pope was possible at the time of Malines. Had it been possible the result might have been more fruitful.

'Looking to the future the Holy Fr. stressed the importance of the spiritual in this field and he then launched into a long history of his own spiritual development. He said that he was most happy as a Pastor and that he disliked ambition. He told the Archbp. that from his Ordination as a Priest he had tried to have three guides for his own spiritual life (a) a love and desire to serve others always; (b) to accept cheerfully whatever was sent; (c) to wish for less more and more. He said (with a twinkle) that those who never asked for anything were never disappointed.

'A long account followed by the Holy Fr. of how he became Pope much to his own surprise. [This was not dictated by the Archbp. as it bore no relevance to anything else]. In return the Archbp. himself felt called upon to speak of the foundations upon which his own spiritual life had been based. He said that from his own experience he knew that no-one could really command unless he really understood how to obey himself.

'At this juncture the Archbp. asked if he could introduce his Chaplains and the Pope rang a bell at the table. The Revd. F. Temple and I were then brought in and the Chamberlains retreated. There was no chance of making customary genuflections though we did kneel and kiss his ring.

'The Archbp. introduced his Senior Chaplain as a nephew of his predecessor and the Pope said he remembered the name. I was then introduced and the Archbp. said I was the equivalent of the Pope's Cardinal Bea. The Holy Fr. thought this was a great joke in considering the difference in our ages.

'The Archbp. repeated that this would remain a great event in his life and that he would like to leave a small reminder of the visit. He asked the Pope whether he would accept a copy of the Coronation Service – as it had a special significance. It follows the ancient Catholic Consecration Rite – Queen Elizabeth herself . . . had been crowned by the Archbp. according to the Rite. The Pope said he would be delighted to receive it – and the book together with a large illustrated copy of English cathedrals was given to the Archbp. by the Chaplains who had carried them in.

'The Pope himself after thanking the Archbp. said that he had some small presents; and as they were rather heavy he would arrange to have them sent to His Grace before we left.

'Before saying our farewells the Holy Fr. repeated how grateful he was for the visit, that he, the successor of Gregory the Great, should after so many dividing years be receiving the successor of Augustine of Canterbury. He said that in his meditations earlier that morning he had again thought of the two Disciples on the road to Emmaus in the presence of their Risen Saviour.

'As we took our leave, the Pope himself came to the Library door and waved to us until we disappeared through the outer door of the South Throne Room.'

The Archbishop himself expressed his complete satisfaction with the meeting and said that never once had there been a moment 'lacking in the rapport'. As to the audience John Satterthwaite commented that the Chamberlain who remained with the Reverend F.S. Temple and himself in the Throne Room became a little restive after the first twenty minutes as that was the usual length of a long private audience. Satterthwaite had a long conversation with Signor Filipo Spandi, Chamberlain of Cape and Sword who confessed that everyone in Italy was delighted that such a visit had been made possible. To all of them it was obvious that a new day was dawning in Church relations.

We turn now briefly to the only other account of the audience which survives in England which the Archbishop includes in his taped autobiography dictated some eight or nine years after the event. It gives a more colourful and personal reaction to the occasion than does that already quoted. 'We greeted each other at once', Geoffrey Fisher writes, 'in the ordinary, friendly way – we shook hands and smiled at each other, and straight away we started as any two friendly people would start, talking about one thing or another and breaking the ice.' However, once seated they got bogged down in an elaborate and rather pointless story about General Eisenhower until the Archbishop felt he must take an initiative and interjected, 'Yes, Your Holiness, that reminds me of something', after which a genuine 'to and fro' conversation began. 'So we talked as two happy people who'd seen a great deal of the world and of life and of the Churches, glad to talk together.' Quoting from one of his own Addresses the Pope referred to the time 'when our separated brethren should return to the Mother Church' evoking the response from the Archbishop 'Your Holiness, not return', to which a puzzled Pope replied: 'Not return, why not?' 'None of us can go backwards', came the reply, 'we are each now running on a parallel course, but we are looking forward until in God's good time our two courses come – approximately – and meet.' After a pause the Pope responded 'You are right' and Geoffrey Fisher comments: '. . . and from that moment, so far as I know, he and the Vatican have never talked about our returning to something in the past'.

When the audience was over Robert Hornby was still detained in the Vatican waiting for the arrival of Monsignor Samori to finalise the statement. When he eventually came – he had been unwell – the Archbishop's Press Secretary urged him 'to get a move on' and to bring the corrected version to the Minister's villa as rapidly as possible. The Monsignor carried out Hornby's instructions to the letter. The result was that at the villa, Sir Peter's private residence – the use of the Press Club was forbidden – there assembled some twenty leading correspondents to hear further details of this eventful week. The Audience with the Pope ended at 1.20 pm and not many minutes after there suddenly appeared at the villa the Archbishop 'red hot' from the Vatican. He admitted – this is clearly not true – to being a 'happy' and 'relieved' man, though in deference to Cardinal Tardini no Roman Catholic ecclesiastics attended the celebratory lunch.

For Geoffrey Fisher the last few days had been gruelling in the extreme, so much so that both Hornby and Beloe were deeply impressed with his strength of will, tenacity and leadership when everything hung in the balance. The news brought by Hornby that the statement had been approved – his Holiness adding a short paragraph on the place of religious experience in the life of the Christian – must have been welcome indeed. The crisis was now at last over and the tension removed. The Archbishop's mood at the villa, consequent upon the release of stress, was one of 'gaity and boyishness', almost flippancy. His own recollection of the Press conference was that of a relaxed, almost high-spirited affair. When asked how in fact he greeted the Pope when they first met he replied, 'Oh, of course, Dr Livingstone, I presume'; at which point Robert Hornby chipped in: 'Off the record'. Later Geoffrey Fisher volunteered the information that they 'didn't kiss each other as one does the Oecumenical Patriarch'. The Archbishop realised that he must on no account break the confidentiality as to the substance of their talks. Hence he admits to giving 'a cheerful and humorous reply to all their questions; the whole thing was very natural and they said nothing in their reports which they were not meant to say'.

In the afternoon, much to his delight and in spite of an earlier prohibition by Tardini, he called on Cardinal Bea at his residence. The Archbishop recorded in his diary that they had a 'lovely, helpful conversation, each one promising to keep the other in full touch'. What was not publicised in *The Times* the next morning which recorded this meeting was an agreement that the Archbishop should send an Anglican priest to live unobtrusively in Rome to serve as a link between Lambeth and the Secretariat. In a message to Geoffrey Fisher on the eve of the latter's retirement, Cardinal Bea recalled their conversation characterised by 'a good Christian Spirit' and greatly enjoyed. 'As you know,' he wrote, 'your confident hope is also mine that the Lord will bestow his blessing upon all human endeavours in the cause of unity.'

The long day was not yet over for at 6.00 pm Sir Ashley Clarke gave a large reception which the Archbishop described as 'very cordial'. Sir Ashley had invited leading members of the various Churches – Anglican, Methodist, Scottish, American, British Roman Catholics; and representatives of the Seminarists. The Archbishop's old friend, Archbishop Matthew was also present. After the reception there was a dinner party when Sir Ashley said nice things about the Primate of All

England to which he suitably responded. His diary for the day ends, not surprisingly, 'So to bed'.

The morning of Saturday 3 December was free from formal business. The Archbishop collected his presents from the Pope which included a bound copy of his sermons together with a book on Vittoria's music, and also from Cardinale a portfolio of Raphael's Cartoons. This latter presentation was a slightly cloak-and-dagger affair as it was held, not in the Library, but for various reasons in the Minister's Office.

Finally Geoffrey Fisher was invited to go on a grand tour by car around the city which he accepted with alacrity and enthusiasm. He describes it as 'wonderful in every way, crammed with all the best that makes for fullness of life'. And so the time came for him to go to the airport leaving on Flight BE131 and arriving in Heathrow at 1.50 pm.

On the whole the reception by the rank and file of the Church of Rome, in spite of traumas and some official hostility was not unfriendly. Only one dignitary, Cardinal Heard, it would seem intimated that he did not wish to be invited to the final reception. Indeed, Sir Peter Scarlett commented that there was 'none of the apartheid characteristic of the Roman Catholic Church a few years ago'. Some who might have been 'stand-offish' were won over by the Archbishop's 'unfeigned affability and simplicity'.

Responsible Roman Catholic comment was not long in forthcoming. On the morning of 3 December *Il Quotidiano*, a Catholic Action newspaper printed in Rome, carried an unsigned editorial which reflected the cautious attitude of the Secretary of State and the Holy Office. It stressed the divergence between the Roman and the Anglican Communion and contrasted Dr Fisher's conception of unity with that of the Pope's *Ad Petram Cathedram*. However, the general mood of the article was generous suggesting that no changes in mutual relations could be expected in the near future. That same morning the Pope, in an Address to the Cardinals and Prelates at the close of the Advent retreat, spoke as if possible consequences flowing from the Archiepiscopal visit might not prove to be so remote. Just as it was the privilege of Gregory the Great to send evangelists to northern lands so now it might be the privilege of his distant successor through the Second Vatican Council to renew to the Christians of the Separated Communities the invitation to pledge themselves lovingly to the cause of unity in faith that so many hearts longed for in all parts of the world.

A third comment came from the pen of Cardinale in a long article in the *Civitate Catholica* which was summarised in the *Osservatore Romano* of 16 December 1960. This carefully written and in a measure authoritative article in view of Cardinal Bea's chairmanship of the Secretariat for Unity laid down the principles which ought to determine the way forward. The Roman Church had a duty to uphold orthodoxy since Christian faith could not be served by betraying truth. On the other hand there rested upon it the obligation to display charity. All validly baptised Christians were members of the mystical Body of Christ and it was in this capacity that the Supreme Pontiff addressed members of the Separated Churches as 'brethren' and 'sons'. In the delicate situation created by the visit of the Head of a Separated Community it was necessary not only to preserve the faith but to avoid any ambiguity damaging to both parties or a false indifferentism which tended to gloss over divergencies. If the duty to preserve orthodoxy made it necessary for the Church at times to act severely this did not mean it should act brusquely, suspiciously or with a lack of charity.

Cardinal Bea's own personal assessment of the visit was that it had brought to the surface and symbolised the more favourable atmosphere which now existed between the Anglican and Roman Churches. It was significant, he believed, that the initiative for the late visit came entirely from the Archbishop of Canterbury himself though later approved by the responsible leaders of his Church. The Archbishop's great merit was to have sensed the new atmosphere of change. Cardinal Bea concluded with the hope that the event of 2 December would bear 'salutory fruit' though he preferred not to forecast what its final outcome would be.

Sir Peter Scarlett, so intimately involved and contributing so much to its success, wrote of the visit as follows:

'I sincerely believe that this visit went well from every point of view. The Archbishop saw the Vatican as it really is and departed with no illusions as to the practical difficulties involved in any attempt to improve relations between Christians. By expressing his own views, clearly and unequivocally, not only in Jerusalem and Istanbul but in Rome itself, his Grace left the Vatican and Roman Catholics in general with no excuse for misunderstanding his own position. Far more so than the insipidity and vagueness of the authorised communiqués in the conversations with the Pope his Grace's public assertions of his own point of view made it impossible for the world to think that he and His Holiness had joined in a fundamental discussion of the problem in which they are both interested. It was also for the best that the arrangements for the visit should have been removed from the slightly High Church or the Romanising context of Monsignor Cardinale's contacts and dealt with by the people who most matter in the Secretariat of State as the unique event that it really was. I still think that Cardinal Tardini went too far in virtually forbidding me to invite guests from the Vatican to meet the Archbishop and in excluding the Press from the Palazzo of St Peter as well as from the interior of the Vatican, but on the whole a happy balance was struck between excessive display of enthusiasm and the ceremonial frigidity of an ordinary private audience. Finally, in view of the general belief that the Pope is a Head of the Church in his attitude towards Christians outside his fold it was probably an excellent thing that the senior official of the Secretariat of State after Cardinal Tardini should have been present throughout the conversations and thus have been in a position to know what was said.'

It is now some thirty years since Geoffrey Fisher paid his visit to Pope John XXIII and both have departed from this terrestial scene. The Archbishop greeted, on his return, with congratulatory letters, official and unofficial, from the many who at a purely personal level saw the visit as a significant break-through, thereby paving the way later for doctrinal discussions of Faith and Order. Though the Anglican Roman Catholic International Commission (ARCIC), for example, had set itself the goal of organic unity in respect of which Geoffrey Fisher remained sceptical or even hostile, this does not minimise the long term significance of the encounter of Pope and Archbishop in 1960. Without right personal relations and the spirit of friendliness as in a family, theologians unaided are not likely to get very far. Geoffrey Fisher helped in the process of understanding which must undergird and inform ecumenical relations.

To the Church Assembly, as seemed appropriate, the Archbishop gave his personal report. He described his threefold itinerary as exhibiting one of the 'courtesies' of the Kingdom. It was understandable that the visit to Rome, for many, would appear the most significant. This instinct was a sure one, particularly as the Church of England had entered into an inheritance derived from the Catholic Church of the Middle Ages as well as the Continental Reformation. It was impossible, in the Archbishop's view, and a folly, to attempt to estimate what the precise consequences of his meeting with Pope John XXIII would be. In the longer sweeps of history cause and effect are not easily discerned. It was the hope of Geoffrey Fisher that his travels in December 1960 would do something to keep up a momentum which began with the Edinburgh Conference of 1910.

There were, of course, some who shrank from Rome as did their forebears, but a more general verdict on his calling in on Jerusalem, Istanbul and Rome was favourable and in some quarters enthusiastic.

Once back in Lambeth the Archbishop ran into a spate of work but this did not prevent his expressing gratitude to all those who had helped him to cope successfully with many pitfalls. To Sir Peter Scarlett he wrote a letter which gives a vivid picture of the general ambience of his visit to Rome. 'I want to thank you and Lady Scarlett immensely,' he began, 'for your kindness to me and my party when we were in Rome. I think we all got a great deal of amusement out of the course of events but it did mean, I am afraid, a good deal of work for you and

McDermott – to which I would add a great deal of enjoyable conversation with your wife. In the end everything went superbly well. I cannot tell you how much I myself owed to the high-spirited and resolute support which carried me along all the time. Thank you so much for your hospitality and your encouragement.'

In the same vein he wrote to Sir Ashley Clarke with whom he had discussed the visit before setting out. It gave him great confidence, he wrote, to have him at the Embassy, helping to make 'the whole thing really splendid'.

To the Pope Geoffrey Fisher dispatched a letter on 21 December which, maybe, deserves quotation more or less in full. 'I write to thank Your Holiness with all my heart for the friendliness of your reception of me and for the happiness of our spiritual discourse together. As we talked in such harmony I felt the richness of the fellowship which the Holy Spirit imparted to us.' The Archbishop particularly expressed his thanks to Cardinal Bea, and much appreciated, so he told His Holiness, the conversation he had with him. 'The way forward' he wrote, 'will often be hard to find or beset with difficulties but the Pope's establishing the New Secretariat and the encouraging wisdom of the Cardinal will enable them to join together in mapping out the way. The first enemy to be met with is ignorance; and by the exchange of information now made possible we can happily go forward to banish ignorance and to let the light of the knowledge and the love of God shine forth through all obscurities.'

It was not until mid-January, 1961, that His Holiness responded to Geoffrey Fisher's letter which caused the Supreme Pontiff a little embarrassment but was due, so he explained, to 'the many grave cares of our apostolic mandate' and his 'increased pastoral commitments over Christmas'. He concluded his epistle: 'Your Grace's visit, we are well aware, has had reverberations the world over. We presume now to have confidence that, for the praise and glory of God and His Church, the good impulses aroused by Our frequent clear invitations to Our separated brethren may mature and bear fruit. From Our heart we thank you for the prayers which you raise for Us and Our ministry. In return we would assure you that we shall not fail to recommend you when we stand at the Altar of the Lord.'

Geoffrey Fisher was a pattern in the meticulous care which he devoted to writing his 'Thank You' letters. Like the elephant he never forgot. They usually bear the impress of his personality. Amongst the many letters he sent off subsequent to his travels we may select just three for partial quotation.

To Sir Bernard Burrows, the United Kingdom Ambassador at Ankara, he wrote thanking him for making the journey to Istanbul so easy: also, he expressed his appreciation to the Consul-General who, with his wife, 'looked after me enabling me to use your house as a bedroom and a waiting room, an office and everything else'. Looking back on his visit, he could say that 'in spite of its inevitable sadnesses to anyone who remembers the part of the Orthodox Church, I found it helpful and encouraging'.

To Archbishop MacInnes in Jersualem and his wife he expressed deep gratitude for the 'wonderful way' they had cared for him, thus making 'the whole experience quite unforgettable'. 'All I can say,' he added, 'is that however exciting, and even exhausting the various experiences were, at the heart of them was your lovely hospitality, and the kindly, friendly and wise insight of your wife. For all those things I thank you most heartily.' Characteristically there was a significant postscript. He had forgotten to give a word of encouragement to St George's College on the eve of its profound changes. Would the Archbishop do this for him?

There was one person, always modestly at work behind the scenes, to whom Geoffrey Fisher recognised that he owed an incalculable debt – Canon John Satterthwaite, General Secretary of the Church of England Council on Foreign Relations. 'There are several people,' he wrote to him, 'without whom this tour could not have taken place: one, I suppose, is myself; another is Hornby and his management of the Press; the third is yourself, the essential hyphen between all the other participants. I have admired intensely the way in which you have conducted the whole operation from the very start, and would both thank you and congratulate you that the whole thing worked without any major hitch at all.'

'Also would you thank Miss Wallace and the rest of the staff?'

His episcopal colleagues were lavish in their praise but one tribute in particular from an Old Reptonian destined to be his successor at Canterbury – their mutual relations were at times somewhat 'edgy' – must have given him unique satisfaction. It ran as follows: 'I hope that this Christmas at Canterbury will be gloriously happy for you. You have been doing great things. It was very hard to predict what form the benefits of your visit to Rome would take; and it is now clear that a widespread loosening of relations between us and the Romans has happened, and a charity and brotherhood, long waiting to find expression and long inhibited, have broken loose. It will now be a task of some few years to make wise and good use of this but certainly it has happened. It has also affected the impression of the world around that Christendom is a real and possible thing. *Laus Deo!*'

A wish which was dear to the Archbishop's heart was that his visit to Rome might lead to a closer relationship with the Catholic hierarchy in England, particularly as the Pope wished that a more 'friendly understanding should grow up between Anglicans and the Church of

Rome'. In this context he believed that Cardinal Heenan might well prove a key man. On acknowledging the Archbishop of York's appreciative letter, he asked whether a meeting at Lambeth might promote this end – but nothing specific seems to have resulted from this enquiry.

It may seem somewhat incongruous to end this chapter with a further reference to Cardinal Tardini who does not appear to have come out very well from the story here narrated. However, a sense of charity if not justice may serve to remind us that it is possible too easily to be critical of Cardinal Tardini. He saw himself as a conscientious civil servant interpreting the traditional mind of the Catholic Church *vis à vis* ecumenical relations. That Tardini was unaware of a newly emerging ecclesiastical scene, or, if aware, set his face steadily against it, ought not to expose him to criticism. That he was unable to maintain the restrictions he wished to impose on the Archbishop's visit was due, in the main, to such as Cardinal Bea and Willebrands who took a contrary view – and had the ear and support of the Supreme Pontiff himself.

In the summer of 1963 vivid and poignant memories of his historic journey must have come vividly back to him. The reference is to the death of His Holiness Pope John XXIII. Immediately Geoffrey Fisher responded to an invitation to broadcast a panegyric over the European Service of the BBC. His words were indeed moving and perceptive. Due to His Holiness, he claimed, 'the Church of Rome can never be the same again. There will be, there already is, a change of spirit and a renewal of ecumenical life'. The Pope, he said, obeying the impulse of the Holy Spirit, had taken the initiative and what he began cannot be halted by his death. 'God will continue to give it increase.' In his 'storming barriers' and breaking a way through he had shown the 'vitality, the impetuosity, the youthfulness of a very wise and single-minded old man'.

This assessment was greatly appreciated by Roman Catholics and the Apostolic Delegate to Britain described it as a 'beautiful tribute'.

PART ELEVEN:

THE FINAL YEARS

CHAPTER 59

Resignation

GEOFFREY Fisher was born on 5 May 1887, so that on his birthday in 1961 he had reached the age of seventy-four. In the light of his immediate predecessors this did not necessarily of itself suggest retirement. Frederick Temple died in office at the age of eighty-one, Randall Davidson resigned at eighty; Cosmo Lang at seventy-eight. (William Temple died in office aged sixty-three). From such precedents it might well have been thought that Geoffrey Fisher had still at least a few years to go at Lambeth. In so busy a life he had probably not thought seriously about his own retirement though on many occasions he had persuaded a number of office holders, often most reluctantly, to step down. However, the years had taken their toll and as he entered into his middle seventies he confessed to being too easily irritated, too prone to excitement and to talk overmuch. This was increasingly evident at Bishops' Meetings where he tended more and more to be domineering, unwilling to allow others to speak their mind; and to dislike any opposition to his own views. With great courage one of his chaplains drew the Archbishop's attention to this unhappy situation with a degree of emphasis which could not be ignored. Nor was such behaviour confined to meetings of the Episcopate. There was, on one occasion, a somewhat embarrassing scene at a meeting of the Canterbury Diocesan Synod. The circumstances were as follows. Canon Bennett, Vicar of Maidstone (the son of a former Dean of Chester) in a debate on the parson's freehold supported this life tenancy on the grounds that to get rid of it would be to increase the power of the bishop. Immediately the Archbishop sprang to his feet and there was an unseemly struggle as he endeavoured to wrench the microphone out of Bennett's hand. Fortunately he made an immediate apology in these words: 'If I showed any undue excitement in answering Canon Bennett I apologise. But when a person has been shot at and trampled on for many years it is not easy for him to listen in silence when a fresh attack is made on him.'

The Archbishop, however, was a big enough person to recognise the seriousness of his chaplain's criticisms and he frankly admitted that this admonition from one of his own staff 'shook him a great deal', the more so because he was 'a great friend, a great ally and a man of very sound judgement'. 'I took all this to heart,' he wrote later, 'and tried, as far as that went, to modify any failing of that kind;' but he was forced to admit that he could not change his whole approach if he were to remain 'quick on the ball'.

From these comments it is clear that Geoffrey Fisher had begun to contemplate at least the possibility of retirement. He had busy months ahead of him in 1960 which included an exacting visit to the Far East and his famous pilgrimage to Jerusalem, Istanbul and finally Rome. This last tour certainly might well be conceived as a fitting *finale* to a distinguished archiepiscopate. So it was that his chaplain's words, and those of others, bore fruit and finally led him to take action. Thus before he set off for Japan, Geoffrey Fisher informed his legal secretary, David Carey, when they were both on holiday in Scotland that, to quote his own words, 'resignation is much in my mind'.

However, there were other factors that persuaded Geoffrey Fisher to come to this decision, all of which were saying powerfully that the world was changing. There were heavy responsibilities round the corner, which the Archbishop felt that he could not face so enthusiastically as in previous years. For example, the World Council of Churches was due to assemble shortly in New Delhi, an occasion which needed most laborious preparation. There was looming up the Anglican Congress in Toronto and already a large correspondence in connection with this event was flooding in to Lambeth. As he contemplated seriously what these would mean for him personally, he indulged in an uncharacterisitic fit of nostalgia. He was oppressed with the thought that old friends such as 'the cheerful' Henry Sherrill would no longer be around. A younger generation which 'knew not Joseph' was waiting in the wings and Geoffrey Fisher felt that he just could not personally face up to these oncoming responsibilities. Also he admits to fearing lest Stephen Bayne, the Anglican Executive Officer whom, incidentally, he greatly admired and had appointed, should wish to do things in a more highly organised, expensive and grandiose style, more American than English.

So it was that Geoffrey Fisher stuck to his original intention, and before Christmas 1960 gave advance notice to the Prime Minister, Harold Macmillan, of his intention to resign.

It was only natural that he should be interested in the appointment of his successor though determined not to make any positive single recommendation himself. To this sensible resolution he adhered firmly, though it is questionable how wise he was to lay on a straw vote among the diocesan bishops who came up with three names – Michael Ramsey, Donald Coggan and Faulkner Allison – which he passed on to the Patronage Secretary for dispatch to the Prime Minister.

In January 1961 the Archbishop himself went to Downing Street to see Harold Macmillan. From the Archbishop's account – we have no other – it was a near disaster. The Prime Minister had never warmed to the Archbishop, remembering doubtless his slashing attack in the

House of Lords on his Premium Bonds which he described as this 'squalid enterprise', and his equally severe criticism of his much reported claim: 'You've never had it so good'. So when the two sat side by side in the large Cabinet room, Mr Macmillan, so Geoffrey Fisher later recalled, was at his 'very worst', basically because he did not wish an interview with the Archbishop having already made up his mind for Michael Ramsey as his successor. Dr Fisher's own account of this 'encounter' deserves a brief mention particularly as it lingered long and unhappily in his memory. 'I sat beside him,' he writes, 'and he talked in the kind of impersonal way that he could sometimes, not really paying any attention to me but asking the necessary questions and taking the answers I gave with hardly a comment. It was a truly frigid proceeding. All the right things were said. I made it perfectly clear that I could not back any one of the two (*sic*) obvious candidates – each had very great merits and it wasn't for me to decide between them. How could I? I did say that while Michael's claims as a theologian were far better than anybody else's on the Episcopal Bench, he had some very odd traits which might cause difficulty – more than that I couldn't obviously say. There I left it.'

Certainly this was not an enthusiastic commendation: and as they got up and were walking out together the Prime Minister, according to Geoffrey Fisher, said in a very 'ungracious manner' that he supposed the Archbishop would like to be given a life peerage to provide a platform from which he could go on talking. To this the Archbishop replied simply that he thought it was 'suitable'. The Prime Minister's final remark as they parted was, to say the least, unfortunate. 'Of course,' he said, 'this will mean a lot of changes when you go, there will be York to be filled.' This seemed a clear indication that the Prime Minister had already made up his mind, before he saw the Archbishop, as to who should follow him at Canterbury. Suddenly realising his mistake he added: 'That is to say if Ramsey is appointed'. The Archbishop then asked that they might have another conversation since he did not feel that they had explored the whole situation with sufficient thoroughness. They did in fact meet again later at what the Archbishop himself described as a 'rather easier interview' when they talked a little more freely about possibilities. But the Prime Minister insisted that haste was now needed since the Queen was going on her travels and he wished to settle this matter before she went – an explanation which the Archbishop felt ignored the fact that this could have been done easily through correspondence. However, the Archbishop was gracious enough, though he believed he had received very cavalier and discourteous treatment at the hands of the Prime Minister, to comment: 'Anyhow, the decision was made and if I had been in Macmillan's place I should have made the same decision'.

Michael Ramsey long remembered the talk he had with the Prime Minister a few days after the announcement of his appointment to Canterbury. The latter introduced their conversation with these words: 'Well, Fisher seems to disapprove of you'. Michael Ramsey, in jest, replied: 'Yes – he was my headmaster and headmasters often know the worst'. To this Macmillan snorted: 'He may be your headmaster, but he is not going to be mine'.

It has to be said that Geoffrey Fisher was by no means happy with the way in which he was treated *vis-à-vis* the appointments which needed to be made pursuant to Michael Ramsey's appointment to Canterbury. He believed that there was quite unnecessary haste and that he was deliberately being bypassed. True, he agreed, there was much to be said for Donald Coggan, Bishop of Bradford, going to York but equally there might be a strong case for his going to London for which hc had exceptional gifts and which in the life of the Church and Nation was more significant than the Primacy of the Northern Province. Geoffrey Fisher's frustrations spilt over into a letter which he dispatched to Michael Ramsey on 19 January 1961; 'Is not this unfair to me and the Church?', he asked. 'Appointment to York is a question on which I have a right to be heard, and since I have not considered the question you have no means of knowing what I should think! I need time to consider and, if necessary consult others.' And so the correspondence went on though Geoffrey Fisher was pleased to have a protracted conversation with Donald Coggan who sought his advice – and who went to York!

CHAPTER 60

An Assistant Parish Priest

WHEN Geoffrey Fisher ceased to be Archbishop of Canterbury in 1961 neither he nor Rosamond had made definite plans about their future. They remained at work discharging their mutual roles right up to the last moment. Maybe, as they began to look ahead, Geoffrey recalled that when he left Repton after being its Headmaster for sixteen years and Archbishop Temple asked him what he wished to do next, his immediate reply was 'to be a country clergyman'. And so it was that on his retirement he turned instinctively to the countryside, to the rock whence he was hewn, and when they were offered a cottage on their beloved Exmoor, familiar from many a holiday, they accepted with alacrity. Afterwards, however, they moved to Sherborne, a small town in the heart of rural Dorset, and renowned during the Middle Ages for its Benedictine Abbey. This choice was in part determined by a desire to be near their son Charles who joined the staff at Sherborne School in September 1961 after having taught in Rhodesia. For a year they rented a house of considerable antiquity in the High Street and greatly enjoyed their many local contacts, not least with two schools. However, knowing his love for the countryside, the Bishop of Bath and Wells suggested that Geoffrey and Rosamond might like to occupy the redundant rectory of the parish of Trent, a small and delightful village of some 300 inhabitants. They moved there in 1962 and it was there that Geoffrey spent the remaining ten years of his life, Rosamond remaining there for another decade after his death. Of his life in this village, the Archbishop writes: 'If we searched England, we could not have found any place at all which would have suited us better. All is just what it should be: true country and a pure country village. Both Rosamond and I were born in the country and our heart is always there. We are near Sherborne which is a country town. All this is coming back into our lives at last. And there is also the charm of the church and of the surroundings which are exquisite. The house is just what anybody who cares for the history of England and the history of English domestic life would want. It is comely: it is half the old Rectory, just a little bit short of space, but what does that matter? The staircase, which is often a great test, has low risers so that as one's legs get more feeble it is still easy to mount the staircase. The rooms are beautifully proportioned and there in the church, one feels one is in the quiet, graceful atmosphere of the Church of England as it has grown through the 18th and 19th centuries changing its image and its relation to the world but always its strong and splendid self. I have been wonderfully blessed in the whole thing. I'm allowed to take services, two or it may be three, every Sunday in our own church or at Nether Compton or Over Compton. That is a joy. The other thing I've discovered is that the fact of having no responsibility gives one a completely new and happy approach to people in the village and elsewhere.'

These words seem to echo the sentiments of a former 18th century Rector of Trent, Barnabas Smyth: 'Were a person who loves retirement to choose a place for himself, where he might hope to pass the latter part of his life in peace and plenty, he could scarcely find a situation more agreeable to his wishes than Trent will afford him'.

Walking had always been a favourite pastime and here Geoffrey Fisher had ample opportunity to indulge it. 'I walk up Compton Hill sometimes', he writes, 'and then I look to Yeovil, pleasant in the distance and then further to the right the spire of Trent church, and between the two the Mendips and Glastonbury Tor. What could be more eloquent of the glory of England!'

In return for occupying the rectory for life, Geoffrey Fisher conducted such services as he could, consonant with his being from time to time away in London undertaking other commitments. When he was thus not available the Reverend T.F. Taylor, Rector of the neighbouring parishes of Over and Nether Compton, deputised for him. This arrangement worked well for some three years until Mr Taylor went off to read for a doctorate at Oxford. The Reverend T.C.Brook, then a housemaster and chaplain at Sherborne School, became rector of the combined three parishes and felt it a privilege to have the permanent help of the former Archbishop.

It was not to be expected that Geoffrey Fisher would be forgotten even though he was now living 'far from the madding crowd'. Indeed, the BBC sought him out, and produced a programme giving a picture of his changed estate. The *Radio Times* referred to his new lifestyle in these words: 'Most afternoons in the Dorset village of Trent a few miles from Sherborne an elderly man in a cloth cap can be seen going along to the village shop or off to post some of the many letters he writes every day'. 'My correspondence is voluminous', he explains, adding with his famous chuckle: 'And some of the people who get it don't like it'. In retirement he still spoke out in letters to *The Times*; in correspondence with theologians and politicians; in the pulpit every Sunday in one of the local churches; in friendly conversation. 'I don't much want to read New Theology', he confessed 'because in the end it's merely the old one re-hashed with a little modern psychology thrown in, and I can get on without all that'.

The summer of 1967 was a time of great rejoicings not only for the Fishers and their family but for the whole village since it was then that Geoffrey and Rosamond celebrated their golden wedding and Geoffrey his 80th birthday. The festivities began in London when the Queen and Prince Philip entertained them at Windsor Castle on 11 April, this being followed by a reception at the Drapers' Hall at which the Very Reverend Ian White-Thompson, Dean of Canterbury and a former chaplain to the Archbishop at Lambeth, gave an address. To many in the village the climax came on 5 May when a reception was laid on in the hall of the local church school. When Geoffrey Fisher was asked what form the celebration should take he replied without any hesitation: 'An Edwardian old-fashioned concert' – and so it was. The venue was packed beyond capacity and many of the villagers dressed themselves up in period costumes. The Fishers were presented with a set of antique chairs and a table. A special parish newsletter, extending to some twenty-two pages, was produced which contained tributes from those who had known Geoffrey and Rosamond over long years – that is from Marlborough days to Canterbury. A local worthy wrote 'The Ballad of Trent', the chorus of which was sung lustily by all present. This masterpiece concluded with the following stanzas:

> But more wonderful still this event
> Of which we shall never repent,
> Which gave us a Curate – long may he endure it –
> Lord Fisher of Lambeth in Trent.

> He's won all our hearts. Everyone
> Takes pride in our Trent's greatest son.
> The youngest, the oldest, the warmest, the coldest
> And so let our ballad be done.

> Lord Fisher, the night is far spent,
> So all of your neighbours in Trent –
> The big and the small, the short and the tall –
> Wish both of you every content.

All, however, was not yet quite over, for two days after this village event the Bishop of Bath and Wells, Jock Henderson as he was affectionately known, preached at the morning service to a packed congregation and the Archbishop celebrated Holy Communion. It was singularly appropriate that this year Lady Fisher should open the parish Summer Fête in the rectory garden when a record sum was raised for church funds.

To the two principals in this village commemoration, the setting, the general character of it all, and the involvement of the whole village must have given a unique if somewhat nostalgic satisfaction. The spontaneous spirit of affection and friendship which characterised these festivities reveals only too plainly, as the Rector wrote later, the esteem and love which the village entertained for the two Fishers and their grown-up family.

Not every day, of course, at Trent was lived at so high a level. During his ten years there Geoffrey Fisher settled easily into an orderly pattern of life which had earlier become almost second nature to him. After breakfast he resorted to his study where he dealt with his correspondence and, of course, digested *The Times* newspaper. The Rector usually called in at mid-morning when over a cup of coffee Dr Fisher read out to him some of the letters which had occupied him earlier. How far the Rector offered any critical comments or tried to exercise a restraining influence history does not record. Lunch was followed by a brief period of rest, after which Dr Fisher went the rounds of the parish talking to everyone he met and usually opening the conversation when he 'spied a stranger' with the greeting: 'And who are *you*?' His approach to all and sundry was easy and natural and he saw himself as a genuine member of the village community. Walking was always, as we have before mentioned, both a stimulus and relaxation and he used to say that there were fourteen ways into and out of the village. He knew the names and circumstances of nearly all Trent's inhabitants and would often knock at the door of one of the cottages for a cup of tea and was uniformly welcomed warmly – as he had done at Higham sixty or so years earlier.

As to the liturgical side of church life, the Rector and his assistant curate discussed this together on Monday morning, the latter putting himself unreservedly at the disposal of the former. The Rector was well aware that Dr Fisher preferred the 1662 Book of Common Prayer (or the 1928 for some offices) which meant that services according to the Series I, II and III booklets were undertaken by the Rector. His assistant curate took a great deal of time preparing his sermons, the result being that they were simple, straightforward and relevant to the life of those in the three parishes to which he ministered. Typical was a course on the Ten Commandments. With the same intelligibility in view he devised a new lectionary: and occasionally made his own translations of the text when he felt that the Authorised Version too obscure. Sometimes when conducting services a delightful informality could creep in. For example, it was not beyond him to forget a name when he was calling the banns and to redeem this omission by indicating that Mrs X seated in the congregation could supply the additional information that had eluded him. The former Archbishop was happy to be called in from time to time to conduct adult confirmations; to preach on special occasions; and to baptise and marry Trent parishioners. With the Rector – his relations with him were excellent indeed intimate – he attended meetings of the Sherborne Rural Deanery: sampled religious lectures at the Somerset Adult Conferences: and was present at discussions on Anglican-Methodist Union when it is unlikely that he remained silent. For Geoffrey Fisher his ministry at Trent was full and fulfilling and he was privileged to discharge it more or less to the end of his life.

CHAPTER 61

Post-Retirement Ecumenicity

GEOFFREY Fisher, as we have just seen, derived a unique satisfaction in ministering to a small village community. However, this is not the whole story of his retirement since he felt unable to confine his interests solely to shepherding his rural flock. The ecumenical bug which had bitten deeply over the years did not go away but continued to spur him into action. In particular he played a controversial part in the debate on Anglican/Methodist relations, thereby expending a great deal of energy in writing a plethora of letters; seeing many people; and drawing up countless memoranda and articles. This led to his being widely criticised by those who felt that having resigned office he should gracefully bow his way out of the controversial ecclesiastical scene. Can anything be said to explain if not to justify this continuing involvement? Is it that Geoffrey Fisher, in his old age, convinced himself that the Church of England was being led astray and that he still had a responsibility to set it right? Here maybe he had a blind spot in not seeing this activity as necessarily prejudicing former friendships and being unfair to his successor. Those who knew him best tried to restrain him; Lady Fisher and members of the family endeavoured to bring their influence to bear upon him but largely in vain. Some recipients ceased to reply to his letters and to many it seemed a tragedy that his closing years should have been clouded in this way. In this context, perhaps a letter sent by John Taylor, later Bishop of Winchester, to Lady Fisher at the time of Geoffrey's death is relevant:

'Of course I was aware of the almost excessive anxiety which gripped him in regard to the method of achieving Church union. I appreciated enormously the wisdom with which you guarded him in this. My own feeling was one of deep dismay that so great a man should be so hurt, and, in a way, isolated from many of his former colleagues. Yet it was wonderful to know how readily he could switch off from that whole world of anxiety and draw upon the simple affection with which he was surrounded in the Trent parish and in the vast circle of friendships with which he had literally ringed the world.'

It was understandable, of course, that Geoffrey Fisher should retain an interest in the ecumenical cause which he had championed so consistently but quite another that he should publicly commend or oppose any particular policy with which the Church was actively at the moment concerned such as, for example, the scheme for Anglican-

Methodist Union which many hoped would be finally approved by the General Synod. Geoffrey Fisher by no means welcomed this expectation, indeed quite the reverse, for he believed that the means taken to secure this end were ill-conceived and hence bound to cause doubt and confusion. Thus he could not keep silent; but publicly campaigned against the proposals, even becoming a member in Trent of a small Faith and Order Group consisting of clergy and ministers, schoolmasters and one Plymouth Brother. An independent society *Veritas* was set up, the purpose of which was to secure the rejection of this reunion scheme. As to his own views Geoffrey expressed them publicly in these forthright terms '. . . for the Church of England and the Methodists to come together in a United Church in the form proposed had no attraction for anyone and to call on the post-war Churches to start working again on this kind of model would lead nowhere.'

In 1968 the plan for Anglican-Methodist Union, approved by the Methodist Conference was rejected by the General Synod of the Church of England, the motion commending it failing to secure the necessary two-thirds majority – and this in spite of the support given to it by Michael Ramsey, Archbishop of Canterbury. Geoffrey Fisher was relieved at the result expressing himself as 'thankful that along that line the Church of England had got nowhere' and the scheme was 'dead'. Perhaps it is significant that now, more than twenty-two years later, no other scheme along these lines has been submitted either to the Methodist Conference or to the General Synod.

The rejection in 1968, however, did not, so far as Geoffrey Fisher was concerned, close the controversy or inhibit his own private correspondence or actions. Indeed this verdict in the General Synod convinced him, more than ever, that the Ecumenical Movement was 'running out of steam', largely because it was wrong in its basic assumption that organic union was the only way forward. In fact Christians were already, so he used to assert, organically united with each other in and through their Baptism which was the divinely appointed channel of entering into the universal Church militant. To set up as the final goal a 'Unified Catholic Church Militant for all Christendom is either a lunacy or a nightmare, or both.' In this respect he was particularly aggrieved with members of the English Episcopate whom he blamed for forcing him to assume the 'burdensome task of trying to *make* Bishops of the Church of England think like Anglicans'. He thus saw his task as 'trying to win not victory but success in the struggle for truth'. At the moment it was hard going on the ecumenical Anglican-Methodist front with all its Church of England's 'high-ups ranged on one side and that the wrong side'.

Geoffrey Fisher did not lack sympathisers in the Church of England even if they disapproved of his continued open involvement in Anglican-Methodist ecumenical affairs. What is more surprising is that he received a letter from a monk at Ampleforth at the time of the collapse of the Anglican-Methodist scheme for reunion in the General Synod urging him 'to go on teaching people, it is the *sapientia* of the grey-headed that bears some of the best fruit in advice and guidance'.

That Geoffrey Fisher should have actively associated himself with opposition to the Anglican-Methodist scheme must be regretted, indeed condemned, not because he was necessarily on the wrong side – he may have been right – but because as a retired Archbishop he should have seen himself precluded from personal participation in this sensitive controversy domestic to the Church of England and in which his successor at Canterbury was intimately involved.

However, we now turn to another area of ecumenical relations not, it is true, so closely integrated with the day-to-day life of the Church of England but one in which Geoffrey Fisher showed a marked interest. It may be that in this area of ecumenicism to which I now very briefly call attention a more indulgent, less judgemental view may be taken.

From his own experience of reunion negotiations with the Free Churches, Methodists and Presbyterians in the United Kingdom, Geoffrey Fisher was deeply conscious of their having been shipwrecked on the nature and relevance of the episcopal office. Indeed his Cambridge sermon was an effort to bypass this obstacle. This lack of success here caused Geoffrey Fisher great frustration, so much so that he questioned the presuppositions on which these negotiations had hitherto been based and broken down. Was it not possible for the Church of England, he asked himself, to seek closer relations with a Church already episcopal? Thinking along the same lines was a small group of Roman Catholics, their immediate background being the loosening-up process inspired by Pope John XXIII. This included Alberic Stacpole, a monk of Ampleforth and editor of its influential journal, together with John Todhunter, a distinguished Roman Catholic layman, and a former alumnus of Trinity College, Cambridge. These came to know Geoffrey Fisher intimately which led to an extensive correspondence between them and a sharing of ideas. Also there were a few others much more cautiously involved such as, for example, Bishop Butler, Abbot of Downside. They saw the Church of England and the Church of Rome as two indigenous episcopal communions in Britain, the former derivative from the latter, as providing an opportunity for a new approach to ecumenicity and a further way of breaking through the *impasse* which had hitherto hindered any closer coming together of these two churches. John Todhunter, more ambitiously, in a letter to Geoffrey Fisher, maintained that it was 'urgent' that an understanding should be reached between Rome and Canterbury. He believed that this could be achieved without any violation or conflict of principle. From a purely practical standpoint these optimistic views may strike the detached observer as both highly surprising and certainly wishful in their thinking even though the winds of change were certainly blowing through the corridors of ecclesiastical institutions. Geoffrey Fisher corresponded extensively with Stacpole and Todhunter; wrote articles which appeared in the Ampleforth Journal; and dispatched letters to Church papers as well as *The Times*. It was his deep conviction that too often the dialogue between churches was bedevilled by a serious confusion in the use of language so that the same word was frequently employed with different meanings and in a wide variety of contexts. To use his own colourful language he himself in his own researches had needed to press on 'trying to find a further way through the brambles and briars of theological ambiguities and contrary purposes'. This stumbling block particularly applied to such designations as 'auto-cephalous churches'; 'inter-communion'; 'unification'; 'full communion'; 'collegiality'; 'organic union' – to quote but a few. In order to assist clear thinking Geoffrey Fisher published a booklet *A Clarification of some Terms and Ideas connected with Church Unity* in which he went to great lengths to suggest a clearly defined vocabulary as a guide and discipline for ecumenical discussion. As to autocephalous churches which, he writes, 'have not attempted to define any objective goal for the Church militant' they have not considered together whether it was possible or even desirable to look beyond the existence of separate churches to some kind of United Church constituted so as to embrace all Churches.

Geoffrey Fisher was in many respects a life-long optimist in spite of past disappointments and he threw himself with energy into these conversations with his Roman Catholic friends believing that something practical might come out of them. He was helped in thinking this way by recognising that though truth questions are necessarily involved in religious statements, he did not believe all such statements could be expected to constrain universal assent. It was 'chimerical' – this is his own word – 'to suppose that the Church of England could ever accept the Primacy or the infallibility of the Pope, or that there could ever be a root and branch doctrinal agreement between Canterbury and Rome'. A new intellectual and theological climate increasingly suggested the near impossibility of determining what beliefs were, or were not, essential to Christian faith. Thus only by 'a gracious plurality of theologies could integrity be preserved'. 'The Churches very wisely,' he commented, 'leave the theologians to work out their own salvation with the help of all kinds of specialist mysteries and metaphysics. They are interesting to them that can follow them perfectly but the ordinary churchman need not grapple with what will certainly pass his understanding.' These remarks illustrate again his suspicion of philosophy 'when mixed up with Christian doctrine'. His mind worked historically rather than teleologically, practically rather than theoretically. Indeed there was that in him, even if only subliminally, which made him fight shy of making absolute religious statements. Life was larger than logic and the very existence of a number of autocephalous churches brought together through a quirk of history – or was it by divine providence? – represented on the whole a truer picture of the total life of the Christian Church than did a united *Ecclesia* argued into existence round a table by nice calculations of 'less or more'. In this spirit Geoffrey Fisher sent a congratulatory letter to Bishop Butler on an article he wrote for the *Ampleforth Journal* under the title 'Unity not Absorption'.

Thus, when John Todhunter, Stacpole and Dr Fisher got together asking where they ought to begin their discussions it was on this basic fact of baptism that relations between the Church of England and the Church of Rome must be built. It was, therefore, idle to spend time debating 'Organic Union' since members of these two Churches were already in this relationship with one another. The structure and the integrity of each Church could, therefore, be fully respected because the 'barriers which had hitherto fenced them in were already broken down'. There was nothing to prevent these two episcopal churches living together in full fellowship and communion as two expressions of the one Catholic Apostolic Church militant here in earth.

This may appear to many as far too simplistic; far too short a route to a glittering prize. Might it not be, however, that an agreement to differ, while meeting together around the Lord's table, could give elbow room for the Spirit to engage in his eirenic work. True, one finds it hard to believe that Geoffrey Fisher would have fought for this *modus vivendi* had he still been Archbishop of Canterbury and titular Head of the Anglican Communion. Certainly a large area of Anglican opinion would not have supported him in so radical a view. Thus the Archbishop of Wales dismissed it in a couple of sentences on 9 August 1972: 'The idea of a number of Churches all in full communion with one another but maintaining their separate existence and organisation, just doesn't make sense . . . when we look at the way our smallest rural communities are divided between so many different denominations all hard put to it to maintain their existing work let alone cope with the rapid change taking place in the community.'

However, the triumvirate – Geoffrey Fisher, John Todhunter and Alberic Stacpole – remained convinced not only of the rightness of their position but its practicality. As part of their on-going deliberations a conference took place at Ampleforth in July 1972. Geoffrey Fisher determined to attend but as the day came nearer it was clear that his health was beginning to deteriorate with increasing rapidity. Thus he confessed that his article on 'Clarification' would probably be the last of its kind to proceed from his pen. The conference duly took place without him, though his *Tractate on Full Communion* was delivered orally on his behalf. It well illustrated the clarity and application to detail with which Geoffrey Fisher could still prosecute the cause of full communion with Roman Catholics.

Can Geoffrey Fisher be equally condemned for his part in co-operating with a minute group of Roman Catholics in advocating full communion between the Churches of Canterbury and Rome while at the same time preserving the identity of both? I think the answer must be 'no' and to compare this involvement as on a level with his participation in the Anglican-Methodist discussions after his retirement cannot reasonably be sustained. Geoffrey Fisher and John Todhunter, *et alii* were concerned with the fundamental principles as to the nature of the Church and how two Episcopal Communions within the universal Church militant here in earth could relate themselves to each other. This was a proper subject for inquiry and in no sense could embarrass members of ARCIC teasing out the problems connected with organic union. I suspect that the vast bulk of Roman Catholics and Anglicans did not even know that such discussions were taking place. Perhaps the former Archbishop might have been wiser to avoid any engagement of any kind in ecclesiastical affairs – but perhaps this would have been to ask too much and to deprive the *Ecclesia Anglicana* of a clear expression of a point of view, not usually commended verbally or by the pens of theologians. It may well be that at the end of the day this concept of re-union will be found the only practical way forward – if not the end of the road.

CHAPTER 62

Requiescat in Pace

GEOFFREY Fisher remained remarkably fit for most of his retirement but as 1972 went on it was clear that his health was rapidly declining. On the Sunday before his death he was worshipping as usual in the parish church of Trent; but his final illness was mercifully brief. On Thursday 14 September, he suffered a slight stroke, and when Rosamond came to assist him as he lay prostrate he said to her whimsically: 'Don't bother me, dear, I'm busy dying'. He was taken into the Yeatman Hospital, in Sherborne, and it was a matter of grief to Rosamond, who had tended him with such great love over the years, that she was not present when he died peacefully in his sleep early the next day.

On Wednesday, some five days later, the funeral service was held in Trent church early in the afternoon. It was indeed a family occasion. To the parishioners Rosamond Fisher wrote later: 'The service was just what he had asked for, and very lovely; and you all came to join with us his own family – you people of Trent and Adber, who were indeed in a very real sense his 'family' too. Thank you for coming and for your lovely singing and thank you for all the beautiful bunches of flowers from your gardens.' It was singularly appropriate that the bearers of the coffin were nine villagers from Trent and the Comptons. Resting on the coffin was the Bishop's mitre. His cope, a gift from the Anglican Church in Japan, was borne in procession, as was the Archbishop's staff, given him by the Episcopal Church of the United States of America when Henry Sherrill was Presiding Bishop. Memorial services were held in Canterbury Cathedral when Dr Ramsey gave the Address and at Sherborne Abbey where three Bishops (Exeter, Truro and Sherborne) who had been consecrated during Archbishop Fisher's Primacy, participated. Later, on 10 October, a memorial service was held in Westminster Abbey when the preacher was Canon Max Warren.

Telegrams and letters of condolence flooded in to Lady Fisher literally from all over the world. These came from leading statesmen; Commonwealth personalities; churchmen of all denominations; those who had known him at various periods during his long life spanning the years from Repton to Trent. Many of these messages breathed more than a merely formal tribute, being warm and deeply appreciative of a life so well lived. Dr Michael Ramsey stressed that he was 'far

more than the schoolmaster-archbishop, as he was so often described'
– indeed he showed a 'deep pastoral care and concern for people'. Dr
Hcenan, the Cardinal Archbishop of Westminster, affirmed that 'probably more than any other man, Lord Fisher had been responsible for
the speed with which the Ecumenical Movement had developed in the
Roman Catholic Church because with great courage and on his own
initiative he was received by Pope John in the Vatican'. The Reverend
John Huxtable, Moderator Elect of the Free Church Federal Council,
stressed his 'immense service to the Ecumenical Movement and the
British Council of Churches'. Dr Immanuel Jakobovits, the Chief
Rabbi, said he would be remembered for his distinguished work as a
President of the Council of Christians and Jews and 'his defence of
Britain's moral and social values'.

Lady Fisher was to spend another ten years in Trent rectory, after
which she went to live with a member of her family near Wimbledon.
The years in rural Dorset were indeed no anti-climax either for
Geoffrey or Rosamond and no one could have been more helpful or
indeed more appreciative of all that they did together in the parish than
the rector, Timothy Brook. This was as it should be since Geoffrey
Fisher had always maintained that central to the life-blood of the
Church of England was the parish priest. It was as a parish priest that
he died.

It might have been thought that Geoffrey Fisher, following precedents set by his immediate predecessors, would have been buried in the
precincts of Canterbury Cathedral but he himself and Lady Fisher had
some time earlier decided otherwise. Two years previously he told the
rector that he hoped to be buried in Trent. The first suggestion was
that a vault should be made under the south transept, but there were
difficulties about this and a second suggestion was then produced,
namely that the south transept should become a baptistry and a vault
beneath the cross in the churchyard used for a burial. Both of these
proposals were put into effect. The churchyard vault was ready by
Easter 1971, and the baptistry dedicated by the Bishop of Bath and
Wells in December of the same year. So it was in the heart of rural
England and in a parish where he had ministered that the remains of
all that could be mortal of Dr Geoffrey Fisher and of Lady Fisher –
some years later – were laid to rest.

Though electing to be buried in Trent, it was felt right that Geoffrey
Fisher should be memorialised in Canterbury Cathedral among his
peers and predecessors. The first intention was to erect a window there
depicting the Archbishop with Pope John XXIII but this was turned
down by the Cathedral Advisory Committee. It was then decided to
beautify and refurbish the chapel of St Gregory in the South Transept
and to place there a memorial tablet inscribed with these words:

IN THIS CHAPEL DEDICATED TO SAINT GREGORY
REMEMBER WITH THANKFULNESS
GEOFFREY FRANCIS FISHER
ARCHBISHOP 1945 – 1961
A FOUNDER PRESIDENT OF THE
WORLD COUNCIL OF CHURCHES
BY HIS VISIT IN 1960 TO POPE JOHN XXIII HE RENEWED FRIENDSHIP
BETWEEN ROME AND CANTERBURY AFTER 400 YEARS
LAUS DEO

This plaque was dedicated, along with a cross and two candlesticks, on 15 September 1979, the preacher on this occasion being Canon Ian White Thompson, a dear and lifelong friend who was his chaplain during the first two years of his archiepiscopate. Most appropriately he took as his text, 'There is a diversity of gifts'.

EPILOGUE

Geoffrey Fisher – The Man and his Faith

(i)

I HAVE tried in this biography to be as objective as possible in my understanding and interpretation of the vast collection of letters, memoranda and papers which are deposited in the Library at Lambeth Palace. To achieve full objectivity in the writing of history is impossible and the claim to have secured it a dangerous delusion. However, I confess to having come away from my researches more convinced than I was before of Geoffrey Fisher's high significance in the continuing history of the *Ecclesia Anglicana* during a most critical period.

I propose now to suggest a few thoughts on Geoffrey Fisher simply as a human being, that is the man who lies behind and informs his works. I believe this to be important since he has suffered severely over the years from the media which have tended to create a stereotype image – greatly to his disadvantage – which has persisted across the years. There are various reasons for this. The Beaverbrook press, for example, for many years indulged an anti-Church of England stance going back to the time of Cosmo Lang and his alleged major role in securing the abdication of King Edward VIII. The image thereby foisted upon Geoffrey Fisher in the popular mind was that of the routine operator par excellence, the quintessential, rule-obsessed head-master concerned to deprive others of their natural enjoyment. Undoubtedly there were particular reasons helping to promote this caricature which is a gross distortion. The Church of England's marriage discipline in refusing remarriage in church to divorcees whose former partner was still living, angered many and Archbishop Fisher, in particular, became identified with this deprivation. Also, it must be allowed that now and again he made *ad hoc* impromptu statements, unhappily phrased and easily misunderstood. Such was, for example, that it might be within the Providence of God that mankind should destroy itself by nuclear bombs. Equally provocative was his assertion that though all people were equal in the love of God, they were not necessarily equal in the sight of God.

Few, I am confident, who knew Geoffrey Fisher at first hand would think of him as egocentric or in any way an intellectual snob. Indeed in his taped autobiography he makes no reference whatever to his academic record at Oxford – three firsts! In fact he was remarkably modest. Those who met him for the first time were charmed by his friendliness and approachability. His usual response to people – and this was no affectation – was one of genuine concern as if he or she alone mattered and deserved his whole attention. His staff, and this applied to all his chaplains, felt themselves to be working with rather than for him. True he could on occasions, if rarely, explode but it soon subsided. For example, after a fracas with Canon John Collins over South Africa when tempers became frayed, the Archbishop wrote to him that neither of them came out of this tussle very well and it was therefore better for both to forget it. Ideas were important, but more so were the people who embodied and expressed them. Thus his letters often contained little personal references which must have meant much to the recipients, many of whom, in the Far East, were lonely, cut off by war and some imprisoned. Certainly he made maximum use of what Dr Eric Abbott used to call his 'ministry of the post'. Never was he at the receiving end of hospitality without acknowledging it to the host(ess) in a warm and gracious way. It was one of his oft-repeated sayings, sometimes maybe a little naive, that the solution of many thorny problems, not least in liturgical practices, lay simply in good manners and ordinary courtesy.

Young people were instinctively drawn to him. Typical, for example, was his correspondence with a Winchester schoolboy who solemnly informed him that he had squared the circle, an ambition which had defied mathematicians across the centuries. The consequent exchange of letters only ceased when the Archbishop was forced to admit that his own expertise in this field was too limited for him to pursue the argument any further.

In the same way he carried on a correspondence with a young coloured conscript whom he encountered quite casually – though he claimed that their 'eyes met' – as he was leaving a church in the United States. When this young man was later blown up in a tank accident on the Continent, one letter alone was found in his wallet. It was from the Archbishop!

Lady Fisher used to say that, though he was unaware of it, Geoffrey Fisher possessed gifts of healing however we may account for such an endowment. She quotes an instance which came her way. The Archbishop was processing down the aisle at the end of a service when he caught sight of a disabled lady in a wheelchair. He immediately 'broke ranks' and put his hands upon her shoulders – a characteristic gesture. She confessed to feeling an infusion of power and a sense of release.

In spite of his undoubted self-assurance which gave a general impression that he was completely on top of things he was yet sensitive to criticism even if he seldom publicly showed it. An example of this is the excessive length of some of the replies to complaining letters which many a bishop would almost automatically have referred to his chaplain. At no time in his historic pilgrimage in 1960 was he more upset than in Jerusalem when he was accused by the English press of attacking the policy of Britain in the Middle East which was not the 'done thing' in a foreign land. The Archbishop was cut to the quick and in his private diary indulged a veritable orgy of self immolation. Was there any point in his carrying on his tour? Did it really matter?

Geoffrey Fisher never had any desire to parade the trappings of office and in this he had little in common – and he said so – with Archbishop Lang whose portrait by Orpen was thought to depict him as 'proud, pompous and prelatical', thus evoking the comment from the caustic Hensley Henson: 'To which of those epithets does your Grace take objection?' Often he would show off to visitors his spacious study hoping it might impress them with the greatness of the Church of England. (In fact Lang was a much more complex and subtle character than this passing reference might seem to suggest.) A working journalist calls attention from his own experience to Geoffrey Fisher's 'easy and natural manner'. 'He has', he writes, 'never attempted to set himself up as a great Prince of the Church. His manner is friendly; his speeches unpompous; he admits on television that he reads detective stories. The consequence of the Archbishop's manner is that many people noting what is clearly a human being in the Chair of St Augustine have tended to assume that the Archbishop is no better equipped than themselves to make moral judgements.' From what we have said perhaps it was to be expected that when Geoffrey Fisher 'unbuttoned' himself so far as to smoke a pipe in public Cosmo Lang was shocked. Later in life he gave up the habit absolutely and got rid of all his pipes.

Though the Archbishop was described by Canon Waddams as a 'workaholic' he certainly relaxed on holiday but it is significant that he took pleasure in making himself physically tired, hence, earlier, his predilection for squash. His favourite hobby was walking, and many were the holidays spent with the family at Minehead trekking across Exmoor, the route being carefully mapped out by the Archbishop. Indeed there was one summer when he occupied himself almost exclusively by taking a billhook and slashing away at the heather which blocked his favourite walk. Equally years later at Canterbury he complained to the local authority that a favourite right of way had been rendered unusable by a local farmer. It was soon reopened!

One of Geoffrey Fisher's saving graces which could prove a safety valve in situations of stress was a highly developed sense of humour. Certainly this lightened many a load; defused many a tricky situation, not least when he was chairing meetings of Convocation, the Church Assembly, the Diocesan Synod – or a Lambeth Conference. To dissolve into laughter at a solemn ecclesiastical gathering can at times be therapeutic. It could also serve to stifle a deep emotion which he wished to conceal.

Two typical examples of his humour may be quoted.

On one occasion when doubt was expressed as to whether clergyman X was tough enough to take on a most difficult parish the Archbishop clinched the matter by saying: 'If the Reverend X had the courage to marry Mrs X then he can cope with anything'.

At a Pilgrims' Dinner in the United States on 16 November 1954, he informed his fellow diners, though he realised what a bitter disappointment it would be to them, that in spite of considerable pressure brought to bear on him he had finally decided not to run for the Presidency against General Eisenhower.

Until he went to London and the war broke out he enjoyed a richly satisfying family life. Hence one of his sons writes:

'I am sure that the family was very important to him. It is true that he left the running of it to my mother but he liked to be in the middle of it. He would always join the family circle in the evening even if he brought some solid piece of reading to do when we embarked upon noisy card games or such like. He never joined in these and was fully able to concentrate on what he was reading despite the din. We once had occasion to move all the furniture out of the room we were sitting in in preparation for a dance and when he finished his book he realised for the first time that his chair was the only piece of furniture left! In music he liked to sing a bass part in family carols and he had his musical favourites which included, surprisingly, Peter Grimes.'

His son also remembers how he took a delight in talking to all and sundry whether it were schoolboys or workmen on the reconstruction at Lambeth Palace. He also loved finding out, with a perennial curiosity, what people did, who they were and when they told him he tended to say 'Quite right' as if he had known all along. The habit of a lifetime persisted when he went into retirement at Trent and had more time and opportunity to indulge it. On one evening in the week he went regularly to play chess with one of the village boys. Such a simple act reinforces Dean Ian Thompson, who knew him intimately and describes him as 'an immensely loving man'.

The war years, with most of the sons in the Forces, were a period of great stress and strain. Rosamond never forgot the poignant moment when she heard that one of the family, reported missing, was alive. In respect of one of Geoffrey's brothers, Leonard, who became a Bishop in South Africa, geographical distance was not allowed to separate them and their relationship remained close and intimate. They saw each other at Lambeth Conferences and sometimes Geoffrey would break a journey abroad to meet up with him.

Geoffrey Fisher, unlike Dr Johnson, was not really a clubbable man and he seldom visited the Athenaeum except for a particular purpose. This did not mean that he had few personal friends. It did mean, however, that his close friends tended to be drawn from a narrow circle. Thus a son writes: 'He had the great gift of promoting many people with whom he was working to the level of a friend'. Perhaps number one amongst them was Henry Sherrill, the Presiding Bishop of the Protestant Episcopal Church of America, to whom many references have been made in the course of this biography.

(ii)

No one I suspect can write a full-length biography and in the process live with his subject over a number of years without putting to himself the question: 'What makes him tick? What influences have proved most formative in creating him the man that he was?'

Geoffrey Fisher's early *curriculum vitae* conforms to the conventional pattern of a middle class upbringing in the rectory of a rural parish. Perhaps one endowment he inherited from his family was genetic, namely an astonishing physical energy which enabled him to work long hours; to transfer easily from one area of interest to another; and to keep going. On his long and arduous tours his resilience proved invaluable and those who witnessed it at first hand, not least journalists, were deeply impressed and admiring.

No endeavour to see Geoffrey Fisher 'steadily and to see him whole' can fail to recognise the strong influence brought to bear upon him by the parish of Higham on the Hill where members of his family had ministered, in direct succession, as incumbents for over one hundred years. Doubtless in very early days this conditioning was subliminal but it was none the less real. Here the young Geoffrey, *ab initio*, absorbed without conscious effort the general *ethos* of the Church of England right at its heart – in a parish. It set for him the dominant pattern around which nearly everything else revolved. Family prayers; grace before meals; regular worship Sunday by Sunday in the parish church; the village school which he attended in his earliest years; the general landscape and the churchyard wherein 'the rude fore-fathers of the hamlet sleep'; an accepted but not divisive social hierarchy – these were fixed points as natural to him as the air he breathed. Certainly, not even embryonically, was there any apparent sign of an 'angry young man', frustrated and protesting. When he left for Marlborough and then Exeter College, Oxford, the influence of the *Ecclesia Anglicana* was still strong even if this Indian summer was on the wane.

But what, at its roots, did this Church of England dimension mean to Geoffrey Fisher? What, to put it crudely, did he 'take on board' through this early conditioning? As I let my mind play around this question so I would remind the reader of two most significant experiences, already referred to, and which he himself records in some detail though he probably never envisaged that these descriptions would be read by others. The first refers to the spiritual travail and heart-rending anguish he went through on being offered the bishopric of London during Holy Week. The other relates to his moving – or more accurately his being propelled – along the Via Dolorosa in Jerusalem during his visit to the Holy City in 1960.

Geoffrey Fisher, unlike the poet Byron, had no desire to trail his bleeding heart across Europe. Rather, he distils his inmost thoughts into an *aide-memoire* and a private diary both contemporary with the experience they record.

As Geoffrey ponders over, and meditates in prayer upon his summons to London so he identifies himself with the sufferings and final commitment of Jesus until in the end he utters: 'Not as I will but as thou wilt'. He is glad that the call has come to him during Holy Week so that he may identify himself with his Lord in his total self-giving.

Equally along the *Via Dolorosa* his indidual consciousness merges itself into a deep awareness of his Lord. Though he has travelled far from the Christo-centricity which he first learnt at his mother's knees in Higham rectory yet its basic character, deepened and more mature, remains central. Hence discipleship of Jesus is for him no contrived following of his example. His situation was not ours. Rather, in the power of his Spirit, we must respond to our own contemporary challenges as we seek to follow whither leads us. It is within this context that Geoffrey Fisher understands his membership of the Church of England – a Church liberal in its *ethos*, and to quote his oft repeated words equally conscious of what it does not know as what it does; a Church, moreover, which does not rush to unchurch others.

One of his sons writes: 'I would say that his religious faith sprang from early experience but it became very profound and personal and comprehensive. I always regarded his faith as powerful and absolutely unchanging. If there were any reasons for doubts I would only imagine they would have sprung from some awful things that go on in the world that God made. At Chester we all turned and knelt on our knees before breakfast but that dropped out in the war years. He certainly worried about things in the sense of concentrating his mind upon them for lengthy periods and there would also be significant conversation between him and my mother at bedtime.'

When I concluded my biographical study of Bishop Thomas Sherlock (1678–1761) I wrote these words: 'It is, perhaps, as much the task of the reader as the author to estimate the contribution which he made to the life of his times'. In the same spirit, therefore, I leave it to the present reader to reflect upon the facts which I have placed before him or her and, as a consequence, to accept, qualify or reject my considered view which is that Geoffrey Fisher served the Church of England througout a critical period in its post-war history; that he gave a high priority to assist the growth and self understanding of the multi-racial Anglican Communion; that he showed both courage and insight in 'leaping over the wall' to embrace the congregation of Christian people dispersed throughout the world; and that he kept firmly in his sights and concerns the secular society around him.

It is appropriate, I think, that I should now end with a favourite quotation of the Archbishop from the Epistle to the Hebrews: 'For he looked for a city which hath foundations, whose builder and maker is God'.

APPENDICES

APPENDICES

APPENDIX I

Note on Sources

When I took over the responsibility of writing this biography of
Geoffrey Fisher, I was soon made aware of the lavishness of the
available material for his tenure of the office of Primate of All England.
The Fisher Papers, now housed in Lambeth Palace Library, contain
every letter and document which was received by the Archbishop
during his sixteen years in office, together with the letters, memoranda,
pronouncements, speeches and sermons written by himself. It is this
huge volume of material which forms the essential source for this
biography. When I worked through the collection, it was housed in
over 400 large boxes, but was otherwise un-numbered and undes-
cribed. Since that time the papers have been meticulously catalogued
by the staff at the Library. With some reluctance, however, I have
decided not to return to Lambeth in order to secure precise references
to the material which I have used. This explains why the book is
without footnotes. To have provided detailed footnotes would have
delayed even further a book already long delayed; would have meant
reducing the length of the text in order to make way for them; and
would, to some extent, have been superogatory since the basic sources
are not scattered and arcane but consolidated and accessible. I do not
think that it will be very difficult for the reader, who wishes to follow
up particular points, to locate at Lambeth the material which I have
used.

The sources for Geoffrey Fisher's London episcopate are as bare as
those for his Archiepiscopate are abundant. I was able to inspect a few
boxes of London papers, which survive at Lambeth, but, for the rest,
the archives of that period have disappeared, indeed have probably
been destroyed. Geoffrey Fisher was a compulsive letter writer and a
most conscientious and hard working diocesan bishop. His episcopate
in London coincided with the years of the Second World War which
constituted a unique period in the history of the great metropolis. His
pastoral letters to his own clergy must have told an unforgettable story,
and one can only deplore that it can never now be told. However, all is
not lost for there still exist the minutes of various committees set up
through the exigencies of war and of which Geoffrey Fisher was
chairman. I refer, *inter alia*, to the Bishop of London's Committee for
the City Churches; The Archbishops' War Committee; and the Joint
Standing Committee, the membership of which was ecumenical.

I was fortunate in being able to use the diary in which he pondered over what he should do *à propos* his nomination to Canterbury; the letters he wrote to Rosamond Fisher during her evacuation from London in the war; his Coronation Diary; and the diary which he kept while in Jerusalem. Likewise, William Purcell kindly made available a transcript of the Archbishop's taped autobiography. It will be evident from the text where I am using these sources. A word is necessary on the taped autobiography. It was recorded after Fisher's retirement in the late sixties and shows only too clearly that as he approached his eighties his judgement became erratic and his emotional involvement with colleagues somewhat combative. Thus I have referred to this source sparingly, although it is valuable for his early years at Higham on the Hill.

Archival material, of course, can only give a limited impression of the impact which Geoffrey Fisher made on his contemporaries. Naturally I have followed his career in the pages of the press. But above all I am indebted to countless people, who came to know him well both in England and overseas, and who shared their views with me in conversations and correspondence. Their willingness to talk and write freely, informally and frankly has been invaluable in giving me a 'full' picture of the man.

APPENDIX II

Geoffrey and Lady Fisher's last annual circular letter

TRENT RECTORY

SHERBORNE

JANUARY 1972

Once again we have had the great joy of hearing at Christmas from very many friends, and now have the almost equal pleasure of writing to thank you for all the cards and letters, and to tell you our news.

We are both very well indeed, rather less mobile but keeping going.

A new car (second-hand) and a lovely new carpet in the Drawing-room, a present from one of our sisters, indicate our continuing capacity for enjoyment of life and looking forward. Geoffrey has now given up assisting at the services and much enjoys being just one of the congregation.

Rosamond still takes her place in the choir to give support (moral rather than musical) to its few members.

In 1971 we did not undertake any exciting journeys, our furthest being to Cornwall to spend a week in lovely May weather in Frank's holiday house at Trebetherick. We also visited four sons at different times at Larchmere, Wellington, New Malden and Bilton Grange, and we had a few happy days in London with our old friends Bishop and Mrs. Sherrill who were paying a short visit to England in celebration of their golden wedding.

Our family news is cheerful - Harry enjoys being a banker (Schroeder Wagg) and his family of four are growing up delightfully. I can only mention particularly Emma who did so well at Oxford, and who is now working for a publisher in an editorial capacity.

And Thomas, who entered Marlborough exactly forty years after his father and seventy after his grandfather.

Frank made a splendid tour of several places in Africa, and in Mauritius en route for Australia, and their Headmasters Conference to which he was a delegate from the English H.M.C.

Charles who is Headmaster of the C. of E. Grammar School in Brisbane with 1400 boys is Secretary of the Australian H.M.C. and the Conference took place in Brisbane. So Frank spent two weeks with him and Anne and their six children (their eldest Jane not quite 19, has just completed her second year at Brisbane University with Distinction). Frank also stayed with Humphrey and Diana in Sydney. He is head of Outside Broadcasting in the Australian Broadcasting Corporation. He and Diana joined the Brisbane party for a very happy family holiday at a seaside place in Queensland.

Bobbie is still in the big group practice (nine doctors) in South London. He and Jill are delighted that their eldest, David, has got into

- 2 -

Kings College, Wimbledon (Junior) he is also a keen chorister at their
Church. Tim and Clare are kept very busy with the 190 boys at Bilton Grange
Preparatory School (8 yrs. - 13) but find enormous pleasure and relaxation
with their little son Paul aged 21 months. He is our fourteenth grandchild.

During 1971 we had a succession of visitors, both staying with us, and
just calling in. Some of them were from the U.S.A. and Canada, Australia,
Africa and from Ireland. It gave us great pleasure to see them all and to
be able to return a little of the generous hospitality which they have
extended to us on many occasions. The highlight of the year in our Parish
was the Dedication of a new Baptistry in the Church.

Thanks to generous gifts from an American friend and from members of
our family the south transept has been cleared and re-furnished and the font
moved into it, where its beautiful Pre-Reformation carved cover can be seen
to advantage, and adequate space round for Godparents and Parents of those
being baptised. The Bishop of Bath & Wells came to dedicate it during our
annual carol service, and one of our former Chaplains now vicar of Yeovil
and Rural Dean - Michael Percival-Smith was also present.

And in mentioning him I must also say that we were most happy to see
two other chaplains recently Eric Jay with Margaret from Montreal, and
Michael Adie with Anne from Louth in Lincolnshire. We also see Priscilla
Lethbridge from time to time.

With best wishes from us both.

Geoffrey (Archbishop)

and

Rosamond Fisher

APPENDIX III

Entry in Who's Who, 1972

*(Reproduced with permission of A & C Black Limited,
publishers of Who's Who)*

FISHER OF LAMBETH, Baron *cr* 1961,
of Lambeth (Life Peer); **Most Rev. and Rt.
Hon. Geoffrey Francis Fisher;** PC 1939;
GCVO *cr 1953; Royal Victorian Chain,
1949; Hon. DD, LLD, and DCL; MA; b*
5 May 1887; *y s* of late Rev. H. Fisher,
Rector of Higham on the Hill, Nuneaton;
m 1917, Rosamond Chevallier, *d* of late
Rev. A. F. E. Forman, and *g d* of Dr S. A.
Pears, once Headmaster of Repton; six *s.
Educ:* Marlborough Coll., Exeter Coll.,
Oxford (open scholar); First Class Hon-
ours in Moderations, 1908; Lit Hum 1910;
Theology, 1911; Liddon Scholarship,
1911; Wells Theological Coll., 1911.
Deacon, 1912; Priest, 1913. Hon. Fellow,
Exeter Coll., Oxford, 1939; Asst Master,
Marlborough Coll., 1911–14; Headmaster
of Repton Sch., 1914–32; Bishop of
Chester, 1932–39; Bishop of London,
1939–45; Archbishop of Canterbury,
1945–61. Dean of the Chapels Royal,
1939–45; Prelate of Order of British
Empire, 1939–45; Prelate, 1946, and Bail-
iff Grand Cross, 1947, of Order of S John
of Jerusalem; President of the World Council of Churches, 1946–54. Select Preacher,
Oxford Univ., 1925–27, Cambridge Univ.,
1937 and 1940; Freeman of Cities of
London and Canterbury, 1952; of Croydon, 1961. Hon. Doctor of Laws (Universities of Pennsylvania and Columbia, 1946,
Yale and British Columbia, 1954); Hon.
DD; Oxford, 1933; Cambridge and Princeton, 1946, Edinburgh, 1953; Montreal,

1962; TCD 1963; Hon LLD: Pennsylvania
and Columbia, 1946; London 1948; Man-
chester, 1950; Yale and BC, 1954; Rikkyo,
Japan, 1959; Yonsel, Korea, 1959; Hon.
DCL (Roman Catholic) University of the
Assumption, Windsor, Canada; Hon. STD,
Northwestern, Evanston, 1954; Doctor of
Theology, General Theological Seminary,
New York, 1957. Grand Cross of Greek
Order of the Redeemer, 1947; Grand Cross
of St Olav (Norway), 1947; Czechoslovak
Order of the White Lion (II Class), 1948.

List of books written by Geoffrey Fisher, or to which he contributed

Anglican-Methodist Conversations and Problems of Church Unity, The. Some personal reflections by Lord Fisher of Lambeth, formerly Archbishop of Canterbury. (Oxford University Press, London, 1964)

Archbishop Speaks, The. Addresses and Speeches by the Archbishop of Canterbury, The Most Reverend Geoffrey Francis Fisher, PC, GCVO, DD. Selected by Edward Carpenter. (Evans Brothers Limited, London, 1958)

Archbishop Talks to the Forces, The. Six talks broadcast in the B.B.C. Overseas Services in March 1946. (Reprinted by the B.B.C.)

Canterbury Speaks. With Foreword by the Primate of Australia. Addresses delivered by the Archbishop during his visit to Australia in October and November 1950. (Published by Canon Ernest Cameron, Diocesan Church House, George Street, Sydney)

Church Today, The. Geoffrey Francis Fisher . . . being the *McMath Lectures* delivered at the Cathedral Church of St Paul, Detroit, Michigan, in October 1962.

Covenant and Reconciliation – A critical examination. Archbishop Lord Fisher of Lambeth. (A. R. Mowbray, London & Oxford, 1967)

Faith. G. F. Fisher, DD, Bishop of London. (Frederick Muller Ltd, London W.C.1, 1942)

Feeling Our Way. Three sermons by the Archbishop of Canterbury preached in Jerusalem, Istanbul and Rome. (C.I.O., Church House, Westminster, 1960)

'I Here Present unto You'. Six addresses interpreting the Coronation of Her Majesty Queen Elizabeth II, given on various occasions by His Grace the Archbishop of Canterbury (*S.P.C.K.*, London, 1953)

Pattern Makers by the Archbishop of Canterbury.
> Contents: 1. *The Key Industry*. Text of a sermon before members of the Duke of Edinburgh's Study Conference on the Human Problems of Industrial Communities within the Commonwealth and Empire, on Sunday 22 July 1956, in the University Church of St Mary-the-Virgin, Oxford.
> 2. *A More Excellent Way*. Text of a sermon given by His Grace at a Service of Dedication for the Trades Union Congress at St Peter's Church, Brighton, on Sunday 2 September 1956. (The Industrial Christian Fellowship, 195 New Kent Road, London, S.E.1)

Redeeming the Situation. Occasional sermons, 1947, by the Archbishop of Canterbury. (S.P.C.K., London, 1948)

Standards of Morality, Christian and Humanist by Archbishop Lord Fisher of Lambeth. (A. R. Mowbray, London and Oxford)

Survey of Church Relations, A by Lord Fisher of Lambeth. (S.P.C.K. London 1967)

Touching on Christian Truth – The Kingdom of God, The Christian Church and the World – by Archbishop Lord Fisher of Lambeth. (A. R. Mowbray London and Oxford)

APPENDIX V

Chaplains who served Archbishop Fisher

Senior:
Prebendary Christopher Cheshire
Prebendary Stanley Eley   (Prebendary of St Paul's Cathedral)
The Reverend Eric Jay   (later Dean of the Theological Faculty of McGill
    University, Canada)
The Reverend Frederick (Freddie) Temple   (later Bishop of Malmesbury)

Resident (or Domestic) Chaplain:
Michael Adie   (later Bishop of Guildford)
John Long   (later Archdeacon of Ely)
Michael Percival-Smith   (later Archdeacon of Maidstone)
Simon Ridley
Ian White-Thomson   (later Dean of Canterbury)

(Canon Herbert Waddams also acted as Senior Chaplain between
    appointments)

APPENDIX VI

Bishops during Geoffrey Fisher's Archiepiscopate

PROVINCE OF CANTERBURY

London
1945 John William Charles Wand
1956 Henry Montgomery Campbell
1961 Robert Stopford

Winchester
1942 Mervyn Haigh
1952 Alwyn Williams
1961 Falkner Allison

Bath & Wells
1943 John William Charles Wand
1946 Harold Bradfield
1960 Edward Henderson

Birmingham
1924 Ernest Barnes
1953 Leonard Wilson

Bristol
1933 Clifford Woodward
1946 Arthur Cockin
1959 Oliver Tomkins

Chelmsford
1929 Henry Wilson
1951 Falkner Allison
1962 John Tiarks

Chichester
1929 George Bell
1958 Roger Wilson

Coventry
1943 Neville Gorton
1956 Cuthbert Bardsley

Derby
1936 Alfred Rawlinson
1959 Geoffrey Allen

Ely
1941 Harold Wynn
1957 Noel Hudson

Exeter
1936 Charles Curzon
1949 Robert Mortimer

Gloucester
1923 Arthur Headlam
1946 Clifford Woodward

1954 Wilfred Marcus Askwith
1962 Basil Guy

Guildford
1934 John Macmillan
1949 Henry Montgomery Campbell
1956 Ivor Watkins
1961 George Reindorp

Hereford
1941 Richard Parsons
1949 Tom Longworth
1961 Mark Hodson

Leicester
1940 Guy Vernon Smith
1953 Ronald Williams

Lichfield
1937 Edwards Woods
1953 Arthur Stretton Reeve

Lincoln
1942 Henry Skelton
1946 Leslie Owen
1947 Maurice Harland
1956 Kenneth Riches

Norwich
1942 Percy Mark Herbert
1959 Launcelot Fleming

Oxford
1937 Kenneth Kirk
1955 Harry Carpenter

Peterborough
1927 Claude Blagden
1949 Spencer Leeson
1956 Robert Stopford
1961 Cyril Eastaugh

Portsmouth
1942 William Anderson
1949 Launcelot Fleming
1960 John Phillips

Rochester
1939 Christopher Chevasse
1961 Richard David Say

St Albans
1920 Michael Furse

1944   Philip Loyd (Eric)
1950   Michael Gresford Jones

St Edmundsbury & Ipswich
1940   Richard Brook
1954   Arthur Harold Morris

Salisbury
1936   Ernest Lovett
1946   Geoffrey Lunt
1949   William Anderson

Southwark
1941   Bertram Simpson
1959   Mervyn Stockwood

Truro
1935   Joseph Hunkin
1951   Edmund Morgan
1960   John Key

Worcester
1931   Arthur Perowne
1941   William Wilson Cash
1956   Mervyn Charles-Edwards

PROVINCE OF YORK

York
1942   Cyril Garbett
1956   Arthur Michael Ramsey
1961   Frederick Donald Coggan

Durham
1939   Alwyn Williams
1952   A. M. Ramsey
1956   Maurice Harland

Blackburn
1942   Wilfred Askwith
1954   Walter Baddeley
1960   Charles Claxton

Bradford
1931   Alfred W. F. Blunt

1956   Frederick Donald Coggan
1961   Clement St Michael Parker

Carlisle
1920   Henry Williams
1946   Thomas Bloomer

Chester
1939   Douglas Crick
1955   Gerald Ellison

Liverpool
1944   Clifford Martin

Manchester
1929   Frederic Guy Warman
1947   William Greer

Newcastle
1927   Harold Bilbrough
1941   Noel Hudson
1957   Hugh Ashdown

Ripon
1935   Geoffrey Lunt
1946   George Chase
1959   John Moorman

Sheffield
1939   Leslie Hunter
1962   Francis Taylor

Sodor & Man
1928   William Jones
1942   John Taylor
1954   Benjamin Pollard

Southwell
1941   Frank Russell Barry

Wakefield
1938   Campbell Richard Hone
1946   Henry McGowan
1949   Roger Wilson
1958   John Ramsbotham

APPENDIX VII

Bibliography

Manuscript Sources

Archives:
    Church Missionary Society
    Society for the Propagation of the Gospel
    National Society
Lambeth Palace Library:
    Fulham Papers: Fisher
    Fisher Papers
    Douglas Papers
    Church of England Council on Foreign Relations
Parish Records:
    Higham on the Hill

Selective Bibliography

ADY, C.M. *The English Church*. Faber & Faber, 1940
ALUMNI OXONIENSIS. ed. J. Foster, 1892
ALUMNI CANTABRIGIENSIS. ed. J & J. A. Venn, 1926
Ampleforth Journal
BATTISCOMBE, G. *Queen Alexandra*. Constable, 1969
JOOST E BLANK. *Bartha de Blank*, 1977
BELL, G. K. A. *Randall Davidson, Archbishop of Canterbury*. O.U.P., 1935
BINNS, J. S. P. *Bishop Blunt 1879–1957*. Mountain Press
BOWEN, D. *The Idea of the Victorian Church*. McGill, University Press, Montreal, 1968
BROOKE, Z. M. *The English Church and the Papacy*. O.U.P., 1931
BROWNE, J. C. *Lambeth Palace & its Associations*
The Canon Law of the Church of England being the Report of the Archbishop's Commission on Canon Law. S.P.C.K., 1947
The Canons of the Church of England. S.P.C.K., 1969
Canterbury Diocesan Notes
CARMICHAEL, J. D. and GOODWIN, H.S. *William Temple's Political Legacy*. Mowbray, 1963
CARPENTER, S.C. *Biography of Winnington Ingram*. Hodder & Stoughton
CARPENTER, EDWARD, *Cantuar*, Cassell & Co Ltd, 1971, Mowbray 1988
CARPENTER, EDWARD, *The Archbishop Speaks*, Evans Bros Ltd, 1958
CARPENTER & HART. *The Nineteenth Country Parson*, Wilding
CHADWICK, OWEN, *Victorian Church Part 1*, 1966; *Part II*, A & C Black 1970
CHADWICK, OWEN, *Biography of Michael Ramsey*. O.U.P., 1990
Chester Diocesan Gazette

Chronicle of the Convocation of Canterbury
Chronicle of the Convocation of York
Church Assembly Reports and proceedings
Church and State – Reports of Commissions. C.I.O.
Church Congress Reports
Church Membership and Inter Communion. Darton Longman and Todd,
   1973
Church Times
Coronation of Her Majesty Queen Elizabeth: The Order of Divine Service
The English Church and the Continent, The Faith Press Ltd, 1959
Life and Letters of Mandell Creighton D.D. by his wife. 2 Vols. Longmans,
   1906
Marjorie Cruikshank. *Church and State in English Education 1870–1965*
DALE, W. L. *The law of the Parish Church*. Butterworth, 1957
DARK, S. *Seven Archbishops*. Eyre & Spottiswoode, 1944
DAVIDSON, R. T. *Five Archbishops, a Sermon*. S.P.C.K., 1911
DAVIDSON AND BENHAM. *Life of Archbishop Campbell Tait*. 2 Vols.
   Macmillan, 1891
Oxford Dictionary of the Christian Church. Ed. F. L. Cross, O.U.P., 1966
Dictionary of English Church History. Ed. Olland and Cross
Dictionary of National Biography, O.U.P., 1919
DUFF, EDWARD, *The Social Thought of the World Council of Churches*.
   Longmans, 1956
EDWARDS, DAVID. *The future of Christianity*. Hodder & Stoughton, 1987
ELLIOTT AND SOMERSKILL. *A Dictionary of Politics*. Penguin Books, 1964
Ecumenical Prayer Cycle – for all God's People. S.P.C.K. & Catholic Truth
   Society, 1978
ELLIS, RUTH. *Victor Gollancz, Biography*. Gollancz Ltd, 1987
The Family in Contemporary Society. S.P.C.K., 1958
FOX, ADAM. *Dean Inge*. John Murray, 1960
HASTINGS, ADRIAN. *A History of English Christianity 1920–1985*. Collins,
   1986
HEWETT, G. H. *Leslie Hunter Strategist of the Spirit*. Becket, 1985
HOWARD, ANTHONY. *RAB, The life of R. A. Butler*. Jonathan Cape, 1987
Hansard, Parliamentary Debates
HENSON, H. B. *Retrospect of an Unimportant Life*. 3 Vols. O.U.P., 1943
HOLTBY, R. *Robert Wright Stopford*. The National Society, 1988
HUDSON, DARRIL. *The World Council of Churches in International Affairs*.
   The Faith Press, 1977
HUNTER, LESLIE S. *The English Church: A New Look*. Penguin Books,
   1966
INGE, W. R. *Diary of a Dean*. Hutchinson, 1949
Inter-Communion Today, Report of the Archbishop's Commission. C.I.O.,
   1968
IREMONGER, F. A. *William Temple*. O.U.P., 1948
INGLES, B. A. *Abdication*. Hodder & Stoughton, 1966
JASPER, R. C. D. *George Bell, Bishop of Chichester*. O.U.P., 1967
JOHNSON, HEWLETT. *Searching for Light*. Michael Joseph, 1967
KEMP, E. W. *The Anglican-Methodist Conversations: A comment from
   within*. 1964

A King's Story, The Memoirs of H.R.H. The Duke of Windsor, K.G., Casell, 1951

KIRK-SMITH, H. *William Thomson, Archbishop of York*. S.P.C.K., 1958

LAQUEURAND RUBIN, *The Israel Arab Reader*, Penguin Books, 1987

Lambeth Conference 1948. S.P.C.K., 1948

Lambeth Conference 1958. S.P.C.K., 1958

Lambeth Palace Order for Service for the Rededication of the Chapel

LAMB, J. W. *The Archbishop of York*. The Faith Press, 1967

LEE, SIR S. *King Edward VII, a biography*, Macmillan, 1925

LOCKHART, T. G. *Cosmo Gordon Lang*. Hodder and Stoughton, 1949

London Diocesan Leaflet

London Diocesan Gazette

London Diocesan Conference

LLOYD, R. *The Church of England in the Twentieth Century*. S.C.M. Press

MATTHEWS, W. R. *Memories and Meanings*. Hodder and Stoughton

MATTHEWS, W. R. and others. *William Temple, an Estimate and Appreciation*. James Clarke, 1946

The Life of Frederick Denison Maurice. Ed. Frederick Maurice. 4th edition, 2 Vols. Macmillan, 1885

MARSH, P. T. *The Victorian Church in Decline*. Routledge, 1968

MOSELEY, NICHOLAS. *The life of Raymond Raynes*. The Faith Press, 1961

MURPHY, JAMES. *Church, State and Schools in Britain 1800–1970*. Routledge and Kegan Paul, 1971

PATON, ALAN. *Apartheid and the Archbishop – the Life and Times of Geoffrey Clayton*. Jonathan Cape, 1974

PAYNE, EARNEST. *Thirty Years of the British Council of Churches 1942–1972*, BCC, 1972

PARR, STEPHEN. *Canterbury Pilgrimage*. Simpson and Williams Ltd, 1951

PERKINS, J. *The Crowning of the Sovereign*. Methuen, 1937

PHILLIMORE, W. G. F. *The Ecclesiastical Law of the Church of England*. Sweet and Maxwell and Stephen's and Son, 1895

POWYS, A. R. *The English Parish Church*. Longmans Green & Co, 1930

PURCELL, W. E. *Fisher of Lambeth*. Hodder and Stoughton, 1969

The Report of the Commission on Religious Education in Schools, S.P.C.K., 1970

RAE, JOHN. *The Public School Revolution*. Faber and Faber, 1981

Report of the Anglican Methodist Union Commission. S.P.C.K., 1968

Repton School Terminal Letters

SAVIDGE, ALAN. *The Foundations and early years of Queen Anne's Bounty* S.P.C.K., 1955

SIMPSON, J. and STORY, E. *The Long Shadows of Lambeth X*. McGraw Hill Book Company, 1969

SMITH, ARNOLD with SANGER, CLYDE. *Stitches in Time*. Andre Deutsch, 1981

STEPHENSON, A. M. G, *The First Lambeth Conference 1967*. S.P.C.K., 1967

STEPHENSON, A. M. G. *Anglicanism and the Lambeth Conference*. S.P.C.K., 1978

STOCK, E. *A History of the Church Missionary Society*, C.M.S., 1899

Theology

THOMPSON, H. P. *Into all Lands*, S.P.C.K., 1951

Trent and Abder News Letter, October 1972 in Memoriam

VISSER'T HOOFT, W. A. *Memoirs*, S.C.M. Press

WEDDERSPOON, ALEXANDER. *Religious Education 1944–1984*

WELSBY, P. A. *A History of the Church of England 1945–1980*, O.U.P., 1984

WEST, W. M. S. *To be a Pilgrim – A Memoir of Ernest A. Payne.* Lutterworth Press, 1983

WHITE, J. L. *Abdication of Edward VIII.* Routledge, 1951

Who's Who at Lambeth 1968. Church Missions Publishing Company U.S.A.

Index

Abbott, Judge Charles 358
Abbott, Dr Eric 291, 768
Abdullah, King 589
abortion 363, 682
Abyssinia 52
Accra Diocese 504, 506
Acland, Sir Richard 163
Act of Praemunire 215, 232, 235
Acts of Convocation 117
Ad Petram Cathedram Encyclical 732, 739
Addleshaw, Dr 209
Adeane, Sir Michael 276, 277, 280, 283
Adelaide 482
Aden 603, 611, 612
African Christian Council 565
air travel 444
air-raids 64, 66, 81–2, 93, 117
Alamein memorial 369–70
Albert Hall 154
Alexandra, Queen 55, 272, 279
Alexis, Patriarch 140
Alice, Princess 285
All Saints Church, Fulham 115
All Saints Church, Margaret Street 118, 333
Allen, Chappie 12
Allen, Geoffrey, Bishop in Egypt 228, 610–13
Allen, Godfrey 79, 81, 82
Allen, Lord 143
Allison, Faulkner, Bishop 222, 748
Alport, Lord 512
American Commission of Public Affairs 558
Ampleforth Abbey 349, 356, 758, 760
Ampleforth Journal 759, 760
Amsterdam 147, 171–82, 499
Amulree, Lord 362–3
ancestors of Geoffrey Fisher 3
Andrew, Prince 269
Andrews, Linton 414
Andrews, Mr (Treasurer, Chester Board of Finance) 46
Anglican Advisory Committee on

Missionary Strategy 460, 461, 468, 473, 474, 692
Anglican Communion 443–4, 449, 463, 468, 600, 682
Anglican Congress, Minneapolis 183, 460–1, 463, 468, 657
Anglican Congress, Toronto 748
Anglican Cycle of Prayer 457
Anglican Roman Catholic International Commission (ARCIC) 351, 741, 761
Anglican-Methodist Union 755, 756–8
Anglo-Catholic revival 4
Anglo-Catholics 13; attitude to Book of Common Prayer 116–20; committee work 121; opposition to appointments of Bishops 236; opposed to Service of Blessing 388; in Australia 483
Anglo-Indians 643
Anglo-Presbyterian Report 280
Anglo-Soviet Friendship League 140
Anne, Princess 269, 482
Ansari, Sheik Mustafu 714
Ansell, W.H. 78, 84
Anson, Lady 284
anti-semitism 581, 582, 584, 585
'Any Questions' 377
apartheid 176, 188, 228, 229, 357; condemned by Archbishop Fisher 550, 552, 555; African opposition 559; origins 545; *see also* Dutch Reformed Church; South Africa
Apostolic Delegate 361–2, 367, 708, 719, 720, 727, 744
Arab Evangelical Episcopal Church 595, 599–601
Arab Legion 587–9
Arabic Councils 596–605
Arabs 577–94; Holy Places in Jerusalem 585–94; Christian Arabs 595–606, 613, 713, 722; opposition to Jewish immigration into Palestine 577–80; *see also* Jerusalem; Palestine
Archbishops' War Committee 85–102, 105; formation 85; chaplains 94–7; complaints regarding Home Guard

86–93; demobilisation 96–7; domestic problems 93–4; moral problems of War 98–102; Sunday observance 95–6
Archbishops' War Damage Committee 69–70, 71
Argentina 693
Armadale 482
Armitage, Reverend Cyril 410–11
Armitstead, Archdeacon 35, 36
Armstrong-Jones, Anthony 269, 290, 291–2
Army chaplains 94–7, 103, 155, 161, 167, 466
Army Scripture Readers' Association 96
Army Service Books 93
artificial insemination 391–2, 399
Ashton, Sir Hubert 212
Asmussen, Pastor 156
Asquith, Herbert Henry 11
assistant curates 123
Association of Vergers 123
Assumption of the Blessed Virgin Mary 351–2
Astor, Lord 349–50, 586
Athenagorus, Oecumenical Patriarch of Constantinople 626, 633, 709, 712, 725–9, 734
Attlee, Clement 143, 548; episcopal appointments 215, 216, 220–2, 224, 234; leadership of Labour Party 152, 162–3, 164; support for appointment of Canon Collins 229; supports canon law revision 208; proposes extending Homage at Coronation service 252; forewarned of atomic attack on Japan 373; reform of episcopal representation in House of Lords 396; relations with Archbishop Fisher 401–2; Palestine policy 578, 581
Attlee, Mary 401
Aubrey, Reverend M.E. 105, 106, 316, 579
Auckland 493–4
Australia 479–91; tour of Archbishop Fisher 468, 479–85; constitutional position of Church of England 484, 485–91
Austria 162
autocephalous churches 759, 760

Babington, Miss 138
Baillie, Dr 320–2, 325
Baines, Henry, Bishop 685–7, 689, 690
Bairstow, Sir Edward 34
Baker, Dr 317

Baker-Wilbraham, Sir Philip 133, 398
Balfour Declaration 578, 582
Balkans 141
Ballantrae, Lord 167
Bancroft, Richard, Bishop 205
Banks, Lord 84
Bantu Education Act (1953) 549, 552, 554
baptism 757, 760
baptism of Geoffrey Fisher 4
Baptismal Reform Movement 274
Baptist Union 105, 317, 579
Baptists 105–6
Barbados 279
Bardsley, Cuthbert, Bishop of Coventry 96, 167, 239, 369
Barfoot, Dr 466
Baring, Sir Evelyn 523
Barker, Sir Ernest 233, 392
Barnes, Dr E.W., Bishop of Birmingham 295–304, 421, 610
Barnes, Sir John 304
Barnes, Sir Thomas 209, 212
Barry, Dr F.R., Bishop of Southwell 110, 455, 456
Barth, Karl 179
Baslow 13
Bathurst Diocese 485–6
Bathurst, Reverend W. 298
Batty, Bishop of Newcastle (Australia) 485–7, 489, 490
Bayne, Stephen, Bishop of Olympia 688, 691, 695, 748; at 1958 Lambeth Conference 472–5; appointed Executive Officer of Advisory Council 473–4; attends meeting of South African bishops 565–7; proposes draft statement on deportation of Bishop Reeves 570; in preparations for visit of Archbishop Fisher to Rome 706, 708
Bea, Cardinal 365, 366, 708; heads Secretariat for Unity 707, 711, 735; holds conference on visit of Archbishop Fisher to Pope 712; favours visit of Archbishop Fisher 730, 740, 744; agrees Archbishop Fisher's statement to Press 731; meeting with Archbishop Fisher opposed by Cardinal Tardini 732; visited by Archbishop Fisher 738, 742
Beales, A.C.F. 103, 104, 108, 111
Beaverbrook, Lord 324
Beaverbrook press 767
Beck, G.A. 348

Beecher, Leonard, Bishop of Mombasa
523
Begbie, Archdeacon 486, 487
Beirut 612, 613, 713, 724, 725
Bell, G.C. 8, 9
Bell, George, Bishop of Chichester 423,
522; on Joint Standing Committee 104,
106–10, 112, 113; supports Bishop
Fisher on approach to Anglo-Catholics
119; considered as successor to
Archbishop Temple 129, 130;
encourages Bishop Fisher to accept
bishopric of London 60; visit to
postwar Germany 158, 163; criticises
Archbishop Temple's letter to Bishop
Hall on woman priest 661; in WCC
177, 178, 181, 183–6; sceptical of
canon law revision 206; rejected by
Churchill as Bishop of London
217–19; rejected by Eden as Bishop of
London 225; criticises hasty translation
of Bishop of Fulham 226–7; criticises
Archbishop Fisher's episcopal
appointments 236; criticises Bishops'
Meetings 242; conducts prayers on
death of George VI 246; views on
Coronation service 250, 263; supports
action over *Rise of Christianity* 297,
299; opposes Roman Catholic
propaganda 355; suggests statement by
Queen on Roman Catholic subjects
358–9; on committee to consider
atomic weapons 376; opposes mass
bombing 379; opposes Central African
Federation 399; supports Archbishop
Fisher on Education Bill 430; at 1958
Lambeth Conference 469; visit to
Australia 480; co-ordinates appeal for
funds for South African schools 554;
supports Visser't Hooft on deportation
of Archbishop Makarios 622; discusses
Cyprus crisis with King of Hellenes
631–2; deplores H-bomb tests 673–4;
contacts with Roman Catholics 706
Bellew, Sir George 256, 260
Beloe, Robert 317, 537, 539; appointed
Lay Secretary 192, 196; organises
attendance of bishops in House of
Lords 598–9; in Rome for Archbishop
Fisher's visit 733, 738
Belsen 153
Benedict XIV, Pope 351
Bennett, Bishop Augustus, of Aotearoa
492, 494
Bennett, Canon 747

Bennett, Dean Selwyn Macaulay 34, 35,
36, 43, 59
Bennett, Frank 149
Benson, Edward, Archbishop 190, 595
Berlin 158, 159, 165, 167
Berlin Airlift 140, 165
Bermondsey 40
Bermuda 698–702
Bernstein, Dr 580
Berry, Dr 107
Bethlehem 714
Betjeman, Sir John 482
Betts, Stanley, Bishop of Maidstone 146
Bevan, Aneurin 198
Bevan, Mr (Treasurer of Chester
Diocesan Conference) 47, 48
Beveridge Committee on Broadcasting
418
Beveridge, Lord 152, 164, 362, 426
Beverley, Dr R.A., Bishop of Toronto
447, 611
Bevin, Ernest 164, 588, 670
Bevir, Anthony 215–17, 219, 220, 229
Bewes, Canon 522, 523
Bexhill 96
Bezzant, Canon 301
biblical scholarship 13, 295–7, 301, 754
Bickersteth, Canon Edward M. 601, 603,
604, 612
Bickersteth, Julian 136
Billhurst, Dr 562, 565
Birkenhead 40, 63
Birley, Sir Robert 438
Birmingham 299, 316, 550, 551
birth control 361, 362, 453, 472, 682
birth of Geoffrey Fisher 4, 41, 747
Bishop, Major-General 167
bishops 176, 215–44, 325–6;
appointments by Archbishop Fisher
216–31, 236, 599; Crown
appointments 232–6; in House of
Lords 185, 196, 395–8; nominations
215, 232, 395; relationships with
Archbishop Fisher 236–44; residential
conference 243–4; Roman Catholics
241, 256; stipends 230; suffragans
136–7, 146, 148, 230–1; see also
episcopacy
Bishops' Meetings at Lambeth 312,
336–7, 355, 391, 419; origins 241;
conduct of meetings 242; Bishop
Barnes not invited 297–8; dominated
by Archbishop Fisher 242, 243, 747;
secrecy condemned 241
Bishopscourt 483

Bishopsthorpe 121
Blackburn 42, 228–9
Blackburn Diocesan Council for
  Religious Education 159
blackout regulations 93, 95
Blackpool 140
Blagden, Dr Claude, Bishop of
  Peterborough 94, 458
Blantyre 518
blitz 63–8, 117, 122, 429
Blomfield, H.G. 274
Blunt, Dr, Bishop of Bradford 274, 301
Board of Deputies of British Jewry 579
Board of Supervisors 42, 44
Boegner, Pastor Marc 94, 156, 169, 171,
  179, 358
Boggis, Reverend R.J.E. 72
Bonhoeffer, Dietrich 155
Boon, Miss (headmistress) 6
Booth, Alan 565
Boothby, Lord 289
Boult, Sir Adrian 254
Bouquet, Dr 351
Boy Scouts 156, 719
Brandeth, Fr 367
Brazil 696
Bridgeman, Lady 199
Bridgeman, Lord 87
Brinstead, Norman, Bishop of the
  Philippine Islands 669
Brisbane 482
British Broadcasting Corporation (BBC)
  377, 392, 752; religious broadcasting
  417–22, 615; Schools Broadcasting
  Council 420
British Columbia 446
British Council 479, 615
British Council of Churches 188, 328,
  368, 466; in Second World War 109,
  111–13; Bishop Fisher's chairmanship
  of Executive Committee 112, 169;
  reconciliation with Germany 155, 157,
  164; report on nuclear weapons 376;
  disarmament conference 379, 380;
  views on Television Bill 425–6;
  statement on Central African
  Federation 512; resolution on High
  Commisssion Territories 549; address
  by Archbishop Fisher condemns
  apartheid 550; opposition to apartheid
  553, 561; resolutions on Cyprus crisis
  624; interview with Colonial Secretary
  on Cyprus crisis 626; resolution on H-
  bomb tests 674
British Hygiene Council 99

British Israelites 96
British Museum 406–7
British-China Friendship Association 143
British Weekly 313, 548
Brodie, Israel 589
Brook, Reverend Timothy 752, 763
Broomfield, Canon G.W. 520, 521
Brown, Gordon, Bishop in Jerusalem 596
Brown, Hefer, Bishop of Bermuda 698,
  699
Brown, Leslie, Bishop of Uganda 526,
  527, 531, 536–8, 541–3
Brownrigg, Captain 419
Bruce, Michael 177, 336
Brunner, Emil 179
Buchman, Frank 255
Buckingham Palace 281, 526; domestic
  staff 281
Buddhism 275–7, 668, 678
Buganda 527, 532, 536, 539; *see also*
  Mutesa II; Uganda
Bulawayo 515
Bulaya, Canon 524
Bulgaria 141
Bullock, Sir Ernest 254
Bulmer-Thomas, Ivor 398
Burger, The 550
Burne, Reverend R.H. 36
Burrows, Sir Bernard 742
Butler, Bishop, Abbot of Downside 758,
  760
Butler, R.A. 203, 363, 405, 407, 436;
  Education Act 196, 428–30; sets up
  Fleming Committee 437
Buxton, Bishop 165
Buzzard, Sir Anthony 378

Cadogan, Sir Alexander 165
Cairo 609, 612, 613
Calcutta 642–4, 647
Caldecote, Lord 72, 73
Callaghan, James 236
Cambridge sermon of Archbishop Fisher
  310, 316, 449, 468, 471, 649; reaction
  313; context for talks with Church of
  Scotland 320–3; problem of
  episcopacy 341, 758
Campbell, Montgomery, Bishop of
  Guildford 226, 239, 475
Campbell-Bannerman, Sir Henry 11
Canada 185, 270; tours of Archbishop
  Fisher 444–7, 463–7
Canadian Council of Churches 622
Canadian Pacific Railway 463, 464
Canberra 482–3

canon law revision 205–14, 387–8, 486–7; report of commission to Convocation 206; procedure laid down by Archbishop Fisher 207–8; reform of ecclesiastical courts 211–12

Canterbury Archbishopric, nomination and Enthronement of Bishop Fisher 129–32, 146, 150, 152, 169

Canterbury Cathedral 135–9, 260, 762, 763; Chapter 136, 137; choir 138; Dean 135–7, 140–5; Friends of the Cathedral 138; King's School 136, 142, 479, 483; order of precedence 136–7; Statutes 137

Canterbury City 144

Canterbury Diocese 129–34, 146–51, 191, 479; Board of Finance 150; clergy conference at Dymchurch 149; clerical stipends 150–1; Diocesan Conference 150, 163, 202, 306, 581; parish visitations 146–8; Rural Deans 148

Canterbury, New Zealand 479

Cape Town 479, 545

Cardinale, Monsignor 711, 734, 739, 740

Carey, David 748

Carey, Francis, Bishop 656

Carleton Green, Sir Hugh 424

Caroe, Sir Olaf 250

Carpenter, Dr S.C. 272

Carpenter, Harry 224

Carrington, Dr Philip, Archbishop of Quebec 473

Cash, William, Bishop 612

Catholic Herald 357

Catholic Leader 364

Catholic Times 359

Catholic Truth Society 111

censorship 305, 425

Central Africa 467, 509–19; Provincial organisation 501, 502, 509–15; visit of Archbishop Fisher and inauguration ceremony 515–19

Central African Federation 509–15, 538; Constitutional Conference 513

Central Council for the Care of Churches 80

Central Hall, Westminster 61, 491

Central Religious Advisory Committee (CRAC) 420, 423, 425, 426

Ceylon 275–8, 335, 340–2

Chadwick, Henry 310

Chalmers (representative of War Graves Commission) 369, 370

Chamberlain, Neville 55, 60

Chang, Bishop 652, 656

Chao, Professor J.C. 174–5, 182

Chaplain-General 369; in Second World War 94, 96, 97–8, 101; in postwar Germany 157, 159, 161

Charles, Prince of Wales 269, 274, 292

Charles-Edwards, Reverend Mervyn 419

Charterhouse School 30

Charteris, Sir Martin 275, 276, 709

Chavasse, Christopher, Bishop of Rochester 13, 409

Chen, Robin, Bishop of Shanghai 647, 655–8

Chester City 32

Chester Council of Free Churches 52

Chester Diocese 29–30, 32–52, 381, 446; Consecration of Geoffrey Fisher as Bishop 30, 34; Enthronement of Geoffrey Fisher as Bishop 34–5; Board of Education 42, 44; Board of Finance 46; Church schools 44–6, 431; churchmanship 37–8; Diocesan Conference 35, 41, 47–8, 59; Diocesan Gazette 33, 38–9, 42, 44, 52, 59; Diocesan Office 47; Diocesan Youth Council 46; finance 47–50; Geoffrey Fisher nominated as Bishop 29–30; incomes of parish clergy 48–9; Missionary Council 50; parish visitations 41–2, 62, 148; training college 42–4, 45

Chester Infirmary 58

Chester Training College 42–4, 45

Chiang Kai-Shek 650, 657

Chief Rabbi 579, 584

childhood of Geoffrey Fisher 3–7

China 182, 443, 470, 645, 647, 648–67; fund raising 648; under Communist regime 650–4; ordination of woman priest 649, 653, 659–67; absence of bishops from 1958 Lambeth Conference 657–8; *see also* Hall, Bishop; Hong Kong

choir boys 12, 138, 495

Christchurch, NZ 493, 496

Christian Action 229, 554

Christian International Service 160

Christian Reconstruction in Europe Committee 157, 162

Christie, John 29

Chung Hua Sheng Kung Hui (CHSKH) 653, 654, 655, 663

Chung Yang Leafi, Reverend 653

Church Advisory Council for Training for the Ministry 97

Church Assembly: Archbishop Fisher's report on clerical stipends 200, 202; Archbishop Fisher's report on visit to Jerusalem, Istanbul and Rome 741; Boards 239, 242, 243; canon law revision 207; debate on training colleges 70–7; donation to UNRRA 162; Ecclesiastical Advisory Committee 234; Fund 49; Liturgical Committee 239; Measures 70–7, 207, 208; participation of Archbishop Fisher 122; resolution on establishment of Church 232; resolutions on postwar food shortage 163; selection of representatives to WCC 178; reluctant to provide funds for press relations 410; control of religious education 433–4; addressed by Archbishop Fisher on Ugandan problem 531; statement by Archbishop Fisher on invitation of Archbishop Makarios to Lambeth Conference 633; report by Archbishop Fisher on visit to Jerusalem, Istanbul and Rome 741

Church Commissioners 196, 198, 202, 203, 204; capital investments 203, 204; Scheme K 201

Church Demobilization Board 97

Church of England Assembly (Powers) Act (1919) 71

Church of England Council for Education 433

Church of England Council on Foreign Relations 191, 357, 623, 632, 706, 710

Church of England Council for Social Work 394

Church of England Missionary Council 50

Church of England Moral Welfare Council 101, 385, 392

Church of England Newspaper 278, 337, 416, 528

Church of England in South Africa 483, 485

Church Information Board 355, 409

Church Information Office 691

Church Missionary Society 4, 452, 457, 538, 541; consulted by Archbishop Fisher 523, 609; Evangelical tradition 335, 501; grant of Constitution to Arabic Evangelical Episcopal Church 595, 596, 598, 599, 600; hospital in Gaza 611

Church schools 44–6, 48, 428, 431–5, 552–4

Church of Scotland 167, 247, 274, 319–30; in Second World War 111, 320; represented at enthronement of Archbishop Fisher 131; represented at Coronation service 264, 267; conversations on inter-communion 320–30; establishment 131, 266, 280, 319, 346; General Assembly 158, 281; representation in House of Lords 396, 397; religious broadcasting 422, 426; attitude to Central African Federation 512; in WCC 174

Church of South India 183, 331–43, 415, 456; Archbishop Fisher's statement to Convocation 333–5; grants by SPG 335–7; status of episcopacy 331–5, 338

Church Times 278, 660; on Archbishop Fisher's speech to WCC on Cyprus crisis 625; on churchmanship in London Diocese 119; on Coronation Rite 252; on CSI 339, 340–1; on enthronement of Bishop Fisher as Archbishop of Canterbury 131; on episcopacy and Free Churches 313; on Geoffrey Fisher 59; on *Lady Chatterley's Lover* 305; letters from Archbishop Fisher on ecclesiastical allegiance 414–15; 5000th issue 415–16

church towers 87–90

Church Training Colleges 42

Church Union 12, 13, 120, 284, 342, 419

Churchill, Sir Winston: dislike of Bishop Bell 130, 217–19, 400; episcopal appointments 129, 130–1, 215; Fulton speech 173; loses 1945 election 153, 220, 401; insists on televising of Coronation 257–8; rejects appointment of Bishop Bell as Bishop of London 217–19, 225; on Sunday observance 95–6; support for United Europe 154; advises Queen on visit to Ceylon 276–7; urges ringing of church bells on return of Queen from Commonwealth tour 282; relations with Archbishop Fisher 400–1; election victory in 1951 401, 402; supports religious education 430; demands end of British Mandate in Palestine 585

churchmanship of Geoffrey Fisher 37–8, 238, 483, 754

churchyards 87–92

City Churches' Committee 83
City Improvement Committee 84
City of London churches, war damage 78–84
City Parish Assessors 83
civic services 345
civil defence 82, 91
Civitate Cattolica 739
Clare, Mother Mary 258, 288
Clarification of some Terms and Ideas connected with Church Unity, A (Fisher) 759
Clarke, Sir Ashley 730, 731, 734, 738, 742
Claxton, Charles, Bishop of Blackburn 229, 570
Clayton, Geoffrey, Archbishop of Cape Town, Bishop of Johannesburg 545–6; concern to Africanise Church 569; advises Archbishop Fisher 547, 548, 550, 552, 553, 560; condemns racial policy of South Africa 550, 555–6; death 556, 557, 558
Clayton, Reverend Tubby 14
Clements, Dom Bernard 118
Clements, Mr A.J., (secretary at Lambeth Palace) 192
clergy 41, 71, 84, 92–3, 380; *see also* stipends of clergy
Clutterbuck, Sir Alexander 445
Clutton Brock, Guy 161
Cockin, F.A., Bishop of Bristol 221, 227, 301, 419, 420
Coggan, Donald, Bishop of Bradford 121, 239, 310, 526, 748, 750
Cohen, Sir Andrew 527, 530, 532, 535
Colchester 96
Cold War 140
Coleman, Reverend F.R. 419
Collins, John, Canon of St Paul's 178, 229, 374, 548, 549, 554, 768
Collins, Norman 425
Colville, Lady Cynthia 287
Comfort, Alexander 418
Commission of Churches 106
Commissioner, Senior 199, 201, 203
Commonwealth Party 163
Communism 135, 144
confirmation services 41, 93, 117, 148, 728, 754
Congregationalists 327
conscientious objection 20
conscripts 159–60
Consecration of Geoffrey Fisher as Bishop 30

Consistory courts 209
Constantinople (Istanbul) 726
contraceptives 98–102, 383, 392, 393, 472
conversion 109, 156
Convocation of Canterbury 93, 121–2, 150, 206, 207, 662; Archbishop Fisher's statement on CSI 333–5; statement by Archbishop Fisher on *Rise of Christianity* controversy 299–300, 303; resolutions on inter-communion conversations 323, 326; debate on CSI 332; regulations on divorce 388; motion on atomic weapons 377; address by Archbishop Fisher on apartheid 564; address by Archbishop Fisher on Palestine problem 588
Convocation of York 88, 121, 206, 207; condemnation of *Rise of Christianity* 301; statement by Archbishop Temple on ordination of women 660; debate on CSI 332; regulations on divorce 388
Cooper, Charles John, Bishop of Korea 679
Coote, Roderick, Bishop of Gambia 507
Coptic Church 612, 613
Corbishly, Fr 344
Coronation of Queen Elizabeth II 245–68, 269, 283, 508, 676; Coronation Rite 248–53, 261, 265, 736; Commonwealth participation 250–2, 266, 526, 550, 551; invitations 255–6, 526, 550, 551; music 254, 265; televising 256–8, 263, 416; rehearsals 259–60; the ceremony 261–3; appraisals 263–8; copy of Service presented to Pope 736
corporate worship 177, 186
Corr, Reverend Gerard 712, 731
Cottesloe Conference of WCC 568, 571–2
Council of Christians and Jews 581, 584, 763
Council for the Protection of Ancient Buildings 80
Courcy, Kenneth de 250
Coventry 50
Cragg, Kenneth 582, 722
Craig, Dr A. (Archie) C. 104, 105, 162, 324–5
Craske, Tom 160
Craven, Bishop 344
Crawford, Lord 84, 407
Creech-Jones, Arthur 618

Creighton, Mandell, Bishop of London 55, 60, 63, 116, 215
Crewe 39
cricket 481, 483, 697
Criminal Law Amendment Bill 549, 550
Cripps, Sir Stafford 220
Crockford's Clerical Directory 207
Crossland, G.H. 270
Crossthwaite, Sir Philip Moore 713, 724, 725, 728, 729
Crowley, A.H., Bishop of Michigan 554
Crown Patronage 216, 233
Croydon Parish Church 148, 407–8
Cry the Beloved Country (Paton) 546
Cuba'in, Canon Najib Ataliah: conversation with Archbishop Fisher on Arab Council 598–9; frustration over Constitution problem 600, 602; heads delegation to Lambeth 603; at enthronement of Archbishop McInnes 605; consecrated Bishop 606; attends 1958 Lambeth Conference 606; meets Archbishop Fisher in Tel Aviv 713; meets Archbishop Fisher in Jerusalem 714, 716–17; attends conference in Beirut 724, 725
Cunningham, Sir Andrew 584
Curtis, Bishop 650–1
Curzon, Lord 11, 397, 643
Cyprus 368, 617–35, 681; Governor's veto on election of Archbishop 617; election of Makarios as Archbishop 618; deportation of Makarios 619–20; debates in House of Lords 620–1, 627, 630, 634, 635; reaction to deportation 619–27; release of Makarios 629; Lord Radcliffe's constitution 627, 629–31; independence granted 633–5; partition 635; *see also* Makarios
Czechoslovakia 176

Daily Express 324, 361, 412, 414, 632
Daily Herald 386
Daily Mail 153
Daily Mirror 288, 289
Daily Sketch 143, 414
Dale, Basil, Bishop of Jamaica 697–8
Dalton, Hugh 200
Daly, John, Bishop of Gambia 506, 679–80
Darbyshire, Russell, Archbishop of Cape Town 545
Daryngton, Lord 61
Dashwood, Sir Henry T.A. 90, 92, 197, 208, 286, 605, 696

Davey, Noel 119, 194, 259, 355
Davidson, Randall, Archbishop of Canterbury 40, 85, 295, 520, 736; appeal for Church unity 309; at Lambeth Palace 129, 133, 190, 195; on lawful authority 206; relationship with George V 268; resignation 747
Davies, Clement 378
Dawe, Sir Hugh 592–3
de Blank, Joost, Archbishop of Cape Town: Bishop of Stepney 229, 558–9; elected Archbishop of Cape Town 558–9; calls for WCC Churches to dissociate from Dutch Reformed Church 561–6; sends sermon on South Africa jubilee to Archbishop Fisher 566–7; opposes Archbishop Fisher and Visser't Hooft on apartheid 568; invites Archbishop Fisher to Bishopscourt 568, 571; regrets departure of Bishop Ambrose Reeves 570; at Cottesloe Conference of WCC 572–3
de Cheux, Hero 358
de Jong, Cardinal 171
de la Warr, Earl 424, 425
de Mel, Bishop Lakdasa 563, 572
de-requisitioning of church property 97
deaconesses 661, 665
Dead Sea Scrolls 717
Deal, Kent 147
Deane, Canon Anthony 81
death of Archbishop Fisher 635, 762
Defence of the Realm Act 89
demobilisation 96–7, 154, 160, 390
Denman, R.D. 75
Denning, Dr 112
Denning, Lord 207, 382, 383, 386
Department of Reconstruction 162
Dewey, John 451
Dibelius, Bishop 182
Dillistone, F.W. 121
Dimbleby, Richard 289, 416
Diocesan Reorganisation Areas Measure (1943) 75, 76
Diocesan Reorganisation Committee Measure (1941) 71
Diocesan Reorganisation Committees 70–3, 84, 151
Diocesan War Damage Committees 71
disarmament 379–80
discipline 15, 19, 20
Disraeli, Benjamin 130
divorce 284, 286, 288–90, 381–94, 472–3; clergy 390; litigation 382, 394;

reconciliation 382; remarriage after divorce 385, 387–90, 472, 697, 767; report of Archbishop's conference at Lambeth 387; Royal Commission on 385, 386; statistics 381

Divorced Wife's Sister Bill 383, 386

Dix, Dom Gregory 309, 311–12, 315, 332

Don, Dr Alan, Dean of Westminster 130, 131, 246, 247, 359–60, 486; in revision of Coronation Rite 249, 267

doodle bugs 68, 122

Douglas, John, Bishop of Nassau 287

Douglas, Reverend C.E. 70, 75, 241, 272

Doukaris, Phedias 630, 631

Duesberg 167

Duncan-Jones, Andrew, Dean of Chichester 165

Duncannon, Lord 425

Dunedin, NZ 497

Dunlop, Colin, Bishop of Jarrow 239

Dunning, T.C. 104, 106

Dunstan, Canon Gordon 394, 472

Duppa, Bishop 92–3

Durham Diocese 222–3

Dutch Reformed Church 175–6, 545; membership of WCC 175–6; support for apartheid 545, 553, 554; conversations with Protestant Churches 549, 550; reaction to Sharpeville massacre 561; repudiation of apartheid demanded by Archbishop Joost de Blank 561–5; Archbishop Fisher attempts to maintain relations 566–8; at WCC Cottesloe Conference 572–3

Dykes Bower, Wilfrid 246, 254

Dymchurch, Kent 149

Dyson, George 15

Earl Marshal 248, 256, 260, 262–3, 266

East Africa 501, 502, 520–3

East Anglia 466

East End 65, 66

East Germany 162

Eastern Orthodox Churches 173, 333, 627

Eastman, Lieutenant-General 86, 87, 91

Eastman, Philip 512

Ecclesiastical Commissioners 71, 83, 123, 133, 200, 201, 204

Ecclesiastical Committee 74, 75, 76

ecclesiastical courts 211, 212, 298, 381, 383, 389

Ecclesiastical Jurisdiction Measure 212

Ecumenical Commission of the Churches for International Friendship and Social Responsibility 104

ecumenical movement 309–18; Archbishop Fisher's dedication 169–70, 309, 465, 610, 756; in wartime 103–14; Cambridge sermon of Archbishop Fisher 310, 313, 316, 320–3, 341, 449, 468, 471, 649; discussions with Free Churches and Methodists 309–18; problem of episcopacy 310–15, 318, 330

Ede, Chuter 252

Eden, Sir Anthony 608; episcopal appointments 215, 224, 227; rejects Bishop Bell as Bishop of London 225; ruling on use of Church property in war time 88, 89, 90, 92; policy on nuclear weapons 377–8; succeeds Churchill as Prime Minister 402; Suez crisis 402–5; condemnation of Nasser 614; defends Foreign Service against bishops 615–16; writes to Archbishop Fisher on Government's Cyprus policy 625–6; succeeded by Harold Macmillan 629

Edinburgh Conference (1910) 13, 104, 169, 741

education 44–6, 428–39; Church schools 432–5; independent and maintained schools 435–8; secularization 438–9; in South Africa 553, 554, 557

Education Act (1936) 44

Education Act (1944) 196, 428–32

Edward VII, King 279

Edward VIII, King 51, 287, 324, 413, 767

Eels, Dr Francis 80

Egypt 369, 399, 402–5, 598, 601, 607–16; legislation against foreigners 607; financial problems 608, 611, 613; retirement of Bishop Gwynne 608–9; appointment of Bishop Allen 609–10; uncertain future of diocese 609–16; appointment of Bishop Johnstone 613

Eisenhower, General Dwight 185, 628, 734, 737

Eley, Stanley 115

Eliot, T.S. 104, 108, 112, 142, 310

Elizabeth, consort of George VI, later Queen Mother 246, 259, 279, 281, 293, 470; Silver Wedding 269; at Coronation of Elizabeth II 261, 262

Elizabeth, Princess 245, 246, 271, 272;

marriage 269, 272–4, 299; visit to Ceylon 275–8; tour of Canada 270–1

Elizabeth II, Queen 51, 246, 268; tour of Commonwealth 282; attends Church of Scotland celebrations in Edinburgh 328–30; corresponds with Archbishop Fisher on his visit to Rome 709–10; entertains Archbishop Fisher and Mrs Fisher at Windsor Castle 753; *see also* Coronation of Queen Elizabeth

Elliot, W.H. 421

Ellis, Ruth 412

Ellison, Randall 25

Elphinstone, Elizabeth 288

Ely Diocese 216–17

Emmerson, Sir Harold 257

Enabling Act (1929) 207

Engineering Industries' Association 94

Enosis 618, 622, 625

ENSA 99

Eoka 619, 628

episcopacy 310–15, 318, 319, 322, 323–5, 758; in Canada 465; in CSI 331–8; *see also* bishops

Episcopal Church of Scotland 285, 320–2, 324, 328–30, 338

Esher, Lord 80

establishment of Church of England 207, 208, 289, 317, 358, 500, 615; effect on episcopal appointments 232–3, 235, 236

Ethiopia 611

eulogies 36

European Economic Community 154

evacuees 65–6, 123, 428, 429

Evander, Dr Sven 667

Evangelical Fellowship for Theological Literature 121

Evangelicals 13, 120–1, 211

Evans, D.L., Bishop of Brazil 693–6

Evans, Reverend J.B.H. 87

Evanston Congress of World Council of Churches 180, 182–9, 443, 463, 555, 561

Exeter College, Oxford 10–14, 344, 771

faith of Geoffrey Fisher 767–72

Faith and Order Commission 184, 188, 315

Falkland Islands 402, 693, 694

family planning 392–3, 472, 675

famine 162–3

Farndale, W.E. 271

Federation of Catholic Priests 118, 120

Festival of Britain (1951) 421

ffrench-Beytagh, G.A., Dean of Salisbury 515

fire-watching 81–2

First World War 4, 17, 18, 20–2, 98, 234

Fisher, Charles (son of Geoffrey) 66, 138, 751

Fisher, Edith (sister of Geoffrey) 4–5, 14

Fisher, Frank (son of Geoffrey) 66

Fisher, Harry (brother of Geoffrey) 4

Fisher, Henry (father of Geoffrey, rector of Higham on the Hill) 4, 5, 14

Fisher, Henry (son of Geoffrey) 27, 263–4

Fisher, Herbert (brother of Geoffrey) 3, 4

Fisher, Humphrey (Huff) (son of Geoffrey) 63, 64, 68

Fisher, John (grandfather of Geoffrey) 3

Fisher, John (great-grandfather of Geoffrey) 3

Fisher, John (Prior of Benedictine Abbey) 3

Fisher, Katie (sister of Geoffrey) 4, 60, 718, 720

Fisher, Legh (brother of Geoffrey) 4

Fisher, Leonard, Bishop of Natal (brother of Geoffrey) 4, 30, 60, 479, 516, 569, 770

Fisher, Lucy (sister of Geoffrey) 4

Fisher, Mabel (wife of Leonard) 30

Fisher, Katherine (*née* Richmond, mother of Geoffrey) 3, 5–6, 14, 772

Fisher, Robert (son of Geoffrey) 64

Fisher, Rosamond (*née* Forman, wife of Geoffrey) 17, 39, 717, 718, 768, 770; at Lambeth 192, 193; at Repton 26–7, 29, 31; marriage 27; move to Chester 32, 34; in Chester Diocese 39, 59; move to London 56, 57, 58, 61, 133; stays in Minehead with children 63–8; visits Archbishop Temple 129; move to Lambeth 133, 134; in Canterbury 138–9, 193; at marriage of Princess Elizabeth 272, 273; visits Windsor before Coronation 259; letter on Princess Margaret's visit to Lambeth Palace 290; at wedding of Princess Margaret 292; celebrates restoration of Lambeth Palace chapel 293; received at Buckingham Palace 295; tours of Canada 444, 445, 463; tour of USA 451; heads Hospitality Committee at 1958 Lambeth Conference 469; tour of Australia 479–84, 491; tour of New Zealand 492–8; tour of Central Africa

516–19; tour of Nigeria 543; tour of
Pakistan 640, 641; tour of India
642–4; tour of Hong Kong 646; tour
of Japan 674–9; tour of Korea
679–81; in retirement 751, 753, 756,
763; golden wedding 753; widowed
762; death 763
Fisher, Tim (son of Geoffrey) 64
Fishponds (Bristol) Training College 42
Fleet Street 348, 410, 411, 413
Fleming, Archibald, Bishop of the Arctic
447
Fleming Committee 437, 438
Fleming, Launcelot, Bishop of Norwich
228
Fletcher, Colonel 141
Fletcher, Frank 9, 15, 16, 28, 30, 60, 181
Flew, Newton 180
Foot, Sir Hugh 631, 632, 697
Ford, Major Edward 245
Ford, Sir Edward 278, 295
Foreign Office 141, 350, 607, 632, 640,
710
Forman, Peggy 66, 67, 68, 134
Forman, Rosamond *see* Fisher,
Rosamond
Fort Augustus 482
Foxell, Reverend Maurice 281
France, Canon 461
Franciscans 715–17, 735
Franco, General 470
Free Church Federal Council: in
ecumenical movement 104–5, 174,
313; represented at enthronement of
Archbishop Fisher 131; represented at
Coronation service 247; in Second
World War 97, 105, 158, 160;
representation in House of Lords 396;
religious broadcasting 422; attitude to
Central African Federation 514
Free Churches 51, 69, 91, 94, 99
Freeth, Bishop 7
Fremantle 480
Fry, Dr Franklin 181, 182, 620
Fulham Palace 63–8, 133, 595
Fuller, Fr R.C. 287
funeral service of Archbishop Fisher 762

Gage-Brown 118, 119, 120
Gainsey, David 490
gaiters 242, 450
Gaitskell, Hugh 212
gambling 271, 405–6
Garbett, Cyril, Archbishop of York 152,
203, 279, 284, 351, 466, 491;

considered for appointment as Bishop
of London 58, 60; choice of
representatives for WCC 178;
chairman of canon law review
commission 206, 211; supports
nomination of Bishop Ramsey as
Archbishop of York 225; episcopal
appointments 217–19, 221, 230, 232,
234; considered for appointment as
Archbishop of Canterbury 129, 130,
132; relationship with Archbishop
Fisher 237; deputises for Archbishop
Fisher on death of George VI 246;
objects to broadcasting Coronation
service 257; declines to give address at
royal wedding 272; supports action on
Rise of Christianity controversy 297,
299, 301; policy on CSI 332, 333;
refuses to sign below Cardinal Griffin
347; supports Archbishop Fisher's
policy towards Roman Catholics 355,
358; views on abortion 363; supports
Archbishop Fisher on Table of Affinity
383; visit to Chicago 451; at 1948
Lambeth Conference 456; at 1958
Lambeth Conference 469; letter to
Times on Jerusalem 586; retirement
224; illness 238; memorial service 238
Garvin, J.L. 28
Gaskin, Wat 24
Gaza Strip 611
Gelsthorpe, Alfred, Assistant Bishop in
Egypt 608, 611
General Ordination Examination 303
General Synod of the Church of England
757, 758
Geneva 173, 176, 184, 186
Geneva Convention 165
George V, King 51, 246, 247, 268, 281,
395
George VI, King 51, 268, 284, 479, 496,
506; Coronation 248–9, 254, 259,
263; Silver Wedding 269; at wedding
of Princess Elizabeth 273; receives
Lambeth bishops 457; admiration for
Bishop Wilson 685; death 245–6, 276;
funeral 269; Lying-in-State 246–7
germ warfare 143, 144
German Evangelical Churches 157
Germanos, Archbishop 174, 271–2, 617,
705
Germany 130, 152–61, 428; broadcast
to people by Archbishop Fisher 158–9;
non-fraternisation policy 161–2;
postwar condition 152, 156, 163;

postwar visit of Archbishop Fisher 166–8, 300; Reformed Churches 155
Giles, Canon 626
Glamis Castle 284, 286
Godfrey, Cardinal 287, 365, 594
Gold Coast 509
Gollancz, Victor 20–2, 162
Goodall, Dr Norman 540, 590, 601
Gore, Charles, Bishop 31, 458, 501
Gothic, HMS 281
Governing Bodies Association 435, 437
Grace, H.B. 271
Grafton, Australia 482, 491
Great Fire of London (1666) 78
Greats 12
Greece 174, 622, 728
Greek Orthodox Church 174, 175, 271–2, 610, 727, 729; in Cyprus 617, 619–20, 624, 630
Greenford 118
Greer, William, Bishop of Manchester 419
Greeves, Reverend Derrick 553
Gregg, Sir James 164
Gresford Jones, Michael, Bishop of St Albans 222, 561
Grey, Earl 43, 76
Griffin, Cardinal 111, 164, 256, 344–7, 359, 360, 363
Griffin, J.B. 533
Grigg, Sir James 91
Grimstead, Reverend J. 713
Grisewood, Freddie 377, 423
Grivas, General George 628, 635
Groser, Fr John 161, 345
Group Ministries 76
Grubb, Sir Kenneth 409, 540, 622, 623
Guardian (Church newspaper) 278, 416
Guild Churches 76
Guildford Cathedral 279, 283, 698
Guj Ranwala 641
Guyana 700
Gwynne, Llewellyn, Bishop in Egypt 607–9, 611

Hague Conference (1948) 154
Hahn, Kurt 153
Haigh, Dr Mervyn, Bishop of Winchester 77, 194, 239, 455
Hailsham, Lord (Quintin Hogg) 210, 384, 399, 405, 406
Haley, Sir William 257, 385, 420
Halifax, Lord 279
Halifax, Nova Scotia 445, 446

Hall, Reverend E.F. 434
Hall, Ronald, Bishop of Hong Kong: meets Archbishop Fisher in Hong Kong 647, 681; ordains woman priest 649, 653, 659–60; criticised by David Paton 652; resignation sought by Chinese bishops 653; opposed to Hong Kong becoming separate diocese 654, 655; visits Archbishop Fisher at Lambeth 656, 662; attends 1958 Lambeth Conference 658, 665–7; ordination of woman priest condemned by Archbishop Fisher 661–2, 664; defends ordination of woman priest 663; declines Bishopric of Singapore 688
Hamilton, Eric, Bishop 516
Hamilton, Bermuda 698
Hamilton, Canada 447
Hamilton, NZ 493, 495
Hammer, Reverend R.J. 673
Hancock, Sir Keith 531–4
Hancock, Sir Patrick 719
Harding, Field Marshal Sir John: deports Archbishop Makarios 619, 624; opposes negotiations with Archbishop Makarios 622, 625, 626; determined to maintain bases in Cyprus 618, 625; discussions with Archbishop Fisher and Lennox-Boyd 628–9
Harland, Maurice, Bishop of Lincoln 89, 226
Harris, Reverend Donald 118
Harris, Sir William 254
Harrison, D.E.W. 121
Harthill, Venerable Percy 194
Hay, Ian 28
Hayter, Sir William 632
Hayward, H.L. 31
Headmasters' Conference 28, 436
Heard, Cardinal 739
Heaslett, Bishop 670
Heathcote Smith, Sir Stafford 164
Heenan, Cardinal 359, 360, 364, 708, 743; comments on Dr Jay's booklet 348; supports visit of Archbishop Fisher to Rome 711–12, 763
Hemingford, Lord 76
Henderson, Bernard 12, 13
Henderson, E.B. ('Jack'), Bishop of Bath and Wells 228, 288, 753
Henderson's of Charing Cross Road 21
Henneker, Reverend G. 74
Henriques, Sir Basil 392
Henry VIII, King 215, 286, 364

Henson, Hensley, Bishop 30, 312, 452
Herbert Act (1937) 210, 384, 386
Herbert, Dr Percy 228, 246
Herklots, Canon Hugh 149
Hewitt, John 216, 234
Hicks, Joynson 207
Higham on the Hill, Leicestershire 3–7,
  8, 49, 344, 754, 771, 772; school 6,
  44, 344, 771; departure of Fisher
  family 14
Hilliard, N.G., Bishop Co-adjutor of
  Sydney 488
Hinsley, Cardinal 103–7, 113–14, 345,
  346, 357
Hiorne, Mr (architect) 80
Hirohito, Emperor 675
Hiroshima 222, 373, 639, 648, 668, 671,
  684
Hobart 482
Hobson, His Honour Judge 212
Hodgson, Dr Leonard 297
Hogg, Quintin (*see* Hailsham, Lord)
Hokkaido 681
Holland 152, 162
Holocaust 577
Holy Communion 117, 119, 281, 389,
  472
Home, Sir Alec Douglas 686
Home Guard 66, 67, 85; Sunday training
  86–7; use of Church property 87–92
homosexuality 19, 393, 399
Honest to God (Robinson) 231
Hong Kong 639, 656, 662, 681; separate
  diocese suggested by Archbishop Fisher
  652–4; Synod asks Archbishop Fisher
  to act as Metropolitan 655; Bishop
  Hall's views of future of Church
  658–9; tour of Archbishop Fisher
  646–7; Bishop Hall ordains woman
  priest 649, 653, 659–60; withdrawal
  from WCC 654
Horder, Lord 64, 101
Horison, Canon 285, 286
Hornby, Colonel Robert 197, 413, 414,
  730; Press Secretary for Archbishop
  Fisher's visit to Rome 730, 731, 733,
  737, 738, 743
Horstead, John, Bishop of Sierra Leone
  506
Horton, Dr 670
House of Commons 397–8
House of Lords 69, 76, 129, 130, 154;
  denominational representation 396–7;
  episcopal representation 195, 196,
  395–8; speeches by Archbishop Fisher

375–6, 383, 391, 399–400, 413–14,
  424, 426–7, 552, 620–3, 627; women
  members 397; debate on Sharpeville
  massacre 560; debates on Cyprus crisis
  620–1, 627, 630, 634, 635
House, Reverend Francis 324, 418, 421,
  422
Houston family 447–8
Howells, Canon 503
Howells, Herbert 254
Howick, Lord 520
Howick Commission 234
Hromadka, Professor Josef 176, 179
Huddleston, Trevor, Bishop 520–1, 548,
  549, 550, 555
Hudson, Noel 217
Huggins, Sir Godfrey 511, 513
Hultgren, Gunnar, Archbishop of
  Uppsala 667
humanism 451
Hungary 142, 162, 186–7, 360
Hunkin, Dr 86
Hunter, Leslie 91, 129, 242
Huxtable, Reverend John 763

imperialism 20
India 639; tour of Archbishop Fisher
  642–5
inflation 198, 204, 437
Inge, Dean W.R. 81
Inge, Mrs (wife of Dean) 81
Innes, Dom Bennett 711
Institutions 41, 44, 243
Inter-Church Aid 162
inter-communion 317, 471, 728, 759
International Commission for Friendship
  and Social Responsibility 110
International Missionary Council 183
International Red Cross 164
International Students Day 159
Iona Community 325
Iran 598, 600, 601, 611
Iremonger, F.A. 190
Iron Curtain 140, 173, 181
Islam 582, 607, 614, 616, 639
Isle of Dogs 65
Israel 402–4, 585, 594, 720; *see also*
  Palestine
Istanbul: pilgrimage of Archbishop Fisher
  244, 705, 706, 721, 725–9, 748;
  Christ Church 727; St George's Church
  728; Saint Sophia 726

Jackson, Lady 103, 113, 114
Jackson, Reverend W.W. 10

Jacob, Professor 232
Jacob, Sir Ian 263, 377, 422–3, 424
Jago, Dr, Bishop of Bermuda 699–701
Jakobovits, Dr Immanuel 763
Jalland, Dr 232
Jamaica 697–8
James, Dr Marcus 656
James I, King 205, 268
Japan 373, 443, 639, 668–79, 684;
  Amalgamated Church 668–9, 672;
  bishops attend 1958 Lambeth
  Conference 671–2; opposition to H-
  bomb tests 673–4; visit of Anglican
  delegation 670; tour of Archbishop
  Fisher 674–9
Jarrett-Kerr, Martin 305
Jasper, Dr 130
Jay, Dr Eric 194, 261, 348, 350, 415,
  468, 561
Jericho 720
Jerusalem: under League of Nations
  Mandate 577; visit of Chief Rabbi
  579; postwar administration 585–94;
  Anglican Church in 580–2;
  internationalisation 589–94;
  pilgrimage of Archbishop Fisher 244,
  522, 705, 706, 713–23, 729, 748;
  Church of the Holy Sepulchre 715,
  720, 723; Dome of the Rock 714;
  Gethsemane 714, 717; Hebrew
  University 592; Holy Places 585–94,
  722; Mount of Olives 592, 714, 718,
  720; Pool of Bethesda 720; Rockefeller
  Museum 717; St George's Cathedral
  587, 604, 605, 612, 713–14, 721; St
  George's College 722, 743; Via
  Dolorosa 714, 723, 772
Jerusalem Bishopric 461–2, 595–606,
  608, 612; history 595–6, 717;
  Archbishop's Advisory Committee
  proposes new regulations 596–7;
  discussions on new Constitution
  598–601; successor to Bishop Stewart
  602–6; Archbishop Fisher proposes
  Middle East Province 603–6
Jewish Agency 581, 589
Jewish Christians 587
Jewish Chronicle 592
Jews 109, 112, 396, 577; *see also*
  Jerusalem; Palestine; refugees
Jinnah, Mohammed Ali 540
Joad, Dr C.E.M. 301
Johannesburg Diocese 546, 549, 553
John XXIII, Pope 411, 763; Apostolic
  Delegate in Istanbul 726–7; elected

Pope 363–4; concern for Church unity
  365, 706, 758; sets up Secretariat for
  Unity 707; audience with Archbishop
  Fisher arranged 707, 708, 711, 712;
  Ad Petram Cathedram Encyclical 732,
  739; audience with Archbishop Fisher
  197, 730, 733–7, 741; correspondence
  with Archbishop Fisher on visit 742;
  death 741, 744; broadcast panegyric
  by Archbishop Fisher 744
Johnson, Dr Hewlett 131, 135–6,
  140–5, 304; Dean of Canterbury
  135–7; absences abroad 135–6,
  141–3, 709; brings Malenkov to
  Canterbury 145
Johnson, Dr Samuel 3, 192, 457, 770
Johnstone, Archdeacon of Cairo 609,
  610, 613
Joint Standing Committee 104–14, 152
Jones, Sherwood, Bishop of Lagos 503
Jordan 603, 605, 606, 611, 720, 722
Joseph, Keith 588
Jowett, Lord William 208, 220, 382,
  384, 404

Kalgoorlie 481, 487
Kampala 524, 535, 543
Karachi 640, 641
Katakirro 536, 537, 538
Keble, John 38
Kemp, Canon 356
Kent, Sir Harold 233
Kenya 467, 522–3
Kenyatta, Jomo 523
Kerensky, Aleksandr 21
Key, J.M. 228
Khama, Seretse 539–40
Khartoum 612
Khrushchev, N.S. 193, 379–80, 624
Killick, Reverend E.T. 97
Kilmuir, Viscount 212, 386, 403–4
King, Martin Luther 558
King's School, Canterbury 136, 142,
  479, 483
Kingston, G.P., Bishop 447
Kirk, Kenneth, Bishop of Oxford 223,
  297, 334, 363, 383, 486
Knight, Dr Gerald 138, 293
Knight, Margaret 418
Knox, Ronnie 13
Knutsford Training College 36
Kobe 674, 676, 677, 681
Koechlin, Dr Alphons 169
Koh, Roland Peck-Chiang, Bishop 691;
  considered for appointment as Bishop

of Singapore 687–92; appointed
Assistant Bishop of Singapore 691
Kollek, Teddy 720
Korea 181, 467, 639, 655; tour of
Archbishop Fisher 679–83
Kotelawala, Sir John 276–7
Kuala Lumpur 689, 691
Kyodan 668, 669
Kyoto 676, 678

Labour Party 152, 220, 395–7, 578
Lady Chatterley's Lover 304–5
Lagos 543
Lahore 641
laity 207, 209
Lambeth Conference, origin 190, 452,
492
Lambeth Conference (1920) 320, 458,
472, 661, 692
Lambeth Conference (1930) 177, 332,
339, 452–3, 458, 692
Lambeth Conference (1948) 147, 170,
239, 317, 452–62, 503, 649;
preparation 468; Archbishop Fisher
encourages US and Canadian Bishops
to attend 444, 448, 451, 465; agenda
454–5; opening speech by Archbishop
Fisher 455; committees 454–5;
Archbishop Fisher meets overseas
bishops 479, 487, 492, 503, 671, 692;
attendance of Japanese bishops 671–2;
attitude of *Church Times* 415; debate
on Church in Japan 671; discussion of
CSI 338, 453, 456; resolution on
ordination of women 665–6;
resolution on regional liaison officers
473; statement on contraception 393;
talks on Church in Australia 487;
criticism 458–9; outcome 459–62
Lambeth Conference (1958) 318,
468–76, 606, 645, 679; agenda 470;
committees 470–3; appointment of
Executive Officer 473–5; Cardinal
Godfrey declines invitation to social
event 364; condemnation of apartheid
561; discussions on CSI 339, 341, 342;
invitation to Archbishop Makarios
632; resolutions on relations with
Church of Scotland 326; statement on
birth control 361–2, 683; absence of
Chinese bishops 657–8
Lambeth Conference (1968) 457
Lambeth Consultative Body 459, 473,
474
Lambeth Palace 133–4, 295, 453–4,

468–9; Library 454, 468; restoration
292–4, 415, 454, 468–9, 770; staff
190–7, 293, 469
Lambeth Quadrilateral (1920) 309
Lamont, Daniel 347
Lanchester Tradition, The (Bradby) 28
Lang, Cosmo, Archbishop of
Canterbury: at 1930 Lambeth
Conference 452, 458; in Archbishops'
War Committee 85, 86, 90, 95–6, 99,
101, 107; at Coronation of George VI
259; Bishops' Meetings 242; in Church
Assembly 77; in Convocation 121,
122; criticises morality of Armed
Forces 98; encourages Bishop Fisher to
accept Bishopric of London 55;
encourages Bishop Fisher to accept
Archbishopric of Canterbury 132; on
Lambeth Palace 133, 190; support for
Bishop Bell 219; role in Abdication of
Edward VIII 324, 767; relationship
with George VI 268; attitude to royal
family 288; concern for Bishopric of
Jerusalem 596; working habits 195;
letters to *The Times* 374; portrait 769;
retirement 102, 747; memorial service
359
Las Palmas 479
Lasbury, Bishop of Nigeria 505
Lascelles, Sir Alan 359; dissuades Duke
of Windsor from attending Coronation
255; at meeting on televising
Coronation 257; on Princess
Elizabeth's tour of Canada 270, 271;
on Princess Margaret's visit to Vatican
275; on Queen's visit to Ceylon 276;
denies story of conversion of Edward
VII 279; on Glamis wedding 284, 285,
286; ascertains procedure during
absence of Archbishop Fisher 479; on
health of George VI 245
Latham, Lord 355
Lausanne, Treaty of 726
Law Lords 72
Lawrence, D.H. 304–5
lay readers 94, 117, 123
Lay Secretary 192, 195, 196, 398, 537,
539
League of Nations 20, 52, 112, 152, 153,
577
Leander Rowing Club 12
Lebanon 605, 606, 658, 713, 724, 725
Lee, Mr (headmaster) 6
Leeson, Spencer, Bishop of Peterborough
242, 433, 434

Leigh, Sir Piers 281
Lennox-Boyd, Alan 511, 532, 538, 628–9, 632; corresponds with Archbishop Fisher on restrictions on Anglican clergy in Malta 368; negotiates agreement with Lukiko of Uganda 534, 535; approves deportation of Archbishop Makarios 619; disagrees with Archbishop Fisher on Cyprus policy 623–5, 628; protests against invitation to Archbishop Makarios to attend 1958 Lambeth Conference 632
Leontios, Bishop of Paphos 617
Lethbridge, Priscilla 192, 196
Lidgett, Dr Scott 392
Lie, Trygve 588
Life of Faith, The 108
Life and Liberty Movement 16
Life and Liberty Weeks 104, 112, 344
life peerages 396–7, 749
Life of Raymond Raynes, The (Mosley) 334
Lighter Side of School Life, The (Hay) 28
Lincoln Training College 42
Lindley Lodge preparatory school 6–7, 8
Listowel, Lord 529, 530
Little, Dr Graham 392
liturgical change 116, 117, 205, 316, 768
Liverpool 24, 42
Llewellyn, Lord 515
Lloyd, Roger 149, 310, 313, 459
Lloyd, Selwyn 379
London County Council 79, 80, 95, 429
London Diocese 55–62, 115–25, 310, 432; Bishop Fisher nominated as Bishop 55–9, 130, 132, 771, 772; churchmanship 121; Diocesan Conference 61, 91, 122–4; Diocesan Fund 123; Diocesan Leaflet 122, 123, 124; Diocesan Office 123; Moral Welfare Council 98
London Docks 64
London Missionary Society 522, 541
London School of Economics 103
Long, John 261
Longley, Archbishop 452, 492, 493
Lordani, Mgr Francesco 734
Lord's Day Observance Council 271
Lowe, John 223
Loyd, Phillip, Bishop of St Albans 222, 302
Luckraft, Reverend C.R. 684
Lutheran Church 155, 157, 595
Lyon, Hugh 434

Lyttelton, Oliver 522–3, 527–30
Lyttleton, NZ 492, 496, 497

Macclesfield 36, 39, 63
McCulloch, Joseph 129
McDermott, Brian 731, 732, 733, 741
McDonald, Dr 84
McDonald, Malcolm 645, 685
MacDonald, Ramsay 29
MacInnes, Archbishop 584, 587, 590, 606; appointed Archbishop of Jerusalem 603–6; arranges Archbishop Fisher's visit to Jerusalem 705; meets Archbishop Fisher in Jerusalem 713, 717, 720, 722; accompanies Archbishop Fisher to Beirut 724, 725; thanked by Archbishop Fisher 743
McKay, Fr 13
McKay, Reverend Roy 419, 423
McKie, Dr William 254–5, 265
MacKinnon, Professor Donald 178, 376
Maclagan, Sir Eric 81
McLean, Dr Norman 583
McLeod Campbell, Canon John 460, 473, 509, 612, 648
McLeod, George 325
Macleod, Iain 702
Macmillan, Sir Harold 215, 227, 379, 389; succeeds Eden as Prime Minister 212, 405, 406, 629; introduces Premium Bonds 405–6, 749; discusses British Museum with Archbishop Fisher 406–7; 'You've never had it so good' speech 407–8, 749; 'wind of change' speech 518, 563–4; rejects Archbishop Fisher's offer to mediate in Cyprus crisis 629–30; reaction to invitation of Archbishop Makarios to Lambeth Conference 632; informed of Archbishop Fisher's visit to Rome 710; receives notice of Archbishop Fisher's resignation 748; unpleasant meeting with Archbishop Fisher 748–9; appoints Michael Ramsey to succeed Archbishop Fisher 749–50
McQueen, Malcolm 211
Maidstone 148
maisons tolérées 99, 101
Makarios, Archbishop 368, 468, 539, 618–35; elected Archbishop 618; declines to condemn violence 619, 620; deported to Seychelles 619, 620; deportation condemned by Greeks 622–3; left out of negotiations on constitution 628–9; released from

Seychelles 630; invited to 1958
Lambeth Conference 632–3; meets
Archbishop Fisher at Lambeth Palace
633–4; deposed by coup 635; elected
President 634
Malan, Dr D.F. 545, 548, 551, 556
Malaya 690, 691
Malenkov, G.M. 145
Malik, Dr Charles 590–1, 614
Malim, F.B. 9
Malines Conversations 735–6
Malta 283, 349, 367–70
Malthens, Dr Z.K. 560
Manchester 42, 111, 725
Manchester Guardian 143, 163, 253,
412, 624
Mancroft, Lord 386
Mann, J.C., Bishop 374, 648, 670
Manning, Bishop 94
Manson, Professor 297, 321, 322
Mao Tse-Tung 650, 655
Maoris 494–5, 497
Margaret, Princess 240, 286; relations
with Group Captain Townsend 224,
288–90, 385; visit to Vatican 274–5;
engagement 290; wedding 269, 292–3
Marie Louise, Princess 278
Marlborough 8
Marlborough College 96; education of
Geoffrey Fisher 8–10, 14, 344, 404,
771; teaching career of Geoffrey Fisher
15–16, 141, 428; visited by Queen
Elizabeth II 279
marriage 51, 117, 205, 289, 290,
381–94, 697, 767; bigamous 93; civil
382–3, 472; Royal Commission on
385, 386
marriage of Geoffrey Fisher 27
Marriage Guidance Council 390
marriage licences 93
Mary, Queen 246, 269, 282, 287, 418
Masasi Diocese 520–2
Mascall, Dr Eric 342, 454
Maschwitz, Eric 27
Masterman, J.C. 11
materialism 498, 507
mathematics 9, 15, 16
Matthew, David, Cardinal 346, 369,
370, 511, 738
Matthews, Dean Walter 58, 210, 214,
272, 329
Mau Mau 517, 522–3
Maud, John Redcliffe 184
Maurice, F.D. 13, 373, 455
Mauritius 583–4

Maxwell, Alan, Assistant Bishop in West
Szechwan 649
media *see* Press; radio; television
Medical Defence Union 392
Medical-Legal Society 383
Melbourne, Australia 482
Melcher, Bishop 695
memorial services for Archbishop Fisher
762
memorial tablet to Archbishop Fisher
763–4
Menzies, Robert 483, 484
Merriman, Lord 84, 384
Merritt, Prebendary 116, 118
Merseyside Crusade 39–40
Messel, Oliver 292
Methodist Church Union 270
Methodist Conference 271, 757
Methodists: conversations on inter-
communion 311–13, 318, 756–8, 761;
in CSI 332; Faith and Order committee
318, 352
Michael, Archbishop 622
Middle East, Province envisaged by
Archbishop Fisher 601–6
Milford, Reverend C. S. 600, 602
Minehead, Somerset 63, 64, 769
Minister of Works and Building 69
Ministry of Information 64, 409, 627
Minneapolis 183, 460, 461, 463, 468,
657
missionary activity of the Church 49–51
mixed marriages 352–5, 368, 572
Mo Yung, Bishop 653
Moberly Commission on Crown
Appointments 233, 235
Modern Churchmen's Union 298, 416
Moline, Dr R.W.H., Archbishop of Perth
480
Mombasa 612
monarchy 51, 358
Monckton Report 515
money-consciousness of Geoffrey Fisher
47–9, 151, 199, 608
monogamy 525
Monteath, Dean 494
Montgomery, Field Marshal 155, 156,
159, 160, 370; visit to Canada 444,
445, 447
Montreal 446
Moorman, John 216
Moral Rearmament 256, 397
Morland, Sir Oscar 674
Morley, Reverend Fenton 553
Morris, Bishop A.H. 223

Morrison, Herbert 252, 385
Mortimer, Robert C., Bishop of Exeter 232, 240, 310, 326
Morton of Heryton, Lord 385
Moscow 140
Moscow Patriarchate 173, 174, 186
Mosley, Nicholas 334
Mothers' Union 34, 59, 285, 338, 389, 391; in Canada 464; in Korea 680; in New Zealand 493–5, 497
Mott, Dr John R. 171, 181, 449
Mott, J.R. 13, 49
Mottistone & Paget 454
Mottistone, Lord 134, 292
Mountbatten, Lady 640
Mountbatten, Lord 684
Mowll, Dr H.W.K., Archbishop of Sydney 480, 483
Mukerjee, A.N., Metropolitan of India 642
Mulieri 531–3, 535
Munich 52
Munster, Earl of 536, 538
Murray, Fr John 104, 108
Murray, Fr Victor 103, 108
Mussolini, Benito 52, 363, 428
Mutesa II, Kabaka 524–39, 541; matrimonial situation 525–6; visits England and attends Coronation 525–6; deportation to Britain 527–34; returns to Uganda 535; elected President 539; expelled by Obote 539
Myers, Bishop 346

Nablus 718
Nagasaki 222, 373, 639, 648, 668, 671, 884
Najadanna, Dr 165–6
Nambiremi Bishopric 536, 543
Napier, NZ 495
Nash, N.B., Bishop of Massachusetts 455, 456
Nassau 287
Nasser, President 402, 614, 692, 720, 722
National Clergy Association 131
National Council of Social Services 94
National Day of Prayer 86, 245, 362, 514, 584
National Emergency Precautions Measure 82
National Service 97
National Society 430–5
National Union of Czechoslovak Students 159

National Union of Protestants 206
nationalism 607, 614, 644, 668, 687, 692
Native Laws Amendment Bill 557
NATO 368, 630, 631
Navy 95
Nazareth 592
Nazism 157, 578
Nehru, Pandit 252, 640, 644, 645
Neill, Stephen 170, 183, 342
Nelson, Dr Robert 188
Nelson, NZ 495
Nether Compton 752, 762
New Delhi 748
New English Bible 473
New Statesman 258
New York 448, 451, 464, 588
New York Board of Rabbis 588
New York Herald 562
New Zealand 468, 479, 686–7; tour of Archbishop Fisher 492–9, 687
Newbigin, Bishop 339
Newbolt, Canon 36
Newcastle, Australia 482
News Chronicle 289, 413
Nickolae, Metropolitan 173
Niebuhr, Reinhold 179, 380
Niemöller, Pastor 158, 182
Nigeria 280, 502, 505, 509, 536; visit of Archbishop Fisher 543–4
Nippon Sei Ko Kai (NSKK) 668–9, 671–3, 682
No Chip on my Shoulder (Maschwitz) 27
Noel-Baker, P.J. 626
Noel-Baker, Mrs 376
Nolde, Dr O. Frederick 590, 622
Norfolk, Duchess of 259–60, 262
Norfolk, Duke of 262, 362
North India re-union scheme 342–3, 645
North Korea 174
Northern Rhodesia 509–15
Norwich Diocese 86, 92, 228
Nottingham 110
nuclear weapons 373–80, 450, 459, 767; protests to Archbishop Fisher 374–6; reaction of Archbishop Fisher 374–9; tests 673–4; used against Japan 373, 673
Nugent, Lord 291
nullity decree 286, 381, 383–4
Nuneaton 3
Nyasaland 467, 509–15

obliteration bombing 130, 156, 218, 379
Obote, Milton 539

Observer, The 28, 411, 528, 553, 699
O'Donovan, Fr 716
Oestreicher, Paul 563
O'Hara, Monsignor 361
Oldham, J. (Joe) H. 13, 179
Oman 603
Omukana of Toro 524, 527–8
Ontario 466
'Open Communions' 176–7
Orchard, Reverend K.K. 540
order of precedence 136
ordinands 202, 304, 466, 641
ordination of Geoffrey Fisher 25–6
ordinations 41, 240, 303, 340–3; of
  women 649, 653, 659–67
Orthodox Churches 173–4, 176, 179,
  271–2, 666; in Cyprus 617–20, 622,
  633; in Palestine 596, 604, 705; in
  WCC 619
Orthodox Russian Church 172–4, 709
Osaka 676, 678, 681, 683
Osborne, Sir Francis 171
Osservatore Romano 733, 739
O'Sullivan, Richard 104
Ottaviani, Cardinal 734
Ottawa 445, 447
Outward Bound School, Abergavenny
  436
Over Compton 752, 762
Overseas Christian Council 560–1
Owen, Bishop Leslie 333
Owen, R.H., Archbishop of New
  Zealand 475, 687
Oxford and Bermondsey Mission 40
Oxford Diocese 223–4, 459
Oxford Movement 4, 38, 333
Oxford University 10–14, 40, 223

Paddington Station 63
Paget, Dr H.L. 29, 30, 34, 37, 46
Paget, Edward, Bishop of Mashonaland
  514, 517
Paget, Mrs (wife of Dr H.L.) 32
Paget, Paul 134, 292
Paige-Cox, Archdeacon 35, 36
Paisley, Reverend Ian 709
Pakenham, Lord 357, 366, 367, 437
Pakistan, creation of state 639; tour of
  Archbishop Fisher 640–2
Palestine 577–94; British Mandate
  577–8, 582, 583; postwar situation
  577–8; plight of Jews in Germany
  577–9; role of Archbishop Fisher
  579–82; refugees interned in Mauritius
  583–4; renunciation of Mandate 585;

control of Jerusalem 585–94; *see also*
  Arabs; Jerusalem; Jerusalem Bishopric
Palestinian Arabic Evangelical Episcopal
  Community (PAEEC) 596
Palestinian Christianity 713
Palmer, Bishop 501, 503, 596
Panapa, Metana, Bishop of Aotearoa 494
Pare, Reverend Clive 138, 479
Parfitt, Bishop of Madagascar 630
Paris 270
Parish Church Councils 41, 50
Parker, John 398
Parker, Wilfred, Bishop of Pretoria 509
Parkes, James 589, 594
Parochial Church Councils 47, 147
parochial quotas 123
parochial system 72, 76, 116
parsonages 4, 83, 198, 302, 747
Parsons, Bishop 94
Parsons, Canon 26
parson's freehold 747
Partridge, Dr 43
Pass Laws 559
Paton, Alan 546, 568
Paton, Canon David 28, 652, 656
Paton, Dr William 104, 109
Patronage Secretary 215, 220
patronage system 72
Patterson, Cecil, Archbishop of West
  Africa 505
Paul VI, Pope 367
Pavlidis, Sir Paul 626, 627
Pawley, Reverend Bernard 411
Payne, Dr Ernest 186, 621
Peake, Sir Charles 625
Pearl Harbor 373, 650, 668, 671
Pears, Dr Steuart Adolphus 16, 17, 27
Peel Commission 581
peerages 395–6
Penn, Arthur 280
pensions 97–8, 123, 193, 203
Pensions Board 48
Pepys, Samuel 8
Perham, Margery 513, 530
Perkins, Benjamin 312
Perth, Australia 480, 481
petrol rationing 93, 164
Philadelphia 447, 448, 450
Philip, Prince (Duke of Edinburgh) 245,
  246, 753; reception into Church of
  England 271–2; at Lambeth Palace
  reception 293; letter on retirement of
  Archbishop Fisher 294; role in
  Coronation service 248, 251, 253, 262
Phillip, J.R. 264

Phillips, Samuel, Assistant Bishop of Lagos 504
Pike, James, Bishop 558
Pike, Victor 369
Pilcher, C. Vernon, Bishop Coadjutor of Sydney 583
Pitt, Valerie 305
Pius XII, Pope 103, 350–1, 363, 590
politics 11, 20, 33, 135, 498
Pollock, Dr 86
Poole, Joseph 138
Pope-Hennessy, Sir John 288, 367
Poperinghe 161
Port, Sir John 17
Portal, Lord 350
postwar Europe 152–68
Potsdam Conference 163
Potts, Margaret 258
poverty 39, 47, 641, 642, 646
Powell, Enoch 212
praemunire 215, 232, 235
Prayer Book 60, 120, 143, 240, 486; 39 Articles 143; attitude of Anglo-Catholics 116–20; irregularities in use 205; in Japan 673; in West Indies 700
Prayer Book (1662) 119, 239, 274, 327, 515, 517; preferred by Archbishop Fisher 754; Table of Affinity 117, 383
Prayer Book (1928) 33, 116, 207, 239, 316, 388, 754
Premium Bonds 405–6, 749
preparatory school 6
Presbyterian Church of Scotland 301
Presbyterianism 314, 319, 320, 326
Press 379, 380, 409–16; praise for Coronation 264; reports on royalty 270, 277, 284, 288; *Rise of Christianity* controversy 302; Archbishop Fisher addresses Press Club 411; ecclesiastical papers 414–16; criticised by Archbishop Fisher 411–12; hostility to Archbishop Fisher 632–3; coverage of Archbishop Fisher's visit to Rome 730–3, 737–8; in Canada 445, 446; *see also under names of newspapers*
Press Bureau of Church of England 352, 665
Press Club 410–11
Press Council 412, 413
press officer 194, 197, 410; *see also* Hornby, Robert
Princeton University 450
Privy Council 72; Coronation Committee 252

Profumo, John 635
Protestant Episcopal Church of America 94, 131, 172, 185, 187, 256, 448; in Far East 669, 672–3; representation at 1948 Lambeth Conference 453, 459; interest in Middle East 598, 611; in South America 694–6
Provinces of Church of England 443, 500–2; formation encouraged by Archbishop Fisher 443, 509–10, 686; *see also under names of Provinces*
Public School looks at the World, A ('Pubbers') 21, 22
public schools 437–8
Publicity, 1947 410
Purchas, Miss 655
Pusey House, Oxford 13

Quebec 445, 446
Queen Anne's Bounty 200, 202, 204
Queensland 482
Quickswood, Lord 71–6

Radcliffe, Lord 626–7, 629–31
Radcliffe, Major 102
radio 257, 273, 416–22
Radio Times 261, 752
Ramallah 718
Ramsey, Archbishop Michael: at Repton School 26, 223, 238; episcopal appointments 216, 217, 228; on canon law revision 213; appointed Bishop of Durham 222–3, 224; appointed Archbishop of York 224–6, 238; at residential meeting of bishops 243–4; chairs High Anglican committee on conversations with Free Churches 310, 315; in talks on inter-communion with Church of Scotland 321; plan for Church in North India 343; criticises Archbishop Fisher's attack on Roman Catholics 357; opposes Deceased Wife's Sister Bill 386; chairs commission on education 434; heads committee on Scriptures at 1958 Lambeth Conference 473; at 1968 Lambeth Conference 455; on apartheid 563; approves return of Bishop Reeves to England 569–70; congratulates Archbishop Fisher on visit to Rome 743; appointed Archbishop of Canterbury 749–50; succeeded at York by Archbishop Coggan 750; supports Anglican-Methodist Union

757; gives address at funeral of
Archbishop Fisher 762–3
Ramsgate 147, 185
Ratcliffe, Professor 249, 263, 342
Raven, Dr Charles 160, 249–50, 298,
312
Ravensdale, Lady 397
Rawlinson, Bishop of Derby 336, 337,
341, 585
Raynes, Fr Raymond 302, 332–3, 552
Rea, Canon 711
Record 337
Reeves, Ambrose, Bishop of
Johannesburg: declines secretaryship of
Advisory Council on Missionary
Strategy 474; appointed Bishop of
Johannesburg 546; writes to
Archbishop Fisher on South African
situation 549, 559, 560; opposes Bantu
Education Act 552, 554; supports
Archbishop Fisher on Dutch Reformed
Church and WCC 566; supports
Archbishop Joost de Blank on Dutch
Reformed Church and WCC 562; loss
of son 569; flies to London 569–70;
returns to Johannesburg 570; deported
to England 570–2; considered for
appointment as Bishop of Blackburn
228–9
Reformation 205, 319, 327–30, 381
Reformed Churches 173
refugees 130, 162, 164–6, 362; Arab
611; in Far East 639, 641, 643, 644;
Jewish 577–82
Refugees Defence Committee 164
Regina, Canada 463
registry offices 382–3, 388
Reindorp, George, Bishop of Guildford
240
Reith, Lord 427
Relevance of Christianity, The (Barry)
455
religious freedom 108, 182, 345, 555,
585, 607, 651
Reorganisation Areas Measure (1943) 73
Repton Priory 17, 24, 31
Repton School: history 17; headship of
William Temple 16, 33, 130; headship
of Geoffrey Fisher 17–31, 33, 57, 133,
206, 223, 238, 435; departure of
Geoffrey Fisher 30–1, 751; Archbishop
Fisher's chairmanship of governing
body 436; Chapel 18, 26, 31, 344;
discipline 19–20; Gollancz-Somervell
row 20–2; homosexual practices 19;

Officer Training Corps 22;
scholarships 23, 24
Repton village 3, 17, 21, 28
resignation of Archbishop Fisher 747–50
retirement of Archbishop Fisher 294,
379, 424, 542, 594, 611, 751–64;
unfinished business 207, 212, 326,
330, 543, 659, 712; reminiscences 227,
234, 288, 394, 399; works as assistant
parish priest 751–5; ecumenicity
756–64; international events 515, 594
Rhee, Syngman 680
Rhodes, Dennis 286
Rhodes, Reverend Clifford 416
Rhodesia 399, 467
Rhys Williams, Lady 425
Richardson, Canon 298
Richmond, Bruce 3
Richmond, Reverend Legh 3
Riley, Harold 284
Rinkel, Anreas 226
Rio de Janeiro 695, 696
Rise of Christianity, The 295–305, 421
Robbins, A.P. 412
Roberts, Bishop 336, 547, 645, 654
Roberts, Brian 412–13
Roberts, Dr Howard 314
Robertson, General Sir Brian 166–7
Robertson, Sir Ian 167
Robinson, John, Bishop of Southwark
230, 304–5, 570–1
Rogers, Murray 375
Roleston, Captain C.H. 417
Roman Catholics 344–70, 666, 759; in
ecumenical movement 103–14, 710,
759, 760; in Germany 155;
representation at WCC 171–2, 181;
bishops decline to attend Coronation
service 247, 256, 359; Cardinal Griffin
rejects Ecumenical Committee 344–5;
support for Archbishop Fisher's visit to
Rome 710–12; Asian priests 688;
bishops 241, 256; Church schools 429,
431, 554; civic services 345; mixed
marriages 352–5, 368; pilgrimages in
memory of martyrs 327; representation
in House of Lords 396, 397;
Secretariat for Unity 707, 712, 739,
742; teaching on family planning 393;
territorial titles of bishops 356; use of
media 418, 419, 420; in Canada 446;
in USA 449; in Australia 483, 484; in
New Zealand 497; war damage 69; *see
also* John XXIII; Vatican
Rome, pilgrimage of Archbishop Fisher

244, 730–44, 748; preparation
705–12; support from Roman
Catholics in England 710–12; arrival
in Rome 730–1; Press coverage
730–1; Archbishop Fisher's statement
to Press 731–3; audience with Pope
John XXIII 733–7; Archbishop Fisher
visits Cardinal Bea 738; reactions to
visit 739–44
Roosevelt, Eleanor 558
Roosevelt, President 448
Roper, Dr Stanley 254
Roper, Justice 485–6
Rowallen, Lord 699
rowing 11–12
Roy, Dr B.C. 643
Royal Air Force 89, 350
royal events 51
royal family 268–94; baptisms 268, 274;
domestic staff 281; marriages 272–4,
284–6; relationships of Archbishop
Fisher 268–70, 289; travels 274–80;
*see also under names of members of
royal family*
Royal Institute of British Architects 78
Royal Medical Corps 98
rugby 11
Rumania 141
Runcie, Robert, Archbishop of
Canterbury 667
Rupertsland 466
Rupp, Gordon 157
Russian Revolution 21

Sabiti, Bishop 724
St Augustine's theological college,
Canterbury 461–2
St Bride's, Fleet Street 79, 410, 411, 414
St Clement's, Fulham 118
St Cuthbert's, Philbeach Gardens 118
St Dunstan's, Fleet Street 84
St Edmundsbury and Ipswich Diocese
223
St George's Chapel, Windsor 247
St George's Church, Cannon Street 161
St George's Church, Edinburgh 302
St Giles, Edinburgh 329
St James, Piccadilly 16
St John the Baptist, Tottenham 115
St John's, Folkestone 147
St John's, Smith Square 218
St Margaret's Church, Westminster 682
St Mary-le-Bow 61
St Mary's Church, Oxford 190

St Michael and All Angels, Bedford Park
118
St Paul's Cathedral 61, 79, 115, 247,
263, 415, 422; Dean 154, 157, 330
St Paul's Church, Birkenhead 39
St Paul's, Knightsbridge 288, 480
St Peter's School, Adelaide 136
Salisbury, Lord 282, 346, 362, 396
Salisbury, Rhodesia 516, 517
Samori, Monsignor 734, 735, 737
San Francisco Conference 152
Sandringham 228, 245, 246
Sandwich 148
Sansbury, Kenneth, Bishop of Singapore
461, 640, 642, 689–92
Sargent, Canon Alec 132, 136
Satterthwaite, Reverend John 364, 366,
623, 633; in preparations for
Archbishop Fisher's visit to Rome
705–8, 711, 713; present at meeting of
Archbishop Fisher and Oecumenical
Patriarch 728; accompanies
Archbishop Fisher to Vatican 733, 734,
736–7; praised by Archbishop Fisher
743
Savage, Sir Alfred 700
Say, David, Bishop of Rochester 184,
186, 187, 239
Scarbrough, Lord 283
Scarlett, Lady 732, 741
Scarlett, Sir Peter, informs Archbishop
Fisher of Press blackout on visit to
Rome 730; committed to success of
visit 730; receives Archbishop Fisher
on arrival in Rome 731; entertains
Archbishop Fisher at Legation 732;
approves Archbishop Fisher's
statement to Press 733; holds Press
conference in villa 737; assessment of
visit 739, 740; thanked by Archbishop
Fisher 741
school-leaving age 44
Sclater, Reverend J.R.P. 465–6
Scott, Dr A. T., Chairman of House of
Bishops in China 648, 659, 663, 664,
665
Scott, John Guillum 77
Scott, Reverend Michael 514, 547, 548
Scottish Church Union 302
Scottish Presbyterian Church in England
322, 324
Second World War 453; Archbishop's
War Committee 85–102; blitz 63–8,
117, 122; damage to churches 69–84;
Holocaust 577

Seely and Paget 133
Selborne Committee 433, 434
Selborne, Lord 233, 433
Selwyn, Dr 232, 297, 303
Selwyn, George Augustus, Bishop of New
    Zealand 492, 493, 496
Sempe, Kaluli 531
Seoul 679, 680
sermons of Geoffrey Fisher 26–7, 132,
    721, 754; *see also* Cambridge sermon
service of blessing 388, 390
sex 472, 473, 677
sex education 98–102
Sexton, Dr H.E., Bishop of British
    Colombia 465
Shanghai 654
Shape of the Liturgy (Dix) 309
Sharpe, Ernest, Archdeacon of London
    79, 120
Sharpe, Kenneth 542
Sharpeville massacre 559–62, 569
She, George 652
Shedden, Roscow 301
Sheffield 91
Sheffield Morning Post 91
Shen Fann, Reverend 657
Sheppard, Dick 16, 221
Sherborne 751, 752, 762
Sherrill, Bishop Henry 172, 256, 563,
    673, 702, 762; at First WCC Assembly
    182; at Second WCC Assembly 187,
    189; at 1948 Lambeth Conference 453,
    458, 460, 673; at 1958 Lambeth
    Conference 475; discussions with
    Archbishop Fisher on Middle East 598;
    concern over Episcopal Church in
    Brazil 696–7; friendship with
    Archbishop Fisher 748, 771
Shinwell, Emmanuel 160, 362
Shirley, Canon 136, 142
Sierra Leone 506
Silsoe, Lord 195, 196, 203
Simeon, Charles 501
Simkin, W.J., Bishop of Auckland 492
Simmonds, Lord 212
Simon, Lord 72, 382
Simpson, Canon 36
Simpson, Bertram, Bishop of Southwark
    119, 227, 303
Simpson, W.W. 581
Simpson, Wallis 288
Singapore, postwar situation 684–5;
    appointment of Bishop Baines 685–6;
    appointment of Bishop Koh 687–91
Six Days War 594

Skelton, Henry, Bishop of Lincoln 241
Slack, Kenneth 556, 621, 629
Slater's Hall, Canterbury 144
Sleaford 89
Slokenburg, Pastor 165
Smith, Guy Vernon, Bishop of Leicester
    239
Smith, Reverend C.R. 118, 119
Smithers, Sir Waldron 143, 418
smoking 10–11, 769
Smuts, General 273, 545, 557
Smyth, Canon Charles 17, 18, 25, 26,
    27, 298
Society for Promoting Christian
    Knowledge (SPCK) 111, 119, 259,
    355, 410
Society for the Propagation of the Gospel
    (SPG) 335–8, 452, 554, 649
Soldier's Welfare, The 101
Somervell, David 18, 20–1
Soper, Dr Donald 376
South Africa 4, 30, 188, 500, 545–73;
    apartheid policy 545–9; oppressive
    legislation 549–50, 555–7; Sharpeville
    massacre 559–62; reaction of
    Churches to Sharpeville 560–8;
    referendum on secession from
    Commonwealth 571; Cottesloe
    Conference of WCC 572–3; *see also*
    apartheid
South African war 6
South America 693–70
South American Missionary Society 694,
    695
South Indian Re-Union Scheme 315, 453,
    458; *see also* Church of South India
South West Africa 547
South West Australia 482
Southern Rhodesia 509–12
Spandi, Signor Filipo 737
Spanish Episcopal Church in Madrid 470
Spectator, The 252, 289
Spender, Stephen 713
Spens, Sir Patrick 209
spiritual development of Geoffrey Fisher
    10
Stacpole, Alberic 758–60
Stanley, Oliver 583
Stapeldon, Walter 10
Statement on Religious Co-operation
    105–6
Stephens, David 215–17, 227
Stephenson, P.W., Bishop of Nelson 492
Stepney 64
Stern Gang 582

Stewart, Sir Campbell 349

Stewart, Weston, Bishop in Jerusalem 595; discusses Jerusalem Bishopric with Archbishop Fisher 595, 601; informs Archbishop Fisher of situation in Palestine 578; not Bishop 'of' Jerusalem 596–7; jurisdiction over Anglicans of all races in diocese 599; in talks with Arabic Church Council 599–600; in discussions on revised Constitution of Bishopric 604; resignation 600, 602, 603

stipends of clergy 48–9, 83, 123, 150–1, 198–204; bishops 230, 231; concern of Archbishop Fisher 198–204; CSI 335–6; report of Archbishop Fisher to Church Assembly 200–2; in Egypt and Sudan 608, 722; in South America 695; in Uganda 542

Stockholm Peace Conference 174

Stockport 39

Stockwood, Mervyn, Bishop of Southwark 227, 230, 240, 242, 244; rebuked by Apostolic Delegate 361–2; audience with Pope 706, 708

Stone, Dr 13

Stopes, Dr Marie 384

Stopford, Bishop Robert 226–7, 239, 468

Streeter, Reverend 13

Strijdom, J.G. 556, 568

Strutt, Sir Arthur 709

Strutt, Sir Austin 280

Stuart, Cyril, Bishop of Uganda 524, 526, 528

Student Christian Movement 149, 391

Stuttgart Conference 158, 163

Sudan 601, 608

Suez Canal 142, 402–5, 601, 613, 634, 677

Suffragan Bishops 136–7, 146, 148, 230–1, 542

Suiliel, Metropolitan 725

Sullivan, Martin 499

Sun 375

Sunday Despatch 301

Sunday Express 237, 286, 625, 721

Sunday observance 95–6, 615

Sunday Pictorial 301

Sunday Schools 45

Sunday Times 275, 632

Swanwick 13

Sweden 108, 165, 341, 667

Swinton, Lord 252, 514, 551

Sword of the Spirit movement 104, 107, 109, 111, 112, 344, 345

Sydney 479, 482, 483, 484, 487, 490–1; Jewish community 580, 583

Sykes, Professor Norman 232, 252, 298, 329

synagogue 719

Synge, Reverend F.C. 115

Syria 605, 606

Table of Affinity 117, 383

Tablet 360

Tait, Archbishop 60, 130, 395, 452

Takasi, A.T., Bishop 672

Tanganyika 541–2

Tardini, Cardinal 364, 366; restrictions on Archbishop Fisher's visit to Rome 711, 730, 738, 740, 741; tries to change Archbishop Fisher's Press statement 732, 733; attitude explained 744

Task for the Laity, A 201

Tasmania 482

Taylor, Reverend F.J. 321

Taylor, H.S. 414

Taylor, J.R.S., Bishop of Sodor and Man 121

Taylor, John, Bishop of Winchester 529, 756

Taylor, Myron 172

Taylor, P.W. 9

Taylor, Prebendary 79

Taylor, Robert, Bishop of Pretoria 516

Taylor, Dr Ralph 242

Taylor, Reverend T.F. 752

teaching 15

Team Ministries 76

technology 391, 452, 677, 682

Tel Aviv 713

television 256–8, 470; Independent Television 424–7; religious broadcasting 416–27; training for clergy 419–20

Temple, Frances 129, 133, 261, 457

Temple, Reverend Freddie 317, 647, 681, 686, 688, 713; accompanies Archbishop Fisher to audience with Pope 733, 736, 737

Temple, Archbishop William 13, 43, 130, 408, 450, 608, 751; headmaster of Repton 16, 18, 20, 33, 133; governor of Repton 29; nominates Geoffrey Fisher as Bishop of Chester 29; at consecration of Geoffrey Fisher 34; Bishops' Meetings 242; in

Convocation 121, 122; in Merseyside Crusade 39; nominations for episcopal appointments 220, 221; encourages Bishop Fisher to accept bishopric of London 56, 57, 58; in Church Assembly 77; opposes wartime violation of churchyards 88–90; radicalism 13; working habits 195; support for religious co-operation 104, 105, 170; dedication to WCC 169, 170; belief in Virgin Birth 296; policy on CSI 332, 334; supports Butler's Education Bill 428; at 1930 Lambeth Conference 452, 453; suggests Province of West Africa 503; disturbed by ordination of women priests 659–61, 663, 664; illness 111, 129, 661; retirement 130; death 102, 113, 124, 129, 169, 430, 662, 747; funeral 129; memorial service 359

Templewood, Lord 316

Tenison, Archbishop 268, 319

terrorism 581, 582, 584, 622, 628

Theology 458

Thetis (submarine) 52

Thomas, A.F.W. 98

Thomas, Canon 42, 43

Thomas, Howard 420

Thorne, Frank, Bishop of Nyasaland 518

Thorpe, Archdeacon 36

Times, The 275, 278, 359, 360, 754; in nineteenth century 409; on Archbishop Fisher's meeting with Cardinal Bea 738; on Archbishop Fisher's plan for Jerusalem 592; on Archbishop Fisher's speech to Lukiko of Uganda 534; on Archbishop Fisher's speech to Medical-Legal Society 384; on Archbishop Fisher's speeches on Cyprus crisis 621, 625; on Archbishop Makarios 635; on Butler's Education Bill 428; on Chester Cathedral 35; on Church of Scotland 324; on Coronation Rite 249, 250, 264; on invitation of Archbishop Makarios to Lambeth Conference 632; on Kenya 523; on Khrushchev's disarmament speech 380; on London Diocese 60; on nomination of Bishop Fisher as Archbishop of Canterbury 131; on non-fraternisation policy in Germany 161; on Princess Margaret 288; on procession at 1958 Lambeth Conference 470; on Roman Catholicism 348–50; on schools broadcasting 420; on threat of famine 163; statement of Kabaka Mutesa II 533; letter from Dr Barnes 295; letters from Archbishop Fisher 405, 511, 512, 581, 586, 589, 640, 752, 759; letter from Archbishop Lang 374; letter from Robert Menzies 484; letter from Margery Perham 513; letter from Brian Roberts 412; letter from Roman Catholic Bishop of Nottingham 356; letter from Sword of the Spirit and Commission of Churches 104, 107, 108; letters on church restoration 78, 81; joint letter on Central African Federation 514; joint letter from Archbishop Fisher and Cardinal Griffin 346

Tindall, Professor 155, 156, 157, 709

Ting, Reverend K. 656

tithe 48, 83, 204

Tithe Acts (1936) 48, 199

Tithe Clerks 83

Todhunter, John 710–12, 758–61

Tokyo 669, 670, 673, 675–6, 679, 681

Tomkins, Oliver 157, 239, 711; on Bishops' Meetings 242; in discussions on relations with German Churches 157; on Faith and Order Commission of WCC 170, 171, 178, 184, 188, 227; nominated as Bishop of Bristol 227; relationship with Archbishop Fisher 239; predicts growth of *Enosis* 618

Tomkinson, Reverend 333–4

Tomuda Sugati, Bishop 670

Toronto 446, 464, 748

Towards the Conversion of England 409

Townsend, Group Captain Peter 224, 288–9, 385

Tractate on Full Communion (Fisher) 761

trade unions 156

tradition 15

training colleges 43

Transport Bill (1948) 199, 200

Trent, Dorset 401, 751, 752, 755–7, 762, 770

Trevelyan, Mary 523, 552

Trivett, Reverend Alexander 656

Truman, President 172, 578, 580

Trustram Eve, Malcolm 203–4

Truth magazine 33

Tsen, Lindel, Bishop of Honan 649, 652, 666

Tsi, Sister Litimoi 659–60, 662–4, 666–7

Tsu, Bishop 664

Tubbs, Bishop 36, 41
Tucker, St J., Bishop 669
Turkey 617, 622, 630, 635

Uganda 467, 502, 524–44; retirement of
    Bishop Stuart 524–6; appointment of
    Bishop Brown 526; Kabakaship
    problem 524–39; Lukiko 527, 530,
    533–5, 539; inauguration of Province
    540–3; *see also* Buganda; Mutesa II
Uganda Relationship Commission 537–8
Ugandan Advisory Council 526
Union of the All Orthodox Rabbis in
    America and Canada 588
Union of Benefices Act 72
United Church of Canada 465
United Council of Churches in Egypt 607
United Nations 375, 399, 634;
    inauguration 152, 153, 454; in
    Palestine 585–6, 589–91; General
    Assembly decides on
    internationalisation of Jerusalem
    593–4; Suez crisis 402–5, 677
United Nations Conciliation Commission
    590, 591
United Nations Relief and Rehabilitation
    Administration (UNRRA) 161, 162,
    717
United States of America, tour of
    Archbishop Fisher 447–51, 580, 770;
    Palestine policy 580, 586, 591, 603
Universities Mission to Central Africa
    452, 501, 520, 538, 541, 542
Upper Nile Diocese 542–3

Vaisey, Lord Justice 206, 207, 232–3,
    235
Vandemoore, Dr 572
Vassal, Henry 24
Vatican 171, 179, 181, 275, 351, 362,
    363–4, 706; visit of Archbishop Fisher
    733, 737, 740; visit of Princess
    Margaret 275
Vatican Council, second 706, 712, 735
Vaughan Williams, Ralph 254
venereal disease 100, 159–60
Verwoerd, Dr H.F. 560, 564, 568–9
vestments 38, 93, 210–11, 515–16
Victoria, Australia 482
Victoria, Canada 463
Victoria, Queen 6, 254, 259, 260, 265,
    268, 595, 643
Vidler, Dr Alec 236, 297, 661
Vining, L.G., Bishop of Lagos 506, 508
Visser't Hooft, negotiations with member

Churches of WCC 171–5; at First
    Assembly of WCC 177–81; role in
    Second Assembly of WCC 182, 185–7;
    writes to Archbishop Fisher on appeal
    of Pope John XXIII 365; visits
    Archbishop Fisher at Lambeth
    169–70; opposes proposed withdrawal
    of Province of South Africa from WCC
    562, 564; role in controversy over
    Dutch Reformed Church in WCC 565,
    566, 567–8, 570; reaction to
    deportation of Archbishop Makarios
    619–20; reprimanded by Archbishop
    Fisher 621–2; interview with
    Archbishop Fisher on Cyprus problem
    626; anxiety over Cyprus crisis and
    Orthodox Churches 627–8; justifies
    WCC delegation visit to Cyprus 633;
    primes Archbishop Fisher on visit to
    Oecumenical Patriarch 706, 728
Vodden, Henry, Bishop of Hull 94

Waddams, Canon Herbert 363, 364,
    593, 769; accompanies Archbishop
    Fisher on visit to Germany 168;
    seconded to Lambeth 191, 193, 196; in
    preparations for First Assembly of
    WCC 174, 178; move to Canada 194;
    omitted from Church of England
    delegation to Second Assembly of
    WCC 184–5; views on relationship of
    Church of England and WCC 184;
    visits Foreign Office on behalf of
    Archbishop Fisher 141; paper on
    Roman Catholic bishops' territorial
    titles 356; criticises Archbishop Fisher
    for attack on Roman Catholics 357;
    interview with French priest 358; in
    discussions on new plans for Bishopric
    of Jerusalem 604; advises Archbishop
    Fisher on Cyprus problem 618, 631,
    632
Waldorf Hotel 107
Walker, Reverend J.A. 47
walking, hobby of Archbishop Fisher
    752, 754, 769
Wallasey 39, 40
Walton, Sir William 254, 260
Wand, William, Bishop of London 187,
    337; on committee for canon law
    revision 206; nominated as Bishop of
    London 219; resigns from commission
    on ecclesiastical courts 212; resignation
    224, 225, 229; appointed canon of St

Paul's 229–30; committee chairman at 1948 Lambeth Conference 456
Wanganui, NZ 495
Wanstall, Canon D.J.N. 731
war damage 69–84, 123–5
War Damage Act (1940) 69, 70
War Damage Commission 70, 71, 84, 203
War Graves Commission 369–70
War Office 21–2, 64, 89, 99, 101, 102
Warburton, Miss 590
Ward, Barbara 103, 104, 107, 112, 113
Warren, Canon Max 394, 501, 523, 594, 604, 656; founds Evangelical Fellowship for Theological Literature 121; at Second Assembly of WCC 183, 187; in discussions with Free Churches 310; declines to become Bishop 236, 602–3; advises Archbishop Fisher on Ugandan problems 526, 529, 531; advises Archbishop Fisher on Egyptian crisis 607, 609; rejects Bishop Allen's proposals on Egypt 612; urges restraint over attendance of Chinese bishops at 1958 Lambeth Conference 657; preaches at memorial service for Archbishop Fisher 762
Washington 449–50
Watkins-Jones, Dr H. 352
Watson, Dr Pitt 267
Weatherhead, Dr Leslie 313
Wedgwood Benn, Anthony 377
Week of Prayer and Giving 123
Weizman, Dr 589
Welenski, Sir Roy 513
Welfare State 152, 401, 498
Wellard, Prebendary 79–83
Weller, Bishop 693, 694
Wellington, Bishop of Shantung 650, 651
Wellington, NZ 495, 687
Wells, H.G. 25, 69
Wells Theological College 26
Welsby, Canon Paul 212, 214
West Africa 500–8; Provincial Constitution 500–6; visit of Archbishop Fisher and inauguration ceremony 506–8
West Kirby 39
West-Watson, C., Archbishop of New Zealand 492
Westcott House, Cambridge 213, 243
Western Australia 480–2
Westgate 101
Westminster Abbey 250, 261, 485, 762
Westminster, Archbishop of 157, 158

Westminster Cathedral 422
Westminster Hall 250, 251
Westminster Hotel 16
Wetheridge, G.C. 726
Wheeler, Monsignor Gordon 305
Wheeler, Reverend W.T.P. 317
White, John 144
White-Thompson, Ian, Dean of Canterbury 261, 753, 764, 770
Whitehorn, Ethel 699
Whitehorne, Dr 323
Whiteman, Reverend H.G. 278–9
widows of clergy 49, 97–8
Wilbraham, Sir Philip Baker 199, 202, 203
Wilkinson, Green, Bishop of Northern Rhodesia 519
Willan, G. Healey 254
Willebrands, Monsignor 707, 708, 731, 744
Williams, A.L.E., Bishop of Bermuda 701
Williams, Alwyn, Bishop of Durham 222, 666
Williams, Dr A.T.P., Bishop of Winchester 473
Williams, N.P. 12, 13, 34
Williams, Paul 409
Williams, Dr R.R. 178, 409
Willink, Henry 184
Willis, Frederick, Bishop of Delhi 531
Willis, Sir Frank 160
Wilson, Henry, Bishop 222
Wilson, Leonard, Bishop of Singapore 243, 684, 691
Windsor, Duke of 255–6, 287
Winnington-Ingram, Bishop 55, 60–1, 116, 278, 463
Winnipeg 446, 447, 448, 463, 464
Winster, Lord 618, 620
Winterton, Lord 400
Wishart, Reverend J.H. 316
With One Accord 50
Wittenbach, Reverend Harry 657
Wolfenden Report 393
Wollogong 483
Wolsey, Cardinal 8
women in life of the Church 480, 491; *see also* Mothers' Union
women priests 649, 653, 659–67
Women's Offering 123
Women's Voluntary Service 65, 66
Wood, Reverend C.T. 9
Wood, C.T., Archdeacon of Cape Town 560, 565
Wood, Richard 520

Woodruff, Fr Douglas 104, 109, 112, 360
Woods, Edward, Bishop of Lichfield 88
Woodward, Clifford, Bishop of Bristol 218, 219
Wordsworth, Christopher, Bishop 367
World Council of Churches 164, 169–89; origins 129, 152, 454; inception 162, 169–70, 227, 468; .Churches represented 171–8, 184; Executive Committee deliberations interrupted by death of George VI 246; First General Assembly (Amsterdam) 147, 171–82, 185, 499; new building in Germany visited by Archbishop Fisher 166; Praesidium 180–3, 187, 705; Provisional Committee 169, 170, 173, 174, 180; Second General Assembly (Evanston) 180, 182–9, 443, 463, 561, 562; use of Archbishop Fisher to approach British government 164; New Delhi Assembly 180, 748; response to Pope John XXIII 365; hosts to Archbishop Fisher in USA 448, 449; hosts to Archbishop Fisher in Australia 480, 482; opposition to apartheid 554, 555, 561–2; controversy over Dutch Reformed Church and apartheid 561–8; Cottesloe Conference 568, 571–2; policy on Palestine 588, 591, 592; reaction to deportation of Archbishop Makarios 619–21, 628; delegation visits Cyprus 633; withdrawal of Hong Kong diocese 654; observers invited to Vatican II 706; Cardinal Willibrands attends meeting in Scotland 707; representatives at Vatican II 712; support of Oecumenical Patriarch encouraged by Archbishop Fisher 729
World-wide Church, The 50
Wren, Sir Christopher 78
Wurm, Bishop of Stuttgart 156, 158

Yanagihara, Bishop of Osaka 672
Yashiro, Bishop of Kobe 639; in NSKK 669, 673; leads Japanese bishops at 1948 Lambeth Conference 671–2; opposes H-bomb tests 673–4; meets Archbishop Fisher in Japan 674–5, 681; at consecration of Kobe cathedral 678; writes to Archbishop Fisher 683
York Minster 34
Yorkshire Post 413
Young Men's Christian Association 160, 720
Young, Reverend A.D. 118
youth councils 45

Zionism 578, 585